THE OXFORD HANI

LAW AND POLITICS

THE
OXFORD
HANDBOOKS
OF
POLITICAL
SCIENCE

GENERAL EDITOR: ROBERT E. GOODIN

The Oxford Handbooks of Political Science is a ten-volume set of reference books offering authoritative and engaging critical overviews of all the main branches of political science.

The series as a whole is under the General Editorship of Robert E. Goodin, with each volume being edited by a distinguished international group of specialists in their respective fields:

POLITICAL THEORY
John S. Dryzek, Bonnie Honig & Anne Phillips

POLITICAL INSTITUTIONS
R. A. W. Rhodes, Sarah A. Binder & Bert A. Rockman

POLITICAL BEHAVIOR
Russell J. Dalton & Hans-Dieter Klingemann

COMPARATIVE POLITICS
Carles Boix & Susan C. Stokes

LAW & POLITICS
Keith E. Whittington, R. Daniel Kelemen & Gregory A. Caldeira

PUBLIC POLICY
Michael Moran, Martin E. Rein & Robert E. Goodin

POLITICAL ECONOMY
Barry R. Weingast & Donald A. Wittman

INTERNATIONAL RELATIONS
Christian Reus-Smit & Duncan Snidal

CONTEXTUAL POLITICAL ANALYSIS
Robert E. Goodin & Charles Tilly

POLITICAL METHODOLOGY
Janet M. Box-Steffensmeier, Henry E. Brady & David Collier

This series aspires to shape the discipline, not just to report on it. Like the Goodin–Klingemann *New Handbook of Political Science* upon which the series builds, each of these volumes will combine critical commentaries on where the field has been together with positive suggestions as to where it ought to be heading.

THE OXFORD HANDBOOK OF

LAW AND POLITICS

Edited by

KEITH E. WHITTINGTON
R. DANIEL KELEMEN

and

GREGORY A. CALDEIRA

OXFORD
UNIVERSITY PRESS

OXFORD

UNIVERSITY PRESS

Great Clarendon Street, Oxford OX2 6DP
United Kingdom

Oxford University Press is a department of the University of Oxford.
It furthers the University's objective of excellence in research, scholarship,
and education by publishing worldwide.

Oxford is a registered trade mark of Oxford University Press in the UK
and in certain other countries

British Library Cataloguing in Publication Data
Data available

Library of Congress Cataloging in Publication Data
Data available

ISBN 978-0-19-958557-1

CONTENTS

About the Contributors   x

PART I   INTRODUCTION

1. The Study of Law and Politics   3
   KEITH E. WHITTINGTON, R. DANIEL KELEMEN
   & GREGORY A. CALDEIRA

PART II   APPROACHES

2. Judicial Behavior   19
   JEFFREY A. SEGAL

3. Strategic Judicial Decision-making   34
   PABLO T. SPILLER & RAFAEL GELY

4. Historical Institutionalism and the Study of Law   46
   ROGERS M. SMITH

PART III   COMPARATIVE JUDICIAL POLITICS

5. The Rule of Law and Courts in Democratizing Regimes   63
   REBECCA BILL CHAVEZ

6. The Global Spread of Constitutional Review   81
   TOM GINSBURG

7. Establishing and Maintaining Judicial Independence   99
   GEORG VANBERG

8. The Judicialization of Politics 119
RAN HIRSCHL

9. Comparative Federalism and the Role of the Judiciary 142
DANIEL HALBERSTAM

10. Legal and Extralegal Emergencies 165
KIM LANE SCHEPPELE

PART IV INTERNATIONAL AND SUPRANATIONAL LAW

11. International Law and International Relations 187
BETH SIMMONS

12. The European Court and Legal Integration:
An Exceptional Story or Harbinger of the Future? 209
KAREN J. ALTER

13. War Crimes Tribunals 229
GARY J. BASS

14. The Globalization of the Law 245
BRYANT G. GARTH

PART V FORMS OF LEGAL ORDER

15. Civil Law and Common Law: Toward Convergence? 267
UGO MATTEI & LUCA G. PES

16. Constitutionalism 281
KEITH E. WHITTINGTON

17. Constitutional Law and American Politics 300
MARK A. GRABER

18. The Legal Structure of Democracy 321
RICHARD H. PILDES

19. Administrative Law 340
DANIEL B. RODRIGUEZ

20. Legislation and Statutory Interpretation 360
ELIZABETH GARRETT

21. Informalism as a Form of Legal Ordering 378
CHRISTINE B. HARRINGTON

PART VI SOURCES OF LAW AND THEORIES OF JURISPRUDENCE

22. Natural Law 399
ROBERT P. GEORGE

23. Rights in Legal and Political Philosophy 414
MATTHEW H. KRAMER

24. Formalism: Legal, Constitutional, Judicial 428
FREDERICK SCHAUER

25. Feminist Theory and the Law 437
JUDITH A. BAER

26. The Racial Subject in Legal Theory 451
SHEILA R. FOSTER & R. A. LENHARDT

PART VII THE AMERICAN JUDICIAL CONTEXT

27. Filling the Bench 469
DAVID A. YALOF

28. The U.S. Supreme Court 487
LEE EPSTEIN

29. Relations among Courts 503
SUSAN HAIRE

30. Litigation and Legal Mobilization 522
MICHAEL MCCANN

31. Legal Profession 541
RICHARD L. ABEL

PART VIII THE POLITICAL AND POLICY ENVIRONMENT OF COURTS IN THE UNITED STATES

32. Judicial Independence   557
FRANK CROSS

33. Law and Regulation   576
SUSAN ROSE-ACKERMAN

34. Law as an Instrument of Social Reform   595
CHARLES R. EPP

35. Criminal Justice and the Police   614
WESLEY G. SKOGAN

36. Law and Political Ideologies   626
JULIE NOVKOV

37. Courts and the Politics of Partisan Coalitions   644
HOWARD GILLMAN

38. Understanding Regime Change: Public Opinion, Legitimacy, and Legal Consciousness   663
SCOTT BARCLAY & SUSAN S. SILBEY

PART IX INTERDISCIPLINARY APPROACHES TO LAW AND POLITICS

39. Law and Society   681
LYNN MATHER

40. The Analysis of Courts in the Economic Analysis of Law   698
LEWIS A. KORNHAUSER

41. Psychology and the Law   711
TOM R. TYLER

42. Law and History   723
CHRISTOPHER TOMLINS

PART X   OLD AND NEW

43. The Path of the Law in Political Science: De-centering Legality
    from Olden Times to the Day before Yesterday   737
    STUART A. SCHEINGOLD

44. Reflections about Judicial Politics   752
    HAROLD J. SPAETH

45. Law and Politics: The Problem of Boundaries   767
    MARTIN SHAPIRO

Index   775

About the Contributors

Richard L. Abel is Michael J. Connell Professor of Law at the University of California at Los Angeles.

Karen J. Alter is Associate Professor of Political Science at Northwestern University.

Judith A. Baer is Professor of Political Science at Texas A&M University.

Scott Barclay is Associate Professor of Political Science and Public Administration and Policy at the State University of New York at Albany.

Gary J. Bass is Associate Professor of Politics and International Affairs at Princeton University.

Gregory A. Caldeira is Distinguished University Professor and Ann and Darrell Dreher Chair in Political Communications and Policy Thinking at the Ohio State University.

Rebecca Bill Chavez is Associate Professor of Political Science at the United States Naval Academy.

Frank Cross is Herbert D. Kelleher Centennial Professor of Business Law at the University of Texas at Austin.

Charles R. Epp is Associate Professor of Public Administration at the University of Kansas.

Lee Epstein is Beatrice Kuhn Professor of Law and Professor of Political Science at Northwestern University.

Sheila R. Foster is Albert A. Walsh Professor of Law and Co-Director of the Stein Center for Law and Ethics at Fordham University.

Elizabeth Garrett is Sydney M. Irmas Professor of Public Interest Law, Legal Ethics, Political Science and Policy, Planning, and Development at the University of Southern California.

Bryant G. Garth is Dean and Professor of Law at Southwestern Law School.

Rafael Gely is Judge Joseph P. Kinneary Professor of Law at the University of Cinncinati.

Robert P. George is McCormick Professor of Jurisprudence and Director of the James Madison Program in American Ideals and Institutions at Princeton University.

Howard Gillman is Dean of the College of Letters, Arts and Sciences and Professor of Political Science, History, and Law at the University of Southern California.

Tom Ginsburg is Professor of Law and Political Science and Director of the Program in Asian Law, Politics, and Society at the University of Illinois at Urbana-Champaign.

Mark A. Graber is Professor of Law and Government at the University of Maryland School of Law and the University of Maryland, College Park.

Susan Haire is Associate Professor of Political Science at the University of Georgia.

Christine B. Harrington is Professor of Politics at New York University.

Daniel Halberstam is Professor of Law and Director of the European Legal Studies Program at the University of Michigan at Ann Arbor.

Ran Hirschl is Professor of Political Science and Law and Canada Research Chair in Constitutionalism, Democracy, and Development at the University of Toronto.

R. Daniel Kelemen is Associate Professor of Political Science at Rutgers University.

Lewis A. Kornhauser is Alfred B. Engelberg Professor of Law at the New York University School of Law.

Matthew H. Kramer is Professor of Legal and Political Philosophy at the University of Cambridge and a Fellow of Churchill College, Cambridge.

R. A. Lenhardt is Associate Professor of Law at Fordham University School of Law.

Lynn Mather is Professor of Law and Political Science and Director of the Baldy Center for Law and Social Policy at the State University of New York at Buffalo.

Ugo Mattei is Alfred and Hanna Fromm Chair in International and Comparative Law at the University of California Hastings College of the Law.

Michael McCann is Gordon Hirabayashi Professor for the Advancement of Citizenship at the University of Washington.

Julie Novkov is Associate Professor of Political Science and Women's Studies at the State University of New York at Albany.

Luca G. Pes is a Ph.D. candidate in anthropology at the London School of Economics and Political Science.

Richard H. Pildes is Sudler Family Professor of Constitutional Law at New York University.

Daniel B. Rodriguez is Minerva House Drysdale Regents Chair in Law at the University of Texas School of Law.

Susan Rose-Ackerman is Henry R. Luce Professor of Jurisprudence at Yale University.

Frederick Schauer is Frank Stanton Professor of the First Amendment at Harvard University.

Stuart A. Scheingold is Professor Emeritus of Political Science at the University of Washington.

Kim Lane Scheppele is Laurence S. Rockefeller Professor of Public Affairs in the Woodrow Wilson School and the University Center for Human Values as well as Director of the Program in Law and Public Affairs at Princeton University.

Jeffrey A. Segal is SUNY Distinguished Professor and Chair of Political Science at Stony Brook University.

Beth Simmons is Clarence Dillon Professor of International Affairs in the Department of Government at Harvard University.

Martin Shapiro is James W. and Isabel Coffroth Professor of Law at the University of California at Berkeley.

Susan S. Silbey is Professor of Sociology and Anthropology at the Massachusetts Institute of Technology.

Wesley G. Skogan is Professor of Political Science at Northwestern University.

Rogers M. Smith is Christopher H. Browne Distinguished Professor of Political Science at the University of Pennsylvania.

Harold J. Spaeth is Research Professor of Law and Emeritus Professor of Political Science at Michigan State University.

Pablo T. Spiller is Jeffrey A. Jacobs Distinguished Professor of Business and Technology and Professor of Business and Public Policy at the University of California at Berkeley.

Christopher Tomlins is Senior Research Fellow at the American Bar Foundation.

Tom R. Tyler is University Professor of Psychology at New York University.

Georg Vanberg is Associate Professor of Political Science at the University of North Carolina at Chapel Hill.

Keith E. Whittington is William Nelson Cromwell Professor of Politics at Princeton University.

David A. Yalof is Associate Professor of Political Science at the University of Connecticut.

PART I

INTRODUCTION

CHAPTER 1

THE STUDY OF LAW AND POLITICS

KEITH E. WHITTINGTON
R. DANIEL KELEMEN
GREGORY A. CALDEIRA

Law is one of the central products of politics and the prize over which many political struggles are waged. The early American jurist James Wilson observed that law is the "great sinew of government" (Wilson 1896, 1: 314). It is the principal instrument by which the government exerts its will on society, and as such it might be thought to lie (at least indirectly) close to the heart of the study of politics. But law is also the means by which the government organizes itself. It is law in this second mode, sometimes called public law, that has attracted independent attention. Here law is not only the product of politics but also constitutive of politics.

The study of law and politics is a varied and multidisciplinary enterprise. From its starting point in political science of studying constitutional and administrative law, the field soon added courts, lawyers, and related legal actors to its purview. And the substantive scope of the field is broader now than it has ever been. Although the U.S. Supreme Court has always been the center of gravity within the field in American political science, the politics of law and courts in the international arena and in other countries is receiving growing attention and thriving communities of scholars continue to explore other aspects of law and courts beyond constitutional courts and peak appellate tribunals. The interdisciplinary connections of the study of law

The editors thank Rob Hunter for his able assistance his preparing the manuscript for publication.

and politics have varied over time, but, like the discipline of political science, the field of law and courts has readily borrowed concepts and methods from other disciplines. Active scholarly communities concerned with various aspects of law and politics in various disciplines make this a particularly good time for cross-disciplinary conversations among those in political science, and those in the humanities, the other social sciences, and the law schools.

This *Oxford Handbook of Law and Politics* is designed to reflect the diversity in the field today. With increasing diversity comes specialization, and there is always the danger that specialist scholars who are broadly concerned with law and politics will nonetheless find themselves sitting at Gabriel Almond's (1990) "separate tables," having separate conversations and missing some of the productive cross-fertilization that can take place across the field as a whole. Although we have not forced the individual authors in this volume to launch those new conversations, we hope readers will benefit from the breadth of the offerings.

Our starting point, however, is with the study of law *and* politics, or the political analysis of law and courts. Law, as an autonomous field of study as taught in schools of law, is centrally concerned with the substance of law and the practices of legal professionals. For the professional craft of law, the politics of law can often be bracketed. For scholars concerned with law and politics, it is the professional craft of law that is bracketed. We need not deny that legal reasoning and skill are real and matter in the determination and application of the law and in the actions of legal institutions. But the starting point for the study of law and politics is that politics matters and that considerable analytical and empirical leverage over our understanding of law and legal institutions can be gained by placing politics in the foreground.

1 THE DEVELOPMENT OF THE STUDY OF LAW AND POLITICS

The study of law and politics held a prominent place within the discipline of political science as academic disciplines and departments developed in the late nineteenth century. It was the narrow professionalism of the law school that spurred Columbia University in 1880 to create a separate School of Political Science, the progenitor of the discipline, under John Burgess, to develop and teach a "science of jurisprudence" that would provide better preparation for the new federal civil service. Within the school, a distinct Department of Public Law and Jurisprudence quickly emerged and was only decades later renamed the Department of Political Science. The first dissertations in political science, reflecting the strength of its faculty and the fact that most of its students had first passed through the law school, were dominated by constitutional and legal history (Hoxie et al. 1955; Somit and Tanenhaus 1967).

As the discipline developed internally, the study of law and politics, although prominent, became a distinct specialty within political science. The 1915 report of an American Political Science Association (APSA) committee on college instruction was chaired by Charles Grove Haines (1915, 356–357), one of the leading constitutional scholars of the period, and five of its twelve recommended core courses were on legal subjects (with a sixth dedicated to judicial administration and organization). Despite this endorsement, recommended courses such as commercial law and Roman law did not survive long in political science departments; and international law was soon crowded out by international relations, just as administrative law already had been by public administration. Constitutional law and jurisprudence became the core of the study of law and politics in political science, with legislation, administrative reports, and other legal materials the raw material of political science generally and other substantive areas of law being either absorbed into broader fields within the discipline or left entirely to the law schools.

The leading public law scholars prior to World War II were primarily constitutional scholars, often with an emphasis on history. With law schools by and large continuing to leave constitutional law in relative neglect, Edward Corwin, Charles Grove Haines, Thomas Reed Powell, and Robert E. Cushman were the leading constitutional scholars of their day, as well as leaders within the discipline (each served as president of the APSA). From 1917 to 1961, the association's flagship journal, the *American Political Science Review* (*APSR*), published an annual overview of the constitutional decisions of the U.S. Supreme Court, written by Cushman during much of that period, often supplemented with a separate review of state constitutional law decisions.

Their constitutional scholarship and teaching was simultaneously realist and normative in its sensibilities. As Corwin (1929, 592) understood it, the purpose of political science was to cultivate an understanding of "the true ends of the state and how best they may be achieved." A 1922 *APSR* article on constitutional law teaching reported that law school classes in constitutional law were generally regarded as too technical and too focused on litigation to be suitable to the training of graduate students, who required a better grasp of the "historical, philosophical, and comparative aspects of the subject" and how "fundamental principles" of American constitutionalism evolved over time. The undergraduate classes in constitutional law brought political action and behavior to the political science curriculum. The formal and descriptive character of courses in American and comparative government might be the starting point for understanding American politics, but constitutional law was the class in which students could see how principles, beliefs, actors, and social conditions interacted and developed; and a "problem method" of instruction could teach students the valuable skill of how to draft legislation that could address a given social problem while adhering to constitutional limitations (Hall 1922).

Constitutional scholarship of this sort continued in political science after World War II, but under increasing competitive pressure. A new generation of constitutional lawyers in the law schools was more prominent and more sophisticated than their predecessors. Political scientists such as Carl Swisher, Alpheus Mason, David Fellman, and John Roche continued this humanistic tradition of constitutional studies well into the 1960s, but their successors were fewer and increasingly marginal to the discipline.[1] Others such as Martin Diamond, Herbert Storing, Walter Berns, and again Alpheus Mason drifted further into political theory and American political thought. It is telling that in a 1958 volume on the state of the discipline, two prominent constitutional scholars, Robert McCloskey (1958) and Carl Friedrich (1958), were invited to discuss "political theory" rather than public law.

Within the discipline, the study of law and politics was generally shifting away from constitutional law and thought and toward judicial politics. Although there were some tentative earlier efforts to pursue quantitative studies of judicial behavior and to consider the political and social influences on judicial decision-making, C. Herman Pritchett (1948, 1954) pushed the field in a significant new direction with his statistical studies of voting behavior on the Supreme Court in the 1930s and 1940s (Murphy and Tanenhaus 1972, 17–20). With a different methodological and conceptual approach, Jack Peltason (1955, 1961) likewise sought to open the field up by looking beyond constitutional decisions and the Supreme Court and focusing more broadly on the judicial process as it related the courts as policy-makers and administrators to one another, the broader political system, and the relevant political environment. These emerging works in judicial politics had in common a single-minded focus on the political behavior of judges and those with whom they interacted, analyzed as other political actors might be analyzed and largely stripped of substantive legal content, historical development, or philosophical implication.

Works on the political behavior of judges and associated actors proliferated in the 1960s and soon dominated the field (Pritchett 1968; Schubert 1966). Among others, Pritchett and Walter Murphy gave close study to the rising hostility in Congress to the federal judiciary and its decisions. David Danelski, Sheldon Goldman, and Joel Grossman unpacked the judicial recruitment and selection process. Martin Shapiro resuscitated administrative law and the policy-making role of the courts outside of constitutional law. Walter Murphy, Alpheus Mason, and J. Woodward Howard uncovered the internal operations of the courts. Clement Vose focused attention on litigants and the relevance of interest groups to the judiciary. In-depth studies of the implementation of and compliance with judicial decisions were undertaken. Glendon Schubert, Harold Spaeth, Sidney Ulmer, and a host of others followed directly on Pritchett and built sophisticated statistical analyses of judicial voting behavior. Several scholars made tentative efforts at

---

[1] Carl Swisher in 1960, Charles Hyneman in 1962, and Carl Friedrich in 1963 were the last constitutionalists to be honored with the APSA presidency. The last law and politics scholar to serve as APSA president was C. Herman Pritchett in 1964.

public opinion research and comparative analysis. Although the use of statistical techniques received the most attention and was most controversial, the methodologies employed were varied and included archival research, judicial biographies, field studies, game theory, and more.

Subsequent movements have deepened and broadened these developments in the study of law and politics in political science. The interdisciplinary law-and-society movement reinforced the behavioralist turn in political science but added a greater interest in the operation of law and courts closest to the ground—criminal justice, the operation of the trial courts, juries, dispute resolution, the behavior of lawyers, the informal penetration of law into the social, economic, and cultural spheres—and fostered new conversations about law and politics across the social sciences. The empirical study of tribunals and law in the international arena and outside the United States has grown rapidly in recent years, fostering connections between the study of law and courts and the study of comparative politics and international relations. Historical institutionalist studies have recovered an interest in constitutional ideas and historical development and wedded it to the post-behavioralist concern with political action and the broader political system. Game theoretic accounts of political strategy have come forth and provided new perspectives on judicial behavior and new approaches to linking courts with other political institutions.

2 THE STRUCTURE OF THE FIELD

There is no single best way to divide up the field of law and politics. Literatures overlap, and it is possible to view those literatures at different levels of aggregation or with different points of emphasis so as to highlight commonalities or differences. Indeed, the prior discussion suggests a basic bifurcation in the field, between constitutional law and jurisprudence on the one side and judicial process and politics on the other. But this basic bifurcation better reflects the historical evolution of the field than it does the current structure of the study of law and politics. We offer below one map of the field.

2.1 Jurisprudence and the Philosophy of Law

Jurisprudence and the philosophy of the law is the oldest aspect of the study of law and politics and stands conceptually at its foundation. Jurisprudence is concerned with the basic nature of law. It has sought to identify the essential elements of law, distinguishing the realm of law from other aspects of the social order and other forms of social control. In an older tradition, jurisprudence hoped to systematize legal knowledge, extracting and refining the central principles of the law and the logical coherence of the legal system as a whole. In this mode, jurisprudence was to be an essential tool of the legal teacher, scholar, and practitioner and the starting point of a legal science. When wedded to normative commitments and theories, jurisprudence was also a tool of legal reform, identifying where the law needed to be worked pure and how best to do so.

A primary task of jurisprudence is to answer the question: What is law? It seeks to identify the common features of a legal system and clarify the logical structure of law. To do so requires distinguishing law from other normative systems of social ordering, such as custom and religion. Basic to this inquiry has been the effort to identify the conditions that would render a norm legally valid. Two well-established schools of thought have developed around these questions, with natural lawyers contending that the legal validity of a rule depends in part on its substantive morality and legal positivists arguing that legal validity is potentially independent of morality and solely a function of social convention. Related to this issue are such concerns as clarifying the nature of legal concepts such as rights and duties, identifying the kinds of reasons by which legal authority is established and legal obligations are created, and explicating the process of legal reasoning. Supplementing analytical approaches to these issues are distinctively normative jurisprudential theories, which are concerned with which legal rights and obligations are most justified, how best to reason about the law, and the like.

These predominant branches of jurisprudence have been periodically challenged by self-consciously realist theories of law that attempt to ground the basic features of law in social conditions. From Roscoe Pound's sociological jurisprudence onward, realist theorists have questioned whether law can be profitably analyzed in the abstract, apart from its relationship with external conditions, whether economic relations, human behavior, or something else. The linkage of legal theory with such empirical concerns has supported both critical theories aimed at subverting dominant jurisprudential models and more positive theories concerned with developing their own understandings of the law.

2.2 Constitutional Law, Politics and Theory

Constitutional law is often paired with jurisprudence. The subfields share interests in the substance of law and ideas surrounding law. They also share an interest in normative aspects of law. But where jurisprudence is concerned with the conceptual underpinnings of law writ large, constitutional law is concerned with the legal and theoretical foundations of a particular, and a particular kind of, political order.

The subfield has long been concerned with constitutional law itself. In this vein, political scientists have, along with legal scholars, explored the doctrinal developments in particular areas of law. In addition, however, political scientists have been somewhat more likely to examine the intellectual history of constitutional concepts and modes of thought, the normative underpinnings of constitutional principles, the constitutional philosophies of individual justices or historical eras, and the relationship between constitutional law and broader political and social currents. Political scientists have been attracted to constitutional law as intellectual historians, normative political theorists, and social theorists, as well as legal doctrinalists.

In recent years, the study of constitutional law per se has been submerged within the broader subject of constitutional politics. Although there have been notable exceptions, constitutional law has traditionally been the particular subject area within which political scientists have explored the origin, development, and application of legal principles and the interaction of courts and judges with other institutions and actors on the political stage. Whether taking the form of individual case histories or broader analyses, the making of constitutional law can be studied like the making of other forms of public policy. Constitutional politics highlights the ways in which the creation of constitutional law is situated within a broader political, institutional, and intellectual context and the significance of actors other than judges in contributing to constitutional policy-making.

2.3 Judicial Politics

The field within political science that studies law and politics was once widely known as "public law." For many, it is now known as "judicial politics." The behavioral revolution of the 1960s shifted the disciplinary center of gravity from the study of constitutional law and doctrine to the study of courts, judges, and company. The political process by which courts are constituted and legal decisions are made and implemented is central to empirical research in the field.

Originally, the study of the voting behavior of individual judges, in particular the justices on the Supreme Court, formed the core of the study of judicial politics: Why do judges vote as they do, as opposed to the how and the why of the reasons they give in opinions? What do the patterns of votes within the Court and other collegial courts tell us about these institutions as political actors? Now, judicial voting is but a part, albeit an important part, of the study of judicial politics. Scholars increasingly are taking a broader view, and are attempting to study the behavior of judges and courts in the political process, as just one more group or political actor among many others, including other courts and judges, executives, legislatures, interest groups, lawyers, and ordinary citizens.

2.4 Law and Society

Law and society is not a subfield within political science, but rather an interdisciplinary enterprise that has long invited political scientists to explore a broader range of legal phenomena and to employ a broader range of methodologies. Law and society scholarship explores the reciprocal impact of law on society and of society on law—with some scholars focusing on the role of law as an instrument of social change or social control and others focusing on how social mobilization, culture, and legal consciousness determine the actual impact of law. With its roots in the legal realism scholarship of the 1950s, law and society scholarship proliferated in the 1960s with the founding of the Law and Society Association in the United States. Today the field of law and society includes a vibrant mix of scholars from political science, sociology, anthropology, history, and law who draw on a variety of methods and epistemological premises.

Law and society scholarship has served as an important antidote to the tendency of most political scientists interested in law and courts to focus almost exclusively on the upper echelons of the judicial hierarchy and the storied battles between high courts and other branches of government. The law and society perspective has encouraged many political scientists to turn their gaze to the local level, to explore how law is mobilized, how it is experienced, and what impact it has across society in fields as diverse as criminal law, civil rights, and business regulation. Such contributions are perhaps most obvious in studies of legal mobilization and the impact of law, where law and society scholarship has shed light on the conditions under which social movements mobilize law in pursuit of their aims. Law and society has also encouraged a comparative perspective, with the field shifting from its roots in studies of the American legal system to embrace an increasingly wide range of scholarship on comparative and transnational socio-legal issues. Some scholars (Provine, 2007) suggest a growing rift between much of political science and the field of law and society, as the latter shifts away from an interest in formal institutions of law and government and from positivist social science. Given the fruitful engagement of political science and law and society over the past half-century, the growth of any such rift would be unfortunate.

2.5 Comparative and International Law and Courts

Until recently, the subfield of comparative politics largely ignored law and politics, while the subfield of law and politics largely ignored law and courts outside the US. Today change is coming from both directions. Comparativists are taking greater interest in the politics of law and courts, and scholars in the law and politics subfield are increasingly doing comparative work. Current scholarship builds on the work of such pioneers as Murphy and Tanenhaus (1972), Schubert and Danelski

(1969), Shapiro (1981), Kommers (1989), Stone (1992), and Volcansek (1992), who set out a research agenda, calling on others to examine and compare the influence of courts on politics and the influence of politics on courts across democracies. Although most of the early work focused exclusively on the politics of constitutional courts in established democracies, more recent work has expanded in two directions. First, the transitions to democracy in the 1980s and 1990s gave birth to a host of new constitutional courts in Latin America, Eastern Europe, and Asia which have spawned a new wave of scholarly research (see for instance Ginsburg and Chavez, this volume). Second, in studying the widespread "judicialization" of politics, comparativists have moved beyond an exclusive focus on constitutional courts to examine the role of the full range of administrative and civil courts in policy-making and implementation.

In the study of international law, the growing dialogue between legal scholars and political scientists has generated a rich literature. The institutionalist turn in international relations theory and the proliferation of international courts and law-based regimes have drawn more and more political scientists to the study of international law and legal institutions. Meanwhile, recognizing the limits of a strictly legal analysis, legal scholars have turned to international relations theory to help explain the design, operation, and impact of international rules and legal institutions. Finally, research on themes such as the globalization of law (see Garth, this volume) and European legal integration (see Alter, this volume) tie together comparative and international approaches, examining how international institutions and networks may spread legal norms and practices across jurisdictions.

3 THE ORGANIZATION OF THE VOLUME

The organization of *The Oxford Handbook of Law and Politics* is related to but does not strictly follow the basic structure of the field. Parts of the field, primarily as it exists outside the discipline of political science, have been adequately covered or covered in more detail elsewhere (Coleman and Shapiro 2002; Cane and Tushnet 2003; Sarat 2004), and we have not sought to replicate those efforts here. Additionally, it is useful to provide perspective on some issues that cut across the field as a whole and not only burrow into its various components.

We should also explicitly note that the organization of the volume does not simply mirror the existing distribution of research on law and politics within the discipline. There is little question that the empirical study of various aspects of the U.S. Supreme Court, and more broadly the federal appellate courts in the United States, has occupied more scholarly attention in recent decades than has any other single aspect of law and courts. We have consciously downsized the Supreme Court in order to reflect the conceptual diversity of the field and the emergence in recent years of new areas of study that are of broad interest.

Approaches reviews three prominent traditions of empirical analysis of law and politics and, indeed, politics more broadly: judicial behavior, strategic action, and historical institutionalism. These traditions have provided some basic conceptual approaches to identifying and examining problems in law and politics, though in practice they are not mutually exclusive or obvious rivals. They do, however, offer different perspectives on what about law and courts is of interest and importance and which aspects of politics are likely to be relevant and useful to understanding the development of law and the behavior of courts and associated actors.

Comparative Judicial Politics focuses on questions of law and courts in a global context. In some instances, the tools and questions that have been used to study American courts have simply been exported for use in studying courts elsewhere. Significantly, however, the global context raises distinctive issues for consideration and offers new opportunities for theoretical and methodological development. Issues that have been given some historical consideration but that have less immediate salience in the American context, such as the role of courts and the rule of law in economic development and democratization, are of immediate importance in many parts of the world. In the wake of recent waves of democratization and economic liberalization, these topics are now receiving greater scholarly attention within political science and cognate fields. Other issues of contemporary relevance in the United States, such as the foundations of judicial independence, have in the past nonetheless received only limited attention in the American context. The global context has both increased interest in such issues and provided new leverage for analyzing them and sometimes alerted us to the importance of these issues in the United States. This section raises issues of law and politics common to many countries.

International and Supranational Law gives attention to several issues involving international law and tribunals. The study of international law was present at the origins of the discipline, but was quickly pushed to its margins. Recent developments in the international arena have drawn political scientists back into the study of international law. The sovereignty and political autonomy of nation states have been challenged and modified in various ways by new international institutions, changing norms and political pressures, and the transformation of global economic relationships. These changes clearly implicate law and courts, which have been both the instruments and sometimes the cause of the shifting international order.

Forms of Legal Order focuses on some aspects of how law constitutes and orders political and social relationships. Traditionally the study of law and courts in political science has not attended to the myriad ways in which law is used to structure and shape society. The policy consequences of different regimes of tort law, criminal law, business organization, tax law, and the like have largely been left to others, with the partial exception of how such legal regimes might themselves have political consequences, as with the growing interest in felon disenfranchisement. How law structures politics and how law is used to govern the government itself are of traditional concern, though they have often been in eclipse. Recent years have seen a resurgence of scholarly activity in this area, often operating at the disciplinary boundaries between political scientists and lawyers, and the future promises further advances with political scientists as both producers and consumers.

Sources of Law and Theories of Jurisprudence incorporates the philosophy of law into the *Handbook*. American political science has often been a somewhat languid consumer of jurisprudence. Both scholarship and teaching in this area have gradually migrated out of political science departments and into philosophy departments and law schools. Outside the United States, however, jurisprudence remains a thriving field for politics faculty, and important pockets of activity remain within the United States, with public law and political theory remaining a natural pairing for many. Indeed, jurisprudence is a natural point of connection between philosophical and empirical pursuits and addresses fundamental conceptual and normative features of politics and the state. As such, it is a subfield to which political science as a discipline should have much to contribute and from which it should be able to learn.

The American Judicial Context embraces aspects of both judicial politics and law and society, where much of the empirical work in law and politics has been done. It focuses on various features of the immediate institutional environment of the courts and the participants in the judicial process, including the recruitment of judges to the federal and state benches, several of the central questions in the study of the Supreme Court, empirical and theoretical perspectives on the vertical and horizontal relations among appellate courts, how and why lawyers and litigants do and often do not use the law to achieve their purposes, and the roles of lawyers and the legal profession in the politics of law.

The Political and Policy Environment of Courts in the United States examines further aspects of how courts, politics, and society have intersected in the United States. Whereas the prior section focused on particular institutions and actors that engage the courts, this section examines the broader environment within which courts operate and situates the actions of the courts within policy and ideological contexts. These two sections consider some of the central issues and concerns in the contemporary empirical literature on law and politics in the United States.

Interdisciplinary Approaches to Law and Politics reviews several recent interdisciplinary movements in the study of law and politics and how they intersect with and are of interest to political science. Each of these movements has spawned organized scholarly societies and journals of its own and linked the law schools to other disciplines and departments within the universities. Although political scientists have been the most prominent participants in the law-and-society movement, each offers bridges to aspects of political science as well as to other disciplines.

Old and New offers more personal perspectives on how the study of law and politics has developed over the past generation and where it might be headed in the next. Stuart Scheingold, Martin Shapiro, and Harold Spaeth have long operated on different frontiers of the field, helping to make and consolidate the behavioral revolution in law and politics and to realize its promise over the past decades. To conclude the volume, they bring to bear that experience in assessing how the field has developed.

REFERENCES

ALMOND, G. A. 1990. *A Discipline Divided: Schools and Sects in Political Science.* Newbury Park, Calif.: Sage.

CANE, P., and TUSHNET, M. 2003. *The Oxford Handbook of Legal Studies.* New York: Oxford University Press.

COLEMAN, J., and SHAPIRO, S. 2002. *The Oxford Handbook of Jurisprudence and Philosophy of Law.* New York: Oxford University Press.

CORWIN, E. S. 1929. The democratic dogma and the future of political science. *American Political Science Review*, 23: 569–92.

FRIEDRICH, C. J. 1958. Political philosophy and the science of politics. In *Approaches to the Study of Politics*, ed. R. Young. Evanston, Ill.: Northwestern University Press.

HAINES, C. G. 1915. Report of the committee of seven on instruction in colleges and universities. *American Political Science Review*, 9: 353–74.

HALL, A. B. 1922. The teaching of constitutional law. *American Political Science Review* 16: 486–96.

HOXIE, R. G. et al. 1955. *A History of the Faculty of Political Science, Columbia University.* New York: Columbia University Press.

KOMMERS, D. 1989. *The Constitutional Jurisprudence of the Federal Republic of Germany.* Durham, NC: Duke University Press.

McCLOSKEY, R. G. 1958. American political thought and the study of politics. In *Approaches to the Study of Politics*, ed. R. Young. Evanston, Ill.: Northwestern University Press.

MURPHY, W. F., and TANENHAUS, J. 1972. *The Study of Public Law.* New York: Random House.

PELTASON, J. W. 1955. *Federal Courts in the Political Process.* New York: Random House.

——— 1961. *Fifty-Eight Lonely Men.* New York: Harcourt, Brace and World

PRITCHETT, C. H. 1948. *The Roosevelt Court.* New York: Macmillan.

——— 1954. *Civil Liberties and the Vinson Court.* Chicago: University of Chicago Press.

——— 1968. Public law and judicial behavior. *Journal of Politics*, 30: 480–509.

PROVINE, D. M. 2007. Law & society symposium: on separate paths. *Law and Courts, Newsletter of the Law and Courts Section of the American Political Science Association*, 17: 6–8.

SARAT, A. 2004. *The Blackwell Companion to Law and Society.* Malden, Mass.: Blackwell.

SCHUBERT, G. A. 1966. The future of public law. *George Washington Law Review*, 34: 593–614.

—— and DANELSKI, D. J., eds. 1969. *Comparative Judicial Behavior: Cross-Cultural Studies of Political Decision Making in East and West.* New York: Oxford University Press.

SHAPIRO, M. 1981. *Courts: A Comparative and Political Analysis.* Chicago: University of Chicago Press.

SOMIT, A., and TANENHAUS, J. 1967. *The Development of Political Science: From Burgess to Behavioralism.* Boston: Allyn and Bacon.

STONE, A. 1992. *The Birth of Judicial Politics in France.* New York: Oxford University Press.

VOLCANSEK, M. 1992. *Judicial Politics and Policy-Making in Western Europe.* London: Cass.

WILSON, J. 1896. *The Works of James Wilson,* ed. J. DeWitt Andrews, 2 vols. Chicago: Callaghan.

PART II

APPROACHES

JUDICIAL BEHAVIOR

JEFFREY A. SEGAL

WHAT do judges do and why do they do it? The answers to these questions fall within the realm of judicial behavior, the study of which consists of systematic, empirical, theoretically based attempts to explain what courts and judges do. It is open to theoretical approach—legal, strategic, institutional, attitudinal, whatever—but excludes descriptive doctrinal approaches (i.e. what the law is), prescriptive norma- tive approaches (what the law should be), and purely deductive formal approaches.[1]

So what then is it that judges do? Legal realists commonly assert that judges act like "single minded seekers of legal policy" (quoted in George and Epstein 1992, 325). Nevertheless, the extent to which judges *choose* to act in such a manner and the extent to which they *can realize their goals* by acting in such a manner is the subject of much debate. Thus, Gibson notes, "judges' decisions are a function of what they prefer to do, tempered by what they think they ought to do, but constrained by what they perceive is feasible to do" (1983, 7).

The extent to which judges choose to move beyond their policy preferences divides the field of law and politics. Normatively, influences over what judges ought to do include evaluating legal rules such as precedent or legislative intent, in an attempt to find the best answers to cases before them. Thus, in addition to the judges' own preferences, legal influences should be useful in explaining judicial

I thank Elyce Winters for research assistance.

[1] These approaches may, among other things, provide invaluable hypotheses, but any such work that provides formal proofs without more is not a study of judicial behavior.

Table 2.1 A typology of judicial decision-making models on the merits

Source of influence	Temporal influence	
	Past	Present
Legislators	Text and Intent	Separation of Powers
Judges	Horizontal or Vertical Precedent	Attitudinal Model

behavior, though the extent to which it does undoubtedly varies throughout the judicial system.

Similarly, strategic approaches deal with what is feasible for judges to do. Voting their sincere preferences may not, in many cases, further judges' policy goals. Because courts do not make policy in isolation from judicial superiors or other branches of government, strategic judges must temper their decisions by what they *can* do or else risk being overturned.

These models can be usefully depicted according to the schematic in Table 2.1. Sources of influence include legislators and judges. When judges rely on previous judicial decisions, whether vertically from hierarchical superiors, or horizontally, from courts at their own level, they are following legal precedent. But, when judges follow their own (present) preferences, they behave consistently with their political attitudes. When judges rely on the preferences of the lawmakers of the statutes and constitutional provisions under consideration, they follow legal text and intent. But, when they defer strategically to the constraints imposed by current legislative majorities, they behave consistently with the separation-of-powers model.

Judicial politics can be law or politics, but frequently it is both, with the mixture dependent on the type of court and the context of the case.

1 MODELING LAW

Modeling law causes practical difficulties: we must be able to measure it. The arguments against empirically modeling law come from two sources: those who lacked the requisite imagination (e.g. Segal and Spaeth 1993, 33), and those philosophically opposed to the idea on the ground that legal decision-making is nothing more than "a sincere belief that their decision represents their best understanding of what the law requires" (Gillman 2001, 486).

Thus, under the latter approach, virtually any decision *can be* consistent with the legal model; and any decision *is* consistent with it so long as the judge has sincerely convinced herself that the decision is legally appropriate. The most basic problem with this approach is clear: the model is not falsifiable. Thus, by accepted standards of scientific research, the model cannot provide a valid explanation of what judges actually do.

It is impossible to know whether judges believe they are judging in good faith. The extensive psychological literature on motivated reasoning suggests that plausible arguments are all that decision-makers need to create an overlap between prior views and a subjective belief in correct results (Braman 2006), suggesting that good faith will not be all that difficult to come by.

Thus, those interested in modeling law must hold judges to a higher standard than "a sincere belief" in the appropriateness of their decisions; legal modelers must show that law has an independent and measurable influence. This does not, however, require a deterministic or mechanical approach to judicial decision-making and is not much different than viewing law as a gravitational force on decision-making.

To determine the impact of law is not much different to determining the impact of other social phenomena. Simply put, judges' decisions should change—not deterministically, but at the margins—as law changes, holding alternative phenomena constant.[2] This is easiest to see in the case of vertical *stare decisis*, where the strategic implications can be quite complex, but the essence of testing them requires little more than determining how lower court decisions change as higher court decisions change after controlling for other relevant factors such as case characteristics and the preferences of lower court judges. For example, it would not suffice simply to show that lower courts became more conservative during the Burger and Rehnquist courts, because Republican appointees during this era undoubtedly made both the upper and lower courts more conservative.

1.1 *Stare Decisis*

Despite early research showing substantial noncompliance with Supreme Court decisions (see Baum 1978), recent evidence indicates that judges on lower courts follow the preferences of judges on higher courts (Benesh and Martinek 2002). Overtly noncompliant decisions by Court of Appeals judges are exceedingly rare.

Why judges so frequently comply is a matter of dispute. According to legalistic accounts, the overwhelming number of lower court decisions that the Supreme Court must oversee, and the very few cases it chooses to hear, means that lower court judges have little fear of reversal. And to the extent that judicial decisions are binary, overturned outcomes are likely to be no worse than if the lower court had done the higher court's bidding in the first place. Thus judges presumably comply

---

[2] Nor should it change as legally irrelevant factors, such as the parties to a suit, change.

with the Supreme Court out of a belief that such behavior is legally appropriate (Cross 2005; Klein and Hume 2003). Strategic accounts, alternatively, argue that if judicial policy-making actually occurs over a continuous spectrum, the policy costs of reversal are real. Moreover, frequent reversal can limit the prospects for promotion. Since the likelihood of being reversed is a function of the lower court's level of compliance, fear of getting overturned can lead to a "compliance cascade" (Cross 2005) whereby lower courts compete to avoid being overturned by pushing their decisions closer and closer to the preferences of the higher court (Songer et al. 1994; McNollgast 1995). Certainly, the Supreme Court strategically uses both its certiorari jurisdiction (Cameron et al. 2000) and citations to its own precedents (Hansford and Spriggs 2006) as a means of obtaining compliance from lower courts.

One potential way through these competing explanations is with a thought experiment. What would happen if Congress denied the Supreme Court appellate jurisdiction over an issue? The legal reliance on Supreme Court precedent would arguably be the same, but the fear of override would literally be driven down to zero. If the issue area were abortion, would conservative lower court panels continue to uphold such rights? My hunch is that in salient issues such as this, the answer is no. In less salient areas, my hunch is still no, but with considerably less certainty.

Although tests for vertical *stare decisis* demonstrate compliance, testing for the horizontal impact of precedent poses substantially more difficulty. Once again, the task is to see how judges' behavior changes as law changes. Thus, we could try to determine how the behavior of Supreme Court judges changed on abortion rights following the massive change in law created by *Roe v. Wade* (1973). The problem, of course, is that we would be looking for this impact on the judges who created *Roe*. One way around this problem is to examine the impact of horizontal *stare decisis* on judges who dissented from the original ruling (cf. Gillman 2001). As Jerome Frank accurately stated, "Stare decisis has no bite when it means merely that a court adheres to a precedent that it considers correct. It is significant only when a court feels constrained to stick to a former ruling although the court has come to regard it as unwise or unjust" (*United States v. Shaughnessy* 1955, 719). This view equally applies to those who dissented on the original case but are faced with similar issues in subsequent cases. Thus, when Justice Stewart reversed his view in *Griswold v. Connecticut* (1965) and accepted the right to privacy in *Eisenstadt v. Baird* (1972), we have a *prima facie* case that *stare decisis* influenced the justice. Tests using this standard find that *stare decisis* influences the decisions of Supreme Court justices only about 10 percent of the time (Segal and Spaeth 1996; cf. Brenner and Stier 1996; Songer and Lindquist 1996), but it is worth noting that this percentage nearly doubles for the least salient of the Court's decisions (Spaeth and Segal 1999), suggesting the contingent nature of *stare decisis*, even within a court.

Alternatively, Richards and Kritzer (2002) proposed a "jurisprudential regime" approach to modeling law. This approach begins with fact-pattern analysis—using

case stimuli to predict judicial decisions—to argue that certain cases create jurisprudential regimes that shift the manner in which the Supreme Court treats
those stimuli. They show that the impact of different case stimuli, such as the
level of government involved or the identity of the speaker, on the likelihood of a
liberal decision vary before and after *Grayned v. City of Rockford* (1972), the First
Amendment decision requiring content neutrality. Although the impact of First
Amendment case stimuli vary significantly before and after 1972, the results also
show that they vary before and after 1960, 1961, 1962 etc.; and the differences are
higher in the years before *Grayned* than in the year of *Grayned*. Additionally, the
authors do not test alternative functional forms for the change. That a case fact had
a greater impact on the Court's decision after 1972 than before 1972 does not
indicate that the change occurred in 1972, and indeed, it does not indicate that
there was a discrete change at any time point. The impact of these case stimuli
could be changing steadily over time, rather than abruptly, as required by their
theory. Nevertheless, with further testing, this original line of research could readily
answer questions about horizontal *stare decisis* that clearly need to be answered.

1.2 Text and Intent

Assessing the impact of text and intent, like the impact of precedent, poses
difficulties, but not insurmountable ones. At least for text, we can start with the
notion that judicial behavior should change as the text of law changes. This sounds
trivial, but judicial behavior does not necessarily conform to obvious expectations.

Testing for the impact of text at the federal level poses certain problems, since
many of the laws we are interested in have not changed in over 200 years. This
problem makes the states a more natural laboratory to study such influence, and we
could examine the impact of text either diachronically or cross-sectionally. Neither
approach is without problems. Diachronically, judicial behavior should change over
time as statutory or constitutional text changes, and cross-sectionally, judicial behavior should change over space as different jurisdictions have different laws.

Testing the impact of text across jurisdictions, Baldez, Epstein, and Martin
(2006) find the presence of a state-level Equal Rights Amendment does not
influence the likelihood of ruling in favor of litigants pressing sex-discrimination
claims.[3] Moreover, there appears to be no impact of educational rights provisions
in state constitutions on the decision of state supreme courts to strike down
unequal funding provisions for public schools (Lundberg 2000). But constitutional
rights to privacy significantly increase the likelihood that state supreme courts will
nullify anti-abortion statutes (Brace, Hall, and Langer 1999).

---

[3] It does indirectly influence the probability that a court will use the strict-scrutiny standard by
about .12.

Cross-sectional analyses cannot be conducted at the federal level, and diachronic analyses will not be very helpful for the sort of constitutional provisions that interest public law scholars. How, then, through *a priori* measures and falsifiable tests can we systematically assess, text and intent as potential explanations for the justices' behavior? One possibility is to measure *legal arguments* rather than "law." If, for example, Justice Scalia is truly a textualist, he should be more willing to support a litigant who makes an textual claim—e.g. an undisputed claim that the plain meaning of the statutory text supports his side—than a litigant who makes no such claim, *ceteris paribus*.

In fact, while Justices Scalia and Thomas support liberal textual claims in less than half of the cases (45.3 and 47.6 percent respectively), these numbers are higher than their support for liberal parties lacking textual claims (Segal and Howard 2002). Similarly, Scalia and Thomas are more likely to support defendants' rights in criminal-justice disputes when those rights are supported by originalist arguments (Barkow 2006). For legislative or constitutional intent, though, Segal and Howard (2002) find little evidence that the justices respond to such claims.

Overall, though, these and other approaches have led to some conditional positive findings on the impact of law on judicial behavior, particularly in the lower courts. Yet, even where we would expect the influence of law to be the greatest, in vertical *stare decisis*, the results are mixed; and elsewhere, the impact has generally been minimal.

2 ATTITUDES

The attitudinal model holds that judges decide cases in light of their sincere ideological values juxtaposed against the factual stimuli presented by the case. Consider a search and seizure whose constitutionality the Court must determine. Assume that the police searched a person's house with a valid warrant supported by probable cause and there were no extenuating circumstances. The search uncovers an incriminating diary. Now imagine a second search, similar to the first in that probable cause existed, but in which the police failed to obtain a warrant.

We can place these searches in ideological space. Since the search with a warrant can be considered less intrusive than the search without the warrant, we place the first search to the left of the second search. This is diagrammed in Figure 2.1, where A represents the first search and B the second. Presumably, any search and seizure can be located on the line; the more invasive the search, the further to the right the search will fall. Points on the line where the searches lie are j-points.

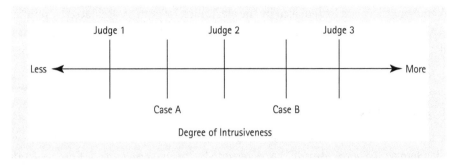

Fig. 2.1 Justices and cases in ideological space

Next, place the judges in ideological space. Consider three judges, 1, 2, and 3, respectively, liberal, moderate, and conservative. Judge 1 is so liberal that he would not even uphold the search in the first case. Thus we could place Judge 1 to the left of Case A. Judge 2 might not be quite so liberal as Judge 1; she would uphold the search of the home with a warrant, but would not uphold the warrantless search. Thus, we could place Judge 2 to the right of Case A but to the left of Case B. Finally, Judge 3 might find the warrant relatively unimportant and would uphold any search he considered reasonable, including Case B. Figure 2.1 places the justices in ideological space, with the markers for the judges representing their indifference points (i-points). Judges uphold all searches to the left of their indifference point, reject all searches to the right of their indifference point, and are indifferent about whether searches at that point are upheld or overturned.

Numerous behavioral implications follow from this model. At the case level, a court's decisions should depend in part on the factual stimuli in the case. This implication is consistent with, but not unique to, the attitudinal model. At the judge level, differences in judges' attitudes should influence aggregate and individual levels of ideological voting. Finally, the votes of particular judges in particular cases should depend on the interaction between the case stimuli and the judge's attitudes.

The likelihood of judges behaving consistently with the attitudinal model will depend on institutional incentives and disincentives for ideological behavior. Attitudinal behavior should be at its apogee for a court at the top of the judicial hierarchy and which therefore cannot be overruled by higher courts; where public opinion supports an independent judiciary, limiting legislative attempts to strike at the court; when the court has docket control and thus can weed out frivolous cases that no self-respecting judge could decide only on her ideology; when the judges enjoy life tenure; and when the judges lack ambition for higher office and thus have no incentive to placate others (Sisk, Heise, and Morriss 1998). Although legal realists might argue that discretion inheres in all judging, judges will have less discretion when judges can be overruled by higher courts, political culture disfavors judicial independence, legally determinate cases fill the docket, or when judges seek higher office, can be replaced by the electorate, or even assassinated by political enemies (Helmke 2002). "Your i-point or your life" should be an easy decision to make when threats are real.

2.1 The Supreme Court

The attitudinal model well fits behavior on the U.S. Supreme Court. At the case level, changes in case stimuli have repeatedly been shown to influence Court decisions (see Segal and Spaeth 2002, 312–20 for a review).

At the level of individual judges, the relationship between the justices' ideology (Segal and Cover 1989) and their behavior on the Court is quite strong. Ideally, the measure of the justices' behavior would be based on the policies they supported in the Court's written opinions, but such measures are not yet available (see Conclusion, below). Figure 2.2 thus shows the relationship between ideology and votes for all justices appointed since Earl Warren. The correlation coefficient, 0.78, demonstrates that the justices' ideology explains exceedingly well their aggregate voting behavior.

As for the juxtaposition between the justices' ideology and case stimuli, the model well predicts the Court's search and seizure decisions. A model combining

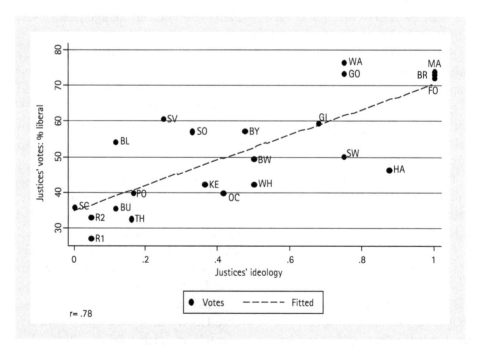

Fig. 2.2 Justices' votes by justices' ideology

the justices' attitudes and a series of case stimuli predicts 71 percent of the justices' votes correctly (Segal and Spaeth 1992, ch. 8).

2.2 Lower Courts

For various reasons, attitudes are unlikely to have the same impact on lower court judges' decisions that they do on Supreme Court justices' decisions. Consider, for example, the U.S. Courts of Appeals. First, and foremost, Court of Appeals judges are undoubtedly influenced by the decisions and preferences of the U.S. Supreme Court. When Samuel Alito voted as a Court of Appeals judge to strike New Jersey's partial birth abortion law, he was undoubtedly expressing the Supreme Court's preference, not his own. Second, the Courts of Appeals have mandatory jurisdiction and undoubtedly hear many cases where they simply lack decisional discretion. Third, the composition of panels matters, i.e. Court of Appeal judges appear to be substantially influenced by those who sit with them on particular panels. Democrats (Republicans) sitting on a panel with a Republican (Democratic) majority are much more likely to vote conservatively (liberally) than they otherwise would, at least on less salient issues (Revesz 1997; Sunstein, Schkade, and Ellman 2004). Yet, in other situations, the minority on the panel, a "whistleblower," can influence the majority by threatening to reveal doctrinal deviation to the higher court (Cross and Tiller

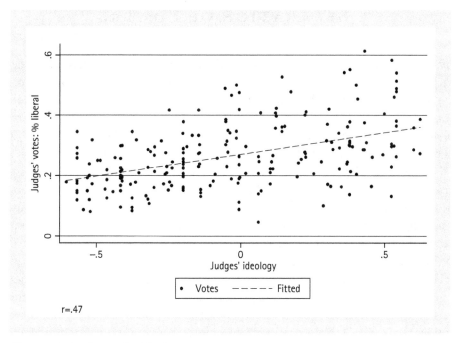

Fig. 2.3 Judges' votes by ideology

1998). And the presence of women and minorities on panels independently influences the decisions of those who sit with them (Farhang and Wawro 2004).

Figure 2.3 examines the relationship between ideology and liberal voting percentages on the U.S. Courts of Appeals. The data come from Songer's United States Court of Appeals database for all judges who voted in twenty or more civil liberties cases (criminal procedure, First Amendment, civil rights, due process and privacy). The ideology of judges on the Courts of Appeals comes from the well-validated scores created by Giles, Hettinger, and Peppers (2001), rescaled so that liberal scores have higher values and the predicted relationship between attitudes and votes is positive. Although the fit is pretty good—indeed, it would be hard to imagine any other variable that explains so substantial a proportion of the judges' voting behavior—obviously much more is at work on the Court of Appeals than just ideology.

Reliable measures of judges' attitudes are much more difficult to create for state courts, so partisanship is frequently used as a proxy for ideology (cf. Brace, Langer, and Hall 2000). Pinello's (1999) meta-analysis reports substantially lower relationships than reported here for federal courts, and indeed, at the state trial-court level, there appears to be no correlation between the judges' ideology and behavior (Gibson 1978; Narduli, Fleming, and Eisenstein 1984).

3 SEPARATION OF POWERS

Separation of powers (SoP) models examine the degree to which courts must defer to legislative majorities in order to prevent overrides that result in a policy worse than what the court might have achieved through sophisticated behavior. Consider the example in Figure 2.4, where the Court must decide a case in two-dimensional policy space. The game is played as follows. First, the Court makes a decision in (x_1, x_2) policy space. Second, the House and Senate can override the Court's decision if they agree on an alternative. H, S, and C represent the ideal points of the House, Senate, and Court, respectively. The line segment HS represents the set of irreversible decisions, i.e. no decision on the line can be overturned by Congress because improving the position of one chamber by moving closer to its ideal point necessarily worsens the position of the other. Alternatively, any decision off of HS, call it x, can be overturned, because there will necessarily be at least one point on HS that H and S prefer to x. Imagine, for example, a decision at the Court's ideal point, C. The arc I_S represents those points where the Senate is indifferent to this decision, with the Senate preferring any point inside the arc to any point on or outside the arc. Similarly, I_H represents the points where the House is indifferent to the Court's decision. Thus, both the House and Senate prefer any point between

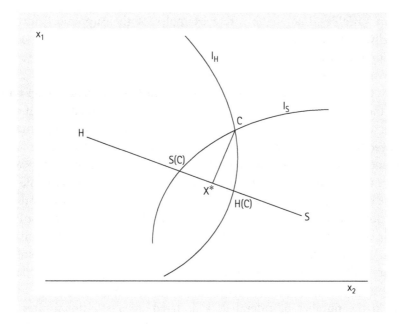

Fig. 2.4 The SoP model
H=House ideal point; S=Senate ideal point; C=Court ideal point; I_H=House indifference curve; I_S=Senate indifference curve; S(C)=Point on Set of Irreversible Decisions where Senate is indifferent to Court ideal point; H(C)=Point on Set of Irreversible Decisions where House is indifferent to Court ideal point; X*=equilibrium.

S(C) (the point on the set of irreversible decisions where the Senate is indifferent to the Court's decision) and H(C) (the point on the set of irreversible decisions where the House is indifferent to the Court's decision) to a decision at C.

What, then, should a strategic Court do in this situation? If the Court rules at its ideal point or, indeed, any place off the set of irreversible decisions, Congress will overturn the Court's decision and replace it with something that is worse from the Court's perspective. For example, if the Court rules at C, then Congress's response will be someplace between S(C) and H(C). The trick for the Court is to find the point on the set of irreversible decisions closest to its ideal point. By the Pythagorean Theorem, the Court accomplishes this by dropping a perpendicular onto the line. Thus, rather than ruling sincerely at C and ending up with a policy between S(C) and H(C), the Court rules at X*, the point between S(C) and H(C) it most prefers.

Separation-of-powers games vary in a variety of details, such as the number of issue dimensions, number of legislative chambers, influence of committees, existence of a presidential veto, etc. Regardless of the specific assumptions made, these models generally assume that the Court will construe legislation as close to its ideal point as possible without getting overturned by Congress (Ferejohn and Shipan 1990).

Despite its elegance, empirical support for the SoP model is not so clear-cut. Many articles on the SoP model are simply case studies—often selected on the dependent variable—that demonstrate examples of the Supreme Court acting strategically. Systematic analyses, though, report mixed results at best (Eskridge 1991), with the vast majority of studies reporting no impact (see Segal and Spaeth 2002, ch. 8 for a thorough review.)

Perhaps one reason the results typically do not work is that these studies typically examine the SoP model at the court that is perhaps most insulated from external influence: the U.S. Supreme Court. Judges on the Argentinian Supreme Court (Iaryczower, Spiller, and Tommasi 2006), Japanese lower court (Ramseyer and Rasmussen 2001), and U.S. state supreme courts (Brace and Hall 1990) appear more responsive to their political environments than justices on the U.S. Supreme Court.

Despite the lack of success in explaining the Supreme Court's statutory decisions as a function of congressional preferences, scholars have expanded the SoP model to include constitutional cases, at least theoretically (Rosenberg 1992). Empirically, although Whittington (2005) suggests that judicial review can be a tool of the dominant coalition, there is little systematic evidence to support strategic deference by the Court in constitutional cases. Friedman and Harvey (2003) argue that the increase in the number of federal laws declared unconstitutional after 1994 is evidence that a strategic, conservative Court found itself free to overturn legislation following the 1994 Congressional elections. But this increase in activism also came, with a short lag, after the Court gained a fifth vote for conservative activism with the appointment of Clarence Thomas in 1991. Thus, Segal and Westerland (2005) find that the conservatism of the Court, not its ideological distance from the current Congress, best explains the annual number of federal statutes that the Court struck down between 1949 and 2001.

4 CONCLUSION

There is of course much more to judicial behavior than covered in this chapter, which has focused on judges' decisions on the merits, with particular attention on four important models of judicial behavior. My focus has excluded important merits-related topics such as public opinion and the effect of the solicitor general, and broader studies on granting discretionary review (Caldeira, Wright, and Zorn 1999; Brenner 1979) and opinion writing (Epstein and Knight 1998; Hettinger, Linquist, and Martinek 2006; Maltzman, Spriggs, and Wahlbeck 2000).

A persistent complaint about virtually all of the "merits" work cited above is that it measures votes, e.g. a judge's decision to vote liberally or conservatively in a case or a series of cases, but what we're really interested in is the policy established by the judge or court (Friedman 2006). Nevertheless, there is a substantial relationship between the votes judges cast and the policies set forth in their opinions (Wenzel 1995). Yet Wenzel's findings are limited, and thus should not assuage us.

Recent work by McGuire and Vanberg (2005) opens up the possibility of more accurate and reliable recordings of judicial policy-making. Utilizing the computer-based Wordscore program, which has been used to map the ideology of political parties, McGuire and Vanberg have mapped the ideological positioning of Supreme Court opinions. The application of this technology should have a huge impact on our ability to better understand judicial behavior.

References

BALDEZ, L., EPSTEIN, L., and MARTIN, A. D. 2006. Does the U.S. Constitution need an ERA? *Journal of Legal Studies*, 35: 243–83.

BARKOW, R. 2006. Originalists, politics, and criminal law on the Rehnquist Court. *George Washington Law Review*, 74: 1043–77.

BAUM, L. 1978. Lower court response to supreme court decisions: reconsidering a negative picture. *Justice System Journal*, 3: 208–19.

BENESH, S. C., and MARTINEK, W. L. 2002. State supreme court decision-making in confession cases. *Justice System Journal*, 23: 109–34.

BRACE, P., and HALL, M. G. 1990. Neo-institutionalism and dissent in state supreme courts. *Journal of Politics*, 52: 54–70.

—— —— and LANGER, L. 1999. Judicial choice and the politics of abortion: institutions, context, and the autonomy of courts. *Albany Law Review*, 62: 1265–300.

—— LANGER, L., and HALL, M. G. 2000. Measuring the preferences of state supreme court justices. *Journal of Politics*, 62: 387–413.

BRAMAN, E. 2006. Reasoning on the threshold: testing the separability of preferences in legal decision-making. *Journal of Politics*, 68: 308–21.

BRENNER, S. 1979. The new certiorari game. *Journal of Politics*, 41: 649–55.

—— and STIER, M. 1996. Retesting Segal and Spaeth's *stare decisis* model. *American Journal of Political Science*, 40: 1036–48.

CALDEIRA, G., WRIGHT, J. R., and ZORN, C. J. W. 1999. Strategic voting and gatekeeping in the Supreme Court. *Journal of Law, Economics and Organization*, 15: 549–72.

CAMERON, C. M., SEGAL, J. A., and SONGER, D. 2000. Strategic auditing in a political hierarchy: an informational model of the Supreme Court's certiorari decisions. *American Political Science Review*, 94: 101–16.

CROSS, F. B. 2005. Appellate court adherence to precedent. *Journal of Empirical Legal Studies*, 2: 369–405.

—— and TILLER, E. H. 1998. Judicial partisanship and obedience to legal doctrine: whistle-blowing on the federal courts of appeals. *Yale Law Journal*, 107: 2155–76.

EPSTEIN, L., and KNIGHT, J. 1998. *The Choices Justices Make*. Washington, DC: Congressional Quarterly Press.

ESKRIDGE, Jr., W. N. 1991. Reneging on history? Playing the Court/Congress/President civil rights game. *California Law Review*, 79: 613–84.

FARHANG, S., and WAWRO, G. 2004. Institutional dynamics on the U.S. Court of Appeals: minority representation under panel decision-making. *Journal of Law, Economics and Organization*, 20: 299–330.

FEREJOHN, J., and SHIPAN, C. 1990. Congressional influence on bureaucracy. *Journal of Law, Economics and Organization*, 6: 1–20.

FRIEDMAN, B. 2006. Taking law seriously. *Perspectives on Politics*, 4: 261–76.

—— and HARVEY, A. 2003. Electing the Supreme Court. *Indiana Law Journal*, 78: 123–52

GEORGE, T. E., and EPSTEIN, L. 1992. On the nature of Supreme Court decision-making. *American Political Science Review*, 86: 323–37.

GIBSON, J. L. 1978. Judges' role orientations, attitudes, and decisions: an interactive model. *American Political Science Review*, 72: 911–24.

—— 1983. From simplicity to complexity: the development of theory in the study of judicial behavior. *Political Behavior*, 5: 7–49.

GILES, M. W., HETTINGER, V. A., and PEPPERS, T. 2001. Picking federal judges: a note on policy and partisan selection agendas. *Political Research Quarterly*, 54: 623–41.

GILLMAN, H. 2001. What's law got to do with it? Judicial behavioralists test the "legal model" of judicial decision-making. *Law and Social Inquiry*, 26: 465–504.

HANSFORD, T. G., and SPRIGGS, J. F., II. 2006. *The Politics of Precedent on the U.S. Supreme Court*. Princeton, NJ: Princeton University Press.

HELMKE, G. 2002. The logic of strategic defection: court-executive relations in Argentina under dictatorship and democracy. *American Political Science Review*, 96: 291–303.

HETTINGER, V. A., LINDQUIST, S. A., and MARTINEK, W. L. 2006. *Judges on a Collegial Court: Influence on Federal Appellate Decision Making*. Charlottesville: University of Virginia Press.

IARYCZOWER, M., SPILLER, P. T., and TOMMASI, M. 2006. Judicial lobbying: the politics of labor law constitutional interpretation. *American Political Science Review*, 100: 85–97.

KLEIN, D. E., and HUME, R. J. 2003. Fear of reversal as an explanation of lower court compliance. *Law and Society Review*, 37: 579–606.

LUNDBERG, P. J. 2000. State courts and school funding: a fifty-state analysis. *Albany Law Review*, 63: 1101–46.

MALTZMAN, F., SPRIGGS, J. F. II, and WAHLBECK, P. J. 2000. *Crafting Law on the Supreme Court: The Collegial Game*. New York: Cambridge University Press.

McGUIRE, K. T., and VANBERG, G. 2005. Mapping the policies of the U.S. Supreme Court: data, opinions, and constitutional law. Presented at the annual meeting of the American Political Science Association.

McNOLLGAST. 1995. A positive theory of judicial doctrine and the rule of law. *Southern California Law Review*, 68: 1631–89.

NARDULLI, P. F., FLEMMING, R. B., and EISENSTEIN, J. 1984. Unraveling the complexities of decision-making in face-to-face groups: a contextual analysis of plea bargained sentences. *American Political Science Review*, 78: 912–28.

PINELLO, D. R. 1999. Linking party to judicial ideology in American courts. *Justice System Journal*, 20: 219–54.

RAMSEYER, J. M., and RASMUSSEN, E. B. 2001. Why is the Japanese conviction rate so high? *Journal of Legal Studies*, 30: 53–88.

REVESZ, R. L. 1997. Environmental regulation, ideology, and the D.C. Circuit. *Virginia Law Review*, 83: 1717–72.

RICHARDS, M. J., and KRITZER, H. M. 2002. Jurisprudential regimes in Supreme Court decision-making. *American Political Science Review,* 96: 305–20.

ROSENBERG, G. N. 1992. Judicial independence and the reality of judicial power. *Review of Politics,* 54: 369–98.

SEGAL, J. A., and COVER, A. D. 1989. Ideological values and the votes of U.S. Supreme Court justices. *American Political Science Review,* 83: 557–65.

—— and HOWARD, R. M. 2002. An original look at originalism. *Law and Society Review,* 36: 113–38.

—— and SPAETH, H. J. 1993. *The Supreme Court and the Attitudinal Model.* New York: Cambridge University Press.

—— —— 1996. The influence of *stare decisis* on the votes of U.S. Supreme Court justices. *American Journal of Political Science,* 40: 971–1003.

—— —— 2002. *The Supreme Court and the Attitudinal Model Revisited.* New York: Cambridge University Press.

—— and WESTERLAND, C. 2005. The Supreme Court, Congress, and judicial review. *North Carolina Law Review,* 83: 101–66.

SISK, G. C., HEISE, M., and MORRISS, A. P. 1998. Charting the influences on the judicial mind: an empirical study of judicial reasoning. *New York University Law Review,* 73: 1377–1500.

SONGER, D. R., and LINDQUIST, S. A. 1996. Not the whole story: the impact of justices' values on Supreme Court decision-making. *American Journal of Political Science,* 40: 1049–63.

—— SEGAL, J. A., and CAMERON, C. M. 1994. The hierarchy of justice: testing a principal-agent model of Supreme Court–circuit court interactions. *American Journal of Political Science,* 38: 673–96.

SPAETH, H. J., and SEGAL, J. A. 1999. *Majority Rule vs. Minority Will: Adherence to Precedent on the U.S. Supreme Court.* New York: Cambridge University Press.

SUNSTEIN, C. R., SCHKADE, D., and ELLMAN, L. M. 2004. Ideological voting of federal courts of appeals: a preliminary investigation. *Virginia Law Review,* 90: 301–54.

WENZEL, J. P. 1995. Stability and change in the ideological values in Supreme Court decisions. Presented at the annual meeting of the Midwest Political Science Association.

WHITTINGTON, K. E. 2005. "Interpose your friendly hand:" political supports for the exercise of judicial review by the United States Supreme Court. *American Political Science Review,* 99: 583–96.

CASES

Eisenstadt v. *Baird.* 1972. 405 U.S. 438.

Grayned v. *City of Rockford.* 1972. 408 U.S. 104.

Roe v. *Wade.* 1973. 410 U.S. 113.

United States v. *Shaughnessy.* 1955. 234 F. 2d 715.

CHAPTER 3

STRATEGIC JUDICIAL DECISION-MAKING

PABLO T. SPILLER
RAFAEL GELY

The Supreme Court is a political court. The discretion that the justices exercise can fairly be described as legislative in character, but the conditions under which this "legislature" operates is different from those of Congress. Lacking electoral legitimacy, yet wielding Zeus's thunderbolt in the form of the power to invalidate actions of the other branches of government as unconstitutional, the justices, to be effective, have to accept certain limitations on their legislative discretion.... They have to be seen to be doing law rather than doing politics.

(Posner 2003)

1 INTRODUCTION

IN his incomparable style, Judge Posner describes what is perhaps the issue of most interest to scholars in the strategic tradition to judicial decision-making: under which conditions do judges behave more like "legislators" or more like "judges?" Judge Posner's description of the role of judges suggests that judges' behavior can be modeled in the same fashion we model other rational actors—politicians, activists, managers:

driven by well-defined preferences, behaving in a purposive and forward-looking fashion. The strategic approach seeks to sort out the various competing interests faced by judges when making decisions. In essence, the strategic approach explores the role politics play in judicial decision-making. In this chapter we provide a brief overview of the strategic approach, offering some concluding thoughts about the future of positive analyses of judicial decision-making.

2 THE STRATEGIC APPROACH

2.1 Antecedents

Most of the positive literature on judicial decision-making, to which the strategic approach belongs, can be traced back to the work of political scientists such as C. Herman Pritchett, whose analysis of Supreme Court justices is based on the understanding that, at its core, "the essential nature of the task of a Supreme Court Justice" is "not unlike that of a Congressman" (Pritchett 1942, 491). According to Pritchett, both politicians and judges decide important public policy issues, formulate opinions, and issue a vote, enjoying substantial discretion. In addition the work of modern congressional scholars, such as Mayhew (1974), Fiorina (1982), Becker (1983), Shepsle and Weingast (1987), and Weingast and Marshall (1988) among many others, was of critical importance to the early development of the strategic approach. In particular, the concepts of rationality—each legislator acts to advance his or her own particular interest—and strategic behavior—individuals recognize the interdependency of their actions in a forward-looking way—were fundamental in further developing Pritchett's notion of a judge as a politician.

2.2 The First Wave

It is appropriate to place Marks (1988) as one of the pioneers of the strategic approach to judicial decision-making. Although Marks (1988) does not derive a full-fledged strategic framework, he formalizes the effect of constraints imposed on the courts by the institution of separation of powers. Marks focuses on the potential for Congress to reverse a judicial decision. Thus, he looks at the set of conditions under which Congress could not modify (reverse) a Court decision. Following congressional scholars, Marks also discusses how different institutional arrangements within Congress affect the Court's flexibility to impose its preferred policy alternative.

The strategic approach assumes that judges have a sophisticated understanding of the legislative process and of congressional policy preferences (Gely and Spiller 1990; Eskridge and Ferejohn 1992). This assumption allows the strategic approach to make simple and empirically testable propositions. A fundamental early result of the strategic approach is that, in equilibrium, Congress will tend to acquiesce to judicial decisions (Gely and Spiller 1990). The rationale is simple. As long as justices' preferences are policy-based, they are better off selecting policy decisions that are reversal proof.

Consider a bargaining framework consisting of three stages, in a political setting such as depicted in Figure 3.1. In the first stage, an agency interprets a statute. In the second stage, the Court determines the legal status quo. The final stage consists of bargaining between the two chambers of Congress for an alternative policy outcome. The outcome of the final stage is the final policy outcome. If the House and the Senate agree on an alternative to the Court's policy, then the congressional decision becomes the law. The feasible equilibria to this game comprise the contract set between the House and the Senate (i.e. the area between their ideal points). Since the Court anticipates the bargaining outcome from any feasible decision, it will make its decision strategically, so that the median justice maximizes his or her utility and Congress does not reverse the Court. That is, the Court will pick a policy outcome in the contract curve between the House and the Senate. A decision outside the legislative contract set will trigger a legislative bargain with an outcome strictly within the contract set. So, if the ideal point of the median justice is outside the contract set, its optimal decision is the closest boundary of the contract set. Thus, under the strategic model, one would expect the Supreme Court to hand down only decisions that, in general, Congress and the President will not overturn. That is, justices maximize their utility subject to the constraints imposed by the preferences of the

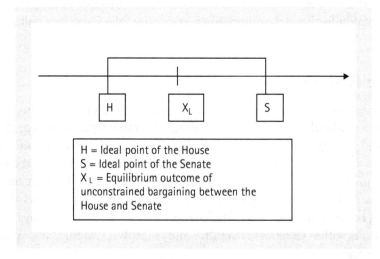

Fig. 3.1 Set of feasible equilibria

relevant political players. In an early survey of congressional overrides of Supreme Court interpretations of federal statutes, Eskridge (1991) finds that in interpreting statutes the Court is more responsive to the expectations of the current Congress (as well as the Court's own preferences) than those of the enacting Congress.

A second type of fundamental result arising from this simple model of strategic judicial behavior is that judicial decisions depend on the location of the Court in relation to the position of the relevant politicians. For example, were the Court's preferences to the right (in a policy line, such as in Figure 3.1) of the most liberal relevant member of Congress, the only relevant political constraint to its decision would be that politician's ideal policy outcome. Thus, as in the Congressional Dominance Hypothesis (Weingast and Moran 1983), judicial decisions are either unconstrained—when the Court's median justice's preferences fall within the congressional contract set—or constrained by the extreme boundaries of that set. This finding is methodologically important, because it suggests that a linear empirical specification (e.g. a linear regression) will not accurately capture the dynamics of the Court–Congress interaction, as the relevant constraint varies depending on the relative location of the Court.

Spiller and Gely (1992) provide the first empirical test of the strategic approach using Supreme Court statutory decisions in the area of labor relations. Like Eskridge, Spiller and Gely find that the preferences of both legislators and justices matter. In particular, the manner in which the preferences of the Court and Congress interact is consistent with the predictions of the strategic approach.

The topic of statutory interpretation received careful consideration in the earlier years. Ferejohn and Weingast (1992a; 1992b), for example, sketch a positive theory of statutory interpretation showing the interaction between the Court and the enacting and future legislatures.[1] McNollgast (1992; 1994) further explores how the organization of Congress affects the ability of the Court to act strategically when engaging in statutory interpretation; the Court is able strategically to use legislative history to give a statute an expansive reading.

2.3 The Second Wave

Over the next several years, scholars from a variety of disciplinary backgrounds expanded the focus of the strategic approach in multiple directions. Spiller and Spitzer (1992) analyze the Court's choice between making a decision on constitutional or non-constitutional grounds. Spiller and Spitzer use a strategic representation that includes Congress, the courts, the President, the agency, and state legislatures to explain the Court's putative reluctance to base its decisions on constitutional grounds. It is not surprising, they conclude, to find that courts are reluctant to use the

---

[1] See also Schwartz et al. (1994) and de Figueiredo et al. (1999) for related, and formal, developments.

constitutional instrument, because the threat of statutory interpretation is generally sufficient to restrain agency decisions, and that the Court's preferences would have to be significantly different from those of the political mainstream for a constitutionally restrictive decision to constitute equilibrium (Spiller and Spitzer 1992).

Tiller and Spiller (1999, 351) elaborate on the issue of choice of legal rules in analyzing why agencies might choose a particular regulatory instrument (e.g. adjudication) over another (e.g. rulemaking), and why courts of appeal might reverse agencies by focusing on procedural challenges to agency action rather than issues of statutory interpretation. They find that by strategically choosing a combination of policy outcomes and regulatory instruments, administrative agencies and lower courts impose higher decision costs on the reviewing court and thus minimize the chances of reversal. In a related article, Cross and Tiller (1998, 2159) illustrate the effects of raising decision costs within the context of intra-court of appeals panel. They find that increasing transaction costs forces court of appeals panels to act less along ideological or political lines than they would otherwise like to.

Spiller and Tiller (1997) look at the power of Congress to change the structure of interaction among agencies and the courts, and in so doing exercise control over policy outcomes. Congress has the ability of influence the judiciary either through the manipulation of the decision-making process that the agency must follow (e.g. cost–benefit analysis) or by changing the standard of review a court must apply when reviewing an agency action (e.g. the Bumpers Amendment 1975). Congress can influence the courts by various other means as well. De Figueiredo and Tiller (1996; 2000) explore Congress's ability to influence the federal judiciary through the expansion of judgeships; and Toma (1991; 1996) provides evidence that Congress uses the budget appropriations as an instrument to signal its preferences to the Supreme Court, similar to what it does in its interactions with administrative agencies (Weingast and Moran 1983).

The strategic approach to the study of judicial behavior, and in particular, to judicial independence, outside the U.S. has received substantial recent attention.[2] Spiller (1996) develops the basic comparative logic to understand the raise of the doctrine of judicial independence. In environments characterized by a strong and unified polity—such as in two-party parliamentary systems—attempts to exercise judicial independence will trigger political conflict and retaliation. When it is difficult for the polity to overturn or to retaliate against the judiciary, a doctrine of judicial independence would naturally evolve.

This insight has been applied to a multiplicity of political environments across almost all continents. Cooter and Ginsburg (1996), for example, follow this approach by examining the impact of political institutions on judicial independence across twenty-one countries. Consistent with the basic precepts of the strategic approach, they find that, when it is easier for the legislature to override the court and when a "dominant disciplined party" controls the governing coalition, the discretion of the

---

[2] State Courts have also provided a natural comparative setting for rational choice analyses. See e.g. Spiller and Vanden Bergh (2003) and references therein.

courts is limited. Epstein et al. (2001) also apply this framework to understand the behavior of European constitutional courts in their interaction with the relevant political actors. They analyze the decisions of the Russian Constitutional Court following the collapse of the Soviet Union. They find that consistent with the strategic approach, as the political environment in Russia became more stable and unified, the Court began to show more deference to the political branches.

Garrett et al. (1998) apply the strategic approach to the European Court of Justice (ECJ). The ECJ is in the difficult position of "being seen as enforcing the law impartially by following the rules of precedent" and at the same time not making "decisions that litigant governments refuse to comply with" (174). They identify the conditions under which the ECJ is more likely to rule against a litigant government and, in turn, those conditions when member governments are likely to respond to the ECJ's rulings.

In his study of three Asian countries, Ginsburg (2003) reach similar conclusions. In the context of constitutional design, increased political uncertainty leads to the adoption of judicial review as a form of protecting the constitutional bargaining. In a comparative study of Japan and the U.S., Ramseyer (1994) finds that independent courts are likely to be supported by elected officials when they believe they are likely to lose in a future election. Under such conditions, it is in the interest of the existing ruling elite to create independent courts to protect the policy that has just been enacted into law. Similarly, Ramseyer and Rasmusen (1997; 2006) in studying judicial independence in Japan conclude that, in Japan, politicians seek to achieve the "ideal judge" by exercising more control over judges during their careers, rather than at appointment time, finding evidence that political bias played a role in the career advancement of judges.

Iaryczower et al. (2002) find that, despite an inhospitable environment, the judiciary in Argentina has shown some measure of judicial independence. Similar to Ramseyer and Rasmusen (2006), the authors find that judicial independence depends on the political environment, and that in periods with a more fragmented polity, the Court is more willing to challenge legislative and executive actions.[3]

3 THE ATTITUDINAL APPROACH

3.1 The Basic Hypothesis

At its most basic level, the attitudinal approach holds that judges decide disputes based on their "sincere" ideological preferences and values, unconstrained by outside or inside institutions (Segal and Spaeth 2002, 86). Because various

---

[3] See also Helmke (2002) for a related result.

institutional devices insulate them from outside influences, scholars working within this framework model justices' behavior as influenced by their sincere ideological preferences.[4] Scholars in this tradition have provided evidence that both case-facts and justices' attitudes play a significant role in justices' decisions. Segal and Cover (1989), for example, report an 80 percent correlation between their measure of justices' attitudes and their measure of aggregated voting tendencies in civil liberties cases (Segal et al. 1995 extended the study to include economic cases), suggesting that attitudes are good predictors of their decisions in the two areas that constitute a significant portion of the Supreme Court's docket (Segal 1997).

3.2 The Attitudinal and Strategic Approaches Face Each Other

In a series of papers beginning in the late 1990s, scholars in both the strategic and attitudinal camps carefully explored the claims made by each model. In 1997 Segal compared the attitudinal (sincere) and strategic (sophisticated) approaches. Although Segal does not reject the strategic account outright, he concludes that the evidence unambiguously favors the attitudinal model. A few years later, Segal and Spaeth (2002) reached the same conclusion: "If the overwhelming majority of statistical models find no support for the separations-of-powers model, if the few statistical models supporting the separations-of-powers model are seriously flawed, and if the model's foremost advocate [William Eskridge] concludes that the Warren, Burger and Rehnquist courts all ignored legislative preferences, there is little need to say more" (2002, 349).

Segal and Spaeth, however, go on to say more: "one might imagine a spectrum along which the separation-of-powers model might be relatively true" and "it should hardly be surprising that institutional structures matter" (2002, 349–50). These statements are interesting because they are consistent with Spiller and Gely (1992) who suggest that there are ranges in which the Court is constrained and ranges in which the Court is not, and thus ranges where the justices are able to impose their own preferences.

In fact, Bergara et al. (2003) apply Spiller and Gely's (1992) model to Segal's (1997) data. Consistent with both the attitudinal and strategic approaches, they find that justices' ideologies matter. Consistent with the strategic approach, they find that the Court is often, but not always, constrained by Congress and the extent to which the Court is constrained by politics varies significantly over time, a finding consistent with that of Rosenberg (1992). Finally, and also consistent with the strategic model, Bergara et al. (2003) find that when the Court is constrained by

---

[4] Going back to Figure 3.1 above, the attitudinal approach operates in an environment in which the Court is always located within the contract set of the legislature—i.e. the court is always in the political mainstream—while the strategic approach becomes relevant when the Court's preferences deviate from the political mainstream.

politics, it seems to respond strategically. The point is, as Jacobi (2006, 265) puts it: "If judges are policy-motivated individuals, why would they not pursue those policies in a sophisticated manner?"

4 STRATEGY IN THE CHAMBERS

4.1 Brief Overview

Another interesting stream is what we call the "Internal Strategic Approach." This approach focuses on the decision-making process within the Court.[5] Until fairly recently, scholars applying strategic models to judicial decision-making have focused primarily on the final vote on the case. With a few exceptions (e.g. Schubert 1962; Provine 1980) scholars have generally ignored the strategic implications of judicial decisions made prior to the final outcome of the case. Justices can behave strategically at any of the following five stages: on certiorari; at the "conference vote," where a preliminary vote on how the case should be decided takes place; in the assignment, by the Chief Justice or by the most senior associate justice in the majority, of the writing of the majority opinion; in the writing itself, so as to garner majority support; and finally, at the decision to join, concur, or dissent.

Since justices have the opportunity to engage in strategic behavior at each stage, failure to model these stages might result in incomplete understanding of judicial behavior. Epstein and Knight (1998, 65) find evidence of strategic behavior at the certiorari stage, particularly with the use of the dissent of cert tool. Modeling yet a different stage, Hammond et al. (2005) find that, under some conditions, it is optimal for the opinion assigner "to assign the opinion to some justice who is not the closest ideologically." This result may explain why Chief Justice Burger systematically assigned opinions to less ideologically compatible colleagues.

4.2 Strengths

The Internal Strategic Approach presents a number of exciting opportunities to the study of judicial decision-making. Not only can we focus on the various stages of the

---

[5] The hierarchy of the court has been also extensively analyzed. For example, Songer et al. (1994) analyzed the incentives of appeal courts to follow supreme court policies. Spiller (1992) analyzes agency independence given the hierarchy of judicial review. He shows how the judicial hierarchical process further limits agency independence. The strategic choice of cases has been analyzed by, among others, Cameron et al. (2000) and Lax (2002).

internal game, but we can also model legal issues and policies. Lax (2006), for example, has transformed Kornhauser's (1992) mostly normative work on legal rules into analyses of doctrine as equilibrium to internal games. Lax (2006) analyzes rule-based games, showing that equilibrium to rule games have more robust properties than equilibrium to policy games (e.g. while there may not be a median justice, there is always a median rule equilibrium). Doctrine can also be seen as a means of political control, both in the game between a Supreme Court and lower courts (Cohen and Spitzer 1994), and between the Court and politicians (Spiller and Spitzer 1995).

Refocusing the discussion on the various stages of decision-making should motivate the collection and codification of new sources of data, such as courts' procedures that, although obscure or rarely used (e.g. an order by the Court dismissing a writ of certiorari as improvidently granted, i.e. a DIG), may be used by justices in a strategic manner (e.g. Solimine and Gely 2005).

5 THE STATE OF THE STRATEGIC APPROACH

To some extent, we have just started to develop comprehensive, and empirically testable, theories of judging (e.g. Hammond et al. 2005). Although perhaps no model will ever be able to capture the complexities of judging, the strategic approach provides a useful general framework to study judicial decision-making.

Consistent with the attitudinal model, the strategic model recognizes that there is a range of policy alternatives over which justices may vote their preferences without fear of reversal by the legislature (Spiller and Gely 1992). The strategic model goes further, however, by systematically accounting for other forces (e.g. judicial norms) that could affect judicial decision-making. The possibility of greater integration between the two approaches is perhaps at its apex now, as scholars have begun to explore more carefully the internal strategies justices engage in as they decide cases. In particular, it is likely that, in some stages, the justices have more room to impose their preferences and in others might be more constrained by political forces. Similarly, the type of case (e.g. statutory vs. constitutional) might influence the justices' calculus and even within a given type of case, the cases' salience may affect other political actors' responses, and thus the ability of justices to impose their own preferences

In sum, the strategic approach to judicial decision-making, rooted in rationality and sophistication, is alive and well. It has evolved from a relatively simple framework to include concepts such as doctrines, rules, internal decision-making, and vertical relations among levels of the judiciary, and it has traveled overseas and brought back fascinating ideas about the impact and growth of judicial institutions.

We have pried open the lid on knowledge about how justices make decisions in the United States, at least at the federal level; but we still have very little systematic knowledge about their strategic choices in other developed countries and, more fundamentally, in emerging and developing economies where institutions are more varied and where the impact of institutions on judicial decision-making can sometimes be seen more starkly.

REFERENCES

BECKER, G. 1983. A theory of competition among pressure groups for political influence. *Quarterly Journal of Economics*, 98: 371–400.

BERGARA, M., RICHMAN, B., and SPILLER, P. T. 2003. Modeling Supreme Court strategic decision-making: the congressional constraint. *Legislative Studies Quarterly*, 28: 247–80.

CAMERON, C. M., SEGAL, J. A., and SONGER, D. 2000. Strategic auditing in a political hierarchy: an informational model of the Supreme Court's certiorari decisions. *American Political Science Review*, 94: 101–16.

COHEN, L., and SPITZER, M. 1994. Solving the *Chevron* puzzle. *Law and Contemporary Problems*, 57: 65–110.

COOTER., R. D., and GINSBURG, T. 1996 Comparative judicial discretion: an empirical test of economic models. *International Review of Law and Economics*, 16: 295–313.

CROSS, F. B., and TILLER, E. H. 1998. Judicial partisanship and obedience to legal doctrine: whistleblowing on the federal courts of appeals. *Yale Law Journal*, 107: 2155–76.

DE FIGUEIREDO, J. M., and TILLER, E. H. 1996. Congressional control of the courts: a theoretical and empirical analysis of expansion of the federal judiciary. *Journal of Law and Economics*, 39: 435–62.

—— —— 2000. Congress and the political expansion of the U.S. District Courts. *American Law and Economics Review*, 2: 107–25.

—— SPILLER, P. T., and URBIZTONDO, S. 1999. An informational perspective on administrative procedures. *Journal of Law, Economics and Organization*, 15: 283–305.

EPSTEIN, L., and KNIGHT, J. 1998. *The Choices Justices Make*. Washington, DC: CQ Press.

—— —— and SHVETSOVA, O. 2001. The role of constitutional courts in the establishment and maintenance of democratic systems of government. *Law and Society Review*, 35: 117–64.

ESKRIDGE, W. N. 1991. Overriding Supreme Court statutory interpretation decisions. *Yale Law Journal*, 101: 331–455.

—— and FEREJOHN, J. 1992. Making the deal stick: enforcing the original constitutional structure of lawmaking in the modern regulatory state. *Journal of Law, Economics and Organization*, 8: 165–89.

FEREJOHN, J., and WEINGAST, B. 1992a. Limitation of statutes: strategic statutory interpretation. *Georgetown Law Review*, 80: 565–82.

—— —— 1992b. A positive theory of statutory interpretation. *International Review of Law and Economics*, 12: 263–79.

FIORINA, M. P. 1982. Legislative choice of regulatory forms: legal process or administrative process. *Public Choice*, 39: 33–66.

GARRETT, G., KELEMEN, R. D., and SCHULZ, H. 1998. The European Court of Justice, national governments, and legal integration in the European Union. *International Organization*, 52: 149–76.

GELY, R., and SPILLER, P. T. 1990. A rational choice theory of Supreme Court statutory decisions with applications to the *State Farm* and *Grove City* cases. *Journal of Law, Economics and Organization*, 6: 263–300.

GINSBURG, T. 2003. *Judicial Review in New Democracies*. New York: Cambridge University Press.

HAMMOND, T. H., BONNEAU, C. W., and SHEEHAN, R. S. 2005. *Strategic Behavior and Policy Choice on the U.S. Supreme Court*. Stanford, Calif.: Stanford University Press.

HELMKE, G. 2002. The logic of strategic defection: judicial decision-making in Argentina under dictatorship and democracy. *American Political Science Review*, 96: 291–303.

IARYCZOWER, M., SPILLER, P. T., and TOMMASI, M. 2002. Judicial independence in unstable environments, Argentina 1935–1998. *American Journal of Political Science*, 46: 699–716.

JACOBI, T. 2006. The impact of positive political theory on old questions of constitutional law and the separations of powers. *Northwestern Law Review*, 100: 259–78.

KORNHAUSER, L. A. 1992. Modeling collegial courts II: legal doctrine. *Journal of Law, Economics and Organization*, 8: 441–70.

LAX, J. R. 2002. Certiorary and compliance in the judicial hierarchy: discretion, reputation and the rule of four. *Journal of Theoretical Politics*, 15: 61–8.

—— 2006. Median rules with a median judge: the collegial politics of legal doctrine. Unpublished manuscript, Columbia University.

MARKS, B. 1988. A model of judicial influence on congressional policy-making: *Grove City College v. Bell*. Working Paper in Political Science P-88-7, Hoover Institution.

MAYHEW, D. R. 1974. *Congress: The Electoral Connection*. New Haven, Conn.: Yale University Press.

McNOLLGAST. 1992. Positive canons: the role of legislative bargains in statutory interpretation. *Georgetown Law Journal*, 80: 705–42.

—— 1994. Legislative intent: the use of positive political theory in statutory interpretation. *Law and Contemporary Problems*, 57: 3–37

POSNER, R. 2003. The anti-hero. *New Republic*, February 24, review of B. A. Murphy, *Wild Bill: The Legend and Life of William O. Douglas*.

PRITCHETT, C. H. 1942. The voting behavior of the Supreme Court, 1941–42. *Journal of Politics*, 4: 491–506.

PROVINE, D. M. 1980. *Case Selection in the United States Supreme Court*. Chicago: University of Chicago Press.

RAMSEYER, J. M. 1994. The puzzling (in)dependence of courts: a comparative approach. *Journal of Legal Studies*, 23: 721–47.

—— and RASMUSEN, E. B. 1997. Judicial independence in a civil law regime: the evidence from Japan. *Journal of Law, Economics and Organization*, 13: 259–86.

—— —— 2006. The case for managed judges: learning from Japan after the political upheaval of 1993. *University of Pennsylvania Law Review*, 154: 1879–930.

ROSENBERG, G. N. 1992. Judicial independence and the reality of political power. *Review of Politics*, 54: 369–98.

SCHUBERT, G. 1962. Policy without law: an extension of the certiorari game. *Stanford Law Review*, 14: 284–327.

SCHWARTZ, E. P., SPILLER P. T., and URBIZTONDO, S. 1994. A positive theory of legislative intent. *Law and Contemporary Problems*, 57: 51–74.

SEGAL, J. A. 1997. Separation-of-powers games in the positive theory of Congress and courts. *American Political Science Review*, 91: 28–44.

—— and COVER, A. D. 1989. Ideological values and the votes of U.S. Supreme Court justices. *American Political Science Review*, 83: 557–65.

—— EPSTEIN, L., CAMERON, C. M., and SPAETH, H. J. 1995. Ideological values and the votes of U.S. Supreme Court justices revisited. *Journal of Politics*, 57: 812–23.

—— and SPAETH, H. 2002. *The Supreme Court and the Attitudinal Model Revisited*. New York: Cambridge University Press.

SHEPSLE, K., and WEINGAST, B. 1987. The institutional foundations of committee power. *American Political Science Review*, 81: 85–104.

SOLIMINE, M., and GELY, R. 2005. The Supreme Court and the DIG: an empirical and institutional analysis. *Wisconsin Law Review*, 2005: 1421–78.

SONGER, D. R., SEGAL, J. A., and CAMERON, C. M. 1994. The hierarchy of justice: testing a principal–agent model of Supreme Court–circuit court interactions. *American Journal of Political Science*, 38: 673–96.

SPILLER, P. T. 1992. Rationality, decision rules and collegial courts. *International Review of Law and Economics*, 12: 186–90.

—— 1996. A positive political theory of regulatory instruments: contracts, administrative law or regulatory specificity? *University of Southern California Law Review*, 69: 477–515.

—— and GELY, R. 1992. Congressional control or judicial independence: the determinants of U.S. Supreme Court labor relations decisions, 1949–1988. *Rand Journal of Economics*, 23: 463–92.

—— and TILLER, E. H. 1997. Decision costs and the strategic design of administrative process and judicial review. *Journal of Legal Studies*, 26: 347–70.

—— and SPITZER, M. T. 1992. Judicial choice of legal doctrine. *Journal of Law, Economics and Organization*, 8: 8–46.

—— —— 1995. Where is the sin in sincere? Sophisticated manipulation of sincere judicial voters (with applications to other environments). *Journal of Law, Economics and Organization*, 11: 32–63.

—— and VANDEN BERGH, R. G. 2003. Toward a positive theory of state supreme court decision-making. *Business and Politics*, 5: 7–43.

TILLER, E. H., and SPILLER, P. T. 1999. Strategic instruments: legal structure and political games in administrative law. *Journal of Law, Economics and Organization*, 15: 349–77.

TOMA, E. F. 1991. Congressional influence and the Supreme Court: the budget as a signaling device. *Journal of Legal Studies*, 20: 131–46.

—— 1996. A contractual model of the voting behavior of the Supreme Court: the role of the Chief Justice. *International Review of Law and Economics*, 16: 433–47.

WEINGAST, B. R., and MORAN, M. J. 1983. Bureaucratic discretion or congressional control? Regulatory policymaking by the Federal Trade Commission. *Journal of Political Economy*, 91: 765–800.

—— and MARSHALL, W. J. 1988. The industrial organization of congress; or why legislatures, like firms, are not organized as markets. *Journal of Political Economy*, 96: 132–63.

HISTORICAL INSTITUTIONALISM AND THE STUDY OF LAW

ROGERS M. SMITH

1 THE EMERGENCE OF HISTORICAL INSTITUTIONALISM

THERE are two chief motives to formulate academic "isms," one higher, one lower. The higher goal is to define an understanding of what and how to study that can illuminate significant and neglected or misunderstood features of existence. The lower but defensible aim is to be part of a "school" which administrators, funders, and other scholars see as worthwhile. Both motives gave rise to historical institutionalism in political science and public law in the 1990s.[1] By 2006, scholars had made progress toward each end. And if the second, more attainable aim has been more fully realized so far, recent works show that the promise of historical institutionalism to provide new theoretical and substantive insights is increasingly being fulfilled, in public law and in political science generally.

[1] The focus here is on how public law scholars have employed historical institutionalist approaches. For a valuable analysis of how other historical institutionalists have dealt with law that calls for "increased attention" to law and courts, see Skrentny (2006, 214).

In 1984 James March and Johan Olsen published a landmark article, "The New Institutionalism: Organizational Factors in Political Life." It saw in political science "a resurgence of concern with institutions" that challenged prevailing notions of politics as "the aggregate consequences of individual behavior," motivated by self-interested conduct that resulted in efficient historical processes (March and Olsen 1984, 734). Instead, more scholars portrayed institutions as playing a relatively autonomous role in shaping individual behavior, even individual senses of interests and identities (738–39). Sometimes, this shaping produced conduct that was more dutiful than self-interested, or simply more routinized than efficient (741). Examples of new institutionalist scholarship included rational choice work on legislative rules (Shepsle and Weingast 1983); comparative and American politics studies "bringing the state back in" (Skocpol 1979; Skowronek 1982); research on corporatism (Berger 1981); on states and foreign policies in international relations (Krasner 1978); and more (734–35).

March and Olsen did not cite any works focused on law, but they suggested the relevance of new institutionalist approaches to legal scholarship by arguing that "Constitutions, laws, contracts, and customary rules of politics . . . develop within the context of political institutions" (740). They also stressed the significance of "normative structures" defining "duties, obligations, roles and rules," and how "consistency and inconsistency in beliefs affect . . . political meaning" and the creation of "social order" (744). Subsequently they endorsed jurisprudential views holding that judges, like other institutional actors, actively gave "meaning to the values they espouse" in politically consequential ways (March and Olsen 1989, 128).

After March and Olsen wrote, institutionalist approaches proliferated in political science and other disciplines. Political scientists soon distinguished "rational choice" institutionalism from "historical/interpretive" or, before long, "historical institutionalism" (e.g. Thelen and Steinmo 1992, 7; Hall and Taylor 1996).[2] To be sure, many have sought and still seek to blend these new institutionalisms (e.g. Katznelson and Weingast 2005). But in the 1990s, most historical institutionalists contrasted their approaches to much rational choice scholarship on several grounds. They saw institutions as constructing the "bounded rationality" of "satisficing" actors, instead of simply providing the strategic contexts for rationally "maximizing" actors. They saw "sticky," enduring institutions as producing "path dependent" behavior, "unanticipated consequences," and perhaps most importantly, structural inequalities of power that made historical processes less than functional and efficient for all involved. And they saw institutions as playing a "generative" or "constitutive" role, helping to provide the content of the identities,

---

[2] Thelen and Steinmo attributed the term historical institutionalism to Theda Skocpol (1992, 28 n. 4), originally a political sociologist. Other sociologists developed "new institutionalist" approaches that displayed kinship with historical/interpretive political science (e.g. DiMaggio and Powell 1991). But many sociological institutionalists minimize personal political agency in favor of action seen "as the enactment of broad institutional scripts rather than a matter of internally generated and autonomous choice, motivation and purpose" (Meyer, Boli, and Thomas 1987, 13).

preferences, and interests that actors could embrace and express (Thelen and Steinmo 1992, 7–10; Smith 1992, 9, 20–5; Hall and Taylor 1996, 939–42).

It took no great insight to realize that these emphases on the importance of rules in bounding action and constituting actors, while simultaneously enabling rule-interpreters to make choices that shaped outcomes, might aid scholars of law and courts. Early on an argument to that effect appeared in the *American Political Science Review* (Smith 1988). Thereafter the receptivity of top journals to this new institutionalism encouraged public law scholars critical of behavioralism to identify themselves first as "new," then as "historical institutionalists." Just what that meant remained unclear. Some new institutionalists defined institutions as only the "formal or informal procedures, routines, norms and conventions embedded" in the organizations that comprise "the polity or political economy" (Hall and Taylor 1996, 938). Others defined institutions as also including "overarching structures of state" and a "nation's normative social order" (John Ikenberry, cited in Thelen and Steinmo 1992, 2).

Many of the early public law new institutionalists favored broader definitions. They challenged pluralist and attitudinal models that portrayed courts and all other institutions simply as instruments of dominant political forces that appointed judges who voted their political ideologies. They argued that although judicial behavior did involve such factors, the specific doctrines and the broader conceptions of institutional roles that the judicial system embodied also shaped judicial decision-making. In some ways, these specifically legal ideas and discourses provided bounds to plausible judicial decisions; but they also provided credible authority claims and interpretive leeway that gave judges some relative autonomy from broader political forces, indeed real power to affect political results. These discourses might, to be sure, be included among the "norms" and "routines" that comprised judicial institutions even on narrower definitions of institutions, and some legal new institutionalists warned against venturing too far beyond institutionalized doctrines into studies of a nation's whole "normative social order" (Stone 1992, 15; Clayton 1999, 34–5). But most also felt that legal doctrines had to be grasped as expressions of broader political ideologies, institutionalized in ways that constrained judges but also empowered them to give specific meaning to more general political outlooks (e.g. Smith 1988, 94–6; Stone 1992, 6–15; Gillman 1993, 15–18; Bussiere 1997, 11–22; Clayton and Gillman 1999, 3–5).

These scholars hoped a focus on institutionalized doctrines as simultaneously restricting and enabling might achieve what Martin Shapiro argued to be a goal of all political scientists studying law: "to strengthen our skills at doctrinal analysis while also maintaining an outsider's perspective"—taking doctrine seriously without treating the law as simply "there" to be discovered by judges, nor as grist for "analyses" that were mere advocacy for preferred legal results (Shapiro 1989, 99). New institutionalists tried to show empirically how pressures to be consistent with existing doctrines sometimes constrained judicial reasoning and generated "path dependent" behavior as well as unanticipated consequences, even as their inter-pretive duties sometimes enabled judges to stall, or further social change.

Thus in a pioneering effort to apply new institutionalist perspectives to courts outside the U.S., Alec Stone argued that the French Constitutional Council gained meaningful autonomous power in the 1980s in part through demonstrating its soothing conformity to judicial norms (Stone 1992). Howard Gillman showed how legal doctrines entrenching Jacksonian notions of "no special privileges" hindered judicial acceptance of labor legislation in the *Lochner* era (1993). Susan Burgess suggested that the rhetoric of judicial supremacy worked to limit capacities and practices of constitutional interpretation outside of courts (1993). Elizabeth Bussiere argued that doctrines stressing procedural rather than substantive impli-cations of equal protection had been used to resist extending subsistence rights to politically marginal Americans (1997). Related projects proliferated, so that by 1999, Cornell Clayton and Gillman were able to put together two edited collections of new institutionalist judicial scholarship that did much to show that a school was emerging (Clayton and Gillman 1999; Gillman and Clayton 1999).

2 THEORIZING HISTORICAL INSTITUTIONALISM

Though the substantive contributions of these works helped to win recognition for historical institutionalist public law scholarship, many in and outside the camp questioned whether historical institutionalism was as yet a full-fledged theoretical perspective. Some feared it was a new name for the old wine of doctrinal analysis as a mix of history and advocacy, or an umbrella label for a hodgepodge of unconnected works. Similar anxieties haunted historical institutionalists in other parts of polit-ical science, generating further efforts at theory building.

Amid a fast-growing forest of contributions, two agendas of theoretical develop-ment stand out. Comparativist historical institutionalists, especially, have sought to flesh out the concept of path dependence, none more carefully than Paul Pierson. He argues that at certain "critical junctures" in historical processes, many paths of development are open. As a public law example (not Pierson's), many scholars think the future of slavery was unclear when the Constitution was adopted, even with the new constitutional protections for it (Amar 2005, 18–21, 91–8). Some framers thought it would endure, some thought it would decline, some preferred not to think about it. But contingent circumstances—including the advent of the cotton gin, making slavery more economical in the South—combined with political accommodations for slaveholders so that in the early nineteenth century, investments not only in slaves, but in judicial doctrines, public policies, policing practices, religious and scientific understandings, and social and cultural institutions and practices supportive of slavery, all increased. These developments provided "positive feedback" to slavery: for many in power, the economic and political benefits of maintaining slavery and all the arrangements that facilitated it grew, and so did the costs of seeking to transform it. But wage-labor systems and cognate institutions also proliferated in the North, creating conflicts in which marginal groups like territorial inhabitants and abolitionists could play prominent roles in bringing a massive war, a new "critical juncture."

This view of "politics in time" prompts analysts to look for certain types of political phenomena. *Timing* and *sequence* matter greatly. If the technology that made slavery profitable had come earlier, the Constitution might have resembled that later written by the Confederacy. If it had come later, the emancipatory movements triggered by the Revolution in the North might have extended to the South. *Long-term patterns* of economic and social development also matter enormously, for they can build to intense conflicts. But the short-term, institutionally situated choices of political agents in addressing those conflicts matter as well. And both institutional and policy choices can have *unintended consequences*, so that Pierson prefers to speak of institutional "development" rather than institutional "design" (2004, 103–66). The creation of a national republic led to the development of a party system that few framers expected; conflicts over slavery then tore that party system apart. A Supreme Court decision aimed at solidifying legal protection for slavery instead mobilized political opposition against it.

Such examples show why many public law institutionalists agree with Pierson that analysts must identify critical junctures and contingencies that produce path-dependent lines of development. Bruce Ackerman has influentially interpreted the whole of American constitutional history as resting on such critical junctures, or "constitutional moments" (Ackerman 1991). Such accounts attend both to the long-term, causal processes that sometimes lead to transformative moments and to the short-term responses of political institutions, actors, and voters to the challenges these processes throw up. Those responses may include resistance, inefficiency, and unanticipated choices (Pierson 2004, 10–16). These core concepts are now generating far more intriguing lines of research than I can canvass here.

But not all historical institutionalists give the same centrality to path dependency that Pierson does. The overlapping but somewhat contrasting theory-building efforts of Karen Orren and Stephen Skowronek have particularly influenced those studying American political development. Orren and Skowronek doubt whether path dependency accounts can theorize the sources of critical junctures and, especially, reasons for change. They contend that if junctures are explained in terms of "exogenous shocks that disrupt established patterns," then path dependence reduces to the unhelpful claim that "politics follows a particular course until something happens that changes the course." But if "exogenous shocks" are instead "informed by structures, identities, cleavages, programs, agendas present in the prior period," then we need analyses of those structures, identities, cleavages, and programs to identify which occurrences reinforce established patterns of governance and which are "redirecting" (Orren and Skowronek 2004, 103).

Orren and Skowronek think we can best achieve such accounts by exploring the interactions or "intercurrence" of multiple "political orders" (17). These orders are arrays of institutions and constituencies with broadly shared agendas and some internal tensions that can foster true "development" or "durable shifts in governing authority." These authors particularly stress that "development" can occur when different institutions come into conflict with each other or reinforce each other in new, transformative ways (Orren and Skowronek 2004, 123–31). In regard to the slavery example, they argue that "in antebellum America, politics was framed by the competing entailments and mutually threatening movements" of two "orders," "southern slavery" and an "expanding democracy for white male citizens" centered in the North (17). Eventually the mounting collisions of those orders led to the Thirteenth Amendment's ban on slavery, launching Reconstruction. That era was a critical juncture that produced real development, the ending of a "legal relation that confined four million individuals to servitude." Yet much structural racial inequality persisted: "those freed were isolated, impoverished, denied equal rights, and left without means for collective or personal advancement" (134). How to understand this historic mix of continuity and change, path dependence and disjuncture?

Orren and Skowronek note that few anti-slavery reformers in the antebellum period thought through all that might be involved in ending slavery, an "entrenched political order" that was "wound tightly" into innumerable features of American governance, including federalism, the separation of powers, civil and criminal justice systems, and family law (2004, 134). The central question of Reconstruction thus became, "how much political authority needed to shift" to culminate slavery's demise? Orren and Skowronek see the federal judiciary as institutionally structured to preserve existing legal rights and governmental relations, and so as the supporter of the former masters' view that ending slavery should change as little as possible. In contrast, the Congress, charged with giving legislative effect to the Thirteenth Amendment, was institutionally situated to advance the cause of the former slaves. The Presidency had conflicting institutional roles of lawmaking and rights enforcement—but executive actions therefore resisted the most radical Reconstruction measures. Orren and Skowronek argue that, with the judiciary and the Presidency often allied against change, congressional reformers could uphold voting rights for the relatively few blacks in the North, but they did not have the power to transform the South. As a result, formal constitutional grants of equal political and civil rights never took hold there (Orren and Skowronek 2004, 134–42).

Though objections can be raised to this account (Smith 2006), it exemplifies well the multiple orders, intercurrence-centered theory of development. Slavery was a political order that had conflicts within it between masters and slaves, and that clashed with the increasingly distinct institutions that predominated outside the South, as path-dependency accounts would argue. But once the paths of these rival institutions led to war and an indefinite range of new possibilities opened up, it was struggles among federal institutions that determined the sources and substance of empowering changes (for blacks in the North) and dispiriting continuities (for blacks in the South).

These differences in emphasis are no great chasm. Pierson admits the limitations of earlier formulations of path dependency in accounting for change, and he agrees with Orren and Skowronek that "overlapping processes" can involve abrasions that are "sources of dynamism" (2004, 135–6). He adds that analyses focused on path dependency can also identify other spurs to development (137–66). While decrying the "impoverished state of theorizing" on institutional change, Wolfgang Streeck and Kathleen Thelen have recently mapped out many ways institutions can generate development, including *displacement* of one institution by another, the *layering* of new institutions on older ones, *drift* in institutional functions, *conversion* of institutions to other purposes, and *exhaustion* as institutional endeavors reach their limits (Streeck and Thelen 2005, 19–30). These categories incorporate the main arguments of Pierson, Orren and Skowronek, and other major contributors to historical institutionalist scholarship.

3 HISTORICAL INSTITUTIONALISM AND PUBLIC LAW TODAY

Although the arguments of many public law scholars exemplify these sorts of theoretical explanations for continuity and change, scholars have only begun to make those connections explicit. In part this is because early on, many public law historical institutionalists focused more than their counterparts in other subfields on structures of ideas: the ideas that comprise legal doctrines, broader notions of the proper role of the judiciary, sometimes the general political outlooks with which doctrinal and institutional conceptions are associated (Gillman 1999). Even so, the analyses that resulted often had strong path-dependent flavors, while also suggesting how ideational "stickiness" can be part of meaningful change. These writings stressed how entrenched ideas like "no special privileges," judicial nonpartisanship, judicial supremacy, and procedural justice shaped and constrained judicial conduct, even though they did not wholly determine judicial decisions, and even though, in new settings, applications of old doctrines sometimes produced novel results.

Many early public law institutionalist works also were strongly court-centered, giving limited attention to other "political orders."

Things have changed, partly from efforts to work through the implications of Mark Graber's prize-winning essay, "The Nonmajoritarian Difficulty: Legislative Deference to the Judiciary" (1993). Graber argued that generally the Supreme Court has not declared state and federal practices unconstitutional unless "the dominant national coalition" was "unable or unwilling to settle some public dispute," so that "prominent elected officials" consciously invited "the judiciary to resolve" controversies they could not or "would rather not address" themselves (1993, 36). Graber's work encouraged scholars to analyze the Court's decisions and doctrines in relation to the positions of the dominant political party, of Congress, and of the Executive Branch—in effect, to attend to intercurrence between the judiciary and other major institutions and actors.

In this vein, Howard Gillman argues that late nineteenth-century Republicans expanded the federal courts' jurisdiction to establish legal frameworks conducive to economic nationalism (Gillman 2002). George Lovell maintains that Congress has written ambiguous labor statutes in order to stick courts with responsibility for controversial labor decisions (Lovell 2003). Mitchell Pickerill argues that judicial review leads Congress to attend to constitutional issues, though in court-constrained ways (Pickerill 2004). Ran Hirschl contends that many countries have established new bills of rights and given courts power to enforce them in order to protect neoliberal economic policies and other elite interests (Hirschl 2004). Kevin McMahon shows how FDR's administration helped restructure the federal judiciary to make it more receptive to civil rights claims (McMahon 2004). Keith Whittington has detailed the variety of ways resort to the judiciary can help strong but not omnipotent political actors to overcome entrenched interests and fractious, cross-pressured coalitions (Whittington 2005).

To some degree, these analyses are but variations on Martin Shapiro's behavioralist "political jurisprudence," which explains judicial decisions as services to interest groups and other political actors (Shapiro 1964). That is not surprising: to participants in the law and courts subfield, Shapiro's work has loomed far larger than scholarship in comparative politics or even American political development. Public law historical institutionalists have continued to stress, however, that even when engaged in "friendly judicial review," courts do not "simply do the bidding of political leaders" (Whittington 2005, 585). The judges' concerns about doctrinal consistency and their own institutional power, along with their sometimes distinct understandings of principles they share with "prominent elected officials," mean that their rulings often give such officials less, more, and other than what the officials desired. That is why "the delegation of power to the courts involves considerable long-term risks" for politicians, though today more politicians in more places are taking those risks (Hirschl 2004, 15). Paul Frymer adds, in good historical institutionalist fashion, that sometimes legislators have expanded judicial power in ways that have had unintended consequences. He argues that 1960s legisla-tors adopted what they saw as uncontroversial technical reforms to civil procedure rules sought by leading sectors of the legal community—but they ended up enabling courts to promote racial integration in labor unions (Frymer 2003, 484).

But even as they use forms of intercurrence and path dependence to grasp judicial conduct, many public law institutionalists still also explain what judges do and why by analyzing the role of ideas. Julie Novkov argues that, in partly unanticipated fashion, lawyers, interests groups, and judges built a path to universal protective labor laws in the Progressive and New Deal eras by shifting the doctrinal focus from *work* that needed protection to *workers* that needed protection. This change led to determinations first that women, and then all materially vulnerable workers, might legally benefit from state regulatory aid (Novkov 2001). Thomas Keck contends that the presence on the Rehnquist Court of activist conservatives, activist liberals, and centrist incrementalists collectively generated wide-ranging judicial activism despite much talk of restraint (Keck 2004). These accounts continue to employ fruitfully the focus on structures of ideas that first attracted many public law scholars to historical institutionalism, even as they also highlight external institu-tions and actors affecting the judiciary and the often unintended consequences of the institutionalization of diverse, frequently conflicting perspectives.

4 PUBLIC LAW AND HISTORICAL INSTITUTIONALISM TOMORROW

Their attention to ideas remains a distinctive strength, but as public law institution-alists become more self-consciously theoretical, it may prove to be in jeopardy. The dominant theoretical emphases in other historical institutionalist literatures rarely feature what some term "ideational" or "ideological" structures. To be sure, compar-ativists including Hall (1997), Berman (1998), and Blyth (2002), among others, address the role of ideas, and Pierson applauds such work on how "emerging worldviews" and "mental maps" may generate "institutions, organizations, and specialized actors." He also notes that once institutionalized, "basic outlooks on politics ... are generally tenacious. They are path dependent" (2004, 39–40). His stress remains, however, on identifying forms of positive feedback and unintended consequences, not on analyzing how the pursuit of agendas defined by complex, often internally inconsist-ent world-views might shape development. Similarly, Orren and Skowronek define institutions as having "*purposes*" and "mandates" that "carry on through time," contributing to intercurrent clashes as they often "riddle the political world with obsolescent and incongruous controls" (2004, 82, 86). But their focus is rarely on the substance of these purposes or institutional "reasons for being." They attend chiefly to conflicts among institutional orders seen as behaving in largely path-dependent fashions, in ways that produce collisions over time. Many leading historical institutionalists seem to resist giving too much analytical primacy to "values, norms, ideas . . . systems of meaning or normative frameworks" out of fear of moving inquiry beyond what is empirically determinable (Skocpol 1995, 105). Partly because public law institutionalists have had similar worries, many now favor an "institutional-systems" or "political regime" approach, centered on the relationships of courts to other institutional and group actors, rather than idea-centered work.

Yet precisely because courts are so prominently constrained and empowered by their duty to argue in terms of legal precedents and doctrines, public law scholars are still giving more attention to "patterns of purpose and meaning" than other historical institutionalists (Clayton 1999, 38). This attention, I submit, is desirable. When scholars such as March and Olsen, Thelen and Steinmo, and Hall and Taylor first began elaborating what might make historical institutionalism a valuable approach to the study of politics, they featured the role of institutions in shaping identities, values, preferences, and therefore behavior. But this role cannot be understood without close attention to ideas. However much institutional development may involve unintended consequences, unexpected collisions with other institutions, drift, layering, exhaustion, and more, the tasks of understanding the purposes that institutions embody, and of the consequences of the internal tensions and the transformative demands that those purposes exhibit, are inescapable. The real difficulties of studying ideas cannot justify shrinking from exploration of elements that are deeply constitutive of institutions, according to the leading definitions of what institutions are and what they do.

If public law scholars stopped attending to the pressures for development generated by institutionalized ideas, they would also lose a feature of their work that has distinguished them from behavioralist as well as some traditional legal accounts. They would be less able to defend the claim that courts possess some meaningful relative autonomy, rather than being purely instruments of external political forces, or mechanical articulators of either "the law" or judges' own fixed ideological attitudes. And they would be less able to argue that judicial deliberation involves some sincere efforts to make sense of legal materials, along with efforts to pursue institutional and ideological objectives strategically. Historical institutionalists studying law, then, cannot minimize the study of ideas without risking undue minimization of the role of courts in politics.

Greater attention to ideas, however, only compounds the leading difficulty besetting historical institutionalist analyses. We are to examine path-dependent institutions and intercurrences among institutional orders, and I am adding that we must examine "normative orders" and other structures of ideas. But there are so many institutions, so many orders, so many ideas! How can historical institutionalism hope to foster scholarship that accumulates, that tests and builds on existing work, rather than generating an assortment of loosely related studies?

These difficulties are versions of a problem haunting all social science. It is often impossible to include all the independent variables that might affect outcomes, without having so many as to preclude meaningful statistical relationships with the available "n's" for the dependent variables. Nothing can eliminate that problem, but there are ways to cope with it. Independent variables must be theoretically justified to gain entry into analyses; their existence must be empirically supported; and then scholars can over time weigh the power of some against others, accumulating evidence that certain variables have been most potent in certain circumstances.

It is not difficult, for example, for institutionalists to justify theoretically the claim that Congress, the Presidency, political parties, and interest groups are likely to be the institutions and actors that interact with the federal judiciary most consequentially. It is then possible in empirical investigations to show *how* these institutions and actors have interacted with the judiciary, and to demonstrate fairly conclusively that some actors, perhaps pro-civil rights members of FDR's Justice Department or ABA officials seeking the restructuring of federal rules of civil procedure, had more impact on the judiciary than others, perhaps political parties. It may be more difficult to identify empirically the presence of structures of ideas, such as conceptions of women's place and needs or of the legitimacy of conservative activism. But the work of scholars like Gillman, Bussiere, Novkov, Keck, and others gives reason to believe that these ideational factors can be well specified, located empirically in judicial opinions, advocacy briefs, and similar sources, and that their impact can be weighed systematically against other influences.

Undeniably, more has to be done to realize fully the promise of historical institutionalism. Theoretically, institutionalists need to formulate hypotheses or "middle-level" theories about what sorts of factors are most likely to disrupt path dependency under what circumstances, building on the categories suggested by Streeck and Thelen. Similarly, scholars must formulate and test accounts arguing that some institutions or institutional orders—perhaps legislative, executive, and judicial institutions; federal structures; parties; legal orders of class, race, and gender—are more consistently influential in certain contexts than others. And they must further develop how best to capture the role of ideas, perhaps as purposes embedded in existing institutions, perhaps as independent variables in their own right. Until we do more, it will remain premature to make grand claims for historical institutionalist scholarship in law and politics.

But to say that there is a lot still to do is not to deny that historical institutional scholars have already accomplished a lot, or that their work has great potential to achieve still more. It is rather to say that in the academy, as in politics, the fate of "isms" is generally determined only over many years, as early agendas are pursued and sometimes improved, sometimes discredited and abandoned, and as external factors also affect success. In legal studies, the growth of historical institutionalist scholarship seems rapid and promising. But fittingly, the future remains uncertain; scholarly agency will matter; and only time will tell.

REFERENCES

ACKERMAN, B. 1991. *We the People: Foundations.* Cambridge, Mass.: Harvard University Press.

AMAR, A. R. 2005. *America's Constitution: A Biography.* New York: Random House.

BERGER, S. (ed.) 1981. *Organizing Interests in Europe: Pluralism, Corporatism, and the Transformation of Politics.* Cambridge: Cambridge University Press.

BERMAN, S. 1998. *The Social Democratic Movement: Ideas and Politics in the Making of Interwar Europe.* Cambridge, Mass.: Harvard University Press.

BLYTH, M. 2002. *Great Transformations: Economic Ideas and Institutional Change in the Twentieth Century.* Cambridge: Cambridge University Press.

BURGESS, S. R. 1993. Beyond instrumental politics: the new institutionalism, legal rhetoric, and judicial supremacy. *Polity,* 25: 445–59.

BUSSIERE, E. 1997. *(Dis)entitling the poor: The Warren Court, welfare rights, and the American political tradition.* University Park: Pennsylvania State University Press.

CLAYTON, C. W. 1999. The Supreme Court and political jurisprudence: new and old institutionalisms. Pp. 15–41 in *Supreme Court Decision-Making: New Institutionalist Approaches,* ed. C. W. Clayton and H. Gillman. Chicago: University of Chicago Press.

—— and GILLMAN, H. (eds.) 1999. *Supreme Court Decision-Making: New Institutionalist Approaches.* Chicago: University of Chicago Press.

DIMAGGIO, P. J., and POWELL, W. W. 1991. Introduction. Pp. 1–38 in *The New Institutionalism in Organizational Analysis,* ed. P. J. DiMaggio and W. W. Powell. Chicago: University of Chicago Press.

FRYMER, P. 2003. Acting when elected officials won't: federal courts and civil rights enforcement in U.S. labor unions, 1935–85. *American Political Science Review,* 97: 483–99.

GILLMAN, H. 1993. *The Constitution Besieged: The Rise and Demise of Lochner Era Police Powers Jurisprudence.* Durham, NC: Duke University Press.

—— 1999. The Court as an idea, not a building (or a game): interpretive institutionalism and the analysis of Supreme Court decision-making. In Clayton and Gillman 1999: 65–87.

—— 2002. How political parties can use the courts to advance their agendas: federal courts in the United States, 1875–1891. *American Political Science Review,* 96: 511–24.

—— and CLAYTON, C. 1999. *The Supreme Court in American Politics: New Institutionalist Interpretations.* Lawrence: University of Kansas Press.

GRABER, M. A. 1993. The nonmajoritarian difficulty: legislative deference to the judiciary. *Studies in American Political Development,* 7: 35–73.

HALL, P. A., and TAYLOR, R. C. R. 1996. Political science and the three new institutionalisms. *Political Studies,* 44: 936–57.

—— 1997. The role of interests, institutions, and ideas in the comparative political economy of the industrialized nations. In *Comparative Politics: Rationality, Culture, and Structure,* ed. M. I. Lichbach and A. S. Zuckerman. Cambridge: Cambridge University Press.

HIRSCHL, R. 2004. *Toward Juristocracy: The Origins and Consequences of the New Constitutionalism*. Cambridge, Mass.: Harvard University Press.

KATZNELSON, I., and WEINGAST, B. R. 2005. Intersections between historical and rational choice institutionalism. In *Preferences and Situations: Points of Intersection Between Historical and Rational Choice Institutionalism*, ed. I. Katznelson and B. R. Weingast. New York: Russell Sage Foundation.

KECK, T. M. 2004. *The Most Activist Supreme Court in History: The Road to Modern Judicial Conservatism*. Chicago: University of Chicago Press.

KRASNER, S. D. 1978. *Defending the National Interest: Raw Materials, Investments and the U.S. Foreign Policy*. Princeton, NJ: Princeton University Press.

LOVELL, G. I. 2003. *Legislative Deferrals: Statutory Ambiguity, Judicial Power, and American Democracy*. New York: Cambridge University Press.

MCMAHON, K. J. 2004. *Reconsidering Roosevelt on Race: How the Presidency Paved the Road to Brown*. Chicago: University of Chicago Press.

MARCH, J. G., and OLSEN, J. P. 1984. The new institutionalism: organizational factors in political life. *American Political Science Review*, 78: 734–49.

———— 1989. *Rediscovering Institutions: The Organizational Basis of Politics*. New York: Free Press.

MEYER, J. W., BOLI, J., and THOMAS, G. M. 1987. Ontology and rationalization in the western account. In *Institutional Structure: Constituting State, Society, and the Individual*, ed. J. W. Meyer, J. Boli, and G. M. Thomas. Newbury Park, Calif.: Sage.

NOVKOV, J. 2001. *Constituting Workers, Protecting Women: Gender, Law, and Labor in the Progressive Era and New Deal Years*. Ann Arbor: University of Michigan Press.

ORREN, K., and SKOWRONEK, S. 2004. *The Search for American Political Development*. New York: Cambridge University Press.

PICKERILL, J. M. 2004. *Constitutional Deliberation in Congress: The Impact of Judicial Review in a Separated System*. Durham, NC: Duke University Press.

PIERSON, P. 2004. *Politics in Time: History, Institutions, and Social Analysis*. Princeton, NJ: Princeton University Press.

SHAPIRO, M. 1964. *Law and Politics in the Supreme Court*. New York: Free Press.

—— 1989. Political jurisprudence, public law, and post-consequentialist ethics: comment on Professors Barber and Smith. *Studies in American Political Development*, 3: 88–102.

SHEPSLE, K., and WEINGAST, B. 1983. Institutionalizing majority rule: a social choice theory with policy implications. *American Economic Review*, 73: 357–72.

SKOCPOL, T. 1979. *States and Social Revolutions: A Comparative Analysis of France, Russia and China*. New York: Cambridge University Press.

—— 1995. Why I am an historical institutionalist. *Polity*, 28: 105.

SKOWRONEK, S. 1982. *Building a New American State*. New York: Cambridge University Press.

SKRENTNY, J. D. 2006. Law and the American state. *Annual Review of Sociology*, 32: 213–44.

SMITH, R. M. 1988. Political jurisprudence, the "new institutionalism," and the future of public law. *American Political Science Review*, 82: 89–108.

—— 1992. If politics matters: implications for a "new institutionalism." *Studies in American Political Development*, 6: 1–36.

—— 2006. Which comes first, the ideas or the institutions? Pp. 91–113 in *Rethinking Political Institutions: The Art of the State*, ed. I. Shapiro, S. Skowronek, and D. Galvin. New York: New York University Press.

STONE, A. 1992. *The Birth of Judicial Politics in France: The Constitutional Council in Comparative Perspective*. New York: Oxford University Press.

STREECK, W. and THELEN, K. 2005. Introduction: institutional change in advanced political economies. Pp. 1–39 in *Beyond Continuity: Institutional Change in Advanced Political Economies*, ed. W. Streeck and K. Thelen. New York: Oxford University Press.

THELEN, K., and STEINMO, S. 1992. Historical institutionalism in comparative politics. Pp. 1– 32 in *Structuring Politics: Historical Institutionalism in Comparative Analysis*, ed. S. Steinmo, K. Thelen, and F. Longstreth. New York: Cambridge University Press.

WHITTINGTON, K. E. 2005. "Interpose your friendly hand:" political support for the exercise of judicial review by the United States Supreme Court. *American Political Science Review*, 99: 583–96.

PART III

COMPARATIVE JUDICIAL POLITICS

THE RULE OF LAW AND COURTS IN DEMOCRATIZING REGIMES

REBECCA BILL CHAVEZ

THE fortification of the rule of law is increasingly seen as a necessity for nascent democracies across the globe. The past decade has witnessed a growing recognition by political scientists that an independent judiciary can bolster both political and economic development. This recognition is central to the young but growing body of literature that addresses how emerging democracies build the rule of law and autonomous courts. As nations struggle to consolidate democracy, we have witnessed a surge of promising new scholarship on the conditions under which the rule of law emerges and endures. This movement in academia has accompanied the emphasis by influential sources of development funds, including the World Bank, the Inter-American Development Bank, and the International Monetary Fund, on the importance of independent judicial systems that have the capacity to encourage investment, protect rights, and bolster democracy.

In many third wave democracies, the judicial branch remains unable to place real constraints on the executive or other government actors. Countries such as Argentina, Russia, and Taiwan instituted open electoral competition before developing the rule of law. A myopic focus on elections is partly to blame for the fragility of the democratic scaffolding in many nascent democracies. Competitive elections have masked the fact that other essential components of democracy have not taken root (Dahl 1971; Karl 1986). For instance, weak political institutions and the remnants of authoritarianism have impeded the development of the rule of law, resulting in "illiberal" or "delegative" democracies (Diamond 1996; Larkins 1998; O'Donnell 1994; Zakaria 1997). Without the rule of law, democratic consolidation may never occur. Judicial independence and the rule of law constitute important bulwarks against the erosion of democratic institutions.

1 INDEPENDENT COURTS AND THE RULE OF LAW

The rule of law is a broad concept that encompasses many areas including judicial autonomy, access to justice, human rights, and property rights. It entails the equality of all citizens under the law and predictability in the application of rules and regulations. Although political scientists increasingly list the rule of a law as a critical element of liberal democracy, they have only recently begun to define, seriously examine, and empirically research the concept. With the rise of scholarship on the rule of law in democratizing regimes during the past decade, the precise meaning of the rule of law has become the subject of much debate (Tamanaha 2004). Peerenboom laments the lack of literature on alternate conceptions of the rule of law. In his analysis of China, he concludes that although China may not develop a liberal democratic rule of law, we should not abandon the rule of law or reserve it for liberal democracies. The rule of law, he argues, may look different in China, but it has the potential to meet the minimal requirement of restraint on the state (Peerenboom 2002b).

Merryman's definition provides a starting point: the rule of law is "a system of government in which the acts of agencies and officials of all kinds are subject to the principle of legality, and in which procedures are available to interested persons to test the legality of governmental action and to have an appropriate remedy when the act in question fails to pass the test" (Merryman 1985, 40–1). In cases of concentration of power in a single person or group, however, there is no way to ensure that those who wield power act within the law. Instead, the individual or group can make, change, and enforce laws but is not bound by those laws. Berman writes: "[I]t [the rule of law] meant that the respective heads of each body would be bound by the law which they themselves had enacted; they could change it lawfully, but until they did so they must obey it—they must rule *under* law" (Berman 1983, 292).

The rule of law requires an effective system of horizontal accountability that is composed of government institutions that hold one another accountable to the law and to the public. Such a system is necessary to constrain arbitrary government action and to ensure that state actors comply with the constitution. As O'Donnell argues, horizontal accountability is a critical ingredient of democracy: "In institutionalized democracies, accountability runs not only vertically, making elected officials answerable to the ballot box, but also horizontally, across a network of relatively autonomous powers (i.e., other institutions) that can call into question, and eventually punish, improper ways of discharging the responsibility of a given official" (O'Donnell 1994, 61–2). State agencies with the autonomy, the authority, and the will to act as controls on other government agencies and on the private sector are a necessary condition for horizontal accountability. Where power is dispersed and embedded in multiple institutions that act as horizontal accountability agencies, the rule of law is possible. Without these agencies, dominant actors have little or no incentive to obey constitutional constraints on their exercise of power but rather have incentives to ignore or eliminate these constraints. An independent judicial branch is part of a larger system of overlapping and mutually reinforcing agencies of horizontal accountability.

An autonomous judiciary on its own is not enough to ensure the rule of law, but it can help in its construction by binding powerful actors. In addition to being efficient, accessible, well funded, and well staffed, the courts must be independent from all actors that tend to monopolize power. In order to function as a horizontal accountability agency, the judiciary cannot be subordinate to the other branches of government, to the military, or to powerful elements in the private sector. An independent judiciary can help build the rule of law by guaranteeing that those who wield power submit to the rules. Only a judiciary that is independent of pressure, inducement, and manipulation can check abuses of power. Judicial independence requires impartiality and "political insularity" (Fiss 1993, 56). Judges must not be biased in favor of or fear to challenge the powers that be.

Without effective constraints such as an independent judiciary, countries are trapped in what Weingast calls "asymmetric equilibrium." Here, the sovereign has incentives to transgress formal limits on its power (Weingast 1997, 7). Williamson argues that *ex ante* arrangements ensuring compliance with formal limits can prevent costly *ex post* opportunistic behavior or shirking. In his discussion of transaction cost economics, he writes, "Rather than reply to opportunism in kind, therefore, the wise prince [governing regime] is one who seeks both to give and receive "credible commitments." Incentives may be realigned, and/or superior governance structures within which to organize transactions may be devised" (Williamson 1985, 48–9). An autonomous judicial branch is one institutional means of organizing transactions to achieve credible commitments and to prevent transgressions. By placing costs on *ex post* opportunism, an independent judiciary creates incentives that prevent abuses of power.

England prior to the Glorious Revolution and Old Regime France illustrate the negative consequences of the failure to develop independent judicial institutions. These historical cases are predecessors of today's democratizing regimes that have yet to construct the rule of law. North and Weingast use the case of England prior to 1689 to demonstrate the disastrous effects of failing to limit the Crown's authority. Until the Revolution Settlement, an elite pact that served as a coordinating device, sovereign transgressions were common. The Revolution Settlement introduced parliamentary supremacy, abolished many royal powers, and established the rule of law. The development of a constitution that established the supremacy of common law effectively tied the king's hands (North and Weingast 1989). Root shows that only with the development of institutions capable of checking the king's power was France able to establish the conditions necessary for economic and political stability (Root 1989). As seventeenth-century England and Old Regime France illustrate, institutions condition the behavior of governments. In particular, autonomous judicial institutions can compel state actors to rule according to law, introducing greater liberty, predictability, and political stability.

Scholars often limit their definition of the rule of law to constraints on state actors. A complete definition must go a step further. The rule of law requires that not only state agents but also any individual or sector that exercises significant power be subject to legality. Otherwise, these actors can use their economic or political power to violate the formal rules of the game. Threats to the rule of law can come from a diverse group of powerful actors that includes executive functionaries, legislators, military officials, wealthy businessmen, religious leaders, and union representatives. Any actor who wields political, economic, or military power must submit to the law.

Threats to the rule of law vary across and within regions. Different countries face different dangers depending on where economic and political power is concentrated. For instance, in the England described by North and Weingast and the France described by Root, the Crown represented the principal danger. In Russia and other post-Communist nations in Central and Eastern Europe, including Albania, Belarus, Kazakhstan, and Romania, the major challenge is the presidency, which may be elected democratically but is thereafter subject to few constraints (Herron and Randazzo 2003; Schwartz 1998). Executive dominance is also a threat to the rule of law in Tanzania and Zambia (Gloppen 2003). In Bulgaria, the parliament has interfered with judicial autonomy (Melone 1996). In the case of Hungary, it is the state administrative apparatus that violates the rule of law (Örkény and Scheppele 1999). In Pakistan, the military and extremist religious groups represent a challenge. In China, it is Communist Party dominance that poses a danger (Lubman 1999). In many nascent democracies, members of the private sector with a monopoly on the means of production are a major threat. In the case of El Salvador, for instance, the judiciary has been more focused on preserving the privileges of the economic elite than on protecting the rights of all citizens (Popkin 2000).

Variation also exists within regions. In Venezuela, the armed forces remain a potential hazard alongside the executive, even though for most of Latin America the major challenge to the rule of law is no longer a military coup. In Colombia, drug lords along with guerilla and paramilitary groups present a danger to established political institutions. Across Latin America as a region, however, the concentration of power in the president is a principal challenge to the rule of law. As a result of executive supremacy, other state actors lack effective checks on the president. In the context of Latin American ultrapresidentialism, judges must have the capacity to act as controls on the executive (Kapiszewski and Taylor 2006).

The emerging literature on the rule of law in nascent democracies highlights that a country's position on the judicial autonomy continuum depends on more than constitutional guarantees of life tenure or of protections against salary reduction. In order to determine the degree of judicial independence in a given country, a consideration of informal practices must accompany the analysis of the rules outlined in national constitutions, what Madison calls "parchment barriers" (Madison 1937, 321). Informal practices that allow elected officials to control the courts often overshadow formal guarantees of judicial independence. Institutionalized subconstitutional practices can shape the incentive structure facing judges in such a way that they are unlikely to oppose government policies. These subconstitutional practices can include withholding funds from the judiciary, imposing limitations on the jurisdiction of the courts, or more drastic measures such as removing judges and court packing. An understanding of informal practices that shape behavior and incentives is essential where actual behavior is inconsistent with constitutional provisions. Nevertheless, many scholars mistakenly limit their analysis to formal guarantees of judicial autonomy. Actual practices may reveal that the formal institutions are mere façades that hide the subordination of the courts (Chavez 2004).

As a result of the prevalence of informal practices, scholars have begun to focus their attention on how to bolster judicial independence and build the rule of law in new democracies. Although scholars agree that judicial autonomy is an important component of the rule of law, there are competing views about the circumstances under which independent courts emerge and endure. Two of the most fruitful areas of scholarship are the separation of powers approach and research that highlights the role of nonstate actors.

2 BUILDING THE RULE OF LAW: THE SEPARATION OF POWERS FRAMEWORK

Over the past decade, much of the literature dealing with the construction of the rule of law in new democracies argues that independent courts arise from the strategic choices of relevant actors. Rulers abide by the law only when the costs of disobeying the law outweigh the benefits. According to the separation of powers approach, the rule of law becomes possible when no single actor or group of actors has sufficient power to dominate. This school of thought considers the impact of the broader political context on judicial independence. In particular, the distribution of power is what matters.

The party competition thesis is a variant of the literature that focuses on power relations and political fragmentation. Increasingly, scholars are finding that party competition can foster independent courts. In those nascent democracies where a ruling party foresees that it will remain in power indefinitely, the development of judicial autonomy is unlikely. In contrast, where two or more parties compete aggressively with one another, a ruling party is likely to accept and even promote autonomous courts. In-depth single case studies and comparative studies from different regions, including Asia, Eastern Europe, Latin America, the Middle East, and the United States, support the claim that the degree of party competition provides a persuasive explanation for the waxing and waning of judicial autonomy.

In his groundbreaking comparative study of Japan and the United States, Ramseyer employs the party competition thesis, arguing that judicial autonomy depends on whether politicians expect elections to continue indefinitely and that if elections do indeed continue, whether the ruling party expects to win indefinitely. An independent judiciary is likely to emerge only when there is a high likelihood of continued elections and a high likelihood of the ruling party being defeated. In the case of Japan, for instance, continuous rule by the Liberal Democratic Party (LDP) for close to four decades beginning in 1955 created a climate in which the courts were easily manipulated (Ramseyer 1994). A similar phenomenon occurred in Mexico where the Institutional Revolutionary Party (PRI) controlled the government for close to seventy years. Prolonged PRI dominance led to executive subordination of the courts. (Domingo 2000). The case of Argentina also supports the argument that when a party foresees its displacement, it has incentives to fortify the judiciary. Organs that protect the opposition today may protect the ruling party tomorrow, when it becomes the opposition (Chavez 2004).

As part of his insurance thesis, Ginsburg persuasively uses party competition to explain the varying levels of judicial autonomy in three new Asian democracies: Korea, Mongolia, and Taiwan. When parties compete for power, rulers support judicial independence as a form of insurance in the face of possible electoral defeat. In Korea, intense competition among three parties of relatively equal strength permitted the creation of an independent constitutional court in 1988. The risk-averse parties favored a court that would have the autonomy to act as political insurance in a climate of electoral uncertainty. In Mongolia, although the former Communist Party was in a dominant position, the recent emergence of viable opposition parties led to the 1992 creation of a constitutional court that enjoys a surprisingly high degree of autonomy. In contrast, Taiwan's hegemonic party system led to a weak and subordinate court; the dominant Kuomintang party was able to prevent the creation of an independent constitutional court (Ginsburg 2003).

Finkel also makes an insurance policy argument, which she skillfully applies to the case of Mexico. Following close to seven decades of dominance by a single party, the PRI, President Ernesto Zedillo in 1994 introduced a series of reforms that increased the independence of the judicial branch. Zedillo's willingness to create a judiciary capable of checking the power of the president and of his dominant PRI appears to counter political logic, but it makes sense as an insurance policy to protect the ruling party from its rivals. As PRI leaders discovered that they were unlikely to retain their dominant position, they opted to empower the Mexican Supreme Court as a hedge against the loss of office (Finkel 2005).

The insurance thesis and party fragmentation argument also provide an explanation for variation in judicial independence in the nascent democracies of Eastern Europe. In their study of eight post-Communist countries in Eastern Europe, Smithey and Ishiyama use the level of party system fragmentation to explain the variation in judges' ability to exercise political power (Smithey and Ishiyama 2002). In his explanation for the variation found among Bulgaria, Hungary, and Poland, Magalhaes argues that electoral uncertainty encourages self-interested political actors to accept autonomous courts (Magalhaes 1999). Moravcsik uses a similar logic to explain the creation of international human rights regimes in postwar Europe. He finds that emerging democracies are more likely to support binding human rights regimes than are mature democracies. Nascent democracies favor human rights regimes because such regimes lead to an independent court, which serves as a form of insurance that locks in democratic institutions in the face of future political uncertainty. The international judicial body responsible for enforcing a human rights regime creates judicial constraints on future governments that may attempt to weaken democracy (Moravcsik 2000).

In his compelling comparative study of Canada, New Zealand, Israel, and South Africa, Hirschl argues that the global shift toward judicial empowerment stems from the self-interested behavior of strategic actors. According to his theory of hegemonic preservation, when a ruling party foresees its replacement, it is willing to transfer power to the courts and to enact constitutional reforms that will constrain those who will replace it. As the threatened political elites see their popular support begin to erode, they seek to lock in their policy preferences by transferring policy-making power to the courts (Hirschl 2004).

In his study of subnational constitutional courts in Russia, Trochev employs the strategic actor assumption but challenges the claim that the political elite create independent judicial institutions in response to electoral uncertainty. Instead, he finds that dominant political actors create autonomous constitutional courts as means of consolidating their ruling status. Like Hirschl, Trochev highlights how judicial review allows political elites to retain their power (Trochev 2004). Furthermore, Trochev's work on judicial politics at the regional level in Russia serves as an important reminder that subnational analysis is a powerful tool for comparativists who seek to understand the role of courts in democratizing regimes.

Brown applies a strategic actor argument to the Middle East. He asserts that leaders in Egypt and the Gulf states constructed an independent judiciary that constrained their authority as part of their effort to create a more centralized and intrusive state. According to Brown, the political elite were willing to build a system that would reduce their control over specific cases in exchange for insurance that their regulations would be enforced across society (Brown 1997).

The separation of powers or political fragmentation framework has been useful in explaining the changing level of judicial independence in other countries, including the United States, Russia, Mexico, and Argentina (Shapiro 1986; Ferejohn 2002; Epstein, Knight, and Shvetsova 2001, Epstein and Knight 2003). In his persuasive study of Mexico, Ríos-Figueroa uses fragmentation to explain the emergence of Supreme Court autonomy. When the PRI lost its majority in the House in 1997, the Court began to rule against the government (Ríos-Figueroa 2007).

Evidence from both the federal level and the provincial level in Argentina shows that party competition creates a climate in which an independent judiciary can emerge. Party balance encourages divided government, which permits the legislature to check the president. Without a majority in Congress, a president cannot push through legislation that subordinates the judiciary (Chavez 2004). In their study of the Argentine Supreme Court from 1935 through 1998, Iaryczower, Spiller, and Tommasi argue that justices are strategic actors. The likelihood that a justice will rule against the government decreases the stronger the president's control over Congress (Iaryczower, Spiller, and Tommasi 2002). In their comparative study of Argentina and the United States, Chavez, Ferejohn, and Weingast use a spatial model to show that when significant and sustained disagreements arise among elected officials, such as occur under divided government, judges have the ability to challenge the state and sustain an independent course, with little fear of political retribution (Chavez, Ferejohn, and Weingast 2003). Helmke employs the separation of powers approach to explain why non-independent Supreme Court justices acting rationally have ruled against the Argentine government. In order to avoid being purged by an incoming administration, justices strategically defect and rule against the current government as its power wanes. The strategic defection model contrasts Dahl's depiction of the legal-political cycle in the United States where justices who were appointed by the previous administration rule against the government at the beginning of a new administration (Dahl 1957). In Argentina, the high level of institutional instability leads to a reverse cycle (Helmke 2005).

The separation of powers or strategic actor approach conflicts with political culture explanations. In her well-argued analysis of Chile, Scribner focuses on whether there is a political majority or coalition support for the president, which challenges the literature that attributes the deference of the Chilean Supreme Court to a particular judicial culture (Scribner 2004; Hilbink 1999). Couso also challenges the argument that the Chilean judiciary's deference to the political branches stems from a nondemocratic political culture. He asserts that the Chilean courts' reluctance to exercise their power of judicial review represents the continuation of a long-held strategic stance of avoiding politically controversial cases. This reluctance has allowed the judiciary to preserve its independence (Couso 2003). In his case study of Chile under General Augusto Pinochet (1973–90), Barros argues that even autocratic rulers are sometimes bound by law. Despite the impression of unlimited military power during the Pinochet dictatorship, the rule of law was possible because the armed forces were divided into distinct services that were potential checks on one another. The military acted as a collective sovereign rather than a unified entity. In order to ensure that no single service dominated, the different groups agreed upon a set of rules that limited their power. Like a democracy, if an authoritarian government is comprised of a plurality competing actors, it will create rules that ultimately constrain the rulers (Barros 2003).

3 Building the Rule of Law: The Role of Civil Society and the International Community

The burgeoning literature on the construction of the rule of law includes impressive scholarship on the key role of nonstate actors, particularly of civil society and the international community. Reform coalitions composed of domestic civil society and external actors can be central to progress toward judicial autonomy in new democracies. In nations where those with a monopoly on power have hardened against the rule of law, dense interaction between civil society and political actors is necessary for change. Ultimately, in order to alter the status quo, the legislature must adopt reform and the executive branch must either approve reform or be overridden. By providing alternative sources of information and increasing the demand for change, reformist networks can foster vertical accountability, which is secured through the electoral process. A reform coalition can impose electoral costs on subordination of the courts by mobilizing public opinion against state actors that subordinate the courts and by advancing the cause of opposition parties.

The experiences of a wide variety of countries, including Argentina, Canada, Egypt, El Salvador, Guatemala, India, Indonesia, Malaysia, Mexico, South Africa, the United Kingdom, and the United States, demonstrate that the creation of reform networks of nonstate actors is a dynamic process that relies heavily on information politics and leverage politics. Information and material leverage are sources of power for reform coalitions that seek to establish the rule of law (Keck and Sikkink 1998, 16–25). The documentation and dissemination of data about subordination of the courts draws domestic and international groups into the coalitions. The economic vulnerability of many nascent democracies allows external actors to use material leverage to push government to enact reforms. Outside actors can impose sanctions and employ conditionality to pressure for change.

Domestic civil society groups typically serve as the foundation for reform coalitions. Across the globe, civil society groups have acted as watchdogs that expose the subordination of the courts. In order to attract members, the coalition must demonstrate that a deliberate wrongdoing has harmed a shared value (Keck and Sikkink 1998, 26–9, 206–8). By showing how a pliant judiciary undermines shared values such as human rights and economic development, the coalitions can recruit a diverse group of local actors with an interest in an independent judicial branch, including human rights groups, lawyers, judges, and business associations. In the United States, public opinion and civil society were critical in the struggle that blocked President Franklin D. Roosevelt's court-packing initiative (Friedman 2000). In his work on Egypt, Moustafa shows that by developing ties to civil society groups, the courts helped direct those groups to focus on reform efforts that bolstered judicial independence (Moustafa 2003). In Guatemala and Mexico, nongovernmental organizations have been key actors in the push for judicial reform (Sieder 2003; Domingo 2004). In his impressive study of judicial politics in Mexico, Staton shows how public support for the courts creates pressure for officials to comply with adverse rulings (Staton 2004). In Tanzania where most citizens view the courts as irrelevant, civil society has not provided the social support that would make it costly for the executive to undermine judicial autonomy (Gloppen 2003).

Lawyers and judges are often on the front line of reform coalitions. Lawyers and judges provide coalitions with valuable expertise, and their deep commitment to the rule of law contributes to their effectiveness. Judicial autonomy is a central concern for these actors who work within the judiciary. For those attorneys and judges who resist pressure, an independent judiciary is necessary for a successful career. When trying cases, attorneys rely on predictable and unbiased application of laws. Attorneys who engage in the fight for an independent judiciary represent an important strain of "cause lawyering" (Sarat and Scheingold 1998). As the cases of Indonesia and Malaysia demonstrate, lawyers can be valuable players in the struggle to create and defend the rule of law (Lev 1998). Judges who challenge the interests of those with a monopoly on power must not fear retribution. The experiences of Tanzania and Argentina illustrate how individual judges can move the cause of judicial autonomy forward (Widner 2001; Chavez 2004).

In his thoughtful comparative study of the United States, Canada, Britain, and India, Epp demonstrates the central role that can be played by a supportive bar.

In both Canada and the U.S., well-organized and ideologically diverse lawyers' associations were critical actors in the struggle to establish rights-protecting regimes. Although lawyers in Britain are a more homogeneous group, their growing numbers and increasing diversification allowed them to work alongside other civil society groups to overcome the traditionally conservative judiciary and wage a modest rights revolution. In contrast, the fragmented and individualized legal profession in India hindered a rights revolution (Epp 1998).

In recognition of the economic costs of executive subordination of the courts, powerful business organizations can help establish the rule of law. In the case of Argentina, for instance, business groups joined the national reform coalition and rallied around the call for "*seguridad jurídica*," or judicial security. National associations of corporate executives and entrepreneurs lobbied for a predictable judicial environment to encourage investment, protect property rights, and enforce contracts (Chavez 2004). The demand for protection of property rights also created pressure for reform in Mexico (Domingo 2000).

Without the support of a vibrant and well-organized domestic civil society, international actors are limited in their ability to push for judicial reform in democratizing regimes. Indeed, external actors are most successful when they join forces with local civil society. The support of domestic groups legitimizes the international presence. In her case study of El Salvador, Popkin attributes the failure of international judicial reform efforts to the fact that domestic civil society did not play a supportive role. After emerging from a twelve-year civil war, civil society in El Salvador was not strong enough to exert pressure effectively on the state for reform of the criminal justice system (Popkin 2000).

The international community works alongside domestic civil society groups to promote the rule of law in new democracies. External funding sources increasingly recognize the importance of judicial reforms that bolster the rule of law and have placed these reforms high on their development agendas. The economic vulnerability of many democratizing nations permits external actors to use material leverage to push governments to enact reforms. Nascent democracies that rely on foreign aid are likely to respond to pressure from international agencies that advocate judicial autonomy. For example, the World Bank and International Monetary Fund have effectively employed aid conditionality and threatened economic sanctions to push for reform. In the case of Argentina, domestic civil society actors built relationships with influential international organizations that exerted external pressure on the executive branch to push for judicial autonomy. The international component amplified the call for the rule of law. Pressure from outside Argentina's borders countered President Carlos Menem's initial unresponsiveness to local groups. International organizations aided the reform coalition in two primary ways: they provided material leverage, and they bolstered domestic coalition members by providing training and funding (Chavez 2004).

International investors can also serve as an important source of pressure and leverage. In the Middle East and Asia, for instance, the need to attract foreign investment has been central to the push for legal reform. Moustafa attributes Egypt's ability to establish an independent constitutional court despite the authoritarian political system in large part to the need for foreign investment during the shift to a market-driven economy (Moustafa 2003). Jordan, Lebanon, and Kuwait have sought reform in the arena of commercial law as a way to attract foreign investment. The rule of law is essential for the nations of Asia that are striving to deepen economic liberalization and consolidate market reforms (Carothers 1998). In China, market-oriented reforms bolstered efforts to protect property rights, attract investment, and encourage trade (Peerenboom 2002a; Potter 2004). The European Union and Japan also illustrate how economic liberalization encourages judicial empowerment (Keleman and Sibbitt 2004).

In his insightful study of South Africa's creation of a bill of rights protected by judicial review through an independent judiciary, Klug demonstrates the key role played by the international community. While not discounting the uniqueness of the South African context, Klug emphasizes the impact of global forces. In order to reintegrate itself into the international economy and gain legitimacy in the eyes of the global community, post-apartheid South Africa had no choice but to accept reforms. Klug argues persuasively that the United Nations along with non-governmental organizations and transnational corporations created the pressure that shaped the emerging democracy's new legal framework, which included an independent judiciary. South Africa was also influenced by the international political culture, which embraced the notion of constitutional supremacy (Klug 2000).

4 Conclusions

As Iraq, Afghanistan, and other democratizing regimes across the globe struggle to establish the rule of law, the scholarship on judicial autonomy in new democracies will undoubtedly continue to grow. As indicated above, a substantial research effort is already under way. A positive trend has been the use of diverse methodologies to address the question of how nascent democracies build the rule of law. The use of qualitative, in-depth case studies and the application of the comparative method have proved fruitful in theory-building. Moreover, an increasing number of scholars are employing the rational choice framework with the tools of positive political theory.

Many scholars who study the development of independent judiciaries in nascent democracies use the separation of powers approach. Despite the many strengths of this framework, it is not without limitations. The separation of powers framework is an "external" account of judicial behavior in the sense that it claims that conditions outside of the courts and the law shape the incentives of judges and, consequently, their behavior. However, one can imagine other external explanations that do not focus on the composition of the political branches but rather concentrate on the dispositions of powerful social groups such as the military, regional governments, labor unions, ethnic groups, or social movements. With the exception of the work on the role of social movements or reform coalitions, such alternative external accounts remain under-represented in the literature.

In addition, many of the strategic actor models discussed in this chapter are formulated for separation of powers systems in which the judicial branch is supposed to enjoy constitutional independence from the legislature and executive. However, in parliamentary systems, the notion of judicial independence is different, as the exercise of judicial and executive authority in such systems is supposed to be subordinate to the legislature. Judicial independence in parliamentary systems is typically protected by requiring judges to give literalist interpretations for legal codes with the expectation that the legislature can quickly alter codes that lead to unacceptable results. Nevertheless, one can imagine operationalizing political fragmentation in ways that would fit the realities of parliamentary government. For example, coalition or minority governments might have a weaker capacity to respond to adverse judicial rulings and therefore provide judges with more scope for autonomous action. In addition, the emergence of powerful supranational judicial institutions, such as the European Court of Justice, the European Court of Human Rights, and the Inter-American Commission on Human Rights, present further arenas in which judges are able to act independently.

External theories stand in some opposition to internal accounts of judicial behavior. Part of the very idea of legality or the rule of law is the notion that there is an explanation for any proper judicial ruling that refers only to sources internal to law, including statutes, regulations, prior judicial decisions, and accepted principles of legal interpretation. Thus, it is not surprising that in virtually all cases in which the separation of powers approach is used, there is a plausible internal explanation for the result. The question arises then of the relationship between internal and external explanations, a question that has not yet been addressed adequately by the literature. Both internal and external factors place limits on decisions without strictly determining them (Chavez, Ferejohn, and Weingast 2003).

Future research should include further study of the way in which external and internal explanations interact. In the case of Chile, two plausible alternative theories coexist, yet there remains insufficient discussion on how cultural or ideological explanations of judicial behavior might interact with the strategic actor model put forward by Scribner and Couso. In her excellent study, for instance, Hilbink argues that the nondemocratic culture and illiberal ideology of the judiciary, which equate judicial professionalism with apoliticism, have resulted in passive judges who do not assert their independence (Hilbink 1999). Case studies of China also illustrate the importance of considering the impact of resilient local norms on legal reform initiatives (Lubman 1999; Peerenboom 2002*a*; Potter 2004). In her study of judicial reform in Guatemala, Sieder cautions against focusing solely on institutional factors and stresses the importance of considering the complex interaction of a country's specific historical legacy and cultural context (Sieder 2003). In his analysis of the constitutional courts of Eastern Europe, Schwartz suggests that political culture and tradition have contributed to the success of the courts in Slovakia (Schwartz 1998).

In addition, most of the literature on building the rule of law in democratizing regimes overlooks the impact of domestic economic factors. Although the scholarship on reform coalitions considers the role of international sources of financial aid to new democracies, there is very little research on how patterns of economic power at the domestic level impact the rule of law. For instance, the case of Argentina suggests that socioeconomic complexity increases the likelihood of disputes that pave the way for the emergence of an independent judiciary. When there is plurality of strong domestic economic actors in competition with one another, they require a secure way to protect property rights, to enforce contracts, and to mediate economic disputes. Competing economic groups that vie for power push for a mechanism of adjudication. In contrast, the concentration of assets stands in the way of the rule of law; there is no need for a body to adjudicate. In countries where a dominant elite is unified, concentrated ownership of the means of production obstructs the emergence of a neutral referee (Chavez 2004).

There is also need for further research on the relationship between economic inequality and the rule of law in democratizing regimes, in particular on how inequity impacts access to justice. Many nascent democracies face pervasive income inequality and poverty. In countries characterized by widespread economic hardship and social distress, the wealthy tend to have advantages in the legal system while the courts often fail to protect vulnerable groups. In their study of democratizing regimes, scholars would do well to expand their conception of the rule of law to include greater emphasis on access to justice (Méndez, O'Donnell, and Pinheiro 1999; Ungar 2002).

Despite gaps in the literature, the body of work on the rule of law in nascent democracies is a strong one. This achievement is especially notable in light of the fact that as recently as the early 1990s, there was very little research on the role of the judiciary in democratizing regimes. Not just the subfield of democratization, but the field of comparative politics more generally had overlooked law and courts (Gibson, Caldeira, and Baird 1998, 343). Fortunately, over the past decade, there has been increasing recognition of the importance of independent courts for democratic consolidation. As more countries move along the spectrum toward democracy, there will be greater opportunity to generate theory and to study additional cases that will make this new focus of scholarship even richer.

REFERENCES

BARROS, R. 2003. Dictatorship and the rule of law: rules and military power in Pinochet's Chile. Pp. 188–219 in *Democracy and the Rule of Law*, ed. J. M. Maravall and A. Przeworski. New York: Cambridge University Press.

BERMAN, H. J. 1983. *Law and Revolution: The Formation of the Western Legal Tradition.* Cambridge, Mass.: Harvard University Press.

BROWN, N. J. 1997. *The Rule of Law in the Arab World: Courts in Egypt and the Gulf.* New York: Cambridge University Press.

CAROTHERS, T. 1998. The rule of law revival. *Foreign Affairs*, 77: 95–106.

CHAVEZ, R. B. 2004. *The Rule of Law in Nascent Democracies: Judicial Politics in Argentina.* Stanford, Calif.: Stanford University Press.

—— FEREJOHN, J. A., and WEINGAST, B. R. 2003. A theory of the politically independent judiciary. Presented at the annual meeting of the American Political Science Association, Philadelphia.

COUSO, J. A. 2003. The politics of judicial review in Chile in the era of democratic transition, 1990–2002. *Democratization*, 10: 70–91.

DAHL, R. A. 1957. Decision-making in a democracy: the Supreme Court as a national policy-maker. *Journal of Public Law*, 6: 279–95.

—— 1971. *Polyarchy: Participation and Opposition.* New Haven, Conn.: Yale University Press.

DIAMOND, L. 1996. Democracy in Latin America: degrees, illusions, and directions for consolidation. Pp. 52–104 in *Beyond Sovereignty: Collectively Defending Democracy in the Americas*, ed. T. Farer. Baltimore: Johns Hopkins University Press.

DOMINGO, P. 2000. Judicial independence: the politics of the Supreme Court in Mexico. *Journal of Latin American Studies*, 32: 705–35.

—— 2004. Judicialization of politics or politicization of the judiciary? Recent trends in Latin America. *Democratization*, 11: 104–26.

EPP, C. R. 1998. *The Rights Revolution: Lawyers, Activists, and Supreme Courts in Comparative Perspective.* Chicago: University of Chicago Press.

EPSTEIN, L., and KNIGHT, J. 2003. Constitutional borrowing and nonborrowing. *International Journal of Constitutional Law*, 1: 196–223.

—— —— and SHVETSOVA, O. 2001. The role of constitutional courts in the maintenance and establishment of democratic systems of government. *Law and Society Review*, 35: 117–63.

FEREJOHN, J. 2002. Judicializing politics, politicizing law. *Law and Contemporary Problems*, 65: 41–68.

FINKEL, J. 2005. Judicial reform as insurance policy: Mexico in the 1990s. *Latin American Politics and Society*, 47: 87–113.

FISS, O. 1993. The right degree of independence. Pp. 55–72 in *Transition to Democracy in Latin America: The Role of the Judiciary*, ed. I. P. Stotzky. Boulder, Colo.: Westview.

FRIEDMAN, B. 2000. The history of the countermajoritarian difficulty, part four: law's politics. *University of Pennsylvania Law Review*, 148: 971–1064.

GIBSON, J. L., CALDEIRA, G. A., and BAIRD, V. A. 1998. On the legitimacy of national high courts. *American Political Science Review*, 92: 343–58.

GINSBURG, T. 2003. *Judicial Review in New Democracies: Constitutional Courts in Asian Cases.* New York: Cambridge University Press.

GLOPPEN, S. 2003. The accountability function of the courts in Tanzania and Zambia. *Democratization*, 10: 112–36.

HELMKE, G. 2005. *Courts Under Constraints: Judges, Generals, and Presidents in Argentina*. New York: Cambridge University Press.

HERRON, E. S., and RANDAZZO, K. A. 2003. The relationship between independence and judicial review in post-communist countries. *Journal of Politics*, 65: 422–38.

HILBINK, E. 1999. Legalism against democracy: the political role of the judiciary in Chile, 1964–1994. Ph.D. dissertation, University of California at San Diego.

HIRSCHL, R. 2004. *Towards Juristocracy: The Origins and Consequences of the New Constitutionalism*. Cambridge, Mass.: Harvard University Press.

IARYCZOWER, M., SPILLER, P. T., and TOMMASI, M. 2002. Judicial independence in unstable environments, Argentina 1935–1998. *American Journal of Political Science*, 46: 699–716.

KAPISZEWSKI, D., and TAYLOR, M. M. 2006. Doing courts justice? Studying judicial politics in Latin America. Presented at the annual meeting of the American Political Science Association, Philadelphia.

KARL, T. L. 1986. Imposing consent? Electoralism versus democratization in El Salvador. Pp. 9–36 in *Elections and Democratization in Latin America, 1980–1985*, ed. P. W. Drake and E. Silva. San Diego: Center for Iberian and Latin American Studies and Center for U.S.–Mexican Studies, University of California.

KECK, M. E., and SIKKINK, K. 1998. *Activists Beyond Borders: Advocacy Networks in International Politics*. Ithaca, NY: Cornell University Press.

KELEMAN, R. D., and SIBBITT, E. C. 2004. The globalization of American law. *International Organization*, 103–36.

KLUG, H. 2000. *Constituting Democracy: Law, Globalism, and South Africa's Political Reconstruction*. New York: Cambridge University Press.

LARKINS, C. 1998. The judiciary and delegative democracy in Argentina. *Comparative Politics*, 30: 423–42.

LEV, D. 1998. Lawyers' causes in Indonesia and Malaysia. Pp. 431–52 in *Cause Lawyering: Political Commitments and Professional Responsibilities*, ed. A. Sarat and S. Scheingold. New York: Oxford University Press.

LUBMAN, S. B. 1999. *Bird in a Cage: Legal Reform in China after Mao*. Stanford, Calif.: Stanford University Press.

MADISON, J. 1937. Federalist No. 48. In *The Federalist: A Commentary on the Constitution of the United States*. New York: Random House; originally published 1788.

MAGALHAES, P. C. 1999. The politics of judicial reform in Eastern Europe. *Comparative Politics*, 32: 43–62.

MAGALONI, B. 2003. Authoritarianism, democracy and the Supreme Court: horizontal exchange and the rule of law in Mexico. Pp. 266–305 in *Democratic Accountability in Mexico*, ed. S. Mainwaring and C. Welna. New York: Oxford University Press.

MARAVALL, J. M., and PRZEWORSKI, A. (eds.) 2003. *Democracy and the Rule of Law*. New York: Cambridge University Press.

MELONE, A. P. 1996. The struggle for judicial independence and the transition toward democracy in Bulgaria. *Communist and Post-Communist Studies*, 29: 231–43.

MÉNDEZ, J. E., O'DONNELL, G., and PINHEIRO, S. (eds.) 1999. *The (Un)rule of Law and the Underprivileged in Latin America*. Notre Dame, Ind.: University of Notre Dame Press.

MERRYMAN, J. H. 1985. *The Civil Law Tradition: An Introduction to the Legal Systems of Western Europe and Latin America*, 2nd edn. Stanford, Calif.: Stanford University Press.

MORAVCSIK, A. 2000. The origins of human rights regimes: democratic delegation in postwar Europe. *International Organization*, 54: 217–52.

MOUSTAFA, T. 2003. Law versus the state: the judicialization of politics in Egypt. *Law and Social Inquiry*, 28: 883–930.

NORTH, D., and WEINGAST, B. 1989. Constitutions and commitment: the evolution of institutions governing public choice in seventeenth-century England. *Journal of Economic History*, 49: 803–32.

O'DONNELL, G. 1994. Delegative democracy? *Journal of Democracy*, 5: 55–69.

ÖRKÉNY, A., and SCHEPPELE, K. L. 1999. Rules of law: the complexity of legality in Hungary. Pp. 55–76 in *The Rule of Law after Communism: Problems and Prospects in East-Central Europe*, ed. M. Krygier and A. Czarnota. Brookfield, Vt.: Ashgate.

PEERENBOOM, R. P. 2002a. *China's Long March Toward Rule of Law*. New York: Cambridge University Press.

——— 2002b. Let one hundred flowers bloom, one hundred schools contend: debating rule of law in China. *Michigan Journal of International Law*, 23: 471–544.

POPKIN, M. 2000. *Peace Without Justice: Obstacles to Building the Rule of Law in El Salvador*. University Park: Pennsylvania State University Press.

POTTER, P. B. 2004. Legal reform in China: institutions, culture and selective adaptation. *Law and Social Inquiry*, 29: 465–95.

PRILLAMAN, W. C. 2000. *The Judiciary and Democratic Decay in Latin America: Declining Confidence in the Rule of Law*. Westport, Conn.: Praeger.

RAMSEYER, J. M. 1994. The puzzling (in)dependence of courts: a comparative approach. *Journal of Legal Studies*, 23: 721–47.

RÍOS-FIGUEROA, J. 2007. Fragmentation of power and the emergence of an effective judiciary in Mexico, 1994–2002. *Latin American Politics and Society*, 49: 31–57.

ROOT, H. 1989. Tying the king's hands: credible commitments and royal fiscal policy during the old regime. *Rationality and Society*, 1: 240–58.

SARAT, A., and SCHEINGOLD, S. 1998. *Cause Lawyering: Political Commitments and Professional Responsibilities*. New York: Oxford University Press.

SCHWARTZ, H. 1998. Eastern Europe's constitutional courts. *Journal of Democracy*, 9: 100–14.

SCRIBNER, D. L. 2004. The Chilean Supreme Court: political isolation and institutional stability—stable judicial tenure and judicial decision-making. Presented at the Latin American Studies Association Meeting, Las Vegas.

SMITHEY, S., and ISHIYAMA, J. 2002. Judicial activism in post-communist politics. *Law and Society Review*, 36: 719–41.

SHAPIRO, M. 1986. *Courts: A Comparative and Political Analysis*. Chicago: University of Chicago Press.

SIEDER, R. 2003. Renegotiating "law and order:" judicial reform and citizen responses in post-war Guatemala. *Democratization*, 10: 137–60.

STATON, J. K. 2004. Judicial policy implementation in Mexico City and Mérida. *Comparative Politics*, 37: 41–60.

STOTZKY, I. P. (ed.) 1993. *Transition to Democracy in Latin America: The Role of the Judiciary*. Boulder, Colo.: Westview.

TAMANAHA, B. Z. 2004. *On the Rule of Law: History, Politics, Theory*. New York: Cambridge University Press.

TROCHEV, A. 2004. Less democracy, more courts: a puzzle of judicial review in Russia. *Law and Society Review*, 38: 513–48.

UNGAR, M. 2002. *Elusive Reform: Democracy and the Rule of Law in Latin America.* Boulder, Colo.: Lynne Rienner.

WEINGAST, B. 1997. The political foundations of democracy and the rule of law. *American Political Science Review*, 91: 245–63.

WIDNER, J. A. 2001. *Building the Rule of Law: Francis Nyalali and the Road to Judicial Independence in Africa.* New York: W.W. Norton.

WILLIAMSON, O. E. 1985. *The Economic Institutions of Capitalism: Firms, Markets, Relational Contracting.* New York: Free Press.

ZAKARIA, F. 1997. The rise of illiberal democracy. *Foreign Affairs*, 6: 22–43.

CHAPTER 6

THE GLOBAL
SPREAD OF
CONSTITUTIONAL
REVIEW

TOM GINSBURG

CONSTITUTIONAL review, the power of courts to strike down incompatible legislation and administrative action, is an innovation of the American constitutional order that has become a norm of democratic constitution writing. Whereas before World War II, only a small handful of constitutions contained provisions for constitutional review, as of this writing, 158 out of 191 constitutional systems include some formal provision for constitutional review.[1] Some political systems, such as the United States, have developed vigorous constitutional review even without an explicit textual mandate. How did this institution, whose democratic foundations are so often questioned in its birthplace, become a norm of democratic constitution writing?

The spread of constitutional review has both ideational and institutional underpinnings. Constitutional review is closely associated in the popular mind with what

---

[1] Seventy-nine written constitutions had designated bodies called constitutional courts or councils. Another sixty had explicit provisions for judicial review by ordinary courts or the supreme court. Finally, a small number of constitutions (China, Vietnam, and Burma) provide for review of constitutionality by the legislature itself. This data comes from the *University of Illinois Comparative Constitutions Project,* available at http://netfiles.uiuc.edu/zelkins/constitutions.

has been characterized as the most important idea of the twentieth century, the notion of human rights (Henkin 1990). But political scientists looking at constitutional review have emphasized its origin in a functional need for dispute resolution. This chapter traces the spread of constitutional review and evaluates the various political explanations for the establishment, development, and spread of the institution, emphasizing the mutually reinforcing roles of ideas and institutions. The chapter also suggests lines for future inquiry in the burgeoning field of comparative constitutional studies.

1 THREE WAVES

1.1 The Founding

Although conventionally traced back to John Marshall's famous decision in *Marbury v. Madison* (1803), the practice of judicial review was well known to the earlier colonial governments (Snowiss 1990; Marcus 1995; Rakove 1997; Treanor 2005). Underpinning the practice were a number of distinct ideas that came together around the time of the American Revolution. One crucial background idea drew on Judeo-Christian notions of higher law (Cappelletti 1989). If a normative system divides rules into higher law and lower law, then there is an inherent need to limit lower laws that conflict with higher principles. Another crucial idea was the Lockean notion of government as social contract, so that citizens conceived of government as a bearer of duties and themselves as bearers of rights. If government was in a contract with its citizens, then citizens ought to be able to enforce the contract. This seemed even more natural when the contract was embodied in a written constitution, one of the innovations of the American founding. These three ideas of higher law, the social contract, and the written constitution all contributed to the notion of constitutional supremacy in the early American milieu.

Simply accepting that the constitution is supreme, however, does not itself dictate a precise institutional mechanism for ensuring supremacy in practice. Here judges drew on an institutional legacy distinct to the Anglo-American legal tradition, for common law judges had established a long tradition of institutional autonomy in England. Autonomy is not itself supremacy. Indeed, Lord Coke's opinion in *Bonham's Case*,[2] calling on judges to overturn laws that were contrary to common law and reason, had not been followed during the ascendancy of Parliament in seventeenth-century Britain. But the natural law notions embodied in

---

[2] 8 Coke Reports 114 (1609–10).

Coke's opinion were embraced by young American lawyers, who naturally had less respect for the notion of *British* parliamentary supremacy. The long tradition of institutional autonomy and the natural law overtones of common law adjudication gave the judges a resource to become the guardians of higher legality in the newly independent United States.

Judicial review thus originates as an expression of Anglo-American natural law tradition in an age of positive legislation; it could not or at least did not emerge in the same manner in the Islamic, Chinese, or Romanist political-legal traditions. The Islamic tradition had a strong emphasis on religiously-rooted natural law constraints on temporal rulers, but lacked a general theory of legislation (Shapiro 1981) and so avoided the problem of lower law in conflict with divine law. The Chinese tradition, on the other hand, had a theory of legislation but no notion of institutional constraint on the Emperor, who stood at the center of the cosmological system (Ginsburg 2003).

The above account explains the necessary ideological underpinnings of constitutional review, but not the particular details of its emergence in the late eighteenth century. One set of political accounts of the origin of judicial review emphasizes game theory and the particular strategic constraints on Marshall and Jefferson in the context of *Marbury* (Clinton 1989, 31–42; 1994; Epstein and Knight 1998, 151–3). Marshall, in deciding whether to order Jefferson to deliver a commission he did not want to deliver, faced uncertainty about the prospects of compliance. Jefferson too faced uncertainty with regard to reactions of other political actors to his various possible responses to Marshall. This set up a game theoretic situation in which alternative outcomes might easily have resulted. Marshall could have declined to claim the power of judicial review, or delivered it stillborn by ordering an action that would generate presidential defiance. Instead, Marshall's decision, to decline to order the delivery of Marbury's ill-fated commission but to establish judicial review, fit the strategic logic of the situation and established a new institutional equilibrium.

This view of *Marbury* as central is challenged somewhat by Graber (1999) who takes a more gradualist political approach to constitutional review, arguing that it was not until the election of the more moderate Madison that Marshall could truly issue the key decisions empowering the Court. Graber's account emphasizes context and long-term historical interactions among various branches in establishing the practice of review, rather than a single great case.

Another series of accounts emphasizes the federal logic of judicial review in the early United States (Shapiro 1992; 1999; Rakove 1997; Ackerman 1997). There are two basic rationales or complementarities between federalism and judicial review. First of all, whenever there are two lawmaking bodies or levels with different lawmaking jurisdictions, there is the potential for conflicts over jurisdiction. A neutral third body can serve both levels of government in resolving these disputes as they arise (Shapiro 1981). Indeed, federal systems would seem to require some sort of mechanism for resolving jurisdictional disputes, and the affinity of judicial review with federalism is illustrated by the large number of federal systems with some form of judicial review. This branch of federalist logic is structural and functionalist in character, emphasizing the need to deal with inevitable disputes in countries with complex political structures and multiple lawmakers.

The second complementarity between federalism and judicial review is related to free trade (Shapiro 1992). In a free trade system with multiple lawmakers, states face a collective action problem with regard to their own legislative powers. There is the threat that each state will put up protectionist barriers. If every state does so, then trade will not be free at all. States thus have a problem committing to a free trade system on their own. A written constitution with a neutral body in the form of a court that can evaluate state legislation can help make states' commitments to free trade federalism more credible (Qian and Weingast 1997). Indeed, the early history of the United States Supreme Court illustrates this logic, focusing as it did on consolidating national power.

These functionalist accounts (game theory, federalism) could be used to develop a theory of the spread of constitutional review. Presumably the logic in the founding case might have something to do with later cases. Outside the United States, constitutional review was rarely provided for and even more rarely utilized before World War II. Norway's Supreme Court had the power but refrained from exercising it (Slagstad 1995; Smith 2000). Portugal introduced judicial review in 1909 (Vanberg 2005, 10). The initial polities with active judicial review were indeed all common law federal polities, namely the United States, Canada, and Australia.[3] Mexico developed a form of constitutional review, the *amparo* suit, which restricted the remedy for unconstitutionality to individual cases; at times in its early history, *amparo* cases focused on federal–state relations as well (Baker 1971, 36).

Affinities between constitutional review and federalism, as well as free trade, may have some power in explaining dynamics of constitutional review outside the founding case (especially in the second wave case of the European Union). The federalist account suggests that one reason constitutional review was relatively limited before the twentieth century was that there were relatively few federal systems. However, the adoption of constitutional review after World War II in so many countries without federalism or internal problems of committing to free trade suggests that these dynamics may be at best sufficient but not necessary conditions for its establishment.

---

[3] In the Canadian example, much of the early judicial review was exercised by the Privy Council in London. See Bednar et al. (2001, 246–9).

1.2 The Second Wave

The second wave of judicial review began in earnest with the development of Hans Kelsen's model of constitutional review, originally embodied in the Austrian constitution of 1920. This model rested on a strong theoretical orientation of judges as subordinate to the parliament. Therefore, constitutional interpretation needed to be done by a designated body outside of the ordinary judicial power. This led to the creation of a special Constitutional Court to safeguard the constitutional order. The Austrian case seems to fit the federalism logic of constitutional review, for in its original formulation it only had jurisdiction to resolve jurisdictional disputes among different levels of government.

This model of a designated constitutional court became the basis of the post-World War II constitutional courts in Europe. Though many mistakenly assert that most European countries have designated constitutional courts, in fact there were only five of the Kelsen model in Western Europe: Austria, Germany, Italy, Portugal, and Spain. It is no accident that these are the post-fascist countries: the conventional account traces these developments to a new postwar awareness of rights and natural law limitations on the power of legislatures (Cappelletti 1989). The courts were adopted along with constitutions that had extensive rights provisions, and constitutional review became associated with the protection of rights.

Designated constitutional courts make a good deal of sense in new democracies where the ordinary judiciary has low status or capacity, as in post-fascist and later in post-Communist contexts. This contrasts with the founding case of the early nineteenth-century United States, when John Marshall was able to draw on the stock of legitimacy in the ordinary courts of the common law tradition to explain how it was only natural that the courts possessed a power to disregard statutes that contradicted constitutional requirements (Shapiro 1999, 211).

Outside Europe, the wave of decolonization and constitutional reconstruction led other countries to adopt constitutional review. India's new democracy adopted a model of judicial review in which the Supreme Court had a carefully circumscribed power of review. Japan's American-drafted constitution also contained provision for judicial review on the American model. In these and other cases, constitutional review spread to new democracies where rights traditions were relatively underdeveloped.

These second wave institutions varied in their levels of activity, but several courts emerged as major forces in their societies. Over time, the Indian Supreme Court transformed the original constitutional scheme to greatly expand its power (Baxi 1980). Volcansek (1994) has emphasized the role of the Italian Court in striking down pieces of fascist legislation one at a time, maintaining the legitimating fiction that the Italians had won the War. Germany proved to be exceptionally fruitful soil for constitutional review, combining as it did a federal system with a post-fascist yearning for rights. Germany's Constitutional Court is arguably the most influential court outside the U.S. in terms of its institutional structure and jurisprudence (Ackerman 1992, 101–4; Kommers 2001; Vanberg 2005).

Separately, Charles de Gaulle in France was developing a distinct model of constitutional review. Frustrated by the ineffectual parliament in the Fourth Republic, de Gaulle's prerogative was to set up a separate realm of executive lawmaking. De Gaulle's constitution created a new body, the *Conseil Constitutionel,* which was empowered to conduct only pre-promulgation, abstract review (Stone 1992). Fearing encroachment by the legislature on the executive, de Gaulle allowed the *Conseil* to hear challenges to unconstitutional legislation before it took effect. The orientation was less toward the protection of rights than toward the maintenance of divided and separated powers. Access to constitutional review was limited to the executive branch, leaders of the legislature, and certain other designated officials, and the institution was designed to constrain the legislature on behalf of the executive rather than on behalf of citizens directly. As in the earlier federalist cases, constitutional review was a functionalist response to a division of powers, but it was a horizontal division of powers rather than a vertical one. Both horizontal and vertical divisions of powers were at play in the establishment and expansion of supranational review in the European Union (Hirschl 2005; Kelemen 2004; Stone Sweet 2004; Conant 2002; see Alter, this volume).

Even in polities without explicit constitutional authorization for constitutional review, courts were in some instances able to repeat Marshall's trick in *Marbury* and claim the power for themselves. Israel is the paradigmatic example here: Its assertions were ultimately blessed by the passage of Basic Laws that explicitly authorized judicial review (Jacobsohn 1993; Hirschl 2000). The French *Conseil* read the Declaration of the Rights of Man, incorporated into the preamble of the French constitution, into a judicially enforceable set of rights, greatly expanding its bases of review (Stone 1992).

These were the second wave cases of constitutional review that were by and large successful, and they generally involved countries that were democratic and industrialized (with India a notable exception from the latter condition). In more unstable or authoritarian political environments, courts were more constrained. One pattern saw courts falling on their swords, in what Helmke (2002; 2005) has called the logic of "strategic defection" against political elites. Strategic defection is motivated by the desire of judicial actors to maintain institutional capital when they think regime change may occur. By openly challenging elites in the endgame of authoritarianism, courts and judges risk the imposition of short-term costs in exchange for mid-term legitimacy. A similar dynamic has been observed in Pakistan (Newberg 1995), Indonesia (Bourchier 1999), and might explain recent moves in Egypt (Moustafa 2007). This move preserves the institutional capital of the judiciary after the eventual return to democracy. It may also itself play a role in hastening democracy, as judges can signal to other actors that the end of the regime is nigh, provide institutional resources for regime opponents through supportive decisions, and make judicial independence a political issue around which to organize.

These various institutional dynamics are important for understanding and evaluating the overall success of constitutional review. The postwar spread of the international human rights movement, with its normative attachment to judicial forms of protection, meant that constitutional review was seen as an important bulwark against arbitrary government, and courts were able to draw on this legitimacy in constraining the state. No doubt the actual performance of review varied, depending on local political circumstances, but the successful courts were emulated and became an ideal to which others aspired.

1.3 The Third Wave

The third wave of democratization (Huntington 1991), and particularly the fall of the Berlin Wall, corresponded with a new wave of constitution-writing. This led to the creation of a whole new set of constitutional courts. Indeed, every post-Soviet constitution has some provision for a designated constitutional court, save Estonia which adopted the American model (Ishiyama-Smithey and Ishiyama 2000; 2002; Schwartz 2000). Elsewhere, countries in Africa and Asia, from Mali to Korea, also created new courts or reinvigorated old ones (Ginsburg 2003). The result is the current situation in which the vast majority of constitutions have some provision for judicial review, by either a designated constitutional court or the ordinary court.

Clearly the rights story was an important part of the spread of the institution in the post-Soviet bloc countries. Judges were closely identified with constraining government and protecting rights. Indeed, the inherent legitimacy of the constitutional judiciary was such that in post-apartheid South Africa, the Constitutional Court was entrusted with authority to approve the draft Final Constitution, and its initial rejection of the draft did not provoke significant negative reaction. Constitutional review was seen as an inherent and valuable constraint on democracy, and the so-called counter-majoritarian difficulty was hardly raised.

A final point worth noting is the spread of quasi-constitutional review to the international system, a topic to be covered by other chapters in this *Handbook*. When a NAFTA tribunal reviews national legislative or administrative measures for conformity with Chapter 11, or when an ad hoc arbitration tribunal does the same acting under a Bilateral Investment Treaty, they are evaluating government action and legislation for conformity with higher law. They do so upon direct application from a private party, unlike the traditional state-to-state mechanisms of public international law. These tribunals are subject to pressure from interest groups that seek to file *amicus* briefs. When the tribunals find treaty violations, they typically produce an order to modify the legislation or administrative action, or threaten externally imposed costs. While they do not have the authority to strike the legislation, neither as a formal matter do certain supreme courts exercising constitutional review. These developments might herald a fourth wave, though it is too early to say how robust these practices will be in the face of legitimacy concerns.

In summary, constitutional review has evolved from an institution primarily directed at enforcing structural provisions of constitutions, such as federalism, to a close identification with rights and democracy. It has served to help spread liberal and democratic values to new constitutional cultures. This remarkable institutional success begs for explanation. We now consider various political accounts of the proliferation of constitutional review.

2 Explaining Institutional Proliferation

2.1 Federalism and Rights

We can characterize the traditional theories for the spread of constitutional review as institutional–functional or ideational in character. Of course, the various theories are hardly mutually exclusive. In some cases, they clearly reinforce one another, such as the iconic German case that involved both federalism and rights rationales. It is likely that the ultimate political account explaining constitutional review has both ideational and institutional elements (see also Ferejohn 2002, 55–61).

Ideational accounts of the early development of judicial review have to grapple with the fact that the founding case did not much emphasize rights in its first century of existence. Shapiro (1999) discusses what he calls the "rule of law" theory, suggesting that judicial review will flourish in countries with stronger allegiances to judicial neutrality. Judicial review is more likely in cultures where judges are associated with the liberal ideal of limited government. Because the English common law tradition emphasized this idea, English colonies were particularly receptive environments for judicial review.

While the federalism and rule of law hypotheses look quite powerful in the founding case of the United States and its common law relatives such as Australia, neither of these accounts seems to be wholly adequate given the adoption of constitutional review as a norm in other countries after World War II. We then turn to a second ideational account, the "rights hypothesis" (Shapiro 1999, 200), which focuses on the growing national and international concern with individual rights. A rights ideology, evident in advanced industrial economies since World War II and embodied in international human rights instruments, has spread globally. The spread of a rights culture and rights ideology, accompanied by support structures (Epp 1998), leads to greater demand for constitutionalization. The long association of courts with protecting individual rights has made judicial review the institution of choice to protect these crucial interests. Constitutional review in this account is a dependent variable with demand for rights as the key independent variable.

An early and formalistic version of this hypothesis suggested that the written constitution was dispositive. That is, judicial review would be greater in countries that had written rights provisions in the constitution (such as India and the United States) than in countries with unwritten constitutions (such as England). Ishimaya-Smithey and Ishiyama (2002), in a study of Eastern Europe, did not find a positive relationship between formal rights and judicial review, suggesting that a rights culture is a more informal and ideological phenomenon.

Shapiro (1996; 1999) roots the growth of rights ideology in increasing complexity of governmental processes. Demand for judicial review stems from common conditions in advanced industrial societies, namely distrust of the ubiquitous and essential technical bureaucracies. Citizens demand protection from all kinds of harms, but this entails delegation of immense power to unelected government experts. Citizens naturally fear unchecked governmental power. Judges, in Shapiro's view, become the generalist guardians of the public interest, by demanding reasons for administrative and legislative action, by enforcing participatory rights, and by ensuring transparency. Sometimes these judicially imposed constraints are framed in constitutional terms.

Shapiro sees this as a strong, if not inevitable, trend that triggers a dialectic. If courts succeed they generate greater demands for constraining government, leading them to become, inevitably, deeply involved in policy-making. Shapiro is deeply skeptical about the possibility of courts limiting themselves to the "proper" level of constitutional review. Courts making policy in turn may generate a backlash from legislative and executive actors who charge unelected judges with overstepping their mandates. There is a kind of grammar to constitutional contestation, but also dynamics of limitation and constraint that operate over time (Vanberg 2005). The driving factors, however, are cultural and ideological.

2.2 Beyond Rights: The Domestic Logics of Constitutional Review

However powerful the role of rights may be in creating demands for judicial review, rights ideology alone simply cannot explain the patterns of institutional diffusion that we observe. The rights hypothesis is a demand-side theory that posits judicial review as an institutional response to social forces. There are, however, evidentiary problems with this account. The level of demand for "rights" is difficult to assess across countries. Furthermore, courts play an important role in *generating* demand for rights through their decisions. Disentangling demand from judicial supply of rights is difficult.

Demand-side theories also tend to be underspecified. They neither account for variation in institutional design of constitutional review, nor for the different levels of activism that various courts engage in. They have trouble dealing with forms of constitutional review, such as the French, in which individuals do not have access to make claims about rights-protections. And they cannot explain the particular timing of the adoption of constitutional review (Hirschl 2000, 99–100).

To examine variation in form and substance, an institutionalist approach is more helpful. Institutionalism assumes that institutions "matter" and that the variety of institutional structures is not random (March and Olsen 1984; Gillman and Clayton 1999). Both the existence and operation of constitutional review are to be explained and not assumed by political analysis. A recent set of theories roots constitutional review in *domestic* political logics, which in turn suggests more theoretical payoff in terms of explanatory power to account for variation.

The basic institutional story begins with political fragmentation (Ferejohn 2002). As the discussion of waves of judicial review illustrated, several accounts of the emergence of judicial review are built on the fragmentation of power vertically (as in federalist polities) or horizontally (as in presidential systems like the United States and France). Political fragmentation creates the potential for conflict among different institutions and therefore demand for a third party to resolve disputes (Shapiro 1981). Since this is what courts do, they are a logical place to turn when disputes concern constitutional allocation of policy-making power.

Fragmentation also creates the potential for political gridlock as institutional veto players make it difficult to shift policies from the status quo. In turn, this expands the space for judicial policy-making. When the political system cannot deliver policies because of gridlock, those who seek to advance particular interests will turn to the courts to obtain those policies. Constitutional review is a particularly entrenched form of judicial policy-making that may be utilized in such instances.

This basic institutional story has been supplemented in recent years. Drawing on a theory of judicial independence put forward by Ramseyer (1994), Ginsburg (2003) argues that the spread of democracy is a factor in the spread of constitutional review. Judicial review, he argues, is a solution to the problem of political uncertainty at the time of constitutional design. Parties that believe they will be out of power in the future are likely to prefer constitutional review by an independent court, because the court provides an alternative forum for challenging government action. Constitutional review is a form of political *insurance* that mitigates the risk of electoral loss. On the other hand, stronger political parties will have less of a desire for independent judicial review, since they believe they will be able to advance their interests in the post-constitutional legislature. Ginsburg provides some large-n and case study evidence for this proposition that the design and functioning of courts reflects political insurance and is related to features in the party system (see also Finkel 2001; Stephenson 2003; Chavez 2004).

Hirschl (2004) offers a complementary political account of judicialization that he calls *hegemonic preservation*. His view is that judicialization, including establishment of constitutional review, is a strategy adopted by elites that foresee themselves losing power. In the final stages of their rule, it makes sense to set up courts to preserve the bargains embodied in legislation and constitutionalized rights. This account has the great strength of shedding light on the *timing* of the adoption of review. It fits the classic understanding of the American experience establishing judicial review, in which the Federalists spent the months after losing the 1800 election putting their supporters into the courts. Hirschl extends the account to judicialization in other common law jurisdictions, including Canada, Israel, New Zealand, and South Africa. More recently, the last parliamentary session of the Palestinian Authority before the takeover of Hamas passed a law establishing a constitutional court empowered to strike legislation, a conspicuous case of hegemonic preservation (though the immediate response of the new parliament was to supersede this law). Mexico's empowerment of its Supreme Court in the waning years of PRI rule may also make sense as a case of hegemonic preservation, and certainly fits the insurance model (Finkel 2001; Magaloni 2006).

Hirschl and Ginsburg's theories both rely on intertemporal electoral uncertainty as the primary theoretical driver for the adoption of constitutional review. Hirschl's hegemonic preservation seems to make strong assumptions about the information available to elites; but it has the virtue of accounting for situations where a declining power adopts the institution that then ends up hastening the party's demise. Ginsburg's insurance model is broader, as it can account for the support for the establishment of constitutional review by new, nonhegemonic political parties (as in Eastern Europe) when they think they may not win the post-constitutional election. Both, however, are political theories that are not purely functional in character, but consider the party system and the "political vectors" (Hirschl 2000, 91–5) of establishing review.

These political theories also link with the literature on democratization. Declining hegemons and electoral uncertainty are the core of the democratization dynamic. While the focus of the new political accounts of judicial review is on domestic politics, they suggest that a primary cause for the spread of the institution is the spread of democracy.

Both insurance and hegemonic preservation theses, then, are rooted in exogenously specified domestic political incentives. Institutions are the dependent variable. One area in which further work is needed concerns the feedback effects of these institutional choices. When adopted by a declining authoritarian regime, for example, an independent constitutional court can hasten the regime's demise through strategic decision-making and diffusing political power. Ginsburg (2003) makes the point that, as political insurance, constitutional review lowers the potential costs of losing for the electoral losers, making it more likely that they will respect the constitutional order even when out of power. Constitutional review is not only reinforced by democracy, but itself reinforces democracy.

In general, the dominant counter-majoritarian paradigm has been supplemented in recent years through work elucidating the majoritarian political functions of courts (Whittington 2005; Hofnung and Dotan 2005). Whittington (2005) discusses judicial activism by a relatively friendly court and notes that courts can help overcome obstacles to direct political action. The entrenchment function emphasized by Ginsburg and Hirschl, in other words, is not the only role for courts. This suggestion has not been adequately assimilated in comparative work (but see Hofnung and Dotan 2005).

2.3 New Directions

The comparative study of constitutional review is just beginning. This section considers issues that deserve greater attention as the field goes forward. One set of cases that has not adequately been theorized or studied concerns the establishment of constitutional review in authoritarian contexts. These authoritarian cases, in which review serves functional needs in the political system, clearly have little to do with the rights hypothesis, and are better accounted for by the political theories of judicial empowerment. For example, Iran's Council of Guardians exercises review for Islamicity and has served to constrain the democratically elected political institutions in the Islamic Republic. This draws on long religious traditions of Islamic constraint on the state, but with the twist that it now serves to preserve a particular faction and is used by the illiberal elements of the regime to maintain control (Shambayati 2004). The basic idea of using the courts to limit a competing faction because of political uncertainty seems to fit this case.

Barros (2003) develops a fascinating account of the role a constitutional court can play in an authoritarian regime, with examples from Chile under the Pinochet dictatorship (1973–90). Barros notes that the junta was not a unitary actor, and faced a need for internal coordination among the different branches of the military. This coordination role was effectively played by the new constitutional court set up under Pinochet. This account resonates with much of the division of powers argument, illustrated by the federal cases and Fifth Republic France, but suggests an interesting extension: even informal divisions of power in an oligarchy can generate a role for constitutional review.

Another area for future work is to further examine the underexplored ideological reasons for the adoption of legal forms of political restraint. That is, the political theories of constitutional review explain why it is that temporally insecure political agents may wish to constrain future political institutions, but they do not provide a complete explanation for why *courts* are the institution that is chosen. Other minoritarian institutions, such as bicameralism and supermajority requirements, might be able to play the same role. We as yet have no thorough account of the institutional trade-offs in the process of constitutional design. No doubt there is a kind of economy of possible constraining devices, but we have little awareness of the trade-offs that constitutional designers engage in, or how various institutions supplement and complement each other.

To answer the question of why courts have become the focal institutions for constitutional designers, ideational elements are likely important. One prominent theory of institutional change tracks the diffusion of ideas and institutions to countries that have similar characteristics such as language, geographic region, legal tradition, and ethnic connections (Elkins and Simmons 2005). Diffusion emphasizes transnational and ideational elements rather than the domestic political logics of the new accounts of constitutional review.

While no general diffusion-based study has yet been undertaken to examine the spread of constitutional review, casual empiricism suggests there is a good deal of diffusion or institutional isomporphism with regard to structures of constitutional review. For example, nearly every country with a "constitutional council" exercising only abstract pre-promulgation review is a former French colony. After a wave of new constitutions in Eastern Europe, the German model of a designated constitutional court appears to be the dominant form of constitutional review, although the scope of powers vary with local political conditions (e.g. Solyom and Brunner 2000). An account that combines institutional considerations with some of the recent diffusion-based approaches may be a more fruitful direction than either approach alone. Isolating the factors that push towards adoption or retardation of particular elements of institutional design would advance our understanding a good deal.

Even diffusion studies do not always account for the particular pathways or processes by which institutions are adopted. Casual observers attribute a good deal of weight to the role of foreign governments and advisers in the process of constitutional design (Boulanger 2003, 13). We have very few microstudies of constitutional design processes, and so the association of constitutional review with particular foreign influence or advice remains speculative. We do, however, observe a good deal of constitutional borrowing among courts when deciding particular cases, suggesting that the operation if not the adoption of constitutional review is increasingly a transnational process.

3 MEASURING PERFORMANCE

To the extent that constitutional review spreads because of its perceived success, the operation of constitutional courts must be part of our inquiry. Why is it that some constitutional courts fail and others succeed?

Comparative work on variations in performance is hampered by lack of a common metric of judicial power. While courts may look alike, each is embedded in a particular institutional environment. Evaluating failure is relatively easy, for there is typically evidence of a conflict between courts and other branches of government; but identifying success is harder conceptually. All in all, the variables of number and importance of cases and compliance with decisions do seem to be indicators of judicial power. But a very powerful court may decide relatively few cases because legislators already accommodate its preferences. Furthermore, a court with very broad standing rules might have a large volume of cases, but a relatively small number of valid claims, so it may have a lower rate of striking legislation. One cannot therefore rely on simple strike rates as a metric of success or power (cf. Herron and Randazzo 2003).

While in the American context many scholars utilize the attitudinal model to study the Supreme Court, the strategic model has been most successful in explaining the success of courts abroad. Attitudinalism is a particularly problematic method for comparative work because it depends on coding separate opinions of individual judges and linking them to their appointing authorities. Because of variations in procedures for appointing judges to constitutional courts and the fact that many courts issue single "consensus" opinions, rather than signed majority opinions and dissents, the attitudinal model is unlikely to work as a basis for comparative research.

We are left with the strategic approach. Any political account of courts assumes that they operate within political constraints, and that these constraints can vary across time and space. Much recent work draws on this insight to elucidate the conditions under which courts can succeed or fail. Whether explicitly or implicitly utilized, the strategic model (Epstein, Knight, and Shvetsova 2001; Ginsburg 2003; Vanberg 2005) underpins these accounts.

Further research is also needed into the interactions between constitutional courts, legislatures, and governments, along with further theoretical refinement of effective strategies by courts. The strategic perspective implies some constraints on constitutional decision-making, as the other political actors retain means of punishing courts, reducing jurisdiction, budget, and powers. Consistent with this framework, Herron and Randazzo (2003, 434) find that presidential power is negatively associated with judicial review for the intuitive reason that concentrated executive power facilitates punishment of wayward courts. Iaeyczower and Spiller show that in Argentina, antigovernment decisions rise during periods of divided government in part because leaders have les ability to sanction courts (Iaeyczower, Spiller, and Tommasi 2002; Rosenberg 1992).

Vanberg's (2005) account of Germany emphasizes the importance of public support and transparency as crucial factors in a game of executive-judicial relations. Public support can insulate the constitutional court from criticism and counterattack. Public support for constitutional review depends not just on structural factors such as access to the court but on a substantive ideology of rights. A public that demands rights protection will avail itself of a constitutional court more than a public that does not care about rights. Thus a rights framework, while it cannot explain the adoption of constitutional review on its own, does have some power to account for the operation of a particular court and its acceptance by the public.

Much work remains to be done in the comparative examination of constitutional review. The vast majority of studies to date have been country-specific, which is understandable given the particularities of each institutional context. But truly comparative work should become increasingly possible as national studies accumulate. Possible dimensions of comparison include the different functioning of courts in presidential and parliamentary systems; comparisons of situations wherein the court is the embodiment of a clear founding moment (Ackerman 1997) with more gradualist political transitions; and situations wherein the court itself takes the power of constitutional review or significantly expands it versus situations where that power is clearly granted in a constitutional text (Hofnung 1996). The connection of constitutional review to particular political cultures, or what might be called national styles of constitutional review (Ginsburg 2002) may also become apparent as more studies are concluded.

4 CONCLUSION

From its origins in colonial America, constitutional review has become a global institutional norm. It has spread to nearly every democracy as well as a number of authoritarian regimes, and increasingly, transnational contexts as well. Traditional political accounts of the spread of the practice, focusing on federalism and rights, no doubt identified some of the important dynamics, but have been refined by a richer set of theories that emphasize the interests of political actors in adopting constitutional review. These institutional explanations have advanced our understanding significantly and provided useful frameworks for understanding constitutional review in particular national contexts. But ideational factors which are often casually linked to the spread of constitutional review remain poorly understood and inadequately tested.

No doubt the future of constitutional review will be determined by the strategic dynamics of judicial power that have been observed in many national contexts. Judges will continue to decide central questions of social, political, and economic life as matters of constitutional law. They will do so subject to constraints by external political forces. Judicial skill and daring will determine whether the judges are subjected to the various forms of punishment that politicians have at their disposal, and whether judicial review can maintain its institutional reputation as a device of choice for constitution-drafters in the twenty-first century.

References

ACKERMAN, B. 1992. *The Future of Liberal Revolution.* New Haven, Conn.: Yale University Press.

—— 1997. The rise of world constitutionalism. *Virginia Law Review,* 83: 771–97.

BAKER, R. 1971. *Judicial Review in Mexico: A Study of the Amparo Suit.* Austin: University of Texas Press.

BARROS, R. 2003. Dictatorship and the rule of law: rules and military power in Pinochet's Chile. Pp. 188–222 in *Democracy and the Rule of Law,* ed. J. M. Maravall and A. Przeworski. New York: Cambridge University Press.

BAXI, U. 1980. *The Indian Supreme Court and Politics.* Lucknow: Eastern Book Company.

BEDNAR, J., ESKRIDGE, JR., W. N., and FEREJOHN, J. 2001. A political theory of federalism. Pp. 223–70 in *Constitutional Culture and Democratic Rule,* ed. J. Ferejohn J. Rakove, and J. Riley. New York: Cambridge University Press.

BOULANGER, C. 2003. Beyond significant relationships, tolerance intervals and triadic dispute resolution: constructing a comparative theory of judicial review in post-communist societies. Presented at the Law and Society Association Meeting, 5–8 June, Pittsburgh.

BOURCHIER, D. 1999. Magic memos, collusion and judges with attitude: notes on the politics of law in contemporary indonesia. Pp. 233–52 in *Law, Capitalism, and Power in Asia: The Rule of Law and Legal Institutions,* ed. K. Jayasuriya. New York: Routledge.

BURLEY, A.M., and MATTLI, W. 1993. Europe before the Court: a political theory of legal integration. *International Organization,* 47: 41–76.

CAPPELLETTI, M. 1971. *Judicial Review in the Contemporary World.* New York: Bobbs-Merrill.

—— 1989. *The Judicial Process in Comparative Perspective.* Oxford: Clarendon Press.

CHAVEZ, R. B. 2004. *The Rule of Law in Nascent Democracies: Judicial Politics in Argentina.* Stanford, Calif.: Stanford University Press.

CLINTON, R. L. 1989. Marbury v. Madison *and Judicial Review.* Lawrence: University of Kansas Press.

—— 1994. Game theory, legal history, and the origins of judicial review: a revisionist analysis of *Marbury v. Madison. American Journal of Political Science,* 38: 285–302.

CONANT, L. 2002. *Justice Contained: Law and Politics in the European Union.* Ithaca, NY: Cornell University Press.

ELKINS, Z., and SIMMONS, B. 2005. On waves, clusters and diffusion: a conceptual framework. *Annals of the American Academy of Political Science,* 598: 33–51.

EPP, C. 1998. *The Rights Revolution.* Chicago: University of Chicago Press.

EPSTEIN, L., and KNIGHT, J. 1998. *The Choices Justices Make.* Washington, DC: CQ Press.

—— KNIGHT, J., and SHVETSOVA, O. 2001. The role of constitutional courts in the establishment and maintenance of democratic systems of government. *Law and Society Review,* 35: 117–63.

FEREJOHN, J. 2002. Judicializing politics, politicizing law. *Law and Contemporary Problems,* 65: 41–68.

FINKEL, J. 2001. Judicial reform in Latin America: market economies, self-interested politicians, and judicial independence. Ph.D. dissertation, UCLA.

—— 2003. Supreme Court decisions on electoral rules after Mexico's 1994 judicial reform: an empowered court. *Journal of Latin American Studies*, 35: 777–99.

GILLMAN, H., and CLAYTON, C. (eds.) 1999. *The Supreme Court in American Politics*. Lawrence: University of Kansas Press.

GINSBURG, T. 2002. Confucian constitutionalism? Globalization and judicial review in Korea and Taiwan. *Law and Social Inquiry*, 27: 763–800.

—— 2003. *Judicial Review in New Democracies: Constitutional Courts in Asian Cases*. New York: Cambridge University Press.

GRABER, M. 1999. The problematic establishment of judicial review, Pp. 28–42 in *The Supreme Court in American Politics*, ed. H. Gillman and C. Clayton. Lawrence: University of Kansas Press.

HALMAI, G. (ed.) 2000. *The Constitution Found? The First Nine Years Of The Hungarian Constitutional Review Of Fundamental Human Rights*. Budapest: Indok, Human Rights and Information Documentation Center.

HELMKE, G. 2002. The logic of strategic defection: court–executive relations in Argentina under dictatorship and democracy. *American Political Science Review*, 96: 291–303.

—— 2005. *Courts under Constraints: Judges, Generals, and Presidents in Argentina*. Cambridge: Cambridge University Press.

HENKIN, L. 1990. *The Age of Rights*. New York: Columbia University Press.

HERRON, E. S., and RANDAZZO, K. A. 2003. The relationship between independence and judicial review in post-communist courts. *Journal of Politics*, 65: 422–38.

HILBINK, E. 2002. An exception to Chilean exceptionalism? The historical role of Chile's judiciary and prospects for change. In *The Politics of Injustice in Latin America*, ed. S. E. Eckstein and T. Wickham-Crowley. Berkeley: University of California Press.

HIRSCHL, R. 2000. The political origins of judicial empowerment through constitutionalization: lessons from four constitutional revolutions. *Law and Social Inquiry*, 25: 95–139.

—— 2004. *Towards Juristocracy: The Origins and Consequences of the New Constitutionalism*. Cambridge, Mass.: Harvard University Press.

—— 2005. Preserving hegemony? The political origins of the European Constitution. *International Journal of Constitutional Law*, 3: 269–91.

HOFNUNG, M. 1996. The unintended consequences of unplanned constitutional reform: constitutional politics in Israel. *American Journal of Comparative Law*, 44: 585–604.

—— and DOTAN, Y. 2005. Legal defeats—political wins: why elected representatives go to court. *Comparative Political Studies*, 38: 75–103.

HUNTINGTON, S. 1991. *The Third Wave*. Norman: University of Oklahoma Press.

IAEYCZOWER, M., SPILLER, P., and TOMMASI, M. 2002. Judicial independence in unstable regimes: Argentina 1935–1995. *American Journal of Political Science*, 46: 699–716.

ISHIYAMA-SMITHEY, S., and ISHIYAMA, J. 2000. Judicious choices: designing courts in post-communist politics. *Communist and Post-Communist Studies*, 33: 166–82.

—— —— 2002. Judicial activism in post-communist politics. *Law and Society Review*, 36: 719–41.

JACOBSOHN, G. 1993. *Apple of Gold: Constitutionalism in Israel and the United States*. Princeton, NJ: Princeton University Press.

KELEMEN, R. D. 2004. *The Rules of Federalism*. Cambridge, Mass.: Harvard University Press.

KOMMERS, D. 2001 *The Constitutional Jurisprudence of the Federal Republic of Germany*, 2nd edn. Durham, NC: Duke University Press.

MAGALONI, B. 2006 *Voting for Autocracy: Hegemonic Party Survival and its Demise in Mexico*. Cambridge: Cambridge University Press.

MARCH, J., and OLSEN, J. 1984. The new institutionalism and organizational factors in public life. *American Political Science Review*, 78: 734–49.

MOUSTAFA, T. 2007. *The Struggle for Constitutional Power: Law, Politics and Economic Development in Egypt*. New York: Cambridge University Press.

NEWBERG, P. 1995. *Judging the State: Courts and Constitutional Politics in Pakistan*. New York: Oxford University Press.

QIAN, Y., and WEINGAST, B. 1997. Federalism as a commitment to market incentives. *Journal of Economic Perspectives*, 11: 83–92.

RAKOVE, J. 1997. *Original Meanings*. New York: Vintage.

RAMSEYER, J. M. 1994. The puzzling (in)dependence of courts: a comparative approach. *Journal of Legal Studies*, 23: 721–47.

ROSENBERG, G. 1992. Judicial independence and the reality of political power. *Review of Politics*, 54: 369–98.

SCHWARTZ, H. 2000. *The Struggle for Constitutional Justice in Post-Communist Europe*. Chicago: University of Chicago Press.

SHAMBAYATI, H. 2004. A tale of two mayors: courts and politics in Turkey and Iran. *International Journal of Middle East Studies*, 36: 253–75.

SHAPIRO, M. 1981. *Courts*. Chicago: University of Chicago Press.

—— 1992. Federalism, the race to the bottom and the regulation-averse entrepenuer. In *North American and Comparative Federalism*, ed. H. Scheiber. Berkeley, Calif.: Institute of Governmental Studies Press.

—— 1996. The globalization of judicial review. In *Legal Culture and the Legal Profession*, ed. H. Scheiber and L. Friedman. Boulder, Colo.: Westview.

—— 1999. The success of judicial review. Pp. 193–219 in *Constitutional Dialogues in Comparative Perspective*, ed. S. Kenney, W. Reisinger, and J. Reitz. London: Macmillan.

SLAGSTAD, R. 1995. The breakthrough of judicial review in the Norwegian system. In *Constitutional Justice Under Old Constitutions*, ed. R. Slagstad and E. Smith. The Hague: Kluwer Law International.

SMITH, C. 2000. Judicial review of parliamentary legislation: Norway as a European pioneer. *Public Law*, 45: 595–606.

SNOWISS, S. 1990. *Judicial Review and the Law of the Constitution*. New Haven, Conn.: Yale University Press.

SOLYOM, L., and BRUNNER, G. (eds.) 2000. *Constitutional Judiciary in a New Democracy: The Hungarian Constitutional Court*. Ann Arbor: University of Michigan Press.

STEPHENSON, M. 2003. "When the devil turns…:" the political foundations of independent judicial review. *Journal of Legal Studies*, 32: 59–81.

STONE, A. 1992. *The Birth of Judicial Politics in France*. New York: Oxford University Press.

STONE SWEET, A. 2004. *The Judicial Construction of Europe*. New York: Oxford University Press.

TREANOR, W. M. 2005. Judicial review before *Marbury*. *Stanford Law Review*, 58: 455–562.

VANBERG, G. 2005. *The Politics of Constitutional Review in Germany*. New York: Cambridge University Press.

VOLCANSEK, M. 1994. Political power and judicial review in Italy. *Comparative Political Studies*, 26: 492–509.

WHITTINGTON, K. E. 2005. "Interpose your friendly hand:" political supports for the exercise of judicial review by the United States Supreme Court. *American Political Science Review*, 99: 583–96.

CHAPTER 7

ESTABLISHING AND MAINTAINING JUDICIAL INDEPENDENCE

GEORG VANBERG

A CHARMING (but apocryphal) story in an anonymous biography of Frederick the Great provides a poignant illustration of the central role of judicial independence in Western conceptions of the rule of law. Bothered by the incessant noise generated by a windmill located close to his summer palace of *Sanssouci*, Frederick offered to buy out the miller, who steadfastly refused to sell. Frustrated, the king resorted to threats: "Don't you know that I can use my powers to take your mill without paying anything for it?" Unimpressed, the miller replied: "With all due respect, your majesty might well do that—if it were not for the judges in Berlin." Grudgingly, Frederick relented.[1] The notion of judicial independence is pivotal in the story: the miller's decision to reject the royal demand is based on the expectation that he can get a fair hearing in front of independent judges who will decide

---

[1] The actual historical circumstances surrounding the origin of this legend, concocted out of several different events, are far less flattering to Frederick's respect for judicial independence. Having intervened in a legal dispute, the king removed and jailed a panel of judges that had refused to overturn a verdict he disagreed with.

on the basis of law, unimpressed by the king's interests. The king shares this assessment and therefore acquiesces in the noise of the mill. This ideal of independent courts that police the constitutional boundaries of the polity and constrain political power has assumed a central place in Western constitutional thought (see Cappelletti 1989). While normatively appealing to many, this vision of the judicial role raises significant positive questions about how constitutional politics functions. How is judicial independence established and maintained in practice?

Before attacking this question, it is useful to highlight a number of important distinctions. Judicial independence refers to an abstract, conceptual as well as a formal, institutional dimension. At the broadest level, the ideal of judicial independence expresses the aspiration that judicial decisions should not be influenced in an inappropriate manner by considerations judged to be normatively irrelevant. Typically, judicial independence in this sense is associated with independence from the political interests of current office-holders.[2] Judges are independent when threats of sanctions or promises of rewards by public officials in return for favorable decisions do not have inappropriate sway over their decisions. The desire to reduce the impact of inappropriate considerations gives rise to a formal, institutional dimension of judicial independence that identifies it with specific institutional safeguards that can serve to insulate judges against these influences. For example, constitutional features such as fixed, non-renewable appointments for judges or protections against reductions in judicial salaries diminish the incentives for judges to be mindful of the interests of other policy-makers and are therefore thought to enhance their independence.[3]

The distinction between these two dimensions of judicial independence implies several caveats. First, there is considerable room for disagreement over what judicial independence requires, especially in its institutional dimension. Different normative understandings of the kinds of considerations that judges ought to take into account, and different judgments about when particular influences become inappropriate, imply that reasonable people can disagree about what judicial independence is, whether particular institutional safeguards promote it effectively, and whether a given judiciary enjoys sufficient autonomy.

Second, judicial independence must be distinguished from the closely related concept of judicial accountability. The notion that judges should be independent does not imply that they should be free to decide on the basis of whims, with no need for justification and no accountability. Rather, independence is desirable

---

[2] Naturally, one might also be concerned with the independence of judges from powerful private interests. Since most of the literature on judicial independence focuses on independence from the other branches of government, I do not explore independence from private actors here but focus on judicial independence in a political sense.

[3] In a series of papers with various co-authors, Stefan Voigt has worked to develop empirical, cross-national indicators of de facto and *de jure* judicial independence which roughly map onto this distinction (e.g. Feld and Voigt 2003).

precisely because it frees judges from inappropriate considerations, thereby allowing them to decide based on considerations judged to be relevant. A commitment to judicial independence is thus fully compatible, at least in the abstract, with a commitment to judicial accountability, that is, to mechanisms that can ensure that judges will, in fact, be guided by appropriate considerations in reaching decisions. As with independence, institutional provisions, including the appointment process, impeachment provisions, or in some countries, the possibility of legislative review of judicial decisions, play an important role in securing judicial accountability.

Importantly, efforts to increase judicial independence can conflict with attempts to secure judicial accountability. In particular, independence and accountability often involve trade-offs in institutional design. For example, judges with life tenure are more independent than judges with fixed terms who can be reappointed or must face reelection, and are therefore more likely to be sensitive to the political interests of current majorities. But judges with life tenure are also freer to disregard systematic developments in public attitudes that perhaps they ought to be responsive to under some normative conceptions.[4] This trade-off has long been recognized and plays a prominent role in arguments over constitutional design. During the debates over the U.S. Constitution, it was at the heart of the dispute between the Federalists and Anti-federalists concerning the role of the judiciary. A central argument advanced by Brutus against the work of the constitutional convention alleged that:

they have made the judges *independent*, in the fullest sense of the word. There is no power above them, to controul any of their decisions. There is no authority that can remove them, and they cannot be controuled by the laws of the legislature. In short, they are independent of the people, of the legislature, and of every power under heaven. Men placed in this situation will generally soon feel themselves independent of heaven itself. (Ketcham 1986, 305)

Thus, precisely the same institutional features of the U.S. Constitution that Alexander Hamilton identifies as safeguards for judicial independence (see his argument in *Federalist 78*) primarily serve to undercut the accountability of judges for Brutus, creating a judiciary that is "subject to no control." I return to this connection between judicial accountability and independence, and the role that accountability may play in preserving independence, below. First, however, it is time to turn to the heart of this chapter: How can judicial independence be established, and how can it be maintained?

---

[4] For example, much opposition to the Supreme Court in the 1930s was based on the belief that a majority of the justices were "holding on" to a jurisprudence judged to be out of touch with contemporary political realities.

1 THE PUZZLE OF JUDICIAL INDEPENDENCE

Judicial independence is not valued for its own sake. Instead, the presence of an independent judiciary in the political process is believed to be instrumental in securing central values of constitutionalism. Constitutional government is limited government, and scholars and constitution-writers alike have typically regarded judicial review as a central mechanism for the enforcement of constitutional constraints on political power. To be effective, this mechanism requires a judiciary that is sufficiently autonomous to overturn statutes or executive decisions (Ferejohn 1998, 366). That is, an independent judiciary is valued primarily for the limits it can place on the exercise of political power by current officeholders (see also Burbank 2002).

To the extent that judicial independence is valued because it can serve to constrain political power, it poses a puzzle. Constitutional systems typically provide specific institutional safeguards for judicial independence (e.g. secure tenure for judges, prohibitions against reducing judicial salaries, etc.). At the same time, most constitution-writing processes, especially in the post-World War II era, are dominated by politicians and parties that expect to play a significant role in the political system that is being constituted. Why would these actors consent to, and even actively support, the creation of an independent judiciary that is intended to constrain political power?[5]

Once established, the maintenance of an independent judiciary continues to pose a challenge. While constitutions can incorporate institutional features that promote judicial independence, these provisions do not necessarily guarantee that a judiciary will be independent de facto once politics begins to unfold. For current political majorities that are dissatisfied with particular judicial decisions, or anticipate unwelcome judicial opposition, there "remain myriad loopholes that determined elected officials might use to punish the judiciary for its actions and reduce its independence" (Whittington 2003, 446). One feature that makes maintaining judicial independence potentially problematic is that constitutions typically cannot fully specify all aspects of judicial structure. As a result, legislative majorities often retain control over important details, such as the size of the

---

[5] The West German constitutional convention of 1949 provides an illustrative example. During the negotiations over the establishment of a constitutional court, Konrad Adenauer advocated the creation of a strong court because "there is also dictatorship by a parliamentary majority. And we want protection against such dictatorship in the form of a constitutional court" (Vanberg 2005, 1). At the time, Adenauer must have known that he was likely to be the leader of such a parliamentary majority. He did indeed go on to lead the largest legislative faction in subsequent elections and became Germany's first postwar Chancellor. Once the court began to attack central parts of his legislative agenda, he became a much less enthusiastic supporter of the court and attempted to subvert its independence in several respects (see Vanberg 2000).

judiciary, its jurisdiction, and budget. Moreover, implementation of judicial decisions often requires the cooperation of other policy-makers, opening the door to resistance to judicial demands. Elected officials who are dissatisfied with past decisions or hope to secure favorable outcomes in pending cases may be tempted to use these tools to threaten judicial independence and to make the judiciary more pliant. Understanding how independent courts can come to play a central role in a constitutional system thus requires an explanation of the mechanisms that lead powerful political actors to establish, and to maintain, an institution that is primarily (at least at first glance) intended to constrain their power.

2 EXPLAINING JUDICIAL INDEPENDENCE

Although the establishment and the maintenance of judicial independence are conceptually, and perhaps empirically, separate issues (see Friedman 2004), the explanations that scholars have offered for both largely overlap. The key in accounting for an independent judiciary is to explain why elected officials (politicians and political parties) will not want to, or will not be able to, undermine judicial autonomy. It is useful to conceptualize this problem in a simplified model, adapted from Whittington (2003), that highlights the essential trade-offs.

Any political system identifies political actors that can potentially threaten an independent judiciary. For example, the most prominent political actors that can undermine the independence of the federal judiciary under the U.S. Constitution are the bicameral Congress and the executive branch. At any moment in time, each of these actors has preferences regarding the continued existence of an independent judiciary. At least in principle, they can derive benefits from an independent judiciary. From the executive's point of view, for example, an effective, independent judiciary may restrain legislative majorities in ways that the executive finds desirable. As a shorthand, denote the benefit that actor i perceives from the continued independence of the judiciary by $B_i \geq 0$. On the other hand, an independent judiciary may impose costs on political actors, most obviously by blocking a policy they favor that would have been realized in the absence of the judicial veto (I will treat these benefits and costs in more detail below). These costs are symbolized by $C_i \geq 0$.

Significantly, it is typically impossible for political actors to reap the benefits that flow from an independent judiciary without also tolerating the costs that it may impose when judicial independence results in undesirable outcomes. Judicial independence is a "package." The reason for this, as Whittington (2003, 449) notes, is that "the political power to sanction the Court is a blunt instrument." Attempts by elected officials to resist unwelcome decisions or to retaliate against the court affect not only those particular decisions, but the *institution* of judicial independence, and therefore obliterate the benefits of judicial autonomy along with its costs.[6] Whether a particular actor prefers the continued existence of an independent judiciary therefore depends not on any particular decision (all officials are likely to be confronted by decisions they do not approve of from time to time), but on the *balance* of costs and benefits she perceives. When $B_i - C_i > 0$, the benefits of judicial independence, at least in the long run, outweigh the costs of particular, unpleasant decisions. Even if dissatisfied with particular decisions, the actor is supportive of an independent judiciary as an institution. But when an elected official concludes that C_i outweighs B_i, she will be tempted to threaten the judiciary.

An actor who has concluded that maintaining an independent judiciary is no longer in her interest may not necessarily have a preference for attacking judicial autonomy. Undertaking court-curbing activities can be associated with significant costs (I provide a more detailed account of these costs below.) To continue our stylized representation, denote the costs that an actor must incur to discipline the court by $D_i \geq 0$. An elected official who prefers to see an independent judiciary abolished is only willing to engage in court-curbing if the net costs of tolerating an independent judiciary become so prohibitive as to outweigh the political price of reducing it. In terms of our symbolic representation, there are thus three cases of interest:

(1) $B_i - C_i \geq 0$

Under this first scenario, the political actor—while on occasion dissatisfied with particular judicial decisions—derives sufficient benefits from an independent judiciary on balance to prefer maintenance of the system. She is supportive of judicial independence.

(2) $B_i - C_i < 0$ and $D_i \geq C_i - B_i$

Under this scenario, considering only the benefits and the costs of particular judicial decisions over time, the actor would prefer not to be subject to an independent judiciary. But the costs of actually undermining judicial independence are sufficiently high to induce the actor to be willing—grudgingly—to tolerate judicial independence.

(3) $B_i - C_i < 0$ and $D_i < C_i - B_i$

Finally, under this last scenario, an independent judiciary imposes sufficient net cost on the actor (relative to the costs of attacking it), that the actor prefers to undermine judicial autonomy.

---

[6] Below, I discuss the implications of relaxing the assumption that policy-makers are unable to resist particular decisions without threatening the institution of judicial independence. Once the decision to respect particular decisions is decoupled from the decision to maintain an independent judiciary, additional complications arise.

Judicial independence can be maintained as long as all relevant political actors find themselves in scenarios 1 or 2. It is unlikely to be maintained if there is an actor with the ability to attack judicial independence successfully whose preferences correspond to scenario 3. Thus, this simple model suggests that explaining how judicial independence is maintained requires explaining why policy-makers with the ability to challenge judicial autonomy will generally have preferences that correspond to scenarios 1 and 2, rather than scenario 3. (Conversely, explaining lack of judicial autonomy involves explaining why at least one actor with the ability to undermine independence has preferences that fall under the third scenario.)

These three, admittedly stylized, scenarios provide a convenient road map for organizing the disparate theoretical answers that have emerged in the scholarly literature to explain the puzzle of judicial independence. For the most part, this literature addresses a handful of systematic concerns, including structural conditions that favor judicial independence, the political benefits that elected officials can derive from independent judicial review, the political costs of court-curbing activities, and strategic interactions between judges and other policy-makers that correspond directly to the terms B_i, C_i, and D_i in our inequalities. Naturally, any particular argument rarely falls cleanly into one of the categories of explanations I outline below, and individual accounts often contain arguments that cross the boundaries between these types of explanations. Nonetheless, it is useful to separate these categories conceptually to gain greater clarity about the nature of the theoretical arguments.

3 CONSTITUTIONAL STRUCTURE AND JUDICIAL INDEPENDENCE

One set of arguments concerning conditions that favor the maintenance of judicial independence focuses on the institutional structure within which a judiciary is embedded. In particular, constitutional systems that separate power across institutions in such a way as to necessitate coordinated action by several political actors in order to attack the judiciary increase the security of courts.[7] Adopting the language of the model laid out above, separated powers generally increase the costs of subverting judicial independence because they make it necessary to secure agreement among several actors. Securing such agreement is likely to be prohibitively

---

[7] In the American context, Whittington (2003) and Friedman (2004) among many others highlight this point. Vanberg (2000) provides a detailed account of the importance of separation of powers in explaining the establishment of an independent constitutional court in postwar Germany.

costly when the preferences of actors diverge across institutions (i.e. under "divided" government).

Once again, consider the U.S. Constitution as an example. An effective attempt at court-curbing—at least involving the most effective tools for doing so—necessitates coordinated action by both houses of Congress and the President. Legislative majorities in one house may, on occasion, have an interest in introducing court-curbing legislation. But the costs of securing the other chamber's and the President's consent (that is, the concessions or reciprocal favors that would be required to secure agreement) will often be prohibitive.[8] Contrast this with the position of courts under the British constitution. Here, political power is fused in the cabinet, supported by a majority in the House of Commons, and typically composed of a single party. In this institutional setting, a government that favors reigning in judicial independence faces few costs in securing the necessary legislation. Courts, as a result, find themselves in a more precarious situation (Shapiro 1981).

Importantly, the conclusion to be drawn from these considerations is not that separation of powers can guarantee judicial independence or that an independent judiciary cannot be maintained under the kind of unified institutional structure exemplified by the British constitution. The institutional structure within which a judiciary is embedded affects D_i, the cost of successfully attacking a court. Institutional frameworks that divide powers, such as bicameralism and a presidential system, raise these costs and therefore decrease, *all other things being equal,* the likelihood of scenario 3. In this sense, they tend to promote judicial independence. But, as the approaches that we turn to next remind us, all other things typically are not equal. Whether judicial autonomy can be maintained depends critically on conditions that affect B_i and C_i.

4 ENDOGENOUS EXPLANATIONS FOR JUDICIAL INDEPENDENCE

Some of the most interesting and counterintuitive arguments provide what one might call *endogenous* explanations for judicial independence. At first glance, an independent judiciary appears to pose an unwelcome limitation on the power of other political actors. Framing the issue in this light (much as this chapter does in

---

[8] Whittington (2003) argues that court-curbing in the U.S. is most successful when a dominant political coalition controls all branches of government, effectively negating much of the protection usually afforded by separated powers. Rosenberg (1992) provides a detailed account of court-curbing initiatives in the U.S. that highlights the same lesson.

its opening pages), poses judicial autonomy as a puzzle: Why would elected officials in other branches tolerate an independent judiciary when they could undermine it? Endogenous explanations for judicial independence turn this argument on its head. The central feature of these accounts is the claim that—occasional examples to the contrary notwithstanding—an independent judiciary, rather than imposing costs on other political actors, serves their purposes. Judicial independence provides benefits to elected officials that they could not secure in other ways. These benefits are so significant that these officials prefer an independent judiciary, even if they disapprove of particular decisions on occasion. In the language of the model presented above, we find ourselves in scenario 1.

William Landes and Richard Posner's seminal 1975 piece on "The Independent Judiciary in an Interest Group Perspective" is an early example of literature in this tradition. Approaching the problem of judicial independence from a public choice perspective, Landes and Posner argue that the expected durability of legislation (the time period for which a statute is expected to be in force) poses a central concern in interactions between legislators and interest groups. If interest groups expect that legislation they are able to secure to promote their interests is easily undone by subsequent legislative or judicial action, the value of legislation for interest groups declines—and along with it the "payments" that groups are willing to make to legislators in order to secure it. To increase the value of legislation, legislators therefore have an interest in "tying their own hands" in ways that increase the durability of legislation. Delegation to an independent judiciary is one way of doing so because it diminishes the influence of legislative majorities over the interpretation and enforcement of past legislative deals. Under this argument, it is precisely because it constrains legislators that judicial independence (paradoxically) improves the position of legislators by raising the value of the "product" they are able to supply to interest groups.

While the particulars of Landes and Posner's account have come under attack,[9] the article is seminal in providing the foundation for an important strand of literature that places issues of "credibility" at the heart of explaining judicial independence. In Landes and Posner's argument, legislators wish to enhance the credibility of legislative agreements, and it is the desire to enhance credibility that induces them to create and to maintain an independent judiciary. More generally, elected officials often face incentives to commit to certain courses of action, but need to make these commitments *credible* in order to reap their benefits. Simply promising to adopt a responsible fiscal policy that holds down inflation may not be credible. Transferring control over monetary policy to an independent central bank may do the trick. Similarly, it may often be in the interest of public officials to

---

[9] Theoretically, it is not clear what would motivate judges to enforce legislative deals in accordance with the preferences of the enacting legislature. For an empirical critique of the argument, see Boudreaux and Pritchard (1994).

commit to other courses of actions or principles and these commitments may be made credible through the creation and maintenance of an independent judiciary that can enforce them.

Douglass North and Barry Weingast's (1989) account of the origins of judicial independence in seventeenth-century England provides an illustrative example. By establishing appropriate incentives for investment and entrepreneurship, a firm commitment that a government will respect and enforce property rights creates conditions that are favorable to economic development. However, while any ruler will generally have an incentive to claim to be committed to respecting property rights, the benefits of secure property are only going to accrue when this commitment becomes credible. North and Weingast argue that the establishment of an independent judiciary provides an important mechanism for achieving this. Like Ulysses, who could hear the sirens sing and live by tying himself to the mast, so public officials can secure the benefits of credible commitment to property by establishing and maintaining an independent judiciary that can protect citizens against encroachments on their property. As in Landes and Posner, judicial independence serves the long-run interests of political actors precisely because it provides a roadblock to their short-term temptations.[10] Constrained power is preferred by officeholders to unconstrained power.

The ability to make credible commitments constitutes only one benefit that may lead elected officials to favor an independent judiciary. A second reason scholars have identified concerns incentives for elected officials to delegate difficult or unpopular decisions to other policy-makers (see Whittington 2003; Ura 2006). Rather than make decisions that carry an electoral risk, officials may prefer to pass such issues off to someone else, including the judiciary. However, this strategy of "passing the buck" only works if the other actor is *independent*, thus providing a reason for elected officials to support judicial autonomy.

A final set of arguments that provide an endogenous explanation of judicial independence does not focus on the interests of political actors qua officeholders, but on the parties and politicians that occupy those offices at different times. These arguments are rooted in the logic of cooperation in repeated games. They place primary emphasis on the incentives to support judicial independence that emerge if there is sufficient electoral uncertainty and parties and politicians expect to rotate in and out of office.

Democratic politics typically involves alternation in power, and political parties and politicians generally cannot expect to control the levers of power permanently (although, as will be important below, there may be considerable variation in the rate of alternation). In such a setting, actors are likely to care not only about what

---

[10] Mancur Olson (1993) makes a closely related point, arguing that democratic institutions, including an independent judiciary, make commitments by rulers to constraints on their power credible, thus serving the long-run interests of rulers and citizens alike.

they can accomplish while they are in government, but also about the protection of their interests while out of power. As a result, they may be inclined to favor limits on political power, and enforcement of these limits through an independent judiciary. In maintaining an independent judiciary, parties thus face a situation that can be captured by the logic of the repeated Prisoner's Dilemma. While each party would prefer not to be subject to judicial control while in office, it may be willing to tolerate this constraint in the expectation that other parties will similarly respect an independent judiciary when they come to power. Judicial autonomy is maintained by reciprocity among political actors trying to protect their interests while out of power.[11]

Importantly, this argument depends—as its proponents note—on several conditions. First, parties and politicians must value the future sufficiently. Reciprocity cannot induce current policy-makers to defer to an independent judiciary unless they value future occasions on which the judiciary may protect their interests sufficiently. Second, the argument depends on electoral volatility. It is the threat of losing power that induces respect for an independent judiciary. If a party becomes dominant and can expect to retain power for the foreseeable future, the incentives to tolerate an independent judiciary vanish and judicial independence is unlikely to survive. Thus, Ramseyer posits the relative dominance of the Liberal Democratic Party in the postwar era as the primary explanation for the relative lack of independence of the Japanese judiciary. Similarly, Whittington (2003) explains the variation in court-curbing efforts by Congressional majorities by considering the uncertainty confronting current majorities about their future ability to control policy-making. Stephenson (2003) provides cross-national data that suggest that political competition enhances judicial independence.

The unifying theme of the endogenous explanations for judicial independence reviewed here—whether they focus on issues of credibility or reciprocity—is that an independent judiciary is created and maintained primarily because it serves the interests of those in a position to undermine it. In the language of the model that opened this section, for each actor that could threaten it, an independent judiciary secures a benefit B_i that is significant enough to move us into scenario 1. It is crucial to note that these arguments do not deny that an independent judiciary constrains the exercise of political power. Paradoxically, it is *precisely* the fact that judicial oversight constrains current officeholders that makes the independent judiciary so valuable to other political actors.[12]

---

[11] There are numerous variations on this general type of argument, including Ramseyer (1994), Ginsburg (2003), Whittington (2003), and Stephenson (2003).

[12] Rogers (2001) argues that elected officials may also value judicial review because of the unique informational perspective that courts—which review legislation in light of its actual results rather than projected consequences—bring to bear. While Rogers' argument highlights an important dimension of judicial review, it does not bear directly on support for an *independent* judiciary. To

5 Exogenous Explanations for Judicial Independence

The arguments just reviewed focus on the benefits that policy-makers can derive from the existence of an independent court. In this sense, these explanations are endogenous. They illustrate why the actors whose room to maneuver is constrained by courts might prefer to establish and maintain them nonetheless. In contrast, the literature we turn to now focuses on exogenous reasons that may lead policy-makers to refrain from threatening judicial independence. In particular, these explanations highlight the fact that attempts at court-curbing can be costly for policy-makers who engage in them. If these costs are sufficiently high, we find ourselves in scenario 2. Policy-makers who would prefer to see judicial independence abolished will grudgingly respect it because the costs of moving against the judiciary are prohibitive.

The most important source of political costs confronting policy-makers for attacking judicial independence that scholars have identified is public support for an independent judiciary (e.g. Caldeira 1986; Staton 2006). If a sufficiently large number of citizens believes that respect for judicial independence is an important constitutional value, and may withdraw support from elected officials who threaten it, powerful incentives for elected officials to tolerate an independent judiciary emerge. For example, Vanberg (2000) demonstrates that attempts by the first postwar West German government to undermine the independence of the German Constitutional Court failed only when a clear public reaction convinced the government that persisting in attacking the court would be electorally costly.

Given the central role that public support is likely to play in preserving judicial authority, it is not surprising that a large body of literature has investigated public support for courts empirically. Generally, courts appear to enjoy higher levels of support than other political institutions, especially in advanced democracies (see Gibson, Caldeira, and Baird 1998). No clear scholarly consensus exists about the foundations of public support, although several clear trends appear. Thus, citizens who know more about courts tend to be more supportive (see Gibson, Caldeira, and Baird 1998; Caldeira and McGuire 2005). Similarly, individuals who support broad, constitutional values such as individual liberty, and who perceive courts as procedurally fair, appear to be more supportive of courts (Caldeira and Gibson 1992; Shapiro 1981). Evidence on the relationship between satisfaction with particular

---

maximize the information gain from judicial review, legislative majorities would prefer a judiciary that shares their preferences exactly, i.e. a *dependent* judiciary. Whittington (2005) argues that in a fragmented political system, particular political actors can make use of judicial review by an allied court to advance their policy agenda. While this argument calls attention to an important (and underappreciated) benefit of judicial review, it also does not connect immediately to support for an *independent* judiciary.

judicial decisions and support for courts is more mixed, with some scholars concluding that support for courts is linked to approval of decisions while others find little evidence for this connection (see Mondak 1992; Caldeira and Gibson 1992). Nonetheless, most scholars agree that public support for courts declines in response to decisions that are consistently out of line with prevailing public attitudes (see Durr, Martin, and Wolbrecht 2000; Caldeira 1986).

Theoretical approaches to understanding public support for courts highlight benefits that citizens can derive from an independent judiciary that they cannot secure directly from democratically elected policy-makers. Such arguments generally adopt a principal–agent framework that views courts as tools that citizens can use in order to enforce constitutional limits on policy-makers. Two versions are worth highlighting. The lynchpin for Rogers (2006) is the observation that democratic politics raises a problem of delegation: citizens must be able to hold elected officials accountable in order to prevent abuses of power. Using a simple game-theoretic model, he demonstrates that if direct monitoring of elected officials is costly, and legislators may be tempted to pursue "special interest" legislation that harms majority interests, citizens may prefer the creation of a judiciary with a veto over legislation that can police the legislature directly. Judicial authority in the model derives from public support, which is in turn contingent on public perceptions that the court acts to protect the public against legislative abuses. Under this argument, the judiciary becomes a majoritarian, rather than a countermajoritarian tool.[13] Judicial decisions that frustrate policy demands of a democratic majority are possible, but they are incidental and unintended consequences of a system that generally promotes majoritarian influence.

A second argument for public support for courts that is rooted in the benefits that citizens can derive from the existence of an independent judiciary takes off from an argument made by Weingast (1997). Weingast argues that effective constraints on political power require coordination of citizen expectations about the appropriate limits of the state. Only if a sufficient number of citizens has the same expectations about which actions by a government constitute a violation of these limits, and if they are willing to act on these expectations, do limits on power become self-enforcing. Expecting effective resistance in response to certain actions, rulers will refrain from violating those limits in the first place.

Although Weingast does not discuss an independent judiciary explicitly in this context, it is not difficult to see how extending his argument provides citizens with reasons to value an independent judiciary. Coordination of citizen expectations about which actions are "out of bounds" is facilitated by mechanisms that reduce ambiguity and create focal points. Thus, for Weingast, the Revolution Settlement following the Glorious Revolution, with its detailed list of limits on royal power,

---

[13] See Friedman (2002) for a rich, sophisticated discussion of the "countermajoritarian difficulty" in arguments about judicial review.

served as such a coordination device. Coordination around *institutional* rules provides an even more unambiguous device because it reduces the need to find agreement on substantive questions. All that citizens require is agreement on the proposition that policy-makers are subject to review by an independent judiciary, and that opposition to judicial decisions or an attempt to manipulate the judiciary signals a threat to the constitutional order that requires citizen reaction. In short, citizens may value judicial independence as an institutional solution to limiting political power because the presence of an independent court can serve as a signal that other policy-makers are no longer committed to adhering to constitutional boundaries, irrespective of agreement with particular decisions (see also Sutter 1997).

Arguments that root judicial independence in public support for courts place primary emphasis on the term D_i in the simple model laid out above. The threat of a public backlash for undermining judicial independence increases the costs of moving against the judiciary for political actors that might be inclined to do so. Scenario 3 becomes less likely.

6 Law as a Public Good

Up to this point, the argument has assumed that attempts by policy-makers to resist particular rulings or to pressure the court undermine judicial independence wholesale, thus forcing policy-makers to consider whether judicial independence is "worth it" in the long run, even if they disagree with particular outcomes. In many contexts, this is a sensible substantive assumption. As Whittington has argued, disciplining a court is often a blunt instrument. Nevertheless, in some circumstances at least, policy-makers may be able to engage in "targeted resistance" that aims to circumvent or counteract individual decisions without attacking the judiciary as an institution. If this is possible, the decision to resist particular decisions is decoupled from the decision to maintain an independent judiciary. As a result, even policymakers who regard independent judicial review on balance as a beneficial institution may be tempted to resist individual decisions.

Such "decoupling" poses a challenge because it implies that maintaining judicial independence acquires many of the characteristics of a public goods problem. Even if all policy-makers agree that an independent judiciary is desirable (for some of the reasons outlined above), each policy-maker recognizes that her own "contribution" to independent judicial review (in the sense of complying with individual decisions) is no longer pivotal for the maintenance of the institution. Yet, as in the classic story of the commons, the institution of effective, independent judicial review breaks down in the aggregate if too many policy-makers act on these incentives and choose to oppose decisions with which they disagree. To solve this problem—which emerges because choosing not to comply with a particular decision is not equivalent to undermining judicial independence in one fell swoop—it is necessary to account for factors that drive the decision to comply with individual decisions.

Scholars who have attacked this problem have largely argued that compliance with particular decisions depends on the prospect that *exogenous* costs will be imposed on policy-makers who engage in attempts at resistance. Importantly, the imposition of such costs requires that the actors who impose them—be they citizens through an electoral backlash or political elites—are aware of attempts at noncompliance and can coordinate on punishing policy-makers who oppose specific decisions. Consequently, factors in the political environment that raise awareness of decisions and make it easier to police compliance are likely to strengthen judicial independence. Such factors include the constellation of interest groups (Epp 1998), the complexity of issues (Vanberg 2005), the salience of a decision (Staton 2006), as well as the specificity of an opinion (Baum 1976; Spriggs 1997). While these studies have begun to provide some insight into the forces that shape compliance with particular decisions, more concerted theoretical efforts are needed in explaining how judicial independence can be maintained in the face of the "collective action problem" that emerges if resisting particular decisions does not (on its own) lead to a subversion of judicial independence.

7 THE ROLE OF STRATEGIC JUDGES IN MAINTAINING JUDICIAL INDEPENDENCE

The literature reviewed so far explains judicial independence by highlighting the benefits that independent judicial review may provide for political actors that could move to threaten the judiciary or by pointing to the costs that these actors may confront in trying to undermine judicial autonomy. In both types of explanation, the actions of judges have been implicit. A final strand of the literature on judicial independence places explicit emphasis on judicial behavior and points to the prominent role of judges in maintaining judicial independence. In the context of the model laid out above, these explanations focus on the manner in which judicial decisions affect parameters B_i, C_i, and D_i.

Arguments that rely on public support to maintain judicial independence already suggested a first dimension of this literature. To the extent that public support for courts can be undermined by decisions that systematically run counter to prevailing public opinion, courts that rely on public support for their authority and independence are likely to be more sensitive to public attitudes in their rulings than is usually assumed under the "countermajoritarian" vision of courts. It is important to note that authors in this tradition generally do not argue that courts do not or cannot issue unpopular rulings. However, their ability to do so is constrained. Courts cannot consistently buck clear trends in public attitudes and expect to maintain their independent status. Empirical work on the U.S. Supreme Court has long suggested that judicial decisions do not generally and systematically run counter to clear trends in public opinion (Dahl 1957; Murphy 1964; McCloskey 1994), a finding that continues to be borne out by more recent research not only in the American case but in the comparative context as well (see McGuire and Stimson 2004; Vanberg 2005). In the logic of our simple model, the need to maintain public support (a principal component of D_i) requires that judges anticipate and accommodate public opinion if they want to maintain judicial independence.

Similarly, strategic judges may anticipate the interests of powerful political actors in specific decisions and accommodate those interests in order not to provoke a direct confrontation (see Murphy 1964). That is, judges may consciously attempt to reduce C_i (the burden imposed on political actors by judicial review) in order to reduce the likelihood of scenario 3. Courts have a number of tools available for this purpose, including "compromise solutions" that split the difference between parties (see Shapiro 1981), procedural rules that allow them to avoid deciding cases that are politically sensitive, or other mechanisms that reduce the costs of particular decisions. The German Constitutional Court's practice of declaring statutes unconstitutional but not void (thus allowing continued application of the law, often for a period of years) provides a useful example. As Donald Kommers has argued, "the practice of declaring a legal provision unconstitutional but not void is...used by the court to soften the political impact of its decisions" (Kommers 1997, 53).

A number of authors have recently argued that such sensitivity to the interests of powerful political actors is particularly important during the initial establishment of an independent judiciary (see Ginsburg 2003; Carrubba and Rogers 2003; Epstein, Knight, and Shvetsova 2001). By strategically accommodating other actors early on, courts may be able to build legitimacy and support among the public (and political actors) that is sufficient to allow them to exercise their powers more aggressively in the future. The common interpretation of the establishment of judicial review in the United States fits this argument. The Marshall court famously decided *Marbury v. Madison* in a manner that imposed no positive obligations on the Jefferson administration, thus avoiding an open conflict (see Clinton 1994). Several scholars have argued that, more generally, the Marshall court was careful in its jurisprudence to establish certain principles, but to do so in a manner that would not tread too closely on the interests of the other branches. For example, Mark Graber (1998, 232) concludes that this early era "evinces a court desperately avoiding clashes with a potentially hostile administration." More broadly, systematic cross-national evidence suggests that courts are more hesitant to exercise their full power in the early years of their existence and become increasingly willing to confront other policy-makers as they establish themselves (Ginsburg 2003, 71).

The argument that judges strategically anticipate both trends in public opinion and the interests of powerful political actors, and adjust their decisions accordingly, has a number of significant implications. On the one hand, these arguments highlight the fact that judges themselves—by acting prudently—play an important role in the establishment and maintenance of judicial autonomy. Judges that fail to pay attention to the constraints imposed by their environment may quickly provoke a confrontation that puts an effective end to judicial independence. The experience of the first post-Soviet Russian Constitutional Court, which aggressively confronted President Yeltsin over his use of the decree power, provides a poignant example. In 1993, Yeltsin suspended the court and replaced a number of judges, establishing a court that is so lacking in independence from the executive that Alexander Solzhenitsyn dubbed it a "mere plaything" (Schwartz 2000, 162).

On the other hand, one might legitimately ask to what extent the need by judges to be sensitive to public opinion and to the interests of powerful political actors is not itself a sign of the *lack* of judicial independence. There are a number of ways to think about this issue. One is to highlight the dynamic nature of the process: Strategic accommodation of justices during the early history of a court sets the stage for later exercises of judicial power that need to be less sensitive to the interests of other policy-makers. Another, perhaps more interesting, way to resolve this tension is to recall the distinction between judicial independence and judicial accountability. Arguments that stress the need for judges to be sensitive to the preferences of the public and of elected policy-makers do not conclude that these preferences are determinative of outcomes in particular cases. Judges do enjoy discretion, and can issue decisions that run counter to public attitudes or the preferences of public officials in specific cases. However, they typically cannot do so consistently over a large number of cases and over time. Even independent courts operate in a zone of discretion that is constrained by the interests of citizens and other policy-makers. In this sense, courts are subject to an indirect check that provides some judicial accountability, and may be normatively appealing.

8 CONCLUSION

A number of general themes emerge from the literature that examines the conditions that lead to the establishment and the maintenance of judicial independence. Perhaps the most overarching conclusion that scholars have reached is that establishing and maintaining judicial independence requires that political actors with the ability to attack or undermine judicial autonomy do not find it in their interest to do so. Under this general heading, the most significant distinction between theoretical approaches concerns the question why it is in the interest of political actors to respect judicial independence. Some approaches place primary emphasis on the benefits that political actors can derive from the existence of an independent judiciary. These accounts typically do not deny that courts constrain current holders of political power. Instead (some might say paradoxically), they demonstrate that those constraints actually serve the long-run interests of actors in those positions (either by allowing them to commit credibly to certain courses of action or because they provide insurance against losing power). In contrast, other accounts conclude that independent courts may well pose an unwelcome constraint on the other branches. For these authors, public officials choose to tolerate judicial autonomy because it is costly to attempt to attack the judiciary, either because doing so risks a costly public backlash, or because it requires the consent of other political actors that is too costly to secure.

Under both scenarios, two important implications emerge. First, judicial independence cannot be taken for granted. Maintaining a system of effective judicial checks depends on the right external circumstances. In the language of the simple model that opened this chapter, courts will remain independent only as long as scenarios 1 and 2 prevail. Second, even independent judges are not unconstrained. The foundations of judicial independence imply that judges need to be at least minimally sensitive to the interests of powerful political actors and to public opinion. While courts can and do make genuinely unpopular decisions, it is probably not useful to think of them as primarily countermajoritarian institutions.

While much progress has been made in understanding the foundations of judicial independence, important open questions remain. One particularly pressing issue is the need to integrate the various theoretical approaches that have emerged over the last decade. Many of these explanations are not mutually exclusive or incompatible. But to date, most scholars have focused on one or two of the dimensions outlined. We need a more coherent understanding of how these complex considerations interact, and under what conditions each explanation is likely to be particularly important. Second, while we have developed a workable static conception of judicial independence (the notion that judges remain independent as long as no powerful actor finds it in her interest to undermine judicial independence), we do not yet understand the dynamics of establishing judicial independence well. How do courts build support over time? What are the strategies that allow them to emerge as powerful actors? And how does judicial independence, once established, break down? While we have some suggestive theorizing on these questions, much more remains to be done.

REFERENCES

BAUM, L. 1976. Implementation of judicial decisions. *American Politics Quarterly*, 4: 86–114.

BOUDREAUX, D., and PRITCHARD, A. C. 1994. Reassessing the role of the independent judiciary in enforcing interest group bargains. *Constitutional Political Economy*, 5: 1–21.

BURBANK, S. 2002. What do we mean by judicial independence? *Ohio State Law Journal*, 64: 322–39.

CALDEIRA, G. 1986. Neither the purse nor the sword: dynamics of public confidence in the Supreme Court. *American Political Science Review*, 80: 1209–26.

—— and GIBSON, J. 1992. The etiology of public support for the Supreme Court. *American Journal of Political Science*, 36: 635–64.

—— and McGUIRE, K. 2005. What Americans know about the courts and why it matters. In *Institutions of American Democracy: The Judiciary*, ed. K. L. Hall and K. T. McGuire. New York: Oxford University Press.

CAPELLETTI, M. 1989. *The Judicial Process in Comparative Perspective*. Oxford: Clarendon Press.

CARRUBBA, C., and ROGERS, J. 2003. National judicial power and the dormant commerce clause. *Journal of Law, Economics and Organization*, 19: 543–70.

CLINTON, R. 1994. Game theory, legal history, and the origins of judicial review: a revisionist analysis of *Marbury v. Madison*. *American Journal of Political Science*, 38: 285–302.

DAHL, R. 1957. Decision-making in a democracy: the Supreme Court as a national policy-maker. *Journal of Public Law*, 6: 279–95.

DURR, R., MARTIN, A., and WOLBRECHT, C. 2000. Ideological divergence and public support for the Supreme Court. *American Journal of Political Science*, 44: 768–76.

EPSTEIN, L., KNIGHT, J., and SHVETSOVA, O. 2001. The role of constitutional courts in the establishment and maintenance of democratic systems of government. *Law and Society Review*, 35: 117–64.

EPP, C. 1998. *The Rights Revolution: Lawyers, Activists, and Supreme Courts in Comparative Perspective*. Chicago: University of Chicago Press.

FELD, L., and VOIGT, S. 2003. Economic growth and judicial independence: cross-country evidence using a new set of indicators. *European Journal of Political Economy*, 19: 497–527.

FEREJOHN, J. 1998. Independent judges, dependent judiciary: explaining judicial independence. *Southern California Law Review*, 72: 353–84.

FRIEDMAN, B. 2002. The birth of an academic obsession: the history of the countermajoritarian difficulty, part five. *Yale Law Journal*, 112: 153–228.

—— 2004. History, politics, and judicial independence. In *Judicial Integrity*, ed. A. Sajo. Amsterdam: Koninklijke Brill NV.

GIBSON, J. 1991. Institutional legitimacy, procedural justice, and compliance with Supreme Court decisions: a question of causality. *Law and Society Review*, 25: 631–6.

—— CALDEIRA, G., and BAIRD, V. 1998. On the legitimacy of national high courts. *American Political Science Review*, 92: 343–58.

GINSBURG, T. 2003. *Judicial Review in New Democracies: Constitutional Courts in Asian Cases*. Cambridge: Cambridge University Press.

GRABER, M. 1998. Establishing judicial review? *Schooner Peggy* and the early Marshall Court. *Political Research Quarterly*, 51: 221–39.

KETCHAM, R. 1986. *The Antifederalist Papers and the Constitutional Convention Debates*. New York: Mentor Books.

KOMMERS, D. 1997. *The Constitutional Jurisprudence of the Federal Republic of Germany.* Durham, NC: Duke University Press.

LANDES, W., and POSNER, R. 1975. The independent judiciary in an interest group perspective. *Journal of Law and Economics,* 18: 875–901.

McCLOSKEY, R. 1994. *The American Supreme Court,* ed. S. Levinson. Chicago: University of Chicago Press.

McGUIRE, K., and STIMSON, J. 2004. The least dangerous branch revisited: new evidence on Supreme Court responsiveness to public preferences. *Journal of Politics,* 66: 1018–35.

MONDAK, J. 1992. Institutional legitimacy, political legitimacy, and the Supreme Court. *American Politics Quarterly,* 20: 457–77.

MURPHY, W. 1964. *Elements of Judicial Strategy.* Chicago: University of Chicago Press.

NORTH, D., and WEINGAST, B. 1989. Constitutions and commitment: the evolution of institutions governing public choice in seventeenth-century England. *Journal of Economic History,* 49: 803–32.

OLSON, M. 1993. Dictatorship, democracy, and development. *American Political Science Review,* 87: 567–76.

RAMSEYER, M. 1994. The puzzling (in)dependence of courts: a comparative approach. *Journal of Legal Studies,* 23: 721–47.

ROGERS, J. 2001. Information and judicial review: a signaling game of legislative–judicial interaction. *American Journal of Political Science,* 45: 84–99.

—— 2006. The majoritarian basis for judicial countermajoritarianism. Presented at the annual meeting of the Midwest Political Science Association.

ROSENBERG, G. 1992. Judicial independence and the reality of political power. *Review of Politics,* 54: 369–98.

SCHWARTZ, H. 2000. *The Struggle for Constitutional Justice in Post-Communist Eastern Europe.* Chicago: University of Chicago Press.

SHAPIRO, M. 1981. *Courts: A Comparative and Political Analysis.* Chicago: University of Chicago Press.

SPRIGGS, J. 1997. Explaining federal bureaucratic compliance with Supreme Court opinions. *Political Research Quarterly,* 50: 567–93.

STATON, J. 2006. Constitutional review and the selective promotion of case results. *American Journal of Political Science,* 50: 98–112.

STEPHENSON, M. 2003. "When the devil turns:" the political foundations of independent judicial review. *Journal of Legal Studies,* 32: 59–90.

SUTTER, D. 1997. Enforcing constitutional constraints. *Constitutional Political Economy,* 8: 139–50.

URA, J. D. 2006. The effects of judicial review in american politics. Ph.D. dissertation, Department of Political Science, University of North Carolina.

VANBERG, G. 2000. Establishing judicial independence in West Germany: the impact of opinion leadership and separation of powers. *Comparative Politics,* 32: 333–53.

—— 2005. *The Politics of Constitutional Review in Germany.* Cambridge: Cambridge University Press.

WEINGAST, B. 1997. The political foundation of democracy and the rule of law. *American Political Science Review,* 91: 245–63.

WHITTINGTON, K. E. 2003. Legislative sanctions and the strategic environment of judicial review. *International Journal of Constitutional Law,* 1: 446–74.

—— 2005. "Interpose your friendly hand:" political supports for the exercise of judicial review by the United States Supreme Court. *American Political Science Review,* 99: 583–96.

CHAPTER 8

THE JUDICIALIZATION OF POLITICS

RAN HIRSCHL

THE judicialization of politics—the reliance on courts and judicial means for addressing core moral predicaments, public policy questions, and political controversies—is arguably one of the most significant phenomena of late twentieth and early twenty-first century government. Armed with newly acquired judicial review procedures, national high courts worldwide have been frequently asked to resolve a range of issues, varying from the scope of expression and religious liberties, equality rights, privacy, and reproductive freedoms, to public policies pertaining to criminal justice, property, trade and commerce, education, immigration, labor, and environmental protection. Bold newspaper headlines reporting on landmark court rulings concerning hotly contested issues—same sex marriage, limits on campaign financing, and affirmative action, to give a few examples—have become a common phenomenon. This is evident in the United States, where the legacy of active judicial review recently marked its bicentennial anniversary; here, courts have long played a significant role in policy-making. And it is just as evident in younger constitutional democracies that have established active judicial review mechanisms only in the last few decades. Meanwhile, transnational tribunals have become the main loci for coordinating policies at the global or regional level, from trade and monetary issues to labor standards and environmental regulations.

However, the growing political significance of courts has not only become more globally widespread than ever before. It has also expanded its scope to become a manifold, multifaceted phenomenon that extends well beyond the now "standard" concept of judge-made policy-making, through ordinary rights jurisprudence and judicial redrawing of legislative boundaries between state organs. The judicialization of politics now includes the wholesale transfer to the courts of some of the most pertinent and polemical political controversies a democratic polity can contemplate. Recall such matters as the outcome of the American presidential election of 2000 or the Mexican presidential election in 2006, the war in Chechnya, the Pervez Musharraf-led military *coup d'état* in Pakistan, Germany's place in the EU, restorative justice dilemmas in post-authoritarian Latin America, post-Communist Europe, or post-apartheid South Africa, the secular nature of Turkey's political system, Israel's fundamental definition as a "Jewish and Democratic State," or the political future of Quebec and the Canadian federation: all of these and many other "existential" political controversies worldwide have been framed as constitutional issues. And this has been accompanied by the concomitant assumption that courts—not politicians or the demos itself—are the appropriate fora for making these key decisions.

Despite the increasing prevalence of this trend, academic discourse addressing the judicialization of politics worldwide remains surprisingly sketchy. With a few notable exceptions (e.g. Tate and Vallinder 1995; Goldstein et al. 2001; Hirschl 2002; 2004a; 2006; Ferejohn 2002; Shapiro and Stone Sweet 2002; Pildes 2004; Sieder et al. 2005), the judicialization of politics is often treated as an obvious byproduct of the global convergence toward constitutional supremacy and the prevalence of rights discourse. What is more, the judicialization of politics is often used indiscriminately to refer to what in fact are several distinct phenomena: these range from judicial activism and rights jurisprudence to debates over judicial appointments and the politicization of the judiciary—the inevitable flip side of judicialization.

This chapter presents a lucid vocabulary and a coherent framework for analyzing the scope, nature, and causes of the judicialization of politics as we now know it. I begin with a classification of the various categories and instances of the trend that is broadly referred to as the judicialization of politics. I illustrate the distinct characteristics of each of these groupings of judicialization through recent jurisprudence of courts and tribunals worldwide. Special attention is given to the judicialization of "mega" or "pure" politics—by this I mean the transfer to courts of contentious issues of an outright political nature and significance. In the chapter's second part, I explore the main theories that purport to identify the central institutional, societal, and political conditions that are conducive to the judicialization of politics.

1 WHAT IS THE JUDICIALIZATION OF POLITICS?

The "judicialization of politics" is an often umbrella-like term referring to what are really three interrelated processes. At the most abstract level, the term refers to the spread of legal discourse, jargon, rules, and procedures into the political sphere and policy-making fora and processes. The ascendancy of legal discourse and the popularization of legal jargon is evident in virtually every aspect of modern life. It is perhaps best illustrated by the subordination of almost every decision-making forum in modern rule-of-law polities to quasi-judicial norms and procedures. Matters that had previously been negotiated in an informal or nonjudicial fashion have now come to be dominated by legal rules and procedures (Sieder et al. 2005, 5). The proliferation of legalistic discourse and procedures seems to reflect the common translation of fundamental justice into what is predominantly procedural fairness. Judicialization of this type is inextricable from law's capture of social relationships and popular culture and its expropriation of social conflicts (Teubner 1987; Habermas 1988). Related aspects of this type of "juridification" of modern life have also been identified by early legal sociologists—for example, Henry Maine and Emile Durkheim's "from status to contract" thesis (Maine 2000 [1861]; Durkheim 1964 [1893]); or Max Weber's emphasis on the rise of a formal, unambiguous, and rational legal system in Western societies (Weber 1978 [1914]).

A second, more concrete aspect of the judicialization of politics is the expansion of the province of courts and judges in determining public policy outcomes, mainly through administrative review, judicial redrawing of bureaucratic boundaries between state organs, and "ordinary" rights jurisprudence. Not a single week passes by without a national high court somewhere in the world releasing a major judgment pertaining to the scope of constitutional rights protections or the limits on legislative or executive powers. Of these, the most common are cases dealing criminal due process rights and other aspects of procedural justice. Also common are rulings involving classic civil liberties, various aspects of the rights to privacy, and formal equality—all of which expand and fortify the boundaries of the constitutionally protected private sphere, often perceived as threatened by the long arm of the encroaching state and its regulatory laws (Hirschl 2004a, 103–18). This ever-expanding body of civil liberties jurisprudence has essentially redefined the boundaries of the private sphere in constitutional democracies, and has transformed numerous policy areas involving individual freedoms.

The proliferation of administrative agencies in the modern welfare state has expanded the scope of administrative review by courts. More often than not, such judicial involvement in public policy-making is confined to procedural aspects, focusing on process rather than substance. Drawing upon basic norms from contract law, constitutional law, and mainly administrative law, courts oversee and enforce the application of due process, equal opportunity, transparency, account-ability, and reasonableness in public policy-making. It is therefore not surprising that judicialization of this type dominates the justice system itself, from civil procedure to criminal due process; it is particularly noticeable in other process-heavy policy areas such as immigration, taxation, or public tenders. But it is also clearly evident in countless other areas, from urban planning and public health to industrial relations and consumer protection. In short, whereas the first type of judicialization may be described as "juridification of social relations," judicializa-tion of this second type manifests itself mainly in the domain of procedural justice and formal fairness in public policy-making processes.

Over the last two decades, the judicialization of public policy-making has also proliferated at the international level (Romano 1999; Slaughter 2000; Goldstein et al. 2001), with the establishment of numerous transnational courts and quasi-judicial tribunals, panels, and commissions dealing with human rights, trans-national governance, trade, and monetary affairs. Perhaps nowhere is this process more evident than in Europe (e.g. Weiler 1999; Stone Sweet 2000). The European Court of Justice (ECJ) interprets the treaties upon which the European Union is founded and the enormous body of EU secondary legislation, and has been awarded an increasingly important status by legislators, executives, and judiciaries in the now eastward-expanded EU, particularly with respect to interstate legal and economic disputes. The European Court of Human Rights in Strasbourg, the judicial arm of the Council of Europe, has in effect become the final court of appeal on human-rights issues for most of Europe. The judgments of these courts (as well as of other supranational tribunals such as the Inter-American Court of Human Rights) carry great symbolic weight and have forced many countries to incorporate transnational legal standards into their domestic legal system.

A similar process has taken place with respect to international trade disputes. Decisions by the World Trade Organization's (WTO) dispute settlement mechan-ism have had far-reaching implications for trade and commerce policies at the national level. This is also the case even in the United States, where compliance with unfavorable rulings by foreign tribunals has always been a tough sell. The 1994 North America Free Trade Agreement (NAFTA) also establishes quasi-judicial dispute resolution processes regarding foreign investment, financial services, and antidumping and countervailing instances. Similar arrangements were established by the MERCOSUR agreement in South America and ASEAN in the Asia-Pacific region. In short, a large-scale transfer of crucial policy-making prerogatives—from policy-making bodies and majoritarian decision-making arenas at the national level to relatively insulated transnational entities and tribunals—has been rapidly established over the last few decades. This trend has been described as nothing short of a new world order (Slaughter 2004).

A third emerging class of the judicialization of politics is the reliance on courts and judges for dealing with what we might call "mega-politics:" core political controversies that define (and often divide) whole polities. The judicialization of mega-politics includes a few subcategories: judicialization of electoral processes; judicial scrutiny of executive branch prerogatives in the realms of macroeconomic planning or national security matters (i.e. the demise of what is known in constitutional theory as the "political question" doctrine); fundamental restorative justice dilemmas; judicial corroboration of regime transformation; and above all, the judicialization of formative collective identity, nation-building processes and struggles over the very definition—or *raison d'etre*—of the polity as such—arguably the most problematic type of judicialization from a constitutional theory standpoint. These emerging areas of judicialized politics expand the boundaries of national high-court involvement in the political sphere beyond the ambit of constitutional rights or federalism jurisprudence, and take the judicialization of politics to a point that far exceeds any previous limit. More often than not, this trend is supported, either tacitly or explicitly, by powerful political stakeholders. The result has been the transformation of supreme courts worldwide into a crucial part of their respective countries' national policy-making apparatus. Elsewhere I have described this process as a transition to juristocracy (Hirschl 2004a).

It is difficult to overstate the profoundness of this transition. Whereas oversight of the procedural aspects of the democratic process—judicial monitoring of electoral procedures and regulations, for example—falls within the mandate of most constitutional courts, questions such as a regime's legitimacy, a nation's collective identity, or a polity's coming to terms with its often less than admirable past, reflect primarily deep moral and political dilemmas, not judicial ones. As such, they ought—at least as a matter of principle—to be contemplated and decided by the populace itself, through its elected and accountable representatives. Adjudicating such matters is an inherently and substantively political exercise that extends beyond the application of rights provisions or basic procedural justice norms to various public policy realms. Judicialization of this type involves instances where courts decide on watershed political questions that face the nation, despite the fact that the constitution of that nation does not speak to the contested issues directly, and despite the obvious recognition of the very high political stakes for the nation. It is precisely these instances of judicialization of watershed national questions involving the intersection of very high political stakes with little or no pertinent constitutional guidelines that make the democratic credentials of judicial review most questionable. For it is ultimately unclear what makes courts the most appropriate forum for deciding such purely political quandaries.

The difference between the second and third face of judicialization is subtle, but it is important. It lies in part in the qualitative distinction between mainly procedural justice issues on the one hand, and substantive moral dilemmas or watershed political quandaries that the entire nation faces on the other. In other words, there seems to be a difference between the political salience of judicialization of public policy-making and the judicialization of mega-politics. Ensuring procedural fairness in public tenders is an important element of corruption-free public administration. But its political salience is not nearly as significant as that of purely political issues such as the place of Germany in the European Union, the future of Quebec and the Canadian federation, the constitutionality of the post-apartheid political pact in South Africa, or that of the boundaries of the Jewish collective in Israel.

But the difference between the second and third level of judicialized politics goes beyond the question of political salience. It depends on our conceptualization of the "political." What counts as a "political" decision is not an easy question to answer. A political decision must affect the lives of many people. However, many cases that are not purely political (e.g. large class-action lawsuits) also affect the lives of many people. More importantly, since there is no plain and simple answer to the question "what is political?"—for many social theorists, the answer to that question would be "everything is political"—there cannot be a plain and simple definition of the judicialization of politics either. Likewise, what may be considered a controversial political issue in one polity (say, the right to have an abortion in the United States) may be framed as a clash between domestic law and supranational law in another country (e.g. Ireland), or may be a nonissue in yet another polity. That said, there seems to be a qualitative difference between the political salience of (for example) a court ruling refining the boundaries of the right to fair hearing or reviewing the validity of federal quotas on agricultural export, and a landmark judgment determining the legitimacy of a polity's regime or a nation's collective identity and membership boundaries. Indeed, few decisions may be considered more "political" than authoritatively defining a polity's very *raison d'être*. That elusive yet intuitive distinction is what differentiates the judicialization of mega-politics form the first two levels of judicialization. Consider the following examples—all are seldom addressed by American constitutional theory, often preoccupied with rights jurisprudence and with matters American.

2 A New Frontier: The Judicialization of "Mega-politics"

The judicialization of mega-politics includes several different types of controversies, not all of which are equally problematic from the standpoint of canonical constitutional theory. One emerging subcategory of judicialized mega-politics is the increased judicial scrutiny of core prerogatives of legislatures and executives in foreign affairs, fiscal policy, and national security. The Supreme Court of Canada was quick to reject the "political question" doctrine (nonjusticiability of explicitly political questions) following the adoption of the Canadian Charter of Rights and Freedoms in 1982. In its landmark ruling in *Operation Dismantle* (1985)—a challenge to the constitutionality of U.S. missile testing on Canadian soil—the Supreme Court of Canada held unanimously that "[i]f a case raises the question of whether executive or legislative action violated the Constitution, then the question has to be answered by the Court, regardless of the political character of the controversy... [d]isputes of a political or foreign policy nature may be properly cognizable by the courts."

In the *Chechnya Case* (1995), the Russian Constitutional Court agreed to hear petitions by a number of opposition members of the Duma, who challenged the constitutionality of three presidential decrees ordering the Russian military invasion of Chechnya. Rejecting Chechnya's claim to independence and upholding the constitutionality of President Yeltsin's decrees as *intra vires*, the majority of the judges of this court stated that maintaining the territorial integrity and unity of Russia was "[a]n unshakable rule that excludes the possibility of an armed secession in any federative state." In a similar fashion, the Israeli Supreme Court ruled in 2004 on the constitutionality and compatibility with international law of the West Bank barrier—a controversial network of fences and walls separating Israel from Palestinian territory. It also heard arguments concerning the constitutionality of matters such as the Oslo Peace Accords or Israel's unilateral pullback from the Gaza Strip. In recent years, constitutional courts in many countries have also begun the scrutiny of "process-light" measures adopted by governments to combat terrorism in the so-called "war on terror" era. In 1999, the Israeli Supreme Court banned the use of torture in interrogations by Israel's General Security Services. In late 2006 it ordered the weighing of security considerations against potential harm to civilians in determining the legality of "targeted killings" (the controversial practice of assassinating suspected Palestinian terrorists by Israel's security forces).

A slightly different, yet equally telling manifestation of judicial scrutiny of core executive prerogatives—this time in the context of national fiscal and welfare policy—can be found in the 1995 *Austerity Package Decisions* (the so-called "Bokros cases") by the Hungarian Constitutional Court. Here, the Court drew upon the concepts of reliance interest and legal certainty to strike down twenty-six provisions of a comprehensive economic emergency plan introduced by the government, the major thrust of which was a substantial cut in the government's expenditures on welfare benefits, pension allowances, education, and health care in order to reduce Hungary's enormous budget deficit and foreign debt. An equally significant manifestation of the judicialization of contentious macroeconomic matters is the Supreme Court of Argentina's October 2004 ruling (the so-called *Corralito Case*) on the constitutionality of the government's "pesification" plan (total convergence of the Argentine economy into pesos) and the corresponding freezing of savings deposits nominated in U.S. dollars—a fall-out of Argentina's major economic crisis of 2001.

A second area of increased judicial involvement in mega-politics is the corroboration of regime change. The most obvious example here is the "constitutional certification" saga in South Africa: This was the first time a constitutional court refused to accept a national constitutional text drafted by a representative constitution-making body. Other recent manifestations of this type of judicialization of mega-politics include the 2004 dismissal by the Constitutional Court of South Korea of the impeachment of President Roh Moo-hyun by South Korea's National Assembly (the first time in the history of modern constitutionalism that a president impeached by a legislative body has been reinstated by a judicial body); the rarely acknowledged yet astonishing restoration of the 1997 Fijian constitution by the Fijian Court of Appeals in *Fiji v. Prasad* 2001 (the first time in the history of modern constitutionalism that a polity's high court restored a constitution and the democratic system of government created by it); and the crucial yet seldom recognized involvement of the Pakistan Supreme Court in political transformation in that country (since 1990 Pakistan has known five regime changes and the Pakistan Supreme Court has played a key role in each of these radical transitions).

The judicialization of mega-politics is also increasingly evident in a third area: judicial oversight of electoral processes, or what may be referred to as "the law of democracy" (Miller 2004). The most prevalent subcategory here is the judicial scrutiny of the pre-electoral process in virtually all countries where elections, referenda, or plebiscites take place. In some instances this is done via scrutiny, at times compulsory, of candidates and voter registry by electoral commissions that often comprise judges. In terms of jurisprudence, courts are frequently called upon to decide on matters such as party funding, campaign financing, and broadcast advertising during election campaigns; the redrawing of electoral districts; and the approval or disqualification of political parties and candidates. Over the last decade, courts in a number of countries, notably Bangladesh, Belgium, India, Israel, Spain, Thailand, and Turkey, have banned (or come close to banning) popular political parties from participating in national elections. During the last decade alone, constitutional courts in over twenty-five countries have been called upon to determine the political future of prominent leaders through impeachment or disqualification trials. Courts approved (or disapproved) the extension of Colombia's President Alvaro Uribe, Uganda's President Yoweri Museveni, and Russia's President Boris Yeltsin's terms in office. Pakistan's former prime ministers Benazir Bhutto and Nawaz Sharif, and the Philippines' President Joseph Estrada— to give a few examples—have all had their political fate determined by courts. To that list one could add corruption indictments against heads of state (e.g. Italy's Silvio Berlusconi, Peru's Alberto Fujimori, or Thailand's Thaksin Shinawatra), and "political trials," in which prominent opposition candidates and leaders have been disqualified or otherwise removed from the race by a politicized judiciary.

Courts have also become ultimate decision-makers in disputes over national election outcomes, for example in Taiwan (2004), Georgia (2004), Puerto Rico (2004), Ukraine (2005), Congo (2006), Italy (2006), where the Constitutional

Court approved a win of fewer than 25,000 votes by center-left leader Romano Prodi in one of Italy's closest elections. Likewise, a series of election appeals and counter-appeals culminated in Mexico's Federal Electoral Court's dismissal of leftist runner-up Andres Manuel Lopez Obrador's claim for a massive fraud by right-wing candidate and election winner Felipe Calderon in the July 2006 presidential election in that country. Calderon won the election by a less than 0.6 percent margin. Constitutional courts have also played key roles in deciding election outcomes in states and provinces. Even the fate of elections in the exotic island nations of Madagascar and Trinidad and Tobago has been determined by judicial tribunals. Clearly, the *Bush v. Gore* courtroom struggle over the fate of the American presidency was anything but an idiosyncratic moment in the recent history of comparative constitutional politics.

A fourth emerging area of mega-politics that has been rapidly judicialized over the past few decades is that of transitional or restorative justice. Quasi-judicial "truth commissions" or special tribunals dealing with core issues of transitional justice have been established in dozens of countries from El Salvador to Ghana. Recall, for example, the judicialization of restorative justice in the early years of the post-apartheid era in South Africa: Here, the "amnesty-for-confession" formula had been given a green light by the South African Constitutional Court in *AZAPO* (1996) allowing establishment of the quasi-judicial Truth and Reconciliation Commission. Similarly, the Pinochet affair can be thought of as an example of the judicialization of restorative justice dilemmas in post-authoritarian Latin America. Another example would be the major role played by the newly established constitutional courts in post-Communist Europe: these courts have played a central role in confronting their respective countries' pasts through the trials of former office-holders who committed what are now considered to be human rights violations during the Communist era. A paradigmatic case here is the 1993 decision of the constitutional court of the Czech Republic to uphold a law that declared the entire Communist era in the former Czechoslovakia illegal. These courts also made landmark rulings pertaining to Holocaust-related reparative justice and restitution policies. Yet another example would be the wholesale judicialization of the battle over the status of indigenous peoples in so-called "settler societies," particularly Australia, Canada, and New Zealand.

The judicialization of restorative justice is also evident at the transnational level. Here too there are many examples. The International Criminal Court (ICC) (ratified by ninety countries as of 2006) was established in 1998 as a permanent international judicial body with potentially universal jurisdiction pertaining to genocide, crimes against humanity, war crimes, and so on. The International Criminal Tribunal for the former Yugoslavia (ICTY) in The Hague was established in 1993. Another example here is the International Criminal Tribunal for Rwanda (ICTR) in Arusha, Tanzania, established in 1995. Also included in this category are the "hybrid courts" in Cambodia, East Timor, Kosovo, and Sierra Leone, which are all tribunals working within the rules and regulations of the domestic legal system, and applying a compound of international and national, substantial and procedural, law. Notorious leaders such as Slobodan Milosevic, Charles G. Taylor, and Saddam Hussein, were all put to trial before this new nexus of war crime tribunals.

But the clearest manifestation of the wholesale judicialization of core political controversies—arguably, the type of judicialization of politics that is the hardest to reconcile with canonical constitutional theory concerning the role of courts in a democracy—is the growing reliance on courts for contemplating the very definition, or *raison d'être*, of the polity as such. This type of judicialized "mega-politics" is common in fragmented polities facing deep ethnic, linguistic, or religious cleavages. A few examples of this phenomenon include: the central role the Turkish Constitutional Court has played in preserving the strictly secular nature of Turkey's political system, by continually outlawing antisecularist political forces and parties; the landmark jurisprudence of the Supreme Court of India pertaining to the status of Muslim and Hindu religious personal laws; the crucial role of courts in Egypt, Pakistan, Malaysia, or Nigeria in determining the applicability of Islamic *Shari'a* law in public life; the wholesale transfer of the deep secular/religious cleavage in Israeli society to the Israeli judiciary through the judicialization of the question of "who is a Jew?" and the corresponding entanglement of the Israeli Supreme Court in interpreting Israel's fundamental definition as a "Jewish and Democratic State." An example here is the German Federal Constitutional Court's key role in the creation of the unified Germany, illustrated for example in the *Maastricht Case* (1993): here, the Court drew upon Basic Law provisions to determine the status of post-unification Germany vis-à-vis the emerging European supranational polity. Another "textbook" illustration is the unprecedented involvement of the Canadian judiciary in dealing with the status of bilingualism and the political future of Quebec and the Canadian federation, including the Supreme Court of Canada's landmark ruling in the *Quebec Secession Reference* (1998)—the first time a democratic country had ever tested in advance the legal terms of its own dissolution. Following a slim loss by the Quebecois secessionist movement in the 1995 referendum, the federal government was quick to draw upon the reference procedure to ask the Supreme Court to determine whether a hypothetical unilateral secession declaration by the Quebec government would be constitutional. The court accepted the challenge with open arms and took the liberty to articulate with authority the fundamental pillars of the Canadian polity in a way no other state organ has ever done before.

In short, "nothing falls beyond the purview of judicial review; the world is filled with law; anything and everything is justiciable," as Aharon Barak, the former Chief Justice of the Supreme Court of Israel, once said; and this appears to have become a widely accepted motto by courts worldwide. While many public policy matters still remain beyond the ambit of the courts (Graber 2004; Schauer 2006), in numerous countries throughout the world, there has been a growing legislative deference to the judiciary, an increasing (and often welcomed) intrusion of the judiciary into the prerogatives of legislatures and executives, and a corresponding acceleration of the process whereby political agendas have been judicialized. Together, these developments have helped to bring about a growing reliance on adjudicative means for clarifying and settling fundamental moral controversies and highly contentious political questions, and have transformed national high courts into major political decision-making bodies.

The wave of judicial activism that has swept the globe in the last few decades has not bypassed the most fundamental issues a democratic polity ought to address—whether it is the corroboration of new political regimes, coming to terms with its own (often not so admirable) past, or grappling with its embedded collective identity quandaries. Although foundational political questions of this nature may have certain important constitutional aspects, they are neither purely, or even primarily, legal dilemmas. As such, one would think, they ought to be resolved, at least on the level of principle, through public deliberation in the political sphere. Nonetheless, constitutional courts throughout the world have gradually become major decision-making bodies for dealing with precisely such dilemmas. Fundamental restorative justice, regime legitimacy, and collective identity questions have been framed in terms of constitutional claims (often for rights and entitlements), and as such have rapidly found their way to the courts.

3 WHY THE JUDICIALIZATION OF POLITICS?

Scholars have identified a number of possible reasons and explanations for the judicialization of politics. Akin to any other major sociolegal phenomenon, no simple or single explanation can account for its wide range of manifestations. Given that a confluence of elements must exist, it is most productive to consider the factors that are, *ceteris paribus*, conducive to the judicialization of politics. These may be grouped into three main categories: institutional features, judicial behavior, and political determinants.

3.1 Institutional Features

As a bare minimum, the judicialization of politics requires the existence of a reasonably independent judiciary, with a well-respected and fairly active apex court. It is also generally agreed that there is a close affinity between the existence of a constitutional catalogue of rights and viable judicial review mechanisms in a polity, and judicial activism on the part of that polity's judiciary. If the constitution does not list tangible and defensible rights that individuals hold against the state, then judicial review is based on limited *ultra vires* principles, and is generally confined to procedural matters. In these circumstances, intervention by the judiciary in fundamental moral controversies or in highly political or politicized issues is generally unlikely. On the other hand, the existence of a constitutional catalogue of rights and judicial review mechanisms not only provides the necessary institutional framework for courts to become more vigilant in their efforts to protect the fundamental rights and liberties of a given polity's residents; it also enables them to expand their jurisdiction to address vital moral dilemmas and political controversies of crucial significance to that polity.

What is more, the existence of a constitutional framework that facilitates judicial activism may provide political actors who are unable or unwilling to advance their policy preferences through majoritarian decision-making arenas with an alternative institutional channel (the courts) for accomplishing their policy goals. Likewise, the existence or adoption of a constitutional catalogue of rights is likely to increase the public's "rights awareness." It also allows for what may be referred to as "judicialization from below"—legal mobilization by groups and movements that aim to advance social change through constitutional rights litigation. Therefore, in countries where bills of rights and active judicial review procedures have been adopted, one can expect a significant growth in the frequency and scope of the exercise of judicial review, and a corresponding intrusion by the judiciary into the prerogatives of both legislatures and executives. Likewise, the adoption of multilateral treaties and international agreements that contain justiciable provisions, and the accompanying establishment of adjudication or arbitration tribunals at the supranational level, are preconditions for the judicialization of international trade disputes.

Models of judicial review employed by constitutional democracies vary significantly in their procedural characteristics—a fact that has important implications for the scope and nature of judicial review in these countries. A pertinent distinction here is between a priori or *abstract* review and a posteriori or *concrete* review—whether the constitutionality of a law or administrative action is determined before or after it takes effect, or whether a declaration of unconstitutionality can be made in the absence of an actual case or controversy; in other words, the distinction is between hypothetical "what if" scenarios ("abstract" review) and judicial review that may take place only in the context of a specific legal dispute ("concrete" review). In the United States, only a posteriori and *concrete* judicial review is allowed. Judicial review of legislation, whether exercised by lower courts or by the Supreme Court, is a power that can only be exercised by the courts within the context of concrete adversary litigation; i.e. when the constitutional issue becomes relevant and requires resolution in the decision of the case. In France, by contrast, judicial review is limited to an a priori and *abstract* judicial review. The *Conseil Constitutionnel* has pre-enactment constitutional review powers, but no power to nullify a law after it has been enacted by the legislature.

A number of leading democracies feature combined a priori/a posteriori, abstract *and* concrete review systems. In the latter capacity, national high courts in such countries could outlaw a statute before it was formally enacted on the basis of hypothetical constitutional arguments about its potential effect. Judicial review in Canada, for example, is not limited to review within the context of concrete adversary litigation. The reference procedure allows both the federal and provincial governments in Canada to refer proposed statutes or even questions concerning hypothetical legal situations to the Supreme Court or the provincial courts of appeal for an advisory (abstract) opinion on their constitutionality. It is hardly surprising therefore that some of the most contentious issues in Canadian politics of the last few decades have reached the Supreme Court through the reference procedure.

Moreover, unlike in the United States, most countries that employ an a priori and abstract review model allow public officials, legislators, cabinet members, and heads of state to initiate judicial scrutiny of proposed laws and hypothetical constitutional scenarios, thereby providing a constitutional framework hospitable to the judicialization of politics and the accompanying politicization of the judiciary. In France and Italy, for example, the initiation of constitutional litigation in constitutional courts is limited to elected politicians. In other countries (Germany and Spain, for example) elected officials may challenge proposed legislation through the abstract a priori review. In short, a system that permits a priori and abstract review initiated by politicians would appear to have a greater potential for generating high levels of judicialized policy-making using the process of constitutional review (Stone 1992). That said, scholars have correctly pointed out that "the apparently more restrictive combination of *a posteriori* and concrete review has hardly relegated the U.S. Supreme Court to a minor policy role" (Tate 1992, 6).

Another pertinent distinction is that which exists between *decentralized* (all courts) and *centralized* (constitutional court) review. In a decentralized system (for example, in the U.S.), judicial review is an inherent competence of almost all courts in nearly any type of case and controversy. The centralized judicial review system (often referred to as "constitutional review") is characterized by having only a single state organ (a separate judicial body in the court system or an extrajudicial body) acting as a constitutional tribunal. This model of judicial review has been adopted by many European countries that follow various branches of the civil law tradition (such as Germany, Austria, Italy, and Spain), as well as by almost all new democracies in post-Communist Europe. Some new constitutionalist countries (such as Portugal) employ a combined decentralized/centralized model of judicial/constitutional review.

Other variables being equal, the impact of the judiciary on public policy outcomes is likely to be more significant under a decentralized, all-court review system. As Tate points out, "restricting the power to declare legislation and regulations unconstitutional to a constitutional court ... sharply reduces the number of occasions and range of policy issues on which courts can be invited (or can invite themselves) to exercise judicial review" (1992, 7). That said, administrative review—however limited—is always available to the courts in most centralized review countries. Moreover, the symbolic importance of landmark high-court decisions in such countries is at least as significant as that of national high-court rulings in countries employing a decentralized review system. Germany's Federal Constitutional Court and the youthful Hungarian Constitutional Court are perhaps the most frequently mentioned examples of centralized judicial bodies that not only fulfill the sole function of judicial review in their respective countries, but have also become crucial policy-making bodies at the national level (Kommers 1997; Sólyom and Brunner 2000).

Another important aspect of judicial review that has implications for the judicialization of politics is the question of standing (*locus standi*) and access rights: Who may initiate a legal challenge to the constitutionality of legislation or official action; and at what stage of the process may a given polity's supreme court become involved. In the United States, standing rights have been traditionally limited to individuals who claim to have been affected by an allegedly unconstitutional legislation or official action. The U.S. Supreme Court will not hear a challenge to the constitutionality of legislation unless all other possible legal paths and remedies have been exhausted. Moreover, the Court has full discretion over which cases it will hear—its docket therefore consists of "discretionary leave" cases, rather than appeals by right. However, constitutional democracies that employ a priori and abstract judicial review (such as France) allow for, and even encourage, public officials and political actors to challenge the constitutionality of proposed legislation. Several polities authorize their constitutional court judges, in an *ex-officio* capacity, to initiate proceedings against an apparently unconstitutional law. Other countries (South Africa, for example) impose mandatory referrals of constitutional questions by lower courts to a constitutional tribunal. And yet other countries, most notably Israel and India, allow private-person constitutional grievances to be submitted directly to their respective high courts. In addition to legislative frameworks, constitutional courts in most liberal democracies have continuously liberalized the rules of standing and expanded intervener (e.g. *amicus curiae*) status. Other variables being equal, liberal standing and accessibility rights along with lowered barriers of nonjusticiability provides an important institutional channel through which ordinary citizens can challenge what they regard as infringements upon their constitutionally protected rights before a country's judicial system, thereby increasing the likelihood of judicial involvement in public policy-making.

3.2 Judicial Behavior

The rise of "philosopher king courts" cannot be attributed solely or even primarily to the existence of a constitutional framework conducive to the judicialization of politics. It depends to a large extent upon judicial willingness to engage in public policy-making. In that respect, an increasing number of scholars suggest that judges do not behave or reach decisions in a way that is fundamentally different from other branches of government. Courts are political institutions not merely because they are politically constructed, but also because the determinants of judicial behavior are not distinctly different from the determinants of decision-making by other public officials. Judicial behavior, especially by constitutional courts in cases involving politically charged issues, may be driven by adherence to national meta-narratives, responsiveness to public opinion, personal ideological preferences, collegial considerations, prevalent attitudes within the legal profession, or strategic considerations vis-à-vis other national decision-making bodies.

Of particular relevance to the judicialization of politics are some insights drawn from the strategic approach to the study of judicial behavior. Like most other institutions, courts and judges are strategic actors to the extent that they seek to maintain or enhance their institutional position vis-à-vis other major national decision-making bodies or simply expand the ambit of their political influence and international profile. Accordingly, constitutional court rulings may not only be analyzed as mere acts of professional, apolitical jurisprudence (as doctrinal legalistic explanations of court rulings often suggest), or reflections of judicial ideology (as "attitudinal" models of judicial behavior might suggest), but also a reflection of judges' own strategic choices (Epstein and Knight 1998; 2000).

Courts may realize that there are circumstances—such as the changing fates or preferences of other influential political actors, or gaps in the institutional context within which they operate—in which they may be able to strengthen their own position by extending the scope of their jurisprudence and fortifying their status as crucial national policy-making bodies. The establishment of a supranational rule of law in Europe, for example, was driven in no small part by national judges' attempts to enhance their independence, influence, and authority vis-à-vis other courts and political actors (Alter 2001), as well as by a corresponding and continuous judicial activism by the ECJ (Mattli and Slaughter 1998; Weiler 1999). Conversely, credible threats on the court's autonomy and harsh political responses to unwelcome activism or interventions on the part of the courts have chilling effects on judicial decision-making patterns (Epstein et al. 2001; Helmke 2005; Vanberg 2005). Courts must be responsive to the political environment in which they operate in other respects as well. Because justices do not have the institutional capacities to enforce their rulings, they must take into account the extent to which popular decision-makers will support their policy initiatives (McGuire and Stimson 2004). Judges seem to care about their reputation within their close social milieu, court colleagues, and the legal profession more generally (Baum 2006). And with the increasing internationalization of constitutional discourse, the judicialization of politics (primarily through constitutional rights litigation) may also support the interests of a supreme court seeking to increase its symbolic power and international prestige by fostering its alignment with a growing community of liberal democratic nations engaged in judicial review and rights-based discourses.

The centrality of judicial will in explaining the judicialization of politics is often emphasized by constitutional theorists critical of judicial activism. With a few exceptions, these critics often blame "power hungry" courts and judges for being too assertive and excessively entangled with moral and political decision-making, subsequently disregarding fundamental separation of powers and democratic governance principles. Even the more politically astute critics of the US Constitution's expropriation by the United States Supreme Court are more concerned with the Supreme Court's "imperialist" impulse than with the political conditions that promote the transition to juristocracy (e.g. Tushnet 1999; Bork 2001; Kramer 2004).

In my opinion, portraying courts and judges as the main source of judicialization is misguided. Courts are first and foremost political institutions. Like any other political institutions, they do not operate in an institutional or ideological vacuum. Their establishment does not develop and cannot be understood separately from the concrete social, political, and economic struggles that shape a given political system. Indeed, constitutionalization, political deference to the judiciary, and the expansion of judicial power more generally, are an integral part and an important manifestation of those struggles, and cannot be understood in isolation from them. And this brings us to the final category, political determinants of judicialization.

3.3 Political Determinants

A favorable constitutional framework and an active judiciary are important contributors to the judicialization of politics. However, this unprecedented level of political jurisprudence cannot develop, let alone be sustained, without the receptiveness and support, tacit or explicit, of the political sphere itself. Recent studies of comparative judicial politics propose a number of explanations for the expansion of judicial power and the corresponding judicialization of politics. These may be grouped into three subcategories: macro sociopolitical trends, the prevalence of rights discourse and litigation, and finally strategic maneuvering by powerful political stakeholders.

The proliferation of democracy worldwide is a main cause of judicialization and the expansion of judicial power more generally. By its very nature, the establishment of a democratic regime entails the establishment of some form of separation of powers among the major branches of government, as well as between the central and provincial/regional legislatures. It also entails the presence of a set of procedural governing rules and decision-making processes to which all political actors are required to adhere. The persistence and stability of such a system, in turn, requires at least a semi-autonomous, supposedly apolitical judiciary to serve as an impartial umpire in disputes concerning the scope and nature of the fundamental rules of the political game. Active judicial review is both a prerequisite and a byproduct of viable democratic governance in multilayered federalist countries (Shapiro 1999). In other words, more democracy equals more courts. However, the "proliferation of democracy" thesis cannot provide a full explanation for the significant variations in levels of judicialization among new democracies. And it does not provide an adequate explanation for increased levels of judicialization in polities that have not undergone any apparent changes in their political regime.

From a functionalist standpoint, judicialization may emanate from the proliferation in levels of government and the corresponding emergence of a wide variety of semi-autonomous administrative and regulatory state agencies as the main driving forces behind the expansion of judicial power over the past few decades (Shapiro and Stone Sweet 2002). According to this thesis, independent and active judiciaries armed with judicial review practices are necessary for efficient monitoring of the ever-expanding administrative state. Moreover, the modern administrative state embodies notions of government as an active policy-maker, rather than a passive adjudicator of conflicts. It therefore requires an active, policy-making judiciary (Feely and Rubin 1998). Along the same lines, the judicialization of politics may emanate from a general waning of confidence in technocratic government and planning, and a consequent desire to restrict the discretionary powers of the state, resulting in a diffusion of judicial power (Shapiro 1999). It may also stem from the increasing complexity and contingency of modern societies (Luhmann 1985), and/or from the creation and expansion of the modern welfare state with its numerous regulatory agencies (Teubner 1987; Habermas 1988). Some accounts of the rapid growth of judicialization at the supranational judicial level portray it as an inevitable institutional response to complex coordination problems deriving from the systemic need to adopt standardized legal norms and administrative regulations across member states in an era of converging economic markets (Stone Sweet 2000). In some instances, economic liberalization may be an important pro-judicialization factor. In the regulatory arena, the combination of privatization and liberalization may encourage "juridical regulation" (Vogel 1998; Kelemen and Sibbitt 2004).

A second approach emphasizes the prevalence of rights discourse or greater awareness to rights issues, which is likely to yield what may be termed "judicialization from below." Charles Epp (1998) suggests that the impact of constitutional catalogues of rights may be limited by individuals' inability to invoke them through strategic litigation. Hence bills of rights matter to the extent that a support structure for legal mobilization—a nexus of rights-advocacy organizations, rights-supportive lawyers and law schools, governmental rights-enforcement agencies, and legal-aid schemes—is well developed. In other words, while the existence of written constitutional provisions is a necessary condition for the effective protection of rights and liberties, it is certainly not a sufficient one. The effectiveness of rights provisions in planting the seeds of social change in a given polity is largely contingent upon the existence of a support structure for legal mobilization, and more generally, sociocultural conditions that are hospitable for "judicialization from below."

Legal mobilization from below is aided by the commonly held belief that judicially affirmed rights are self-implementing forces of social change removed from the constraints of political power. This belief has gained a near-sacred status in public discussion. The "myth of rights" as Stuart Scheingold (1974) termed it, contrasts the openness of judicial proceedings to the secret bargaining of interest group pluralism so as to underscore the integrity and incorruptibility of the judicial process. "The aim, of course, is to enhance the attractiveness of legal and constitutional solutions to political problems" (1974, 34). This is turn may lead a spread of populist "rights talk" and the corresponding impoverishment of political discourse (Glendon 1991).

Similarly, an authentic, "bottom up" judicialization is more likely to occur when judicial institutions are perceived by social movements, interest groups, and political activists as more reputable, impartial, and effective decision-making bodies than other bureaucracy-heavy government institutions or biased majoritarian decision-making arenas (Tate and Valinder 1995). An all-encompassing judicialization of politics is, *ceteris paribus*, less likely to occur in a polity featuring a unified, assertive political system that is capable of restraining the judiciary. In such polities, the political sphere may signal credible threats to an overactive judiciary that exert a chilling effect on courts. Conversely, the more dysfunctional or deadlocked the political system and its decision-making institutions are in a given rule-of-law polity, the greater the likelihood of expansive judicial power in that polity (Guarnieri et al. 2002, 160–81). Greater fragmentation of power among political branches reduces their ability to rein in courts, and correspondingly increases the likelihood of courts asserting themselves (Ferejohn 2002).

A more "realist" approach suggests that the judicialization of politics is largely a function of concrete choices, interests, or strategic considerations by self-interested political stakeholders. From the politicians' point of view, delegating policy-making authority to the courts may be an effective means of shifting responsibility, and thereby reducing the risks to themselves and to the institutional apparatus within which they operate. The calculus of the "blame deflection" strategy is quite intuitive. If the delegation of powers can increase credit or legitimacy, and/or reduce the blame placed on the politician as a result of the delegated body's policy decision, then such delegation can benefit the politician (Voigt and Salzberger 2002). At the very least, the transfer to the courts of contested political "hot potatoes" offers a convenient retreat for politicians who have been unwilling or unable to settle contentious public disputes in the political sphere. It may also offer refuge for politicians seeking to avoid difficult or "no win" decisions and/or avoid the collapse of deadlocked or fragile governing coalitions (Graber 1993). Conversely, political oppositions may seek to judicialize politics (for example, through petitions and injunctions against government policies) in order to harass and obstruct governments (Tate and Vallinder 1995). At times, opposition politicians may resort to litigation in an attempt to enhance their media exposure, regardless of the actual outcome of litigation (Dotan and Hofnung 2005). A political quest for legitimacy often stands behind the transfer of certain regime-change questions to courts. (Consider the aforementioned Pakistani Supreme Court legitimization of the 1999 military *coup d'état* in that country). Empirical studies confirm that national high courts in most constitutional democracies enjoy greater public legitimacy and support than virtually all other political institutions. This holds true even when courts engage in explicit manifestations of political jurisprudence (Gibson et al. 2003).

Judicial empowerment may also reflect the competitiveness of a polity's electoral market or governing politicians' time horizons. According to the "party alternation" thesis, for example, when a ruling party expects to win elections repeatedly, the likelihood of an independent and powerful judiciary is low. However, when a ruling party has a low expectation of remaining in power, it is more likely to support a powerful judiciary to ensure that the next ruling party cannot use the judiciary to achieve its policy goals (Ramseyer 1994; Ginsburg 2003). Likewise, judicial empowerment may be driven by "hegemonic preservation" attempts taken by influential sociopolitical groups fearful of losing their grip on political power (Hirschl 2004a). Such groups and their political representatives—who possess disproportionate access to, and influence over, the legal arena—are more likely to delegate power to the judiciary when they find strategic drawbacks in adhering to majoritarian decision-making processes or when their world-views and policy preferences are increasingly challenged in such arenas. For example, constitutional courts have become key guardians of secular or moderate interests against the increasing popularity of principles of theocratic governance (Hirschl 2008). Likewise, when elected politicians are obstructed from fully implementing their own policy agenda, they may favor the active exercise of constitutional review by a sympathetic judiciary to overcome those obstructions (Hirschl 2004b; Whittington 2005). Powerful national high courts may allow governments to impose a centralizing "one rule fits all" regime upon enormous and diverse polities (Morton 1995; Goldstein 2001). (Think of the standardizing effect of apex court jurisprudence in vast and exceptionally diverse polities such as the United States or the European Union).

Perhaps the clearest illustration of the necessity of political support for the judicialization of mega-politics is the political sphere's decisive reaction to instances of unwelcome judicial activism. Occasionally, courts may respond to counter-establishment challenges by releasing rulings that threaten to alter the political power relations in which the courts are embedded. However, as the recent history of comparative constitutional politics tells us, recurrent manifestations of unsolicited judicial intervention in the political sphere in general—and unwelcome judgments concerning contentious political issues in particular—have brought about significant political backlashes, targeted at clipping the wings of over-active courts. These include legislative overrides of controversial rulings, political tinkering with judicial appointment and tenure procedures to ensure the appointment of "compliant" judges and/or to block the appointment of "undesirable" judges, "court-packing" attempts by political power holders, disciplinary sanctions, impeachment or removal of "objectionable" or "over-active" judges, the introduction of jurisdictional constraints, or clipping jurisdictional boundaries and judicial review powers. In some instances (e.g. Russia in 1993, or Ecuador in 2004, or Pakistan in 2007) they have resulted in constitutional crises leading to the reconstruction or dissolution of high courts. To this we may add another political response to unwelcome rulings: more subtle, and possibly more lethal, sheer bureaucratic disregard for, or protracted or reluctant implementation of, unwanted rulings (Rosenberg 1991; 1992; Garrett et al. 1998; Conant 2002). In short, the judicialization of politics is derivative first and foremost of political, not judicial, factors.

In sum, over the last few decades the world has witnessed a profound transfer of power from representative institutions to judiciaries, whether domestic or supranational. One of the main outcomes of this trend has been the transformation of courts and tribunals worldwide into major political decision-making loci. Over the last two decades, the judicialization of politics has extended well beyond the now "standard" judicialization of policy-making, to encompass questions of pure politics—electoral processes and outcomes, restorative justice, regime legitimacy, executive prerogatives, collective identity, and nation-building. These developments reflect the demise of the "political question" doctrine, and mark a transition to what I have termed "juristocracy." Akin to any other transformation of that scope and magnitude, the judicialization of politics is not derivative of a single cause. Instead, a confluence of institutional, societal, and political factors hospitable to the judicialization of politics is necessary to create and sustain it. Of these factors, three stand out as being crucial: the existence of a constitutional framework that promotes the judicialization of politics; a relatively autonomous judiciary that is easily enticed to dive into deep political waters; and above all, a political environment that is conducive to the judicialization of politics.

REFERENCES

ALTER, K. 2001. *Establishing the Supremacy of European Law.* Oxford: Oxford University Press.

BAUM, L. 2006. *Judges and Their Audiences: A Perspective on Judicial Behavior.* Princeton, NJ: Princeton University Press.

BORK, R. H. 2002. *Coercing Virtue: The Worldwide Rule of Judges.* Toronto: Vintage Canada.

CONANT, L. 2002. *Justice Contained: Law and Politics in the European Union.* Ithaca, NY: Cornell University Press.

DOTAN, Y., and HOFNUNG, M. 2005. Legal defeats—political wins: why do elected representatives go to court? *Comparative Political Studies*, 38: 75–103.

DURKHEIM, E. 1964 [1893]. *The Division of Labor in Society.* New York: Free Press.

EPP, C. 1998. *The Rights Revolution: Lawyers, Activists and Supreme Courts in Comparative Perspective.* Chicago: University of Chicago Press.

EPSTEIN, L., and KNIGHT, J. 1998. *The Choices Justices Make.* Washington, DC: CQ Press.

—— —— 2000. Towards a strategic revolution in judicial politics: a look back, a look ahead. *Political Research Quarterly*, 53: 625–61.

—— —— and SHVETSOVA, O. 2001. The role of constitutional courts in the establishment and maintenance of democratic systems of government. *Law and Society Review*, 35: 117–63.

FEELEY, M., and RUBIN, E. 1998. *Judicial Policy Making and the Modern State: How the Courts Reformed America's Prisons.* Cambridge: Cambridge University Press.

FEREJOHN, J. 2002. Judicializing politics, politicizing Law. *Law and Contemporary Problems*, 61: 41–68.

GARRETT, G. et al. 1998. The politics of judicial integration in the European Union. *International Organization*, 49: 171–81.

GIBSON, J. L., CALDEIRA, G., and SPENCE, L. K. 2003. The Supreme Court and the U. S. presidential election of 2000: wounds, self-inflicted or otherwise? *British Journal of Political Science*, 33: 535–56.

GINSBURG, T. 2003. *Judicial Review in New Democracies: Constitutional Courts in Asian Cases.* Cambridge: Cambridge University Press.

GLENDON, M. A. 1991. *Rights Talk: The Impoverishment of Political Discourse.* New York: Free Press.

GOLDSTEIN, J. et al. (eds.) 2001. *Legalization and World Politics.* Cambridge, Mass.: MIT Press.

GOLDSTEIN, L. 2001. *Constituting Federal Sovereignty: The European Union in Comparative Context.* Baltimore: Johns Hopkins University Press.

GRABER, M. 1993. The nonmajoritarian difficulty: legislative deference to the judiciary. *Studies in American Political Development*, 7: 35–73.

—— 2004. Resolving political questions into judicial questions: Tocqueville's thesis revisited. *Constitutional Commentary*, 21: 485–545.

GUARNIERI, C., and PEDERZOLI, P. 2002. *The Power of Judges: A Comparative Study of Courts and Democracy.* New York: Oxford University Press.

HABERMAS, J. 1988. Law as medium and law as institution. In *Dilemmas of Law in the Welfare State*, ed. G. Teubner. Berlin: Walter De Gruyter.

HELMKE, G. 2005. *Courts under Constraints: Judges, Generals, and Presidents in Argentina.* New York: Cambridge University Press.

HIRSCHL, R. 2002. Repositioning the judicialization of politics: *Bush v. Gore* as a global trend. *Canadian Journal of Law and Jurisprudence*, 15: 191–218.

—— 2004a. *Towards Juristocracy: The Origins and Consequences of the New Constitutionalism.* Cambridge, Mass.: Harvard University Press.

—— 2004b. Constitutional courts vs. religious fundamentalism: three Middle Eastern tales. *Texas Law Review*, 82: 1819–60.

—— 2006. The new constitutionalism and the judicialization of pure politics worldwide. *Fordham Law Review*, 75: 721–53.

—— 2008. Juristocracy vs. theocracy: constitutional courts and the containment of religious fundamentalism, *Middle East Law and Governance*.

KELEMEN, D., and SIBBITT, E. 2004. The globalization of American law. *International Organization*, 58: 103–36.

KOMMERS, D. 1997. *The Constitutional Jurisprudence of the Federal Republic of Germany.* Durham, NC: Duke University Press.

KRAMER, L. 2004. *The People Themselves: Popular Constitutionalism and Judicial Review.* New York: Oxford University Press.

LUHMANN, N. 1985. *A Sociological Theory of Law.* London: Routledge.

MAINE, H. 2000 [1861]. *Ancient Law.* Washington, DC: Beard Books.

MATTLI, W., and SLAUGHTER, A.-M. 1998. Law and politics in the European Union: a reply to Garrett. *International Organization*, 49: 182–90.

McGUIRE, K., and STIMSON, J. 2004. The least dangerous branch revisited: new evidence on Supreme Court responsiveness to public preferences. *Journal of Politics*, 66: 1018–35.

MILLER, R. A. 2004. Lords of democracy: the judicialization of "pure politics" in the United States and Germany. *Washington and Lee Law Review*, 61: 587–662.

MORTON, F. L. 1995. The effect of the Charter of Rights on Canadian federalism. *Publius*, 25: 173–88.

PILDES, R. 2004. The Supreme Court, 2003 term—foreword: the constitutionalization of democratic politics. *Harvard Law Review*, 118: 29–160.

RAMSEYER, J. M. 1994. The puzzling (in)dependence of courts: a comparative approach. *Journal of Legal Studies*, 23: 721–48.

ROMANO, C. 1999. The proliferation of international judicial bodies: the pieces of the puzzle. *New York University Journal of International Law and Politics*, 31: 709–51.

ROSENBERG, G. 1991. *The Hollow Hope: Can Courts Bring About Social Change?* Chicago: University of Chicago Press.

—— 1992. Judicial independence and the reality of political power. *Review of Politics*, 54: 369–98.

SCHAUER, F. 2006. The Supreme Court, 2005 Term-foreword: the Court's agenda—and the nation's. *Harvard Law Review*, 120: 4–64.

SCHEINGOLD, S. 1974. *The Politics of Rights: Lawyers, Public Policy, and Political Change.* New Haven, Conn.: Yale University Press.

SHAPIRO, M. 1999. The success of judicial review. In *Constitutional Dialogues in Comparative Perspective*, ed. S. Kenney. New York: Palgrave Macmillan.

—— and STONE SWEET, A. 2002. *On Law, Politics, and Judicialization.* New York: Oxford University Press.

SIEDER, R., SCHJOLDEN, L., and ANGELL, A. (eds.) 2005. *The Judicialization of Politics in Latin America.* New York: Palgrave Macmillan.

SLAUGHTER, A.-M. 2000. Judicial globalization. *Virginia Journal of International Law*, 40: 1103–24.

—— 2004. *The New World Order.* Princeton, NJ: Princeton University Press.

SÓLYOM, L., and BRUNNER, G. 2000. *Constitutional Judiciary in a New Democracy: The Hungarian Constitutional Court.* Ann Arbor: University of Michigan Press.

STONE, A. 1992 *The Birth of Judicial Politics in France: The Constitutional Council in Comparative Perspective.* New York: Oxford University Press.

STONE SWEET, A. 2000. *Governing with Judges: Constitutional Politics in Europe.* Oxford: Oxford University Press.

TATE, C. N. 1992. Comparative judicial review and public policy: concepts and overview. In *Comparative Judicial Review and Public Policy,* ed. D. Jackson and C. N. Tate. Westport, Conn.: Greenwood Press.

—— and VALLINDER, T. (eds.) 1995. *The Global Expansion of Judicial Power.* New York: New York University Press.

TEUBNER, G. 1987. *Juridification of the Social Spheres.* Berlin: Walter de Gruyter.

TUSHNET, M. 1999. *Taking the Constitution Away from the Courts.* Princeton, NJ: Princeton University Press.

VANBERG, G. 2005. *The Politics of Constitutional Review in Germany.* Cambridge: Cambridge University Press.

VOGEL, S. 1998. *Freer Markets, More Rules.* Ithaca, NY: Cornell University Press.

VOIGT, S., and SALZBERGER, E. 2002. Choosing not to choose: when politicians choose to delegate powers. *Kyklos,* 55: 289–310.

WEBER, M. 1978 [1914]. *Economy and Society: An Outline of Interpretive Sociology.* Berkeley: University of California Press.

WEILER, J. H. H. 1999. *The Constitution of Europe: Do the New Clothes have an Emperor?* Cambridge: Cambridge University Press.

WHITTINGTON, K. E. 2005. "Interpose your friendly hand:" political supports for the exercise of judicial review by the United States Supreme Court. *American Political Science Review,* 99: 583–96.

CHAPTER 9

COMPARATIVE FEDERALISM AND THE ROLE OF THE JUDICIARY

DANIEL HALBERSTAM

1 INTRODUCTION

FEDERALISM means the coexistence within a single polity of multiple levels of government each with constitutionally grounded claims to some degree of organizational autonomy and jurisdictional authority. Federal systems may result from a devolutionary bargain struck within a previously unified system (as in Belgium or the United Kingdom) or from an integrative project among previously separate jurisdictions (as the European Union, Germany, Switzerland, or the United States) (Lenaerts 1990; Stepan 1999). Federal systems may be organized in two basic ways. In horizontal systems (as in the United States), central and constituent governments are organizationally distinct, each with a full complement of legislative, executive, judicial, and fiscal powers. In vertical systems (such as Germany and the European Union), in contrast, the central government mostly acts through the constituent states while sharing a significant array of other powers (such as judicial and fiscal powers). Finally, federalism may be enshrined in a formal constitution

I would like to thank Jenna Bednar, Rick Hills, Ellen Katz, Chris McCrudden, Don Regan, Eric Stein, Scott Shapiro, and Walter Van Gerven for comments and discussions.

(as in the United States and Spain), organic or basic laws (as in Canada or Germany), treaties (as in the European Union), or even ordinary laws that acquire a privileged status through custom and tradition (as may yet happen in the United Kingdom). But regardless of its particular origin, form, or mode of denotation, federalism's distinctive feature is to locate the central and constituent governments' respective claims of organizational autonomy and jurisdictional authority within a set of privileged legal norms that are beyond the arena of daily politics.

Federalism is a "constitutional" bargain. It is constitutional in the sense of running deeper than daily politics—legal norms, customs, and culture place federalism beyond easy renegotiation (Filipov et al. 2004; Ferejohn, Rakove, and Riley 2001). And it is constitutional in the sense of constituting the framework within which daily politics takes place. Federalism is thus neither a simple contract among parties in static relation to one another nor a plain device of negative precommitment (cf. Elster 1979, 94–5; S. Holmes 1988). Instead, like constitutionalism, federalism is a creative commitment that enables governance as much as it limits governments.

The precise content of the federal bargain will necessarily be incomplete. The authors cannot foresee all the contingencies that an effective system of governance must confront. Federal bargains will be struck on particulars without consensus on an underlying theory; and federal bargains will be struck on more abstract principles without agreement on the particulars that the principles entail (Bellamy and Schönlau 2004; Sunstein 1995; Stone Sweet 2004, 24–5). Federalism and constitutionalism therefore present a common difficulty: They must remain beyond ordinary politics and yet they stand in steady need of completion.

A successful federal system must remain flexible enough to allow for effective governance and yet be stable enough to prevent radical centripetal or centrifugal shifts of power that undermine the principle of shared rule. Numerous interrelated factors—from the size, number, and relative resources of the constituent states to the social, political, and cultural commitments of the population and the design and functioning of the political institutions of governance—are important to sustaining this balance. This chapter focuses on only one particular factor, the significance of which has been debated since the American birth of modern federalism over 200 years ago: the role of the central judiciary.

There is much disagreement about the central judiciary's role in federalism. Whereas some scholars view a central judicial umpire as a defining feature of federalism (Lenaerts 1990, 263), others find courts acting as arbiters of federalism to be unnecessary, ineffective, or even marginally harmful (Thayer 1893; Wechsler 1954; Dahl 1957; Choper 1980; Tushnet 1999, 123). Yet others would agree with Justice Holmes, who famously remarked: "I do not think the United States would come to an end if we lost our power to declare an Act of Congress void. I do think the Union would be imperiled if we could not make that declaration as to the laws of the several States" (Holmes 1920, 295–6).

For the most part, the debate about the role of the judiciary as federal umpire has taken place within two separate disciplinary compartments: comparative politics and law. Almost hermetically sealed off from one another, the two disciplines have largely avoided cross-pollination (Friedman 2005; Whittington 2004). The legal side of the debate has overwhelmingly focused on normative theory, with a particular penchant for originalism in the United States. Empirical investigations, as well as positive political theory, are frequently neglected in academic legal scholarship on federalism and constitutional law. Normative constitutional scholarship has also shunned comparative inquiry. After all, why look abroad, when the normative framework of the inquiry is rooted at home? Comparative politics, in contrast, is inherently comparative (at least when not practiced as area studies). And it is inherently empirical, even as it reaches for theory. And yet, comparative politics frequently treats the law as a black box with extreme skepticism of any claims of the autonomy of legal discourse.

Building on recent efforts to bring these two disciplines closer, this chapter provides a fresh look at three common criticisms of granting the central judiciary power to protect federalism. First, that federalism can and should be protected by politics not law. Second, that the central judiciary is biased toward the central legislature. And third, that the judiciary is, in any event, unable to perform a meaningful functional inquiry into whether the balance of federalism has been breached. The comparative and interdisciplinary analysis offered here concludes that political safeguards of federalism are insufficient, that concerns about judicial bias are overstated, and that the particular limitations on the judiciary's ability to implement the principles of substantive subsidiarity, instrumental subsidiarity, and integration should inform judicial doctrine more systematically than they currently do.

2 Horizontal Federalism, Vertical Federalism, and the Power of Politics

The classic argument against judicial involvement in intergovernmental power disputes is Herbert Wechsler's insistence in the U.S. context that there are sufficient "political safeguards" protecting the states from federal overreaching. Larry Kramer has recently revived this argument as a matter of original design, emphasizing the negligible attention that judicial review received in the debates at the American Founding (Kramer 2004). Kramer has also enhanced Wechsler's functional argument by revealing additional characteristics of the political structure of U.S. federalism that should render the federal government amply solicitous of state interests.

A comparative glance abroad can provide new insight into this well-worn U.S. controversy. There is irony in the claim that judicial arbitration of federalism disputes is superfluous in the United States. Even in Germany and the European Union, where constituent units' political control of the central government is far stronger, constituent governments have deliberately opted for judicial review of central government activities.

Consider the formal structure of the U.S. system. Along with Canada, the United States is what we may call a "horizontal" federal system: Central and constituent state governments are independent political organizations sitting alongside one another, each with a full complement of powers. Each level of government has an independent democratic base, an independent fiscal base, as well as the ability to formulate, execute, and adjudicate its own policies.

Contrast this with what may be termed a "vertical" system of federalism (as in Germany, the European Union, or Switzerland), in which the central government largely acts through the constituent units of government and in which decision-making and fiscal powers are, to use Fritz Scharpf's word, "intertwined" (Scharpf et al. 1976). In such systems, the central government frequently needs the constituent governments to transpose central government policies into more specific constituent state laws, administer central government policies, and adjudicate central government law. Moreover, in a vertical system of federalism, constituent units of government also take part in the central government's process of decision-making, as, for example, in the case of the European Council, the *Bundesrat* (Germany), or the *Ständerat* (Switzerland). Finally, in contrast to horizontal systems, in which each level of government collects and spends its own tax revenue, vertical systems share fiscal resources.

Vertical federalism protects state government interests differently and far more securely than does horizontal federalism (Halberstam and Hills 2001; Halberstam 2001*b*). Indeed, vertical systems protect state government interests so formidably as to create significant inefficiencies. By creating a "joint decision trap," vertical federalism frequently favors the status quo and provides incentives for overspending (Scharpf 1988). In any event, a vertical system of federalism protects constituent state interests more robustly against central government encroachment than does a horizontal system.

Horizontal systems of federalism give rise to competition among the different levels of government (Breton 1996) as well as to a good deal of cooperation (Grodzins 1966; Halberstam and Hills 2001). Despite the formal separation of the various levels of governance, horizontal systems, in practice, feature a significant amount of vertical coordination, such as indirect revenue sharing and constituent state implementation of federal policy. This, in turn, fosters the creation of an intergovernmental bureaucracy and a fair amount of vertically integrated political coordination. In the United States, moreover, even after the Seventeenth Amendment introduced the popular election of U.S. Senators, the continued equal representation of the states in the U.S. Senate (especially when coupled with the filibuster rule) skews federal decisions in favor of interests organized at the state level. So, too, the election of the U.S. President through an electoral college, instead of directly by the voters at large, increases the voice of interests organized within small states. Political parties link the fortunes of central and constituent politicians. And an intergovernmental lobby may help represent constituent states effectively at the central level (Wechsler 1954; Choper 1980; Kramer 2004; Riker 1975). In Canada, informal mechanisms of vertical integration (such as the First Ministers' Conference) similarly soften the central detachment contemplated by the formal system of horizontal federalism (Elazar 1987, 217).

But reliance on the informal mechanisms of vertical coordination as a means to preserve federalism rests on the shifting sands of politics. As a matter of politics, decentralization depends on the opportunities left open by the fragmentation of political power and ineffective coordination at the central level of government (Bednar, Eskridge, and Ferejohn 2001). When the central government is strong and united across its various branches, politically motivated decentralization wanes. Even the formal separation of powers at the central level of government, which indirectly promotes decentralization by fragmenting central power, may be overcome by politics. Political alliances counteract fragmentation. They may overcome the institutionalized separation of powers (Tsebelis 2002, 145; Levinson and Pildes 2006), consolidate power, and coordinate from the top down as well as from the bottom up. To be sure, as Max Weber already noted, U.S. political parties have been notoriously weak. But to the extent that political parties become strong and centralized, central party figures may control, rather than be controlled by, constituent state politicians (Frymer and Yoon 2002).

For example, William Riker has shown that prior to passage of the Seventeenth Amendment in the United States, the relative salience and importance of federal politics meant that U.S. senatorial choices were not determined by state legislators as Article I formally required. It was the other way around. Through the "public canvass" method, voters would elect state legislators based on which U.S. Senator those state legislators would support (Riker 1955, 463). Although recent institutional decentralization within Congress has mitigated the power and national stature of committee chairs in Washington (Chubb 1985), this, too, may change again. Similarly, in Germany scholars have argued that strong national parties and the formation of national coalition governments have at times transformed the *Bundesrat* from an institution representing *Länder* interests into one simply representing the national political opposition (Lehmbruch 1976). To be sure, these phenomena all foster a species of vertical integration. But they represent top-down integration. In short, they amount to informal centralization.

It should come as no surprise, then, that we find judicial review not only in horizontal systems, but also in vertical federal systems with their characteristically greater structural protections of constituent state interests. Moreover, in vertical systems such as the European Union and Germany, this is clearly a deliberate choice. In Germany, constituent states lobbied for over twenty years for an increase in the *Bundesverfassungsgericht*'s role in limiting the central government's exercise of powers (Oeter 1998*a*). The measure finally passed due to the persistence of the constituent state parliaments. The sole exception is Switzerland, in which an exceptionally strong tradition of popular referenda has led to the consistent rejection of judicial review. Aside from Swiss exceptionalism, however, juxtaposing horizontal and vertical systems indicates that even in systems of vertical federalism, which have far stronger and constitutionally embedded political safeguards of federalism, constituent states nonetheless do not view the political safeguards of federalism as sufficient.

3 Bias, (In)dependence, and the Central Judiciary

K. C. Wheare once observed that "[i]n spite of the formal dependence of the supreme courts on the executive and legislature of the general government, they have exhibited a considerable impartiality in the exercise of their function as interpreters of the division of powers" (Wheare 1964, 60–1). Contemporary scholars have taken issue with Wheare's assessment, maintaining that the central judiciary is not independent enough to serve as a meaningful umpire of federalism. The worry is that the central government's role in creating the central judiciary, supplying financial resources, and controlling appointments renders the central judiciary a natural ally of the central government in the control of the states. Add to this that the central judiciary is generally charged with interpreting central government laws, and you have a structural bias in favor of an expansive interpretation of central government law. Some scholars argue that this has produced nothing short of a "failure of judicial review in the modern federal state," which exposes that the central judiciary is little more than a "particip[ant] in the exercise of central political control over member states" (Bzdera 1993, 28; see also Shapiro 1981, 24).

Would that it were so easy. A vast literature develops the many factors that motivate judges and the institutional dynamics that constrain their decisions (e.g. Llewellyn 1960; Coffin 1980; Shapiro 1981; Burley and Mattli 1993; Posner 1993; Garrett, Kelemen, and Schulz 1998; Slaughter, Stone Sweet, and Weiler 1998; Segal and Spaeth 2002; Friedman 2005; Halberstam 2005; Levinson 2005; Solberg and Lindquist 2006). Even these sources, however, provide only a partial list of judicial motives and constraints. Let us briefly sketch ten points to consider:

1. Central courts might have an interest in expanding their jurisdiction. This might incline them toward expansive interpretations of central government law and upholding central governmental law over the laws or policies of constituent states.
2. Central courts have an interest in retaining fiscal and logistical support. Thus, to the extent that the central government has discretion in providing such support, the central judiciary might favor the central government to retain that support.
3. If individual judges' pay, retention, or promotion depends on the approval of certain institutions of governance, judges may seek to avoid displeasing those actors. This factor is significantly limited, however, whenever pay and tenure is protected, as it is, to varying degrees, in the United States, Canada, Germany, and the European Union.
4. Judges may be interested in controlling their workload. This would temper the expansionist aspirations of courts without discretionary dockets. Even when a high court can control its own docket, that court may become an advocate of the overburdened lower courts that do not enjoy such discretion (e.g. Rehnquist 1999).
5. Judges might seek to increase the proportion of interesting cases they hear. This, in turn, would lead to a bias in favor of certain subject matters, as opposed to the general expansion of federal jurisdiction across the board.
6. Judges might be interested in asserting their power not only vis-à-vis state courts and state governments, but also vis-à-vis the central legislature. This would push them to strike down central, as well as constituent government, laws.
7. Judges might seek to advance their personal substantive policy preferences. This would lead judges to disregard institutional interests at either level of governance (especially those arising only in the aggregate) in furtherance of their personal preferences in any particular case.
8. Judges will have an interest in maintaining their own authority, their own legitimacy, and a general respect for the law. Accordingly, judges would want to (a) appear neutral as between the competing parties, (b) maintain consistency, predictability, and general public approval of its decisions, (c) avoid being overruled, especially in a manner that questions their original judgment, (d) forestall institutional reforms that undermine its functions, and (e) minimize the possibility of unlawful resistance to their judgments by other government officials as well as citizens.
9. Judges will be interested in gaining the respect of their peers, that is, fellow judges and lawyers. This will give judges an incentive to produce well-crafted opinions that meet the highest standards of their fellow professionals.
10. Last, but certainly not least, judges are trained to believe in the relative autonomy of legal discourse. That is, as professionals they subscribe to the limitations that the law and legal interpretation place on the immediate advancement of simple claims of power, morality, or all-things-considered policy.

Some of these concerns might encourage the central judiciary to hew close to the preferences of the central government. But not all of them do. Even if one were inclined to dismiss the last factor as romantic delusion, many of the remaining, positive claims suffice to complicate the idea that the central judiciary will invariably act to vindicate the central government's interests.

In the light of this expanded view of judicial motives and incentives, the high court practice we observe across federal systems is unsurprising. The record of central judicial review of federalism largely confirms Wheare's assessment. In the United States, for example, there has been a rather steady ebb and flow of Supreme Court endorsement of, and resistance to, the broad assertion of federal powers (e.g. Eskridge and Ferejohn 1994). After an early expansionist phase, the Supreme Court repeatedly rejected Congress's invitation to expand federal jurisdiction in diversity cases, resisted federal attempts to nationalize civil rights, and struck down expansive federal economic legislation. In its most notorious stand-off with the central government, the Court relented on the issue of federal economic legislation only after the President and Congress in a historic moment of political unity threatened to pack the Court. Even as the Court gave in to expanded federal powers in the New Deal, it also expanded the state governments' powers to regulate commerce and drastically restricted federal jurisdiction over state common law claims. Later, the Supreme Court expanded federal powers again, this time over civil rights and criminal procedure. Finally, the recent Rehnquist Court issued a flurry of decisions limiting federal review of state criminal convictions, federal intrusions on state autonomy, and the scope of federal legislation under the Commerce Clause and the Civil War Amendments.

One thing seems clear. On matters of federalism, the Supreme Court cannot, for extended periods of time, resist a mobilized and fully unified federal government. Federalism ultimately depends not on parchment but on a commitment of the populace to maintaining a division of powers (Livingston 1956, 2). But this may be less troubling than might appear at first. The legitimacy of federalism ultimately rests on popular consent. Accordingly, it may well be legitimate to heed the clear and sustained expression of popular will that the balance currently being struck by the Court, which itself is partly based on past political mobilization, is in need of correction (Ackerman 1991). This brings us back to the idea of federalism as constitutionalism, and the idea, expressed by Elazar and others, that federalism is not an end-state but a process. Federalism is a precommitment to the principle of divided powers, which is not reexamined in daily politics, but which nonetheless must remain flexible as societies search for the proper jurisdictional scope for government activity (Nicolaidis 2001).

Beyond the clear situation of sustained unified politics, the political and institutional environment in which the U.S. Supreme Court operates allows for considerable independence (cf. Ramseyer 1994). To be sure, the sustained capture of the Presidency and the Senate will allow those institutions to remake the federal judiciary in their own image. But here, as elsewhere, creation is not control. Even small amounts of political fragmentation at the central level of government will prevent the emergence of the supermajorities necessary to threaten removal or otherwise curb the political discretion of the Court.

For example, the Court may play one institution off against another, as it did in *Gonzales v. Oregon* (2006) by striking down Attorney General Ashcroft's attempt to use federal drug control laws to preempt state initiatives on physician assisted suicide. The Court in this case was well aware that Congress had failed to pass such preemptive measures directly (in part due to the filibuster rules in the Senate). The Court may also undo legislation that was part of a larger political compromise, which may be difficult to cobble together a second time around. Or it may outlaw the policy in its entirety based on the Constitution. In any event, the Supreme Court is not an "agent" of the federal government. If anything, it is more of a trustee (cf. Majone 2001; Stone Sweet 2004, 28–9). Indeed, given its broad audience and the possibility of shifting politics and national popular mobilization, the Court is best seen not as a trustee of any single government, but of the citizens as a whole.

Other high courts confirm this picture. To be sure, the Canadian Supreme Court's rulings might be viewed as more centrist than those of its arguably more neutrally situated predecessor, the Privy Council. And yet, contrary to some claims (Bzdera 1993), in several references the Canadian Supreme Court refused simply to support the national government. In the *Patriation Reference* (1981), for example, the Supreme Court did not legally bar patriation of the Constitution and yet provided a serious impetus to the central government to continue negotiating with the provinces on the Charter of Fundamental Rights and Freedoms (Bednar 2007, 295–301). As a result, to appease the provincial governments, the drafters included a provision allowing for the legislative override of certain fundamental rights. Similarly, the *Secession Reference* (1998) was not a purely nationalizing decision, but "provided both federalists and separatists with congenial answers" (Hirschl 2004, 181–2).

In this vein, the sustained lobbying efforts of the German *Länder* for an increased role of the *Bundesverfassungsgericht* in federalism disputes are once again instructive (see Oeter 1998a). It would demonstrate a remarkable degree of self-deception on the part of the *Länder*, if there were truly no hope that the German high court would resist the expansion of central government powers. (To be sure, the *Länder* formally control the appointment of half the judges on that court. But this feature has long been neutralized by national party politics.) It would seem odd for the *Länder* parliaments to expend political capital if the central high court were, as Martin Shapiro has suggested, "principally designed to hold and exploit the countryside for the central regime" (Shapiro 1981, 24).

Consider also the European Court of Justice (ECJ). That court has been a spectacularly centralizing institution for most of its history, but it has done so not at the behest of a strong central government. To the contrary, the ECJ has consistently stepped into the breach left by a weak center that was hobbled by unanimity rules and political gridlock. And the ECJ has done so frequently against the express wishes of the member states, which control central judicial appointments (Stein 1981). Streams of scholarship have sought to document, explain, justify, or criticize this development. For the moment, let us focus on the fact that the ECJ's actions fall within the pattern that some scholars have identified as common to several federal systems: the expansive interpretation of central government powers during the early years of the federal system (e.g. Kelemen 2004, 13–14). Let us dub this the idea of "infant system protection."

The pattern of infant system protection undermines the claim that central governments exercise undue influence over the central judiciary. If the judiciary were biased as a result of central government influence, we would expect mature central governments to create more of a judicial bias in favor of centralization than fledgling central governments ever could. But we observe exactly the opposite. In the European Union and elsewhere, it appears that as the central level of governance gains in power and stature, the judiciary will become less—not more—inclined to rule in favor of the central government.

To be sure, during the infancy of a newly minted federal system the central judiciary may see its fortunes linked with the basic survival of the central government. But this suggests, conversely, that once the central government is up and running, the central judiciary will no longer feel compelled to play the predictable role of supporting actor. Instead, as we have seen in the United States, the judiciary in a mature federal system will exploit even small amounts of central political fragmentation to become a policy entrepreneur in the opposite direction, and initiate—or participate in—a "velvet revolution" on behalf of the states (Whittington 2001).

In conclusion, high court judges face a wide array of incentives based on personal preference, professional ethos, and the institutional environment in which they operate. For every centralizing incentive, there is likely to be one pulling the other way—not to mention those orthogonal to the issue of federalism. Perhaps most important, a successful high court must appear to be neutral as between the parties. To be sure, many devices, from black or red robes to "legalese" and issuing a consolidated "Opinion of the Court" might be used to help conceal illicit judicial preferences. (Gold stripes are occasionally employed for emphasis in plays and real life as well.) But as Cicero suggested in the case of friendship and Pascal did in the course of his wager, the best way to appear to act on principle is to act on principle. And the best way to come to act on principle is to act as if one were acting on principle. In this vein, judicial success ultimately depends "[n]ot simply [on] rhetorical but [on] some degree of real neutrality and independence in federal conflicts" (Shapiro 2002, 167). As a general matter, high courts—whether attached to the central government or appointed by the constituent states—strive to bring that about.

4 Federalism Theory in a Nutshell

Even if federal courts are necessary and reasonably neutral, can they do the job? This depends, of course, on what we are asking them to do. To be sure, whenever the rules of federalism are reasonably clear, courts may serve federalism well. But what about the cases in which courts must resort to functional principles to assess whether a unit or level of government has overstepped its bounds? Here courts will frequently draw on the principles of subsidiarity and integration. But they do so too often only implicitly and without a proper understanding of the promise and perils of the underlying theory.

4.1 Subsidiarity: Instrumental or Substantive?

Democratic theory suggests that the exercise of powers in a federal system should be based on subsidiarity. All things being equal, democracy at the local level, especially when coupled with citizen mobility, is more representative of citizens' interests, allows for a greater satisfaction of diverse preferences, and is therefore more legitimate than democracy at a more distant level of governance. In addition, the diffusion of power reduces the risk of tyranny and allows for experimentation that may benefit all. For these reasons, we begin with a presumption in favor of local governance, which is expressed in the principle of subsidiarity: The central level of government should play a supporting role in governance, acting if and only if the constituent units of government cannot do so on their own (e.g. Bermann 1994; McConnell 1987). Although the concept is frequently treated as synonymous with decentralization, it is important to note that subsidiarity may function as either a limit on, or a justification for, central government intervention. Since Edmund Randolph's introduction of the Virginia Plan in the U.S. constitutional convention, subsidiarity in this bidirectional sense (albeit not necessarily by name) has served as a guide for the allocation of powers in modern federal systems.

Subsidiarity suggests the need for central governance with regard to two kinds of issues. First, constituent units will be unable to act or to serve as appropriate fora of political decision-making in the presence of externalities and other kinds of collective action problems. Whenever the effects of a given decision radiates beyond the deciding jurisdiction or when disaggregate decision-making leads to an incentive structure that tends to prevent outcomes that could be achieved by coordinated strategies, the decision should be moved to a higher level of governance. The second kind of shortcoming of constituent unit governance may be termed a problem of internalities, that is, problems such as majoritarian oppression, corruption, or minority capture that skew or undermine the democratic legitimacy of the political process of the constituent units. Here, the costs of isolated decision-making by the constituent governments fall entirely on groups within those sub-units of govern-ment. And yet, this problem, too, may sometimes be remedied by moving the decision to a higher level of governance on the theory that a more diverse political process will not suffer from the same flaw (and will not introduce some counter-vailing deficiency) (Madison 1787).

Although the idea of subsidiarity has guided much federal design, the results are far from uniform. Each system reflects instead the moral and cultural commit-ments of whatever society it organizes as well as the practical worries of the day. We should expect no less, since subsidiarity sets forth only the general form of an argument, not its substance.

Externalities, for example, are in the eye of the beholder. Although there may be commonly recognized ones, such as when a constituent state diverts the waters of an interstate river or declares war against a foreign nation, the recognition of many others is hotly contested. After all, one state's felt externalities—be they physical or ideological—may be another state's autonomy. Whether providing abortions, marrying two persons of the same sex, or warming up rivers are constitutionally recognized as producing externalities for individuals in neighboring states, ultim-ately reflects deeply held views about the nature of rights and harms (Herzog 2000). So, too, with internalities. As the literature responding to John Hart Ely's process-based theory of constitutional rights has fleshed out, any theory of ideal process depends on the fixing of baselines of inclusion (e.g. Tribe 1980).

Contrary to the indiscriminate usage in the vast literature on subsidiarity, we should distinguish carefully between two different versions of subsidiarity. Let us call one "instrumental subsidiarity" and the other "substantive subsidiarity" (to echo the distinction between instrumental and substantive rationality). Instru-mental subsidiarity seeks to determine which level of governance is best suited to achieve a given goal. The European Union's subsidiarity clause provides a good example. It demands that, in areas of concurrent competence, the Community act "only if and insofar as the objectives of the proposed action cannot be sufficiently achieved by the Member States" (Article 5 EC). This provision presupposes that the central government has the authority to determine "the objectives of the proposed action" and then asks who can best achieve the centrally specified goal of governance.

Substantive subsidiarity, by contrast, seeks to determine which level of govern-ance is best suited to determine whether a particular objective should be considered a policy goal at all. Somewhat like the perennial European question regarding "competence-competence," the question of substantive subsidiarity is a macro-level inquiry into competence. It asks which level of governance should have the authority to frame certain issues as problems that any level of governance should address.

For example, substantive subsidiarity asks which level of governance may decide whether gay marriage, physician-assisted suicide, or the use of chewing tobacco in one jurisdiction should be recognized as imposing externalities on other jurisdictions. The Canadian Constitution, which authorizes central legislation for the "Peace, Order, and good Government of Canada" (Const. Act. Art. 91), includes just such a substantive component. This "POGG Clause" puts into question not only whether the central government is better equipped to achieve a given goal, but also whether the center is authorized to pronounce a given goal as necessary for the "good" government of Canada.

The question of substantive subsidiarity thus precedes that of instrumental subsidiarity—unless, of course, there is general agreement across the various levels of governance about the policy goal to be achieved or about the presence of externalities or internalities. Put another way, instrumental subsidiarity presumes what substantive subsidiarity expressly puts into focus: the authority to designate the regulatory goal or to declare that externalities or internalities are present.

As we shall see in greater detail below, the distinction between substantive and instrumental subsidiarity helps clarify the nature of the difficulty that courts face in enforcing subsidiarity. Instrumental subsidiarity involves a *technically* complex empirical investigation into the relative capacities and incentives of the various levels of government in tackling a given problem. Here, we ask whether collective action problems exist at the local level and about the relative regulatory resources of each level of governance. Substantive subsidiarity, by contrast, involves a *morally and politically* complex assessment of relative substantive claims of authority. Here, we ask which level of governance has a superior claim to deciding whether a given objective should be considered a goal of governance at all. Both inquiries are difficult. And both challenge the limits of what courts can do. But each is challenging for a different reason.

4.2 The Idea of Constitutional Integration

The second principle underlying federal systems is integration. This term needs to be unpacked as well. In a lexicon in which subsidiarity functions as a synonym for decentralization, integration simply designates the opposite (e.g. Oeter 1998*b*, 1). If we understand subsidiarity as providing arguments both for and against centralization, however, and if we further distinguish between substantive and instrumental subsidiarity, we can better grasp the real meaning and importance of the idea of integration.

Instrumental considerations of subsidiarity are compatible with a fairly modest form of integration. Centralization may serve a collection of disparate governments as long as they happen to share a common policy goal or engage in an arms-length quid-pro-quo bargain among themselves across different issues. Central rule in this case is ultimately based on the unanimous consent of constituent governments whose preferences may be taken as given. In short, central rule as a result of instrumental subsidiarity is simply a matter of efficiency. Much of what in common and scholarly parlance is termed "international economic integration" is of precisely this sort.

Substantive considerations of subsidiarity, however, demand a deeper kind of integration. Arguments about the central government's superior moral and political claim to authority do not depend on constituent government consent. Instead, they are based on the idea of a political community that comprises individuals across the various constituent states. As a member of the larger polity, the individual thus partly escapes the political confines of her constituent state. In the European context, various scholars have discussed this kind of integration in terms of "deep" integration, the emergence of a "transnational society" (Fligstein and Stone Sweet 2002), or simply in terms of a "European political community" (Habermas 2002). Because this kind of integration *constitutes* the political community, I shall call this kind of integration "constitutional integration" regardless of whether it is based on a formal constitution (see Halberstam 2005).

Constitutional integration may be exogenous or endogenous to the federal legal system. Institutions may act based on preexisting constitutional integration or they may act based on a vision of constitutional integration and thereby help bring it about. Either way, only the presence of "constitutional integration" justifies our speaking of federalism in the sense of a continuum of regulatory units and jurisdictional levels that share in the common governance of a polity. Constitutional integration does not demand an intimate affinity among citizens or units of governance. And it can be implemented at varying levels of depth. But constitutional integration does suggest a minimum level of solidarity, mutual tolerance, and common purpose to sustain the federal system as a whole.

5 THEORY MEETS PRACTICE

Once the designers of the federal system have translated their particular vision into law, courts can play their part in helping to sustain and complete it. Because the rules and principles of federalism frequently demand interpretation, courts will resort to a functional understanding of federalism and to the twin ideas of integration and subsidiarity to understand better the scope of powers of the various levels and units of government. Too often, however, a failure to confront these principles openly leads to a jurisprudence that serves federalism only haphazardly.

5.1 The Use and Abuse of Integration in Court

Courts in federal systems draw on the idea of integration most obviously in adjudicating such open-textured provisions as those regarding common citizenship, antidiscrimination, free movement, or even free speech. The ECJ, for example, has used the first three of these aggressively in an attempt to promote the constitutional idea of a common polity with pan-European solidarity among citizens (Halberstam 2005). The U.S. Supreme Court has done the same in the case of free movement of persons (Hills 2000) and free movement of goods (Regan 1986). The Canadian Supreme Court, too, has used the idea of constitutional integration, for example in prohibiting provincial criminal regulation of speech on the theory that the restriction compromised individuals' ability to participate in a nationwide exchange of ideas (Tarnopolsky 1975, 31–46). Courts also implicitly rely upon a certain vision or existing degree of constitutional integration when adjudicating fundamental rights. In this vein, the U.S. Supreme Court found a common right to intimate homosexual relations in *Lawrence v. Texas* (2003), and declined to find a common right to physician-assisted suicide in *Washington v. Glucksberg* (1997).

Courts have also drawn on functional ideas of integration to develop a host of duties of cooperation and mutual respect that bind the various units and levels of governance in the exercise of their assigned powers (Halberstam 2004). The ECJ, for instance, has drawn loosely on Article 10 EC to develop duties of information, consultation, consideration, compliance, implementation, compensation, intervention, and stewardship that bind the member states and the European Union. The *Bundesverfassunggericht*, in turn, has developed similar principles under the rubric of *Bundestreue*, despite the absence of any textual provision.

Courts have not always moved for greater integration. The U.S. Supreme Court, for example, refused to give real substance to the "privileges and immunities" of national citizenship after the Civil War (*The Slaughterhouse Cases* 1873). So, too, certain strands of recent Supreme Court jurisprudence insist on the constituent states' categorical entitlement to refuse to cooperate with the federal government or with sister states (e.g. *Printz v. United States* 1997). And the *Bundesverfassungsgericht* has insisted that the federal government must not control the internal organization of *Länder* governments (*Besoldungsvereinheitlichung* 1972).

Nonetheless, the ECJ, the *Bundesverfassungsgericht*, and the U.S. Supreme Court have each, on occasion, pursued integration with too much zeal. With regard to the free movement of goods, for example, both the ECJ and the U.S. Supreme Court have at times suggested limiting regulatory diversity across constituent states in the name of "balancing" the interests of individuals throughout the federal system, as though those individuals were members of a unitary state (Regan 1986; Maduro 1998). Similarly, the *Bundesverfassungsgericht* and the U.S. Supreme Court have suppressed local initiatives with defense and foreign policy implications simply to preserve an *exclusive* unitary national sphere of decision-making on these matters (Goldsmith 1997; Halberstam 2001*a*; Spiro 1999).

Rarely do courts consciously consider calibrating the degree of integration in the light of principles of federalism. A more deliberate jurisprudence would understand that some degree of integration is necessary to help constitute a common polity but that too much threatens to undermine the principle of shared rule. Vindicating a basic nondiscrimination requirement—of equal treatment of individuals as well as governments across the various levels and units—therefore makes sense. At the same time, courts should help protect the organizational autonomy of the various levels and units of governance. Within these parameters, courts (acting alone without specific legislative warrant) should strive to allow for regulatory and policy-making diversity as long as such policies do not violate the basic rules of nondiscrimination. The commonality of rights must also not be pressed beyond that which truly underpins the creation and maintenance of a common polity. After that, the beacon of integration may become a threat to federalism itself.

5.2 Subsidiarity as Power Definition or Side Constraint: Twin Challenges to Judicial Competence

Courts draw on the idea of subsidiarity in a host of situations. In its most dramatic form, the principle of subsidiarity serves as a basic power definition. As Canada's POGG Clause illustrates, subsidiarity as power definition demands both substantive and instrumental inquiries. Focusing on the latter while obscuring the former, the Canadian Supreme Court has developed the so-called "provincial inability test." The Court asks whether a given problem has the "singleness, distinctiveness and indivisibility clearly distinguishing it from matters of provincial concern and a scale of impact on provincial jurisdiction that is reconcilable with the fundamental distribution of legislative power under the Constitution" (*Crown Zellerbach* 1988, par. 33). Applying this test, the Court held, for example, that the central government could require permits for dumping substances into provincial salt waters as a way of controlling externalities and preventing a race to the bottom in environmental standards. As is implicit in the dissent, the difficulty with such a judgment is not so much the instrumental judgment regarding provincial inability. Instead, the questionable part is the substantive decision to recognize as a constitutional matter that environmental harm creates externalities warranting a comprehensive response, especially given that "[a]ll physical activities have some environmental impact" (*Crown Zellerbach* 1988, par. 70 (La Forest, J., dissenting)). To be sure, the majority's substantive judgment may well be plausible. And yet, the problem with substantive subsidiarity even in such a straightforward context highlights the acute involvement of fundamental policy decisions for which the judiciary may not be well suited.

Subsidiarity may also constrain powers that are already defined elsewhere. When subsidiarity is employed in this manner, i.e. as a "side constraint" on the exercise of otherwise defined powers, the question regarding subsidiarity tends to be an instrumental one. This is because the substantive decision as to which level of government has the authority to define the regulatory goal is already contained in the basic definition of power. For example, in the European Union or in Germany, where the central government has concurrent power over water pollution and subsidiarity functions as a side constraint on the exercise of that power, the central government has the authority to declare standards of water purity as policy objectives. Here, the judiciary is limited to asking only whether the constituent states would be unable (or lack the proper incentives) to address this particular, centrally defined problem.

Even so, both the ECJ and the German *Bundesverfassungsgericht* have shied away from adjudicating instrumental subsidiarity as a side constraint. The ECJ has engaged in only the most perfunctory review of whether Community action was taken in accordance with the EC Treaty's subsidiarity rule in Article 5. The German *Bundesverfassungsgericht*, in turn, expressly refused to adjudicate the original necessity principle in Article 72(2) of the *Grundgesetz*, which tracked concerns about collective action problems, externalities, and integration (*Straffreiheitsgesetz* 1953). The Court relented only recently after Article 72(2) was revised in 1994 to allow the federal government to act only "if and to the extent that the creation of equivalent living conditions in the federal territory or the preservation of legal and economic unity demands, in the interests of the state as a whole, federal regulation." In 2005, the *Bundesverfassungsgericht* for the first time held that the federal legislature had not sufficiently justified the need for federal regulation (*Hochschulrahmengesetz* 2005). According to the court, the federal rule restructuring university hiring practices might well have been superior to that used by many of the *Länder*, but the federal legislature did not put forth any argument to explain the need for a *uniform* rule across the country.

Finally, the invocation of subsidiarity as power definition—in both its substantive and instrumental versions—often enters adjudication as an implicit interpretive guide. Take, for example, the historic cases in the United States and in the European Union, in which the U.S. Supreme Court for the first time in sixty years and the ECJ for the first time ever struck down a central government law as being *ultra vires*. On its face, *United States v. Lopez* (1995) resorted to categorical formalism by distinguishing between "economic" and "non-economic" matters. It held that only the former could bear a "substantial relation to interstate commerce" and accordingly struck down a federal law prohibiting the possession of guns within 1,000 feet of a school. In *Germany v. Parliament and Council* (2000), the European Court of Justice, in turn, held that any market harmonization measure based on then-Article 100a "must genuinely have as its object the improvement of the conditions for the establishment and functioning of the internal market." Given that the Community lacked an independent basis to issue health regulations, the ECJ examined whether the Tobacco Advertising directive actually served to eliminate any obstacles to the free movement of goods or distortions in competition. The Court found that, in this regard, the ban was overly broad.

Both courts here implicitly appeal to subsidiarity to help interpret an otherwise vague definition of powers. Lurking behind the categorical essentialism in *Lopez* may be functional conceptions of substantive subsidiarity, instrumental subsidiarity, and integration. One might reconstruct *Lopez* as holding that "economic" activities, more so than education or the suppression of violent crime, (1) create constitutionally cognizable interstate externalities and collective action problems and (2) help integrate society (Hills 2005). Similarly, the ECJ, having all but rejected subsidiarity review under Article 5 EC, brings instrumental subsidiarity in through the back door to help interpret the definition of Community powers to harmonize the market.

The difficulty with these two judicial appraisals of subsidiarity is readily apparent. Neither appeal to subsidiarity is transparent. And neither court provides much support for its conclusions. As a result, neither judgment lays the foundation for a stable jurisprudence.

Two subsequent decisions provide some brief indication of this difficulty. The first is *Gonzales v. Raich* (2005), in which the U.S. Supreme Court upheld the application of a federal ban on the manufacture, distribution, and possession of marijuana to individuals growing marijuana at home for personal medical consumption approved by the State of California. And the second is *Swedish Match* (2004), in which the ECJ upheld a Community-wide ban on the sale of "snus" tobacco for Community-wide health reasons because some member states had already disrupted the common market by banning the product for health reasons. In *Gonzales*, a consistent focus on subsidiarity would have required Congress to make a more particularized showing that California's regulation of home grown marijuana for medical purposes does not create a separate and wholly intrastate form of production and consumption with only negligible effects on the interstate market. In the European Union, taking subsidiarity seriously would have counseled against accepting the Community's justification of the complete ban of snus on health grounds. Instead, the Community should have been held to demonstrating the necessity of the ban on the grounds of protecting the functioning of the common market. The Community might have done so by pointing to the foreseeable disruption of the common market due to member state self-help measures if some states allowed snus while others did not. Or the Community might have argued that the overall ban was necessary to protect individual member state bans from being undermined by the existence of a common market.

In summary, a more explicit judicial focus on the role of substantive and instrumental subsidiarity in defining and constraining powers would achieve three things. First, it would highlight the question whether a court, such as the U.S. Supreme Court or the European Court of Justice, should be asking about subsidiarity at all, or whether considerations of subsidiarity are restricted to the phase of constitutional design. Second, a distinction between instrumental and substantive subsidiarity would highlight the technical and empirical nature of the former judgment and the moral and political nature of the latter, with useful implications for the kinds of evidence needed to evaluate each. Third, distinguishing between substantive and instrumental subsidiarity would likely yield a more discriminating jurisprudence of deference to the legislature. Courts would be well advised to police subsidiarity not through categorical rules, but through clear statement requirements that force vigorous, transparent political engagement among the relevant stakeholders. Here, the distinction would help courts and legislators understand what kinds of justifications they are looking for and what the relevant political actors are (or should be) arguing and bargaining about.

6 Conclusion: From Politics to Law and Back Again

In a system with functional governments at both the central and constituent level of governance, conflicts are bound to arise. With the exception of Switzerland, federal systems seem to have heeded Madison's advice that "[s]ome ... tribunal is clearly essential to prevent an appeal to the sword, and a dissolution of the compact, and [that] ... it ought to be established under the general rather than under the local Governments" (Madison 1788, 256). Dicey may thus be right when he notes that "[f]ederalism ... means legalism—the predominance of the judiciary in the constitution—the prevalence of a spirit of legality among the people" (Dicey 1959, 175).

Courts can serve a useful role in sustaining the federal system. And central courts are not irredeemably biased in favor the center. But it would be a mistake to understand this as an argument either for judicial supremacy or for the complete autonomy of the law. The promise and limitations of judicial review suggest that the judiciary can help protect and complete federalism. But it must do so with the understanding that the primary determinants of the federal balance lie in politics, and in bargaining over the appropriate jurisdictional scope for government action. Accordingly, the judiciary should control fair play and cohesion among the levels and units of government by enforcing nondiscrimination rules and basic rules of free movement. It should also preserve the organizational integrity of the various levels and units of governments. And courts should impose burdens of justification on the central government to help ensure the salience and transparency of what is ultimately a political determination.

References

Ackerman, B. 1991. *We The People*, vol. 1: *Foundations*. Cambridge, Mass.: Harvard University Press.

Bednar, J. 2007. *The Robust Federation*. Cambridge: Cambridge University Press.

—— Eskridge, Jr., W. N., and Ferejohn, J. 2001. A Political Theory of Federalism. Pp. 223–67 in *Constitutional Culture and Democratic Rule*, ed. J. Ferejohn, J. N. Rakove, and J. Riley. Cambridge: Cambridge University Press.

Bellamy, R., and Schönlau, J. 2004. The good, the bad and the ugly: the need for constitutional compromise and the drafting of the EU Constitution. Pp. 56–74 in *Political Theory and the European Constitution*, ed. L. Dobson and A. Folledal. New York: Routledge.

Bermann, G. 1994. Taking subsidiarity seriously: federalism in the European Community and the United States. *Columbia Law Review*, 94: 331–456.

Breton, A. 1996. *Competitive Governments: An Economic Theory Of Politics and Public Finance*. Cambridge: Cambridge University Press.

Burley, A. M., and Mattli, W. 1993. Europe before the Court: a political theory of legal integration. *International Organization*, 47: 41–76.

Bzdera, A. 1993. Comparative analysis of federal high courts: a political theory of judicial review. *Canadian Journal of Political Science*, 26: 3–29.

Choper, J. H. 1980. *Judicial Review and the National Political Process*. Chicago: University of Chicago Press.

Chubb, J. E. 1985. Federalism and the bias for centralization. Pp. 273–386 in *The New Direction in American Politics*, ed. J. E. Chubb and P. E. Peterson. Washington, DC: Brookings Institution.

Coffin, F. M. 1980. *The Ways of a Judge: Reflections from the Federal Appellate Bench*. Boston: Houghton Mifflin.

Dahl, R. A. 1957. Decision making in a democracy: the Supreme Court as national policymaker. *Journal of Public Law*, 6: 279–95.

—— 1989. *Democracy and its Critics*. New Haven, Conn.: Yale University Press.

Dicey, A. V. 1959. *Introduction to the Study of the Law of the Constitution*, 10th edn. London: MacMillan & Co.; originally published 1885.

Elazar, D. J. 1987. *Exploring Federalism*. Tuscaloosa: University of Alabama Press.

Elster, J. 1979. *Ulysses and the Sirens*. New York: Cambridge University Press.

Eskridge, Jr., W. N., and Ferejohn, J. 1994. The elastic Commerce Clause: a political theory of American federalism. *Vanderbilt Law Review*, 47: 1355–400.

Filippov, M., Ordeshook, P. C., and Shvetsova, O. 2004. *Designing Federalism: A Theory of Self-Sustainable Federal Institutions*. Cambridge: Cambridge University Press.

Fligstein, N., and Stone Sweet, A. 2002. Constructing polities and markets: an institutionalist account of European integration. *American Journal of Sociology*, 107: 1206–43.

Friedman, B. 2005. The politics of judicial review. *Texas Law Review*, 84: 257–337.

Frymer, P., and Yoon, A. 2002. Political parties, representation, and federal safeguards. *Northwestern University Law Review*, 96: 977–1026.

Garrett, G. R., Kelemen, D., and Schultz, H. 1998. The European Court Of Justice, national governments, and legal integration in the European Union. *International Organization*, 52: 149–76.

GOLDSMITH, J. L. 1997. Federal courts, foreign affairs, and federalism. *Virginia Law Review,* 83: 1617–715.

GRODZINS, M. 1966. *The American System: A New View of Government in the United States,* ed. D. J. Elazar. Chicago: Rand McNally.

HABERMAS, J. 2002. Toward a European political community. *Society,* 39: 58–62.

HALBERSTAM, D. 2001*a.* The foreign affairs of federal systems: a national perspective on the benefits of state participation. *Villanova Law Review,* 46: 1015–68.

—— 2001*b.* Comparative federalism and the issue of commandeering. Pp. 213–51 in *The Federal Vision: Legitimacy and Levels of Governance in the United States and the European Union,* ed. R. Howse and K. Nicolaidis. New York: Oxford University Press.

—— 2004. Of power and responsibility: the political morality of federal systems. *Virginia Law Review,* 90: 732–834.

—— 2005. The bride of Messina: constitutionalism and democracy in Europe. *European Law Review,* 30: 775–801.

—— and HILLS, JR., R. M. 2001. State autonomy in Germany and the United States. *Annals of the American Academy of Political and Social Science,* 574: 173–84.

HERZOG, D. 2000. Externalities and other parasites. *University of Chicago Law Review,* 67: 895–923.

HILLS, JR., R. M. 2000. Poverty, residency, and federalism: states' duty of impartiality toward newcomers. *Supreme Court Review,* 1999: 277–335.

—— 2005. *Two Concepts of the Economic: The Underlying Unity of Federalism and Due Process Jurisprudence.* Manuscript.

HIRSCHL, R. 2004. *Towards Juristocracy: The Origins and Consequences of the New Constitutionalism.* Cambridge, Mass.: Harvard University Press.

HOLMES, S. 1997. Precommitment and the paradox of democracy. Pp. 195–240 in *Constitutionalism and Democracy,* ed. J. Elster and R. Slagstad. Cambridge: Cambridge University Press.

HOLMES, W. 1920. *Collected Legal Papers.* New York: Harcourt, Brace and Company.

HOPKINS, W. J., 2002. *Devolution in Context: Regional, Federal and Devolved Government in the Member States of the European Union.* London: Cavendish.

KELEMEN, R. D. 2004. *The Rules of Federalism: Institutions and Regulatory Politics in the EU and Beyond.* Cambridge, Mass.: Harvard University Press.

KRAMER, L. D. 2004. *The People Themselves: Popular Constitutionalism and Judicial Review.* New York: Oxford University Press.

LEHMBRUCH, G. 1976. *Parteienwettbewerb im Bundesstaat.* Stuttgart: Kohlhammer.

LENAERTS, K. 1990. Constitutionalism and the many faces of federalism. *American Journal of Comparative Law,* 38: 205–64.

LEVINSON, D. 2005. Empire-building government in constitutional law. *Harvard Law Review,* 118: 915–72.

—— and PILDES, R. H. 2006. Separation of parties, not powers. *Harvard Law Review,* 119: 2311–86.

LIVINGSTON, W. S. 1956. *Federalism and Constitutional Change.* Oxford: Oxford University Press.

LLEWELLYN, K. N. 1960. *The Common Law Tradition: Deciding Appeals.* Toronto: Little, Brown.

MCCONNELL, M. W. 1987. Federalism: evaluating the founders' design. *University of Chicago Law Review,* 54: 1484–512.

MADISON, J. 1787. The Federalist no. 10. Pp. 56–65 in *The Federalist,* ed. J. E. Cooke. Middletown, Conn.: Wesleyan University Press, 1961.

—— 1788. The Federalist no. 39. Pp. 250–7 in *The Federalist*, ed. J. E. Cooke. Middletown, Conn.: Wesleyan University Press, 1961.

MADURO, M. P. 1998. *We the Court: The European Court of Justice and the European Economic Constitution.* Oxford: Hart.

MAJONE, G. 2001. Two logics of delegation: agency and fiduciary relations in EU governance. *European Union Politics*, 2: 103–22.

NICOLAIDIS, K. 2001. Conclusion: the federal vision beyond the federal state. Pp. 439–81 in *The Federal Vision: Legitimacy and Levels of Governance in the United States and the European Union*, ed. K. Nicolaidis and R. Howse. Oxford: Oxford University Press.

OETER, S. 1998*a*. Artikel 72. Pp. 1795–1864 in *Kommentar zum Grundgesetz*, H. v. Mangoldt, F. Kilen. Munich: Verlag Franz Vahlen.

—— 1998*b*. *Integration und Subsidiarität im Deutschen Bundesstaatsrecht.* Tübingen: Mohr Siebeck.

POSNER, R. A. 1993. What do judges and justices maximize? (The same thing everyone else does). *Supreme Court Economic Review*, 3: 1–41.

RAMSEYER, M. 1994. The puzzling (in)dependence of courts: a comparative approach. *Journal of Legal Studies*, 23: 721–47.

REGAN, D. 1986. The Supreme Court and state protectionism: making sense of the dormant commerce clause. *Michigan Law Review*, 84: 1091–287.

REHNQUIST, W. 1999. 1998 year-end report of the federal judiciary. *Third Branch: Newsletter of the Federal Courts*, 31(1): 2–3.

RIKER, W. H. 1955. The Senate and American federalism. *American Political Science Review*, 49: 452–69.

—— 1975. Federalism. Pp. 93–172 in *Governmental Institutions and Processes*, ed. F. I. Greenstein and N. W. Polsby. Reading, Mass.: Addison-Wesley.

SCHARPF, F. W. 1988. The joint-decision trap: lessons from German federalism and European integration. *Public Administration*, 66: 239–78.

—— REISSERT, B., and SCHNABEL, F. 1976. *Politikverflechtung: Theorie und Empirie des kooperativen Föderalismus in der Bundesrepublik.* Kronberg: Scriptor.

SEGAL, J. A., and SPAETH, H. J. 2002. *The Supreme Court and the Attitudinal Model Revisited.* Cambridge: Cambridge University Press.

SHAPIRO, M. 1981. *Courts: A Comparative and Political Analysis.* Chicago: University of Chicago Press.

—— 2002. The success of judicial review and democracy. Pp. 149–183 in *On Law, Politics, and Judicialization*, ed. M. Shapiro and A. Stone Sweet. New York: Oxford University Press.

SLAUGHTER, A.-M., STONE SWEET, A., and WEILER, J. H. H. (eds.) 1998. *The European Court and National Courts: Doctrine and Jurisprudence Legal Change in Its Social Context.* Oxford: Hart.

SOLBERG, R. S., and LINDQUIST, S. A. 2006. Activism, ideology, and federalism: judicial behavior in constitutional challenges before the Rehnquist Court, 1986–2000. *Journal of Empirical Legal Studies*, 3: 237–61.

SPIRO, P. J. 1999. Foreign relations federalism. *University of Colorado Law Review*, 70: 1223–61.

STEIN, E. 1981. Lawyers, judges, and the making of a transnational constitution. *American Journal of International Law*, 75: 1–27.

STEPAN, A. 1999, Federalism and democracy: beyond the U.S. model. *Journal of Democracy*, 10: 19–34.

STONE SWEET, A. 2004. *The Judicial Construction of Europe*. New York: Oxford University Press.

SUNSTEIN, C. 1995. Incompletely theorized agreements. *Harvard Law Review*, 108: 1733–72.

TARNOPOLSKY, W. S. (ed.) 1975. *The Canadian Bill of Rights*, 2nd rev. edn. Toronto: McClelland and Stewart.

THAYER, J. B. 1893. The origin and scope of the American doctrine of constitutional law. *Harvard Law Review*, 7: 129–56.

TRIBE, L. H. 1980. The puzzling persistence of process-based constitutional theories. *Yale Law Journal*, 89: 1063–4.

TSEBELIS, G. 2002. *Veto Players: How Political Institutions Work*. Princeton, NJ: Princeton University Press.

TUSHNET, M. 1999. *Taking the Constitution Away from the Courts*. Princeton, NJ: Princeton University Press.

WECHSLER, H. 1954. The political safeguards of federalism: the role of the states in the composition and selection of the national government. *Columbia Law Review*, 54: 543–60.

WHEARE, K. C. 1964. *Federal Government*, 4th edn. New York: Oxford University Press.

WHITTINGTON, K. E. 2001. Taking what they give us: explaining the Court's federalism offensive. *Duke Law Journal*, 51: 477–521.

—— 2004. Crossing over: citation of public law faculty in law reviews. *Law and Courts*, 14: 5–10.

CASES

Canada

Reference Re: Resolution to Amend the Constitution (Patriation Reference), [1981] 1 S.C.R. 753.

Reference Re: Secession of Quebec (Secession Reference), [1998] 2 S.C.R. 217.

Regina. v. Crown Zellerbach, [1988] 1 S.C.R. 401.

European Union

Case C-376/98, *Germany v. Parliament and Council*, [2000] ECR-I 8419.

Case C-210/03, Swedish Match, [2004] ECR I-11893.

Germany

BVerfGE 34:9 (1972) (Besoldungsvereinheitlichung).

BVerfG, 2 BvF 1/03, 26.1.2005, not yet reported (Hochschulrahmengesetz).

BVerfGE 2, 213 (1953) (Straffreiheitsgesetz).

United States

Gonzales v. Oregon. 126 S.Ct. 904 (2006).

Gonzales v. Raich. 545 U.S. 1 (2005).

Lawrence v. Texas. 539 U.S. 558 (2003).

Printz v. United States. 521 US 898 (1997).

United States v. Lopez. 514 US 549 (1995).

Washington v. Glucksberg. 521 US 702 (1997).

The Slaughterhouse Cases. 83 US 36 (1873).

CHAPTER 10

....

LEGAL AND EXTRALEGAL EMERGENCIES

....

KIM LANE SCHEPPELE

WHAT should a duly constituted and legitimate government do when political crises threaten the very viability of the state? The usual answers to this question fall into two camps: the legal and the extralegal (Gross 2003; Scheuerman 2006).

The legalists argue that crises of state must be met by entirely legal responses. Such responses may be *different* than they would be in a normal and peaceful situation, but they must be legal all the same (Gross and Ní Aoláin 2006, 17–85). Legalists typically constitutionalize emergency powers by ringing them round with various forms of constraint (Ackerman 2006; Ferejohn and Pasquino 2004). Only in this way, say the legalists, can constitutional government be preserved in the face of serious challenge. To do anything else abandons a constitution just when it may be most needed to ensure that the basic principles of state are preserved (J. Fitzpatrick 1994). Besides, maintaining separation of powers and rights in times of crisis may affirmatively assist a state in fighting the threat (Cole and Lobel 2007).

The extralegalists argue that serious crises of state must be met with responses outside the law. Law, they claim, must operate by rules but the very nature of serious crises is that they cannot be predicted, rationalized, and normalized by rules (Schmitt 2005, 6–7). Constraining the executive by ordinary rules of law when the state faces a mortal challenge is to deprive the state of the wherewithal to protect and defend itself in the ways it may need to in order to survive (Yoo 2005). Moreover, bringing emergencies into the law contaminates the law itself by making it accommodate practices that will of necessity spoil the law (Agamben 2005, 32–3). Better to preserve the integrity of law and the normative coherence of the state, the extralegalists say, by keeping the treatment of emergencies in a different realm altogether. And better to protect the state.

The debate between legalists and extralegalists goes on in the normative realm. But the debate needs empirical context if it is to be well informed, because each argument is animated by premises that are fundamentally predictions about what would happen if each approach were followed. As we will see, actually existing emergencies don't quite map onto the normative debate because most legal traditions as well as the conduct in most real-world emergencies feature both legal and extralegal elements.

The international literature on emergency powers is difficult to grasp because different national traditions use different terminology and pose questions in distinctive ways. To help sort this out, I will examine the major national traditions in the justifications of and legal frameworks for emergency powers. Then, I will review common governmental technologies—how governments actually exercise emergency powers. Though I will attempt a catalogue in both sections, the sheer unruliness of the subject matter means that the categories can be neither mutually exclusive nor exhaustive. But this survey will give us some basis, in the final section, for understanding the debate over emergency powers after 9/11 as many countries deal with what they see as novel and mortal threats from international terrorism.

1 TRADITIONS OF THOUGHT IN EMERGENCY GOVERNANCE

Different language families and legal systems have their own terminologies, legal tools, and conceptual frames to deal with extraordinary threats to the state. The ancient world used the idea of the legal dictator; common law systems use "martial law" or "prerogative power;" the French tradition proceeds under the heading of "state of siege;" the German tradition relies on the "state of exception." And then there is the all-purpose "constitutional reason of state" (Friedrich 1957). To blend them all together misses some very real differences among them, though they also share crucial similarities. First, we will disaggregate the traditions.

1.1 Ancient Models of Constrained Dictatorship

The idea that a crisis can hold the state in a death grip has a long pedigree. Aristotle's *Politics* explained that in ancient Athens an elective tyranny was created to restore the rule of law when the state was too weak to hold itself together (Aristotle, Book IV, 10). But the ancient world's more enduring legal conceptualization for governing states of emergency is the Roman dictator. In fact, the Roman dictator, specifically Cincinnatus, has been romanticized in constitutional political thought, though there were ninety-four other dictators during the 300 years that the institution existed. Given extraordinary powers to repel a threat, Cincinnatus legendarily responded to the call of his countrymen and then, when he successfully fended off the threat, he went back to being an ordinary farmer (Rossiter 2004, 16).

The historical use of the office indicates that it was constitutionally entrenched. When Roman public law fixed the organization of the state with two consuls at its head, it anticipated that the two consuls would conflict or prove indecisive. Moreover executive functions in general were parceled out over an extraordinary range of persons so that, if the state had to act with one voice or quickly, it would be hard to do (Rossiter 2004, 18–19). In a crisis, someone would be named a dictator. His power was absolute and he was responsible to no one. His actions were subject to no veto; his sentences could not be appealed; his decrees held the status of law for the duration of the emergency. His job was to uphold the constitutional order against threats. The only limitation on his power was the strict six-month term of office, a restriction that appears to have never been broken (Rossiter 2004, 23–4). The Roman dictator owes much of its modern allure to the fact that Machiavelli, Montesquieu, Harrington, and Rousseau used the model in their thinking (Ferejohn and Pasquino 2004). But the institution of the constitutional dictator declined along with the Roman republican constitution itself and eventually dictators in the Roman tradition came to carry the modern connotation of rulers without any accountability.

The legal dictator may not be the only legacy that the ancient world bequeaths, however. Agamben's discussion of Roman law calls attention to another institution that could be invoked in emergency situations. The Roman Senate could issue a decree declaring a *tumultus* (public crisis) and therefore invoke a *iustitium* (a "standstill" or "suspension" of the law) (Agamben 2005, 50). Under such circumstances, *all citizens*—and not just the dictator—were empowered to prepare for battle to save the state. The law was temporarily set aside, which gave citizens license to act in ways normally forbidden. There was no creation of a new office, as with the dictator. Instead, the *iustitium* simply removed all legal constraint. If such an institution existed—and Agamben cites only one late nineteenth-century German source who interprets the classical texts this way (Agamben 2005, 45–8)— then there were in the ancient world precedents *both* for handling emergencies inside the law (the dictator) and for suspending the law altogether in times of crisis (the *iustitium*).

1.2 Martial Law and Prerogative Power in Common-law Systems

In common-law systems, emergency powers have historically clustered around claims of prerogative and invocations of martial law. Locke's discussion of prerogative in *Two Treaties of Government* noted that law was often not adequate to the task of governing during crisis (Fatovic 2004). In these situations, the executive should be entrusted to exercise his discretion, even if the law were clear and applicable:

> For since many accidents may happen wherein a strict and rigid observation of the laws may do harm... it is fit the ruler should have a power in many cases to mitigate the severity of the law... This power to act according to discretion for the public good, without the prescription of the law and sometimes even against it, is that which is called prerogative; for since in some governments the law-making power is not always in being and is usually too numerous, and so too slow for the dispatch requisite to execution, and because, also, it is impossible for foresee and so by laws to provide for all accidents and necessities that may concern the public, or make such laws as will do no harm, if they are executed with an inflexible rigour on all occasions and upon all persons that may come in their way, therefore there is a latitude left to the executive power to do many things of a choice which the laws do not prescribe.   (Locke 1689, Book II, ch. XIV, para. 159–60)

Locke saw the dangers in this power, however, and realized that a prince who did not have the good of the community in mind might well abuse it. But what if a parliament and a prince were in conflict over the uses of this power because, for example, there was a bad prince? According to Locke, there was no judge on earth who could mediate (Locke 1689, Book II, ch. xiv, para. 168).

The specter of prerogative, formulated this way, has been the subject of regular recurrence in theory and action in common-law countries. But even by the time Locke wrote, it was already controversial. During the English Civil War, Crown and Parliament each had its own military force and each issued its own Articles of War to its own troops (Madsen 1999, 4). When the Articles of War lapsed, civilian courts reasserted jurisdiction over the military. Starting in 1689, however, the year of Locke's discussion of emergency powers, Parliament began passing annual Mutiny Acts creating a separate branch of military law and binding (at least in the view of the Parliament) the king's actions in time of crisis. By the time of Blackstone, it was possible to distinguish sharply between the absolute powers of the king in wartime with respect to foreign enemies, where prerogative still reigned, and the far more limited uses of martial law at home, where the king could act only pursuant to a grant of powers from the Parliament. Martial law spanned the two realms:

> For martial law, which is built upon no settled principles, but which is entirely arbitrary in its definitions, is... in truth and reality no law, but something indulged, rather than allowed as a law... and therefore it ought not to be permitted in a time of peace, when

the king's courts are open for all persons to receive justice according to the laws of the land.   (Blackstone 1979, Book I, ch. 7 at 400)

By the end of the eighteenth century, royal prerogative had clearly bent before parliamentary sovereignty on the question of who could authorize and maintain law for the military and how far military law could extend at home (Holdsworth 1902). Military law had to be itself derived from civil authority (Dennison 1974). Martial law, always distinguished from military law, was to be used sparingly, if at all. In *Grant v. Gould* (1792), for example, Lord Chief Justice Loughborough ruled that the king could *only* declare martial law under the authority of the annual Mutiny Acts of Parliament. Even then, only soldiers—and not civilians—could come under the king's jurisdiction this way. Within a century of Locke's discussion, martial law in the common-law world was already quite firmly governed within the norms of ordinary lawmaking. And Locke's view that conflicts between Parliament and the king could not be judged on earth had found their earthly judge in an active judiciary that repeatedly announced that the king could not use his prerogative powers in domestic law.

While martial law was generally condemned, it was in fact used as the general form of emergency powers through the end of the nineteenth century, not only in England but even in the differently constitutionalized worlds of the U.S. and Canada (Fairman 1941–2; Scheppele 2006a). Occasionally, however, prerogative claims would return, especially in the U.S. with its strong executive (Franklin 1991; Relyea 1974; Fisher 2004; Scheuerman 2002; Miller 1979–80). Within the common-law tradition, then, one finds both legalist and extralegalist arguments operating side by side.

1.3 State of Siege and the French Constitutional Tradition

In the French tradition, emergency powers have gone under the heading of the *état de siege*. First formalized in the midst of the French Revolution, when the Constituent Assembly issued a legislative decree on July 8, 1791 establishing it, the state of siege was distinguished from a state of peace, when normal laws applied, and a state of war, when civil authorities would still be responsible for the domestic order but security concerns could require them to take special measures. In a state of siege, the civil authorities were to be replaced by military authorities in domestic matters, but only when there was a serious threat of attack or rebellion (Svensson-McCarthy 1998, 36–7). The state of siege was, therefore, a suspension of the normal legal order in its entirety, even as the state of siege was itself regulated by law. As the Revolution went on and constitutional monarchy fell to an anarchic republic and then to various forms of autocracy throughout the 1790s, the siege law also underwent changes. By 1815, it authorized the executive to declare a state of siege virtually at its discretion. The concept of the state of siege also migrated to give rise to two types of the institution: the *actual* state of siege, which would be occasioned by an external military threat challenging the state, and the *constructive* state of siege, which could be occasioned by internal dissent to the regime (Rossiter 2004; Radin 1942).

From the start, the courts in France refused to recognize constructive states of siege. In 1832, for example, during a period of substantial domestic protest, special courts were set up to try people accused of insurrection. The ordinary courts declared the judgments issued by these bodies null and void. By 1849, with a new republican constitution tenuously in place, a new state of siege law gave only the *parliament* the ability to invoke a state of siege, but this power was widely abused. In response to the abuse, the law was again amended in 1878, constraining parliament's powers to declare a state of siege only in circumstances in which there was "imminent peril" and only for a limited time and in a limited physical territory. In addition, citizens were affirmed in all legal rights and privileges that had not been explicitly suspended (Svensson-McCarthy 1998, 39). Even this law, however, proved tempting for those in power, as in 1914 when a presidential declaration of a state of siege lasted for the duration of World War I (Gross and Ní Aoláin 2006, 29).

Against this background, a formal step back toward executive discretion and loosening of legal restraint was taken with the 1958 (current) constitution, written for De Gaulle to accommodate his extraordinarily expansive conception of executive power. The current constitution permits the executive to declare a state of siege

[w]hen the institutions of the Republic, the independence of the nation, the integrity of its territory, or the fulfillment of its international commitments are under grave and immediate threat and when the proper functioning of the constitutional governmental authorities is interrupted. (French Constitution of 1958, Art. 16(1))

The president then may "take the measures demanded by these circumstances," measures not constitutionally specified in any way. The only constraint is that he should consult with the parliament and the Constitutional Council, as well as endeavor to make the state of siege last as short a time as possible. But there are no veto points to challenge his power and no sanctions should he fail to heed the other branches of government.

The French tradition of the state of siege was adopted by many countries in Latin America, with the same promises and problems (Loveman 1993). In such cases, siege powers sometimes come with strict legal regulation and, other times, near-total discretion is given to the executive without constraint. And here too, as in the other traditions, emergencies are seen as alternately inside and outside the law.

1.4 State of Exception and the German Constitutional Tradition

"Sovereign is he who decides on the exception," Carl Schmitt famously declared (Schmitt 2005, 5). Schmitt's *Political Theology* was first published in 1922 when the Weimar Constitution was getting off to a shaky start, and then republished in 1934 after the Nazi government had consolidated its power under the emergency laws that Schmitt had helped to invoke. The experiment with constitutional republicanism under Weimar was full of turmoil and Schmitt's extensive writings on dictatorship, emergency, and other dark corners of liberal states proposed dramatic solutions:

Every general norm demands a normal, everyday frame of life to which it can be factually applied and which is subject to its regulations. ... There exists no norm that is applicable to chaos. For a legal order to make sense, a normal situation must exist, and he is sovereign who definitely decides whether this normal situation actually exists. All law is "situational law."   (Schmitt 2005, 15)

When norms no longer hold, a state of exception fits the reality of chaos, for Schmitt. He saw the exception as the only way to restore normalcy.

Schmitt's writings on the exception were influenced by Bodin's writings on sovereignty (Bodin 1576, Book III, chs. 2 and 3). Bodin's state *officers* were assigned tasks within the law while *commissars* were assigned specific tasks with unlimited powers to achieve them. From this, Schmitt argued that dictators were of two types: the *commissar* whose specific assigned task could be performed outside the law while leaving the legal system intact, and the *sovereign* dictator who had the power to set aside the legal order altogether (Schmitt 1921; Schwab 1970, 30–7). Schmitt argued in academic constitutional debates throughout the 1920s that the Weimar Constitution, while appearing to limit emergency powers to specific competencies in a commissarial way, logically contained the seeds of sovereign dictatorship (Kennedy 2004, 76). When Schmitt offered his support to the Nazis, his position in the theoretical debate became policy.

For Schmitt, the exception demonstrates the sovereign's power to stand outside the law. In arguing this, he drew from Sieyès' (1789) conception of the *pouvoir constitué* (Seitzer 2001). The Constituent Assembly of the French Revolution had claimed the ability to bring a new constitution into being without having to follow the existing law in place to do so. For Schmitt, having this ability to act outside the law to create new power was the very marker of sovereignty. His "exception" differed from a constituent power, however, because an "exception" to law paradoxically requires that what the exception exempts itself from is *law* (Strong 2005, xxi). The effect of the state of exception, therefore, is to allow the executive to rule outside the law in a time of crisis, all the while defining this exceptional power not as "new law" but as "not law."

Schmitt's exceptional sovereign was in many ways nothing new in the German legal tradition. As Stolleis has noted in surveying German legal theory of the state, "The hour of need is in Germany the hour of the executive" (Stolleis 1998, 94). The first strong constitution of a unified German state, the imperial Constitution of 1871, contained an emergency provision that granted the Kaiser sole power to declare war and, as a concomitant, to exercise exclusive powers necessary for conducting the war (German Constitution of 1871, art. 68). This power had itself been taken from a Prussian statute of 1851, adopted in reaction to the revolution of 1848, in which a military commander could take direct control of any civilian administration in his jurisdiction (Caldwell 1997, 54–5).

The 1919 Weimar Constitution, by contrast with the 1871 Constitution, put explicit restrictions on the ability of the president to declare and manage an emergency. Article 48 famously permitted the president to use any measures necessary, including armed force and the suspension of many constitutional rights, to return law and order when "public safety is seriously threatened or disturbed" (Weimar Constitution, art. 48). Though the constitution required the president to cease such measures if the *Reichstag* (lower house of parliament) demanded it, the constitution also permitted the president to dissolve the parliament for any reason (Weimer Constitution, art. 25). When the Nazis consolidated power in 1933, the president first dissolved the parliament and then declared a state of exception (Watkins 1939). As the parliament was not in session, it could not dissolve the emergency.

Hans Kelsen was one of Schmitt's intellectual adversaries in the constitutional debates of Weimar Germany and someone who, in contrast with Schmitt's extra-legalism, was himself a legalist. Kelsen lodged the legitimacy of a legal system in popular acceptance of a *Grundnorm* (basic norm) that itself would specify how a legal system was to be set up. But in the event of an overthrow of the political order, popular approval of a *new Grundnorm* would succeed in creating a new legitimate government, not a government of "no law." In this way, the successful overthrow of one constitutional order would create a new constitution rather than a space outside of law (Kelsen 1949, 115–23; Kelsen 2002, 120–4). But though Kelsen is usually thought of as being on the correct side of the Weimar questions, Kelsen's theory of "revolutionary legality" was picked up by a number of courts around the world to find dubious constitutional legitimation for coups (Mahmud 1993; 1994; Iyer 1973).

The West Germany that emerged, divided, from the ashes of Weimar, feared emergency powers and did not include any provision for them in the Bonn Constitution (The Basic Law 1949; Golay 1958, 131–2). Only in 1968, when the rumbles of revolution again rolled across Europe, did West Germany add emergency powers to its constitution. But this time, the extralegal arguments of Carl Schmitt were used only as evidence of what *not* to do. The Bonn Constitution's emergency powers have never formally been used, though it had a moment of temptation during the Red Army Faction crisis of the 1970s (Müller 2003, 181–93). The 1968 amendments provided for a "state of defense" that must be declared by the parliament or by a specially constituted joint committee that substitutes for the parliament if it cannot meet. Also, the parliament has the ability to undeclare the state of defense as well as to override any specific executive emergency decrees. Only specified powers are given to the Chancellor during the emergency and he may neither dissolve the parliament nor change the operation of the Constitutional Court during this time (Basic Law 1949, ch. X). Clearly, Germany has brought emergencies in from their prior extra-legal status to full constitutionalization. As a result, Germany now has a tradition that shares with all of the others we have seen a history of debate over whether extra-legal measures can be used in an emergency or whether an executive must stay within legal means. Since World War II, the legalists have won.

But now that constitutional debates in Germany have been clearly settled in favor of legalism, Carl Schmitt has been making a comeback, if not as a normative theorist, then as an analyst useful in comparative constitutionalism (Cristi 2000; Müller 2000; Seitzer 2001) and as a keen observer of how states of emergencies work (Gross 2000). In fact, Schmitt's revival as theorist of emergencies has been nothing short of remarkable, with an outpouring of writings on Schmitt in many languages (Caldwell 2005; McCormick 1998). Even in Germany, a justice of the Constitutional Court (Böckenförde 1998) and one of the country's major postwar political theor-ists (Preuss 1999) have considered Schmitt's work important in understanding the weaknesses of liberal states and their susceptibility to emergency governance. Some have even argued that Schmitt's theory of the exception could help liberal rights-conferring democracies find a way to defend themselves from antidemocratic forces, though the dangers of extreme executive power in times of crisis are not trivial (Cristi 1998). Schmitt, despite having lost the normative battle in Germany, remains very much alive in the discussion of modern emergency powers.

As we have seen in our quick review of four different time-and-place-bound theories of emergencies, both legal and extralegal strands exist in each tradition of thought. The legalist/extralegalist debate, then, is not a debate *across* different legal traditions, but a debate *within* each one. In none of these traditions is the debate ever clearly settled for crises almost always bring out both sides.

2 THE TECHNOLOGY OF EMERGENCIES

If emergencies often hover between legal and extralegal in theory, how do they work in practice? Of course, there are many examples of coups, revolutions, absolute defeat in wartime, and other such crises that typically require a comprehensive emergency government until a permanent form of state can be established (International Commission of Jurists 1983). But for states that are already more-or-less constitutional and that face serious internal or external threats, how are emergency powers invoked and what strategies of government are used to cope with crises? And how does the use of emergency powers affect the viability of democratic regimes?

The practice of emergencies, like the theory and the law on the subject, also hovers between the legal and the extralegal. For example, when countries "legalize" states of emergency by embedding them in domestic constitutions, such provisions are almost never used in a formal way (Freeman 2003; Ferejohn and Pasquino 2004). To take only a few: Germany since 1968, Russia since 1993, South Africa since 1996, and Canada after the Charter reforms in 1983 (when an emergency statute was passed requiring consistency of emergency measures with the Charter) have never in fact used their constitutional emergency provisions to deal with any crisis, including 9/11. France has used its constitutional emergency provision only once, in 1961 during the Algerian Crisis (Ferejohn and Pasquino 2004). In the history of the U.S., there have only been two occasions on which suspension of the writ of *habeas corpus*, the primary emergency power named in the U.S. Constitution, has occurred (during the Civil War and currently after 9/11). Open constitutional emergencies, however, are not declared in constitutional states as often as one might expect, even when such a possibility is written into the constitution. Creeping emergencies, in which emergency powers are invoked piecemeal or only in part, are far more common.

Moreover, when emergency powers are used, they are almost never the sort of total emergencies that cover all or even most aspects of political life as one might imagine from the theory. Many fly under the radar of constitutional alarm. Instead, constitutional states tend to deal with actually existing emergencies with what I call methods of *delegation, suspension, deference,* and *partition,* usually of a subconstitutional sort that allows the constitutional questions to be avoided and a veneer of legalism to remain. In most constitutional democracies, this partial use of emergency powers is so astonishingly common that they have become part of normal governance.

2.1 Delegation

The enabling act is the most common vehicle of emergency governance. Enabling acts prospectively delegate a substantial body of legislative power to the executive. The executive is then given the ability to invoke the enabling act when he feels that there is a crisis. As a result, an executive, without any separate legislative approval at a time of crisis, can invoke the crisis laws at his discretion. And all of this happens within the framework of preexisting statutory law, raising no constitutional question other than the limits of the delegation power (Ferejohn and Pasquino 2004).

American courts have typically not touched this question in times of crisis, satisfying themselves that as long as the legislature has consented, extraordinary uses of executive power poses no constitutional problem (Issacharoff and Pildes 2005; Epstein et al. 2005).

From the start of the twentieth century, this has in fact been the dominant method of crisis management in diverse systems like the United States, Canada, France, and Germany. In the United States, for example, most extraordinary powers exercised by presidents during the two World Wars in the twentieth century were exercised pursuant to a formal legislative delegation to the executive in advance of the crisis. And in both wars, attempts to roll back this power at the end of the crisis were resisted and the crisis laws were used extensively after the wars were over (Scheppele 2006*b*). In Canada, the War Measures Act had the same general structure, delegating huge discretionary powers to the executive in times of crisis (Scheppele 2006*a*). In France, an enabling act was used to enable to Poincaré government in 1926 to initiate broad administrative reforms, and after 1934, resort to enabling acts became very common as a way of delegating legislative power to the executive on all manner of issues (Gross and Ní Aoláin 2006, 29–30). The most notorious enabling act was the one approved by the Reichstag on March 23, 1933, declaring a permanent state of emergency and giving dictatorial powers to Hitler (Caldwell 1997, 174–5). And one of the most-used enabling acts is the Stafford Act in the United States, which allows presidents to declare emergencies and then to bypass the constitutionally mandated congressional appropriations process to funnel money to areas where natural disasters have hit (Scheppele 2006*b*). Though this act formally suspends a crucial element of the constitution, it has never been constitutionally challenged. Once an enabling act is passed, the executive simply appears to be following a law enacted by the legislature instead of seizing powers on his own, which minimizes the constitutional disruption. The executive therefore appears to govern in crisis entirely through normal law.

2.2 Suspension

Many constitutions give executives the power to dissolve parliaments for a variety of reasons. Or, they give executives the power to act on their own when legislatures are not in session. Sometimes political bodies suspend themselves when it becomes too hard to govern. Through these perfectly constitutional mechanisms, constitutional checks can dissolve and emergency powers can fill the gaps.

Here, too, Nazi Germany is the famous and extreme case, where the president dissolved the parliament, as the constitution's Article 25 allowed him to do, and then declared a state of emergency, which Article 48 allowed him to do. These actions were clearly permitted in the constitution, except that the check on Article

48—that the parliament could undeclare the emergency—was not in place once the parliament itself was dissolved.

Triggering an emergency through the legal suspension (or self-suspension) of constitutional bodies is more common and more constitutionally ambiguous than the dramatic example of Nazi Germany suggests. For example, in Austria in 1933, the chairman and two vice-chairmen of the parliament resigned in response to major national strikes. The government then announced that parliament had dissolved itself and started to issue decrees under the Emergency Law of 1917. When these decrees were challenged before the Constitutional Court, the government "persuaded" some judges to resign, a second "self-elimination." A new constitution was adopted in 1934 that legimated the new regime (Somek 2003, 363–4). Abdications that trigger emergency provisions are also quite common. The opening act of the Russian Revolution, which launched emergency rule, featured the tsar and all eligible members of his family abdicating at once (S. Fitzpatrick 1984). In the Ukraine in 2007, two Constitutional Court judges resigned rather than rule on controversial decrees of the president that asserted powers beyond those given in the constitution ("Ukraine's Constitutional Court Not 'Politicized,'"—New Chairman, July 27, 2007). In each of these cases, constitutional bodies take themselves out of the political arena and tip a country over into a crisis where emergency powers have little resistance.

2.3 Deference

Without any formal change of law, constitutionally specified checks on executive power may disappear because the bodies in question choose to stay in place but choose not to exercise their power of review during crises. Parliamentary oversight is neglected; courts drop cases for political or jurisdictional reasons.

This is almost a commonplace in thinking about judicial review during emergencies as reflected in the slogan, *inter arma silent leges*. Surely the cases of *Korematsu v. United States* (1944) and its postwar Canadian equivalent *Cooperative Committee on Japanese-Canadians v. Attorney General of Canada* (1946)—both approving extraordinary rights deprivations of people of Japanese origins during wartime—are among the cases that demonstrate that judicial review has its limits where war is involved (Brandon 2005). When the American courts have handled wartime cases, they typically decide on the basis of institutional competency rather than on the basis of rights (Issacharoff and Pildes 2004). National courts in general have not been effective protectors of rights during emergencies (Alexander 1984). Though the European Court of Human Rights performs extensive reviews of emergency declarations, not all commentators have found their jurisprudence sufficiently skeptical of state claims of emergency (Gross 1998).

Since 9/11, however, courts have become less overtly deferential in their holdings, though equally deferential to executives in the remedies they allow (Cole 2003). For example, in the two (so far) Guantánamo cases where the U.S. Supreme Court has reviewed the detentions without trial of presidentially declared "enemy combatants," the detainees have "won" their habeas claims, but they still remain in detention (*Rasul v. Bush* 2004; *Hamdan v. Rumsfeld* 2006). The holding says that they have rights but the remedy does not permit their immediate release. Similarly, in the English torture case (*A. v. Secretary of State* 2005), the Law Lords unanimously agreed that evidence acquired by torture could not be used by courts in assessing whether the indefinite detention of a terrorism suspect was "reasonable," but all of the judges indicated (*a*) that the executive branch could use such information, (*b*) that courts could use evidence acquired by cruel, inhuman, and degrading treatment, and (*c*) that evidence could only be excluded by courts as having been acquired by torture if it could be demonstrated that the particular statement at issue was acquired directly under torture, something nearly impossible to show (Scheppele 2005*b*). Here too, this decision looks like a constraint on government action, but in fact it allowed the British government to go on doing what it had been doing. The face of judicial deference has changed since 9/11. Now courts issue decisions that appear to provide a check on power in the name of rights. But they are still deferring in practice.

2.4 Partition

Emergencies might be more obvious, and therefore more objectionable to many of the citizens of a constitutional democracy, if they affected the whole population or made all prior law invalid. But most emergencies don't affect most people in the societies where they occur. Instead, emergencies are usually more selective, partitioning off the space where the crisis brews from the rest of the political scene, which appears normal. Even in one of the most horrendous classic cases—Nazi Germany—much of the ordinary law remained the same (Stolleis 1998). Ernst Fraenkel famously described it as a "dual state," where a "normative state" obediently following the prior law was acting side-by-side with a "prerogative state" of arbitrary executive power (Fraenkel 1941).

During "the troubles" in Northern Ireland, Britain operated under an emergency regime, but the emergency laws applied only in the North (Finn 1991; Donohue 2001). When Russia tried to crack down on terrorism in the 1880s, they largely did so through separate courts and separate institutions; the recent wars in Chechnya were carried out through geographically partitioned extraordinary powers (Scheppele 2005*a*). Though there have been three national emergencies in India since independence, there are routine declarations of emergency in specific regions, leaving the rest of the country largely unaffected and mobilizing nowhere near the opposition that national emergencies do (Omar 2002; Hussain 2003). Even when there is a national emergency in a country, only certain groups may be affected, like the Muslim men detained after 9/11 in New York (Inspector General, U.S. Department of Justice 2003). When an emergency can partition the political space into those "few" affected by the uses of emergency powers and those "many" who are not, the state can often blunt the impact of criticism and exercise unlimited powers in the emergency zone while maintaining normal governance elsewhere.

From this quick review of actually existing emergencies and the strategies used to produce them, we can see the general theory of emergencies and the constitutional frameworks that regulate them are rather detached from actual practice. Usually, emergency powers are delegated subconstitutionally, exercised in the absence or deference of bodies that might check them, and targeted only at parts of a population. Emergencies usually exist alongside absolutely normal governance and often without any formal suspension of constitutional guarantees. As a result, the practical choice is not between emergencies that are legal and those that are extralegal. Most actual emergencies have elements of both, operating simultaneously. There are spaces of absolutely normal legality that continue even while extralegal powers are invoked for some topics, some places, some people. When the checking bodies look the other way, legality may disappear, but only in targeted places for targeted people. In practical terms, both the legalists and extralegalists tend to prevail during any actually existing emergency.

3 AFTER 9/11: THE LEGALISTS AND THE EXTRALEGALISTS REVISITED

The attacks on the Unites States on September 9, 2001 have produced another generation of debate over emergency powers, not just in the United States, but internationally. Not surprisingly, the abstract debate over state powers to fight terrorism tends to divide, as it has so often before, into legalist and extralegalist camps. The legalists include not just those who defend constitutional integrity (Cole and Lobel 2007; Dyzenhaus 2006) but also those who claim that international law also requires legalism in the face of crisis (International Bar Association Task Force on Terrorism 2003; Duffy 2005). Because the legalist position is so dominant in the theoretical debate, today's extralegalists generally advocate following *some* law, but the law in question is one that has few practical constraints on executive power because legality derives from prerogative power (Paulsen 2004; Yoo 2005; Posner 2006).

The battle is therefore joined between the "strict enforcement" advocates who believe that law should not change during crises and the "accommodationists" who believe that law can be flexible without creating a permanent danger of constitutional collapse (Posner and Vermeule 2003).

The UK, alone among constitutional states, declared a state of emergency after 9/11 and derogated formally from international human rights conventions, while passing new terrorism laws that overtly trenched on rights (Walker 2002; Scheppele 2004*a*). But many other countries also have taken measures to fight terrorism that raise serious questions about compliance with their own constitutional orders and with adherence to international human rights frameworks (Ramraj, Hor, and Roach 2005; Roach 2003). Most other countries, however, are operating without formal declarations of emergencies or overt invocation of crisis laws even as they act as if they are in a full-blown exceptional state (Steinmetz 2003; Scheppele forthcoming).

Since 9/11, a number of writers have found parallels between Schmitt's theory of the exception and the strategies of the Bush administration in fighting the "war on terrorism" as they call attention to the dangers of unchecked executive discretion (Levinson 2006; Tushnet 2006; Scheppele 2004*b*). For these critics, the argument that the commander-in-chief power permits the president to ignore statutes that he believes to trench on his powers, to single-handedly abrogate treaties, and to insist his policies remain unreviewed by courts (see Office of Legal Counsel memos reproduced in Greenberg and Dratel 2005) amounts to the declaration that the president can stand outside the law in a time of crisis in just the way that Schmitt advocated. But other writers have called more positively upon the Lockean conception of prerogative to justify extraordinary measures taken in the name of emergency (Paulsen 2004; Yoo 2005).

That said, 9/11 has produced relatively few empirical studies of how emergency powers are being invoked. Much of this is because the uses of emergency powers are often secret during the emergency, which makes them hard to study. But there are some aspects of the reactions of states to 9/11 that can be studied empirically even while the crisis continues. As we have seen from the handling of past emergencies, the practices of delegation, dissolution, deference, and partition are prevalent during emergencies, and many of these practices will be visible even as the details of emergency operations are secret. Has there been more sweeping enabling legislation after 9/11, as one would expect? Are bodies that might check executive power putting themselves into effective suspension in the fight against terrorism? Are courts and legislatures deferring to executive claims on power since 9/11? Are states after 9/11 partitioning their domestic space so that constitutional protections are seriously eroded for some sectors of the population while remaining untouched in others? These have been the markers of emergency governance in the past, and finding an increase in each of these practices could well signal that states are acting as if they are in an emergency, even when such emergencies are not formally declared. One of the important services that empirical scholarship can provide is to document changes in state practices and to compare them with well-known actually existing emergencies in the past to diagnose when actual emergency government is in effect, despite state protestations to the contrary.

While there is a certain density of writing on theoretical approaches to emergencies and constitutional frameworks for limiting them, there is much less empirical work on the details of actual emergency governance. The post-9/11 world, sadly, provides many opportunities to consider how emergencies work. In studying these new emergencies, the parallel case studies compiled by the International Commission of Jurists (1983) contain much useful information about how emergencies work as a matter of detailed legal practice. Studies by Finn (1991), Loveman (1993), Dyzenhaus (1991), Roach (2003), Hussain (2003), the authors collected by Ramraj, Hor, and Roach (2005), and of course Rossiter (2004) can also provide good models for the study of emergency government.

As we have seen, all traditions of emergency thinking have elements that both allow complete executive direction and that routinize and legalize emergencies. In actual emergencies, it is often hard to tell which theoretical tradition is being used because the actual practices are often suspended between the two, with elements of both in the mix. In short, the debate between legalists and extralegalists is a fine one in theory, but it tends to disguise how the two approaches are blended in practice. More empirical work is necessary to sort out how the categories of the normative debates actually work in actually existing emergencies.

REFERENCES

ACKERMAN, B. 2006. *Before the Next Attack: Civil Liberties in an Age of Terrorism*. New Haven, Conn.: Yale University Press.

AGAMBEN, G. 2005. *State of Exception*, trans. K. Attell. Chicago: University of Chicago Press.

ALEXANDER, G. J. 1984. The illusory protection of human rights by national courts during periods of emergency. *Human Rights Law Journal*, 5: 1–69.

ARISTOTLE 1998 [350 BC]. *Politics*, trans. C. D. C. Reeve. Indianapolis: Hachett.

BLACKSTONE, W. 1979 [1765]. *Commentaries on the Laws of England*. Vol I: *Of the Rights of Persons*. Chicago: University of Chicago Press.

BÖCKENFÖRDE, E.-W. 1990. The origin and development of the concept of the *Rechtsstaat*. Pp. 47–70 in *State, Society and Liberty: Studies in Political Theory and Constitutional Law*, trans. J. A. Underwood. New York: Berg.

—— 1998. The concept of the political: a key to understanding Carl Schmitt's political theory. Pp. 37–55 in *Law as Politics: Carl Schmitt's Critique of Liberalism*, ed. D. Dyzenhaus. Durham, NC: Duke University Press.

BODIN, J. 1955 [1576]. *Six Books of the Commonwealth*. Oxford: Basil Blackwell.

BONN CONSTITUTION (The Basic Law, 1949), with amendments to the present, available at www.jurisprudentia.de/jurisprudentia.html.

BRANDON, M. 2005. War and the constitution. Pp. 11–38 in *The Constitution in Wartime: Beyond Alarmism and Complacency*, ed. M. Tushnet. Durham, NC Duke University Press.

CALDWELL, P. 1997. *Popular Sovereignty and the Crisis of German Constitutional Law: The Theory and Practice of Weimar Constitutionalism*. Durham, NC: Duke University Press.

—— 2005. Controversies over Carl Schmitt: a review of recent literature. *Journal of Modern History*, 77: 357–87.

CRISTI, R. 1998. *Carl Schmitt and Authoritarian Liberalism: Strong State, Free Economy*. Cardiff: University of Wales Press.

—— 2000. The metaphysics of constituent power: Schmitt and the genesis of Chile's 1980 constitution. *Cardozo Law Review*, 21: 1749–75.

COLE, D. 2003. Judging the next emergency: judicial review and individual rights in times of crisis. *Michigan Law Review*, 101: 2565–95.

—— and LOBEL, J. 2007. *Less Safe, Less Free: Why America is Losing the War on Terror*. New York: New Press.

DENNISON, G. M. 1974. Martial law: the development of a theory of emergency powers, 1776–1861. *American Journal of Legal History*, 18: 52–79.

DONOHUE, L. 2001. *Counter-terrorist Law and Emergency Powers in the United Kingdom 1922–2000*. Dublin: Irish Academic Press.

DUFFY, H. 2005. *The "War on Terror" and the Framework of International Law*. Cambridge: Cambridge University Press.

DYZENHAUS, D. 1991. *Hard Cases in Wicked Legal Systems: South African Law in the Perspective of Legal Philosophy*. Oxford: Oxford University Press.

—— 2006. *The Constitution of Law: Legality in a Time of Emergency*. Cambridge: Cambridge University Press.

EPSTEIN, L., HO, D. E., KING, G., and SEGAL, J. A. 2005. The Supreme Court during crisis: how war affects only non-war cases. *New York University Law Review*, 80: 1–116.

FAIRMAN, C. 1941–2. The law of martial rule and the national emergency. *Harvard Law Review*, 55: 1253–302.

FATOVIC, C. 2004. Constitutionalism and contingency: Locke's theory of prerogative. *History of Political Thought*, 25: 276–97.

FEREJOHN, J., and PASQUINO, P. 2004. The law of the exception: a typology of emergency powers. *International Journal of Constitutional Law*, 2: 210–39.

FINN, J. 1991. *Constitutions in Crisis: Political Violence and the Rule of Law*. New York: Oxford University Press.

FISHER, L. 2004. *Presidential War Power*, 2nd edn. Lawrence: University Press of Kansas.

FITZPATRICK, J. 1994. *Human Rights in Crisis: The International System for Protecting Rights During States of Emergency*. Philadelphia: University of Pennsylvania Press.

FITZPATRICK, S. 1984. *The Russian Revolution 1917–1934*. New York: Oxford University Press.

FRAENKEL, E. 1941. *The Dual State: A Contribution to the Theory of Dictatorship*, trans. E. Shills, E. Lowenstein, and K. Knorr. Oxford: Oxford University Press.

FRANKLIN, D. 1991. *Extraordinary Measure: The Exercise of Prerogative Powers in the United States*. Pittsburgh, Pa.: University of Pittsburgh Press.

FREEMAN, M. 2003. *Freedom or Security: The Consequences for Democracies Using Emergency Powers to Fight Terror*. Westport, Conn.: Praeger.

FRIEDRICH, C. J. 1957. *Constitutional Reason of State: The Survival of the Constitutional Order*. Providence, RI: Brown University Press.

FRENCH CONSTITUTION, 1958, with amendments to present, available at www.servat. unibe.ch/law/icl/fr00000_.html.

GERMAN CONSTITUTION of 1871, available in Hucko, E. (ed.) 1987. *Four German Constitutions*. New York: Berg.

GOLAY, J. F. 1958. *The Founding of the Federal Republic of Germany*. Chicago: University of Chicago Press.

GREENBERG, K., and DRATEL, J. (eds.) 2005. *The Torture Papers: The Road to Abu Ghraib*. New York: Cambridge University Press.

GROSS, O. 1998. "Once more unto the breach:" the systemic failure of applying the European Convention on Human Rights to entrenched emergencies. *Yale Journal of International Law*, 23: 437–501.

—— 2000. The normless and exceptionless exception: Carl Schmitt's theory of emergency powers and the "norm-exception" dichotomy. *Cardozo Law Review*, 21: 1825–66.

—— 2003. Chaos and rules: should responses to violent crises always be constitutional? *Yale Law Journal*, 112: 1011–34.

—— and NÍ AOLAÍN, F. 2006. *Law in Times of Crisis: Emergency Powers in Theory and Practice*. Cambridge: Cambridge University Press.

HOLDSWORTH, W. S. 1902. Martial law historically considered. *Law Review Quarterly*, 18: 117–32.

HUSSAIN, N. 2003. *The Jurisprudence of Emergency: Colonialism and the Rule of Law*. Ann Arbor: University of Michigan Press.

INSPECTOR GENERAL, U.S. Department of Justice. 2003. The September 11 detainees: a review of the treatment of aliens held on immigration charges in connection with the investigation of the September 11 attacks. Available at www.ccrny.org/v2/reports/docs/OIGReport.pdf.

INTERNATIONAL BAR ASSOCIATION TASK FORCE ON TERRORISM 2003. *International Terrorism: Legal Challenges and Responses*. Ard, NY: Transnational.

INTERNATIONAL COMMISSION OF JURISTS. 1983. *States of Emergency: Their Impact on Human Rights*. Geneva: International Commission of Jurists.

ISSACHAROFF, S., and PILDES, R. 2004. Emergency contexts without emergency powers. *International Journal of Constitutional Law*, 2: 296–333.

—— —— 2005. Between civil libertarianism and executive unilateralism: an institutional process approach to rights during wartime. Pp. 161–97 in *The Constitution in Wartime: Beyond Alarmism and Complacency*, ed. M. Tushnet. Durham, NC: Duke University Press.

IYER, T. K. K. 1973. Constitutional law in Pakistan: Kelsen in the courts. *American Journal of Comparative Law*, 21: 759–71.

KALYVAS, A., and MÜLLER, J.-W. (eds.) 2000. Carl Schmitt: legacy and prospects. *Cardozo Law Review*, 21: 1469–902.

KELSEN, H. 1949 [1945]. *General Theory of State and Law*, trans. A. Wedberg. Cambridge, Mass.: Harvard University Press.

—— 2002 [1934]. *Introduction to Problems of Legal Theory*, trans. B. Litschewski Paulson and S. L. Paulson. Oxford: Oxford University Press.

KENNEDY, E. 2004. *Constitutional Failure: Schmitt in Weimar*. Durham, NC: Duke University Press.

LEVINSON, S. 2006. Constitutional norms in a state of permanent emergency. *Georgia Law Review*, 40: 699–751.

LOCKE, J. 1960 [1689]. *Two Treatises of Government*. Cambridge: Cambridge University Press.

LOVEMAN, B. 1993. *The Constitution of Tyranny: Regimes of Exception in Spanish America*. Pittsburgh, Pa.: University of Pittsburgh Press.

McCORMICK, J. 1998. Political theory and political theology: the second wave of Carl Schmitt in English. *Political Theory*, 26: 830–54.

MADSEN, C. 1999. *Another Kind of Justice: Canadian Military Law from Confederation to Somalia*. Vancouver: University of British Columbia Press.

MAHMUD, T. 1993. Praetorianism and common law in post-colonial settings: judicial response to constitutional breakdown in Pakistan. *Utah Law Review*, 1993: 1226–305.

—— 1994. The jurisprudence of successful treason: coup d'état and the common law. *Cornell Journal of International Law*, 27: 51–140.

MILLER, A. S. 1979–80. Reason of state and the emergency constitution of control. *Minnesota Law Review*, 64: 585–633.

MÜLLER, J.-W. 2000. Carl Schmitt and the constitution of Europe. *Cardozo Law Review*, 21: 77–1795.

—— 2003. *A Dangerous Mind: Carl Schmitt in Post-War European Thought*. New Haven, Conn.: Yale University Press.

OMAR, I. 2002. *Emergency Powers and the Courts in India and Pakistan*. New York: Kluwer Law.

PAULSEN, M. 2004. The constitution of necessity. *Notre Dame Law Review*, 79: 1257–98.

POSNER, R. 2006. *Not a Suicide Pact: The Constitution in Times of National Emergency*. New York: Oxford University Press.

—— and VERMEULE, A. 2003. Accommodating emergencies. *Stanford Law Review*, 56: 605–44.

PREUSS, U. 1999. Political order and democracy: Carl Schmitt and his influence. Pp. 157–65 in *The Challenge of Carl Schmitt*, ed. C. Mouffe. New York: Verso.

RADIN, M. 1942. Martial law and the state of siege. *California Law Review*, 30: 634–47.

RAMRAJ, V., HOR, M., and ROACH, K. (eds.) 2005. *Global Anti-Terrorism Law and Policy*. Cambridge: Cambridge University Press.

RELYEA, H. 1974. *A Brief History of Emergency Powers in the United States*. A Working Paper Prepared for the Special Committee on National Emergencies and Delegated Emergency Powers, United States Senate, 92rd Congress, 2nd Session, July 1974. Reprinted by University Press of the Pacific, 2005.

ROACH, K. 2003. *September 11: Consequences for Canada*. Montreal: McGill-Queen's University Press.

ROSSITER, C. 2004 [1948]. *Constitutional Dictatorship: Crisis Government in the Modern Democracies*. Princeton, NJ: Princeton University Press.

SEITZER, J. 2001. *Comparative History and Legal Theory: Carl Schmitt in the First German Democracy*. Westport, Conn.: Greenview Press.

SCHEPPELE, K.L. 2004a. Other people's PATRIOT Acts: Europe's response to September 11. *Loyola Law Review*, 50: 89–148.

—— 2004b. Law in a time of emergency: states of exception and the temptations of 9/11. *University of Pennsylvania Journal of Constitutional Law*, 6: 1001–83.

—— 2005a. "We forgot about the ditches:" Russian constitutional impatience and the challenge of terrorism. *Drake Law Review*, 53: 963–1027.

—— 2005b. Evidence from torture: dilemmas for international and domestic law. *Proceedings of the American Society of International Law*, 99: 271–7.

—— 2006a. North American emergencies: the uses of emergency powers in the United States and Canada. *International Journal of Constitutional Law*, 4: 213–43.

—— 2006b. Small emergencies. *Georgia Law Review*, 40: 835–62.

—— forthcoming. *The International State of Emergency*.

SCHEUERMAN, W. E. 2002. Rethinking crisis government. *Constellations*, 9: 492–505.

—— 2006. Emergency powers. *Annual Review of Law and Social Science*, 2: 257–77.

SCHMITT, C. 1921. *Die Diktator*. Berlin: Duncker & Humblot.

—— 2005 [1992]. *Political Theology: Four Chapters on the Theory of Sovereignty*, trans. G. Schwab; intro. T. Strong. Chicago: University of Chicago Press.

—— 2007 [1928]. *Constitutional Theory*, trans. J. Seitzer. Durham, NC: Duke University Press.

SCHWAB, G. 1970. *The Challenge of the Exception*. Berlin: Duncker & Humblot.

SIEYÈS, E.-J. 1789. *What Is the Third Estate?* trans. M. Bloudel. New York: Praeger.

SOMEK, A. 2003. Authoritarian constitutionalism: Austrian constitutional doctrine 1933–1938 and its legacy. Pp. 361–88 in *The Darker Legacies of Law in Europe*, ed. C. Joerges and N. S. Ghaleigh. Oxford: Hart.

STEINMETZ, G. 2003. The state of emergency and the revival of American imperialism: toward an authoritarian post-Fordism. *Public Culture*, 15: 323–45.

STOLLEIS, M. 1998. *The Law of the Swastika*. Chicago: University of Chicago Press.

STRONG, T. 2005. Introduction to *Carl Schmitt, Political Theology: Four Chapters on the Theory of Sovereignty*, trans. G. Schwab. Chicago: University of Chicago Press.

SVENSSON-MCCARTHY, A.-L. 1998. *The International Law of Human Rights and States of Exception*. The Hague: Martinus Nijhoff.

TUSHNET, M. 2006. Meditations on Carl Schmitt. *Georgia Law Review*, 40: 877–88.

"Ukraine's Constitutional Court Not 'Politicized' "—New Chairman. July 27, 2007. *Financial Times L.*, BBC Monitoring International Reports.

U.S. CONSTITUTION, 1787 with amendments to present, available at www.yale.edu/lawweb/avalon/usconst.htm.

WALKER, C. 2002. *Blackstone's Guide to the Anti-Terrorism Legislation (UK)*. Oxford: Oxford University Press.

WATKINS, F. M. 1939. *The Failure of Constitutional Emergency Powers under the German Republic*. Cambridge, Mass: Harvard University Press.

WEIMAR CONSTITUTION, a.k.a. Reich Constitution of August 11, 1919, with amendments to 1933, available in Hucko, E. (ed.) 1987. *Four German Constitutions*. New York: Berg.

YOO, J. 2005. *The Powers of War and Peace: The Constitution and Foreign Affairs after 9/11*. Chicago: University of Chicago Press.

CASES

A and Others v. Secretary of State for the Home Department (A and others II). 2005. Law Lords. [2005] UKHL 71.

Cooperative Committee on Japanese-Canadians v. Attorney General of Canada. 1946. [1947] 1 D.L.R. 577.

Grant v. Gould (1792) 2 Henry Blackstone's Reports 69–108.

Hamdan v. Rumsfeld. 2006. 126 S. Ct. 2749.

Korematsu v. United States. 1944, 323 U.S. 214.

Rasul v. Bush. 2004. 542 U.S. 466.

PART IV

INTERNATIONAL
AND
SUPRANATIONAL
LAW

INTERNATIONAL LAW AND INTERNATIONAL RELATIONS

BETH SIMMONS

1 SCOPE AND BACKGROUND

INTERNATIONAL law can be thought of as the set of rules that are intended to bind states in their relationships with each other. The overwhelming share of research by political scientists has been on public international law, or the rules which states create to regulate and order their own behavior (in contrast with private international law, or international agreements about which rules should apply to private transactions such as contracts, etc.). International law is largely state-made, although as with all law, private actors and organizations can have significant input into the national positions and diplomatic processes that produce it. International law is largely designed to apply to states, both to constrain (the laws of war) and to empower them (law of sovereignty). Increasingly, international law has been codified, so that today most international obligations are contained in treaty form, although historically customary international law played a relatively more important role than it does today.

The role of international law in informing foreign policy decision-making has waxed and waned over the course of the past century. It has also varied significantly across countries. The acknowledged role for international law in American foreign policy-making provides an interesting example. Steinberg and Zasloff point out the crucial role that the paradigm of law played in American foreign policy thinking toward the end of the nineteenth century. As they point out, "Every American secretary of state from 1889 to 1945 was a lawyer; the same could be said of only one British foreign secretary during the same period" (2006, 66). Historically, United States Republicans in particular were committed to law as a basis for foreign policy-making. President Coolidge asserted in the 1920s that Republican public policy "represents the processes of reducing our domestic and foreign relations to a system of law" (Steinberg and Zasloff 2006, 67).

For many, however, the lesson of the 1930s and 1940s was that of misplaced trust in international law as a touchstone for foreign policy-making. Hitler's cunning use of the rhetorical language of international legal justification to "mislead his enemies, avoid alienating neutrals, and pacify opposition" (Goldsmith and Posner 2005, 168) while engaging in the most flagrant violations of legal commitment demonstrated to many the patently inappropriate—and dangerous—appeal to law in the conduct of international affairs. The post-World War II period unleashed some of the harshest critical scholarship on the (misplaced) role of law in international affairs (see below); ironically, however, it was also a period in which international law was ever more deeply woven into the texture of international affairs in such areas as the use of force and collective security, international trade and monetary relations, and international human rights.

It is striking the extent to which international interactions have become reflected in and regulated by formal state-to-state agreements. Multilateral treaties have proliferated over the course of the past century. Figure 11.1 demonstrates this proliferation graphically. A burst of diplomatic activity in the quarter century after World War II gave rise to nearly 2,000 new multilateral interstate agreements, many of which were key to the establishment of the postwar economic, security, and human rights order. The last quarter of a century saw a slight reduction in the number of new multilateral treaties, but the expansion of international agreements into new areas, such as environmental protection. At the same time, the postwar proliferation of state actors post-decolonization has meant that these rules bind more players, extending the scope of law practically worldwide. To these multilateral agreements, it is important to add bilateral treaties (not reflected in Figure 11.1), which have proliferated in many areas, such as the protection of investment, regulation of air traffic, criminal extradition, and market access for trade. Currently, the United Nations Treaty Series (UNTS) lists about 3,500 multilateral treaties and

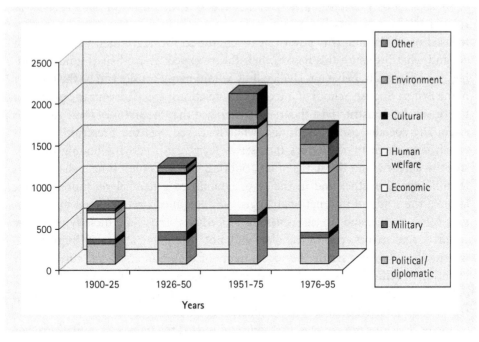

Fig. 11.1 Number of new multilateral treaties concluded

50,000 bilateral treaties (this latter figure may be even larger considering the greater tendency for bilateral agreements to be under-reported).[1]

That treaties have proliferated and that states have participated in the "legalization" of their mutual relations over the past century is not a controversial claim. What it means for the study and practice of international law and international relations, however, is hotly contested. One debate, which has proved sterile for social scientists but which has animated a philosophical discussion among legal scholars, is whether these agreements among states constitute "law" properly understood, and whether the set of such agreements can be characterized as an international "legal system." One pole in this debate has become associated with the position of John Austin, who held that enforcement was integral to the conception of law; without it, agreements were little more than expressions of intentions (2006). H. L. A. Hart (1961) wrote at length about what constitutes a "legal system" and expressed the idea that such systems were composed not only of primary rules (substantive proscriptions or prescriptions for behavior) but also secondary rules (rules about how substantive rules should be created, amended, terminated, adjudicated, and enforced). Few would claim that international law matches domestic legal systems by either of these criteria.

---

[1] These numbers were provided by the UN Office of Legal Affairs, Treaty Section.

Social scientists have been less concerned about whether we want to call these rules "law," "agreements," "conventions," or something else. They have been more focused on explaining why governments choose to formalize their agreements at all, and what influence this has on their future expectations, beliefs, understandings, and especially, behavior. Hedley Bull, whom many consider to be the founder of the British English School of international relations, as well as an early precursor to present day constructivist theorists, recognized that the status of these rules was essentially socially constructed, and what mattered was the prescriptive status attached to them by the actors themselves (1977, 136). Perhaps hoping to sidestep the debate about the status of law, political scientists for a time eschewed this terminology altogether and in the 1970s established a parallel yet more positive agenda: the study of international "regimes." "Regimes" were defined to encompass rules, norms, and decision-making procedures, and while these typically are codified agreements, regime scholars did not explicitly link their inquiries to international law per se. By the 1990s, many of these same scholars turned their attention specifically to the "legalization" of international relations, which they defined as the increasing precision, obligation, and delegation to be found in treaties and international custom (Goldstein et al. 2000).

Today, divisions remain over the value and indeed the scope of international law for the purposes of social scientific studies. Some scholars focus on treaties and other legal instruments explicitly; these scholars tend to be concerned about why actors demand formal arrangements (Abbott and Snidal 2000), why these agreements have particular provisions (Koremenos 2005), and the effect of making formal legal commitments on state behavior and other outcomes (Simmons 2000). Others are more concerned with the normative underpinnings of international relations, whether or not these are contained in hard law agreements (Finnemore and Toope 2001). Some, such as Jeffrey Legro (1997), purport to look at norms but look to the texts of treaties as authoritative evidence of the content of norms. Thus, the scope of study is quite broad, including the development and spread of norms, soft law, hard law, treaties, and international customary law. How we should think about these phenomena varies considerably depending on one's theoretical approach to international relations more generally.

2 Political Theories of International Law

International law as studied by political scientists is typically embedded in theories of international relations. There are two major questions that can help to organize the dominant theoretical orientations to international law. The first divide is over what motivates actors in international relations. Realism along with various rationalist approaches focus on the material incentives for certain behaviors. They look for the incentives states and other actors may (or may not) have to create rules and to comply with them. Traditional realists take a dim view of the ability of legal agreements fundamentally to alter the incentives states face in their mutual relationships with one another. Rationalists give more play to the equilibrium behavior rules can induce in the long run, and often see a positive role for enforcement via reciprocity. Quite different in orientation are constructivist approaches, which emphasize the social nature of international law, the extent to which it reflects normative expectations, and the persuasive rhetoric as well as identity politics that inform law creation and compliance.

A second divide is over the relevant actors on which our analyses should primarily focus. The study of international law is influenced by the state-centric focus of international relations generally. Liberal theories, however, place civil society at the center of the analysis. They understand international law's development and influence as flowing from the interaction of state and civil society (domestic and transnational).

These "divides" hardly do justice, of course, to the diversity and complexity of existing international law research. Many scholars are willing to acknowledge the relative usefulness of different approaches depending on the issue area under study. Some strive to integrate approaches, emphasizing the strategic uses of law for example, for normative purposes. Realist scholars of international relations tend to ignore international law in their analyses precisely because they see no compelling theoretical reason to do otherwise; as a consequence, realist studies of international law are few compared to the much wider array of studies with rationalist, constructivist, and liberal theoretical moorings. Nonetheless, realist theory deserves attention because it is typically the "null hypothesis" against which a variety of alternative approaches compare their insights. For this reason, in the following section, I first consider theories that reject an important role for international law in international affairs, and then consider the debate over how and why law does indeed matter to the study of international politics.

2.1 Realism

Realism's hostility to international law—both positive and prescriptive—is well known. The analytic focus here is on state power and state interests. International law reflects the power and the interests of the states that take part in its generation, but it does little to tame the use of power in the name of interests (prescriptively: nor should it). Realists do not have a fully elaborated explanation for the proliferation of legal agreements, presumably because there is no need to theorize phenomena that have no central bearing on the fundamental questions of world politics. Governments may appear to comply with such agreements, but only when law does not engage a national interest, or if it does, only if it is consistent with that interest. Compliance against the grain of interests is interpreted as the result of coercion on the part of more powerful states or other actors.

These views are well represented among academic realists (Mearsheimer 1994–5). The early post-World War II years saw a spate of extended critiques of international law in response to the legal idealism perceived to have pervaded the interwar years. The decentralized nature of the international legal system was typically presented as its prime defect. International agreements lacked restraining power, as Hans Morgenthau argued, since governments generally retain the right to interpret and apply the provisions of international agreements selectively. While Morgenthau was ready to admit that "during the four hundred years of its existence international law ha[d] in most instances been scrupulously observed" he thought that this could be attributed either to convergent interests or prevailing power relations (1985, 295). Governments make legal commitments cynically, and "are always anxious to shake off the restraining influence that international law might have upon their foreign policies, to use international law instead for the promotion of their national interests" (Morgenthau 1985).

Traditional realism split in two different directions by the 1970s. The British English School of international relations absorbed the centrality of power and interest into their account of international order, but began to acknowledge a place for "international society" and the role of shared social purposes among states, without which international law was unlikely to provide much stability (Bull 1977; Carr 1964). But just as intersubjectivity was becoming of growing analytical importance to one branch of thought, spare objective structuralism was becoming more central to another. Neorealism as advanced by Kenneth Waltz (1979) stripped the essential political structure down to the bare bones of power relationship among states, though efforts have since been made to restore norms to the relevant international "structure" (Kocs 1994). These views inform the present-day realist position that international law is inconsequential and epiphenomenal (Mearsheimer 1994–5) as well as a long-standing policy opposition to subjecting national interests to international legal constraints.[2]

Despite or perhaps because of their skepticism, realists have made an important contribution to the way scholars from other theoretical perspectives have come to study international law. Realist challenges for evidence that international law matters—and is not merely epiphenomenal to interests—have forced researchers to confront problems of endogeneity and selection bias in their empirical studies. "High compliance rates," George Downs and others have reminded researchers,

---

[2] George F. Kennan (1951, 127) and other "applied" realists made the normative case that this was the only way to properly formulate foreign policy.

should not be mistaken for important treaty effects, since most treaties just reflect the "easy" commitments governments were willing to implement, even in the treaty's absence (Downs et al. 1996). Jana von Stein writes that treaties primarily "screen," and that it is difficult to show that they also constrain (von Stein 2005); that is, treaty commitments may separate willing compliers from resistors, without much effect on either. Oona Hathaway argues that in the absence of enforcement, international law commitments are often cynical or at most symbolic (2002), which many have noted often results in a "radical decoupling" of principle and practice (Hafner-Burton and Tsutsui 2005). Jack Goldsmith and Eric Posner represent the mainstream realist view: international law compliance is largely explained by coercion or coincidence of interest (2005). Realist skepticism has made a genuine contribution to the improvement of empirical studies of law's effects, which I discuss below. But first it is important to acknowledge two theoretical counterthrusts to the realist's unremitting focus on power and unidimensionally defined interest.

2.2 Rational/Functionalist Theories

For reasons that are not quite clear—possibly the withering critique of realism, coupled with the doubts often expressed by legal scholars about the status of international rules—one of the most important theoretical developments in the political study of international law in the last quarter century eschewed the word "law" altogether. Instead, a cluster of scholars developed a research agenda on "international regimes:" rules, norms, and decision-making procedures, around which actors' expectations converge in a given issue area (Krasner 1983, 1). The most innovative theoretical contribution to the understanding of international regimes—which has since been taken up enthusiastically by some international legal scholars—was the idea that the "demand for international regimes" (Keohane 1983) could largely be theorized to result from a nonmyopic understanding of the need for rules in order to enjoy the fruits of cooperation over time.

Robert Keohane's functional theory of international regimes has had a profound impact on the study of international law and institutions (1984). The main contribution was to explain something the realists could not: why the world had become so extensively organized into cooperative structures, especially since World War II. Accepting the central realist tenet of rational egoism, Keohane theorized longer time horizons and denser transactions than realists were willing to assume, and his approach yielded a rational explanation for rules that generate joint gains by reducing uncertainty, minimizing transactions costs, creating focal points, and raising expectations of compliance. Keohane's approach has been the theoretical workhorse for decades of research into international economic law, especially the development of international trade, investment, and monetary agreements.

Functionalist theories akin to those pioneered by Robert Keohane dominate much current theorizing in international law. Despite their great variety, rationalist models of law and institutions owe a good deal to Keohane's insights about self-interested actors' motives to design laws and institutions that solve various kinds of collective action problems. Lisa Martin and others have exploited the distinction between collaboration problems and cooperation problems to explain the kinds of legal institutional features one might expect rational actors to design (Martin 1992). Ken Abbott and Duncan Snidal have used the concepts of transaction costs and negotiating costs to develop predictions of when soft law versus hard law instruments will be negotiated (2000), while Beth Simmons (2002) has appealed to the "opportunity costs of disputing" to explain governments' willingness to settle their territorial disputes using various forms of international judicial settlement. Even those who primarily expound on "the limits of international law" have used what has come to be known as "institutionalist theory" (essentially, functionalist logic to explain international institutions) to show that cooperation happens independently of law itself (Goldsmith and Posner 2005). Eric Posner (2003) has striven to develop a rationalist explanation for the laws of war that rests exclusively on states' mutual interest in limiting the efficiency of military technology, rather than a humanitarian interest in the populations these technologies devastate.

Rational functionalist theories have been applied in a sustained way to study why international institutions have the peculiar design provisions they do. Barbara Koremenos (2005) has analyzed the problem of uncertainty for the design of international legal agreements. Her model and data suggest that states rationally negotiate agreements of finite duration when they face higher degrees of uncertainty and to the degree that they are risk averse. An entire volume edited by Koremenos, Lipson, and Snidal (2004) is devoted to the "rational design of international institutions." The "rational design" approach can also be used to understand the demand for delegation to international organizations (created by law) to perform various functions that governments themselves would prefer not to perform (Abbott and Snidal 1998, 18).

While rationalist approaches to international law and institutions have spawned a fruitful research agenda, the functionalist logic underlying this approach has not been without serious criticism. The most sustained and intellectually coherent has come from constructivist perspectives, discussed below. The primary criticism of constructivists scholars is that rational approaches are not providing a sufficiently deep "explanation" for the formation of international law and institutions. The true explanations, they suggest, lie in the reasons states have for wishing to pursue certain outcomes in the first place; in the legitimacy of the actors involved in the negotiating process (taken for granted by rational functionalists); and in the social purposes these actors are collectively pursuing. The form legal arrangements will take, as a positive matter, will be highly influenced by these deeper and more subjective understandings (Wendt 1999).

Rational approaches to international law have recently drawn inspiration from theories of signaling[3] and reputation-building to help understand why governments choose to enter into more or less binding international agreements among themselves. One branch of theorizing assumes that formal agreements impose costs on actors that ultimately are useful in overcoming their cooperative dilemmas. Some scholars emphasize the *ex ante* costs that formalizing international agreements imposes on governments. Lisa Martin's research (2000) on the nature of international agreements in democratic countries is an example of this research stream. She shows that governments who face higher and more transparent ratification hurdles are ultimately more able to make credible commitments than are governments whose ratification hurdles are essentially pro forma and hence costless. This argument dovetails with Kurt Taylor Gaubatz's findings that democracies seem able to make more credible commitments (Gaubatz 1996). Similarly, when U.S. presidents choose between executive agreements and ratified treaties they select the mode of commitment that will most efficiently convey to other governments their intent to comply with the terms of the agreement. When strong assurances of an intent to comply are needed—in trade or security relationships, for example—Martin (2005) finds that governments turn to formal treaties rather than executive agreements. This is an example of how the decision to pay steep *ex ante* costs effectively separates those who intend to comply from those who may not. Only the former are expected to be willing to pay such costs in the first place.

Another related branch of recent rationalist theorizing involves the ways in which international law functions to increase a government's credibility *ex post*. That is, legal agreements can be designed to raise the costs of noncompliance, essentially by raising the "reputational stakes" in the event of noncompliance. Andrew Guzman for example argues that states rationally choose to make agreements that include "credibility enhancing" mechanisms—such as hard-law obligations, mandatory dispute settlement procedures, and monitoring capacity—into their international agreements to reduce the likelihood of noncompliance, but that these design elements must also be balanced against the net costs they impose on the contracting parties in the case of noncompliance (Guzman 2005). Guzman and many others have argued that international legal agreements have credibility-enhancing qualities, in comparison to other forms of commitment making that are less visible, less public, and less formal. According to Guzman, "by allowing states to establish clear rules and pledge their reputations, treaties cause the behavior of states to change" which he claims constitutes an "independent binding force" (Guzman 2002, 59; see also Lipson 1991). The idea that international legal commitments raise audience costs and engage reputational concerns inform a broad range of empirical

---

[3] While his work does not deal explicitly with international law, many of these theories regarding the notion of domestic audience costs draw intellectual inspiration from Fearon (1994).

studies, from the public international law of money (Simmons 2000) to foreign direct investments (Elkins et al. 2006) to the implementation of peace agreements (Fortna 2003).

Rational functional approaches have primarily tackled the theoretical puzzle of why international law exists at all; the answer is that law tends to solve cooperation problems that states would have difficulty solving in other ways. The form agreements take is assumed to be chosen rationally to address such goals in a relatively efficient way. But exactly why international law is a rational response to such dilemmas may well depend on the significance and meaning the major actors attach to law itself. These are the central issues taken up by constructivist thinkers, to which we now turn.

2.3 Constructivist Approaches

The other important perspective to come out of the early regimes literature was the application of social constructivist ideas to international law and institutions. John Ruggie's intersubjective approach to the rise, evolution, and change of international regimes opened up a more sociological and contextual, and less materialistic and strategic, possibility for theorizing international law and institutions (1982). Whereas Robert Keohane proceeded to reason as an economist might about the demand for international regimes, Ruggie proceeded in a more sociological mode: he sought an understanding of international agreements in the context of commonly held meanings of the actors (governments and states, in relationship with the goals of their societies). Along with Fritz Kratochwil, Ruggie was among the first political scientists to draw attention to the inherently sociological nature of the development of international regimes. An understanding of actors' purposes and intentions, they argued, is central to understanding the existence and operation of international institutions (Kratochwil and Ruggie 1986). This approach was in accordance with the emerging British School of International Relations, and would provide a good deal of inspiration to constructivist scholars of international law in the decades to come.

What did the constructivists see in analyzing international law to which the realists and rationalists were apparently blind? Much, according to a recent review by Christian Reus-Smit (2004). Every step in the creation of legal rules and norms must be understood as broadly political. Politics itself is an inherently social activity. It is largely about who will be accepted as a legitimate actor and what will pass as rightful conduct. Debates over who is a legitimate actor and the kinds of purposes that are socially acceptable frame the "rational" pursuit of interests. Thus, the central insight in this approach is that international law reflects and informs struggles over international legitimacy. Sovereignty itself is a construct to delimit who is a legitimate participant in the project of public international lawmaking (states). Rules and norms are crucial because they have become a key focal point for discursive struggles over legitimate political agency and action (internationally and domestically). Rules should therefore be viewed as critical resources in the international politics of legitimacy. As Reus-Smit has put it, "legal right is as much a power resource as guns and money, and juridical sovereignty, grounded in the legal norms of international society, is becoming a key determin-ant of state power" (2004, 2).

In contrast to realist theory, constructivists view international law not only as epiphenomenal of power, but also as reflection of social purpose. The development of international law and states' relationship to it is not conditioned as much by the material interests central to rational choice analyses, as by normative and ideational structures, which themselves change as states and other actors interact. Construc-tivists insist that international law and politics are mutually constitutive of one another: International law should not simply be thought of as a constraint on state behavior; it also defines the social and political system which gives rise to the further elaboration and legitimation of such rules (Sandholtz and Stone Sweet 2004). For some, international law is an ideology which is integral to the inter-national political system and helps stabilize the power relationships within that system (Arend 1999; Scott 1995).

International law, as a reflection of norms and social purpose, can have a profound effect on actors and outcomes according to most constructivists. But international law operates in a fundamentally different way in this theory than in most rationalist analyses. While many constructivists acknowledge the rational utilitarian ways in which actors use legal norms, their unique contribution is their understanding of law's persuasive normative influence (Checkel 2001). Inter-national rules are significant to the extent that they shape understandings of interests, perceptions of legitimate behavior, and the nature of the justificatory discourse in international affairs (Goodman and Jinks 2004). All of this occurs in a specific social context, in sharp contrast to the individual calculations on which rationalist theories focus.

2.4 Legal Commitments

The three theoretical approaches developed above provide differing explanations for why sovereign governments choose to limit their actions through international legal agreements. Realists tend to believe that these agreements are made cynically, with little expectation of compliance. Rational functionalist theories suggest states make commitments in order to realize joint future gains. Both of these approaches assume that the costs of committing are, in expectation, lower than the benefits to be gained. Constructivists believe governments ultimately commit because they become persuaded of the appropriateness of such actions. In the latter conception, the logic of appropriateness dominates the logic of consequences.

The most puzzling international treaty commitments for both realists and rational functionalists are those relating to human rights. These theories do not have the conceptual tools to explain why it is that sovereign states would agree to the monitoring of the treatment of their own citizens by the international community. Neither power nor joint gains through reciprocity persuasively address the phenomenon of the proliferation of human rights treaties and the near universal ratification in some cases (Simmons forthcoming). The "puzzling" ratification of such treaties has therefore dominated the recent empirical literature. Oona Hathaway believes the pattern of ratifications reflects low costs associated with doing so, and supports this point with evidence that democracies (no surprise) are much more likely to ratify the major treaties granting legal rights to individuals (Hathaway 2003; see also Landman 2005). Yet her theory—that many of the worst rights practitioners also ratify because they enjoy the symbolic benefits and the low risk of enforcement—has been taken to task as logically incoherent by Ryan Goodman and Derek Jinks (2003) who point out the implausibility that international audiences would be "fooled" in anything but the shortest run by insincere ratification. More plausible may be rational theories that embed treaty ratification in struggles within domestic polities for policy stability into the future. Andrew Moravscik, for example, has written persuasively that one reason governments make international legal commitments that include enforcement mechanisms is that they are concerned to lock in a particular legal rule as insurance against efforts of a future government to renege on human rights protections (Moravcsik 2000).

Ratification of human rights treaties has a very different explanation for constructivists. In their account, the "rights frame" has become central to the modern paradigm of what it means to be a legitimate nation state. Governments have become socialized to view ratification as the appropriate thing for them to do in the past few decades. Consequences do not figure in this explanation in any explicit way. Through their connections with the rest of the modern world polity—through international organizations, conferences, and increasingly dense contact with international civil society—governments become persuaded that the ratification of these agreements is an important part of their desired identity. Scholars working in this vein have shown empirically that the ratification of rights treaties is associated in time and across countries with the intensification of these socialization influences (Cole 2005; Wotipka and Ramirez forthcoming).

3 THE INFLUENCE OF INTERNATIONAL LAW: IMPLEMENTATION, COMPLIANCE, AND EFFECTIVENESS

For decades, realists dismissed international law as not very relevant to the conduct of international affairs. The patent inability of international law to avert or contain some of the most tragic events of the twentieth century relegated research in this area to a very low priority. Yet the puzzle of its very existence—why would governments spend so much effort in creating international rules if they were of no use?—has stimulated new theoretical and empirical research into whether and how international law influences outcomes of significance to governments and their people.

A growing literature from a multiplicity of theoretical perspectives has developed to explain the extent to which international law has had important consequences. Some of this literature considers the direct consequences of making legal commitments, while others consider the broader influences that the spread of legal norms has had on actors, whether governments have officially committed to those norms or not.

3.1 Implementation

One of the key influences on outcomes may be the ways in which international legal rules become enmeshed in domestic legal and political systems. One step in understanding international legal effects is to examine the extent of implementation in domestic law. "Implementation" is usually understood as the integration of international rules into domestic law and institutions. Some scholars (especially those who believe that international law works primarily through domestic politics and institutions) view implementation as crucial to eventual compliance (Victor et al. 1998).

Implementation is shaped by the nature and activities of domestic political and legal institutions. First, different legal systems absorb international legal obligations with varying levels of automaticity. Many civil law systems tend to be monist in conception; in these cases international law is much more likely to have direct domestic effect. Common law systems tend to be dualist in conception, and require the passage of explicit implementing legislation in order for international law to be enforceable in domestic courts (Harland 2000). Federations may find it more difficult to fully implement international legal agreements, if the subject matter they are designed to govern is the legislative purview of sub-national governments. This is a common theme of much research on the United

States's non-implementation of international human rights obligations, for example (Bradley and Goldsmith 2000). Judicial implementation is another possible mechanism. In this case, the judiciary can be influenced by foreign judicial interpretations that effectively import international legal interpretations into domestic law. Anne Marie Slaughter points to "transjudicial dialog" and Harold Koh to "transnational legal processes" as mechanisms through which international legal obligations are implemented in domestic law (Koh 1999; Slaughter 1995).

3.2 Compliance

"Compliance" refers to behavior that is or comes into relative conformity with prescribed or proscribed behavior (Young 1979).[4] In the context of international law, it usually refers to the behavior of governments or their official agents (we consider the broader effects involving other actors below). First-order compliance refers to compliance with the substantive provisions of a rule, while second-order compliance refers to actions in accordance with the ruling of an authoritative body charged with the interpretation or adjudication of a primary rule (the Dispute Settlement Body of the World Trade Organization, the International Criminal Court, the International Court of Justice, for example). Opportunities to observe second-order compliance are relatively rare, as very few disputes in international law are actually adjudicated. Nonetheless, many scholars (often not taking into account the biased nature of the sample they are examining) have concluded that second-order compliance is pretty high (Bulterman and Kuijer 1996).

Formal international mechanisms to enforce international law are notoriously weak. Certainly no legal system has foolproof law enforcement, but this is especially true of the multilateral system of law sovereign states have created among themselves. Outside of the European Union, authoritative supranational enforcement is nearly nonexistent. Where it does exist—for certain purposes, for example, in the Security Council of the United Nations—politics and collective action problems have often made enforcement late, inadequate, or lacking completely. International trade disputes may be adjudicated by the World Trade Organization's Dispute Settlement Body, but the WTO itself does not enforce its decisions. This is up to the aggrieved party, who is authorized to "retaliate" with trade sanctions equivalent to the harm done by the violator. While the U.S., Europe (which acts as a bloc), and Japan may be in a good position to "enforce" the law, smaller states are quite obviously not. The international human rights regime is perhaps the best example of formal enforcement mechanisms that are inherently—and probably intentionally—weak (Donnelly 1986). Self-reporting, volunteerism with respect to oversight, and the lack of follow up with respect to the findings of treaty oversight bodies are

---

[4] For a review of theories of compliance see Simmons (1998).

often cited as key weaknesses. This has led many scholars to conclude that unless international agreements are self-enforcing—represent an equilibrium from which no party has an incentive to defect—they are doomed to failure.

What conditions make compliance with international agreements more likely? One set of explanations relate to coercion and enforcement (Downs et al. 1996), usually by actors external to the state itself. Emilie Haffner-Burton (2005) for example finds that international human rights norms are more likely to be complied with when obligations are tied to concrete economic benefits, such as trade. A similar carrot and stick dynamic may be at work in the European Union's manipulation of material incentives to bring prospective trade partners into compliance with a number of international norms (Schimmelfennig et al. 2003). Material incentives, but especially technical and political *capacities* to comply, tend to be central in studies of environmental treaties (Weiss and Jacobson 1998).

Rational functionalist theories focus on the role of reputation and reciprocity in enhancing international law compliance. James Morrow (2002) argues that laws of war support reciprocity by specifying when reciprocal sanctions are appropriate and by delimiting the nature of acceptable responses. Beth Simmons (2002) finds that compliance with international arbitration awards over territory is much more likely when the government in power is the government who committed to arbitration, indicative of a concern to preserve a reputation to follow through on legal promises to be bound by the decisions of third parties. As a general proposition, however, reputation can hardly account for all international law compliance. Governments often want to cultivate multiple reputations—sometimes for law abidingness, sometimes for toughness—and it is not at all obvious that a reputation for the respect for law is fungible across issue areas or even across treaty partners (Downs and Jones 2002).

Some of the newest research on compliance focuses on the domestic political mechanisms the make it more likely. Three domestic mechanisms can be singled out, though the variations on these are many. One is the constraint on behavior posed by domestic audiences, who prefer compliance and have explicit constitutional mechanisms to hold their government to their legal commitments. Litigation referring to international law is one possible strategy (Tolley 1991) which is dependent on judicial independence and competence, as well as the relationship between international law and domestic law. Domestic groups may also make use of the information international oversight organs—created by treaty arrangement—to hold governments accountable through electoral mechanisms. Xinyuan Dai (2005), for example, has developed a game theoretical model in which information generated by even "weak" oversight mechanisms gives domestic electorates the leverage they need to hold leaders accountable for their environmental policies.

Contructivists link international law compliance with the development of inter-subjective meanings and normative expectations, notably norm coherence, legitimacy, and persuasion. Legal scholars have tended to view international law itself as providing the legitimacy necessary to sustain a "culture of compliance" (Franck 1990; Henkin 1995, 46). Many have recognized the process of international law-making as an essentially persuasive activity and view compliance as largely an issue of management and negotiation (Chayes and Chayes 1993). When confronted with the reality that various international norms are observed quite differentially, constructivists offer a range of explanations. Some argue that the quality of the norm itself matters. Margaret Keck and Kathryn Sikkink have argued that human rights norms that are the most universal in nature—those protecting innocent women and children—are the most widely held and have a special compliance pull (see also Hawkins 2004; Keck and Sikkink 1998). In his examination of arms control treaties during the interwar years, Jeffry Legro (1997) argues that qualities such as norm specificity, durability, and concordance improve prospects for compliance. Others argue that norms will be more or less influential depending on how they mesh with domestic norms and institutions (Checkel 2001; Cortell and Davis 1996). Whether because of their persuasive function or their information providing function (or both) constructivists often agree with rational theorists that pressures applied by (often transnational) civil society tend to bring governments into compliance with their international legal obligations, especially in issue areas in which official pressure is likely not to be forthcoming (Hafner-Burton and Tsutsui 2005). Like rationalists, constructivists recognize that "reputation" surely matters to governments and their constituencies, but reputational concerns themselves are hardly exogenously given constructs; they are the result of intense socialization among state elites within a particular region (Lutz and Sikkink 2000).

3.3 Effectiveness

Scholars of international law generally distinguish broader treaty effects from compliance (Raustiala and Slaughter 2002, 539). Sometimes international treaties do not achieve their goals, even if all actors are in substantial compliance. Oona Hathaway (2002) for example shows that, whether or not governments have complied with its specific provisions, the Convention on the Political Rights of Women has not been effective in increasing the representation of women in parliaments around the world. On the other hand, careful studies of international environmental agreements often reveal improvements in environmental impact, but ones that are far short of what would be collectively optimal (Helm and Sprinz 2000). On the one hand, international agreements, like all forms of law, can be weak, flawed, or just poorly designed to achieve specific ends, even when governments comply with the letter of the law. On the other hand, Paige Fortna (2003) has found that specific provisions of peace agreements—ones that help the parties make credible commitments, such as the creation of demilitarized zones, third-party guarantees, and dispute settlement—enhance a durable peace.

Research into the broader distributive effects of international legal agreements has begun to reveal interesting (if predictable) consequences. Relative to most domestic political systems, international relations remains the realm of power politics, and the distributive consequences of those power relations are visible in many areas governed by international rules. International trade is an example. As Richard Steinberg (2002) has noted, market share has traditionally granted the largest countries disproportionate influence in designing international trade law, despite the apparent mechanisms of "consensus" decision-making formally built into the General Agreement on Tariffs and Trade and the World Trade Organization. The consequence has been worldwide trade growth, but the benefits of liberalization have flowed disproportionately to the more highly developed industrialized countries (Subramanian and Wei 2003).

International law is subject to many of the problems of unanticipated (or undesired) consequences found in other regulated polities. Even if they "comply," actors sometimes substitute one undesirable behavior for the banned or regulated activity. One consequence of the Convention Against Torture, for example, has been for government agents to use horrific forms of physical and psychological coercion that do not involve permanent bodily harm (Ron 1997). International law can also be used simply to divert the form tragedy takes. The laws of war, for example, have been somewhat successful in reducing direct civilian targeting, but have legitimated the use of high tech methods to devastate human settlements more generally (Smith 2002). The effectiveness of prosecuting war crimes—for example in the new International Criminal Court—has stimulated hot debate over the wisdom of a "prosecutorial model" and the strategic behavior it could encourage to the detriment of more durable forms of peaceful reconciliation (Snyder and Vinjamuri 2003–4). Some studies have warned of the backlash to the overlegalization of issues ranging from human rights (Helfer 2002) to trade (Goldstein and Martin 2000).

4 Conclusions

Competing visions of the role of international law in international relations have given rise to a lively debate about how law orders relationships among states and other actors in the international setting. This is a setting that most analysts continue to believe is short on centralized authority to enforce international rules. Over the last few years, theories have developed about the ways in which international legal commitments influence cooperation by buttressing credible commitments among states as well as through the use of legal rhetoric to facilitate persuasion and legitimation.

The study of international law remains a small part of the study of international relations. Nonetheless, it is one of the fastest growing areas of international research. From its roots in the regimes literature, the theoretical work has developed in fruitful ways, both rationalist and constructivist. The former has been most useful in the areas of international economic relations, while the latter has had far more influence in research relating to international human rights law (Schmitz and Sikkink 2002). International law relating to peace and security and to environmental agreements tend to draw from both theoretical traditions.

The hallmark of international research in the past decade has been the turn to systematic empirical studies. Yet there remains a good deal of theoretical and empirical work to do to get the right concepts and measures for studying the relationship between international law and domestic and international politics. One of the central debates—as yet unresolved—is the relative importance of treaties as mechanisms that constrain behavior versus mechanisms that merely screen participants in the regime itself (von Stein 2005). While there is no theoretical reason to believe that treaties do not perform both of these functions (Simmons and Hopkins 2005), it is important to understand which mechanism contributes most to observed compliance with treaty commitments. Much more work needs to be done to understand the relationship between international law and domestic legal systems. Why for example is it more difficult—politically and institutionally—for international law to gain traction in some legal and political systems than in others? Another area in which good empirical work would be quite valuable is in the testing of various theories of domestic audience costs. Does international law really increase the reputational stakes with domestic audiences? Survey research might be useful in order to ascertain the plausibility of such a mechanism. Furthermore, relatively little work has been done to look at treaty commitments beyond ratification. Yet implementation is arguably one of the most important steps in the compliance process.

Finally, much more should be done to elucidate the distributive consequences of international legalization. Who has benefited and how from the greater legalization of multilateral trade and bilateral investment treaties, changing legal conceptions of the use of force (including humanitarian intervention), and the internationalization of environment regulation? Who has paid the costs? These remain important yet little studied aspects of the process of the legalization of international relations over the past half century.

REFERENCES

ABBOTT, K., and SNIDAL, D. 1998. Why states act through formal international organizations. *Journal of Conflict Resolution*, 42: 3–32.

—— —— (2000), Hard and soft law in international governance. *International Organization*, 54: 421–56.

AREND, A. C. 1999. *Legal Rules and International Society*. Oxford: Oxford University Press.

AUSTIN, J. 2006. *The Austinian Theory of Law: Being an Edition of Lectures I, V, and VI of Austin's "Jurisprudence", and of Austin's "Essay on the Uses of the Study of Jurisprudence,"* ed. G. T. Gale. London: Thomson Gale.

BRADLEY, C. A., and GOLDSMITH, J. L. 2000. Treaties, human rights, and conditional consent. *University of Pennsylvania Law Review*, 149: 399–469.

BULL, H. 1977. *The Anarchical Society: A Study of Order in World Politics*. New York: Columbia University Press.

BULTERMAN, M. K., and KUIJER, M. (eds.) 1996. *Compliance with Judgments of International Courts*. The Hague: Martinus Nijhoff.

CARR, E. H. 1964. *The Twenty Years' Crisis, 1919–1939: An Introduction to the Study of International Relations*. New York: Harper and Row.

CHAYES, A., and CHAYES, A. H. 1993. On compliance. *International Organization*, 47: 175–205.

CHECKEL, J. T. 2001. Why comply? Social learning and European identity change. *International Organization*, 55: 553–88.

COLE, W. M. 2005. Sovereignty relinquished? Explaining commitment to the International Human Rights Covenants, 1966–1999. *American Sociological Review*, 70: 472–96.

CORTELL, A. P., and DAVIS, J. W. J. 1996. How do international institutions matter? The domestic impact of international rules and norms. *International Studies Quarterly*, 40: 451–78.

DAI, X. 2005. Why comply? The domestic constituency mechanism. *International Organization*, 59: 363–98.

DONNELLY, J. 1986. International human rights: a regime analysis. *International Organization*, 40: 599–642.

DOWNS, G., ROCKE, D., and BARSOOM, P. 1996. Is the good news about compliance good news about cooperation? *International Organization*, 50: 379–406.

—— and JONES, M. A. 2002. Reputation, compliance, and international law. *Journal of Legal Studies*, 33: S95–114.

ELKINS, Z., GUZMAN, A., and SIMMONS, B. 2006. Competing for capital: the diffusion of bilateral investment treaties, 1960–2000. *International Organization*, 60: 811–46.

FEARON, J. D. 1994. Domestic political audiences and the escalation of international disputes. *American Political Science Review*, 88: 577–92.

FINNEMORE, M., and TOOPE, S. J. 2001. Alternatives to "legalization:" richer views of law and politics. *International Organization*, 55: 743–58.

FORTNA, V. P. 2003. Scraps of paper? Agreements and the durability of peace. *International Organization*, 57: 337–72.

FRANCK, T. M. 1990. *The Power of Legitimacy Among Nations*. New York: Oxford University Press.

GAUBATZ, K. T. 1996. Democratic states and commitments in international relations. *International Organization*, 50: 109–39.

GOLDSMITH, J. L., and POSNER, E. A. 2005. *The Limits of International Law.* New York: Oxford University Press.

GOLDSTEIN, J., KAHLER, M., KEOHANE, R. O., and SLAUGHTER, A.-M. 2000. Introduction: legalization and world politics. *International Organization*, 54: 385–99.

—— and MARTIN, L. L. 2000. Legalization, trade liberalization, and domestic politics: a cautionary note. *International Organization*, 54: 603–32.

GOODMAN, R., and JINKS, D. 2003. Measuring the effects of human rights treaties. *European Journal of International Law*, 13: 171–83.

—— —— 2004. How to influence states: socialization and international human rights law. *Duke Law Journal*, 54: 621–701.

GUZMAN, A. 2005, The design of international agreements. *European Journal of International Law*, 16: 579–612.

—— 2002. International law: a compliance based theory. *California Law Review*, 90: 1823–88.

HAFNER-BURTON, E. M. 2005. Trading human rights: how preferential trade agreements influence government repression. *International Organization*, 59: 593–629.

—— and TSUTSUI, K. 2005. Human rights in a globalizing world: the paradox of empty promises. *American Journal of Sociology*, 110: 1373–411.

HARLAND, C. 2000. The status of the International Covenant on Civil and Political Rights (ICCPR) in the domestic law of state parties: an initial global survey through UN Human Rights Committee documents. *Human Rights Quarterly*, 22: 187–260.

HART, H. L. A. 1961. *The Concept of Law.* New York: Oxford University Press.

HATHAWAY, O. 2002. Do human rights treaties make a difference? *Yale Law Journal*, 111: 101–99.

—— 2003. The cost of commitment. *Stanford Law Review*, 55: 1821–62.

HAWKINS, D. 2004. Explaining costly international institutions: persuasion and enforceable human rights norms. *International Studies Quarterly*, 48: 779–804.

HELFER, L. R. 2002. Overlegalizing human rights: international relations theory and the commonwealth Caribbean backlash against human rights regimes. *Columbia Law Review*, 102: 1832–911.

HELM, C., and SPRINZ, D. 2000. Measuring the effectiveness of international environmental regimes. *Journal of Conflict Resolution*, 44: 630–52.

HENKIN, L. 1995. *International Law: Politics and Values.* Dordrecht: Martinus Nijhoff.

KECK, M. E., and SIKKINK, K. 1998. *Activists Beyond Borders: Advocacy Networks in International Politics.* Ithaca, NY: Cornell University Press.

KENNAN, G. F. 1951. *American Diplomacy, 1900–1950.* New York: New American Library.

KEOHANE, R. O. 1983. The demand for international regimes. Pp. 141–72 in *International Regimes*, ed. S. D. Krasner. Ithaca, NY: Cornell University Press.

—— 1984. *After Hegemony: Cooperation and Discord in the World Political Economy.* Princeton, NJ: Princeton University Press.

KOCS, S. A. 1994. Explaining the strategic behavior of states: international law as system structure. *International Studies Quarterly*, 38: 535–57.

KOH, H. H. 1999. How is international human rights law enforced? *Indiana Law Journal*, 74: 1397–417.

KOREMENOS, B. 2005. Contracting around uncertainty. *American Political Science Review*, 99: 549–65.

KOREMENOS, B., LIPSON, C., and SNIDAL, D. (eds.) 2004. *The Rational Design of International Institutions.* Cambridge: Cambridge University Press.

KRASNER, S. D. 1983. Structural causes and regime consequences: regimes as intervening variables. Pp. 1–21 in *International Regimes*, ed. S. D. Krasner. Ithaca, NY: Cornell University Press.

KRATOCHWIL, F., and RUGGIE, J. G. 1986. International organization: a state of the art on an art of the state. *International Organization*, 40: 753–75.

LANDMAN, T. 2005. *Protecting Human Rights: A Comparative Study.* Washington, DC: Georgetown University Press.

LEGRO, J. W. 1997. Which norms matter? Revisiting the "failure" of internationalism. *International Organization*, 51: 31–63.

LIPSON, C. 1991. Why are some international agreements informal? *International Organization*, 45: 495–538.

LUTZ, E. L., and SIKKINK, K. 2000. International human rights law and practice in Latin America. *International Organization*, 54: 633–59.

MARTIN, L. L. 1992. *Coercive Cooperation: Explaining Multilateral Economic Sanctions.* Princeton, NJ: Princeton University Press.

—— 2000. *Democratic Commitments: Legislatures and International Cooperation.* Princeton, NJ: Princeton University Press.

—— 2005. The president and international commitments: treaties as signaling devices. *Presidential Studies Quarterly*, 35: 440–65.

MEARSHEIMER, J. 1994–5. The false promise of international institutions. *International Security*, 19: 5–26.

MORAVCSIK, A. 2000. The origins of human rights regimes: democratic delegation in postwar Europe. *International Organization*, 54: 217–52.

MORGENTHAU, H. 1985. *Politics Among Nations: The Struggle for Power and Peace*, 6th edn. New York: Alfred Knopf.

MORROW, J. D. 2002. The laws of war, common conjectures, and legal systems in international politics. *Journal of Legal Studies*, 33: S41–60.

POSNER, E. A. 2003. A theory of the laws of war. *University of Chicago Law Review*, 70: 297–317.

RAUSTIALA, K., and SLAUGHTER, A.-M. 2002. International law, international relations, and compliance. Pp. 538–58 in *Handbook of International Relations*, ed. W. Carlsnaes, T. Risse, and B. A. Simmons. London: Sage.

REUS-SMIT, C. 2004. The politics of international law. Pp. 14–44 in *The Politics of International Law*, ed. C. Reus-Smit. New York: Cambridge University Press.

RON, J. 1997. Varying methods of state violence. *International Organization*, 51: 275–300.

RUGGIE, J. G. 1982. International regimes, transactions, and change: embedded liberalism in the postwar economic order. *International Organization*, 36: 379–415.

SANDHOLTZ, W., and STONE SWEET, A. 2004. Law, politics, and international governance. Pp. 238–71 in *The Politics of International Law*, ed. C. Reus-Smit. New York: Cambridge University Press

SCHIMMELFENNIG, F., ENGERT, S., and KNOBEL, H. 2003. Costs, commitment and compliance: the impact of EU democratic conditionality on Latvia, Slovakia and Turkey. *Journal of Common Market Studies*, 41: 495–518.

SCHMITZ, H. P., and SIKKINK, K. 2002. International human rights. Pp. 517–37 in *Handbook of International Relations*, ed. W. Carlsnaes, T. Risse, and B. A. Simmons. New York: Sage.

SCOTT, S. V. 1995. Explaining compliance with international law: broadening the agenda for enquiry. *Australian Journal of Political Science*, 30: 288–99.

SIMMONS, B. A. 1998. Compliance with international agreements. *Annual Review of Political Science*, 1: 75–93.

—— 2000. International law and state behavior: commitment and compliance in international monetary affairs. *American Political Science Review*, 94: 819–35.

—— 2002. Capacity, commitment, and compliance: international institutions and territorial disputes. *Journal of Conflict Resolution*, 46: 829–56.

—— forthcoming. *International Human Rights: Law, Politics, and Accountability.*

—— and HOPKINS, D. J. 2005. The constraining power of international treaties: theory and methods. *American Political Science Review*, 99: 623–31.

SLAUGHTER, A.-M. 1995. A typology of transjudicial communication. *University of Richmond Law Review*, 29: 99–138.

SMITH, T. W. 2002. The new law of war: legitimizing hi-tech and infrastructural violence. *International Studies Quarterly*, 46: 355–74.

SNYDER, J. L., and VINJAMURI, L. 2003–04. Trials and errors: principle and pragmatism in strategies of international justice. *International Security*, 28: 5–44.

STEINBERG, R. H. 2002. In the shadow of law or power? Consensus-based bargaining and outcomes in the GATT/WTO. *International Organization*, 56: 339–74.

—— and ZASLOFF, J. M. 2006. Power and international law. *American Journal of International Law*, 100: 64–87.

SUBRAMANIAN, A., and WEI, S.-J. The WTO promotes trade, strongly but unevenly. NBER Working Paper 10024.

TOLLEY, H. 1991. Interest group litigation to enforce human rights. *Political Science Quarterly*, 105: 617–38.

VICTOR, D. G., RAUSTIALA, K., and SKOLNIKOFF, E. B. 1998. *The Implementation and Effectiveness of International Environmental Commitments: Theory and Practice.* Laxenburg: International Institute for Applied Systems Analysis.

VON STEIN, J. 2005. Do treaties constrain or screen? Selection bias and treaty compliance. *American Political Science Review*, 99: 611–22.

WALTZ, K. N. 1979. *Theory of International Politics.* Reading, Mass.: Addison-Wesley.

WEISS, E. B., and JACOBSON, H. K. (eds.) 1998. *Engaging Countries: Strengthening Compliance with International Accords.* Cambridge, Mass.: MIT Press.

WENDT, A. 1999. *Social Theory of International Politics.* Cambridge: Cambridge University Press.

WOTIPKA, C. M., and RAMIREZ, F. O. 2008. World society and human rights: an events history analysis of the Convention on the Elimination of All Forms of Discrimination Against Women. In *The Global Diffusion of Markets and Democracy*, ed. B. A. Simmons, F. Dobbin, and G. Garrett. Cambridge: Cambridge University Press.

YOUNG, O. 1979. *Compliance with Public Authority.* Baltimore: Johns Hopkins University Press.

CHAPTER 12

THE EUROPEAN COURT AND LEGAL INTEGRATION: AN EXCEPTIONAL STORY OR HARBINGER OF THE FUTURE?

KAREN J. ALTER

1 INTRODUCTION

ESTABLISHED as part of the European Coal and Steel Community in 1950, and later adapted as part of the 1957 Treaty of Rome, three design features distinguished the European Court of Justice (ECJ) from international courts of the time. First, member countries could be compelled to participate in proceedings (in the parlance of international law, the ECJ had "compulsory jurisdiction"). Second, the ECJ's "preliminary ruling mechanism" provided a means for private actors to access the ECJ via national court references. Third, there was process whereby a supranational actor (the Commission) could raise noncompliance charges against states. There were reasons for these design features, but neither the Treaty negotiators, the governments who signed the Treaties founding the European Communities, nor European Community officials anticipated how legally, politically, or institutionally transformative these design features would be.

The most important feature proved to be the "preliminary ruling mechanism." This mechanism was intended to provide national courts with technical support in interpreting complex European law. In practice, preliminary ruling references provided a means for the ECJ to insert itself into national debates regarding the relationship of European law to national law, and to harness national courts as enforcers of ECJ decisions. The "Transformation of the Europe" began in 1962 when a Dutch Tariff Commission sent a preliminary ruling reference to the ECJ, asking if the article of the Treaty of Rome in question could be seen as self-executing. Whether or not treaty provisions are self-executing is a question of domestic law, not European law, and the governing Dutch law implied that the particular provision in question was not self-executing (Claes and De Witte 1998, 172–8). The Dutch government argued that the reference should be rejected as inadmissible, because it concerned a question of domestic law. The ECJ disagreed, issuing a provocative ruling that turned traditional legal reasoning on its head. Whereas in the past a direct internal effect of treaty provisions was an exception that had to be shown to be implicitly intended (Donner 1968, 72), the ECJ argued that provisions reasonably capable of having direct internal effects should be presumed to have it. Its *Van Gend en Loos* ruling made the case as follows:

The objective of the EEC Treaty, which is to establish a Common Market, the function of which is of direct concern to interested parties in the Community, implies that this Treaty is more than an agreement which merely creates mutual obligations between the contracting states. . . . the Community constitutes a new legal order of international law for the benefit of which the states have limited their sovereign rights, albeit within limited fields, and the subject of which comprise not only Member States, but also their nationals . . . Independent of the legislation of Member States, Community law therefore not only imposes obligations on individuals but is also intended to confer upon them rights which become part of their legal heritage. These rights arise not only where they are expressly granted by the Treaty, but also by reason of obligations which the Treaty imposes in a clearly defined way upon individuals as well as upon Member States and upon the institutions of the Community.   (*Van Gend en Loos v. Nederlandse Administratie Belastingen*)

Two years later, an Italian citizen challenged his $3 electricity bill because, he claimed, the Italian electricity company ENEL had been nationalized in contravention of the Treaty of Rome. The small claims court sent its reference simultaneously to the ECJ and the Italian Constitutional Court. The Italian Court ruled first, finding the reference invalid. The ECJ accepted the case anyway, issuing a ruling that challenged the Italian doctrine that the "last law passed" takes precedence. The ECJ asserted that:

By contrast with ordinary international treaties, the EEC Treaty has created its own legal system which, on entry into force of the Treaty, became an integral part of the legal systems of the Member States and which their courts are bound to apply. By creating a Community of unlimited duration, having its own institutions, its own personality, its own legal capacity and capacity of representation on the international plane and, more particularly, real powers stemming from the limitation of sovereignty or a transfer of powers from the States to the Community, the Member States have limited their sovereign rights, albeit within limited fields, and have thus created a body of law which binds both their nationals and themselves.

...It follows from all these observations that the law stemming from the Treaty, an independent source of law, could not, because of its special and original nature, be overridden by domestic legal provisions, however framed, without being deprived of its character as Community law and without the legal basis of the Community itself being called into question.   (*Costa v. ENEL*)

These early rulings were remarkable in their audacity, but if one looked at the full picture of ECJ authority in the 1960s, this is what it would have looked like. On paper, there was an ECJ with unusual jurisdiction and authority. But states fully controlled the process of making European law, and were quite capable of stopping integration where they did not want it. While the ECJ had asserted the direct effect and supremacy of European law, the rulings themselves were of little practical import. The ECJ avoided substantive rulings that would upset states, meanwhile in the 1960s the Italian Constitutional Court and the French *Conseil d'État* had both rejected the ECJ's doctrinal assertions.

These ECJ rulings, however, worked their way into national doctrines regarding the relationship of European law to national law (Alter 2001), and the ECJ became more willing to make substantive rulings affecting important state interests. The ECJ's 1979 *Cassis de Dijon* ruling declared that member states must recognize as valid one another's product standards. In 1987 the ECJ struck down Germany's historic Beer Purity Law as an impediment to trade (*Commission v. Germany*). Three years later the ECJ forced the Conservative government of Margaret Thatcher to equalize its retirement age for men and women (*Barber v. Guardian Royal Exchange Group*). In 1991 the ECJ ruled that Ireland could not stop the advertisement of British Abortion Clinics' services (*SPUC Grogan*). In 2000 the ECJ found that provisions of the German Basic Law limiting the types of roles women could fulfill in the military contradicted European rules regarding gender equality (*Tanja Kreil v. Bundesrepublik*). Each of these rulings triggered fundamental shifts in national policies that would not have otherwise occurred.

This transformation of the European legal system is the stuff of fairytales. Off in the Grand Duchy of Luxembourg, supranational judges teamed up with lawyers in contrived cases to turn an international convention into a constitution for a new supranational polity. They did this in contradiction to the will of member states, whose leaders were in the 1960s busy making deals designed to put a halt to the process of European integration (Weiler 1991, 2424–31). They did this in a political context in which only a handful of European courts—national or supranational—even had authority to undertake judicial review of government policy (Stone 1990).

The question for this chapter is: How do we understand the ECJ's role in European integration? Section 2 summarizes a vast scholarship regarding the role of the ECJ in European integration. Section 3 locates the ECJ's remarkable experience in the larger context of international courts and international law.

2 SCHOLARSHIP ON THE ECJ AND EUROPEAN INTEGRATION

The literature on the ECJ puts forward three different narratives about its role in European integration. Legalist scholarship puts the ECJ at the center of their narrative, portraying the ECJ as a heroic actor capable of pushing European governments and institutions in the direction of greater European integration. International relations scholars assume that states are at the center of international relations in the EU, thus they examine the ECJ as a tool of states to accomplish their objectives. Comparative politics approaches focus on the relationship between the ECJ and actors above and below the state that use the European legal system to promote their own objectives. There is an element of truth in all three narratives, though today the comparative politics approach is the most widely shared of the narratives.

2.1 The Legalist Narrative: The ECJ as the Hero Driving European Integration

Legalist accounts are correct in that the European legal system was transformed by a relatively small group of judges and lawyers. But legalist accounts of the 1960s and 1970s were disembodied from the actors involved, using a positivist logic that supported a myth that the ECJ was merely using legal interpretation to work out the details agreed in the Treaty of Rome. Asked to comment on a typical legalist analysis of the period, Martin Shapiro characterized the scholarship this way:

Professor Barav's Article is a careful and systematic exposition of the judicial review provision of the "constitution" of the European Economic Community, an exposition that is helpful for a newcomer to these materials. But it represents a stage of constitutional scholarship out of which American constitutional law must have passed about seventy years ago (although remnants of it are still to be found). It is constitutional law without politics. Professor Barav presents the Community as a juristic idea; the written constitution (the treaty) as a sacred text; the professional commentary as a legal truth; the case law as the inevitable working out of the correct implications of the constitutional text; and the constitutional court (the ECJ) as the disembodied voice of right reason and constitutional teleology.... we must bear in mind that particularly in the European tradition, professional writing is simultaneously an act of scholarship and an act of law-making—that is to say an act of politics. In this light there is much to be said for Professor Barav's unspoken, but none the less emphatic, assertion of the autonomy of law and the teleological inevitability of the Community's legal system... To treat the law as autonomous is to accentuate the positive; that sort of accentuation is important to institutional building.   (Shapiro 1980)

Today we know that there was a social movement backing the ECJ in its efforts (Madsen and Vauchez 2005; Saeriste and Vauchez 2007; Alter 2007). The transformation of Europe began when Robert Lecourt was essentially exiled to the Duchy of Luxembourg because French president Charles De Gaulle did not want him in Paris. Ensconced in the irrelevant ECJ, Lecourt penned the *Van Gend en Loos* and *Costa v. ENEL* rulings described above, in an intentional strategy to promote integration through law.[1] Lecourt was joined in his mission by Pierre Pescatore[2] and Federico Mancini, a firm Euro-federalist, who also penned legal rulings, wrote articles, gave speeches, and told tales of Champagne brunches wherein national judges were convinced of the endeavor of constructing Europe through law.[3] The work of these judges, and the promulgation of "heroic" narrative, was facilitated by national associations of academics and practitioners. Each

[1] An ECJ Judge from 1962 to 1976, Lecourt published articles explaining how he saw the role of judges in promoting integration through law. See: Le rôle du droit dans l'unification européenne, *Gazette du Palais* (1964), 49–54; La dynamique judiciaire dans l'édification de l'Europe, *France Forum*, 64 (May 1965), 20–2. *L'Europe des Juges*, Brussels: Établissements Émile Bruylant (1976); Le rôle de la Cour de Justice dans le développement des Communautés, *European Yearbook*, 24 (1976), 19–41; Quel eut été le droit des communautés sans les arrêts de 1963 et 1964? In *Mélanges en Hommage à Jean Boulouis: L'Europe et le Droit*, Paris: Edition Dalloz (1991).

[2] As Luxembourg's appointee to the ECJ, Pescatore served on the ECJ from 1967 to 1985. In addition to legal rulings, Pescatore wrote articles and books addressing issues of concern within national legal systems. A small sample of his writing includes: Die Menschenrechte und die europäische Integration, *Integration* (1969), 103–36; L'attitude des juridictions nationales à l'égard du problème des effets direct du droit communautaire, *Revue trimestrielle de droit européen*, 2 (1970), 296–302; Aspects of the court of justice of the European communities of interest from the point of view of international law, *Zeitschrift für Ausländisches Öffentliches Recht und Völkerrecht*, 32 (1972), 239–52; Community law and the national judge, *Law Guardian* (January 1973); L'executif communautaire: justification du quadripartisme institué par les traités de Paris et de Rome, *Cahiers de droit européen*, 4 (1978), 387–406; The doctrine of "direct effect:" an infant disease of community law, *European Law Review*, 8 (3) (1983), 155–77.

[3] F. Mancini was appointed as an Avocat General in 1982, and was a judge from Italy from 1988 to 1999. His writings include: Politics and the judges—the European perspective, *Modern Law Review*, 43 (1) (1979), 1–17; The incorporation of community law into the domestic laws of the member states of the European Communities presented at the International Uniform Law in Practice, Rome September 7–10, 1987; The making of a constitution for Europe, *Common Market Law Review*, 24 (1989), 595–614. With D. Keeling: From cilfit to erta: the constitutional challenge facing the European Court, *Yearbook of European Law*, 11 (1992), 1–13; and Democracy and the European Court of Justice, *Modern Law Review*, 57 (2) (1994), 175–90.

country had its own association, and collectively associations came together as part of the umbrella Fédération de Droit Européen (FIDE). As lawyers and judges, FIDE members helped create cases that the ECJ could rule on. They debated legal ideas with ECJ judges and Legal Service advisers. They founded legal journals dedicated to European law, wrote articles in national journals to inform national legal communities about European law, wrote critical analyses of national court rulings that challenged ECJ doctrine, and even engaged in private diplomacy with skeptical national judges.

In the 1960s and 1970s, just about the only scholarship regarding European law was legal positivist in nature. A less involved group of scholars, coming from countries that were not part of the original European integration project, began writing about European legal integration in the 1980s (Stein 1981; Rasmussen 1986; Weiler 1981). While one can still find "law without politics" accounts of ECJ jurisprudence in contemporary scholarship, the legal debate has mostly moved beyond legalist accounts. For example, Renaud Dehousse's (1998) analysis of the European Court and legal integration takes as given that the ECJ is a strategic political actor, and that political forces shape legal integration. It is also now widely accepted that ECJ rulings take political mediation before they become a reality, that not all ECJ rulings do become instigators of change, and that it is not the quality of the rulings or the boldness of the ECJ that determines which rulings become instigators of change and which do not. To the extent that scholars continue to put the ECJ in the center of their narrative, "sophisticated legalists" examine how the ECJ uses its office as part of a political and legal strategy to build the foundations of its own political authority (Burley and Mattli 1993; Helfer and Slaughter 1997; Slaughter 2000).

2.2 International Relations Narrative: The ECJ as States' Agent

Probably because the scholarship on the ECJ was so heavily tilted towards the heroic apolitical legalist narrative of the ECJ, a counter narrative was championed by political scientists. Geoffrey Garrett and Barry Weingast adopted the ontology of principal–agent theory, asserting that ECJ, like all courts, was an "agent" of the actors that delegated authority to it. If courts were simply agents of their "principal" masters, the challenge was merely to define the hidden "tools" states were using as their levers of control. Garrett and Weingast's analysis amounted to an assertion:

Courts whose rulings are consistently overturned typically find themselves and their role in the political system weakened. As a consequence, the actions of the courts are fundamentally "political" in that they must anticipate the possible reactions of other political actors in order to avoid their intervention...Embedding a legal system in a broader political structure places direct constraints on the discretion of a court, even one with as much constitutional independence as the United States Supreme Court. This conclusion holds even if the constitution makes no explicit provisions for altering a court's role. The reason is that political actors have a range of avenues through which they may alter or limit the role of courts. Sometimes such changes require amendment of the constitution, but usually the appropriate alterations may be accomplished more directly through statue, as by alteration of the court's jurisdiction in a way that makes it clear that continued undesired behavior will result in more radical changes.... the possibility of such a reaction drives a court that wishes to preserve its independence and legitimacy to remain in the area of acceptable latitude.   (Garrett and Weingast 1993, 200–7)

Garrett originally believed that the ECJ based its decisions on the interests of the most powerful states (Garrett 1995). In subsequent writings, he distanced himself from his most strident claims, recognizing that ECJ doctrine can provide an element of political autonomy as do institutional rules that make reversing ECJ decisions difficult (Garrett, Kelemen, and Schulz 1998). The tradition of applying principal–agent theory is still alive in international relations scholarship, but now the focus is more on the determinants and limits of state control over agent decision-making (Tsebelis and Garrett 2001; Hawkins et al. 2006).

Garrett and Weingast's assertion of state control spawned an extensive effort to examine the extent to which state preferences shape the ECJ's docket and its decision-making. Bernadette Kilroy set out to test the principal–agent expectation that the ECJ responded to sanctioning threats, coding ECJ decisions to see if they were biased in favor of the more powerful states (Kilroy 1999; 1995). Kilroy herself found that the ECJ responded more to the threat of noncompliance than the threat that states might sanction the ECJ. Considering Kilroy's analysis, Mark Pollack finds that despite her efforts Kilroy cannot rule out other explanations of ECJ decision-making—such as the argument that the ECJ decides the case purely on the basis of law, without varying its rulings according to the power or intransigence of member states, or the likelihood of state compliance (Pollack 2003, 200).

Pollack investigated Garrett, Kelemen, and Shultz's claim that the *Barber Protocol* forced the ECJ to retreat from activism (Garrett, Kelemen, and Schulz 1998). The *Barber Protocol* was inserted into the 1993 Maastrict Treaty with the intent of limiting the impact of the ECJ's *Barber v. Guardian Group* ruling equalizing pension policies for men and women. While not a legislative reversal of the Barber ruling, the protocol was seen as a political rebuke of the ECJ because political bodies were acting before the ECJ had a chance to itself address the issue of retrospective effects, and because it emerged at the same time that efforts to sanction the ECJ were under way (Tallberg 2003, 118–22). Reviewing the ECJ's pre- and post-*Barber* rulings regarding gender equality, Pollack finds "only partial support for Garrett, Kelemen and Schultz's claim that the Court has "retreated" following the Barber protocol... Indeed one might argue that the Court's post-Barber jurisprudence, rather than constituting a generalized retreat, represents a return to the pre-Barber pattern in which the Court generally, but not always, opts for a broad interpretation of Article 141, most often over the objections of one or more . . . member governments." Pollack suggests that the political factor shaping ECJ decision-making is a concern for noncompliance, but he also acknowledges that it is equally plausible that legal factors and not concerns about noncompliance shape ECJ decisions (Pollack 2003, 200).

Derek Beach also finds limited support for Garrett, Kelemen, and Schultz's hypotheses that variations in the legal clarity of European law, variation in the potential cost of adverse rulings, or institutional barriers explain variation in ECJ decision-making. Where Pollack suggests that compliance concerns provide a tool of state influence, Beach argues that the ECJ mainly is responding to concerns voiced by national courts—which are the ECJ's crucial constituency (Beach 2001).

Jonas Tallberg examines the mixed messages states convey to the ECJ, noting that at the same time states were complaining about ECJ activism, they were also giving it more power. Tallberg argues that states want to stop ECJ decisions they do not like, but they also want the European legal system to help enforce compliance with EU law. Like Pollack, Tallberg finds that principal–agent factors can account for the Commission's lesser autonomy compared to the ECJ. Tallberg argues that principal–agent factors also explain why the Commission and ECJ are best able to impart their vision at the interpretive stage compared to the legislative stage. While Tallberg believes that principal–agent analysis is useful and insightful, he admits up front that it doesn't explain ECJ decision-making (Tallberg 2003, 12).

At this point, all that is left of the Garrett–Weingast state control thesis is that concerns about noncompliance with ECJ decisions may shape ECJ decision-making. Tanja Börzel finds the problem of noncompliance is overstated—compliance with EU law is generally high. Her findings based on reviewing Commission enforcement of European law, combined with quantitative studies of national court reference rates, suggest that the Commission is not skewing its investigations based on the power of the state, and that there is little relationship between the overall level of compliance and whether a country undertakes to sanction the ECJ for activism (Börzel 2001; Stone Sweet and Brunell 1998).[4]

Despite a lack of empirical support, Garrett and Weingast's arguments about states influencing the ECJ remain widely cited to support the claim that principal–agent theory is explaining ECJ decision-making. Elsewhere I have examined more systematically why the tools of political control are not as influential as Garrett and Weingast expected them to be (Alter 1998; 2006a; 2008a).

---

[4] Britain spearheaded the efforts to sanction the ECJ (Tallberg 2003). France and Germany at different times supported efforts to sanction the ECJ. These efforts are discussed in Alter (2001).

2.3 Comparative Politics Narrative: The ECJ as an Interlocutor

The hardest forms of the "heroic ECJ" and "agent-ECJ" have been repudiated. There is now a convergence around the view that both legal and political considerations influence ECJ jurisprudence, and that the European legal system provides a legal mechanism that other actors—private litigants, national courts, or EU institutions—can use to promote their policy objectives (Weiler 1994). In some respects, this convergence represents the maturation of European law scholarship. It is no longer necessary to construct myths that justify the ECJ's authority. Meanwhile, since the ECJ now has a lot in common with other constitutional courts, it makes sense to examine the ECJ's role as one examines that of other constitutional courts.

If the ECJ is mainly an interlocutor for the efforts of other actors, then the actions or nonactions of potential litigants and those actors who channel cases to the ECJ will shape where the ECJ expands European law and influences national policies. There are four distinct steps involved in the ECJ influencing European politics. First, since the ECJ only rules in concrete cases, some actor must first raise a complaint before the ECJ can insert itself into the political process. Because cases raised in national courts or brought to the attention of the Commission are not necessarily referred to the ECJ, the second step is to understand which cases get referred to the ECJ for resolution. Third, one must understand when the ECJ is willing to provoke a political response through its rulings, and when it refrains from interjecting itself in areas where the law is not fully clear. Fourth, we must understand when and how other actors "follow through" on legal victories, creating pressure on political bodies to respect ECJ jurisprudence (Alter 2000).

The "hero-ECJ" and "agent-ECJ" narratives only focused on step three, implicitly suggesting that the key to legal expansion is how the ECJ rules in cases. The "intelocutor-ECJ" narrative tells you that steps one, two, and four are equally if not more important in understanding the ECJ's role in legal integration. There is extensive scholarship on each of these questions. I have previously discussed most of this scholarship (Alter 2000), and the factors influencing ECJ decision-making above. Here I will focus only on more recent scholarly developments regarding the first, second, and fourth links in the litigation chain.

Step 1: Raising a case involving European Law. With respect to domestic mobilization around European litigation strategies, Carol Harlow, Joseph Jupille, and James Caparoso argued that a "goodness of fit" between the opportunities offered by European law and the interests of substate actors explained when private litigants embrace European litigation strategies (Harlow 1992*a*; 1992*b*; Harlow and Rawlings 1992; Caporaso and Jupille 2001). Critics of this view have observed that "goodness of fit" was both ill defined and not enough to explain variation in when substate actors invoked European law. Lisa Conant argued that many actors who might benefit from the European legal system never raise a case; there need to be big payoffs for fairly well-resourced actors before a litigation strategy emerges (Conant 2002). Conant also observed that in some countries actors litigate more as a tool of policy promotion compared to other countries, thus cultural differences could influence whether or not judges would be likely to refer a case to the ECJ and whether actors mobilize around European law (Conant 2001). More recently Nicole Richardt has found that the political strategies of actors on the ground are shaped by domestic political structures. In some countries, actors pursue gender equality through soft law European tools, which by definition do not create justiciable rights within the European legal system. Even where justiciable rights exist, equality promoting actors may not invoke them as tools to influence policy. In other contexts, domestic actors prefer hard European law that can become a wedge they can use in courts to promote their objectives (Richardt 2006).

Step 2: Referring a case to the ECJ: The scholarship regarding which cases national courts refer to the ECJ has developed in two ways. There are a number studies that employ quantitative methods to test ideas that were suggested in qualitative studies of legal integration (Stone Sweet and Brunell 1998; Carrubba and Murrah 2005; Nyikos 2000). There are also studies that situate references to the ECJ in the larger terrain of national court rulings regarding European law (Chalmers 2000; 2004*a*; Conant 2006; 2002; Green Cowles, Caporaso, and Risse-Kappen 2001; Börzel 2006). This second group of studies shows that the cases referred to the ECJ are a minority of the cases involving European law which appear in front of national courts. As of now we have little sense how European law is treated in cases that are not referred, and thus what these cases say about national court willingness to enforce European law. Damian Chalmers implies that in most cases the decision whether or not to refer a cases is technical—if the judge is confused about the issue of law and the plaintiffs are willing to wait for a ruling, a reference is made (Chalmers 2004*b*). My own work implies that national judges may refuse to refer cases that may undermine or affect their own prerogatives (2001). Jonathan Golub suggests that sometimes judges do not refer cases because they want to keep the ECJ out of an issue of domestic importance (Golub 1994). These are not contradictory claims; rather probably different reasons matter at different times.

The Commission can also raise cases in front of the ECJ. There are now extensive studies examining the practice of the Commission in pursuing infringements (Tallberg 2002; Börzel 2001; Schmidt 2000). These studies mostly describe what the Commission does pursue; there is little investigation of which cases the Commission settles out of court compared to which cases make it to the ECJ for resolution.

Step 4: The influence of ECJ decision-making on European politics: I have argued that ECJ decisions need "follow through" in order to have a political influence, suggesting that legal victories do not on their own translate into political victories (2000). But it is also true that a legal body can have influence even if a case never makes it to court. A new scholarship focuses on the Commission's use of the ECJ legal threat to influence compliance, something Jonas Tallberg has labeled "compliance bargaining" (Tallberg 2002; 2003; Tallberg and Jönsson 1998). This concept of compliance bargaining has been primarily applied to studies involving the Commission, but it also probably applies to suits raised by private litigants.

3 THE EUROPEAN COURT OF JUSTICE: THE EXCEPTION OR THE RULE?

Scholars disagree on whether the European experience could occur elsewhere. As long as the ECJ was itself *sui generis*, one could not get traction on this question. But the end of the cold war ushered in a period of expansive legalization of international politics that has clarified many international rules and led to a proliferation of international legal mechanisms to enforce these rules (Goldstein et al. 2001; Romano 1999). I started this chapter noting design features that were unique to the ECJ when it was created. A recent study of the design of twenty-six international adjudicatory bodies shows a growing trend of designing these bodies to be more like the ECJ (Helfer and Slaughter 2005). By my count, there are now eighteen International Courts (ICs) with compulsory jurisdiction, sixteen of which allow private actors to be a party to the suit either directly in front of the IC or in national courts that will refer the case to the IC, and seventeen that hear noncompliance suits raised against state actors (Alter 2006*b*). The scholarship on the factors leading to IC effectiveness is in its infancy, making it hard to draw firm conclusions about why the ECJ has been able to play this role where other international courts have not. One can, however, look to the various stories about the ECJ as potential explanations worthy of examination.

The early explanations of the transformation of the European legal system were heroic narratives about astute judges transforming a legal system through their rulings. Anne-Marie Slaughter and Laurence Helfer drew insights from the ECJ's experience, crafting a proto-"Theory of Effective Supranational Adjudication." Effective supranational courts, they argue, are able to convince domestic political institutions to comply, either through direct persuasion or via pressure from supra- and substate actors. Helfer and Slaughter create a list of steps that states can take in setting up an IC to aid its effectiveness (such as appointing judges with strong reputations and aiding the court in making sound legal rulings) and factors that the judges themselves can control (such as how they craft their rulings to build their own authority and to reach out to potential interlocutors) (Helfer and Slaughter 1997). Their instructions create a checklist of factors one could examine as potential sources of variation in the impact and influence of international courts.

The checklist is a start, but not enough in that certain courts may intentionally not be given the tools they could use to be effective. For example, the creators of the Inter-American Court of Human Rights emulated the European Court of Human Rights, but they left out the key feature of making the court's jurisdiction compulsory because they felt unready for such a step. Meanwhile other courts, such as the Andean Court of Justice, may have every tool on the checklist, yet operate in a political context that creates inherent limitations on how activist or effective they may be. We must control for endogeneity—the probability that supranational courts may not be given what they need to succeed—while at the same time remembering the ECJ experience where the court became influential in ways the creators never envisioned.

Before looking at International Court outputs, however, the ECJ experience suggests that we need to examine which cases get litigated. This is currently a hot topic of debate in scholarship on the World Trade Organization (WTO), a context where states are the only authorized litigants (Busch and Reinhardt 2000; Reinhardt 2001; Guzman and Simmons 2004). The ECJ's transformation was orchestrated in cases brought by private litigants. A number of scholars have expected private access to be important in creating effective ICs elsewhere (Helfer and Slaughter 1997, 314–18; Alter 2001, 188–9; Slaughter, Keohane, and Moravcsik 2000, 482).[5] The reason is that private actors are more numerous, more likely to raise cases that serve their interests compared to state actors, and more likely to follow through with legal victories until they achieve satisfaction. Indeed it is clear that ICs with private access have far larger caseloads compared to ICs without private access. It is not clear, however, that having more cases means that courts are more effective in the basic sense that their rulings help induce changes in state behavior.[6] Table 12.1 shows which ICs have private access

---

[5] Eric Posner and John Yoo offer an alternative argument whereby factors that contribute to IC independence from states undermine IC effectiveness (measured in terms of compliance with IC rulings). This argument has generated a lively debate. See Helfer and Slaughter (2005); Posner and Yoo (2005).

[6] Like Helfer and Slaughter, I do not measure a court's effectiveness in terms of compliance with its rulings; for an excellent summary of the difference between compliance and effectiveness see Raustalia (2000).

Table 12.1   International courts' design & caseloads organized within each section by
date established

International court	Date established	Compulsory jurisdiction	Private actor access	Total cases (last year included in figures)[a]
Courts without private access				
International Court of Justice (ICJ)	1945	Optional protocol		104 contentions cases filed, 80 judgments, 23 advisory opinions (2003)
Benelux Court (BCJ)	1965	X	Indirect*	**
Inter-American Court of Human Rights (IACHR)	1969	Optional protocol	Commission is a gate keeper	104 judgments, 18 advisory opinions, 148 orders for provisional measures (2003)
Judicial Tribunal for Organization of Arab Petroleum-Exporting Countries (OAPEC)	1980	So qualified as to be meaningless[b]	Only if defendant state consents	2 cases (1999)
International Tribunal for the Law of the Seas (ITLOS)	1982	Optional protocol	Seabed authority & seizing of vessels only	12 cases, 11 judgments (2003)
Court of Justice for the Arab Magreb Union (AMU)	1989	X (but not yet established)		Not yet in operation
General Agreement on Tariffs and Trade (GATT)[d]	1953–93	–		229 cases, 98 rulings
World Trade Organization Permanent Appellate Body (WTO)	1994	X		304 disputes formally initiated, 59 appellate rulings, 115 panel reports (2003)
Courts with private access				
European Court of Justice (ECJ)	1952	X	X	2304 infringement cases by Commission, 5044 cases referred by national courts (2003)
European Court of Human Rights (ECHR)	1950	X	X (as of 1998)	8810 cases deemed admissible, 4145 judgments (2003)

(continued)

Table 12.1   (*continued*)

International court	Date established	Compulsory jurisdiction	Private actor access	Total cases (last year included in figures)[a]
Tribunal of Justice of the Cartagena Agreement (Andean Community) (ATJ)	1981	X	X	32 nullifications, 96 infringement cases, 563 rulings regarding interpretive questions (2003)
European Court of First Instance (CFI)	1988	X	X	1823 decisions from 2507 cases filed (figures exclude staff cases) (2003)
Central American Court of Justice (CACJ)	1991	X (some exceptions)[c]	X	49 rulings (2003)
European Free Trade Area Court (EFTAC)	1992	X	X	59 opinions (2003)
Economic Court of the Common-Wealth of Independent States (ECCIS)	1993	X	X	47 cases, not clear if they are ruled on yet (2000)
Court of Justice for the Common Market of Eastern and Southern Africa (COMESA)	1993	X	X	**
Common Court of Justice and Arbitration for the Organization for the Harmonization of Corporate Law in Africa (OHADA)	1993	X	X	4 opinions, 27 rulings (2002)
International Criminal Tribunal for the Former Yugoslavia (ICTY)	1993	X	Defendant only	75 public indictments, 18 completed cases, 11 judgments in various stages of appeal (2003)
International Criminal Tribunal for Rwanda (ICTR)	1994	X	Defendant only	58 cases in progress, 17 completed cases (2003)
International Criminal Tribunal for Sierra Leone (ICTSL)	2002	X	Defendant only	11 indictments proceeding, 2 withdrawn due to death (2003)

Adapted from Alter (2006c, 26–7). I have excluded from consideration private access when it only includes suits brought by employees of the IO. * Indirect means that cases with private litigants would come through national courts references to the IC. ** = no data.

[a] Data compiled by author, based on the best information available on the PICT website, updated by visiting the websites of the international courts and consulting scholarship where available. ECCIS data from (Dragneva 2004).

ᵇ There is an implicit compulsory jurisdiction, but only so long as the disputes do not infringe on the sovereignty of any of the countries concerned. Also, for cases involving firms, jurisdiction must be consented to by the state.

ᶜ As a general rule, consent to the CACJ contentious jurisdiction is implicit in the ratification of the Protocol of Tegucigalpa. However, consent must be explicitly given in the case of: (i) territorial disputes (in which case consent to jurisdiction has to be given by both states party to the dispute); (ii) disputes between states member of the Central American Integration System and states which are not members; (iii) cases in which the Court sits as arbitral tribunal.

ᵈ GATT does not meet PICT's definition because there was no permanent court. This is also the reason that NAFTA is not included on the table.

and compulsory jurisdiction. Most of these courts seem unlikely to replicate the ECJ's experience.

Private access may not be enough, however, to allow an international court to play a large role in the international political system. On the one hand, as Keohane, Slaughter, and Moravcsik argue, cases are the fodder courts can use to promote their legitimacy—suggesting that private access will make a big difference to the role an IC comes to play (Keohane, Moravcsik, and Slaughter 2000, 482). On the other hand, the ECJ did not only have private access, it had national courts playing a supportive role enforcing ECJ rulings. Is Europe unique in the willingness of national courts to enforce European law?

Looking in the area of human rights, Andrew Moravcsik argues that supra-national legal systems are far more likely to be effective if members are liberal democracies (Moravcsik 1997). His argument gains strength when one compares the European Court of Justice to the Andean Court of Justice. Today's Andean Court is almost identical in design to the ECJ—it has compulsory jurisdiction, a preliminary ruling mechanism that allows national courts to send questions of interpretation for the Andean Court to rule on, and a supranational Secretariat that can raise infringement suits. Yet while the Andean Court had issued 1200 rulings by the end of 2006, the vast majority of which have been issued in cases raised by private litigants, none of its rulings rival in importance or effect the ECJ's rulings (Alter 2008b). Does this difference derive from a lack of legal acumen and audacity on the part of Andean Court judges? Or does perhaps the liberal context of the ECJ account for much of what makes the ECJ exceptional? The answer is not clear, but it is clear that private access to international courts is in itself insufficient, and that Europe is exceptional in the willingness of private actors to use international legal mechanisms to promote personal and public policy objectives (Alter 2006b).

There remain a number of unanswered questions raised by the ECJ's experience. It is now "taken for granted" that the ECJ has political autonomy, and can influence European politics. Is the same true of other ICs, or is the ECJ unusually autonomous? If the ECJ is unusual, why is it more autonomous than other courts? After all, there is little in the appointment mechanism of ECJ judges, or the terms they serve in office, that separate the ECJ from other ICs. Are the mechanisms of "follow-through" different in the European context, where ECJ legal rulings are applied by national courts, from those in other contexts, so that the ECJ's legal rulings have a different impact compared to rulings by other ICs?

The debate about what the ECJ's incredible experience implies for other courts is just beginning. There is a general recognition that a "rule of law" is a key element in the promotion of democracy and economic development. We are witnessing the proliferation of constitutional courts in newly emerging democracies (Unger 2002; Schwartz 2000), and of the types of rules and institutions that have contributed to the development of judicial autonomy and of the rule of law in Europe. The World Bank is funding research on what makes some rule of law systems work, while identical institutions fail to lead to the emergence of a rule of law in other cases. Thus the question of why the European Court was able to develop its authority and influence is perhaps even more relevant today than it was when the ECJ was embarking on its own revolution.

References

ALTER, K. J. 1998. Who are the masters of the Treaty? European governments and the European Court of Justice. *International Organization*, 52: 125–52.

—— 2000. The European legal system and domestic policy: spillover or backlash? *International Organization*, 54: 489–518.

—— 2001. *Establishing the Supremacy of European Law: The Making of an International Rule of Law in Europe.* Oxford: Oxford University Press.

—— 2006a. Delegation to international courts and the limits of recontracting power. Pp. 312–38 in *Delegation and Agency in International Organizations*, ed. D. Hawkins, D. A. Lake, D. Nielson, and M. J. Tierney. Cambridge: Cambridge University Press.

—— 2006b. Private litigants and the new international courts. *Comparative Political Studies*, 39: 22–49.

—— 2007. Jurist social movements in Europe: the role of Euro-law associations in European integration (1953–1975). Presented at the Historical Roots of European Legal Integration converence, October 26, Copenhagen.

—— 2008a. Agent or trustee: international courts in their political context. *European Journal of International Relations*, 14.

—— 2008b. Exporting the European Court of Justice model: the experience of the Andean Common Market Court of Justice. Manuscript on file with author.

BEACH, D. 2001. *Between Law and Politics: The Relationship Between the European Court of Justice and EU Member States.* Copenhagen: DJØF Publ.

BÖRZEL, T. 2001. Non-compliance in the European Union: pathology or statistical artifact? *Journal of European Public Policy*, 8: 803–24.

—— 2006. Participation through law enforcement: the case of the European Union. *Comparative Political Studies* 39: 128–52.

BURLEY, A.-M., and MATTLI, W. 1993. Europe before the Court. *International Organization*, 47: 41–76.

BUSCH, M., and REINHARDT, E. 2000. Testing international trade law: empirical studies of GATT/WTO dispute settlement. In *The Political Economy of International Trade Law: Essays in Honor of Robert Hudec*, ed. D. L. M. Kennedy and J. D. Southwick. Cambridge: Cambridge University Press.

CAPORASO, J., and JUPILLE, J. 2001. Transforming Europe: Europeanization and domestic change. In *Europeanization and Domestic Structural Change*, ed. M. Green Cowles, J. Caporaso, and T. Risse. Ithaca, NY: Cornell University Press.

CARRUBBA, C. J., and MURRAH, L. 2005. Legal integration and use of the preliminary ruling process in the European Union. *International Organization*, 59: 399–418.

CHALMERS, D. 2000. A statistical analysis of reported decisions of the United Kingdom invoking EU laws 1973–1998. Jean Monnet Paper, Harvard Law School 1/2000.

—— 2004*a*. The dynamics of judicial authority and the Constitutional Treaty. Jean Monnet Working Paper 5/04.

—— 2004*b*. The satisfaction of constitutional rhetoric by the European judiciary. Presented at "Alteneuland: The Constitution of European in an American Perspective," April 28–30, New York.

CLAES, M., and De WITTE, B. 1998. Report on the Netherlands. In *The European Courts and National Courts*, ed. A.-M. Slaughter, A. Stone-Sweet, and J. Weiler. Oxford: Hart.

CONANT, L. 2001. Europeanization and the courts: variable patterns of adaption among national judiciaries. In *Transforming Europe: Europeanization and Domestic Change*, ed. J. Caporaso, M. G. Green Cowles, and T. Risse-Kappen. Ithaca, NY: Cornell University Press.

—— 2002. *Justice Contained: Law and Politics in the European Union*. Ithaca, NY: Cornell University Press.

—— 2006. Individuals, courts, and the development of European social rights. *Comparative Political Studies*, 39: 76–100.

DEHOUSSE, R. 1998. *The European Court of Justice: The Politics of Judicial Integration*. New York: St. Martin's Press.

DONNER, A. 1968. *The Role of the Lawyer in the European Communities*. Evanston, Ill.: Northwestern University Press.

DRAGNEVA, R. 2004. Legal institutions for economic integration in the Commonwealth of Independent States. Presented at the Annual Meeting of the Comparative Law and Economics Forum, June 25–6, Zurich.

GARRETT, G.. 1995. The politics of legal integration in the European Union. *International Organization*, 49: 171–81.

—— KELEMEN, D., and SCHULZ, H. 1998. The European Court of Justice, national governments and legal integration in the European Union. *International Organization*, 52: 149–76.

—— and WEINGAST, B. 1993. Ideas, interests and institutions: constructing the EC's internal market. In *Ideas and Foreign Policy*, ed. J. Goldstein and R. Keohane. Ithaca, NY: Cornell University Press.

GOLDSTEIN, J., KAHLER, M., KEOHANE, R., and SLAUGHTER, A.-M. 2001. *Legalization in World Politics*. Cambridge, Mass.: MIT Press.

GOLUB, J. 1994. Using the judiciary to preserve sovereignty. D.Phil., Oxford University.

GREEN COWLES, M., CAPORASO, J., and RISSE-KAPPEN, T. 2001. *Transforming Europe: Europeanization and Domestic Change.* Ithaca, NY: Cornell University Press.

GUZMAN, A. T., and SIMMONS, B. 2004. Power plays and capacity constraints: the selection of defendants in WTO disputes. *Journal of Legal Studies,* 34: 557–98

HARLOW, C. 1992*a*. A community of interests? Making the most of European law. *Modern Law Review,* 55: 331–51.

—— 1992*b*. Towards a theory of access of the European Court of Justice. *Yearbook of European Law,* 12: 213–48.

—— and RAWLINGS, R. 1992. *Pressure Through Law.* London: Routledge.

HAWKINS, D., NEILSON, D., TIERNEY, M. J., and LAKE, D. A. 2006. *Delegation Under Anarchy.* Cambridge: Cambridge University Press.

HELFER, L., and SLAUGHTER, A.-M. 2005. Why states create international tribunals: a response to Professors Posner and Yoo. *California Law Review,* 93: 899–956.

—— —— 1997. Toward a theory of effective supranational adjudication. *Yale Law Journal,* 107: 273–391.

KEOHANE, R., MORAVCSIK, A., and SLAUGHTER, A.-M. 2000. Legalized dispute resolution: interstate and transnational. *International Organization,* 54: 457–88.

KILROY, B. 1995. Member state control or judicial independence: the integrative role of the Court of Justice. Presented at the American Political Science Association Conference, August 31–September 3, Chicago.

—— 1999. Integration through law: ECJ and governments in the EU. Ph.D. dissertation, Department of Political Science, UCLA, Los Angeles.

MADSEN, M. R., and VAUCHEZ, A. 2005. European constitutionalism at the cradle: law and lawyers in the construction of a European political order (1920–1960). In *In Lawyers' Circles: Lawyers and European Legal Integration,* ed. A. Jettinghoff and H. Schepel. The Hague: Elsevier Reed.

MORAVCSIK, A. 1997. Explaining international human rights regimes: liberal theory and Western Europe. *European Journal of International Relations,* 1: 157–89.

NYIKOS, S. 2000. The European Court of Justice and national courts: strategic interaction within the EU judicial process. Ph.D. dissertation, Department of Political Science, University of Virginia.

POLLACK, M. 2003. *The Engines of Integration: Delegation, Agency, and Agency Setting in the European Union.* Oxford: Oxford University Press.

POSNER, E. A., and YOO, J. C. 2005. A theory of international adjudication. *California Law Review,* 93: 1–72.

RASMUSSEN, H. 1986. *On Law and Policy in the European Court of Justice.* Dordrecht: Martinus Nijhoff.

RAUSTIALA, K. 2000. Compliance and effectiveness in international regulatory cooperation. *Case Western Reserve Journal of International Law,* 32: 387–440.

REINHARDT, E. 2001. Adjudication without enforcement in GATT disputes. *Journal of Conflict Resolution,* 45: 174–95.

RICHARDT, N. 2006. Transforming Europe's welfare regimes: policy innovation through European gender equality laws in the United Kingdom and in Germany. Ph.D. dissertation, Department of Political Science, Northwestern University.

ROMANO, C. 1999. The proliferation of international judicial bodies: the pieces of the puzzle. *New York University Journal of International Law and Politics,* 31: 709–51.

SACRISTE, G., and VAUCHEZ, A. 2007. The force of international law: lawyer's diplomacy on the international scene in the 1920s. *Law and Social Inquiry* 32: 83–107.

SCHEPEL, H., and WESSELING, R. 1997. The legal community: judges, lawyers, officials and clerks in the writing of Europe. *European Law Journal*, 3: 165–88.

SCHMIDT, S. 2000. Only an agenda setter? The European Commission's power over the Council of Ministers. *European Union Politics*, 1: 37–61.

SCHWARTZ, H. 2000. *The Struggle for Constitutional Justice in Post-Communist Europe.* Chicago: University of Chicago Press.

SHAPIRO, M. 1980. Comparative law and comparative politics. *Southern California Law Review*, 53: 537–42.

SLAUGHTER, A.-M. 2000. Judicial globalization. *Virginia Journal of International Law Association*, 40: 1103–24.

—— KEOHANE, R., and MORAVCSIK, A. 2000. Legalized dispute resolution, interstate and transnational. *International Organization*, 54: 457–88.

STEIN, E. 1981. Lawyers, judges and the making of a transnational constitution. *American Journal of International Law*, 75: 1–27.

STONE, A. 1990. The birth and development of abstract review: constitutional courts and policymaking in Western Europe. *Policy Studies Journal*, 19: 81–95.

STONE SWEET, A., and BRUNELL, T. 1998. The European Court and the national courts: a statistical analysis of preliminary references, 1961–95. *Journal of Public European Policy*, 5: 66–97.

TALLBERG, J. 2002. Paths to compliance: enforcement, management and the European Union. *International Organization*, 56: 609–43.

—— 2003. *European Governance and Supranational Institutions: Making States Comply.* London: Routledge.

—— and JÖNSSON, C. 1998. Compliance and post-agreement bargaining. *European Journal of International Relations*, 4: 371–408.

TSEBELIS, G., and GARRETT, G. 2001. The institutional foundations of intergovernmentalism and supranationalism in the European Union. *International Organization*, 55: 357–90.

UNGER, M. 2002. *Elusive Reform: Democracy and the Rule of Law in Latin America.* Boulder, Colo.: Lynne Rienner.

WEILER, J. 1981. The community system: the dual character of supranationalism. *Yearbook of European Law*, 1: 257–306.

—— 1991. The transformation of europe. *Yale Law Journal*, 100: 2403–83.

—— 1994. A quiet revolution: the European Court of Justice and its interlocutors. *Comparative Political Studies*, 26: 510–34.

CASES

Barber (Douglas Harvey) v Guardian Royal Exchange Assurance Group. ECJ case 262/88 [1990] ECR I-1889.

"Cassis de Dijon" *Rewe Zentral AG v. Bundesmonopolverwaltung für Branntwein.* Case 120/78 ECR 1979: 649.

Commission v. Germany. Case 178/84 [1987] ECR 1227–1277.

Costa v. ENEL & Soc. Edisonvolta. Italian Constitutional Court Decision 14 of 7 March 1964, [1964] CMLR 425, [1964] I Il Foro It. 87 I 465.

Society for the Protection of Unborn Children Ireland Ltd. v. Grogan. Case C-159/90 *SPUC v Grogan* [1991] 3 Common Market Law Review 849J.

Tanja Kreil v. Bundesrepublik Deutschland. Case C-285/98, 2000 E.C.R. I-69.

Van Gend en Loos v. Nederlandse Administratie Belastingen. ECJ 26/62 [1963] ECR 1. [1963] CMLR 105.

CHAPTER 13

WAR CRIMES TRIBUNALS

GARY J. BASS

As LONG as there has been war, there have been laws to civilize it. Thucydides recounts with horror the story of the Thracian conquest of Mycalessus. Although Mycalessus was a weak city that could not have possibly have resisted Thrace, the Thracians

burst [in] . . . sacked the houses and temples, and butchered the inhabitants, sparing neither the young nor the old, but methodically killing everyone they met, women and children alike, and even the farm animals and every living thing they saw. For the Thracian race, like all the most bloodthirsty barbarians, are always particularly bloodthirsty when everything is going their own way. . . . Among other things, they broke into a boys' school, the largest in the place, into which the children had just entered, and killed every one of them. Thus disaster fell upon the entire city, a disaster more complete than any, more sudden and more horrible.   (Thucydides 1972, 495)

This was not a massacre out of necessity, not the result of self-defense or battle stress or panic; the Thracians did what they did because they wanted to do it. Thucydides here appears not just as the dispassionate historian, but also as the judge in the name of Greek civilization. This same kind of notion of civilizing warfare comes up in Clausewitz too. Although Clausewitz famously sees war as escalating, he has to admit that civilized states fight differently: "If, then, civilized nations do not put their prisoners to death or devastate cities and countries, it is because intelligence plays a larger part in the methods of warfare and has taught them more effective ways of using force than the crude expression of instinct" (Clausewitz 1976, 76).

The idea of legal norms in war also goes back to the dawn of history. When Plataea, an Athenian ally, was besieged by Spartan troops, the Plataeans only agreed to surrender on the condition that the guilty alone would be punished, after a fair trial. But as Thucydides recounts, the Spartans sent out five judges, who were not really judges: "On the arrival of these judges, no formal accusation was drawn up. Instead the Plataeans were called forward and simply asked this one question: 'Have you done anything to help the Spartans and their allies in the present war?' " (Thucydides 1972, 224–5). This was a question about alliance politics, not about justice. So the Plataeans complained that this was not proper Greek justice (Thucydides 1972, 225):

we did not expect to face a trial of this sort, but one more in accordance with usual practice.... We have reason to suspect that the issue at stake is nothing less than life or death and that you yourselves are not going to act impartially. Our evidence is in the fact that no accusation has been brought forward for us to answer... [I]n order to gratify another state [Plataea's enemy city, Thebes] you are giving us the kind of trial in which the verdict has already been decided in advance.

The Plataeans and Spartans clearly share a common understanding of what a fair trial is, and the Plataeans can thus accuse the Spartans of not pursuing those legalistic standards: "If you are going to take as your standards of justice your own immediate advantage and their hatred for us, you will stand confessed as people who are more interested in pursuing your own interests than in judging sincerely between right and wrong" (Thucydides 1972, 227). The final outcome was an early instance of what has since become an old story (Thucydides 1972, 235):

the Spartan judges decided that their question—whether they had received any help from the Plataeans in the war—was a proper one to ask.... They therefore brought the Plataeans before them again one by one and asked each of them the same question. "Have you done anything to help the Spartans and their allies in the war?" As each man replied "No," he was taken away and put to death, no exceptions being made. Not less than 200 of the Plataeans were killed in this way, together with twenty-five Athenians who had been with them in the siege. The women were made slaves. As for the city, they gave the use of it for one year to some political refugees from Megara and to those of the pro-Spartan party among the Plataeans who still survived. Afterwards they razed it to the ground from its very foundations.

Such was the way of the world, even then. The Greeks knew full well what law meant, and hoped to see it applied in foreign policy; but military exigencies trumped. Although Thucydides tells the story without editorializing, he is obviously appalled by Sparta's trickery and thuggery.

The laws of war can stand in the way of grand strategy and petty tactics, which is precisely why legal advocates like them, and why they are always under siege. The Spartans are with us still. War crimes tribunals aim to change when and how states fight. The sheer ambition is what makes the whole project so precarious. Still, today international justice is a fact of life in the modern successors to doomed

Mycalessus: in Bosnia, Cambodia, Congo, Darfur, East Timor, Kosovo, Rwanda, Sierra Leone, and Uganda.

This chapter will look at the state of the field in three crucial issues about war crimes tribunals: victors' justice, outlawing war, and the trade-off between peace and justice. In all three, the tension between the partiality of politics and the impartiality of law is stark and enduring.

1 VICTORS' JUSTICE

Who judges? Although international tribunals are often billed as simply the extension of the domestic rule of law, there is no set legitimate authority in place in international relations. Even the permanent International Criminal Court is brand new, and its permanence is hardly guaranteed. So prior war crimes tribunals have been ad hoc affairs, hastily thrown together to respond to some fresh bloodbath. Usually, the judges are drawn from the ranks of the victorious powers—from the ranks of independent lawyers if all goes well, or the ranks of political hacks if not.

The question of who judges is particularly salient because of the weak consensus on underlying values in the international system. The basic societal consensus that is present in well-functioning domestic polities is nowhere in evidence in global politics (Kennedy 1964, 231–44). Even the recourse to customary international law or to natural law—a favorite move of human rights advocates of many stripes—does not always resolve the problem (Ratner and Abrams 1997, 45–77; see also Bork 1989, 3–10). This is not to say that cultural relativism proves that there are no such things as inviolable rights. As Judith Shklar wrote,

Unless and until we can offer the injured and insulted victims of most of the world's traditional as well as revolutionary governments a genuine and practicable alternative to their present conditions, we have no way of knowing whether they really enjoy their chains. There is very little evidence that they do. The Chinese did not really like Mao's reign any more than we would, in spite of their political and cultural distance from us. The absolute relativism, not merely cultural but psychological, that rejects the liberalism of fear as both too "Western" and too abstract is too complacent and too ready to forget the horrors of our world to be credible. (Shklar 1998, 16)

But Shklar also warned, "When...the American prosecution at the Tokyo Trials appealed to the law of nature as a basis for condemning the accused, he was only applying a foreign ideology, serving his nation's interests, to a group of people who neither knew nor cared about this doctrine" (Shklar 1986, 128).

In the absence of a stable international legal order, law will matter only when it is backed by some kind of politics. As Shklar correctly noted, "Law does not by itself generate institutions, cause wars to end, or states to behave as they should" (Shklar 1986, 131). This means that war crimes tribunals are torn between effectiveness and legitimacy. The closer they are linked to state power, the greater their chance of enforcing their edicts; but the closer they are linked to state power, the less impartial they look.

Since many war crimes tribunals come in the immediate aftermath of wars, they are often tagged as victors' justice (Bass 2000). The judges often hail from the victorious countries. Some diplomats have noticed the high-handed nature of their own justice; after the Great War, David Lloyd George, the British prime minister, privately suggested the inclusion of German judges (British Public Records Office, Kew, London, CAB 23/43, Imperial War Cabinet 37, November 20, 1918, noon, p. 7). But the bitter end of a war is not usually a moment of reflection and self-criticism. At Nuremberg, the judges represented the four European victors of World War II; at Tokyo, they represented eleven victors of World War II in Asia. There were no judges from neutral countries on either panel. (There were also no judges at Tokyo from some of the countries that had suffered the most from imperial Japan: Korea, Malaysia, Vietnam, Indonesia, and Burma.) To this day, some Japanese question or resent this imposition of foreign justice (Yutaka 2006; Buruma 1994). Even some liberal Japanese, who are deeply opposed to nationalism and militarism and champion a tough look at the imperial past, have reservations about the legitimacy of the trial (Hosoya et al. 1986). As one respected left-wing University of Tokyo academic wrote, "The raison d'être of law should lie in its universal applicability" (Onuma 1984). But to date, universal applicability remains a faint dream, leaving human rights advocates painfully torn between ideals of prosecution and ideals of impartiality.

These themes are shot through the debate over the new International Criminal Court (ICC), which has a universal mandate (Chayes and Slaughter 2000).[1] Unlike the previous ad hoc tribunals for specific parts of the globe (the former Yugoslavia and Rwanda), the ICC has an unlimited geographical ambit—unless governments refuse to sign up. But in practice, the ICC faces many of the same problems as its predecessors. Without the support of America, Russia, or China, it is weakened. For now, the ICC is essentially an African court—dealing with cases in places like Uganda and Sudan.

To date, the great powers have not had to subordinate themselves to international courts (Koh 2005, 111–43; see also Hersh 2005 and Danner 2004). Even America, the *hyperpuissance*, has had limited success pressuring a country as powerful as China into improving its human rights record (Tyler 1999, 343–79, 383–411; Santoro 2000, 1–32; Foot 2000, 251–73). More often, if there is judgment at all for war crimes committed by the strongest states, it has to come from within— in particular, in liberal states where domestic groups can protest against their own

---

[1] For critiques of the ICC, see Bolton (1999), Helms (2000–1), Wedgwood (1998), Rabkin (1998), and Rieff (1998).

government's brutality (T. Taylor 1970, 11–17, 123–53, 183–207). But more often, international justice—when it happens at all—remains a matter of bigger powers putting pressure on smaller powers to bring thugs to book.

In the end, the ICC has been created with an inherent crisis of legitimacy. If it tries to appease the great powers in order to make itself functional and viable, then it loses legitimacy by showing partiality toward the powerful. But if it tries to take on great powers—for instance, by something like accusing British officers of war crimes in Iraq—then it risks being quietly gutted behind the scenes. Either way, it loses its legitimacy. These are the deep inherent problems of war crimes tribunals in a world without a consensus on who judges.

2 OUTLAWING WAR

There is, at least for some, a progressive narrative of international justice, with Nuremberg as a founding moment birthed by far-sighted New Dealers,[2] followed by a slow forward march of international law. This is a kind of "Whig history" of war crimes tribunals (Butterfield 1965).

In fact, in a crucial sense, the ambit of war crimes trials has been shrinking since the end of World War I, not growing. At the end of World War I, the Allies strove to put Kaiser Wilhelm II of Germany on trial for starting the war. When asked in November 1918 what precisely Wilhelm II would be charged with, David Lloyd George, Britain's prime minister, told his cabinet: "The crime for which he is responsible is plunging this world into war" (British Public Records Office, Kew, London, CAB 23/43, Imperial War Cabinet 37, November 20, 1918, noon, p. 7). This was meant to be an enduring precedent. As Lloyd George said, "I think rulers who plunge the world into all this misery ought to be warned for all time that they must pay the penalty sooner or later" (ibid.). In the Treaty of Versailles, Article 227 read: "The Allied and Associated Powers publicly arraign William II of Hohenzollern, formerly German Emperor, for a supreme offence against international morality and the sanctity of treaties." Nuremberg was, as Justice Robert Jackson, the American chief prosecutor, put it in his magnificent opening statement, "the first trial in history for crimes against the peace of the world" (Jackson 1946, 3).

---

[2] See, e.g Borgwardt (2005, 236–9, 285–94). Borgwardt, while extremely serious and thoughtful, writes, "The Morgenthau Plan shared a certain reformist sensibility with the New Deal" (2005, 207). Aside from the conflation of destroying a country with rebuilding one, the other problem here is that the key New Dealers—Franklin Delano Roosevelt, Henry Morgenthau Jr., Cordell Hull, and Harry Hopkins—initially firmly opposed Nuremberg, which was championed by the Republican war secretary, Henry Stimson.

This was not an unmitigated blessing. All prosecutions involve opportunity costs, and the emphasis on Axis aggression could give shorter shrift to charges of crimes against humanity. At Tokyo, the prosecution concentrated on imperial Japanese aggression, subsuming the Japanese atrocities in China—including the Nanjing massacre—into an accusatory narrative of a Japanese drive toward waging war from 1941 on (Eykholt 2000, 19). At Nuremberg, most strikingly, the focus on German aggression even extended to Jackson's prosecution of Nazi racism. Having stipulated that Germany's aggressive designs were sufficiently heinous that they required international punishment, he rolled in the Holocaust with those plans. Ordinarily, Jackson knew, Nazi Germany's persecution of German Jews would be cloaked by national sovereignty. To get around that, he made the historical misstep of treating the segregation and mass murder of the Jews as a part of the overall Nazi war plan. As he said at Nuremberg, "That attack upon the peace of the world is the crime against international society which brings into international cognizance crimes in its aid and preparation which otherwise might be only internal concerns" (Jackson 1946, 11). Nazi domestic terror was lumped together as part of the overall war conspiracy. Jackson told the court that the domestic Nazi assault on the Social Democrats, the churches, and the Jews was meant "to clear their obstruction to the precipitation of aggressive war" (Jackson 1946, 48). It is plausible to see the Social Democrats and the churches as possible centers of anti-Nazi opposition, and thus a likely target for Hitler's jackboot. But it is only in the Nazi mental universe that one can say the same thing about the Jews. Germany's Jews were no real threat to the Nazi regime. Here, Jackson tied himself in knots.

In cases beyond World War II, the road to war tends to be a convoluted one (Shklar 1986, 170–9). Here, as is often the case, the Nuremberg example can be the wrong one. Hitler's war was extraordinarily premeditated (Bullock 1967; Trevor-Roper 1961). But while wars are hardly the same as traffic accidents, the assignation of blame is a task that can flummox historians as much as judges. Even if one accepts, for instance, the Fischer thesis that lays the blame for World War I squarely at the feet of Germany (Fischer 1976), that might not translate into the kind of judicial convictions that the Allies sought for Kaiser Wilhelm II after the war (see Keegan 1999; Ferguson 1999; Fromkin 2004; Steiner 2003). In the 1918 cabinet debate, Winston Churchill warned that a juridical account of the outbreak of the Great War would raise uncomfortable questions about the role of British allies: "Russia has been given very many hundreds of millions by the French to complete strategic railways, and if Russia was in the hands of a couple of women they might persuade her either this way or that" (British Public Records Office, Kew, London, CAB 23/43, Imperial War Cabinet 37, November 20, 1918, noon, p. 7). It is easy to see why war crimes tribunals might hesitate before plunging into the run-up to, say, the wars between India and Pakistan since partition. Such a ruling would have to be extraordinarily judicious.

The ad hoc tribunals for the former Yugoslavia and Rwanda did not formally include aggression in their charters, although the role of Slobodan Milosevic in the destruction of Yugoslavia—including Serb nationalist aggression against Bosnia, a UN member state—was a major theme of his protracted yet abortive trial. The ICC has a special working group trying to hammer out a way to prosecute aggression, but so far the prosecutor's office has shown modest instincts in interpreting its mandate. The world is thus in the bizarre position of pursuing an international legal order that enshrines the key tenets of *jus in bello*, while largely ignoring *jus ad bellum*.

3 PEACE VS. JUSTICE?

Political life is often about agonizing choices between competing goods. For war crimes tribunals, the starkest trade-off is between democracy or peace on the one hand, and justice (Bass 2004, 404–6). As Raymond Aron asked, "Would statesmen yield before having exhausted every means of resistance, if they knew that in the enemy's eyes they are criminals and will be treated as such in case of defeat? It is perhaps immoral, but it is most often wise, to spare the leaders of the enemy state, for otherwise these men will sacrifice the lives and wealth and possessions of their fellow citizens or their subjects in the vain hope of saving themselves. If war as such is criminal, it will be inexpiable" (Aron 1967, 115). Once a leader has committed crimes against humanity, that leader will surely demand some kind of amnesty as a precondition to ending a war or a tyranny.

Thus amnesties became a standard part of the ending of a war. In 1827, as the Greek revolt against Ottoman rule was raging on, Metternich, who wanted to crush the Greeks, did not mind offering the Greek insurgents a generous amnesty if they would just lay down their arms: "The remedy applicable to the past is forgetting. The known form of that is an amnesty put out by the sovereign authority" (Metternich to Esterhazy, March 25, 1827, in Metternich 1881, 360).

To this day, the temptation of amnesty is strong, as many authors have argued. Samuel P. Huntington wrote, "virtually every authoritarian regime that initiated its transformation to democracy also decreed an amnesty as a part of that process" (Huntington 1991, 215). Huntington has no illusions about these amnesties. They are made at gunpoint, to protect people who, by any normal moral standard, richly deserve prosecution and punishment. But he nevertheless argues in favor of accepting them—in the name of democratization, or at least of a less violent democratization. If not for amnesty-for-democracy bargains, Huntington argues, "possibly half of the pre-1990 third wave transitions would not have occurred. To reject amnesty in these cases is to exclude the most prevalent form of democratization" (Huntington

1991, 217). Priscilla Hayner (2001, 12) and Jon Elster (2004, 188–98) made similar arguments.[3] So have Alfred Stepan, Guillermo O'Donnell, and Philippe Schmitter. In pacted transitions, they argue, the military was able to secure its own amnesty against prosecution (O'Donnell and Schmitter 1986, 37–47; Stepan 1986). The worse the brutality, the likelier it is that the killers will demand amnesty (O'Donnell and Schmitter 1986, 29):

> The more brutal, inhumane, and extensive were the repressive actions, the more their actual perpetrators—the institutions involved and those persons who collaborated in them or supported them—feel threatened and will tend to form a bloc opposing any transition. Where they cannot prevent the transition, they will strive to obtain iron-clad guarantees that under no circumstances will "the past be unearthed;" failing to obtain that, they will remain a serious threat to the nascent democracy.

The people who least deserve amnesty are the ones who are most likely to demand it.

Many of these amnesties result in the creation of a halfway measure: truth commissions. These quasi-judicial measures cannot provide real accountability, but they are the most that can be extracted from an outgoing regime (Hayner 2001). The Archbishop Desmond Tutu is totally frank about the way that South Africa's famed Truth and Reconciliation Commission grew out of a deadlock. A Nuremberg in South Africa, he writes (Tutu 1999, 19–23),

> was not really a viable option at all, perhaps mercifully for us in South Africa. In World War II the Allies defeated the Nazis and their allies comprehensively and were thus able to impose what has been described as "victor's justice." . . . Neither side [in South Africa] could impose victor's justice because neither side won the decisive victory that would have enabled it to do so, since we had a military stalemate. . . . There would have been no negotiated settlement and so no new democratic South Africa had the negotiators on one side insisted that all perpetrators be brought to trial. . . . We could very well have had justice, retributive justice, and had a South Africa lying in ashes—a truly Pyrrhic victory if ever there was one.[4]

In other words, the choice for a truth commission was taken out of political necessity (Rotberg and Thompson 2002). On the alternatives to truth commissions see Barkan (2000) and Minow (1998).

How should we view such amnesties? On the one hand, realists prefer to capitulate to the demands of the war criminals, in the name of stability or balance-of-power politics. Some realists prefer to avoid moral judgment, because it could interfere with alliance politics, and criticize "[human] rights activists' assault on the granting of amnesty" (Snyder and Vinjamuri 2003–4, 12, 26, in reference to Saddam Hussein). Jack Goldsmith and Stephen Krasner warn that the new International Court "suppresses considerations of power;

---

    [3] See also Ackerman (1992, 72–80); Pion-Berlin (1994); and Snyder and Vinjamuri (2003–4).
    [4] See also Asmal et al. (1997, 12–27); Rosenberg (1996, 86–95); Krog (1998); and Gibson (2004).

it lacks democratic accountability; and it cannot reliably balance legal benefits against possible political costs" (Goldsmith and Krasner 2003, 53). They continue:

the ICC...lacks the institutional capacity to identify and balance properly the consequences of a prosecution on potentially affected groups. The ICC treaty insists that "the most serious crimes of concern to the international community as a whole must not go unpunished and their effective prosecution must be ensured." Here again we see modern international idealism's commitment to individual accountability at the expense of national amnesties and other forms of political reconciliation....The ICC could initiate prosecutions that aggravate bloody conflicts and prolong political instability in the affected regions. Relatedly, the possibilities for compromise that exist in a political environment guided by prudential calculation are constricted when political deliberation must compete with an independent judicial process. Many believe that the threat of prosecution by the international tribunal in The Hague made it practically impossible for NATO to reach an early deal with Milosevic, thereby lengthening the war and the suffering in the Balkans in the summer of 1999. The best strategy for stability often depends on context and contingent political factors that are not reducible to a rule of law.   (2003, 54–5)

On the other hand, such amnesties are deeply unpopular with human rights activists—and with many of the victims themselves. For many human rights advocates, an amnesty-for-democracy or amnesty-for-peace exchange is fundamentally illegitimate. Such purists reject the notion that one must choose between democracy and justice. They argue that there is no possibility of real democracy without justice—that is, without establishing the rule of law with the grand founding gesture of human rights trials, any democracy will be compromised and tainted. Such a democracy is born in sin, and its development will be stunted by its ignoble origins. "There are almost always prudent reasons for going along with them," writes Aryeh Neier, who, as the head of the Open Society Institute and as a former leader of Human Rights Watch and the American Civil Liberties Union (ACLU), is one of the most respected human rights advocates in the United States. "[Y]et the effect has been to create a culture of impunity" (Neier 1998, 103).

Huntington is surely right to point to relative power as fundamental. But on that score, realists may be giving up too easily. Outside actors can weigh in to change that balance of relative power (Elster 2004, 191). So long as war crimes trials are seen as part of an overall reconstruction process that rests on some measure of outside pressure, the forces of human rights can potentially be strengthened. It was victory in World War II that made Nuremberg and Tokyo possible. The irony is that realists usually warn of the dangers of total war—that the quest for purity will result in wars that are longer and harsher than they had to be (Kennan 1984, 101; Taylor 1955, 79; and, with a critique of Nuremberg as a byproduct of total war, Hankey 1950, 53–69). But those warnings are oddly forgotten by realists when it comes to war crimes tribunals, where realists now overlook the possibility of outside pressure.

To take the most salient example, in the case of the former Yugoslavia, the relative power balance was subject to change by foreign pressure—either for the Serb nationalists (by Russia) or against them (by NATO). For liberals, taking relative power seriously means seeing legal institutions as only one part of an overall settlement of a conflict. For realists, taking relative power seriously should mean a less enthusiastic view of amnesty. Such impunity would only make sense in a situation where the perpetrators of human rights violations permanently had substantially more power than the advocates of the rule of law. In Goldsmith and Krasner's own case of the Kosovo war, they do not offer any empirical evidence that Milosevic was driven away from peace by The Hague; indeed, the empirical record suggests that he was worried about being prosecuted, which could have moderated his behavior.

On top of that, realists tend to overlook the possibility of a regime falling without a negotiated settlement (Snyder and Vinjamuri 2003–4). As Carlos Santiago Nino notes, "When the transition [to democracy] is more coercive, a new balance of power contributes positively to the prospects of retroactive justice" (Nino 1996, 118). Where a dictatorship collapses suddenly, the realist case for impunity is generally not particularly compelling. There is a long dishonor roll of authoritarians whose regimes bit the dust without much opportunity to negotiate any kind of protections for themselves. In 1979, Idi Amin of Uganda, who had invaded Tanzania, had to flee Kampala as the Tanzanian army closed in on the capital. Amin first went to Libya and then Saudi Arabia, where he died in 2003. In 1979, Muhammad Reza Pahlavi fled the Iranian revolution to Sadat's Egypt, and later wound up in Morocco, the Bahamas, and Mexico, as well as a brief medical visit in the United States. In 1986, Ferdinand Marcos fled from the Philippines to Hawaii and was later indicted for embezzlement. The same year, Jean-Claude "Baby Doc" Duvalier of Haiti fled to France without a promise of amnesty, on an eight-day visitor's visa which he has rather massively overstayed, although the French government now says they are not sure where he is. In 1989, Alfredo Stroessner of Paraguay, best known for making his country a haven for Nazi war criminals, was toppled in a coup, with barely enough time to flee to Brazil. In 1991, Mengistu Haile Mariam of Ethiopia fled to Zimbabwe just before Addis Ababa fell to the rebels, and since has, along with seventy-one other senior Derg officials, been charged by Ethiopia with war crimes and crimes against humanity. In 1997, as Laurent Kabila's rebel troops stormed unstoppably toward Kinshasa, Mobutu Sese Seko fled what was then Zaire. He first went to Togo, where he was given only a ride on the presidential jet of the Togolese dictator to Rabat, Morocco. He evidently wanted to get to his estate on the French Riviera, reportedly asking the French government to let him go there for medical treatment, and Morocco had said he could only stay for a few days. But he wound up stuck in Morocco, and died there of prostate cancer a few months later. There are clearly many cases where a dictator falls fast and hard. Mobutu and Baby Doc arrived in exile with the promise of only a few days' safe berth from their reluctant hosts. These leaders are not in a position to extract any concessions from anyone. They are lucky to be alive.

The Metternichian case for amnesty is predicated on a deep concern about spoilers—dissatisfied extremists who will destroy a peace settlement rather than face punishment themselves. But for realists, the spoilers are usually the perpetrators. This overlooks the fact that victims can be spoilers too. As Jon Elster and José Alvarez note, transitional justice must provide some kind of restitution for victims (Elster 2004, 166–87; Alvarez 1999; see also Rosenberg 1996). Most members of a victimized group desperately want to see some kind of punishment. Victim groups may be held back by the lack of political opportunity to realize justice, but their goal is clear. According to a July 2005 report on northern Uganda, an overwhelming majority wanted justice. Some 76 percent of respondents wanted to see war criminals punished. Some 66 percent wanted to deal with the Lord's Resistance Army (LRA) by trial or killing, against 22 percent for forgiveness and reconciliation. If there was no other choice, most of those surveyed would have accepted an amnesty. Asked if they would accept amnesty if it was the only road to peace, 29 percent of respondents said no. Even so, they definitely wanted the amnesties to be conditional on some kind of retribution or acknowledgment of guilt from the guilty. There was 65 percent support for some kind of amnesties for the LRA, but only 4 percent support for unconditional amnesty (Pham et al. 2005).

Another powerful recent example comes from Iraq. In June and July 2003, Physicians for Human Rights, a Boston-based group, did a randomized population-based survey of over 2,000 households in southern Iraq, as well as a series of more targeted interviews with victims of human rights abuses under the Saddam regime. They concentrated on the predominantly Shia cities of Najaf, Nasiriyah, and Amarah. Their basic findings were that there were widespread human rights abuses of the kind we are morbidly familiar with: disappearances, torture, sexual assault, beatings, shootings, and the forced amputation of the ear of deserters from the Iraqi army. There was virtual unanimity among the Iraqis that those responsible for war crimes and crimes against humanity should be punished—fully 98 percent. So what kind of punishment? Twenty-two percent went for what could be called extralegal methods of punishment: execution, torture, hanging, revenge killing, or "eye for an eye" principles. Many of the respondents suggested punishments: "execution as a severe punishment, but in the city for all to see," "I myself want to punish them," "execute them," and "torture them just as they tortured me then kill them." (A spokesman for Muqtada al-Sadr, the Shia former insurgent leader, said that Saddam did not deserve a trial.) The rest wanted some kind of court: 24 percent for secular Iraqi courts; 23 percent Shari'a courts (which could include some variation on revenge killing); 18 percent an unspecified kind of court; and 12 percent an international war crimes tribunal. This strongly suggests that, at least for the Shia in the south, the Shia-dominated Iraqi government is carrying out the wishes of its political base: a national Iraqi court, with the death penalty as a sop for those 22 percent who wanted some kind of revenge killing (Amowitz et al. 2003). It is hard to imagine any accountable Iraqi government ignoring this kind of sentiment. A political process that freezes out the victims will often be unstable too.

Finally, the Metternichian call for amnesty ignores the potential shifts in public opinion that can be created by war crimes trials. Of the Milosevic trial, Jeremy Rabkin has written: "The tribunal for the Balkans has managed to make Slobodan Milosevic popular again in Serbia" (Rabkin 2002). In fact, Milosevic was consistently stunningly unpopular in Serbia even while in the dock (International Republican Institute 2002; Bass 2003). But this image of backlash is even less accurate in Rwanda. In a 2002 survey, it turned out that Hutu were actually more favorably inclined than Tutsi to the UN war crimes tribunal in Arusha as an alternative to Rwandan justice (Longman 2004, 214–15). This suggests that there are times when a variety of options for justice are preferable—even in the eyes of a group in whose names the atrocities were committed.

4 Looking Forward

Some of the most influential work on war crimes tribunals after the cold war came from the legal academic establishment. In recent years, a variety of social scientists have joined the debate, looking at the empirical determinants of government support for tribunals and at the impact of these courts. Despite increasing sophistication and insight, the study of international justice seems most in need of further work in at least three areas.

First, we need a better understanding of the individual-level microfoundations of the politics around war crimes trials. When will individuals accept or reject the verdicts of foreign judges? When will victims turn away from vengeance? When will perpetrators renounce their ferocity? Answering these questions is less a task for the legal academics and social scientists who have so far dominated the debate, and more a task for social psychologists. Many of the arguments for judicial or quasi-judicial processes rest on psychological premises that are not yet proven. Do war crimes trials really bring catharsis and healing? As Hayner (2001, 6) notes, "Though little scientific evidence is yet available on this question, it is clear that the notion of healing is a bit overstated, at least." These are all empirical questions, in need of empirical answers.

Second, we need a better understanding of the aggregate impact of war crimes trials. In more general terms, Oona Hathaway has argued that human rights treaties do not improve the actual behavior of repressive governments (Hathaway 2002; see also Moravcsik 2000, 217–52; Keck and Sikkink 1998). This might suggest a certain caution about what tribunals could do for reconciliation, even if one does not accept realist warnings of the perverse consequences of pursuing justice. Still, there have been only a limited number of in-depth investigations of the actual effects of justice (see Stover and Weinstein 2004; Gourevitch 1999, 242–55; Segev 1994, 323–66; Neuffer 2001; Meernik 2005, 271–89). In a study of postwar ethnic reconciliation in Mostar and Prijedor, in Bosnia, and Vukovar, in Croatia, Dinka Corkalo et al. found skepticism about the impartiality and competence of both national courts and the UN's war crimes tribunal for the former Yugoslavia. Serbs, Croats and Bosnians all criticized The Hague as biased against their ethnic group (2004, 143–61). In a statistical study of attitudes in Prijedor and Mostar, in Bosnia, and Vukovar, in Croatia, Miklos Biro et al. found that ethnic grudges had receded somewhat since the end of the war, but had not dropped to prewar levels— suggesting that a certain modesty is in order about what war crimes tribunals could hope to do (2004, 183–91). Understandably, Bosnians had the warmest attitudes toward The Hague, while Serbs and Croats were sure that the tribunal was biased against their group. More strikingly, Serbs in Vukovar and Bosnians generally were the most open to accepting their own side's responsibility for war crimes, while Croats in Mostar and Serbs in Prijedor were the most resistant (Biro et al. 2004, 193–5). Those who were personally traumatized in the war did not particularly want war crimes trials (Biro et al. 2004, 200–1). These are fascinating and rich findings—but ones that we do not fully understand.

Finally, anyone who is serious about building a better world will have to look beyond war crimes tribunals. As Shklar wisely wrote, "The idea that all international problems will dissolve with the establishment of an international court with compulsory jurisdiction is an invitation to political indolence. It allows one to make no alterations in domestic political action and thought, to change no attitudes, to try no new approaches and yet appear to be working for peace" (Shklar 1986, 134). The proliferation of war crimes tribunals is not really a sign of progress; real progress would be preventing the war crimes in the first place, rather than judging them afterward.

References

Ackerman, B. 1992. *The Future of Liberal Revolution*. New Haven, Conn.: Yale University Press.

Alvarez, J. E. 1999. Crimes of state/crimes of hate: lessons from Rwanda. *Yale Journal of International Law*, 24: 365–483.

Amowitz, L., et al. 2003. Southern Iraq: reports of human rights abuses and views on justice, reconstruction and government. Boston: Physicians for Human Rights.

Aron, R. 1967. *Peace and War: A Theory of International Relations*, trans. R. Howard and A. Baker Fox. New York: Praeger.

ASMAL, A., ASMAL, L., and SURESH ROBERTS, R. 1997. *Reconciliation Through Truth: A Reckoning of Apartheid's Criminal Governance*. New York: St. Martin's Press.

BARKAN, E. 2000. *The Guilt of Nations: Restitution and Negotiating Historical Injustices*. New York: Norton.

BASS, G. J. 2000. *Stay the Hand of Vengeance: The Politics of War Crimes Tribunals*. Princeton, NJ: Princeton University Press.

—— 2003. Milosevic in the Hague. *Foreign Affairs*, 82: 82–111.

—— 2004. Jus post bellum. *Philosophy and Public Affairs*, 32: 384–412.

BIRO, M., et al. 2004. Attitudes toward justice and social reconstruction in Bosnia and Herzegovina and Croatia. In Stover and Weinstein 2004.

BOLTON, J. R. 1999. The global prosecutors: hunting war criminals in the name of utopia. *Foreign Affairs*, January–February: 157–64.

BORK, R. H. 1989. The limits of "international law." *National Interest*, 18: 3–10.

BORGWARDT, E. 2005. *A New Deal for the World: America's Vision for Human Rights*. Cambridge, Mass.: Belknap Press of Harvard University Press.

BULLOCK, A. 1967. Hitler and the origins of the Second World War. *Proceedings of the British Academy*, 53: 125–43.

BURUMA, I. 1994. *The Wages of Guilt: Memories of War in Germany and Japan*. New York: Meridian.

BUTTERFIELD, H. 1965. *The Whig Interpretation of History*. New York: Norton.

CHAYES, A., and SLAUGHTER, A.-M. 2000. The ICC and the future of the global legal system. In *The United States and the International Criminal Court*, ed. S. B. Sewall and C. Kaysen. Cambridge, Mass.: American Academy of Arts and Sciences.

VON CLAUSEWITZ, C. 1976. *On War*, trans. M. Howard and P. Paret. Princeton, NJ: Princeton University Press; originally published 1832.

CORKALO, D. et al. 2004. Neighbors again? Intercommunity relations after ethnic cleansing. In Stover and Weinstein 2004.

DANNER, M. 2004. *Torture and Truth: America, Abu Ghraib, and the War on Terror*. New York: New York Review of Books.

ELSTER, J. 2004. *Closing the Books: Transitional Justice in Historical Perspective*. Cambridge: Cambridge University Press.

EYKHOLT, M. 2000. Aggression, victimization, and Chinese historiography of the Nanjing massacre. In *The Nanjing Massacre in History and Historiography*, ed. J. A. Fogel. Berkeley: University of California Press.

FERGUSON, N. 1999. *The Pity of War: Explaining World War I*. New York: Basic.

FISCHER, F. 1976. *Germany's Aims in the First World War*, trans. H. Holborn and J. Joll. New York: Norton.

FOOT, R. 2000. *Rights Beyond Borders: The Global Community and the Struggle over Human Rights in China*. Oxford: Oxford University Press.

FROMKIN, D. 2004. *Europe's Last Summer: Who Started the Great War in 1914?* New York: Knopf.

GIBSON, G. 2004. *Overcoming Apartheid: Can Truth Reconcile a Divided Nation?* New York: Russell Sage.

GOLDSMITH, J., and KRASNER, S. D. 2003. The limits of idealism. *Daedalus*, 132: 47–63.

—— and POSNER, E. 2005. *The Limits of International Law*. Oxford: Oxford University Press.

GOUREVITCH, P. 1999. *We Wish to Inform You That Tomorrow We Will Be Killed with Our Families: Stories from Rwanda*. New York: Farrar Straus and Giroux.

HANKEY, L. 1950. *Politics, Trials and Errors*. Chicago: Henry Regnery.

HATHAWAY, O. 2002. Do human rights treaties make a difference? *Yale Law Journal*, 111: 1935–2042.

HAYNER, P. 2001. *Unspeakable Truths: Confronting State Terror and Atrocity*. New York: Routledge.

HELMS, J. 2000–1. American sovereignty and the UN. *National Interest*, 29: 31–4.

HERSH, S. M. 2005. *Chain of Command: The Road from 9/11 to Abu Ghraib*. New York: Harper.

HOSOYA, C. et al. (eds.) 1986. *The Tokyo War Crimes Trial: An International Symposium*. Tokyo: Kodansha.

HUNTINGTON, S. P. 1991. *The Third Wave: Democratization in the Late Twentieth Century*. Norman: University of Oklahoma Press.

INTERNATIONAL REPUBLICAN INSTITUTE 2002. Serbia poll. November.

JACKSON, R. H. 1946. *The Case Against the Nazi War Criminals: Opening Statement for the United States of America*. New York: Knopf.

KECK, M. E., and SIKKINK, K. 1998. *Activists Beyond Borders: Advocacy Networks in International Politics*. Ithaca, NY: Cornell University Press.

KEEGAN, J. 1999. *The First World War*. New York: Knopf.

KENNAN, G. F. 1984. *American Diplomacy*. Chicago: University of Chicago Press.

KENNEDY, J. F. 1964. *Profiles in Courage*. New York: Harper and Row.

KOH, H. H. 2005. America's Jekyll-and-Hyde exceptionalism. In *American Exceptionalism and Human Rights*, ed. M. Ignatieff. Princeton, NJ: Princeton University Press.

KROG, A. 1998. *Country of My Skull: Guilt, Sorrow, and the Limits of Forgiveness in the New South Africa*. New York: Times Books.

LONGMAN, T. 2004. Connecting justice to human experience: attitudes toward accountability and reconciliation in Rwanda. In Stover and Weinstein 2004.

MEERNIK, J. 2005. Justice and peace? How the International Criminal Tribunal affects societal peace in Bosnia. *Journal of Peace Research*, 42: 271–89.

METTERNICH, K. VON. 1881. *Mémoires, documents et écrits divers: L'Ère de paix, 1816–1848*, vol. 4. Paris: Plon.

MINOW, M. 1998. *Between Vengeance and Forgiveness: Facing History after Genocide and Mass Violence*. Boston: Beacon.

MORAVCSIK, A. 2000. The origins of human rights regimes: democratic delegation in postwar Europe. *International Organization*, 54: 217–52.

NEIER, A. 1998. *War Crimes: Brutality, Genocide, Terror, and the Struggle for Justice*. New York: Times Books.

NEUFFER, E. 2001. *The Key to My Neighbor's House: Seeking Justice in Bosnia and Rwanda*. New York: Picador.

NINO, C. S. 1996. *Radical Evil on Trial*. New Haven, Conn.: Yale University Press.

O'DONNELL, G., and SCHMITTER, P. C. (eds.) 1986. *Transitions from Authoritarian Rule: Tentative Conclusions about Uncertain Democracies*. Baltimore: Johns Hopkins University Press.

PHAM, P., et al. 2005. Forgotten voices: a population-based survey on attitudes about peace and justice in northern Uganda. New York: International Center for Transitional Justice.

PION-BERLIN, D. 1994. To prosecute or to pardon? Human rights decisions in the Latin American Southern Cone. *Human Rights Quarterly*, 16: 105–30.

RABKIN, J. 1998. Courting disaster. *American Spectator*, 31.

—— 2002. "Don't tread on us!" How to handle the International Criminal Court. *Weekly Standard*, 7: 11.

RATNER, S. R., and ABRAMS, J. S. 1997. *Accountability for Human Rights Atrocities in International Law: Beyond the Nuremberg Legacy*. Oxford: Clarendon.

RIEFF, D. 1998. Court of dreams: a nice idea that won't work. *New Republic*, 219: 16–17.

ROTBERG, R., and THOMPSON, D. (eds.) 2002. *Truth vs. Justice: The Morality of Truth Commissions*. Princeton, NJ: Princeton University Press.

ROSENBERG, T. 1996. Recovering from apartheid. *New Yorker*, November 18: 86–95.

SANTORO, M. A. 2000. *Profits and Principles: Global Capitalism and Human Rights in China*. Ithaca, NY: Cornell University Press.

SEGEV, T. 1994. *The Seventh Million: The Israelis and the Holocaust*, trans. H. Watzman. New York: Hill and Wang.

SHKLAR, J. N. 1986. *Legalism: Law, Morals, and Political Trials*. Cambridge, Mass.: Harvard University Press.

—— 1998. The liberalism of fear. In *Political Thought and Political Thinkers*, ed. S. Hoffmann. Chicago: University of Chicago Press.

SNYDER, J., and VINJAMURI, L. 2003–4. Trials and errors: principle and pragmatism in strategies of international justice. *International Security*, 28: 5–44.

STEINER, Z. S. 2003. *Britain and the Origins of the First World War*. New York: Palgrave Macmillan.

STEPAN, A. 1986. Paths toward redemocratization: theoretical and comparative considerations. In O'Donnell and Schmitter 1986.

STOVER, E., and WEINSTEIN, H. M. (eds.) 2004. *My Neighbor, My Enemy: Justice and Community in the Aftermath of Mass Atrocity*. Cambridge: Cambridge University Press.

TAYLOR, A. J. P. 1955. *Bismarck: The Man and Statesman*. New York: Knopf.

TAYLOR, T. 1970. *Nuremberg and Vietnam: An American Tragedy*. Chicago: Quadrangle.

THUCYDIDES 1972. *History of the Peloponnesian War*, trans. R. Warner. London: Penguin (originally written *c.* 431–410 BCE).

TREVOR-ROPER, H. R. 1961. A. J. P. Taylor, Hitler and the war. *Encounter*, 17: 88–96.

TUTU, D. M. 1999. *No Future Without Forgiveness*. New York: Doubleday.

TYLER, P. E. 1999. *A Great Wall: Six Presidents and China*. New York: Public Affairs.

WEDGWOOD, R. 1998. Fiddling in Rome. *Foreign Affairs*, 77: 20–5.

YUTAKA, S. 2006. Legitimacy of Tokyo war crimes tribunal still debated 60 years after the fact. *Asahi Shimbun*, May 17.

C H A P T E R   14

THE GLOBALIZATION OF THE LAW

BRYANT G. GARTH

THE "globalization of the law" became a central topic in legal and social science scholarship in the 1980s. The topic refers to "legalization" diffused into two related kinds of domains. First, it refers to the development of and enhanced role for legal rules and procedures in *transnational* political and economic matters. Second, it refers to the increased importance of the *domestic* "rule of law" in countries throughout the world. The growing role for law and lawyers posited by legal globalization means as a corollary that other forms of authority—for example, the state, families, religions, and political parties—have become relatively less important. The globalization of law means that legal authority has become more prominent in the governance of the state and the economy at the national and international level.

The theme of much of the scholarly literature is that the trend toward the globalization of law is inevitable, responding to technological changes and a growing demand by citizens and businesses for democracy and the rule of law. That theme can be traced in the literature on the rise of the international human rights movement, on the one hand, and on international business transactions on the other. This theme can also be traced in much of the literature on the growing role of courts in regulating political affairs—suggested by the term "juristocracy" by Ran Hirschl (2004). The literature, mainly from political science, on transnational norms and advocacy networks provides a further support for the literature on the globalization of law. Political scientists and lawyers have joined in promoting the emergence of global norms with the potential to become legal rights that are universally accepted and enforceable globally (Sikkink 2004; Goldstein et al. 2000). Finally, there are increasing areas of the law where the standards that emerge in domestic states reflect a global state-of-the-art, including securities law and corporate governance, environmental law, antitrust, and intellectual property.

The faith in a growing consensus encompassed by the globalization of law was characteristic especially of the 1990s. The faith has given way partially to the theme of a contested choice between "internationalists" favoring the global rule of law and "unilateralists" seeking to promote a foreign policy that avoids concessions to transnational legal institutions or supposedly global norms. According to this perspective, the administration of President Bill Clinton could be identified with the promotion of the globalization of law, but the administration of George W. Bush, in dramatic contrast, has emphasized unilateralism. Dean Harold Koh of Yale, for example, who served in the Clinton administration, in 2005 called the U.S. a "member of the axis of non-obedience" of international law (Koh 2005). Similarly, from the British side, a leading barrister and human rights champion, Philippe Sands, published a book in 2005 entitled *Lawless World: America and the Making and Breaking of Global Rules* (Sands 2005). Sands exemplifies how critics of the United States castigate the Bush administration for betraying globalized legal norms that seemed just a short while ago to offer much promise for a more peaceful and prosperous world.

This debate between unilateralism and the multilateralism associated with law and legal institutions is in part a continuation of earlier debates in the United States about the role of law and legal ideals in foreign policy. The so-called realists of the 1950s and 1960s in particular, including Hans Morgenthau and George Kennan, blamed Wilsonian idealism and faith in international law for the foreign policy problems that led to World War II. The approach of the Bush administration in Iraq, however, has not fit well into the dichotomy of realists versus idealists, since the Bush administration drew on the positions of the idealists—in particular, human rights and democracy proponents—in order to promote an essentially unilateral foreign policy. The rule of law was proclaimed a central goal in Iraq from the start of the invasion, but the ideals of the international legal community that had built the consensus supporting legal globalization were of little or no concern to the Bush administration in relation to Iraq or to the so-called war on terror more generally.

The apparent paradox is that the globalization of law rejected by the Bush administration is both multilateralism and a form of Americanization. This dual nature can best be understood by tracing the role of law in U.S. foreign policy from the Wilsonian period during and after World War I to the present. Many of the major institutions and approaches identified recently with the globalization of law came from that period, including the International Chamber of Commerce in Paris and the League of Nations as a forerunner of the United Nations. Because of the significance of the United States in defining the globalization of law, it makes particular sense to trace the emergence of law in U.S. foreign policy and the relationship of U.S. law to other legal approaches and traditions. Instead of focusing on details of substantive law and how they have changed over time, this approach highlights the processes that produce globalization and its legal components. In particular, events associated with the end of the cold war—including increased trade and investment on one side, and a decline in the importance of win/lose cold war decision-making—provided an opportunity for U.S. power to flow into the "softer" forms of hegemony associated with legal approaches and institutions.

Scholarship on the globalization of the rule of law continues to raise questions about the sources and staying power of global legalization. Some of the debates are normative, raising questions linked to the long-standing debates about realism and idealism, interests and norms (e.g. Sands 2005; Koh 2005). Another body of research, linked to historical and sociological approaches, seeks to relate the expansion of legal technologies and approaches to issues of empire and hegemony. Contests in the colonial or hegemonic powers, according to this approach, help determine whether power is exerted through force or through methods linked more to the purported ideals of the dominant country—including law (Pitts 2005). Avenues for future inquiry include the differences and similarities between the British imperial approach of the 19th century, exemplified by the development of legal institutions in India, and U.S. approaches associated with the post-cold war period of U.S. dominance. Research questions from the economic and policy literature also continue to attract considerable scholarly attention. Many would argue, for example, that there are "best practices" requiring legal institutions in order to promote the development of liberal democracies facilitating global peace and prosperity. A scholarly agenda with this policy focus might then examine how desired practices are best implemented—for example, an independent judiciary (Russell and O'Brien 2001) or a judicial system that protects property rights (North 2005). Much of the output of organizations such as the World Bank tends to take this policy-oriented approach associated with the "Washington Consensus" as it evolves over time (Williamson 2000).

1 BUILDING BLOCKS OF LEGAL GLOBALIZATION: COLONIALISM AND LAW

The prominence of the United States in the recent story of the globalization of law supports the analogy between the globalization of law and the history of colonialism. The European colonial powers—in particular France, Great Britain, the Netherlands,

Portugal, and Spain—invested in legitimating their colonial ventures through law (Benton 2001; Mommsen and de Moor 1992). The so-called "legal families"—common law versus civil law—were the outgrowth of the different colonial regimes. Globalization took place through the export of laws and legal approaches from the European colonial centers to the colonies they controlled in the South.

The establishment of colonial legal systems served initially to co-opt and integrate local elites. As it turned out, however, the local elites—in Latin America typically the descendants of the colonizers—educated in the European faculties of law became the leaders of the movements for independence. When they took power, moreover, they typically sought to keep the essentials of the legal systems that represented a good part of their local authority. Latin American elites, for example, continued to send their children to Paris and elsewhere to gain credentials and connections that defined them as gentlemen and also justified their rule at home. Recent law graduates would bring back the latest legal ideas to show that they were at the forefront of modernization and progress.

There was therefore a kind of legal globalization in the relationships of import and export that continued long after the formal colonial relationships ended. The relationships were both country specific—Indonesia and the Netherlands, India and Great Britain, Brazil and Portugal, for example—and within the so-called legal families, civil law and common law. Law graduates—typically coming from the landowning elite and educated abroad in one of the legal capitals—tended to occupy most of the leading positions in the governments.

The globalization of law associated with the late twentieth century, however, should not be seen mainly as the progressive integration of the various legal traditions or families into one with claims to universality. There was a major transformation in the period after World War II that redefined the global market in legal approaches and technologies. The transformation involved a number of related events. In Europe, the prominence of law and lawyers diminished as countries focused increasingly on social issues and the welfare state (Abel-Smith and Stevens 1967). Lawyers in these countries also suffered from their identification with conservative groups that tended to oppose the welfare state. The role of law and the prominence of law graduates declined both in Great Britain and on the European continent in the era of the welfare state. In the former colonies, similarly, the activities of "developmental states" also encountered resistance among legal elites identified with landowning classes. In Latin America, for example, lawyers complained that they had been replaced by economists in the major governing positions (Dezalay and Garth 2002), while in India the legal elite identified with the movement for independence lost prestige as leading advocates fought against the moderate socialist policies of the Congress Party (Dezalay and Garth 2006).

In contrast, in the United States, the position of lawyers, while seemingly threatened by the New Deal, which many corporate lawyers resisted, ended up bolstered in what scholars later termed a "lawyers' deal" (Shamir 1995). In the period after World War II, accordingly, the United States was in a very strong position in the world because of its role in securing the Allied victory, and the position of law within the United States was also quite strong. The globalization of law that accelerated with the end of the cold war can be understood as the product of that key historical juxtaposition.

2 LAWYERS AND U.S. ANTICOLONIAL COLONIALISM

Both the strong position of lawyers after World War II in the United States and their ideological orientation reflected an historical pattern that manifested itself early in U.S. foreign policy. What became the globalization of law after World War II was built on these earlier orientations developed as part of a U.S. "colonial strategy" early in the twentieth century. The legal dimension can be traced initially by examining the careers of a relatively small group of corporate lawyers who became involved in foreign policy at the turn of the twentieth century. The descendants and protégées of this early group came to be characterized in the United States as the "foreign policy establishment." A brief sociological examination of the characteristics of this group helps to explain both their success and the shape of the recent phenomenon of the globalization of law.

Elihu Root became Secretary of War under McKinley in 1899 in the period of the Spanish American War while the United States was trying to consolidate its power in the Philippines. Root at the time of his appointment was already quite prominent as a corporate lawyer. His clients included the infamous Sugar Trust, which he helped to survive the threat embodied in antitrust legislation. As a generalist lawyer with cosmopolitan connections and a reputation for good judgment, Root made sense as a troubleshooter for the new and problematic colonial ventures. Root initiated the prominent role for corporate lawyers—then just emerging into prominence in New York City in particular—in U.S. foreign policy throughout the twentieth century.

Root had to deal with the continued resistance in the Philippines to the U.S. occupation and in the United States to the idea that colonialism was inconsistent with U.S. legal and moral values. McKinley and Root enlisted Judge William Howard Taft to help respond to the challenge. Taft, then the presiding judge of the Sixth Circuit Court of Appeals and dean of the law school of the University of Cincinnati, took charge of the Philippines effort. He drew on U.S. legal ideas to invest the occupation with a secular mission akin to the religious civilizing missions associated with the Europeans. Instead of making a permanent colony, however, he sought to legitimate U.S. dominance by training the Philippine people eventually to govern themselves. There were, of course, real economic interests and concerns underlying this U.S. assertiveness in the Philippines and elsewhere around this time, but the business interests were combined with an idealism that these corporate lawyers encouraged and expressed. Foreign involvement was an opportunity to transplant the universal U.S. values which they represented— including democracy, openness to trade, and a broad scope for private enterprise.

Some sense of this idealistic role of law can be garnered from testimony of one of the dominant "civilizers" in the Philippines. George Malcolm was a young law graduate of the University of Michigan who went to the Philippines in order to "see my country initiate a system of ever increasing self-government for the Philippines... [and] to take a stand in favor of resolute adherence to America's revolutionary anti-colonial policy" (Malcolm 1957, 23). Through entrepreneurial initiative, he helped to establish the University of Philippines College of Law in 1911, and became the first dean. His goal with the law school was "the training of leaders for the country. The students were not alone tutored in abstract law dogmas; they were inculcated with the principles of democracy." One of the graduates in 1913 was Manual Roxas, who became the first President of the Philippine Republic. U.S. imperial domination was therefore to be justified through law and democracy.

The U.S. leaders used their Philippines experience to build their arguments for comparable approaches in U.S. foreign policy more generally. Expressing hostility to European-style colonial empires, for example, Taft as president of the United States sought to open markets for U.S. business through "dollar diplomacy" through trade and investment rather than new colonial conquests (Rosenberg 2003). Dollar diplomacy was part of a move to promote elections, encourage liberal economic reform, and facilitate U.S. investment in the form of loans and private enterprise. It led the way to the policies of Woodrow Wilson, who succeeded Taft as president. The ideals were consistent with a world-view in which both the corporate lawyers and their clients would prosper under a legitimate anticolonial relationship that at the same time entrenched U.S. dominance.

After World War I and the failure of the U.S. to join the League of Nations, a group of elite lawyers and others formed the Council on Foreign Relations (CFR) to keep alive the case for active U.S. engagement with the international community. They maintained their interest in the ideals that they saw consistent with freedom and a major place in the world for the U.S. and its businesses. These lawyers worked closely with counterparts in Europe as well to support international law and institutions. As indicated by the early leadership of Elihu Root and John W. Davis, these activists were also leading corporate lawyers. Davis himself was J. P. Morgan's lawyer. In the era of so-called isolationism, the Council on Foreign Relations continued to promote interest in a strong role for the United States in international relations.

This group of closely integrated corporate lawyers was fortified with a world-view grounded in legal ideals, opposed to European colonialism, and consistent with the prosperity of clients seeking opportunities abroad. They kept these ideals alive through the Depression, World War II, and the advent of the cold war. During the cold war, the Council of Foreign Relations became the source of virtually all the foreign policy leaders, including Dean Acheson, John Foster and Allan Dulles, and John J. McCloy. The period of greatest influence came in the Kennedy administration. The central figure of the Kennedy administration, for example, was McGeorge Bundy, the principal organizer of Kennedy's elite group and later adviser to the president for foreign affairs. Bundy was not a lawyer himself, but his father and brother were and he was the son-in-law of Dean Acheson. Bundy's career included service as a very young dean of the Harvard College of Arts and Sciences, the Council of Foreign Relations, National Security Advisor, and finally the leadership of the Ford Foundation, which he directed from 1967 to 1979. Bundy's generation and close circle of friends also included Cyrus Vance, then in his first government service with the Department of Defense (and whose father figure was John W. Davis).

The brief account of the names and influence of elite corporate lawyers attests to the importance afforded to lawyers and legal training in U.S. governance and foreign relations, especially after World War II. They envisioned a world of U.S. influence legitimated by law and legal ideology. Their specific behavior in the cold war, however, was not directly tied to the law. They were fighting the cold war, and they drew mainly on traditional European-style diplomacy backed by force. They in fact scoffed at the idea that international relations might be based on international law and legal institutions. Even as late as 1968, for example, Dean Acheson scolded an audience at the American Society of International Law for confusing what the law is with what they wanted it to be by invoking international human rights. The justification for an active U.S. foreign policy was in part to defend freedom from communism, but it was also grounded in the more limited justification of the national interest of the United States.

The fight against communism, moreover, made law relatively unnecessary to the activist foreign policy that the U.S. maintained after World War II. Law could also have been a constraint on U.S. behavior if taken too literally or made more easily enforced globally. As the cold war came to an end, the legal justification for U.S. imperial actions gained in importance. Law gained in authority in relation to personal relations and diplomacy. Increased trade and investment, for example, helped promote the spread of the U.S. model of corporate law firms into the major cities of the world. The loss of legitimacy of authoritarian states that had been sustained by the cold war helped give rise to the international human rights movement. The transformation can be seen in three areas chosen as representative of legal globalization in politics and economics. The first topic is international commercial arbitration for business transactions. The second is trade law governing the rules for international trade. The third is international human rights law with respect to the rules binding states.

3 GLOBALIZED DISPUTE RESOLUTION: INTERNATIONAL COMMERCIAL ARBITRATION

International commercial arbitration in the 1980s came to be the default method for resolving international business disputes (Dezalay and Garth 1995). It is a form of private justice that allows the disputing parties to select notables to handle the disputes, typically a panel of three arbitrators. International commercial arbitration can be traced to the generation of lawyers promoting internationalization early in the twentieth century. Elihu Root, in particular, won the Nobel Peace Prize in part for his role in establishing the Hague Court of International Arbitration prior to World War I. After World War I, the group of individuals that established the Council of Foreign Relations, including Root and his disciples, helped to promote the International Chamber of Commerce (ICC), established in Paris in 1919 by business leaders from the allied countries in order to encourage trade and open markets. The ICC International Court of Arbitration was established right away, in 1923, in order to encourage the development of commercial arbitration for transnational business disputes.

The business of international commercial arbitration began relatively slowly, consistent with a reliance on personal relations before entrusting the dispute to one or more of the notables acting as arbitrators. The ICC had some 3,000 requests for arbitration in the period from 1923 to 1976, and then business rose dramatically with the next 3,000 arbitrations coming in the following eleven years. The commercial arbitration was centered especially on French and Swiss professors serving as arbitrators, but there were important ties with the elite lawyers in the United States. Still, international commercial arbitration was a relatively marginal—even if elite—activity until the 1980s.

The oil nationalizations that occurred increasingly in the post-World War II period were resolved mainly through state pressure and personal relations, but they also provided an opportunity for the small arbitration community to build its international business reputation and show its commitment to a private law—the so-called *lex mercatoria* (customary commercial law)—that would protect business investments against state action. The ICC also led the charge for the creation and adoption of the New York Convention of 1958, which made arbitration awards more enforceable than litigation in court. The relatively small field of arbitration thrived under the umbrella of the ICC and the *lex mercatoria* in the 1960s. Disputes were resolved through a legal process more like today's mediation than the litigation-like processes now associated with arbitration.

A number of factors came together to put pressure on the system as it had operated to handle major disputes involving developed and developing countries. There was a proliferation of infrastructure projects that drew on the abundance of petrodollars after the oil crisis of 1973. Disputes arising out of the projects turned into major arbitrations. Within the United States, in addition, law firms led by Skadden Arps and Wachtell Lipton pioneered in aggressive litigation as part of a new business strategy both for general competition and for preventing or facilitating mergers and acquisitions. There was also a "third worldism" in the South that helped make it more difficult to manage disputes through personal relations and negotiation. In the field of international commercial arbitration, the caseload of the ICC and others started to expand dramatically in the 1980s. The relative decline in the cold war also meant that private commercial transactions were less dependent on state-to-state negotiations with cold war implications.

As commercial arbitration gained prominence, in addition, a number of developing countries began to employ U.S. law firms, especially those located in Paris and socialized to the elite world of the International Chamber of Commerce. In part, the decision to pick U.S. firms related to the U.S. support for independence from colonialism. Sonnetrach, the Algerian oil and gas company, for example, hired Shearman and Sterling for their arbitrations. As the field expanded and commercial litigation began to further expand in importance in the United States, litigators and their new aggressive tactics began to be found in international commercial arbitration. Instead of gentlemanly proceedings conducted under the legal doctrine of the *lex mercatoria*, the U.S. lawyers pushed for cross-examination, extended efforts at discovery, motions, and above all mountains of documents.

The established European pioneers of arbitration—associated with the *lex mercatoria* and relatively informal proceedings—resisted what they saw as the "proceduralization" and "bureaucratization" of arbitration that went with this increased caseload and adversarial approach. A new group of self-conscious "technocrats" typically with advanced legal degrees from the United States, led the transition from the *lex mercatoria* and relatively informal arbitration to "off-shore litigation" typically governed not by the European *lex mercatoria* but rather by the commercial law of New York or England.

U.S. law firms, which had long shopped among legal forums in the United States, also helped to multiply the number of arbitration centers, creating a competition and a pressure for all countries to join the international commercial arbitration mainstream. The market for international commercial arbitration spread, and different places—Cairo, Hong Kong, London, New York, Stockholm, Vienna, and elsewhere—competed with the established sites of Paris and the leading

Swiss cities. Commercial arbitration became central to China trade as well and became established in Latin America in the 1990s—helped in Mexico by the provisions of the NAFTA Treaty.

In sum, international commercial arbitration, now handled as offshore litigation, U.S. style, has replaced the world of personal relationships on the one hand, and a kind of informal arbitration on the other. The soft law of the European-centered *lex mercatoria* has also given way largely to transnational contracts that list the law of England or New York as the governing law. Globalization in this instance is the diffusion of largely U.S. legal technologies and litigation approaches into business transactions the world over.

The success can be seen in two respects. First, the prominence of international commercial arbitration reflects an increase in the importance of private law and legal authority as compared to family or personal relations more generally, or state-to-state negotiation. Second, with respect to law itself, the development led to a privileged place for transnational as opposed to domestic legal systems. The transnational arena, however, is made up of national ingredients that above all now reflect the dominant contribution by U.S. approaches and technologies. The system developed largely through the influence initially of senior European scholars in the field of international law, but it matured through the market power and legal sophistication of U.S. corporate law firms and their litigation departments as private commerce began to overshadow cold war diplomatic concerns.

4 Trade and the World Trade Organization

One of the tenets of "dollar diplomacy" and Wilsonian idealism early in the twentieth century, seen in part in the support of commercial arbitration, was a faith that free trade would lead to economic growth and world peace. The long U.S. hostility to a European-style empire was consistent with an opposition to systems of colonial exploitation that also closed markets to U.S. exports. This ideal was often expressed but faced difficulties in practice. High tariffs characterized U.S. policies throughout most of the first half of the century as the more particular interests of business overcame the general sentiments of the New York legal elite. The legal elite's traditional preserve in the executive branch—the State Department—was long identified with free trade, but it was not a value that took precedence over diplomacy. Truman and Acheson, for example, did not fight for the establishment of an International Trade Organization after World War II to go along with the other proposed Bretton Woods institutions, the International Monetary Fund (IMF) and the World Bank. They settled for the General Agreement on Tariffs and Trade (GATT).

The situation began to change in the Kennedy administration with the GATT tariff negotiations termed the Dillon Round. When Kennedy chose not to push too far to promote free trade to pry open European markets, the Department of Commerce, which was much closer to business, complained and began to push for a stronger formal trade policy. The bill that passed in 1962 reflected growing business clout. Kennedy agreed to appoint a Special Trade Representative (later termed the U.S. Trade Representative or USTR) who would negotiate further trade issues. Economic difficulties and a growing awareness of the imbalance in trade with the increasingly powerful Japanese economy began to galvanize the Trade Representative to a more active approach. Trade was beginning to gain a priority that a focus on the cold war had delayed. President Nixon, encouraged by Treasury Secretary John Connally, finally became more confrontational. Under the leadership of William Eberle, a Harvard JD-MBA and former business executive, the Office of the Trade Representative was retooled with the idea of actively promoting trade liberalization outside the United States, not simply promoting tariff reductions through new GATT rounds. The Trade Act of 1974, signed by Gerald Ford, ratified and reinforced this transformation in the position of the Trade Representative.

The Trade Act also provided the Section 301 remedy for U.S. businesses who claimed that they were excluded unfairly from foreign markets. U.S. businesses could make their arguments legally without depending on the good graces of the executive branch. This and other more aggressive and pro-business positions on trade created opportunities for legal practitioners to move away from the European-centered diplomatic approach to free trade that had long been promoted by the legal elite and the Department of State.

As Dryden notes in a detailed study of the transformation that took place in the U.S. and ultimately abroad, "starting with the Trade Act of 1974, representatives of American business were notably successful in engineering changes in the dumping laws and other trade regulations that virtually required foreign companies and governments to hire small armies of Washington-based experts" (Dryden 1995, 344). There were opportunities for both sides of the trade practice as law increasingly gained importance. Those who traditionally resisted opening U.S. markets to foreign competition could make a case through the doctrine of "antidumping," while the new generation of business—including the new financial services industries—aggressively seeking new markets and places to invest, could use the legal weaponry created by Section 301.

Adversarial trade practice began to flourish, helping to sustain the traditional legal elite's orientation toward more free trade, now bolstered with more demanding clients, but also giving legal doctrines that could be invoked by the more traditionally oriented businesses. The size of the U.S. trade bar increased dramatically from the mid

1970s, when only a few Washington lawyers did any work in trade, until the end of the Tokyo Round at the end of that decade.

According to one lawyer who was active at the time, "I would view the major change in that as being the Tokyo round GATT negotiations, and the 1979 Trade Agreements Act. What that did was to greatly judicialize the practice. Ninety percent of the practice of trade law is dumping and countervailing duties.... And so it went from being this wildly informal procedure where you never saw the other side's facts, and the files are literally this thick, to being everyone saw everyone else's facts. The files are now infinite" (cited in Dezalay and Garth 2007). The work of two prominent U.S. law professors, John Jackson and Robert Hudec, also pushed developments in the law. GATT gradually moved from the realm of European-style diplomacy and politics to a specifically legal instrument. As with respect to the growth of business litigation in the United States, trade was legalized in the United States and then U.S. lawyers helped transform the transnational field (Shaffer 2003; Stone Sweet 1997).

The WTO, established finally after the Uruguay Round and the support of the Clinton administration, protected the key elements of U.S. trade practice, including antidumping, and provided a natural forum for U.S. trade lawyers to push further in the direction of legalization. In addition, through the efforts of a coalition of U.S. businesses heavily invested in the "knowledge industry"—drug companies, software companies, the film industry—aggressive lobbyists succeeded first in making the Section 301 remedy available with respect to intellectual property protection and then in moving the key forum for the protection of intellectual property from the World Intellectual Property Organization to the WTO (Drahos and Braithwaite 2002), thereby entrenching and legalizing the rules that favor the U.S. and a few other countries.

One of the negotiators of the WTO agreement, more generally, noted "there was general support for a more effective dispute resolution" that would eliminate the state veto process found in the GATT (cited in Dezalay and Garth 2007). And despite nearly universal opposition to U.S.-style antidumping laws, long tainted as protectionist, the U.S. took the position that it was politically impossible for negotiators to agree to any provision that would restrict the scope of antidumping laws. The negotiations thus produced a further increase in the legalization of U.S.-style free trade.

Now, reminiscent of the developing countries retaining law firms to enter the world of international commercial arbitration, other parties including Europe and now even some developing countries such as India and Brazil are building the legal credibility and adversarial structure themselves by taking advantage of the strategic opportunities presented by the legal structure (Shaffer 2005). They learn from and employ U.S. law firms as well. Further, even opponents of globalization have themselves treated the WTO as a quasi-legal forum, criticizing it for a lack of transparancy, lack of independent appellate review, and above all for lacking mechanisms to provide standing to environmental groups (Wallach and Sforza 1999).

The result is that the international field of trade law has a very strong momentum both to enforce rules that promote the free trade part of U.S. ideology and to perpetuate U.S. approaches—built through U.S. politics and law—toward defining how to enforce such policies and provide outlets for important businesses harmed by international competition. There is now an active body of panelists schooled in trade law and practice and eager to continue to develop trade as a global legal field. The strong U.S. position in favor of open markets abroad is now enshrined in global law.

5 International Human Rights

International human rights concerns and organizations played a relatively small role in the first two decades of the cold war. As with respect to trade and international commercial arbitration, elite lawyers in the United States generally identified themselves with the cause of human rights and democracy abroad, rather than colonialism, but they had not acted to entrench that ideology in autonomous legal institutions. The priorities of the cold war took precedence over legal ideals as the bases for U.S. activities abroad.

The Universal Declaration of Human Rights of 1948 provided a strong symbolic endorsement promoted by the United States, but there was no machinery for enforcement. The next major development from the U.S. side began after the cold war got under way. Indeed, it came mainly in response to the Soviet support of the International Association of Democratic Jurists (IADJ), which had been very critical of McCarthyism in the early 1950s. John J. McCloy, then the High Commissioner for Germany, joined with a small group of political lawyers close to him—including Allen Dulles, then President of the Council on Foreign Relations and Deputy Director of the CIA—to respond to the IADJ (Tolley 1994, 29). With funding and administrative support provided by the CIA, they created the International Commission of Jurists (ICJ), located it in Geneva, and entrusted it to the management of a group of notables mainly from Europe. The ICJ recruited well-known persons from the academic or diplomatic worlds in Europe to serve as secretaries-general. Those who served included Sean McBride, one of the founders of the Council of Europe and a signatory of the European Convention on Human Rights. McBride was especially active until his dismissal in 1967 when the CIA's involvement was made public.

As part of a cold war strategy, the ICJ spoke out against injustices associated with communism. Despite the relative lack of importance of the law except for the legitimacy and cover it might provide for politically motivated activities, the ICJ did promote the development and circulation of legal expertise and a group of individuals schooled in principles of international human rights. At the same time, in addition, under the influence of the United States and the cold war, European institutions led by the Conseil d'Europe began to build up a European body of human rights law (Madsen 2004; 2007).

The move from the ICJ (and a few related organizations) to a greater international institutionalization of human rights outside of Europe and the United States came from a variety of investments and circumstances. First, there was the group of individuals who tried to take the ostensible ideals of the ICJ more seriously. Several, for example, were active in the establishment of Amnesty International in 1961 in Great Britain. Seeking to remedy some of the perceived inadequacies of the ICJ, the founders of Amnesty International sought to gain more influence for human rights arguments through a mass organization financed exclusively by activists, and characterized by strict neutrality in the cold war. They gave priority to prisoners of conscience punished for the expression of their opinions, and they excluded those who had committed or encouraged acts of violence. The growing legitimacy of this approach helped put Amnesty and others who had increased their investment in human rights ideals into a position to take advantage of a series of events and crises that occurred in the late 1960s and early 1970s. These events related to a relative decline in cold war pressures as well.

Although beneath the radar screen of the cold war at the time, there was also some academic investment in a positive law of international human rights. Much of the initial scholarship came from Europe. The first U.S. casebook on international human rights was published in 1973 (Sohn and Buergenthal 1973). The authors were two scholars born in Europe, Louis Sohn and Thomas Buergenthal, both somewhat out of the legal mainstream. They drew extensively on European developments and quite self-consciously pulled together whatever might contribute to build law. The authors of the second casebook, Richard Lillich and Frank Newman (Lillich and Newman 1979), followed the same strategy. These works of legal idealism and promotion began to gain some academic respectability in the 1970s.

The election of Richard Nixon in 1968 led to a toughening of the U.S. cold war position, and the so-called doves who were opposing the Vietnam War began to focus on legal issues in the conduct of the cold war. Reacting to the revelations of the role of the CIA in the fall of Allende, in particular, some activist members of Congress joined with the pioneer academics, including Frank Newman, to challenge the resulting dictatorship. Drawing extensively also on Amnesty International and the now revitalized International Commission of Jurists, congressional staffs produced a report on "Human Rights and the World Community" (1974) which led to legislation calling for the State Department to deny certain assistance to countries "committing serious violations of human rights" (Foreign Assistance Act of 1973, section 32).

In Chile, at the same time, the political elite removed from power and persecuted by Pinochet searched for legal arguments that would gain international support.

They found that the invocation of international human rights gained credibility with the *New York Times* and others, including the Chilean representatives of the Ford Foundation, who had made friends with and supported many of those now persecuted by Pinochet. The idealists in the Ford Foundation offices caught the attention of MacGeorge Bundy, head of the Ford Foundation since 1966, and persuaded him that the public interest law he was supporting at home should also be implemented abroad. Ford proceeded to fund organizations in the United States and in many other countries to support this legalization, and it required the same kind of links to establishment boards and corporate law firms that Ford had required of the public interest law firms in the United States to ensure their respectability. The Ford Foundation became the leading provider of funds to human rights organizations, thus spreading the movement further and strengthening the legal legitimacy of at least one strand of U.S. foreign affairs.

President Jimmy Carter picked up the human rights mantle and incorporated it into his foreign policy—with some notable cold war exceptions, such as the Philippines under Marcos. The election of Ronald Reagan, however, was especially notable in bringing the human rights field to maturity internationally. In 1982, with funding from the Ford Foundation and others, Human Rights Watch, along with a new branch termed Americas Watch, became formally established. The director was Aryeh Neier, a prominent former leader of the ACLU, and the early board included leading corporate lawyers identified with opposition to the Vietnam War. These new organizations were quite entrepreneurial and were also directed against the Reagan administration's policies.

Growing competition in the field promoted its development and professionalization. In many respects, the prosperity of the human rights field in the 1980s—and the conversion of the Reagan administration with respect to Chile, where they supported an election that toppled Pinochet—came from the widely reported debates between Reagan administration officials, especially Elliot Abrams, and human rights advocates such as Aryeh Neier and Michael Posner. The adversarial media campaign organized around human rights gave legitimacy and importance to law and to lawyers in debates around foreign policy. The legal expertise of the new generation of lawyers became central to the enterprise. As with respect to trade and arbitration, legal adversarialism gained prominence and built the field within the United States. International human rights law became central to U.S. foreign policy and closely defined in relation to U.S. politics. Again, as with respect to trade and arbitration, aspiring leaders in developing countries and elsewhere—including, for example, South Africa—worked with the emerging norms and the leading U.S. legal actors—now a group of NGOs centered in New York and Washington, DC—to fight their legal and political battles.

U.S.-based NGOs, the U.S. media, and U.S. campuses became central to the international agenda. The international agenda depended on issues with credibility in the United States such as violence against women, elections, a media free from government domination, and more recently trafficking in women—an issue that could mobilize women's groups and the Christian right in the United States. Human rights organizations modeled on those originally funded by the Ford Foundation based on the model in Chile now exist throughout the world. Sarat and Scheingold characterize this aspect of globalization as the spread of "cause lawyering" (Sarat and Scheingold 2001). The approaches that are taken, the strategies adopted, and even the particular norms that have salience, however, take their cues from an *international* legal field oriented very strongly toward the United States.

6 Processes of Import and Export

The preceding sections describe first the development of a strong legal role in U.S. foreign policy as corporate lawyers on Wall Street took the lead in finding a place for the U.S. as an emerging global power in a world already carved up by European colonization. The legal approach that they developed was built on their role and image of the United States as a democratic government, a large open market, and a place with considerable freedom available to private enterprise. They supported the growth of international law as a matter of principle, but the globalization of law early in the twentieth century would have meant the adoption of legal principles produced mainly in Europe. Similarly, the actual conduct of foreign affairs tended also to follow European-style diplomacy, which was only loosely connected to legal norms. It is not surprising, therefore, that the notable lawyers who developed the U.S. approach to colonialism and foreign affairs and then took over the leadership role in foreign policy tended also to rely on personal relations and diplomacy in the areas of dispute resolution, trade, and human rights. The exigencies of the cold war, in addition, tended to lead them to downplay the importance of legal ideals and institutions. The turn toward legal globalization therefore took place at the time the cold war itself was coming to an end. Elite groups came to believe that the cold war tactics above the law were no longer defensible as a source of U.S. power abroad, and more generally the end of the cold war opened up a space for institutions to apply legal standards without the looming presence of cold war pressures and ideologies.

The three examples of legal globalization show this rapid movement in the period after the 1970s (Shapiro 1993). The prominence of a legal elite in the United States in foreign affairs helped translate trends in the U.S. legal profession—the development of business litigation, public interest law, and the trade bar, for example—into key ingredients of legal globalization. In each setting, the U.S. intersected with areas that developed initially out of European law and diplomacy and reoriented them toward U.S. legal approaches and agendas. As the cold war basis for an active U.S. foreign policy led by corporate lawyers declined, the legal basis accelerated and globalized. The examples could be multiplied. Anne-Marie Slaughter, for example, has focused attention on the exchange that has developed between U.S courts and high courts abroad (Slaughter 2000).

The trend toward the globalization of law can be stated more generally. U.S. norms and approaches have become the major components of emerging global norms—even those that the U.S. has specifically rejected recently such the Kyoto accords on global warming, and criminal law in the International Criminal Court. The importance of the United States in this new era of globalization is in part a reflection of U.S. power, but the process relates more specifically to the prestige of law in the United States and the U.S. academy globally (Kelemen and Sibbitt 2004; Wiegand 1991).

The role of law in Europe and in the former European colonies declined generally in the period just before and continuing after World War II. Lawyers looking to build their position and prestige naturally took an interest in U.S. approaches, and indeed U.S. lawyers gained strong footholds in Europe. Law graduates throughout the world, but especially in developing countries, began to see greater prestige from graduate study in the United States than from the traditional stint in Europe. When they returned to their own countries fortified with U.S. degrees and the credibility that they brought, they invested their imported ideas and technologies in their own legal professions and countries, multiplying the influence of U.S. law. They were the natural agents to build U.S. legal influence in national legal settings and also to support U.S. approaches in transnational arenas. U.S. law degrees served to legitimate the governance of local elites just as European degrees had for earlier generations. The force of this import and export process was enhanced by organizations operating to build the rule of law and human rights globally—the World Bank, the IMF, the Ford Foundation—that also were dominated by the prestige and power of U.S. legal approaches. Instead of the cold war or the earlier European hegemony build on colonial relationships as well as European law, the position of the United States and its law firms, NGOs, and businesses came to be built on law.

7 THE FUTURE OF ANTICOLONIAL COLONIALISM AS THE GLOBALIZATION OF LAW

The processes that have produced the globalization of law relate closely to the prestige and power of the United States and U.S. law. U.S. law and U.S. legal approaches spread through a largely consensual process because of their legitimacy around the world. Local elites gain local stature because of their link to this store of legitimacy and credibility. As long as the United States and the ideas produced there are treated with that kind of respect, the globalization of law will likely continue.

The Bush administration has tested that prestige in two ways. First, it has shown relatively little respect for the law as a constraint on its behavior. Second, recalling the relationship of legal globalization to imperial logic, it has invested very little in law as a legitimating basis for its own behavior abroad. To the extent that elites from around the globe seek power and prestige by opposing the United States, the globalization of law is threatened. Models for the governance of the state and the economy legitimated in the United States will lose their influence. Similarly, to the extent that local elites seek not the prestige and credibility of U.S. *law* but rather to be seen as combatants in the war against terror, there will also be diminished investment in legal norms and legal globalization. Foreign policy in the first decades of the cold war, in fact, was controlled largely by corporate lawyers, but their policies did not focus very much on building the rule of law or promoting global legal norms to legitimate U.S. activities abroad. Law ascended only as the cold war declined in importance. The war on terror could therefore have a pronounced impact on the processes and incentives that led to the success of the globalization of law in the 1980s and 1990s and oriented it toward the ideals of the United States and the elite corporate lawyers who helped define its role in the world.

REFERENCES

ABEL-SMITH, B., and STEVENS, R. 1967. *Lawyers and the Courts: A Sociological Study of the English Legal System, 1750–1965*. Oxford: Heinemann Educational.

BENTON, L. 2001. *Law and Colonial Cultures: Legal Regimes in World History, 1400–1900*. Cambridge: Cambridge University Press.

DEZALAY, Y. 1992. *Marchands de Droit*. Paris: Fayard.

—— and GARTH, B. 1995. *Dealing in Virtue: International Commercial Arbitration and the Construction of a Transnational Legal Order*. Chicago: University of Chicago Press.

—— —— 2002. *The Internationalization of Palace Wars: Lawyers, Economists, and the Contest to Transform Latin American States*. Chicago: University of Chicago Press.

—— —— 2006. The legal construction of a politics of notables: the double game of the patricians of the Indian Bar in the market of civic virtue. *Retfærd: Nordic Legal Journal*, 29: 42–63.

—— —— 2007. From the foreign policy establishment to the legalization of foreign policy. In *Cambridge History of American Law*, ed. M. Grossberg and C. Tomlins. Cambridge: Cambridge University Press.

DRAHOS, P., and BRAITHWAITE, J. 2002. *Information Feudalism: Who Owns the Knowledge Economy?* New York: New Press.

DRYDEN, S. 1995. *Trade Warriors: USTR and the American Crusade for Free Trade*. Oxford: Oxford University Press.

GOLDSTEIN, J., KAHLER, M., KEOHANE, R. O., and SLAUGHTER, A.-M. 2000. Legalization and world politics. *International Organization*, 54: 385–703.

HIRSCHL, R. 2004. *Towards Juristocracy: The Origins and Consequences of the New Constitutionalism*. Cambridge, Mass.: Harvard University Press.

KELEMEN, R. D., and SIBBITT, E. C. 2004. The globalization of American law. *International Organization*, 58: 103–36.

KOH, H. 2005. The value of process. *International Legal Theory*, 11: 27–38.

LILLICH, R., and NEWMAN, F. E. 1979. *International Human Rights: Problems of Law and Policy*. Boston: Little, Brown.

MADSEN, M. 2004. France, the United Kingdom and the "boomerang" of the internationalisation of human rights (1945–2000). In *Human Rights Brought Home: Socio-Legal Perspectives on Human Rights in the National Context*, ed. S. Halliday and P. Schmidt. Oxford: Hart.

—— 2007. From cold war instrument to supreme European court: the European Court of Human Rights at the crossroads of international and national law and politics. *Law and Social Inquiry*, 23: 137–59.

MALCOLM, G. A. 1957. *American Colonial Careerist*. Boston: Christopher.

MOMMSEN, W. J., and de MOOR, J. A. (eds.) 1992. *European Expansion and Law: The Encounter of European and Indigenous Law in 19th and 20th Century Africa and Asia*. Oxford: Berg.

NORTH, D. 2005. *Understanding the Process of Economic Change*. Princeton, NJ: Princeton University Press.

PITTS, J. 2005. *A Turn to Empire: The Rise of Imperial Liberalism in Britain and France*. Princeton, NJ: Princeton University Press.

ROSENBERG, E. 2003. *Financial Missionaries of the World: The Politics and Culture of Dollar Diplomacy 1900–1930*. Durham, NC: Duke University Press.

RUSSELL, P. H., and O'BRIEN, D. M. (eds.) 2001. *Judicial Independence in the Age of Democracy*. Charlottesville: University Press of Virginia.

SANDS, P. 2005. *Lawless World: America and the Making and Breaking of Global Rules*. New York: Penguin.

SARAT, A., and SCHEINGOLD, S. (eds.) 2001. *Cause Lawyering and the State in the Global Era*. Oxford: Oxford University Press.

SHAFFER, G. 2003. *Defending Interests: Public–Private Partnerships in WTO Litigation*. Waashington, DC: Brookings Institution.

—— 2005. The challenges of WTO law: strategies for developing country adaptation. *World Trade Review*, 5: 177–98.

SHAMIR, R. 1995. *Managing Legal Uncertainty*. Durham, NC: Duke University Press.

SHAPIRO, M. 1993. The globalization of law. *Indiana Journal of Global Legal Studies*, 1: 37–64.

SIKKINK, K. 2004. *Mixed Signals: U.S. Human Rights Policy and Latin America*. Ithaca, NY: Cornell University Press.

SLAUGHTER, A.-M. 2000. Judicial globalization. *Virginia Journal of International Law*, 40: 1103–24.

SOHN, L., and BUERGENTHAL, T. (eds.) 1973. *International Protection of Human Rights*. Indianapolis: Bobbs-Merrill.

STONE SWEET, A. 1997. The New GATT: dispute resolution and the judicialization of the trade regime. In *Law Above Nations*, ed. M. Volcansek. Gainesville: University of Florida Press.

TOLLEY, H. 1994. *The International Commission of Jurists: Global Advocates for Human Rights*. Philadelphia: University of Pennsylvania Press.

WALLACH, L., and SFORZA, M. 1999. *Whose Trade Organization? Corporate Globalization and the Erosion of Democracy*. Washington, DC: Public Citizen.

WIEGAND, W. 1991. The reception of American law in Europe. *American Journal of Comparative Law*, 39: 229–48.

WILLIAMSON, J. 2000. What should the World Bank think about the Washington Consensus? *World Bank Research Observer*, 15: 251–64.

PART V

FORMS OF LEGAL ORDER

CHAPTER 15

CIVIL LAW AND COMMON LAW: TOWARD CONVERGENCE?

UGO MATTEI

LUCA G. PES

1 INTRODUCTION

CONVERGENCE between the common law and the civil law tradition is a well established topic of the academic discipline known as comparative law (Cappelletti 1971, 66–8, 84, 100; Cappelletti 1981, 381; Schlesinger 1998, 390–1, 402, 422–3, 644, 690; Zweigert and Kötz 1998, 308–32). In order to analyze analogies and differences between the common law and the civil law systems, comparative lawyers have developed a number of tools, among which convergence is quite an important one. In this chapter we will try to critically introduce this notion for the use of outsiders to our discipline.

First we try to work out a definition of convergence, offering examples of the various meanings that convergence has been given in comparative legal literature in different contexts. Secondly, we offer some illustration of both current and classic debates, in comparative legal literature, on the convergence of common law and civil law. At the end of the chapter we will attempt some conclusions on the forces that can actually explain convergence at play in the current international legal scenario.

The first part of the chapter unveils deterministic logic as one of the constitutive elements of the notion of convergence, sometimes conveying the idea of a process of evolution of a legal system towards solutions that are presented in a positive way, either because they constitute a sound middle ground between different legal traditions or because they are perceived as improvements of some kind. However, as the rest of the chapter aims to show, such evolutionary flavour, though ideological in its nature, does not make us reject the notion of convergence. On the contrary, legal processes described by the notion of convergence, when critically analyzed in their historical and political context, may unveil power dynamics that are crucial for an understanding of the law in context.

2 The Idea of Convergence in Comparative Law

Broadly speaking, a phenomenon of legal convergence between two or more legal systems happens when, starting from different or very different stated rules, they evolve meeting somewhere at a middle ground (Schlesinger 1995, 477). An example is that of the legal rules on attorneys' fees. The majority of civil law countries follows a rule known as "loser pays" according to which the loser in litigation must pay the fees of his own attorneys as well as those of the attorneys of the counterpart. Other systems, mostly part of the common law tradition, follow the so-called "American rule" according to which after litigation, independently of the outcome, each party has to pay his or her attorneys' fees (for details, see Schlesinger 1998, 365–70). These rules are divergent, offering opposite solutions to the same problem. Over time, however, they have quite substantially evolved. In America, a variety of "fee shifting" devices (statutory or based on case law) have been introduced. The American rule seemed unfair in case of winners in a number of "public interest" matters having nevertheless to pay attorneys despite having produced a substantial benefit to society as a whole through litigation. For similar reasons of fairness, in most civil law countries adhering to the "loser pays" rule, judges can and actually do "compensate" the costs in cases that proved to be a "close call" in order not to be too harsh on loser that might have litigated or resisted in good faith. This is an example of convergence.

As this example shows, convergence is neither a static event nor a phenomenon occurring to a legal system on the whole and affecting all its elements in the same way. An analytical definition of convergence must emphasize the aspect of time, showing a process by which two or more legal systems "become," rather than "are," more alike. The definition must also emphasize the need to differentiate among the various aspects, layers, and elements of a legal system that are converging. Convergence may happen at substantive, procedural, or institutional level and, more frequently, it consists of a combination of these elements. Convergence, like "legal transplants" (Watson 1974), is a complex and multifaceted phenomenon, happening in legal systems that are not monolithic entities (Sacco 1991).

One should observe that the idea of convergence in comparative law betrays a deterministic logic, a strong evolutionary flavor conveying the sense of an incremental, almost natural evolution of the law towards a *sound middle ground* between extremes. Take as an illustration another classic example often discussed by comparative lawyers, that of the binding nature of court decisions. Here two extremes are usually portrayed: *extreme (a)* the position of the English courts between late nineteenth century and 1966 in which a single decision of the House of Lords, however "mistaken" was to be followed by everybody below and by the House of Lords itself, because only such a strict *stare decisis* could be coherent with a legal and political theory by which the whole Parliament and not the House of Lords alone has the power to change the law; *extreme (b)* the position of the French system by which the *Cour de Cassation* could only annul decisions coming from below and send back its annulment to the lower judge. The lower judge, however, was *not bound* by the *Cassation* decision, which could begin a tournament of table tennis between the two that was extremely difficult to resolve. In French legal and political theory, judges must be bound only by the written law and not by other judges and therefore could and should independently interpret statutes (for details, see Schlesinger 1998, 597 ff.; Cappelletti 1981, 381). Today the House of Lords has freed itself of the absurd duty to obey its own wrong or obsolete precedents, and the lower French judges now have to follow the *renvoi* of the *Cassation*. This is a *sound middle ground*, incrementally reached, between irreasonable, ideologically motivated policy extremes.

The central idea behind the notion of convergence thus seems to be that all systems should and would eventually reach similar "natural" results that are dictated by "reason" and certainly not by ideological or political choices. This deterministic, evolutionary, and ultimately unilinear approach is highly problematic since convergence is also used in a broader sense in comparative law, showing legal systems moving at different paces to the same results. Extremes do not need to be on the two sides of comparison, and one system could already be right out there, offering a light of civilization that all the others will "naturally" reach. For example, the Romans professionalized the law, by "inventing" independent jurists as a class more than 2,000 years ago. Over time, the law has been professionalized through the Western legal tradition and even beyond it. The United States (whose theory of precedent already made them the sound middle ground between England and France) invented the institutional device known as "constitutional adjudication" as early as 1803. Since then, many other legal systems in the world at different paces have followed the lead—some after World War II and others after the fall of the Berlin Wall—so that today most legal systems of the world are "converging" or have already converged towards an idea of governance in which judges have the power to interpret constitutions declaring "unconstitutional" legislation or other official activity that they regard as contrasting with the supreme law.

These two examples show how convergence, in this broader systemic sense, might display the seeds of hegemonic ideology, like any evolutionary unilinear model. It is too easy to see how today "professionalization" of the law as well as the development of "independent courts of law" as watchdogs of the constitution are strongly pressed upon so-called developing countries, being even introduced in the conditionality part of development loans. In this scenario, convergence (towards the professionalized mainstream) becomes a word loaded with positive meaning, while the actual processes that that notion pretends to describe appear very differently under a more critical light. In fact, the imposition of laws, policies, and institutional settings by international financial institutions in conditions of critical unbalances of bargaining power are far from being a "natural" evolution of the legal systems of developing countries. Nevertheless, there is a recent trend in social sciences (one ultimately associated with conservative theories) presenting such power dynamics as cases of "natural" convergence. According to "the end of history" view, for example, social systems are naturally converging toward market-based, liberal, capitalist democracies after having abandoned aberrations such as communism (Fukuyama 2006). Here, the idea of convergence is used to present power dynamics as the outcome of "natural" evolutions, suggesting that such transformations are ultimately legitimate (and not only in a cultural perspective, but, more effectively, on a strictly legal plane).

A similar use of convergence inevitably runs the risk of an ideological decline, depriving the notion of analytical significance. This observation, however, should not lead to a straightforward rejection of convergence as an analytical tool. To the contrary, it pushes comparative lawyers to consider both the role of politics in the realm of law as well as the contribution that other social sciences can offer their discipline in this field. The study of policy convergence or diffusion, for example, is a well-established topic in comparative politics (Elkins and Simmons 2005; Levi-Faur 2005a), and it allowed some political scientists to unveil the ideological and political aspects of the dynamics of policy convergence or diffusion, offering a critical anatomy of a variety of "convergence theories" (Bealey 1999; Bennett 1991). Recent literature in comparative politics and international relations has applied the models used to explain policy "diffusion" or "convergence" into the field of law (Kelemen and Sibbitt 2004; 2005; Levi-Faur 2005b). This literature may certainly offer comparative law a number of interesting insights into the study of the civil–common law opposition.

As these caveats have tried to suggest, an analysis of the convergence of the common law and the civil law traditions should seriously consider the fact that the middle ground reached by these two major families of legal systems can become a crucial ideological factor, presenting the merger between the "more advanced" professionalized solutions as *natural* points of arrival of any system wishing to evolve toward "civilization."

We can now turn to an illustration of convergence between common law and civil law in a number both of current debates and of classic *loci oppositionis* in comparative law, in order to discover the most promising future directions.

3 Convergence in Some Current Debates

Convergence maintains both a favorable and an evolutionary flavor which we know can hardly be clearly severed. Scholars of the common law and civil law opposition are thus divided both as to the existence of convergence and as to its desirability. Such division justifies the question mark on the title of the present chapter. Recently, strong cases have been made for both positions. Basil Markesinis entitled his book devoted to the meeting between English law and Continental law consequent to the common European institutional setting as "The Gradual Convergence" (Markesinis 1993). To the opposite pole, Pierre Legrand has published a broadly cited article, devoted to the same topic, with the title "European Legal Systems Are Not Converging" (Legrand 1996).

Similar polarized positions are easy to detect in the ongoing debate on European private law, another area in which it is difficult to deny that some harmonization and thus some convergence is certainly happening, not only as the result of European normative production but also as the impact of certain scholarly ideology which has characterized the debate (see, for example, Zimmermann 2001). In front of the younger generation polarized in what is clearly becoming a pointless tournament of scholars, it is always sound to look at the classics of the discipline. A late master such as Rudolf B. Schlesinger devoted his last published piece to exactly this issue (Schlesinger 1995). In this reconstruction, Schlesinger observes the issue of convergence between civil law and common law as a deeply cultural experience that should be understood in connection with scholarly and political events in which it is embedded. This points to different historical phases in which, because of the political and cultural contexts in which it is called to operate, legal scholarship emphasized at times convergence and at times divergence by following what Schlesinger calls "contrastive" or "integrative" approaches from the beginning of the discipline of comparative law (Schlesinger 1995, 477). While before the era of codification integrative approaches emphasizing convergence allowed the diffusion and unfolding of the *ius commune*, the contrastive

vision followed the nationalistic and state-centric ideology that produced codification. According to the late master, a new wave of exaggerated integrative vision
emerged in the mid-1990s—what he regarded as a simplistic vision that sophisticated
comparative law was well equipped to criticize.

To be sure, the debate over convergence between civil law and common law as it
unfolded in comparative law is tainted both by ideological worries and by a
disturbing attitude towards universalistic generalization. From the first perspective, proponents of convergence theory seem fascinated by the possibility of
building a notion of Western rule of law cutting across the great historical divide
of legal traditions, thus participating in the ideological and hegemonic construction of "the end of history." Opponents of the idea of convergence, to the contrary,
are partisans of postmodern notions of difference and incomparability, thus
participating in the hermeneutical shift of some parts of contemporary philosophy
and social science. Both these approaches overlook the fact that law and (a fortiori)
legal traditions are not monolithic entities, so that convergence might be observed
and experienced at certain levels of the legal systems and not at others. The issue of
convergence or divergence thus has to be approached as a dynamic process of legal
transformation that can be understood, at least in part, only by following its
historical evolution in different contexts.

The current homogeneity both of the common law and civil law traditions is not
at all a settled issue. For example, one could argue that English law is "converging"
towards the civil law idea of administrative law as a consequence of its participation
to the European Union system (Craig, Harlow, and Rawlings 2003; Schwarze 1996).
One can thus see in Europe the civilian majority as the strong player of the
comparative relationship with a common law minority in need of protection, an
argument which is often used against codification of European private law which
would mean yet another step towards the hegemony of a civil law approach. It is
nevertheless true that, if one looks at the law in a global perspective, the leading
force today is certainly one system traditionally "belonging" to the common law
tradition; that is, U.S. law whose style, philosophy, and institutional solutions are
exported worldwide by means of a variety of agencies. Among such exporters are
the mega law firms of New York City, the aggressive jurisdiction of U.S. courts of
law in extraterritorial issues, the policy of IMF, World Bank, and other "global"
legislators, the preeminent worldwide standing of legal institutions of high culture,
such as the leading U.S. law schools, and many other factors (Kelemen and
Sibbitt 2004; Mattei 2003; Shapiro 1993; Wiegand 1991). The outcome of this
process of "diffusion" (another word used, mostly in political science, as a synonym for convergence, and sharing its depoliticizing flavour) is that many civilian
jurisdictions worldwide, including some of the traditional leading countries,
see their legal systems more or less visibly Americanized. Thus the possible
vision (opposite to the one that would emerge if the focus was kept only on
European countries) that convergence is happening towards the common law as

represented by the U.S. This evident contradiction (the common law at the same time in danger of civilian-ization and a worldly hegemonic family of law) can be solved either by denying that the common law is today a significant analytical box including both England and the U.S., or that nothing significant on the issue of convergence can be learned at this excessively broad level of generalization.

4 SOME CLASSIC *LOCI OPPOSITIONIS*

Perhaps the best way to explore the issue of convergence between civil law and common law is thus that of observing a few classic *loci oppositionis* between the two families of legal systems, trying to detect trends of some relevance. With only limited exceptions, the classic *loci oppositionis* are located in the domain of sources of law so that some separate observations might be in order.

While both the civil law and the common law official theories agree that statutes are the politically legitimized sources of law, traditionally civil law countries are those in which this ideal has produced generalized codification of the law. Case law, to the contrary, has been the key tenet of the common law tradition, to the point that cases and precedents can be considered de facto if not *de iure* the main repositories of Anglo-American law. In 1982, Guido Calabresi observed that, because of the growth of welfare state legislation through the first two-thirds of the twentieth century, common law has entered an "age of statutes" with a great production of a legislation including ambitious pieces of model legislation in the form of codes, such as the Uniform Commercial Code or the Model Penal Code in the United States (Calabresi 1982). During the same time, in the civil law tradition judges have been emboldened by the need to adapt the quite rigid structure of codes to new circumstances, so that case law has more successfully claimed a role in the making of the civil law tradition (for a classic discussion, see Dawson 1968; for a sophisticated critique, see Lasser 1995). This general observation, certainly pointing to some "convergence," needs however to be understood in context. There is still no comparison between the importance that cases enjoy in the common law as opposed to the civil law where their importance, while increasing, is still generally limited. Moreover, the role of judges in the common law tradition is still much more important sociologically than that of their civilian colleagues. The role of codes cannot be considered the same even in the age of statutes. Common law codes are still exceptions in a panorama of the sources of law in which the grand scheme of legal interpretation is still contained in the common law tradition. One could observe as to the common law, that should all the statutes be abolished overnight there still would be a viable legal system, since all the general doctrines that can be used for principled application of the law to the multiple facts of life are all judge-made and contained in case law. To the contrary, should the case law be repealed in common law jurisdictions, statutes would not offer a coherent and principled body of law to apply. In the civil law, the opposite holds true. The abolition of codes would leave the system in total disarray, while the ban on utilizing all published case law would be all but irrelevant. Here again, all depends from the point of observation and from the biases of the observer to decide whether the glass is half empty or half full.

The role of legal doctrine (i.e. scholarly writings about the law) tells a similar story. Also in this area quite relevant distinctions are at play, both within the civil law and within the common law, where U.S. scholarship has always been much more influential than English. Generally speaking, one could say that legal academics have been the most influential players in the making of the civil law tradition and that scholarly commentary to enacted legislation and case law is still today an unavoidable component of the everyday work of a lawyer (Dawson 1968). In the common law tradition, to the contrary, academic commentary of the law has traditionally played an almost irrelevant practical and theoretical role, since legal education was the domain of practitioners and not of law professors. Again, things might have changed, showing some degree of convergence. Not only has academic legal education since the late nineteenth century become the rule in the United States, with consequent production of some highly influential literary genres (Gilmore 1977), but even in England, in the last forty years or so, academic institutions have been able to take over from the Inns of Court as the most diffused venues of lawyers' education (Braun 2006). Thus a bigger role for legal scholarship in the common law world than was traditionally the rule.

On the other side, from the time of codification, the influence and prestige of law professors in the civil law tradition has considerably declined. While in the era of the *ius commune*, academic writings were universally considered sources of law, because they were understood as capable of discovering "what the law is" no more and no less than judicial reasoning at the time of the "declaratory theory of the common law" (Blackstone 1766), with the enactment of general codification their influence dramatically changed. Other factors, such as the democratization of access to university with the consequent multiplication of academic institutions, have also contributed to the decline in quality, and thus in prestige and influence, of scholarly writings, so that today one could argue that comparatively speaking some convergence can be observed (Mattei 2004). Again, such a clear-cut picture has to be put in context by considering not only the tremendous variations on this theme in different civil law jurisdictions, but also a certain increase more recently of influence in scholarly writings in connection with the great transformation caused by the rise of European Union law (Hesselink 2001).

Outside of the domain of sources, we might look for some other classic *loci comparationis*. The existence or absence of the institution of *trust* is one such.

Trust developed in the very peculiar setting of the common law of property. Its unfolding as an institution has been historically determined by the complex and at times conflicting relationship between common law and equity courts beginning in fifteenth-century England. From that date, the Englishman could enjoy both legal rights (enforced by courts of law) and equitable rights (protected by the Chancellor in equity courts) to protect his property rights. Nothing of the like evolved in civil law jurisdictions, so that trust, living in the intersection between law and equity, can be seen as a genuinely endemic creature received only where reception of the common law has been substantive and deep enough. The gulf between the common law, endowed with a dualistic theory of property, and the civil law with its unitary doctrine of ownership of Roman origins, was enlarged by the French Revolution and by the polemic against feudal rights and the legal system stemming from it (modern continental civil law).

Trust reached the status of a classic comparative opposition when comparative law was born as a discrete academic discipline early in the twentieth century. With the globalization of market transactions and the opening of legal frontiers, trust proved to be a highly adaptable and efficient institution, thanks to its flexibility and capability to serve the needs of modern commercial transactions (Mattei 2002). Today, trust-like institutions are detectable in many other jurisdictions as the unitary theory of property indebted to symbolic reasons rather than supported by a fully articulated rationale. Recent data obtained in the *Common Core of European Private Law* (Graziadei, Mattei, and Smith 2005) might prove some convergence at least in some substantive areas of trust law as applied to commercial transactions. However, one should consider that the dual theory of property rights has never been articulated in the civil law and that, while trust is an institution of very broad and general use by the common law lawyer, it is still a quite exotic institution, viewed with a degree of suspicion even by those lawyers in continental systems that have ratified the convention on the ratification of the effects of trust in civil law, negotiated in the framework of The Hague Convention in Private International Law (Gambaro 1984; 1994).

What could arguably be considered signs of a process of convergence in the domain of trust law should not nevertheless be exaggerated. Schlesinger pointed out as early as the 1950s that the real difference that matters in this domain, as in many other differences in the opposition between common law and civil law, is in procedure and institutions rather than in substantive rules; so that, once again, we can see convergence or seeds of it happening at a certain level of the legal system but not at others.

Procedure would offer some interesting new examples of ambiguous answers to the question of convergence. Both in civil and in criminal procedure, deeply historically rooted comparative oppositions are used by comparative law scholars contrasting the "inquisitorial" nature and origins of the civil law as opposed to the "adversarial" nature and origins of the common law (Damaska 1986). While the civil law process was born in the secret chambers of Romano-canonistic procedure, exemplified by the "Inquisition" and reminding us of terrible medieval witch-hunts, the common law stemmed from the very special dynamic between the judge and the jury and its symbol is today the flamboyant attorney in a U.S. trial. The fundamental difference of a trial with law and facts allocated to different institutions (judge and jury), rather than concentrated in the hands of a bureaucrat judge as in the civil law, explains the high variety of procedural alternatives that creates yet another major gulf between the civil and the common law. Recently, some converging trends might be seen even in this area. While some countries have imported the adversarial model of criminal procedure (Italy), and others have made steps in the direction of introducing the jury (Spain, Russia), common law judges both in England and the U.S. are incrementally abandoning their position of neutral tennis court "umpires" and developing a variety of managerial devices, making them more proactive in the preparation of the trial and thus similar to the "inquisitorial judge" (Christensen and Wise 2005; Resnik 2001).

Here again, the devil is in the details. Many scholars have pointed out how the transplantation of U.S. informed institutions has been a failure in civil law countries (Grande 2000b) or, at best, what has been defined as a mistranslation (Langer 2004; Teubner 2001). One should also observe that the very terms of the common law–civil law opposition in this domain can be seen as ideological, because an adversarial trial conveys an idea of highly developed civilization while the idea behind the notion of inquisition is rather the opposite (Grande 2000a). This opposition thus serves an ideological or even hegemonic strategy because it erases the fact that more than 90 percent of cases at common law never reach the trial phase and are decided by settlement under the fear of very intrusive discovery (in civil trial) or of the overwhelming power of the prosecutor. In other words, the pre-trial phase of the common law process is highly inquisitorial and determines the vast majority of cases. It also erases the historical fact that civilian systems reacted against the horrors of the Inquisition early during the Enlightenment age, so that today the civilian defendant has similar if not stronger guarantees than his common law counterpart (Schlesinger 1976). Once again, this example shows how far from full convergence we are, and how carefully these kinds of questions should be handled.

5 CONCLUSION

We could indeed offer other examples, but the story emerging would not really change. Common law and civil law are deeply rooted historical experiences through which the Western legal tradition has institutionalized its relationship between individuals, the state, and social classes. The issue of convergence between these two dominant legal experiences of the world must then consider not only the internal "Western" relationship between them, but also the domination project that has always characterized the relationship of the West with the rest (Twining 2000).

One of the most promising future developments of legal literature comparing the common law and the civil law tradition is precisely to develop a set of analytical tools, such as the notion of convergence, allowing the comparativist to consider this problematic relationship. In fact, from one side, convergence may offer the analytical ground for a notion of Western rule of law cutting across the common law civil law opposition (Gambaro 1998). On the other side, however, convergence may also describe the processes by which the common middle ground reached by these two major legal traditions is presented, in a highly idealized form, as a "model" of legal civilization in non-Western contexts through a variety of means (Mattei 2003).

A more critical understanding of convergence, as a notion employed in comparative legal literature to describe such processes, may unveil an ideological and political dimension which is essential to put the law in context. In particular, it may contribute to the understanding of the processes, widely studied by other social sciences, through which power dynamics become "institutionalized" receiving some form of cultural and legal legitimacy (Ferguson 1990; Nader 2002). In order to adopt such a perspective, ultimately allowing oneself to consider the role of politics in the realm of the law, an opening of legal knowledge to the contribution of other social sciences, in particular political science, appears crucial.

Comparative legal analysis should understand the processes of convergence between the common law and the civil law tradition in both their historical and their political context. As in any process of that kind, convergence between these two traditions leaves winners as well as losers, and critical scholarship should make special efforts to detect the latter and give voice to their concerns. The very distinction of legal families into *civil law* and *common law* is problematic and must be understood in context. A critical analysis of the topic of convergence should approach this issue too, because many oppositions between the two families are already cast in biased language and often are by no means even present within them. For example the role and prestige of legal scholarship and of case law varies sensibly both within the civil law and within the common law, and every generalization in broad areas such as "sources of law," "property," or "procedure" should be handled with the utmost care.

A variety of other elements that can be considered as part of the context of convergence, may improve our grasp of the problem. The understanding of a convergence between the common law and civil law traditions could be enlightened considering, for example, linguistic patterns. The common law with practically no exception is a tradition that used English; that is, the dominant language of power worldwide. By contrast, the civil law is highly divided linguistically. Because in the law, as Arthur Leff once said, "form is substance" and because legal form expresses itself in a language, the connection of the common law with the dominant language is a crucial factor that might suggest as a general statement, not so much convergence or diffusion as rather hegemony and domination of the common law (mostly in its American version) allied with economic forces in the making of an institutional structure of current capitalism, that is not only Western but also distinctively imperialistic. Thus the search for a full-fledged theory of power and of language in comparative law seems to open the next frontier of research in the domain of convergence.

REFERENCES

BEALEY, F. 1999. *Blackwell Dictionary of Political Science*. Oxford: Blackwell.

BENNETT, C. J. 1991. What is policy convergence and what causes it? *British Journal of Political Science*, 21: 215–33.

BLACKSTONE, W. 1766. *Commentaries on the Laws of England*. Oxford: Clarendon Press.

BRAUN, A. 2006. *Giudici e Accademia nell'Esperienza Inglese*. Bologna: Il Mulino.

Calabresi, G. 1982. *A Common Law for the Age of Statutes*. Cambridge, Mass.: Harvard University Press.

CAPPELLETTI, M. 1971. *Judicial Review in the Contemporary World*. Indianapolis: Bobbs-Merrill.

——— 1981. The doctrine of stare decisis and the civil law: a fundamental difference—or no difference at all? In *Festschrift für Konrad Zweigert*, ed. H. Bernstein, U. Drobnig, and H. Kotz. Tubingen: Mohr (Paul Siebeck).

CHRISTENSEN, R. K., and WISE, C. R. 2005. A full and fair capacity: federal courts managing state programs. *Administration and Society*, 37: 576–610.

CRAIG, P. P., HARLOW, C., and RAWLINGS, R. 2003. *Law and Administration in Europe: Essays in Honour of Carol Harlow*. Oxford: Oxford University Press.

DAMASKA, M. R. 1986. *The Faces of Justice and State Authority: A Comparative Approach to the Legal Process*. New Haven, Conn.: Yale University Press.

DAWSON, J. P. 1968. *The Oracles of the Law*. Ann Arbor: University of Michigan Law School.

ELKINS, Z., and SIMMONS, B. 2005. On waves, clusters, and diffusion: a conceptual framework. *Annals of the American Academy of Political and Social Science*, 598: 33–51.

FERGUSON, J. 1990. *The Anti-Politics Machine: "Development," Depoliticization, and Bureaucratic Power in Lesotho*. Cambridge: Cambridge University Press.

FUKUYAMA, F. 2006. *The End of History and the Last Man*. New York: Free Press.

GAMBARO, A. 1984. Problemi in materia di riconoscimento degli effetti del trust nei paesi di civil law. *Rivista di Diritto Civile*, 1: 93 ff.

——— 1994. Il "trust" in Italia e Francia. In *Studi in Onore di Rodolfo Sacco: la comparazione giuridica alle soglie del terzo millennio*, ed. P. Cendon. Milan: Giuffré.

——— 1998. Western legal tradition. In *The New Palgrave Dictionary of Economics and the Law*, ed. P. Newman. London: Palgrave Macmillan.

GILMORE, G. 1977. *The Ages of American Law*. London: Yale University Press.

GRANDE, E. 2000a. *Imitazione e Diritto: ipotesi sulla circolazione dei modelli*. Turin: Giappichelli.

—— 2000b. Italian criminal justice: borrowing and resistance. *American Journal of Comparative Law*, 48: 227–59.

GRAZIADEI, M., MATTEI, U., and SMITH, L. D. 2005. *Commercial Trusts in European Private Law*. New York: Cambridge University Press.

HESSELINK, M. W. 2001. *The New European Legal Culture*. Deventer: Kluwer.

KELEMEN, R. D., and SIBBITT, E. C. 2004. The globalization of American law. *International Organization*, 58: 103–36.

—— 2005. Lex Americana? A response to Levi-Faur. *International Organization*, 59: 463–72.

LANGER, M. 2004. From legal transplants to legal translations: the globalization of plea bargaining and the Americanization thesis in criminal procedure. *Harvard International Law Journal*, 45: 1–64.

LASSER, M. 1995. Judicial (self-)portraits: judicial discourse in the French legal system. *Yale Law Journal*, 104: 1325–410.

LEGRAND, P. 1996. European legal systems are not converging. *International and Comparative Law Quarterly*, 45: 52–81.

LEVI-FAUR, D. 2005a. "Agents of knowledge" and the convergence on a "new world order:" a review article. *Journal of European Public Policy*, 12: 954–65.

—— 2005b. The political economy of legal globalization: juridification, adversarial legalism, and responsive regulation. *International Organization*, 59: 451–62.

MARKESINIS, B. S. 1993. *The Gradual Convergence: Foreign Ideas, Foreign Influences, and English Law on the Eve of the 21st Century*. Oxford: Oxford Univeristy Press.

MATTEI, U. 2002. Should Europe codify trust? In *Themes in Comparative Law: In Honor of Bernard Rudden*, ed. B. Rudden, P. Birks, and A. Pretto. New York: Oxford University Press.

—— 2003. A theory of imperial law: a study on U.S. hegemony and the Latin resistance. *Indiana Journal of Global Legal Studies*, 10: 383–448.

—— 2004. *Il Modello di Common Law*. Turin: Giappichelli.

NADER, L. 2002. *The Life of the Law: Anthropological Projects*. Berkeley: University of California Press.

RESNIK, J. 2001. Categorical federalism: jurisdiction, gender and the globe. *Yale Law Journal*, 111: 619–80.

SACCO, R. 1991. Legal formants: a dynamic approach to comparative law (instalment I of II). *American Journal of Comparative Law*, 39: 1–34.

SCHLESINGER, R. B. 1976. Comparative criminal procedure: a plea for utilizing foreign experience. *Buffalo Law Review*, 26: 361–86.

—— 1995. The past and future of comparative law. *American Journal of Comparative Law*, 43: 477–81.

—— 1998. *Comparative Law: Cases, Text, Materials*. New York: Foundation Press.

SCHWARZE, J. 1996. *Administrative Law Under European influence: On the Convergence of the Administrative Laws of the EU Member States*. London: Sweet and Maxwell.

SHAPIRO, M. 1993. The globalization of law. *Indiana Journal of Global Legal Studies*, 37: 37–64.

TEUBNER, G. 2001. Legal irritants: how unifying law ends up in new divergencies. Pp. 417–41 in *Varieties of Capitalism: The Institutional Foundations of Comparative Advantage*, ed. P. A. Hall and D. Soskice. Oxford: Oxford University Press.

TWINING, W. 2000. Comparative law and legal theory: the country and western tradition. In *Comparative Law in Global Perspective*, ed. I. Edge. New York: Transaction.

WATSON,. A. 1974. *Legal Transplants: An Approach to Comparative Law*. Edinburgh: Scottish Academic Press.

WIEGAND, W. 1991. The reception of American law in Europe. *American Journal of Comparative Law*, 39: 229–48.

ZIMMERMANN, R. 2001. *Roman Law, Contemporary Law, European Law: The Civilian Tradition Today*. Oxford: Oxford University Press.

ZWEIGERT, K., and KÖTZ, H. 1998. *Introduction to Comparative Law*. Oxford: Oxford University Press.

CHAPTER 16

CONSTITUTIONALISM

KEITH E. WHITTINGTON

CONSTITUTIONALISM is the constraining of government in order to better effectuate the fundamental principles of the political regime. It can be argued that in a sense (often associated with Aristotle) every country has a constitution. That is, every country has a governmental framework that can be described and categorized. Alternatively, constitutions might be identified specifically with a written document that formalizes the framework of government. But it has been strongly argued that "constitutionalism" should be distinguished from the mere possession of a constitution, whether in an Aristotelian or a written sense. Written constitutions may provide few effective constraints on government or may be ignored, and governments may be effectively constrained without a written constitution, with Great Britain being the classic example. Constitutionalism has often been associated specifically with liberalism, with the protection of individual rights against the state. The distinguishing feature of a constitutional state, in this view, would not be its possession of a written document called a constitution but its effective protection of individual rights—though there still may be disagreements about whether any particular institutions or practices, such as judicial review, are essential features of a meaningful constitutional system (Friedrich 1968; Sartori 1962; Bogdanor 2003). But individual rights provide only one set of fundamental principles that might impose meaningful limits on the power of the state and the discretion of government officials. The tools of constitutionalism have also been used, for example, to constrain power holders to care for the common weal or adhere to particular conceptions of national identity or religious law.

The great examples of constitutional scholarship from an earlier generation were primarily works of intellectual history. Sweeping studies of Western political thought,

Roman law, and the British legal tradition provided detailed arguments on the origins and development of the idea of constitutionalism (Friedrich 1941; Wormuth 1949; McIlwain 1947). Although significant, if less sweeping, historical studies have recently emerged, they no longer characterize the field (Pennington 1993; Gelderen and Skinner 2002). After a period of some pessimism about the value of constitutionalism itself, let alone constitutional scholarship, recent decades have seen a remarkable rebirth of the field (Wheeler 1975). Constitutional studies are no longer occupied with historical debates of primarily antiquarian interest, but are actively engaged in debating and understanding ongoing constitutional disputes. This chapter reviews some of those developments in three sections: normative constitutionalism, conceptual constitutionalism, and empirical constitutionalism.

1 NORMATIVE CONSTITUTIONALISM

Constitutional theory has largely been a normative enterprise. For a great deal of the postwar period, constitutional theory was predominantly American and particular in its focus. The U.S. Supreme Court had, somewhat sporadically and with the support of national conservative politicians, imposed constitutional constraints on the expanding progressive state in the early twentieth century, leading some scholars and activists on the left to develop critiques of both constitutionalism and judicial review as ill-suited to modern industrial democracy. The conflict, of course, came to a head in the constitutional struggle over the New Deal, and the Court beat a retreat in 1937 even as President Franklin Roosevelt introduced a legislative plan to pack the Court with his own allies by expanding the size of the bench beyond the traditional nine justices (the "switch in time that saved nine"). Roosevelt and his successors soon filled the bench with ideological allies through the normal process of attrition and replacement, setting the stage for the modern academic debate (Friedman 2000).

For liberals emerging from the New Deal and World War II, attitudes toward judicial review diverged into two broad camps. Some such as Justice Felix Frankfurter and Judge Learned Hand argued, consistent with their pre-New Deal critiques of the conservative Court, that judges should exercise restraint in exercising the power of judicial review and defer to the will of elected representatives in most circumstances. Others such as Justices William O. Douglas and Frank Murphy instead accepted the idea that the courts should be active in defining and enforcing constitutional limits on the other branches of government but simply thought that the pre-New Deal Court had been enforcing the wrong set of substantive values. For the first camp, the New Deal was about democracy and institutional authority within a democracy. For the second, it was about substantive values and gaining control over the levers of power, including the power of judicial review.

The agenda for the modern scholarly debate in normative constitutional theory was set with the U.S. Supreme Court's decision in *Brown v. Board of Education* in 1954, the school desegregation case. The case was high-profile and substantively controversial. It overturned deeply entrenched policies with ongoing electoral support in many states in the nation. It was difficult to reconcile the outcome of the case with the available legal materials as traditionally understood, the Court overturned long-standing precedent to reach the result in the case, and it made little effort to provide a persuasive legal explanation for its decision. Although Frankfurter reluctantly signed on to the decision, *Brown* soon inspired Learned Hand (1958, 73) to deliver the Holmes Lecture at Harvard Law School questioning whether the United States needed a "bevy of Platonic Guardians" to rule the country from the bench. Herbert Wechsler (1959, 12), a Columbia Law School professor and a young lawyer during the New Deal, responded the next year in the Holmes Lecture by defending active judicial review, but only when doing so meant behaving like "courts of law" and not like a "naked power organ." The *Brown* Court, he feared, failed that test by not adhering to neutral legal principles and careful legal reasoning. Not all constitutional scholars agreed with Wechsler's complaint about the Court's actions and reasoning in cases like *Brown*. Nonetheless, post-Wechslerian constitutional theory has been centrally concerned with answering the progressive challenge voiced by Hand. It seeks to legitimate the practice of activist judicial review while providing substantive guidance as to how judges should interpret the Constitution so as both to vindicate that institutional practice and to realize the proper constitutional values. As Alexander Bickel (1962) famously framed the problem, normative constitutional theory seeks to answer the "countermajoritarian difficulty," and it does so by offering guidance to the Court in how judicial review ought to be exercised and how constitutional law ought to be constructed.

At least four notable developments further shaped the debate between its origins in the aftermath of the *Brown* decision and today. The first was again provided by the Supreme Court. Over time, a new generation of scholars came to the fore and their formative experiences and key reference points were not the struggle *against* the Supreme Court over the New Deal but the struggle *with* the Supreme Court over segregation and the broader civil rights and civil liberties revolution of the 1960s. For these scholars, judicial review was a force for social justice to be cherished, and they constructed increasingly bold theories to justify an active role for the courts within the American constitutional system. This generation's *Brown* came in the form of *Roe v. Wade*, the 1973 abortion decision. *Roe* was substantively controversial and troubling to many, generating new efforts to think through the foundations of judicial review (Ely 1973). The second development was the rise of Ronald Reagan and the conservative legal movement. Academic constitutional theory had largely been the project of political liberals, though there were a handful of exceptions to this general tendency. The 1980s saw a flowering of conservative contributions to academic constitutional theory even as the Reagan administration and attendant interest groups and political activists made academic theory a matter of serious public debate (Keck 2004; O'Neill 2005; Teles 2008). The third development was internal to the scholarship itself. Post-Wechslerian constitutional theory has produced an enormous and complex literature. In addition to responding to external events such as judicial opinions and presidential initiatives, scholars of course reacted to the arguments and ideas being developed within the active constitutional theory literature itself while also integrating ideas (and sometimes scholars) from a variety of cognate disciplines. Over the course of decades of debate, some broad schools of thought have risen and fallen, but many approaches have been refined in the course of argument (Kalman 1996). A fourth development broadened the scope of constitutional theory. The fall of the Berlin Wall set off a new wave of constitution-making and, in the process, drew the attention of a new group of political philosophers to the basic question of how to balance democracy and rights (Loughlin 2005). Although not framed in terms of American constitutional law and the particular countermajoritarian difficulty of justifying judicial review, the questions being asked and the answers being provided by this new international and philosophical wave of normative constitutional theorizing mirror the traditional American arguments. Unfortunately, the two literatures have largely been developed along separate tracks with few points of contact or engagement between them.

Broadly speaking, normative constitutionalism remains centrally concerned with the problem of how to reconcile constitutionalism (the protection of minority and individual rights and particular substantive political values) and democracy (a mode of government that places ultimate political authority in popular majorities). Subsumed within that broad problem are a variety of more particular questions, including how best to legitimate the specific institutional practice of judicial review, how should constitutional texts in general or a particular constitutional text best be interpreted, what set of constitutional rights are most worthy of recognition, and what is the best conception of democracy.

There are four general approaches to reconciling constitutionalism and democracy. One is for constitutional commitments to receive democratic authorization. Recent originalist theories have emphasized this approach. In the 1980s, scholars and politicians who advocated that judges be guided by the original intent of the founders or the original meaning of the constitutional text (and many originalist theories eventually shifted their emphasis from the former to the latter) tended to justify their approach with arguments based on judicial deference to current legislative majorities. Recent originalist theories have generally disavowed any particular connection to judicial deference (Whittington 2004). Instead they have usually appealed to popular sovereignty as explaining why later interpreters should adhere to the meaning of the constitutional rules that the authorized lawgivers thought they were laying down (Whittington 1999*b*; Alexander and Prakash 2004). Others have added arguments for originalism grounded in an appeal to natural rights (Barnett 2004) or the substantively desirable results that are thought to follow from rules adopted through the supermajoritarian procedures characteristic of constitutions (McGinnis and Rappaport 2007). Still others have explored the possibilities of a politically progressive originalism (Balkin 2007). The originalism debates continue to be an active site for the further development of theories of textual interpretation, though the normative questions of whether judges or others must be faithful to original meaning or limit themselves to interpreting the constitutional text are separate issues (Alexander and Prakash 2004; Solum 2007).

Other scholars who would not identify themselves as originalists have also turned to the democratic authorization of constitutional commitments as a way of reconciling constitutionalism and democracy. Perhaps the most notable of these has been Bruce Ackerman (1991; 2007). In an ambitious and sprawling project, he has sketched out both a normative theory of "dualist democracy" and a sweeping reinterpretation of American constitutional history that illustrates that theory. Moments of explicit constitutional change invite and require wide and deep democratic deliberation and approval before old governing commitments are abandoned and new ones are made. By contrast, Ackerman argues, "normal politics" can reasonably operate with a lowered threshold of democratic deliberation as citizens focus on their private lives and expect policy decisions to be made within the confines of the constitutional boundaries previously established by more deliberate democratic choice. Ackerman connects this theoretical framework to a historical narrative that argues that such authoritative constitutional moments can and have occurred without making any formal changes in the constitutional text, and that judges should incorporate such episodes of nontextual "higher lawmaking" into their constitutional jurisprudence.

The appeal to democratic authorization for constitutional commitments raises at least two issues that have been the subject of increasing scholarly attention. One issue is the possibility that the democratically authorized constitution will become antiquated or fall out of favor. Those working within this tradition have attempted to address this concern in various ways. Ackerman's theory is one innovative example, as he has offered a theory that makes it potentially easier to alter the U.S. Constitution by democratic means and expands the number of episodes in which "the people" might have authorized constitutional change. Others have argued that the principles that have been democratically adopted are in fact consistent with a "living constitution" because of their capacious terms (Balkin 2007), or that the interpretable rules of the Constitution need to be and have been supplemented over time by additional practices and principles that give shape to the effective constitution of any particular historical era (Whittington 1999*a*). Relatedly, there are sharp intramural debates, only now being explored, among originalists over the normative significance of *stare decisis* (Lawson 2007; Nelson 2001;

Lash 2007; Griffin 2007). But these general debates point to a general question of how—and whether—constitutions and constitutional foundings that claim to govern into the future can ever be legitimate (Michelman 1998; Habermas 1996; Marmor 2007). A second issue is the possibility that the democratically authorized constitution might be morally inadequate. This approach to reconciling constitutionalism and democracy gambles that "reason" and democratic "will" can be brought together and produce a substantively desirable, or at least acceptable, outcome (Kahn 1993). But that leaves open the possibility that the gamble may not pay off. The people may authorize a bad, imperfect, or even an "evil" constitution, which in turn raise questions of constitutional legitimacy, the purposes of constitutions, and the circumstances under which constitutions should be regarded as authoritative in whole or in part (Balkin 1997; Barnett 2003; Graber 2006).

A second approach attempts to reconcile constitutionalism and democracy by emphasizing a procedurally oriented constitutionalism that facilitates the operation of democratic government. This approach is still most closely associated with John Hart Ely's (1980) *Democracy and Distrust*, which argued that the U.S. Constitution was largely concerned with procedural rather than substantive values. Judges who exercised the power of judicial review so as to advance fair democratic procedures, such as protecting voting rights or free speech rights, did not face the countermajoritarian difficulty and the associated legitimacy problems, Ely argued, that judges who sought to impose contested substantive values such as abortion rights did. Ely's particular defense of a proceduralist theory of constitutionalism and judicial review was often criticized as undertheorized and too quick to assume that the meaning of democracy itself was beyond contestation (see e.g. Tribe 1980; Tushnet 1980).

Recent scholars have followed up on Ely's effort to conceptualize a constitutionalism that reinforces democracy. One important justification for constitutional rules, on this reading, would be to protect the citizenry from the self-interested behavior of politicians. In particular, constitutions and constitutional devices such as judicial review might embody "anti-entrenchment" principles designed to prevent incumbent power-holders from exploiting their position to resist forces for political change (Klarman 1997; Charles 2007). Particular substantive debates over such issues as gerrymandered legislative districts and campaign finance have fed recent interest, primarily among legal scholars, in whether constitutional rules can and should limit legislative discretion in these areas (Karlan 2002; see also Pildes, this volume). Various forms of "legislative entrenchments," ranging from the U.S. Senate's cloture rules to efforts to regulate congressional budgeting, may not be designed to protect incumbent politicians from electoral competition but raise related questions for normative constitutionalism (Posner and Vermeule 2002; McGinnis and Rappaport 2003). Although many recent scholars working in this vein have eschewed broad theorizing for more particular inquiries, Michael Louis Seidman (2001) has argued on behalf of a broad-ranging theory of constitutional law and judicial review that would urge judges to routinely "unsettle" political outcomes so as to prevent the possibility of perpetual and disaffected political losers. Instead of authorizing a free-ranging judiciary to unsettle political outcomes in the name of constitutional law, sympathetic political scientists have tended to emphasize the multiple values embedded in the constitutional text and the complex institutions created by it that tend to make political resolutions difficult to achieve and maintain (Thomas 2004; Zeisberg 2007).

Influenced by various theoretical developments including civic republicanism, Habermasian visions of deliberative democracy, and public choice theory, scholars have also tried to provide a more elaborate account of how democratic institutions should be understood and justified and ultimately meshed with constitutionalism. Cass Sunstein's (1993; 1999) work developing a normative neorepublican vision of the Constitution operated in this vein. It abandoned Ely's claim that constitutional law could be politically neutral and was more explicit about the liberal values that Sunstein was building into his vision of a democratic society, but like Ely he emphasized a "minimalist" judiciary that facilitated democratic deliberation on many substantive political principles. Rather differently, Christopher Eisgruber (2001, 48) has provocatively emphasized the "complex, non-majoritarian" character of democracy. For Eisgruber politically insulated institutions such as judicial review (or a central bank) are an alternative mechanism by which the people attempt to govern themselves so as to best achieve an optimal mix of constitutional and policy outcomes. The ultimate justification for constitutionalism is to foster "democratic flourishing," but here democratic flourishing may well require expansive intervention by courts in substantive disputes on issues such as abortion that Ely thought should be decided directly by elected representatives. Such arguments stray a long way from Ely's initial efforts to restricting judicial review to enforcing democratic procedures, but they reflect the continued attraction and vitality of procedurally oriented constitutionalism.

A third approach emphasizes a substantive constitutionalism that trumps democratic processes. At least in some circumstances, substantive values such as individual rights are argued to take priority over democratic values of majority rule, and the legitimacy and authority of the political system and unelected judges exercising the power of judicial review is to be found in the proper vindication of those substantive values. There is little question that Ronald Dworkin has been the most prominent proponent of this view in recent decades. In his influential metaphor, individual rights should be regarded as "trumps" over either the policy preferences or the social welfare of political majorities (Dworkin 1985, 359). When possible, judges should pursue a "moral reading of the Constitution" (Dworkin 1996). When interpreting and applying the rights provisions of the Constitution to controversial social issues, judges should refer directly to the underlying moral questions so as to impose a resolution in the hard constitutional cases in front of them. The "deepest, most fundamental conflicts between individual and society" are to be withdrawn from the realm of politics and made a matter of "law" or "justice" to be decided by politically insulated courts. Although far more extensively developed on the political left (e.g. Fleming and Barber 2007; Hershovitz 2006), such arguments have also been played out from the political right with a different set of answers to how judges ought to resolve those hard constitutional cases (Epstein 2003).

A final approach to be considered reconciles constitutionalism and democracy by favoring democracy across the board. Constitutional values are to be the subject of ongoing democratic deliberation and decision-making, and constitutional choices are not to be entrenched in supermajoritarian or countermajoritarian institutions. Parliamentary supremacy within Westminster democracies has a long pedigree as both a normative theory and a political practice, but the reliance on legislatures and democratic institutions to interpret, maintain, and implement constitutional commitments has been under pressure at least since World War II. There were few modern robust defenses of that classic tradition, and even many Westminster democracies have through treaty or domestic reform debated or adopted constitutional or quasi-constitutional modifications to parliamentary supremacy. These political challenges to the vitality of the tradition of parliamentary sovereignty have spurred new scholarly debate over the meaning and value of that tradition (Goldsworthy 2001; Allan 2003).

Jeremy Waldron (1999) has mounted the most philosophically developed recent defense of legislative sovereignty and the priority of democracy over constitutionalism. Waldron's signal contribution is his emphasis on the reality of political disagreement and the constitutional implications that follow from that fact. At the core of Waldron's project, in this regard, is to examine the theoretical foundations for constitutional institutions like legislatures and judicial review and to ask what purposes they serve or might serve within a properly constituted political system. Given the "circumstances of politics" in which we find ourselves, circumstances in which we have good faith and reasonable disagreements about such matters as abortion rights, economic liberties, free speech, and affirmative action, he argues that the only way to treat our fellow citizens with equal concern and respect is to allow them to be equal participants in making the decision as to what to do on such contested issues—that is, to subject such questions to democratic decision-making. Removing such issues to the realm of constitutional law and courts does not render them any less controversial and politically contestable, it simply means that a smaller, less representative body gets to decide them. Waldron's argument invites closer analysis of how political institutions work empirically, which may shape our assessment of what work constitutions and judicial review might do within a democratic political system (Whittington 2002b; Waldron 2006).

A related move (or set of moves) in the specifically American context goes under a variety of labels: "popular constitutionalism" (Kramer 2004; Reed 1999), "constitution outside the courts" (Tushnet 1999), "extrajudicial constitutional interpretation" (Whittington 2002*a*), and "democratic constitutionalism" (Post and Siegel 2007). At the extreme, such theories have favored minimizing or even eliminating the judicial role in interpreting and enforcing constitutional rules and values. More often, such theories have focused greater attention on the question of who should decide, or which institution should decide, contested constitutional issues. Normative constitutional theory had long worked on an implicit assumption that the courts would and should settle all genuine contested constitutional issues (there being some debate as to whether claims that the courts heard and resolved raised genuine constitutional issues at all). Judicial supremacy in constitutional interpretation has been defended as essential to the stability and clarity of constitutional meaning, as well as more likely to achieve substantively desirable outcomes (Alexander and Schauer 1997). The constitutionalism outside the courts literature challenges this judicial supremacy assumption, arguing that courts should often be more deferential to the constitutional judgments made by the other branches of government for democratic, pragmatic, and other reasons. This has been one of the biggest new developments in the normative constitutional theory literature over the past decade, shifting the debate from how constitutions ought to be interpreted to which institutions ought to take the lead in shaping constitutional understandings.

2 CONCEPTUAL CONSTITUTIONALISM

Normative constitutional theory has received the most attention from scholars over time, and it seemed to have the most immediate potential payoffs in terms of responding to the perceived legitimacy crisis of active judicial review and of directing the course of constitutional law. But those tasks have always been closer to the professional concern of American constitutional law professors than to other constitutional scholars, and even academic constitutional lawyers were inclined to expand their agenda as the Warren Court faded into memory and a wave of new constitutions were being written across the globe.

Conceptual constitutionalism is not concerned with the legitimacy of constitutions or their proper content, as normative constitutionalism is. Conceptual constitutionalism is concerned with what constitutions are, what functions they serve within a political system, and how they work analytically. A variety of approaches have been taken to conceptualizing the functions that constitutions serve within a political order.

What are constitutions? The answers that have been offered to that question depend in part on how societies are thought to be structured and what the central problems of politics are to be solved. One, not very prominent option is to consider constitutions as a kind of collective promise. In this mode constitutions might be understood to primarily perform a kind of ideological and symbolic work. At minimum, they might remind an already united people of their higher ideals when they face future moments of temptation to deviate from those ideals. More substantially, they might remake the very people who adopt them. A people might help constitute itself as such precisely by making the promises embodied in the constitution, and the placement of collective ideals and aspirations in a constitutional text may create a dynamic that eventually alters political and legal understandings of what the nation's most basic commitments really are (Norton 1993; Harris 1992; Habermas 2001).

A second, more prominent model within the literature has been to consider constitutions as precommitment devices. The precommitment approach shares significant similarities with the constitutions-as-promises approach. Both assume largely unified, collective peoples, and both see constitutions as primarily future-oriented. As promises, constitutions are primarily about articulating and representing collective ideals. As precommitment devices, constitutions are about creating institutional mechanisms that help effectuate our own current plans in the future (Elster 2000). Constitutions entrench our current preferences and put in place devices to help ensure that those preferences will be implemented in the future despite changing circumstances. A simple example at an individual level is that if one were to decide to lose weight, one could simply resolve not to eat the chocolate cake or one could take the further step of throwing the cake away. Likewise, constitutions can be seen as entrenching a current consensus against a variety of potential future political threats. Generally speaking, however, the assumption is not necessarily that the constitutional drafters are more virtuous than those who will be living under the constitution, but that the former will be differently and perhaps better situated. Constitutional drafters might well look to entrench favored commitments against the shifting or more partial preferences of future political officeholders, for example. They might look to remove particularly divisive issues from the political arena, or control the forum within which they are discussed (Holmes 1995). One concern with the precommitment approach is that it assumes initial consensus in order to focus on the problem of how to effectuate those commitments across time, but the initial constitutional decisions may themselves be controversial and contested which might in turn suggest that the constitutional entrenchment is serving a different purpose than guarding against temptations. Indeed, on some issues, constitutions may not be entrenching a settled outcome at all but may simply be carrying the debate into the future (Waldron 1999; Whittington forthcoming).

By contrast, contractarian approaches assume that there is current disagreement among the members of a given society and a constitution serves as a contract among those divergent interests. This is, of course, a classic model of thinking about the ordering of political societies with roots in political theorists such as

Thomas Hobbes, John Locke, and David Hume. It provided a common way of thinking about the origin of societies and their own revolutionary experience for the founding generation in the United States.[1] More immediately, contract metaphors have played a prominent role in some recent works in political theory and political economy (Rawls 1999; Buchanan and Tullock 1962). Despite the divergent interests of the members of society, the contractual approach argues that constitutions provide the basis for general agreement and consent precisely because they offer potential benefits to all (Mueller 2000; Buchanan 2001). But also because constitutions rest on divergent, even conflicting, interests, enforcement of the constitutional contract is a persistent and serious issue.

A related model relevant to at least some constitutional features is that of credible commitments. Whereas precommitment devices are concerned with carrying our own current preferences into the future, credible commitments are concerned with making promises believable to someone else—they are about sending signals of credibility. Thus, in an economic context, offering security for a loan makes promises for repayment more credible and less risky, and credit is more readily available and on better terms if repayment is less risky. In the constitutional context, particular constitutional features such as expanded suffrage, specific rights provisions, or judicial review might be integrated into a political system in order to satisfy some powerful internal or external constituency. Without such credible constitutional commitments, those powerful actors might either withdraw benefits from the state or engage in politically destabilizing behavior (North and Weingast 1989; Moustafa 2007).

Finally, constitutions may be understood as coordination devices. The coordination approach argues that constitutions provide the ground rules that facilitate and enable cooperative political and social action on the part of those who live under them. The primary virtue of a constitution is that it settles disputes and provides a stable and reliable order, allowing individuals to make meaningful plans with others. Because the constitution primarily facilitates cooperation, those operating under the constitution generally have an incentive to foster and uphold its terms rather than subvert it. Moreover, because the costs of deviating from social conventions are high once those conventions are established, constitutional rules and practices are likely to be relatively stable and self-enforcing (Hardin 1999; Ordeshook 1992; Voigt 1999).

Across these various approaches, constitutions are understood to achieve their effects in different ways. Constitutions entrench rules and commitments. Judicially enforceable constitutional rights provisions are perhaps the most familiar, and

---

[1] Although the early state constitutions were often conceptualized as social contracts of the classic Lockean type, the national constitution was understood to be a negotiated agreement among various important interests in the early republic. A school of thought associated with the Jeffersonian and antebellum Democratic parties characterized the U.S. Constitution as a "compact" among the states.

often the most controversial, examples of such entrenchments. But these are not the only "hardwired" provisions of a constitution that can entrench initial interests or values. The equal-state apportionment of the U.S. Senate is just one example (Levinson 2006). Constitutions can establish common standards and expectations about acceptable political behavior. By making relatively clear what would constitute a violation of community expectations, constitutions help deter violations and help clarify when violations have occurred (Weingast 1997). Finally, constitutions can help establish a "grammar," "language," or "discourse" of political debate and legitimacy (Harris 1992; Goldford 2005; Schweber 2007). To the extent that the constitution successfully does so, political actors reproduce the terms of the constitutional text through their ongoing rhetoric and actions.

This still leaves open the question of what constitutions can do within a political order. A number of possibilities exist. A little studied possibility is that constitutions are thought to help legitimate a political regime, whether in the eyes of domestic or international constituencies. Constitutions and constitutional decisions have clearly served a public relations purpose even for established democracies, and the act of drafting a constitution may well serve to win support for a new regime (Dudziak 2002; Widner 2007). Constitutions authorize government action. They empower government against a background of private actors and rights and potentially against a background of other governmental actors as well. In authorizing government action, a constitution may also direct government toward favored goals and mark out the purposes to which government power is to be put (Elkin 2006; Edling 2003). Constitutions also structure government powers. They define the offices of government and distribute powers among them. Finally, of course, constitutions limit government powers.

3 Empirical Constitutionalism

A third branch of literature relating to constitutionalism focuses on empirical issues of how constitutions operate in practice. There is, of course, a great deal of work on how particular political institutions or political systems operate. One can, to some degree, infer something about constitutional features from such studies that are not explicitly concerned with analyzing constitutions. More valuable, however, are studies that are specifically focused on empirically investigating constitutions and their components.

One large question is whether constitutions even matter. The question is of obvious interest, but the problems associated with answering the question are daunting. The behavioralists long ago raised the question of whether institutional features of political systems such as constitutions had significant effects on political outcomes or whether social and cultural factors determined whether nations developed and maintained free democratic systems or not. Although the behavioralist challenge has been met on many fronts by showing that institutions do indeed matter in politics, the macro effects of constitutions remain the subject of debate. The issue has become all the more pressing as constitutional design becomes a matter of practical concern for nations across the globe (Murphy 2007; Lutz 2006).

Constitutions might matter for various political outcomes that we care about. Economists have recently begun to examine the empirical consequences of different constitutional designs, and unsurprisingly they have been particularly interested in the consequences for economic outputs. Of particular concern, for example, is whether presidentialist systems are more capable of engaging in economic reform and trade liberalization, or whether presidentialist systems have smaller governments (Persson and Tabellini 2003; Nielson 2003). It remains an open question of whether particular constitutional institutions—such as separation of powers, federalism, or judicial review—generally increase the freedom of the citizens who live under those institutions (Lane 1996). More work needs to be done on that issue, as well as the question of whether such institutions have value in particular contexts even if they need not be universal features of meaningful constitutions.

Constitutional design may also matter for the consolidation and maintenance of democracy. Certain constitutional features help create different kinds of democratic regimes. Fundamental electoral rules and the basic design of representative institutions help determine the type and size of political coalitions that will form within a country. Basic features of the constitutional design may also help determine the longevity of a democratic regime and whether the democratic system will ultimately be subverted from within (Barros 2002; Cheibub and Limongi 2002; Samuels and Shugart 2003).

If one large set of empirical issues involve the consequences of constitutions, another large set of empirical issues involve the internal operation of constitutions. Scholars working from both positive and normative traditions have increasingly begun to examine assumptions about how constitutions work. The political foundations of an independent judiciary has received a great deal of attention (see Vanberg and Cross, both in this volume). Such studies provide insight into how particular constitutional institutions develop and are maintained, and they ultimately also have implications for thinking about the consequences of constitutional designs. A great deal of normative constitutional scholarship has been driven by the apparent conflict between democracy and judicial review, but empirical scholarship suggests that the exercise of judicial review is often favored by political leaders and that the relationship between democratic politics and judicial review is far more complicated than the traditional emphasis on the countermajoritarian veto wielded by the courts would suggest (Whittington 2007).

A related issue is how and why constitutional change occurs. The alteration of constitutions to entrench rights and empower judiciaries is one example of constitutional change that has attracted empirical analyses, and these have provided a basis for examining the motivations and triggers for constitutional changes (Hirschl 2004; Erdos 2006; Rittberger and Schimmelfennig 2006). Constitutions differ in how high of a threshold they establish for formal constitutional change, which has consequences for how often constitutions are amended and how easily constitutional change can be used to trump the decisions of government officials such as judges (Lutz 1994; Reed 1999). Formal constitutional amendment is only one vehicle for constitutional change, however. Scholars have increasingly emphasized the importance of informal constitutional changes, some of which may eventually be formalized in the constitutional text but many of which are not (Ackerman 1991; Whittington 1999; Strauss 2001; Graber 2005). The empirical theories of constitutional change are not yet well developed, however, and there is a great deal of room for development both theoretically and empirically in this area.

4 Conclusion

Constitutional scholarship has grown and changed substantially in recent years, and there is room for substantial additional growth in coming years. Even in the area of normative constitutionalism, where the literature over the past half-century has been extensively developed, there are numerous live debates. More striking than the new arguments in the old debates perhaps has been the emergence of entirely new areas of research. Many are still in their infancy. The new and growing literature on the constitution outside the courts or on empirical theories of constitutional adoption and change, for example, raise fundamental issues about how constitutions work and are growing but remain theoretically and empirically underdeveloped. Too little is known about how constitutions can contribute to the stability of democratic regimes, the freedom of the citizenry, and other political outcomes that we might care about.

The three areas of constitutional scholarship outlined in this chapter are unfortunately often isolated from one another. In recent years, there has been an increasing appreciation of the benefits of interdisciplinary conversations in normative constitutional theory. In coming years, there is likely to be an increasing appreciation for the benefits of research and conversations that cross the boundaries between the several areas of constitutional scholarship. In particular, the normative constitutional theorists who drive a great deal of explicit interest in constitutional institutions often rest their arguments on assumptions about constitutions that require greater conceptual and empirical work to adequately unpack and examine. Recent work on the constitution outside the court and on the countermajoritarian character of judicial review provide encouraging examples of bodies of research that cross these divides. Constitutional scholarship in each of these divergent areas has responded to its own separate traditions and problems, and these will undoubtedly continue to motivate their development. But progress can also be made by recognizing that these different bodies of work are addressing a common subject matter and form a common literature on constitutionalism.

References

ACKERMAN, B. A. 1991. *We the People*, vol. 1: *Foundations*. Cambridge, Mass.: Harvard University Press.

—— 2007. The Holmes Lectures: the living constitution. *Harvard Law Review*, 120: 1727–812.

ALEXANDER, L., and SCHAUER, F. 1997. On extrajudicial constitutional interpretation. *Harvard Law Review*, 110: 1359–87.

—— and PRAKASH, S. 2004. "Is that English you're speaking?" Some arguments for the primacy of intent in interpretation. *San Diego Law Review*, 41: 967–95.

ALLAN, T. R. S. 2003. *Constitutional Justice: A Liberal Theory of the Rule of Law*. New York: Oxford University Press.

BALKIN, J. M. 1997. Agreements with Hell and other objects of our faith. *Fordham Law Review*, 65: 1703–38.

—— 2007. Abortion and original meaning. *Constitutional Commentary*, 24.

BARNETT, R. E. 2003. Constitutional legitimacy. *Columbia Law Review*, 103: 111–48.

—— 2004. *Restoring the Lost Constitution: The Presumption of Liberty*. Princeton, NJ: Princeton University Press.

BARROS, R. 2002. *Constitutionalism and Dictatorship: Pinochet, the Junta, and the 1980 Constitution*. New York: Cambridge University Press.

BICKEL, A. M. 1962. *The Least Dangerous Branch: The Supreme Court at the Bar of Politics*. Indianapolis: Bobbs-Merrill.

BOGDANOR, V. (ed.) 2003. *The British Constitution in the Twentieth Century*. New York: Oxford University Press.

BUCHANAN, J. M. 2001. *Choice, Contract, and Constitutions*. Indianapolis: Liberty Fund.

—— and TULLOCK, G. 1962. *The Calculus of Consent: Logical Foundations of Constitutional Democracy*. Ann Arbor: University of Michigan Press.

CHARLES, G.-U. 2007. Democracy and distortion. *Cornell Law Quarterly*, 92: 601–77.

CHEIBUB, J., and LIMONGI, F. 2002. Democratic institutions and regime survival: presidentialism and parliamentarism reconsidered. *Annual Review of Political Science*, 5: 151–79.

DUDZIAK, M. L. 2000. *Cold War Civil Rights: Race and the Image of American Democracy*. Princeton, NJ: Princeton University Press.

DWORKIN, R. 1985. *A Matter of Principle*. Cambridge, Mass.: Harvard University Press.

DWORKIN, R. 1996. *Freedom's Law: The Moral Reading of the Constitution.* Cambridge, Mass.: Harvard University Press.

EDLING, M. M. 2003. *A Revolution in Favor of Government: Origins of the U.S. Constitution and the Making of the American State.* New York: Oxford University Press.

EISGRUBER, C. L. 2001. *Constitutional Self-Government.* Princeton, NJ: Princeton University Press.

ELKIN, S. L. 2006. *Reconstructing the Commercial Republic: Constitutional Design after Madison.* Chicago: University of Chicago Press.

ELSTER, J. 2000. *Ulysses Unbound: Studies in Rationality, Precommitment, and Constraints.* New York: Cambridge University Press.

ELY, J. H. 1973. The wages of crying wolf: a comment on *Roe v. Wade. Yale Law Journal,* 82: 920–49.

—— 1980. *Democracy and Distrust: A Theory of Judicial Review.* Cambridge, Mass.: Harvard University Press.

EPSTEIN, R. A. 2003. *Skepticism and Freedom: A Modern Case for Classical Liberalism.* Chicago: University of Chicago Press.

ERDOS, D. O. 2006. National Bill of Rights institutionalization: a study of Westminster democracies. Ph.D. dissertation, Princeton University.

FLEMING, J. E., and BARBER, S. A. 2007. *Constitutional Interpretation: The Basic Questions.* New York: Oxford University Press.

FRIEDMAN, B. 2000. The history of the countermajoritarian difficulty, part four: law's politics. *University of Pennsylvania Law Review,* 148: 971–1064.

FRIEDRICH, C. J. 1941. *Constitutional Government and Democracy: Theory and Practice in Europe and America.* Boston: Little, Brown.

—— 1968. Constitutions and constitutionalism. Pp. 318–26 in vol. 3, *International Encyclopedia of the Social Sciences,* ed. D. L. Sills. New York: Macmillan.

GARRETT, E. 2003. Is the party over? Courts and the political process. *Supreme Court Review,* 2002: 95–152.

GELDEREN, M. VAN, and SKINNER, Q. (eds.) 2002. *Republicanism: A Shared European Heritage.* New York: Cambridge University Press.

GOLDFORD, D. J. 2005. *The American Constitution and the Debate over Originalism.* New York: Cambridge University Press.

GOLDSWORTHY, J. 2001. *The Sovereignty of Parliament: History and Philosophy.* New York: Oxford University Press.

GRABER, M. A. 2005. Settling the West: the annexation of Texas, the Louisiana Purchase, and Bush v. Gore. In *The Louisiana Purchase and American Expansion, 1803–1898,* ed. L. Levinson and B. H. Sparrow. Lanham, Md.: Rowman and Littlefield.

—— 2006. *Dred Scott and the Problem of Constitutional Evil.* New York: Cambridge University Press.

GRIFFIN, S. M. 2007. Rebooting originalism. Tulane public law research paper.

HABERMAS, J. 1996. *Between Facts and Norms: Contributions to a Discourse Theory of Law and Democracy.* Cambridge, Mass.: MIT Press.

—— 2001. Why Europe needs a constitution. *New Left Review,* 11: 5–26.

HAND, L. 1958. *The Bill of Rights.* Cambridge, Mass.: Harvard University Press.

HARDIN, R. 1999. *Liberalism, Constitutionalism, and Democracy.* New York: Oxford University Press.

HARRIS, W. F., II. 1992. *The Interpretable Constitution.* Baltimore: Johns Hopkins University Press.

HERSHOVITZ, S. (ed.) 2006. *Exploring Law's Empire: The Jurisprudence of Ronald Dworkin.* New York: Oxford University Press.

HIRSCHL, R. 2004. *Towards Juristocracy: The Origins and Consequences of the New Constitutionalism.* Cambridge, Mass.: Harvard University Press.

HOLMES, S. 1995. *Passions and Constraint: On the Theory of Liberal Democracy.* Chicago: University of Chicago Press.

KAHN, P. W. 1993. *Legitimacy and History: Self-Government in American Constitutional Theory.* New Haven, Conn.: Yale University Press.

KALMAN, L. 1996. *The Strange Career of Legal Liberalism.* New Haven, Conn.: Yale University Press.

KARLAN, P. S. 2002. Exit strategies in constitutional law: lessons for getting the least dangerous branch out of the political thicket. *Boston University Law Review,* 82: 669–98.

KECK, T. M. 2004. *The Most Activist Supreme Court in History: The Road to Modern Judicial Conservatism.* Chicago: University of Chicago Press.

KLARMAN, M. J. 1997. Majoritarian judicial review: the entrenchment problem. *Georgetown Law Journal,* 85: 491–553.

KRAMER, L. 2004. *The People Themselves: Popular Constitutionalism and Judicial Review.* New York: Oxford University Press.

LANE, J.-E. 1996. *Constitutions and Political Theory.* Manchester: Manchester University Press.

LASH, K. 2007. Originalism, popular sovereignty, and reverse stare decisis. *Virginia Law Review,* 93: 1437–81.

LAWSON, G. 2007. Mostly unconstitutional: the case against precedent revisited. *Ave Maria Law Review,* 5: 1–22.

LEVINSON, S. 2006. *Our Undemocratic Constitution: Where the Constitution Goes Wrong (and How We the People Can Correct It).* New York: Oxford University Press.

LOUGHLIN, M. 2005. Constitutional theory: a 25th anniversary essay. *Oxford Journal of Legal Studies,* 25: 183–202.

LUTZ, D. S. 1994. Toward a theory of constitutional amendment. *American Political Science Review,* 88: 355–70.

—— 2006. *Principles of Constitutional Design.* New York: Cambridge University Press.

McGINNIS, J., and RAPPAPORT, M. B. 2003. Symmetric entrenchment: a constitutional and normative theory. *Virginia Law Review,* 89: 385–445.

—— —— 2007. A pragmatic defense of originalism. *Northwestern University Law Review,* 101: 383–98.

McILWAIN, C. H. 1947. *Constitutionalism, Ancient and Modern.* Ithaca, NY: Cornell University Press.

MARMOR, A. 2007. Are constitutions legitimate? *Canadian Journal of Law and Jurisprudence,* 20: 69–94.

MICHELMAN, F. I. 1998. Constitutional authorship. In *Constitutionalism: Philosophical Foundations,* ed. L. Alexander. New York: Cambridge University Press.

MOUSTAFA, T. 2007. *The Struggle for Constitutional Power: Law, Politics, and Economic Development in Egypt.* New York: Cambridge University Press.

MUELLER, D. C. 2000. *Constitutional Democracy.* New York: Oxford University Press.

MURPHY, W. F. 2007. *Constitutional Democracy: Creating and Maintaining a Just Political Order.* Baltimore: John Hopkins University Press.

NELSON, C. E. 2001. *Stare decisis* and demonstrably erroneous precedents. *Virginia Law Review*, 87: 1–84.

NIELSON, D. L. 2003. Supplying trade reform: political institutions and liberalization in middle-income presidential democracies. *American Journal of Political Science*, 47: 470–91.

NORTH, D. C., and WEINGAST, B. R. 1989. Constitutions and commitment: the evolution of institutions governing public choice in seventeenth-century England. *Journal of Economic History*, 49: 803–32.

NORTON, A. 1993. *Republic of Signs: Liberal Theory and American Popular Culture*. Chicago: University of Chicago Press.

O'NEILL, J. 2005. *Originalism in American Law and Politics: A Constitutional History*. Baltimore: Johns Hopkins University Press.

ORDESHOOK, P. C. 1992. Constitutional stability. *Constitutional Political Economy*, 3: 137–75.

PENNINGTON, K. 1993. *The Prince and the Law, 1200–1600: Sovereignty and Rights in the Western Legal Tradition*. Berkeley: University of California Press.

PERSSON, T., and TABELLINI, G. 2003. *The Economic Effects of Constitutions*. Cambridge, Mass.: MIT Press.

POSNER, E. A., and VERMEULE, A. 2002. Legislative entrenchment: a reappraisal. *Yale Law Journal*, 111: 1665–706.

POST, R., and SIEGEL, R. B. 2007. *Roe* rage: democratic constitutionalism and backlash. *Harvard Civil Rights–Civil Liberties Law Review*, 42: 373–434.

RAWLS, J. 1999. *A Theory of Justice*, rev. edn. Cambridge, Mass.: Harvard University Press.

REED, D. S. 1999. Popular constitutionalism: toward a theory of state constitutional meanings. *Rutgers Law Journal*, 30: 871–932.

RITTBERGER, B., and SCHIMMELFENNIG, F. 2006. *The Constitutionalization of the European Union*. London: Routledge.

SAMUELS, D. J., and SHUGART, M. S. 2003. Presidentialism, elections and representation. *Journal of Theoretical Politics*, 15: 33–60.

SARTORI, G. 1962. Constitutionalism: a preliminary discussion. *American Political Science Review*, 56: 853–64.

SCHWEBER, H. H. 2007. *The Language of Liberal Constitutionalism*. New York: Cambridge University Press.

SEIDMAN, M. L. 2001. *Our Unsettled Constitution: A New Defense of Constitutionalism and Judicial Review*. New Haven, Conn.: Yale University Press.

SOLUM, L. B. 2007. Constitutional texting. *San Diego Law Review*, 44: 123–51.

STRAUSS, D. A. 2001. The irrelevance of constitutional amendments. *Harvard Law Review*, 114: 1457–505.

SUNSTEIN, C. R. 1993. *The Partial Constitution*. Cambridge, Mass.: Harvard University Press.

—— 1999. *One Case at a Time: Judicial Minimalism on the Court*. Cambridge, Mass.: Harvard University Press.

TELES, S. M. 2008. *The Rise of the Conservative Legal Movement*. Princeton, NJ: Princeton University Press.

THOMAS, G. 2004. Recovering the political constitution: the Madisonian vision. *Review of Politics*, 66: 233–56.

TRIBE, L. 1980. The puzzling persistence of process-based constitutional theories. *Yale Law Journal*, 89: 1063–80.

TUSHNET, M. V. 1980. Darkness on the edge of town: the contributions of John Hart Ely to constitutional theory. *Yale Law Journal*, 89: 1037–62.

—— 1999. *Taking the Constitution Away from the Courts*. Princeton, NJ: Princeton University Press.

VOIGT, S. 1999. *Explaining Constitutional Change: A Positive Economic Approach*. Cheltenham: Edward Elgar.

WALDRON, J. 1999. *Law and Disagreement*. New York: Oxford University Press.

—— 2006. The core of the case against judicial review. *Yale Law Journal*, 115: 1346–406.

WECHSLER, H. 1959. Toward neutral principles of constitutional law. *Harvard Law Review*, 73: 1–35.

WEINGAST, B. R. 1997. The political foundations of democracy and the rule of law. *American Political Science Review*, 91: 245–63.

WHEELER, H. 1975. Constitutionalism. In *Handbook of Political Science*, ed. F. I. Greenstein and N. W. Polsby. Reading, Mass.: Addison-Welsley.

WHITTINGTON, K. E. 1999*a*. *Constitutional Construction: Divided Powers and Constitutional Meaning*. Cambridge, Mass.: Harvard University Press.

—— 1999*b*. *Constitutional Interpretation: Textual Meaning, Original Intent, and Judicial Review*. Lawrence: University Press of Kansas.

—— 2002*a*. Extrajudicial constitutional interpretation: three objections and responses. *North Carolina Law Review*, 80: 773–851.

—— 2002*b*. An indispensable feature? Constitutionalism and judicial review. *New York University Journal of Legislation and Public Policy*, 6: 21–33.

—— 2004. The new originalism. *Georgetown Journal of Law and Public Policy*, 2: 599–613.

—— 2007. *Political Foundations of Judicial Supremacy: The Presidency, the Supreme Court, and Constitutional Leadership in U.S. History*. Princeton, NJ: Princeton University Press.

—— forthcoming. Constitutional constraints in politics. In *The Supreme Court and the Idea of Constitutionalism*, ed. M. R. Zinnman. Philadelphia: University of Pennsylvania Press.

WIDNER, J. A. 2007. Constitution writing in post-conflict settings. *William and Mary Law Review*, 49.

WORMUTH, F. D. 1949. *Origins of Modern Constitutionalism*. New York: Harper.

ZEISBERG, M. A. 2007. Constitutional war powers: beyond the zone of twilight. Manuscript.

CONSTITUTIONAL LAW AND AMERICAN POLITICS

MARK A. GRABER

CASUAL spectators follow politics and law the same way they follow sports and entertainment. During sporting events, the camera and average fan obsessively follow the ball and scoreboard. Millions tune in each week to discover who gets voted off the island or remains in the American Idol competition. During political and legislative campaigns, the media provides citizens with numerous opinion polls and legislative scorecards. Litigants and court-watchers count judicial votes and determine the winning percentages of the leading litigants before the Supreme Court.

Afficionados of sports and politics recognize that the crucial events which determine outcomes often take place away from the camera's eye. Players on successful teams create scoring opportunities by moving without the ball. Producers and directors conduct extensive off-camera investigations that ensure viewers will be entranced by the televised product. Students of congressional elections are similarly aware that the private campaign for dollars frequently determines the public campaign for votes (Herrnson 2004). Power accrues to those who control the political agenda, not to those who win particular votes (Riker 1986; Bachrach and Baratz 1970). Public law scholars, by comparison, too rarely "look off the ball."

"The scholarly focus," Keith Whittington (2000, 601) observes, remains "on individual justices and how they cast their votes."

Public law scholars whose scholarship focuses primarily on the public conflicts between constitutional authorities fail to appreciate how constitutional law influences American politics and judicial decision-making. Legal norms better explain how constitutional controversies are structured than how they are resolved. Basic principles of constitutional law help secure legal agreement in the face of political disagreement. Political actors who reason constitutionally do not dispute numerous matters that they dispute vigorously when employing other justificatory logics. Citizens who disagree about the merits of a recent Supreme Court nomination nevertheless agree that the nominee will legitimately serve on the bench if confirmed by the Senate. When political disagreements are resolved into legal disagreements, basic principles of constitutional law alter the terrain on which those conflicts are fought. Political actors who reason constitutionally debate different matters than they do when they employ other justificatory logics. Elected officials and interest groups during the New Deal debated the merits of national legislation mandating collective bargaining. The justices on the Hughes Court debated whether various industries covered by the resulting laws were engaged in interstate commerce.

The following pages detail how and why constitutional law influences both judicial and public decision-making. Section 1 discusses the tendency for political scientists to first claim that constitutional law is no different to other forms of policy-making, observes how those claims are almost always qualified in practice, and points to problems with the standard qualifications. Too often concerned only to demonstrate the political components of judicial decision-making, many scholars explore only those aspects of judicial decision-making best explained by policy commitments. Section 2 highlights political science and legal scholarship which detail how constitutional norms and standards generate legal agreements among persons who dispute the underlying merits of particular policies under constitutional attack. These norms and standards explain constitutional criticism, why only a small proportion of the political questions that occupy Americans are normally resolved into constitutional questions, and how legislatures by making constitutionally "safe" choices may immunize their decisions from judicial scrutiny. Section 3 focuses on another line of scholarly inquiry which describes how constitutional law structures those constitutional controversies that do take place. Constitutional debates are often quite different from other political debates. Constitutional norms and standards require constitutional decision-makers to treat as important phenomena that are of less interest to policy-makers and attach little significance to those phenomena crucial to the underlying policy decision. Section 4 briefly comments on aspects of constitutional decision-making obscured by too sharp a distinction between law and policy. Recent work in both law and political science suggest that scholars who neatly divide the justificatory world into legal norms and policy norms implicitly take sides in hotly contested interpretive debates and overlook the most important differences between elected officials and judges as constitutional decision-makers.

Law may constrain or constitute rather than motivate. Behaviorally oriented political scientists may correctly describe justices as consciously motivated when deciding cases primarily by a desire to make good policy, rejecting Howard Gillman's (1999, 67–8) claim that "Supreme Court justices may sometimes view themselves as stewards of institutional missions, and that this identity generates *motivations* of duty and professional responsibility" (emphasis added). Chess players, after all, are routinely described as motivated by a desire to win games, not by some institutional mission to maintain the rules of the game. Still, one cannot explain what justices, other constitutional decision-makers, and chess players do without reference to the norms of their respective practices. Whether players perceive a choice and what choices they perceive as legitimate are often a consequence of what choices can be justified within the rules, even if a commitment to playing by those rules does not explain what choice is made.

1 POLICY AND LAW IN CONSTITUTIONAL DECISION-MAKING

Many political scientists make claims which suggest that constitutional law has little influence on political practice, the practices of justices on the Supreme Court of the United States in particular. Jeffrey Segal and Harold Spaeth, the leading proponents of the attitudinal model of judicial decision-making, insist that Supreme Court Justices exercise "virtually untrammeled policy-making authority" (2002, 86). *Stare decisis*, original meanings, and textualism, crucial passages in their writings apparently assert, serve only to mask judicial rulings reached on entirely different grounds. Segal and Spaeth declare, "precedent ... provides no guide to the justices' decisions" and does not "limit ... the operation of judicial policy preferences" (2002, 81). They further insist that "no one has systemically demonstrated that legislative or framers' intent influences the decisions of Supreme Court justices" (2002, 75), and that "no one has systemically demonstrated that plain meaning influences the decision of Supreme Court justices" (2002, 59). In their view, scientific proof that precedent, history, and text matter does not exist. "No proponent," Segal and Spaeth contend, "has even suggested a falsifiable test for th[ese] component[s] of the legal model" (2002, 59, 75).

Similar assertions litter the political science literature. "Most justices, in most cases," the leading work on the strategic model of judicial decision-making contends, "pursue policy; that is, they want to move the substantive content of law as close as possible to their preferred position" (Epstein and Knight 1998, 23). Gregory Caldeira and John Wright (1988, 1111) "propose that justices of the U.S. Supreme Court are motivated by ideological preferences for public policy and they pursue their policy goals by deciding cases with maximum potential impact on political, social, or economic policy." Andrew Martin (2006, 4, 6) states that "(a) key tenet of the modern study of Supreme Court decision-making is that justices are policy-seeking political actors, ... who use their resources to pursue preferred policies given political constraints." Lee Epstein, when Head of the Law and Courts Section of the American Political Science Association, described the legal model of judicial decision-making as "trivial" (1999, 3).

These bald claims are usually, but not always, modified subsequently. Caldeira and Wright (1988, 1111) "recognize that the justices maximize their positions subject to a complicated matrix of legal rules, social norms, and institutional constraints." Segal and Spaeth demonstrate that the attitudinal model explains judicial *votes* only in "hard cases." They concede the existence of "meritless" legal claims that "no self-respecting judge would decide solely on the basis of his or her policy preferences" (2002, 93). "[P]recedents lie on both sides of most every controversy," in their view, only "at the appellate level" (2002, 77). Epstein and Jack Knight believe that policy-minded justices have strategic reasons for making legal decisions. "[J]ustices who wish to establish policy that will govern the future activity of the society in which their Court exists," they (1998, 45) state, "will be constrained to choose from among the set of rules (precedent and the like) that the members of that society will recognize and accept."

The tendency to understate dramatically the role of constitutional law in judicial decision-making nevertheless has a baneful influence on scholarship, even when the text later adopts a more sophisticated understanding of legal factors. The argument that justices have strategic reasons for adhering to legal norms assumes that elected officials and the general public have commitments to those legal norms independent of their policy commitments. Otherwise, justices could predict that their rulings were be implemented only to the extent that outside actors supported the underlying policy. No empirical study, however, has attempted to prove the intuitively doubtful claim that Supreme Court justices are the political actors least constrained or motivated by accepted legal norms.[1] Younger scholars who read works concluding that the justices are "strengthening [their] position as king of the government hill" (Segal and Spaeth 2002, 432) or "that justices' ideological

---

[1] Social science studies have concluded that ordinary people often obey laws that they disagree with, even when they have no strategic reason for compliance (e.g. Tyler 2006). No study, however, has directly compared the tendencies for citizens, elected officials, and justices to reason legally.

predilections affect their decisions in much the same way that other elite political actors are motivated by their personal ideological agendas" (Caldeira and Wright 1988, 1120–1) may perhaps be forgiven for forgetting how these blunt assertions about the judicial practice were previously qualified.

Empirical political science scholarship tends to focus on those aspects of the judicial decision process in which constitutional law matters the least, often to the exclusion of those aspects of the judicial process in which law plays a more significant role. Segal, Spaeth, and other proponents of the attitudinal model tend to count judicial votes, even though a good case can be made that judicial opinions both are far more influenced by legal factors and have far greater policy impacts (Friedman 2006, 266–7). The terrain of "easy" cases is rarely mapped by commentators looking at the influence of policy on decisions in "hard cases." The extent to which justices exercise "virtually untrammeled policy-making authority," however, depends on the ratio of easy to hard constitutional cases. If, as Friedman (2006) suggests, most statutory questions do not present analogous constitutional questions, then justices may be limited to making policy in a relatively small domain, at least when compared to elected officials.

Proponents of legal models of judicial decision-making have sometimes confused matters by conceding that crucial elements of the legal model are not testable or by providing vague standards for determining whether law influenced constitutional decisions. Segal and Spaeth (2002, 432–3) correctly point out that such claims as "decisions are considered legally motivated if they represent a judge's sincere belief that their decision represents their best understanding of what the law requires" (Gillman 2001, 486) are hardly testable. The legal model is capable of scientific testing. Herbert Kritzer and Mark Richards (2003; Richards and Kritzer 2002), as noted below, have demonstrated that judicial voting patterns change in response to landmark precedents. Jeb Barnes (2006) found that legal disagreements over the meaning of federal statutes were substantially reduced when, in response to judicial decisions, Congress rewrote crucial provisions.

Legal models perform particularly well when some judicial phenomenon other than differences in judicial voting patterns is studied. Some tests are so obvious that no respectable journal would think the results worth publishing. Judges who oppose capital punishment sometimes declare unconstitutional legislation mandating the death penalty, but as the legal model would predict, judges who favor the death penalty do not interpret federal or state constitutions as mandating that sanction. Other tests have been run which demonstrate that law matters, but they have been used for other scholarly purposes. Frederick Schauer's (2006) analysis of the judicial agenda was not directed at models of judicial decision-making, but the results tend to confirm the significance of constitutional law as a constraint on judging. Finally, as noted in Section 3, students of American constitutional development have noted how law has structured particular episodes in American history. Looking at all this evidence as a whole may help both legalists and behaviorists gain a more nuanced understanding of the contributions each school of thought has to make on the role of constitutional law in American politics.

2 CREATING AGREEMENT

The strength of practices such as law is best measured by determining the extent to which practitioners agree on the appropriate norms and application of those norms. That doctors do not always agree on the proper diagnosis or treatment in "hard cases" hardly entails that medicine is entirely subjective. Constitutional criticism, the remarkably limited agenda of constitutional courts, and the existence of safe harbors on almost every constitutional question all indicate that constitutional law similarly constrains legal practitioners and decision-makers. Constitutions and constitutional law consistently secure agreements where agreements would otherwise not exist. People who reason constitutionally agree on numerous legal standards, even when they dispute the merits of the contested policy. Some constitutional agreements help forge normative agreements. Americans may favor the Electoral College because they revere a constitution which mandates the Electoral College.

The practice of constitutional criticism in the United States illustrates the agreement function of constitutional law. Antifederalists, abolitionists, populists, progressives, and contemporary citizens have alleged numerous flaws in the constitutional order. Sanford Levinson (2006, 21) penned a polemic describing the constitution as "both insufficiently democratic, in a country that professes to believe in democracy, and significantly dysfunctional, in terms of the quality of the government we received." The subjects of his scorn include equal state representation in the Senate, the Electoral College, a life-tenured judiciary, the presidential veto, the limited grounds for impeachment, and the supermajoritarian requirements for constitutional amendment (Levinson 2006, 6–7). Yet, as is the case with previous constitutional critics, Levinson agrees that these pernicious constitutional provisions are presently the law of the land. He does not insist, the text of Article I to the contrary, that the Patriot Act is illegal because the Senate which approved that measure is undemocratically constructed.

The rules Levinson challenges have consequences that would almost certainly guarantee intense constitutional debate were constitutional debate little more than a stylized version of policy or political debate. Presidential campaigns would be quite different had the Constitution mandated that the winner gain a majority of the popular vote rather than a majority of the Electoral College votes. Constitutional structures explain why the Kerry and Bush campaigns in 2004 spent almost half their funds on Florida and Ohio, ignoring such states as New York and California (Levinson 2007, 15). The practice of electing all members of the national legislature from states or districts located entirely within states contributed significantly to political polarization during the 1850s and to polarization at present (Graber 2006a, 159). Presidential parties do notoriously poorly during the second midterm election, but no president has ever received a vote of no confidence after such an adverse result. The constitutional rule limiting impeachments to "high crimes and misdemeanors" restricts the capacity of partisan majorities in Congress to remove an unpopular president whose party was decisively rejected during the most recent national election. Federal spending on matters as different as highways and terror prevention grossly favor low population western states. Equal state representation in the Senate guarantees that Wyoming will garner (almost) as much transportation funding as New York (Lee and Oppenheimer 1999). Numerous popular constitutional amendments, ranging from prohibitions on child labor to permissions for school prayer, have failed to meet the supermajoritarian requirements for ratification (Kyvig 1996). Nevertheless, although the "hardwired" provisions of the Constitution create political winners and losers, their meaning is rarely controversial. Californians and Rhode Islanders agree that each state is to be represented by two senators and that this arrangement significantly benefits Rhode Island.

These agreements on constitutional law may better explain important preferences or beliefs about best political practices than those preferences or beliefs explain agreements on constitutional law. Persons socialized in a particular constitutional order may develop relatively unthinking commitments to the constitutional procedures of their native polity. Whether persons favor a parliamentary or presidential regime may largely be a function of whether they live and have been educated in a parliamentary or presidential regime. Some Americans wax poetic over constitutional institutions with very clouded historical pasts. The framers adopted the Electoral College largely to provide additional political protections for slavery. Madison and others observed that selecting the president by popular vote would leave southern states with "no influence in the election on the score of the Negroes" (Farrand 1966, 57; Finkelman 2002). No democratic nation subsequently constitutionalized and maintained a practice resembling the Electoral College for electing the national executive. Given these dubious origins and the utter lack of imitation, continued American support for the Electoral College (McGinnis 2007; Lowenstein 2007) ultimately may reflect reverence for the Constitution rather than claimed virtues of that practice that did not occur to the framers and have not occurred to constitutionalists in any other regime (Levinson 2007, 28–9). Had constitutional law mandated different rules for electing the national executive, those rules would almost certainly enjoy the same degree of public acclaim.

Constitutional law generates agreements on the legality of controversial public policies as well as on the legality of potentially controversial political procedures. Tocqueville (1945, 280) grossly distorted both the plasticity of constitutional law and the influence of courts on public policy when he asserted, "scarcely any political question arises in the United States that is not resolved, sooner or later, into a judicial question" (Tocqueville 1945, 280). Two recent studies, the first on contemporary politics (Schauer 2006), the second on politics in the Jacksonian age (Graber 2004), detail how the majority of political questions that arise in the United States remain, in whole or in large part, political questions. Intense political debates are no more likely to be constitutionalized than issues less salient to most voters. The political questions that have historically divided the two major political parties in the United States are rarely resolved into constitutional questions and even more rarely settled by judicial decree. This would not be case were constitutional law a mere mask for policy preferences and Supreme Court justices unalloyed policy-makers.

Professor Frederick Schauer's comparison of judicial and political agendas casts doubt on common impressions "that the Constitution, constitutional law, and the Supreme Court not only occupy a major role in American policymaking, but also in fact make a great deal of American policy" (2006, 11). He found that the justices tend to resolve only political questions of relatively low interest to the general public, at least when compared to political questions being resolved elsewhere in the political system. Schauer's analysis of newspapers and public opinion surveys revealed that such "hot button issues for the court" as "race, sexual orientation, and abortion . . . turn out to generate an unexpectedly low amount of attention" (Schauer 2006, 27) when attention was measured by newspaper headlines, newspaper stories, and responses to questions about the most important political issues facing the country. Judicial rulings on the constitutionality of the Bush administration's antiterrorism policies influence the concerns of the general public only at the margins. *Hamdan v. Rumsfeld* (2006), Schauer observes, is not "much more than a footnote to the war on terrorism" and has "little to do with Iraq—the topic the public and their representatives now care most about" (2006, 27). The issues off the judicial agenda are far more important to the general public than the issues on it. Schauer (2006, 31–2) points out that the justices have not ruled on

fuel prices, the minimum wage, income taxes, the estate tax, Social Security, inflation, interest rates, avian flu, or the nuclear capabilities of Iran and North Korea, while taking on issues related to healthcare, employment, and education that could not seriously be described as in any way connected with current or past policy debates on these topics.

This tendency for the Court to operate at the periphery of American politics has been true for the past half-century. "[T]he Court's noninvolvement, with few exceptions," Schauer details (2006, 44),

encompassed almost all of World War II, European postwar recovery, the occupation of Japan, the Berlin Airlift, the Cold War, the Korean War, nuclear disarmament, Cuba, farm policy and agricultural subsidies, recession, the creation of the interstate highway system, the establishment of Medicare, the war in Vietnam, double-digit inflation, severe gas shortages, and military operations in the Dominican Republic, Panama, Somalia, Lebanon, Kosovo, and Iraq, among others.

That courts making decisions on the basis of constitutional law do not intervene in these matters belies claims that "the extent to which either representative or democratic elections have force and effect depends on the will of a majority of the nine unelected, lifetime-serving justices" (Segal and Spaeth 2002, 2). Comparisons of the judicial and political agendas consistently find that "the people and their elected representatives can nevertheless be understood as still making the vast bulk of decisions that are most important to the people themselves" (Schauer 2006, 53; see Graber 2004, 531–4). Many of these political questions were not resolved into judicial questions because they were not first resolved into constitutional questions. Elected officials, on issues as diverse as the annexation of Cuba and the privatization of social security, have agreed that government may constitutionally make the controversial political choice. Disagreement was limited to policy considerations. Supreme Court justices apparently support this consensus. Although each justice writes approximately thirty to forty opinions a year, no contemporary justice has sought to lay the precedential foundations for making their policy views the law of the land on tax cuts or troop strength in Iraq.

Constitutional law matters even when political questions are resolved into constitutional questions. The Constitution, in most cases, establishes legal floors or ceilings on government policy, but not both.[2] The Eighth Amendment forbids "cruel and unusual punishment." No constitutional provision bans "unusually compassionate punishment." Elected officials may have constitutional obligations to punish crime adequately, but most commentators (e.g. Sager 1993) who champion such duties treat them as not legally enforceable. This feature of constitutional law typically provides elected officials making binary policy choices with a constitutional safe harbor. Although one policy choice is constitutionally controversial, rejecting that choice is not. Constitutional lawyers debate whether government may outlaw flag-burning, impose capital punishment, and condemn land for private development. General agreement exists that government may constitutionally permit flag-burning, refrain from imposing capital punishment, and outlaw condemnations for private development.

Constitutional safe harbors sharply constrain judicial capacity to influence public policy and shape constitutional development. Persons deciding exclusively on policy logics are free to choose whether to outlaw burning the flag, impose capital punishment, or condemn land for private development. Persons deciding exclusively on constitutional logics may intervene only when policy-makers select

---

[2] The potential conflicts between the free exercise and establishment clauses of the First Amendment, and between the press clause of the First Amendment and due process clause of the Fifth Amendment, are the two most important exceptions to the discussion in the text.

the constitutionally controversial alternative. Justices who believe the death penalty morally evil and unconstitutional strike down legislative efforts to mandate capital punishment. Justices who believe the death penalty a moral necessity and constitutionally permitted have no constitutional grounds for intervention when policy makers refuse to punish murder by death. The Marshall Court found this limit on constitutional adjudication particularly frustrating. Shortly after handing down *McCulloch v. Maryland* (1819), the justices wrote a letter to President Monroe declaring that their opinion upholding the national bank provided the necessary legal precedent for sustaining the internal improvements bill under presidential consideration (see Warren 1947, 596–7). Nevertheless, when Monroe (1897) vetoed that bill on constitutional grounds, constitutional law did not provide the Marshall Court with the authority to reverse that constitutional mistake (Graber 2000, 34). A constitutional disagreement could not be fully translated into a legal disagreement because while both the decision to sign and the decision to veto would have been controversial policy choices, only the decision to sign would have been a controversial constitutional choice.

The Marshall Court was one of many constitutional decision-makers whose influence on public policy was sharply limited by their obligation to justify decisions legally. Decision-makers limited to constitutional logics do not participate in debates over the merits of the Constitution. They do not participate in the numerous policy debates, ranging from the proper strategy in Iraq to the structure of national education testing, that are not resolved into constitutional debates. Justices do not participate in constitutional debates whenever elected officials choose the constitutionally uncontroversial policy.

These limits on constitutional decision-making hardly leave constitutional authorities with a dull agenda. Abortion, affirmative action, environmental regulation, and the status of detainees during the war on terrorism are examples of the hot political questions that constitutional logics permit to be resolved into judicial questions. These issues are bitterly contested by prominent interest groups, even if they tend not to be among the first members of the general public think about when asked about their most pressing political concerns. Moreover, much political science scholarship (Epp 1998; Hirschl 2006) suggests that vital political questions are far more likely than in the past to be resolved into constitutional and judicial questions. Still, we should not make "the fallacious leap from the accurate premise that much of what the Supreme Court does is important to the erroneous conclusion that much of what is important is done by the Supreme Court" (Schauer 2006, 8). When keeping one eye on the judicial agenda, students of constitutional politics should keep their other eye firmly on the rest of the political agenda. As the Bible reminds us, understanding that David has slain "his ten thousands" puts in better perspective claims that "Saul has slain his thousands."

3 STRUCTURING DISAGREEMENT

Law structures constitutional conflicts when constitutional conflicts break out. Persons who reason from constitutional norms have different disagreements than persons who reason from other norms. Ideology often explains the differences between persons engaged in a constitutional debate, but law usually explains the debate they are having. Policy disputes over whether the president's economic policies are wise are quite different from constitutional disputes over whether national economic policies regulate interstate commerce, even if both pit liberals against conservatives.

Thinking about "jurisprudential regimes" provides a helpful way of understanding how constitutional law influences constitutional disputes. As detailed by Mark Richards and Herbert Kritzer (2002, 305), "jurisprudential regimes structure Supreme Court decision-making by establishing which case factors are relevant for decision-making and/or by setting the level of scrutiny or balancing the justices are to employ in assessing case factors." The presence of a jurisprudential regime does not guarantee that all justices will reach the same conclusions. Rather, jurisprudential regimes encourage justices to ask the same questions. Justices making decisions in the jurisprudential regime instituted by *Plessy v. Ferguson* (1896) focused on the extent to which the separate facilities offered to white persons and persons of color could be said to be equal. When constitutional decision-makers disagreed, their dispute was over whether the law was a race distinction or a race discrimination (Stephenson 1910; *Plessy v. Ferguson* 1896). Justices making decisions in the jurisprudential regime instituted by *Brown v. Board of Education* (1954) focused on the extent to which laws made justifiable race distinctions. When constitutional decision-makers disagreed, their dispute was over whether government had a sufficiently compelling reason to make a conceded race distinction/discrimination (*Johnson v. California* 2005; *Korematsu v. United States* 1944).

Initial studies indicate that the establishment of a jurisprudential regime influences judicial voting. Richards and Kritzer (2002) found that individual justices were likely to be influenced by different factors after an important precedent established clear case law. Judicial voting patterns changed when the Supreme Court in *Chicago Police Department v. Mosley* (1972) and *Grayned v. Rockford* (1972) ruled that time, place, and manner regulations had to be content neutral. Justices of all political persuasions were more likely to protect "racial minorities, alleged communists, and businesses" after *Mosley* and *Grayned* were decided (2002, 314). Although the existence of a content neutral regulation had no statistical impact on judicial voting before 1972, that factor was statistically significant afterwards. "[A]fter the adoption of the speech-protective part of the regime that applies to content-based regulations," Richards and Kritzer (2002, 314) detail, "the justices were likely to be more supportive of speakers who were regulated based on the content of their speech relative to speakers whose expression fell within the less protected categories."

Lemon v. Kurtzman (1971) had a similar impact on judicial voting in religion cases. That decision held that laws passed constitutional muster only if they had a secular purpose, were neutral between different religions, and avoided excessive government entanglement with religion. Before that decision, secular purpose and religious neutrality were not statistically associated with judicial voting, while government monitoring statistically increased the probability that a justice would vote to sustain the law under constitutional attack. After *Lemon* was handed down, lack of a secular purpose, lack of religious neutrality, and government monitoring statistically increased the probability that a justice would strike down the law under constitutional attack. Ideology mattered before and after *Lemon*. Conservative justices were more likely than liberal justices to reject establishment clause claims. Nevertheless, *Lemon* shifted the terrain of judicial debate. Before *Lemon*, conservative and liberal justices disputed whether a law was supported by historical practice. After *Lemon*, conservative and liberal justices disputed whether the law had a secular purpose, was religiously neutral, and required excessive government entanglement with religion. Laws sustained in one regime were struck down in the other, even though no significant change in judicial membership had taken place (Kritzer and Richards 2003, 835–7).

Jurisprudential regimes include all legal materials that constitutional decision-makers, be they judges or elected officials, consider when resolving controversies. The language of constitutional provisions structures constitutional disagreements as do shared understandings about constitutional history. Understood this broadly, the impact of jurisprudential regimes on constitutional decision-making is obvious. Consider the post-Civil War Amendments. Americans disputed the constitutional status of persons of color before and after the Civil War. Before the Civil War, whether persons of color were citizens was a central constitutional issue (e.g. *Dred Scott v. Sandford* 1856). After the Civil War, disputes were over what rights persons of color enjoyed as citizens (e.g. *Civil Rights Cases* 1883). Before joining the bench in 1859, Nathan Clifford was on record as supporting the result in *Dred Scott* (Clifford 1922, 271–3). While on the bench, Clifford interpreted narrowly Fourteenth Amendment protections for persons of color (e.g. *Strauder v. West Virginia* 1880), but he nevertheless recognized that the "one pervading purpose" of the post-Civil War constitution was "the freedom of the slave race, the security and firm establishment of that freedom, and the protection of the newly-made freedman and citizen from the oppressions of those who had formerly exercised unlimited dominion over him" (*Slaughter-House Cases* 1873, 71).

Howard Gillman's (1993) acclaimed *The Constitution Besieged: The Rise and Demise of Lochner Era Police Powers Jurisprudence* provides another important case study of how law influences the terrain of constitutional debate. Gillman demonstrates that two distinctive debates over business regulation took place during the late nineteenth and early twentieth centuries. The political debate was over the merits of laissez-faire, over whether government intervention promoted liberty and efficiency. The legal debate was over the application of the constitutional animus to class legislation. Participants in these distinctive controversies employed distinctive justificatory logics. Federal and state judges and justices consistently employed legal logics and those legal logics explain why they consistently made legal distinctions between cases when there was no corresponding policy distinction. As Gillman (1993, 199) concludes:

that the justices were by and large motivated by a principled commitment to the application of a constitutional ideology of state neutrality, as manifested in the requirement that legislation advance a discernible public purpose...explains a good deal more of the dependent variable (judicial behavior) than do hypotheses that suggest the justices were basing decisions on a blind adherence to laissez-faire or on a desire to see members of their class win specific lawsuits or on an interest in imposing their idiosyncratic policy preferences on the country.

Policy commitments influenced how different justices applied the constitutional commitment to state neutrality. Justices who were more sympathetic to state regulation in general were more likely to find a discernible public purpose than those who were not (e.g. *Lochner v. New York* 1905; *Holden v. Hardy* 1898). For this reason, analyses limited to explaining differences between justices would find ideology the most significant variable. Such analyses ignore how judicial battles over class legislation were structured differently to political struggles over the administrative state. The justices sustained hundreds of laws that political conservatives insisted were economically unwise (McCloskey 2005, 100–5). No policy-maker in the legislature or the White House came close to mirroring any judicial preference. Persons who based decisions on the "constitutional ideology of state neutrality" behaved differently than those who based decisions on the night watchman state.

Several lesser-known decisions handed down during the "Constitutional Revolution of 1937" provide another window into the way in which constitutional struggles are often fought over different terrains than related policy struggles. On the same day the Supreme Court by 5–4 votes ruled that the Wagner Act could be constitutionally applied to businesses manufacturing steel and clothing (*NLRB v. Jones & Laughlin Steel Corp.* 1937; *NLRB v. Friedman-Harry Marks Clothing Co.* 1937), the justices unanimously held that Congress could regulate the hours and wages of persons employed by a bus company that operated a line running between Maryland, the District of Columbia, and Virginia (*Washington, Virginia & Maryland Coach Co. v. NLRB* 1937). Two weeks earlier, conservatives and liberals on the Hughes Court unanimously held that Congress could regulate labor relationships in the railroad business (*Virginia R. Co. v. System Federation* 1937). No one in the nonlegal world suggested employees who worked on trains and buses should be treated differently than persons employed by steel and clothing magnates. The relevant policy debates were over the merits of minimum wages and collective bargaining. Conservative justices making decisions on the basis of constitutional law, by comparison, could consider only whether the affected business was engaged in interstate commerce. The constitutional distinction between steel workers and bus drivers reflected a conservative constitutional commitment to the distinction between production and commerce that had no conservative policy analogue.

Constitutional law constrained the liberals on the New Deal Court as well as conservatives. Unions generally won legislative struggles during the 1930s, but Congress after World War II increasingly favored management. Liberals particularly abhorred the Taft–Hartley Act, which placed sharp limits on strikes. Nevertheless, although President Harry Truman's veto message (1947, 7500) described Taft–Hartley as "a dangerous stride in the direction of a totally managed economy," he and his political allies regarded the bill as within the enumerated powers of Congress. Having committed themselves to a substantial effects test which permitted the national government to regulate labor relations, New Deal constitutionalists lacked the tools to distinguish between pro-union and anti-union legislation. When the Supreme Court debated the constitutionality of Taft–Hartley, the justices focused entirely on the Communist registration provisions (*American Communication Ass'n v. Douds* 1950), a matter that did not occupy much legislative attention.

Much political science scholarship on American constitutional development explicitly or implicitly highlights sharp differences between political and constitutional controversies. Prominent examples include Pamela Brandwein's (2006) analysis of how inherited understandings about the nature of rights influenced the origins of the state action doctrine, Julie Novkov's (2001) history of how categories taken from gender influenced New Deal constitutional law, and Ken Kersch's (2004) work on the evolution of privacy law. None of these scholars insist that justices shed their policy preferences once they joined the bench. The argument is simply that these preferences had to be expressed in legal language and were subtly altered by the "requirement of translation" (Schweber 2007, 14). Sometimes justices found that commitments made in one area of the law constrained other constitutional decisions. New Deal protections for speech were truncated in large part because of previous commitments progressives had made when opposing the freedom of contract (Graber 1991). Some justices concluded that what they believed were pressing policy commitments could not be translated into legally enforceable norms. Elizabeth Bussiere (1997) details the difficulty Great Society liberals had finding welfare rights in the constitution. Judicial liberals were more inclined to support welfare rights than judicial conservatives, but they provided far less support for welfare rights than liberals with the same policy commitments in the legislative and executive branches of the national government.

4 BEYOND THE LAW/POLITICS DISTINCTION

Too sharp distinctions between policy and law obscure how constitutional decision-making may incorporate both in ways that cannot be fully separated. Prominent constitutional thinkers maintain that constitutional decision-makers are sometimes obligated to engage in value voting, basing decisions partly on beliefs about political philosophy and the general welfare. Ronald Dworkin (1986, 379) and other leading proponents of aspirational theories of constitutional interpretation maintain that justices and others have an obligation "to interpret the Constitution to make it the best it can be" (Barber and Fleming 2007, xiii). Justices who refuse to make value judgments, they believe, act *illegally*, violating their obligation to be faithful to the law (Dworkin 1986, 215). Justice Antonin Scalia agrees that justices in certain narrowly defined circumstances may let political principles influence judicial decisions. He approves how "the inevitable tendency of justices to think the law is what they would like it to be . . . cause(s) most errors in judicial historiography to be made in the direction of projecting upon the age of 1789 current, modern values" (1987, 864). This brief excursion into constitutional theory suggests the crucial issue is when constitutional decision-makers are legally entitled to engage in value voting, and not whether value voting is legitimate legally. Investigation is likely to reveal broad agreements that value voting is permissible in some circumstances, impermissible in other instances, and controversial on those matters on which constitutional decision-makers disagree.[3]

Distinctions between law and policy do not capture distinctions between how elected officials and justices make decisions. Constitutional decision-making takes place in all governing institutions. "Immortal principles fly their standards in judicial opinions," Thomas Reed Powell (1918, 647–8) observed, "(b)ut so they do in the common every-day talk of the butcher and the banker, of the suffragists and the anti-suffragist, the pacifist and the militarist, the Socialist and the individualist." Much recent political science literature (e.g. Fisher 1988; Whittington 1999) details how presidents and members of Congress have made principled constitutional arguments when engaged in heated constitutional debates. Nevertheless, elected officials making constitutional decisions may have different constitutional commitments than justices. These distinctive constitutional orientations *may* help explain important distinctions between legislative and judicial decision-making patterns.

Professor Tom Keck's research demonstrates how institutional affiliations influence constitutional decision-making. He compares the judicial coalitions respon-

---

[3] The same is true of strategic decision-making. Some instances of strategic decision-making are legal, some are illegal, and some are controversial. See Graber (2006*b*).

sible for declaring fifty-three federal laws unconstitutional between 1980 and 2004 with the legislative and executive coalitions responsible for passing those measures. Judicial voting patterns proved distinctive. Justices neither voted as liberals or conservatives did in the national legislature, nor as did Republicans or Democrats. On a tribunal that "never included more than two Democratic appointees," Keck (2007, 336) observes,

more than 70% of its judicial review decisions were issued by bipartisan coalitions and more than 80% invalidated statutes that had been enacted with substantial Republican legislative support. Similarly, more than sixty percent of the decisions are inconsistent with a model of policy-motivated judging, either because they were joined by both liberal and conservative justices or because they reached results that are difficult to place in ideological space.

Scholars aware of these findings would attend more carefully "to the possibility of institutionally motivated action," in particular, the influence of law on judicial decisions (2007, 337). Keck concludes, "(s)o long as the justices think the purpose of an independent judiciary is to defend certain fundamental principles against majoritarian interference, that normative commitment is likely to shape at least some of their decisions" (2007, 337).

One should not confuse "institutional motivations" with a commitment "to defend settled law against majoritarian override," as Keck (2007, 337) sometimes does. The elected officials who voted for the Religious Freedom Restoration Act and for the Americans with Disabilities Act thought they were protecting fundamental constitutional principles from (local) majoritarian interference. Many prominent constitutional scholars (e.g. Post and Siegel 2003; Colker and Brudney 2001) side with Congress, insisting that the Supreme Court decisions declaring those measures unconstitutional are inconsistent with both the original meaning of the Fourteenth Amendment and settled precedents. Institutional affiliation may matter, such cases as *City of Boerne v. Flores* (1997) and *Board of Trustees of University of Alabama v. Garrett* (2001) indicate, because justices have different beliefs about constitutional authority and constitutional interpretation than elected officials, and not because the former are more prone to be motivated by law. Judicial rulings on constitutional authority may also be rooted in institutional commitments to preserving judicial power, commitments not clearly identifiable as either purely political or purely legal. Keck's (2007, 331–6) evidence suggests that justices are more likely than elected officials to be committed to libertarian understandings of constitutional rights, formalist interpretations of the separation of powers, and judicial supremacy. These findings cast important light on the consequences of giving justices the power to declare laws unconstitutional, even if they do not reflect the traditional law/politics distinction.

5 TOWARD A BETTER RESEARCH AGENDA

Judge, later Justice, Benjamin Cardozo's famous Storrs lectures still provide the best starting place for scholars interested in understanding the influence of law on judging and constitutional decision-making. When considering how to "decide a case," Cardozo (1921, 10, 14) first noted that "[t]here are times when the [decision] is obvious" because either the text or precedent plainly resolved a legal dispute. These pure legal logics were insufficient when there were "gaps in the law." In such instances, "justice and general utility" were "the two objectives" Cardozo thought should influence judicial votes (1921, 75). Significantly, Cardozo added, on most matters the law was fairly clear. Quoting Justice Oliver Wendell Holmes (*Southern Pacific Co. v. Jensen* 1917, 221), he (1921, 69) insisted,

I recognize without hesitation that judges must and do legislate, but they do so only interstitially; they are confined from molar to molecular motions. A common-law judge could not say, I think the doctrine of consideration a bit of historical nonsense and shall not enforce it in my court.

Cardozo's observations highlight how law often settles matters before substantial controversies arise. Controversies take place only in legal gaps. The geography of these gaps is largely determined by legal texts, legal precedents, and legal history. Behavioral analysis that focuses entirely on disagreements among legal authorities over the precise application of "the doctrine of consideration" cannot appreciate the central role consideration plays in contract law. A similar obsession with explaining controversies over the meaning of the First Amendment overlooks all the controversies Americans do not have because of the First Amendment.

Much good empirical work will be done once public law scholars acknowledge the relative autonomy of constitutional law. We need more extensive research on the nature of constitutional reasoning. On some accounts (Gillman 1999, 78–86), constitutional decision-makers make self-conscious decisions to follow the Constitution rather than their policy preferences. Other accounts (Brigham 1996; Whittington 2000, 615–16) suggest constitutionalism is constitutive, that persons occupying certain roles are simply socialized to think constitutionally. Whether a constitution is "a machine that would go of itself" (Kammen 1986) may depend partly on which account of constitutional reasoning is correct. We need more extensive research on how constitutional questions arise and are settled. Americans in the nineteenth century thought protective tariffs raised constitutional questions. Free trade, at present, is considered entirely a policy choice. No current approach to constitutional decision-making explains this transformation. Most important, we need more extensive research into the different ways in which persons in different institutional settings make constitutional decisions. A good deal of contemporary scholarship indicates that judicial review is unnecessary as a means for ensuring decisions are made on the basis of constitutional principle (e.g. Kramer 2004). All governing coalitions act on the basis of constitutional visions that structure their policy choices. Nevertheless, much contemporary scholarship also suggests that justices act on different constitutional principles than other governing officials (Hirschl 2004; Graber 2005, 447–8). What those principles are and whether their articulation is desirable should be central to the next generation of constitutional law scholarship.

References

BACHRACH, P., and BARATZ, M. S. 1970. *Power & Poverty: Theory & Practice.* New York: Oxford University Press.

BARBER, S., and FLEMING, J. E. 2007. *Constitutional Interpretation: The Basic Questions.* New York: Oxford University Press.

BARNES, J. 2006. *Overruled? Legislative Overrides, Pluralism, and Contemporary Court-Congress Relations.* Stanford, Calif.: Stanford University Press.

BRANDWEIN, P. 2006. The civil rights cases and the lost language of state neglect. In *The Supreme Court & American Political Development,* ed. R. Kahn and K. I. Kersch. Lawrence: University Press of Kansas.

BRIGHAM, J. 1996. *The Constitution of Interests: Beyond the Politics of Rights.* New York: New York University Press.

BUSSIERE, E. 1997. *Distitling the Poor: The Warren Court, Welfare Rights, and the American Political Tradition.* University Park: Pennsylvania State University Press.

CALDEIRA, G. A., and WRIGHT, J. R. 1988. Organized interests and agenda setting in the U.S. Supreme Court. *American Political Science Review,* 82: 1109–27.

CARDOZO, B. N. 1921. *The Nature of the Judicial Process.* New Haven, Conn.: Yale University Press.

CLIFFORD, P. G. 1922. *Nathan Clifford: Democrat.* New York: G. P. Putnam's Sons.

COLKER, R., and BRUDNEY, J. J. 2001. Dissing Congress. *Michigan Law Review,* 100: 80–144.

DWORKIN, R. 1986. *Law's Empire.* Cambridge, Mass.: Harvard University Press.

EPP, C. R. 1998. *The Rights Revolution: Lawyers, Activists, and Supreme Courts in Comparative Perspective.* Chicago: University of Chicago Press.

EPSTEIN, L. 1999. The comparative advantage. *Law and Courts,* 9: 1–6.

—— and KNIGHT, J. 1998. *The Choices Justices Make.* Washington, DC: CQ Press.

FARRAND, M. 1966. *The Records of the Federal Convention of 1787,* vol. II. New Haven, Conn.: Yale University Press.

FINKELMAN, P. 2002. The proslavery origins of the Electoral College. *Cardozo Law Review,* 23: 1145–57.

FISHER, L. 1988. *Constitutional Dialogues: Interpretation as Political Process.* Princeton, NJ: Princeton University Press.

FRIEDMAN, B. 2006. Taking law seriously. *Perspectives on Politics,* 4: 261–76.

GILLMAN, H. 1993. *The Constitution Besieged: The Rise and Demise of Lochner Era Police Powers Jurisprudence.* Durham, NC: Duke University Press.

GILLMAN, H. 1999. The Court as an idea, not a building (or a game): interpretive institutionalism and the analysis of Supreme Court decision-making. In *The Supreme Court Decision-Making: New Institutionalist Approaches*, ed. C. W. Clayton and H. Gillman. Chicago: University of Chicago Press.

—— 2001. What's law got to do with it? Judicial behavioralists test the "Legal Model" of judicial decision-making. *Law and Social Inquiry*, 26: 465–504.

GRABER, M. A. 1991. *Transforming Free Speech: The Ambiguous Legacy of Civil Libertarianism*. Berkeley: University of California Press.

—— 2000. The Jacksonian origins of the Chase Court. *Journal of Supreme Court History*, 25: 17–39.

—— 2004. Resolving political questions into constitutional questions: Tocqueville's thesis revisited. *Constitutional Commentary*, 21: 485–545.

—— 2005. Constructing judicial review. *Annual Review of Political Science*, 8: 425–51.

—— 2006a. *Dred Scott and the Problem of Constitutional Evil*. New York: Cambridge University Press.

—— 2006b. Legal, strategic, or legal strategy: deciding to decide during the Civil War and reconstruction. In *The U.S. Supreme Court and American Political Development*, ed. R. Kahn and K. I. Kersch. Lawrence: University Press of Kansas.

HERRNSON, P. S. 2004. *Congressional Elections: Campaigning at Home in Washington*. Washington, DC: CQ Press.

HIRSCHL, R. 2004. *Toward Juristocracy: The Origins and Consequences of the New Constitutionalism*. Cambridge, Mass.: Harvard University Press.

—— 2006. The new constitutionalism and the judicialization of pure politics worldwide. *Fordham Law Review*, 75: 721–53.

KAMMEN, M. 1986. *A Machine That Would Go of Itself: The Constitution in American Culture*. New York: Knopf.

KECK, T. M. 2007. Party, policy, or duty: why does the Supreme Court invalidate federal statutes? *American Political Science Review*, 101: 321–38.

KERSCH, K. I. 2004. *Constructing Civil Liberties: Discontinuing in the Development of American Constitutional Law*. New York: Cambridge University Press.

KRAMER, L. D. 2004. *The People Themselves: Popular Constitutionalism and Judicial Review*. New York: Oxford University Press.

KRITZER, H. M., and RICHARDS, M. J. 2003. Jurisprudential regimes and Supreme Court decisionmaking: the lemon regime and establishment clause cases. *Law and Society Review*, 37: 827–40.

KYVIG, D. E. 1996. *Explicit and Authentic Acts: Amending the U.S. Constitution, 1776–1985*. Lawrence: University Press of Kansas.

LEE, F. E., and OPPENHEIMER, B. I. 1999. *Sizing Up the Senate: The Unequal Consequences of Equal Representation*. Chicago: University of Chicago Press.

LEVINSON, S. 2006. *Our Understanding Constitution: Where the Constitution Goes Wrong (And How We the People Can Correct It)*. New York: Oxford University Press.

—— 2007. Debating the Electoral College. *University of Pennsylvania Law Review*, Pennumbra, 156: 11–15, 25–30.

LOWENSTEIN, D. H. 2007. Five inconceivable reasons to support the Electoral College. *University of Pennsylvania Law Review*, Pennumbra, 156: 20–5, 33–7.

McCloskey, R. G. 2005. *The American Supreme Court*, 4th edn., rev. S. Levinson. Chicago: University of Chicago Press.

McGinnis, J. 2007. Two cheers for the Electoral College (and two cheers is all that can be expected for an electoral system). *University of Pennsylvania Law Review, Pennumbra*, 156: 16–20, 30–2.

Martin, A. D. 2006. Statutory battles and constitutional wars: congress and the Supreme Court. In *Institutional Games and the U.S. Supreme Court*, ed. J. R. Rogers, R. B. Flemming, and J. R. Bond. Charlottesville: University of Virginia Press.

Monroe, J. 1897. Veto message. In *A Compilation of the Messages of the Presidents (Volume II)*, ed. J. Richardson. Washington, DC. Government Printing Office.

Novkov, J. 2001. *Constituting Workers, Protecting Women: Gender, Law, and Labor in the Progressive Era and New Deal Years*. Ann Arbor: University of Michigan Press.

Post, R., and Siegel, R. 2003. Protecting the Constitution from the people: juricentric restrictions on Section Five power. *Indiana Law Journal*, 78: 1–45.

Powell, T. R. 1918. The logic and rhetoric of constitutional law. *Journal of Philosophy, Psychology, and Scientific Methods*, 15: 645–58.

Richards, M. J., and Kritzer, H. M. 2002. Jurisprudential regimes in Supreme Court decision-making. *American Political Science Review*, 96: 305–20.

Riker, W. H. 1986. *The Art of Political Manipulation*. New Haven, Conn.: Yale University Press.

Sager, L. G. 1993. Justice in plain clothes: reflections on the thinness of constitutional law. *Northwestern Law Review*, 88: 410–35.

Scalia, A. 1987. Originalism: the lesser evil. *University of Cincinnati Law Review*, 57: 849–65.

Schauer, F. 2006. Foreword: the Court's agenda—and the nation's. *Harvard Law Review*, 120: 4–64.

Schweber, H. 2007. *The Language of Liberal Constitutionalism*. New York: Cambridge University Press.

Segal, J. A., and Spaeth, H. J. 2002. *The Supreme Court and the Attitudinal Model Revisited*. Cambridge: Cambridge University Press.

Stephenson, G. T. 1910. *Race Distinction in American Law*. New York: D. Appleton.

Tocqueville, A. de. 1945. *Democracy in America* (vol. 1), ed. B. Phillips. New York: Vintage.

Truman, H. 1947. President's message on veto of Taft–Hartley Bill. *Labor Relations Reference Manual*, 20: 22–30.

Tushnet, M. 1995. Policy distortion and democratic debilitation: comparative illumination of the countermajoritarian difficulty. *Michigan Law Review*, 94: 245–301.

Tyler, T. R. 2006. *Why People Obey the Law*. Princeton, NJ: Princeton University Press.

Warren, C. 1947. *The Supreme Court in United States History* (vol. 2). Boston: Little, Brown.

Whittington, K. E. 1999. *Constitutional Construction: Divided Powers and Constitutional Meaning*. Cambridge, Mass.: Harvard University Press.

—— 2000. Once more unto the breach: postbehavioralist approaches to judicial politics. *Law and Social Inquiry*, 25: 601–34.

Cases

American Communication Ass'n v. Douds, 339 U.S. 382 (1950).
Board of Trustees of University of Alabama v. Garrett, 531 U.S. 536 (2001).
Brown v. Board of Education, 347 U.S. 483 (1954).
Bush v. Gore, 531 U.S. 536 (2001).
Chicago Police Department v. Mosley, 408 U.S. 92 (1972).
City of Boerne v. Flores, 512 U.S. 507 (1997).
Civil Rights Cases, 109 U.S. 3 (1883).
Dames & Moore v. Regan, 453 U.S. 654 (1981).
Dred Scott v. Sandford, 60 U.S. 393 (1856).
Gratz v. Bollinger, 539 U.S. 244 (2003).
Grayned v. Rockford, 408 U.S. 104 (1972).
Grutter v. Bollinger, 539 U.S. 306 (2003).
Hamdan v. Rumsfeld, 126 S. Ct. 2749 (2006).
Holden v. Hardy, 169 U.S. 366 (1898).
Johnson v. California, 543 U.S. 499 (2005).
Korematsu v. United States, 323 U.S. 214 (1944).
Lemon v. Kurtzman, 403 U.S. 602 (1971).
Lochner v. New York, 198 U.S. 45 (1905).
McCleskey v. Kemp, 481 U.S. 279 (1987).
McCulloch v. Maryland, 17 U.S. 316 (1819).
NLRB v. Friedman-Harry Marks Clothing Co., 301 U.S. 58 (1937).
NLRB v. Jones & Laughlin Steel Corp., 301 U.S. 1 (1937).
Planned Parenthood of Southeastern Pennsylvania v. Casey, 505 U.S. 833 (1992).
Plessy v. Ferguson, 163 U.S. 537 (1896).
Slaughter-House Cases, 83 U.S. 36, 71 (1873).
South Carolina v. Dole, 483 U.S. 203 (1987).
Southern Pacific Co v. Jensen, 244 U.S. 205, 221 (1917).
Strauder v. West Virginia, 100 U.S. 303 (1880).
United States v. Lopez, 514 U.S. 549 (1995).
Virginia R. Co. v. System Federation, 300 U.S. 515 (1937).
Washington, Virginia & Maryland Coach Co. v. NLRB, 301 U.S. 142 (1937).

CHAPTER 18

....

THE LEGAL STRUCTURE OF DEMOCRACY

....

RICHARD H. PILDES

THE institutional structure and legal framework that organize democracy can dramatically shape the practice and experience of democracy. This is true for the most visible, macro-scale institutional choices, such as whether the legislature should be chosen through proportional representation or first-past-the-post elections, and whether the executive–legislative relationship should be a parliamentary or separated powers one. It is also true for many less visible choices, such as the way legal rules structure and regulate political parties; the way in which election districts are designed (in systems that use districts); the institutional structures and rules by which elections are administered and potentially explosive election disputes are resolved; the methods by which the law permits elections to be financed; or the way institutions and law address the tension between majoritarianism and recognition of minority interests. The "new institutionalism" in political science and legal studies over the last two decades has generated important insights into the theoretical and empirical dimensions of these effects (Filippov et. al. 2004; Pierson 2004; Shepsle 1989).

Two developments over the past two decades have played a role already in catalyzing research on these issues. These developments are even more likely to define the frontiers of academic work in the coming years. The first is the doubling of the number of recognized democracies since 1985. The self-conscious creation of these democracies, in contexts ranging from South Africa, to the states of the former Soviet Union, to Latin America and elsewhere, has given renewed urgency to foundational questions in the design of democratic institutions, such as the likely effects of structuring legislative elections in particular ways. Moreover, this proliferation of new democracies (as well as attempts at democratization in places where the verdict is still out) makes greater comparative study of the legal structure of democracy more possible, more interesting, and more necessary.

Second, during this same period, courts are being asked to play a more active role around the world in overseeing the structure of democratic institutions and processes (Hirschl 2004). The United States Supreme Court initiated this new role for courts in the 1960s, with the requirement that nearly all representative institutions in the United States be restructured in accord with the newly announced constitutional principle of one person, one vote. Applying the United States Constitution, the Supreme Court has, over the last two decades or so, taken on a more and more central role in determining the essential structures of democracy in the United States. Similarly, the domestic courts of other countries, and supranational courts such as the European Court of Human Rights, have been asked to judge and revise the basic structures of democratic governance. I call this general development "the constitutionalization of democratic politics" (Pildes 2004). Issues concerning the structure of democracy that for generations had been the subject of political compromise, negotiation, conflict, and settlement are now being transformed into matters for judicial resolution. The intersection of law and political science is thus becoming all the more important for both normative and empirical analysis of the practice of democracy.

This chapter first turns to several discrete issues likely to be the focus of research in the coming years: political parties; the design of election districts, including gerrymandering; election administration; and campaign finance. In each case, the major focus is on the American context, but the analysis then broadens to suggest the future role of comparative work. The last section focuses on some of the most pressing issues at the macro level in the design of democratic institutions today.

1 Political Parties: The Effect of Law on Polarized Politics

In modern democracies, political parties remain the central organizational vehicle through which voters are integrated into politics. Parties are also the central form through which government is effectively organized. Although the political sphere is more fragmented in the current era, with the greater role of nonparty ideological groups and the rise of the internet, political parties remain the most important organizational entity through which democracy is organized, mobilized, and made effective.

The central fact about political parties in the United States today is their dramatic polarization. Ironically, just a few decades ago the literature was dominated by "the decline of parties" narrative, with some political scientists declaring the parties all but dead in their ability to control the behavior of elected officials (Wattenberg 1998; Fiorina 1980). But currently the Republican and Democratic parties are both more internally coherent ideologically and more strongly differentiated and polarized than at any time since the start of the twentieth century (Bond and Fleisher 2000; Poole and Rosenthal 1997). The consequences for the functioning of Congress and the relationship between Congress and the president have been dramatic (Levinson and Pildes 2006). The question is what causes account for this fact and what role law might play in contributing to it.

In the United States, political parties have long been subject to greater legal regulation than in any other Western democracy (Epstein 1986). This regulation reflects a progressive-era fear that parties had become controlled by corrupt "bosses." The most visible manifestation of this distrust was the creation of the state-mandated political primary, early in the twentieth century, as the means by which parties became legally required to nominate their candidates. In recent years, however, the Supreme Court has begun to grant parties broad constitutional autonomy as the Court has more expansively interpreted the scope of the First Amendment "associational rights" of party members. As parties become more immune from state regulation, important research questions arise regarding the way this immunity affects the nature of elections and governance.

The legal rules by which states conduct primary elections have important consequences. These rules are a good example of how less visible regulations of the political process can profoundly shape the actual experience of democracy. By law, state-mandated primaries can be closed, open, or somewhere in-between. Closed primaries (used in twelve states) permit only previously-registered party members to vote; open primaries, used in about half the states in some form, permit at least some nonparty members, such as independents, to vote as well (Persily 2001). Primary elections tend to have lower turnout than general elections; those who turn out are the most active and the most ideological party members. In closed primaries, the winners are therefore likely to reflect the views of the median party activist, rather than of the median voter in the general electorate. Closed primaries might therefore contribute to selection of more extreme candidates, and hence greater polarization of the parties and of officeholders.

Nonetheless, the Supreme Court has imposed new constitutional limits on the ability of states, or voters in the states, to open up primary election structures. Voters in California, dissatisfied with closed primaries that produced candidates viewed as being from the extreme wings of both parties, used a ballot initiative to change the system to a fully open one. The main justification for doing so was that this change would lead to more moderate candidates being chosen from the two parties, which would give the general electorate more centrist candidates from whom to choose in the general election. Indeed, empirical studies of the two elections conducted under this system tend to confirm that it indeed had this effect (Gerber 2002). But, in the landmark *California Democratic Party v. Jones* decision, the Supreme Court held it unconstitutional to force political parties to permit all nonparty members to vote in a party's primary election. The full implications of *Jones* will be worked out in coming years. Taken to its most expansive reach, *Jones* might require states to register voters by party and forbid states from using anything other than a closed primary-election structure. Because about half of states use open primaries of some form, this would amount to a dramatic change in the structure of primary elections.

As the structure of primary election changes, partly in response to *Jones*, these changes will provide fertile ground for research assessing the effects of the legal structure of elections on candidates, parties, voters, and officeholders. To the extent that closed primaries contribute to more polarized politics, or that opening up primary-election participation provides a counter to party polarization produced by other forces, the ongoing effect of *Jones* merits careful attention.

At least three other legal changes might also contribute to the polarization of the parties. First, gerrymanders have increasingly rendered election districts overwhelmingly "safe" for incumbents of one party or the other. Because safe districts are not competitive on general election day, primary elections effectively determine who represents the district. For the reasons noted above, this means that safe districts are more likely to be represented by the wings, not the centers, of the parties. The next section will explore this issue in more detail. Second, recent changes in the internal rules and practices of the House and Senate have centralized power in the hands of party leaders; as a result, leaders have greater capacity to enforce party discipline (Rohde 1991). Third, campaign-finance laws have created incentives for the formation of leadership political-action committees (PACs), through which legislative leaders have become major fundraisers and contributors to other candidates, which also enhances the capacity for effective party discipline (Eilperin 2006). Determining the relative contribution of these variables—closed primaries, safe districts, internal governance rules, and campaign finance—to party polarization is a difficult task.

In addition to these more contingent influences, there is a long-term secular change to consider as well. The nature of political parties before the 1965 Voting Rights Act might have reflected the artificiality of a Southern electorate from which black voters were largely excluded. The Act, and related civil-rights laws, initiated a process by which black voters have become full participants in American elections. For that same reason, the Act also triggered a fundamental realignment of the national political parties, a realignment that worked its way through the state and local level during the 1990s (Black and Black 2002). The question is whether the current polarization of the parties reflects a "maturation" of the American party system as the transition to a fully inclusive democratic electorate has "purified" the parties and made them more ideologically coherent. From the New Deal until the Act, the Democratic Party was a fragmented coalition of Southern and Northern Democrats linked on economic issues but fundamentally divided on any issue perceived to touch on race. As the effects of the Act have ramified through the political system, the Democratic Party has become more unified and ideologically coherent, as has the Republican Party. Whether current party polarization is the steady state of American politics for years to come or a short-term phase will depend, in part, on the relative contribution of more contingent factors versus this long-term secular change. The effects of legal regulation versus this secular change on party polarization remains an important subject of study.

2 GERRYMANDERING

Among well-established democracies that use individual election districts, in whole or in part, to constitute their legislative bodies, only the United States leaves the power to design election districts in the hands of elected officials (Pildes 2004). Typically once a decade in the wake of a new census, these districts are redesigned to keep up with the constitutional requirement that the districts be consistent with the one-vote, one-person standard. Both congressional districts and state legislative districts are overwhelmingly crafted through the state political process—although eleven states now use commissions of various sorts, which stand at least at some remove from the direct control of partisan elected officials. Partisan gerrymandering and bipartisan gerrymandering are the two principal focal points of public debate and academic study concerning the effects on democracy of this institutional structure that puts the power to design election units in the hands of self-interested political actors.

2.1 Partisan Gerrymandering

For many decades, partisan gerrymandering had been the exclusive concern of scholars and litigants. This issue arises when unified party control of the state political process (the house, the senate, and the governor's office) exists after a new census, when districts are redesigned. The concern is that the party in power will manipulate the design of districts so that it gains control of more than its "fair share" of seats. Three principal academic issues dominate current analysis of partisan gerrymandering.

First, there is the central question of defining a partisan gerrymander, which requires defining what would constitute a non-gerrymandered set of election districts for any particular state. Put in other terms, this requires defining a "neutral" baseline of fair districting or determining what a party's "fair share" of seats ought to be, in light of its political support among voters (Lowenstein and Steinberg 1985). Social scientists have sought primarily to develop outcome-oriented standards for answering these questions; these standards compare the seat/vote ratio for the political parties, where the vote denominator is tied to the number of votes a party receives statewide. The most important innovation in these formulas developed recently is the "partisan symmetry standard" (King and Grofman 2007).

The basic concept underlying this partisan symmetry standard is that an electoral system should treat similarly-situated political parties equally, so that each party receives the same percentage of legislative seats as the other would receive if it had received the same percentage of the vote. Thus, if the Democratic Party receives 55 percent of the vote statewide, but 70 percent of the seats, this is not necessarily a violation; if the Republican Party would also receive 70 percent of the seats if it received 55 percent of the statewide vote, the mere fact that the winning party receives a "bonus" in a single-member districting plan does not condemn that plan as a partisan gerrymander. There is increasing consensus among social scientists that this standard provides the best means to operationalize the concept of a "fair share" of seats for a party in a representative body, given a certain number of votes.

In contrast, legal scholars have focused more on developing process-oriented means to constrain partisan gerrymandering; these constraints do not seek to define fair outcomes but to provide prophylactic means to check *ex ante* the capacity of political actors to engage in such gerrymandering. These process-oriented means include suggestions that districts must respect various external constraints: that they be reasonably compact, for example, and/or that they respect preexisting political subdivisions, such as towns, cities, and counties (Niemi and Pildes 1993). Other process-oriented suggestions include that legislators must precommit in advance to specific and transparent criteria by which districting will be done (Issacharoff 1993). The differences in approach between social scientists and legal academics likely reflects the tendency of legal scholars to look for solutions courts might adopt, accompanied by the belief that courts are more likely to prefer process-oriented to outcome-oriented standards for limiting partisan gerrymandering.

Second, the capacity to gerrymander has become greater in recent years as a result of the information and technology revolution, as well as the greater party polarization of American democracy (Pildes 1997). Dramatic advances in computer technology now enable district designers to move increasingly fine-grained groups of voters, down to the level of individual blocks, and project immediately the partisan consequences of doing so. Moreover, if voters have become more reliably partisan across time and level of election, as is the case (Abramowitz 2006), projections of future voting behavior based on past election return data are likely to be more accurate. In turn, this has implications for a third central issue: how stable partisan gerrymanders are over time. Some (including justices on the Supreme Court: *Davis v. Bandemer*) have argued that such gerrymanders are inherently unstable, and hence less a concern for public policy, because overly aggressive partisan gerrymanders can backfire if gerrymanderers cut their margins of safety too thin. On this view, the fact that districting plans must be in place for a decade, that demographics will change over that period, and that predicting voting behavior is always fraught with uncertainty, creates inherent and effective constraints on the process.

The motivation and incentive to engage in partisan gerrymandering of congressional districts is, in part, a function of how closely balanced partisan control is of the United States House. Because the partisan margin of control has been closer for a longer period of time over the last decade or so than in over 100 years, partisan battles over congressional districting in the states have been exceptionally intense. The most recent round of districting witnessed the emergence for the first time in the twentieth century of what came to be called "re-redistricting," in which state legislatures redistricted even after courts had already put into place valid redistricting plans after the 2000 census. The Colorado legislature re-redistricted but the state courts held doing so illegal; the Texas legislature also re-redistricted, and the United States Supreme Court held that the federal Constitution did not bar such action (*Salazar v. Davidson*).

There have been many efforts over the last twenty years to draw the courts more deeply into this issue, and the Supreme Court has held that partisan gerrymandering can, at some extreme point, violate the Constitution (*Davis v. Bandemer*). But this has been an abstract principle with no practical effect; before the 2000s, no federal court had ever held the design of congressional or state legislative districts to violate this principle (Issacharoff, Karlan, and Pildes 2007, 836). After the 2000 round of redistricting, the Supreme Court agreed to hear two cases that sought to give some practical bite to the abstract constitutional principle against excessive partisan gerrymandering. But in both cases, the Court concluded that there had been no constitutional violation. In the aftermath of these decisions, several points became clear: a majority of the Court appears deeply troubled by partisan gerrymandering; some justices would tackle the issue through more aggressive judicial doctrine; but a majority of the Court is uncertain about whether there are clear, judicially manageable standards to address the problem. Hence, constitutional law, while nominally condemning excessive partisan gerrymandering as unconstitutional, has generated no practical remedy for it. Several members of the Court did, however, discuss proposals to adopt the partisan symmetry standard, which has given proponents of that standard a degree of continuing optimism.

2.2 Bipartisan or "Sweetheart" Gerrymandering

More recently, particularly in the 2000 round of districting, the practice of bipartisan gerrymandering has become more common. In these "sweetheart" gerrymanders, incumbents of both parties enter into a nonaggression pact in which they agree to stock each of their own districts with such a large number of same-party voters that the districts are "safe" against challenges from the other party. These pacts can be driven by incumbents seeking to protect themselves against the rigors of electoral competition or by risk-averse party leaders seeking to maintain the existing partisan distribution of seats. Seats gerrymandered to be safe for both parties necessarily reduce competition in general elections.

The newer practice of bipartisan gerrymandering has raised three main questions for social scientists and legal academics. First, to what extent does this practice account for the general decline in recent years of electoral competition? Normally, elections immediately after a redistricting are the most competitive, given the way newly designed districts destabilize the status quo. But the post-redistricting congressional elections in 2002 were the least competitive in American history (Jacobson 2003). Some social scientists conclude that sweetheart gerrymandering in the 2000 round of redistricting was a significant cause of this decline (McDonald 2006a; 2006b). Others resist this conclusion, however, and point to different factors, such as the greater consistency with which voters vote along party lines; the greater geographical concentration of voters by party affiliation independent of the way election districts are designed; and the increasing cost of elections, which disadvantages challengers (Abramowitz et al. 2006). The academic literature has not yet incorporated analysis of the 2006 congressional elections into this debate. Because those elections did result in a change of partisan control of the House, they might suggest that the system is more responsive and competitive than the decade's earlier elections had suggested. One initial study, however, suggests that seats remain more insulated from change than at any previous time, even if they cannot be made wholly safe: The magnitude of the shift in voter preferences between parties necessary to shift partisan control of a certain number of seats, such as the fifteen seats that determined partisan control in 2006, is now much greater than in the past. On this view, only the concatenation of a long, unpopular war; an off-year election with a president receiving some of the lowest approval ratings in history; and congressional scandals, generated enough of a shift in voter preferences to make as many seats vulnerable as in 2006 (Nagler and Issacharoff 2007). To the extent parties and voters are more polarized today, however, perhaps large shifts between the parties will become more common than they have been in the past.

Second, there is a normative debate about whether bipartisan gerrymanders cause significant systemic harms. This debate involves the relationship between the democratic values of electoral competition, representation, and political responsiveness. Though safe districts are not competitive, absent exceptional changes in circumstance, they can produce legislatures that are fairly representative (Persily 2002). In a state in which 55 percent of voters tend to vote for Democratic House candidates, a sweetheart gerrymander that aims to give Democrats 55 percent of the seats would entail fair representation in the seats-to-vote sense (unlike a partisan gerrymander). In essence, such gerrymanders faithfully transfer divisions in the electorate up to the level of representative institutions. How troubling, then, should such gerrymanders be? Critics assert that one negative effect is that sweetheart gerrymanders contribute to the extreme polarization of politics (Issacharoff 2002). When primary elections become the locus of effective political choice, more extreme candidates and officeholders are likely to emerge, given that party activists dominate primary elections. In addition, there is concern that safe districts will make the House insufficiently responsive even to significant shifts in public opinion; if 60 percent of the voters in many districts are reliably Republican or Democratic, then even a 5 percent shift nationwide in party preferences might not have much effect on the composition of the House. Finally, competitive elections tend to increase turnout, itself a democratic value, and generate more debate during the election process over issues.

Third, there are questions about the role courts and constitutional law should play in response to the rise of sweetheart gerrymanders. From a judicial point of view, the problem is even more difficult than that of partisan gerrymandering. There is no outcome-oriented standard, such as seat-to-vote ratios, for determining, even in principle, when a sweetheart gerrymander is "unfair." By definition, the outcome of these gerrymanders is to produce legislatures that are fair in representational terms, in the seats-to-vote sense. Nor is it easy to imagine courts requiring that all districts be designed to meet some optimal standard of competitiveness.

2.3 Institutional Design and Comparative Issues

Addressing gerrymandering is likely to require new institutional solutions. Among the most important research questions is how these institutions ought to be designed. A small number of states now use commissions of some sort to design districts. Initial studies suggest that commission-drawn plans do produce somewhat more competitive elections than plans drawn by legislative bodies (Carson and Crespin 2004). Commissions can be structured in a number of ways, with greater or lesser ties to partisan elected officials. Determining the effects of commissions designed in different ways remains an important subject of inquiry. In addition, research into why commissions have been successfully adopted in some states but not others, as a result of what kinds of political processes, is an important subject.

Comparative studies on both these issues also provide a promising direction for future work (Pildes 2004, 78–80). Great Britain initiated the independent commission approach in 1944; among other countries that use single-member districts, Australia, Canada, and New Zealand have since followed Great Britain in adopting the commission approach. Indeed, in a study of sixty countries that regularly design election districts, 73 percent assigned this responsibility to an election management body or a boundary commission specifically created for this purpose (Handley et al. 2006, 20). There are country-specific studies of these commissions, but no work that provides a synthesis from which general design lessons can easily be drawn. Comparative analysis can illuminate the different ways these commissions might be designed; their effects on outcomes, such as how competitive election districts are; and the circumstances in which countries are likely to replace politically self-interested approaches to districting with ones that use intermediary institutions, such as boundary-drawing commissions.

3 ELECTION ADMINISTRATION

The 2000 presidential election exposed an array of problems with the micro-level administration of U.S. elections: ballot design; proper voting technology; valid recount processes; problems in voter registration and voter purging practices; differences between counties regarding many of these issues, particularly which kinds of voting technology are used and the variation in error rates among these technologies; and many others. More recently, disputes over whether voters should be required to show identification at the polls, and if so, what kind, have roiled state legislatures and the courts (Overton 2007).

Seen from a broader perspective, many of these issues have their source in two fundamental features of the way elections are organized in the United States. First, even national elections are administered through exceptionally decentralized structures. Ballot design, for example, even in presidential elections, is primarily handled at the county level. Second, most election administration is in the hands of partisan elected officials (Saltman 2006). During the 2000 election dispute, this produced the surreal context of partisan-elected county canvassing boards having the power to decide how to count disputed ballots; at the same time, the chief election officer of the State of Florida, the elected Secretary of State, was the chair of the campaign committee in the state for one of the candidates, while the chief law enforcement officer of the state, the elected Attorney General, was the chair for the other candidate's committee. Compared to other long-established democracies, both this partisan control and extreme decentralization of election administration in the United States are unique.

Since 2000, there has been a flood of research on many of these issues involving the micro-mechanics of election administration, such as issues of voting technology and vote-counting processes (Alvarez 2004; Brady 2001; Kimball et. al. 2006; Tokaji 2005*a*; 2005*b*; Electionline.org 2006). There will continue to be much work in this vein. But two of the broadest issues for research stem from these two central characteristics of the American regime.

One of the most important subjects is the issue of partisan election administration. This is another area where comparative study is likely to be particularly illuminating, as more is learned about the success and failure of various institutional structures other countries have created to take election administration out of the hands of elected officials (Massicotte et al. 2004). Academics have long lamented that the professionalization of other disciplines that began in the late nineteenth century never developed a professional field of election administration (Harris 1934). Questions about the causes for the creation of nonpartisan election administration structures in other countries, the optimal structures for these institutions, and the effects of such bodies in areas like resolution of disputed elections, are likely to be fruitful subjects for research. One of the few such studies argues that the most successfully stable long-term democracies in Central and South America—Costa Rica, Chile, and Uruguay—owe their success to the fact that they had established independent electoral commissions to resolve disputed elections, thus taking the power to do so out of the hands of the executive and legislative branches (Lehoucq 2002). On this view, among the greatest challenges to democratic stability are elections whose outcome is disputed. Unlike other countries, those with independent electoral commissions were able to resolve these disputes in ways that generated enough social legitimacy to underwrite settlement of the dispute. That the intensely disputed recent election for Mexico's president appears to have been successfully settled by a unanimous decision of the Electoral Tribunal of the Federal Judiciary might add credence to this intriguing hypothesis.

The second promising area of broad import will be research into the effects on election administration of initial legislative and judicial efforts to bring greater centralization and uniformity to the process. Legislatively, the most significant development thus far is the Help America Vote Act of 2002 (HAVA). That Act mandates or encourages greater centralization and uniformity in voting technology, provisional voting, state registration databases, and photo identification—although many of the details remain to be implemented at the state and local level. National regulation of voting has always been the exception, not the rule, in the United States, and much of the national regulation that exists has been targeted at prohibiting racially discriminatory voting rules and practices, such as the 1965 Voting Rights Act (amended, most recently, in 2006). HAVA thus represents a less-common model of national legislation that aims at general protection for the right to vote as such (Pildes 2006). Study of the effects of HAVA will therefore be important to judgments about what kinds of additional national legislation are necessary and likely to be effective (Tokaji 2005a). Efforts to use the courts to bring about greater uniformity in election administration attempt to expand on the Supreme Court's decision in the 2000 presidential election dispute. Such efforts include attempts to get the courts to require uniform statewide practices in areas such as the use of particular voting technologies. Thus far, this litigation has not generated many successes, but it is too early to reach a definitive verdict and ongoing study of these litigation efforts and their consequences is warranted (Foley 2007).

4 DEMOCRACY IN DIVIDED SOCIETIES: MAJORITARIANISM VS. POWER-SHARING ARRANGEMENTS

The most urgent practical and academic problem in the design of democratic institutions today is how best to design such institutions in the midst of profound heterogeneity, conflict, and group difference. As the most recent wave of democratization has spread, not only states transitioning from authoritarianism, but even states emerging from civil war and explosive conflict, have come to view democracy as the preferred institutional structure going forward. Although theorists in the nineteenth century viewed a high degree of prior social cohesion and homogeneity as a necessary precondition for democracy, democracies today are being forged in the midst of extraordinary group differences—religious, racial, linguistic, tribal, regional, cultural, or of other forms. The delegitimation of forcibly moving populations to achieve greater ethnic or national homogeneity has contributed to the need for democracies to address group conflict and difference. Even in long-established democracies, such as Great Britain and Canada, demands for greater recognition and protection of distinct groups within those societies have increased. The problem of designing democratic institutions to address group differences— some potentially explosive and destabilizing of democracy itself—has thus become of great moment.

Since the 1970s, academic studies and debate on these issues have been dominated by "consociationalists" and their critics, sometimes labeled "integrationists." The pathbreaking work of Lijphart brought conceptual clarity and articulation to the consociational vision (Lijphart 2002; 1995; 1985; 1977; 1969; 1968). Lijphart and his followers offered this vision for states riven with group conflicts of potentially extreme divisiveness. The central institutional feature of consociational democracies, according to its proponents, is a power-sharing executive structure in which the different relevant groups all have a stake (a "grand coalition," or at least a coalition that requires some degree of power sharing across relevant groups). In addition, consociational democracies are organized around ideas of community autonomy and allocation of various public goods, such as political representation and public employment, in proportion to the relevant groups' share of the population. To generate widespread acceptance and general stability for a democratic state, consociationalists urge that much of the public sphere—the legislature, the judiciary, and the administrative bureaucracy (including, in some contexts, the police and army)—be structured to ensure fair representation of the particular, relevant groups in any particular society. Lijphart also favors list-PR elections in order to empower party elites and thus make negotiated deals across groups more likely; and some consociational systems explicitly set aside a percentage of seats for particular groups. Consociational theory and practice also tends to entail granting formal powers to geographic sub-units or particular communities over certain domains, such as education, or certain social issues, such as marriage, divorce, and inheritance, and perhaps separately funded public media. Finally, minority-group veto rights over policy are also commonly present (McGarry, O'Leary, and Simeon 2008). Consociational theorists aspire to a context in which political elites of the various groups will be able to negotiate among themselves, which is the key mechanism through which these theorists believe consociational structures will ensure stability and success of a democratic regime.

The principal antagonists, frequently called integrationists, have perhaps been Horowitz and, in a more purely theoretical vein, Barry (Horowitz 2000; 1991; 1985; Barry 1989; 1975). Integrationists argue that consociationalism has a poor track record; that consociational structures harden and rigidify preexisting group differences; and that the central assumption of consociationalism is mistaken, for there is no reason to believe political elites will be any more accommodating, or will have the latitude to be, than their supporters. Integrationists argue that the group-based structures of consociationalism actually inflame group conflict and exacerbate political instability. Integrationists favor electoral systems that encourage moderation, a kind of moderation in which voters have some incentive to vote across group lines. Integrationists tend to support executive branches designed to favor candidates who must stand above the group conflicts that dominate deeply divided societies. Such scholars disfavor democratic structures that give substantial autonomy to sub-groups of defined identities; and, to the extent integrationists support federalism, it is typically a federalism in which the constituent units are *not* dominated by any single nationality or religious, linguistic, tribal, or similar community.

The debate between these positions has grown more robust as more new democracies in deeply divided societies face basic institutional design choices (Reynolds

2002). It is difficult to imagine any general scholarly or practical consensus emerging across democracies, even on the more instrumental or empirical dimensions of these debates—at the very least, not at this stage of knowledge and experience. No general, comprehensive analysis that attempts to explain when consociational democracies manage to arise has yet been done (O'Leary 2006). Two particularly promising lines of research and practice are likely to enrich understanding of these issues greatly.

First, recent years have seen a flourishing of works that emphasize the fluidity and malleability of the group identities central to the problem of how to design democratic institutions in deeply divided societies (Brubaker 2004; Laitin 1998). Some of this work presents striking findings about the extent to which the design of democratic institutions and the structures of political competition can shape the expression and mobilization of group identities (Posner 2005). Thus, rather than viewing group identities as fixed, and attempting to determine how to design democratic institutions on the foundation of those identities, more recent research has suggested that the design of these institutions can encourage or diminish the tendency for certain identities to find expression in the political sphere. Future efforts to address this important problem in the design of democratic institutions, both academic and practical efforts, ought to avoid too static an approach. The dynamic and interactive nature of the relationship between group identities and the design of democratic institutions must be central to further work on these questions (Pildes 2008).

Second, the all-or-nothing choice between full-blown consociationalism and purely integrationist institutions is an artificial choice. In response to particular configurations of power and concerns at the moment, different newly-formed democracies in recent years have adopted some power-sharing features without adopting Lijphart's approach across the board. Academic studies have begun to catch up to these practical developments (Choudry 2008). Instead of a broad debate between consociationalism and its critics, research should focus more on particular power-sharing arrangements and their consequences for various democratic concerns and values.

In the American context, a mild form of power sharing has been built into the design of representative institutions through the Voting Rights Act (VRA). To the extent the United States has the kind of group conflicts that animate tensions between majoritarianism and accommodation of minority-group interests, those conflicts have centered on the issue of race. First enacted in 1965 to dismantle the legal barriers to black political participation in the American South, the VRA in the years since has also come to require, in certain circumstances, the creation of "safe" minority election districts. These are districts intentionally designed so that a racial or ethnic minority (primarily black or Hispanic voters) will be the majority of the electorate. The justification for such districts is that, in certain contexts, minority groups as such should have control over the choice of representative. The VRA can be viewed as a mild form of power-sharing or consociationalism for the American context.

These "safe" minority districts have always been opposed by those who view the explicit drawing of election districts on a racial basis as inappropriate or unconstitutional on normative grounds. Over the last decade, however, a different set of issues, grounded more in political science and empirical debate, has come to the fore. These issues center on the consequences of these districts for the democratic system as a whole.

One issue arises as a byproduct of creating individual safe minority election districts: surrounding districts are necessarily drained of minority voters. Because black voters are overwhelmingly liberal and Democratic, surrounding districts therefore become whiter and more Republican. There is thus a trade-off between "descriptive" and "substantive" representation (Pildes 1995). Intentionally designed safe minority districts enhance the former, in that they lead to many more minorities being elected; they detract from the latter, in that such districts have the effect of producing legislative bodies as a whole that are more conservative—and hence less likely to adopt the substantive policies most black voters report themselves to prefer. More study of the magnitude of this trade-off, as well as debate about what to do in light of how significant it is, will be important. In addition, "safe districts" (as their name implies) are not competitive in general elections. Districts in which black voters form a majority of the electorate do not elect Republicans; if there is any competition, it is limited to Democratic primaries. Such districts tend to make surrounding districts less competitive, too, since the former concentrate liberal voters into a few districts rather than spreading them over many. Because issues concerning the decline of electoral competition in districted elections have become central in recent years, as discussed above, the relationship between the VRA, safe districting, and the values of political competition are likely to be important subjects of study and public-policy debate in the coming years. Finally, the great rise in the Hispanic population over the last decade will shift the focus of the VRA. Historically, the focus of the VRA has been tied to issues of race and much of VRA law and scholarship has been built on assumptions or facts that emerge from that racial context. Given that the Hispanic community is less politically cohesive than the black community, and that so many Hispanics are recent arrivals, the question of how the VRA should apply to Hispanic voters will inevitably raise profound new challenges for the future of the law of democracy in this area (de la Garza and DeSipio 2006; Nagler and Alvarez 2004; Baretto, Segura, and Woods 2004).

5 CONCLUSION

At both the macro and micro levels, law and political science have become increasingly intertwined in understanding the causes and effects of democratic institutions and processes. Recent years have spawned greater attention to the way in which the "nature" of democracy in different states, including the United States, is shaped by the specific ways in which the institutional and legal framework of democracy is designed. As noted throughout, comparative research on these issues is becoming one particularly fertile point of entry into these issues. The focus of promising academic research ranges from the broadest issues of how different forms of power sharing among groups in deeply-divided societies affect the stability, acceptance, and performance of democracies, to much less visible issues that nonetheless have considerable influence on the nature of democratic politics, such as how election districts are designed, how political parties choose their candidates, how elections are administered, and how election disputes are resolved.

REFERENCES

ABRAMOWITZ, A. I., ALEXANDER, B., and GUNNING, M. 2006. Incumbency, redistricting, and the decline of competition in U.S. House elections. *Journal of Politics*, 68: 75–88.

ALVAREZ, R. M., and HALL, T. E. 2004. *Point, Click and Vote: The Future of Internet Voting*. Washington, DC: Brookings Institution Press.

BARRETO, M., SEGURA, G., and WOODS, N. 2004. The mobilizing effect of majority-minority districts on Latino turnout. *American Political Science Review*, 98: 65–76.

BARRY, B. 1989. *Democracy, Power, and Justice*. Oxford: Clarendon Press.

—— 1975. The consociational model and its dangers. *European Journal of Political Research*, 3: 393–412.

BLACK, E., and BLACK, M. 2002. *The Rise of Southern Republicans*. Cambridge, Mass.: Belknap Press.

BOND, J. R., and FLEISHER, R. (eds.) 2000. *Polarized Politics: Congress and the President in a Partisan Era*. Washington, DC: CQ Press.

BRADY, H., BUCHLER, J., JARVIS, M., and McNULTY, J. 2001. *Counting All The Votes: The Performance Of Voting Technology in The United States*. Berkeley: Department of Political Science, Survey Research Center, and Institute of Governmental Studies, University of California. Available at: http://ucdata.berkeley.edu:7101/new_web/countingallthevotes.pdf.

BRUBAKER, R. 2004. *Ethnicity Without Groups*. Cambridge, Mass.: Harvard University Press.

CARSON, J. L., and CRESPIN, M. H. 2004. The effect of state redistricting methods on electoral competition in United States House of Representatives races. *State Politics and Policy Quarterly*, 4: 455–69.

CHOUDRY, S. (ed.) 2008. *Constitutionalism in Divided Societies*. Cambridge: Cambridge University Press.

COLLIE, M. P., and MASON, J. L. 2000. The electoral connection between party and constituency reconsidered: evidence from the U.S. House of Representatives, 1972–1994. In *Continuity and Change in House Elections*, ed. D. W. Brady, J. F. Cogan, and M. P. Fiorina. Stanford, Calif.: Stanford University Press.

DE LA GARZA, R. O., and DESIPIO, L. 2006. Reshaping the tub: the limits of the VRA for Latino electoral, politics. In *The Future of the Voting Rights Act*, ed. D. L. Epstein, R. Pildes, R. de la Garza, and S. O'Halloran. New York: Russell Sage Foundation.

EILPERIN, J. 2006. *Fight Club Politics: How Partisanship is Poisoning the House of Representatives.* Lanham, Md.: Rowman and Littlefield.

ELECTIONLINE.ORG 2006. *Election Reform: What's Changed, What Hasn't and Why 2000–2006.* Available at: http://www.electionline.org/Portals/1/Publications/2006.annual.report.Final.pdf.

EPSTEIN, L. D. 1986. *Political Parties in the American Mold.* Madison: University of Wisconsin Press.

FILIPPOV, M., ORDESHOOK, P. C., and SHVETSOVA, O. 2004. *Designing Federalism: A Theory of Self-Sustainable Federal Institutions.* Cambridge: Cambridge University Press.

FIORINA, M. P. 1980. The decline of collective responsibility in American politics. *Daedalus,* Summer: 25–45.

FLEISHER, R., and BOND, J. R. 2004. The shrinking middle in the U.S. Congress. *British Journal of Political Science,* 34: 429–51.

FOLEY, E. B. 2007. The future of *Bush v. Gore? Ohio State Law Journal,* 68: 925–1006.

GERBER, E. R. 2002. Strategic voting and candidate policy positions in a blanket primary. In *Voting at the Political Fault Line,* ed. B. E. Cain and E. R. Gerber. Berkeley: University of California Press.

—— and MORTON, R. B. 1998. Primary election systems and representation. *Journal of Law, Economics and Organization,* 14: 304–24.

GROFMAN, B., and KING, G. 2007. The future of partisan symmetry as a judicial test for partisan gerrymandering after LULAC v. Perry. *Election Law Journal,* 6: 2–35.

HANDLEY, L., GRACE, J., SCHROTT, P., BONEO, H., JOHNSTON, R., MALEY, M., MCROBIE, A., ATTIE, C., ROSSITER, D., and WATSON, P. 2006. *Delimitation Equity Project: Resource Guide.* Washington, DC: IFES. Available at: http://www.ifes.org/publication/a6daa78465c4907 cd23912e3429d333a/Delimitations_Manual_full.pdf.

HARRIS, J. P. 1934. *Election Administration in the United States.* Washington, DC: Brookings Institution.

HIRSCHL, R. 2002. Resituating the judicialization of politics: *Bush v. Gore* as a global trend. *Canadian Journal of Law and Jurisprudence,* 15: 191–218.

—— 2004. *Toward Juristocracy: The Origins and Consequences of the New Constitutionalism.* Cambridge, Mass.: Harvard University Press.

HOROWITZ, D. L. 1985. *Ethnic Groups in Conflict.* Los Angeles: University of California Press.

—— 1991. Electoral systems for a divided society. Pp. 163–95 in *A Democratic South Africa? Constitutional Engineering in a Divided Society,* ed. D. L. Horowitz. Berkeley: University of California Press.

—— 2000. Constitutional design: an oxymoron? Pp. 253–84 in *Designing Democratic Institutions,* ed. I. Shapiro and S. Macedo. New York: New York University Press.

ISSACHAROFF, S. 1993. Judging politics: the elusive quest for judicial review of political fairness. *Texas Law Review,* 71: 1643–703.

—— 2002. Gerrymandering and political cartels. *Harvard Law Review,* 116: 593–648.

ISSACHAROFF, S., KARLAN, P. S., and PILDES, R. H. 2007. *The Law of Democracy: Legal Structure of the Political Process*. New York: Foundation Press.

—— and NAGLER, J. 2007. Protected from politics: diminishing margins of electoral competition in U.S. Congressional elections. *Ohio State Law Journal*, 68: 1121–37.

JACOBSON, G. C. 2003. Terror, terrain, and turnout: explaining the 2002 midterm elections. *Political Science Quarterly*, 118: 1–22.

KIMBALL, D. C., KROPF, M., and BATTLES, L. 2006. Helping America vote? Election administration, partisanship, and provisional voting in the 2004 election. *Election Law Journal*, 5: 447–61.

LAITIN, D. D. 1998. *Identity in Formation: The Russian-Speaking Populations in the Near Abroad*. Ithaca, NY: Cornell University Press.

LEHOUCQ, F. E. 2002. Can parties police themselves? Electoral governance and democratization. *International Political Science Review*, 23: 29–46.

—— and MOLINA, I. 2002. *Stuffing the Ballot Box: Fraud, Electoral Reform, and Democratization in Costa Rica*. Cambridge: Cambridge University Press.

LEVINSON, D. J., and PILDES, R. H. 2006. Separation of parties, not powers. *Harvard Law Review*, 119: 2311–86.

LIJPHART, A. 1968. *The Politics of Accommodation: Pluralism and Democracy in the Netherlands*. Berkeley: University of California Press.

—— 1969. Consociational democracy. *World Politics*, 21: 207–25.

—— 1977. *Democracy in Plural Societies: A Comparative Exploration*. New Haven, Conn.: Yale University Press.

—— 1985. Consociational theory and its critics. Pp. 83–117 in *Power-Sharing in South Africa*, ed. A. Lijphart. Berkeley: University of California Press.

—— 1995. Self-determination versus pre-determination of ethnic minorities in power-sharing systems. In *The Rights of Minority Cultures*, ed. W. Kymlicka. Oxford: Oxford University Press.

—— 2002. The wave of power-sharing democracy. Pp. 37–55 in Reynolds 2002.

LOWENSTEIN, D. H., and STEINBERG, J. 1985. The quest for legislative districting in the public interest: elusive or illusory? *UCLA Law Review*, 33: 1–75.

MASSICOTTE, L., BLAIS A., and YOSHINAKA, A. 2004. *Establishing the Rules of the Game: Election Laws in Democracies*. Toronto: University of Toronto Press.

McDONALD, M. P. 2006. Drawing the line on district competition. *PS: Political Science and Politics*, 39: 91–4.

McGARRY, J., O'LEARY, B., and SIMEON, R. 2008. Integration or accomodation? The enduring debate in conflict-regulation. In *Constitutionalism in Divided Societies*, ed. S. Choudry. Cambridge: Cambridge University Press.

—— 2006b. Re-drawing the line on district competition. *PS: Political Science and Politics*, 39: 99–102.

NAGLER, J., and ALVAREZ, R. M. 2004. Latinos, Anglos, voters, candidates, and voting rights. *University of Pennsylvania Law Review*, 153: 393–432.

OVERTON, S. 2007. Voter identification. *Michigan Law Review*, 105: 631–81.

PERSILY, N. 2001. Toward a functional defense of political party autonomy. *NYU Law Review*, 76: 750–824.

—— 2002. In defense of foxes guarding henhouses: the case for judicial acquiescence to incumbent-protecting gerrymanders. *Harvard Law Review*, 116: 649–83.

PIERSON, P. 2004. *Politics in Time: History, Institutions and Social Analysis*. Princeton, NJ: Princeton University Press.

PILDES, R. H. 1995. The politics of race. *Harvard Law Review*, 108: 1359–92.

—— 1997. Principled limitations on racial and partisan redistricting. *Yale Law Journal*, 106: 2505–61.

—— 2004. The Supreme Court, 2003 term—foreword: the constitutionalization of democratic politics. *Harvard Law Review*, 118: 29–154.

—— 2006. The future of voting rights policy: from anti-discrimination to the right to vote. *Howard Law Journal*, 49: 741–65.

—— and NIEMI, R. G. 1993. Expressive harms, "bizarre districts," and voting rights: evaluating election-district appearances after Shaw v. Reno. *Michigan Law Review*, 92: 483–587.

POOLE, K. T., and ROSENTHAL, H. 1997. *Congress: A Political-Economic History of Roll Call Voting*. New York: Oxford University Press.

POSNER, D. 2005. *Institutions and Ethnic Politics in Africa*. New York: Cambridge University Press.

REYNOLDS, A. (ed.) 2002. *The Architecture of Democracy: Constitutional Design, Conflict Management, and Democracy*. Oxford: Oxford University Press.

ROHDE, D. W. 1991. *Parties and Leaders in the Postreform House*. Chicago: University of Chicago Press.

SALTMAN, R. G. 2006. *The History and Politics of Voting Technology: In Quest of Integrity and Public Confidence*. New York: Palgrave Macmillan.

SHEPSLE, K. A. 1989. Studying institutions: some lessons from the rational choice approach. *Journal of Theoretical Politics*, 1: 131–47.

TOKAJI, D. P. 2005a. Early returns on election reform: discretion, disenfranchisement, and the Help America Vote Act. *George Washington Law Review*, 73: 1206–53.

—— 2005b. The paperless chase: electronic voting and democratic values. *Fordham Law Review*, 73: 1711–836.

WATTENBERG, M. P. 1998. *The Decline of American Political Parties, 1952–1996*. Cambridge, Mass.: Harvard University Press.

CASES

California Democratic Party v. Jones, 530 U.S. 567 (2000).

Davis v. Bandemer, 478 U.S. 109, 152 (1986) (O'Connor, J., concurring in the judgment).

League of United Latin American Citizens v. Perry, 126 S. Ct. 2594 (2006).

People ex rel Salazar v. Davidson, 79 P.3d 1221 (2003), *cert. denied*, 541 U.S. 1093 (2004).

CHAPTER 19

···

ADMINISTRATIVE LAW

···

DANIEL B. RODRIGUEZ

ADMINISTRATIVE regulation through specialized agencies is a ubiquitous and rather permanent characteristic of modern policy-making. These agencies wield enormous power and, although their respective architectures are arguably in tension with our bedrock constitutional principles of separation of powers and representative democracy, the administrative state seems rather entrenched. Surely, if there was ever a significant fork in the road where we might have limited the nature and scope of policy-making by this so-called headless fourth branch of government, that time has long passed (see Rubin 2005). Instead, the pertinent challenge for contemporary administrative law is how best to control and manage these complex processes. This chapter focuses on the ways in which the modern study of administrative law has tackled these challenges; and, especially in the last section, it describes the leading effort to tie together the law and politics of administration through the use of positive political theory.

1 GOVERNANCE AND LEGALITY IN ADMINISTRATION

···

The central objective of administrative law is to reconcile two major aims: the successful exercise of regulatory power by the bureaucracy and the tethering of

For excellent comments on earlier versions of this chapter, I thank, in addition to the editors of this volume, Lisa Bressman, David Law, and Barry Weingast.

administrative agencies to the rule of law. The first goal is concerned fundamentally with regulatory *governance*; the second is concerned with *legality*. Although administrative law has always grappled with each of these goals, the tension between governance and legality has grown over the course of the last hundred years, a time period congruent with the development of the modern administrative state (Rabin 1986; Skowronek 1982).

In the first major era in administrative regulation, beginning roughly in the late nineteenth century and continuing through the New Deal, the key academic defenders of the administrative state viewed the bureaucracy optimistically and had a bold commitment to expanding the scope of national regulatory power. Advocates of these innovative administrative strategies insisted on a separation between administration and politics; they declared that "there is no Democratic or Republican way to pave a street." Accordingly, regulatory agencies were modeled after scientific bureaus; the aim was to configure "something far better and nobler than politics" (Shapiro 1986, 464), namely, technocratic, apolitical government organizations responsible only to the public interest and invested with broad authority to regulate and manage.

The task of administrative law in that era was seen as a limited one. Agencies could be trusted to regulate "in the public interest;" no more specific regulatory mandates were necessary; nor were elaborate administrative procedures warranted. Agencies should be flexible, aggressive, and scientific. By contrast, political authorities and the judiciary deserved less solicitude. "The administrative process," wrote prominent New Dealer James Landis in 1938, "is, in essence, our generation's answer to the inadequacy of the judicial and the legislative processes" (Landis 1938, 14). The elements of American administrative law were created in the shadow of this emerging managerial ideology.

Though limited in scope, administrative law was necessary to establish adequate legality, that is, to ensure that agencies would not abuse their power (Jaffe 1965). Two legal developments were critical in this era. First, the Supreme Court approved the use of delegated administrative power in areas that had previously been subject solely to adjudication among private parties (see *Crowell v. Benson*, 285 U.S. 22). Thereafter, agencies would be permitted wide latitude to manage actively the distribution of resources and rights (see Stewart and Sunstein 1982). Second, Congress enacted the Administrative Procedure Act (APA) in 1946. The APA, forged in the battles between conservatives and liberals during the New Deal, reflected in the end a rather thin administrative law. Although it did establish procedural rights in formal administrative adjudications and created a template for agency rulemaking, it did not expand substantially the federal courts' role in superintending the regulatory process through judicial review (Rodriguez 1997). Nonetheless, it was an omnibus reiteration of the imperative of legality in administrative performance and also a reminder that legal controls were purposefully interstitial and modest (Shapiro 1986).

With time and experience came change in perspectives on legality and regulatory administration. Faith in neutral expertise began to fade in the face of emerging skepticism about the behavior of administrative officials and the performance of regulatory agencies (Schiller 2000; Merrill 1997). The second major era in administrative law scholarship began in the 1960s as scholars began to look with growing concern at the performance of regulatory agencies. Central to this skepticism was an extended critique of bureaucracies by prominent political economists. These influential scholars described the many ways in which regulatory agencies were captured by pressure groups; public interest was thereby sacrificed to private interests (Becker 1983; Lowi 1969; Peltzman 1976; Stigler 1971). This sacrifice was manifest in under-regulation of certain segments of the economy (Mendeloff 1988) and in the enactment of regulations which distorted the market and reflected the undue influence of powerful industries (Kahn 1988). A distinct strand of scholarship in the positive political theory (PPT) tradition emphasized the persistence of political strategizing and legislative choice in the management of regulatory processes. Instead of seeing the basic problem as agencies departing from legislative will and from the public interest, these scholars explained that agencies were behaving more or less as Congress imagined them behaving (McCubbins et al. 1987; Moe 1990; Mitnick 1980). Regulatory agencies, in this view, were involved in small and large ways in redistributing governmental resources from one group of legislative clients to another; in other words, they were means to discrete political ends (Weingast and Moran 1983). Faith in administrative expertise had seriously eroded in the years following the New Deal. And, along with this eroding faith, came skepticism that the thin administrative law reflected in the APA and in key cases could deal adequately with the problem of legality in regulatory administration (Rodriguez 1997).

During this period, a second major development helped push administrative law and its scholarship in a more skeptical direction. The 1960s and early 1970s brought a watershed collection of important regulatory initiatives. This was the era of the new social regulation and, in a relatively short time, Congress greatly expanded the scope of national regulation of social policy. These statutes created powerful agencies to protect and regulate civil rights, voting rights, occupational health and safety, motor vehicle safety, the environment, and other problems which called for federal intervention. Unlike the progressive and New Deal era regulatory statutes, these new statutes were considerably more detailed, requiring more deliberate regulatory processes. Furthermore, these statutes revealed a growing belief on the part of Congress in the value of public participation and in regulatory administration (Rossi 1997; McGarity 1991).

Administrative law mirrored this development through judicial doctrines which broadened the scope of public involvement and limited the scope of agency discretion through more intrusive legal rules. In a seminal article, Richard Stewart (1975) described the emergence in the 1970s of a more avowedly political conception of administrative regulation, whereby "the exercise of agency discretion is inevitably seen as the essentially legislative process of adjusting the competing claims of various private interests affected by agency policy" (1975 1683). Correspondingly, administrative law was tasked with the function of assuring that these "competing claims" were adequately considered; that stakeholders were represented at one or another place in the administrative process; and, finally, that agency discretion was cabined by the terms and policies of the legislative delegation.

Although the characteristics of this new administrative law were diffuse, they could be lumped into two broad categories: internal and external. Internal rules dealt with recreating the procedural elements of agency decision-making in order to maximize public participation, to improve administrative rationality, and to improve judicial review (Melnick 1992; Davis 1969). For example, the federal courts construed the APA to require agencies, even in informal adjudicatory proceedings, to disclose *ex parte* contacts with agency officials (*HBO v. FCC* 1977). This aimed to create a more level playing field among regulated entities and beneficiaries. Similarly, agencies were obliged to respect a rather formalistic separation of roles among legislative, executive, and adjudicatory functions in undertaking administrative decisions (*Ash Grove Cement v. FTC* 1978). While most of these judicial decisions were purportedly grounded in existing statutes, including the APA and the agencies' organic statutes, most scholars rightly saw these developments as growing directly from the courts' skepticism about the willingness of agencies to curtail their own discretion and to resist the entreaties of powerful rent-seeking interest groups (Sunstein 1986; Garland 1985). Indeed, it was from the fear that agencies might behave essentially as transmission belts for various pressure groups who sought governmental assistance in the form of "good" or "less" regulation, that courts—particularly the influential, liberal DC Circuit—imposed an increasingly heavy hand on agencies.

Alongside the development and enforcement of these internal procedural restrictions on agency actions, courts developed external limits through aggressive "hard look" judicial review. These interventions represented what Colin Diver described as the shift from incremental to synoptic decision-making in administrative law (Diver 1981). Although Stewart had described in 1975 the courts' review role in rather modest terms, declaring "[t]he court's function is one of containment," the DC circuit took a much more expansive view of the court's responsibilities. "The function of the court," announced Judge Harold Leventhal in a key 1971 case, "is to assure that the agency has given reasoned consideration to all the facts and issues" (*Greater Boston Television Corp. v. FCC*). Hard look review imposed more severe "reasonableness" constraints—in a word, more legality—on agency actions (Mashaw and Harfst 1990). The result was a considerable transformation in the relationship between the judiciary, the legislature, and courts (Shapiro 1988).[1]

The third major era in the scholarly effort to reconcile administrative law's twin objectives of governance and legality began in 1980 with the election of Ronald Reagan as U.S. president. The Reagan administration had two profound effects on the conduct of administrative policy and law. First, agency officials were appointed

---

[1] In commenting on the chapter, Lisa Bressman notes that one key strand of "hard look review" might properly be viewed as internal, namely, the requirement that agencies take a hard look at their decision-making process and that this hard look be transparent to courts upon review.

with a mandate by the new administration to curtail governmental regulation, a mandate that carried over, as well, into the subsequent Bush administration of 1989–93. Second, President Reagan appointed conservative judges to influential federal courts. These judges proved, as expected, much more skeptical about administrative law's hard look at agency behavior. These twin developments came together in the Court's lodestar decision in *Chevron v. Natural Resource Defense Council* (1984). In *Chevron*, the Court accepted the Environmental Protection Agency's decision to limit the scope of its regulatory commands on companies under the Clean Air Act; in the course of doing so, the Court announced an influential rule of deference to agency statutory interpretations, a rule of deference which had the effect of significantly curtailing the role of lower federal courts in reviewing administrative agency decisions (Miles and Sunstein 2006; Shuck and Elliott 1990). This decision supported, whether deliberately or not, the Reagan administration's agenda of supporting agencies' deregulatory initiatives; however, the consequences on judicial–agency relations were more important and long-lasting.

Chevron was merely the most notable example of the gradual turn away from strong judicial intervention into administrative agency decision-making (Barron and Kagan 2001); lower federal courts somewhat backed away from the hard look approach beginning in the mid-1980s. Under *Chevron* and other doctrines, federal courts deferred to agency regulations and administrative orders, often struggling to reconcile this augmented deference with standard administrative law doctrine. Few were ready by the end of the century to write the obituary on hard look review; but the relationship between courts and agencies had, by any measure, gone through a significant adjustment in the Reagan and post-Reagan era.

Prominent administrative law scholars raised a large number of objections to this turn, proclaiming that the essential principles of legality that underlay the *quid pro quo* of broad administrative delegation were being sacrificed to deregulatory goals, goals principally vented through doctrines of agency deference (Sunstein 1990), restrictions on citizen standing (Suntein 1992), and other forms of judicial abstemiousness. Moreover, critics noted that the president was asserting greater prerogatives of control over the regulatory processes (Shane 1995; Seidenfeld 1992; Farina 1989). This new presidential activism pushed, too, in the direction of deregulation. In particular, administrative orders requiring agencies to evaluate the costs and benefits of regulations before enactment, along with other related orders and, in the case of the Bush I administration, a moratorium on regulations and active presidential control, all represented the encroachments of presidential will—and, indeed, presidential ideology—into the machinery of regulatory administration. Commentators described how these arguably novel strategies disrupted agency performance and endangered procedural fairness and due process. To critics, both of the essential aims of administrative law—*governance* and *legality*—were being undermined by this reenvisioned administrative law. These vigorous disputes among scholars and advocates over the proper priorities of the administrative state marked this era of administrative law scholarship, an era that carried over into the administrations of Presidents Clinton and Bush II.

From the beginning, administrative law struggled to reconcile governance and legality. In different eras, one or another of these goals were more prominent in the courts and in the literature. Scholarship at the founding of the administrative state (1880s to 1930s) generally accepted the imperative of legality and judicial oversight and proffered an optimistic model of administrative discretion and regulatory expertise. The next two generations of administrative law scholars were more ambivalent about the governance–legality trade-off, first urging more judicial intervention and then, later, retreating somewhat in the face of influential critiques that the regulatory process had become "ossified" by elaborate procedures and aggressive judicial oversight (Landis 1938). We are in the early stages of a distinctive era of administrative law scholarship, one that confronts the enduring tension between governance and legality, but one that promises new insights from the application of novel methodologies and more eclectic approaches to the enduring questions. In particular, scholars have applied the insights of "positive political theory" (PPT), described loosely as the application of non-normative tools of rational choice theory, to the study of governmental institutions to these recurring questions of regulatory policy and administrative law. In the rest of this chapter, we consider, first, the standard dilemmas and, next, the contributions of PPT to addressing these dilemmas.

2 The Dilemmas of Regulatory Administration and, therefore, of Administrative Law

The questions that remain central to administrative law scholarship today are similar to the questions central to scholarship in the late nineteenth century. Scholars ask, in various ways: What are the most appropriate structures of legal control to support the agenda of legality while also facilitating sound governance (Edley 1990)? In considering these structures and their consequences for effective regulation, administrative law scholars grapple with a series of fundamental dilemmas of which we consider four here: delegation, discretion, fairness, and regulatory unreasonableness.

2.1 Delegation

An enduring predicament for administrative regulation has been how—or even whether—agencies should wield substantial power, given that the federal bureaucracy cannot be readily accommodated into one of the three branches of government in the U.S. Constitution. Traditionally, this predicament has been framed formalistically: Agencies are viewed with skepticism because they cannot be accommodated within the formula of purely executive, legislative, and judicial power. Such a view has been criticized vigorously as premodern (Rubin 2005), impractical (Posner and Vermeule 2002), and welfare-reducing (Mashaw 1985). Two brute facts loom critical to this debate: First, agencies exercise power that is simultaneously executive, legislative, and judicial; and, second, the Supreme Court has more or less abandoned serious scrutiny of federal legislation under the Constitution's nondelegation doctrine.

Nonetheless, a strand of skepticism endures about delegation in the modern scholarship on public administration and administrative law. Delegation of broad power to unelected agency officials, it is argued, splinters authority from responsibility (Ely 1980); moreover, it illegitimately separates elected representatives from fundamental policy choices, to the overall detriment of democratic accountability (Schoenbrod 1993; Lowi 1969). How can we assess whether and to what extent administrators are acting consistently with principles of legality if Congress has passed the buck to agencies to create regulatory policy?

Although the effort to rein in delegation through external constitutional standards has largely failed, the effort to control agencies through other devices continues in different forms. In recent years, emphasis in the courts has shifted decisively from a close scrutiny of legislative delegations to questions of whether agencies have complied adequately with applicable procedures. The proceduralization of the delegation issue has two sources, both growing out of themes prominent in the administrative law literature. First, requiring agencies to proceed through specific procedural means arguably limits the capacity of agencies to dislodge policy choice from legality (Davis 1969). Second, relying on procedural mechanisms instead of the nondelegation doctrine to ameliorate delegation's threats reflects a more modest, interstitial role for the federal courts in superintending public administration. After all, the nondelegation doctrine is a rule of constitutional review. The effect of a judicial ruling against delegation was to invalidate a duly enacted federal statute; the doctrine was a blunderbuss for a complex policy problem. Subconstitutional devices for restraining delegation would be a more suitable strategy for judicial intervention (Bressman 2004). Insistence on procedural regularity, then, goes hand in hand with narrowing statutory interpretations—what Cass Sunstein has called "antidelegation canons"—in manifesting only moderately intrusive judicial scrutiny (Sunstein 1990).

2.2 Discretion

The problem of discretion always looms in the shadow of debates over the nature and scope of administrative power. Unmitigated discretion, so the argument goes, is antidemocratic; and misuse of agencies' discretionary powers defeats the object-ives of sound governance (Davis 1969). In each of the eras surveyed above, discretion was a central predicament in both the positive and the normative evaluation of regulation and administrative law. Still, we lack a settled account of what exactly we mean by discretion and, moreover, how the project of limiting discretion serves the twin objectives of governance and legality.

The relationship between doctrinal administrative law and the practical exercise of administrative discretion is a complex one. A growing number of scholars emphasize the need to steer the argument away from the dangers of administrative discretion to focus on the possibilities for improved governance through bold administrative action. The challenge is to improve administrative "substance" rather than to remain preoccupied with administrative "procedure" (Sunstein 1990). Dean Edward Rubin argues for abandoning altogether the "pre-historic" conceptions of discretion and accountability, urging administrative law to focus primarily on improving of the capacity of agencies as instruments of active govern-ment to realize modern social and economic goals (Rubin 2005, 84). Legal rules are important, but they are merely one set of implementation mechanisms beside other resources available to public officials to realize government objectives in regulation (2005, 334). Less radically, Jerry Mashaw argues for a reconfiguration of the endur-ing "discretion" debate into a more systematic, empirically-informed analysis of accountability as part of the "grammar of governance" (Mashaw 2005a; 2005b). "The challenge," suggests Mashaw, "is to design administrative institutions that creatively deploy multiple modalities of accountability for the pursuit of complex public purposes" (2005a, 35). Likewise, scholarship in the so-called "new govern-ance" tradition argues for recreating the discretion-as-problem conception of agency power into something more supple, taking account of local knowledge and of emerging public-private governance regimes and networks (Lobel 2007; Metzger 2003; Freeman 2003; 2000). These disparate veins of administrative theory share in common their scrupulous focus on improved governance as the overriding objective of control mechanisms and also the absorption of the discretion question into larger agendas of agency performance and responsiveness, and, lastly, the deemphasis of traditional legal regimes to compel active agency governance.

Nonetheless, many informed scholars continue to worry about under-regulated administrative discretion. Libertarian skeptics fret about the tendency of agencies to use discretion to expand the role of government (Ruhl and Salzman 2003); and, in parallel, progressives worry about the tendency of "free market-oriented" bureaucrats to do precisely the opposite. Moreover, scholars of various ideological stripes point to the admixture of temptations and incentives that drive agencies away from the public interest (Stewart 1990; Pildes and Sunstein 1995). Discretion has not vanished as a dilemma for administrative law; rather, contemporary public law scholars have noted the controversial assumptions underlying the debate over bureaucratic discretion.

2.3 Fairness

Beyond the concerns with accountability as a means of constraining the scope and performance of administrative government, we also worry about the ways in which agencies treat individuals. After all, administrative agencies are in the retail justice business. This is inexorably true of agencies ranging from the Social Security Administration to the Immigration and Naturalization Services at the federal level, to the various bureaus at the state level that deal with issues such as un-employment compensation, health care administration, automobile driving, and attendance at public schools. The challenge is how best to balance the public's interest in just, efficient distribution of the resources and values of the local, state, and national governments and individuals' interest in fair administration in the particular cases (Mashaw 1983). Although the post-New Deal administrative phil-osophy accorded wide deference to government authorities in striking this balance, a major shift appeared to take place in the 1970s as the Supreme Court, in *Goldberg v. Kelly* (1970) and other cases, insisted on various trial-type procedures to be followed in administrative adjudications. Over the past quarter century, however, the trend has been to limit the interventions of the judiciary in requiring a type or level of administrative justice (Mashaw 1983). In *Vermont Yankee v. NRDC* (1978), for example, the Court instructed the lower federal courts to leave the question of which procedures are necessary to Congress and the agencies and, therefore, to decline to impose *Goldberg*-like procedures in the administration of regulatory programs. And the due process revolution in benefit administration was curtailed sharply by a series of major decisions in which the Supreme Court limited the domain of procedural due process and required the federal courts to balance the advantages of more trial-type procedures with the costs to the regulatory scheme.

What scope is left for fairness in administrative law? Most of the requirements for administrative fairness in individual cases are found in the structure of the agencies' organic acts, along with the Administrative Procedure Act as interpreted by the federal courts (notwithstanding the Court's watershed decision in *Vermont Yankee*). Despite the excoriations of critics of administrative activity in the 1970s and 1980s, agency mandates do contain a variety of procedural restrictions designed to ensure a measure of fairness in the administration of benefit programs and other regulatory decisions. The struggles in the federal courts in recent years have involved less the question of whether a regulatory program complies with the Constitution's require-ments of due process, than the question whether and to what extent the agency has complied with its procedural mandates—its designed standards of fairness—in the statute or administrative rule at issue (see Rodriguez and Weingast 2007).

That said, administrative law scholars continue to debate whether administrative decision-making sufficiently ensures procedural fairness. And, where such decision-making fails on this score, scholars proffer various, imaginative solutions to this fairness deficit. Among the most conspicuous recent efforts to address these supposed deficits are proposals that there be more deliberation in traditional venues of regulatory decision-making (see Cuellar 2005) and, moreover, more use of avowedly collaborative mechanisms, for example, regulatory negotiation (Freeman and Langbein 2000).

2.4 Reasonableness

To many contemporary commentators, the dilemmas addressed above are just elements in the more general project of ensuring that agencies act in ways that foster sound governance (Stewart 2003). Thus, scholars urge courts to look more closely at whether and to what extent agency decisions are adequately reasoned. In some limited contexts, this responsibility grows squarely out of the APA's standards for judicial review in formal proceedings. There, agency decisions must be based upon substantial evidence; and, even in informal regulatory proceedings, agency decisions are reviewed to ensure that they are neither arbitrary nor capricious. Yet, it has only been in the last three decades or so that courts and scholars have viewed these statutory requirements as essentially akin to a general requirement of agency reasonableness (Shapiro 1988; Diver 1981). This approach represents perhaps the single most important development in administrative law over the last half century. By disentangling the strands of this judicial approach, we can better understand the tensions in contemporary views of public administration and administrative law.

Reasonableness review is based upon skepticism about agency discretion and confidence in the capability of courts. The critique of agency discretion has been shaped largely by influential political economists of the Chicago School and its kin, public choice theory (Farber and Frickey 1991). These scholars view agencies as rent-seeking and detached from the public interest; aggressive judicial review, then, was justified as a means for restraining the deleterious effects of regulation. Likewise, progressives view agencies as frequently unworthy of public trust (Bressman 2004; Sunstein 1990). Insofar as agencies could not be trusted to implement progressive social policies, policies encoded in the watershed statutes of the 1960s and 1970s, courts must ride herd on agency officials to make sure that they were doing their jobs.

Reasonableness review reflects, as well, confidence in the capacity of courts to ensure sound governance through close scrutiny of agency decisions. In a noted "hard look review" case in the DC Circuit (*Ethyl Corp. v. EPA* 1978), two influential appellate court judges debated whether judges should be expected to act as surrogate experts, as amateur scientists of a sort, when they examined administrative records under the APA. From one perspective, such expertise is essential—and entirely possible—in order to sort out satisfactorily sensible from senseless decisions. From another perspective, such role-playing is inapt; instead, judges could and should closely scrutinize agency decisions using standard legal techniques to satisfy themselves that the agency's decision was sustainable upon the assumptions and standards developed in the administrative record and, critically, in the decision-making rules laid out in past administrative law cases. Although this disagreement frames much of the debate over how hard "hard look" should be, the tacit assumption underlying both perspectives is that, in whatever form, searching "reasonableness" review is both possible and proper. No longer would courts be limited to determining whether agency actions are within or outside the scope of the statute—what Stewart called the "constraining" function; rather, judges should look closely at agency records and rationales to satisfy themselves that the agency decisions are the result of a rational process.

As Martin Shapiro (1988) describes this searching review, scholars concerned with regulatory unreasonableness would require agencies to engage in more thorough deliberation. These scholars "do not want administrators to play the purely passive political role of registering and implementing group preferences" (1988, 144). Instead, administrators would ideally, "consult and debate with their fellow administrators to hammer out collective prudential judgments about public affairs, judgments that would best serve the common good" (1988, 145). This vision harkens back to the "expertise" model celebrated by commentators at the founding of the administrative state; yet, unlike the expertise model, deliberation requires sustained democratic participation; it asks of agencies a process to reach consensus among interested and affected participants over the content and implementation of the public good.

Other critics view this new administrative law from a more practical standpoint, describing how hard look contributes to the "ossification" of administrative rule-making (Pierce, Jr. 1995; McGarity 1992). Reasoned deliberation comes at the price of efficient governmental performance—in particular, slow scrutiny by federal courts of agency decision-making to ensure the sufficiency of both procedures and rationales—undermines the efficacy of administrative regulation (Breyer 1993; Mashaw and Harfst 1990). In three separate, influential studies from the 1980s, scholars described in detail how the federal courts, in requiring increasingly stringent explanations and procedural steps to justify certain regulatory strategies, undermined the objectives of social regulation in the areas of clean air (Melnick 1983), occupational health and safety (Mendeloff 1988), and motor vehicle safety (Mashaw and Harfst 1989). Robert Kagan (2001) describes this phenomenon as the triumph of "adversarial legalism," that is, the replacement of traditional policy analysis involving collaboration among salient interest groups and pertinent governmental institutions with court-centered regulatory commands driven by profligate litigation.

The critique of searching reasonableness review and the new administrative law is not a universal one. Some have suggested that the claims of ossification are exaggerated, pointing to data which reveal agencies methodically managing their regulatory responsibilities notwithstanding episodic judicial interventions (Jordan 2000; Seidenfeld 1997). Others that explained why and how searching review is valuable and efficient notwithstanding the costs to the regulatory system (Garland 1985). In the end, the debate is impossible to settle by mere arguments over whether and to what extent administrative rulemaking is ossified. The costs of judicial review can be assessed, if at all, only in light of what we believe to be the values of administrative efficiency. Moreover, a fully informed analysis of the judiciary's capacity to review successfully administrative decision-making requires a developed positive theory of judicial performance (how do the courts behave in light of its complex institutional structure and incentives?) and an empirical analysis of judicial decision-making in practice, topics taken up in the last part of this chapter.

3 The Political Foundations of Administrative Law

Administrative law has historically been concerned with legal, not political, control of agencies. More aspirationally, administrative law has typically been seen as an antidote to politics, and perhaps a means of protecting agencies from the baleful influence of partisan influences of legislators and the president. This dichotomy between administrative law and administrative politics is a false one. First, law affects political outcomes and, therefore, any effort to create a sensible administrative law must be acutely aware of the political consequences of certain legal rules and doctrines. Second, political economists point to the strategic elements of court/legislature/agency interactions. In a number of provocative recent works, scholars have described how administrative law can be used to accomplish ideological objectives, whether on the part of courts, Congress, or both institutions. For these reasons, contemporary administrative law scholars influenced by positive political theory appreciate to a greater degree than before the intractable inter-institutional relationships among Congress, the president, courts, and agencies. The implications of this greater attention to the political foundations of administrative law are both positive and normative (see Rodriguez and Weingast 2007).

Early work in this vein helpfully described the origin and functions of regulatory agencies and the ubiquitous strategies of political control over agency performance. Terry Moe describes the regulatory process as a "political firm," that is, a public bureaucracy consisting of the "entire two-tiered hierarchy linking politicians, interest groups, and bureaucrats" (1990, 122). This firm exercises power in pursuit of an admixture of public and private goals. Moreover, as McCubbins et al. (1989; 1987) explain, Congress creates these administrative organizations in order to fulfill and further political agendas; and legislators will structure internal administrative procedures (for example, "notice and comment" rulemaking) in order to improve the capacity of legislators to govern. The key insight of this burgeoning literature is this: Elected officials use administrative agencies strategically to implement discernible goals. To be sure, these goals will shift over time (see Shepsle 1992), as will the interests of the various groups making up the elements of the "political firm." Yet, the overriding objective of Congress and the president is to manage the administrative process purposively and with the resources available to politicians in modern government (see Rodriguez 1994).

The implications of this view for administrative governance are manifold. Viewed broadly, agency procedures can be better understood in light of these diffuse, but persistent political strategies. For example, the choice of whether and how much to delegate is, too, refracted through the lens of strategic choices by political officials (Epstein and O'Halloran 1999; Kiewiet and McCubbins 1991). The essential challenge for Congress is to limit "bureaucratic drift" (Shepsle 1990), that is, "the ability of an agency to enact outcomes different from the policies preferred by those who originally delegated power" (Epstein and O'Halloran 1999, 25). Oversight, a classic form of *ex post* legislative control, can ameliorate this drift (Aberbach 1990; Weingast and Moran 1983). The usual sorts of political checks include oversight hearings, appropriations limits, and various informal checks on the behavior of agency officials—all techniques that can be described (per McCubbins and Schwartz 1984) as "police patrols" and "fire alarms."

Not to be neglected in the arsenal of legislators are various forms of *ex ante* controls established through the mechanisms of agency design and procedural rules. For example, Congress in the APA established the system of notice and comment rulemaking and thereby mandated that agencies disclose their agendas before the end of the rulemaking process. Thus, while ostensibly a mechanism for citizen participation (the APA gives comment opportunities to all "interested parties"), this requirement fulfills an important legislative oversight objective as well. McCubbins et al. (1989; 1987) point that this strategy of *ex ante* control through procedural design is particularly useful because it enables Congress to tether courts to this larger political strategy since, after all, courts will be responsible to enforce these procedural rules through ordinary rules of administrative law.

A further positive implication of this positive political perspective on administrative law is that Congress will likewise constrain the courts in their objective—if it is indeed an objective—to combat political influence over administration. More generally, courts will be constrained by Congress *whatever* their objectives in agency policy-making. Courts are not the last movers in the sequence of decision-making (Rodriguez 1994). Congress and the president can react to judicial decisions; and, more to the point, the threat of such reactions disciplines courts and ensures that administrative law and statutory interpretation decisions will be within the boundaries of the policy space represented by pertinent congressional and presidential preferences. Through simple and more complicated game theoretic models, scholars in the PPT tradition have usefully described the dynamics of court/legislature/agency relations (Ferejohn and Shipan 198). Though vulnerable to the critique that these abstract models oversimplify reality, the essential insight of the PPT logic, that agencies will make choices in the shadow of congressional and judicial preferences and strategies and the other relevant institutions will act purposively as well, reflects a significant advance in understanding. The normative implications for administrative law of this understanding are being shaped in recent scholarly work (see e.g. Rodriguez and Weingast 2007; Bressman 2007).

Perhaps one reason why this model of regulatory governance and administrative law has become enormously influential in recent years is that it often has testable implications for both the performance of agencies and the decisions of federal courts. For example, Linda Cohen and Matthew Spitzer (1994) focus squarely on the *Chevron* doctrine; building on the PPT model, they explain how and why courts would calibrate their deference to agency statutory interpretations depending upon how closely the agency decisions track the ideological preferences of the Supreme Court. Where the Court and agencies are more closely aligned than are the agencies and the lower federal courts, higher courts, acting strategically in pursuit of policy goals, should increase deference to agency interpretations; the reverse should happen when the alignment between agencies and the lower federal courts is closer. More recently, Matthew Stephenson (2004, 755) finds that the opposite from what Cohen and Spitzer hypothesized happened in the years beginning with the Clinton administration. The Supreme Court, suggests Stephenson, may be inclined to support the president's mandate for leadership, even where this mandate is distant from the justices' preferences (2004, 755).

Stephenson brings PPT insights to bear in evaluating another administrative law doctrine: the requirement that agencies provide a suitably extensive explanation of their regulatory decisions. This requirement was created by courts in the heyday of the "hard look" review era; legal scholars have typically connected this requirement to the general imperative of agency reasonableness. Stephenson offers a different explanation, one drawn directly from the economics literature on signaling. He shows how "judicially-imposed explanation requirements can help reviewing courts overcome their comparative informational disadvantage for reasons that are independent of the (in)ability of courts to understand or verify the substantive content of the justifications advanced by government decision-makers" (2004). In essence, Stephenson sees agencies as signaling through their elaborate explanations to the courts about how much the agencies value their outcomes. The thesis, as with most other PPT perspectives on administrative law doctrines, rests on key, controversial assumptions. A central assumption here is that "the expected benefit of a proposed policy from the reviewing court's perspective is positively correlated with the benefit of that policy to the government" (2004).

Administrative law is, after all, an omnibus legal category that includes a mix of different judicially imposed control devices. One important implication of PPT is that courts will choose from a menu of doctrines and rules in order to implement more effectively their aims (Spiller and Tiller 1997). These doctrines include reasonableness review, scrutiny of agency procedures and the fidelity by the agency to these procedures, and statutory interpretation. Through strategic use of one or another of these doctrinal substitutes, courts can navigate around some of the shoals of political influence; they can, for instance, raise the costs to politicians of reversing judicial decisions. Moreover, courts can rely on certain doctrines as proxies for variables that the court deems important but cannot observe directly. The motivations for judges to structure rules strategically are, broadly speaking, equivalent to the motivations of other "political" actors—to realize certain objectives through the purposive use of the regulatory process. But, the "game" continues beyond the decisions of the courts; and agencies and Congress can adapt in their own decision-making procedures and institutional structures to cabin judicial influence (Stephenson 2006a; 2006b; Cuellar and Weingast 2006). It is essential to scrutinize carefully the dynamics of court/agency/legislative/executive politics and policy-making; for it is only when we see these complex institutions operating in the shadow of one another that we can better understand the structure and strategy of contemporary administrative law.

Legal scholars have drawn interesting normative implications from this work. For example, Daniel Rodriguez, Barry Weingast, and Mathew McCubbins have described how PPT insights can ground certain prescriptive approaches to statutory interpretation of complex regulatory statutes (Rodriguez and Weingast 2007; 2003; McCubbins and Rodriguez 2005). McNollgast (1987; 1989) and Rodriguez and Weingast argue that attention to the strategic incentives of legislators to engage in self-serving rhetoric through fashioned legislative histories can assist courts in separating costly signals—and, therefore, trustworthy information—from cheap talk. In a similar vein, McCubbins and Rodriguez criticize the Supreme Court's injunction that legislative changes to regulatory statutes through the appropriations process should be disfavored in statutory interpretation. They explain how the appropriations process provides a venue for fairly reliable information about the scope of legislator preferences in regulatory implementation; therefore, if anything, courts should pay particular attention to how legislators reconfigure policy implementation through the appropriations process.

Several prominent scholars, including Lisa Bressman (2004), Jonathan Macey (1992), and Terry Moe (1987), and have highlighted the especially important role of the president in regulatory implementation. Drawing from PPT, they consider how certain legal doctrines can help decrease the opportunities for the president to micromanage agency policy-making at the expense of Congress and its constituents. This line of work raises a more fundamental issue to be sure: What is the proper role of courts in superintending the "tug of war" between Congress and president over regulatory policy-making? While this is not a new issue, of course, PPT's emphasis on the strategic incentives of political officials and the resources available to officials to intervene *ex ante* and *ex post* in regulatory decision-making sheds interesting light on this enduring debate (Kagan 2001; Macey 1992; Eskridge and Ferejohn 1992).

Legal scholars working within the PPT tradition have drawn different conclusions on the largest normative question; that is, whether courts should be more or less interventionist in agency policy-making. Some have argued that hard look review, in either its traditional form or modified in ways that take into account more sophisticated understandings of the Congress/agency process, is especially justified where we fear ubiquitous political influence and strategic behavior (see Bressman 2007). Particular objectives, such as sorting out low-value from high-value regulations (Johnston 2002) or fostering democratic participation in regulatory processes (Cuellar 2005), arguably counsel more vigorous judicial scrutiny of agency performance. Others argue, however, that PPT teaches us that more aggressive judicial scrutiny is unwarranted (Tiller 2002; Cross 1999). While the reasons for these objections differ, the basic problem identified is that judicial interventions just push agencies in directions that ultimately undermine the goals of regulatory efficiency while not accomplishing the normative goals that motivated aggressive judicial review in the first instance. Given the prominence of PPT in modern administrative law debates, we can expect to see more thorough theoretical and empirical analyses of these central questions. Indeed, PPT provides an especially rich set of tools for novel exploration of normative considerations.

At base, a richer understanding of the political foundations of administrative law and attention to the role of politics and political strategy in regulatory decision-making better explains certain patterns in contemporary administrative law. Likewise, it helps justify more effectively particular prescriptive suggestions about how courts and agencies should implement their objectives. Such efforts echo, then, a theme that Judge Richard Posner raised in a decade-old essay entitled "The rise and fall of administrative law" (1997), an essay in which he commented that the "interesting questions of administrative law... can be answered well only by administrative lawyers who... are willing to cast beyond law's traditional limits for methods of analysis and sources of insight" (1997, 963).

4 CONCLUSION

The objectives of administrative law—governance and legality—remain properly central to the enterprise of the field. Scholars in a variety of intellectual traditions and with a large tool kit of methodologies have furnished many provocative perspectives on these enduring objectives. Regulation and public administration are means of governance that tap deeply into the most contested issues of social, economic, and political ideology; and with high stakes come grand controversies. Many of the main controversies have involved disagreements about how effective are agencies at accomplishing the tasks accorded to them by Congress. The common wisdom has shifted back and forth over the decades, with different eras bringing greater or lesser confidence in the motivations and capacity of regulatory agencies to govern effectively. Meanwhile, the standard issues—delegation, discretion, fairness, and reasonableness—have framed the debates over these eras.

Administrative law as an intellectual field has evolved in recent years primarily through its use of various methods of analysis outside of the four corners of law. Particularly influential have been economic analysis, social science more generally (including, especially, careful empirical analyses of regulation and administrative processes), and the emerging positive political theory of administrative law. With these methodological advancements has come a more sustainable connection between the positive understanding of the role of administrative agency decision-making and normative efforts to shape the processes of policy-making to realize key social objectives.

References

ABERBACH, J. D. 1990. *Keeping a Watchful Eye.* Washington, DC: Brookings Institution.

BARRON, D., and KAGAN, E. 2001. Chevron's nondelegation doctrine. *Supreme Court Review*, 2001: 201–65.

BECKER, G. 1983. A theory of competition among pressure groups for political influence. *Quarterly Journal of Economics*, 98: 371–400.

BRESSMAN, L. 2004. Judicial review of agency inaction: an arbitrariness approach. *New York University Law Review*, 79: 1657–718.

—— 2007. Procedures as politics in administrative law. *Columbia Law Review*, 107: 1749.

—— and VANDENBERG, M. 2006. Inside the administrative state: a critical look at the practice of presidential control. *Michigan Law Review*, 105: 47–99.

BREYER, S. 1993. *Breaking the Vicious Circle: Toward Effective Risk Regulation.* Cambridge, Mass.: Harvard University Press.

COHEN, D., CUELLAR, M., and WEINGAST, B. 2006. Crisis bureaucracy: homeland security and the political design of legal mandates. *Stanford Law Review*, 59: 673–760.

COHEN, L., and SPITZER, M. 1994. Solving the Chevron puzzle. *Law and Contemporary Problems*, 57: 65–110.

CROSS, F. 1999. Shattering the fragile case for judicial review of rulemaking. *Virginia Law Review*, 85: 1243–334.

CUELLAR, M. F. 2005. Rethinking regulatory democracy. *Administrative Law Review*, 57: 411–99.

DAVIS, K. 1969. *Discretionary Justice: A Preliminary Inquiry.* Baton Rouge, La.: LSU Press.

DIVER, C. 1981. Policymaking paradigms in administrative law. *Harvard Law Review*, 95: 393–434

DUFFY, J. 1998. Administrative common law in judicial review. *Texas Law Review*, 77: 113–214.

EDLEY, C. 1990. *Administrative Law: Rethinking Judicial Control of Bureaucracy.* New Haven, Conn: Yale University Press.

ELY, J. 1980. *Democracy and Distrust: A Theory of Judicial Review.* Cambridge, Mass.: Harvard University Press.

EPSTEIN, D., and O'HALLORAN, S. 1999. *Delegating Powers: A Transaction Cost Politics Approach to Policy Making under Separate Powers.* New York: Cambridge University Press.

ESKRIDGE, W., and FEREJOHN, J. 1992. The Article I, Section 7 game. *Georgetown Law Journal*, 80: 523–64.

FARBER, D., and FRICKEY, P. 1991. *Law and Public Choice: A Critical Introduction.* Chicago: University of Chicago Press.

FARINA, C. 1989. Statutory interpretation and the balance of power in the administrative state. *Columbia Law Review*, 89: 452–528.

FEREJOHN, J., and SHIPAN, C. 1990. Congressional influence on bureaucracy. *Journal of Law, Economics and Organization*, 6: 1–20.

FREEMAN, J. 2000. The private role in public governance. *New York University Law Review*, 75: 543–675.

—— 2001. The contracting state. *Florida State University Law Review*, 28: 155–212.

—— and LANGBEIN, L. 2000. Regulatory negotiation and the legitimacy benefit. *New York University Environmental Law Journal*, 9: 60–151.

GARLAND, M. 1985. Deregulation and judicial review. *Harvard Law Review*, 98: 505–91.

JAFFE, L. 1965. *Judicial Control of Administrative Action*. Boston: Little, Brown.

JOHNSTON, J. 2002. A game theoretic analysis of alternative institutions for regulatory cost–benefit analysis. *University of Pennsylvania Law Review*, 150: 1343–410.

JORDAN, W. 2000. Ossification revisited: does arbitrary and capricious review significantly interfere with agency ability to achieve regulatory goals through informal rulemaking? *Northwestern University Law Review*, 94: 393–450.

KAGAN, E. 2001. Presidential administration. *Harvard Law Review*, 114: 2245–385.

KAHN, A. 1988. *The Economics of Regulation: Principles and Institutions*. Cambridge, Mass.: MIT Press.

KIEWIET, R., and MCCUBBINS, M. 1991. *The Logic of Delegation: Congressional Parties and the Appropriations Process*. Chicago: University of Chicago Press.

LANDIS, J. 1938. *The Administrative Process*. New Haven, Conn.: Yale University Press.

LOBEL, O. 2007. The paradox of extralegal activism: critical legal consciousness and transformative politics. *Harvard Law Review*, 120: 938–88.

LOWI, T. 1969. *The End of Liberalism: Ideology, Policy, and the Crisis of Public Authority*. New York: Norton.

MACEY, J. 2002. Separated powers and positive political theory: the tug of war over administrative agencies. *Georgetown Law Journal*, 80: 671–703.

MASHAW, J. 1983. *Bureaucratic Justice: Managing Social Security Disability Claims*. New Haven, Conn.: Yale University Press.

—— 1985. Prodelegation: why administrators should make political decisions. *Journal of Law, Economics and Organization*, 1: 81–100.

—— 1994. Improving the environment of agency rulemaking: an essay on games, management and accountability. *Law and Contemporary Problems*, 1994: 185–257.

—— 2005. Structuring a "dense complexity:" accountability and the project of administrative law. *Issues in Legal Scholarship*, 2005: 1–38.

—— and HARFST, D. 1990. *The Struggle for Auto Safety*. Cambridge, Mass.: Harvard University Press.

MCCUBBINS, M., and RODRIGUEZ, D. 2005. Canonical construction and statutory revisionism: the strange case of the appropriations canon. *Journal of Contemporary Legal Issues*, 14: 669–716.

—— and SCHWARTZ, T. 1984. Congressional oversight overlooked: police patrols versus fire alarms. *American Journal of Political Science*, 2: 165–79.

—— et al. 1987. Administrative procedures as instruments of political control. *Journal of Law, Economics and Organization*, 3: 243–77.

—— et al. 1989. Structure and process, politics and policy: administrative arrangements and the political control of agencies. *Virginia Law Review*, 75: 431–82.

MCGARITY, T. 1991. *Reinventing Rationality: The Role of Regulatory Analysis in the Federal Bureaucracy*. New York: Cambridge University Press.

—— 1992. Some thoughts on "deossifying" the rulemaking process. *Duke Law Journal*, 41: 1385–462.

MELNICK, R. S. 1983. *Regulation and the Courts: The Case of the Clean Air Act.* Washington, DC: Brookings Institution.

—— 1992. Administrative law and bureaucratic rationality. *Administrative Law Review,* 44: 245–59.

MENDELOFF, J. 1988. *The Dilemma of Toxic Substance Regulation: How Overregulation Causes Underregulation.* Cambridge, Mass.: MIT Press.

MERRILL, T. 1997. Capture theory and the courts, 1967–1983. *Chicago–Kent Law Review,* 72: 1039–117.

METZGER, G. 2003. Privatization as delegation. *Columbia Law Review,* 103: 1367–502.

MILES, T., and SUNSTEIN, C. 2006. Do judges make regulatory policy? An empirical investigation of Chevron. *University of Chicago Law Review,* 73: 823–81.

MITNICK, B. 1980. *The Political Economy of Regulation: Creating, Designing, and Removing Regulatory Forms.* New York: Columbia University Press.

MOE, T. 1990. The politics of structural choice: towards a theory of public bureaucracy. In *Organization Theory: From Chester Barnard to the Present and Beyond,* ed. O. E. Williamson. Berkeley: University of California Press.

PELTZMAN, S. 1976. Toward a more general theory of regulation. *Journal of Law and Economics,* 19: 211–40.

PIERCE, R. Jr. 1995. Seven ways to deossify agency rulemaking. *Administrative Law Review,* 47: 59–95.

PILDES, R., and SUNSTEIN, C. 1995. Reinventing the regulatory state. *University of Chicago Law Review,* 62: 1–129.

POSNER, E., and VERMEULE, A. Interring the nondelegation doctrine. *University of Chicago Law Review,* 69: 1721–61.

POSNER, R. 1997. The rise and fall of administrative law. *Chicago–Kent Law Review,* 72: 953–63.

RABIN, R. 1986. Federal regulation in historical perspective. *Stanford Law Review,* 38: 1189–326.

RODRIGUEZ, D. 1994. The positive political dimensions of regulatory reform. *Washington University Law Quarterly,* 72: 1–150.

—— 1997. Jaffe's law: an essay on the intellectual underpinnings of modern administrative law theory. *Chicago–Kent Law Review,* 72: 1159–86.

—— and WEINGAST, B. 2003. The positive political theory of legislative history: new perspectives on the 1964 Civil Rights Act and its interpretation. *University of Pennsylvania Law Review,* 151: 1417–542.

—— 2007. The paradox of expansionist statutory interpretations. *Northwestern University Law Review,* 101: 1207–56.

ROSSI, J. 1997. Participation run amok: the costs of mass participation for deliberative agency decisionmaking. *Northwestern University Law Review,* 92: 173–249.

RUBIN, E. 2005. *Beyond Camelot.* Princeton, NJ: Princeton University Press.

RUHL, J. B., and SALZMAN, J. 2003. Mozart and the red queen: the problem of regulatory accretion in the administrate state. *Georgetown Law Journal,* 91: 757–850.

SCHILLER, R. 2000. Enlarging the administrative polity: administrative law and the changing definition of pluralism 1945–1970. *Vanderbilt Law Review,* 53: 1389–453.

SCHOENBROD, D. 1993. *Power Without Responsibility.* New Haven, Conn.: Yale University Press.

SCHUCK, P., and ELLIOTT, E. D. 1990. To the Chevron station: an empirical study of federal admininistrative law. *Duke Law Journal,* 1990: 984–1077.

SEIDENFELD, M. 1992. A civic republican justification for the bureaucratic state. *Harvard Law Review,* 105: 1511–76.

—— 1997. Demystifying deossification: rethinking recent proposals to modify judicial review of notice and commence rulemaking. *Texas Law Review*, 75: 483–524.

SHANE, P. 1995. Political accountability in a system of checks and balances: the case of presidential review of rulemaking. *Arkansas Law Review*, 48: 161–214.

SHAPIRO, M. 1986. APA: past, present, future. *Virginia Law Review*, 72: 447–92.

—— 1988. *Who Guards the Guardians?* Athens: University of Georgia Press.

SHEPSLE, K. A. 1992. Bureaucratic drift, coalitional drift, and time inconsistency: a comment on Macey. *Journal of Law, Economics and Organization*, 8: 111–18.

SKOWRONEK, S. 1982. *Building a New American State: The Expansion of National Administrative Capacities, 1877–1920*. New York: Cambridge University Press.

SPILLER, P., and TILLER, E. 1997. Decision costs and the strategic design of administrative process and judicial review. *Journal of Legal Studies*, 26: 347–70.

STEPHENSON, M. 2004. Mixed signals: reconsidering the political economy of judicial deference to administrative agencies. *Administrative Law Review*, 56: 657–731.

—— 2006a. Legislative allocation of delegated power: uncertainty, risk, and the choice between agencies and courts. *Harvard Law Review*, 119: 1035–70.

—— 2006b. The strategic substitution effect: textual plausibility, procedural formality, and judicial review of agency statutory interpretations. *Harvard Law Review*, 120: 528–72.

STEWART, R. 1975. The reformation of American administrative law. *Harvard Law Review*, 88: 1667–813.

—— 2000. Madison's nightmare. *University of Chicago Law Review*, 57: 335–56.

—— 2003. Administrative law in the twenty-first century. *New York University Law Review*, 78: 437–60.

—— and SUNSTEIN, C. 1982. Public programs and private rights. *Harvard Law Review*, 95: 1193–322.

STIGLER, G. 1971. The theory of economic regulation. *Bell Journal of Economics and Management Science*, 2: 3–21.

SUNSTEIN, C. 1986. Factions, self-interest, and the APA: four lessons since 1946. *Virginia Law Review*, 62: 271–95.

—— 1990. Law and administration after Chevron. *Columbia Law Review*, 90: 2017–120.

—— 1992. What's standing after Lujan? Of citizen suits, "injuries," and Article III. *Michigan Law Review*, 91: 163–236.

TILLER, E. 2002. Resources based strategies in law and positive political theory: cost–benefit analysis and the like. *University of Pennsylvania Law Review*, 150: 1453–72.

WEINGAST, B. R., and MORAN, M. J. 1983. Bureaucratic discretion or congressional control: regulatory policymaking by the FTC. *Journal of Political Economy*, 91: 765–800.

CASES

Ash Grove Cement v. FTC, 577 F.2d 1368 (9th Cir. 1978).

Chevron v. NRDC, 467 U.S. 837 (1984).

Crowell v. Benson, 285 U.S. 22 (1932).

Ethyl Corp. v. EPA, 541 F.2d 1 (D.C. Cir. 1976) (*en banc*).

Goldberg v. Kelly, 397 U.S. 254 (1970).

Greater Boston Television Corp. v. FCC, 463 F.2d 268 (D.C. Cir. 1971).

Home Box Office v. FCC, 567 F.2d 9 (D.C. Cir. 1977).

Vermont Yankee v. NRDC, 435 U.S. 519 (1978).

CHAPTER 20

LEGISLATION AND STATUTORY INTERPRETATION

ELIZABETH GARRETT

THE study of statutory interpretation moved to the forefront of scholarly attention in the 1980s in large part because legal scholars began to use insights and methodologies from political science—most fruitfully, from public choice and other positive theories of politics. Not only did this interdisciplinary approach transform legal scholarship, but it also was adopted by leading jurists. Justice Scalia (1997, 13) proclaimed that "[w]e live in an age of legislation" and tirelessly worked to convince all interpreters to adopt his method of interpretation, textualism, which was influenced by public choice.

At the outset of this renaissance of statutory interpretation scholarship, positive theories of politics were primarily used to cast into doubt two of the foundational theories of interpretation—intentionalism, the dominant theory with origins in Blackstone, and purposivism, primarily associated with Hart and Sacks' *Legal Process* materials (1994 [1958]). Some who were convinced by the pessimistic vision espoused by the first wave of public choice scholarship advocated exclusive use of the third foundational method: textualism. The aspiration of textualists to use their method of interpretation to force Congress to pay more attention to legislative drafting and consider difficult questions of policy rather than punting them to the less democratic judiciary has been drawn into question by sophisticated understandings of the legislative process inspired by political science. Scholars have also recently deployed the tools of political science to provide more nuanced approaches to intentionalism; others who have been greatly influenced by public choice have developed theories that have an affinity to purposivism.

In this chapter, I describe the interaction of positive theories of politics with the foundational theories of statutory interpretation, discussing how political science has been used to challenge these theories and how it has sometimes provided a more nuanced and convincing version of interpretive techniques. This latter development has been particularly noticeable in recent work aiming to resurrect intentionalism by using positive political theory to determine which signals of legislative intent are credible and which are "cheap talk." Although I discuss all three theories, I particularly focus on intentionalism because it remains the dominant interpretive method. I conclude by suggesting that future scholarship should focus on two emerging areas of study, in addition to continued work to revise the foundational theories. First, scholars should produce more empirical studies on the effect of interpretive strategies on the behavior of legislators, judges, and agency administrators. Second, more attention must be paid to statutory interpretation by agencies—both how they interpret now and how they should deploy interpretive tools—because agencies, not courts, are the primary expositors of statutory meaning.

1 INTENTIONALISM

Intentionalism has long been the most widely accepted theory of statutory interpretation. Blackstone (1765, 59) opined that "[t]he fairest and most rational method to interpret the will of the legislator, is by exploring his intentions at the time when the law was made." In the United States, many have argued that judges must seek to implement the meaning that legislators intended because of constitutional separation of powers. Attention to the legislature's will is required by the Constitution's "democratic purpose" (Breyer 2005, 99) because the power to set policy has been delegated to the legislature by the people. In the policy-making realm, the Constitution mandates that legislators are the superiors of judges, who should act as the lawmakers' faithful agents when interpreting unclear statutory commands (Posner 1986). If agency officials, rather than judges, are interpreting statutory language, they do so as part of their responsibility to execute the policy set by Congress. Thus, no matter which branch—judicial or executive—is faced with the interpretive question, the argument from constitutional structure suggests it is bound by Congress' intent.

The problem, recognized long before political science's recent influence on legal scholarship, is that Congress is a multimember body that must act collectively.

Thus, it is difficult to determine an "intent" that fairly captures the varied motivations of those who might support a particular bill. Blackstone ignored this issue by
referring to only one legislator when identifying the intent relevant to interpretation. Not only is this approach unrealistic, but it also overlooks one of the aspects
of a legislature that provide its commands legitimacy, compelling even those who
disagree with the law to obey it. A law merits this kind of respect because it
represents the collective action of a representative body in the face of the *circumstances of politics*, i.e. "action-in-concert in the face of disagreement" (Waldron
1999, 108). Although Radin (1930) offered one of the first attacks on the possibility
of discerning a single, coherent intent of a multimember body, the objection
became one of the major criticisms of intentionalism mounted by political scientists writing in the public choice tradition.

This attack is best summed up by the title of Shepsle's influential article: *Congress
is a "They," Not an "It:" Legislative Intent as Oxymoron* (1992). The argument is
more than just an observation that many legislators are apt to have many ideas of
the meaning of statutory language; the problem of a collective body's intent is more
intractable. Drawing on the work of Arrow and others, public choice scholars have
contended that the available methods of aggregating legislators' views into a
decision are subject, among other things, to cycling and strategic manipulation.
They contend it is impossible to ascribe rationality to any legislative outcome, and
it certainly cannot be presumed that the outcome necessarily represents the
majority's sentiment (Ordeshook 1986; Farber and Frickey 1991). The possibility
of cycling and other voting pathologies also means that the procedural rules
shaping the choices put before legislators become crucial to determining outcomes;
in particular, the group controlling the agenda has disproportionate influence over
legislative output. For some, that challenges the legitimacy of the decisions of
democratic bodies; these decisions are either chaotic and meaningless or the
product of agenda manipulation by a few, a reality that undermines majoritarianism (Riker 1982). Other less pessimistic scholars still conclude that decision theory
leads to a sobering bottom line: "Voting theory teaches that majoritarian democracy is necessarily a compromised process and that any institutional design chosen
to promote democracy will have a problematic relationship to our normative
aspirations" (Mashaw 1997, 15).

One way in which legislators manipulate the process, according to the bleak
public choice view, is through the manufacture of legislative history that does not
reflect the views of the majority enacting the law. Since the Supreme Court
indicated a willingness to look at congressional materials to ascertain the meaning
of vague or ambiguous legislative text in *Holy Trinity Church v. Unites States* (1892),
judges have turned to committee reports, floor debate, and other materials for
evidence of what enacting lawmakers understood text to mean. The problem
identified by public choice theorists is that legislative history is particularly susceptible to manipulation by those who did not succeed in enacting their objectives

and who produce a sort of "loser's history." They then have a second and perhaps a third chance to prevail when they use the manufactured legislative history to convince agencies and judges to interpret language in a way that a congressional majority was unwilling to legislate. Indeed, under this conception of the legislative process, enormous amounts of legislative history will be produced—some by losers, some by the winners to respond to the anticipated behavior by losing legislators, and some in the ordinary course of lawmaking to provide information to members as they decided how to vote. Judges will find themselves relatively unconstrained in interpreting statutes because they can always find some legislative materials to support their decision. Interpreting therefore inevitably becomes policy-making, undermining the constitutional order as well as leading to uncertainty about the meaning of legal commands.

Many interpretive theorists have rejected intentionalism as a hopeless enterprise, turning to either textualism or a dynamic interpretive method akin to purposivism; I will discuss each of these moves below. Other scholars, however, have attempted to develop a more nuanced intentionalist theory. They note that the extremely pessimistic claims of public choice theorists are overstated. Although Arrow's Theorem suggests that collective decision-making may lead to irrational outcomes and other social choice work points to the possibility of instability in collective bodies, neither demonstrates that all collective choice will be meaningless (Mackie 2003). Indeed, we do not observe tremendous instability in Congress because institutional design leads to "structure-induced equilibrium" (Shepsle and Weingast 1981). Some political scientists argue that this stability is not entirely the result of institutional arrangements—which themselves could be subject to instability if chosen by strategic players—but also the consequence of exogenous factors that are not easily manipulated. In short, "to destabilize a standing social decision, a group of individuals must *have both the ability and the desire* to force a change. Scarcity and uncertainty can drain them of both" (Lupia and McCubbins 2005, 601). For example, an institution cannot cycle through alternatives without cost; thus, the group may meaningfully choose to stick with a policy and achieve stability. Mackie's analysis of case studies of cycling calls into question virtually all "published and developed example[s] of cycling and manipulation" finding alternative explanations or consequences of "little practical importance" (2003, 21).

Not content just to mitigate the extreme claims drawn from social choice work, scholars working to rehabilitate intentionalism also focus on procedures and institutions to discern a legislative intent that can illuminate textual meaning. Positive political theory (PPT) and communication theory provide methods to distinguish cheap talk by legislators trying solely to influence subsequent interpretations from credible, costly signals by lawmakers constructing a deal that will successfully navigate through legislative vetogates (McNollgast 1994). Legislative materials are not always, and perhaps not primarily, produced with an eye to interpretation by courts or agencies; instead, these materials are crucial tools for assembling a legislative majority. Some Congress members who play key roles in enacting legislation must communicate truthfully with colleagues to convince them to support bargains; if they dissemble or misrepresent, they will find it more difficult in the future to pass legislation. Of particular importance in this analysis are the signals sent by key players at stages in the legislative process necessary for a bill's enactment, especially those by repeat players who need to develop reputations for truthfulness. In addition, statements revealing the views of pivotal lawmakers whose support is necessary for enactment are apt to more fairly represent the bargain than the statements of ardent supporters or opponents, who have incentives to provide extreme interpretations (Rodriguez and Weingast 2003).

PPT, therefore, focuses attention on the statements of credible repeat players communicating with pivotal voters at points in the legislative process vital to the law's enactment. It suggests that determining a coherent intent from the actions of a collective body is not hopeless but requires a sophisticated understanding of the legislative process, the key veto gates in the system, and the institutional arrangements allowing lawmakers to discriminate between trustworthy bargaining and cheap talk. It is informed by social choice theory because it focuses on procedures used to bring order to collective decision-making and on the entities controlling the legislative agenda and thus shaping the resulting bargains. PPT has been supplemented by communication theory, a natural move because of the importance of signals being sent and decoded. Legislating entails communications among lawmakers, and those conversations are shaped by constitutional and other procedures that can provide interpreters information about how the pivotal lawmakers understood what they were enacting (Boudreau et al. 2007).

These scholars view the role of interpreters as reconstructing the legislative communication process and sorting credible signals that motivated pivotal lawmakers to vote for the bill from strategic signals sent by ardent supporters. Only in this way can courts fulfill their role as the faithful agents of the legislature. Indeed, the argument goes, if interpreters ignore the more moderate interpretation of statutory language that an emphasis on pivotal actors yields and adopt instead the expansionist interpretation favored by ardent supporters, then legislative compromise will be more difficult in the future. Congressional moderates will be unwilling to support legislation because they will fear that subsequent interpretation will allow more sweeping change than they were willing to agree to, and those seeking to craft compromise cannot credibly promise that judges will stick to the terms of the agreement (Rodriguez and Weingast 2007).

Moreover, PPT supports the notion that judges can get away with imposing more extreme interpretations that might not have been able to pass the legislature in the first place. The procedures providing legislative stability entrench the status quo; as long as some ardent supporters are in a position to block any attempts to reestablish the understanding that drove the original enactment, it will be difficult for Congress to override an expansive interpretation (Eskridge and Ferejohn 1992). A determined minority can block legislation, particularly if its members control a veto gate, such as a committee, or if they can take advantage of supermajoritarian aspects of the legislative process, such as the Senate filibuster.

Even if judges do not ignore the signals sent by pivotal lawmakers in order to "enact" their own view of the right policy, they may misinterpret the legislative bargain because they are not competent to discriminate between reliable signals and strategic talk. Although agency officials may be sufficiently well-versed in the intricacies of the legislative process to accurately decode the signals, generalist judges who have little familiarity with the often convoluted legislative process are likely to make mistakes as they sift through voluminous legislative history. The intentionalist strategy developed by those using PPT and communication theory seems likely to require high judicial decision costs and result in significant error costs. For example, Rodriguez and Weingast (2003) work to decode the signals sent by Congress when it enacted the Civil Rights Act of 1964 in order to construct meanings for unclear provisions that disregard the views of ardent supporters and put more weight on pivotal lawmakers. The resulting analysis would be difficult for interpreters to replicate with every piece of legislation subject to litigation, or even with every piece of major legislation that is the subject of interpretive dispute.

The reality of the institutional constraints shaping judicial interpretation has led some to adopt a textualist stance for pragmatic reasons rather than for the more formalist considerations discussed below (Vermeule 1998). Others have attempted to provide courts with rules of thumb with respect to legislative history, such as Eskridge's "hierarchy of legislative history sources" (1990, 636) designed to help interpreters discern generally which kinds of materials can be given weight and which should be disregarded. The difficulty with these shortcuts is that they are often based on simplistic views of the legislative process, which is sufficiently complex and variegated that no one size can fit all, or even most, enactments (Garrett 2002).

This discussion, whether informed by the pessimistic public choice vision of the legislature as rife with social choice pathologies, or by the recent work seeking to construct a coherent legislative intent by replicating the legislative bargain, assumes that the intent being discovered is that of the enacting legislature. A different approach to interpretation, also strongly influenced by PPT, is based on the notion that the relevant intent is that of the legislature sitting at the time the court interprets the statute (Elhauge 2002). In some cases, the current legislature will be made up largely of the original enactors, but in others, its composition will be entirely different—and a majority of its members may have very different preferences to the enacting body. This argument does not rest on the realist grounds that interpreters can only offer interpretations that align with the preferences of the current law-makers who have the power to override the judicial decision. Instead, Elhauge argues that the enacting legislature will rationally prefer interpreters to try to track current legislative preferences, i.e. "enactable preferences," because this approach allows them to influence not only the legislation they pass but all legislation being interpreted while they are in office. Elhauge identifies several techniques used by interpreters to ascertain enactable preferences (rather than to determine the enacting coalition's preferences), such as considering subsequent legislative enactments and deferring to reasonable statutory interpretations by administrative agencies. At the least, this work on "preference-estimating" interpretative methods underscores the reality that interpreters are influenced not only by the legislative intent of the original enactors, but they may also be very conscious of the preferences of current lawmakers who will decide how to react to any interpretation. (See also Ferejohn and Weingast 1992a.)

2 TEXTUALISM

Some of the most prominent scholars and judges influenced by public choice have eschewed intentionalism as a hopeless endeavor that inevitably leads to unconstrained judicial interpretation. They have embraced instead a second foundational theory of interpretation: textualism. Some defenders of textualism do so on formalist grounds: The Constitution sets out the exclusive mechanism for enacting policy, and any legislative materials that have not gone through those procedural hoops cannot be given the status of legislation. That position, however, does not necessarily rule out using legislative materials that reveal the political context surrounding enactment as evidence of meaning when textual provisions are unclear. The textualist rejects even this use of legislative history for the reasons provided above: Legislative history is manipulated by strategic political actors who could not enact their preferences, and legislative materials provide clues only to the motivations of a few lawmakers, not the intent of a collective body, which itself is an inherently unintelligible concept.

Political science also casts some doubt on textualism, however. First, a sophisticated understanding of the legislative process throws into question one of the main goals of textualism: to provide incentives for Congress to legislate more precisely and clearly, thereby avoiding the need for extensive interpretation. Not only would this improve the quality of statutes and meet rule of law concerns, but also, textualists argue, more attention to memorializing the legislative deal clearly in the text would improve decision-making in the politically accountable branches. The realities of the legislative process cast serious doubt on whether this part of the textualists' project can succeed. The few empirical studies focused on determining how aware members of Congress and their staff are of statutory decisions and strategies suggest that awareness is relatively low, even among expert staff (Katzmann 1997). A case study of the Senate Judiciary Committee and associated staff revealing a relatively high level of knowledge of interpretive strategies, including some of the key canons of construction, also discovered that legislative drafting nonetheless often fails to live up to textualists' expectations (Nourse and Schacter 2002). The authors conclude that drafters are driven more by "constitutive virtues," i.e. "action and agreement, reconciling political interests, and addressing the pragmatic needs of those affected by legislation," rather than by the "interpretive virtues" of drafting precision and clarity of language (2002, 615).

Even if drafters are aware of textualism, they may rationally decide not to incur the costs of greater textual clarity—costs that can include failure to reach a compromise necessary for enactment—because they gamble that the provision will not be subject to litigation or, if it is, that the judge interpreting it will not be a textualist. Just like legislatures, courts comprise many judges who employ different approaches and reasonably reach different conclusions about difficult questions (Vermeule 2005). The success of textualism's discipline depends on the strength of its incentive effect, and institutional realities suggest that effect will be weak. That has led some to argue that this justification for textualism is merely a veneer to cover the true objective of textualism: to allow conservative judges to constrain the legislature from pursuing a broad regulatory agenda (Marmor 2005).

A second interaction between textualism and political science occurs because of textualists' enthusiastic use of canons of construction to give meaning to unclear terms. Textualists are not limited to the four corners of the statute when discerning meaning; instead, in Scalia's words, they "find the ordinary meaning of the language in its textual context; and . . . *using established canons of construction,* ask whether there is any clear indication that some permissible meaning other than the ordinary one applies" (*Chisom v. Roemer*, 1991, 404, emphasis added). Although Scalia (1997) has expressed reservations about the use of some canons, particularly ones loading the dice in favor of particular policy outcomes, textualists routinely use the canons to determine how "a skilled, objectively-reasonable user of words" (Easterbrook 1988, 65) would have understood the statutory text, in the context of the entire statute and the body of statutory law. Some public choice scholars have also been attracted by canons because they believe that, when consistently applied and clearly formulated, canons can serve as a more certain interpretive regime against which laws can be drafted (McNollgast 1992). Much like contract default rules, canons can predictably fill gaps, allowing lawmakers to focus attention on the language necessary to enact details of particular bargains that deviate from normal expectations.

Some of the linguistic canons, like the use of dictionaries, serve to illuminate how words are ordinarily used, although perhaps capturing usage in the more formal context of legislation than in casual everyday conversation. To judge the validity of these syntactic canons, interdisciplinary work in linguistics and law can be helpful (Cunningham et al. 1994). Linguistics alone, however, is insufficient to discover whether the textual canons can be used to discover meaning because "ordinary" meaning in the legislative context can be different from commonplace meaning understood by average people. For example, the canon to avoid surplusage and the canon of *expressio unius est exclusio alterius* do not accurately capture the way we talk in everyday conversation, but they may be norms internalized by drafters writing in formal statutory language. If they reflect ordinary legislative usage, these canons can illuminate the meaning that lawmakers were likely to impute to statutory text when they passed it.

Other canons of construction, part of a group of canons classified as "substantive," are justified because they take account of legislative realities and work to reduce any consequences of failures in the deliberative process. These canons are not neutral; they are designed to ratify one vision of the legislative process and limit the scope of legislation passed under conditions that deviate substantially from that ideal. Some political scientists would take issue with that ideal vision of a legislature; but if one accepts some element of deliberation as necessary for a well-functioning lawmaking body, political science scholarship can be used to ensure that the canons are appropriate to meet that goal. Consider, for example, the relatively uncontroversial canon that courts narrowly construe substantive riders to appropriations bills. This canon has been used frequently by the Supreme Court and lower courts, most notably to protect the snail darter that was threatened by the Tellico Dam being built by the Tennessee Valley Authority (*TVA v. Hill*, 1978). Because of the dam's deleterious effect on the snail darter's habitat, continued construction would arguably have violated the Endangered Species Act (ESA), which requires federal agencies to ensure that their actions do not jeopardize the continued existence of endangered species or destroy their habitat. However, those advocating the completion of the dam pointed to continued congressional support through the appropriations process, which might be understood to have repealed the ESA to this extent.

To decide the case, the Supreme Court invoked two canons: first, repeals by implication are disfavored, and, second, such repeals found in appropriations bills are particularly disfavored. The Court explained its approach through a description of the congressional appropriations process. It noted that appropriations committees do not have jurisdiction over substantive legislation and suggested that these committees do not pay the same close attention to the issues raised by substantive legislation as do committees with specialized expertise in the programs. It also stated that there is less legislative awareness of appropriations riders; in other words, the lawmakers voting for the appropriations bill were probably either unaware of the provision or did not fully understand the impact of funding the dam on the mandates of the ESA. The Court justified the use of the canon because of its view of the appropriations process as "hurried, opaque, and, on the whole, nondeliberative" (McCubbins and Rodriguez 2005, 688). Thus, the Court ruled that continued work on the Tellico Dam violated the ESA's mandates.

Political science can shed light on whether the Court's view of the federal appropriations process is an accurate one that can support the use of a canon limiting the power of Congress and the scope of statutory language. Contrary to the assumptions made by the Supreme Court, McCubbins and Rodriguez find that the appropriations process is actually closer to the deliberative ideal valued by those who deploy this canon than is the path traveled by other legislation. Appropriations bills command the attention of many stakeholders—including interest groups, party leaders, and executive branch officials—vitally concerned about the allocation of limited governmental resources; the appropriations committees are more representative than many substantive committees, which can be primarily populated by lawmakers with intense preferences on the subject matter; and appropriations bills are the most frequently amended, suggesting a high level of legislative attention and activity.

Substantive canons are not neutral in the way that textual canons are: they systematically promote some outcomes over others. Thus, each requires sustained analysis and justification, often using the tools of political science, particularly because of the canons' increased importance with the rise of textualism. Not all of the substantive canons require a close examination of the legislative process to determine their legitimacy. Some of the canons work to instantiate other sorts of values, such as protecting constitutional principles not necessarily protected through more aggressive judicial invalidation of statutes. These canons, which include the canon to construe legislation to avoid raising federalism concerns or to favor Native Americans, are legitimate if the values, constitutional or otherwise, are those that should guide interpreters (Garrett 2005). But the subset of substantive canons that are linked to a particular view of the legislative process should be measured against the reality of the legislative process, and modified or discarded if appropriate.

3 PURPOSIVISM

The third foundational theory is purposivism, which has its roots in the "mischief rule" articulated in *Heydon's Case* (1584). Interpreters should identify both the mischief that prompted Parliament's action and the remedy chosen to attack the mischief. "[T]he office of all the Judges is always to make such construction as shall suppress the mischief, and advance the remedy" (*Heydon's Case*, 638). The notion that interpreters should construe legislation so that it achieves its purpose is hardly controversial; all three foundational theories incorporate some purposive analysis. What distinguishes the theories is how the purpose is identified. For intentionalists, the relevant purpose is that of the enactors; for textualists, the purpose is determined by examining the language of the statute and how it fits into the body of law. Purposivists, writing in the *Legal Process* tradition, assume "unless the contrary unmistakably appears, that the legislature was made up of reasonable persons pursuing reasonable purposes reasonably" (Hart and Sacks 1994 [1958], 1378). Inferring this purpose includes a close examination of text and other sources of meaning, although the process does not aim necessarily to capture the subjective intent of the enactors. Instead, purposivists create a "reasonable" legislator and determine how she might have attacked the mischief targeted by the legislature.

Just as the infusion of political science into the statutory interpretation literature undercut many of the assumptions of intentionalism, it also challenged the legitimacy of using the "reasonable legislator" as the focus for interpretation. Public choice led many to believe that the actual legislative process is not populated by reasonable legislators, and, even if it was, it is not likely to achieve reasonable results. The real legislative process was seen as a forum for rent-seeking by contending interest groups, which take advantage of the power of the agenda setter and legislative procedures to block laws that would harm them and obtain legislation that transfers benefits to them even if the result is not welfare-enhancing from society's perspective. Because the constellation of interest groups is disproportionately skewed to favor well-organized groups with money, laws serving the public interest are unlikely to emerge from the political process. Contrary to Hart and Sacks' rosy vision of a legislature pursuing reasonable goals reasonably, some viewed Congress as full of self-interested legislators sending government benefits to groups who in turn reward them with campaign funds, post-service employment, and lavish trips and gifts (Eskridge, Frickey, and Garrett 2006).

It is not clear from the *Legal Process* materials whether the authors thought the "reasonable legislator" accurately represented the actual legislative process. Certainly, they "expressed no caveat along these lines, much less attempted any elaborate normative justification for these assumptions if they were deemed unrealistic, [so] it appears that at least some of the legitimacy of their approach depends upon the empirical accuracy of these assumptions" (Eskridge and Frickey 1990, 334). The leading modern judicial proponent of an interpretive method similar to Hart and Sacks' purposivism is Justice Breyer. Breyer (2005, 99) argues that interpretation should be viewed primarily as a way to ensure that legislation meets the general purpose underlying it because that is consistent with our "delegated democracy" where legislators, as the representatives of the people, determine policy. Norms of accountability are also served because citizens think broadly in terms of general purposes and do not focus on the precise details of the legislative language. Breyer's justification for purposive interpretation seems to depend crucially on a link between the purpose that would drive a reasonable legislator and the purpose that drives the actual legislator—a link undermined by public choice, decision theory, and interest group realities. In a nod to this reality, Breyer calls the construct of a reasonable legislator a "fiction" (99); he seems to view his approach as a pragmatic solution, terming it "a workable method of implementing the Constitution's democratic objective" (101). Whether it is "workable" is not clear, but sophisticated political science work certainly undermines the notion that this fiction accurately captures the real legislative process, which should be the basis on which elected officials are held accountable.

With the increasing awareness of the large gap between the purposivist's reasonable legislator and the real lawmaker, many view purposivism as a judicial power grab. The malleable concept of "reasonableness" allows an extraordinary range of judicial discretion. Judges construct the fiction of reasonable legislators, and judges determine what purposes are reasonable. Although Hart and Sacks emphasized that the text of the statute should cabin the range of the discretion, vague or ambiguous language often provides no substantial restriction. Given human nature, it should not surprise us that a judge, faced with determining what a reasonable legislator might have intended with unclear statutory language, often relies on what the judge himself thinks is the right answer. Purposivism allows him to cloak a decision to implement his own policy objectives in the language of obedience to Congress, albeit to a fictive legislature characterized by reasonableness. Textualism is a reaction to this formulation of purposivism and an attempt to constrain judges by focusing on the enacted text and denying access to legislative history materials.

Disillusionment with the ability of Congress to behave reasonably led those writing in the public choice tradition to different approaches. Some, in addition to being attracted by textualism as a way to constrain willful judges and ensure the primacy of the elected branches, advocated narrow constructions of statutory language. If legislation is merely a deal among interest groups and unlikely to enhance social or economic welfare, then statutes should be narrowly construed to limit their effects as much as the text makes possible. Courts should acknowledge the reality that, in many cases, legislation is a contract between interest groups and legislators; therefore, an interpreter should seek to implement only the terms of the deal (Easterbrook 1984). Often Congress seeks to hide the reality of interest group deals by using language that invokes the public interest; Easterbrook argues that courts should disregard these broad statements of principles and hew to the terms of the deal. Other scholars contend that the way to discourage private-regarding deals is to adopt purposive methods of interpretation that discourage rent-seeking and do not necessarily stick to the terms of the legislative bargain. Thus, Macey (1986), who accepts the economic vision of legislation, concludes that judges should interpret statutory language in a public-regarding way where possible— even if the underlying legislation is purely an interest group bargain—because by denying the interest groups the deal they "bought," interpreters will discourage future rent-seeking. Only if interest groups can convince Congress to legislate their deals clearly will they be sure to reap the benefits they seek, and lawmakers will be loath to enact such explicit bargains because of fear of voter backlash.

A final set of interpreters influenced by public choice have blazed a third trail which resonates with the original purposivists in its optimism. Eskridge's (1994) theory of dynamic statutory interpretation is informed by political science; indeed, he was one of the scholars who first approached interpretation from this avowedly interdisciplinary perspective. Dynamic statutory interpretation is not only premised on a realistic view of the legislature and the limitations of collective choice, but also incorporates the insights of PPT, viewing the court as one institution among many, including agencies and subsequent legislatures, that affect a statute's interpretation. Judges should approach the interpretive task pragmatically, seeking to adopt interpretations that are consistent with the text and political context of enactment, but that also take account of changed circumstances since passage (Ferejohn and Weingast 1992b). Other dynamic interpretive values emphasize the need for statutory coherence so that a particular law is understood in a way that fits it smoothly into the fabric of statutory law.

Eskridge's theory, which grew from his work with Frickey, is both descriptive and normative. Eskridge (2002) argues that political science teaches that judges will inevitably interpret statutes pragmatically and dynamically, and he contends that some element of dynamism in interpretation is attractive because judges have "*comparative advantages* in ensuring that ... statutes are adapted to new social and legal circumstances [and dynamic interpretation] enhance[s] the legitimacy of the polity as a whole" (17). Although Eskridge draws heavily on the purposive approach of Hart and Sacks and provides an unabashedly normative defense of the exercise of some judicial discretion in interpretation, his theory is grounded in pragmatism, rejecting any one foundational theory of interpretation.

4 New Scholarly Directions

As the foregoing discussion has demonstrated, tools provided by PPT are producing new ways to ascertain intent and to scrutinize traditional tools of statutory construction, such as canons. This work has also uncovered a gap in the scholarship—the need for systematic, rigorous empirical work to determine whether the assumptions grounding the various foundational theories are consistent with the reality of policy-making. In addition, a few scholars are turning their attention away from courts to the forum where the most statutory interpretation occurs: administrative agencies. Interdisciplinary work in law and politics will be necessary to determine accurately how agency interpretation differs from judicial interpretation and how agency practices diverge from one another.

4.1 Empirical Scholarship and Statutory Interpretation

Much of the theoretical work done at the intersection of law and politics demands empirical underpinnings. Scholarship working to discern the signals sent by legislators in order to interpret unclear language consistently with the message that was sent by the enactors requires a sophisticated understanding of the legislative process—both generally and specifically as it pertains to that legislation. Generalizations drawn from the legislative history of one bill about the enactment of other laws should be subjected to empirical assessment. The institutional dynamics described by positive political theorists lead to hypotheses concerning the behavior of political actors in those institutions, and these can be confirmed or discarded through studying each branch's response in particular instances. Understanding the reality of the legislative and judicial processes is crucial for assessing interpretive methods and the tools used. For example, if textualism's defense rests on the expectation that the legislature will respond by drafting laws more carefully and precisely, then it is important to determine whether that is possible given institutional constraints. If clear statement rules are used to ensure that Congress deliberates on specific areas of constitutional concern, then their legitimacy rests in part on whether such deliberation occurs. If various canons are used because they are seen as neutral reflections of legislative expectations, then political science must be deployed to confirm that they track expectations rather than undermine them.

Some empirical work of this type has been done, but it is still in its infancy compared to the theoretical work inspired by public choice and PPT. An area of relatively robust empirical analysis concerns congressional overrides of statutory interpretation decisions (see e.g. Eskridge 1988; Barnes 2004). Other promising empirical work—legislative case studies or analyses of the accuracy of assumptions undergirding particular canons of construction—has been described above. Nourse and Schacter (2002) have conducted a rich analysis, using interviews with lawmakers and relevant staff, of the process of legislative drafting in the Senate Judiciary Committee. Although promising, this study is limited to a particular, probably atypical committee at a particular time and thus cannot easily be generalized to other committees, the other chamber, or other time periods. Thus, more work of this type is required to assess claims about the extent of legislative knowledge of judicial interpretive strategies and the norms and practices of legislative drafters.

Empirical work has been done on the interpretive practice of courts, but this scholarship is also relatively scanty compared with the outpouring of theoretical work that makes testable descriptive claims and controversial normative claims. Some scholars have worked to measure textualism's influence on courts (e.g. Zeppos 1992); others have attempted to determine whether courts interpret more dynamically and how they shift interpretations in response to changed circumstances (e.g. Farber 2005); still others have focused on the judicial use of canons to test whether they serve as a stable interpretive regime (e.g. Brudney and

Distlear 2005). One challenge for those drafting and interpreting legislation is how to determine the right strategies before the empirical landscape has been clarified. Accordingly, Vermeule (2006, 289) has constructed an "interim interpretive theory" designed to guide judges during this period of empirical uncertainty. Vermeule's proposals—counseling judges "to adopt an unassuming posture of rule-bound, relatively inflexible decision-making, using a small set of interpretive tools and deferring to agencies and legislatures" on unclear text (289)—will spark reactions from others proposing different intermediate pragmatic responses to the reality of empirical uncertainty. Debating and constructing such pragmatic approaches to judicial interpretation while the empirical work is being done is a necessary and complementary scholarly agenda.

4.2 Interpretation by Administrative Agencies

This chapter, like the bulk of scholarship on interpretation, has been primarily focused on courts as interpreters and on the institutional relationship between Congress and the judiciary. This emphasis reflects the court-centrism of legal scholars who tend to study all issues through the prism of judicial opinions. It does not reflect the reality of interpretation where that task falls mostly to administrative agencies, with their decisions reviewed only occasionally by judges. Scholars have primarily been interested in statutory interpretation by agencies only as it affects judicial interpretation; thus, a great deal has been written about the deference that judges should accord to agencies' statutory interpretation under the doctrine articulated in *Chevron v. Natural Resources Defense Council* (1984). Much of the empirical work on interpretation has concerned the use of the *Chevron* doctrine and has attempted to measure whether judges really do defer to agency interpretations when they might independently reach a different conclusion (Schuck and Elliott 1990; Merrill 1992). Little, however, has been done on the interpretive practices employed by agencies as they determine the meaning of unclear language in the process of implementing policy set by Congress.

Thus, the second promising avenue of study lies in an increased focus on statutory interpretation by administrative agencies. One would expect that there are differences in interpretive methods used by courts and agencies, as well as differences among agencies. For example, while federal judges are relatively independent of influence by the other branches, agency officials work for the president and play a role in implementing his policy agenda, and they have to be aware of the preferences of the current Congress which controls the appropriations process and other oversight mechanisms (Mashaw 2005). With respect to relatively recent enactments, agency officials are likely to have played key roles in the drafting process itself and thus have a more nuanced understanding of the legislative history than a generalist judge will ever develop (Strauss 1990).

The institutional differences between agencies and courts—for example, the former have more political accountability, and they have greater expertise in the substance of the regulatory area and the legislative process—suggest that the two institutions will use different interpretive methods and tools. Moreover, they may be justified in choosing different approaches, although any differences in method produce interactions among all three branches. At this point, we have many more questions than answers about statutory interpretation by agencies; Mashaw's (2005) recent work attempts to provide a preliminary framework for descriptive and normative analysis. He argues that a focus on methods that are sensitive to institutional design leads to different sets of canons for courts and agencies. He suggests that an agency might legitimately adopt strategies to interpret unclear language to "give energy and breadth to all legislative programs within [its] jurisdiction" (522), while a court should be more attentive to coherence between a statute and the body of statutory law, including enactments outside the agency's jurisdiction.

This work is preliminary and demands more sustained attention by those studying both statutory interpretation and administrative law. This research should be part of the empirical project I urge above, as scholars use political science methodology to determine how particular agencies interpret laws. It must also have a normative component, as those familiar with the institutional characteristics of agencies and courts develop and justify the interpretive methods and tools each should use. Just like the influential work in judicial statutory interpretation over the last two decades, both research agendas will draw heavily on the methods and insights of political science.

References

BARNES, J. 2004. *Overruled? Legislative Overrides, Pluralism, and Contemporary Court-Congress Relations.* Stanford, Calif.: Stanford University Press.

BLACKSTONE, W. 1765. *Commentaries on the Laws of England,* 8th edn. Oxford: Clarendon Press.

BOUDREAU, C., LUPIA, A., McCUBBINS, M. D., and RODRIGUEZ, D. B. 2007. What statutes mean: interpretive lessons from positive theories of communication and legislation. *San Diego Law Review,* 44: 957–92.

BREYER, S. 2005. *Active Liberty: Interpreting our Democratic Constitution.* New York: Alfred A. Knopf.

BRUDNEY, J. J., and DITSLEAR, C. 2005. Canons of construction and the elusive quest for neutral reasoning. *Vanderbilt Law Review,* 58: 1–116.

CUNNINGHAM, C. D., LEVI, J. N., GREEN, G. M., and KAPLAN, J. P. 1994. Plain meaning and hard cases. *Yale Law Journal,* 103: 1561–625.

EASTERBROOK, F. H. 1984. The Supreme Court, 1983 term—foreword: the Court and the economic system. *Harvard Law Review,* 98: 4–60.

—— 1988. The role of original intent in statutory construction. *Harvard Journal of Law and Public Policy,* 11: 59–66.

ELHAUGE, E. 2002. Preference-estimating statutory default rules. *Columbia Law Review*, 102: 2027–161.

ESKRIDGE, W. N., JR. 1988. Overruling statutory precedents. *Georgetown Law Journal*, 76: 1361–439.

—— 1990. The new textualism. *UCLA Law Review*, 37: 621–91.

—— 1994. *Dynamic Statutory Interpretation*. Cambridge, Mass.: Harvard University Press.

—— 2002. The dynamic theorization of statutory interpretation. *Issues in Legal Scholarship*, 3: art. 16.

—— and FEREJOHN, J. 1992. The Article I, Section 7 game. *Georgetown Law Journal*, 80: 523–64.

—— and FRICKEY, P. P. 1990. Statutory interpretation as practical reasoning. *Stanford Law Review*, 42: 321–84.

—— —— and GARRETT, E. 2006. *Legislation and Statutory Interpretation*, 2nd edn. New York: Foundation Press.

FARBER, D. A. 2005. Earthquakes and tremors in statutory interpretation: an empirical study of the dynamics of interpretation. *Minnesota Law Review*, 89: 848–89.

—— and FRICKEY, P. P. 1991. *Law and Public Choice: A Critical Introduction*. Chicago: University of Chicago Press.

FEREJOHN, J., and WEINGAST, B. R. 1992a. Limitation of statutes: strategic statutory interpretation. *Georgetown Law Journal*, 80: 565–82.

—— 1992b. A positive theory of statutory interpretation. *International Review of Law and Economics*, 12: 263–79.

GARRETT, E. 2002. Attention to context in statutory interpretation: applying the lessons of *Dynamic Statutory Interpretation* to omnibus legislation. *Issues in Legal Scholarship*, 3: art. 1.

—— 2005. Step one of *Chevron v. Natural Resources Defense Council*. Pp. 55–84 in *A Guide to Judicial and Political Review of Federal Agencies*, ed. J. F. Duffy and M. Herz. Chicago: American Bar Association.

HART, JR., H. A., and SACKS, A. M. 1994 [1958]. *The Legal Process: Basic Problems in the Making and Application of Law*, ed. W. N. Eskridge, Jr. and P. P. Frickey. Westbury, NY: Foundation Press.

KATZMANN, R. A. 1997. *Courts and Congress*. Washington, DC: Brookings Institution.

LUPIA, A., and McCUBBINS, M. D. 2005. Lost in translation: social choice theory is misapplied against legislative intent. *Journal of Contemporary Legal Issues*, 14: 585–617.

MACEY, J. R. 1986. Promoting public-regarding legislation through statutory interpretation: an interest group model. *Columbia Law Review*, 86: 223–68.

MACKIE, G. 2003. *Democracy Defended*. Cambridge: Cambridge University Press.

MARMOR, A. 2005. The immorality of textualism. *Loyola Law Review*, 38: 2063–79.

MASHAW, J. L. 1997. *Greed, Chaos, and Governance: Using Public Choice to Improve Public Law*. New Haven, Conn.: Yale University Press.

—— 2005. Norms, practices, and the paradox of deference: a preliminary inquiry into agency statutory interpretation. *Administrative Law Review*, 57: 501–42.

McCUBBINS, M. D., and RODRIGUEZ, D. B. 2005. Canonical construction and statutory revisionism: the strange case of the appropriations canon. *Journal of Contemporary Legal Issues*, 14: 669–715.

McNOLLGAST. 1992. Positive canons: the role of legislative bargains in statutory interpretation. *Georgetown Law Journal*, 80: 705–42.

—— 1994. Legislative intent: the use of positive political theory in statutory interpretation. *Law and Contemporary Problems*, 57: 3–37.

MERRILL, T. W. 1992. Judicial deference to executive precedent. *Yale Law Journal*, 101: 969–1041.

NOURSE, V. F., and SCHACTER, J. S. 2002. The politics of legislative drafting: a congressional case study. *New York University Law Review*, 77: 575–624.

ORDESHOOK, P. C. 1986. *Game Theory and Political Theory: An Introduction*. Cambridge: Cambridge University Press.

POSNER, R. A. 1986. Legal formalism, legal realism, and the interpretation of statutes and the Constitution. *Case Western Reserve Law Review*, 37: 179–217.

RADIN, M. 1930. Statutory interpretation. *Harvard Law Review*, 43: 863–85.

RIKER, W. H. 1982. *Liberalism Against Populism: A Confrontation Between the Theory of Democracy and the Theory of Social Choice*. San Francisco: W. H. Freeman.

RODRIGUEZ, D. B., and WEINGAST, B. R. 2003. The positive political theory of legislative history: new perspectives on the 1964 Civil Rights Act and its interpretation. *University of Pennsylvania Law Review*, 151: 1417–542.

—— 2007. The paradox of expansionist statutory interpretations. *Northwest University Law Review*, 101: 1207–55.

SCALIA, A. 1997. *A Matter of Interpretation: Federal Courts and the Law*. Princeton, NJ: Princeton University Press.

SCHUCK, P. H., and ELLIOTT, E. D. 1990. To the *Chevron* station: an empirical study of federal administrative law. *Duke Law Journal*, 1990: 984–1077.

SHEPSLE, K. A. 1992. Congress is a "they," not an "it:" legislative intent as oxymoron. *International Review of Law and Economics*, 12: 239–56.

—— and WEINGAST, B. R. 1981. Structure-induced equilibrium and legislative choice. *Public Choice*, 37: 503–19.

STRAUSS, P. L. 1990. When the judge is not the primary official with responsibility to read: agency interpretation and the problem of legislative history. *ChicagoKent Law Review*, 66: 321–53.

VERMEULE, A. 1998. Legislative history and the limits of judicial competence: the untold story of *Holy Trinity Church*. *Stanford Law Review*, 50: 1833–96.

—— 2005. The judiciary is a they, not an it: interpretive theory and the fallacy of division. *Journal of Contemporary Legal Issues*, 14: 549–84.

—— 2006. *Judging Under Uncertainty: An Institutional Theory of Legal Interpretation*. Cambridge, Mass.: Harvard University Press.

WALDRON, J. 1999. *Law and Disagreement*. Oxford: Clarendon Press.

ZEPPOS, N. S. 1992. The use of authority in statutory interpretation: an empirical analysis. *Texas Law Review*, 70: 1073–137.

CASES

Chevron v. Natural Resources Defense Council, 467 U.S. 837 (1984).

Chisom v. Roemer, 501 U.S. 380 (1991) (Justice Scalia, dissenting).

Heydon's Case, 76 Eng. Rep. 637 (Exch. 1584).

Holy Trinity Church v. United States, 143 U.S. 457 (1892).

Tennessee Valley Authority v. Hill, 437 U.S. 153 (1978).

CHAPTER 21

....

INFORMALISM AS A FORM OF LEGAL ORDERING

....

CHRISTINE B. HARRINGTON

AMONG the many forms of ordering discussed in this book, "informalism" is perhaps the most difficult to pin down. Informal dispute processes, such as mediation, are found in a wide range of institutions (Figure 21.1), across different societies, in Western and non-Western states—including capitalist, Communist, and socialist countries—and over time. The early twentieth-century Small Claims Court reform movement in the U.S., for example, eschewed adversarial procedures in favor of informal settings where magistrates spoke directly with the parties without lawyers present. Dean of the Harvard Law School, Roscoe Pound, among other prominent progressives, hailed informal processes, like those used in small claims courts, as both "efficient and fair" ways of resolving "petty" disputes (1906). The Americanization Movement, acting in harmony with legal elites, also praised the informal side of law, viewing it as a less coercive and more effective way of socializing and assimilating new immigrants to "American" legal norms (Harrington 1985, 20–2). Similarly, James Q. Wilson characterized the, "night watchman style of policing" as an approach to law enforcement that relies on building informal relationships of trust, familiarity, and shared values between the police and the neighborhood (1968). Informalism in these particular contexts is perceived of as a form of order maintenance, a way of getting people to follow legal norms without directly coercing them to do so. Whether in fact informalism does,

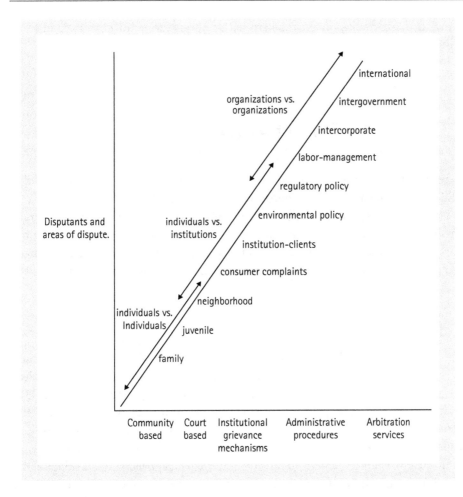

Fig. 21.1 Type of informal forms of legal ordering

or does not, function to maintain order by securing agreement from the affected parties, is an empirical question to be addressed in the context of social science research on informalism.

The central focus of this chapter is not on whether the promises of informalism are realized. Rather my objective is to analyze informalism as a form of legal ordering embedded in judicial and administrative institutions. The chapter begins by identifying what I take to be the major approaches to informalism (Section 1). The central "technologies" of informalism within judicial and administrative settings, such as mediation and negotiated rulemaking, are discussed next (Section 2). I then discuss research on informal law in the law and politics field and what these studies of informalism tell us about the politics of law and legal institutions more generally (Section 3).

1 APPROACHES

There are three distinctive approaches to informalism in the field of law and politics: (1) judicial hierarchy approach; (2) ongoing relationship approach; and (3) legal pluralist approach. In general, all three approaches have similar descriptions of informal forms of orderings, be they *institutions*, such as small claims courts, or *procedures*, such as mediation. The approaches differ in terms of how each treats the relationship between informal and other forms of ordering.

1.1 Judicial Hierarchy

The most conventional and familiar approach, what I call a "judicial hierarchy approach," comprehends legal institutions and legal procedures in terms of a hierarchy of authority. Institutions, such as the United States Supreme Court in the U.S. context, are placed on top of the hierarchy, with the federal appellate courts, the federal trial courts, and federal administrative agencies following in descending order. While there may be exceptions within the hierarchy, such as the fact that appeals from administrative agencies tend to go directly to the federal appellate courts skipping the federal trial courts in most matters, the *logic* of a judicial hierarchy approach rests on the legal convention that parties must exhaust lower court remedies before appealing to a "higher" court. Parties move up the institutional hierarchy from agencies to courts, from trial courts to appellate courts. The scope of jurisdiction that institutions have also tends to expand as parties and their cases move up a judicial hierarchy.

Informalism is relegated to the "lower courts" in a judicial hierarchy approach. Judges in these courts have access to *extra-judicial resources*, such as "pre-trial diversion programs," to assist in the disposition of cases. From the late 1960s onward in the U.S., one way lower court judges have exercised their discretion is by referring defendants to diversion programs (e.g. alcohol abuse programs, aggression management training, etc.) instead of hearing the case. To the extent that a formal-legal process exists in the everyday workings of these courts, it is put on hold and cases are classified as "pending" while defendants go to diversion programs. The principle substantive justification for diversion alternatives is rehabilitation. Attention to "treatment" versus "innocence or guilt" is thus one aspect of informal forms of ordering practiced in these courts.

Informalism is also relegated to administrative agencies in a judicial hierarchy approach. It is the case that the federal administrative agencies, subject to the Administrative Procedure Act (APA 1946), are in general governed by less legalistic procedures than those that govern federal courts (Carter and Harrington 2000). "Negotiated rulemaking" is an example of a post-1980 reform in U.S. administrative rulemaking that employs the informal legal practices of negotiation and consent agreements. Administrative agencies may exercise their discretion to convene Federal Advisory Committees made up of actors they designate to be the principle "stakeholders" in the area that the agency chooses to make a rule about. The negotiation and eventual consent among the parties takes place *before* the agency submits the rule to the traditional APA "notice and comment" procedure. I will discuss this in more detail later, but for now the point is to understand that a judicial hierarchy approach, whereby courts are at the top of the scale of authority, associates informalism with institutions "below" courts, such as administrative agencies.

A judicial hierarchy approach deems *flexible informal procedures* to be more appropriate for resolving disputes in lower courts and for crafting administrative rules in agencies than the application of formal-legal rationality, which this approach associates with the "upper courts." The claim is that formal legal procedures, such as procedural due process rules, impose external rules restricting the ability of the disputants' individual circumstances, histories, and incentives within the disputants' relationship from playing a role in reaching an accommodation or compromise (Fuller 1971; 1978). Informal procedures are less adversarial; the third-party mediators or arbitrators have less coercive authority over disputing parties, enabling the person who is mediating the dispute to draw out information from the parties that may assist in getting the parties to reach an agreement, a "consent agreement" (versus issuing a legal judgment). Thus Max Weber's famous distinction between "substantive rationality" and "formal-legal rationality" is embedded in a judicial hierarchy approach.[1] Informal forms of ordering are open to substantive rationality—the values in the resolution or *outcome*—while formal-legal rationality—the impersonal procedures or *means*—is the modus operandi of adjudication.

Where the line should be drawn between who is governed by, or subject to, formal versus informal ordering is controversial. The Juvenile Court Reform Movement of the late nineteenth century in the U.S. advocated informality for children versus adults, building a special court out of informal norms at every turn to the point that some argued it was an "anti-legal" reform movement (Platt 1977). Juveniles were not allowed legal representation in these courts until 1967 when the Supreme Court ruled that they were "persons" within the meaning of the Fourteenth Amendment

---

[1] For a comprehensive and comparative analysis of forms of legal rationality based on Weber's conceptualization, see Heydebrand (2003).

entitled to notice of the charges against them and counsel to represent them, as well as the constitutional protection against self-incrimination and right to cross-examine their accusers. In the majority opinion, Justice Fortas wrote that, "Juvenile Court history has once again demonstrated that unbridled discretion, however benevolently motivated, is frequently a poor substitute for principle and procedure" (*In re Gault*, 387 U.S. 1, 1967: quoted in Cooper, Puritz, and Shang 1998, 653). In this instance the upper rungs of a judicial hierarchy brought formal-legal rationality to bear on perceived abuses (i.e. the denial of procedural due process) in the exercise of discretion by juvenile courts. Informal forms of ordering can be and are subject to judicial scrutiny by a "higher judicial authority."

1.2 Ongoing Relationship Approach

This approach focuses on the nature of the *relationship between the parties* as a principle determinant of whether informal or formal forms of ordering apply.[2] Two claims about informalism and related-party cases are characteristics of this approach: (1) ongoing relationship disputes are *complex* and so too are the kinds of remedies they call for; and (2) the closer parties are to one another the more likely it is that they will choose *flexible informal processes* for dispute resolution. Cases involving disputants in ongoing relationships, or what are also termed "related-party" cases, such as family members, neighbors, landlord–tenant relationships, are often reluctant to take their disputes to formal-legal institutions, it is argued, because they feel they will lose control over shaping a resolution in court—the judge will make a decision. This "ongoing relationship" informal dispute resolution phenomenon is also present in business disputes resolution (Macaulay 1963). Further, if these disputes are adjudicated, the ongoing relationship will likely terminate, according to this approach.

An ongoing relationship approach assumes that informal orderings are more confidential, off the record, and *private*. The degree of procedural informality (versus formality) tends to correspond to the degree to which the process is private—meaning the process is less transparent, less accountable to substantive and procedural norms or rules, and has limited ability to imposed or enforce sanctions, unless permitted to so do by the state. For example, state arbitration statutes often have provisions to enforce private arbitration agreements. Some state contract laws can be used to enforce agreements reached though private mediation processes, such as family mediation (Schneider 1993). Since the 1990s, U.S. law increasingly permits

---

[2] There are both normative arguments and empirical accounts in the literature on informalism as a mode of dispute resolution for parties in ongoing relationships. Anthropologists, more so than political scientists, have studied the cultural bases for the more frequent association of informal forms (versus formal) of disputing with parties who know one another. For an interesting analysis of this association see Yngvesson (1989) and her ethnography of the practice (1993), as well as Nader and Todd (1978).

regulated entities to privatize the disputing forum by inserting mandatory arbitration clauses in their contracts. Studies have found that these clauses are "virtually immune from regulation; so regulated entities have near-complete freedom to design the forum in which litigation will occur" (Weidemaier 2007, 1).

1.3 Legal Pluralist Approach

A legal pluralist approach seeks to illuminate informalism in the context of what is understood to be a complex dynamic of multiple and partial forms of ordering. The standpoint from which a legal pluralist approach comprehends informalism is characteristically more dynamic than the two previous approaches. It challenges approaches that assume forms of ordering necessarily emanating from a central unified positive authority (the state). Instead, a legal pluralist approach is interested in examining the blending of legal orderings.

Traditionally "legal pluralism" was defined by anthropologists as the coexistence of different legal orders in the same political space, perhaps at different "levels," but as distinct systems of knowledge and practice (Pospisil 1967). In the early 1970s, Sally Falk Moore argued for a more unified analysis of legal pluralism, based on the concept of "semi-autonomous fields" where a particular political space can generate rules and practices internally, "but is also vulnerable to rules and decisions and other forces emanating from the larger world by which it is surrounded" (1973, 55). Today, scholars working on informalism from a legal pluralist approach are studying the *vulnerability* of legal orderings, be they more formal or informal in character. Law is theorized as the "unsettled [results] of relations with a plurality of social forms and in this law's identity is constantly and inherently subject to challenge and change" (Fitzpatrick 1983, 138, cited by Merry 1988, 884; also in Harrington and Merry 1988).

The concept of "interlegality" (Santos 1987) refers to the blurring and crystallization of difference *between* ordering forms, how they may overlap, intersect, and reinforce one another. As does the proliferation of "hybrid" orderings (see Latour 1993), which is not purely informal in character as the invention of the Juvenile Court prophesized, this conceptualization directs attention to the partial achievement, or existence, of unified forms of ordering. Indeed, the legal pluralist approach challenges the positivist assumption that all legal authority emanates from a central unified power—the state; it challenges the notion that forms of legal ordering can be usefully understood only in an hierarchical arrangement. Instead, it postulates that forms of ordering are *polycentric*, in that they consist of a dynamic and unstable space of mixed legal codes, legal practices, and legal geography (local, regional, national, global) that may operate simultaneously. A legal order, like the concept of "lived hegemony," is thus "always a process. It is not, except analytically, a system or a structure. It is a realized complex of experiences, relationships, and activities, with specific and changing pressures and limits" (Williams 1977, 112).

A legal pluralist approach also focuses on the production of political and cultural systems of knowledge and power in forms of ordering (Santos 1987; Harrington and Merry 1988; Fitzpatrick 1993). This means that a legal pluralist approach pays attention to nonstate-centered forms of legality *and* their relationship to state legality. For example, a legal pluralist approach to informalism developed in an empirical study of community mediation program in the U.S., found three analytically distinguishable projects within community mediation: (1) the delivery of dispute resolution services; (2) social transformation; and (3) personal growth. Each appropriated pieces of the other, borrowing the language of community participation to expand mediation as a judicial service, mobilizing arguments about personal growth and satisfaction behind institutionalized mediation services, leaning on the coercive power of justice system referrals to direct cases into socially transformative programs. Nevertheless, the central symbol of "consensual justice" presses toward uniformity (Harrington and Merry 1988).

2 TECHNOLOGIES OF INFORMAL LAW

While distinctions between criminal and civil, official and nonofficial legal norms, and formal and informal dispute processes, to name a few, are taken for granted by many disciplines, research on informalism documents the fuzziness, if not breakdown, of these dichotomies in practice. The law enforcement policy shift from coercion to incentives, emanating from the U.S. Attorney General's Office in the late 1970s, spawned a new set of legal technologies that were designed to secure compliance through self-regulation. Attorney General Griffin Bell oversaw the creation of the Office on Legal Policy and supported experimental projects that brought "voluntary" incentives, associated with civil litigation, to the lower courts handling "minor" criminal cases (Harrington 1985; also see Brigham and Brown 1980). In collaboration with local bar associations and community organizers, a legal reform movement, known as the "alternative dispute resolution" (ADR) movement, set up new dispute institutions throughout the U.S. on a scale not seen since the progressive era reform movements, which produced the Juvenile Courts and the Small Claims Courts (Harrington 1985).

From the perspective of the early twenty-first century, we can now see more clearly how this policy shift helped to constitute a much larger transformation from the welfare-state civil-rights protectionist policies to the neoliberal state program of "deregulation," "delegalization." However, scholars have found that ADR, in its many forms that we will turn to in a moment, does not tend to replace existing "formal" legal or regulatory mechanisms (i.e. adjudication, plea bargaining, settlement, administrative rulemaking) as the reformers' term "delegalization" implies. It is a "movement in law;"[3] a form of legal ordering that has even impacted legal education,[4] well noted by legal historians as rather intractable. Sociolegal scholars, including many political scientists, have theorized a relationship between informal and formal dispute processes, and empirically established dispute processing as an *interdependent sociolegal phenomenon* (McEwen and Maiman 1984; Harrington 1985; Hofrichter 1987; Pavlich 1996; Hartley 2002; Kagan, Krygier, and Winston 2002; Olson and Dzur 2004). From the plethora of contemporary informal forms of ordering, I have chosen to focus on three areas of research: 1) alternative dispute resolution in lower counts; 2) information in regulating agencies; and 3) comparative and global developments.

2.1 Alternative Dispute Resolution in Lower Courts

Neighborhood Justice Centers (NJCs) are court deferral programs designed to mediate minor civil and criminal disputes between parties who had, or continue to have, ongoing relationships (e.g. family members, neighbors, landlords–tenants). In most jurisdictions, mediation is mandatory upon filling a domestic civil complainant. In others, a judge will order the parties to go to mediation as part of the court's ruling. The location of NJCs varies from inside court buildings with other deferral programs, to separate locations such as neighborhood centers and office buildings.

NJCs were established in the early 1980s as part of a worldwide reform movement called "alternative dispute resolution" or "access to justice." According to the reformers, mediation by lay-citizens trained in the skills of labor-mediation, promised efficiency: specialized forums for particular kinds of problems and the rational allocation of judicial resources. Reformers also claimed that mediation is a consensus-building process that parties prefer over the adversarial model of adjudication. There is little sound empirical evidence to support this claim; indeed what was once a "voluntary" service, has been turned largely mandatory because parties were not willing to go voluntarily to NJCs. In the U.S., the legal profession's interest in rationalizing, streamlining, and fine-tuning the judicial system to cope more effectively with a wide range of problems has been a theme in court administration and court reform throughout the twentieth century. In the United States,

---

[3] For an articulation of other movements in the sociological legal tradition, see Hunt (1978).

[4] For a description of the general theory and approach to teaching ADR in U.S. law schools and information on casebooks in the field, see Nolan-Haley (2001).

the U.S. Attorney General's Office created pilot NJCs, which then served as models for local bar associations and community groups to replicate. Within a decade of their development, NJCs became as prevalent as Small Claims Courts in the U.S. court system. These court-related mediation programs are the most typical kind of NJCs.

The term "neighborhood justice center" is also a generic term for mediation programs not affiliated with courts or focused on rationalizing dispute processing. In the contemporary U.S. movement, there is talk of "community empowerment," the creation of a new sense of community through self-governance or neighborhood control, decentralized judicial decision-making, and the substitution of community members for professional dispute resolvers. Proponents of this type of program turn to socialist experiments conducted under revolutionary conditions for inspiration, deliberately taking on the social transformation agenda that accompanied these movements. Advocates view community mediation as completely independent of the judicial system and locate its authority in the local neighborhood rather than the state (see Milner and Merry 1993).

Another kind of neighborhood justice center are those that emphasize "personal growth and development" and view mediation as a process of consensual dispute settlement that "empowers" individuals, permits them to take greater control over their own lives by enhancing their personal skills in dealing with conflict, and endows them with techniques which they can apply to other situations. These neighborhood justice centers use psychological approaches instead of labor-mediation approaches in their dispute process training sessions. There are religiously inspired mediation programs that argue that learning to settle differences through sharing ideas and talking will diminish dependence and improve spiritual wellbeing (Tomasic and Feeley 1982; Auerbach 1983; Beer 1986).

Local programs typically spin off from a single ideological project, but there are interesting mixes among them. Some programs emphasize social and personal transformation; others advocate increased efficiency as well as greater personal satisfaction. While the court-related NJCs espouse a close working relationship with the judicial system, the social transformation neighborhood justice programs may reject all ties with it, and the personal growth programs may cooperate with the state judicial system but derive ideological inspiration from the helping professions rather than the judicial system. To some extent, however, a therapeutic approach to problem solving is already well entrenched in the judicial system (Harrington and Merry 1988).

2.2 Informalism as a Regulatory Reform

Beginning in the early 1980s, informal negotiation processes, along with other reforms such as cost–benefit analysis, were hailed by regulatory reformers as workable solutions. The most notable practice of informal negotiation in administrative procedure was the creation of "negotiated rulemaking"—allegedly a consensus process to craft an administrative rule before the traditional "notice and comment" procedure as outlined in Section 553 of the Administrative Procedure Act. Legal services entrepreneurs, such as the Harvard Program on Negotiation, and corporate spin-offs, like NDispute, claimed that by bringing together parties affected by, or interested in, particular regulations, informal negotiations between them would practically eliminate the "distance" between the regulators, the regulated, and the public. Alleging that "consensus" among "stakeholders" would alleviate an accountability deficit they perceived with traditional "notice and comment" procedure, advocates of negotiated rulemaking (led by the Administrative Conference of the United States, ACUS) urged administrative agencies to experiment with negotiated rulemaking during the 1980s. The institutionalization of this procedure then followed in 1990 with an amendment to the Administrative Procedure Act titled "The Negotiated Rulemaking Act of 1990" (NRA).

As with other proposals for alternative dispute resolution (ADR), the advocates are very enthusiastic about the advantages of rulemaking through negotiation. Specifically, they see the following advantages: (1) negotiated rulemaking offers the parties direct participation in the process; (2) the mediator is more active in "outreach" to the parties affected by regulation than in the "customary rulemaking route;" (3) the parties are engaged in direct substantive decisions rather than appearing as expert witnesses providing testimony before the agency; (4) the costs of participation are reduced because the parties need not prepare "defensive research;" (5) the quality of participation is richer because the parties are in a setting that provides incentives to rank their concerns; and (6) according to reform activists, regulatory negotiations cannot fail: "[a]t the very least, conflicts can be clarified, data shared, and differences aired in a constructive way. Even if consensus is not achieved the negotiation process will still have narrowed the issues in disputes" (Susskind and MacMahon 1985, 159; for a deconstruction of this ideology see Harrington 1988). Negotiated regulation is most successful, according to its proponents, when the agency participates, because interested parties are more likely to participate than without the agency to avoid the uncertainty of agency review (Harter 1983; for a critique see Coglianese 1996).

The empirical studies of negotiated rulemaking tell us about the political consequences of informalism in regulatory rulemaking on government accountability. The practice of accountability appears to be significantly different in a negotiated rulemaking setting compared to traditional methods. Negotiated rulemaking produces a more open and transparent regime, for the invited private actors who have greater opportunities to circulate their views, as evident in a market-based model of accountability. Yet, challenges to who is allowed to participate in negotiated rulemaking—who are the stakeholders, the private parties that meet with government agencies and whether these groups or individuals have any representative capacity, and thus accountability—are signs that this market model may only produce accountability for those who get to participate, leaving open the potential for a crisis of legitimacy.

The traditional understanding of regulatory accountability formally recognizes a public, which holds the right to keep elected politicians accountable. And elected politicians are supposed to oversee the appointed bureaucrats. There is no such chain of accountability, however, in the "ordering" of negotiated rulemaking. Agencies may exercise broader discretion as a result of the law (NRA). Informalism, here, is one element of a much larger neoliberal regulatory regime. Courts, in the traditional model of regulatory accountability, completed the circuit of accountability, by providing a forum for citizens to challenge allegedly unfair exclusion from the rulemaking system. Now that this forum appears to be no longer available, the checks and balances system within the state may be destabilized. Together with the opening up of new spaces of discretion through the vehicle of informalism, this destabilization is likely to produce a legitimacy crisis (Harrington and Turem 2006).

2.3 Informalism from Comparative and Global Perspective

Comparative research on informalism reveals much sharper and deeper political divisions over the meaning of informal forms of ordering, such as community mediation, to those apparent in the U.S. experience. For example, in the Soviet Union, China, Cuba, Chile, and Portugal "popular justice" is associated with periods of upheaval and revolution. Informalism was harnessed to the task of reshaping society according to a new, revolutionary vision. Neighborhood justice has been part of broader social transformation experiments in Cuba, Chile, and Portugal after the 1974 revolution, where the public theater of the lower courts is seen as a powerful socialization experience (Abel 1982b). In the early postrevolutionary years, the Cuban government viewed local justice as a form of public theater to be carried out on the streets with a clear articulation of the new moral order. Similarly, in Portugal after the 1974 revolution, popular justice played a role in social transformation. The 1971 proposal in Chile to establish neighborhood courts was promoted by Allende's recently elected party, designed to establish a nationwide system of elected, neighborhood, lay-staffed courts, framed in the critique that the poor had no access to the existing legal system and that the professional judiciary was part of the legal order that discriminated against the poor. However, by the late 1980s and in other Global South countries, neighborhood justice reforms were mandatory in foreign aid packages and explicitly designed to promote modernization by pulling marginal and obstreperous elements into the center (for an analysis see Dezalay and Garth 2002).

The terms of debate over informalism in the United States are not as stark; the underlying political meanings are more subdued and camouflaged. It is harder in the U.S. context to find sharp divisions between self-government and state power, working class control and professional control, the use of legal metaphors and relationship metaphors (Milner and Merry 1993). Although the political ideologies of U.S. inform-alism projects discussed above are analytically distinct, the boundaries between them are ambiguous, with considerable borrowing of ideas and central symbols. Indeed, the use of symbols in the community mediation movement lies in their very ambiguity, in the multiplicity of interpretations which are possible and which are mobilized as resources for the reform movement and within local programs.

There is little question that informalism is a major technology in creating and building global governmentality, such as it exists today. The proliferation of informalism in new international tribunals (Slaughter 2004; Kingsbury, Krisch, and Stewart 2006), the establishment of informal governmental and nongovernmental commissions for standards setting (Courville 2006), and so forth, are operating to forge a web of what is call "transnational governance" (Shapiro 2001). The term "soft law" refers to informally organized (nonstate) forms of legal order standards or guidelines, as well as informal dispute processes (Trubek and Trubek 2005). Typically soft law is the name given to regulatory proposals produced by networks of NGOs working in a particular substan-tive policy field, such as water (Morgan 2006). Usually, NGOs in the international field design procedures for global regulation without the formal backing of sovereign states and then work to integrate soft law into the world of "hard law," the law of sovereign nations, through transnational institutions like the World Trade Organization (WTO), North American Free Trade Association (NAFTA), and European Union (EU).

The circulation of informal forms of ordering already operating within the U.S., such as community mediation, is now so pervasive worldwide that it is a global phenomenon. Whether U.S. models will become the "global standard" is of course a major political, economic, and cultural debate. Research on this process (sometimes referred to as "legal transplates") is tracking the allocation of both foreign and domestic resources to the establishment of U.S. mediation forums particularly in the Global South (Cohen 2006).

So, too, we are witnessing the expansion of informal administrative orderings in recent calls for and debates over a "global administrative law." The precise informal features of a global administrative law are not yet clearly identifiable, but there are some who have advocated for what they view to be the virtues of informal forms in the U.S. administrative law model (Aman 2001; Stewart 2005).

3 INFORMALISM AND THE POLITICS OF LAW AND LEGAL INSTITUTIONS

As should be clear by this point, I do not embrace the view that informalism is an "alternative" to law; indeed I take the position that informalism exists in relation to multiple forms of ordering. From a legal pluralist approach we might refer to these forms as "legalities" while also attempting to specify what kind of legality we are speaking about (formal, informal, private, public, and so on). Power operates through and in the multiple forms of orderings that we recognize as sociolegal norms and institutions. This view of informalism requires us to grapple with the practices of ordering forms, rather than just cycle through the paradoxes present in laws and juridical institutions embodying multiple orderings.

Attention to informal legal orderings from this view, I think, brings a new set of theoretical questions to light for the study of law and politics: (1) Is disputing a forum for political participation? (2) What political meanings are produced through the intersection of forms of ordering, such as those we recognize as more or less informal? (3) What are the cultural politics of various hybrid forms of ordering? These questions reoriented research on law and politics, challenging us to go beyond the behavioralist judicial decision-making paradigm. They ask us to think about the context and social forces (political, economic, and cultural) that constitute what is taken to be "the law" and shape how it operates.

Research on informalism underscores the theoretical limits of the so-called "upper court myth" that was articulated earlier in U.S. Law and Society circles and demonstrated most formidability by work such as Malcolm Feeley's *The Process is the Punishment* (1979). If legal realists and judicial process scholars had earlier called for a move away from focusing on U.S. Supreme Court decision-making, then political scientists doing dispute-processing research called for a move beyond behavioralist assumptions motivating those studies (Harrington 1984). Put simply, how we understand the place of law and courts *in society* informs our thinking about what constitutes "law" and affects our research agendas (Shapiro and Stone Sweet 2004, ch. 1). Not all studies of informalism, however, consciously embrace this epistemological shift. Yet a significant number are engaged in lively theoretical discussions about critical epistemologies in law (Brigham and Harrington 1989; Harrington and Yngvesson 1990; Whittington 2000; Cotterrell 2001).

In the early 1980s, Lynn Mather and Barbara Yngvesson (1980–1) provided theoretical insight and empirical evidence about how institutional actors (lawyers, court officials) frame problems and shape conflicts that come to courts. Building on judicial process research, their work shifted attention to the importance of studying how the meaning of law gets produced in encounters between legal actors and disputing parties. This study (and those that followed on dispute processing practices) helped reorient the field away from judicial decision-making studies to research on the politics of framing disputes. From a poststructuralist perspective, framing is a form of power and can be treated as an *effect* of law and legal institutions. Similarly when the Civil Litigation Research Project (CLRP) at the University of Wisconsin-Madison emphasized the importance of treating "dispute" as the unit of analysis, it laid the groundwork for an alternative to the judicial decision-making paradigm. Among other things, CLRP found that whether a grievance becomes a claim depends on the type of dispute (e.g. tort, post-divorce, discrimination) and type of access claimants have to various dispute processing channels (e.g. administrative remedies, private insurance bureaus, courts); see CLRP research by Miller and Sarat (1981); Grossman et al. (1982); and Bumiller (1988).

At the same time, the problem of law's relationship to political development—that very large question about the rule of law and modernity—can be examined from the angle of informal forms of orderings. The traditional and usually the operative explanation for the use of third-party dispute processes (i.e. litigation) was grounded in a Weberian economic and political development theory until research on disputing produced contradictory historical and empirical evidence (Grossman and Sarat 1975). While there is some evidence from local trial court studies to support this environmental theory, it is not robust (McIntosh 1983; Stookey 1992).

In addition, as political science joined with sociology and history to build the scholarly study of "neoinstitutionalism"[5] there now is some work on forms of ordering, such as civil litigation, that offers an institutional interpretation and explanation for litigation trends. This work turns the usual question about litigation—what explains changing rates of demand for litigation over time?—around, looking instead at the supply side (courts): How do courts affect the changing patterns of litigation rates over time? What characteristics of courts (or what might be called "institutional properties") are themselves agents, operating within particular political, economic, and institutional contexts, that have the capacity to signal lawyers and litigants, and thus shape the processes of encouraging and discouraging civil litigation (Heydebrand 1990; Harrington and Ward 1995)? Howard's (1981) study of the U.S. Courts of Appeals is an important influence on shaping this approach.

4 CONCLUSION

Informalism is a political resource, mobilized in symbolic and instrumental ways, by the legal profession, entrepreneurs, and social movements as well as political elites. Sociolegal theory continually reminds us that the mobilization of law—or what is taken to be "law"—is a social phenomenon (e.g. as expressed through rights

---

[5] I am referring to work such as that by Orren (1991); Gillman (1993); Graber (1993); Brandwein (1999); Clayton and Gillman (1999); Novkov (2001); Frymer (2003); Jensen (2003); Sterett (2003); Keck (2004); Pickerill (2004); Morag-Levine (2005); Frymer (2005); Kahn and Kersch (2006).

movements in Brigham (1996); labor strikes in Brisbin (2002); media coverage of tort reform in Haltom and McCann (2004); tribal acknowledgment processes in Cramer (2005); hate-speech regulation in university administrations in Gould (2005); the impact of economic libertarians on regulation in Hatcher (2005)). This should caution scholars against substituting academic assumptions that there is a determinate legal logic for an explanation (or expectation) of social change. Through the study of informal legal orderings we have found reason to believe that interdependent legal forms constitute law. This work not only expands our understandings about what constitutes "law," but it also makes more transparent the struggles to determine what is law.

REFERENCES

ABEL, R. L. (ed.) 1982a. *The Politics of Informal Justice: The American Experience*, vols. 1–2. New York: Academic Press.

—— 1982b. *The Politics of Informal Justice: Comparative Studies*, vol. 2. New York: Academic Press.

AMAN, A. C. 2001. The limits of globalization and the future of administrative law: from government to governance. *Indiana Journal of Global Legal Studies*, 8: 379–401.

AUERBACH, J. S. 1983. *Justice Without Law?* New York: Oxford University Press.

BEER, J. E. 1986. *Peacemaking in Your Neighborhood: Reflections on an Experiment in Community Mediation*. Philadelphia: New Society.

BRANDWEIN, P. 1999. *Reconstructing Reconstruction: The Supreme Court and the Production of Historical Truth*. Durham, NC: Duke University Press.

BRIGHAM, J. 1996. *The Constitution of Interests: Beyond the Politics of Rights*. New York: NYU Press.

—— and BROWN, D. (eds.) 1980. *Policy Implementation: Penalties or Incentives?* Beverly Hills, Calif.: Sage.

—— and HARRINGTON, C. B. 1989. Realism and its consequences: an inquiry into contemporary socio legal research. *International Journal of the Sociology of Law*, 17: 41–62.

BRISBIN, R. A. 2002. *A Strike Like No Other Strike: Law and Resistance During the Pittston Coal Strike of 1989–1990*. Baltimore: Johns Hopkins University Press.

BUMILLER, K. 1988. *The Civil Rights Society*. Baltimore: Johns Hopkins University Press.

CARTER, L., and HARRINGTON, C. B. 2000. *Administrative Law and Politics*, 3rd edn. New York: Addison-Wesley Longman.

CLAYTON, C. W., and GILLMAN, H. (eds.) 1999. *The Supreme Court in American Politics: New Institutionalist Interpretations*. Lawrence: University of Kansas Press.

COGLIANESE, C. 1996. Litigating within relationships: disputes and disturbance in the regulatory process. *Law and Society Review*, 30: 735–65.

COHEN, A. J. 2006. Debating the globalization of U.S. mediation: politics, power, and practice in Nepal. *Harvard Negotiation Law Review*, 11: 295–353.

COOPER, N. L., PURITZ, P., and SHANG, W. 1998. Fulfilling the promise of *In Re Gault*: advancing the role of lawyers or children. *Wake Forest Law Review*, 33: 651–79.

COTTERRELL, R. (ed.) 2001. *Sociological Perspectives on Law: Contemporary Debates*. Aldershot: Ashgate.

COURVILLE, S. 2006. Understanding NGO-based social and environmental regulatory systems: why we need models of accountability. In *Public Accountability: Designs, Dilemma and Experiences*, ed. M. Dowdle. New York: Cambridge University Press.

CRAMER, R. A. 2005. *Cash, Color, and Colonialism: The Politics of Tribal Acknowledgment*. Norman: University of Oklahoma Press.

DEZALAY, Y., and GARTH, G. B. 2002. *The Internationalization of Palace Wars*. Chicago: University of Chicago Press.

FEELEY, M. 1979. *The Process is the Punishment: Handling Cases in a Lower Criminal Court*. New York: Russell Sage.

FITZPATRICK, P. 1983. Law, plurality and underdevelopment. In *Legality, Ideology and the State*, ed. D. Sugarmann. London: Academic Press.

—— 1993. The impossibility of popular justice. In *The Possibility of Popular Justice*, ed. N. Milner and S. Merry. Ann Arbor: University of Michigan Press.

FRYMER, P. 2005. Racism revised: courts, labor law and the institutional construction of racial animus. *American Political Science Review*, 99: 373–87.

FULLER, L. L. 1971. Mediation—its forms and functions. *Southern California Law Review*, 44: 305–39.

—— 1978. The forms and limits of adjudication. *Harvard Law Review*, 92: 353–409.

GILLMAN, H. 1993. *The Constitution Besieged: The Rise and Demise of Lochner Era Police Powers Jurisprudence*. Durham, NC: Duke University Press.

GOULD, J. B. 2005. *Speak No Evil: The Triumph of Hate Speech Regulation*. Chicago: University of Chicago Press.

GRABER, M. A. 1993. The non-majoritarian difficulty: legislative deference to the judiciary. *Studies in American Political Development*, 7: 35–73.

GROSSMAN, J. B., and SARAT, A. 1975. Litigation in the federal courts: a comparative perspective. *Law and Society Review*, 9: 321–46.

—— KRITZER, H. B., BUMILLER, K., SARAT, A., and McDOUGAL, S. 1982. Dimensions of institutional participation: who uses the courts and how? *Journal of Politics*, 44: 86–114.

HALTOM, W., and McCANN, M. 2004. *Distorting the Law: Politics, Media and the Litigation Crisis*. Chicago: University of Chicago Press.

HARRINGTON, C. B. 1984. The politics of participation and nonparticipation in dispute processes. *Law and Policy*, 6: 203–30.

—— 1985. *Shadow Justice: The Ideology and Institutionalization of Alternatives to Court*. Westport, Conn.: Greenwood Press.

—— 1988. Regulatory reform: creating gaps and making markets. *Law and Policy*, 10: 293.

—— and MERRY, S. E. 1988. Ideological production: the making of community mediation. *Law and Society Review*, 22: 709–37.

—— and YNGVESSON, B. 1990. Interpretive sociolegal research. *Law and Social Inquiry*, 15: 135–48.

—— and WARD, D. S. 1995. Patterns of appellate litigation, 1945–1990. In *Contemplating Courts*, ed. L. Epstein. Washington, DC: Congressional Quarterly Press.

—— and TUREM, Z. U. 2006. Accounting for accountability in neoliberal regulatory regimes. In *Public Accountability: Designs, Dilemma and Experiences*, ed. M. Dowdle. New York: Cambridge University Press.

HARTER, P. J. 1982. Negotiating regulations: a cure for malaise. *Georgetown Law Journal*, 71: 1–118.

—— 1983. The political legitimacy and judicial review of consensual rules. *American University Law Review*, 32: 471–96.

HARTLEY, R. E. 2002. *Alternative Dispute Resolution in Civil Justice Systems*. New York: LFB Scholarly Press.

HATCHER, L. J. 2005. Economic libertarians, property and institutions: linking activism, ideas and identities among property rights advocates. In *Worlds Cause Lawyers Make*, ed. S. Scheingold and A. Sarat. Palo Alto, Calif.: Stanford University Press.

HEYDEBRAND, W. 1990. Government litigation and national policymaking: from Roosevelt to Reagan. *Law and Society Review*, 24: 477–95.

—— 2003. Process rationality as legal governance: a comparative perspective. *International Sociology*, 18: 325–49.

HOFRICHTER, R. 1987. *Neighborhood Justice in Capitalist Society: The Expansion of the Informal State*. Westport, Conn.: Greenwood Press.

HOWARD, J. W. 1981. *Courts of Appeals in the Federal Judicial System: A Study of the Second, Fifth, and District of Columbia Circuits*. Princeton, NJ: Princeton University Press.

HUNT, A. 1978. *The Sociological Movement in Law*. London: Macmillian Press.

In re Gault, 387 U.S. 1 (1967).

JENSEN, L. 2003. *Patriots, Settlers, and the Origins of American Social Policy*. New York: Cambridge University Press.

KAGAN, R. A., KRYGIER, M., and WINSTON, K. (eds.) 2002 *Legality and Community: On the Intellectual Legacy of Philip Selznick*. Lanham, Md.: Rowman and Littlefield.

KAHN, R., and KERSCH, K. I. (eds.) 2006. *The Supreme Court and American Political Development*. Lawrence: University of Kansas Press.

KECK, T. M. 2004. *The Most Activist Supreme Court in History*. Chicago: University of Chicago Press.

KINGSBURY, B., KRISCH, N., and STEWART, R. B. 2005. The emergence of global administrative law. *Law and Contemporary Problems*, 68: 1–13.

LATOUR, B. 1993. *We Have Never Been Modern*. Cambridge, Mass.: Harvard University Press.

MACAULAY, S. 1963. Non-contractual relations in business: a preliminary study. *American Sociological Review*, 28: 55–67.

MCEWEN, C., and MAIMAN, R. J. 1984. Mediation in small claims courts: achieving compliance through consent. *Law and Society Review*, 18: 11–49.

MCINTOSH, W. 1983. Private use of a public forum: a long range view of the dispute processing role of courts. *American Political Science Review*, 77: 991–1010.

MATHER, L., and YNGVESSON, B. 1980–1. Language, audience, and the transformation of disputes. *Law and Society Review*, 15: 775–822.

MERRY, S. E. 1988. Legal pluralism. *Law and Society Review*, 22: 869–96.

MILLER, R., and SARAT, A. 1981. Grievances, claims, and disputes: assessing the adversary culture. *Law and Society Review*, 15: 525–66.

MILNER, N., and MERRY, S. (eds.) 1993. *The Possibility of Popular Justice*. Ann Arbor: University of Michigan Press.

MOORE, S. F. 1973. Law and social change: the semi-autonomous social field as an appropriate subject of study. *Law and Society Review*, 7: 719–46.

MORAG-LEVINE, N. 2003. *Chasing the Wind: Regulating Air Pollution in the Common Law State*. Princeton, NJ: Princeton University Press.

MORGAN, B. 2006. Turning off the tap: urban water service delivery and the social construction of global administrative law. *European Journal of International Law*, 17: 215–46.

NADER, L., and TODD, H. L. (eds.) 1978. *The Dispute Process: Law in Ten Societies*. New York: Columbia University Press.

NOLAN-HALEY, J. M. 2001. *Alternative Dispute Resolution: In a Nut Shell*, 2nd edn. St. Paul, Minn.: West Group.

NOVKOV, J. 2001. *Constituting Workers, Protecting Women: Gender, Law and the Progressive Era and New Deal Years*. Ann Arbor: University of Michigan Press.

OLSON, S. M., and DZUR, A. W. 2004. Revisiting informal justice: restorative justice and democratic professionalism. *Law and Society Review*, 38: 139–76.

ORREN, K. 1991. *Belated Feudalism: Labor, the Law, and Liberal Development in the United States*. New York: Cambridge University Press.

PAVLICH, G. 1996. The power of community mediation: government and formation of self-identity. *Law and Society Review*, 30: 707–33.

PICKERILL, J. M. 2004. *Constitutional Deliberation in Congress: The Impact of Judicial Review in a Separated System*. Durham, NC: Duke University Press.

PLATT, A. M. 1977. *The Child Savers: The Invention of Delinquency*, 2nd edn. Chicago: University of Chicago Press.

POSPISIL, L. 1967. Legal levels and multiplicity of legal systems in human societies. *Journal of Conflict Resolution*, 11: 2–26.

POUND, R. 1906. The causes of popular dissatisfaction with the administration of justice. *American Bar Association Reports*, 29: 395–417.

SANTOS, B. DE S. 1987. Law: a map of misreading; toward a postmodern conception of law. *Journal of Law and Society*, 14: 279–302.

SCHNEIDER, C. E. 1993. The tension between rules and discretion in family law: a report and reflection. *Family Law Quarterly*, 27: 229–53.

SHAPIRO, M. 2001. Administrative law unbounded: reflections on government and governance. *Indiana Journal of Global Legal Studies*, 8: 369–77.

—— and STONE SWEET, A. 2004. *On Law, Politics, and Judicialization*. New York: Oxford University Press.

SLAUGHTER, A. M. 2004. Global government networks, global information agencies, and disaggregated democracy. In *Public Governance in the Age of Globalization*, ed. K. H. Ladeur. London: Ashgate.

STERETT, S. M. 2003. *Public Pensions: Gender and Civil Service in the States, 1850–1937*. Ithaca, NY: Cornell University Press.

STEWART, R. 2006. U.S. administrative law: a model for global administrative law? New York University School of Law, NYU Public Law and Legal Theory Working Papers, 13.

STOOKEY, J. 1992. Trying times: a sociopolitical history of litigation during the first half of the twentieth century. *Social Science History Review*, 16: 23–61.

SUSSKIND, L., and MACMAHON, G. 1985. Theory and practice of negotiated rulemaking. *Yale Journal on Regulation*, 3: 133–65.

TOMASIC, R., and FEELEY, M. (eds.) 1982. *Neighborhood Justice: Assessment of an Emerging Idea*. New York: Longman.

TOMLINS, C. L., and MANN, B. H. (eds.) 2001. *The Many Legalities of Early America*. Chapel Hill: University of North Carolina Press.

TRUBEK, D. M., and TRUBEK, L. G. 2005. Hard and soft law in the construction of social Europe: the role of the open method of coordination. *European Law Journal*, 11: 343–64.

Weidemaier, W. M. C. 2007. Private law: the public nature of private disputing. SSRN paper, University of North Carolina, Chapel Hill.

Whittington, K. E. 2000. Once more unto the breach: post behavioralist approaches to judicial politics. *Law and Social Inquiry,* 25: 601–34.

Williams, R. 1977. *Marxism and Literature.* New York: Oxford University Press.

Wilson, J. Q. 1968. *Varieties of Police Behavior.* Cambridge, Mass.: Harvard University Press.

Yngvesson, B. 1989. Inventing law in local settings: rethinking popular legal culture. *Yale Law Journal,* 98: 1689–709.

—— 1993. *Virtuous Citizens, Disruptive Subjects: Order and Complaint in a New England Court.* New York: Routledge.

PART VI

SOURCES OF LAW AND THEORIES OF JURISPRUDENCE

CHAPTER 22

....

NATURAL LAW

....

ROBERT P. GEORGE

1 NATURAL LAW AND PRACTICAL REASONING

....

THEORIES of natural law propose to identify fundamental aspects of human well-being and fulfillment ("basic human goods") and norms of conduct entailed by their integral directiveness or prescriptivity ("moral norms"). Propositions picking out basic aspects of human flourishing are directive (prescriptive) in our thinking about what to do or refrain from doing (our practical reason)—they are or provide more than merely instrumental reasons for action and restraint. When these foundational principles of practical reflection are taken together they entail norms that may exclude some options and require others in situations of morally significant choosing. Moral norms provide *conclusive* reasons for choice and action in circumstances in which one has an intelligible reason to do X, but also an intelligible reason (or some subrational motive) not to do X, perhaps because one has a reason or other motive to do Y, where one's doing Y is incompatible, here and now at least, with doing X.

Although all choosing involves emotion, basic practical principles provide motivation that is more than merely emotional. Basic human goods—such as friendship, knowledge, critical aesthetic appreciation, and personal authenticity and integrity—are possible objects of volition where the will is regarded, as in the thought of St. Thomas Aquinas and other leading figures in the tradition of natural-law thinking, as a rational appetite—an appetite for intelligibilities in data presented to the intellect of the person who is deliberating about a question with a view to choosing and acting. An agent as a choosing subject has a reason to act where one grasps the possibility of bringing into being a state of affairs that does not exist but which, one supposes, can be brought into existence by one's choice; and where one's deliberation and choice *have a point* by virtue of the intelligibility of the basic form(s) of human good (i.e. aspect(s) of human well-being and fulfillment) that one, in deliberating, has in view (for a recent survey of various "objective list" theories of basic goods, see Oderberg 2004, 127–65).

Following Aristotle, Aquinas distinguishes, and rigorously respects the distinction, between "practical" and "speculative" (or "theoretical") reasoning. Practical reasoning is reasoning about *what is worth doing and what ought to be done*. Its principles guide choices and the conduct that executes those choices. Theoretical reasoning is reasoning about *what is the case* concerning the natural world, including human deliberation, choosing, and acting; supernatural realities, if such exist; human society and history; and so forth. Natural-law theories are fundamentally theories of *practical* reasoning, even though, like practical reasoning itself, such theories of (or about) practical reasoning necessarily include certain premises that are the fruit of theoretical, rather than practical, awareness, insight, and reasoning. (As to whether the first principles of practical reason that are the most basic precepts of natural law are underived foundational principles, as John Finnis says in *Natural Law and Natural Rights* (1980), or principles that are derived from methodologically antecedent theoretical truths about nature—particularly human nature, as Russell Hittinger maintains in *A Critique of the New Natural Law Theory* (1987)—a lively dispute exists among scholars of natural law.) To avoid misunderstanding, it is important to see that in distinguishing these two types of reasoning, natural-law theorists are not supposing that a person possesses two separate minds or intellects. Rather, each of us possesses a single, complex but unified intellect that can be directed to comprehending different types of objects. On the one hand, inquiry can be directed toward uncovering facts about nature, God or the gods, society, history, and other subjects. On the other hand, inquiry can be directed towards grasping the point, if any, of (for example) pursuing intellectual knowledge as something worthwhile in itself, or making and being a friend, or seeking critically to appreciate this or that work of literature, art, or music.

Natural-law theorists typically understand the human good as variegated. There are many basic aspects of human well-being and fulfillment. People can flourish, or fail to flourish, along many dimensions of their lives. Since these dimensions—the bodily, the rational, the emotional, the spiritual—cannot be reduced to each other or to some common factor, natural-law theorists speak of human *goods*, in the plural; and goods, as they shape options for morally significant choices, are in important respects incommensurable. Choices have costs as well as benefits. Moral norms that guide choices (thus characteristically bringing them into a certain type of commensurability in the concrete circumstances of decision-making) cannot be of the utilitarian or consequentialist sort that presuppose the possibility of identifying a morally right choice that contains all the good available in other options plus some more. According to natural-law theory, there is no such possibility.

At a crucial juncture in his formal treatment of natural law, Aquinas asks whether the first principles of practical reason (which are, he says, the most basic precepts of natural law) are several, or whether there is only one such principle. He concludes that there are several, precisely because the human good is variegated. There are many basic human goods—irreducible aspects of human well-being and fulfillment—and each is the referent of a practical principle which Aquinas frames in terms of a first, entirely generic principle: "good (*bonum*) is to be done and pursued (*prosequendum*), and bad (*malum*) is to be avoided." He makes clear that his view of *malum* is privative. Ignorance and other evils are privations of human goods. The "bads" or "evils" that "are to be avoided"—ignorance, disease, animosity—are privations of the goods that "are to be done and pursued." However, neither this first, formal principle nor the several substantive first principles of practical reason and basic precepts of natural law are, strictly speaking, *moral* principles. They direct choice and action toward what is intelligibly desirable and away from what is not. But, in so doing, they do not resolve moral problems. Indeed, it is the plurality and diversity of these principles (and the opportunities for their instantiation as the fruit of human deliberation, choice, and action) that generate moral problems and require the identification of specifically moral principles in the shape of norms to guide free choice where an agent's grasp of attractive but incompatible options makes choosing necessary (for more on incommensurability and choice, see Chang 1997). These moral principles specify what is required for one to be responsive to the *integral* directiveness of the first practical principles—that is, to the directiveness they have when taken together. That directiveness is toward integral human fulfillment, i.e. the well-being and fulfillment of all human persons and communities across the range of dimensions of their flourishing.

Of course, no choice or series of choices can bring about such fulfillment. Integral human fulfillment is an ideal; it cannot be an operational objective. There can be no five billion year plan to bring about the complete fulfillment of all human beings and all communities. The open-endedness of human living and the opportunities it presents precludes any such possibility. But the principle that one should choose and act only in ways compatible with a will toward integral fulfillment is no mere ideal. When specified, it is capable of guiding action by, for example, excluding choices that violate the Golden Rule of fairness or the Pauline Principle that evil may not be done even for the sake of good consequences. Still, moral norms cannot always narrow the fully reasonable and, in that sense, morally available options to a single, uniquely correct choice. Often choices are between options, both or all of which are fully compatible with what might be called the first principle of morality: that one's willing be always compatible with a will toward integral human fulfillment.

In sum, the relationship between the first principles of practical reason and moral norms, understood as specifications of the first principle of morality, is this:

moral principles such as the Golden Rule, like other, more specific moral norms, are norms of conduct entailed by the integral directiveness or prescriptivity of the basic human goods to which the first principles of practical reason direct choice and action. To take these principles of reasonableness in choosing together, and to choose in line with them and not in defiance of any of them (despite emotional or other subrational motives one might very well have for making contrary choices), is to respect their integral directiveness. A choice that is compatible with this directiveness is a fully reasonable, and thus morally upright, choice.

This is not to suggest that immoral choices are simply *irrational*. Most immoral choices are made for reasons. As immoral, however, they fall short of *all* that reason requires. Thus, they are "unreasonable"—practical reasonableness being the criterion of morality on the natural-law account of the matter—even when they are not simply irrational. Consider the case of a wealthy father whose beloved daughter is afflicted with a life-imperiling heart ailment. Let us suppose that she could be saved by a heart transplant, but no transplantable heart is available to her. So, in desperation, her father is driven by love and concern for his child to a desperate act. He identifies a corrupt cardiac surgeon who is willing to transplant a heart without asking where it came from. The father then contracts with an organized criminal element to secure a heart from a homeless demented person who will be murdered to obtain it. Now, wicked though it is, this is hardly an irrational act. Although the father is deflected by powerful emotion from conforming his conduct to what morality stringently requires, the ultimate motivating purpose of his action is undeniably a basic human good: the life and health of his daughter. So he is acting on one of the first principles of practical reason, but not in a way that respects the integral directiveness of these principles. On the contrary, his action violates moral norms that are what they are as entailments of this directiveness and as specifications of the requirement of reason (and, thus, of morality) that one choose compatibly with a will toward integral human fulfillment. His act's rationality is flawed in a way best summarily expressed as *unreasonable*, and unreasonableness in matters of choice involving basic human goods is immoral.

2 NATURAL LAW, MORALITY, AND VIRTUE

The foregoing should make clear the ways that natural-law theories are both like and unlike utilitarian and other consequentialist approaches to morality, on the one hand, and Kantian or "deontological" approaches, on the other. Like utilitarian approaches, and unlike Kantian ones, natural-law theories are fundamentally concerned with human well-being and fulfillment and, indeed, take basic human goods as the starting points of ethical reflection. Unlike utilitarian approaches, however, they understand the basic forms of human good, as they figure in options for morally significant choosing, as incommensurable in ways that render senseless the utilitarian strategy of choosing the option that overall and in the long run promises to conduce to the net best proportion of benefit to harm (however "benefit" and "harm" may be understood and defined). Natural-law theorists share the Kantian rejection of aggregative accounts of morality that regard the achievement of sufficiently good consequences or the avoidance of sufficiently bad ones as justifying choices that would be excluded by application of moral principles in ordinary circumstances.

Unlike Kantians, however, they do not believe that moral norms can be identified and justified apart from a consideration of the integral directiveness of the principles of practical reason directing human choice and action toward what is humanly fulfilling and away from what is contrary to human well-being. Natural-law theorists do not believe in purely "deontological" moral norms. Practical reasoning is reasoning about *both* the "right" and the "good," and the two are connected. The content of the human good shapes moral norms inasmuch as such norms are entailments of the basic aspects of human well-being and fulfillment considered integrally. A leading area of research for contemporary scholars of natural law is to identify with greater precision than has been achieved heretofore what is entailed in various areas of moral controversy by the integral directiveness of human goods. Scholars seek to make progress both by more rigorous logical analysis, and by attaining a phenomenologically richer understanding of basic forms of human good as these can be realized by the deliberation, judgment, and choice of human agents.

The natural-law understanding of morality presupposes the possibility of free choice—choosing that is the pure product of neither external nor internal forces but subrational motivating factors, such as sheer desire. So a complete theory of natural law will include an account of principles of practical reason, including moral norms, as principles for the rational guidance of free choices, and a defense of free choice as a genuine possibility. This entails the rejection of forms of rationalism, according to which all phenomena are viewed as caused. It understands human beings—some human beings, at least sometimes—as uncaused causings of realities they bring into existence for reasons by free choices. In the natural-law account of human action, freedom and reason are mutually entailed. If people were not really free to choose among options—free in the sense that nothing but the choosing itself settles what option gets chosen—then truly rationally motivated action would not be possible. Conversely, if rationally motivated action were not possible, the experience we have of freely choosing would be illusory.

Another feature of the natural-law account of human action is its carefully delineated distinctions between various modes of voluntariness. Morality is fundamentally about rectitude in willing. In sound moral judgments and upright choices and actions, the will of the agent is oriented positively toward the human good, integrally conceived. In choosing and acting, one is not, of course, pursuing every human good—that is not possible—but one is pursuing at least one basic human good well; and if one is choosing and acting in a morally upright way, one is respecting the others. Yet, is it not obvious that many upright choices—choices of good ends sought by morally good means—have some bad consequences? For example, do we not know with moral certainty that by constructing a system of highways on which drivers of automobiles are authorized to drive at a speed of, say, sixty-five miles per hour, we are permitting a circumstance to exist in which several thousand people each year will be killed in driving accidents? Indeed, we do. But, according to the natural-law understanding of human action, there is a real and sometimes morally critical distinction between *intending* harm to a basic human good (and thus to a person, since human goods are not mere abstractions, but are aspects of the well-being of flesh-and-blood persons) and accepting harm as a *side effect* of an otherwise morally upright choice. One can intend harm in two different ways: as an end-in-itself or as a means to some other end. One intends harm as an end when, for example, one seeks to injure or kill someone out of hatred, anger, or some similarly powerful emotion. One intends harm as a means when, for example, one seeks to kill a person in order to recover on the victim's life insurance policy. The key thing to see is that intending death (whether as end or means) is distinct from accepting death as a side effect (even if the side effect is clearly foreseen, as we foresee, for example, the deaths of motorists and passengers on the highways in ordinary accidents).[1]

Natural-law theorists emphasize the fact that by our choices and actions we alter states of affairs in the world external to us and at the same time constitute ourselves—for better or worse—as persons with a certain character. Recognition of this self-shaping or "intransitive" quality of morally significant choosing leads to a focus on virtues as habits born of upright choosing that orient and dispose us to further upright choosing—especially in the face of temptations to behave immorally. People sometimes ask: Is natural law about rules or virtues? The answer is that it is about *both*. A complete theory of natural law identifies norms for distinguishing right from wrong as well as habits or traits of character whose cultivation disposes people to choose in conformity with the norms and thus compatibly with what we might call, borrowing a phrase from Kant, a good will, viz., a will towards integral human fulfillment. Although natural-law theorists reject what might be called a "pure" virtue ethics—a theory of morality which proposes to identify virtues, and to treat them as action-guiding, entirely independently of substantive

---

[1] Although the distinction between intending, on the one hand, and accepting bad side effects, on the other, is often pertinent to moral evaluation on a natural-law account, one should not suppose that it is impossible to violate moral norms in accepting side effects. On the contrary, one may behave *unjustly*, for example, in accepting bad side effects, even where one has not run afoul of the norm against intending, say, the death or injury of an innocent human being (see e.g. George 1999a, 106).

moral norms—they hold that the identification and analysis of virtues is critical to a sound and reasonably comprehensive account of moral life. Hence, natural-law theorists, beginning with Aristotle and Thomas Aquinas, have contributed to the study of virtue and the virtues, and their contemporary followers have fruitfully engaged the work of modern virtue ethicists.

3 POLITICAL MORALITY AND POSITIVE LAW

So far, the focus of this discussion has been the individual human being as a deliberating, acting, and choosing subject. We have been talking, one might say, about "personal" morality. But there is also what might be called "political" morality—and the relationship between personal and political morality, as Christopher Wolfe shows in *Natural Law Liberalism* (2006), is tight in the tradition of natural-law theorizing. Choices bearing, for better or worse, on the basic goods of human nature are made by and for communities, as well as individuals. People live not as isolated individuals, but in families, kinship groups, clans, and various forms of political association. And among the aspects of human flourishing are various forms of harmony or unity with others. And so natural-law theories propose accounts of the common good of communities, including political communities. Characteristically, the political common good is not some additional human good alongside the others, but, rather, the securing of conditions in which people can flourish in respect of their integral good by cooperating with each other as fellow citizens. There is a common good because (*a*) the basic human goods are aspects of the flourishing of each and every member of the human family; (*b*) many of these goods can be enjoyed, or enjoyed more fully, by common action to secure them; and (*c*) common action itself can be intrinsically fulfilling inasmuch as humans are indeed "political animals" whose integral good includes intrinsically social dimensions.

The common good of any human society demands that governments be established to make and enforce laws. Law and government are necessary not merely because human beings may treat one another unjustly and even behave in a predatory manner toward each other, but, more fundamentally, because human activity must often be coordinated by authoritative stipulations and other exercises of authority to secure common goals (see Finnis 1980; Ullmann-Margalit 1977). Consider the simple case of regulating highway traffic. Even in a society of perfect saints, law and government would be necessary to establish and maintain a system of traffic regulation for the sake of the common good of motorists, cyclists, pedestrians, and everyone who benefits from the safe and efficient transportation of goods and persons on the highways. Since it is often the case that there is no uniquely reasonable or desirable scheme of regulation—only different possible schemes with different benefits and costs—governmental authority must be employed to choose by stipulating one from among the possible schemes. Authority in such a case is necessary because unanimity is impossible. Authority serves the common good by making a stipulation and enforcing its terms. Assuming that there is no corruption or other injustice involved in the choice of a certain scheme of traffic regulation or the enforcement of its terms, we can regard this as a focal case of legal authority under a natural-law account of the matter. Of course, the complete account would begin by identifying the human goods that schemes of traffic regulation are meant to advance and protect—including, but not limited to, the protection of human life and health—and the evils they seek to allay. It would observe that, in the absence of a legally stipulated and enforced scheme of regulation, these goods would be in constant jeopardy as motorists—even motorists of good will who were doing their best to exercise caution—crashed into each other or created traffic gridlock of the sort that often could easily be avoided by the prudent stipulation of coordinated schemes of driving norms. It would then defend the legitimacy of governmental authority to make the required stipulations not by reference to the unique desirability of the scheme it happens to choose, but rather by appeal to the need for *a* scheme to be given the standing of law.

Lawmaking and law enforcement are central functions and responsibilities of legitimate political authority. The justifying point of law is to serve the common good by protecting the goods of persons and the communities of which they are members. Where the laws are just and effective, political authorities fulfill their obligations to the communities they exist to serve. To the extent the laws are unjust or ineffective, they fail in their mission to serve the common good. As Aquinas says, the very point of the law is the common good (Aquinas ST 1–2, q. 96 a. 1). Law is, as he defined it, "An ordinance of reason for the common good given by him who has the responsibility to care for the community" (Aquinas ST 1–2, q. 90 a. 4). Inasmuch as the moral point of law is to serve the good of human beings, laws against many of the sorts of wrongdoing common, alas, in human societies are necessary and proper. Aquinas's definition of law also requires that there be some individual, group, or institution exercising authority in political communities and fulfilling this authority's moral function by translating certain principles of natural law into positive law and reinforcing these principles with legal sanctions, i.e. the threat of punishment for law-breaking. In this sense, we can say that morally valid authorities derive the law they make (positive law) from the natural law, or equivalently, translate natural-law principles of justice and political morality into the rules of positive law.

Following Aquinas, who was himself picking up a lead from Aristotle, natural-law theorists hold that all just positive law is "derived" from natural law, although there are two types of derivation corresponding to different types of law. In certain cases, the legislator, for the sake of justice and the common good, simply and directly forbids or requires what morality itself forbids or requires. So, for example, the legislator in making murder a criminal offense puts the force and sanctions of positive law behind a principle by which people are bound as a matter of natural law even in the absence of positive law on the subject, namely, the principle forbidding the direct or otherwise unjust killing of one's fellow human beings. Aquinas noted that, in acting in this way, the legislator derives the positive law from the natural law in a manner akin to deducing conclusions from premises in mathematics or the natural sciences. For other types of positive law, however, such a "deductive" approach is not possible. Here, again, traffic regulation is illustrative. In choosing a scheme from among a possible range of reasonable schemes, each with its own costs and benefits, the legislator moves not by a process akin to deduction, but rather by an activity of the practical intellect that Aquinas called "*determinatio.*" Although, unfortunately, no single word in English captures all that the Latin term denotes and connotes, the concept is not difficult to understand. Aquinas explained it by analogy with the activity of a craftsman commissioned to build a house—what we would probably call an architect. There is, of course, no uniquely correct way to design a house. Many different designs are reasonable. Certain design features will be determined by the needs of the person or family that will occupy the dwelling; others are simply matters of style and taste and others, again, of optional compromises between expense and risk. So, in most cases, the architect will exercise a significant measure of creative freedom within a wide set of boundaries. Consider the question of ceiling height. Although some possibilities are excluded by practical considerations—for example, ceilings of only four feet in height would make living in the house intolerable for most people; and ceilings of forty feet in height would ordinarily be impractically expensive—no principle of architecture fixes ceiling heights at seven feet four inches or nine feet or anything in between or a bit higher or lower. In executing his commission, the architect will endeavor to choose a height for the ceilings that harmonizes with other features of his design, including features such as door heights that are themselves the fruit of determinations.

Like the architect, the lawmaker will in many domains exercise a considerable measure of creative freedom in working from a grasp of basic practical principles directing his actions toward the advancement and protection of basic human goods and away from their privations to concrete schemes of regulation aimed at coordinating conduct for the sake of the all-round well-being of the community, viz., the common good. Among the considerations a good legislator will always bear in mind is the fairness of the distribution of burdens and benefits attending any scheme of regulation. Because, on the natural-law account, all persons have a profound, inherent, and equal dignity, the interests (i.e. the well-being) of each and every person must be taken into account; and no one's interests may be unfairly or otherwise unreasonably favored or disfavored. The common good is not the utilitarian's "greatest good of the greatest number;" rather, it is the shared good of all, including the good of living in a community where the dignity and rights of all—including the right to have one's equal basic dignity respected—are honored in the exercise of public authority.

4 Natural Law and Legal Interpretation

Although the natural law sets the translation/derivation of laws as the task of the legislator—and it is only through his efforts that the natural law can become effective for the common good—it is important to note that the body of law created by the legislator is not itself the natural law. The natural law is in no sense a human creation. Positive law, by contrast, is created, posited, put in place—and not just implemented—by humans. This point is telling about the metaphysical status of the positive law. Following Aristotle, we might say that the positive law belongs to the order of "making" rather than the order of "doing." It is thus fitting that the positive law is subject to technical application and is analyzed by a sort of technical reasoning. Hence, law schools do not (or do not just) teach their students moral philosophy, but focus the attention of students on distinctive techniques of legal analysis, e.g. how to identify and understand legal sources, how to work with statutes, precedents, and with the (often necessarily) artificial definitions that characterize any complex system of law. Nonetheless, we must be careful to distinguish a different metaphysical order that attaches to the moral purpose of the law. It is in the order of "doing" (the order of free choice, practical reasoning, and morality) that we identify the need to create law for the sake of the common good. The legislator creates a cultural object, viz. the law—which is deliberately and reasonably subject to technical analysis—for a purpose that is moral and not merely technical.

That the law is a cultural object created for a moral purpose engenders much confusion about the role of moral philosophy in legal reasoning. For instance, a hotly-debated question in American constitutional interpretation is the scope and limits of the power of judges to invalidate legislation under certain allegedly vague or abstract constitutional provisions. Some constitutional theorists, such as Ronald Dworkin (1986), defend an expansive role for the judge by arguing that the conscientious judge must bring judgments of moral and political philosophy to bear in deciding hard cases. Others, such as Robert Bork (1990, 251–9), fear such a role for the judge and hold that a sound constitution—at any rate, the Constitution of the United States—does not give the judge any such role. They maintain that moral philosophy has little or no place in judging, at least within the American legal system. Where should natural-law theorists stand on this complex issue? Natural-law theory treats the role of judge as itself fundamentally a matter for *determinatio* and not for direct translation from the natural law. Accordingly, it does not presuppose that the judge enjoys (or should enjoy) as a matter of natural law a plenary authority to substitute his own understanding of the requirements of the natural law for the contrary understanding of the lawmaker in deciding cases at law. On the contrary, the rule of law (ordinarily understood as a necessary but insufficient condition for a just system of government) morally requires—obligates as a matter of natural law—the judge to respect the limits of his own authority as it has been allocated to him by way of an authoritative *determinatio*. This entails a hypothetical solution to the puzzle that confronts us: If the law of the judge's system constrains his law-creating power in the way that Judge Bork believes American fundamental law does, then he is obliged—legally and, presumptively, morally—to respect these constraints, even where his own understanding of natural justice deviates from that of the legislators (or constitution-makers and ratifiers) whose laws he must interpret and apply. Hence, we see that the question of what degree of law-creating power our law places in the hands of the judge rests on the antecedent of the solution, itself clearly a matter of positive law and not of natural law. At the same time, natural-law theorists such as Lon Fuller (1965), Hadley Arkes (1992), and Harry Jaffa (1993) have in different ways argued that the strict separation of legal from moral inquiry, even in the context of legal interpretation, is not possible. Positive law itself contains an "inner morality" or a "moral logic" which, if missing, marks the absence of anything that can fulfill even formally the purposes and functions of law.

5 NATURAL LAW, POSITIVE LAW, AND LEGAL INJUSTICE

Two questions naturally arise from the foregoing discussion: (1) Does the natural law require that every moral obligation be enforced by the positive law? (2) Are unjust "laws" actually laws?

All natural-law theorists believe that certain moral obligations (such as the obligations not to murder or rape or steal) must be enforced by law. And no natural-law theorist believes that every moral obligation must be enforced by law. As a practical matter, it would be impossible to enforce all moral obligations; and there are some moral obligations, such as the duty to be grateful to benefactors, that are in principle unenforceable. There are natural-law theorists (some of whom speak primarily in terms of "natural rights") who tend toward a more or less strict libertarianism on social or economic matters or both, and others who believe that, for the sake of the common good, law must play a robust part in establishing and maintaining (i) a moral ecology generally conducive to virtue and inhospitable to at least the grosser forms of vice; and (ii) robust institutions to encourage productivity, exchange, and distribution of economic goods and also to protect against unfair or inhuman indigence. As to (i), Aquinas defended a moderate position, noting with evident approval that human law does not seek to prohibit every vice, but mainly suppresses those forms of vice that tend to hurt others. But, he did not reject as intrinsically unjust laws designed precisely to protect public morals. As to (ii), he vigorously upholds private appropriation as well as public property, and is open to a measure of redistribution where the demands of justice and the common good require it.

Many critics of natural-law theory, including H. L. A. Hart (1961) and Hans Kelsen (1949), have seized upon the slogan, found in St. Augustine and echoed by Aquinas that "an unjust law is not (or seems not to be) a law," (ST 1–2, q. 96 a. 4). They claim that the proposition expressed in this slogan, which they regard as being at the heart of natural-law thinking, is utterly implausible. Either it sanctifies injustice by entailing that any law possessing validity by reference to the criteria of a positive system of law is morally good and therefore creates an obligation to obey, or it contradicts plain fact by suggesting that what everyone takes to be laws (i.e. rules possessing validity by reference to the criteria of a positive system of law) are in fact not laws if they are unjust. But this line of criticism is misguided, as will be evident from the following explication of the connection between morality and the law.

A careful reading of natural-law theorists through the ages shows that many of them drew a distinction between the moral validity and the systemic validity—the property of belonging to a legal system—of a law. For instance, in the *Summa Theologiae*, Aquinas treats the distinction between natural and civil law as a distinction within positive law, i.e. law considered in virtue of the social fact that it is humanly laid down. As such, proponents of natural law need have no difficulty accepting the central thesis of legal positivism, viz. that the existence and content of the law depends on social facts and not on its merits. Indeed, it is hard to see how one would otherwise make sense of the locution "an unjust *law*." Note, however, that accepting this thesis is independent of denying other modal connections between morality and the law. In particular, it is unlikely that we would be able to understand significant aspects of the law if we were unable to grasp moral reasons. This is so because the reasons people have for establishing and maintaining legal systems are often moral reasons that issue from normative practical deliberation that is aimed at the common good. Far from threatening the thesis of positivity, such explanatory connections are necessary to provide any fine-grained descriptive account of the law. How else would we home in on the focal cases of the law or appreciate the standards by which laws are judged to be defective qua laws (as we surely do, for example, in the case of laws embodying doctrines of racial superiority and inferiority)? A particularly fundamental connection in this vein is the way in which the normativity of practical reasoning and its directiveness towards human well-being and fulfillment explains the normativity and the action-guiding character of the law's authority. Thus, we see that while natural-law theory preserves a descriptive characterization of the law, it does not commit the fallacy of explaining prescriptive features by reference to nothing but descriptive features.

Having clarified some of the relations between law and morality on a natural-law account, we are now ready to defend the dictum that "an unjust law is not a law." It is certainly possible that an unjust law may at the same time be systemically valid and yet morally invalid; this is precisely the state of affairs that is being identified here. But, this fact alone—absent more specific information about the case at hand—does not necessarily militate either for or against one's obligation to obey the law. On the one hand, one's *prima facie* obligation to obey the law remains intact where its injustice is relatively minor and it would be unfair to others if one disregarded the law. On the other hand, a gravely unjust law may provide one with an overriding all-things-considered reason to disobey the law. The dictum, then, does not deny the significance of the law's positivity. Rather, it expresses the conditional nature of the complex relations that hold between moral obligations and the positive law (for a more detailed investigation of the relationship between natural law and positive law, see George 1999*b*).

The notion of an "obligation" is sometimes understood as being (in some sense or in some cases) correlative to the notion of a "right." How do natural-law theorists analyze the notion of rights? They hold that the concept of natural rights—or, to use a more contemporary idiom, human rights—can be used to express or analyze many of the requirements of practical reasonableness, especially in the political domain. As in the case of law, the explanatory justification of rights-claims, and the resolution of conflicting claims of right, may well require identifying values and principles that belong to the logical space of reasons. Finnis has pointed out that the modern grammar of rights bears witness to "the viewpoint of the 'other(s)' to whom something (including, *inter alia*, freedom of choice) is owed or due, and who would be wronged if denied that something" (Finnis 1980, 206). To better understand a natural-law account of such "rights talk," let us consider the manner in which Aquinas treats the notion of "jus" (that is, the classical precursor of our word "right"). Aquinas holds that the primary meaning of "jus" has to do with "the just thing in itself" or "the fair." In this context, he is clearly referring to certain acts, objects, and states of affairs. The secondary and derivative meaning of "jus" he gives is "the art by which one knows and determines what is just." For Aquinas, the principles and rules of this art simply are the law. Thus far, his notion seems to differ markedly from our notion of a right. But, equally prominently, he defines justice (including the justice of fulfilling one's legal obligations) precisely as giving to others "jus suum," their *right*, or translated with a little more freedom but no loss of accuracy, their *rights*. Thus, his notion of "jus" does not differ in conceptually essential ways from our general concept of "a right." Although some aspects of Aquinas' analysis of rights differ substantially from various contemporary theories (especially those that focus on the "choice" or "will" aspect of rights), it serves as an illuminating prototype for understanding more recent natural-law accounts.

6 NATURAL LAW AND RELIGION

Finally, the following remarks should make it clear that natural law is not—as is sometimes thought—a religious doctrine, though it is, to be sure, embraced by some religious traditions (most notably the Catholic Church). Most natural-law theorists (along with Aquinas) hold that the *ultimate* ground for human beings having moral duties (and rights) is that their specific nature as human persons is what it is, and is what it is by virtue of being created so, prior to any human choice or action. As discussed in an earlier section of this chapter, human nature is to be understood in terms of those essential features of our species that make it such that human flourishing is constituted by certain objective goods, as well as the capacity to pursue these goods in a practically reasonable way. There is nothing in any of this to suggest supernaturalism in either epistemology or ontology. As a theological matter, however, theorists in the natural-law tradition—not least pre-Christian thinkers such as Plato—typically hold that God directs people to their proper ends, not by instinct (as in the case of brute animals) but rather by their faculty of practical reason (understood by Aquinas and others as a sharing in a species of divine power by creatures fashioned by their Creator in his very image and likeness). Christian natural-law theorists interpret St. Paul's reference to a "law inscribed on the hearts even of the Gentiles, who do not have the law [revealed through Moses]" (Romans 2: 14–15) as alluding to a possible—at least in principle—mode of epistemic access to the moral law that is rational and unaided by revelation. According to St. Paul, such natural knowledge of the moral law is sufficient for an ultimate transcendent evaluation of a whole life—"divine judgment." Pope John Paul II further reaffirmed this when he taught in the encyclical letter *Veritatis Splendor* (1993) that the way of salvation open to those who do not have biblical faith is to act in conformity with the moral requirements of the natural law.

REFERENCES

AQUINAS, ST THOMAS 1993. *The Treatise on Law*: Summa Theologiae i, Qq. 90–7. Notre Dame, Ind.: University of Notre Dame Press.

ARKES, H. 1992. *Beyond the Constitution*. Princeton, NJ: Princeton University Press.

BORK, R. 1990. *The Tempting of America: The Political Seduction of the Law*. New York: Free Press.

CHANG, R. (ed.) 1997. *Incommensurability, Incomparability and Practical Reason*. Cambridge, Mass.: Harvard University Press.

DWORKIN, R. 1986. *Law's Empire*. Cambridge, Mass.: Harvard University Press.

FINNIS, J. 1980. *Natural Law and Natural Rights*. Oxford: Clarendon Press.

FULLER, L. 1965. *The Morality of Law*. New Haven, Conn.: Yale University Press.

GEORGE, R. 1999*a*. *In Defense of Natural Law*. Oxford: Clarendon Press.

—— 1999*b*. The natural law doctrine. In *Twenty-Five Year Commemoration to the Life of Hans Kelsen*, ed. G. O. Mazur. New York: Semenko Foundation.

HART, H. L. A. 1961. *The Concept of Law*. Oxford: Clarendon Press.

HITTINGER, R. 1987. *A Critique of the New Natural Law Theory*. South Bend, Ind.: University of Notre Dame Press.

JAFFA, H. 1993. *Original Intent and the Framers of the Constitution*. New York: Regnery.

JOHN PAUL II, POPE 1993. *Veritatis Splendor* (The splendor of truth: encyclical regarding certain fundamental questions of the Church's moral teaching), August 6.

KELSEN, H. 1949. The natural-law doctrine before the tribunal of science. *Western Political Quarterly*, 2: 481–513.

ODERBERG, D. 2004. The structure and content of the good. Pp. 127–65 in *Human Values: New Essays on Ethics and Natural Law*, ed. T. Chappell and D. S. Oderberg. London: Palgrave Macmillan.

ULLMANN-MARGALIT, E. 1977. *The Emergence of Norms*. Oxford: Clarendon Press.

WOLFE, C. 2006. *Natural Law Liberalism*. Cambridge: Cambridge University Press.

CHAPTER 23

RIGHTS IN LEGAL AND POLITICAL PHILOSOPHY

MATTHEW H. KRAMER

WITHIN legal philosophy, issues concerning rights are numerous and variegated but are classifiable into two broad categories: analytical matters and normative matters. Some theorists maintain that all of those issues are normative and that the distinction between the two categories is a difference in levels of concreteness or specificity. However, few if any theorists doubt the reality of the analytical/normative divide—even if that divide is thought by some to be a difference of degree rather than a difference of kind.

Analytical questions about legal rights concern matters such as the fundamental characteristics of those rights, the relationships between those rights and other legal positions such as liberties and powers and duties, and the basic functions of those rights. Normative questions about legal rights concern matters such as the proper distribution and contents of those rights, the appropriate procedures whereby those rights are to be established and conferred, and the drawbacks and benefits of organizing people's interaction in ways that are structured by rights. Whereas the analytical questions concerning legal rights are squarely within the domain of the philosophy of law, the normative questions belong at least as much to political philosophy as to jurisprudence. Distinctions between those two disciplines, and between the two categories of questions, are by no means always as clear-cut in practice as they are when stated at a high level of abstraction; nonetheless, a persistent awareness of those distinctions is of considerable value as an aid to clear thinking about legal rights.

The preceding paragraph's lists of issues relating to rights are far from exhaustive. Hence, this short chapter will have to be highly selective in what it covers. We shall look first at some analytical matters relating to the fundamental features and functions of legal rights, and we shall then turn to some normative debates relating to the suitable means by which the basic legal rights in a society are to be settled. Although the disputes surrounding these two sets of issues are only a small sampling of the controversies about rights in which legal and political philosophers have engaged, they should serve to illustrate the complexity and diversity of the field.

1 ANALYSES OF LEGAL RIGHTS

The most famous and influential analysis of legal rights ever propounded is that developed by the American jurist Wesley Hohfeld in the early twentieth century (Hohfeld 1923, 23–114; Kramer 1998, 7–60; Jones 1994, 12–25; Cruft 2004, 349–52; Edmundson 2004, ch. 5; Harel 2005, 192–3). Hohfeld maintained that the term "rights" is commonly applied to four distinct types of legal entitlements: claims, liberties, powers, and immunities. Only claims, he contended, are properly designated as "rights." That designation should be withheld from each of the other entitlements in strict juridical and philosophical discourse, in order to avert the confusion that ensues when the term is applied indiscriminately.

In Hohfeld's analytical framework, a legal right or claim is a position of legal protection for some person against the uncooperativeness or interference of somebody else. (The Hohfeldian analysis of rights can extend straightforwardly to rights held by groups or animals. However, for ease of exposition, the present discussion will concentrate on rights—and other entitlements—that are held by individual human beings.) Every right is held vis-à-vis some person, who is under a duty to abide by the terms of the right. Thus, for example, if John has a right against being punched in the face by Jim, then Jim is under a duty to abstain from punching John in the face. This relationship between rights and duties was designated by Hohfeld as one of "correlativity" or mutual entailment. Any person X holds a right vis-à-vis some other person Y, with a specified content z, if and only if Y owes a duty to X with that same content. Whereas a right is a position of protection, a duty is a position of requirement. Someone who bears a legal duty to ϕ is required to ϕ, in that he or she will be contravening the terms of some legal mandate if he or she does not ϕ. Such a contravention will render him or her liable to undergo penalties.

In Hohfeld's schema, a legal liberty consists in the absence of a legal duty. If Joe is legally at liberty to walk along Grange Road, then he is not under any legal duty to abstain from walking along Grange Road. More generally, someone who has a legal liberty to φ is under no legal duty not to φ. His or her φ-ing will not render him or her liable to undergo any legal penalties. The legal position correlative to a liberty is a no-right. (Though this hyphenated neologism by Hohfeld is rather awkward, no one has devised a handy alternative.) If Joe is legally at liberty vis-à-vis Andrew to walk down Grange Road, then Andrew has a legal no-right concerning Joe's walking down Grange Road. More idiomatically expressed, Andrew does not have any legal right against Joe's walking down Grange Road. Now, someone can have a legal liberty to φ without being able to φ. Moreover, even if the immediate cause of his or her inability to φ is somebody else's conduct, there may well have been no breach of a legal duty involved. Though some types of interference with people's exercises of legal liberties are almost always legally impermissible, many other types are not. Suppose, for example, that a large vehicle is temporarily obstructing Grange Road in such a way that no pedestrians can get past it. Joe almost certainly does not have a legal right against this sort of interference with his walking. Consequently, his ability to exercise his liberty to φ has been permissibly stymied by somebody else.

A legal power as understood by Hohfeld is an ability of a person to effect some change(s) in other people's legal relations or in the person's own legal relations. Correlative to any legal power is a legal liability: namely, one's susceptibility or exposure to the bringing about of a change in one's entitlements by oneself or by somebody else. If Helen has a legal power to endow George with some legal right, then he is liable to acquire that right through her exercise of her power. Now, whereas the contents of most rights and liberties are specified by reference to people's conduct—for example, the content of John's right against being punched in the face by Jim is specified by reference to any actual or potential act whereby Jim would punch John's face, and the content of Joe's liberty to walk down Grange Road is specified by reference to any actual or potential act whereby Joe would walk down that road—the contents of powers are specified by reference to other legal positions. For instance, the content of Helen's legal power to enter into a binding contract with George is specified by reference to her own entitlements and his entitlements. For this reason, powers (and immunities) are often designated as "higher-order" entitlements, while typical rights and liberties are designated as "first-order" entitlements.

A legal immunity, the final type of entitlement which Hohfeld delineated, is the negation of a liability. That is, it is an insusceptibility to some change in one's entitlements. Correlative to any legal immunity is a legal disability; whenever somebody is insusceptible to the effecting of a change in his or her entitlements by somebody else, the latter person is legally disabled from bringing about that change. Though immunities have not generally received as much attention from

philosophers as have the other Hohfeldian entitlements, they are of huge importance. Most (though not all) of the entitlements conferred by so-called bills of rights
are in fact immunities. For example, the First Amendment to the U.S. Constitution
protects various legal liberties by disabling Congress from restricting or removing
those liberties. Under that constitutional amendment, each person in the United
States enjoys an immunity vis-à-vis Congress concerning liberties such as freedom
of speech, freedom of assembly, free exercise of religion, and so forth. Moreover,
immunities are also of crucial importance because of their role in stabilizing other
legal entitlements. For instance, if John has a legal right against being punched
in the face by Jim, and if he has no immunities against being divested of that right
through countless elementary means (for example, through Jim's looking at him or
through Jim's utterance of any word in his presence), then John's right is hollowly
nominal rather than genuine. His right-against-being-punched-by-Jim in such
circumstances will offer him barely any greater legal protection than he would
enjoy if he altogether lacked a right with that content. Only because legal rights are
almost always accompanied by immunities against most types of divestiture, do
they provide solid legal protection against interference or uncooperativeness.

Hohfeld's analytical matrix—the many subtleties and intricacies of which cannot
be explored here—has undergone a variety of criticisms over the century since it
was put forward, but nearly all of those criticisms have been misconceived (Kramer
1998, 22–49, 101–11). The Hohfeldian framework has withstood the test of time, and
it is invoked widely by legal philosophers and political philosophers and moral
philosophers alike. Among its many virtues is its capacity to lend rigor and clarity
to the most prominent debate over the essential features of legal rights: the debate
between the Interest Theory (or Benefit Theory) and the Will Theory (or Choice
Theory). This debate, which dates back to the nineteenth century in various guises,
has in recent decades been pursued with the aid of the Hohfeldian categories
(Kramer 1998, 60–101; Simmonds 1998; Kramer 2001).

Legal and political philosophers have come up with many variants of each of the
two main theories named above, and it is impossible to capture all the different
versions of those theories in any pithy formulations. However, the gist of the
strongest versions of the Interest Theory of legal rights can be summarized in the
following two theses:

(I-1) Necessary though insufficient for the holding of some specified legal right by X
is that the right, when actual, protects some aspect of X's situation that is
normally in the interest of a human being or collectivity or nonhuman animal.

(I-2) Neither necessary nor sufficient for X's holding of some specified legal right is
that X is competent and authorized to demand or waive the enforcement of
the duty that is correlative to the right.

The gist of the strongest versions of the Will Theory of legal rights can be summarized in the following thesis:

(W-1) Both necessary and sufficient for X's holding of some specified legal right is that X is competent and authorized to demand or waive the enforcement of the duty that is correlative to the right.

The "X" variable in the formulations of the two theses of the Interest Theory is more wide-ranging than the corresponding variable in the formulation of the Will Theory's thesis. Whereas the latter variable ranges only over adult human beings whose rational faculties are broadly sound, the former variable ranges over all human beings (including dead and future human beings) and also over collectivities and many nonhuman animals.

On one point, the Interest Theory and Will Theory are agreed. That is, each theory accepts that the mere fact that a certain right would tend to benefit X is not sufficient for X's holding of that right. Also needed is the existence of some law—a statute, a judicial ruling, an administrative regulation, a contract, or some other authoritative legal norm—that bestows the specified right on X.

In all other respects, however, the two theories of legal rights clash directly. For example, whereas the Interest Theory maintains that the tendency of some specified type of legal right to benefit people or creatures like X is necessary for X's holding of a right of that type, the Will Theory rejects any such necessary condition. The disagreements between the two theories can be very roughly encapsulated along the following lines. For the Interest Theorists, the essence of a legal right consists in its tendency to safeguard some aspect of the well-being of its holder; for the Will Theorists, contrariwise, the essence of a legal right consists in its provision of opportunities for its holder to make significant choices. In the eyes of the Interest Theorists, the chief desideratum accruing to the holder of a legal right is security. In the eyes of the Will Theorists, the chief desideratum is control.

Note that the disagreements between the Interest Theorists and the Will Theorists can be stated precisely in Hohfeldian language. Interest Theorists join Hohfeld in regarding "right" and "claim" as interchangeable designations. As far as such theorists are concerned, a Hohfeldian claim will count as a legal right even if it is not accompanied by any other legal entitlements in the hands of the claim-holder (though it will be an emptily nominal right if it is not accompanied by immunities that protect it from being extinguished). By contrast, the Will Theorists contend that a legal claim has to be accompanied by a legal power of enforcement/waiver—in the hands of the claim-holder—if it is to count as a legal right. Some Will Theorists further submit that, if the claim and power are to qualify as a right, they must also be combined with a legal liberty to exercise the power. In other words, according to the Will Theory, X holds a legal right only if X holds a legal claim, a legal power of enforcing or waiving the duty correlative to that claim, and a legal liberty to exercise that power. All or most Will Theorists would also insist that each Hohfeldian element of a legal right must be accompanied by legal immunities that protect each element from being terminated. A Will-Theory right, then, is a complex of all four Hohfeldian entitlements.

Although Interest Theorists and Will Theorists concur when identifying many legal rights as such, the divergences between them concerning other legal rights are striking. Perhaps most noteworthy among those numerous divergences is the much greater expansiveness of the class of potential right-holders under the Interest Theory. For the Will Theory, as has been suggested, the only potential holders of legal rights are adult human beings with sound rational faculties. The Interest Theory significantly expands the class of potential right-holders. It extends that status to all human beings, to collectivities, and to some animals. In so doing, the Interest Theory confronts its proponents with the problem of delimiting the aforementioned class in order to keep it from encompassing too much (Kramer 2001, 29–57).

Consider, for example, a municipal ordinance that forbids people to walk on the grass in public parks. Does the "Keep Off the Grass" mandate confer legal rights on the lawns in those parks? Does it confer legal rights on the individual blades of grass? The principal purpose of such a mandate is to promote the flourishing of the grass by deterring people from trampling it with their feet. Consequently, Interest Theorists might appear to be obliged to identify the grass as the holder of the legal right that is correlative to each person's legal duty to abstain from walking thereon. They might likewise appear to be obliged to identify buildings as the holders of legal rights that are correlative to the legal duties imposed by antivandalism laws and other laws designed to protect the buildings against damage and deterioration. Many other similarly silly ascriptions of legal rights might seem to follow from the Interest Theory.

Fortunately, the tenets of the Interest Theory do not logically commit its proponents to such ridiculous ascriptions of legal rights. Although those ascriptions are not ruled out by the Interest Theory, they are not entailed by it, either. Before the Interest Theory can be applied, the class of potential right-holders has to be demarcated; the task of demarcating that class has to be undertaken on the basis of factors outside the Interest Theory itself. Such a task is a moral endeavor, albeit at a high level of abstraction. The best way of proceeding is to single out some subset of potential right-holders as paradigmatic, and to reflect on the morally pregnant similarities and dissimilarities between those paradigmatic occupants of the right-holding status and the sundry other candidates for that status. For all or most Interest Theorists, the paradigmatic class of potential right-holders is that of adult human beings with sound rational faculties. (For Will Theorists, of course, such human beings are the *only* potential right-holders.) Other potential holders of legal rights, such as children and lunatics and senile people and foetuses and animals and trees and dead people, are to be classified or not classified as potential right-holders by reference to the adult human beings just mentioned. Among the factors on which the relevant comparisons may focus are animateness; sentience; the capacity to experience pleasure and pain; the capacity to think, at least at a primitive level; the capacity to communicate and to receive communications; and the capacity to adjust one's behavior. Not all of these factors would be viewed by every Interest Theorist as dispositive or even relevant, but at least some of them would figure in virtually any effort to delimit the domain of potential holders of legal rights.

The Will Theorists, of course, would look askance at any such effort, since their theory begins by confining the range of potential right-holders to adult human beings who are sound of mind. Still, although their theory may be simpler in that respect, it encounters many other complexities and potential pitfalls. Not least among the disadvantages of the Will Theory is its inconsistency with the proposition that children and mentally infirm people are endowed with various legal rights. Also inconsistent with the Will Theory is the proposition that each person has a legal right (enforceable through criminal prosecutions) against being murdered. Yet another strange conclusion entailed by the Will Theory is that minimum-wage laws do not confer any legal rights upon workers, because the duties imposed by those laws on employers are not waivable.

In addition to generating a number of unappealing conclusions, the Will Theory gives rise to some vexing difficulties that have to be resolved if its central tenet is to be generally applicable. In particular, exponents of the theory will have to specify when a legal power to enforce/waive a legal duty is or is not held by someone. Suppose, for example, that each of two people must assent before a certain legal duty will be waived (or, alternatively, before it will be enforced). Does each of those people hold a legal right correlative to that duty, or does only one of them hold such a right, or does neither of them hold such a right? Similarly, suppose that somebody has the legal power to waive a certain duty simply by not exercising the legal power to enforce that duty, and suppose further that he is entirely ignorant of the fact that he possesses each of those powers. Does his unwitting exercise of his power of waiver qualify as an instance of the control that is associated by Will Theorists with legal rights? These and many other perplexing questions pose challenges for Will Theorists who hope to draw on the general theses of their doctrine in order to identify right-holders.

Fed up with the debates between Interest Theorists and Will Theorists, some philosophers have sophisticatedly attempted in recent years to develop analyses of rights that do not belong to either of those camps (Cruft 2004; Sreenivasan 2005; Wenar 2005). However, their efforts—though piquantly illuminating—have not met with success. What these philosophers have really shown is that both the Interest Theory and the Will Theory stand in need of refinement. That endeavor of refinement, rather than the blazing of an entirely new trail, appears to be the way ahead for philosophical expositions of the nature of legal rights (Kramer and Steiner 2007).

The cardinal values at stake in the debates between Interest Theorists and Will Theorists are theoretical–explanatory: clarity, precision, comprehensiveness, parsimony, adequacy, and so forth. However, those debates also carry certain political implications. On the one hand, the political implications are not as clear-cut as they might initially appear. For example, some philosophers have presumed that the

Interest/Will controversy is an offshoot of the broader controversies between utilitarians and Kantians (Wenar 2005, 224, 250–1); yet, although some Will Theorists have indeed been Kantians, hardly anyone among the main exponents of the Interest Theory is a utilitarian. On the other hand, notwithstanding that the political valences of the Interest Theory and Will Theory are less straightforward than has sometimes been supposed, the political prestige attaching to the language of "rights" ensures that the disputes between the proponents of those theories are vested with political significance. For instance, somebody who hopes to ascribe legal rights to animals or infants or senile people will have to rely explicitly or implicitly on some version of the Interest Theory. Although anyone can perfectly coherently espouse the Interest Theory while declining to attribute any legal rights to beings of the sorts just mentioned, most proponents of that theory embrace it partly because it allows such attributions. Many Interest Theorists favor those attributions on moral–political grounds. In response, most Will Theorists contend that the language of "rights" is devalued by ascriptions of legal rights to creatures devoid of moral agency. According to such a line of thinking, the language of "rights" will lose any distinctive role if it is not confined to people who are capable of deciding whether to assert their own entitlements. Legal rights themselves, so the Will Theorists warn, will lose their special esteem if the Interest Theorists' conception of them gains currency. On both sides of the Interest/Will dispute, then, many of the participants are motivated at least in part by considerations of political morality. Though the dispute is primarily a quest for philosophical clarification and precision and explanatory power, its normative undercurrents render it peculiarly worthy of attention from political philosophers as well as from legal philosophers.

2 By Whom Should Rights be Defined?

Normative questions about legal rights can be roughly divided into substantive concerns and procedural concerns. Among the many procedural issues relating to such rights, the most prominent and contentious is probably the matter of determining who should have a decisive say over the identification of people's legal rights and other legal entitlements. Controversy over that matter tends to be focused especially on the basic civil liberties and civil rights that are protected or conferred by so-called bills of rights in quite a few national constitutions. (As has already been noted, many of the legal entitlements bestowed by the provisions in constitutional bills of rights are immunities which protect the rights and liberties and powers that are explicitly mentioned in those provisions. In addition, however, a number of those rights and liberties and powers are themselves conferred—rather than merely presupposed—by some of the aforementioned provisions.)

Roughly stated, the chief point of contention in the debates under consideration here pertains to the competing merits of unelected officials (especially judges) and elected officials (especially legislators) as the people responsible for determining the contents of fundamental rights and liberties and powers. Such a thumbnail description of the controversy is misleading, however, for it suggests that the positions therein are neatly dichotomous. In fact, both at a theoretical level and at a practical institutional level, quite a number of positions have been adopted. At one end of the spectrum, largely associated with the American legal system, the courts are authorized to invalidate procedurally correct legislative enactments on substantive grounds of political morality enshrined in constitutional provisions. Unless the invalidating decisions are reversed by the courts themselves, they can only be overturned by constitutional amendments. At the other end of the spectrum, largely associated with the English legal system until recently, the courts are unauthorized to question the legal validity of procedurally correct legislative enactments. Between those two positions are sundry alternatives, some of which are instantiated in countries such as Canada and New Zealand (Waluchow 2005, 211 n. 7). For example, courts can be authorized to pronounce upon the constitutionality of legislative enactments, while not being authorized to decline to give effect to any enactments that have been deemed by them to be unconstitutional. Similarly, courts can be authorized to request the legislature to reconsider enactments that are of doubtful constitutionality; unless the legislature reaffirms its support for an impugned enactment within a certain span of time, the courts will subsequently treat that enactment as devoid of legal validity. Yet another possibility is that the courts are authorized to invalidate legislative enactments on grounds of unconstitutionality, but only for a limited period in each case. If an invalidated enactment has not been repealed by the relevant legislature within the set period, then the courts are obligated subsequently to give effect to it. These and many other possible arrangements lie between the American and English ends of the spectrum. Participants in the debates over judicial review versus legislative supremacy sometimes lose sight of the diversity of the options, but that diversity should be kept in mind by anyone seeking to gauge the cogency of the contributions to those debates.

Among the prominent philosophers who have written in favor of judicial prerogatives are David Brink, Thomas Christiano, Ronald Dworkin, and Wil Waluchow (Brink 1988; 2001; Christiano 2000; Dworkin 1996; Waluchow 2005), while Jeremy Waldron has been the most prominent philosopher to write strongly in favor of legislative supremacy (Waldron 1999). Their exchanges are focused not on specifying the legal rights which people should possess, but on identifying the forum within which the contents of those rights should be settled. With regard to the legal rights which people should possess, these philosophers do not disagree; or, at any rate, they *need* not disagree over that matter in order to take up opposing views on the procedural issue that divides them.

Some of the considerations that bear on the disputes between the critics and the supporters of judicial review are empirical matters that cannot be settled purely through philosophical reflection (Waluchow 2005, 244, 247). Those considerations relate, for example, to the competing virtues of legislative institutions and adjudicative institutions as guardians of the fundamental entitlements with which most bills of rights are concerned. Assessments of the relative strengths of those institutions will hinge partly on factors that can only be pinned down empirically. Such factors include, for example, the effects of judges' political disengagement on their decision-making processes, and the effects of various types of legislative representation on the responsiveness of legislators to the interests of disadvantaged minorities. Those and many other factors pertaining to the contingencies of officials' conduct cannot be known through abstract speculation detached from detailed empirical enquiries. Philosophers can offer intelligent and credible conjectures about such matters, and they can delineate the principal reasons for action that are likely to countervail one another as determinants of the officials' behavior. Nonetheless, important though such analyses are, they ultimately have to be supplemented by empirical studies. In regard to such issues, then, the collaboration of political philosophers and political scientists is essential.

Quite a few other aspects of the debates over judicial review do not center on any heavily empirical elements, however. They center instead on complex normative and philosophical questions. Indeed, one should be wary of laying great stress on the empirical dimension of the debates, since an emphasis on that dimension is tilted in favor of the advocates of judicial review. For those advocates, the location of the appropriate forum for the specification and protection of people's fundamental entitlements will hinge primarily on the reliability of the judiciary in accurately perceiving and vigilantly effectuating those entitlements. In other words, although the advocates of judicial review certainly do not altogether ignore noninstrumental concerns, they concentrate chiefly on the instrumental role of the courts. Critics of judicial review, by contrast, train their attention principally on the intrinsic importance of allowing people to decide highly controversial matters for themselves (through their elected representatives). Such critics do not disregard empirical findings and instrumental considerations entirely, of course, but they attach greater weight to the value of democratic self-realization. In their eyes, the cardinal question is not who will make the wisest decisions. Rather, the cardinal question is how decision-making power should be located in order to reflect the basic equality of human beings—including the basic equality between ordinary citizens and juridical officials. Given a situation in which people fiercely disagree with one another about the fundamental entitlements with which each of them is endowed, the only egalitarian resolution lies in the adoption of appropriate democratic procedures that enable each person to have a say. Attempts to enshrine those entitlements in constitutional bills of rights that subject legislative enactments to judicial review are misguided in two key respects. First, they elevate the opinions of judges and other legal officials to a position of unwarranted authority; those officials do not enjoy any special access to moral truth, and their views thus have no special claim to trump the numerous dissenting views of other people. Second, the attempts to use the devices of constitutional provisions and judicial review in order to safeguard people's basic entitlements wrongly presuppose that the general substance of those entitlements is not itself an object of intense controversy. Far from amounting to fixed points that can be taken as given, any formulations of those entitlements will be contestable contributions to debates which they will help to perpetuate. Once the image of constitutional provisions as fixed points beyond the reach of political controversy is abandoned as a mirage, however, we should wonder why unelected officials are authorized to invoke those provisions in order to invalidate the enactments of democratically elected legislatures. We should also wonder why important issues of political morality are mulled over not by direct reference to relevant moral principles, but by direct reference to formulations in a hoary document. For example, instead of worrying whether some activity counts as "speech" under the wording of the U.S. Constitution's First Amendment, we should concentrate on the moral considerations at stake in the regulation of communicative conduct. So, at least, the critics of the institution of judicial review maintain.

Supporters of that institution respond along several lines. They argue, for example, that democratic procedures do not carry any determinative moral weight unless the fundamental rights and liberties of citizens have been upheld. In the absence of adequate opportunities for citizens to express themselves on matters of political importance and to exchange views with their fellow citizens, their judgments about such matters will generally not be properly informed or properly responsive to others' concerns. They will not have had satisfactory opportunities to develop into autonomously reflective moral agents. Some citizens may nonetheless so develop, but the likelihood of any particular person's succeeding (or even endeavoring) is significantly impaired. Citizens' contributions to political processes will therefore be tainted. When preferences have been formed under oppressive conditions, democratic procedures for translating those preferences into political outcomes do not warrant the respect that would be paid to such procedures in circumstances where preferences have been allowed to evolve through deliberation and informed reflection. Hence, if those procedures are to merit esteem and deference, they will have to be subject to safeguards that restrict the range of legitimate outcomes. Such safeguards will ensure that the outcomes do not eliminate basic rights and liberties, and will thus ensure that people's inputs into the democratic procedures are endowed with moral weight. Although judicial review is not the only means by which such safeguards could be imposed, it is peculiarly suitable. It will conflict with legislative supremacy in the sense that legislatures will sometimes be thwarted from doing what they seek to do, but it will not conflict with the moral principle of legislative supremacy. That principle, which affirms the moral obligatoriness of governmental arrangements that enable people to determine the present and future course of their society through their elected representatives, does not countenance arrangements whereby people's participation in political processes is tarnished and skewed through the absence of basic rights or liberties. If the basic entitlements are satisfactorily in place, then the outcomes of democratic procedures that do not themselves threaten those entitlements are vested with great moral weight; however, that weight will have dissipated if basic rights or liberties are lacking. Hence, when legislative supremacy is understood as a veritable moral ideal, it is not at odds with the institution of judicial review. So long as the power of judicial review is exercised within its appropriate bounds, it upholds rather than transgresses that ideal.

Champions of judicial review also seek to rebut the critics' argument which points to serious disagreements among people and which concludes that the legislature should be favored over the judiciary as the forum for the identification of fundamental entitlements. Supporters of judicial review accept the premise of such an argument, but turn it against the argument's conclusion. Intense disagreements among people extend to the ways in which those disagreements are to be resolved. Judicial review is of course a controversial approach to the matter, but so is an abandonment of judicial review; indeed, at least in some countries, an abandonment of judicial review would be even more heatedly controversial than judicial review itself. Hence, when opponents of judicial review advert to widespread disagreements and maintain that the differences among people should be worked out legislatively, they are failing to note that their position is vulnerable to their own strictures. Recourse to the legislative arena would not constitute some neutral ground on which the various disputants can fight their battles. Rather, the advisability of any such recourse is one of the principal matters over which those battles are waged. Hence, simply from the observation that people disagree sharply over some of the basic entitlements that are typically conferred or presupposed by bills of rights, we cannot reach a conclusion concerning the apposite way of dealing with that disagreement. Any conclusion will itself be the object of ferocious disagreements, and will thus embody the problem which it purports to handle.

Theorists who support judicial review and constitutional bills of rights additionally point out, partly as an empirical matter, that such bills of rights can partake of great symbolic significance. Even if fundamental entitlements such as freedom of speech and freedom of assembly are continually re-understood, the explicit recognition of them in a bill of rights can bespeak and promote a society's respect for the dignity and autonomy of individuals. On the one hand, admittedly, a bill of rights is neither necessary nor sufficient for a society's adherence to liberal values. Despotic governments (such as that of the former Soviet Union) can cloak their heinous doings in fine-sounding constitutional provisions, while much worthier governments (such as that of the United Kingdom) can uphold liberal-democratic values admirably without relying on any such formal provisions. On the other hand, a bill of rights in a country that does cleave to liberal-democratic values can distill and reinforce those values. It can become a cynosure for the allegiance of citizens and can thus help to cement their commitment to liberal-democratic ideals. This symbolic role is perhaps most evident in the United States, where the Constitution (including its Amendments) is of huge importance in holding together a country with a vast territory and a heterogeneous population. In many other countries as well, however, the symbolic status of a bill of rights is important and salutary. For example, although the esteem enjoyed by the European Convention on Human Rights within Europe is not fully comparable to the veneration deservedly bestowed on the American Constitution within the United States, the Convention does play a saliently unifying role.

Finally, the supporters of constitutional bills of rights contend that such documents are not nearly as rigid and confining as the opponents have suggested. Although the broad moral principles articulated in bills of rights are determinate and constant in their implications, a society's understanding of those implications will evolve over time. A suitably flexible practice of successive reinterpretations can incorporate and reflect that evolution. Through the case-by-case method of judicial review, collective understandings of general principles can be fleshed out and (where appropriate) modified. Although the practitioners of such a method will address themselves to the formulations contained in relevant constitutional provisions, those formulations—if properly drafted—are expressive of basic values of political morality. Consequently, a focus on them is not a distraction from the real issues on which people should be concentrating; rather, such a focus will lie precisely on those issues.

Perhaps the upshot of the debates over bills of rights and judicial review is that, within liberal-democratic countries, the advisability of each of those institutions is to a large degree a context-specific matter. In a country such as the United States, where the institution of judicial review is long-standing and where it has often been salutary, the insecurities occasioned by its abandonment would outweigh any benefits of electoral accountability that might be gained. In a country such as the United Kingdom, by contrast, where there has been no explicit bill of rights (at least until very recently) and where liberal-democratic values have nonetheless flourished, the drawbacks of moving to a system of judicial review—drawbacks in the form of increased litigiousness and the evanescence of democratic accountability, for example—may well exceed the benefits thereof. Although many problems of political morality call for broadly uniform solutions across societies, many other such problems do not. The procedural problem of coming up with the proper mechanisms for concretely defining people's basic rights and liberties is probably best addressed by reference to the historical specificities of each liberal-democratic polity. Future work on that procedural problem should devote more attention to these context-specific considerations, which are closely related to some of the empirical matters that were broached earlier. Also deserving of far more attention in the future are the numerous intermediate possibilities between the American and English extremes (of judicial supremacy and legislative supremacy, respectively). In regard to those alternative possibilities, practice has run well ahead of theory. Political philosophers and legal philosophers need to reflect sustainedly on the merits of the many potential compromises between the conflicting values that are at stake in this much-contested area of constitutional design.

References

BRINK, D. 1988. Legal theory, legal interpretation, and judicial review. *Philosophy and Public Affairs*, 17: 105–48.

—— 2001. Legal interpretation, objectivity, and morality. Pp. 12–65 in *Objectivity in Law and Morals*, ed. B. Leiter. Cambridge: Cambridge University Press.

CHRISTIANO, T. 2000. Waldron on law and disagreement. *Law and Philosophy*, 19: 513–43.

CRUFT, R. 2004. Rights: beyond interest theory and will theory? *Law and Philosophy*, 23: 347–97.

DWORKIN, R. 1996. *Freedom's Law*. Cambridge, Mass.: Harvard University Press.

EDMUNDSON, W. 2004. *An Introduction to Rights*. Cambridge: Cambridge University Press.

HAREL, A. 2005. Theories of rights. Pp. 191–206 in *The Blackwell Guide to the Philosophy of Law and Legal Theory*, ed. M. Golding and W. Edmundson. Oxford: Blackwell.

HOHFELD, W. 1923. *Fundamental Legal Conceptions*. New Haven, Conn.: Yale University Press.

JONES, P. 1994. *Rights*. Basingstoke: Macmillan.

KRAMER, M. 1998. Rights without trimmings. Pp. 7–111 in *A Debate Over Rights*, M. H. Kramer, N. E. Simmonds, and H. Steiner. Oxford: Oxford University Press.

—— 2001. Getting rights right. Pp 28–95 in *Rights, Wrongs, and Responsibilities*, ed. M. H. Kramer. Basingstoke: Palgrave Macmillan.

—— and STEINER, H. 2007. Theories of rights: is there a third way? *Oxford Journal of Legal Studies*, 27: 281–310.

SIMMONDS, N. E. 1998. Rights at the cutting edge. Pp 113–232 in *A Debate Over, Rights*, M. H. Kramer, N. E. Simmonds, and H. Steiner. Oxford: Oxford University Press.

SREENIVASAN, G. 2005. A hybrid theory of claim rights. *Oxford Journal of Legal Studies*, 25: 257–74.

WALDRON, J. 1999. *Law and Disagreement*. Oxford: Oxford University Press.

WALUCHOW, W. 2005. Constitutions as living trees: an idiot defends. *Canadian Journal of Law and Jurisprudence*, 18: 7–47.

WENAR, L. 2005. The nature of rights. *Philosophy and Public Affairs*, 33: 223–52.

CHAPTER 24

FORMALISM: LEGAL, CONSTITUTIONAL, JUDICIAL

FREDERICK SCHAUER

FORMALISM is a style of adjudication and an approach to constitutional interpretation that is often caricatured (Schauer 1988) but rarely described, let alone defended. The goal of this chapter is to explain what formalism is, and then to present a version of it in its most favorable light, and then finally to show where it most defensibly exists and where it most defensibly might be employed.

1 FALSE FORMALISM: THE DENIAL OF CHOICE

The *Oxford English Dictionary* defines "formalism" as the "strict or excessive adherence to prescribed forms," and even this definition strongly suggests that to describe a person or some behavioral or decision-making approach as "formalist" is no compliment. And this common definition helps to explain why the ubiquitous uses of "formalism" or "formalist" in constitutional commentary are almost invariably pejorative. Indeed, for years the most common target for accusations of formalism has been the Supreme Court's 1905 decision in *Lochner v. New York*, and a close look at *Lochner* may help us to understand formalism at its worst.

The central question in *Lochner* was whether a New York statute setting the maximum working hours for employees at sixty per week unconstitutionally interfered with the argued right of employees (in this case, bakers) and their employers to contract on and for whatever conditions to which they might mutually agree. Writing for a majority of the Supreme Court, and over the famous dissent of Justice Holmes arguing that "the Fourteenth Amendment does not enact Mr. Herbert Spencer's Social Statics," Justice Peckham concluded that the Fourteenth Amendment's prohibition on state deprivation of "liberty... without due process of law" was violated by the New York maximum hours law. For Justice Peckham, the case turned on the meaning of the word "liberty," and thus hinged on the array of activities encompassed by that word. And on that particular question, Justice Peckham confidently concluded that the liberty to contract on whatever terms were agreed to by employer and employee was self-evidently an instantiation of the word "liberty." To Justice Peckham it was as if a person could not be deemed to have understood what the word "liberty" meant unless they understood that it applied to this form of unconstrained contracting, just as we might say that any person who understands what the word "dog" means understands that it applies to Australian Shepherds.

But of course there is a difference between the extension (in the philosophical sense) of the word "dog" and the extension of the word "liberty." Although the former admittedly has fuzzy edges (wolves and hyenas, for example), it remains the case that throughout most of the word's range of applications there is little doubt whether something is or is not a dog. But with the word "liberty," the situation is different. Not only are there contested cases of the word's application, but in fact *most* of the applications of the word are plausibly contestable, and throughout its range the application of the word hinges on contestable and contested political, economic, moral, cultural, and institutional considerations. One can say that an Australian Shepherd is a dog without having a view on the merits of Australian Shepherds, but to say that governmentally unconstrained contracting between employer and employee is an example of liberty is necessarily to take a position on a deeply contested political, moral, and economic question.

Seen from this vantage point, Justice Peckham's formalism consisted of the vice of treating a political question as if it were a linguistic one, and treating what was in reality a genuine choice by the Supreme Court as if the justices had no choice in the matter at all. This variety of formalism is a form of deception (Raz 1996), whether of one's self or others, and it is not at all clear that it is even very close to the dictionary definition of the word. If formalism is the strict adherence to prescribed form, and if in the context of constitutional interpretation the "prescribed form" is the plain (or, perhaps, historical, as will be discussed below) meaning of the words in the document, then Justice Peckham was not in fact strictly adhering to the plain meaning of the words, because the words either had no plain meaning in this context, or the words had a plain meaning that did not dictate an outcome with respect to this particular controversy. In either event, it may be important to distinguish the alleged vice of formalism with the alleged vice of deception, or lack of judicial candor, and here and elsewhere it may be that the epithetical use of the word "formalism" is much more about candor and deception and facing up to judicial choice and legal variability and indeterminacy than it is about adherence to prescribed forms.

2 "Real" Formalism and the Possibility of Interpretive Constraint

But if Justice Peckham's formalism is exposed as not a genuine formalism, then what is? And to answer that question we need to depart from vague constitutional provisions such as the "liberty" clause of the Fourteenth Amendment (and, for further examples, the prohibitions on "cruel and unusual punishments" in the Eighth Amendment and on "unreasonable" searches and seizures in the Fourth). So consider now the requirement in Article II that the President of the United States be, among other things, "thirty-five years of age," or the right, under the Seventh Amendment, to a trial by jury in any suit at common law in federal court in which the "amount in controversy" is "twenty dollars" or more, or the provision, again in Article II, that in the event of death or other unavailability to serve by both the President and the Vice-President, the presidency shall devolve to the "Speaker of the House of Representatives." Unlike words such as "liberty," "unusual," and "unreasonable," the words of these provisions, both individually and as components of larger phrases or sentences, are, like "dog," moderately precise, and are largely uncontestable and uncontested throughout most of their range. Admittedly, there might be vagueness around the edges, as there is potentially for *every* term in every language, in some cases, and there might be grounds for argument were someone to have been born while crossing the International Date Line exactly thirty-five years before his or her inauguration as president. Similarly, there might be in unusual cases some cause for disagreement about what a "dollar" was, or who the "Speaker of the House of Representatives" is, but such instances, although imaginable, are bizarre. In almost every real case, we know who is thirty-five years old and who is not, we know whether a suit is for more or less than twenty dollars, and we know whether the person stepping forward to take the oath of office as President following upon the death of the President and Vice-President is or is not at the time the Speaker of the House of Representatives.

Given this degree of common linguistic clarity, the more plausible definition of "formalism" is the practice (and perhaps it is not necessarily a vice, as we shall see) of following, as in the instances just described, the plain meaning of the words of the document in the face of plausible arguments for doing otherwise. These plausible arguments might take any of numerous forms. Perhaps most common is the argument that following the plain meaning of the words might produce outcomes inferior to those reached by making the best all-things-considered decisions in light of current pragmatic realities and in light of changes that have taken place in the relevant world since the words were first written. With respect to separation of powers, for example, the formalist position is the position that the tripartite division in the constitutional text, including the Constitution's requirements of presentment and bicameralism, is inviolable absent a constitutional amendment, even if there are powerful arguments that vast changes in the scope of government have made strict compliance with the constitutional forms profoundly impractical. So when the Supreme Court majority in *Immigration and Naturalization Service v. Chadha* invalidated the so-called one-house veto because it was incompatible with the bicameralism requirements of Article I, and over Justice White's strong dissent on the grounds of the necessities of modern government, the majority can be understood as having taking the formalist side as against Justice White's antiformalist argument from practical reality and pragmatic necessity.

Although the antiformalist position in *Chadha* was expressed by Justice White in terms of current pragmatic necessity, at other times the formalist argument for adhering strictly to the plain meaning of the words will be opposed to something else. Thus, it is sometimes the case that exactly following the words in a constitutional or legal text will look either illogical, or inconsistent with other or larger legal and constitutional values, or obsolete (Calabresi 1982), and once again the formalist is inclined to disregard those arguments from other values and adhere closely to the plain meaning, come what may. In the 1890 case of *Hans v. Louisiana* and the 1934 case of *Principality of Monaco v. Mississippi*, for example, the Supreme Court accepted the antiformalist argument that allowing people to sue their own states in federal courts but not allowing them to sue other states in federal courts would be inconsistent with the spirit of the Eleventh Amendment and inconsistent with larger federalism and federal courts values, even though the Eleventh Amendment's prohibition is expressly limited to citizen suits against "another" state. And when Justice Hugo Black insisted for years that the Fourteenth Amendment incorporated and thus applied to the states all and only the rights designated in the first eight amendments of the Bill of Rights (Massaro 1988), he followed the formalist position of taking the written words in their most obvious meaning as supreme, even in the face of political, pragmatic, and moral arguments for recognizing nonlisted rights—privacy being of course the most discussed—and even at times in the face of political, pragmatic, and moral arguments for refusing to incorporate and thus apply to the states under the Fourteenth Amendment those rights that might now seem substantially less fundamental and important, such as the rights to keep and bear arms under the Second Amendment, to prevent troops from being quartered in private homes under the Third Amendment, to have a trial by jury in civil cases according to the Seventh Amendment, to have criminal charges initially brought by a grand jury under part of the Fifth Amendment (Curtis 1986).

At times the position opposed to formalism draws not on practical reality but on ascertainable or likely original intent. To depart from constitutional law for an example, consider the Supreme Court's oft-criticized (Posner 1989) 1985 decision in *United States v. Locke*. Locke had filed with the federal Bureau of Land Management his petition to preserve his mining claim under a statute requiring that filings of this variety to be valid must have been submitted "prior to December 31" of the relevant year. Locke, however, submitted his petition *on* and not before December 31. Writing for the majority in rejecting Locke's argument, Justice Thurgood Marshall took the formalist position that "prior to December 31" meant before December 31, and he did so over the dissent of Justice Stevens, joined by Justices Powell and Brennan, who argued that Congress obviously *intended* that the filing deadline be "*on or* prior to December 31," and that sticking to the literal meaning of the words in the face of obvious legislative intent to the contrary was an unacceptable formalism.

Although the formalist position is most commonly expressed in terms of following the plain meaning of the words against pragmatic and other arguments to the contrary, the "form" that the formalist follows might at times be something else. So when constitutional theorist Raoul Berger argued (Berger 1997) that the unmistakable intention of the drafters and congressional approvers of the equal protection clause of the Fourteenth Amendment was to permit racially segregated public schools, he treated the evidence of original intent rather than the text as the formalist benchmark, and indeed was known often to argue that unmistakable evidence of original intent would trump even the contrary indications of constitutional text. Similarly, when Justice Scalia, who often explicitly defends his methods as formalistic (Scalia 1997), treats *historical* meaning (which is not the same, Justice Scalia properly insists, as the intentions of the drafters (Scalia 1997)) as inviolate, he departs from those formalists who would treat contemporary plain meaning with the highest respect, but both positions are formalist in taking a more-or-less clear legal indicator as prevailing against arguments from morality, politics, pragmatics, or anything else.

3 THE CASE FOR FORMALISM

With formalism having been explained, we can turn to its evaluation. And that evaluation is one that can now take on board the best case for formalism. That best case, then, is not that there is something about the nature of law or the nature of constitutional law that *requires* a formalist resolution of each of the controversies described in the previous section. After all, not only are numerous dimensions of law not formalist at all—consider the traditional use in family law custody disputes of the "best interests of the child" formulation, or the Sherman Antitrust Act's prohibition of "[a]ny contract, combination, or conspiracy... in restraint of trade or commerce," as well as Lon Fuller's well-known arguments (Fuller 1969) that much of law hinges far more on purpose than on plain meaning—but the same is also true of much of constitutional law. Even to write provisions such "free exercise of religion" or "unreasonable searches and seizures" or "due process of law" acknowledges that a formal approach may often be excessively resistant to the unexpected complexities of human existence and the inability of lawmakers to predict the future. Moreover, the fact that American constitutional law has survived an antiformal approach to the Eleventh Amendment and to the Contract Clause (*Keystone Bituminous Coal Association*, 1987) shows that formalism is not a necessary condition for a moderately well-functioning system of constitutional law and judicial review. Formalism is thus best seen as itself a product of systemic choice. If there is a case for formalism, it must be argued on normative grounds, just as, of course, the case for antiformalism must also be argued on normative grounds.

Although formalism has been defended as a matter of democratic theory (Scalia 1997), the principal and strongest normative argument for formalism is best understood as a species of the principal and strongest normative argument for rules (Schauer 1991). Although it is true that rigidly following the plain indications of legal or constitutional language will sometimes produce results worse than those that would be produced by ideal decision-makers not so rigidly constrained, not all decision-makers are ideal. The formalism with respect to unenumerated constitutional rights expressed by Justice Black in the incorporation cases, and then by Justice Stewart dissenting in *Griswold v. Connecticut*, appears politically and morally deficient to those who believe that the moral necessity of recognizing a right to privacy is more important than allegedly blind obeisance to the constitutional text. But for Justices Black and Stewart, among others, the power to depart from the most obvious meaning of the text was a power that could not so easily distinguish between the ideal and the nonideal, between the enlightened and the unenlightened, between those who are right and those who are wrong. The power to infuse the due process clause with substantive rights not enumerated in the document is thus not only the power to recognize the right to privacy, but also the power to recognize the virtually absolute freedom of contract recognized in *Lochner*, and the power to recognize a constitutional right to life for the unborn.

The same perspective applies to bulk of other formalist/antiformalist controversies. Justice White may have been correct in *Immigration and Naturalization Service v. Chadha* in concluding that following the strict requirements of the bicameralism provisions of the Constitution would stifle the ability of government to adapt itself to the realities of the modern bureaucratic state, but the question then turns to the one of who shall determine what the realistic requirements of the modern bureaucratic state are. The nation has survived the rewriting of the Eleventh Amendment to preclude federal court jurisdiction for suits against a citizen's own state as well as for suits against another state, but those who argue for formalism worry about the scope of a power in five justices to rewrite the plain words of the document whenever five justices think the actual language illogical or obsolete or inconsistent with higher or deeper legal or constitutional values. And although the nation has also survived the functional elimination of the contract clause, the formalists again worry about what either individual rights or governmental disabilities will be cast aside when their strict application no longer seems to five justices to be reasonable.

Justice Story observed in *Martin v. Hunter's Lessee* that "[i]t is always a doubtful course, to argue against the use or existence of a power, from the possibility of its abuse," and Justice Holmes echoed the same idea in *Panhandle Oil Co. v. Knox* when he quipped that the power to tax is not the power to destroy "while this Court sits." Behind these observations is a wise caution against overuse of the standard "who decides?" "where do you draw the line?" "thin end of the wedge," "the camel's nose is in the tent," "slippery slope" type of argument (Schauer 1985), an argument that frequently accompanies many of the traditional defenses of formalism. But although such arguments can be and frequently are exaggerated, they highlight the fact that the argument for formalism is ultimately a contextual and empirical one. The task will always be to decide whether in some decision-making environment, in which decision-makers with certain characteristics make decisions of a certain type, there are likely to be more (or more serious) errors when wise and enlightened decision-makers are prohibited by formalist expectations and incentives from reaching wise decisions than there are when misguided or mistaken decision-makers are freed from formalist restrictions to make what seem to *them* to be the best moral or political or pragmatic decisions.

When formulated in this way—and especially once we recognize that the debate about formalism in constitutional law is not only a debate about empowering or disempowering judges but is also one about empowering or disempowering presidents, generals, admirals, sergeants, cabinet officials, members of Congress, regulators, bureaucrats, city councilors, and police officers (Alexander and Schauer 1997)—the question of formalism is seen not only as an empirical (and predictive) one, but as an example of a familiar form of decision theory, the design of decision-making institutions under conditions of uncertainty. When the expected consequences of the errors of mistakenly disabling wise decision-makers from reaching wise decisions, in constitutional law and elsewhere, are greater than the expected errors of mistakenly enabling unwise decision-makers from reaching unwise decisions, then many of the arguments for a formal approach to adjudication and decision-making will and should be unavailing. But when the expected consequences of the errors of mistakenly empowering unwise or misguided or mistaken decision-makers are predicted to be more severe than the expected consequences of the errors of mistakenly tying the hands of genuinely wise decision-makers, including but not limited to genuinely wise judges and justices, then formalism will be seen to have its virtues.

The best evidence of this contingent, contextual, and political dimension of formalism may come from the political shifts in commentary about it. Formalism took on much of its bad odor among academics during a period when the widely revered Warren Court was taken (whether accurately or not is beside the point) to exemplify judicial power and judicial behavior. Freeing that Court, or freeing similarly inclined judges, from the shackles of literal interpretation of obsolete language was thought to be an admirable goal in the service of modern and largely progressive values. But as courts, including the Supreme Court, have moved rightward, and as the Bush administration after September 11, 2001, began to argue that *it* should not be shackled by statutory and constitutional language written in a pre-terrorist, pre-9/11, pre-Al Qaeda, and sometimes pre-nuclear age, arguments from the literal meaning of legal and constitutional texts have become more popular even among those who sneered at them several decades ago. This shift in attitude is neither surprising nor condemnable. It shows only that formalist interpretive norms are themselves a component of institutional design, and that institutional design has an unavoidable political component.

Formalism is thus best not understood as a constitutional necessity, because neither history nor sound principles of institutional design support that conclusion. But nor is it best understood as a jurisprudential mistake or a psychological infirmity. It is neither more nor less than one approach to the design of a decision-making institution staffed by real human beings with real human vices and virtues, and in constitutional law, as elsewhere, it will be seen as a sound approach at some times and in some places and an unsound one in other times and in other places. That this determination of soundness is inescapably political should come as little surprise.

References

ALEXANDER, L., and SCHAUER, F. 1997. On extra-judicial constitutional interpretation. *Harvard Law Review*, 110: 1359–87.

ATAYAH, P. S., and SUMMERS, R. S. 1987. *Form and Substance in Anglo-American Law*. Oxford: Clarendon Press.

BERGER, R. 1997. *Government by Judiciary: The Transformation of the Fourteenth Amendment*. Cambridge, Mass.: Harvard University Press.

CALABRESI, G. 1982. *A Common Law for the Age of Statutes*. Cambridge, Mass.: Harvard University Press.

Curtis, M. K. 1986. *No State Shall Abridge: The Fourteenth Amendment and the Bill of Rights*. Durham, NC: Duke University Press.

Fuller, L. L. 1969. *The Morality of Law*, rev. edn. New Haven, Conn.: Yale University Press.

Massaro, T. M. 1998. Reviving Hugo Black? The Court's "jot for jot" account of substantive due process. *New York University Law Review*, 73: 1086–121.

Posner, R. A. 1989. Legal formalism, legal realism, and the interpretation of statutes and the constitution. *Case Western Reserve Law Review*, 37: 179–217.

Raz, J. 1996. *Ethics in the Public Domain*. Oxford: Clarendon Press.

Scalia, A. 1997. *A Matter of Interpretation: Federal Courts and the Law*. Princeton, NJ: Princeton University Press.

Schauer, F. 1985. Slippery slopes. *Harvard Law Review*, 99: 361–82.

—— 1988. Formalism. *Yale Law Journal*, 97: 509–48.

—— 1991. *Playing by the Rules: A Philosophical Examination of Rule-Based Decision-Making in Law and in Life*. Oxford: Clarendon Press.

Strauss, D. 1996. Common law constitutional interpretation. *University of Chicago Law Review*, 63: 877–935.

Sunstein, C. R. 1999. Must formalism be defended empirically? *University of Chicago Law Review*, 66: 636–70.

Cases

Griswold v. Connecticut, 381 U.S. 479 (1965).

Hans v. Louisiana, 134 U.S. 1 (1890).

Immigration and Naturalization Service v. Chadha, 462 U.S. 919 (1983).

Keystone Bituminous Coal Association v. DeBenedictis, 480 U.S. 470 (1987).

Lochner v. New York, 198 U.S. 45 (1905).

Martin v. Hunter's Lessee, 14 U.S. (1 Wheat.) 304 (1986).

Panhandle Oil Co. v. Knox, 277 U.S. 218 (1928).

Principality of Monaco v. Mississippi, 292 U.S. 313 (1934).

United States v. Locke, 471 U.S. 84 (1985).

C H A P T E R 25

FEMINIST THEORY AND THE LAW

JUDITH A. BAER

AMERICAN feminists have identified law as an instrument of male supremacy since their first national gathering at Seneca Falls, New York in 1848. Modeled on the Declaration of Independence, the conference's Declaration of Sentiments and Resolutions listed the denial of the vote, marriage law that made a wife "civilly dead," and divorce law "wholly regardless of the happiness of women" among the "injuries and usurpations on the part of man toward woman, having in direct object the establishment of an absolute tyranny over her" that had inspired the meeting (Commager 1963, 315–16). Critiques of law thus became an important part of the early feminist movement, which succeeded in eradicating the most blatant examples of legal sexism. The signers of the Seneca Falls document were acting not only as social activists but also as legal theorists. Their thesis that law was designed by men for the purpose of dominating women is not far from the arguments of some contemporary feminist jurists.

Feminist scholarship was a product of the second stage of feminism that began in the late 1960s. This feminism arose from women's growing recognition that earlier victories had not succeeded in establishing equality between the sexes. Yet the successes of the contemporary feminist movement might not have happened without one of those early successes: the opening of higher education to women. Campuses proved to be as fertile a ground for the women's movement as they were for the civil rights, antiwar, and student movements. The enactment in 1972 of Title IX of the Education Amendments to the Civil Rights Act of 1964, which extended the prohibition of sex-based discrimination to educational institutions receiving federal funds, enhanced women's opportunities for postgraduate education and helped enlarge the pool of potential feminist scholars.

Twenty-first century Americans disagree on whether second-stage feminism has succeeded or failed, is alive, dead, or merely sleeping, is in stasis, crisis, or disarray, or is a positive or negative force in society. What no thoughtful and knowledgeable person can dispute is that contemporary feminism has had a profound and lasting impact on intellectual discourse. Many young scholars focused on gender in their research, pursuing the feminist goal "to question everything" (Wishik 1986, 64). These scholars and their successors continue to realize the revolutionary potential of feminist thought. "Feminist jurisprudence," as it came to be called, is law's equivalent of feminist history, feminist psychology, feminist philosophy, and their counterparts. Feminist jurisprudence has borrowed freely and fruitfully from these cognate disciplines. Not only has feminist jurisprudence become an integral part of legal theory, but it has also contributed to real-world legal change.

This is not to imply that feminist jurisprudence has become law's equivalent of the pink-collar ghetto. Women legal scholars have made significant contributions in subfields that do not emphasize gender issues. No woman law professor, whatever her personal opinions about feminism, need choose feminist jurisprudence as her specialty; nor does the subfield exclude men.

Scholars who agree on little else agree that

Feminists have tried to describe for the judiciary a theory of "special rights" for women which will fit the discrete, non-stereotypical, "real" differences between the sexes. And herein lies our mistake: We have let the debate become narrowed by accepting as correct those questions which seek to arrive at a definitive list of differences. In so doing, we have adopted the vocabulary, as well as the epistemology and political theory, of the law as it is.   (Scales 1986, 1375)

Feminist theorists who distrust "the law as it is" share three fundamental premises. First, conventional legal doctrines, developed by men in a society dominated by men, have a fundamental male bias even when they are ostensibly gender-neutral. Secondly, women's lives, for whatever reasons, are so different from men's lives that theory developed by men does not fit women's concrete reality. Finally, the development of feminist theory requires that women produce theory from their own experience and perspective.

1 THE PREMISE AND PRESENCE OF BIAS

Feminist jurists who accept the premise of male bias insist on "asking the woman question ... to identify the gender implications of rules and practices which might otherwise appear to be neutral or objective" (Bartlett 1990, 832). This approach to law is radical, if not revolutionary. Conventional jurisprudence requires that adjudication "must be genuinely principled, resting...on analysis and reasons quite transcending the immediate result that is achieved" (Wechsler 1961, 5). The "woman question," on the other hand, exemplifies the result-oriented jurisprudence that conventional jurisprudence condemns. Feminists are not the first to reject law's claim to neutrality. Marxists and the Critical Legal Studies movement had a head start, not to mention Anatole France: "The law, in its majestic equality, forbids the rich as well as the poor to sleep under bridges, to beg in the streets, and to steal bread" (2002 [1894], ch. 7). Feminist scholars do not accept as equal "a scheme that affords extensive protection to the right to bear arms or to sell violent pornography, but not to control our reproductive lives" (Rhode 1990, 633).

Whether or not male decision-makers conspire to disadvantage women, policies designed for men have fit badly with women's lives. Some scholars have concluded that modern equal protection doctrine on sexual equality has benefited men at least as much as women; for example, by requiring gender-neutral spousal support laws (*Orr v. Orr* 1979) but permitting interpretations of divorce and child custody law that disadvantage ex-wives (Baer 1999, ch. 4). A specialist in contract law asserted that the law's refusal to enforce mutual agreements in nonmarital relationships injured the women plaintiffs by denying them compensation for homemaking and childrearing duties (Dalton 1985). When the second stage of feminism began, the law still allowed the defense to inquire into an alleged rape victim's sexual history.

The problem here is not so much that men are dominant and women subordinate, as that reality is gendered. This generalization, of course, is a restatement of the second premise of feminist jurisprudence that I have identified. Feminist jurists who accept this premise differ widely in their explanations of how and why reality is gendered.

2 FEMINIST JURISPRUDENCE AND GENDERED REALITY

Feminist jurisprudence has not been satisfied with pointing out the historical fact that law was created by men (more precisely, by all-male elites) and citing current examples of legal bias in favor of men (vis-à-vis women). These two observations have scant analytical value without connections between them. Making these connections became the first major project of feminist jurisprudence. Much of this early scholarship centered around what came to be called the "difference debate" (Goldstein 1992). There have been two overlapping versions of this discourse.

The first version, *sameness versus difference,* is essentially a dispute about the meaning of gender equality under law. Wendy Williams (1981; 1984–5; 1991 [1982]) and Ruth Bader Ginsburg (1978) advocated across-the-board gender equality with no special treatment for women.[1] Williams does not distinguish between invidious and benign sex discrimination. Therefore, she regards special benefits for women workers like pregnancy and childbearing leaves as no better than the once common, but now overruled, mandatory maternity leaves and the "fetal protection" policies that excluded women from jobs : "If we can't have it both ways, we need to think carefully about which way we want to have it" (1991 [1982], 26). Some feminist legal scholars regard male supremacist laws as anomalies within an essentially gender-neutral system. Nadine Strossen, for example, rejects the antipornography policies favored by many feminists: "We adamantly oppose any effort to restrict sexual speech not only because it would violate our cherished First Amendment freedoms... but also because it would undermine our equality, our status, our dignity, and our autonomy" (1995, 14.)

Scholars like Williams and Strossen comprise a distinct but vocal minority among feminist legal scholars. Most feminist jurists insist that gender equality cannot be equated with sameness, but demands the recognition of and adaptation to gendered realities like the childbearing function and women's economic disadvantages vis-à-vis men (Finley 1986; Kay 1985; Littleton 1987; West 1997; J. Williams 2000). Antipornography feminist Catharine MacKinnon insists that the First Amendment is one of several "abstract rights" that "authorize the male experience of the world" (1989, 248); giving constitutional protection to pornography effectively gives its consumers and producers license to brutalize and degrade women (1993). These responses to prevailing legal doctrines are among many feminist critiques of legal principles that feminist jurists have produced.

The second version of the debate, confusingly labeled *difference versus dominance,* consists of conflicting explanations of the bad fit between law and women's lives. Participants in this discourse use various labels for the two schools of thought, but the labels establish similar dichotomies. "Difference" or "cultural" feminists posit character differences between men and women that make masculinist theories inherently biased against women, whereas "dominance" or "radical" feminists hold that these differences result from "the perspective that has been forced on women" (MacKinnon 1989, 52). Difference feminism has been heavily influenced by the pathbreaking work of psychologist Carol Gilligan. Her study of moral psychology, *In a Different Voice,* maintains that, while men's moral

---

[1] This characterization refers to Ruth Bader Ginsburg's work as a feminist lawyer and law professor, not to her performance on the U.S. Court of Appeals and the Supreme Court.

development emphasizes "rights and noninterference," women's psychology is "distinctive in its greater orientation toward relationships and interdependence," valuing "attachment" to others over "separation" from them (1982, 2, 151).

Robin West's application of these arguments to jurisprudence stresses physical gender differences. "Virtually all modern American legal theorists," she writes, accept "the 'separation thesis' of what it means to be a human being: a 'human being,' whatever else he is, is physically separate from all other human beings. . . . The cluster of claims that jointly constitute the 'separation thesis'. . . while usually true of men, are patently untrue of women." Why? Because women are "connected to life and to other human beings" through four "critical material experiences:" menstruation, hetero-sexual penetration, pregnancy, and breastfeeding (1988, 1–3). In an effort to unite care and justice, West criticizes conventional law for failing both "to protect and nurture the connections that sustain and enlarge women's lives" and "to intervene in those private and intimate "connections" that damage and injure" women (1997, 14).

The terms "connection thesis" and "ethic of care" have become familiar feminist concepts. The association of justice with men and care with women resonates with the observable reality that, other things being equal, women perform more caring activity than men do. The notion of a female ethic of care and nurturance may also appeal to those who share the belief of some nineteenth-century feminists that women are morally superior to men. Finally, the possibility of incorporating care into the concept of justice appeals to many feminist jurists who remain reluctant to associate care with women (Behuniak 1999). Linda McClain similarly argues for "recognizing and promoting care as a public value" that "should inform public deliberation about the meaning of personal responsibility and about the interplay of personal and public responsibility for social reproduction" and emphasizes "the indispensable role of care in fostering persons' capacities for democratic and personal self-government" (2001, 1730).

However, difference feminism and its focus on care have met with pervasive and persuasive criticism.[2] West's explanation for gender difference now seems simplis-tic, exclusionary, and illogical. While the experiences West mentions are unique to women, they are not common to all women; nor does she explain how these experiences connect women to people who are not connected to them. Feminist theorists have made no better case for gender differences than did pre-feminist or outright antifeminist theorists. Difference feminism reads too much like old arguments justifying male supremacy, such as the Supreme Court's opinion in *Muller v. Oregon* (1908), to gain universal feminist acceptance.

West distinguishes herself and other "cultural feminists" from radical feminists like MacKinnon. For cultural feminists, "the important difference between men and women is that women have children and men don't;" for radical feminists, "the

---

[2] Baer (1999, 40–56); MacKinnon (1987, 38–9); Schneider (1986, 589–652); Williams (1992, 41–98).

important difference between men and women is that women get fucked and men fuck" (West 1988, 13). West does not exaggerate or distort. MacKinnon reasons by analogy with Karl Marx's theory of class struggle to argue that law is designed to facilitate men's sexual access to women: "Sexuality is to feminism what work is to marxism: that which is most one's own, yet most taken away" (1989, 3). Radical feminism accepts the premise of the Seneca Falls delegates that men designed the legal system to establish, or at least to preserve, male power.

MacKinnon is by far the most controversial of today's feminist jurists. Her extreme position has provoked considerable feminist criticism.[3] She has been accused both of vilifying men by depicting them as sexual predators and of denigrating women by denying their agency and autonomy (Baer 1999, 58–62). But the fact that a position is extreme does not prove it wrong. The evidence MacKinnon advances to support her thesis includes the fact that the Supreme Court recognized rights to birth control and abortion years before it invalidated fetal protection policies barring women from well-paying blue collar jobs (1989, 190, 226). As we shall see, criticism has not persuaded MacKinnon to moderate either tone or content (MacKinnon; 2005; 2006; Jeffries 2006).

Feminist jurists need not believe that law's *purpose* is to entrench male supremacy in order to argue that law's *effect* is to do this. "Situation jurisprudence" (Baer 1999, 55–8), like radical feminism, emphasizes male power and privilege: men get to choose what they want to do, and women are stuck with whatever is left. Feminist jurists have subjected many ostensibly neutral legal concepts to reexamination and fresh analysis in terms of "what we know as women" (Baer 1999). One example of this type of analysis is Joan Williams's explanation of women's competitive disadvantage in employment. Williams argues that the workplace presumes an "ideal worker" whose other responsibilities take second place to the job. Since most women have greater domestic responsibilities, devoting more time and energy to care for households and dependents than do men, women are less likely to fit the description of the ideal worker (2000).

The difference versus dominance controversy continues in the face of—and in response to—the extensive and trenchant criticism both schools of thought have received. Ironically, feminist jurisprudence has received extensive criticism for doing what it criticizes conventional scholarship for doing. Authors who have asserted that conventional jurisprudence says "person" when it means "man" have been criticized by minority feminists for saying "woman" and meaning "woman plus modifiers:" Caucasian, heterosexual, Western woman.

Angela Harris criticizes both cultural and radical feminists for "gender essentialism—the notion that a unitary, 'essential' woman's experience can be isolated and described" (1990, 604). Harris maintains that race is a central component of the identities of women of color (in Europe and North America, at least), but not

---

[3] Cornell (1991, 139); Feminist Discourse (1985, 75); Smart (1989, 77).

of white women. Therefore, the "critical material experiences" of cultural feminism and the sexual objectification of women emphasized by radical feminists are mediated through a racial context for some women but not for others. "Mainstream" Western feminist jurisprudence has encountered similar challenges made on behalf of lesbians (Brown 1990; Cain 1990) and disabled women (Baer 1999, 34–7).

No consensus exists within feminist theory about the possibility of locating a common essential identity. The same is true of the difference debate in its various manifestations. No one is forced to take sides, and many scholars choose to concentrate on other issues. But legal scholars on both sides and on neither side of these debates embrace the final premise of feminist jurisprudence: the need for scholarship based on women's experience.

3 FEMINIST LEGAL REASONING

The feminist premise of male bias applies as much to methods as to theories. Feminist critiques of method from the humanities and social sciences have influenced legal scholarship. These critiques have characterized conventional methodology as dichotomous, oppositional, hierarchical, abstract, reason-based, and emphasizing separation. Feminist alternative methodology is an intuitive/emotional, holistic, noninvasive, concrete, and contextualized epistemology of connection (Baer 1999, 72–8). It emphasizes "the distinctive features of women's situation in a gender-stratified society" (Harding 1990, 119), "the world of concrete particulars" to which many women are relegated (Smith 1990, 19), and "women's ways of knowing" (Belenky et al. 1986) which applies Gilligan's work to epistemology. For MacKinnon, women's way of knowing is through consciousness raising, "the process through which contemporary radical feminist analysis of the situation of women has been shaped and shared" (1989, 84). Consciousness raising is inductive, not deductive. It came out of the women's discussion groups that flourished in the early years of second-wave feminism. Many members of the founding generation of feminist theory participated in these groups. Feminist jurisprudence has applied the insights of feminist epistemology to the study of legal methods. One scholar credited Gilligan's book with helping her understand "why I felt so uncomfortable in law school" (Feminist Discourse 1985, 1). A study of law students at an Ivy League university discovered that women tended to do less well than comparable men and theorized that the Socratic method of law school teaching is an ordeal for many women (Guinier et al. 1997).

Feminist scholars' distinctions between male and female methods work better in theory than in practice. They do not stand up when applied to concrete, particular analysis of everyday legal decision-making. "Legal feeling" (Baer 1999, 84) is as omnipresent as "maternal thinking" (Ruddick 1989); any follower of the Supreme Court knows that appeals to emotion are a common feature of the justices' opinions. Consciousness raising combines inductive and deductive reasoning. The different versions of the process that developed encouraged participants to use concepts from feminist theory in interpreting their shared experiences. The case for a distinctively *female* epistemology has yet to be made. But *feminist* epistemology has had significant impact on theory and jurisprudence.

4 FROM THE "WOMAN QUESTION" TO "WOMAN ANSWERS"

Feminist jurisprudence has not stopped with pointing out ways in which existing law is hostile to women's interests. Scholars have shown remarkable creativity in devising woman-oriented alternative theories. Twenty-first-century legal doctrine shows the influence of feminist inquiry, although the nexus between cause and effect is neither clear nor simple. Some feminist contributions to legal theory have yet to be put into practice, but others have gained judicial recognition. Since a single article cannot present all of this scholarship, this chapter will focus on three important and controversial innovations. The first two of these, Martha Fineman's work on family law and Catharine MacKinnon's analysis of the law of rape, address specific gendered legal issues. The third innovation is the concept of the "reasonable woman," a theoretical construct that has guided decision-making in both civil and criminal law.

Martha Fineman's studies of family law reflected widespread feminist recognition that gender neutrality might not entail sexual equality. The gradual progression of American family law in the nineteenth and twentieth centuries from traditional male supremacy toward gender-neutrality coincided with, reinforced, and was reinforced by feminism. One major twentieth-century innovation that had some initial feminist support was "no-fault divorce." The old adversarial process of ending a marriage was replaced by "dissolution" premised on the assumption that the decision was mutual. At the same time, maternal preference in child custody decisions yielded to a neutral "best interests of the child" rule. But by the 1980s, feminists had discovered that the new rules often resulted in support judgments that impoverished women and children and custody arrangements that ignored or denied the fact that the mother was almost always the children's primary caregiver (Baer 2002, 134–58.)

Fineman perceives a connection between this legal undervaluing of the mother–child bond and widespread (though decreasing) public hostility toward single and lesbian mothers. She argues that family law presupposed a "sexual family" consisting of mother, father, and children. "The neutered mother" becomes one of two parents and only half of the parental unit; "marriage and family" become inseparable. Fineman proposes abolishing marriage as a legal category and replacing sex with care and dependency as the crucial family bond. This "newly redefined legal category of family" would include "inevitable dependents along with their caregivers. The caregiving family would... be entitled to special, preferred treatment by the state" (1995, 231). While the caregivers could be either women or men, the result of such a change would benefit many women and might even encourage caregiving behavior among men. It would also derail the controversy over same-sex marriage.

Catharine MacKinnon's most recent publications (2005; 2006) apply her theory of law's maleness to criminal law. The radical transformation in the law of sexual assault in the past thirty years represents a landmark victory for second-stage feminism. The modesty of the complainant's appearance, the prudence of her behavior, and the details of her sexual history are no longer before the court. Nonetheless, MacKinnon asserts, "The law of rape protects rapists and is written from their point of view to guarantee impunity for most rapes." She means, she tells an interviewer, "not that all the people who wrote [the law] were rapists, but that they are a member of the group who do." The interviewer continues:

She thinks consent in rape cases should be irrelevant. Women are so unfree that even if a woman is shown to have given consent to sex, that should never be enough to secure an acquittal. Why? "My view is that when there is force or substantially coercive circumstances between the parties, individual consent is beside the point; that if someone is forced into sex, that ought to be enough." (Jeffries 2006)

The classic definition of rape is "carnal knowledge of a woman forcibly *and* (not *or*) without her consent." The prosecution must prove both the presence of force and the absence of consent. Nowhere does the law distinguish between a woman's consent (the commonest defense to a rape charge) and her submission (Schulhofer 1998, ch. 13). The elimination of consent as a defense to sexual assault, like the elimination of legal marriage, would be a change so extraordinary that it brings to mind Ruth Rosen's metaphor for the effects of feminism: "the world split open" (2000). Neither change is even remotely likely in the foreseeable future. But less dramatic developments are bringing both family law and criminal law closer to feminist ideals. Many jurisdictions have adopted a "primary caregiver" preference in child custody cases (Baer 2002, 156–8.) And rape law is showing the effect of the "reasonable woman" standard.

The concept of the "reasonable person" is a crucial component in the law of torts, and is found also in criminal law. To be at fault is to fail to act as a reasonable person would in the same situation. For example, a defendant in a negligence suit can avoid damages by showing by a preponderance of the evidence either that he or she had acted with the "reasonable care" that the context required or by showing that the plaintiff's failure to exercise reasonable care constituted contributory negligence (although statutes have limited or abolished this defense in some instances).

The "reasonable person" concept originated in the common law notion of the "reasonable man." Does the substitution render the concept gender-neutral? Kim Lane Scheppele (2004) insists that in many situations the reasonable person is in effect the reasonable man. She proposes a "reasonable woman" standard for gender-related civil and criminal law.

The question of whether "reasonable person" means "reasonable man" is integral to the criminal law of rape and domestic violence. Scheppele discusses the case of a man who got a ride home with a woman he had just met. He invited her to his apartment and snatched her car keys; she followed him because she feared being out on the street in an unfamiliar neighborhood. After much disagreement within the state appellate courts, the Maryland Supreme Court finally upheld the conviction (*State v. Rusk* 1981.) "Women don't sexualize situations as quickly as men do," Scheppele comments, "and so they may be slower to recognize danger in the first place" (2004, 460).

One tort, sexual harassment, is classified as sex discrimination by Title VII of the Civil Rights Act of 1964 (*Meritor v. Vinson* 1986). The law recognizes two types of sexual harassment. *Quid pro quo* harassment can be summarized as, "sleep with me or I'll fire you," or "sleep with me and I'll promote you." A more common form of harassment is the creation of a hostile environment in the workplace. The typical sexual harassment plaintiff is female; the typical defendant is male.

From the defendant's standpoint, the dispositive question in a hostile environment case becomes whether his behavior was that of a reasonable person or whether the plaintiff's reaction to his behavior met that standard. A defendant who pursues a co-worker after she has rebuffed him may well believe that his behavior is reasonable; after all, he is acting out the plot of countless works of fiction, drama, and comedy, and may even have seen this courtship technique work in real life. A defendant who tells dirty jokes or makes suggestive remarks may argue that the woman who complains about this behavior is unreasonably sensitive. Approaching sexual harassment litigation from these standpoints has the effect of authorizing men's experiences and attitudes.

But suppose that we approach hostile environment cases from the plaintiff's perspective. From her standpoint, the crucial questions become whether a reasonable woman would find the plaintiff's behavior objectionable or threatening enough to create a hostile environment in the workplace. The same year Scheppele published her article, an appellate court ruled in favor of a plaintiff who received unwelcome advances: "We adopt the perspective of a reasonable woman because a sex-blind reasonable person standard tends to be male-biased and tends to systematically ignore the experiences of women" (*Ellison v. Brady* 1991, 880). Plaintiffs who were asked "go to the Holiday Inn" to discuss pay raises, told to fish in the supervisor's pockets for change, or subjected to epithets like "dumb fucking broad" prevailed in court.

The reasonable woman doctrine is not without its defects and dangers. First, the concept conflates gender and role. As women gain power in the workplace, it is likely that some of them, like some men, will abuse their power. Asking what a reasonable woman might do will only confuse matters if aggressor and victim are the same sex (*Oncale v Sundowner Offshore Services* 1998). Might the law better adopt a "reasonable victim" rule? A second difficulty with a reasonable woman rule is that it could do real damage if applied in areas of law that are not overtly gender-sensitive. A jury in a negligence case, for example, might expect more caution and foresight from a reasonable woman than from her male counterpart. And think how a concept like "reasonable mother" might influence a jury!

The concept of the reasonable person has found yet another home in the area of domestic violence. Elizabeth Schneider (2000) points out that legal discourse has long been stuck on the question of why the battered women did not end the abusive relationship. This emphasis on the supposed unreasonableness of the victim's behavior became a rationale for law enforcement agencies and prosecutors to trivialize violence against women much as they once trivialized sexual assault. Feminist scholars have had much success in changing this official behavior.

Lenore Walker, a feminist sociologist, tried to explain victims' toleration of abuse by developing a concept that she labeled the "battered woman syndrome" (1984). Walker argued that long-term abuse taught many women that they were helpless to change their situation. Activists for battered women object that "the image that the concept of learned helplessness conveys . . . is one of passivity and lack of agency" (Downs 1966, 155–7). But the battered woman syndrome defense has won some acquittals in trials of women who kill their abusers, even though it applies the idea of learned helplessness to someone who has displayed considerable aggression. "BWS" is an uneasy combination of two defenses against homicide charges: self-defense and diminished capacity. These two doctrines do not mesh well; the first presumes a rational actor while the latter presumes the opposite.

Efforts to protect oneself, others, or property have long been recognized as exculpating factors in criminal cases. A defendant in a homicide case who pleads self-defense must convince the factfinder(s) that he or she perceived imminent danger of serious injury or death and that this belief was reasonable in the circumstances. Juries have been known to give defendants considerable latitude under the imminent danger rule. For instance, both a Louisiana man who fatally shot a stranger who rang his doorbell by mistake and a Virginia man who killed a neighbor who swore at him during an altercation were acquitted (Baer 1999, 207–8).

Feminists have questioned whether the imminent danger requirement is as neutral as it looks. The rule would lead us to expect a woman whose husband had abused her on numerous occasions to be acquitted after she killed him during yet another violent episode, even without recourse to the battered woman syndrome. When a woman was nonetheless convicted in such a case, the New Jersey Supreme Court ordered a new trial that would include testimony about BWS to show that that the woman could reasonably fear that her life was in danger during the episode (*State v. Kelly* 1984). But most battered women who kill do not do so during an attack, and BWS may have particular significance in those types of cases. The imminent danger rule that can respond so flexibly to male experience is unresponsive to their experience. The battered woman syndrome defense asks factfinders to consider whether the defendant might overreact to a perceived threat because her reasoning capacity is defective, in the same way that an insanity plea makes comparable demands. But, while the logic of the BWS defense is problematic, the defense has entered the legal repertoire.

5 CONCLUSION

Legal doctrine emerges from human experience. When women were excluded from the legal enterprise, man-made law was just that. The growth of feminist jurisprudence has coincided with the entry of more and more women into the lawyering, lawmaking, and judging professions. Relying on women's experiences and perspectives, the first generation of feminist legal scholars has progressed from incisive analyses of law's male bias to the creation of new doctrines, new methods, and new proposals for reform. Activists in the legal arena have changed law to embody these concepts, as the "reasonable person" example shows. The two groups of scholars and activists overlap, and each activity has infiltrated and influenced the other. But law's male bias remains pervasive enough to make legal doctrine more responsive to men's claims than to women's. Both scholars and practitioners know that much work remains for later generations to do.

REFERENCES

BAER, J. A. 1999. *Our Lives before the Law: Constructing a Feminist Jurisprudence.* Princeton, NJ: Princeton: University Press.
—— 2002. *Women in American Law: The Struggle for Equality from the New Deal to the Present.* New York: Holmes and Meier.
BARTLETT, K. T. 1990. Feminist legal methods. *Harvard Law Review,* 103: 829–88.
BEHUNIAK, S. M. 1999. *A Caring Jurisprudence: Listening to Patients at the Supreme Court.* Lanham, Md.: Rowman and Littlefield.
BELENKY, M., CLINCHY, B., GOLDBERGER, N., and TARULE, J. 1986. *Women's Ways of Knowing: The Development of Self, Voice, and Mind.* New York: Basic Books.
BROWN, W. 1990. Consciousness razing. *Nation,* 250: 61–4.

CAIN, P. A. 1991. Feminist jurisprudence: grounding the theories. Pp. 263–80 in *Feminist Legal Theory: Readings in Law and Gender*, ed. K. T. Bartlett and R. Kennedy. Boulder Colo.: Westview.

COMMAGER, H. S. (ed.) 1963. *Documents in American History*, 7th edn. New York: Appleton-Century-Crofts.

CORNELL, D. 1991. *Beyond Accommodation: Ethical Feminism, Deconstruction, and the Law*. New York: Routledge, Chapman and Hall.

DALTON, C. 1985. An essay in the deconstruction of contract doctrine. *Yale Law Journal*, 94: 997–1114.

DOWNS, D. A. 1996. *More Than Victims: Battered Women, the Syndrome Society, and the Law*. Chicago: University of Chicago Press.

DUBOIS, E. C., DUNLAP, M. C., GILLIGAN, C. J., MACKINNON, C. A., MARCUS, I., MENKEL-MEADOW, C. J., and SPIEGELMAN, P. J. Feminist discourse, moral values, and the law: a conversation. 1985. *Buffalo Law Review*, 34: 11–87.

FEMINIST DISCOURSE 1985. Moral values, and the law—a conversation. *Buffalo Law Review*, 55: 11–87.

FINEMAN, M. A. 1995. *The Neutered Mother, the Sexual Family, and other Twentieth Century Tragedies*. New York: Routledge.

FINLEY, L. 1986. Transcending equality theory: a way out of the maternity and the workplace debate. *Columbia Law Review*, 86: 1118–82.

FRANCE, A. 2002 [1894]. *The Red Lily*. Rockville, Md.: Wildside Press.

GILLIGAN, C. 1982. *In a Different Voice*. Cambridge, Mass.: Harvard University Press.

GINSBURG, R. B. 1978. Sex equality and the Constitution. *Tulane Law Review*, 52: 451–3.

GOLDSTEIN, L. F. (ed.) 1992. *Feminist Jurisprudence: The Difference Debate*. Lanham, Md: Rowman and Littlefield.

GUINIER, L., FINE, M., and BALIN, J. 1997. *Becoming Gentlemen: Women's Experience at One Ivy League Law School*. Boston: Beacon Press.

HARDING, S. 1990. *Whose Science? Whose Knowledge? Thinking from Women's Lives*. Ithaca, NY: Cornell University Press.

HARRIS, A. 1990. Race and essentialism in feminist legal theory. *Stanford Law Review*, 42: 581–616.

JEFFRIES, S. 2006. Are women human? Interview with Catharine MacKinnon. *Guardian*, April 12.

KAY, H. H. 1985. Equality and difference: the case of pregnancy. *Berkeley Women's Law Journal*, 1: 1–38.

LITTLETON, C. A. 1987. Reconstructing sexual equality. *California Law Review*, 75: 1279–337.

MACKINNON, C. A. 1987. *Feminism Unmodified*. Cambridge, Mass.: Harvard University Press.

—— 1989. *Toward a Feminist Theory of the State*. Cambridge, Mass.: Harvard University Press.

—— 1993. *Only Words*. Cambridge, Mass.: Harvard University Press.

—— 2005. *Women's Lives, Men's Laws*. Cambridge, Mass.: Harvard University Press.

—— 2006. *Are Women Human?* Cambridge, Mass.: Harvard University Press.

MCCLAIN, L. C. 2001. Care as a public value: linking responsibility, resources, and republicanism. *Chicago-Kent Law Review*, 76: 1673–731.

RHODE, D. L. 1990. Feminist critical theories. *Stanford Law Review*, 42: 617–38.

ROSEN, R. 2000. *The World Split Open: How the Modern Women's Movement Changed America*. New York: Penguin.

RUDDICK, S. 1989. *Maternal Thinking: Toward a Politics of Peace*. New York: Ballantine.

SCALES, A. M. 1986. The emergence of feminist jurisprudence: an essay. *Yale Law Journal*, 95: 1373–403.

SCHEPPELE, K. L. 2004. The reasonable woman. Pp. 456–460 in *Philosophy of Law*, 7th edn., ed. J. Feinberg and J. Coleman. Belmont, Calif.: Wadsworth/Thomson Learning; originally published 1991.

SCHNEIDER, E. 1986. The dialectic of rights and politics: peresspectives from the women's movement. *New York University Law Review*, 61: 589–615.

—— 2000. *Battered Women and Feminist Lawmaking*. New Haven, Conn.: Yale University Press.

SCHULHOFER, S. J. 1998. *Unwanted Sex: The Culture of Intimidation and the Failure of Law*. Cambridge, Mass.: Harvard University Press.

SMART, C. 1989. *Feminism and the Power of Law*. New York: Routledge.

SMITH, D. E. 1990. *The Conceptual Practices of Power: A Feminist Sociology of Knowledge*. Boston: Northeastern University Press.

STROSSEN, N. 1995. *Defending Pornography: Free Speech, Sex, and the Fight for Women's Rights*. New York: Anchor.

TRONTO, J. C. *Moral Boundaries: A Political Argument for an Ethic of Care*. New York: Routledge.

WALKER, L. 1984. *The Battered Woman Syndrome*. New York: Springer.

WECHSLER, H. 1961. *Principles, Politics, and Fundamental Law*. Cambridge, Mass.: Harvard University Press.

WEST, R. 1997. *Caring for Justice*. New York: New York University Press.

—— 1988. Jurisprudence and gender. *University of Chicago Law Review*, 55: 1–72.

WILLIAMS, J. 1992. Deconstructing gender. Pp. 41–98 in *Feminist Jurisprudence: The Difference Debate*, ed. L. F. Goldstein. Lanham, Md.: Rowman and Littlefield.

—— 2000. *Unbending Gender: Why Family and Work Conflict and What To Do about It*. New York: Oxford University Press.

WILLIAMS, W. 1981. Firing the woman to protect the fetus: the reconciliation of fetal protection with equal opportunity goals under Title VII. *Georgetown Law Journal*, 69: 641–704.

—— 1991 [1982]. The equality crisis: some reflections on culture, courts, and feminism. Pp. 15–34 in *Feminist Legal Theory*, ed. K. T. Bartlett and R. Kennedy. Boulder, Colo.: Westview.

—— 1984–5. Equality's riddle: pregnancy and equal treatment. *New York University Review of Law and Social Change*, 13: 325–80.

WISHIK, H. R. 1986. To question everything: the inquiries of feminist jurisprudence. *Berkeley Women's Law Journal*, 1: 64–77.

CASES

Ellison v. Brady. 1991. 924 F. 2d 872.

Meritor Savings Bank v. Vinson. 1986. 477 U.S. 57.

Muller v. Oregon. 1908. 208 U.S. 412.

Oncale v Sundowner Offshore Services. 1998. 523 U.S. 75.

Orr v. Orr. 1979. 440 U.S. 268.

State of Maryland v. Goldberg. 1978. 41 Md. App. 58.

State v. Kelly. 1984. 478 A.2d 364.

State v. Rusk. 1981. 424 A.2d 720.

CHAPTER 26

THE RACIAL SUBJECT IN LEGAL THEORY

SHEILA R. FOSTER

R. A. LENHARDT

As W. E. B. DuBois predicted over a century ago, the problem of the twentieth century would be that of "the color-line" (DuBois 1996 [1903]). Race was a defining feature of American society for most of that century, and remains so today. Curiously, however, neither the subject of race, nor its racialized subjects, played a significant role in legal scholarship for most of the last century. It was not until relatively recently that legal scholars began seriously to engage matters of race and the experiences of people of color in the United States. Exactly why, and when, race moved from being virtually nonexistent to occupying the margins and finally assuming a prominent place in legal scholarship is the subject of this chapter.

In the pages that follow, we map the ways in which scholars have addressed the problem of race in legal theory. In offering this critical overview, we hope to provide context for ongoing debates about the persistence of racial inequality in American society, to underscore the limitations of earlier theories about race and discrimination, and, ultimately, to highlight the promise of engagement with "traditional" legal theories for understanding the nature of racial subordination.

Section 1 explores legal discourse on race in the years preceding the ground-breaking U.S. Supreme Court decision, *Brown v. Board of Education*. Section 2 considers *Brown* and its aftermath, tracking the origins of the legal process theory embraced by scholars during the 1950s, 1960s, and 1970s, as they tried to make sense of judicial intervention in matters of race. Section 3 discusses the rejection of legal process theory that characterized the 1980s and 1990s, and charts the emergence of Critical Race Theory (CRT), a movement that, for the first time in American legal history, made race and the experiences of racial minorities the subject of legitimate intellectual discourse. It highlights CRT's core insights about the function and operation of race and the grounds for its rejection of liberal orthodoxy.

Finally, Section 4 looks at recent scholarly work in the area of race. It documents, among other things, the multiple understandings of race, identity, and subordination now prevalent in many legal communities. Further, this section identifies fruitful areas of future study regarding the place of race in American law.

1 RACE IN THE PRE-*BROWN* ERA

In reflecting on the period of racial unrest and repression that marked Reconstruction and attended the rise of the Jim Crow era, one race commentator remarked, "The slave went free; stood a brief moment in the sun; then moved back again toward slavery" (Du Bois 1992 [1935]). American law reviews developed in the wake of the often violent events that effectuated this sharp reversal in the prospects of newly freed Blacks. Yet the pages of these new journals (the first law review started in the 1850s) appear to have done little to document or analyze the emergence of race-based legislation and legal subordination that undercut efforts to extend the full benefits of citizenship to Blacks. Nor did they bring any significant focus to the long period of slavery that preceded it.

There appear to be surprisingly few turn-of-the-century law review articles that discussed matters of race in any meaningful way. The articles that did address race either explicitly or implicitly endorsed Jim Crow measures or portrayed the subjects of that regime in decidedly negative, almost cartoonish, terms. A 1900 *North Carolina Law Journal* article, for example, emphasized the "criminality" and "bestial bent" of Black men in advocating castration for imagined sexual offenses against white women (Baker 1900 [1901]).

One can only speculate about the reasons for the glaring absence of real analyses of race-based laws during this early period in legal scholarship. Certainly the sense that Blacks and other racial minorities did not merit serious attention as legal subjects explains part of the oversight. So too does the fact that many infringements on black citizenship were essentially uncontested at this time, having been facilitated by local violence, legislative acquiescence, and judicial constraints placed on the interpretation of postwar constitutional amendments.

Race does not make a significant, substantive appearance in legal scholarship until well into the twentieth century. Not until the 1920s and 1930s did scholars expand the range of race-related topics addressed in law reviews—discussing topics such as interracial marriage, jury exclusion, racially restrictive real estate covenants, and the public school segregation of Black and Japanese citizens. Scholarship in this period also began questioning the constitutionality of and judicial approach to racially discriminatory laws (Note 1939).

As social science understandings of race advanced, and as minorities entered the legal academy, more challenges were brought to discriminatory laws which in turn prompted greater interest in the topic among legal scholars. In particular, lawsuits challenging racially restrictive covenants—"a kind of litigation which," as University of Chicago Law School Professor William Ming, the first black faculty member at a majority white law school, noted "had attracted as much public attention and interest as any in our history"—became popular topics in law reviews (Ming 1949). Scholars also began to examine closely statutory definitions of race and to critically explore issues of race-based barriers to citizenship, particularly after the internment of Japanese-Americans and the Supreme Court's decision in *Korematsu v. United States* sustaining the constitutionality of that internment.

The 1950s brought still more change, with articles on segregation in public education becoming more common as the litigation masterminded by Charles Hamilton Houston and former Justice Thurgood Marshall moved closer to the decision in *Brown*. Even with these developments, however, race was not a dominant issue in legal theory. Nor were the actual lives and experiences of African-Americans and other racial minorities featured prominently in law reviews. This would not come until after *Brown* and the desegregation decisions that fundamentally altered our notions of racial equality and the role of courts in effectuating it.

2 RACE AND LEGAL PROCESS THEORY

The post-*Brown* era, particularly the three decades following the decision, thrust race onto the agenda of legal theory. The Court's ruling that racial segregation was unconstitutional, first in education and later in other areas of life, made race the subject of conflicting theories about constitutional interpretation and the role of courts in mediating racial harm. These debates turned, ultimately, not so much on African-Americans themselves, but rather race served as a mechanism for addressing larger, unresolved structural issues of constitutional law.

Herbert Wechsler's famous critique of *Brown* as resting on something other than "neutral principles" embodied the way in which issues of race complicated the relationship between legislatures and the courts. Wechsler's (1959) critique was a direct outgrowth of the "legal process" school that dominated legal theory in the 1940s and 1950s. A rejection of legal realism, legal process theory adhered to the notion of "institutional settlement"—the idea that institutions possessed unique competencies for specific types of decisions. Courts were best at "reasoned elaboration" of existing legal principles, whereas legislatures were deemed the ultimate authority on policy and substantive decision-making (Hart and Sacks 1958).

The Court's increasing attention to racial equality in cases such as *Brown* provoked a spirited debate about how legitimately courts could determine the social status of citizens. On one side, there were those, like Wechsler, who took a *subject neutral* position on judicial intervention in the widespread, legalized racial inequality that marked our nation pre-*Brown*. Under this view, the discrimination cases coming before the Court were less about race per se—its subjects or racialized harm—than about courts' role in choosing between competing social claims, a task presumptively left to legislatures.

On the other side were those who took a *subject specific* view and saw no institutional problem with the Court choosing between group claims in the name of constitutional principles of equality, principles clearly within its domain. A third, moderate position was one aligned ultimately with process theorists in its desire to keep the court above politics by limiting its role to correcting legislative defects, such as racial prejudice, while maintaining as a core concern the subject(s) of legislative policy-making. This latter view became the dominant strain of constitutional theory in the arena of racial equality and continues to reign today (Foster 1998).

Wechsler, the main adherent of the subject neutral position, believed that if there was any constitutional dimension to the issue in *Brown*, it lay not in notions of equality but in the denial by the state of the freedom of Blacks to associate with Whites and concomitantly in the freedom of Whites not to associate with Blacks. Wechsler could not find any neutral principle that could settle whether the Constitution speaks to which of these associational rights should prevail. In effect, the choice was one that fell squarely with the legislature. Courts should defer to this choice unless they could articulate a principled decision, one neutral in applicability to "whatever interest, group, or person may assert the claim." *Brown's* focus on the racial subject—e.g, how segregation affected Blacks—seemed to, according to Wechsler, call into question the Court's legitimacy by implying that "courts are free to function as a naked power organ."

Several theorists defended the *Brown* Court's reasoning as neutral or nonpolitical, and as legitimately subject-specific in its focus on the racial group most affected by segregation. Alexander Bickel, for instance, failed to see the non-neutrality in ruling that a legislative choice in favor of a freedom not to associate is forbidden, "when the consequence of such a choice is to place one of the groups of which our society is constituted in a position of permanent, humiliating inferiority; when the consequence beyond that is to foster in the whites, by authority of the state, ... feelings of racial superiority" (Bickel 1962). Charles Black similarly opined that the "freedom" of Whites to disassociate (publicly) from Blacks must by necessity be curtailed by the Fourteenth Amendment's "directive of equality" which "forbids the disadvantaging of the [black] race by law" (Black 1959). Louis Pollak famously redrafted the *Brown* opinion to emphasize that the "decisive constitutional principles relevant [in the case] are in a vital sense not neutral" and that the history of the Reconstruction amendments was concerned specifically with the emancipation of Blacks. His redrafted opinion recognized that governmentally imposed segregation carries "a stigma directed at the segregated group" and that this form of injury is one against which the Constitution protects (Pollak 1959).

The focus on racial harm and its subjects, however, soon faded as *Brown* gained acceptance and a "second generation" of process theorists, led by John Ely, emerged (Flagg 1994). These theorists embraced a new institutional justification for more active judicial review by focusing on the ways in which the legislative process itself broke down as a result of prejudice and other democratic process defects. According to Ely's theory of judicial review, racial classifications of the type at issue in *Brown* were "suspect" because they disadvantage groups known to be the object of widespread prejudice and that others (e.g. those controlling the legislative process) might wish to injure (Ely 1980). Judicial review could justifiably cleanse the political process of the effects of majoritarian prejudice on minorities by striking down legislation infected by such prejudice. Second generation process theory helped lay the groundwork for a shift in constitutional theory and jurisprudence from "harm to classification talk," motivated in part by a desire to "[insulate] a body of constitutional law concerned with status harm inflicted on blacks against unremitting charges of jurisprudential illegitimacy" (Siegel 2004).

Critical legal scholar Alan Freeman's groundbreaking critique of the Court's antidiscrimination jurisprudence sought to reorient the racial subject in legal theory. Antidiscrimination law, he argued, was hopelessly embedded in a "perpetrator" perspective which focused almost exclusively on identifying bad actors and their illicit motivations. The prohibition on racial classifications, and its normative commitment to "colorblindness," is ultimately indifferent to the "victim[s]" of discrimination and the conditions under which they live. The colorblindness norm had become a "reified abstraction," according to Freeman, "divorced from its origins in the actuality of black–white relations." In other words, "[b]y abstracting racial discrimination into a myth world where all problems of race or ethnicity are fungible, the color-blind theory turns around and denies concrete demands of blacks" (Freeman 1978).

Placing the racial subject at the forefront of antidiscrimination law generally, and constitutional theory more particularly, became the *sine qua non* of an emerging critical legal theory on race. Moving the racial subject from the margins to the center of legal theory was a task that would eventually also extend to the legal academy as well. It was a notable, and ironic, fact that prior to the 1980s the conversation about the place of race in legal theory was one dominated by white men, despite the contributions of scholars of color writing about antidiscrimination law and theory (Delgado 1984). Critical race theory was thus born out of a need for a more explicit subject-consciousness in legal theory, as well as in the halls of the legal academy.

3 RACE AS THE SUBJECT IN LEGAL THEORY

Neither enamored with nor persuaded of the utility of legal process in the area of race, an emerging cadre of scholars began to make race itself their subject in the last two decades of the twentieth century. Beginning in the 1980s, these scholars sought to move questions of substantive racial justice from the sidelines of academic discussions to the center ring of intellectual debate. In doing so, they have grappled not only with the broad topic of racial discrimination and subordination but also with the groups and individuals whose lives are most directly affected by legal theory and judicial decisions such as *Brown*.

3.1 Race, Civil Rights, and Critical Legal Studies

Initial unease about the singular focus on legal process found its strongest voice in the early 1980s among scholars who identified with the Critical Legal Studies (CLS) movement. Comprised of a loosely organized group of legal scholars who embraced a radical political viewpoint, CLS scholars or "crits" embraced three basic "commitments" about the nature and limitations of the law: law is political rather than neutral; necessarily "indeterminate" and manipuable; and highly contingent on the context in which it is rendered (Tushnet 1991; Jones 2002). At its core, CLS saw the deconstruction of the liberal principles reflected in the widespread fealty to legal process as its primary objective.

Sympathetic to Alan Freeman's critique of traditional antidiscrimination law, scholars committed to addressing issues of race in the law endorsed the broad contours of the CLS program and, in many cases, utilized it in developing independent critiques of civil rights doctrine and strategy. For example, in one influential article, Professor Derrick Bell criticized traditional civil rights doctrine and strategy by characterizing blind attorney commitment to school desegregation efforts as a barrier to client representation and the attainment of substantive educational relief sought by African-American parents (Bell 1976). Similarly, in *"Brown v. Board of Education and the Interest Convergence Dilemma,"* Bell interrogated popular beliefs about the overall promise of civil rights law, arguing, *inter alia*, that "the interest of blacks in achieving racial equality will be accommodated only when it converges with the interests of whites" (Bell 1980).

Other scholars of color likewise began to question, as Professor Richard Delgado provocatively framed the issue, whether CLS, at its intellectual core, "ha[d] what minorities want[ed]" (Delgado 1987). Disheartened by the realization that CLS lacked a significant focus on race—after more than a decade of critical engagement with liberal legal norms—these scholars of color crowned CLS's primarily white, male adherents "Imperial Scholars" (Delgado 1984). They took CLS and others to task for excluding minority scholars and for an unwillingness to employ critical analyses on problems of racial hierarchy and subordination.

Scholars of color questioned a number of CLS's specific tenets as detrimental to a scholarly agenda concerned with racial liberation—including CLS's rejection of the transformative possibilities inherent in incremental progress for racial minorities; its embrace of demeaning notions that minorities possessed a "false consciousness" that led them to celebrate "liberal orthodoxy" even as it effectuated their subjugation; and its rejection of legal rights as an indeterminate, political conception designed ultimately to placate rather than to emancipate (Delgado 1987; Jones 2002).

As CLS's limitations became apparent, race scholars began to move concerns about the CLS agenda to the pages of law reviews, turning a critical lens on the purportedly critical stance CLS had assumed with respect to law, power, and hierarchy. Through scholarship that emphasized narrative and a commitment to highlighting the real-life experiences of racial minorities "at the bottom" (Matsuda 1987), scholars such as Richard Delgado, Mari Matsuda, and Patricia Williams sought to underscore the importance of formal rights for racial minorities hoping to secure substantive race reform and to illustrate the limitations of several other CLS principles (Harris 1994). The relationship between CLS and race scholars withered under this focused inquiry. What resulted was the birth of new intellectual movement with strong commitments to critical engagement, oppositional discourse, and race.

3.2 The Emergence of Critical Race Theory

Some debate exists about the precise origins of this new movement, which would become known in the legal academy as Critical Race Theory or CRT. Whether one locates CRT's birth in the student-led protests of majority-white law faculties that marked institutions such as Harvard Law School in the 1980s and 1990s, or describes it as a more organic genesis of themes and commitments refined through conferences and path-breaking scholarship, it is clear that by the early 1990s CRT was on its way to becoming a fixture in the legal academy, with scholars of color securing positions within elite law schools and writing with a CRT affiliation in mind.

The late 1980s and early 1990s were marked by a concerted effort to develop initial critiques of CLS and traditional civil rights law, and to respond to criticisms by more mainstream scholars of color like Professor Randall Kennedy. Kennedy shared CRT's commitment to explicating the legal origins of the American dilemma of race, but took issue with the rejection of the methods of traditional legal scholarship as a vehicle for conducting this inquiry (Jones 2002).

Foundational articles such as Bell's *Racial Realism* and Kimberele Crenshaw's *Race, Reform, and Retrenchment: Transformation and Legitimation in Antidiscrimination Law* confronted both the elusiveness of the change promised by civil rights law and the limitations of the post-Warren Court's focus on intentionality in assessing racial discrimination (Bell 1992; Crenshaw 1988). These works also further interrogated the CLS position on the futility of legal rights.

Significantly, CRT managed during this period also to establish itself as much more than a mere reaction to other theories and programs. Even as they took a critical view, "race crits" introduced new, affirmative theories and strategies designed better to explain the persistence of American racism and inequality, and to counter what many lamented as a judicial retreat from racial justice. For example, Professor Charles Lawrence, drawing on the work of social scientists, advanced the notion of unconscious racism. This cognitive psychology-based theory operated as a rebuke of the doctrinal embrace of intentionality reflected in cases such as *Washington v. Davis*, highlighting its failure to capture indicia of racism in social decision-making (Lawrence 1987). Likewise, Professor Crenshaw, employing feminist insights, developed the concept of intersectionality—a framework that rejected the unidimensionality of prevailing views of race and urged that factors such as gender be incorporated into understandings of racial identity (Crenshaw 1989).

The production of theories such as these made it possible for CRT to begin to address previously unexplored themes and problems. Familiar discussions of CLS and civil rights precedents such as *Brown* were soon joined by theoretical articles addressing topics that ranged from racial essentialism in feminist legal theory to the political geography of race in legal theory. Likewise, CRT scholars drafted articles analyzing the racial aspects of debates on issues as diverse as affirmative action, race-based jury nullification, the incarceration of drug-addicted mothers, and racial profiling.

To be sure, CRT—whose loose organization made it difficult to say precisely who fell within or outside its borders—in no way occupied the entire field of legal scholarship devoted to race. African-American scholars such as Kennedy and Stephen Carter, who had made clear that they did not ascribe to CRT's specific program, also introduced searing appraisals of the scope and impact of American racism. This said, CRT had, by the end of the 1990s, become the dominant vehicle for exploring and understanding the operation of race in law.

3.3 Critical Race Theory: Developing New Tools and Strategies

CRT had successfully challenged the notion that "legal rationality could identify and eradicate the biases of race-consciousness in social decision-making" and had established itself as an oppositional voice for racial liberation within the legal academy (Crenshaw 1988). It had also provided what no previous scholarly enterprise had: a focus on the people directly affected by American racism.

This "reconstruction" of race and racial subjects as a legitimate focus of intellectual inquiry occurred through the theoretical innovations of CRT scholars just described, but also through the deployment of analytical tools that still characterize CRT. Not unlike scholars of race in disciplines such as American literature, race crits of the 1980s and 1990s began to incorporate racial storytelling as a way of raising awareness about the realities of life for Blacks and other racial minorities, and of advancing critiques of prevailing legal orthodoxy. Patricia Williams's pathbreaking book, *The Alchemy of Race and Rights*, and the *Rodrigo's Chronicles* series published by Richard Delgado, which explored issues of race, affirmative action, and law faculty hiring, provide two examples of this (Williams 1990; Jones 2002). The exploits of Geneva Crenshaw, the heroine in Derrick Bell's book *"And We Are Not Saved:" The Elusive Quest for Racial Justice*, who travels through time in order to understand, among other things, slavery and limits on black voting power, constitutes another (Bell 1987).

In addition to narrative, CRT scholars pushed a focus on the structural effects of racial discrimination, white supremacy, and subordination. In this connection, they also highlighted notions of intersectionality in analyzing legal problems. CRT also endorsed multidisciplinarity in legal analysis by incorporating insights from psychology, sociology, anthropology, and even literary theory into assessments of the race effects of doctrine. Finally, CRT scholarship brought postmodernist sensibilities to legal theory (Jones 2002, 228–9). The inclination to deconstruct language and institutional understandings prompted by Jacques Derrida and others distinguished CRT from more traditional approaches, but as the next section details, has also caused disagreement within CRT itself.

4 THE DYNAMIC RACIAL SUBJECT IN LEGAL THEORY

Making race the subject, and theoretical lens, of virtually all areas of law and legal theory came to characterize CRT. With perhaps a handful of notable exceptions, however, the subject of "race" itself was treated as unproblematic by race theorists. Race was a given, something around which histories of subordination were designed and built. Race and racial subordination were also embodied in the experience of African-Americans. Very little attention was paid in early CRT to the different social and legal histories of racial (and racialized) groups. Nor was sufficient attention given to the ways in which race interacts with other marginalized identities like class and gender to complicate narrative(s) of racial subordination.

More recent scholarship on race has complicated the treatment of race in ways that have both destabilized the racial subject and simultaneously made it a more dynamic focus of analysis. The racial subject in contemporary legal theory is one that embodies different racialized histories and identities, and possesses multiple attributes. This dynamism has deepened scholarly writing on race and law while also unmooring the racial subject from its anchor—the historical treatment of African-Americans.

The failure to scrutinize the category of "race" itself changed with a groundbreaking article by Ian Haney-Lopez which analyzed, based on the work of scholars in various disciplines, the legal and "social construction of race" (Haney-Lopez 1994). Race is less a biological fact or a fixed essence, Haney-Lopez argued, than a social phenomenon in which "contested systems of meanings serve as the connections between physical features, races, and personal characteristics." We create, replicate, and re-create the social meanings of race, imposing those meanings on groups of people loosely bound together by common historical, physical, and ancestral attributes. The law helps to create and reinforce these meanings by taking them as a given and building them into legal presumptions and reasoning.

By attending to the ways in which legal rules create and reinforce the social meaning of race, theorists began to call attention to the fluidity of race as a concept and the need to bring unexamined racial norms into theoretical and doctrinal focus. Scholars drew particular attention to the ways in which the law protected "Whiteness" and white identity, for example (Harris 1993). Others pointed out the ways in which immigration laws historically contributed to the construction of race by excluding certain groups from citizenship and reinforcing their racial outsider status (Haney-Lopez 1996; Johnson 2002). Highlighting the various ways in which legal reasoning, legislation, and doctrine helped to create and then enshrine racial categories was further evidence of the fluidity of race.

Once the concept of race itself became destabilized and open to contestation, so too did its proper place in legal theory and history. Scholars from across the ideological spectrum began to bring under intense scrutiny the positioning of race and race scholars in legal scholarship and discourse. Some traditional liberal scholars declared a "radical assault on truth in the law" led by critical race theorists and their embrace of a "socially constructed" reality over "objective" reasoning and concepts such as merit (Farber and Sherry 1997). Likewise, progressive scholars questioned the almost exclusive focus on African-Americans in critical race theory and legal discourse more generally. They urged a move beyond the "black/white binary paradigm of race" to more prominently include the history and role of other groups in shaping legal doctrine (Perea 1997). Eventually, "black exceptionalism"— the claim that Blacks play a unique and central role in American life—ceded ground as black crits recognized the necessity of transcending the black/white paradigm and embracing the full complexity of race (Espinoza and Harris 1997).

The subject of race, and the racial subject itself, had arguably grown to resemble the form of a multiheaded hydra. Legal scholarship about race began to fissure along the lines of identity politics with increased attention to how identity categories, racial and nonracial, contribute to the subordination of people of color. The "LatCrit" movement explicitly sought to move Latino history and experience to the forefront of race scholarship and to create a broader understanding of the structure of racial inequality by more explicitly taking into account language, culture, nationality, and class (Iglesias and Valdes 2001). Asian-American scholars too called for their own corner of legal scholarship and critical theory, pointing to the need for a framework that could "encompass and mediate between the notions of liberalism underlying African American civil rights work and the critical perspectives contained within critical race theory" (Chang 1993).

"Queer" scholars of color likewise pushed for a deeper engagement of race and ethnicity, or racism and ethnocentrism, in understanding better the texture of discrimination and subordination on the basis of sexual orientation (Valdes 1997). Seeking to move beyond the "intersectionality" analysis of earlier critical race theory, scholars began to argue for an approach that recognizes the "multidimensionality" of identity and acknowledges how various forms of identity and oppression are "inextricably and forever intertwined" (Hutchinson 1997; 1999). These scholars seek to understand, and have the law recognize, unlawful discrimination as a product of the convergence of multiple traits and stereotypes.

The turn toward deconstructing "race" and the racial subject has arguably called into question the proper focus and scope of legal scholarship dedicated to race. A recent debate among race theorists highlights the tension between the "discursive" and "materialist" strands that have emerged over the last two decades in the literature. Does the focus on the construction of "race" (the word), rather than race (the real world phenomenon), obscure the importance of "power, history, and similar material determinants of minority-group fortunes" (Delgado 2003)? Or is focusing on the ways law "rationalizes racial subordination created by power disparities" necessary to understanding how racial (and social) inequalities have come to be seen as "fair and natural" (Johnson 2004)? In truth, the tension between modernism and postmodernism is not a new, or irresolvable, one in critical legal theory; indeed, race theorists have long expressed a dual commitment to both traditions (Harris 1994). In the end, adherence to both modernist and postmodernist methodologies has expanded the reach of race theory by bringing under scrutiny a wider spectrum of practices contributing to racial subordination.

5 CONCLUSION: THE FUTURE OF RACE IN/AND LEGAL THEORY

Although there is a growing consensus about the extent to which modernism and postmodernism form a dialectical partnership to advance racial equality, there remains a bit of "subject unrest" among contemporary race theorists (Culp, Harris, and Valdes 2003). For example, some theorists question whether the scholarly focus on race ultimately re-inscribes phenotype and biological markers as the locus of "racial" subordination (Robinson 2000). These theorists call for the use of ethnicity and/or culture to analyze the array of practices that result in group-based discrimination and inequality. Others worry that notions of a common culture or set of ethnic characteristics are prone to the same essentialist lapses and discrimination that created problematic social meanings of race (Ford 2005).

Perhaps there is no way out of the unrest experienced when more people, cultures, and histories become the subject of analysis. Yet, one way out of the insularity in which arguments about race, identity, and culture become mired is through critical engagement with other analytical subjects, methodologies, and avenues of inquiry. This engagement can deepen our understanding and responsiveness to the persistence of race in society and its institutions. It can also foster critical collaborations with other parts of the legal academy that are otherwise not open to the methodologies of critical race theory. For example, some scholars have advocated collaboration between law and economics and critical race scholars. Advocates of such collaboration acknowledge the common critical approach to institutional analysis shared by both fields—the rejection of claims about the neutrality and objectivity of legal rules, albeit for different reasons—and suggest that, if combined, the two fields would produce an exciting new methodology for legal inquiry (Rubin 1996; Carbado and Gulati 2003).

Increasingly, scholars are embarking on comparative analysis of race with other parts of the world to (re)cultivate a basic understanding of the ways in which racial subordination is produced around the world. As one scholar argues, the social construction of race should not obscure the fact that phenotype is *a*, if not *the*, primary vehicle through which social and racial hierarchies are produced: "when we strip away the historical variations in social and political constructions of race in the Americas, one glaring commonality remains: general social discrimination based on skin color" (Hernandez 2002).

Finally, race scholars are more seriously inquiring into how the law can better account for persistent racial inequalities in core areas such as employment and education (Jordan and Harris 2005; Lenhardt 2004). Analyses to date have simplified many of our most entrenched social and political pathologies in ways that fail to do justice to either the complexities of race or its subjects. Scholarship that can fully account for the larger economic structure of contemporary societies, while at the same time keeping race central to the inquiry, can more fully account for the subject of race and the lives of its subjects.

REFERENCES

BAKER, S. C. and SUMPTER, M. D. (1900–1) Negro criminality. *North Carolina Law Journal*, 1: 27–33.

BELL, D. 1976. Serving two masters: integration ideals and client interests in school desegregation litigation. *Yale Law Journal*, 85: 470–517.

—— 1980. *Brown v. Board of Education* and the interest convergence dilemma. *Harvard Law Review*, 93: 518–33.

—— 1987. *And We Are Not Saved: The Elusive Request for Racial Reform*. New York: Basic Books.

—— 1992. Racial realism. *Connecticut Law Review*, 24: 363–80.

BICKEL, A. M. 1962. *The Least Dangerous Branch: The Supreme Court at the Bar of Politics*. Indianapolis: Bobbs-Merrill.

BLACK, C. L. 1960. The lawfulness of the segregation decisions. *Yale Law Journal*, 69: 421–31.

CARBADO, D. W., and GULATI, M. 2003. The law and economics of Critical Race Theory. *Yale Law Review*, 112: 1757–880.

CHANG, R. S. 1993. Toward an Asian American legal scholarship: Critical Race Theory, post-structuralism, and narrative space. *California Law Review*, 81: 1241–324.

CRENSHAW, K. W. 1988. Race, reform, and retrenchment: transformation and legitimation in antidiscrimination law. *Harvard Law Review*, 101: 1331–87.

—— 1989. Demarginalizing the intersection of race and sex: a black feminist critique of antidiscrimination doctrine, feminist theory and antiracist politics. *University of Chicago Legal Forum*, 1989: 139–68.

—— 2002. The first decade: critical reflections, or "a foot in the closing door." *UCLA Law Review*, 49: 1343–94.

—— GOTANDA, N., PELLER, G., and THOMAS, K. (eds.) 1996. *Critical Race Theory: The Key Writings That Formed the Movement*. New York: New Press.

CULP, Jr., J. M., HARRIS, A. P., and VALDES, F. 2003. Subject unrest. *Stanford Law Review*, 55: 2435–52.

DELGADO, R. 1984. The imperial scholar: reflections on a review of civil rights literature. *University of Pennsylvania Law Review*, 132: 561–78.

—— 1987 The ethereal scholar: does Critical Legal Studies have what minorities want? *Harvard Civil Rights–Civil Liberties Law Review*, 22: 301–22.

—— 2003. Crossroads and blind alleys: a critical examination of recent writing about race. *Texas Law Review*, 82: 121–52.

DuBois, W. E. B. 1996 [1903]. *The Souls of Black Folk*. New York: Modern Library.

—— 1992 [1935]. *Black Reconstruction in America*. New York: Atheneum.

ELY, J. H. 1980. *Democracy and Distrust: A Theory of Judicial Review*. Cambridge, Mass: Harvard University Press.

ESPINOZA, L., and HARRIS, A. P. 1997. Embracing the Tar-Baby: Lat-Crit and the sticky mess of race. *California Law Review*, 85: 1585–646.

FARBER, D. A., and SHERRY, S. 1997. *Beyond All Reason: The Radical Assault on Truth in American Law*. Oxford: Oxford University Press.

FLAGG, B. J. 1994. Enduring principle: on race, process, and constitutional law. *California Law Review*, 82: 935–80.

FORD, R. T. 2005. *Racial Culture: A Critique*. Princeton, NJ: Princeton University Press.

FOSTER, S. 1998. Intent and incoherence. *Tulane Law Review*, 72: 1065–176.

FREEMAN, A. D. 1978. Legitimizing racial discrimination through antidiscrimination law. *Minnesota Law Review*, 62: 1049–120.

—— 1988. Racism, rights and the quest for equality of opportunity: a critical legal essay. *Harvard Civil Rights–Civil Liberties Law Review*, 23: 295–392.

HANEY-LOPEZ, I. 1994. The social construction of race: some observations on illusion, fabrication, and choice. *Harvard Civil Rights–Civil Liberties Law Review*, 29: 1–62.

—— 1996. *White By Law: The Legal Construction of Race*. New York: New York University Press.

HARRIS, A. P. 1994. The jurisprudence of reconstruction. *California Law Review*, 82: 741–86.

HARRIS, C. 1993. Whiteness as property. *Harvard Law Review*, 106: 1709–91.

HART, H. M., and SACKS, A. M. 1958. *The Legal Process: Basic Problems in the Making and Application of the Law*. Manuscript.

HERNANDEZ, T. K. 2002. Multiracial matrix: the role of race ideology in the enforcement of antidiscrimination laws, a United States–Latin America comparison. *Cornell Law Review*, 87: 1093–176.

HUTCHINSON, D. L. 1997. Out yet unseen: a racial critique of gay and lesbian legal theory and political discourse. *Connecticut Law Review*, 29: 561–646.

—— 1999. Ignoring the sexualization of race: heteronormativity, Critical Race Theory, and anti-racist politics. *Buffalo Law Review*, 47: 1–116.

IGLESIAS, E. M., and VALDES, F. 2001. LatCrit at five: institutionalizing a post-subordination future. *Denver University Law Review*, 78: 1249–329.

JOHNSON, K. R. 2002. The end of "civil rights" as we know it? Immigration and civil rights in the new millennium. *UCLA Law Review*, 49: 1481–512.

—— 2004. Roll over Beethoven: a critical examination of recent writing about race. *Texas Law Review*, 82: 717–34.

JONES, B. D.-M. 2002. Critical Race Theory: protesting against formalism in the law, 1969–1999. University of Virginia.

JORDAN, E. C., and HARRIS, A. P. 2005. *Economic Justice: Race, Gender, Identity, and Economics*. New York: Foundation Press.

LAWRENCE, C. R. 1987. The id, the ego, and equal protection: reckoning with unconscious racism. *Stanford Law Review*, 39: 317–88.

LENHARDT, R. A. 2004. Understanding the mark: race, stigma, and equality in context. *New York University Law Review*, 79: 803–931.

MATSUDA, M. 1996 Looking to the bottom: Critical Legal Studies and reparations. In Crenshaw et al. 1996.

MING, W. R. 1949. Racial restrictions and the Fourteenth Amendment: the restrictive covenant cases. *Chicago Law Review*, 16: 203–38.

PELLER, G. 1988. Neutral principles in the 1950s. *Michigan Journal of Law Reform*, 21: 561–622.

PEREA, J. 1997. The black/white binary paradigm of race: the "normal science" of American racial thought. *California Law Review*, 85: 1213–58.

POLLAK, L. H. 1959. Racial discrimination and judicial integrity: a reply to Professor Wechsler. *University of Pennsylvania Law Review*, 108: 1–34.

ROBINSON, R. L. 2000. The shifting race-conscious matrix and the multiracial category movement: a reply to Professor Hernandez. *Boston College Third World Law Journal*, 20: 231–90.

RUBIN, E. L. 1996. The new legal process, the synthesis of discourse, and the microanalysis of institutions. *Harvard Law Review*, 109: 1393–438.

SIEGEL, R. B. 2004. Equality talk: antisubordination and anticlassification values in constitutional struggles over *Brown. Harvard Law Review*, 117: 1470–547.

TUSHNET, M. V. 1991. Critical Legal Studies: a political history. *Yale Law Journal*, 100: 1515–44.

VALDES, F. 1997. Queer margins, queer ethics: a call to account for race and ethnicity in the law, theory and politics of "sexual orientation." *Hastings Law Journal*, 48: 1293–342.

WECHSLER, H. 1959. Toward neutral principles of constitutional law. *Harvard Law Review*, 73: 1–35.

WILLIAMS, P. 1990. *Alchemy of Race and Rights*. Cambridge, Mass.: Harvard University Press.

PART VII

THE AMERICAN JUDICIAL CONTEXT

....

FILLING THE BENCH

....

DAVID A. YALOF

1 INTRODUCTION

....

DURING the past quarter century, the subject of judicial recruitment has received considerable attention from scholars of every stripe. Social scientists, historians, law professors, and journalists have all tried to document the politics of recruitment to the American bench. The audience for such research has been growing as well. Sparked first by the controversy surrounding Robert Bork's Supreme Court nomination in 1987, and then four years later by Clarence Thomas's nomination to the Supreme Court, interest in judicial nominations has perhaps never been greater than in the modern era. The recent eleven-year absence of personnel changes on the Supreme Court—the second-longest such period in American history—fueled more intense interest in U.S. Supreme Court appointments in particular. But interest in appointments now extends beyond the high court, as evidenced by the heightened attention paid to President George W. Bush's more controversial appointments to the federal courts of appeals.

Despite the recent increase in attention to the recruitment of judges, the social sciences as a whole—and the discipline of political science in particular—offer an incomplete view of the process. Even as many scholars labor to reveal heretofore undiscovered aspects of judicial recruitment, the literature on recruitment is distorted by various blind spots. Specifically, three biases afflict judicial recruitment scholarship:

1. *A preoccupation with the U.S. Supreme Court.* The controversies surrounding the Bork and Thomas appointments sparked greater interest in judicial appointments by political scientists and others, but they also exacerbated another problem: political scientists interested in the judiciary tend to pay disproportionate attention to the United States Supreme Court. Similarly, scholars have tended to pay an inordinately large amount of attention to U.S. Supreme Court appointments as well. To be sure, the relative infrequency of such high court appointments—one on average every 2.2 years—contributes to a build-up of interest in those vacancies that does not occur elsewhere in the judicial system. Yet given the often idiosyncratic nature of Supreme Court nominations, this emphasis only serves to distort our understanding of how judicial recruitment actually unfolds in the vast majority of cases.

2. *An emphasis on readily available data.* In the eyes of many citizens, a mystical aura surrounds the judiciary and its hidden processes of decision-making. Scholars too must scale a high wall if they wish to go behind the scenes of the nation's courts. Two books that offered an insider's look at the Supreme Court decision-making process, *The Brethren* (1979) and *Closed Chambers* (1998), relied primarily on the memories of Supreme Court clerks to reveal hidden aspects of the process. Because interactions between clerks and justices are normally assumed to be confidential, these controversial treatments of the high court essentially breached traditional norms of institutional secrecy. Whether or not the methods employed in those two instances were justified, any such qualms about exposing behind-the-scenes accounts of the judicial process theoretically do not apply to judicial recruitment studies, where the relevant "inside story" occurs within explicitly political institutions such as the White House, the Governor's Office, the Department of Justice, and the Senate Judiciary Committee. Still, many public law scholars continue to leave such inside analysis of the judicial recruitment process to journalists and others who are more willing to rely on anonymous sources and other less reliable forms of data. Instead, political scientists tend to base the bulk of their analysis of judicial recruitment on data that is already visible to the public: confirmation hearings, Senate votes, interest group participation in the public sphere, the decisions reached by merit plan commissions, etc.

3. *Ignoring connections and comparisons between different recruitment processes.* Most studies of judicial recruitment processes tend to focus on single courts or levels of courts. Nonetheless, findings from such studies provide the raw materials for scholars to explore connections between different recruitment processes, or to draw analytical comparisons among them. For example, recruitment to higher courts (the U.S. Supreme Court and state supreme courts) may be heavily influenced by the recruitment of lower court judges, who eventually make up a large portion of the pool of available candidates for promotion.

1.1 Navigating the Different Streams: A Review of the Literature

Regardless of context, all forms of judicial recruitment have certain elements in common. Unlike recruitment to other positions in government that may be explicitly political in their nature, the myth of judicial independence—whether universally embraced or not—plays a significant role in the process. Unlike candidates for other political offices, judicial candidates (whether competing in elections or vying for appointment and confirmation) recognize that their actions as candidates will be held to a higher standard. Canon 5 of the Model Code of Judicial Ethics promulgated by the American Bar Association proscribes numerous activities by candidates for judicial office (making "pledges, promises or commitments" with respect to cases that are likely to come before the court, soliciting funds to support his or her candidacy, etc.) that would be considered routine for anyone vying for most legislative offices.

Perhaps the most useful way to frame different methods of judicial recruitment at the outset is to place them along a spectrum of two ideal types. As Grossman explains, "at one end is a cluster of variables that might be designated the *professional-independent* model ... at the other end is a cluster that might be labeled the *responsive-accountable-political* model" (2005, 146). In the former model, judges must be able to enforce provisions in the text of the Constitution and statutes, along with more general notions of the "public interest," against transient majorities. This model is easier to maintain in most European systems, where judging is a separate vocation and "is centrally organized along bureaucratic lines" so "there is virtually no political involvement, and no issues of 'democracy' or individual judges' political ideology" (Grossman 2005, 146). American systems may aspire to this ideal as well, but few judicial recruitment methods in the United States avoid becoming steeped in some form of politics.

The responsive-accountable-political model offers a different view of the courts' role in the political system. There is a risk that judges freed from political restraints may pursue their own agendas that are unwise or unfair, leaving the polity defenseless against their abuse. The election of judges is one means of ensuring accountability—the public and its representatives may attempt to ensure judicial responsiveness to the public by overturning decisions (through amendment or referendum), or by directly threatening jurists with recall, impeachment, or removal. Of course as Seidman pointed out, the interests in independence and accountability are "irreducibly contradictory and context-dependent preferences" (Seidman 1988, 1573). Still, judicial recruitment may be best understood according to how specific mechanisms strike a balance between these principles.

Most scholars apply these frameworks to a particular court or level of courts, and make little effort to assess how one type of recruitment system and the values it promotes affects another. Even in those rare instances where scholars have attempted to make intercourt comparisons, most tend to "make direct comparisons either among formal selection systems, or between levels of courts within the same formal system" (Baum 1997, 31). Accordingly, three separate streams of research—investigating U.S. Supreme Court, lower federal court, and state court recruitment practices—have developed. These streams tend to run in different directions, as most scholars submerge themselves in one stream or another, with few systematic efforts to effectively integrate their research and scholarship with other streams, or to search for connections that might be worthy of further exploration.

2 THE WIDEST STREAM: RECRUITMENT TO THE U.S. SUPREME COURT

The amount of scholarly attention to U.S. Supreme Court appointments dwarfs researchers' efforts at studying state or lower federal court appointments. Considerable research on this subject has gone forward despite two significant obstacles: (1) pre-nomination selection dynamics generally occur behind closed doors, rendering most accounts of the process anecdotal, and potentially unreliable; and (2) there exists a relatively small sample of cases. There have been just 114 successful Supreme Court nominations through 2007, with twenty-eight others failing due to Senate defeat, withdrawal, postponement, or inaction. Such a small number of appointments over such a long period of time renders systematic analysis and conclusions elusive.

Most early works on the Supreme Court were case studies that provided valuable insights into the process as it occurred at a single point in time, but suggested little about trends, patterns, or more general implications. Leading judicial biographies typically featured detailed descriptions of the political wrangling that led to the justice's nomination (e.g. Mason 1956a; 1956b; Howard 1968). Only one of these early works concentrated solely on the recruitment process: Danelski's important book on Harding's nomination of Pierce Butler to the Supreme Court, entitled *A Supreme Court Justice is Appointed* (1964). Danelski's research became a landmark in judicial recruitment scholarship (Danelski 1964). Unlike most earlier works on judicial selection, the book's discussion ranged considerably beyond the institutions constitutionally obligated to participate in the process to provide a fuller account of *all* the active players in Butler's appointment including interest groups, business leaders, academicians, and even two sitting members of the Supreme Court. As Thomas Walker notes, Danelski's approach to this subject astutely acknowledged that "outcomes depend on interactions among various players within institutional environments that are shaped by norms and expectations" (Walker 2003, 258). In a similar fashion, McFeeley (1987) documented how the Johnson administration settled upon its three nominations to the high Court.

Meanwhile, most scholarly studies of Supreme Court appointments over a longer period of time made no attempt to provide more systematic analysis. Abraham's *Justices and Presidents* (1974) is notable primarily for its comprehensive coverage of the pre-nomination and confirmation stages of Supreme Court appointments. Until the last decade or so, scholarship on Supreme Court appointments focused either on (1) the characteristics and qualifications of the president's nominees; or (2) the confirmation stage of appointments, perhaps because that phase of the process is so public that its records can be more easily perused and documented.

In the first category, many scholars have weighed in on the changing importance of ideology, party, region, and other variables in nominations and confirmations (e.g. Nemacheck 2007). The failed nomination of Robert Bork in 1987 in particular spurred groundbreaking research about the role that ideology in particular plays in the appointment process (Segal et al. 1988–9; Massaro 1990; Cameron et al. 1990). Additionally, Perry (1991) documented the role that race, gender, and other demographic criteria have played in this process as well.

The confirmation process has also drawn considerable interest. Maltese's research on presidential support for his nominees carefully documents the role that interest groups played in Supreme Court appointments long before the modern era (Maltese 1994). Even so, Maltese admits that the Bork appointment was a watershed moment in terms of the quantity and intensity of interest group mobilization against one nominee. More than a decade after Bork, Caldeira and Wright (1998) documented the important role that organized interests play in shaping senators' confirmation decisions in the modern era.

After Clarence Thomas's controversial 1991 appointment, law professors and social scientists alike soon jumped into the fray with their own analysis of the confirmation process (e.g. Carter 1994; Sinclair 1992). The Thomas hearings proved particularly useful for examining the effect of public opinion and constituency effects on confirmation politics. Caldeira and Smith (1996) argued that dramatic and systematic shifts in sources of opinion mobilization proved crucial in Thomas's case. Mansbridge and Tate (1992) described Thomas's confirmation as a case where "race trumped gender." Overby et al. (1992) determined that the two most significant influences affecting senators' confirmation votes for or against Thomas were the prevalence of African-American constituencies in their home states and the proximity of their upcoming reelection contests. Hutchings (2001) reassessed the Thomas confirmation vote as a case where salience interacted with environmental cues such as the presence of female senate candidates and knowledge of senators' individual votes.

What remains a mystery is the formula for decision-making that leads presidents to choose Supreme Court nominees in the first place. Who influences these decisions, and on what basis are they made? Walter Murphy found that dating back to Chief Justice Taft, Supreme Court justices themselves are often involved in the appointment process (1961, 159). Indeed, ample evidence shows that Chief Justices Taft, Warren, and Burger all influenced the selection process (Yalof 1999). My own research revealed the presence of an elaborate advisory network in recent administrations, with high-ranking executive officers often contesting each other over which nominees should emerge from the administration's shortlists (Yalof 1999, 184–6).

Dahl argued that the Court's decisions are generally consistent with the policy preferences of the dominant political coalition, as presidents have the power to place judges on the Court who represent their own ideological positions (Dahl 1957). Yet it is not clear how much success they enjoy in actually transforming the Court. Many Supreme Court justices—including Warren, Brennan, Blackmun, and Souter—seem to have confounded the presidents who appointed them by taking unexpected positions on high-profile issues and, in modern times, the cohort of appointees named by a particular president has rarely voted together in a cohesive ideological bloc (Lindquist et. al. 2000).

Grossman (1965) first established the significant role of the American Bar Association (ABA) in rating nominees. More recently, Epstein and Segal reminded us of the continuing role that qualifications—as measured by ABA ratings and other information—play in the Supreme Court selection process (Epstein and Segal 2005, 75). As is described later in this chapter, the George W. Bush administration—in an effort to reduce ABA influence over lower court nominations—announced in 2001 that the organized bar would thereafter learn the identity of judicial candidates along with every other interest group, *after* they have been formally nominated. This policy shift has not really affected the significance of ABA ratings: The ABA continues to play an influential role in the process today, albeit alongside these other interest groups. And in the final analysis, perceptions of weak qualifications may still prove devastating to a Supreme Court nominee's chances of confirmation.

The nature of divided party government and its impact on all aspects of the Supreme Court appointment process has also drawn the interest of many scholars. For Silverstein (1994), 1968 marked the turning point in the confirmation of Supreme Court justices, from the point of view of both presidents who now aggressively pursue ideological goals and the senators who are increasingly willing to stand in the president's way.

3 Stream Number Two: Recruitment to Lower Federal Courts

The recruitment of federal district court and circuit court judges has received increased interest from political scientists during the past quarter century. The method of appointing Article III judges—featuring presidential nomination, senatorial advice and consent, and permanent appointments—emphasizes the value of independence over the need for accountability. And yet it has been the nakedly political aspects of the process (presidential motives, the role of political parties, the Senate's strategic delays, etc.) that has attracted the most scholarly attention.

Goldman's *Picking Federal Judges: Lower Court Selection from Roosevelt Through Reagan* (1997) combined comprehensive research from presidential archives with statistical analysis to assess the motivations and accomplishments of nine presidents in their selection of lower federal court nominees. Specifically, Goldman defined three types of presidential agendas:

(1) the *policy agenda*, which refers to the "substantive policy goals of an administration, including its legislative and administrative objectives"; (2) *the partisan agenda*, which refers to the "use of presidential power to shore up political support for the president or his party"; and (3) *the personal agenda*, which means "the use of the president's discretion to favor a personal friend or associate." (Goldman 1997, 3)

Some mix of these three agendas has been at work in every recent administration, although the formula has shifted somewhat in each case. Although Truman's appointments largely reflected a partisan agenda, both Reagan and Roosevelt used the lower court appointment process to help pursue their policy agendas—each wanted judges who shared his own preferences (Goldman 1997, 345). To be sure, some aspects of a personal and policy agenda also crept into Truman's appointments, and Reagan and FDR were certainly cognizant of their own partisan agendas.

What Goldman calls "partisan politics" naturally envisions a role for political parties in the judicial recruitment process. But how great a role? For much of the nineteenth century, the influence of partisanship was a given. From 1829 to 1861 "party was the most significant modernizing force in the selection process... [i]t linked the President, the Congress and the states and territories in a web of commitment" to name particular judges (Hall 1979, 172). Of course party politics still played a role in lower court selections more than a century later. As J. Woodford Howard summed it up: "to the politically active as well as to the party faithful go the prizes" (Howard 1981, 90).

In fact, party affiliation today has become the controlling consideration. Goldman's comprehensive review of the background characteristics of appointments to the federal bench confirms this trend. Between 1976 and 2004, every president appointed members of his own political party to at least 84 percent of the federal district court vacancies, and to at least 82 percent of the federal court of appeals vacancies (Goldman et al. 2005, 269, 274). In the case of courts of appeals, Reagan and George W. Bush were the most partisan of all, appointing Republicans to the courts of appeal in 96 percent and 92 percent of cases, respectively (Goldman et al. 2005, 274).

Much recent scholarship has focused on the interaction between party considerations and activists. For Goldman (1997), lower court judgeships serve as rewards for the most loyal activists, nearly all of whom identify with the president's party. Scherer (2005) concurs, arguing that even during the modern era when the party system has broken down in other contexts, parties continue to use nominations to curry favor and "score points" with the most elite constituency of activists.

Beyond the dominant criteria of party affiliation and party activism, scholarship on lower court appointment politics has also focused on the issue of diversity and, more generally, the question of representativeness. How diverse in race, religion, and ethnicity are the federal courts? Traditionally, senatorial courtesy exerted a dominant influence over the process of choosing lower court judges, with issues of diversity lurking in the background. With the formation of the United States Circuit Judge Nominating Commission at the circuit court level, senators were temporarily stripped of some of this influence in 1977. Its procedures and practices were the subject of extensive research during the late 1970s and early 1980s. At least one study revealed a process permeated with partisanship—the requirement that panel members be individually approved by the White House resulted in a "form of merit selection of Democrats by Democrats" (Berkson et al. 1979, 104; see also Slotnick 1984a, 235).

Slotnick (1984b) found that the Carter administration helped produce a more diverse bench. In just one term, Carter appointed forty women to the federal bench, five times as many as all his predecessors combined, and he appointed thirty-seven African-American judges, nearly double the number of all his predecessors (Epstein and Segal 2005, 58–9). Was this diversity a product of the Commission's procedures, or a result of Carter's personal determination to appoint women and minorities in record numbers? This much is certain: a dramatic change in judicial demographics in the late 1970s would not have been possible had a Democratic Congress not decided to create 144 new judgeships during that period. According to de Figueiredo and Tiller (1996), Congress has traditionally increased the number of judgeships during such periods of political alignment, when the House, the Senate, and the White House are all held by one party.

Another way Congress can exercise control over the judiciary through new appointments is by waiting for vacancies to arise naturally. Barrow and Zuk (1990) argued that the majority of voluntary retirements come from judges who share the same party affiliation as the nominating president (see also Spriggs and Wahlbeck 1995).

The Reagan administration succeeded in making the federal courts more conservative without completely abandoning the Carter administration's interest in a more representative bench. Recruitment to lower courts during the 1980s thus proceeded along two tracks: one, which served the Reagan administration's primary interest in shaping the judiciary to meet its ideological agenda by nominating mostly white males with records of partisan political activities; and a second, in which non-white nominees gained promotion primarily through previous judicial experience (Slotnick 1984*b*, 383).

An administration's success at imposing its ideological will on the federal courts is far harder to pinpoint. Davis compared the voting patterns of Johnson and Carter appointees, and discovered that Carter appointees exhibited a significantly higher percentage of liberal votes (Davis 1986, 340–2). Stidham, Carp, and Songer (1996) found that Clinton appointees exhibited moderate decisional tendencies. By contrast, George W. Bush's judicial appointments through 2004 amassed a record of conservatism matched during the past half century only by President Reagan (Carp, Manning, and Stidham 2004). Yet the relevance of these comparisons among presidents remains open to question, as judges often confront issues that weren't anticipated at the time of their appointment.

The increased prevalence of divided party government since 1969 has had a significant impact on the appointment of federal lower court judges as well, and scholars have been quick to assess the changes. Certainly numerous political scientists have documented the greater length of time it now takes for lower court nominees (especially circuit court nominees) to be confirmed (Hartley and Holmes 1997; Binder and Maltzman 2002). Scherer (2005) documented how an appointment system formerly dominated by patronage is now dominated by policy-oriented strategies, which has led to party-polarized voting on many controversial nominees.

Interest-group mobilization during the confirmation process for lower court nominees has also attracted significant scholarly attention. The number of organized interests that lobby judicial nominations has expanded as the perceived stakes in the federal judiciary as a whole have risen; the technology at interest groups' disposal is also more advanced. Still, Caldeira, Hojnacki, and Wright (2000) suggest that lobbying tactics in the modern era are not all that different from those employed in earlier times; and Flemming et. al. (1998) argue that the most significant interest-group influence occurs behind the scenes, during the early phases of a nomination. Yet there are still relatively few instances of group participation at confirmation hearings for lower court judges. In fact, interest groups do not participate in confirmation hearings more frequently now than they did prior to the Bork nomination, as many no longer see their testimony as useful, especially when compared to other priorities such as grass roots mobilization and publicity for the cause (Bell 2002, 120).

Flemming et. al (1998) found that "organizations with national interests, memberships or constituencies" have displaced local groups and local bar associations in testimony before the Senate Judiciary Committee. One of the constant participants since the 1950s has been the American Bar Association. Grossman reported that "within flexible limits, the ABA's role in the selection of federal judges has been institutionalized," resulting in an in increase in professional lawyers on the federal bench (Grossman 1965, 5). As noted earlier, the ABA's role has shifted, as conservatives criticized the group for favoring liberal nominees. Lindgren used a statistical model to argue that highly credentialed nominees of Republican presidents such as George H. W. Bush actually fared worse in ABA ratings than Clinton nominees with lesser credentials (Lindgren 2001).

By 1988, O'Brien reported that the ABA played no role whatsoever in the initial selection of candidates (O'Brien 1988, 94). The ABA's influence suffered yet another blow in the aftermath of George W. Bush's election to the presidency in 2000. Early in Bush's first term, White House Counsel Gonzales announced a formal shift in policy: the White House would no longer vet candidates for the federal bench through the ABA first. Of course, Gonzales could not exclude the ABA altogether from the process, as the Senate Judiciary Committee has continued to solicit the ABA's recommendations on nominees.

Paralleling the increase in media attention, lower court appointments are receiving greater attention. So far we lack systematic analysis of the relationship between recruitment at either of the two lower levels either to U.S. Supreme Court recruitment, or even to each other. Savchak et al. (2006) has in part addressed this question, identifying the most important variables in the promotion of federal district judges to the federal courts of appeals, including ideological compatibility with the president, previous ABA ratings, and Senate norms of a state's so-called "ownership" of certain judicial seats. The authors concluded that judges have relatively little incentive to slant their decisions in the hope of impressing the president.

4 THE FINAL STREAM: RECRUITMENT TO STATE JUDICIAL SYSTEMS

Students of judicial recruitment in the states have paid significant attention to the ways in which different modes of judicial selection tend to influence the types of judges chosen and, consequently, different types of decisions. The bulk of this research "incorporates the same kind of assumption that underlies studies of judicial background characteristics: recruitment processes are important because they influence the mix of policy preferences on particular courts and sets of courts" (Baum 1997, 31). Many of these studies occurred during the 1960s and 1970s.

Different systems sit in different places on the independence–accountability spectrum. Scholars have tended to place state recruitment methods in at least five different categories. *Partisan elections* are at the extreme end of accountability—parties nominate candidates for judicial office, candidates run with a party label in the general election, and incumbents must run for reelection in either a partisan contest or in a retention election after a given term. *Non-partisan elections* prohibit the mention of party affiliation on the ballot; the top two candidates in a non-partisan primary election then run in the general election and most judges run for reelection in retention elections. *Election by the legislature* is far less common.

Two other schemes sit at the other end of the independence–accountability spectrum. *Gubernatorial appointment* is the method in just a handful of states; and, although governors enjoy the appointment power, a legislative body (normally the state senate) must approve all judicial nominees. A fifth method of judicial recruitment—the so-called *"merit selection system"* (originally called the "Missouri Plan")—attempts to remove partisan forms of politics from judicial selection. It has drawn the most scholarly attention. Emphasizing independence over accountability, it normally starts with a judicial nominating commission featuring lawyers selected by the bar and nonlawyers selected by the governor. The commission then nominates between three and six individuals to fill a judicial vacancy, and from there, the governor makes a selection. After a brief period of judicial service, the judge runs for reelection in a noncontested retention election.

Do judicial elections produce the high level of accountability promised? Many early studies cast doubt on this premise. Following the careers of Louisiana state judges elected from 1945 to 1960, Vines discovered that the judicial election system in most cases secures the initial selection of judges by approval at the polls, but it rarely removes them (Vines 1963, 114–16). A study of Wisconsin judicial elections similarly revealed that the state judiciary maintains a relatively low salience with the electorate (Ladinsky and Silver 1967, 161). And Adamany and DuBois found that voters in nonpartisan spring elections were disproportionately drawn from higher socioeconomic groups and thus tended to be more "respectful" and less "populist" (Adamany and DuBois 1976, 731).

More recent research confirms that judicial elections normally fail to generate public participation and accountability. Hojnacki and Baum (1992, 300), for example, found that election contests do not provide voters with salient cues that generate significant interest and participation; and, even when voters have access to vast amounts of information, issues in judicial election contests usually have only a limited impact. Judicial retention elections in particular tend to be "issueless, colorless and nearly lifeless" (Sheldon and Lovrich 1983); and in Hall and Aspin's (1987) study of retention elections over a twenty-year period, only 1.2 percent of sitting judges were defeated.

What does account for whatever limited accountability is in evidence? According to Bonneau and Hall (2003), institutional arrangements and other environmental factors play a critical role in encouraging electoral challenges to incumbent judges, thus offering some degree of accountability. Yet, if the purpose of judicial elections is to create legitimacy for the judiciary by involving greater numbers of citizens, lawmakers may need to consider reforms, perhaps combining judicial elections with higher-visibility elections for other offices.

Merit plan selection systems also sacrifice significant claims to accountability. Instead, proponents of merit selection systems assert that these plans improve the operation of the judiciary by enabling judges to avoid being beholden to constituencies, and by permitting them to devote full-time attention to their duties without the distractions of reelection campaigns (Schroeder and Hall 1966). Yet the presence of social and economic cleavages in the bar itself can influence judicial selection just as party politics does. As DuBois (1980, 9) found, merit systems merely "changed the nature of that politics to include not only partisan forces but also those relating to the organized Bar, the judiciary, and the Court's 'attentive publics.' " Thus, although some connections to party politics are missing from merit selection, other overt political connections often remain, including most notably the effect of the governor's party affiliation on his choice of committee members.

How are the differences in these judicial recruitment systems most likely to manifest themselves? In the 1960s, Herbert Jacob found that "formal selection procedures . . . are likely to affect the nominating process by establishing certain informal qualifications, by giving access to particular categorical groups, or by placing some individuals at an advantage and others at a disadvantage for particular office" (Jacob 1964, 104–5). Subsequent scholars (e.g. Watson and Downing 1969) applied Jacob's method to explain how merit plan systems in particular produce older, more experienced judges. By contrast, neither Canon (1972) nor Nagel (1973) found significant differences in prestige or competence between elected and appointed judges. In recent decades, scholars have paid increased attention to minority group representation at the state level. According to Graham (1990), more black judges can be found in states that utilize judicial elections. Luskin (1994) discovered that Missouri plan election systems were less likely than other forms of judicial selection to promote African-Americans for the bench. Clearly recruitment procedures have some impact on the nature and characteristics of sitting judges; how much and why will remain a continuing source of debate among scholars.

What influences do recruitment processes have on judicial decision-making? Early research on state judicial selection systems pointed to few, if any differences in outcomes between elected and appointed systems (Nagel 1973, 36–7; Atkins and Glick 1974, 44). Yet, more recent research by Hall and Brace in particular has revealed some important and distinctive decision-making patterns by elected judges, especially in criminal matters. For example, Hall (1992) found that some liberal judges modified their behavior and joined conservative majorities in death penalty cases in anticipation of an election. Other institutional features such as competitive electoral conditions in general increased judicial support for the death penalty (Brace and Hall 1997). Others scholars have also confirmed that elected judges tend to become more punitive in criminal cases as a whole when reelection approaches (Huber and Gordon 2004).

Scholars who study state court recruitment tend to make little effort to integrate their findings with those on federal judicial recruitment. Bratton and Spill (2004) are a recent exception: They identified variables that influence the nomination of state supreme court justices to the federal courts and concluded that state justices from the more prestigious courts were less likely to be nominated to the federal courts, perhaps because they have ruled on more controversial cases (making them more vulnerable during confirmation), or because they may be happier to stay put. Of course, state supreme court justices represent only a slice of the potential recruits from the state judiciary: the only member of the state courts to be nominated to the Supreme Court during the past half century, Sandra Day O'Connor, was not a member of Arizona's highest court. Connections between recruitment to and from these different courts is thus a fascinating and mostly unmined area of future scholarship.

5 THE FUTURE OF SCHOLARSHIP ON JUDICIAL RECRUITMENT

What makes the topic of judicial recruitment so fascinating for so many in the public and the media is what makes it a never-ending source of frustration for scholars. Every few years, events unfold in appointment politics that are, if not unprecedented, certainly quite unusual and unexpected. Consider three recent events in particular: (1) President Bush, backed by a solid Republican majority in the Senate, was forced to withdraw his choice of a Supreme Court nominee due to backlash from his own party; (2) the Democratic minority in the Senate engaged in a series of filibusters against ten of the president's lower federal court nominees; and (3) the Christian Coalition sent interrogatories to candidates in judicial elections, requesting their positions on abortion, parental choice in education, and equal access for theology majors to a state-funded college scholarship program. Are these unusual actions temporary detours off the path of the more traditional recruitment practices, or do they represent a sign of new and long-lasting trends and patterns in recruitment politics?

With only eighteen Supreme Court nominations since 1970, how can one decipher the role that any one variable plays in Supreme Court appointment politics with any confidence? Does the approval of justices such as Roberts and Alito reflect a lack of controversy surrounding meritorious choices, or the strategic selection of candidates who are less likely to invoke political backlash? Is the Democrats' strategy of filibustering what they see as ideological extremists a sign of the future, or is it limited to the current political context?

Despite all these unknowns, scholars continue to focus disproportionate attention on the process of appointing Supreme Court Justices. The confirmation process in particular attracts the bulk of their attention, in part because it is fought primarily before the public. The failure to pay as much attention to judicial recruitment at other levels of courts, and to investigate the less public, more hidden aspects of judicial recruitment in general, combine to distort the picture of judicial recruitment as a whole. Fortunately, scholars in recent years have exhibited an increasing willingness to address these deficiencies.

While numerous excellent studies examine recruitment processes in single courts or court levels, more analysis of the connections between these different processes might prove especially revealing. Does the method by which modern presidents select federal courts of appeal judges further or undermine the goals they wish to pursue when appointing Supreme Court justices some time later? Are state merit-plan selection systems likely to produce judges attractive to the president when he must create a pool of possible federal lower court nominees? Why don't more state supreme court judges receive consideration for slots on the U.S. Courts of Appeal? To date only a handful of studies have even attempted to consider possible connections among formal selection systems, or between levels of courts within the same formal system.

It has become fashionable in recent years for public law scholars to call for more explicit comparisons between United States courts and their foreign counterparts. Yet in considering future paths for the study of judicial recruitment in particular, scholars interested in pursuing comparative research need not feel compelled to look overseas to foreign systems. Comparative perspectives and connections between different recruitment processes within the American judiciary remain largely uncharted territory for political scientists interested in how we select members of the bench.

REFERENCES

ABRAHAM, H. 1974. *Justices and Presidents*. New York: Oxford University Press.
ADAMANY, D., and DuBois, P. 1976. Electing state judges. *Wisconsin Law Review*, 1976: 731–79.
ATKINS, B., and GLICK, H. 1974. Formal judicial recruitment and state supreme court decisions. *American Politics Quarterly*, 2: 427–49.
BARROW, J., and ZUK, G. 1990. An institutional analysis of turnover in the lower federal courts, 1900–1987. *Journal of Politics*, 52: 457–76.

BAUM, L. 1997. *The Puzzle of Judicial Behavior.* Ann Arbor: University of Michigan Press.

BELL, L. 2002. *Warring Factions: Interest Groups, Money and the New Confirmation Process.* Columbus: Ohio State University Press.

BERKSON, L., CARBON, S., and NEFF, A. 1979. A study of the U.S. Circuit Judge Nominating Commission. *Judicature*, 63: 104–29.

BINDER, S., and MALTZMAN, F. 2002. Senatorial delay in confirming federal judges, 1947–1988. *American Journal of Political Science*, 46: 190–9.

BONNEAU, C., and HALL, M. 2003. Predicting challengers in state supreme court elections: context and the politics of institutional design. *Political Research Quarterly*, 56: 337–49.

BRACE, P., and HALL, M. 1997. The interplay of preferences, case facts, context and rules in the politics of judicial choice. *Journal of Politics*, 59: 1206–31.

BRATTON, K., and SPILL, R. 2004. Moving up the judicial ladder: the role of prior judicial experience. *American Politics Research*, 32: 198–218.

CALDEIRA, G., HOJNACKI, M., and WRIGHT, J. 2000. The lobbying activities of organized interests in federal judicial nominations. *Journal of Politics*, 62: 51–69.

—— and SMITH, C. 1996. Campaigning for the Supreme Court: the dynamics of public opinion on the Thomas nomination. *Journal of Politics*, 58: 655–81.

—— and WRIGHT, J. 1998. Lobbying for justice: organized interests, Supreme Court nominees, and the United States Senate. *American Journal of Political Science*, 42: 499–523.

CAMERON, C., COVER, A., and SEGAL, J. 1990. Senate voting on Supreme Court nominees: a neo-institutional model. *American Political Science Review*, 84: 525–34.

CANON, B. 1972. The impact of formal selection processes on the characteristics of judges—reconsidered. *Law and Society Review*, 6: 579–94.

CARP, R., MANNING, K., and STIDHAM, R. 2004. The decisionmaking behavior of George W. Bush's judicial appointees. *Judicature*, 88: 20–8.

CARTER, S. 1994. *The Confirmation Mess: Cleaning up the Federal Appointments Process.* New York: Basic Books.

DAHL, R. 1957. Decisionmaking in a democracy: the Supreme Court as national policy-maker. *Journal of Public Law*, 6: 279–95.

DANELSKI, D. 1964. *A Supreme Court Justice is Appointed.* New York: Random House.

DAVIS, S. 1986. President Carter's reforms and judicial policymaking: a voting analysis of United States courts of appeals. *American Politics Quarterly*, 14: 328–44.

DE FIGUEIREDO, J., and TILLER, E. 1996. Congressional control of the courts: a theoretical and empirical analysis of expansion of the federal judiciary. *Journal of Law and Economics*, 39: 435–62.

DUBOIS, P. 1980. *From Ballot to Bench: Judicial Elections and the Quest for Accountability.* Austin: University of Texas Press.

EPSTEIN, L., and SEGAL, J. 2005. *Advice and Consent: The Politics of Judicial Appointments.* New York: Oxford University Press.

FLEMMING, B., MACLEOD, M., and TALBERT, J. 1998. Witnesses at the confirmations? The appearance of organized interests at Senate hearings of federal judicial appointments. *Political Research Quarterly*, 51: 617–31.

GOLDMAN, S. 1997. *Picking Federal Judges: Lower Court Selection from Roosevelt Through Reagan.* New Haven, Conn.: Yale University Press.

—— SLOTNICK, E., GRYSKI, G., and SCHIAVONI, S. 2005. George W. Bush's judiciary: the first term record. *Judicature*, 88: 244–75.

GRAHAM, B. 1990. Judicial recruitment and racial diversity on state courts: an overview. *Judicature*, 74: 28–34.

GROSSMAN, J. 1965. *Lawyers and Judges: The ABA and the Politics of Judicial Selection*. New York: Wiley.

—— 2005. Paths to the bench: selecting Supreme Court justices in a "juristocratic" world. Pp. 142–73 in *Institutions of American Democracy: The Judicial Branch*, ed. K. Hall and K. McGuire. New York: Oxford University Press.

HALL, K. 1979. *The Politics of Justice: Lower Federal Judicial Selection and the Second Party System 1829–1861*. Lincoln: University of Nebraska Press.

—— 1992. Electoral politics and strategic voting in state supreme courts. *Journal of Politics*, 54: 427–46.

HALL, M., and ASPIN, L. 1987. What twenty years of judicial retention elections have told us. *Judicature*, 70: 340–7.

—— and BONNEAU, C. 2006. Does quality matter? Challengers in state supreme court elections. *American Journal of Political Science*, 50: 20–33.

HARTLEY, R., and HOLMES, L. 1997. Increasing Senate scrutiny of lower federal court nominees. *Judicature*, 80: 274–8.

HOJNACKI, M., and BAUM, L. 1992. Choosing judicial candidates: how voters explain their decisions. *Judicature*, 75: 300–9.

HOWARD, J. 1968. *Mr. Justice Murphy: A Political Biography*. Princeton, NJ: Princeton University Press.

—— 1981. *Courts of Appeals in the Federal Judicial System*. Princeton, NJ: Princeton University Press.

HUBER, G., and GORDON, S. 2001. Accountability and coercion: is justice blind when it runs for office? *American Journal of Political Science*, 48: 247–63.

HUTCHINGS, V. 2001. Political context, issue salience, and selective attentiveness: constituent knowledge of the Clarence Thomas confirmation vote. *Journal of Politics*, 63: 846–68.

JACOB, H. 1964. The effect of institutional differences in the recruitment process: the case of state judges. *Journal of Public Law*, 13: 104–19.

LADINSKY, J., and SILVER, A. 1967. Popular democracy and judicial independence: electorate reactions to two Wisconsin Supreme Court elections. *Wisconsin Law Review*, 1967: 128–69.

LAZARUS, E. 1998. *Closed Chambers: The First Eyewitness Account of the Epic Struggles Inside the Supreme Court*. New York: Crown.

LINDGREN, J. 2001. Examining the American Bar Association's ratings of nominees to the U.S. Courts of Appeals for political bias, 1989–2000. *Journal of Law and Politics*, 17: 1–39.

LINDQUIST, S., YALOF, D., and CLARK, J. 2000. The impact of presidential appointments to the U.S. Supreme Court: cohesive and divisive voting within presidential blocs. *Political Research Quarterly*, 53: 795–814.

LUSKIN, R. C., et al. 1994. How minority judges fare in retention elections. *Judicature*, 77: 316–21.

MALTESE, J. 1994. *The Selling of Supreme Court Nominees*. Baltimore: Johns Hopkins University Press.

MANSBRIDGE, J., and TATE, K. 2001. Race trumps gender: the Thomas nomination in the black community. *PS: Political Science and Politics*, 25: 488–92.

MASON, A. 1956a. *Brandeis: A Free Man's Life*. New York: Viking.

—— 1956b. *Harlan Fiske Stone: Pillar of the Law*. New York: Viking.

MASSARO, J. 1990. *Supremely Political: The Role of Ideology and Presidential Management in Unsuccessful Supreme Court Nominations.* Albany: State University of New York Press.

McFEELEY, N. 1987. *Appointment of Judges: The Johnson Administration.* Austin: University of Texas Press.

MURPHY, W. 1961. In his own image: Mr. Chief Justice Taft and Supreme Court appointments. *Supreme Court Review,* 1: 159–93.

NAGEL, S. 1973. *Comparing Elected and Appointed Judicial Systems.* New York: Sage.

NEMACHECK, C. 2007. *Strategic Selection: Presidential Nomination of Supreme Court Justices From Herbert Hoover Through George W. Bush.* Charlottesville: University of Virginia Press.

O'BRIEN, D. 1988. *Judicial Roulette: Report of the 20th Century Fund Task Force on Judicial Selection.* London: Unwin-Hyman.

OVERBY, M., HENSCHEN, B., STRAUSS, J., and WALSH, M. 1992. Courting constituents? An analysis of the Senate confirmation vote on Clarence Thomas. *American Political Science Review,* 86: 997–1003.

PERRY, B. 1991. *A Representative Supreme Court? The Impact of Race, Religion and Gender on Appointments.* Westport, Conn.: Greenwood Press.

ROWLAND, C. K., CARP, R., and STIDHAM, R. 1984. Judges' policy choices and the value basis of judicial appointments: a comparison of support for criminal defendants among Nixon, Johnson and Kennedy appointees to the federal district courts. *Journal of Politics,* 46: 886–902.

SAVCHAK, E., HANSFORD, T., SONGER, D., MANNING, K., and CARP, R. 2006. Taking it to the next level: the elevation of district court judges to the U.S. Courts of Appeals. *American Journal of Political Science,* 50: 478–93.

SCHERER, N. 2005. *Scoring Points: Politicians, Activists and the Lower Federal Court Appointment Process.* Palo Alto, Calif.: Stanford University Press.

SCHROEDER, R., and HALL, H. 1966. Twenty-five years' experience with merit judicial selection in Missouri. *Texas Law Review,* 44: 1088–97.

SEGAL, J., COVER, A., and CAMERON, C. 1989. The role of ideology in the confirmation of Supreme Court justices. *Kentucky Law Journal,* 77: 485–507.

SEIDMAN, L. 1988. Ambivalence and accountability. *Southern California Law Review,* 61: 1571–600.

SHELDON, C., and LOVRICH, N., JR. 1983. Knowledge and judicial voting: the Oregon and Washington experiences. *Judicature,* 67: 234–45.

SILVERSTEIN, M. 1994. *Judicious Choices: The New Politics of Supreme Court Confirmations.* New York: W. W. Norton.

SINCLAIR, B. 1992 Senate process, congressional politics, and the Thomas nomination. *PS: Poltical Science and Politics,* 1992: 477–80.

SLOTNICK, E. 1984a. Judicial selection systems and nomination outcomes: does the process make a difference? *American Politics Quarterly,* 12: 225–40.

—— 1984b. The paths to the federal bench: gender, race and judicial recruitment. *Judicature,* 67: 370–88.

SPRIGGS, J., and WAHLBECK, P. 1995. Calling it quits: strategic retirement on the Federal Courts of Appeals, 1983–1991. *Political Research Quarterly,* 48: 573–97.

STIDHAM, R., CARP, R., and SONGER, D. 1996. The voting behavior of President Clinton's judicial appointees. *Judicature,* 80: 16–20.

VINES, K. 1963. The selection of judges in Louisiana. In *Studies in Judicial Politics*, ed. K. Vines and H. Jacob. New Orleans: Tulane University Press.

WALKER, T. 2003. David J. Danelski: social psychology and group choice. In *The Pioneers of Judicial Behavior*, ed. N. Maveety. Ann Arbor: University of Michigan Press.

WATSON, R., and DOWNING, R. 1969. *The Politics of Bench and Bar*. New York: Wiley & Sons.

WOODWARD, R., and ARMSTRONG, S. 1979. *The Brethren: Inside the Supreme Court*. New York: Simon and Schuster.

YALOF, D. 1999. *Pursuit of Justices: Presidential Politics and the Selection of Supreme Court Nominees*. Chicago: University of Chicago Press.

CHAPTER 28

THE U.S. SUPREME COURT

LEE EPSTEIN

THE editors assigned me a near-daunting task: to write 8,000 words or so on "central issues on the current research agenda" of students of the U.S. Supreme Court. In the first place, the sheer amount of research on the Court is overwhelming. A search in J-Stor retrieves over 3,245 articles with the "Supreme Court" in the title alone. Our library at Northwestern lists more than 600 books on the Court—and, again, that's just a title search.

Even more daunting is the lack of a singular research agenda. To the study of the Court, social scientists bring diverse substantive interests, competing theoretical frameworks, and methodological approaches ranging from deep study of a single case to sophisticated statistical analyses of several thousand.

Which all goes to say that possible topics and schemata for organizing them abound. Believing, however, that most research ought begin with interesting questions I have chosen to go that route here. Specifically, I focus on three substantive issues of interest to scholars in the field: appointments, agenda setting, and decision-making. For each, I summarize the state of our knowledge but, perhaps more importantly, I highlight areas requiring further attention. Indeed, after reviewing the extensive literature, I have come to believe that while we have made great strides in our quest to explain various features of the Court we still have some distance to travel. The gaps in our understanding may be narrowing, but they nonetheless remain. Moreover, the task of advancing our knowledge, as I suggest below, will profit immensely from a range of theoretical and methodological approaches.

One, perhaps needless, *caveat emptor*: in what follows, I have only skimmed the surface. I did not cover many strains of research in the three areas I chose to cover; and I left out many areas altogether. Of the latter, I particular regret lacking the space to discuss the impact of courts—a subject that is of considerable interest to political scientists, and one that has generated deep debate in recent years. Readers of this volume can take some solace in the fact that Charles Epp does an excellent job in developing one line of inquiry in this literature: law as an instrument of social reform.

1 APPOINTMENTS TO THE COURT

Of all the difficult choices confronting societies when they go about designing legal systems, among the most controversial are those pertaining to the selection and retention of their judges. Some of the most fervent constitutional debates—whether in Philadelphia in 1787 or in Moscow in 1993–4—over the institutional design of the judicial branch implicated not its power or competencies; they involved who would select and retain its members. It is thus hardly surprising to find an immense amount of scholarship on judicial selection and retention, ranging from the primarily normative (e.g. Carter 1994; Cramton and Carrington 2006) to the chiefly empirical (e.g. Segal et al. 1992; Yalof 1999), to work falling between the two (e.g. Davis 2005; Choi and Gulati 2002).

In the context of the U.S. Supreme Court, recent scholarship has shed considerable light on two aspects of the appointments process: presidential nomination and Senate confirmation. On the other hand, our knowledge of the process's triggering mechanism, a vacancy on the Court, remains sketchy.

Turning first to vacancies, although the U.S. Constitution implies that the process of appointing justices starts with the president, it in fact begins with a vacant seat on the Court. In three ways can that void arise: (1) the creation of a new seat, (2) the impeachment and removal or (3) departure of a sitting justice. None has received sufficient attention from political scientists.

The lack of attention to (1) and (2) is understandable. Congress has not altered the size of the Court since 1869; and no justice since Samuel Chase has been impeached and none convicted. Yet, these mechanisms raise too many interesting questions to delegate them to historians. A few suffice to make the point: why did the early Congress establish a norm against (political) impeachments (Knight and Epstein 1996*b*) or, for that matter, any rule that would require justices of one party to resign when a different party came to power, and why have these norms persisted?

That we have paid so little attention to (3), the departure of a sitting justice, is less explicable. Of course it is true that a handful of studies have attempted to model exits from the bench (see e.g. Hagle 1993; Squire 1988) but answers to even basic questions are hardly in abundance. So, for example, while we know from Yoon's (2006) important work that the overall turnover rate for U.S. district court judges jumps to 39 percent in the year they qualify for retirement benefits, that figure is only 13 percent for Supreme Court justices. What other forces are at work? Many commentators posit that justices strategically time their departures to coincide with presidents (and perhaps Senates) who share their partisanship or ideology. But systematic evidence, to the extent it exists, is far from conclusive.

Part of the problem lies in difficult questions of measurement. Thurgood Marshall tried to remain on the Court so that the conservative Ronald Reagan wouldn't replace him; Marshall said as much. But age, health, and the Democratic Party's electoral failure conspired against him. Some might not categorize Marshall's departure (during the George H. W. Bush administration) as "politically timed" but surely his decision to remain was strategic. How to capture that calculus is a challenging enterprise, but one hardly so daunting to render it quixotic.

In contrast to our lack of knowledge about vacancies come the mounds of literature on the next phases of the appointments process, nomination and confirmation. Making use of Goldman's (1997) classic framework, Segal and I (2005) argue that presidents pursue a variety of goals when making Supreme Court appointments but almost all fall under the rubric of politics. In some instances, politics has centered largely on partisan aims—the president attempts to exploit judicial appointments to promote his or his party's interest. In other, perhaps most, cases, politics has been primarily about policy—the president seeks to nominate justices who share his ideological preferences. (Of course, the two are sometimes difficult to separate.)

At least in political science circles the claim that presidents pursue political goals is relatively uncontroversial. More debate arises over the extent to which the Senate acts as a constraint on the president. To be sure, data suggest that presidents are relatively unfettered: fewer than 20 percent of their nominations have failed to gain Senate approval. In an important paper, however, Moraski and Shipan (1999) argue that the low rate of rejection merely shores up the effectiveness of the "advice and consent" clause. When confronted with a hostile Senate, presidents typically modulate their appointments, moving to the right or left as necessary.

The president's inclination to attend to the Senate may well explain why most nominations pass muster. Even so, the Moraski and Shipan result speaks most directly to the question of success within the Senate and not to success with individual senators. In 1993, Ruth Bader Ginsburg's candidacy generated only three nay votes but a decade or so later, Samuel A. Alito Jr. rather narrowly escaped defeat by a vote of 58–42.

In light of this degree of variation, accounting for the votes of senators has become something of a disciplinary cottage industry, though surely almost all contemporary work takes its cues from Cameron et al. (1990)—the first to elaborate and systematically assess a theoretical account of confirmation politics in the United States. Briefly, Cameron and his colleagues assume that electorally oriented senators vote on the basis of their constituents' "principle concerns in the nomination politics" (Cameron et al. 1990, 528). Those concerns primarily center on whether a candidate for the U.S. Supreme Court is (1) qualified for office and (2) sufficiently proximate to the senator (and his constituents) in ideological space. An analysis of data drawn from the votes of individual senators over the twenty-two nominations between 1953 and 1987 supports the account.

Despite the seminal contributions of both the Moraski/Shipan and Cameron et al. papers, it is hardly time to fold up our tents. Many questions remain, and important questions at that. Moraski and Shipan, for example, do not account for the filibuster. That the president may, in practice, need the votes of sixty senators, rather than a simple majority, suggests the possibility of an even greater role for the Senate (but see Johnson and Roberts 2005). By the same token, the Cameron et al. study pays little heed to the changing dynamics of Senate voting over Supreme Court nominees, be it the greater participation of interest groups and the media (see e.g. Davis 2005; Caldeira 1989; Caldeira and Wright 1998) or the increasingly important role of ideology (e.g. Epstein et al. 2006; Yalof 1999).

2 AGENDA SETTING

Just as institutions governing the selection of Supreme Court justices can structure the decisions of presidents and senators, institutions pertaining to access can constrain the choices justices make. As a general matter, justices can only decide issues that come to Court in accordance with jurisdictional rules in the Constitution or in statutes. Yet, even then, the decision-making process does not automatically go into operation. Judges and justices, in the United States and elsewhere, have imposed a series of informal barriers or developed norms that act as barriers to their courtrooms.

The use of formal and informal norms has given rise to many questions, ranging from whether they work to the advantage of particular litigants, to what effect they and other forces may have on the agendas of courts (see e.g. Pacelle 1991; Epp 1998). Here I consider yet another, actually perhaps the most persistent, question about the Supreme Court—what factors, whether norms or others, influence how the justices make decisions over which disputes to hear and resolve and which to reject; that is, how do they go about setting their agenda? This question has fascinated generations of judicial specialists (e.g. Boucher and Segal 1995; Caldeira and Wright

1988; Schubert 1959; Tanenhaus 1963; Ulmer 1972; Caldeira and Wright 1990; Perry 1991*a*)—as well it should. Agenda setting is one of the most important activities undertaken by political actors (e.g. Riker 1993)—and the justices are no exception. Actually, the Court's workload seems truly monumental—over 8,000 requests for review each term—and its discretion equally as high—these days, the justices typically hear and decide fewer than ninety cases per term.

No wonder analyses of agenda setting have burgeoned. And yet—despite immense interest in the subject (see e.g. Perry 1991*b*), the deployment of clever research strategies (e.g. Brenner 1979), and the employment of sophisticated technologies (e.g. Caldeira et al. 1999)—commentators do not agree on why Supreme Court justices make the case-selection decisions that they do. Some offer *legal or jurisprudential* models (Perry 1991*a*; Provine 1980); others see agenda setting as a clear example of *sincere voting to further policy goals* (e.g. Krol and Brenner 1990); still a third set suggest that it is laden with *strategic calculations* (e.g. Caldeira et al. 1999). Finally, there are those who point to the *litigants* themselves (e.g. Ulmer 1978). This disagreement, I should stress, is not a mere matter of emphasis. It is fundamental and it is an impediment to the development of an understanding of a crucial part of the justices' work—the establishment of their institutional agenda. It also impinges on our ability to think more generally about the role of the Court in American society. I return to these points later in the section. For now, let us consider the four basic perspectives with the acknowledgment that while all are influential, no one dominates.

Scholars adhering to a legal or jurisprudential account hold that judges seek to reach principled decisions at the agenda-setting stage—those based largely on various rules governing their review process. For Supreme Court justices, that would be Rule 10, which suggests that the Court prioritizes cases that have generated conflict in the lower courts or that have come into conflict with their own precedents. When justices follow this rule, so the argument goes, they are engaging in principled agenda setting because the rules themselves are impartial as to the possible result over a particular petition. If justices considered only whether conflict existed, their agenda-setting decisions would not reflect their own policy preferences over the substantive consequences of a case but, rather, those of the dictates of the rule itself.

Support for this claim abounds. Based on interviews with U.S. Supreme Court justices and their clerks, Perry (1991*a*, 127) concludes: "All [the justices] are disposed to resolve conflicts when they exist and want to know if a particular case poses a conflict." Flemming's (2004, 99) research reinforces the general importance of "impartial" rules from beyond the borders of the United States. Based on a painstakingly detailed analysis of the Canadian Supreme Court's agenda-setting decisions, he claims that a "jurisprudential account," grounded in the country's "public importance" rule, "offers a persuasive story of how Canada's justices set their agenda."

No doubt virtually all scholars who study case selection attach some importance to the rules governing the process. But equally true is that data raise questions about whether rules provide the sole or even best explanation of agenda-setting decisions. During the 1989 term, for example, the justices declined to review more than 200 petitions that in one way or another possessed real conflict (Baum 2001); likewise, of the 184 cases it agreed to decide during its 1981 term, only 47 (25 percent) met the explicit criteria identified in Rule 10 (O'Brien 2000).

It is thus hardly surprising that Caldeira and Wright (1988) claim Rule 10 provides little aid in understanding "how the Court makes gatekeeping decisions." Or, to put it more charitably, the legal considerations listed in the Rule may act as constraints on the justices' behavior—the Supreme Court might reject petitions lacking genuine conflict—but they do not necessarily further our understanding of what occurs in cases meeting the criteria.

That is why scholars have looked elsewhere, specifically to the justices' policy preferences. Accounts of this sort come in two flavors: sincere (or reversal) and strategic policy models. On the first, justices have policy goals at the review stage— they would like to see the final opinion of the Court reflect their preferred position—and they achieve them by voting sincerely. In operational terms, justices will vote to grant those petitions in which the lower court reached a decision they disliked, such that right-of-center justices will vote to hear cases decided in the liberal direction below and liberal justices will prefer to review those decided conservatively. Why? Segal and Spaeth (2002, 253) provide the conventional answer: "Given a finite number of cases that can be reviewed in a given term, the Court must decide how to utilize its time, the Court's most scarce resources. Certainly, overturning unfavorable lower court decisions has more of an impact—if only to the parties to the litigation—than affirming favorable ones. Thus, the justices should hear more cases with which they disagree, other things being equal."

A good deal of support exists for this proposition, some of which once again comes from the justices themselves. One told Perry (1991a, 270) that the *certiorari* vote is a preliminary vote on the merits in "a majority of cases" and that "[g]enerally when people vote to grant, they feel that it is because [the case was] wrongly decided [below]." More support comes from data showing that, in fact, the Court typically reverses the lower court decisions it reviews—as many as seven out of ten in recent terms—as well as from systematic studies. Krol and Brenner's crosstabular analysis of the aggregated votes of members of the Vinson Court (1946–52), for example, indicates that the justices simply voted against hearing cases with lower court decisions that they liked (ideologically speaking) and voted for hearing those cases with lower court decisions that they disliked. More recent confirmation, though from lower down on the judicial hierarchy, comes in George's (1999) analysis of the determinants of the decision to grant *en banc* review by U.S. Courts of Appeals. Her data show that "extremely conservative courts of appeals...are far more likely to rehear a liberal decision en banc than a conservative one."

In light of these findings, many scholars have come to accept the view that justices are policy-oriented and actively make choices to advance that goal at the review stage and, for that matter, on the merits of cases (Caldeira et al. 1999; Epstein and Knight 1998; Eskridge 1991; Maltzman et al. 2000). Where questions arise is over whether they pursue their policy goals sincerely or with some consideration of the preferences and likely actions of their colleagues. A strategic policy account suggests they do the latter: In deciding whether to review a case, justices consider the likelihood of prevailing at the merits stage. After all, proponents of this account ask, why would policy-oriented justices vote to review a case if they did not think their side could muster sufficient support on the merits?

Does the evidence support this strategic view? Yes but it is mixed. As early as 1959, Schubert relied on inferences from patterns of data (rather than actual *certiorari* votes) to argue that during the 1940s, liberals on the U.S. Supreme Court chose to grant Federal Employees' Liability Act (FELA) cases in which the lower court had decided against the worker and in which the worker would have a good chance of winning on the merits. In contemporary parlance, justices "defensively deny" (when they decline to review cases that they would like to hear because they believe they will not prevail at the merits stage) but they do not "aggressively grant" (when they take a case that "may not warrant review because they have calculated that it has certain characteristics that would make it particularly good for developing a doctrine in a certain way, and the characteristics make it more likely to win on their merits") (Perry 1991a, 208). Boucher and Segal (1995), however, claim that justices pay heed to probable outcomes when they wish to affirm (an aggressive grant strategy) but not when they desire the Court to reverse, while Caldeira and his colleagues (1999) find evidence of both aggressive grants and defensive denials.

Yet a fourth perspective on agenda setting emphasizes the role of particular litigants or their attorneys, whether "repeat players" or "one-shotters," "upperdogs" or "underdogs." McGuire and Caldeira (1993), for example, show that the U.S. Supreme Court is more likely to grant review when an experienced attorney represents the appellant; and Ulmer (1978) demonstrates that upperdogs, under certain conditions, have a clear advantage in the American high court. Along similar lines, numerous studies have concluded that when the U.S. government is a petitioner to a suit, the Court is significantly more likely to grant review (Armstrong and Johnson 1982; Caldeira and Wright 1988; Tanenhaus 1963; Ulmer 1984).

Why the United States (as represented by the Solicitor General), other repeat players, and upperdogs are so successful is open to speculation. What we do know, and what I hope readers can gather from this short review, is why some scholars have deemed the agenda-setting literature a "mess" (Boucher and Segal 1995). Even those who agree on the basic motivation of justices at the review stage—the pursuit of policy—disagree over whether justices advance that goal by always voting sincerely or by making strategic calculations about the eventual outcome at the merits stage.

Compounding matters even further is the existence of other plausible explanations that scholars have yet to consider in any systematic fashion. It is possible, for example, that justices do engage in strategic case selection but not with regard to one another. Rather, they may be attentive to the preferences and likely actions of other relevant actors—such as executives and legislatures—when they go about their agenda-setting task, and this may explain why the government enjoys extraordinary success both at the review stage and on the merits of cases. Consider this comment, not from a U.S. jurist but a justice on the Russian Constitutional Court:

When in December 1995, before the [parliamentary] elections and in the very heat of the electoral campaign, we received a petition signed by a group of deputies concerning the constitutional validity of the five percent barrier for party lists. We refused to consider it. I opposed considering this request, because I believe that the Court should not be itching for a political fight... The Court must avoid getting involved in current political affairs, such as partisan struggles.   (Nikitinsky 1997)

Though this hardly provides proof positive of the existence of yet another explanation of agenda-setting decisions (for additional, though also inconclusive evidence, see Epstein et al. 2002), it is suggestive: This crucial line of inquiry may be in even greater disarray than many scholars think, and the consequences even more disturbing. Surely, the messy state of the literature impinges on our ability to reach a precise understanding of the agenda-setting process, to generate clear-cut predictions. Likewise, to the extent that case selection has implications for the role the Court plays in American society, we are unable to assess it. When the justices emphasize conflict—whether among lower courts, between state and federal courts, or with the Court's own previously decided cases—they convey important information to their judicial inferiors. A desire to reinforce their role as key players in the larger U.S. political system, on the other hand, may manifest itself in an abundance of particularly salient cases on the docket.

What can be done to clean up this "mess?" First, scholars ought refrain from taking certain short cuts that are not just potentially problematic but also may explain the mixed findings in this area. Selection on the dependent variable is particularly rampant: In a non-trivial fraction of published studies the authors analyze only those cases to which the Court granted review rather than the full set of petitions—grants and denials. I understand why scholars invoke this strategy—they may lack the time, resources, or both to take another route. But we also must acknowledge that it is replete with potential pitfalls, the most important being the introduction of bias. Since we know that cases granted review are not representative of the universe of petitions—in fact, a great deal of research has demonstrated that they vary systematically from nongranted cases—it is inappropriate to draw inferences about the way in which justices select cases to review by considering only those petitions they grant.

Second, tricky problems of measurement require creative solutions. Consider jurisprudential approaches. Because the question is not whether conflict is an important consideration but, rather, just how important it is, all studies must incorporate this variable. But how ought they do so? Some rely on the parties' briefs; and others on a project undertaken by law students at New York University in the early 1980s (Estreicher and Sexton 1986, 1984). Neither, for various reasons, is ideal, but alternatives have been difficult to develop. Until now. With the release of Harry A. Blackmun's judicial papers, researchers may be able to make use of the clerk's preliminary (cert.) memos to generate more reliable and valid indicators of conflict.

Finally, as scholars develop better measures and data sources they could make an important addition: expand the reach of their studies to include discretionary courts abroad. As the author of one of the few comparative analyses in this area (Flemming 1997, 1) put it: "Very little is known about agenda setting by courts of final appeal in countries other than the United States. As a consequence, we do not know if the large and well-developed American literature on this topic can be generalized beyond the U.S. Supreme Court." Having just undertaken an extensive review of the relevant literature, I am in complete agreement. Then again, I am not sure we know as much about the American context as Flemming suggests, thereby ensuring that work outside the United States would illuminate practices here.

3 Decision-making

So far I have repeatedly made the claim that "this area has generated an immense amount of research." This is certainly true with regard to appointments and case selection but it is doubly so for judicial decision-making. Over the past six decades, specialists have produced scores of papers and books aimed at explaining Supreme Court decisions on the merits. The result is a vast literature that approaches the subject from normative and positivist perspectives, with theories adopted and adapted from the social sciences and humanities, and with data that are qualitative and quantitative.

Once again no one chapter in this volume, much less a section of one, could consider all this scholarship. And I do not try. Rather, let me highlight a point of agreement, several of departure, and finally some ideas for the future.

The point of consensus is easy to identify: The vast majority of contemporary political scientists hold that justices are by and large motivated to pursue policy; that is, members of the Court want to move the substantive content of the law as close as possible to their preferred political position.

This was not always how political scientists viewed the justices. Much of their early writing on the Court was so highly doctrinal that it was virtually indistinguishable from legal analyses produced by law professors. Indeed, some political scientists who studied the Court went so far as to explicitly reject politics. Cushman's examination of the 1936–7 term, one of the most volatile in history, is exemplary. After acknowledging that the "1936 term . . . will probably be rated as notable, he enumerated some of the facts . . . one should bear in mind"—Roosevelt had won a landslide reelection and had submitted his Court-packing plan. Rather than demonstrate how those "facts" might have affected Court decisions, however, Cushman simply noted "no suggestion is made as to what inferences, if any, might be drawn from them" (Cushman 1938, 278).

Through the efforts of Pritchett (1941; 1948) and later, Schubert (1965), Murphy (1964), and Spaeth (1964), among others, political scientists began to move away from purely doctrinal analyses of the Court and toward the more political explanations that characterize today's work (for an interesting statement about the development of the field, see Whittington 2000). Surely, it was peculiar in Pritchett's day—at least among political scientists, though not legal realists—to write that justices are "motivated by their own preferences" as Pritchett did in 1948 (pp. xii–xiii). But I dare say that nary a political scientist blinked an eye when, five decades later, George and I (1992, 325) characterized justices as "single-minded seekers of legal policy." Nor was the community any more shocked when Gillman (2001) concluded that *Bush v. Gore* (2000) was a partisan decision.

Where more disagreement arises is over whether analyses should incorporate more than the justices' ideological preferences. A juxtaposition of two competing approaches, the attitudinal model and strategic accounts (relatives of the sincere and strategic policy models of case selection), brings this debate into relief. On the first, we need not venture too far beyond the justices' sincerely held ideological responses to cases before them. Or, as two prominent attitudinalists put it, "[Scalia] votes the way he does because he is extremely conservative; Marshall voted the way he did because he was extremely liberal" (Segal and Spaeth 2002, 86). Freeing justices from considerations other than ideology, according to attitudinalists, is the lack of electoral accountability and ambition for higher office, the control justices enjoy over their agenda, and the dearth of judicial superiors (Segal and Spaeth 2002). In stark juxtaposition are strategic accounts, which belong to a class of nonparametric rational choice models as they assume that goal-directed actors operate in strategic or interdependent decision-making contexts. Specifically, these accounts suggest that: (1) justices make choices in order to achieve certain goals (typically but not necessarily policy goals); (2) justices act strategically in the sense that their choices depend on their expectations about the choices of other actors; and (3) these choices are structured by the institutional setting in which they are made (Epstein and Knight 1998).

The distinctions between the two models are many, with two worthy of note here: *interdependency* and *institutions*. Beginning with the role of interdependent choice, on strategic accounts, goal-oriented justices take into account the preferences and likely actions of actors who are in position to thwart or advance their goals—

be it their colleagues, elected officials, or the public. On the attitudinal model, attentiveness to these forces is unnecessary; justices always behave in accord with their sincere preferences.

Both sides, it is worth noting, have developed substantial support for their positions. In a highly influential article (Segal 1997) and later in his book with Spaeth (Segal and Spaeth 2002, 348), Segal is blunt: "the Court's reaction to the ... revelation of congressional preferences is a collective yawn." Armed with equally impressive evidence, Bergara et al. (2003) refute Segal's conclusion asserting that when the Court interprets statutes it in fact "adjusts its decisions to Presidential and congressional preferences." And now several scholars have added fuel to fire by arguing that the justices are not only attentive to the president and Congress in the statutory context but also in the constitutional realm (e.g. Epstein et al. 2001; Harvey and Friedman 2006; Rosenberg 1992)

A second crucial distinction between attitudinal and strategic accounts centers on how they treat institutions. Only a few come into play for attitudinalists, and then only those that allow the justices to vote as they so desire—such as the lack of an electoral connection. By contrast, strategic accounts emphasize the range of institutions but perhaps none more controversial than precedent. To many strategic analysts precedent may not determine judicial outcomes but neither is it, as some attitudinalists contend, completely irrelevant; rather it can serve as a constraint on justices from acting on their personal preferences. In other words, justices have a preferred rule that they would like to establish in the case before them but they strategically modify their position to attend to a normative constraint—a norm favoring *stare decisis.*

Why would justices follow precedent in those situations in which they would prefer to create a different rule? Strategic accounts supply at least two answers: prudential and normative. As to the first, *stare decisis* is one way in which the Court respects the established expectations of a community. To the extent that members of a community base their future expectations on the belief that others will follow existing rules, the Court has an interest in minimizing the disruptive effects of overturning them. If the Court makes a radical change, the community may be unable or unwilling to adapt, resulting in a decision that fails to produce an efficacious rule. As to normative reasons why justices may adhere to precedent rather their own preferences, the logic is this: If a community holds a fundamental belief that the "rule of law" requires the Court to be constrained by precedent, the justices may follow the belief even if they do not personally accept it. The constraint follows from the justices' understanding that the community's belief affects its willingness to accept and comply with the Court's decisions. If the members of the community believe that the legitimate judicial function requires adherence to precedent, then they will reject as normatively illegitimate decisions that regularly and systematically violate precedent. To the extent justices are concerned with establishing rules that the community will accept, they will keep in mind the fact that the community must regard these rules as legitimate. In this way, a norm of *stare decisis* can constrain the actions of even those justices who do not share the view that they should be constrained by past decisions.

Once again, both attitudinalists and strategic analysts have marshaled considerable support for their claims about *stare decisis*. Segal and Spaeth (1996), for example, hypothesize that if precedent matters, it ought to affect the subsequent decisions of members of the Court. In operational terms, if a justice has dissented from a decision establishing a particular precedent, she or he should still feel bound by it and not dissent from its subsequent application. But the data, they argue, suggest otherwise. Of the eighteen justices included in their study, only two occasionally subjugated their preferences to precedent (see also Spaeth and Segal 1999). In a critique of Segal and Spaeth's work, however, Knight and I (1996a) offer substantial evidence of behavior that is consistent with the existence of a norm of respect for precedent. That evidence ranged from the use of precedent in attorneys' briefs, to appeals to precedent made by Supreme Court justices in Conference, to citations to precedent in judicial decisions (see also Brisbin 1996). Newer studies purport to find even more direct evidence of the effect of "law" on the Court's decisions. Richards and Kritzer's (2002, 308) analysis of free expression cases, for example, emphasizes the importance of jurisprudential regimes, or "a key precedent, or set of related precedents, that structures the way in which the Supreme Court justices evaluate key elements of cases in arriving at decisions in a particular legal area."

These and related debates about judging are positive developments. As short as a decade ago, the relationship between the Court and other political actors or even the role of precedent was barely a blip on the radar of political scientists. Today at least we are actively engaged in solving these intellectual puzzles; and, in fact, we are making substantial progress on all fronts. But if the goal is develop a fuller picture of the Court's decisions we can do better. I understand the complicating factors. It is quite difficult, for example, to document the (potential) constraint imposed by legislatures and executives: when justices rule in favor of, say, the existing regime, they may do so because they share the regime's preferences (sincere)—and not because they are attempting to appease that regime (sophisticated). Distinguishing these forms of behavior—sincere and sophisticated—turns out to be no easy task, though recent work has advanced the project. Along these lines, I am particularly taken by analyses of courts abroad (e.g. Helmke 2004; Vanberg 2004). From theoretical, methodological, and substantive perspectives, I have learned a great deal from these studies, and I suspect other Americanists would as well.

Assessing the impact of precedent and other "legal" variables turns out to be equally difficult. Again, I see substantial progress, though, ironically enough, not necessarily in studies of the Supreme Court (e.g. Staudt 2004; Baldez et al. 2006). One exception is an innovative paper by McGuire and Vanberg (2005). Using new technology for mapping texts into policy space, they estimate the relative polarity of particular opinions (e.g. *Lee v. Weisman* registers as more liberal than *Wallace v. Jaffree*). Although the method itself is not flawless (see e.g. Monroe and Maeda 2004) and their application only one among many possibilities, I am taken with the general motivation behind the McGuire and Vanberg (2005) study: to move away from an exclusive focus on the (typically dichotomous) bottom line of a judicial decision (e.g. reverse/affirm, liberal/conservative, winner/loser, uphold/strike down) and to an approach that exploits the entire opinion but eliminates researcher judgment. Indeed, it strikes me as a powerful method for investigating positions in decisions, whether over policy or, possibly, method (e.g. text-, intent-based approaches to interpretation). Ideal point estimation for individual justices based on this method is also possible and just as likely to be informative. Turning to the dynamics of the decision-making process, we may well be able to determine the extent to which areas of the law are interrelated and the degree to which legal decision-making is gradual (as many would argue), abrupt, or both.

References

ARMSTRONG, V., and JOHNSON, C. A. 1982. Certiorari decisions by the Warren and Burger Courts: is cue theory time bound? *Polity*, 15: 141–50.

BALDEZ, L., EPSTEIN, L., and MARTIN, A. D. 2006. Does the U.S. Constitution need an ERA? *Journal of Legal Studies*, 35: 243–83.

BAUM, L. 2001. *The Supreme Court*, 7th edn. Washington, DC: CQ Press.

BERGARA, M., RICHMAN, B., and SPILLER, P. T. 2003. Modeling Supreme Court strategic decision making: the congressional constraint. *Legislative Studies Quarterly*, 28: 247–80.

BOUCHER, R. L., and SEGAL, J. A. 1995. Supreme Court Justices as strategic decision makers: aggressive grants and defensive denials. *Journal of Politics*, 57: 824–37.

BRENNER, S. 1979. The new certiorari game. *Journal of Politics*, 41: 649–55.

BRISBIN, JR., R. A. Slaying the dragon: Segal, Spaeth, and the function of law in Supreme Court decision making. *American Journal of Political Science*, 40: 1004–17.

CALDEIRA, G. A. 1989. Commentary on Senate confirmation of Supreme Court justices: the roles of organized and unorganized interests. *Kentucky Law Journal*, 77: 531–8.

—— and WRIGHT, J. R. 1988. Organized interests and agenda setting in the U.S. Supreme Court. *American Political Science Review*, 82: 1109–28.

—— —— 1990. The discuss list: agenda building in the Supreme Court. *Law and Society Review*, 24: 807–36.

—— —— 1998. Lobbying for justice: organized interests, Supreme Court nominations, and the United States Senate. *American Journal of Political Science*, 42: 499–523.

—— —— and ZORN, C. J. 1999. Sophisticated voting and gate-keeping in the Supreme Court. *Journal of Law, Economics and Organization*, 15: 549–72.

CAMERON, C. M., COVER, A. D., and SEGAL, J. A. 1990. Senate voting on Supreme Court nominees: a neoinstitutional model. *American Political Science Review*, 84: 525–34.

CARTER, S. L. 1994. *The Confirmation Mess: Cleaning Up the Federal Appointments Process.* New York: Basic Books.

CHOI, S., and GULATI, M. 2002. A tournament of judges? *California Law Review,* 92: 299–322.

CRAMTON, R. C., and CARRINGTON, P. D. (eds.) 2006. *Reforming the Court: Term Limits for Supreme Court Justices.* Durham, NC: Carolina Academic Press.

CUSHMAN, R. E. 1938. Constitutional law in 1936–37. *American Political Science Review,* 32: 278–310.

DAVIS, R. 2005. *Electing Justice: Fixing the Supreme Court Nomination Process.* New York: Oxford University Press.

EPP, C. R. 1998. *The Rights Revolution: Lawyers, Activists, and Supreme Courts in Comparative Perspective.* Chicago: University of Chicago Press.

EPSTEIN, L. (ed.) 2005. *Courts and Judges.* Aldershot: Ashgate.

—— and KNIGHT, J. 1998. *The Choices Justices Make.* Washington, DC: CQ Press.

—— —— 2004. Courts and judges. In *The Blackwell Companion to Law and Society,* ed. A. Sarat. Malden, Mass.: Blackwell.

—— —— and MARTIN, A. D. 2001. The Supreme Court as a (strategic) national policy maker. *Emory Law Journal,* 50: 101–29.

—— —— —— 2003. The political (science) context of judging. *St. Louis University Law Journal,* 47: 783–817.

—— LINDSTADT, R., SEGAL, J. A., and WESTERLAND, C. 2006. The changing dynamics of Senate voting on Supreme Court nominees. *Journal of Politics,* 68: 296–307.

—— and SEGAL, J. A. 2005. *Advice and Consent: The Politics of Judicial Appointments.* New York: Oxford University Press.

—— —— and VICTOR, J. N. 2002. Dynamic agenda setting on the U.S. Supreme Court: an empirical assessment. *Harvard Journal on Legislation,* 39: 395–433.

ESKRIDGE, JR., W. N. 1991. Overriding Supreme Court statutory interpretation decisions. *Yale Law Journal,* 101: 331–417.

ESTREICHER, S., and SEXTON, J. 1984. A managerial theory of the Supreme Court's responsibilities: an empirical study. *New York University Law Review,* 59: 681–822.

—— —— 1986. *Redefining the Supreme Court's Role.* New Haven, Conn.: Yale University Press.

FLEMMING, R. B. 1997. Deciding to decide in Canada's Supreme Court. Presented at the annual meeting of the Conference Group on the Scientific Study of Judicial Politics.

—— 2004. *Tournament of Appeals: Granting Judicial Review in Canada.* Vancouver: UBC Press.

GEORGE, T. E. 1999. The dynamics and determinants of the decision to grant en banc review. *Washington Law Review,* 74: 213–74.

—— and EPSTEIN, L. 1992. On the nature of Supreme Court decision making. *American Political Science Review,* 86: 323–37.

GILLMAN, H. 2001. *The Votes that Counted.* Chicago: University of Chicago Press.

GOLDMAN, S. 1997. *Picking Federal Judges.* New Haven, Conn.: Yale University Press.

HAGLE, T. M. 1993. Strategic retirements: a political model of turnover on the United States Supreme Court. *Political Behavior,* 15: 25–48.

HARVEY, A., and FRIEDMAN, B. 2006. The limits of judicial independence: the Supreme Court's constitutional rulings. *Legislative Studies Quarterly,* 31: 533–62.

HELMKE, G. 2004. *Courts Under Constraints: Judges, Generals, and Presidents in Argentina.* Cambridge: Cambridge University Press.

JOHNSON, T. R., and ROBERTS, J. M. 2005. Pivotal politics, presidential capital and Supreme Court nominations. *Congress and the Presidency*, 32: 31–48.

KNIGHT, J., and EPSTEIN, L. 1996a. The norm of stare decisis. *American Journal of Political Science*, 40: 1018–35.

—— —— 1996b. On the struggle for judicial supremacy. *Law and Society Review*, 30: 87–130.

KROL, J. F., and BRENNER, S. 1990. Strategies in certiorari voting on the United States Supreme Court. *Western Political Quarterly*, 43: 335–42.

MALTZMAN, F., SPRIGGS, II, J. F., and WAHLBECK, P. J. 2000. *Crafting Law on the Supreme Court*. Cambridge: Cambridge University Press.

McGUIRE, K. T., and CALDEIRA, G. A. 1993. Lawyers, organized interests, and the law of obscenity: agenda-setting in the Supreme Court. *American Political Science Review*, 87: 717–28.

—— and VANBERG, G. 2005. Mapping the policies of the U.S. Supreme Court: data, opinions, and constitutional law. Presented at the annual meeting of the American Political Science Association, Washington, DC.

MONROE, B. L., and MAEDA, K. 2004. Talk's cheap: text-based estimation of rhetorical ideal-points. Presented at the annual meeting of the Society for Political Methodology, Stanford University.

MORASKI, B. J., and SHIPAN, C. R. 1999. The politics of Supreme Court nominations: a theory of institutional choice and constraints. *American Journal of Political Science*, 43: 1069–95.

MURPHY, W. F. 1964. *Elements of Judicial Strategy*. Chicago: University of Chicago Press.

NIKITINSKY, L. 1997. Interview with Boris Ebzeev, justice of the Constitutional Court of the Russian Federation. *Eastern European Constitutional Review*, 1997: 83–8.

O'BRIEN, D. M. 2000. *Storm Center: The Supreme Court in American Politics*, 5th edn. New York: W. W. Norton.

PACELLE, JR., R. L.. 1991. *The Transformation of the Supreme Court's Agenda*. Boulder, Colo.: Westview.

PERRY, H. W. 1991a. *Deciding to Decide: Agenda Setting in the United States Supreme Court*. Cambridge, Mass.: Harvard University Press.

—— 1991b. Agenda setting and case selection. In *American Courts: A Critical Assessment*, ed. J. Gates and C. Johnson. Washington, DC: CQ Press.

PRITCHETT, C. H. 1941. Divisions of opinion among justices of the U.S. Supreme Court. *American Political Science Review*, 35: 890–8.

—— 1948. *The Roosevelt Court*. New York: Macmillan.

PROVINE, D. M. 1980. *Case Selection in the United States Supreme Court*. Chicago: University of Chicago Press.

RICHARDS, M. J., and KRITZER, H. M. 2002. Jurisprudential regimes in Supreme Court decision making. *American Political Science Review*, 96: 305–20.

RIKER, W. H. (ed.) 1993. *Agenda Formation*. Ann Arbor: University of Michigan Press.

ROSENBERG, G. N. 1992. Judicial independence and the reality of political power. *Review of Politics*, 54: 369–98.

SCHUBERT, G. 1959. The certiorari game. In *Quantitative Analysis of Judicial Behavior*, ed. G. Schubert. New York: Free Press.

—— 1965. *The Judicial Mind: The Attitudes and Ideologies of Supreme Court Justices, 1946–1963*. Evanston, Ill.: Northwestern University Press.

SEGAL, J. A. 1997. Separation-of-powers games in the positive theory of law and courts. *American Political Science Review*, 91: 28–44.

—— CAMERON, C. M., and COVER, A. D. 1992. A spatial model of roll call voting: senators, constituents, presidents, and interest groups in Supreme Court confirmations. *American Journal of Political Science*, 36: 96–121.

—— and SPAETH, H. J. 1996. The influence of stare decisis on the vote of United States Supreme Court justices. *American Journal of Political Science*, 40: 971–1003.

—— —— 2002. *The Supreme Court and the Attitudinal Model Revisited*. New York: Cambridge University Press.

SPAETH, H. J. 1964. The judicial restraint of Mr. Justice Felix Frankfurter—myth or reality? *American Journal of Political Science*, 8: 22–38.

—— and SEGAL, J. A. 1999. *Majority Rule or Minority Will: Adherence to Precedent on the U.S. Supreme Court*. New York: Cambridge University Press.

SQUIRE, P. 1988. Politics and personal factors in retirement from the United States Supreme Court. *Political Behavior*, 10: 180–90.

STAUDT, N. C. 2004. Modeling standing. *New York University Law Review*, 79: 612–84.

TANENHAUS, J., et al. 1963. The Supreme Court's certiorari jurisdiction: cue theory. In *Judicial Decision Making*, ed. G. Schubert. New York: Free Press.

ULMER, S. S. 1972. The decisions to grant certiorari as an indicator to decision on the merits. *Polity*, 4: 429–47.

—— 1978. Selecting cases for Supreme Court review: an underdog model. *American Political Science Review*, 72: 902–10.

—— 1984. The Supreme Court's certiorari decisions: conflict as a predictive variable. *American Political Science Review*, 78: 901–11.

VANBERG, G. 2004. *Constitutional Review in Germany*. Cambridge: Cambridge University Press.

WHITTINGTON, K. E. 2000. Once more unto the breach: post-behavioralist approaches to judicial politics. *Law and Social Inquiry*, 25: 601–34.

YALOF, D. A. 1999. *Pursuit of Justices*. Chicago: University of Chicago Press.

YOON, A. 2006. Pensions, politics, and judicial tenure: an empirical study of federal judges, 1869–2002. *American Law and Economics Review*, 8: 143–80.

CASES

Lee v. Weisman, 505 U.S. 577 (1992).
Wallace v. Jaffree, 466 U.S. 924 (1984).
Bush v. Gore, 531 U.S. 98 (2000).

CHAPTER 29

RELATIONS AMONG COURTS

SUSAN HAIRE

1 INTRODUCTION

THE interactions between judges of different courts are frequently complex, as illustrated in the case of *U.S. v. Sawyer*, 441 F.3d 890 (10th Cir. 2006). The federal government had charged the defendant, Sawyer, with conspiracy to possess stolen property which had traveled in interstate commerce. In response to Sawyer's motion to suppress evidence collected by Kansas law enforcement officers from a search conducted in the state of Oklahoma, the federal district court had certified a question of state law to the Oklahoma Court of Criminal Appeals. After receiving the divided Oklahoma court's response, the federal district judge granted the motion to suppress. The government appealed and the Tenth Circuit panel, made up of judges appointed by Republican presidents, reversed the decision of the district court judge, a Clinton appointee. In addition to suggesting the potential for friction between judges of different courts, this case illustrates how relations among courts are shaped by hierarchical structures and overlapping jurisdictions in the American legal system. By encouraging attention to precedents on factually similar decisions from other courts, the norm of *stare decisis* also structures intercourt communications.

Over the last several decades, a substantial line of scholarly inquiry has been devoted to evaluating the dynamics which characterize intercourt relations. Early scholarship offered rich descriptive accounts of lower-court reaction to controversial

Supreme Court decisions in criminal procedure, equal protection, and civil liberties.[1] Although the behavioral focus in judicial politics research directed attention to individual and case level explanations for variation in judicial responsiveness to upper-court doctrine, by the 1970s and early 1980s, scholars shifted their focus to theories of organizations and communications. More recently, the utilization of formal models, increased availability of data sources on lower-court decision-making, and advances in informational technology have permitted scholars to identify and test propositions which explain patterns of intercourt relations that arise from hierarchical structures as well as those that develop in the transmission of precedents across independent judicial systems.

2 HIERARCHICAL RELATIONSHIPS IN AMERICAN COURT SYSTEMS

2.1 Hierarchical Control and Precedent

The organization of judicial power in the U.S. is frequently conceptualized as a pyramidal structure with the Supreme Court standing at the apex on questions of federal law, including the interpretation of the Constitution.[2] From this perspective, the Supreme Court establishes doctrine by deciding cases, which in turn guide lower courts in disputes involving similar fact patterns. According to the norm of vertical *stare decisis*, decisions rendered by the Supreme Court may not be overruled by a lower court, but rather must be followed until altered or overturned by the Court. If judges sitting in the lower courts do not follow the Court's doctrines, litigants will appeal to ensure compliance. Early on, scholars recognized that reality often fell short of this ideal. In the 1950s, scholars chronicled the reluctance of lower-court judges to implement *Brown vs. Board of Education* (Peltason 1961; Wasby 1970).[3] Nevertheless, a substantial body of scholarship reported that lower-court judges rarely declared that they would not follow unpopular Warren Court's directives in criminal procedure and other areas of civil liberties (Canon 1973; Tarr 1977; Gruhl 1980).

---

[1] For a thorough discussion of scholarly approaches to evaluating the impact of Supreme Court decisions on lower-court policies, see Wasby (1970), Songer (1988), and Canon and Johnson (1999).

[2] Similar hierarchies represent state judicial systems where state courts of last resort are responsible for issuing authoritative precedent with respect to issues of state law.

[3] More recent research suggests that, although *Brown* did not bring about compliance in state supreme courts, lower federal courts were more responsive to the decision of the U.S. Supreme Court (Romero and Romero 2003).

Although defiance appeared to be rare, empirical assessments of the degree to which the Warren Court's precedents influenced lower-court decision-making yielded mixed findings and suggested differing conceptualizations of lower-court responsiveness (Canon and Johnson 1999; Songer 1988). To the extent a consensus emerged in this line of inquiry, scholars tended to conceive of compliance as the proper application of standards established by the upper-court precedent in cases which raise similar questions (Tarr 1977, 35). Using this conceptualization, scholars focused on the lower court's treatment of the upper court's precedent in its opinion, frequently relying on *Shepard's Citations*.[4] "Positive" lower-court citations to upper-court decisions suggest compliance; negative treatment of precedent, noncompliance.

Although lower-court judges generally defer to the norm of *stare decisis*, their preferences over policy may affect their decision-making with conceptions of judicial duty shaping the extent to which he or she decides based on those preferences. Influences in the decision-making environment may also mold lower-court judges' adherence to upper-court directives. Peltason (1961) showed the social pressures faced by federal district court judges during the 1950s in the Deep South when confronted with issues of desegregation; and later research suggested that these judges continued to be reluctant to desegregate school districts in their own communities (Giles and Walker 1975). The local environment also affected responsiveness by state supreme court judges to the Supreme Court's Establishment Clause decisions; compliance with the Court's doctrine tended to be lower in states in which religious practices in schools were entrenched (Tarr 1977).

The effect of precedent on lower-court decision-making may also vary with the clarity of the Court's holding. When the Supreme Court clearly explains its holding, the likelihood of lower-court compliance increases (Canon and Johnson 1999). Building on this premise, scholarship suggests that the precedential value of an upper-court decision is not fixed at the time that the court establishes the rule, but varies over time (Landes and Posner 1976). The vitality of an upper-court precedent may diminish if the court does not refer to the decision in later cases (Hansford and Spriggs 2006). Vitality also appears to shape lower-court use of upper-court precedent. According to a study of lower federal court citations over a span of fifty years, as the number of Supreme Court decisions referring to its own precedent increased, lower-court citations, particularly positive references to that precedent, also increased (Hansford and Spriggs 2006).

---

[4] This reference service lists, by cited case, how that opinion is treated by subsequent courts which cite it. Shepard's categorizes treatment of precedent as: overrule, question, limit, criticize, distinguish, follow, parallel, explain, or harmonize. Although some categories clearly suggest the citing court adopted the holding from the cited case in a positive light (followed, parallel), other categories (harmonize, explained) require further reading of the case before concluding that the treatment is positive. Scholars face even greater difficulty with several of the negative treatment categories, particularly those in which the citing court distinguished the precedent (see Spriggs and Hansford 2000).

Scholarship suggests that judges do not ignore relevant precedent (Benesh and Reddick 2002), but lower courts may dodge potential conflict with higher level tribunals by framing the issues raised in a case so as to avoid the appearance of factual similarity with relevant upper-court precedent (Canon and Johnson 1999). Thus, findings generated from research with a narrow focus on compliance may not be useful for evaluating the impact of an upper-court precedent on lower-court policy (Songer 1988). Empirical assessments report the effects of Supreme Court precedent on outcomes in the lower federal courts to vary by issue area. In obscenity cases, judges on the U.S. courts of appeals tended to adopt a more restrictive posture following the Supreme Court's decision in *Miller* (Songer and Haire 1992); and when the Court held that the federal common law of public nuisance was preempted by legislation, the lower courts halted its earlier expansion under this doctrine (Wahlbeck 1998). In contrast, lower federal court decisions did not exhibit any particular trend in policy outcomes following the Court's decision in *Miranda* (Songer and Sheehan 1990).

2.2 Hierarchical Control and Organizational Design in American Court Systems

Since the 1980s, scholars have reexamined the connections between structural designs of court systems and judicial behavior, increasingly turning to scholarship on bureaucratic politics, including economic approaches to the analysis of organizations (Moe 1984) and principal–agent models advanced as the "dominant framework for the formal analysis of hierarchy" (Moe 1984, 756). Originally conceptualized as an explanation for why private firms behave as they do, these frameworks describe the tensions that arise in organizations when a principal, or supervisor, must delegate tasks to an agent. Agents and principals may have different preferences, which make it less likely that the principal's objectives will be served by the behavior of its self-interested, utility-maximizing agents. Information asymmetries, as a result of the agent's expertise and familiarity with work, will further undermine the principal's task (Moe 1984). Consequently, a rational principal will design monitoring structures to yield information about the activities of the agent and establish incentives which maximize the likelihood of compliance. An agent may divide his or her work among three possible activities, two of which conflict with the principal's desired outcomes: "working, or devoting energy in order to accomplish the policy goals of the principal; shirking, which may be either leisure-shirking or politically motivated shirking; and sabotage, devoting time at work in order to undermine the policy goals of the principal" (Brehm and Gates 1997, 22).

"The circumstances (of the judicial hierarchy) fit the model well" (Songer, Segal, and Cameron 1994, 675). Like other public bureaucracies, American courts are characterized by hierarchical structures with judges on upper courts interested in securing lower-court outcomes which support their preferred policy positions. The agency problem describes the predicament of appellate judges who delegate discretion to trial courts in order to implement rules and standards. Appellate courts also must depend on lower courts for information about the factual context. Informational asymmetries create opportunities for judges on lower courts to make decisions contrary to the views of their principal. In these instances, rational litigants should sound the "fire alarm" and appeal the lower-court ruling; but appellate review consumes an upper court's resources. Thus, upper courts may avoid these "transaction costs" and take shortcuts, relying on easily observable information when deciding whether to scrutinize more closely a lower-court disposition.

Despite the appeal of the principal–agent framework, scholars suggest caution in drawing analogies between the judicial bureaucracy and other hierarchical organizations. "Contrary to the practice in most bureaucracies, those higher up in the judicial hierarchy have no authority over the appointment, removal, promotion, or pay of those below. Sometimes the especially obedient are rewarded by compliments in appellate opinions; sometimes the especially recalcitrant are publicly reprimanded; and sometimes judges high in the hierarchy will be consulted when a judge below seeks to move up. For the most part, however, the hierarchical control over judges is exercised through review of the work product of those below" (Fiss 1983, 1445).

Nonetheless, scholars have employed agency theory in empirical assessments of interactions between upper and lower courts, often conceptualizing the Supreme Court as principal to agents on the federal circuit courts (Brent 1999; Cameron, Segal, and Songer 2000; Cross 2003) and state courts of last resort (Benesh and Martinek 2002; Hoekstra 2005; Kilwein and Brisbin 1997). Principal–agent frameworks have also figured in research which examines interactions between the U.S. courts of appeals and federal district courts (Haire, Lindquist, and Songer 2003; Schanzenbach and Tiller 2007).

Within judicial hierarchies, "principals" include courts at the highest level and intermediate appellate courts responsible for review of trial court or administrative agency decisions in multitiered systems. In the case of the Supreme Court (and other courts of last resort in multitiered hierarchies), monitoring of lower appellate courts begins with the decision to review the case. Today, the docket of the Supreme Court generally includes only those cases which four justices have voted to hear. From the thousands of petitions for *certiorari* filed by litigants each year, the Court currently selects less than 5 percent for review, not including *informa pauperis* cases. Thus, the Court faces a constrained optimization problem. It can only decide a fraction of cert petitions filed from the lower courts on their merits and must therefore allocate its resources so as to maximize its supervisory control and thus ensure general compliance with its decisions. Responsible for ensuring uniformity in federal law, the Supreme Court notes the importance of these institutional considerations in Rule 10, which suggests writs of certiorari are more likely to be granted when:

- (*a*) a United States court of appeals has entered a decision in conflict with the decision of another United States court of appeals on the same important matter; has decided an important federal question in a way that conflicts with a decision by a state court of last resort; or has so far departed from the accepted and usual course of judicial proceedings, or sanctioned such a departure by a lower court, as to call for an exercise of this Court's supervisory power;
- (*b*) a state court of last resort has decided an important federal question in a way that conflicts with the decision of another state court of last resort or of a United States court of appeals;
- (*c*) a state court or a United States court of appeals has decided an important question of federal law that has not been, but should be, settled by this Court, or has decided an important federal question in a way that conflicts with relevant decisions of this Court.

Empirical research suggests this concern for uniformity in federal law is taken seriously by the U.S. Supreme Court. The probability of Supreme Court review is much higher when the appeal raises an actual conflict in doctrine among lower appellate courts (Caldeira and Wright 1990; Perry 1991; George and Solimine 2001). To a lesser degree, conflict between judges who decided the case in the courts below affects the likelihood of *certiorari*. Cases decided by the circuit *en banc* are more likely to be reviewed (George and Solimine 2001). Moreover, in cases where the lower appellate court reversed the trial court, the probability of cert increased (Caldeira and Wright 1990).

When determining which lower-court decisions merit further scrutiny, the Court is at an informational disadvantage, since without hearing the case it cannot be certain that the lower court followed its preferences. To keep down these "review costs," the Supreme Court would be expected to economize and tolerate a certain level of doctrinal deviance in lower-court decisions[5] (McNollgast 1995). The Court will recognize the trade-off between a larger number of relatively undemanding cases and a smaller number of demanding cases (Hellman 1983; McNollgast 1995). Lacking information, the Supreme Court should rely on observed signals to identify a lower-court decision in need of closer scrutiny, including "flags" raised by the filing of *amicus* briefs from the Solicitor General and organized interests (Caldeira and Wright 1988; 1990). Scholars particularly note the tendency of the

---

[5] It is not clear that shirking by agents results in a "cost" to the Supreme Court, unlike principals in private firms. While the Supreme Court may be interested in securing lower-court policy that uniformly promotes its preferences, there appears to be a high tolerance level for lower-court conflict. One study found that the average length of time an intercircuit conflict persisted prior to resolution before the Supreme Court was 8.2 years (Tiberi 1993).

Supreme Court to review cases in which the lower-court outcome was inconsistent with the Court's preferences[6] (Songer 1979; Caldeira and Wright 1988; 1990; George and Solimine 2001).

Cameron, Segal, and Songer (2000) develop the theoretical perspective underlying this premise further and hypothesize that the likelihood of the conservative Burger Court's grant of *certiorari* in search and seizure cases should vary depending on the ideology of the opinion-writer in the lower court. They found that, where a liberal judge excluded evidence from a search, the probability of Supreme Court review was constant regardless of the intrusiveness of the search itself. But when a conservative judge excluded evidence, the probability of review by the Court declined as the intrusiveness of the search increased (2000, 113). In making the decision to audit, the Court was more trusting of decisions to exclude evidence from conservative lower-court judges, particularly when the facts of the case were indicative of illegal police behavior.

Although studies of Supreme Court monitoring often model the lower-court agent as an individual panel, we need to realize that we are dealing with organizations, not superior–subordinate dyads (Mitnick 1992). From an organizational perspective, the Supreme Court may approach appellate supervision with a view toward its expectations and experiences with individual circuits and state supreme courts as separate institutional entities with distinct ideological and jurisprudential identities (Lindquist, Haire, and Songer forthcoming; Scott 2006a). For example, it has been observed that the Ninth Circuit experiences a much higher reversal rate when compared to other courts of appeals (Scott 2006a). Several explanations have been advanced to account for Supreme Court reversals of circuits, including the view that the size of the circuit, as measured by the number of active judges, contributes to the frequency of errant panel decisions that requires monitoring by the Court (Scott 2006b). Goal conflict also appears to affect trends in monitoring: as ideological distance between the Supreme Court majority and the circuit median increases, so too does the reversal rate (Scott 2006b). Moreover, reversal rates of circuits affect *certiorari* decisions in subsequent terms; the Supreme Court devotes greater space on its docket to circuits that have been recently reversed, relative to other more compliant circuits (Lindquist et al. forthcoming).

Whereas courts of last resort often control the composition of their docket, judges sitting on intermediate appellate tribunals must consider cases appealed to them.[7] Monitoring consists of a single-stage review heavily reliant on litigants to

---

[6] Empirical studies also suggest that justices may engage in sophisiticated behavior when evaluating cert petitions and will vote to deny when they would like to reverse if they believe that the majority would not support their position on the merits (Caldeira, Wright, and Zorn 1999; Boucher and Segal 1995).

[7] On the U.S. Courts of Appeals, however, the use of screening devices provides some form of docket control as it winnows down to a smaller set of cases those which will require the "full treatment."

police the actions of trial courts (Shavell 1995). In addition to deciding whether to appeal, litigants frame the issues for the upper court and identify potential legal errors. Not all errors result in reversal; principles of appellate review often require the upper court to distinguish between harmless and reversible lower-court error. Moreover, the standard of review utilized to evaluate findings of fact result in upper courts deferring to the trial courts. In 2005, for example, the U.S. courts of appeals affirmed the lower court in approximately 90 percent of the cases on its docket.[8]

Research on appellate review in civil rights cases litigated in the lower federal courts offers support for several hypotheses suggested by principal–agent frameworks (Haire, Lindquist, and Songer 2003). Goal conflict between the district court and circuit panel shaped the outcome of appellate review: the circuit panel was more likely to reverse district judges who were ideologically distant from it and trial court outcomes inconsistent with the panel majority's policy preferences (Haire et al. 2003). Panels on the appeals courts also appeared to use information about the lower court's ideology strategically. When a district court judge decided a case in a manner apparently contrary to his or her own policy views, the panel was more likely to affirm (Haire et al. 2003). Finally, situated in the middle tier of the judicial hierarchy, circuit courts were influenced by the position of their principal, the Supreme Court, when monitoring district court outcomes, and were therefore more likely to reverse decisions that were inconsistent with Supreme Court preferences (Haire et al. 2003).

The effectiveness of appellate review in maintaining hierarchical control may rest on whether lower-court judges fear the sanction of reversal. Most judges are highly sensitive to being reversed as they value their reputation (Posner 1993). Federal district court judges, however, have additional incentives to avoid reversal. District judges may desire promotion to the circuit bench and frequent reversal might reduce the likelihood of elevation (Cohen 1991). District-court judges also must contend with high caseloads and prefer to avoid the additional work associated with remanded decisions. Their decisions are frequently subject to review as circuit judges must entertain all appeals. In contrast, the exercise of appellate supervision by the Supreme Court over the circuits is sporadic. Interview data suggest that federal appeals court judges are interested in "getting it right" (Klein 2002, ch. 5) but do not attempt to anticipate Supreme Court action (Howard 1981; Klein 2002). For judges on state supreme courts, incentives to avoid reversal are particularly weak as hierarchical supervision by the U.S. Supreme Court is rare and limited to questions of federal law (Kilwein and Brisbin 1997). Moreover, on these courts, the lack of insulation from the state political environment may yield a different incentive structure, where judges must respond to the threat of sanctions from the electorate or other majoritarian institutions (Hoekstra 2005).

---

[8] If one excludes unpublished dispositions, the affirmance rate falls to roughly 65–70 percent.

2.3 Principal–Agent Frameworks and Lower-court Decision-making

Information asymmetries would suggest that lower-court agents will have opportunities to shirk in various ways (e.g. Schanzenbach and Tiller 2007). Empirical support for the hypothesis that lower courts will respond to the preferences of upper courts is mixed. Because of different incentives to avoid reversal as described above, it is not surprising that judicial responsiveness varies by court. In federal district courts, the preferences of the circuit predict trial court determinations in sentencing and patent policy (Baum 1980; Schanzenbach and Tiller 2007); in contrast, the Supreme Court's preferences appear to have no effect on the decision-making of state courts of last resort in confession cases (Benesh and Martinek 2002).

In an analysis of federal circuit-court decision-making, Songer, Segal, and Cameron (1994) concluded that judges were "faithful agents" to the Supreme Court and found that judges responded to changing fact patterns associated with Supreme Court doctrine; but judges also engaged in anticipatory behavior and voted consistently with the changing ideological makeup of the Burger Court. That study and subsequent research made clear that tests of agency theory would require research designs that explicitly incorporate the effects of the preferences of the sitting Supreme Court at the time of the agent's decision and distinguish this effect from deference to previous Courts' precedents. Unfortunately, this requires that the observations include situations in which the preferences of the sitting majority on the Supreme Court diverge from the policy predicted by deference to previous precedent—a task made more difficult when the composition of the U.S. Supreme Court is stable. Comparing the effects of the preferences of the enacting and sitting Supreme Courts, research has found that circuit judges respond to signals from the sitting Court and anticipate the Supreme Court's treatment of its own precedent (Reddick and Benesh 2000). Yet, other studies of circuit court decisions do not find any evidence that the preferences of the sitting Court directly affect circuit court judges' decisions (Klein 2002; Klein and Hume 2003; Cross 2003). These conflicting findings may be due to the effects of other political "principals," including the executive and legislative branches, which control the appointment process for the federal courts and assume important roles in the implementation of judicial policy (Canon and Johnson 1999). Research suggests that the policy preferences of the appointing president and home state senators affect circuit judges' decisions (Giles, Hettinger, and Peppers 2001). Presidential administrations also exercise substantial influence over judicial policy in the circuit courts as repeat-player litigants with substantial resources (Songer, Sheehan, and Haire 1999). Standards of review in certain types of administrative law cases contribute to this effect by encouraging judges to defer to the expertise of the executive agency. Lower federal court judges may also view Congress as a "principal" which possesses the authority to override unfavorable decisions involving statutory interpretation (Brent 1999; Lindquist and Haire 2006).

The mixed findings concerning Supreme Court–circuit court interactions also may be explained by differing measures of judicial ideology. Songer, Segal, and Cameron (1994) relied on background characteristics to identify the policy preferences of circuit judges and a "time counter" to indicate the growing conservatism of the Supreme Court. Others have utilized the policy preferences of the appointing president and home state senator in cases of senatorial courtesy to measure the ideology of appeals court judges.[9] To assess the effect of the preferences of the Supreme Court, scholars have relied on vote-based measures of policy liberalism and the median justice's Segal-Cover score, a measure of ideology based on preconfirmation editorials written at the time of the nomination. Since these measures of the ideological makeup of the two courts are not directly comparable, analyses using measures of ideological distance between the Supreme Court as principal and the circuit court as agent will be limited. In an effort to address this limitation, Epstein et al. (2007) offer a measurement strategy which yields estimates of ideology for Supreme Court justices and Courts of Appeals judges in a common space.

The empirical reality that consensus, rather than conflict, characterizes the relations between judges sitting on upper and lower courts, has hindered efforts to evaluate principal–agent models. An alternative perspective on hierarchical relations emphasizes this lack of conflict among judges and conceptualizes the judiciary as a resource-constrained "team" that seeks to maximize the number of decisions that "get it right" (Kornhauser 1995). From this approach, like-minded lower-court judges decline to apply upper-court precedent in some cases because doing so would result in an outcome that judges on all levels of the court system would agree is a "bad" decision (Caminker 1994). This phenomenon, "underruling," suggests that lower courts learn from the other judges who decided cases prior to them and modify upper-court precedents in a manner that adapts rules to current situations (Caminker 1994). To the extent a consensus emerges among lower-court judges, upper courts need not involve themselves. Empirical research supports this expectation indirectly; a critical predictor of review by the Supreme Court is whether lower courts disagree over doctrine (Caldeira and Wright 1990; Perry 1991). Moreover, in an analysis of Supreme Court decisions on intercircuit conflict in the federal courts, Lindquist and Klein (2006) found that the Court tended to ratify the reasoning process adopted by the majority of circuits involved.

---

[9] Klein (2002) relies on a different measure that includes information reported in a survey of lawyers who are members of the federal bar in the judge's circuit.

3 RELATIONS AMONG PARALLEL COURTS

Judges generally take into account prior rulings from their own court and from the courts above when called upon to formulate solutions to issues raised in the case before them. Yet the search for relevant case law is typically not restricted to binding precedents. Because "judges, in search of convincing answers to legal questions, would be foolish to ignore the work of fellow professionals" (Klein 2002, 28), the doctrinal positions taken by other courts which have addressed similar policy problems are likely to be considered. A court may incorporate, criticize, or ignore relevant holdings from jurisdictions outside its hierarchy. And studies of citation patterns suggest that references to precedents from parallel courts are not random events (Caldeira 1983; Walsh 1997; Harris 1985). Scholars have utilized perspectives from research on communications and diffusion processes to examine intercourt relations and the treatment of parallel precedents.

3.1 Intercourt Relations and Judicial Policy-making

If confronted with an issue uncovered by existing doctrine, courts may respond by creating a new rule or practice. Typically, the need which gave rise to the new judicial doctrine also will fuel diffusion, the "process by which the innovation is then communicated to, and adopted by, other courts" (Baum 1991, 413). As policies spread across courts, judges "reinvent" the innovation to improve upon it, or simply make adjustments for current circumstances (Glick 1992). Judges choose alternatives that have been effective in similar sub-units and, in doing so, save the time and energy needed to craft independent solutions (Berry and Berry 1999). Ultimately, intercourt communication of doctrine contributes to uniformity in the legal system. Thus, for example, communication between judges sitting on fifty independent state court systems played a part in developing a relatively coherent set of state tort law doctrines (Shapiro 1970).

Diffusion in a judicial hierarchy also may take place among sub-units, such as lower courts, as a result of competition within a federal system (Berry and Berry 1999; Boehmke and Witmer 2004). In the federal judicial context, judges are likely to heed the positions of other courts to avoid being perceived as an "outlier." For example, according to one judge, "if [my] circuit hasn't spoken and I see seven circuits have taken a position with a pretty logical argument, I'd probably go along" (Klein 2002, 89). Although a "tournament of judging" among lower courts may work against uniformity within the federal legal system, initial intercourt differences would likely be temporary. Over time, competition between courts will refine the legal issues and arguments. As these issues percolate, many questions will be resolved without the Supreme Court's intervention. With a mutual interest in avoiding Supreme Court review, judges may refer to decisions of other appellate courts to facilitate the development of consensus (Spill Solberg, Emrey, and Haire 2006). And, in cases where lower-court conflict is persistent, the Supreme Court will benefit from the stock of lower-court opinions which provide information on the policy alternatives.

3.2 Parallel Courts and Leadership

Research on state courts' policy innovation incorporates multiple dimensions of the concept of leadership. Early innovators play an important agenda-setting role for sister courts by stimulating litigation in other jurisdictions and framing the con-tours of the policy debate (Glick 1992). But the timing of judicial decisions to adopt innovations depends on the timing of litigants' decisions to bring cases (Canon and Baum 1981). "There is much more to policy leadership than being the first with a novel situation and novel solution" (Glick 1992, 89). The New Jersey Supreme Court was an early innovator in policy-making in right-to-die cases, but its substantive influence on policies in other states was realized only when the reasoning from one of its later decisions, which expanded the scope of the right to die, was adopted by several courts of last resort (Glick 1992). Other research has examined leadership by assessing the reputations of state supreme courts by the frequency with which the court is cited by judges in other states (Caldeira 1985; 1988). State supreme courts were more likely to refer to precedents from out-of-state courts located in populous areas, ranked high on measures of judicial professionalism and prestige, and which produced more opinions (Caldeira 1983; 1985).

In the federal appeals courts, policy leadership by specific circuits has varied with the makeup of the bench and by issue area. For example, the complex issues raised in commercial litigation and the presence of Learned and Augustus Hand likely contributed to the Second Circuit's reputation as "the ablest in the country" in the 1950s (Howard 1981, 142). Interestingly, this reputation has continued in more recent times. An analysis of cross-circuit citations from 1982 to 1995 ranked the Second Circuit just behind the leading Third Circuit in terms of the frequency with which it was cited by other courts of appeals (Landes, Lessig, and Solimine 1998). The role of the DC Circuit in appellate litigation involving federal administrative agencies has contributed to its prominence on matters of administrative law and likely fueled its high ranking in citation analyses (Banks 1999; Landes et al. 1998). Overall, however, federal appellate judges tend to view policy leadership more in terms of individuals than courts (Howard 1981; Klein 2002). In an analysis of circuit decisions in antitrust, search and seizure, and environmental law, the likelihood of adopting a new rule (from another court) increased when the first opinion to announce the rule was authored by a judge who scored high on citation-based measures of prestige (Klein and Morrisroe 1999).

3.3 Intercourt Relations: Judicial Incentives and Cues

Adherence to the norm of *stare decisis* compels appellate panels to follow precedents established by earlier panels of the same court. Thus, there is a tendency for "inward" citations when writing appellate court opinions (Landes et al. 1998; Spill Solberg et al. 2006). Litigants' decisions and the draw of case-facts will also limit the relevant doctrines and policies. Therefore, decisions to adopt the policies of other courts will not be likely unless there are incentives for judges to innovate (Berry and Berry 1999). Several factors facilitate consideration of a judicial policy established by a parallel court. To begin, the availability of legal capital will shape this decision. Judges are more likely to search for positions taken by other courts when confronted with an issue of first impression for which there does not appear to be binding precedent in the forum court (Spill Solberg et al. 2006). Policy preferences also affect receptivity to other courts' precedents. Courts of appeals judges who are ideologically predisposed to another court's rule are more likely to adopt it (Klein 2002). Judicial incentives to use authorities from other jurisdictions may also vary by court. In circuits characterized by dissensus and partisan divisions in the makeup of the bench, opinions were more likely to refer to other circuits' precedent (Spill Solberg et al. 2006).

Policy-makers, including judges, may rely on cues when making a decision to adopt a new policy (Grossback et al. 2004). Research using dyadic data on state supreme courts found that judges are more likely to refer to precedents from geographically close and culturally similar courts (Caldeira 1985). The results of a network analysis testing for reciprocal relationships in citations found similarities in resources and pressures from workloads to be the strongest predictors of "cliques" among state supreme courts (Caldeira 1988). Analysis of cross-circuit citations from 1982 to 1995 in the federal appellate courts also finds support for regional patterns in citation practices; judges in the northeastern circuits (First, Second, and Third) were more likely to cite one another's decisions (Landes et al. 1998). The effect of the breakup of the Fifth Circuit on citation practices was not surprising: nearly one-fourth of the Eleventh Circuit's outside citations referred to precedents decided by the reconstituted Fifth Circuit (Landes et al. 1998, 331).

Research on citation practices is suggestive of intercourt relationships; but scholars are cautious when making generalizations because judges may use precedent for reasons other than acknowledging the substantive influence of the holding. It has been asserted that judges use citations to serve the function of legitimation (Walsh 1997). If concerned about legitimacy, courts are more likely to cite broadly to ensure greater support for their position from an external audience (Harris 1985). Although a single citation may not be evidence of a direct influence of the cited court on decision-making, *patterns of citation practices* suggest structural relationships between parallel courts (Walsh 1997; Caldeira 1988). Employing structural equivalence criteria in network analysis, one analysis found the patterns of citations (both sending and receiving citations) among state supreme courts were predicted by measures of prestige and legal professionalism (Caldeira 1988). A subsequent study found that citation patterns in state supreme courts corresponded to judicial policy outcomes in wrongful discharge precedent-setting cases (Walsh 1997).

Additional research may also inform current policy debates that shape relations among parallel courts, including recent controversies surrounding the use of precedents from foreign courts. In two Supreme Court cases, *Lawrence v. Texas*, 123 S. Ct. 1406 (2003), and *Atkins v. Virginia*, 536 U.S. 304 (2002), the majority's discussion of decisions by European courts fueled a spirited debate, led by Justices Breyer and Scalia, over the appropriateness of incorporating decisions from foreign courts, particularly when interpreting the U.S. Constitution. Supreme Court citations to foreign legal authorities, while relatively rare, have been used more frequently to evaluate issues surrounding the Eighth Amendment and the application of the death penalty (Kommers 2005). Arguments for using foreign law tend to be pragmatic, recognizing trends in globalization and embracing the premise that it is simply more efficient for judges to draw on lessons from other nations (Kommers 2005). Opponents suggest that citations to foreign precedents undermine originalist and textual theories of constitutional interpretation that are designed to minimize judicial activism. Additional studies may explore these opposing arguments by examining how principles of constitutional law diffuse across nation states and exploring factors which influence judicial treatment of foreign court precedents.

4 CONCLUSIONS

Over the last three decades, scholarship on intercourt relations has evolved from analyses of compliance with landmark U.S. Supreme Court decisions to empirical research on horizontal and vertical interactions between judges at varying levels of the court system. Findings from these studies have advanced our understanding of the dynamics that shape relations among courts, but several questions remain. For example, despite widespread compliance with Supreme Court doctrine, there is no clear scholarly consensus on the causal mechanisms underlying lower-court compliance. Given the central importance of norms and institutional design in evaluating this puzzle, our understanding may be limited by the scholarly focus on contemporary courts. As recent scholarship on American political development would suggest, longitudinal research, including studies of earlier eras, potentially offers different insights on the relationship between institutional design and judicial incentives. Moreover, longitudinal investigations would be useful in evaluating the effects of the broader political and social environment. For example, how do lower-court judges respond to attempts by the legislative and executive branches to limit the power of the Supreme Court? One might expect them to "close ranks" within the hierarchy to preserve judicial independence. As an alternative, interbranch conflict may offer an opportunity for lower-court judges to adopt positions contrary to the preferences of the sitting Supreme Court.

Research on intercourt relations has tended to focus on the hierarchical influence of the Supreme Court. Recent studies, however, suggest insights to be gained by studying judicial hierarchies in non-U.S. court systems (Perez-Linan, Ames, and Seligson 2006) and examining other intercourt interactions including those between trial judges and lower appellate courts (Schanzenbach and Tiller 2007) and those between parallel courts (Songer, Humphries, Ginn, and Sarver 2003). Relations among courts will continue to undergo change as advances in information technologies facilitate electronic access to opinions and contribute to the communication of precedent. This development likely contributed to a recent amendment to the federal rules of appellate procedure (FRAP 32.1), permitting litigants to cite unpublished and nonprecedential federal appellate court rulings. With this rule change, judges will have more information available on other courts' decisions, including those without precedential value. Understanding judicial treatment of this growing body of legal authorities will challenge social scientists; but recent methodological innovations over the last several decades suggest this effort offers a promising line of inquiry. Techniques associated with network analysis of citation practices may be used to address critical questions in the study of law and courts that center on assessing the relative influence of specific actors in the emergence, transmission, alteration, and abolition of precedent in the U.S. legal system (Cousins et al. 2005; Fowler et al. 2007).

References

BANKS, C. P. 1999. *Judicial Politics in the D.C. Circuit Court.* Baltimore: Johns Hopkins University Press.

BAUM, L. 1980. Responses of federal district judges to court of appeals policies: an exploration. *Western Political Quarterly,* 33: 217–24.

—— 1991. Courts and policy innovation. In *The American Courts: A Critical Assessment,* ed. J. B. Gates and C. A. Johnson. Washington, DC: CQ Press.

BENESH, S. C., and MARTINEK, W. L. 2002. State supreme court decision making in confession cases. *Justice System Journal,* 23: 109–33.

—— and REDDICK, M. 2002. Overruled: an event history analysis of lower court reaction to Supreme Court alteration of precedent. *Journal of Politics,* 64: 534–50.

BERRY, F. S., and BERRY, W. D. 1999. Innovation and diffusion models in policy research. In *Theories of the Policy Process,* ed. P. A. Sabatier. Boulder, Colo.: Westview.

BOEHMKE, F. J., and WITMER, R. 2004. Disentangling diffusion: the effects of social learning and economic competition on state policy innovation and expansion. *Political Research Quarterly,* 57: 39–51.

BOUCHER, R. L., and SEGAL, J. A. 1995. Supreme Court justices as strategic decision-makers: aggressive grants and defensive denials. *Journal of Politics,* 57: 824–37.

BREHM, J., and GATES, S. 1997. *Working, Shirking and Sabotage: Bureaucratic Response to a Democratic Public.* Ann Arbor: University of Michigan Press.

BRENT, J. 1999. An agent and two principals: U.S. courts of appeals responses to *Employment Division v. Smith* and the Religious Freedom Restoration Act. *American Politics Research,* 27: 236–66.

CALDEIRA, G. A. 1983. On the reputation of state supreme courts. *Political Behavior,* 5: 83–108.

—— 1985. The transmission of legal precedent: a study of state supreme courts. *American Political Science Review,* 79: 178–94.

—— 1988. Legal precedent: structures of communication between state supreme courts. *Social Networks,* 10: 29–55.

—— and WRIGHT, J. R. 1988. Organized interests and agenda setting in the U.S. Supreme Court. *American Political Science Review,* 82: 1109–27.

—— —— 1990. The discuss list: agenda building in the Supreme Court. *Law and Society Review,* 24: 807–36.

—— —— and ZORN, C. J. 1999. Sophisticated voting and gate-keeping in the Supreme Court. *Journal of Law, Economics and Organization,* 15: 549–72.

CAMERON, C. M., SEGAL, J. A., and SONGER, D. 2000. Strategic auditing in a political hierarchy: an informational model of the Supreme Court's certiorari decisions. *American Political Science Review,* 94: 101–16.

CAMINKER, E. 1994. Why must inferior courts obey superior court precedents? *Stanford Law Review,* 46: 817–71.

CANON, B. C. 1973. Reactions of state supreme courts to a U.S. Supreme Court civil liberties decision. *Law and Society Review,* 8: 109–34.

—— and JOHNSON, C. A. 1999. *Judicial Policies: Implementation and Impact,* 2nd edn. Washington, DC: CQ Press.

—— and BAUM, L. 1981. Patterns of adoption of tort law innovations: an application of diffusion theory to judicial doctrines. *American Political Science Review,* 75: 975–87.

COHEN, M. A. 1991. Explaining judicial behavior or what's "unconstitutional" about the Sentencing Commission. *Journal of Law, Economics and Organization,* 7: 183–99.

COUSINS, K., PEARSON-MERKOWITZ, S., SIMONS, S., EVANS, M., KARNES, K., McTAGUE, J., and McINTOSH, W. 2005. Patterns of judicial influence: tracking regulatory takings policy in the lower federal courts. Presented at the Annual Meeting of the American Political Science Association.

CROSS, F. 2003. Decision making in the U.S. Circuit Courts of Appeals. *California Law Review,* 91: 1457–515.

EPSTEIN, L., MARTIN, A. D., SEGAL, J. A., and WESTERLAND, C. 2007. The judicial common space. *Journal of Law, Economics and Organization,* 23: 303–25.

FISS, O. M. 1983. The bureaucratization of the judiciary. *Yale Law Journal,* 92: 1442–68.

FOWLER, J., JOHNSON, T. R., SPRIGGS, J. F., JEON, S., and WAHLBECK, P. J. 2007. Network analysis and the law: measuring the legal importance of Supreme Court precedents. *Political Analysis,* 15: 324–46.

GEORGE, T. E., and SOLIMINE, M. F. 2001. Supreme Court monitoring of the U.S. courts of appeals en banc. *Supreme Court Economic Review*, 9: 171–204.

GILES, M. W., and WALKER, T. G. 1975. Judicial policy making and Southern school segregation. *Journal of Politics*, 37: 917–36.

—— HETTINGER, V. A., and PEPPERS, T. 2001. Picking federal judges: a note on policy and partisan selection agendas. *Political Research Quarterly*, 54: 623–41.

GLICK, H. R. 1992. Judicial innovation and policy re-invention: state supreme courts and the right to die. *Western Political Quarterly*, 45: 71–92.

GROSSBACK, L. J., NICHOLSON-CROTTY, S., and PETERSON, D. A. M. 2004. Ideology and learning in policy diffusion. *American Politics Research*, 32: 521–45.

GRUHL, J. 1980. The Supreme Court's impact on the law of libel: compliance by lower federal courts. *Western Political Quarterly*, 33: 502–19.

HAIRE, S. B., LINDQUIST, S., and SONGER, D. R. 2003. Appellate court supervision in the federal judiciary: a hierarchical perspective. *Law and Society Review*, 37: 143–67.

HANSFORD, T., and SPRIGGS, J. 2006. *The Politics of Precedent on the U.S. Supreme Court*. Princeton, NJ: Princeton University Press.

HARRIS, P. 1985. Difficult cases and the display of authority. *Journal of Law, Economics and Organization*, 1: 209–21.

HELLMAN, A. 1983. Error correction, lawmaking, and the Supreme Court's exercise of discretionary review. *University of Pittsburgh Law Review*, 44: 795–873.

HOEKSTRA, V. 2005. Competing constraints: state courts' responses to Supreme Court decisions and legislation on wages and hours. *Political Research Quarterly*, 58: 317–28.

HOWARD, J. W. 1981. *Courts of Appeals in the Federal System*. Princeton, NJ: Princeton University Press.

KILWEIN, J. C., and BRISBIN, R. A. 1997. Policy convergence in a federal system: the application of intensified scrutiny doctrines by state supreme courts. *American Journal of Political Science*, 41: 122–48.

KLEIN, D. E. 2002. *Making Law in the U.S. Courts of Appeals*. Cambridge: Cambridge University Press.

—— and MORRISROE, D. 1999. The prestige and influence of individual judges on the U.S. Courts of Appeals. *Journal of Legal Studies*, 28: 371–91.

—— and HUME, R. J. 2003. Fear of reversal as an explanation of lower court compliance. *Law and Society Review*, 37: 579–607.

KOMMERS, D. P. 2005. American courts and democracy: a comparative perspective. In *The Judicial Branch*, ed. K. L. Hall and K. T. McGuire. Oxford: Oxford University Press.

KORNHAUSER, L. A. 1995. Adjudication by a resource-constrained team: hierarchy and precedent in a judicial system. *Southern California Law Review*, 68: 1605–29.

LANDES, W. M., LESSIG, L., and SOLIMINE, M. E. 1998. Judicial influence: a citation analysis of federal courts of appeals judges. *Journal of Legal Studies*, 27: 271–332.

—— and POSNER, R. A. 1976. Legal precedent: a theoretical and empirical analysis. *Journal of Law and Economics*, 19: 249–307.

LINDQUIST, S. A., HAIRE, S. B., and SONGER, D. R. Forthcoming. Supreme Court auditing of the United States Courts of Appeals: an organizational perspective. *Journal of Public Administration Research and Theory*.

—— —— 2006. Decision making by an agent with multiple principals: environmental policy in the U.S. Courts of Appeals. In *Institutional Games and the U.S. Supreme Court*, ed. J. Rogers, R. Flemming, and J. Bond. Charlottesville: University of Virginia Press.

LINDQUIST, S. A., and KLEIN, D. E. 2006. The influence of jurisprudential considerations on Supreme Court decision making: a study of conflict cases. *Law and Society Review*, 40: 135–62.

MCNOLLGAST. 1995. Politics and the courts: a positive theory of judicial doctrine and the rule of law. *Southern California Law Review*, 68: 1631–89.

MITNICK, B. M. 1992. The theory of agency and organizational analysis. Pp. 75–96 in *Ethics and Agency Theory: An Introduction*, ed. N. E. Bowie and R. E. Freeman. New York: Oxford University Press.

MOE, T. 1984. The new economics of organization. *American Journal of Political Science*, 28: 739–77

PELTASON, J. 1961. *Fifty-Eight Lonely Men*. New York: Harcourt, Brace.

PEREZ-LINAN, A., AMES, B., and SELIGSON, M. A. 2006. Strategy, careers, and judicial decisions: lessons from the Bolivian courts. *Journal of Politics*, 68: 284–95.

PERRY, JR., H.W. 1991. *Deciding to Decide: Agenda Setting in the United States Supreme Court*. Cambridge, Mass.: Harvard University Press.

POSNER, R. A. 1993. What do judges maximize? (The same things everyone else does). In *Overcoming Law*, ed. R. A. Posner. Cambridge, Mass.: Harvard University Press.

REDDICK, M., and BENESH, S. 2000. Norm violation by the lower courts in the treatment of Supreme Court precedent: a research framework. *Justice System Journal*, 21: 117–42.

ROMERO, D. W., and SANDERS ROMERO, F. 2003. Precedent, parity, and racial discrimination: a federal/state comparison of the impact of *Brown v. Board of Education*. *Law and Society Review*, 37: 809–26.

SCHANZENBACH, M. M., and TILLER, E. 2007. Strategic judging under the United States sentencing guidelines: positive political theory and evidence. *Journal of Law, Economics and Organization*, 23: 24–56.

SCOTT, K. 2006*a*. Supreme Court reversals of the Ninth Circuit. *Arizona Law Review*, 48: 341–54.

—— 2006*b*. Understanding judicial hierarchy: reversals and the behavior of intermediate appellate court judges. *Law and Society Review*, 40: 163–92.

SHAPIRO, M. 1970. Decentralized decision making in the law of torts. In *Political Decision-Making*, ed. S. S. Ulmer. New York: Van Nostrand Reinhold.

SHAVELL, S. 1995. The appeals process as a means of error correction. *Journal of Legal Studies*, 24: 379–426.

SONGER, D. R. 1979. Concern for policy outputs as a cue for Supreme Court decisions on certiorari. *Journal of Politics*, 41: 1185–94.

—— 1988. Alternative approaches to the study of judicial impact: *Miranda* in five state courts. *American Politics Quarterly*, 16: 425–44.

—— HUMPHRIES GINN, M., and SARVER, T. A. 2003. Do judges follow the law when there is no fear of reversal? *Justice System Journal*, 24: 137–62.

—— and HAIRE, S. 1992. Integrating alternative approaches to the study of judicial voting: obscenity cases in the U.S. Courts of Appeals. *American Journal of Political Science*, 36: 963–82.

—— and SHEEHAN, R. 1990. Supreme Court impact on compliance and outcomes: *Miranda* and *New York Times* in the United States Courts of Appeals. *Western Political Quarterly*, 43: 297–319.

──── ──── and HAIRE, S. B. 1999. Do haves come out ahead over time? Applying Galanter's framework to decisions of the U.S. Courts of Appeals, 1925–1988. *Law and Society Review,* 33: 811–32.

──── SEGAL, J. A., and CAMERON, C. M. 1994. The hierarchy of justice: testing a principal–agent model of Supreme Court–circuit court interactions. *American Journal of Political Science,* 38: 673–96.

SPILL SOLBERG, R., EMREY, J. A., and HAIRE, S. B. 2006. Inter-court dynamics and the development of legal policy: citation patterns in the decisions of the U.S. Courts of Appeals. *Policy Studies Journal,* 34: 277–93.

SPRIGGS, J. F., and HANSFORD, T. G. 2000. Measuring legal change: the reliability and validity of Shephard's Citations. *Political Research Quarterly,* 53: 327–41.

TARR, G. A. 1977. *Judicial Impact and State Supreme Courts.* Lexington, Mass.: Lexington Books.

TIBERI, T. 1993. Comment—Supreme Court denials of certiorari in conflicts cases: percolation or procrastination? *University of Pittsburgh Law Review,* 54: 861–92.

WAHLBECK, P. J. 1998. The development of a legal rule: the federal common law of public nuisance. *Law and Society Review,* 32: 613–38.

WALSH, D. J. 1997. On the meaning and pattern of legal citations: evidence from state wrongful discharge precedent cases. *Law and Society Review,* 31: 337–62.

WASBY, S. L. 1970. *The Impact of the U.S. Supreme Court: Some Perspectives.* Homewood, Ill.: Dorsey Press.

CHAPTER 30

....

LITIGATION AND LEGAL MOBILIZATION

....

MICHAEL McCANN

STUDIES of legal mobilization have made important contributions to social science analysis of law over the last three decades. This chapter will begin by briefly reviewing that tradition, emphasizing its basic underlying premises and insights as well as the sources of diversity and even contestation within the legacy. I then examine in greater detail several of these important lines of inquiry within the tradition. Finally, I suggest some of the most fruitful paths of future scholarship regarding litigation and legal mobilization. In my view, this rich tradition of scholarship has been incorporated into the mainstream and thus lost its distinctiveness to some extent, but it remains full of promise for development in many new conceptual, empirical, and geographical directions.

1 THE HISTORICAL CONTEXT OF SCHOLARLY INTEREST IN LEGAL MOBILIZATION

....

It is important to recognize that the rise of scholarly interest in legal mobilization undoubtedly reflected developments in American politics. The legacy of high-profile litigation for social change dating from rulings on racial segregation in *Brown v. Bd. of Education* (1954) and continuing with issues of rights for the accused, privacy rights, affirmative action, women's rights, environmental policy, and the like highlighted the significance of litigation and legal rights claiming in the American constitutional legacy. Moreover, the rapid growth during the 1960s of liberal (and later, conservative) public interest law firms self-consciously committed to the strategic use of litigation for social change further underlined the role of legal advocacy in politics. Indeed, numerous social movements and interest group coalitions touting litigation and rights advocacy as a core strategic resource arose in this period.

These developments along with various political events (Vietnam, Watergate) nurtured disenchantment with partisan electoral politics and a burgeoning alternative faith in lawyers, legal processes, and legal discourses to deliver on promises of social justice. Prominent public figures from Martin Luther King to Ralph Nader not only extolled litigation and rights talk, but pressed for the widespread "judicialization" of government processes (McCann 1986). At the same time, expanded legal standing, liberalized legal rules in civil law, and increased resources for legal counsel promised greater "access to justice" for ordinary, and especially low income, individuals in our nation. All in all, this was the era of expanding "rights consciousness" where the courtroom became as much the center of citizen attention as the voting booth (Schudson 1999). It is thus not surprising that scholars in this period began to develop rigorous frameworks of empirical research for analyzing, understanding, and assessing legal mobilization in practice.

2 LEGAL MOBILIZATION: THE CONCEPTUAL TRUNK AND ITS VARIOUS BRANCHES

The phenomenon of legal mobilization was explored in a host of scholarly inquiries during the 1960s and 1970s (e.g. Scheingold 1974; Lempert 1976). However, it was not until the early 1980s that Zemans (1982; 1983) arguably offered the most elegant and useful definition of legal mobilization and developed the general concept along lines that influenced, or at least anticipated, most subsequent research. "The law is... mobilized when a desire or a want is translated into a demand as an assertion of rights," she wrote (1983, 700). I suggest four core ideas at the heart of the basic logic of analysis focusing on legal mobilization:

1. *Studies of legal mobilization begin with and focus on the actions of legal subjects, especially nonofficial legal actors.* Indeed, much of the earliest literature emphasized the mobilization of law by "private" citizens. Nader (1985) called it a "user

theory" of law and change. This recentering of analysis on legal initiative and action—on "naming, blaming, and claiming" (Felstiner and Sarat 1980–1)—by citizens within civil society thus tends to "decenter" courts and other official state actors and institutions. After all, scholars note, just as the criminal justice system is often mobilized through 911 calls or other acts of citizens, so too are civil claims usually initiated in disputes among private citizens or organizations that may or may not end up seeking legal counsel, much less entering a courtroom. Moreover, although some studies have examined legal activity of business managers, organizations, or elite actors, most legal mobilization studies have focused on "ordinary" citizens, and especially on low income, working class, poor, female, and minority citizens. Studies of legal mobilization thus often are labeled as adopting a "bottom up" view in at least two related regards—beginning with nonofficials rather than officials of law, and focusing on the less powerful or marginalized among the unofficial ordinary people in civil society.[1]

2. *Studies of legal mobilization tend to identify litigation as just one potential dimension or phase of a larger, complex, dynamic, multistage process of disputing among various parties.* Specifically, litigation signals a stage of disputing that generally begins with the official filing of legal claims or charges. Central to this understanding is recognition that only a small percentage of disputes and disputing activity actually ever gets to this formal level of institutional involvement. Indeed, most studies begin with the initial articulation of "grievances" following perceived harms, even if they never reach the litigation phases. Legal mobilization thus only occasionally involves lawyers or other official actors, including the judges, attorneys, and jurors that are central to the litigation process. Finally, disputes often end in the earlier stages of litigation, although they can proceed to trial, judgment, appeals, and beyond to post-appeals interaction. Therefore, the process-based approach to legal mobilization addresses a host of activities and relationships, including those connected to litigation, rarely considered in studies focusing on courts and judicial impact. At the same time, dispute-centered, user-oriented approaches to legal mobilization provide interesting and creative insights into the actions and workings of courts, judges, and other official legal actors. For example, Shapiro (1981) builds his entire theory of "courts" on a quasi-functionalist foundation of third-party intervention in simple disputing processes among social actors. Other scholars similarly draw on legal mobilization to analyze the ways that courts are embedded in complex social and state webs of interaction (Brigham 1996).

3. *Scholars interested in legal mobilization tend to view the choices of actors who generate litigation as well as their effects or impacts as typically complex, indeterminate, and contingent.* Many people who threaten or even initiate litigation have no

---

[1] This identification of "ordinary" legal subjects arguably is problematic and unduly narrow, because it overlooks many of the most important "powerful" legal actors in ordinary life.

intention or hope of going to trial, much less beyond; threatening or starting litigation can often be a very effective tactic in leveraging an informal, out-of-court settlement or simply discouraging continued claims by others. Mnookin and Kornhauser famously referred to this influence as the "shadow" cast by official law and legal processes over informal dispute judgments and negotiations (1979). Indeed, much litigation is initiated precisely with the hope of avoiding trial and ending a dispute informally, preferably with a favorable outcome. Moreover, disputes can be settled or terminated at any point either before or after litigation has begun, including in the post-appeal stages. Thus, avoiding litigation can be a major victory for either or both parties. Conversely, winning in court can often be highly costly in money, delay, and personal pain, and the remedies afforded by legal victories can often fall far short of what is required for justice, either individually or collectively. Moreover, litigation can often divert parties from more productive ways of advancing or resolving conflicts. Rosenberg thus has characterized litigation as a "hollow hope" (1991) for social reformers, and Kagan has identified "adversarial legalism" as an inefficient pathology impeding effective policy responses to basic social problems (2003). Yet, settling disputes prior to or apart from trials may also trade short-term gains for potential long-term gains in legal precedent and new rules governing broader patterns of relationships (Albiston 1999). And for scholars of legal mobilization, these points just scratch the surface of the many ways that litigation can at once shape, advance, discourage, impede, or derail disputing activity.

4. *Virtually all studies of legal mobilization emphasize that the capacity of citizens to mobilize law is highly unequal.* Most scholars begin from the premise that law to a large degree works to sustain the status quo, thus at once enforcing and expressing the unequal relationships among citizens and associations of different wealth, political influence, and organizational power. Not only do legal systems tend to secure and sustain the privileges of unequal power, but also the capacity to mobilize law in disputes and to shape law itself requires many types of social resources, including money, expertise, legal representation, status, political connections, and media access. In fact, most literature on legal mobilization directs interest to the contours of systemic processes—often labeled "hegemony"—that contain, channel, divert, and absorb citizen challenges. But many scholars also recognize the capacity of subaltern groups and relatively powerless citizens on occasion to mobilize the law against more powerful groups and status quo relations. Although nearly all scholars recognize that such mobilization efforts sometimes can advance egalitarian changes, however, experts disagree about how to assess the character of struggles on legal terrain and their implications. Partly out of disaffection with the promises of legal mobilization and litigation, many scholars in recent years have focused primarily on the "resistances" of citizens to law and legal processes as sensible responses to law's hegemonic pact with unequal power and systemic domination (Ewick and Silbey 1998; Gilliom 2001; McCann and March 1996).

2.1 Variations in Overall Approach

There are as well some fundamental differences among types of scholarship in the legal mobilization legacy. We can begin by identifying two general types of framework. First, many of the classic studies in the 1970s were oriented toward citizen *behavior* and framed in largely *positivist* terms. The tendency of most such studies was to focus on documenting and assessing the *instrumental* dimensions of legal mobilization activity. In the simplest terms, instrumental approaches focus on how and to what effect citizens "use" the law. The emphasis was on citizen users as autonomous agents who mobilize law as a discrete, identifiable "tool" for utilitarian purposes of advancing interests or altering institutional relations and practices. The impacts and effects of legal mobilization, whether informal or formal, are often the major focus. Law and society, or at least the social users of law, are relatively independent in this vision, which is often also identified with the "realist" framework.

Second, anthropologists dating back to mid-century tended to view legal mobilization activity instead through a cultural lens, and the interpretive turn in the social sciences generally beginning in the 1980s pushed such approaches to the fore as a leading mode of study. Such cultural studies typically focus on language, discourse, ideology, and the construction of "meaning" as well as on behavior. Most authors in this tradition thus emphasize the *constitutive* rather than instrumental dimensions of law. In this view, law is not separate from and external to subjects, but rather legal discourses constitute subjects, as legal knowledge, logics, language, and values shape the intersubjective worlds citizens inhabit. This framework thus explores how legal conventions routinely prefigure, delimit, and express the expectations, aspirations, and practical world-views of subjects. Attention to "legal consciousness" is an important product of this tradition.

These two general approaches have generated some undeniable rivalry among partisans, but most scholars, whatever their specific emphasis, straddle the divide more than they admit. For one thing, whatever their differences, scholars in both camps similarly emphasize how legal practices often depart from "law on the books." Moreover, most scholars in the post-realist interpretive tradition tend to view the focus on meaning as pushing beyond rather than rejecting realist attention to behavior. As Scheingold announced long ago, "The law is real, but it also is a figment of our imagination" (1974, 3). Subsequent approaches tended to focus on how subjects "think as well as act" in the shadows of law as well as in official legal settings (Ewick and Silbey 1998). Conversely, most realist studies of instrumental behavior include attention to how legal values and understandings shape perceptions, aspirations, and calculations. Finally, as Silverstein (1996) has argued, most studies of law's constitutive power recognize that strategic legal action expresses, reflects, and often deepens the reliance on legal frames of meaning-making.

Constitutive analysts thus do not ignore the importance of instrumental activity and its consequences so much as understand the relationship between law and subjectivity in instrumental activity differently than do behavioral realists.

One further and perhaps clearer division in scholarship on legal mobilization can be drawn between research primarily addressing disputes among individuals and that addressing larger social conflicts among organized groups, especially entailing 'reform-oriented' legal strategies. The remainder of this chapter will be divided between reviews of studies addressing individual and group-based legal mobilization activity.

3 THE MICROPOLITICS OF INDIVIDUAL LEGAL MOBILIZATION: A CLOSER LOOK

By far the greatest amount of scholarship on legal mobilization has focused on the micropolitics of individual disputing. Political scientists in the 1970s and 1980s were highly influential in the development of such studies. Anthropologists and sociologists[2] seized the momentum amidst the interpretive turn in the 1980s, but political scientists continued to contribute important studies. I focus instead on five key contributions of the literature.

1. Perhaps most relevant for political scientists is the recognition that legal mobilization is one of the most important but least studied modes of citizen participation in the U.S. political system and perhaps around the world. Zemans made this argument most expansively and effectively (1982; 1983). As she put it, our civil legal system is grounded in responsiveness to individual action. "The individual citizen can be a true participant in the governmental scheme as an enforcer of the law without representative or professional intermediaries" (1983, 695). Hence, our civil law system "can be considered quintessentially democratic, although not necessarily egalitarian if the competence and the means to make use of this access to governmental authority is not equally distributed" (1983, 693). By focusing on what Nader (1985) called the "users" of law among the citizenry, legal mobilization approaches connect sociolegal study with the core of political science attention to citizen participation and lobbying.

2. The next major contribution was the embrace of the "disputing pyramid" model developed by scholars investigating civil disputing (see Miller and Sarat 1980–1). The graphic representation of the pyramid portrayed a broad base of citizen "grieving"

[2] See e.g. Merry (1990; 2000; 2001); Greenhouse, Yngvesson, and Engel (1994); Ewick and Silbey (1998); Nielsen (2004); Fleury-Steiner and Nielsen (2006).

grounded in legally actionable injuries that narrowed progressively with subsequent stages of potential "claiming," "disputing," "lawyer involvement," and finally, the infrequent "trial" at the tip of the structure. This representation powerfully expressed, among other things, the understanding that a great deal of law is in interactions far from courtrooms and other official legal institutions. Moreover, the image readily captured the dialectical relationship between formal litigation and informal disputing processes, including the metaphorical "shadow" that official law and legal processes cast over everyday interactions and practices. Scores of studies since the 1980s have profitably drawn on this scheme as well as the original Civil Litigation Research Project study to structure empirical research designs and to report research findings (Galanter 1996; Haltom and McCann 2004). And much to the initial model's credit, virtually all subsequent findings confirmed the same basic logic even while refining various elements and adding new dimensions. In short, this model of disputing processes and legal mobilization studies developed together in a close, complementary relationship.

3. The third major achievement of legal mobilization studies, once again owing much to the disputing framework, is to call into question familiar allegations that citizens in the United States are inherently, even obsessively, adversarial, litigious, and rights-obsessed. Miller and Sarat (1980–1), reporting the CLRP, challenged these assumptions directly, if speculatively and cautiously. Zemans (1983) similarly emphasized the prevailing tendency of citizens to mobilize law in ways that stopped far short of formal institutional involvement. In fact, citizen mobilization of law in everyday life was a major reason why more disputes were not formalized through litigation and subjected to direct resolution by legal officials. Fascination with popular assumptions about America's litigious propensities, much of it fueled by the tort reform movement and general turn against law in the post-civil rights era, generated much of the copious empirical research during the 1980s and 1990s about citizen mobilization of, and disputing through, the law (Galanter 1996; Daniels and Martin 1995; Eisenberg and Henderson 1992; for a comprehensive bibliography, see Haltom and McCann 2004). Subsequent research on civil disputing in other nations added important comparative dimensions to this tradition (Wollschlager 1998; Sellers 1995; Kagan 2003). Such studies of legal disputing and mobilization have contributed often, if not always effectively, to debates over public policy.

4. This research tradition also has addressed a host of issues related to *why* citizens in the U.S. and beyond do not mobilize official legal institutions more often, and specifically why most citizens either "lump it" when they are aggrieved or find informal, nonlitigious ways of working toward resolutions of conflicts. This research has focused primarily on informal activity by citizens, but it has also addressed low-level litigation and even rarer incidents of post-trial appeals (Barclay 1999). Indeed, in many ways these latter types of study have been the primary preoccupation of research on individual disputing in the last two decades. Two general types of analyses have been advanced.

The first focuses on the differential resources of money, time, and especially legal counsel available to aggrieved citizens. The concern about inequality was manifest in the earliest research during the 1960s and 1970s on legal "needs" and access to justice for marginalized citizens. Drawing on these early studies, Zemans contended in her classic essays in the early 1980s that citizen mobilization of rights claims and law was democratic but "not necessarily egalitarian if the competence and the means to make use of this access to governmental authority is not equally distributed" (1983, 693). After all, effective legal claiming is potentially expensive, time-consuming, and contingent on effective legal representation. Virtually every study of legal mobilization has underlined how resource inequalities affect not only the capacity to mobilize the law, but the very will to do so. Galanter's argument about "why the haves come out ahead" (1974) was the most sophisticated and theoretically influential development of this insight. He showed how "repeat players"—those powerful corporate institutions with large legal staffs constantly engaged in legal disputing and maneuvering on many fronts—prevail not only in discrete disputes but, more importantly, in shaping the development of substantive legal rules over the long haul. This disparity in power is most dramatic when contrasting repeat players with "one shot" individuals and lesser organizations, but also in understanding the disparate influence among differently situated repeat players over time. Even among one-shotters, of course, disparities in financial resources and legal representation matter a great deal. Citizens with the fewest resources thus often realistically assess that they have little to gain by mobilizing law either against more powerful opponents or, given costs of litigation, against other parties with similarly meager resources.

A second quite different, but often quite closely related, type of inquiry has focused on the study of "legal consciousness" among ordinary citizens. Virtually all scholars in this legacy agree that legal consciousness refers to "the way that people conceive of their 'natural' and normal way of doing things, their habitual patterns of talk and action, and their commonsense understanding of the world" (Merry 1990, 5). Most scholars take individuals as their starting point, but they recognize that individual consciousness is shaped by the patterns of socially constructed and institutionalized discourses, logics, practices, and relationships in which subjects participate. Hence, as Merry adds, quoting Jean Comaroff, legal consciousness is "embedded in the practical constitution of everyday life, part and parcel of the process whereby the subject is constituted by external sociocultural forms" (Merry 1990, 5). However, scholars in this tradition vary in the degree to which they link individual consciousness to social structures (Sarat and Kearns 1993; Engel 1998; Garcia-Villegas 2003; McCann 2006) and the types of socially learned cognitive patterns they identify.

Scholars map legal consciousness in a variety of ways. Some studies focus on how individuals think through logics of law as both substantive principles and as institutionalized processes of interaction. For example, much of the scholarship in the 1960s and 1970s focused on the legal "competence" of differently situated citizens. These studies found both greater knowledge of law and willingness to mobilize legal conventions and processes among middle-class Americans than among the poor (Carlin, Howard, and Messinger 1967; Levine and Preston 1970; Curran 1977). More recently, Laura Beth Nielsen (2004) has provided a fascinating study of legal consciousness among individuals interviewed about ordinary interactions in the streets of several California communities. Her interviews revealed that individuals, and especially minorities and females, were regularly exposed to various types of verbal assault in public street life. While most found these assaults injurious, few saw good reason for pursuing legal remedies and tended to "lump it." Nielsen finds interesting disparities in how citizens of color and women respond relative to white males, although she is careful not to over-generalize from her small sample.

Political scientist Bumiller (1988) took a slightly different approach in her study of why citizens who experienced racial or sexual discrimination did not act on their claims. Bumiller's analysis suggests how mobilizing antidiscrimination claims actually compounds the experience and identification as "victim," exposing one's vulnerability and compromising personal dignity. For relatively powerless victims of injustice, therefore, mobilizing law, and especially litigation, often only aggravates a bad situation and decreases control. Yet other scholars have examined the ways in which legal consciousness at once reflects, expresses, and reinforces dominant ideological currents within society (Sarat 1990; Merry 1990).

The marvelous collection of ethnographic studies by Greenhouse, Yngvesson, and Engel (1994) further developed how romantic norms of "community" encourage avoidance of legal-rights claiming and remedies. Such values are at once enforced by powerful legal actors—court clerks, judges, juries, lawyers, police, and insurance agents—and internalized by citizens seeking respect as insiders to the community, while those lacking status and power are stigmatized as undeserving outsiders when they invoke their rights, mobilize law, and especially, litigate. Marginalized populations thus have a very difficult time even gaining a serious hearing for their claims before officials, thus further discouraging resort to official channels. Haltom and McCann (2004) demonstrate that norms of law avoidance are not just generated by small communities in transition, but rather resonate throughout American mass society. They demonstrate how a combination of well-organized interest group efforts, the sensationalizing proclivities of the mass media, and traditional moralistic values celebrating personal responsibility have stigmatized legal mobilization efforts by aggrieved plaintiffs and their attorneys. These different studies provide powerful arguments about the influence of mass legal culture in discouraging individual citizens from exercising the opportunities for legal mobilization celebrated by scholars like Zemans (1983).

Ewick and Silbey (1998) developed a different but parallel set of understandings about legal consciousness. Their focus is less on how legal logics and discourses relate to broader cultural norms or values than the ways citizens relate to the legal system itself. They identify three general "schemas"—Before the Law, With the Law, and Against the Law—to categorize the orientations of ordinary people to law. The last of these orientations highlighted "resistance" to law, a theme which figured prominently in studies during the 1990s. Perhaps the most significant study is Gilliom's research on resistance by female welfare recipients (2001) toward administrative "overseers of the poor." He documents a variety of survival strategies— e.g. failing to report income from work undertaken to support their children—that not only are against the law, but which reflect an "ethic of care" that eschews rights-based legal mobilization strategies and litigation.

5. Engel and Munger provide yet another angle into individual legal consciousness. *Rights of Inclusion* (2003) explores whether the 1991 Americans with Disabilities Act made much difference. The authors used in-depth interviews to develop personal biographies of sixty persons with disabilities and chart the complexities and changes in their legal consciousness. Generally, the authors find some modest gain in "rights consciousness" among some subjects, but very little actual effort to mobilize the law on their behalf, and no individual litigation at all. Citizen conceptions of their disabilities, identity, and status as rights-bearing subjects are explored in relationship to family, work, gender, and race.

In sum, the bulk of research inquiring as to why so many citizens lump it when injured and refrain from active rights claiming, much less from litigation, paints a paradoxical portrait. Although the U.S. legal system tends to be relatively responsive and open to citizen mobilization, ordinary citizens rarely mobilize law, leaving the bulk of legal mobilization activity to wealthy individuals and, especially, to large organizations. In this sense, the legal system more mirrors the political system than it offers a more responsive or democratic alternative to it. It thus is not surprising that many scholars of legal mobilization and civil disputing use the concept of *hegemony* to make sense of their findings. Hegemony refers to the aggregate of ways, and especially noncoercive ways, that societies produce consent, tame dissent, and secure order. Studies of law in the U.S. demonstrate that relatively open, responsive legal systems can be among the most stable systems for conservatively absorbing, channeling, and containing conflict (McCann 1994; Ewick and Silbey 1998; Lovell and McCann 2004; Fleury-Steiner and Nielsen 2006).

One fundamental source of considerable divergence in studies of individual legal mobilization does merit attention, though. Scholars in this tradition vary widely, although they only sometimes openly disagree, about the terms of how to analyze or "map" the variable features of social *context* and citizen *identity* that figure prominently in different patterns of legal practice. Virtually every scholar in this tradition underlines the importance of social context and identity formation, but there is little commonality of approach and relatively little open exchange or debate about how to advance analysis on these fronts. In particular, the systematic treatment of racial, gender, and class differences has proved a daunting challenge (Seron and Munger 1996).

4 LEGAL MOBILIZATION, GROUP STRUGGLE, AND SOCIAL REFORM

Studies of legal mobilization in group struggles over social reform have produced a robust and prominent legacy. This legacy has primarily emanated from the scholarship of political scientists, although a few sociologists have made important contributions. The divergence in disciplinary focus no doubt explains in part why these studies of group legal mobilization parallel but only rarely engage studies of individual legal mobilization. But other differences also matter greatly. For one thing, if the latter studies focus on disputing in the shadows of law but frequently involving no litigation, studies of legal mobilization in social reform struggles almost always involve litigation campaigns. Moreover, where the litigation at stake in individual studies is mostly in local trial courts, the litigation at stake in reform struggles are usually in state and federal courts, very often in appellate courts, especially the U.S. Supreme Court. In this regard, group-based legal-mobilization studies at once parallel, draw on, and provide an alternative framework to "top-down" studies assessing the judicial impact of social reform litigation, a prominent topic among political scientists (Epstein and Kobylka 1992; Canon and Johnson 1998; Rosenberg 1991).

Scheingold's *The Politics of Rights* (1974) to a large extent initiated the study of macropolitical legal mobilization. His analysis began by debunking the "myth of rights," demonstrating in several chapters why neither federal courts nor civil rights provide reliable protections of freedom and equal opportunity for most citizens. He drew heavily on realist studies of judicial behavior to emphasize the conservative character of courts and their limited capacity to implement their rulings. All in all, he contended, courts are highly unreliable agents of progressive change, but rights, and rights-based litigation, still can be important political resources for group struggles to change public perceptions and to leverage official action. "It is possible to capitalize on the perceptions of entitlement associated with rights to initiate and to nurture political mobilization—a dual process of *activating* a quiescent citizenry and *organizing* groups into effective political units" (1974, 131). Scheingold remained wary about legal avenues to social change, however, and concluded with a skeptical discussion of the "activist bar" and its legalistic inclinations that often undermine a creative politics of rights. His achievement was in outlining the basic tenets for subsequent studies of reform-oriented legal mobilization—a frank awareness about the conservative functions of law, courts, and lawyers; a deep skepticism toward court-centered visions of social change; a tempered faith in "bottom-up" political mobilization of rights that may include but surely transcends litigation; and an emphasis on understanding how legal language constitutes social practice and how politics is about the contestation of meaning as well as of material resources and institutional position.

Scheingold's analysis influenced a number of studies in the 1970s and 1980s. Handler's (1978) multi-case study volume integrated utilitarian theories to show legal mobilization could in part overcome the challenges of collective action for activist entrepreneurs. Other important case studies focused on legal mobilization for disabled persons (Olson 1984), the mentally ill (Milner 1986), Native Americans (Medcalf 1978; Bruun 1982), environmental and consumer groups (McCann 1986), and the early American labor movement (Forbath 1991). Yet other scholars pursued related ideas by using quite different methodologies. Burstein (1991a; 1991b) and Epp (1990) developed large-N statistical studies of large patterns in legal mobilization challenging race and gender discrimination. Conversely, critical race theorists (Crenshaw 1988; Williams 1991) and feminist legal theorists (see Schneider 1986) offered provocative analyses using personal experience to explore the complexities of legally constituted struggles that paralleled legal mobilization approaches to reform struggles.

McCann's *Rights at Work* (1994) at once built on these earlier studies and broke new conceptual ground by integrating contemporary process-based social movement theory and post-structural constructivist theorizing about legal discourse into the dispute-centered legal mobilization approach. His study of union struggles over gender-based wage inequity introduced analysis of group-based legal mobilization in terms of multiple developing phases and social contexts marked by unequal distribution of associational resources and political opportunities. He connected studies of reform-oriented group mobilization of legal rights to various themes developed in studies of individual disputing, including the "constitutive" power of law, "rights consciousness," bargaining in law's shadows, and systemic "hegemony" (see also Hunt 1990; Polletta 2000).

Silverstein's study (1996) of legal mobilization by animal liberation activists showed further how litigation can matter even if unsuccessful at trial and developed a theoretically sophisticated argument about how law's constitutive and instrumental dimensions are interrelated. Brigham's *The Constitution of Interests* (1996) expanded further the "constitutive" approach to legal mobilization, exploring at length how law provides the institutional stage, language, and bounded structure of movement contests. Perhaps most important was his insistence on looking "beyond the politics of rights" to legal manifestations of realism, remedies, and rage. By contrast, Epp advanced the more instrumental side of legal mobilization studies. He undertook a comparative study of legal mobilization in four nations to explain why courts shifted their agendas at particular moments in support of rights claims (1998). Epp demonstrates that a "vibrant support structure" is a necessary condition for the development of judicial support for rights (see also Lawrence 1990; Kessler 1990).

Subsequent studies have developed or amended various facets of the legal mobilization approach. One promising route has drawn on "framing" analysis to identify different strategies of producing and reproducing legal claims for various audiences (see Pedriana 2004). Also interesting is Anderson's study of gay rights (2005), which developed the concept of "legal opportunity structures" to go along with the broader conception of political opportunity structures. Marshall's recent scholarship on sexual harassment has combined individual disputing and social movement dynamics in a productive way (2003).

Perhaps the most innovative recent development in research on reform group legal mobilization has concerned the politics of "counter-mobilization," backlash, and group-based resistances. Scheingold (1974) called attention to the issue of counter-mobilization, and many scholars have addressed it to some extent (Burstein 1991b), but mostly as a secondary dimension of study. Recent works, by contrast, have placed the politics of backlash at the center of analysis. One tradition of research developed how conservative or reactionary groups have appropriated the same basic legal mobilization strategies pioneered by liberal or progressive groups on behalf of marginalized citizens, typically to reverse the currents of politics or restore an imagined status quo (Epstein 1985; Pring and Canon 1996; Den Dulk and Krishnan 2001; Hatcher 2005).

Other studies have expanded the focus to include tactics beyond legal counter-mobilization. Goldberg-Hiller's *The Limits of Union* (2002) focused on the conservative backlash against gay rights, providing an example of social movements that "mobilize *against the law* and seek to transform discourses about rights—particularly civil rights—into exclusionary limits" (2002, 34). Dudas (2003) similarly develops what he labels the "politics of resentment," showing how reactionaries variously stigmatize the character of Native Americans as undeserving subjects, the "special rights" that they claim, and their legal tactics as un-American and corrosive to our very legal traditions. And Haltom and McCann's book *Distorting the Law* (2004) systematically studies the role of mass media in amplifying efforts of big business to roll back progressive legal reforms in tort law. These different studies show two common elements in the politics of counter-mobilization in the U.S: how conservative groups have appropriated and mimicked with great effectiveness tactics pioneered by left-wing or progressive rights-based groups in previous decades; and how arguments about personal responsibility have become the focus of contests over who does or does not qualify as deserving subjects qualifying for rights and meriting respect for their particular rights claims.

Finally, it is worth noting the very closely interrelated legacy of scholarship on "cause lawyering" (see Sarat and Scheingold 1998; 2001; Scheingold and Sarat 2004).

Although the focus of these studies is activist attorneys, the key questions for such scholars are essentially the same ones that concern scholars of legal mobilization and social reform litigation generally. This is most evident in the recent volume on cause lawyers and social movements (Sarat and Scheingold 2006). In sum, any scholar interested in social reform litigation and legal advocacy should be attentive to the literature on cause lawyering.

5 New and Future Developments

I have attempted to map the broad range of studies addressing legal mobilization. Within this tradition, there is much room for innovation and many new avenues of legal activity to explore. I propose here three such promising areas of new study:

1. *Class action and complex litigation.* Despite considerable attention from law professors, social scientists have devoted very little study to class action litigation and other types of "complex" litigation. Given the highly political character and huge consequences of such litigation, it seems like a ripe area for research by social scientists interested in legal mobilization.

2. *Legal mobilization by the powerful.* Most studies focus either on relatively powerless ("ordinary") individuals or on group efforts to challenge prevailing elite institutions. Thus the legal activity initiated by some of the most powerful institutions in society has gone unstudied by legal mobilization scholars. Studies of corporate legal practice are likely to become important.

3. *Integration with historical institutionalism.* Given the methodological and theoretical compatibility of approaches, studies integrating bottom-up legal mobilization with the emphasis of historical institutionalist scholars on horizontal interrelationships among state actors would be most promising (see Skrentny 2006). Frymer (2003) and Lovell and McCann (2004) have demonstrated some interesting possibilities of such integrative efforts.

Promising as these paths may be, however, I envision a rather different overall trajectory of inquiries into legal mobilization. On the one hand, it seems to me that research about legal mobilization arguably has lost its luster in the United States. Two reasons account for this. First, the earlier faith among liberal scholars that legal mobilization activity might promote more responsive politics and progressive agendas has yielded to growing skepticism about the historical record and undeniably conservative trends in current law (see McCann and Dudas 2006). Moreover, many of the most important insights, concepts, and findings of studies about legal mobilization have become integrated into mainstream social science inquiry about law, although their influence in law schools is still limited. The result is a perceived reduction of opportunities for original contributions within this discrete tradition, or at least through explicit identification with the long-established tradition. Instead, it has become more commonplace for scholars to self-consciously synthesize legal mobilization approaches with other frameworks (see Gould 2005) or not to even acknowledge the influence of the familiar legacy at all. The tradition is a casualty of its success.

On the other hand, there is much evidence that the core tenets of legal mobilization analysis are gaining influence among scholars who study regions beyond the United States, especially where we witness increased processes of legalization, influence of judicial institutions, reliance on rights talk, and citizen access to lawyers. Many U.S. scholars have drawn on studies of legal mobilization to inform studies of law and politics in Europe (Cichowski 2006; Conant 2002; Olson 1995), Asia (Diamant, Lubman, and O'Brien 2005), the Middle East (Barzilai 2003), Latin America (Santos and Rodríguez-Garavito 2005; Garcia-Villegas 2003), Russia (Hendley 2004), and South Africa (Abel 1996). Indeed, the legal mobilization framework is very well suited for adaptation to comparative cross-national study of law and politics. Likewise, studies of legal mobilization at the transnational levels hold great promise as well. Some law and society scholars (Santos 1995; Merry 2005; 2001; Bloom 2001) have pointed the way in this regard. All in all, as quasi-Western legal norms, conventions, and institutions become more prominent around the world, we might expect that legal mobilization approaches will become more relevant to studies of politics generally.

REFERENCES

ABEL, R. 1996. *Politics by Other Means: Law in the Struggle against Apartheid, 1980–1994.* New York: Routledge.

ALBISTON, C. 1999. The rule of law and the litigation process: the paradox of losing by winning. *Law and Society Review*, 33: 869–910.

ANDERSON, E. 2005. *Out of the Closets and into the Courts: Legal Opportunity Structure and Gay Rights Litigation.* Ann Arbor: University of Michigan Press.

BARCLAY, S. 1999. *An Appealing Act: Why People Appeal in Civil Cases.* Evanston, Ill.: Northwestern University Press.

BARZILAI, G. 2003. *Communities and Law: Politics and Cultures of Legal Identities.* Ann Arbor: University of Michigan Press.

BLACK, D. 1973. The mobilization of law. *Journal of Legal Studies*, 2: 125–49.

BLOOM, A. 2001. Taking on Goliath: why personal injury litigation may represent the future of transnational cause lawyering. Pp. 96–116 in Sarat and Scheingold 2001.

BRIGHAM, J. 1996. *The Constitution of Interests: Beyond the Politics of Rights.* New York: New York University Press.

BRUUN, R. 1982. The Boldt decision: legal victory, political defeat. *Law and Policy*, 4: 271–98.

BUMILLER, K. 1988. *The Civil Rights Society: The Social Construction of Victims*. Baltimore: Johns Hopkins University Press.

BURSTEIN, P. 1991*a*. Legal mobilization as a social movement tactic: the struggle for equal employment opportunity. *American Journal of Sociology*, 96: 1201–25.

—— 1991*b*. "Reverse discrimination" cases in the federal courts: legal mobilization by a countermovement. *Sociological Quarterly*, 32: 511–28.

CANON, B. C., and JOHNSON, C. A. 1998. *Judicial Policies: Implementation and Impact*, 2nd edn. Washington, DC: Congressional Quarterly Press.

CARLIN, J. E., HOWARD, J., and MESSINGER, S. L. 1967. *Civil Justice and the Poor: Issues for Sociological Research*. New York: Russell Sage Foundation.

CICHOWSKI, R. A. 2006. *The European Court and Civil Society: Litigation, Mobilization, and Governance*. Cambridge: Cambridge University Press.

CONANT, L. 2002. *Justice Contained: Law and Politics in the European Union*. Ithaca, NY: Cornell University Press.

CRENSHAW, K. W. 1988. Race, reform, and retrenchment: transformation and legitimation in antidiscrimination law. *Harvard Law Review*, 101: 1331–87.

CURRAN, B. 1977. *The Legal Needs of the Public: The Final Report of a National Survey*. Chicago: American Bar Foundation.

DANIELS, S., and MARTIN, J. 1995. *Civil Juries and the Politics of Reform*. Evanston, Ill.: Northwestern University Press.

DEN DULK, K. R., and KRISHNAN, J. K. 2001. So help me God: explaining the recent rise in religious group litigation in the U.S. and beyond. *Georgia Journal of International and Comparative Law*, 30: 233–75.

DIAMANT, N. J., LUBMAN, S. B., and O'BRIEN, K. J. (eds.) 2005. *Engaging the Law in China: State, Society, and the Possibilities for Justice*. Palo Alto, Calif.: Stanford University Press.

DUDAS, J. 2003. Rights, resentment, and social change: the politics of treaty rights. Ph.D. dissertation, University of Washington.

EISENBERG, T., and HENDERSON. J. 1992. Inside the quiet revolution in products liability. *UCLA Law Review*, 39: 731–810.

ENGEL, D. 1998. How does law matter in the constitution of legal consciousness? In *How Does Law Matter?* eds. B. Garth and A. Sarat. Evanston, Ill.: Northwestern University Press.

—— and MUNGER, F. 2003. *Rights of Inclusion: Law and Identity in the Life Stories of Americans with Disabilities*. Chicago: University of Chicago Press.

EPP, C. 1998. *The Rights Revolution: Lawyers, Activists, and Supreme Courts in Comparative Perspective*. Chicago: University of Chicago Press.

—— 1990. Connecting litigation levels and legal mobilization: explaining interstate variation in employment civil rights litigation. *Law and Society Review*, 24: 145–63.

EPSTEIN, L. 1985. *Conservatives in Court*. Knoxville: Tennessee University Press.

—— and KOBYLKA, J. F. 1992. *The Supreme Court and Legal Change: Abortion and the Death Penalty*. Chapel Hill: University of North Carolina Press.

EWICK, P., and SILBEY, S. 1998. *The Common Place of Law: Stories from Everyday Life*. Chicago: University of Chicago Press.

FELSTINER, W., ABEL, R., and SARAT, A. 1980–1. The emergence and transformation of disputes—naming, blaming, and claiming... *Law and Society Review*, 15: 631–55.

FLEURY-STEINER, B., and NIELSEN, L. B. (eds.) 2006. *The New Civil Rights Research: A Constitutive Perspective*. Burlington, Vt.: Ashgate–Dartmouth Press.

FORBATH, W. E. 1991. *Law and the Shaping of the American Labor Movement*. Cambridge, Mass.: Harvard University Press.

FRYMER, P. 2003. Acting when elected officials won't: federal courts and civil rights enforcement in US labor unions 1935–85. *American Political Science Review*, 97: 483–99.

GALANTER, M. 1974. Why the "haves" come out ahead: speculations on the limits of legal change. *Law and Society Review*, 9: 95–160.

—— 1996. Real world torts: an antidote to anecdote. *Maryland Law Review*, 55: 1093–160.

GARCIA-VILLEGAS, M. 2003. Symbolic power without symbolic violence. *Florida Law Review*, 55: 157–89.

GILLIOM, J. 2001. *Overseers of the Poor: Surveillance, Resistance, and the Limits of Privacy*. Chicago: University of Chicago Press.

GOLDBERG-HILLER, J. 2002. *The Limits to Union: Same-Sex Marriage and the Politics of Civil Rights*. Ann Arbor: University of Michigan Press.

GOULD, J. B. 2005. *Speak No Evil: The Triumph of Hate Speech Regulation*. Chicago: University of Chicago Press.

GREENHOUSE, C. J., ENGEL, D. M., and YNGVESSON, B. 1994. *Law and Community in Three American Towns*. Ithaca, NY: Cornell University Press.

HALTOM, W., and McCANN, M. 2004. *Distorting the Law: Politics, Media, and the Litigation Crisis*. Chicago: University of Chicago Press.

HANDLER, J. F. 1978. *Lawyers and the Pursuit of Legal Rights*. New York: Academic Press.

HATCHER, L. 2005. Economic libertarians, property, and institutions: linking activism, ideas, and identities among property rights advocates. In Sarat and Scheingold 2005.

HENDLEY, K. 2004. Business litigation in the transition: a portrait of debt collection in Russia. *Law and Society Review*, 31: 305–47.

HUNT, A. 1990. Rights and social movements: counter-hegemonic strategies. *Journal of Law and Society*, 17: 309–28.

KAGAN, R. A. 2003. *Adversarial Legalism: The American Way of Law*. Cambridge, Mass.: Harvard University Press.

KESSLER, M. 1990. Legal mobilization for social reform: power and the politics of agenda setting. *Law and Society Review*, 24: 121–44.

LAWRENCE, S. E. 1990. *The Poor in Court: The Legal Services Program and Supreme Court Decision Making*. Princeton, NJ: Princeton University Press.

LEMPERT, R. O. 1976. Mobilizing private law: an introductory essay. *Law and Society Review*, 11: 173–89.

LEVINE, F., and PRESTON, E. 1970. Community reorientation among low income groups. *Wisconsin Law Review*, 1970: 80–113.

LOVELL, G., and McCANN, M. 2004. A tangled legacy: federal courts and the politics of democratic inclusion. Pp. 257–80 in *The Politics of Democratic Inclusion*, ed. C. Wolbrecht and R. Hero. Philadelphia: Temple University Press.

McCANN, M. W. 1986. *Taking Reform Seriously: Perspectives on Public Interest Liberalism*. Ithaca, NY: Cornell University Press.

—— 1994. *Rights at Work: Pay Equity Reform and the Politics of Legal Mobilization*. Chicago: University of Chicago Press.

—— 2006. Legal rights consciousness: a challenging analytical tradition. In Fleury-Steiner and Nielsen 2006: ix–xxx.

—— and DUDAS, J. 2006. Retrenchment . . . and resurgence? Mapping the changing context of movement lawyering in the United States. In Sarat and Scheingold 2006: 37–59.

—— and MARCH, T. 1996. Law and everyday forms of resistance: a socio-political assessment. *Studies in Law, Politics, and Society*, 15: 207–36.

MARSHALL, A. M. 2003. Injustice frames, legality, and the everyday construction of sexual harassment. *Law and Social Inquiry*, 28: 659–90.

MEDCALF, L. 1978. *Law and Identity: Lawyers, Native Americans, and Legal Practice.* Beverly Hills, Calif.: Sage.

MERRY, S. E. 1990. *Getting Justice and Getting Even: Legal Consciousness among Working Class Americans.* Chicago: University of Chicago Press.

—— 2000. *Colonizing Hawai'i: The Cultural Power of Law.* Princeton, NJ: Princeton University Press.

—— 2001. Rights, religion, and community: approaches to violence against women in the context of globalization. *Law and Society Review*, 35: 1301–50.

—— 2005. *Human Rights and Gender Violence: Translating International Law into Local Justice.* Chicago: University of Chicago Press.

MILLER, R., and SARAT, A. 1980–1. Grievances, claims, and disputes: assessing the adversary culture. *Law and Society Review*, 15: 525–66.

MILNER, N. 1986. The dilemmas of legal mobilization: ideologies and strategies of mental patient liberation. *Law and Policy*, 8: 105–29.

MNOOKIN, R. H., and KORNHAUSER, L. 1979. Bargaining in the shadow of the law: the case of divorce. *Yale Law Journal*, 88: 951–97.

NADER, L. 1969. *Law in Culture and Society.* New York: Academic Press.

—— 1985. A user theory of legal change as applied to gender. *Nebraska Symposium on Motivation: The Law as a Behavioral Instrument*, 33: 1–33.

NIELSEN, L. B. 2004. *License to Harass: Law, Hierarchy, and Offensive Public Speech.* Princeton, NJ: Princeton University Press.

OLSON, S. M. 1984. *Clients and Lawyers: Securing the Rights of Disabled Persons.* Westport, Conn.: Greenwood Press.

—— 1995. Comparing women's rights litigation in the Netherlands and the United States. *Polity*, 28: 189–215.

PEDRIANA, N. 2004. Help wanted NOW: legal resources, the women's movement, and the battle over sex-segregated job advertisements. *Social Problems*, 51: 82–201.

POLLETTA, F. 2000. The structural context of novel rights claims: rights innovation in the southern civil rights movement, 1961–1966. *Law and Society Review*, 34: 367–406.

PRING, F. W., and CANON, P. 1996. *SLAPPs: Getting Sued for Speaking Out.* Philadelphia: Temple University Press.

ROSENBERG, G. 1991. *The Hollow Hope: Can Courts Bring About Social Change?* Chicago: University of Chicago Press.

SANTOS, B. 1995. *Toward a New Common Sense: Law, Science, and Politics in the Paradigmatic Transition.* New York: Routledge.

—— and RODRIGUEZ-GARAVITO, C. A. (eds.) 2005. *Law and Globalization from Below: Towards a Cosmopolitan Legality.* Cambridge: Cambridge University Press.

SARAT, A. 1990. "...The law is all over:" power, resistance and the legal consciousness of the welfare poor. *Yale Journal of Law and the Humanities*, 2: 343–80.

—— and KEARNS, T. R. (eds.) 1993. *Law in Everyday Life.* Ann Arbor: University of Michigan Press.

—— and SCHEINGOLD, S. A. (eds.) 1998. *Cause Lawyering: Political Commitments and Professional Responsibilities.* New York: Oxford University Press.

SARAT, A. 2001. *Cause Lawyering and the State in the Global Era.* Oxford: Oxford University Press.

—— 2006. *Cause Lawyers and Social Movements.* Stanford, Calif.: Stanford University Press.

SCHEINGOLD, S. A. 1974. *The Politics of Rights: Lawyers, Public Policy, and Social Change.* New Haven, Conn.: Yale University Press.

—— and SARAT, A. 2004. *Something to Believe In: Politics, Professionalism, and Cause Lawyering.* Stanford, Calif.: Stanford University Press.

SCHNEIDER, E. M. 1986. The dialectic of rights and politics: perspectives from the women's movement. *New York University Law Review,* 61: 589–652.

SCHUDSON, M. 1999. *The Good Citizen: A History of American Civic Life.* Cambridge, Mass.: Harvard University Press.

SELLERS, J. M. 1995. Litigation as a political resource: courts in controversies over land use in France, Germany, and the United States. *Law and Society Review,* 29: 475–516.

SERON, C., and MUNGER, F. 1996. Law and inequality: race, gender . . . and, of course, class. *Annual Review of Sociology,* 22: 187–212.

SHAPIRO, M. 1981. *Courts: A Comparative and Political Analysis.* Chicago: University of Chicago Press.

SILVERSTEIN, H. 1996. *Unleashing Rights: Law, Meaning, and the Animal Rights Movement.* Ann Arbor: University of Michigan Press.

SKRENTNY, J. D. 2006. Law and the American state. *Annual Review of Sociology,* 32: 213–44

WILLIAMS, P. 1991. *The Alchemy of Race and Rights.* Cambridge, Mass.: Harvard University Press.

WOLLSCHLAGER, C. 1998. Exploring the global landscapes of litigation rates. In *Soziologie des Rechts: Festschrift für Erhard Blankenburg zum 60 Geburtstag,* ed. J. Brand and D. Strempel. Baden-Baden: Nomos.

ZEMANS, F. K. 1982. Framework for analysis of legal mobilization: a decision-making model. *American Bar Foundation Research Journal,* 1982: 989–1071.

—— 1983. Legal mobilization: the neglected role of the law in the political system. *American Political Science Review,* 77: 690–703.

CHAPTER 31

LEGAL PROFESSION

RICHARD L. ABEL

AMERICAN lawyers and courts interact in complex ways. This chapter examines theories of legal representation, interaction between judges and lawyers, alternatives to law, the effects of the size and composition of the legal profession on courts, ensuring the right to counsel, and unresolved tensions between law and politics.

1 THEORIES OF LEGAL REPRESENTATION

Lawyers (especially criminal defense counsel) are often asked: "How can you represent these clients?" (McIntyre 1987). Common law lawyers—especially American—respond by invoking "The Adversary System Excuse" (Luban 1984). They are hired guns, compelled by the "principle of professionalism" to advocate vigorously while being absolved of moral responsibility by the "principle of nonaccountability" (Schwartz 1978; but see Simon 1978). Common law judges endorse this theory because they are more reactive than their civil law counterparts and hence depend on opposing counsel to develop the facts and argue the law (but see Frankel 1975). Nonaccountability is said to encourage lawyers to take unpopular clients and causes: those charged with heinous crimes (e.g. sexual abuse of children) or associated with unpopular groups (e.g. communists, terrorists). English barristers embraced the cab-rank rule, which obligated them to accept any client who could pay their fee in a matter within their competence (Abel 2003, 73, 80–2).

The persistence with which apologists advance this justification suggests that audiences remain skeptical. Clients want lawyers to believe in them, not just be mouthpieces. They have a constitutional right to choose their lawyers (*U.S. v. Gonzalez-Lopez* 2006). Some insist on representing themselves: Zacarias Moussaoui in his federal criminal trial, Slobodan Milosevic before the International Criminal Tribunal for the former Yugoslavia (Simons 2004a; 2004b), and Ali Hamza Ahmed Sulayman al Bahlul before the U.S. Military Commission in Guantánamo (*U.S. Department of Defense* 2004). "Cause lawyers" identify with ideals, not clients (Sarat and Scheingold 1998; 2001; 2003; Scheingold and Sarat 2004; Edwards 2004). The Vatican forbids Catholics to handle divorces (O'Gorman 1963; Henneberger 2002). When lawyers run for public office, voters expect they will remain loyal to their clients: Colorado Democrat Tom Strickland to environmental degraders (Johnston 1996), California Democrat Jane Harman to China (for which she lobbied) (Lesher 1998). Opponents highlighted John Roberts's and Samuel Alito's advocacy to predict their behavior as Supreme Court justices (Kinsley 2006).

Lawyers' amoralism is particularly troubling when law lags behind morality (Abel 1982). Joseph Wilson Kellum represented the two men who murdered Emmett Till, a fourteen-year-old black boy from Chicago, for allegedly acting fresh to a twenty-one-year-old white woman in rural Mississippi in 1955 (Rubin 2005). In his summation, Kellum called the jury "absolutely the custodians of American civilization." "I want you to tell me where under God's shining sun is the land of the free and the home of the brave if you don't turn these boys loose—your forefathers will absolutely turn over in their graves!" It took the white male jury only an hour to acquit. Soon thereafter the killers boasted about the deed to a journalist, who published their confessions in *Look* magazine. Fifty years later Kellum was unrepentant. His clients "told me they did not" do it, and he had "not seen anything where it was supposed to have been an admission of guilt on their part." He invoked the conventional justification for his racist appeal to the jury: "I was trying to say something . . . where they would agree with me . . . because I was employed to defend those fellas. And I was going to defend them as much as I could and stay within the law. . . I received no admonition during the argument from the judge at all." It was "part of the day's work."

Lawyers who do *not* identify with their clients can be equally troubling. Ku Klux Klan member Barry Elton Black burned a thirty-foot cross near a Virginia state highway, prompting terrified blacks to flee and local whites to seek police protection (Holmes 1998). At his arrest, Black declared defiantly: "When is the white man going to stand up to the blacks and the Mexicans in this neighborhood?" A black lawyer volunteered through the ACLU to defend him. "If a white lawyer from a local jurisdiction were to take this case, he would be the subject of all sorts of questions about 'Now we know how old Charlie really feels about things.' With me, there are no questions about that." The NAACP split. The Virginia state director called it "an aberration for a person of African descent to represent a Ku Klux Klan person, in particular for burning a cross." But the national chairman argued that "the First Amendment defense this guy is mounting ought to be precious to all black Americans."

The inauthenticity of role-specific morality can take an enormous toll (Wasserstrom 1975). Robert F. Scamardo was general counsel of the Roman Catholic Diocese of Galveston-Houston for five years (Goodstein 2003). After a jury awarded $119.5 million to eleven sexual abuse victims, Scamardo invoked the statute of limitations and a First Amendment free exercise of religion defense to force others to accept therapy (from Church-selected providers for up to a year) and bind them to secrecy. One plaintiff's lawyer found Scamardo "not overly sympathetic to the victims . . . he just didn't give in." When he was fifteen (thirty years earlier), Scamardo had been sexually abused by an Austin priest. Scamardo confided in the parish lay youth minister, who also abused him. It took Scamardo twenty-seven years to confront his past and three years of therapy to deal with it. Still, he felt good about representing the Church until an elderly woman, victimized as a child, cried when saying she still suffered depression, sexual problems, and marital difficulties. Then a victim he knew committed suicide, and another wrote that he had been abused by the same priest as Scamardo. The lawyer began to contemplate suicide himself. He felt "like the enemy" when a victim walked out of mediation. When he finally reported his abuse to the Austin diocese, it paid for three months of residential treatment. But when he sought $437,500 for medical expenses, lost income, and pain and suffering, the Church pled the statute of limitations, offering only $50,000 for a year's medical expenses because "any financial settlement would be taken from the money that is given by the parishioners on Sunday in the collection." When Scamardo hired a lawyer, the diocese fired him.

Lawyers cannot resolve these tensions by betraying clients. After Russell Tucker was convicted and sentenced to death for murdering a security guard who had caught him shoplifting, David B. Smith was appointed to bring the appeal (Rimer 2000). Smith had practiced more than twenty-five years, eighteen as assistant U.S. Attorney in Greensboro, North Carolina, where he was considered "the best trial lawyer." "At the end of the [first] visit I decided that I did not like Mr. Tucker." Although Smith opposed the death penalty, "I decided that Mr. Tucker deserved to die, and I would not do anything to prevent his execution." While Smith was struggling with this in therapy, he deliberately missed a crucial filing deadline. But when he received notice of the execution date he admitted his behavior to the Center for Death Penalty Litigation.

Almost everyone agrees lawyers must advocate vigorously for criminal accused, regardless of their legal or factual guilt (Curtis 1952; Freedman 1975; Luban 1993; but see Simon 1993). But some refuse to extend that to transactional work, where the adversary may have little or no representation (Pepper 1995; Simon 1998;

Rosenbaum 2004). And what about situations where there is *no* other voice? In the aftermath of 9/11, the U.S. Department of Justice Office of Legal Counsel drafted memoranda advising the president to deny al Qaeda and the Taliban protection under the Geneva Conventions, send "enemy combatants" to Guantánamo because U.S. courts lacked jurisdiction, detain POWs indefinitely without trial (some in secret prisons inaccessible to the Red Cross), try a few in military commissions that disregarded basic due process, employ interrogation techniques that included torture, and "render" detainees to other countries for indefinite detention and torture (Greenberg and Dratel 2005). Should these lawyers be allowed to take refuge in the claim that they were only serving their client? And who is their client: the president or the people?

2 JUDICIAL INFLUENCE ON THE LEGAL PROFESSION

As indispensable intermediaries between civil society and the state, lawyers jealously guard their independence. Yet everywhere legal professions emerged as adjuncts of courts, to which they remain subordinate. As late as the nineteenth century, accused felons were *forbidden* representation for fear lawyers would obstruct conviction. The Bush administration denies lawyers to detainees in the "war on terror" because counsel might render them less vulnerable to pressure and expose abusive interrogation. In civil law regimes, private practice often has lower status than the magistracy (judges and prosecutors) (Abel 1988). In Japan, state lawyers significantly antedated their private counterparts (Rokumoto 1988). Even in the common law world, lawyers remain "officers of the court," which shapes the profession in ways that profoundly affect access to legal services.

Courts typically regulate entry; indeed, governmental restraints on competition have been essential for all professions to emerge and survive. In 2001 New York raised the passing grade on the Multistate Professional Responsibility Examination from 72 to 85 (out of 150), "the most exacting standard set by any of the 52 jurisdictions," in order "to inspire greater attention to the study of legal ethics and standards of professional conduct."[1] In 2002, after three years of study, the state raised the bar examination passing grade from 660 to 675 (out of 1000) "to maintain New York's standard of professional competence and fulfill the public protection function of the bar examination." The existing standard had been "lower than that of 30 of the jurisdictions which administer that test" and "lower than that of states

---

[1] http://www.nybarexam.org/press.htm.

which are New York's geographic neighbors, as well as that of states which are commercially and industrially similar to New York." States have excluded racists (*Hale v. Committee on Character and Fitness* 2000). With the globalization of law practice, jurisdictions have required reciprocity before admitting foreign lawyers (Abel 1994). Specialized courts (for patents or tax) have their own admissions rules.

Courts also protect lawyers' monopoly by prohibiting the "unauthorized practice of law," which they define broadly (Rhode 1981; on nonlawyer advocacy, see Kritzer 1998). Courts and bar associations have restricted software for uncontested divorces and living trusts and lay assistance in filing bankruptcies (Carvajal 1998; Liptak 2002; Hines 2001).[2] The American Bar Association recently considered expanding its definition of the practice of law to include "selecting, drafting, or completing legal documents" (Liptak 2003*a*). The Cleveland Bar Association sought to impose a $10,000 fine on a nonlawyer father who had the temerity to represent his autistic son in seeking an individual educational plan under the federal Individuals with Disabilities Education Act (Liptak 2006). Economists generally find that licensure's heightened costs outweigh any quality gains (Kleiner 2006).

Courts control lawyers in multiple ways. They educate novices, admonish incompetence, prohibit abusive discovery, impose sanctions, disqualify lawyers from representing clients, dismiss lawsuits for lawyer misbehavior, and adjudicate legal malpractice. They generally delegate disciplinary authority to professional associations while retaining appellate review. They can impose sanctions and hold lawyers in contempt for speech that would "impugn the character or integrity of any judicial officer" (Maharaj 1998). They award fees to successful plaintiffs' lawyers in a wide variety of cases and make decisions about damages (remittitur, the availability of punitives), which affect the size of contingent fees. Adversaries strategically complain about ethical violations and conflicts of interest of opposing counsel (Shapiro 2002). Judicial decisions test restrictive practices—on advertising and solicitation, minimum and contingent fees, and multidisciplinary partnerships—against antitrust laws and constitutional guarantees (*Ohralik v. Ohio State Bar Association* 1978; *Florida Bar v. Went for It., Inc.* 1993).

3 LAWYER INFLUENCE ON COURTS

Lawyers influence courts most profoundly by becoming judges. The demography of the profession and its hierarchic structure affect who is eligible for, aspire to, and are elevated to the bench. In England, until recently, only Queen's Counsel—senior

---

[2] *Unauthorized Practice of Law Committee v. Parsons Technology, Inc.*, U.S. D.C. Civil Action 3:97-CV-2589-H (N.D. Texas 1.22.99) (Mem. Op.).

barristers—could be appointed to the higher courts (Abel 2003, 190–5). The growing gap between the salaries of judges and private practitioners affects recruitment and retention. Upon retirement with a sizeable pension, many earn multiples of their government salaries as private judges; this drain aggravates backlog, intensifying demand for speedier justice outside the courts. In common law adversary systems, lawyers educate judges about new sources of law, for instance norms in other countries concerning sodomy (*Lawrence v. Texas* 2003) or the death penalty for juveniles (*Roper v. Simmons* 2005). The initiation and conclusion of litigation is controlled by plaintiffs' lawyers and the pace of litigation by both sides. Fee structures influence lawyers' actions (the different perverse incentives of contingent and hourly fees) (Rubinfeld and Scotchmer 1993). Most appellate judges and all federal trial judges are assisted by recently-graduated law clerks, who introduce the latest academic approaches (Peppers 2006; Ward 2006), as well as by professional clerks, magistrates, special masters, and hearing officers. Professional associations (notably the ABA) evaluate nominees to the federal bench. Websites allow lawyers to comment anonymously (often acerbically) on and rank sitting judges.[3] Lawyers have long contributed to judicial election campaigns; now interest groups representing plaintiffs and defendants in personal injury litigation have huge electoral war chests (Cheek and Champagne 2005; Liptak and Roberts 2006). Lawyers shop for forums and judges: some judges (and juries) are unusually sympathetic to tort victims; the federal government has filed many national security cases in the Fourth Circuit (the most conservative). Lawyers unlucky in the judges assigned move to change venue or recuse them.

Professional associations may seek to influence courts more directly (Halliday 1987; Powell 1988). The American Bar Association has taken positions on such controversial subjects as the death penalty, abortion, affirmative action, military discrimination against gays and lesbians, and the denial of due process to "enemy combatants." Such partisanship creates serious tensions in "unified" bar associations, which compel membership (Schneyer 1983).

4 THE MARKET FOR ADJUDICATION AND LEGAL REPRESENTATION

Because states monopolize the use of force, only courts can prosecute accused or order civil defendants to appear, answer complaints, and satisfy judgments. But courts do not monopolize adjudication nor lawyers representation. Courts eagerly

---

[3] E.g. Los Angeles County Bar Association, "Judge Your Judge," http://www.lacba.org/showpage. cfm?pageid=3538.

shed parts of their dockets or functions, delegating custody and visitation disputes to social workers. They pressure litigants to settle, in part by delaying trials (Resnik 1982). But institutions intended to reduce judicial caseload can impose new burdens. All immigration cases begin in Immigration Courts rather than the U.S. District Courts. However, appeals from the Board of Immigration Appeals now clog the Circuit Courts, consuming *half* of the Ninth Circuit docket (Moore and Simmons 2005). Both case overload and expansion of legal knowledge generate pressures to create specialized courts: family, juvenile, small claims, housing, patent, drugs, security, medical malpractice, etc. This enhances expertise but also invites capture by the litigants (Baum 1977). Courts also lose jurisdiction to competitors, such as arbitration, because of their inadequacies: cost, delay, technicality, lack of relevant expertise (Arthurs 1985; Dezalay and Garth 1996).

Legal professionals face competition from below by independent paralegals, legal document assistants, notarios (Goldschmidt 1998; Moorhead et al. 2003). But the more serious threat comes from those with superior technical expertise and resources (Daly 2002). The best examples are the major accounting firms: ten times larger than the biggest law firm, far more global, highly numerate, better capitalized, more sophisticated in information technology, and permitted to solicit business (*Edenfield v. Fane* 1993). If multidisciplinary partnerships (MDPs) are allowed, accountants are far more likely to dominate lawyers than vice versa. Fortunately for lawyers, the complicity of accountants in the major scandals of the 1990s (epitomized by Enron) seems to have reduced pressures for MDPs (McLean and Elkind 2003; Swartz and Watkins 2003). The same debacles have increased demand for external regulation of lawyers, for instance by the SEC (Glater 2003). As lawyers diversify their activities in an attempt to capture new markets (because they are losing old ones), they inevitably subject themselves to new regulatory agencies.

5 THE CONSEQUENCES OF DEMOGRAPHY

The size and composition of the legal profession have profound consequences for the legal system. Whether or not litigation is "demand driven" (Bevan et al. 1994; Bevan 1996; Cross 1992), it necessarily varies with the number of lawyers, which also affects access to legal services (Sander and Williams 1989). The distribution of lawyers across professional roles is closely articulated with the structure of the legal system. It is no accident that civil litigation rates are significantly higher in common law than civil law countries (but see Wollschlager 1998) or that common law adversary systems have up to twenty times as many private practitioners as judges, whereas those categories are roughly equivalent in civil law inquisitorial systems (Abel 1988, table 1.1). In the United States, private practice is divided into two mutually exclusive hemispheres, one serving ordinary individuals and small businesses, the other wealthy individuals and large corporations (Heinz and Laumann 1982; Heinz et al. 2005). These differ in lawyer background (class and ethnoreligious affiliation), training (law school attended), structure of practice (solo or small firm versus mammoth global firms), status, and remuneration. The last two decades have seen the proportion of lawyer effort devoted to the personal/small-business client sector shrink from 40 to 29 percent while the proportion devoted to the corporate client sector increased from 53 to 64 percent (Heinz et al. 2005, table 2.1). This has obvious consequences not only for access to representation but also for the equality of arms essential for an adversary system to produce justice.

Because the professional project seeks to elevate collective status as well as extract monopoly rents and dampen intraprofessional competition (Larson 1977; but see Karpik 1999), it excludes aspirants on the basis of class, race, and gender. In response to the civil rights and feminist movements, legal professions have recently inverted their goals from exclusivity to representativeness (Abel 2003, ch. 4). Women quickly became half of all entrants, although their progress up the professional hierarchy has been stymied by the difficulty of combining work with parenting (Epstein 1993; Hull and Nelson 1998; Kay and Hagan 1998; Epstein et al. 1999; Schultz and Shaw 2003; Wallace 2004). Despite the success of affirmative action (Bowen and Bok 1998; Lempert et al. 2000) and its qualified support by the Supreme Court (*Grutter v. Bollinger* 2003), racial equality has been more elusive (Chambliss 1997). A diverse legal profession is a necessary but not sufficient condition for a bench that represents the larger population. American judges are recruited from different kinds of law schools: federal from the more elite (with attention to geography), state from the better local schools. Women are overrepresented among civil law judges (though not at the highest levels) (Abel 1989, 118) because appointment is meritocratic (rather than political, as in the United States), motherhood is more compatible with civil service hours than private practice, and judges have less discretion (and less status) when codes rather than precedent govern. Some have argued that women have distinctive styles of moral reasoning and hence of lawyering, which should manifest in judging (Menkel-Meadow 1989).

6 Achieving Justice

The grundnorm of any legal system is justice, symbolized by the blindfolded statute weighing the parties in her scales and the motto on the Supreme Court pediment: "Equal Justice Under Law." But market mechanisms for delivering legal representation necessarily reproduce society's multiple inequalities (Abel 1979). The American legal system has responded to this problem slowly and inadequately (Rhode 2000). Unrepresented defendants faced professional prosecutors in felonies until 1963 (*Gideon v. Wainwright* 1963) and misdemeanors until 1972 (*Argersinger v. Hamlin* 1972). With few exceptions, courts have refused to extend the Sixth Amendment right to counsel from criminal cases to civil (but see Dewan 2005). Even after accused were granted a constitutional right to counsel, governments stinted funding. As New York's mayor, ex-prosecutor Rudolph Giuliani drastically cut legal aid, diverting half of all accused to private counsel (Fritsch and Rohde 2001*a*; 2001*b*; 2001*c*). But at hourly rates of $40 in court and $25 outside, only 1200 lawyers would accept cases. One earned $125,041 in 2000 by taking 1,600 cases, managing his files by throwing them in a pile, so "when the deadline comes for the motions, I miss them." But he was "happy" to be "a .250 hitter."

Before the federal government began funding civil legal aid in 1965, total national expenditure was $5 million (Abel 1985). It peaked at $320 million in 1980 (Carter's last year), before Republicans halved its budget in real dollars and imposed numerous restrictions, prohibiting categories of cases (e.g. voting rights, desegregation, and abortion), lobbying, class actions, and representation of undocumented clients (Abel and Udell 2002). There has been one successful challenge—to the ban on contesting welfare reform (*Legal Services Corporation v. Velazquez* 2001). Although states have increased their funding, even a wealthy liberal jurisdiction like California spent only $13 per eligible client for civil legal services (Weinstein 2002); Mississippi spends $3.19 per capita for criminal defense (Liptak 2003*b*). Conservatives challenged the principal source of state funding—interest on lawyers' trust accounts—for "taking" money from clients without due process (*Brown v. Legal Foundation of Washington* 2003). Business interests convinced the Virginia legislature to eliminate funding for undocumented farmworkers (Weinstein 2001). Industry persuaded the Louisiana Supreme Court to bar Tulane University's Environmental Law Clinic from representing community groups, and federal courts upheld the rule (*Southern Christian Leadership Conference v. Louisiana Supreme Court* 2001). Frustrated by the inefficiencies of dealing with unrepresented litigants, courts have introduced paralegals, *pro se* counselors, and computer terminals, and barred lawyers on both sides (Liu 1999; Morin 2002; Wilgoren 2002). In response to limitations on Legal Services Corporation resources and capabilities, the dramatic growth of corporate law practice (in size and per capita income), and its need to attract and retain law graduates, large firms have greatly expanded and institutionalized their *pro bono* programs (Cummings 2004).

7 THE FUNDAMENTAL CONTRADICTION

Lawyers dream of a world governed by legitimate rules dictating unambiguous outcomes in every case (pandectism). Politicians dream of a world where their unconstrained commands are perfectly implemented (autarchy). To the lawyer, politics is corruption. To the politician, law is a technical obstacle. These visions clash most resoundingly in the courts. We mystify judicial nominations—particularly to the Supreme Court—as a choice of the technically most qualified, as though competence were a unidimensional variable on which there was perfect consensus. But we know politics rules. Nominees walk a tightrope, trying to signal loyalty to supporters without giving ammunition to opponents. Judicial decisions confront the same dilemma: judges seek the outcomes they prefer and then clothe them in the garb of legal necessity. Richard Posner is atypically candid: "The way I approach a case as a judge—maybe you think it heresy—is first to ask myself what would be a reasonable, sensible result, as a lay person would understand it, and then, having answered that question, to ask whether that result is blocked by clear constitutional or statutory text, governing precedent, or any other conventional limitation on judicial discretion" (Posner and Heymann 2006). He sounds refreshingly like the Red Queen: "Sentence first—verdict afterwards" (Carroll 1865, ch. 12). Just as market forces us say how much we are willing to spend for justice, so politics forces us to say how much honesty we can stand.

REFERENCES

ABEL, L. K., and UDELL, D. S. 2002. If you gag lawyers, do you choke the courts? Some implications for judges when funding restrictions curb advocacy by lawyers on behalf of the poor. *Fordham Urban Law Journal*, 29: 873–906.

ABEL, R. L. 1979. Socializing the legal profession: can redistributing lawyers' services achieve social justice? *Law and Policy Quarterly*, 1: 5–51.

—— 1982. Law as lag: inertia as a social theory of law. *Michigan Law Review*, 80: 785–809.

—— 1985. Law without politics: legal aid under advanced capitalism. *UCLA Law Review*, 32: 474–642.

—— 1988. Lawyers in the civil law world. Pp. 1–53 in *Lawyers in Society, Vol. 2: The Civil Law World*, ed. R. L. Abel and P. S. C. Lewis. Berkeley: University of California Press.

—— 1989. Comparative sociology of legal professions. Pp. 80–153 in *Lawyers in Society, VOL. 3: Comparative Theories*, ed. R. L. Abel and P. S. C. Lewis. Berkeley: University of California Press.

—— 1994. Transnational law practice. *Case Western Reserve Law Review*, 44: 737–870.

—— 2003. *English Lawyers between Market and State: The Politics of Professionalism.* Oxford: Oxford University Press.

ARTHURS, H. W. 1985. *"Without the Law:" Administrative Justice and Legal Pluralism in Nineteenth-Century England.* Toronto: University of Toronto Press.

BAUM, L. 1977 Judicial specialization, litigant influence, and substantive policy: the Court of Customs and Patent Appeals. *Law and Society Review*, 11: 823–50.

BEVAN, G. 1996. Has there been supplier-induced demand for legal aid? *Civil Justice Quarterly*, 15: 58–114.

—— HOLLAND, T., and PARTINGTON, M. 1994. *Organising Cost-effective Access to Justice.* London: Social Market Foundation.

BOWEN, W. G., and BOK, D. 1998. *The Shape of the River: Long-Term Consequences of Considering Race in College and University Admissions.* Princeton, NJ: Princeton University Press.

CARROLL, L. D. 1865. *Alice's Adventures in Wonderland.* London: Macmillan.

CARVAJAL, D. 1998. Lawyers are not amused by feisty legal publisher. *New York Times*, C1 (August 24).

CHAMBLISS, E. 1997. Organizational determinants of law firm integration. *American University Law Review*, 46: 669–746.

CHEEK, K., and CHAMPAGNE, A. 2005. *Judicial Politics in Texas: Politics, Money, and Partisanship in State Courts.* New York: P. Lang.

CROSS, F. B. 1992. The first thing we do, let's kill all the economists: an empirical evaluation of the effect of lawyers on the United States economy and political system. *Texas Law Review*, 70: 645–83.

CUMMINGS, S. 2004. The politics of pro bono. *UCLA Law Review*, 52: 1–149.

CURTIS, C. 1952. The ethics of advocacy. *Stanford Law Review*, 4: 3–23.

DALY, M. 2002. Monopolist, aristocrat, or entrepreneur? A comparative perspective on the future of multidisciplinary partnerships in the United States, France, Germany, and the United Kingdom after the disintegration of Andersen Legal. *Washington University Law Quarterly*, 80: 589–648.

DEWAN, S. 2005. Abused children are found entitled to legal aid. *New York Times*, A16 (February 9).

DEZALAY, Y., and GARTH, B. G. 1996. *Dealing in Virtue: International Commercial Arbitration and the Construction of a Transnational Legal Order.* Chicago: University of Chicago Press.

EDWARDS, L. (ed.) 2004. *Bringing Justice to the People: The Story of the Freedom-Based Public Interest Law Movement.* Washington, DC: Heritage.

EPSTEIN, C. F. 1993. *Women in Law,* 2nd edn. Urbana: University of Illinois Press.

—— SERON, C., OGLENSKY, B., and SAUTÉ, R. 1999. *The Part-Time Paradox: Time Norms, Professional Life, Family and Gender.* New York: Routledge.

FRANKEL, M. 1975. The search for truth: an umpireal view. *University of Pennsylvania Law Review*, 123: 1031–59.

FREEDMAN, M. 1975. *Lawyers' Ethics in an Adversary System.* Indianapolis: Bobbs-Merrill.

FRITSCH, J., and ROHDE, D. 2001*a*. Lawyers often fail New York's poor, *New York Times*, A1 (April 8).

—— —— 2001*b*. Caseloads push system to breaking point. *New York Times*, A1 (April 9).

—— —— 2001*c*. On appeals, the poor find little leverage. *New York Times*, A1 (April 10).

GLATER, J. D. 2003. S.E.C. adopts new rules for lawyers and funds. *New York Times*, C1 (January 24).

GOLDSCHMIDT, J. 1998. Crossing legal practice boundaries: paralegals, unauthorized practice of law, and Abbott's system of professions. *Current Research on Occupations and Professions*, 10: 157–91.

GOODSTEIN, L. 2003. Lawyer for church says he hid his own sexual abuse by priest. *New York Times*, A1 (November 25).

GREENBERG, K. J., and DRATEL, J. L. 2005. *The Torture Papers: The Road to Abu Ghraib.* New York: Cambridge University Press.

HALLIDAY, T. C. 1987. *Beyond Monopoly: Lawyers, State Crises, and Professional Empowerment.* Chicago: University of Chicago Press.

HEINZ, J. P., and LAUMANN, E. O. 1982. *Chicago Lawyers: The Social Structure of the Bar.* New York: Russell Sage Foundation.

—— NELSON, R. L., SANDEFUR, R. L., and LAUMANN, E. O. 2005. *Urban Lawyers: The New Social Structure of the Bar.* Chicago: University of Chicago Press.

HENNEBERGER, M. 2002. John Paul says Catholic bar must refuse divorce cases. *New York Times*, A4 (January 29).

HINES, C. N. 2001. Without a lawyer. *New York Times*, C1 (July 31).

HOLMES, S. A. 1998. Klan case transcends racial divide. *New York Times*, A14 (November 20).

HULL, K. E., and NELSON, R. L. 1998. Gender inequality in the law: problems of structure and agency in recent studies of gender in Anglo-American legal professions. *Law and Social Inquiry*, 23: 681–705.

JOHNSTON, M. D. 1996. Shelling out. *Westword* (April 25).

KARPIK, L. 1999. *French Lawyers: A Study in Collective Action, 1274–1994.* Oxford: Oxford University Press.

KAY, F. M., and HAGAN, J. 1998. Raising the bar: the gender stratification of law-firm capital. *American Sociological Review*, 63: 728–43.

KINSLEY, M. 2006. Why lawyers are liars. *Washington Post*, A17 (January 20).

KLEINER, M. M. 2006. *Licensing Occupations: Ensuring Quality or Restricting Competition?* Kalamazoo, Mich.: Upjohn Institute.

KRITZER, H. M. 1998. *Legal Advocacy: Lawyers and Nonlawyers at Work.* Ann Arbor: University of Michigan Press.

LARSON, M. S. 1977. *The Rise of Professionalism: A Sociological Analysis.* Berkeley: University of California Press.

LEMPERT, R. O., CHAMBERS, D. L., and ADAMS, T. K. 2000. Michigan's minority graduates in practice: the river runs through law school. *Law and Social Inquiry*, 25: 395–505.

LESHER, D. 1998. Harman braces for attack on foreign links. *Los Angeles Times*, A3 (April 8).

LIPTAK, A. 2002. Preparing petitions: it irks the lawyers, but is it lawyering? *New York Times*, A1 (August 13).

—— 2003a. U.S. opposes proposal to limit who may give legal advice. *New York Times*, A11 (February 3).

—— 2003b. County says it's too poor to defend the poor. *New York Times*, A1 (April 15).

—— 2006 Nonlawyer father wins his suit over education, and the bar is upset. *New York Times*, A8 (May 6).

—— and ROBERTS, J. 2006. Campaign cash mirrors a high court's rulings. *New York Times* (October 1).

LIU, C. 1999. Pleading their case. *Los Angeles Times*, B2 (January 15).

LUBAN, D. 1984. The adversary system excuse. Pp. 83–122 in *The Good Lawyer*, ed. D. Luban. Totowa, NJ: Rowman and Allanheld.

—— 1993. Are criminal defenders different? *Michigan Law Review*, 91: 1729–66.

MAHARAJ, D. 1998. Judges seek to curb criticism by lawyers. *Los Angeles Times*, A3 (April 20).

McINTYRE, L. 1987. *The Public Defender: The Practice of Law in the Shadows of Repute*. Chicago: University of Chicago Press.

McLEAN, B., and ELKIND, P. 2003. *The Smartest Guys in the Room: The Amazing Rise and Scandalous Fall of Enron*. New York: Penguin.

MENKEL-MEADOW, C. 1989. Feminization of the legal profession: comparative sociology of women lawyers. Pp. 196–255 in Abel and Lewis 1989.

MOORHEAD, R., SHERR, A., and PATERSON, A. 2003. Contesting professionalism: legal aid and nonlawyers in England and Wales. *Law and Society Review*, 37: 765–808.

MOORE, S., and SIMMONS, A. M. 2005. Immigrant pleas crushing federal appellate courts. *Los Angeles Times*, A1 (May 2).

MORIN, M. 2002. Computerized legal assistance is getting its day in court. *Los Angeles Times*, B6 (June 18).

O'GORMAN, H. 1963. *Lawyers and Matrimonial Cases: A Study of Informal Pressures in Private Professional Practice*. New York: Columbia University Press.

PEPPER, S. 1995. Counseling at the limits of the law: an exercise in the jurisprudence and ethics of lawyering. *Yale Law Journal*, 104: 1545–610.

PEPPERS, T. C. 2006. *Courtiers of the Marble Palace: The Rise and Influence of the Supreme Court Law Clerk*. Stanford, Calif.: Stanford University Press.

POSNER, R. A., and HEYMANN, P. B. 2006. Tap dancing. *New Republic Online* (January 31).

POWELL, M. J. 1988. *From Patrician to Professional Elite: The Transformation of the New York City Bar Association*. New York: Russell Sage Foundation.

RESNIK, J. 1982. Managerial judging, *Harvard Law Review*, 96: 374–448.

RHODE, D. L. 1981. Policing the professional monopoly: a constitutional and empirical analysis of unauthorized practice prohibitions. *Stanford Law Review*, 34: 1–112.

—— 2000. *In the Interests of Justice: Reforming the Legal Profession*. New York: Oxford University Press.

RIMER S. 2000. Lawyer sabotaged case of a client on death row. *New York Times*, A27 (November 24).

ROKUMOTO, K. 1988. The present state of Japanese practicing attorneys: on the way to full professionalization? Pp. 160–99 in Abel and Lewis 1988.

ROSENBAUM, T. 2004. *The Myth of Moral Justice*. New York: HarperCollins.

RUBIN, R. 2005. The ghosts of Emmett Till. *New York Times Magazine*, 30 (July 31).

RUBINFELD, D. L., and SCOTCHMER, S. 1993. Contingent fees for attorneys: an economic analysis. *Rand Journal of Economics*, 24: 343–56.

SANDER, R. H., and WILLIAMS, E. D. 1989. Why are there so many lawyers? Perspectives on a turbulent market. *Law and Social Inquiry*, 14: 431–79.

SARAT, A., and SCHEINGOLD, S. A. (eds.) 1998. *Cause Lawyering: Political Commitments and Professional Responsibilities*. New York: Oxford University Press.

—— —— 2001. *Cause Lawyering and the State in a Global Era*. New York: Oxford University Press.

—— —— 2003. *The Worlds Cause Lawyers Make: Structure and Agency in Legal Practice*. Stanford, Calif.: Stanford University Press.

SCHEINGOLD, S. A., and SARAT, A. 2004. *Something to Believe In: Politics, Professionalism, and Cause Lawyering*. Stanford: Stanford University Press.

SCHNEYER, T. J. 1983 The incoherence of the unified bar concept: generalizing from the Wisconsin case. *American Bar Foundation Research Journal*, 8: 1–108.

SCHULTZ, U., and SHAW, G. (eds.) 2003. *Women in the World's Legal Professions*. Oxford: Hart.

SCHWARTZ, M. 1978. Professionalism and accountability of lawyers. *California Law Review*, 66: 669–97.

SHAPIRO, S. P. 2002. *Tangled Loyalties: Conflict of Interest in Legal Practice*. Ann Arbor: University of Michigan Press.

SIMON, W. H. 1978. The ideology of advocacy: procedural justice and professional ethics. *Wisconsin Law Review*, 1978: 29–144.

—— 1993. The ethics of criminal defense. *Michigan Law Review*, 91: 1703–28.

—— 1998. *The Practice of Justice*. Cambridge, Mass.: Harvard University Press.

SIMONS, M. 2004a. Milosevic loses director role in his own courtroom drama. *New York Times*, A3 (September 8).

—— 2004b. Milosevic's lawyers ask to be taken off case. *New York Times*, A8 (October 28).

SWARTZ, M., with WATKINS, S. 2003. *Power Failure: The Inside Story of the Collapse of ENRON*. New York: Doubleday.

U.S. DEPARTMENT OF DEFENSE 2004. Third military commission interrupted by Yemeni detainee request (August 26). http://www.defenselink.mil/releases/2004/nr20040826.

WALLACE, J. E. 2004. *Juggling It All: A Study of Lawyers' Work, Home, and Family Demands and Coping Strategies*. Newton, Pa.: Law School Admission Council.

WARD, A. 2006. *Sorcerers' Apprentices: 100 Years of Law Clerks at the United States Supreme Court*. New York: NYU Press.

WASSERSTROM, R. 1975. Lawyers as professionals: some moral issues. *Human Rights*, 5: 1–24.

WEINSTEIN, H. 2001. Powerful foes of legal aid. *Los Angeles Times*, A1 (May 30).

—— 2002. Legal aid to the poor falls short. *Los Angeles Times*, B1 (November 21).

WILGOREN, J. 2002. Divorce court proceeds in a lawyer-free zone. *New York Times*, A10 (February 9).

WOLLSCHLAGER, C. 1998. Exploring global landscapes of litigation rates. In *Festschrft für Erhard Blankenburg zum 60 Geburtstag*, ed. J. Brand and D. Strempel. Baden-Baden: Nomos.

CASES

Argersinger v. Hamlin 1972. 407 U.S. 25.

Brown v. Legal Foundation of Washington 2003. 538 U.S. 216.

Edenfield v. Fane 1993. 507 U.S. 761.

Florida Bar v. Went for It., Inc. 1993. 115 S.Ct. 1792.

Gideon v. Wainwright 1963. 372 U.S. 335.

Grutter v. Bollinger 2003. 539 U.S. 306.

Hale v. Committee on Character and Fitness 2000. 520 U.S. 1261, 2002 WL 398524 (N.D. Ill. 2002), 335 F.3d 678 (7th Cir. 2003).

Lawrence v. Texas 2003. 539 U.S. 558.

Legal Services Corporation v. Velazquez 2001. 531 U.S. 533.

Ohralik v. Ohio State Bar Association 1978. 436 U.S. 447.

Roper v. Simmons 2005. 543 U.S. 551.

PART VIII

THE POLITICAL AND POLICY ENVIRONMENT OF COURTS IN THE UNITED STATES

CHAPTER 32

JUDICIAL INDEPENDENCE

FRANK CROSS

FEW cows are more sacred than judicial independence. Yet the concept of an independent judiciary is more commonly apotheosized than analyzed. Article X of the Universal Declaration of Human Rights provides that an independent and impartial judiciary is a fundamental human right, but does not define the precise nature of this independence. Much of the existing research on the subject has failed to identify clearly what is meant by judicial independence or to justify why it is inevitably valuable. Some discussions conflate judicial independence with the "rule of law," although the two concepts are distinct and not necessarily even associated. I will explain how the concept of judicial independence is much more complicated and ambiguous than it is often regarded. While judicial independence has real value, it is not a feature to be maximized in all regards.

I review and explicate the literature on judicial independence. I begin with an analysis of the meaning of judicial independence, a crucial issue that is elided by too much of the literature on the subject. There is no single definition of such independence, and the concept is a matter of degree rather than a binary determination of dependent or independent. I next consider the degree to which the judiciary is independent, focusing on the United States federal judiciary. The value of judicial independence is uncertain, because its benefits are accompanied by costs, and some measure of dependence or accountability is optimal. The chapter proceeds to consider the sources of judicial independence. Although constitutional protections may have some value, the root of independence may derive from the interests of other political institutions. Finally, the chapter considers the implications of selection and retention systems on judicial independence, with a focus on the states of the U.S., which provide a convenient testing ground.

1 What Is Judicial Independence?

Any careful analysis of judicial independence must begin with a definition of the concept, but this issue is typically assumed away. Independence is generally defined as something like autonomy or freedom to act as one pleases. The first and most critical aspect of this definition in the context of the judiciary is: "independence from what or whom?" Judicial independence has been called a system in which disputes are resolved by a "neutral third," but this begs the question of neutral of what. Independence assumes a freedom from outside control, but judicial independence need not, and cannot, be absolute. Insofar as "no man is an island," a state of utter independence is probably unrealistic (Russell 2001, 11–12).

The judicial hierarchy itself creates a certain dependence for most judges. The commonplace understanding of judicial independence would have federal district courts and other lower courts free from influence from the president but not free from influence from the U.S. Supreme Court or other relevant courts of last resort. Various other social constraints also inhibit judicial independence. Judge Kozinski of the Ninth Circuit has suggested that if a judge were truly and fully independent he might choose to go to the bench "dressed like Ronald McDonald," or choose to issue all of his or her opinions in French (Kozinski 1998, 862).

Many commentators, such as Justice Breyer, have declared that judicial independence is grounded in decision-making according to law, which implies a lack of judicial independence of the materials and procedures of the law (Breyer 1996). This interpretation, which is not necessarily obvious, makes judges dependent on the materials of the law itself. If judicial independence is not an absolute state in which judges are free to decide cases however they please, there remains the question of what an independent judiciary is to be independent from.

The typical understanding of judicial independence involves the court's freedom from control by other government institutions, such as the executive or legislative branches. The U.S. Supreme Court has defined independence as "judges who are free from potential domination by other branches of government" (*U.S. v. Will* 1980, 218). The rationale for this independence lies in a separation of powers. In the old Soviet Union and Eastern Europe, courts practiced what was sometimes called "telephone justice," in which judges would render decisions after receiving instructions from party leaders. The U.S. constitutional system is designed to prevent such actions through a separation of powers. In *The Federalist*, Hamilton explained that "there is no liberty, if the power of judging be not separated from the legislative and executive powers."

This separation-of-powers aspect of judicial independence is meant to provide something of a bulwark against tyranny (Guarnieri and Pederzoli 2002, 152–4). In the U.S. and other countries, the judiciary has increasingly played an aggressive role in regulating the exercise of legislative and executive authority, policing the political process, and making public policy decisions (Ferejohn 2002). The judiciary appears to be carrying out its independent, separation-of-powers function. There is some quantitative evidence that the separation of powers, including an independent judiciary, effectively reduces governmental corruption and rent-seeking (Panizza 2001). Freedom from control by other government institutions also serves the separate interest of promoting justice according to law. Judges who decide cases on politicians' instructions are probably not deciding according to the law.

The separation-of-powers rationale is commonly invoked as evidence of the importance of judicial independence for protection of individual or minority rights. Yet there is no obvious reason why independent judges would care to protect such rights. Substantive law may not protect the rights, and independent judges may ignore those laws that do. Nothing in the structure of judicial incentives promotes rights protection, though the absence of accountability arguably insulates the judiciary from oppressive majoritarian urges. The existence of majoritarian oppression is not so compelling, though, and there is little evidence that an independent Supreme Court enhances protection of civil rights and liberties (Peretti 2002, 123).

Another theory of judicial independence suggests that judges should be independent of the litigants appearing before them. These litigants may include the government, but this concept is broader and suggests that judges should also be independent from the control or influence of private parties. The rationale for this form of independence is less the separation of powers than fairness and justice and the rule of law. Such fairness means that a litigant should not prevail simply because of its identity, independent of case facts and the law. Fairness requires that a "decision of a case be independent of the *names or identities* of the litigants" (Kornhauser 2002, 49). This is a requisite of judicial impartiality and equality before the law, perhaps of due process of law. The Supreme Court has enforced this precept, vacating a decision because a judge had reason to favor a litigant (*Aetna Life Insurance* 1986). Judges themselves have created codes of conduct to protect this independence and provide for their disqualification when their impartiality might be questioned (Administrative Office of the United States Courts 1990).

Yet another aspect of judicial independence involves freedom from public opinion. An independent judiciary does not take a poll before rendering its decisions. Justice Stevens has emphasized that judging involves deciding cases according to precedent and not "public opinion polls" (*Republican Party of Minnesota v. White* 2002, 799). Through its independence, the judiciary is expected to protect the legal rights of minorities in the face of potential majoritarian oppression. Justice Jackson wrote that one's "right to life, liberty and property, to free speech, free press, freedom of worship and assembly, and other fundamental rights" may not be submitted to vote (*West Virginia State Board of Education v. Barnette* 1943, 638). Thus, federal judges are not subject to election but given life tenure. Some may argue that judicial independence need not be freedom from popular opinion. In a democracy, where judges are invested with political decision-making authority, it is arguably appropriate that this authority be exercised with public sentiment in mind. Although a judge should not be influenced by public opinion in deciding whether a particular defendant deserves the death penalty, public opinion might appropriately be considered in establishing standards for whether the death penalty is permissible and when. In reality, the general public pays relatively little heed to most judicial decisions, so public influence is probably relatively small.

Still another possible aspect of judicial independence involves freeing the judiciary from the constraints of the law. For some, this notion of independence is oxymoronic; judicial independence *means* decision-making according to law. Although judicial independence is surely meant to free judges to decide according to the law, true independence would also allow judges to depart from the dictates of the law.

Making judges beholden to the law limits the separation-of-powers virtues of judicial independence. Giving the legislature control over the content of the law and making judges dependent upon the law inevitably makes judges more dependent on the legislature (though only in statutory and not constitutional issues). If judges "take a positivist attitude toward law and simply follow the rules laid down by the political branches, then they are not really independent of politics but... completely subservient to it" (Scheppele 2002, 269). Congress may not overturn the outcomes of adjudicated disputes, but prospective changes can eliminate much effect of adjudications and arguably infringe upon judicial independence (Salzburger 1992, 349). Judge Kozinski has related how the legislature functionally overruled one of his decisions before he had even finished writing the opinion (Kozinski 1998, 870).

The constraints of law are often regarded as promoting fairness virtues, rather than inhibiting them, but granting legislatures the power arbitrarily to alter the content of law independent of the judiciary might interfere with fairness. Legislation might be arbitrary or unjust, as in the case of segregation laws. To some degree, a written constitution combined with judicial review power can substantially enhance judicial independence, because it empowers judges to disregard statutory commands on the grounds that they violate that constitution (Scheppele 2002, 248–9). Judges who "see themselves as something other than the simple applicants of the regime's law should bode well for a high degree of judicial independence" (Larkins 1996, 612). An independent judiciary might refuse to enforce fascist legislation. This may be more likely when the incumbent political regime is weaker (Helmke 2002).

A separate definitional question is "independence to do what?" Judicial independence need not mean that judges are independent of constraint, free to rape or murder with impunity; rather, judicial independence should be limited to the independence to act "judicially." Such independence might be limited to actions taken in the judge's judicial role, and actions that are consistent with the judicial role and, therefore, do not authorize a judge to exchange rulings for bribes. Independence to act judicially could be accompanied by accountability for non-judicial actions.

Although the limitation of judicial independence to "judicial" actions seems clear in theory, it can be quite complicated in practice. For who is to decide if a judicial action is "judicial" and therefore deserving of independence? If the legislature or executive were permitted to make such decisions, it could eviscerate the independence of all judicial actions, even legitimate ones, because the power could be abused. Indeed, judicial independence may even imply freedom from second-guessing by other judges. For example, judges are not subject to civil liability in court for actions taken in the course of their judging (*Bradley v. Fisher* 1872). Judges therefore are independent and unaccountable for damages, even if their decisions were contrary to law or otherwise illegitimate. Of course, illegitimate decisions might still be vacated by a higher judicial authority.

"Judicial" independence must also have an empowering function. It implies that judges truly have judicial powers. A court without constraint would be practically immaterial if it lacked all power, because it had no jurisdiction or because its rulings were ignored (Kornhauser 2002, 47). The judicial part of judicial independence could be read to mean that judges have the authority to render decisions and have those decisions recognized at law. In Franco's Spain and Pinochet's Chile, the judiciary had a relatively high level of independence from outside control but had so little power that its independence was trivial (Larkins 1996, 612–13).

There is no single, indisputable definition of judicial independence. At its core, judicial independence means freedom from absolute control by other government institutions. Judicial independence also means some degree of freedom from control by litigants and public opinion and even possibly some freedom from positive law. The breadth of this freedom cannot be absolute, though, and it must in some way be limited to judicial functions. The precise degree of independence, from whom and to do what, is not easily defined; but the concept is roughly understood to involve judges' ability to render decisions in cases without fear of retribution. The next section explores the existence of judicial independence in the United States, under the varying interpretations of its meaning.

2 THE REALITY OF JUDICIAL INDEPENDENCE IN THE U.S.

Americans generally and even legal academics often take for granted a belief that our judiciary is independent, at least in the fundamental sense of freedom from interference by other branches. The life tenure of federal judges is invoked as proof of such independence, and the federal judiciary is often considered the paradigmatic case of an independent one. The belief in judicial independence is broadly presumed and not proved, though, because it is difficult to establish measures of judicial independence, in part because the lack of an indisputable definition of the term makes it difficult to conceptualize.

In fact, the executive and legislative branches of the U.S. federal government have considerable power to constrain or influence the federal judiciary. Congress may impeach judges, removing them from office. Although exercise of this power is largely dormant, the threat of impeachment remains and may have an intimidating effect. Such a threat apparently caused federal district court judge Harold Baer to reconsider and reverse a ruling that politicians found especially objectionable (Cross and Nelson 2001, 1461–3).

The judiciary also depends on the other branches of government for its budgetary resources. Although the Constitution prevents Congress from reducing judicial salaries, it may still withhold salary increases or other resources from the federal judiciary and it controls appropriations for supplemental resources that may be material to the interest of judges. Judges have shown considerable concern for their funding, and they regularly appear as supplicants before the legislature (Resnick 1999, 664). Some research suggests that Congress has punished undesirable judicial decisions with budget cuts, and that Supreme Court justices have responded with decisions more amenable to the legislature (Toma 1996). Judge Calabresi reports that budgetary concerns prompted another judge to urge him to rewrite an opinion that might disturb senators (Cross 2003, 207).

The political branches have other sources of influence over the judiciary. For statutory decisions, the Congress may effectively override judicial interpretations, and judges may correspondingly defer to the risk of such an override (Eskridge 1991). The Constitution gives Congress the power to deny the federal judiciary jurisdiction over certain issues. Even if not overridden, the judiciary typically requires assistance from the other branches to implement its decisions, and such assistance may be withheld (Peretti 2002, 112). In the early twentieth century, Congress abolished the newly created Commerce Court due to dislike of its decisions (Dix 1964).

The president and the Senate have the power to promote judges to a higher level of the judiciary and grant higher pay or withhold a possible promotion and salary increases. There is some quantitative evidence suggesting that promotion prospects influence judicial decisions (Sisk, Heise, and Morriss 1998). Congress tends to expand the size of the judiciary when one party has enough political control to ensure that its candidates will fill the newly created vacancies (de Figueiredo and Tiller 1996). The "mere threat of political retribution from Congress seems to have turned the judiciary into an effective self-regulator" (Ferejohn and Kramer 2002, 977). A study of labor relations decisions found that Supreme Court rulings responded to political changes in Congress (Spiller and Gely 1992). Other empirical analyses have shown a varying degree of responsiveness to preferences of other institutions among Supreme Court justices (Cross and Nelson 2001).

The sources of outside influence at the federal level in the United States are relatively crude tools not easily used to target individual judges for rendering disfavored opinions. Although the U.S. federal judiciary does not appear absolutely independent from the political branches, there is ample evidence that it possesses a high level of independence. Segal has conducted a broad empirical analysis of the degree to which the Supreme Court's decisions respond to preferences of Congress, using several different models of congressional decision-making, and he found no effect of legislative preferences (Segal 1997), though some disagree with the findings.

Segal's findings are roughly confirmed by political science research demonstrating that the best determinant of Supreme Court decisions is the justices' own ideology (Peretti 2002, 110–11). Although judicial independence is difficult to measure quantitatively, it may be captured indirectly. If one were to hypothesize how a truly independent judiciary would resolve cases, the most likely determinant would be the individual judges' sense of the just resolution of the case. Their respective senses of a just resolution are contingent on their respective interpretations of justice, which would trace to some degree their respective ideologies. Hence, one would anticipate that an independent judiciary would show an ideological pattern of decision-making.

A wealth of research has demonstrated that judicial ideology is a substantial, if not predominant, determinant of the decisions rendered by the justices of the U.S. Supreme Court. The "attitudinal model" has demonstrated that the decisions of justices are highly correlated with their ideological inclinations (Segal and Spaeth 1993). Nor is there any evidence that other lower courts respond materially to congressional strategic influences in rendering their decisions, as their decisions also are significantly associated with judicial ideology (Pinello 1999). The studies are nearly universal in establishing this statistically significant correlation. These findings presumably underestimate the degree of judicial independence, because they fail to capture nonideological determinants of "justice" and boundary cases where an outcome is too conservative for even a conservative judge, or too liberal for a liberal. Thus, the empirical evidence provides strong support for a finding that the U.S. judiciary is relatively independent. The evidence probably understates the degree of independence, insofar as an independent judiciary would also care about adherence to what they consider to be "correct" legal decisions divorced from their attitudes. There is some evidence, though, that judges are at least somewhat constrained and adapt their decisions to some degree to the preferences of other branches (Epstein and Knight 1998). This constraint may be greater in state judiciaries, where decisions appear to be affected by factors such as judicial tenure and the political makeup of the other branches (Langer 2002, 123).

The second aspect of judicial independence, freedom from the influence of litigants, is also imperfectly operationalized in the judiciary. Litigants use various strategies and tactics to manipulate judicial outcomes. If litigants have greater resources and higher quality legal representation, they may skew outcomes in their favor. Litigants may also strategically settle, so that only cases with the most favorable facts are presented to the judiciary. Research demonstrates that certain litigants, including the government and powerful private parties, are more successful in court (Galanter 1974). Additional evidence indicates that participation in litigation by outsiders, as *amicus curiae*, is associated with greater success in court (Baum 1997, 51). The extent of such influence is not overwhelming, and it is constrained by judicial preferences, but parties clearly do exert some impact on judicial outcomes.

The judiciary may also be influenced by public opinion. Judges live among the public, they read the same media, and they are subject to most of the same influences as the general populace. Judges might also fear for a public backlash against decisions that might compromise their status. Seventh Circuit judge Richard Posner declared that "[j]udges have to worry that if they buck public opinion too strongly," they may suffer punishment (Posner 2002, 739).

Research suggests that federal judicial decisions generally conform to public opinion. Dahl proclaimed that "policy views dominant on the Court are never for long out of line with the policy views dominant among the lawmaking majorities of the United States" (Dahl 1957, 285). Empirical studies of Supreme Court decision-making find that it corresponds with public opinion about as closely as do the elected branches of government (Marshall 1989; McGuire and Stimson 2004). Presidential success before the Court may be linked to presidential popularity (Yates 2002). The evidence is not so strong as to suggest that judges are slaves to public opinion, and it is easy to identify countermajoritarian decisions rendered by courts. Yet, it appears that public opinion may have some impact on judicial decisions.

Independence from the law is not generally considered a feature of the American judiciary. U.S. judges generally do not purport to be independent from the law, but they have implicitly acknowledged the tension between the law and judicial independence and restricted the ability of the legislature to undo judicial decisions. Although the Constitution explicitly prohibits only *ex post facto* criminalization, the Supreme Court has found that Congress cannot reinstate civil claims finally resolved by the courts (*Plaut v. Spend Farm Inc.* 1995).

Empirical analyses have consistently confirmed that lower courts faithfully follow the decisions of the Supreme Court and other aspects of positive law (Klein 2002). However, the findings on the impact of judicial ideology on decisions calls into question the degree to which courts perfectly follow the law. Indeed, some researchers of Supreme Court decisions have questioned whether the law is a significant determinant of that Court's decisions (Segal and Spaeth 1999). The significance of law is confirmed to a degree by the empirical findings on ideological decision-making. Courts of last resort, which are somewhat less bound by the law in the form of prior judicial decisions, are also the most ideological in their decisions (Pinello 1999). American judges plainly are somewhat constrained by law but not to the degree they typically profess. Judicial discretion implies some freedom from the law as well.

In addition, the claim of judicial independence from the law is not terribly meaningful, given the ability of judges to define what the law is. In a common law society, judges themselves create the law; and even after Congress passes a statute, the judiciary declares what that statute means in the context of adjudications. A judge can certainly affect or even alter the meaning of statutes, through his or her interpretation. Even after the legislature attempts to override judicial decisions, the effectiveness of this override may be undermined by judicial interpretation of the overriding legislation (Cross and Nelson 2001, 1455–7).

The judiciary of the United States is plainly somewhat, but not entirely, independent, regardless of the definition of judicial independence. The relative independence of the judiciary is empirically demonstrated by studies showing that the ideological characteristics of judges and perhaps other judicial characteristics influence decisional outcomes. It appears that judges are largely independent of the other branches of government, materially independent of the litigants and public opinion, and at least somewhat independent of the law itself. Moreover, even insofar as the judicial branch is somewhat dependent, individual judges may exercise considerable independence in particular cases (Ferejohn and Kramer 2002). Judicial independence is not a binary condition but exists on a continuum of relative independence and accountability. The next section takes up the question of the desirability of judicial independence along that continuum, which is commonly assumed but seldom demonstrated.

3 THE UNCERTAIN VIRTUE OF JUDICIAL INDEPENDENCE

Independence is generally considered a virtue, but so is accountability; and the two terms are roughly antonymous. An utterly independent judiciary could decide cases on a whim, by a coin flip, or in exchange for personal favors from litigants. Such independence would enable judicial arbitrariness. There is no reason to expect a wholly independent judiciary to abide by the rule of law, and the ideological pattern of federal judicial decisions may suggest that these courts have an excessive degree of independence.

Judicial independence carries the clear virtues associated with the separation of government powers, with some ability to check abuses by other branches of government. This may have the attendant virtue of protecting the rights of individuals. Judicial independence also can further fairness virtues in adjudication, by ensuring that the adjudicator of individual cases is free to decide based on the facts of those cases. This role may be of considerable economic value, as investors can have greater assurance that their economic rights will be protected and their agreements enforced (Barro and Sala-i-Martin 1995). Although these are important values, they do not entirely justify an independent judiciary, which may undermine fairness and fail to protect against government oppression, at least when the judiciary does not oppose or even favors oppressive measures.

Indeed, absolute judicial independence could contradict the very separation-of-powers rationale for which it is typically invoked. A perfectly independent judiciary would be unchecked by other government authority. Unchecked judicial independence could yield judicial tyranny; and, as Barry Friedman has argued, "[t]oo much judicial independence may threaten popular sovereignty" (Friedman 2002, 1). These concerns suggest that judicial independence should not be untrammeled and that the judiciary should be in some way accountable.

The judiciary is often considered the "least dangerous branch," but this is not necessarily so. Thus, the theocratic judiciary of Iran has essentially assumed control of that nation's government, constraining even who may run for elected office (Cross 2003, 199–201). Although the American experience is far from that of Iran, some suggest that the U.S. judiciary has assumed excessive policy-making authority, in decisions such as those striking down laws against abortion. Complaints about "judicial activism" have become common from both the right and the left. Internationally, increased judicial power has been challenged as contrary to democratic policy (Hirschl 2004).

Untrammeled judicial independence may also contravene fairness values. A perfectly independent judiciary is free to be arbitrary or corrupt in its decisions and is likely to become lazy and inefficient (Cross 2003, 198). Unaccountable judges have no external incentive to produce fair rulings and are more likely to produce decisions in accord with their personal and perhaps idiosyncratic preferences. There is no obvious reason to turn over governmental authority to the whims of life-tenured judges.

Although few conceptions of democracy argue that the popular will should govern the outcomes of individual cases, the judiciary does more than simply determine outcomes. Judicial decisions set precedents that establish the law and may determine the meaning of statutes passed by Congress. This form of judicial lawmaking may infringe on democratic preferences about the content of law. The more independent the judiciary, the more able it will be to disregard democratic preferences and even the content of the law passed by elected institutions of government. Independent judges may even arbitrarily strike down statutes as unconstitutional.

Judicial independence is not an unalloyed good. Judge Posner has suggested that independence can simply involve the public's "exchanging one set of tyrants for another" (Posner 1990, 6). The interests of society counsel not the maximization of judicial independence but its optimization on the continuum, though the precise placement of the optimum point is certainly debatable. With this context, I now turn to the sources of judicial independence and how its values may be best implemented.

4 THE SOURCES OF JUDICIAL INDEPENDENCE

Some measure of judicial independence furthers important ends of separation of powers and fairness in administering the law. This leads to the important question of how one may produce a judiciary with an appropriate degree of independence. The typical approach to protecting judicial independence involves constitutional provisions, such as life tenure and protection of compensation. Most nations have created some constitutional protections for judicial independence.

Constitutional guarantees are at times derided as mere "paper guarantees," unable to withstand contrary forces. Formal constitutional protections may be ignored, and the judiciary lacks resources to protect its own independence. In Argentina, the country's supreme court was purged a number of times, notwithstanding constitutional guarantees of tenure for judges. Constitutional protections for Soviet judges did not prevent "telephone justice." By contrast, the United Kingdom and other nations have generally preserved an independent judiciary without written constitutional protections and a structural dependence of the judiciary on the parliament (Russell 2001, 22). Given the judiciary's lack of independent financial and military resources, its authority depends to some degree on the interests of other branches.

Of course, anecdotal examples of constitutional failure do not demonstrate that a constitution is useless in protecting some level of judicial independence. A constitution represents a commitment that is considered part of the "rules of the game" around which individuals coordinate their activities. Once such rules are in place, they can become sticky and difficult to change. Even if constitutionalization is neither a necessary nor a sufficient condition for judicial independence, constitutionalization may facilitate the protection of a measure of independence for judges. A constitution may have its greatest benefit by establishing bright-line rules that expose attempts to infringe on judicial independence.

Beyond constitutional or other legal protections, there may be economic or political bases for judicial independence. Particular judges surely want independence, since it is far more satisfying to make one's own judgments than it is mechanistically to follow the will of others. Consequently, preventing independent decision-making will impose monitoring and enforcement costs on congress, or whatever external force would compromise judicial independence. Given the vast number of cases decided by the courts, considerable judicial independence will result simply from the fact that it is not worth the costs for congress to control the results in most cases. Even in the old Soviet Union, judges were independent for a substantial number of cases (Scheppele 2002, 237). For a few high profile categories of cases, however, congress might choose to bear the considerable monitoring and enforcement costs of compromising judicial independence; and these may be the cases where we might most value judicial independence for separation-of-powers reasons. Even in these cases, however, congress might receive some countervailing benefit from preserving judicial independence.

Economists and positive political theorists have produced various theories why politicians would benefit from creating and protecting an independent judiciary, beyond their own control. Landes and Posner argue that an independent judiciary enables politicians to make credible commitments to interest groups about their bargains (Landes and Posner 1975). Others suggest that politicians have an incentive to create an independent judiciary when their own tenure is uncertain (Ramseyer 1994). An independent judiciary can protect a party's interests when it is out of power and ensure the continued effectiveness of its legislative enactments. An independent judiciary can also provide an informational function, monitoring the bureaucracy and applying general legislation to individual cases, with appropriate discretion. An independent judiciary might also benefit congress as a "punching bag." Elected officials may attempt to shift public blame for governance to the judiciary, which must be independent for this shift to have effectiveness. Elected officials may support independent judicial policy-making to evade political responsibility (Graber 1993, 37).

One additional, commonly overlooked justification for an some level of judicial independence is the "common good." Democratic governments need have a concern for the common good, lest they be thrown out of power (Olson 2000).

An independent judiciary provides adjudicatory fairness and furthers the separation of powers that in turn may encourage investment and economic growth and best satisfy the interests of their constituents (Cooter 2000, 196–7). Although Landes and Posner take a cynical view of the need for credible commitments in interest-group bargains, one could easily take a more generous view of the value of credible commitments to social welfare. As a rising tide lifts all ships, so a commitment to overall public interest may further the private interests of most citizens. This is the logic behind creating independent adjudicators for the World Trade Organization. The maintenance of a system of judicial independence may effectively send a signal to investors and others that the country is committed to certain rights and values (Farber 2002).

Moreover, once a system of judicial independence is in place, for whatever reason, it may become a societal norm. This has been called customary independence, and it arguably explains the high level of judicial independence of the U.K., which lacks written constitutional protection. Customary independence can explain why Congress has rarely used its constitutional authority to discipline the U.S. judiciary. It may explain the vigorous reaction against Roosevelt's 1937 "court-packing" plan. The public seems to value the protection of at least a relatively independent judiciary.

There are various explanations for why judicial independence has arisen and been maintained by government. Constitutional structures presumably play some role in sheltering judicial independence, though they are neither necessary nor sufficient conditions for its fulfillment. The other branches of government may have a self-interest in creating and protecting judicial independence, in part because of its potential benefits to society, including economic benefits.

5 JUDICIAL SELECTION AND RETENTION METHODS

Much of the contemporary controversy over judicial independence involves judicial selection. Although extraconstitutional considerations may insulate judicial independence in a democracy, institutional structures will surely influence the measure and scope of independence. The means by which judges are selected and retained in office are institutional structures that are of concern for judicial independence. Although much of the debate has focused on selection methods, possible methods of judicial removal would pose a greater threat to judicial independence.

At the federal level, judicial selection is highly politicized. Some maintain that this effect compromises judicial independence (Peretti 2002, 104). But if judges, once selected, are outside the control of the Senate, the most salient aspects of judicial independence are not necessarily compromised. The selection process does have some effect on future outcomes, as the choice of conservatives as federal judges will translate into more conservative decisions. Nevertheless, the judge's decision is purely internal and not directly driven by illegitimate external forces. Indeed, the ability of the political branches to exercise some *ex ante* control over who becomes a judge may reduce the need for them to exercise an *ex post* removal control over judges on the bench (Cooter 2000, 196). Political selection could therefore actually enhance independence on the bench.

Other nations have sought to moderate this ideological selection effect by creating a professionalized judiciary that is more like a civil service bureaucracy (Guarnieri and Pederzoli 2002, 34). This approach is absent in the U.S. at both the federal and state levels, but the state governments have adopted a variety of selection and retention methods that may influence the independence of state judges. These selection methods include a partisan election of judges with party affiliations, a nonpartisan election, and selection by elected government officials with or without retention elections after a term in office.

Numerous commentators have argued that certain selection methods, especially those involving elections, compromise judicial independence. Elected judges are obviously not independent of the public that elects them and that may later turn them out of office, although the public is typically relatively uninformed about the candidates when voting (Geyh 2003, 54). In partisan elections, the public will generally cue off party affiliation. Such voting does not ensure judicial accountability, though, as it is largely independent of the decisions of the judicial candidate. Many states have abandoned partisan elections for judges, in favor of nonpartisan or retention elections. In retention elections, reformers have suggested that judicial decisions and qualifications are more likely to matter. In practice, incumbent judges are seldom defeated in such retention elections and typically carry a high percentage of the vote (Hall 2001, 318–19). This success rate may not demonstrate judicial independence, however; it may simply reflect judges' ability strategically to make decisions that ensure their reelection.

Elected judges surely must conform, to some degree, to public preferences in order to gain reelection. There are stories about judges, including but not limited to California's former chief justice Rose Bird, who were defeated because of the content of their opinion or because of a well-funded campaign to defeat them (Geyh 2003, 53). Crime seems to be a key determinant of judicial elections. The state murder rate is a statistically significant determinant of votes for incumbent judges (Hall 2001). Elections and shorter terms for state judges are significantly associated with a greater likelihood of a judge's voting for a defendant to receive capital punishment (Brace and Hall 1995). The findings suggest that, for criminal cases, elections appear to increase accountability to the general public and reduce independence at the level of individual case-decisions.

Elected judges must raise contributions for their electoral campaigns. Doing so may compromise their independence from litigants, who may be their campaign contributors. A survey in Texas found that 99 percent of attorneys and 86 percent of judges themselves believe that campaign contributions have some influence on judicial opinions (Feldman 2000). Elected judges may also be more dependent on political parties even in states with nonpartisan elections (Hanssen 1999, 212). This situation may in turn make such judges less independent of elected politicians.

What may be most "essential for judicial independence is that removal should be very difficult and should be based on a demonstration, judiciously arrived at, that the judge is incapable of discharging the responsibilities of judicial office" (Russell 2001, 15). Under this theory, judges should suffer no personal adverse consequences based on the nature of their decisions. This is the foundation of life tenure for federal judges, and any sort of retention election would seem to compromise this principle.

One study began with the hypothesis that judicial independence would increase outcome uncertainty and that such uncertainty would increase litigation (Hanssen 1999). It found that states with appointed judges indeed had more litigation at a level that was statistically significant for the court of last resort, although not significant at the trial court level. Hanssen concluded that appointing judges protected the judiciary "from political co-option by special interests (or the ruling majority)" (Hanssen, 1999, 232). The common focus on selection methods may be misplaced, however, as judicial retention seems a more relevant measure of independence. Although a "merit" selection system using the bar association was for a time promoted as improving judicial quality and independence, reliance on retention elections has meant that merit plan judges face some of the same pressures as do those subject to partisan elections (Tarr 2003, 1447–8).

The evidence on the compromising effect of judicial elections is not overwhelming. Although researchers have found a significant effect of state selection and retention methods in some circumstances, the magnitude of the effect has not been consistently large or across-the-board. In some ways, elected judges appear more independent of other branches of government. For example, an elected judiciary is somewhat more likely to strike down a state law as unconstitutional than is an appointed judiciary (Cross 2003, 215–16).

An elected judiciary has its own constituency. Jacksonians favored elected judiciaries precisely because they were more accountable to the populace. In its accountability to or dependence on public opinion, an elected judiciary may become somewhat less dependent on the law. An accountable but activist judiciary might advance separation-of-powers values, checking the legislative branch much as an independently elected president is expected to check the legislative branch. Of course, this comes at some cost in terms of independence from public opinion and the parties that may appear in court.

6 CONCLUSION

"Judicial independence" is a far more contested concept than typically recognized. Its meaning and value are uncertain. The judiciary is both a legal institution and a political institution, and judicial independence represents a compromise between these two roles. Independence plays an important role in a system of governance, but it is reasonably compromised to some degree by concerns for judicial accountability.

In the United States, federal judges are essentially, but imperfectly, independent. In the overwhelming majority of cases, such judges are substantially independent of the other branches of government, public opinion, and at least the illegitimate forms of litigant influence, and slightly independent of the law itself. On balance, the federal judiciary has functioned relatively well, to the benefit of the nation, but it is unclear that the current degree of judicial independence is the optimal one. There is a plausible argument that this judiciary has an excess of independence and should be curtailed.

For state courts, the balance is different. Many decry the inappropriate influences on the state judiciary created by electoral demands. Elections inevitably compromise independence in some regard, at least in terms of independence of the public and individuals who may be parties; but they increase judicial accountability, and the trade-off needs to be recognized and analyzed.

The topic of judicial independence warrants additional empirical investigation. We yet have a very limited understanding of the sources of greater levels of judicial independence and of the consequences of such levels. This research requires tools to measure judicial independence, and those tools require researchers to define precisely the nature of the independence they hope to capture.

REFERENCES

ADMINISTRATIVE OFFICE OF THE UNITED STATES COURTS 1990. Judicial code of conduct.

BARRO, R. J., and SALA-I-MARTIN, X. 1995. *Economic Growth*. New York: McGraw-Hill.

BAUM, L. 1997. *The Puzzle of Judicial Behavior*. Ann Arbor: University of Michigan Press.

BRACE, P., and HALL, M. G. 1995. Studying courts comparatively: the view from the American states. *Political Research Quarterly*, 48: 5–29.

BREYER, S. G. 1996. Judicial independence in the United States. *St. Louis University Law Review*, 40: 989–96.

COOTER, R. D. 2000. *The Strategic Constitution*. Princeton, NJ: Princeton University Press.

CROSS, F. B. 2003. Thoughts on Goldilocks and judicial independence. *Ohio State Law Journal*, 64: 195–219.

—— and NELSON, B. J. 2001. Strategic institutional effects on Supreme Court decisionmaking. *Northwestern University Law Review*, 95: 1437–93.

DAHL, R. A. 1957. Decision-making in a democracy: the Supreme Court as a national policy-maker. *Journal of Public Law*, 6: 279–95.

DIX, G. E. 1964. The death of the Commerce Court: a study in institutional weakness. *American Journal of Legal History*, 8: 238–60.

DE FIGUEIREDO, J. M., and TILLER, E. H. 1996. Congressional control of the courts: a theoretical and empirical analysis of expansion of the federal judiciary. *Journal of Law and Economics*, 39: 435–62.

EPSTEIN, L., and KNIGHT, J. 1998. *The Choices Justices Make*. Washington, DC: Congressional Quarterly Press.

ESKRIDGE, W. N. 1991. Overriding Supreme Court statutory interpretation decisions. *Yale Law Journal*, 101: 331–417.

FARBER, D. A. 2002. Rights as signals. *Journal of Legal Studies*, 32: 83–97.

FELDMAN, C. 2000. A state constitutional remedy to the sale of justice in Texas courts. *South Texas Law Review*, 41: 1415–21.

FEREJOHN, J. 2002. Judicializing politics, politicizing law. *Law and Contemporary Problems*, 65: 41–68.

—— and KRAMER, L. D. 2002. Independent judges, dependent judiciary: institutionalizing judicial restraint. *New York University Law Review*, 77: 962–1039.

FRIEDMAN, B. 2002. The history of the countermajoritarian difficulty, part II: reconstruction's political court. *Georgetown Law Journal*, 91: 1–65.

GALANTER, M. 1974. Why the "haves" come out ahead: speculation on the limits of legal change. *Law and Society Review*, 9: 95–160.

GEYH, C. G. 2003. Why judicial elections stink. *Ohio State University Law Journal*, 64: 43–79.

GRABER, M. A. 1993. The nonmajoritian difficulty: legislative deference to the judiciary. *Studies in American Political Development*, 7: 35–73.

GUARNIERI, C., and PEDERZOLI, P. 2002. *The Power of Judges: A Comparative Study of Courts and Democracy*. Oxford: Oxford University Press.

HALL, M. G. 2001. State supreme courts in American democracy: probing the myths of judicial reform. *American Political Science Review*, 95: 315–30.

HANSSEN, F. A. 1999. The effect of judicial institutions on uncertainty and the rate of litigation: the election versus appointment of state judges. *Journal of Legal Studies*, 28: 205–32.

HELMKE, G. 2002. The logic of strategic defection: court–executive relations in Argentina under dictatorship and democracy. *American Political Science Review*, 96: 291–302.

HIRSCHL, R. 2004. *Towards Juristocracy: The Origins and Consequences of the New Constitutionalism*. Cambridge, Mass.: Harvard University Press.

KLEIN, D. 2002. *Making Law in the United States Courts of Appeals*. Cambridge: Cambridge University Press.

KORNHAUSER, L. A. 2002. Is judicial independence a useful concept? Pp. 45–55 in *Judicial Independence at the Crossroads*, ed. S. A. Burbank and B. Friedman. Thousand Oaks, Calif.: Sage.

KOZINSKI, A. 1998. The many faces of judicial independence. *Georgia State University Law Review*, 14: 861–73.

LANDES, W. M., and POSNER, R. A. 1975. The independent judiciary in an interest group perspective. *Journal of Law and Economics*, 18: 875–901.

LANGER, L. 2002. *Judicial Review in State Supreme Courts: A Comparative Study.* Albany: State University of New York Press.

LARKINS, C. M. 1996. Judicial independence and democratization: a theoretical and conceptual analysis. *American Journal of Comparative Law,* 44: 605–26.

MARSHALL, T. R. 1989. *Public Opinion and the Supreme Court.* Boston: Unwin Hyman.

McGUIRE, K. T., and STIMSON, J. A. 2004. The least dangerous branch revisited: new evidence on Supreme Court responsiveness to public preferences. *Journal of Politics,* 66: 1018–35.

OLSON, M. 2000. *Power and Prosperity.* New York: Basic Books.

PANIZZA, U. 2001. Electoral rules, political systems, and institutional quality. *Economics and Politics,* 13: 311–42.

PERETTI, T. J. 2002. Does judicial independence exist? Pp. 103–33 in *Judicial Independence at the Crossroads,* ed. S. A. Burbank and B. Friedman. Thousand Oaks, Calif.: Sage.

PINELLO, D. 1999. Linking party to judicial ideology in American courts: a meta-analysis. *Justice System Journal,* 20: 219–54.

POSNER, R. A. 1990. *The Problems of Jurisprudence.* Cambridge, Mass.: Harvard University Press.

—— 2002. Pragmatism versus purposivism in First Amendment analysis. *Stanford Law Review,* 54: 737–52.

RAMSEYER, J. M. 1994. The puzzling (in)dependence of courts: a comparative approach. *Journal of Legal Studies,* 23: 721–47.

RESNICK, J. 1999. Judicial independence and Article III: too much and too little. *Southern California Law Review,* 72: 657–71.

RUSSELL, P. H. 2001. Toward a general theory of judicial independence. Pp. 1–24 in *Judicial Independence in the Age of Democracy,* ed. P. H. Russell and D. O. O'Brien. Charlottesville: University Press of Virginia.

SALZBERGER, E. M. 1992. A positive analysis of the doctrine of separation of powers. *International Review of Law and Economics,* 13: 349–79.

SCHEPPELE, K. L. 2002. Declarations of independence. Pp. 227–79 in *Judicial Independence at the Crossroads,* ed. S. A. Burbank and B. Friedman. Thousand Oaks, Calif.: Sage.

SEGAL, J. A. 1997. Separation-of-powers games in the positive theory of Congress and courts. *American Political Science Review,* 91: 28–44.

—— and SPAETH, H. 1993. *The Supreme Court and the Attitudinal Model.* New York: Cambridge University Press.

—— 1999. *Majority Rule or Minority Will.* Cambridge: Cambridge University Press.

SISK, G. B., HEISE, M., and MORRISS, J. P. 1998. Charting the influences on the judicial mind: an empirical study of judicial reasoning. *New York University Law Review,* 73: 1377–500.

SPILLER, P., and GELY, R. 1992. Congressional control or judicial independence: the determinants of U.S. Supreme Court labor-relations decisions, 1949–1983. *Rand Journal of Economics,* 23: 463–92.

TARR, G. A. 2003. Rethinking the selection of state supreme court justices. *Willamette Law Review,* 39: 1445–70.

TOMA, E. F. 1996. A contractual model of the voting behavior of the Supreme Court: the role of the chief justice. *International Review of Law and Economics,* 16: 433–45.

YATES, J. 2002. *Popular Justice.* Albany: State University of New York Press.

CASES

Aetna Life Insurance v. Lavoie. 1986. 475 U.S. 813.

Bradley v. Fisher 1872. 13 Wall. 335.

Plaut v. Spendthrift Farm, Inc. 1995. 514 U.S. 211.

Republican Party of Minnesota v. White. 2002. 536 U.S. 765.

United States v. Will. 1980. 449 U.S. 200.

West Virginia State Board of Education v. Barnette. 1943. 319 U.S. 624.

CHAPTER 33

LAW AND REGULATION

SUSAN ROSE-ACKERMAN

THE United States federal courts have been extraordinarily important in constraining and monitoring the development of the modern regulatory state. Their role is broad but shallow. In reviewing the regulatory activities of government, the federal courts almost never provide *de novo* review; they seldom start from the beginning in reviewing agency choices and generally return flawed decisions to the executive to correct mistakes in process or substance.

Considerable controversy surrounds the judicial role in reviewing agency actions, and this is exacerbated by disputes over the value of alternative procedures and decision-making criteria inside agencies. This chapter reviews and reflects on these debates from the contrasting viewpoints of public-policy analysis and rational-choice political economy.

The United States rulemaking process is both more open to public participation and more constrained by law than it is in most other political systems; as a consequence, it is also more time-consuming and more subject to judicial challenge. In addition, the disciplines of public-policy analysis and risk assessment are more fully developed in the United States than in other mature democracies and play an important role in the regulatory process. At a substantive level, the insights of the sciences and social sciences, especially economics, are often incorporated into U.S. regulations. The importance of technical expertise and the inability of nonexpert

judges to evaluate technical material create an ongoing tension in American regulatory jurisprudence; judges are meant to prevent officials from overreaching, but
they themselves have trouble evaluating many decisions.

Politics, of course, has not been banished by either law or technocratic analysis.
Rather, it appears in the language of statutes and rules; in executive branch agenda-
setting; in the interactions between agencies, Congress, the president, courts, and
interest groups. Congress writes statutes and creates legislative history in an effort
to maintain political control of implementation, either directly or indirectly
(Epstein and O'Halloran 1999; Huber and Shipan 2002; McCubbins and Schwartz
1984; McNollgast 1987; 1989). Presidents negotiate with Congress to determine the
degree of agency independence (Lewis 2003). Agency heads, in coalition with
outside networks, sometimes convince Congress to support their own agendas,
even when the policy changes are not those most preferred by the legislative
majority (Carpenter 2001).

Once a law is passed, statutory language is unlikely to be a sufficient constraint
on agencies, even if enforced by the courts. The difficulty of "stacking the deck" in
favor of the enacting coalition has been empirically demonstrated by Hamilton and
Schroeder (1994), Hill and Brazier (1991), Spence (1997; 1999), and Balla (1998).
Both presidents and agency officials attempt to further their agendas, given the
statutory framework. Presidents do this, for example, by appointing allies to top
agency positions, requiring White House review of regulations, issuing signing
statements, and using executive orders and press releases to manage agency actions
and claim credit (Kagan 2001).

Whatever its limits, judicial review is one way for statute writers to create an
ongoing check on agency discretion. Courts are nominally less politically involved
than the other branches and are presumed to provide a neutral forum to challenge
the regulatory process. Nevertheless, empirical research shows that judges sometimes trade off adherence to legal doctrine against their political predilections
(Cross and Tiller 1998; Tiller 1998; Canes-Wrone 2003).

I begin with an introduction to the economic case for regulation of economic
activity and move next to research on the political economy of regulatory policy.
Then I focus on the tension between technical competence and responsiveness to
public concerns. The next section moves to the regulatory process in the United
States concentrating on decisions that mix political and technical issues and that
are bureaucrat-led. After a brief discussion of public participation in other legal
systems, I suggest how a background norm of cost/benefit analysis could be used by
courts as a way to evaluate the quality of regulatory decision-making. The chapter
concludes with some directions for future research.

1 THE ECONOMIC CASE FOR REGULATION

Markets frequently diverge from perfect competition, and these divergences justify government action. There are several common sources of market failure familiar to all economists (Weimer and Vining 2005).

First, positive and negative externalities create distortions. The benefits or costs of economic activities are not always fully reflected in the costs facing firms or individuals. Second, a monopoly firm can restrict output and price above marginal cost. Third, it may be difficult to exclude those who do not pay the marginal cost of using a resource. Fourth, information about a product or about buyers' characteristics may be lacking, and even if information is notionally available, people may make systematic mistakes in using it. Finally, injustices in the distribution of income or of particular goods and services, such as education and health, mean that social beliefs about distributive justice are not translated into market outcomes.

In the design of public programs, policy analysts stress the importance of giving firms and citizens incentives to act efficiently. They urge a move away from command and control regulation toward incentive-based rules that specify outcomes, not inputs, or that create markets that permit firms to trade rights or pay fees that reflect the external costs of their activities. Such systems conserve on the information required by the regulatory agency and rely on the profit motive to accomplish regulatory goals. Of course, market incentives cannot entirely substitute for agency decision-making. The agency must still decide what level of ambient pollution to tolerate and may employ a cost/benefit framework to make that choice (Ackerman and Stewart 1988; Tietenberg 2006).

Antitrust law attempts to split up firms with monopoly power and to constrain the behavior of others. The deregulation of airlines, trucking, telecoms, and banking shows that competitive markets can arise when government constraints are removed. However, new regulatory imperatives may arise as a result of deregulation (Rose-Ackerman 1995, 153–5), and the creation of a market where none existed before has been difficult and demonstrates the continuing need for regulation of some aspects of industry performance.

Congestion and excess use arise when one user cannot exclude others. Here the state might sponsor research to develop technologies of exclusion, provide better enforcement of property rights, or regulate entry to common pool resources such as fisheries and national parks.

If consumers or producers lack information and do not have sufficient incentives to generate it on their own, the government might provide it or require disclosure. If too little information is produced, the state may sponsor research or require firms to do it themselves. Furthermore, behavioral economics shows that people make systematic decision-making errors even when information is available. Sunstein and Thaler (2003) then argue for a liberal paternalism that sets defaults in such areas as retirement savings and allows citizens to opt out.

Finally, the regulation and subsidy of certain goods and services are justified on grounds of fairness and distributive justice. However, considerations of economic efficiency still arise. If the state provides funds for primary education or health care, for example, there is an incentive for beneficiaries to overuse the service. Thus such programs usually include a regulatory component.

2 THE POLITICAL ECONOMY
OF REGULATION

The normative case for regulation contrasts with rational choice analyses of government. Scholars in that tradition argue that democratic decision-making is based on a struggle between interest groups, and they predict that those who experience the most concentrated costs and benefits and who are the best organized and funded will carry the day (Olson 1965). Under this view, most statutes reflect the concerns of narrow, well-funded interests, and even if the laws themselves have broad public-interest rationales, the regulatory agencies that implement them may be captured by the industries they are designed to regulate. These concerns have led some to argue that regulation, far from correcting market failures, often creates inefficiencies not present in unregulated markets (Peltzman 1976; Posner 1974; Stigler 1971). This research focuses on statutes that regulate particular industries such as transportation, electricity, and telecommunications. The rise of new initiatives in environmental protection and occupational health and safety complicate the situation by bringing in interest groups such as environmental nonprofits and labor unions as major political actors (Melnick 1983, 1–23). Such statutes may still be the result of interest-group balancing, but the range of interests covered is larger and includes more of the citizenry.

Political-economic research on Congress helps one to understand the weaknesses of the legislative-drafting process and the consequent need for rulemaking inside the executive branch (Fiorina 1985; 1989; Fiorina and Noll 1978; Huber and Shipan 2002; Epstein and O'Halloran 1999; Wood and Bohte 2004). Statute writing is an exercise in compromise. Efforts to forge a coalition may affect the quality of legislative drafting. Statutes may be internally inconsistent or contain vague language so that each group can claim credit for provisions that satisfy its constituents. Such statutes shift the hard choices to the executive, which promulgates rules designed to clarify the meaning of the statute and articulate policy (Wilson 1973, ch. 16).

Even in the absence of interest groups with differential resources and organizational ability, representative governments are unlikely to follow economists' prescriptions. Legislation will depend not only on preferences and organizational ability but also on the procedural rules under which representatives are chosen and laws are made. The result is a "structure-induced equilibrium" (Shepsle and Weingast 1981). The interactions between the branches of government vary depending upon the precise nature of the separation of powers. In the United States, administrative agencies will have some leeway to make policy without prompting a legislative backlash. Thus, the legislature may create judicial review as a check on executive branch policy-making; but even then, both the courts and the executive will retain some independence (Huber and Shipan 2002; Landes and Posner 1975; Ferejohn and Shipan 1990).

Political-economic research provides an important counterweight to those who assume a functional, public-interest model of government. The functionalists assume that the existence of a market failure is sufficient to produce a rational response from the political system. Rational actor models of government show that this is not necessarily true. But these models, in turn, are limited by their narrow view of the motivations of political actors. This tradition overstates the pathologies of regulatory and political policy-making. It downplays the role of politicians' motives, not only to provide narrow benefits to constituents, but also to satisfy broad public demands. It discounts the professional skills and values of career public officials in the bureaucracy.

3 Rulemaking in a Democracy: Technocracy and Public Accountability

Economics provides clear prescriptions for the substance and form of regulatory policy but has little to say about the process of making policy. Political economy predicts that policy will reflect the impact of powerful interests and well-organized constituents, subject to institutional constraints; but it has little to say about how legal constraints ought to be structured. Both strands of research should take administrative law more seriously. Administrative law seeks to determine the proper role of agencies and bureaucracies in democratic government and the proper separation of powers between the executive, the congress, and the courts.

Are the values of public accountability and open government espoused by U.S. administrative law in deep conflict with the demands of economic efficiency? Any

Table 33.1 Linking process with substance in administration law

SUBSTANCE	PROCESS				
	A. Scientific method	B. Bureaucrat-led			C. Consensual
		1. Courtlike	2. Quasi-legislative	3. Administrative balancing	
A. Technical	X				
B. Individual rights		X			
C. Political			X		
1. Distributive					
2. Net benefits possible					
a. All interests not well represented				X	
b. All interests well represented					X

process requires time and resources; but, over and above such transactions costs, is there a potential for conflict between efficient regulations and democratically legitimate rulemaking procedures? Much past discussion has exaggerated this conflict. Fundamental difficulties arise not so much from the democracy–technocracy trade-off as from a mismatch of techniques and tasks (Breyer 1993). Table 33.1 provides a simple schematic representation of good matchups (Rose-Ackerman 1995, 120–40).

The upper left-hand side of the table matches purely scientific or technical questions (row A) with evaluation methods using the canons of the relevant science (column A). The goal is to establish scientific validity, not to promote fairness or democratic legitimacy. Peer review is the proper evaluative method. Bias is limited by using independent reviewers, giving greater credence to replicated results, and preparing written evaluations. The reviewers' identities are kept secret from the researchers and in some cases the researchers' identities are also hidden from the reviewers. Decision-makers do not use judicialized procedures; rather, impartiality is maintained by a mixture of professional norms and anonymity. The ideal is a balanced assessment of existing research.[1] Even if scientific norms guide the evaluative

---

[1] The US Information Quality Act (44 U.S.C. 3506(b)(1)(C)) seeks to ensure the quality of information disseminated by federal agencies. Guidelines issued by the Office of Management and Budget implementing that Act privilege peer review and the "reproducibility" and "transparency" of data and analysis (67 *Federal Register* 8452). This would seem to be an example of the case discussed in the text, but critics, such as Johnson (2006), argue that it risks misuse in areas that, in my scheme, would fit into the "political" categories discussed below.

process, the choice of topics remains a policy question that must be determined by politically responsible authorities using the methods outlined below.

The protection of individual rights (row B) requires a different procedural framework (column B.1). The aim of a court-like process is a fair decision that permits individuals to defend themselves against arbitrary state authority. Under one familiar variant, individuals have a right to a hearing and to discover the basis of the bureaucracy's decision. They must be able to challenge the state's decisions as unfair or illegal before an independent body. Although the content of rights and the details of the required procedures are controversial, the individualized nature of the proceeding is key. Procedures derived from civil and criminal trials frequently form the basis for such proceedings. The purpose of these procedures is to protect individual rights; they are poorly designed for resolving policy issues.

Regulatory statutes frequently delegate political tasks to the bureaucracy. Here the bureaucracy's job is to balance conflicting interests, not to discover scientific truths or to preserve rights. Science and technology provide a background to many political disputes, and the preservation of individual rights is always a constraint. Nevertheless, neither peer review nor judicial procedures provides a helpful framework.

There are three types of political choice faced by bureaucratic policy-makers. In the easy case (row C.2.b), win-win solutions exist; and all interests have strong and equally balanced representation. In such cases, consensual processes (column C) seem appropriate. The participants will disagree about the division of the gains, but in principle, it is possible for negotiation to produce a unanimous decision. The bureaucracy can structure the process, provide technical advice, clarify the consequences of failure, and select the participants. The state could accept the policy agreed on by the participants and promulgate it as a rule. Publicity and reasoned decision-making are unimportant. If everyone agrees, the outcome is, by definition, legitimate.

The easy case seldom describes reality. If it does not, the process must be "bureaucrat-led." There are no objectively right answers. For distributive choices (row C.1), bargaining will never produce consensus. Instead, bureaucrats must make the choice by balancing the conflicting interests and values (column B.2). The administration should articulate the mixture of principle and political expediency that produced the choice. Politically expedient choices are not per se illegitimate, but they should be acknowledged as such.

In many situations, mutually beneficial solutions exist, but they cannot be reached through negotiation (row C.2.a). Most environmental problems arise from failures of the market system and could be solved with net gains for all. Nevertheless, most are not suitable for regulatory negotiation. The problems of group representation are intractable because some stakeholders are members of extremely diffuse groups, such as consumers or breathers. Public authorities must make the ultimate decision. They must hear representatives of those affected and then apply policy analytic tools to reach a decision. I label this approach "administrative balancing" (column B.3).

In column B.3, even if every group prefers the new policy to the status quo, everyone may be unhappy with his or her share of the gains. Ordinary citizens may prefer policies that impose costs on polluters; dischargers want subsidies and tax concessions. Because of conflicts over the distribution of gains, the government must justify its decision. The aim is not to make everyone happy but rather to obtain an outcome that is consistent with the legislative purpose. For example, a policy designed to correct a market failure could be carried out using principles of cost/benefit analysis. A policy designed to aid the homeless could be implemented under egalitarian principles of distributive justice. The explanation must both articulate the goals behind the policy and clarify the link between the available information and the outcome.

Because direct oversight by the legislature is generally insufficient, authorities must use legitimate procedures to produce a decision. In particular, administrative procedures should permit experts, ordinary people, and organized groups to present their information and views. But openness is not sufficient. If groups are not equally well represented, the bureaucracy must gather data and opinions itself.

Bureaucrats have incentives to avoid the bother of publicly accountable processes and may favor organized groups with large stakes in the outcome. Thus, judicial review is essential. Agencies' expertise is generally superior to that of courts, but agencies may deviate from technically competent and democratically legitimate procedures in order to favor political insiders. Thus, courts can require officials to listen to a wide range of facts and opinions and to explain their decisions. Bureaucratic choices are acceptable because the process assures that no major bodies of knowledge and opinion have been ignored, not because they satisfy everyone (Stewart 1975; Shapiro 1993).

Not all cases fit cleanly into one box or another. Hard cases involve both science and politics, where hybrid procedures are sometimes possible. Negotiations that resolve preliminary issues may be followed by a bureaucratic choice, or preliminary technocratic fact-finding may be followed by negotiation in the light of this information. Scientists, engineers, and social scientists assess the quality of research and technical information, which then forms the basis for policy-makers to ascertain "the state of the art," locate thresholds where human health is "protected," or trade off human lives against economic prosperity. Cost/benefit analysis can be an input into the subsequent balancing process that sets policy (Sunstein 2002; Adler and Posner 1999).

It is often impossible to evaluate the technical material first and then use it to make a policy decision. In such cases, how should the administration proceed? Should it emphasize competence through the use of scientifically acceptable methods, or should it develop a politically legitimate procedure? For bureaucrat-led processes there is often no need to make a choice. Procedures can be designed to further both goals. If hearings provide information, there is no inconsistency between them and the subsequent technocratic exercise used to generate a final rule or standard. If democratic legitimacy requires a statement of reasons, so, too, do scientific canons.

Conflicts will continue, but they will be disputes over values and administrative competence, not over process. Suppose, for example, that officials, operating under an open-ended statute, believe that cost/benefit analysis or risk-assessment is the best way to balance interests. In public hearings, individuals provide information and explain how they will be affected by the policy. Some individuals, however, question the agency's methodology and go on to challenge the ultimate decision in court. Such disputes indicate the lack of a political consensus over how to make competent policy. Challengers may don the mantle of democratic legitimacy in criticizing the agency's decision, but their fundamental complaint is over policy, not procedure.

The remaining conflicts would be prudential—over the cost in time and money of extensive procedures and over bureaucratic capacity. Outsiders may claim that the agency is failing because of laziness, stupidity, or venality. The issue for judicial review would be the agency's failure to live up to legislatively mandated standards. Such cases can produce sharp conflicts between public agencies and outside groups, but they are not conflicts between technocratic decision-making and democracy.

Rulemaking procedures seek to strike a balance between the obligation of the government to make technically competent policy choices under statutory delegations and its obligation to respond to the concerns of citizens and organized groups. With cross-cutting cleavages that do not map neatly onto party labels and with statutes that do not specify in detail how to deal with complex problems, consultation and judicial oversight are one route to public accountability.

In short, for bureaucratic-led processes, the apparent conflicts between competence and democratic legitimacy are frequently the result of underlying disputes over substantive standards and over the way public officials should fulfill their duties. If the democratic legitimacy of the administrative process can be improved with no major sacrifice of policy goals, reform can focus on reforms that further these joint goals and seek to match procedures to the problem to be solved.

4 THE REGULATORY PROCESS IN THE UNITED STATES

In the U.S. notice and comment rulemaking under the Administrative Procedure Act (APA) (5 USC §§ 551–9, 701–6) provides the bare bones of a publicly accountable process. It requires that the preparation of rules with the force of law be reported in the *Federal Register* and include a hearing open to "interested persons." Final rules must be accompanied by a "concise general statement of their basis and purpose" (§ 553(c)). The reach of the APA is broad, and some agencies not subject to its provisions voluntarily comply. Rules can be subject to judicial review for conformity with the authorizing statute and the Constitution and for conformity with APA procedures. A rule can be struck down as "arbitrary and capricious" or in some cases as "unsupported by substantial evidence" (§706).

In spite of recent interest in other procedures such as regulatory negotiation, notice-and-comment rulemaking remains fundamental to the American regulatory process (Coglianese 2002). Between 1994 and 2003 over 4000 rules were issued each year (Crews Jr. 2004, 12). Organized groups representing business, labor, public interest causes, and nonfederal governments view participation as an important part of their strategy to influence public policy-making (Kerwin 2003; Golden 1998; Kerwin and Furlong 1992; Furlong and Kerwin 2005). How do APA procedures mediate the tension between expertise and public accountability? No one has systematically studied this issue, but I review the evidence and come to a guardedly favorable conclusion (based on Rose-Ackerman 2005, 223–33).

The rulemaking process can be costly and time-consuming both for agencies and for interest groups. In the United States, a major rulemaking process at the Environmental Protection Agency (EPA) averages almost three years and requires many hours of input from both bureaucrats and outside interests from industry and the environmental community (Coglianese 1997, 1283–4; Furlong and Kerwin 2005). Court challenges introduce further delay. Yet, some rulemakings attract only a few comments. In one review of eleven rulemaking dockets, rules attracted from 1 to 268 comments (Golden 1998; see also Coglianese 2002, 1125–31). Examination of a random sample of forty-two rulemakings found a median of thirty comments (West 2004). But, if a rulemaking generates public concern, the number of comments can be very large. When the Forest Service was considering a rule on roadless areas in national forests, it received more than 1 million comments, mostly form letters (Mendelson 2003, 623). Both career bureaucrats and political officials may resist increased participation on the grounds that it will delay action and distort choices. The time and trouble of participation may discourage advocates and citizens with little time and money and weak organizational capacities (Schuck 1977).

Long time delays have no simple link to the volume of comments. One study of 150 EPA rules found that the elapsed time between the start of the process and the issuance of the final rule was not associated with either the number of internal participants or the number of comments (Kerwin and Furlong 1992, 125–31). Delay may be strategic and may depend on whether the agency or the White House wants to hold up resolution of an issue or whether members of Congress try to keep the issue from being decided.

Magat, Krupnick, and Harrington's research (1986) assesses participation in EPA rulemakings to determine the "best practical technology currently available" for controlling water pollution. The public comments were dominated by regulated entities, but the results demonstrate the ability of the EPA to resist pressure. Comments that supported weaker standards did not tend to produce weaker standards, and industries with more firms out of compliance with proposed rules did not obtain weaker standards. However, well-organized industry groups with a consistent message were able to influence outcomes in their favor (Magat et al. 1986, 145–7). The latter result suggests the importance of providing assistance to groups whose participation might counter the impact of concentrated industries (Schuck 1977). If nonprofit issue-oriented groups do get their message across, they can have an impact (Mendelson 2003, 628). More recent work by Yackee and Yackee (2006) confirms the predominance of business comments in a broader selection of rulemakings. They conclude that notice and comment rulemaking has done little to democratize the rulemaking process, but their sample specifically omits issues with high public salience.

Many proposed rules change little after the end of the comment period (Golden 1998; Kerwin 2003). Consequently, groups seek access to the agency before proposed rules are announced. In a study of the Mining Act, Strauss (1974) found that agency personnel had little interest in modifying the rule after the public comment period, which was viewed as mostly a formal, public relations requirement (Strauss 1974, 1249–51). However, if a rule is overtly biased toward the regulated industry, the publicity attendant on the notice and comment process will provide unfavorable press for the agency and could lead to a successful judicial challenge. These concerns will feed back to the agency and limit its willingness to buckle under to interest group pressure in the pre-notice period.

Agencies have some freedom to decide whether to regulate through generic rules or case-by-case implementation. If the procedural requirements for rulemaking are too stringent, agencies may use adjudication instead, perhaps combined with guidelines that have no legal force. This may be costly for regulated entities that would benefit from clearly articulated, legal mandates. There is some evidence that this shift has occurred in the United States (Asimov 1992; Mashaw and Harfst 1990), but the continuing importance of rules (Crews Jr. 2004; Coglianese 2002) suggests that the problem, to the extent it exists, is not general or acute. The benefits of general rules for both agencies and regulated entities are simply too substantial.

The value of public participation depends on the way it is managed and used by the bureaucracy. One review of more than 200 environmental decisions covered federal, state, local, and regional processes over a thirty-year period (Beierle and Cayford 2002). The authors conclude that involving the public "not only frequently produces decisions that are responsive to public values and substantially robust, but it also helps to resolve conflict, build trust, and educate and inform the public about the environment" (Beierle and Cayford 2002, 74). The cases ranked highly by the participants in terms of the process used also scored highly on measures of success. In a cautionary note, however, Beierle and Cayford indicate that one-third of the "successes" kept particularly divisive interests off the table or excluded controversial potential participants (2002, 29, 60–1).

The most important problems with participation in rulemaking are delay, bias, displacement to other methods, and irrelevance. These generally appear to be the result of poorly designed and biased procedures and not of participation per se. Of course, consultation does take time. However, the long time between proposed and final rules seems to be driven more by strategic considerations than by cost of the process. As for bias, the case studies suggest that critics have overstated such claims. Displacement leads to nonbinding guidelines and implementation through the adjudication of individual cases. Neither strategy seems to be a general problem given the large number of rules U.S. agencies continue to issue.

The observation that some final rules are very close to the proposed rules is not evidence of irrelevance. Officials draft proposed rules in light of the forthcoming public participation processes. Officials must consider how their proposals will be greeted by the public and the media when they are publicly posted in the *Federal Register* and later, when they are subject to judicial review. They must give reasons to justify their choices. The possibility of subsequent judicial challenges by interested groups on all sides feeds back to the drafting of the initial proposal (West 2004).

Public hearings can raise the salience of an issue with the public and increase public knowledge about a regulatory issue. Furthermore, if the hearing process leads to modifications in the proposed rule, case studies suggest that bureaucrats are not necessarily the captives of well-funded groups. Successful efforts at public involvement can lead to choices that better reflect public values, although of course, fair and open procedures cannot entirely overcome partisan biases.

The normative case for the U.S. rulemaking process is twofold. First, as political economists argue, legislative texts seldom resolve all the policy issues of interest to private individuals and groups. The task of putting laws into effect is not just a technical enterprise but is itself deeply political. Second, given the first claim, modern governments can only make democratically legitimate policies by consulting broadly. If consultation is limited to those with professional expertise or to committees with fixed membership, the agency may ignore concerns from the grassroots and from those affected by rules. These considerations suggest two directions for future research. First, how do agencies balance comments from diverse sources in cases where all interests participate? Second, how are the limited resources of nonprofit and civic groups allocated? Are there important classes of rules where participation is biased because of the limited resources and organizing capacity of some affected interests?

5 PUBLIC PARTICIPATION OUTSIDE THE UNITED STATES

In Europe, most governments are not required to use popular, participatory procedures for the issuance of government rules and guidelines. Consultation concentrates on groups with economic or professional links—business associations, labor unions, and the chambers for medicine and law—and on statutory self-governments—both those with a geographic basis, such as municipalities, and those with an organizational basis, such as university bodies. Only in the area of labor–management relations are formal consultation processes well institutionalized, and these have declined in legitimacy over time with the fall in union membership in many countries. Even when procedural rights exist, they are seldom judicially enforceable. European regulatory reformers are only beginning to think about how to incorporate pluralist elements into high-level government policy-making in the executive. In this context, bureaucrat-led notice-and-comment rulemaking with judicial review may provide some lessons and models (Rose-Ackerman 1995; 2005; Shapiro 1992). Given the continuing need to employ scientific expertise, reforms in the administrative process seem a more valuable direction for democratic reform than the increased use of referenda (as recommended, for example, by Frey 2001, 118–35).

The most comprehensive European experiments in public participation are occurring at the Commission of the European Union (EU) in response to criticism of the EU's "democracy deficit" (Bignami 2004; 2006; Craig 2006). The Commission has also pushed for more participatory procedures in the member states, especially during the accession process for Eastern European countries (Rose-Ackerman 2005, 37–54). Bignami (2004) outlines three stages. First, beginning in the 1970s, the Commission held hearings when it imposed costs on individuals or firms. Next, in the 1990s, Community institutions began to operate with more transparency. Third, at present, there is an ongoing debate about permitting outsiders to participate in Community policy-making processes. Bignami notes the clashing traditions in member states regarding the legitimacy of representation outside of political parties and elections. Without a strong, directly elected executive in the EU, Bignami worries that American-style participation would operate without checks and could be taken over by narrow interests (2004, 80–1). She (2006, 447) suggests that in the EU context perhaps a reformed "old-fashioned European functional participation" could play a constructive role. To my mind, the risk of that strategy is the questionable legitimacy of some of these functional groups—the most obvious being the inability of labor unions to represent the growing number of workers who are not union members (Rose-Ackerman 2005, 126–34). An alternative, which can complement strengthened public participation in rulemaking, is more active review by the European Court of Justice. In fact, Shapiro (1992) suggests that this is likely to occur as Commission rulemaking processes become more transparent and accountable.

6 BACKGROUND NORMS AND THE ROLE OF THE COURTS

So far, I have concentrated on the value of procedural guarantees in bureaucrat-led policy-making and argued that judicial review should assure that these procedures are followed. A major role of the American courts is to police agency procedures for consistency with the APA and other statutes.

Another role of the courts is to check for consistency between agency rules and the substantive regulatory statutes. The legislative process often produces vague statutory language. This leaves agencies and courts with interpretative challenges. A large but inconclusive academic literature and body of judicial opinions deal with this issue and the role of the so-called "canons" of statutory interpretation. I will not deal with this broad issue here except to say that justifications for the canonical status of these principles are often opaque and the canons themselves are internally inconsistent. I concentrate instead on one class of statutes: those that seek to correct market failures.

Even if a market failure justifies regulation, political pressures in the legislature may push drafters toward the provision of special interest benefits. When the government makes rules, it may favor concentrated groups. These biases suggest that courts in reviewing agency action and in interpreting statutes should resist these tendencies. Special-interest legislation is not unconstitutional; but given its failure to benefit the majority, efforts to benefit narrow groups should be stated in unambiguous statutory language in order to be enforced by the courts. Thus, the courts should apply a substantive background norm when they review agency actions under such regulatory statutes. For statutes ostensibly designed to correct market failures and improve economic efficiency, courts could require agencies to use policy analytic methods. Cost/benefit analysis would be a default criterion for regulations designed to improve the efficiency of the economy, subject to override by clear statutory mandates and to constitutional limits. It is superior to an option familiar in Europe, "the precautionary principle," because that principle is not defined clearly enough to provide realistic policy guidance (Sunstein 2003). A presumption in favor of net benefit maximization increases the political costs for narrow groups which must obtain explicit statutory language in order to have their interests recognized by courts and agencies. Nontransparent efforts to induce agencies to benefit narrow interests could not be implemented (Rose-Ackerman 1992, 33–42; see also Hahn and Litan 2005, 501; Sunstein 2002, 191–228).

Judicial review of agency policy analyses would replace tortured attempts to derive legislative intent from legislative history. The words of the statute would be the courts' fundamental guide; but the burden of proof would fall on anyone attempting to show a legislative intent not to maximize net benefits. The use of congressional speeches and committee reports to infer overall legislative intent is problematic; the former may be efforts to obtain publicity in the media; and the latter, may be negotiated deals lacking legislative or popular support.

If goals are not precisely specified in the statute and budgetary appropriations are limited, the agency has leeway to evaluate both benefits and costs. The judiciary should then insist that agencies make this evaluative effort. Of course, cost/benefit analysis cannot always be carried out with precision because of information gaps and unquantifiable harms and benefits. Nevertheless, agencies should be required to make an effort to think through the available options. In line with Table 33.1, agencies should be able to argue that other techniques are more appropriate in particular cases. In some cases, a negotiated bargain between the affected interests may be most likely to produce the best result. In others the agency may create incentives for private individuals and firms to act without specifying the desired result in detail.

This proposal combines policy analysis and political economy to revamp judicial review of the administrative process. It requires a reorientation of the judicial role in favor of encouraging agencies to develop better analytic capabilities. Judges themselves would have to develop some basic competence in these techniques. The judicial role would still be strictly limited and would not impinge on the political and policy-making role of the other branches. Courts would introduce a rebutable presumption in favor of net benefit maximization for those statutes where economic efficiency is a plausible justification for state action.

7 A RESEARCH AGENDA

The existing literature helps one to understand why delegation accompanied by judicial review takes place and how the interests of political, bureaucratic, and judicial actors interact with institutional structures. It illuminates the role of economic analysis in helping politicians and policy-makers design and implement more effective policies. However, there are a number of limitations of this work that suggest directions for future research.

The political-economy literature has exhausted the value of static, one-dimensional models of government. The more discursive legal literature recognizes the complexity of the real world, and some of this richness could be incorporated into formal models without losing tractability. In particular, purely legal considerations are ignored by simple political models where judges' preferences are on the same dimension as legislatures and the executive. Analysts in this tradition need to incorporate judges' views of the law and of their proper role vis-à-vis the other branches. Furthermore, those advocating cost-benefit analysis and other analytic techniques need to take on the potential tensions between democracy and net benefit maximization without giving up the value of careful analysis.

As a normative matter, the rational-choice literature is quite impoverished. Accountability is generally limited to the compatibility between what the congress wants and what the agency does. A full evaluation of the accountability of agencies must bring in the preferences of the public. If the representative character of congressional action is in doubt, then government accountability to citizens may be enhanced by delegation. The rulemaking provisions of the U.S. Administrative Procedures Act, which require notice, open hearings, and reason giving, can be justified not only as a way for Congress to find out about and influence what is happening, but also as a route for those especially concerned with a particular issue to have their say. The final decision is made by the agency, subject to the political oversight of the president and the legislature and to judicial review, but the process gives a role to those outside government with an interest in the matter. Far from being a subversion of democratic principles, these procedures can be a check on agencies and, indirectly, on the legislature as well (Mashaw 1985; Rose-Ackerman 1995; 2005).

Of course, this justification raises a puzzle for rational-choice theorists. Why would Congress and the president support procedural provisions that undermine their ability to make policy? Existing research suggests some partial answers, but those results highlight the importance of examining existing procedures to be sure that they do indeed further the goals of open government with broad public participation. A system that can be explained on the grounds of self-interest may, nevertheless, serve broadly democratic goals of participation and transparency, but that result cannot be taken for granted by those concerned with the continued health of complex modern democracies and of the newly emerging democracies worldwide.

References

ACKERMAN, B. A., and STEWART, R. 1988. Reforming environmental law: the democratic case for market incentives. *Columbia Journal of Environmental Law*, 13: 171–99.

ADLER, M., and POSNER, E. 1999. Rethinking cost-benefit analysis. *Yale Law Journal*, 109: 165–247.

ASIMOV, M. 1992. California underground regulations. *Administrative Law Review*, 44: 43–77.

BALLA, S. J. 1998. Administrative procedures and political control of the bureaucracy. *American Political Science Review*, 92: 663–74.

BEIERLE, T. C., and CAYFORD, J. 2002. *Democracy in Practice: Public Participation in Environmental Decisions*. Washington, DC: Resources for the Future.

BIGNAMI, F. 2004. Three generations of participation rights before the European Commission. *Law and Contemporary Problems*, 68: 61–83.

—— 2006. Rethinking interest representation in the European Union. *Oxford Journal of Legal Studies*, 26: 439–47.

BREYER, S. 1993. *Breaking the Vicious Circle*. Cambridge, Mass.: Harvard University Press.

CANES-WRONE, B. 2003. Bureaucratic decisions and the composition of the lower courts. *American Journal of Political Science*, 47: 205–14.

CARPENTER, D. P. 2001. *The Forging of Bureaucratic Autonomy: Reputations, Networks, and Policy Innovation in Executive Agencies, 1862–1928*. Princeton, NJ: Princeton University Press.

COGLIANESE, C. 1997. Assessing consensus: the promise and performance of negotiated rulemaking. *Duke Law Journal*, 46: 1255–349.

—— 2002. Empirical analysis and administrative law. *University of Illinois Law Review*, 2002: 1111–37.

CRAIG, P. 2006. The locus and accountability of the executive in the European Union. Pp. 315–45 in *The Executive and Public Law: Power and Accountability in Comparative Perspective*, ed. P. Craig and A. Tomkins. Oxford: Oxford University Press.

CREWS, JR., C. W. 2004. *Ten Thousand Commandments: An Annual Snapshot of the Federal Regulatory State*. Washington, DC: Cato Institute.

CROSS, F. B., and TILLER, E. H. 1998. Judicial partisanship and obedience to legal doctrine: whistleblowing on the federal courts of appeal. *Yale Law Journal*, 107: 2155–76.

EPSTEIN, D., and O'HALLORAN, S. 1999. *Delegating Powers: A Transaction Cost Politics Approach to Policy Making under Separation of Powers*. New York: Cambridge University Press.

FEREJOHN, J., and SHIPAN, C. 1990. Congressional influence on bureaucracy. *Journal of Law, Economics and Organization*, 6: 1–20.

FIORINA, M. 1985. Group concentration and the delegation of legislative authority. Pp. 175–199 in *Regulatory Policy and the Social Sciences*, ed. R. Noll. Berkeley: University of California Press.

—— 1989. *Congress: Keystone of the Washington Establishment*, 2nd edn. New Haven, Conn.: Yale University Press.

—— and NOLL, R. 1978. Voters, legislators, and bureaucracy. *American Economic Review—Papers and Proceedings*, 68: 256–66.

FREY, B. S. 2001. *Inspiring Econmics: Human Motivation in Political Economy*. Cheltenham: Edward Elgar.

FURLONG, S. R., and KERWIN, C. M. 2005. Interest group participation in rulemaking: what has changed in ten years? *Journal of Public Administration Research and Theory*, 15: 353–70.

GOLDEN, M. M. 1998. Interest groups in the rule-making process: Who participates? Whose voices get heard? *Journal of Public Administration and Theory*, 8: 245–70.

HAHN, R., and LITAN, R. 2005. Counting regulatory benefits and costs: lessons for the U.S. and Europe. *Journal of International Economic Law*, 8: 473–508.

HAMILTON, J. T., and SCHROEDER, C. H. 1994. Strategic regulators and the choice of rulemaking procedures: the selection of formal vs. informal rules in regulating hazardous waste. *Law and Contemporary Problems*, 57: 111–60.

HILL, J. S., and BRAZIER, J. E. 1991. Constraining administrative decisions: a critical examination of the structure and process hypothesis. *Journal of Law, Economics and Organization*, 7: 373–400.

HUBER, J. D., and SHIPAN, C. R. 2002. *Deliberate Delegation: The Institutional Foundations of Bureaucratic Autonomy*. New York: Cambridge University Press.

JOHNSON, S. M. 2006. Junking the "junk science" law: reforming the Information Quality Act. *Administrative Law Review*, 58: 37–84.

KAGAN, E. 2001. Presidential administration. *Harvard Law Review*, 114: 2245–319.

KERWIN, C. 2003. *Rulemaking: How Government Agencies Write Law and Make Policy*, 3rd edn. Washington, DC: CQ Press.

KERWIN, C. M., and FURLONG, S. R. 1992. Time and rulemaking: an empirical test of theory. *Journal of Public Administration Research and Theory*, 2: 113–38.

LANDES, W. M., and POSNER, R. A. 1975. The independent judiciary in an interest group perspective. *Journal of Law and Economics*, 18: 875–901.

LEWIS, D. E. 2003. *Presidents and the Politics of Agency Design: Political Insulation in the United States Government Bureaucracy, 1946–1997*. Stanford, Calif.: Stanford University Press.

McCUBBINS, M., and SCHWARTZ, T. 1984. Congressional oversight overlooked: police patrols versus fire alarms. *American Journal of Political Science*, 28: 165–70.

McNOLLGAST 1987. Administrative procedures as instruments of political control. *Journal of Law, Economics and Organization*, 3: 243–77.

———— 1989. Structure and process, politics and policy. *Virginia Law Review*, 75: 431–508.

MAGAT, W. A., KRUPNICK, A. J., and HARRINGTON, W. 1986. *Rules in the Making: A Statistical Analysis of Regulatory Agency Behavior*. Washington, DC: Resources for the Future.

MASHAW, J. 1985. Prodelegation: why administrators should make political decisions. *Journal of Law, Economics and Organization*, 1: 81–100.

—— and HARFST, D. 1990. *The Struggle for Auto Safety*. Cambridge, Mass.: Harvard University Press.

MELNICK, R. S. 1983. *Regulation and the Courts: The Case of the Clean Air Act*. Washington, DC: Brookings Institution.

MENDELSON, N. A. 2003. Agency burrowing: entrenching policies and personnel before a new president arrives. *New York University Law Review*, 78: 557–666.

OLSON, M. 1965. *The Logic of Collective Action*. Cambridge, Mass.: Harvard University Press.

PELTZMAN, S. 1976. Toward a more general theory of regulation? *Journal of Law and Economics*, 19: 211–40.

POSNER, R. 1974. Theories of economic regulation. *Bell Journal of Economics and Management Science*, 5: 335–58.

ROSE-ACKERMAN, S. 1992. *Rethinking the Progressive Agenda: The Reform of the American Regulatory State*. New York: Free Press.

—— 1995. *Controlling Environmental Policy: The Limits of Public Law in Germany and the United States*. New Haven, Conn.: Yale University Press.

—— 2005. *From Elections to Democracy: Building Accountable Government in Hungary and Poland*. Cambridge: Cambridge University Press.

SCHUCK, P. 1977. Public interest groups and the policy process. *Public Administration Review*, 37: 132–40.

SHAPIRO, M. 1992. The giving reasons requirement. *University of Chicago Legal Forum*, 1992: 179–220.

SHEPSLE, K. A., and WEINGAST, B. R. 1981. Structure-induced equilibrium and legislative choice. *Public Choice*, 37: 86–108.

SPENCE, D. 1997. Administrative law and agency policy-making: rethinking the positive theory of political control. *Yale Journal of Regulation*, 14: 407–50.

—— 1999. Managing delegation ex ante: using law to steer administrative agencies. *Journal of Legal Studies*, 28: 413–46.

STEWART, R. 1975. The reformation of American administrative law. *Harvard Law Review*, 88: 1667–1813.

STIGLER, G. 1971. The theory of economic regulation. *Bell Journal of Economics and Management Science*, 2: 3–21.

STRAUSS, P. 1974. Rules, adjudications, and other sources of law in an executive department: reflections on the Interior Department's administration of the Mining Law. *Columbia Law Review*, 74: 1231–75.

SUNSTEIN, C. R. 2002. *Risk and Reason*. New York: Cambridge University Press.

—— 2003. Beyond the precautionary principle. *University of Pennsylvania Law Review*, 151: 1003–58.

—— and THALER, R. H. 2003. Libertarian paternalism is not an oxymoron. *University of Chicago Law Review*, 70: 1159–202.

TIETENBERG, T. 2006. *Emissions Trading*. Washington, DC: Resources for the Future.

TILLER, E. H. 1998. Controlling policy by controlling process: judicial influence on regulatory decision-making. *Journal of Law, Economics and Organization*, 14: 114–35.

WEIMER, D., and VINING, A. 2005. *Policy Analysis: Concepts and Practice*, 4th edn. Upper Saddle River, NJ: Prentice Hall.

WEST, W. F. 2004. Formal procedures, informal processes, accountability, and responsiveness in bureaucratic policy making: an institutional analysis. *Public Administration Review*, 64: 66–80.

WILSON, J. Q. 1973. *Political Organizations*. New York: Basic Books.

WOOD, B. D., and BOHTE. J. 2004. Political transaction costs and the politics of administrative design. *Journal of Politics*, 66: 176–202.

YACKEE, J. W., and YACKEE, S. W. 2006. A bias toward business? Assessing interest group influence on the U. S. bureaucracy. *Journal of Politics*, 68: 128–39.

CHAPTER 34

LAW AS AN INSTRUMENT OF SOCIAL REFORM

CHARLES R. EPP

"THERE is, these days, some ambivalence about litigation," Scheingold wrote over thirty years ago. "The civil rights experience has made us all skeptics" (1974, 95). The Supreme Court's apparently bold and decisive rejection of racial segregation in public schools, Scheingold observed, had become mired in continuing political and administrative controversy, and too little had been accomplished. Yet, he also observed, many groups, among them environmentalists, women, prisoners, and the poor, still turned to court in the hope of achieving social reforms. Here I examine why groups seeking social reform in the United States (and elsewhere) commonly have resorted to litigation, and whether (and how) court-made law is an instrument of social reform.

First, what is "law," as posed in the chapter's title, and what is "social reform?" These definitions take on significance in light of the ongoing debate over judicial role and capacity generated first by the Supreme Court's social-policy interventions under the leadership of Chief Justice Warren in the 1950s and 1960s, and, more recently, by the growing role of courts virtually worldwide (see e.g. Keleman 2006; Tate and Vallinder 1995; Stone Sweet 2000) and its close link with civil rights and liberties litigation (Epp 1998; Cichowski 2004; 2006). In this context, when scholars have examined whether "law" may be used as a tool of "social reform," they generally have meant whether judge-made law, particularly in cases brought by social movement litigators, improves the conditions of the disadvantaged groups targeted by such litigation, particularly racial minorities, women, inmates, and people living in poverty (see e.g. Handler, Hollingsworth, and Erlanger 1978; McCann 1994; Rosenberg 1991). I here share this focus on litigation, judge-made law, and social reform targeting particularly disadvantaged groups.

What courts do that may be relevant for social reform is a complicated matter. Arrayed on a continuum, from the most directly intrusive to the least intrusive, their most obvious policy intervention undoubtedly has been the institutional or structural-reform injunction, encompassing a host of tools used for the judicial management of organizational change, most famously in the cases of school desegregation and reform of prisons and mental institutions (see e.g. Chayes 1976; Cooper 1988; Feeley and Rubin 1998). Similarly, courts have intervened in the policy process in direct and obvious ways by declaring new constitutional rights or extending constitutional rights in new ways, generally with the implication that some existing government policy or practice is unconstitutional. Somewhat less intrusively, courts intervene in policy matters whenever they structure incentives for subsequent litigation. Nearly any judicial decision, of course, structures incentives in some fashion; the decision to decline to declare a new right provides fewer incentives to litigate on behalf of the right. But some judicial decisions create policies primarily aimed at structuring such incentives, particularly decisions on standing to sue or access to the federal courts. Similarly, judicial decisions interpreting and applying legislation, by their nature, structure the policy process. Finally, judicial events (hearings, arguments, decisions) have a variety of indirect effects, among them the generation of publicity. Research on tort lawsuits against organizational defendants often finds that organizational managers fear such indirect effects more than the primary output of the event (e.g. damages judgments) (Epp forthcoming). In all of these ways, taken together, judicial activities cast a shadow under which other actors negotiate and machinate for advantage (Mnookin and Kornhauser 1979).

This chapter has three theses. First, the more fragmented and porous the institutional structure of a governing system, the greater the incentives for groups to turn to courts to achieve policy goals; the litigation strategies of disadvantaged groups, like other groups, reflect these incentives. Second, although the institutional characteristics of fragmented governing systems limit the capacity of any agency of government—the courts included—to manage direct, quick, and untroubled implementation of policies, courts are more handicapped than other agencies in this regard. Thus, classic studies on the implementation of public policy generally adopted a mechanistic conception of judicial impact, focusing on particular court orders, courts' limited powers of enforcement, and administrative agencies' capacities for evasion and resistance, and generally concluded that, on balance, courts lacked the capacity to carry out social reform. Third, however, other capacities of courts, particularly institutional authority to create authoritative legal norms and to structure litigation incentives, lend to the courts a capacity to effect relatively fundamental longer-term policy changes. In recent decades, the development of institutional support for social reform litigation and professional networks whose central ideology incorporates legal responsibility have enhanced courts' capacity to influence longer-term policy change. If classic implementation studies focused on judicial power and bureaucratic evasion, a more recent body of research has focused on more diffuse signals from the judiciary in generating law-related perceptions and norms, and their role in mobilizing advocacy coalitions and in generating pressure for normative conformity among other agencies and organizations. The more-recent studies thus find that court-structured law may have a broader social-reform impact than once thought. The remainder of this chapter develops these points via a review of scholarly literature on the role and impact of courts in social reform.

1 CONDITIONS FOR RELIANCE ON COURT-MADE LAW AS AN INSTRUMENT OF SOCIAL REFORM

To the extent that social-reform groups turn to court, they do so in part as the result of structural incentives. Scholars have long recognized that divided or fragmented governing institutions (e.g. a separation of powers) provide incentives for going to court to seek policy change. On the one hand, structural divisions, particularly the separation of powers and federalism, constrain the development of comprehensive administrative programs, thereby channeling some of the pressure for social reform into the courts (Kagan 2001). In such systems, the necessity to build broad legislative coalitions in order to pass legislation contributes to statutory generality and ambiguity, which generates continued struggle over the meaning of statutory language in the administrative and judicial process (Lovell 2003; Melnick 1994). On the other hand, legislatures in systems of separated powers may adopt very precise statutory requirements and authorize private enforcement of those requirements in court in an attempt to control administrative agencies (Burke 2002; Keleman and Sibbitt 2004; McNollgast 1999). Additionally, fragmented governing structures, particularly federalism, contribute to a proliferation of policy-making authorities, thereby creating incentives for courts to address conflicting decisions among competing agencies. The separation of powers also limits the capacity of legislative majorities to overrule decisions made by the courts, thereby giving greater permanence and vitality to judicial decisions (see e.g. Shapiro 1981).

A relatively divided and fragmented governing structure also contributes to a relatively divided and fragmented sphere of political organizations. In contrast to

European political parties, where the governing structure encourages consolidation of political organization in the form of strong, centralized parties and peak business and labor associations, the main American parties are relatively weak and candidate-centered and therefore largely incapable of enacting programmatic social reform or of overriding judicial decisions. This partisan weakness enhances the incentive to go to the courts for social reform. Similarly, the fragmented governing structure provides incentives for these groups to bypass the difficult process of legislative coalition building and instead (or in addition) seek their policy goals in the courts.

The more fragmented and porous are a country's governing institutions, the greater the incentive for seeking social reform in court. Thus, the porous nature of the American political process, and consequently, the almost inevitable involvement by courts in that process, virtually demands that groups seeking policy change must be ready to "play" in all of the key forums of government, among them courts; if they do not, undoubtedly their opponents will. As Sabatier and Jenkins-Smith (1999, 142–3) observe, advocacy coalitions "have a multitude of possible venues," among them legislatures, administrative agencies, and courts, and "coalitions should (and do) spend an enormous amount of time "venue shopping"... pursu[ing] multiple venues at multiple levels, often simultaneously, in a constant effort to find some that will bear fruit."

Admittedly, the dilemma facing social reformers on behalf of disadvantaged groups has sometimes been especially stark: when they have utterly failed in the elected branches of government, is there merit in seeking policy change via the courts? This essentially was the decision facing civil rights advocates in the 1930s and 1940s. At the time, when there was no realistic chance Congress would adopt civil rights legislation—indeed, opponents had blocked even antilynching bills— the dean of Howard University's School of Education observed that it is "no longer a question of whether Negroes *should* resort to the courts, they must resort to the courts. They have no other reasonable, legitimate alternative" (quoted in Lobel 2003, 122; see also Frymer 2007).

2 THE UTILITY OF GOING TO COURT FOR SOCIAL REFORM

To what extent does resort to court pay off for social reformers? The answer is best framed as a paradox identified first in the study of public policy more generally (Sabatier 1986): the greater the change demanded by an official decision, the less likely it will be immediately carried out, due to counter-mobilization by its opponents—but the more likely it may inspire broad-scale mobilization on its behalf, which *may* succeed in effecting significant reform over time.[1] The classic studies of law-led social reform, particularly studies of school desegregation, focused on attempts at massive change of precisely the sort Sabatier (1986) characterized as not amenable to immediate success.

In mobilizing a coalition in favor of law-focused social reform, the first hurdle to cross is getting into court. Litigation requires resources; pursuing several cases through multiple levels of the judicial system may consume substantial resources. Although the chances of victory in court are not a direct reflection of the litigant's resources, higher levels of resources obviously buy more in the legal arena— more skilled attorneys, more legal research, more time devoted to developing a case, and so on. Some groups are better able to bear these costs than others. For disadvantaged groups, particularly those lacking abundant resources, the costs of ongoing litigation may prove prohibitive. Those costs have been more easily met in the last half-century with the development of institutional bases of support for social-reform litigation, sometimes called "support structures" for litigation (Epp 1998).

The second hurdle is convincing a judge to support a social-reform claim. Scholars have long observed that judges are more likely to favor some kinds of requests for social reform than others. Thus Scheingold (1974, 97) observed that "courts are unlikely to take the lead on behalf of goals that are not firmly rooted in constitutional values." He observed (1974, 97–116) specifically that courts tend to support only those claims that are consistent with the "liberal-capitalist" bias of the Constitution, that seek incremental rather than dramatic change, and which are justified in normative, rather than utilitarian, terms. Similarly, Rosenberg (1991, 10–13) argued that the limited nature of constitutional rights is a significant constraint on court-led social reform. Nonetheless, Scheingold observed (1974, 97), courts may easily override the limitations of constitutional rights "when they are swimming with the political tide." Cooper (1988), examining cases in which federal trial judges unexpectedly endorsed social reform causes, observed that federal judges, when presented with facts of egregious injustice, particularly in instances where the other branches of government have ignored the problem, may feel compelled to do *something*. Even Scheingold held a "relatively optimistic" assessment of litigation's ability to alter the "goals" of public policy (1974, 118).

The real question for Scheingold, Rosenberg, and others, then, has been the extent to which altering the goals of public policy via litigation or judge-made law has any meaningful impact on social policy in practice. If judges act, judge-made law and particularly rights, Scheingold argued, may be thought to have one or both of two sorts of effects. The first, postulated by the "myth of rights," is a more-or-less

---

[1] Sabatier (1986) concluded from this observation that the most easily implemented reforms are likely to be those that demand significant but not dramatic change because they will mobilize supporters but not provoke massive counter-mobilizations by opponents.

direct effect on policy in action; Scheingold observed that courts almost entirely lack the tools necessary to force immediate compliance, and so such direct effects depend on widespread support. The second, characterized as the "politics of rights," suggests that rights-claims and judicial decisions announcing law-led social reform produce no automatic policy changes but are more-or-less potent "resources" to be used by proponents of reform in subsequent political struggles. I turn now to an examination of the research on each hypothesis.

3 IMPLEMENTATION

Direct, relatively immediate, and relatively untroubled "implementation" of official decisions of any sort is remarkably rare in fragmented governing systems. In fragmented systems, policy decisions commonly contain significant ambiguity, and there are simply too many agencies with competing authority, too little effective top-down managerial control over the implementation process, and thus too many "veto-points" to facilitate a simple and efficient implementation of policy decisions (see e.g. Baumgartner and Jones 1993; Pressman and Wildavsky 1979; Sabatier 1986). As Sabatier and Jenkins-Smith observe (1999, 143): "A frequent result of venue shopping is policy stalemate: Coalition A dominates one venue, and Coalition B dominates another."

Judicial decisions are no exception. In the 1970s, scholars produced a large body of literature on the implementation of judicial policies, particularly declarations of new rights and court-ordered institutional reform. Although the judicial system itself is remarkably fragmented in divided governing systems, particularly the U.S., one line of research consistently found that higher-court policies are followed in a surprisingly consistent manner in lower courts (Kilwein and Brisbin 1997; Songer, Segal, and Cameron 1994). But courts' ability directly to control other agencies is more limited. The conditions for relatively untroubled, immediate implementation of court-made law are similar to those observed for implementation of policy in general, and may be met even more rarely when the policy is court-mandated. Among other necessary conditions for successful "top-down" implementation of policy in general, Sabatier (1986) identified the following: policy clarity, support from implementing officials, support from interest groups, support from legislative and executive sovereigns, and a favorable socioeconomic climate. These necessary conditions are very similar to those identified by a generation of research on the implementation of judicial decisions (see e.g. Canon and Johnson 1999; Rosenberg 1991). Although it has often been observed that courts, lacking the powers of the purse and the sword, are more handicapped even than other policy-makers, in many instances they have been surprisingly successful in generating increases in appropriations and changes in implementing personnel, which have facilitated broader policy change (see e.g. Feeley and Rubin 1998; Reed 2001). Yet courts *do* lack a crucial power that eases the process of top-down implementation of legislative policy in some cases (Sabatier 1986): the power to create a new agency specifically charged with carrying out the policy. The literature on the implementation of court-mandated policy is large but now somewhat dated, and space precludes a more extended discussion here; Canon and Johnson (1999) provide a valuable summary.

4 LEGAL MOBILIZATION AND INSTITUTIONAL NORMS

Although direct and untroubled implementation of judicial decisions therefore is generally rare, most scholars of the policy process—at least those outside of the field of law and courts—no longer view direct implementation as a valuable test of the effectiveness of social reform. Thus, Sabatier (1986) and Sabatier and Jenkins-Smith (1999) have called for an examination of long-term policy processes, focusing on the mobilization of "advocacy coalitions" that turn to the full range of official forums— legislatures, executives, bureaucracies, and courts—in their strategies to carry out policy change. In sharp contrast to the relatively short windows of implementation typically examined in the judicial literature, the effectiveness of a policy reform, in Sabatier's (1986) analysis, is best gauged over the course of decades. Scheingold (1974, 85) advanced a similar argument, observing, "The authoritative declaration of a right is perhaps best viewed as the beginning of a political process in which power relationships loom large and immediate." Similarly, Galanter (1974) argued that law best serves interests that are organized to compete in the legal system as "repeat players" over the long term.

Three institutional developments in the last half-century have shaped the reception of judicial decisions and social scientific scholarship on that reception. One is the development of support structures for litigation (Epp 1998). Organized groups capable of pursuing sustained litigation have proliferated; the lawyer population has grown considerably and has diversified by race and sex; and shared knowledge of how to pursue social-reform litigation has expanded via "how-to" books, specialist casebooks, law school courses, and formal conferences and training. In some countries, governments have created programs to fund "test cases" or other litigation by disadvantaged groups; and in the U.S., Congress has adopted a number of federal statutes authorizing judges, especially in cases involving federal rights, to require losing defendants to pay the attorneys' fees of winning plaintiffs. As the result of the growth of support structures for legal mobilization in many countries, courts have gained an enforcement arm or a coalition of supporters capable of pressing for application and development of judicial policies.

In addition to more richly developed support structures in civil society, advanced industrialized societies in the last fifty years experienced the birth and substantial growth of administrative professions and professional networks in government agencies and private corporations. Thus, the "human resources" or "personnel administration" profession developed in conjunction with greater attention to the management of employee relations; policing largely completed its shift from a traditional political role to a modern administrative profession; and similar professions developed in association with a vast array of policy areas in the modern state. Edelman (1990; 1992) characterized such administrative professionals as "windows" between bureaucratic organizations and their legal environment, thus allowing for greater influence by the legal environment on organizations (and vice versa). Over time, responsibility to the law and, particularly, to the institutional norms associated with court-focused policy, increasingly has become central to the mission of many administrative professions.

Third, as the federal judiciary has become more politically conservative, judicial interventions into the policy process generally have shifted from injunctive relief and managerial intervention (see e.g. Chayes 1976) to a less dramatic structuring of the incentives of other actors, particularly through remedies modeled after tort damages and statutory interpretation. A number of studies reflect that shift, among them Burke's (2002) on the "litigious policies" enacted by Congress, and Haltom and McCann's (2004) analysis of the media-framed debate over tort liability.

Studies in several fields, reflecting these developments, characterize law's impact in ways that differ sharply in major respects from the older implementation model. Like the "advocacy coalition" theory in the policy field (Sabatier and Jenkins-Smith 1999), these studies focus primarily on the actors and organizations engaged in political and policy struggles and on how they perceive and use the resources and incentives offered by law—and not on discrete judicial orders and their "effects." They view judicial decisions not as interventions independent of the policy process but as steps deeply embedded within that process; and not as commands, but as ideas or as normative resources available for use by participants in that process, or as official ratifications of policy norms favored by some in the policy process. Finally, they characterize subsequent policy processes not as responses to those commands but as continuations of political struggle in light of the newly available resources or judicial imprimatur given to one norm or another. Therefore, they generally avoid the metaphor "implementation" and instead characterize policy activities as ongoing political struggles among multiple affected parties in the shadow of the law.[2] Although these post-implementation studies characterize judicial decisions as deeply embedded in ongoing processes, unlike implementation studies they see judicial decisions (and law more broadly) as potentially effective in contributing to long-term social changes.

One line of research, characterized by a focus on legal mobilization, grew directly out of Scheingold's (1974) argument that law and rights may be best characterized as "resources" available for use in mobilizing political movements of disadvantaged groups, with the ultimate possible effect of transforming relatively narrow or specialized disputes into matters of broad political mobilization and thereby expanding the scope of political conflict and "realigning" political power (1974, 137–9). Thus, judicially-declared rights, he suggested, may be used by movement organizers to "activate the quiescent," particularly by encouraging them to see discontent as a problem subject to political remedy. Similarly, he argued (1974, 139–43), movement organizers may use judicially-declared rights as tools for organizing newly energized people into groups capable of placing pressure on the government. Foreshadowing Sabatier's observation (1986) that far-reaching policy innovations inspire both backlash and mobilization of supporters, Scheingold observed that aspirational rights decisions are unlikely to be straightforwardly implemented but may become the focal point of political organizing. Once mobilized, groups may use judicially-declared rights to undermine the legitimacy of their political opposition, as occurred, Scheingold argued (1974, 143–4), when the South's campaign of massive resistance eroded its legitimacy in the eyes of the wider public.

Rosenberg's *Hollow Hope* (1991) attempted, albeit implicitly, to refute Scheingold's "politics of rights" thesis. Rosenberg argued that key social reform decisions by the Supreme Court *cannot* have had the mobilizing utility ascribed to them by Scheingold precisely because, Rosenberg claimed, judicial decisions have no discernible long-term impact on media coverage and are therefore not associated with expansions of the scope of political conflict and mobilization. In support of this thesis, Rosenberg examined the media and social movement reaction to *Brown*. Based on a count of articles on "blacks in America" reported in the *Reader's Guide to Periodical Literature*, he concluded that *Brown* had no discernible impact on media coverage of the civil rights issue (1991, 111–16). Similarly, although histories of the civil rights movement often give *Brown* credit for providing hope that segregationist policy might be changed, Rosenberg found no contemporaneous accounts from the early civil rights movement that credited *Brown* as an inspiration (1991, 131–50).

It is increasingly hard to credit claims that law and judicial decisions play no substantial role in political mobilization and, in particular, that *Brown* precipitated

---

[2] Although the older implementation studies had significant blind spots, a handful of studies in that line of research (notably Milner 1971; Wasby 1976) integrated some of the newer insights, particularly on the role of perceptions, norms, and professional networks.

no significant change in media coverage. Flemming, Bohte, and Wood (1997), using time-series analysis, demonstrated that several landmark Supreme Court decisions, among them *Brown*, produced significant and very substantial long-term changes in media coverage of the associated policy issues. Indeed, the changes in media coverage reported by the authors are so massive that they may be easily observed without sophisticated statistical methods. Rosenberg failed to observe such changes in the wake of *Brown* primarily because he focused exclusively on the aggregate category "Negroes in America" and did not count articles on school desegregation, most of which the *Reader's Guide* categorized under a different heading, "Public Schools;" and, when all articles associated with desegregation were counted, it became clear that *Brown* triggered "a long-term shift in systemic attention to this issue" (Flemming, Bohte, and Wood 1997, 1229 n. 6 and associated text; quoted, 1237). Flemming et al. concluded that *Brown* and several other landmark decisions "sparked intense national debates that drew in new participants and expanded the scope of conflict through time" (1997, 1247).

More broadly, a rich body of research pioneered by Michael McCann (1994; see e.g. Paris 2001; Pinello 2006) demonstrates that activists for disadvantaged groups commonly use legal rights and law as resources in attempts to advance their causes, sometimes with considerable effect.[3] For instance, McCann (1994) showed that pay equity activists used rights claims to recruit and build local social movements; as leverage to compel concessions from employers; and as bargaining tools during implementation of employers' pay equity policies. Significantly, he observed that ambiguous court decisions, and even *hostile* court decisions, served as potent resources for activists, who creatively reinterpreted those decisions in the service of their interests. Harris (2004) similarly demonstrated that activist lawyers in some jurisdictions were partially successful in pursuing a social reform (provision of housing) for the quintessentially disadvantaged group, the truly impoverished. In each of these cases, law's effectiveness as a tool of social reform depended on preexisting social or labor networks, state-supported legal aid attorneys, or other forms of support for legal mobilization, and on the facility with which policy entrepreneurs in these networks were able to mobilize broader support and shift the terms of the policy debate by use of legal symbols and legal rhetoric. Yet some studies in this genre—notably Brisbin's (2002) poignant analysis of the failure of miners' legal mobilization to achieve significant reform goals during the Pittston coal strike—demonstrate that even when aided by rich networks, organization, and attorneys, law-focused reform may utterly fail, particularly when its goals are far-reaching.

---

[3] The debate between Rosenberg and McCann also generated a valuable discussion of social science methods and the study of judicial impact, which cannot be reviewed here due to space limitations (see esp. Feeley 1992; McCann 1992; 1996; Rosenberg 1992; 1996).

A second line of research, associated particularly with neoinstitutional sociology, focuses on the effect of legal norms on organizational policies and vice versa. A number of studies explore the hypothesis that organizations seek to enhance their legitimacy by demonstrating responsiveness to the normative expectations of the "legal environment" (Edelman 1990; 1992). After the mid-1960s, for instance, the legal environment's norm of nondiscrimination placed intense pressure on employers to demonstrate good-faith efforts in stamping out employment discrimination and respecting employees' rights to due process. Edelman (1990; 1992) hypothesized that organizational responsiveness to these pressures would be greater the more that organizations are exposed to normative pressure from the legal environment. She measured exposure to such pressure by the size of the organization (larger organizations were thought to be more exposed), proximity to the public sector (the closer, the more exposed), and the presence of human resources officials, who act as "windows" between the organization and the legal environment. She found that these factors were strongly associated with the diffusion of several "compliance" policies (e.g. EEO offices, grievance procedures, and the like), even when the compliance policy was not, strictly speaking, legally mandated.

Further, Edelman (1990; 1992; Edelman, Uggen, and Erlanger 1999) argued that the legal environment and responses to it evolve in an interactive manner: new legal-regulatory efforts (e.g. new rights) impose highly significant but highly ambiguous demands on organizations, which spark attempts to demonstrate "compliance," which, in turn, by their construction of the operational meaning of compliance, shape judicial interpretations of what counts as compliance. Edelman has therefore reached pessimistic conclusions about the ability of law to effectuate social reform in organizations, primarily because, in her view, organizational "responses" so greatly shape the operational meaning of what counts as compliance.

By contrast, Dobbin and Sutton (1998) reach more optimistic conclusions. They argue that, in the 1970s, the widespread and justified perception that employee rights under federal law were *expanding* via judicial interpretation—not simply that their requirements were *ambiguous*—encouraged employers to respond with efforts at demonstrating compliance. Significantly, in Dobbin and Sutton's analysis, diffusion of organizational policies *increased* even as federal enforcement abated in the 1980s (measured primarily by the shift to the Reagan administration). Dobbin and Sutton account for this paradox by demonstrating that human resources professionals' justifications for compliance had subtly evolved by the 1980s, from a justification based on legal compliance to a justification based on "good business practice." The authors argue that many legally mandated policies similarly become, over time, justified primarily as good business practices whereupon they take on a self-enforcing life of their own, demonstrating that the American state is "administratively weak but normatively strong."

A handful of studies combines insights from the legal mobilization and neoinstitutional lines of research, focusing on the role of private legal mobilization in contributing to the normative strength of the weak state and, particularly, of courts. The most important of these is Pedriana and Stryker (2004), who show, with an analysis of employment civil rights enforcement in the 1960s and 1970s, that interest-group litigation (specifically by the National Association for the Advancement of Colored People–Legal Defence Fund (NAACP–LDF)), Equal Employment Opportunities Commission (EEOC) recommendations, and Supreme Court decisions, transformed an ambiguous set of employment civil-rights laws into stiff regulatory requirements. In Pedriana and Stryker's (2004) analysis, the NAACP–LDF then used the evolving legal doctrine in "show" cases against major employers, whose managers quickly perceived that the general legal environment was becoming hostile to merely symbolic compliance—that good intentions were not enough—and employers responded by adopting formal offices and antidiscrimination policies. In turn, the Supreme Court later ratified these organizational policies as legitimate signs of organizational compliance. In Pedriana and Stryker's (2004) account, introducing legal mobilization into the analysis and highlighting its interaction with official government policy leads to a conclusion dramatically different to Edelman's: employment civil rights law did not develop primarily along terms set by industry. Similarly, research on the interaction between legal mobilization and official policy in the development of environmental policy generally suggests that judicial interpretation of the Environmental Protection Act (EPA) has broadened and sharpened its impact. Both Sabatier (1975) and Ringquist (1995) concluded that surprisingly vigorous enforcement of the EPA and development of official policy reflected legal mobilization by private litigants.

Comparative studies of sex harassment law and its organizational impact in the U.S. and France (Saguy 2003) and Austria (Cahill 2001) show that, even in the absence of state-centered (administrative) enforcement of sex-harassment policy, policy in the United States is more organizationally demanding and yet employers have adopted associated employment policies much more widely in the United States. The conditions for widespread diffusion appear to be the presence in the United States of a private right to sue and the widespread availability of resources to do so.

Prison reform is an especially telling case of the link among legal norms, professional norms and networks, and judicial decisions. Feeley and Rubin (1998), in perhaps the most persuasive case study of judicial policy-making, examined the development of judge-led prison reform in the 1970s and 1980s. They demonstrated that the earliest judicial efforts at prison reform were precipitated by the contradiction between the new national norm of civil rights and the Southern plantation model of prisons, that judicial models of good prison design and management were drawn from the growing prison management profession, and that judges relied on professional prison managers to conduct the day-to-day management of court-ordered reform. Court-led prison reform, they concluded (1998, 366–80), did not meet the highest hopes of prison-reform radicals—and it was not intended to do so—but extended constitutional rights to prisoners, abolished the South's plantation model, established national standards of prison administration, professionalized prison administration throughout the country, and brought a bureaucratic rule of law to prisons, all in ways that would have been wholly unexpected a few years earlier and would have been unlikely in the absence of judicial intervention.

A number of other studies explore, in one way or another, links among legal mobilization, judicial policy, and professional networks. Mather (1995) examined the role of professional networks in diffusing knowledge about trial court decisions. Similarly, although the earliest studies of the impact of the Warren Court's criminal procedure decisions on policing generally concluded that police systematically evaded the new requirements or implemented them in only the narrowest ways, a substantial body of more recent research suggests that judicial oversight encouraged the development of police professionalism, which together with private litigation and judicial oversight, contributed to a long-term increase in police fidelity to suspects' constitutional rights (see e.g. Orfield 1987; Walker 1993).

Comparative studies of law and policy generally suggest that judicial intervention in the policy process contributes to greater access to that process by disadvantaged groups (see e.g. Cichowski 2004; 2006; Epp forthcoming). Nonetheless, some groups, especially the particularly disadvantaged, lack the capacity to avail themselves of judicial openness (see e.g. Conant 2002); and there is significant debate over whether greater access serves the values of economy and efficiency or even the long-term interests of disadvantaged groups (see e.g. Kagan 2001; Epp 2003).

5 CONCLUDING DISCUSSION

It has sometimes been argued that law is not a useful tool for achieving significant social reform on behalf of disadvantaged groups, largely because of the limited enforcement powers of courts and the limited resource capacities of disadvantaged groups. Disadvantaged groups, these observers say, would do well not to squander their very limited resources on litigation, where they are likely to achieve only symbolic victories at best. The paradigmatic example used to support this observation is, of course, the widespread and successful resistance of Southern school districts to the Supreme Court's desegregation mandate in *Brown v. Board of Education* (1954). Yet, as observed earlier, it is a general observation of policy studies that the greater the social reform, the less likely it will be implemented in the short term because of the backlash commonly occasioned by bold social reforms. School desegregation, in other words, was not unique, nor was the Supreme Court, in comparison to other authorities, especially weak or ineffective.

As the broader policy literature also suggests, bold, aspirational reform policies are more likely than narrower, easier-to-implement policies to broaden the degree of popular mobilization on their behalf, produce realignments in political coalitions, and ultimately, to open the possibility of fundamental policy reorganizations. Baumgartner and Jones (1993) have argued that the American system is characterized by periods of policy inertia punctuated by relatively brief periods of dramatic change that sweep away entrenched policies and interests. Periods of dramatic change commonly are initiated by advocacy mobilizations that succeed in dramatically placing an issue on the public agenda, generally by gaining the imprimatur of a key governing institution. Mobilization unsuccessful in one venue may be successful in another; the availability of multiple venues "is an important part of the process of disrupting policy monopolies" (True, Baumgartner, and Jones 1999, 101–2). "In short, American political institutions were conservatively designed to resist many efforts at change and thus to make mobilizations necessary if established interests are to be overcome. The result over time has been institutionally reinforced stability interrupted by bursts of change" (True, Baumgartner, and Jones 1999, 99). Major changes, True, Baumgartner, and Jones (1999, 103) write, are driven by institutionally centered shifts in attention. *Brown*, as demonstrated by Flemming, Bohte, and Wood (1997), constituted such a shift.

Judicial decisions declaring new rights, as Scheingold (1974, 85) observed, open a "political process" characterized by coalition mobilization and intense policy conflict. Much of the energy naturally focuses on the construction of policies at the administrative level—school enrollment and bussing policies, police use-of-force policies, employment antidiscrimination policies, and so on. The development of such administrative policies, as the advocacy coalition model (Sabatier and Jenkins-Smith 1993) suggests, is conditioned by the relative strengths and capacities of different groups and interests for coalition building, network development, additional litigation, and negotiation over policy in a wide range of official agencies.

In sum, in the fragmented governing systems of the United States and the European Union, social reform advocates commonly turn to courts as part of their repertoire of policy advocacy strategies, are aided by the growth and development of support structures for such litigation, and are rewarded sufficiently often by favorable court decisions to continue their partial reliance on courts. Social reform litigation occasionally has led to major judicial rulings that have transformed the broader policy agenda. More commonly, social reform litigation and court cases are merely incremental steps in a highly fragmented, ambiguous policy process.

Whose interests are best served by law-precipitated social reform? The present system well serves groups that have access to significant financial and organizational resources and who have allies or potential allies among the administrative professions. At times, the disadvantaged groups identified at the outset of this chapter—racial minorities, women, and the poor—have benefited, particularly when organizations advocating their interests have been part of dominant political coalitions. Judicial intervention in the policy process generally does not generate social reform on behalf of groups lacking such resources and allies, particularly the very poor (see e.g. Gilliom 2001). The occasional counter-examples (e.g. Harris 2004) illustrate the difficulty of effectively generating law-centered social reform on behalf of the poor.

Nonetheless, in fragmented governing systems, the availability of court-precipitated reforms generates qualitatively different social reform than in systems where courts play more minor roles. In centralized systems, policies tend to be comparatively more programmatic and administered by centralized, professional administrative systems. In fragmented systems, the policy process is more open to disruption by groups lacking power in dominant political coalitions. The result over time in fragmented systems is a greater tendency toward decentralized reforms that may, by gradual diffusion or endorsement by national policy, come to sweep an entire nation. Principal examples include school desegregation, prison reform, mental institution reform, EEO policy generally, sex-harassment policy in particular, police professionalism, and so on. These reforms are clearly significant and, in each, litigation and judicial decisions played formative roles.

Several issues merit additional research. First, few studies have combined the insights of the legal mobilization and neoinstitutional lines of research. The few that have attempted to do so (e.g. Pedriana and Stryker 2004; Barnes and Burke 2006) suggest the rich possibilities that may lie in such cross-fertilization.

Second, although it has been a theoretical advance to shift the focus from particular judicial decisions to the "legal environment" more generally, more research is needed on understanding and measuring how key actors understand that environment. Some past studies have measured the legal environment in terms of proximity to the public sphere or in terms of the general enforcement stance of presidential administrations. Although these conceptualizations are valuable, they are relatively broad. Arguably, if the general legal environment has regulatory impact, it does so via decision-makers' perceptions of its requirements or norms and the risks related to noncompliance. Implicit in many of the studies on the impact of the legal environment is the assumption that its inducements are felt via the perceived likelihood of being sued (see e.g. Mnookin and Kornhauser 1979). Yet remarkably little systematic empirical research has been conducted on such perceptions, on their impact on bargaining processes or more broadly on policies in practice, or on how these things vary, by jurisdiction or otherwise. Haltom and McCann (2004) have demonstrated that the popular media extensively publish depictions of tort liability, most of which are inaccurate in their characterizations of the underlying legal dispute and its outcome. Similarly, I have begun research on local government managers' perceptions of the risks of legal liability and their anticipatory responses. Additional research is needed on other aspects of the legal environment and actors' understandings of them.

Finally, much of the implementation research of an earlier era focused on the effects of judicial decisions expanding rights. In more recent years, judicial decisions eroding those rights have been equally significant, but there is no body of research on how judicial decisions that limit rights are interpreted, used, and developed in the administrative process. There is much room for research on the topic.

The study of law as an instrument of social reform was once a vibrant part of the field of law and courts but is now somewhat moribund. Ironically, during its heyday, studies of the topic were often confined to narrow conceptions of "law" (focusing primarily on judicial orders) and narrow conceptions of law's impact (focusing primarily on "implementation" of those orders). Perhaps the bias of that time is understandable in light of the era's numerous reform-oriented judicial orders and the battles within bureaucracies (especially the schools and the police) over their meaning and application. But much has changed, both in conceptions of the nature of law's utility and in conceptions of law's impact. Scholars in several disciplines have developed a body of studies, many not clearly linked to each other or to a common discourse, which nonetheless speak directly to the question of law's role in social reform. If researchers can draw together the emerging insights of these diffuse lines of research, the topic of law and social reform has the potential to reemerge as a significant area of inquiry in political science.

References

Baumgartner, F. R., and Jones, B. D. 1993. *Agendas and Instability in American Politics.* Chicago: University of Chicago Press.

Barnes, J., and Burke, T. F. 2006. The diffusion of rights: from law on the books to organizational rights practices. *Law and Society Review*, 40: 493–524.

Brisbin, R. A., Jr. 2002. *A Strike Like No Other Strike: Law and Resistance During the Pittston Coal Strike of 1989–1990.* Baltimore: Johns Hopkins University Press.

Burke, T. F. 2002. *Lawyers, Lawsuits, and Legal Rights: The Battle over Litigation in American Society.* Berkeley: University of California Press.

Cahill, M. L. 2001. *The Social Construction of Sexual Harassment Law: The Role of the National, Organizational, and Individual Context.* Aldershot: Ashgate.

Canon, B. C., and Johnson, C. A. 1999. *Judicial Policies: Implementation and Impact*, 2nd edn. Washington, DC: CQ Press.

Chayes, A. 1976. The role of the judge in public law litigation. *Harvard Law Review*, 89: 1281–316.

Cichowski, R. A. 2004. Women's rights, the European Court and supranational constitutionalism. *Law and Society Review*, 38: 489–512.

—— 2006. Introduction: courts, democracy, and governance. *Comparative Political Studies*, 39: 3–21.

Conant, L. 2002. *Justice Contained: Law and Politics in the European Union.* Ithaca, NY: Cornell University Press.

COOPER, P. J. 1988. *Hard Judicial Choices: Federal District Court Judges and State and Local Officials*. New York: Oxford University Press.

DOBBIN, F., and SUTTON, F. R. 1998. The strength of a weak state: the rights revolution and the rise of human resources management divisions. *American Journal of Sociology*, 104: 441–76.

EDELMAN, L. B. 1990. Legal environments and organizational governance: the expansion of due process in the American workplace. *American Journal of Sociology*, 95: 1401–40.

—— 1992. Legal ambiguity and symbolic structures: organizational mediation of civil rights law. *American Journal of Sociology*, 97: 1531–76.

—— UGGEN, C., and ERLANGER, H. S. 1999. The endogeneity of legal regulation: grievance procedures and rational myth. *American Journal of Sociology*, 105: 406–55.

EPP, C. R. 1998. *The Rights Revolution: Lawyers, Activists, and Supreme Courts in Comparative Perspective*. Chicago: University of Chicago Press.

—— 2003. The judge over your shoulder: the complex evidence of European–American convergence. *Law and Social Inquiry*, 28: 743–70.

—— Forthcoming. The role of tort lawsuits in reconstructing the issue of police abuse in the United Kingdom. In *Fault Lines: Tort Law and Cultural Practice*, ed. M. McCann and D. M. Engel Stanford, Calif: Stanford University Press.

FEELEY, M. M. 1992. Hollow hopes, flypaper, and metaphors. *Law and Social Inquiry*, 17: 745.

—— and RUBIN, E. L. 1998. *Judicial Policy Making and the Modern State: How the Courts Reformed America's Prisons*. New York: Cambridge University Press.

FLEMMING, R. B., BOHTE, J., and WOOD, B. D. 1997. One voice among many: the Supreme Court's influence on attentiveness to issues in the United States, 1947–1992. *American Journal of Political Science*, 41: 1224–50.

FRYMER, P. 2007. *Black and Blue: African Americans, the Labor Movement, and the Decline of the Democratic Party*. Princeton, NJ: Princeton University Press.

GALANTER, M. 1974. Why the haves come out ahead: speculations on the limits of legal change. *Law and Society Review*, 9: 95–160.

GILLIOM, J. 2001. *Overseers of the Poor: Surveillance, Resistance, and the Limits of Privacy*. Chicago: University of Chicago Press.

HALTOM, W., and McCANN, M. 2004. *Distorting the Law: Politics, Media, and the Litigation Crisis*. Chicago: University of Chicago Press.

HANDLER, J. F., HOLLINGSWORTH, E. J., and ERLANGER, H. S. 1978. *Lawyers and the Pursuit of Legal Rights*. New York: Academic Press.

HARRIS, B. E. 2004. *Defending the Right to a Home: The Power of Anti-Poverty Lawyers*. Burlington, Vt.: Ashgate.

KAGAN, R. A. 2001. *Adversarial Legalism: The American Way of Law*. Cambridge, Mass.: Harvard University Press.

KELEMAN, R. D. 2006. Suing for Europe: adversarial legalism and European governance. *Comparative Political Studies*, 39: 101–27.

—— and SIBBITT, E. 2004. The globalization of American law. *International Organization*, 58: 103–36.

KILWEIN, J. C., and BRISBIN, JR., R. A. 1997. Policy convergence in the federal judicial system: the application of intensified scrutiny doctrines by state supreme courts. *American Journal of Political Science*, 41: 122–48.

KINGDON, J. 1984. *Agendas, Alternatives, and Public Policies*. Boston: Little, Brown.

LOBEL, J. 2003. *Success without Victory: Lost Legal Battles and the Long Road to Justice in America*. New York: New York University Press.

LOVELL, G. 2003. *Legislative Deferrals: Statutory Ambiguity, Judicial Power, and American Democracy*. New York: Cambridge University Press.

McCANN, M. W. 1992. Reform litigation on trial. *Law and Social Inquiry*, 17: 715–43.

—— 1994. *Rights at Work: Pay Equity Reform and the Politics of Legal Mobilization*. Chicago: University of Chicago Press.

—— 1996. Causal versus constitutive explanations (or, on the difficulty of being so positive . . .). *Law and Social Inquiry*, 21: 457–82.

McNOLLGAST. 1999. The political origins of the Administrative Procedure Act. *Journal of Law, Economics and Organization*, 15: 180–217.

MATHER, L. 1995 The fired football coach (or, how trial courts make policy). In *Contemplating Courts*, ed. L. Epstein. Washington, DC: Congressional Quarterly Press.

MELNICK, R. S. 1994. *Between the Lines: Interpreting Welfare Rights*. Washington, DC: Brookings Institution.

MILNER, N. A. 1971. *The Court and Local Law Enforcement: The Impact of Miranda*. Beverly Hills, Calif.: Sage.

MNOOKIN, R., and KORNHOUSER, L. 1979. Bargaining in the shadow of the law: the case of divorce. *Yale Law Journal*, 88: 950–97.

ORFIELD, JR., M. W. 1987. The exclusionary rule and deterrence: an empirical study of Chicago narcotics officers. *University of Chicago Law Review*, 54: 1016–69.

PARIS, M. 2001. Legal mobilization and the politics of reform: lessons from school finance litigation in Kentucky, 1984–1995. *Law and Social Inquiry*, 26: 631–84.

PEDRIANA, N., and STRYKER, R. 2004. The strength of a weak agency: enforcement of Title VII of the 1964 Civil Rights Act and the expansion of state capacity, 1965–1971. *American Journal of Sociology*, 110: 709–60.

PINELLO, D. R. 2006. *America's Struggle for Same-Sex Marriage*. New York: Cambridge University Press.

PRESSMAN, J. L., and WILDAVSKY, A. 1979. *Implementation: How Great Expectations in Washington are Dashed in Oakland, or, Why it's Amazing that Federal Programs Work at All*, 2nd edn. Berkeley: University of California Press.

REED, D. S. 2001. *On Equal Terms: The Constitutional Politics of Equal Educational Opportunity*. Princeton, NJ: Princeton University Press.

RINGQUIST, E. J. 1995. Political control and policy impact in EPA's Office of Water Quality. *American Journal of Political Science*, 39: 336–63.

ROSENBERG, G. N. 1991. *The Hollow Hope: Can Courts Bring About Social Change?* Chicago: University of Chicago Press.

—— 1992. Hollow hopes and other aspirations: a reply to Feeley and McCann. *Law and Social Inquiry*, 17: 761–78.

—— 1996. Positivism, interpretivism, and the study of law. *Law and Social Inquiry*, 21: 435–55.

SABATIER, P. A. 1975. Social movements and regulatory agencies: toward a more adequate— and less pessimistic—theory of "clientele capture." *Policy Sciences*, 6: 301–42.

—— 1986. Top-down and bottom-up approaches to implementation research: a critical analysis and suggested synthesis. *Journal of Public Policy*, 6: 21–48.

—— and JENKINS-SMITH, H. C. 1993. *Policy Change and Learning: An Advocacy Coalition Approach*. Boulder, Colo.: Westview.

SABATIER, P. A. 1999. The advocacy coalition framework: an assessment. In *Theories of the Policy Process*, ed. P. A. Sabatier. Boulder, Colo.: Westview.

SAGUY, A. C. 2003. *What is Sexual Harassment? From Capitol Hill to the Sorbonne.* Berkeley: University of California Press.

SCHEINGOLD, S. A. 1974. *The Politics of Rights: Lawyers, Public Policy, and Political Change.* New Haven, Conn.: Yale University Press.

SHAPIRO, M. 1981. *Courts: A Comparative and Political Analysis.* Chicago: University of Chicago Press.

SONGER, D. 1987. The impact of Supreme Court trends on economic policy-making in the United States Courts of Appeals. *Journal of Politics*, 49: 830–41.

—— SEGAL, J. A., and CAMERON, C. M. 1994. The hierarchy of justice: testing the principal–agent model of Supreme Court–circuit court interactions. *American Journal of Political Science*, 38: 673–96.

—— and SHEEHAN, R. 1990. Supreme Court impact on compliance and outcomes: *Miranda* and *New York Times* in the United States Courts of Appeals. *Western Political Quarterly*, 43: 297–319.

STONE SWEET, A. 2000. *Governing With Judges.* Oxford: Oxford University Press.

—— 2004. *The Judicial Construction of Europe.* Oxford: Oxford University Press.

TATE, C. N., and VALLINDER, T. 1995. *The Global Expansion of Judicial Power.* New York: New York University Press.

TRUE, J. L., BAUMGARTNER, F. R., and JONES, B. D. 1999. Punctuated-equilibrium theory: explaining stability and change in public policy making. In *Theories of the Policy Process*, ed. P. A. Sabatier. Boulder, Colo.: Westview.

WALKER, S. 1993. *Taming the System: The Control of Discretion in Criminal Justice, 1950–1990.* New York: Oxford University Press.

WASBY, S. L. 1976. *Small Town Police and the Supreme Court: Hearing the Word.* Lexington, Mass.: Lexington Books.

CHAPTER 35

CRIMINAL JUSTICE
AND THE POLICE

WESLEY G. SKOGAN

MAINTAINING order and bringing offenders to account are among the most important responsibilities of the state, and it is in the operation of the criminal justice system that authority in a democracy makes itself most clearly visible. This chapter focuses on three aspects of criminal justice: policing, criminal sentencing, and the politics of prisons. These are the best-developed bodies of research in the field, and they are subjects of lively and often divisive contemporary political debate. Research has focused on the causes and political consequences of variations in policing, sentencing, and prison policy. The chapter relies on the findings of many empirical studies, and they certainly could not all be cited here. Rather, each section notes examples of research that outline issues in the field and describes key concepts and approaches. I also refer to some of the methodological and data issues involved in the research. This review necessarily excludes areas of research, including studies of media coverage of crime and justice, and also gives a short shrift to the politics of drug policies, and the causes and consequences of yawning race and class disparities in who gets arrested, prosecuted, and imprisoned.

1 Policing

Police departments are among the most political of institutions in American cities. Unlike many nations, policing in the United States is extremely decentralized. The 17,000 or so police departments are locally controlled, funded, and staffed. What police do is highly visible and consequential, and subject to intense public and media scrutiny. Consequently, policing offers a venue for observing the impact of social, economic, and political factors on local governance (Skogan and Frydl 2004). Research on policing falls into two categories. The first examines the impact of politics writ broadly on neighborhood-by-neighborhood, city-to-city, and over-time variation in police personnel, policies, and practices. The second group focuses on the consequences of policing for communities and local politics.

Police are, after schools, the largest local budget item, so decisions about expenditures and staffing levels are significant. How much crime there is affects spending, but its effect is surprisingly small compared to other forces at work in determining law enforcement policy. *Who* gets hired is another issue, for jobs are one of the tangible spoils of political success. Politics also affects the adoption of programs such as community policing and the creation of organizational units, including specialists in sexual assault or domestic violence. In this way departments respond to demands that "something be done" about prominent problems and build legitimacy by showing their responsiveness to public concerns. Politics frames police behavior as well. It helps determine how communities monitor and respond to violence by police and allegations of police corruption. Most recently, police have found themselves embroiled in two of the most significant political divisions of our day, how to respond effectively to terrorism; and demands that they take a more aggressive role in controlling immigration.

A recurring theme in research is that police strength, crime control policies, and practices on the street are driven to an important degree by the fear of dominant racial groups and economic elites that their privileged position is under siege from "the dangerous classes." In this view, the state uses coercion as a means of protecting the current distribution of wealth and power against claims by have-nots for a larger slice of the pie. Empirically, there is a great deal of support for this view, especially when it comes to the presumed threat posed by burgeoning African-American populations at the city, county, and state level (Jacobs and Helms 1997). Net of other factors, jurisdictions hire more and spend more money on police as the size of the black population rises. This effect is blunted somewhat in places where African-Americans are sharply segregated, and variations in the size of the black population do not affect expenditures when the percentages are small and presumably less threatening. The strength of this "racial threat" also appears to have risen following the riots of the late 1960s and early 1970s. Evidence for the threat hypothesis is mixed over the rise of other racial minorities, especially outside the West and Southwest. In practice, measures of class inequality are linked to levels of crime, but have a much weaker relationship to many indicators of criminal justice policies and practices. A much smaller group of studies examining police misconduct (including the use of excessive and deadly force) found that police misconduct is more common in areas characterized by concentrated poverty and with large or growing minority populations.

There is also evidence that, where the have-less gain control, they seize the benefits they can, act to ameliorate the consequences of governance by crime control for their constituents, and focus on other uses of the public treasury. There is a "democratic" spin to the threat-of-the-dangerous-classes hypothesis in an often-replicated curvilinear effect of the size of minority populations on police expenditures and hiring. That is, when racial minorities constitute more than 50 percent of the population, there are signs of a downturn in investments in policing, presumably because the electorate has other priorities. Who the mayor is also makes a difference for big-city policies. Cities with African-American mayors and large black electorates hire more black police officers. Places with African-American mayors are also more likely to have external and civilian review procedures in place to hear complaints against their department. Police in those cities are also less likely to shoot people, and their officers are less likely to be shot, two very concrete policy outcomes (Jacobs and Carmichael 2002; Jacobs and O'Brien 1998). When it was first introduced—before becoming ubiquitous at least on paper—community policing was also more likely to be adopted in cities with significant African-American electorates.

There is a substantial but dated body of research on the distribution of police services at the neighborhood level *within* cities; much of it is reviewed in Skogan and Frydl (2004). Much of this research was conducted by political scientists interested in "who gets what" from government. They examined area-level variations in expenditures, the number of police officers assigned, response time (how quickly police get to the scene of calls), and the time police spend on patrol. The primary goals of this research were to examine the impact of politics on service distribution and to identify race and class bias in the distribution of service, after controlling for measures of service needs such as crime. But, in the main, they found relative equality in the distribution of policing, with crime primarily driving what police did and where they did it. There was sometimes a bit of a bias toward providing extra protection to the best-off and highest tax-paying neighborhoods, but especially in comparison to other services these studies tended to find that police were relatively insulated from political pressures and that police resource allocations are primarily need driven (Lee 1994). The consistency of this finding challenges group threat and elite dominance theories of law enforcement, for their effects should be strongest at the local level where threats are presumably manifested and the politics of city responses are actually played out.

There are few cross-city studies of the impact of more overtly political variables on policing, perhaps due to the paucity of systematic political data at the municipal level. Republican political strength at the state and national level is somewhat correlated with higher employment of police officers, but the money is raised and police hired at the municipal level, where the politics may be quite different. We would like to know about the strength of local interest groups (including police unions), the extent of competition between political factions (traditional parties are not the dividing point in many cities), the place of crime in local political debates, and the tolerance and fears of the electorate. What is available is the form of local government. Compared to cities operating under the reforms that began in the progressive era, "unreformed" cities (those with mayor–council governments, elected mayors, council districts, and partisan elections) spend more on policing (Stucky 2005). In a seminal book on police politics, Wilson (1968) linked policing "styles" to local political cultures. He reported that police in the unreformed cities he studied were more affected by group politics, compared to reformed cities where police tended to operate more bureaucratically. But when representative samples of cities are examined, the skimpy political data available at this level of government have not revealed strong effects of politics on police operations or organizational structure—only on employment. It should be no surprise that, regardless of other factors, the fiscal capacity of cities sets a definite upward bound on their enthusiasm for police hiring. Federal grant money boosted police hiring for a period during the 1990s, but the program was short-lived. And, as in all studies of governance in practice, this year's police budget almost always simply represents an incremental tweaking of last year's budget, so shifts across time in city spending on the police are usually fairly glacial and determined largely by changes in the cost of living (Maguire and Uchida 2000).

A second body of research examines the impact of the police on politics. The police create headaches for politicians on a too-frequent basis, because many of them arise from the unsupervised discretion inevitably exercised by individual officers. There are also formidable barriers to police reform. Charges of police corruption, racial profiling, and discrimination in the application of violence all resonate in city politics. There are frequent demands that review bodies be created to monitor police behavior, but this demand is very infrequently met. In many communities, police officers and their families and friends are a significant force in local elections and have friends in the state legislature as well. Their unions have definite ideas about the policies that should and should not be adopted regarding their members. Labor agreements can sharply curtail the supervisory and disciplinary authority of management. Calls to get tough on crime can overpower concern about police aggressiveness. Groups also take legal action against the policies and practices of police departments. Women have entered the profession in large numbers, for example, not because they were warmly welcomed, but because it was the only way for cities to get out from under a mountain of litigation. Research on these and other aspects of the rough-and-tumble world of police politics has been reported in a small collection of city case studies, most prominently by Scheingold (1984).

2 Courts, Judges, and Sentencing

There is a long tradition of research on the determinants of sentencing in criminal cases. Recent conceptual, statistical, and data developments have enabled researchers to address a wider and more overtly political range of issues associated with criminal sentencing, but the adoption of sentencing guidelines has tempered the significance of the findings.

A key conceptual breakthrough was the recognition that individual criminal defendants—the object of early research—are grouped into dockets of cases decided by a single judge, and that judges are themselves situated in courtroom contexts which are in turn organized by political jurisdiction. This hierarchical "nesting" of cases within judges within court settings within (typically) counties enables analysts to address in tandem a long list of political, legal, social, economic, and organizational issues, and relationships among them as well. Early sentencing studies treated individual defendants in isolation. Characteristics of each case typically were characterized as either "legally prescribed" or "legally proscribed," with research questioning the relative impact of legal and extralegal factors in determining sentencing severity. Not surprisingly, many variables on both lists proved influential. The seriousness of the offense (measured by weapon use, victim injury, and the like), the weight of the evidence against the defendant, and prior record were independently linked to sentencing severity. But so, too, were defendants' race, class, age, gender, and demeanor in the courtroom. Likewise, whether they were in pre-trial detention, if they had a private attorney or a public defender, and if they insisted on going to trial rather than accepting a plea bargain counted as well. The documented importance of many variables on the legally proscribed list was taken as evidence of the unfairness of the criminal process (Nardulli, Eisenstein, and Flemming 1988). Research fueled discussion of strategies to reduce sentencing disparities and to link the outcomes for individual defendants more closely to what they did, rather than who they are.

With time, sentencing studies incorporated other explanatory variables. Measures of the background and experience of judges that could represent their predispositions toward crime and defendants were added to the extralegal list. For example, it made a difference if judges had been prosecutors or public defenders before ascending to the bench. Their age and years of experience as a judge affected sentences as well, these two factors predicting greater leniency. The race and gender of judges were obvious focal points, but except in a few jurisdictions, there simply was not enough *variance* in either to include them in statistical models. One statewide study conducted in the 1980s reported that no minority judge had decided a criminal case (Myers and Talarico 1987). More recent studies enjoy greater diversity in judicial gender, and women judges appear to be somewhat more lenient. But the racial composition of the bench has not changed much overall, and judging is still an overwhelmingly white and male profession. Courts in which there are enough African-American judges to allow race to enter the equation—Detroit was the first well studied—are also obviously operating in a different political and social environment than the judicial mainstream. It appears that African-American judges sentence more leniently, especially when facing black defendants, but political constituency variables are confounded with judicial factors when it comes to race because African-American judges are found in significant numbers only in cities with large minority electorates

There is evidence that constituency racial composition and poverty affect racial disparities in sentencing within courts, with African-American defendants coming off better where they are amply represented in the electorate. At the same time, sentences are stiffer in places with high rates of violent crime and in counties with a tradition of voting for conservative political candidates. There is also evidence that criminal sentencing broadly reflects public opinion and the standards of communities from which judges, prosecutors, and jurors come. Changes in political climate are reflected in subsequent shifts in sentencing patterns, and studies have demonstrated a link between public preferences revealed by referendum voting and local sentencing patterns (Helms and Jacobs 2002). But constituency effects may be confounded by variations in judicial selection and retention procedures. Some of the ways Americans select state judges give the organized bar and the interests they represent more influence; others offer more entry points for groups defined by race and class. A painfully small number of case studies *suggest* that partisan elections produce judges who come from the hurly-burly of political life rather than quiet law offices. As a result, they are less harsh and legalistic in their sentencing and more ready to identify with the "underdog" when other things are equal. However, because most sentencing studies have been conducted in one state and most states have uniform selection procedures, we have no good systematic, comparative studies of the impact of how judges are selected on their sentencing behavior. The best remains Levin's (1977) comparison of Minneapolis and Pittsburgh. He contrasted the politics and decisions of a nonpartisan, business-oriented court with that for an ethnic immigrant, machine-politics town, and found that judges in Pittsburgh gave more lenient and individually tailored criminal sentences.

Over time, sentencing studies also began to examine more outcomes, differentiating between convicting or releasing a defendant, sentencing them to jail versus putting them on probation, and sending them "upstate" to prison versus imposing a spell of jail time. These "in–out" decisions differ somewhat from length of sentence; for example, race matters more when it comes to whether defendants are sent to prison. There is no research on this issue, but the widespread adoption of "alternative sanctions" since the early 1990s has probably increased the race and class correlates of court dispositions, because there is more variance in what can happen to people. Defendants can be sent to boot camps rather than jail, drunk drivers sometimes serve their sentence only on weekends, and probation comes with varying standards for drug testing and supervision. In many jurisdictions, offenders may be sentenced to home detention, with or without work release privileges, and monitored by electronic arrangements of differing cost and effectiveness (Petersilia 1997). In addition, prisons vary famously in stringency and the physical risks associated with confinement, and defendants' attorneys jockey for favorable assignments. I suspect research will reveal that class and race play a large role in determining "who goes where" in the increasingly varied universe of corrections.

Recognition that a substantial fraction of arrestees do not receive a prison or jail sentence in the first place brought into question the findings of studies focusing on sentence length. The "selection bias" inherent in ignoring "non-sentenced" defendants is huge. For example, the apparent impact of legally prescribed variables like "strength of the evidence" is severely underestimated when the weakest cases are (properly) dismissed short of sentencing. As a result of screening decisions we *should* find relatively weak effects of many "legally relevant" case factors, as they have already been taken into account. In response, sentencing studies began to adopt "two-step" statistical models that first ascertain the factors determining the outcome of the "in–out" decision, and then assess impact of those and other variables on sentence severity, doing so in a way that properly represents the characteristics of defendants who did not receive a sentence (Peterson and Hagan 1984). This way of thinking also awoke students of sentencing to a larger array of issues. One was that an earlier filtering mechanism—charging decisions by prosecutors—selectively disposes of a very large proportion of cases short of going to court. Flowcharts of the criminal justice system typically depict large outflows at the felony review stage, when clerks, part-time law school students, and even undergraduate interns examine piles of files to determine who will be held on a felony charge, diverted to a misdemeanor court, or have their case dismissed based on legal or factual issues apparent even to these reviewers. There is no reason to assume that this low-visibility, highly discretionary, virtually unreviewable process is immune to legally proscribed influences either. The effects of this screening are shared by all of the judges in a jurisdiction, so organizing cases into yet another "nest" is clearly called for. It is very rare, however, for sentencing studies to incorporate prosecutors' decisions. Even case studies of prosecutors' offices are few in number, yet it is clear that they have to be incorporated into sentencing research.

So, sentences are now seen as nested within "in–out" decisions, cases share judges, and judges operate within organizations that determine their work flow and set rules and informal norms about how they are to proceed with their business. Courtroom workgroups develop "going rates" for the cases they routinely handle, adding informal uniformity to sentencing at that level. Research finds that judges who have to manage a large volume of cases sentence more leniently. Beyond the courtroom walls lie a further set of constraints. These include the political mechanisms that select judges of differing backgrounds and predispositions. There is also the impact of political and economic factors that determine how much policy-makers are willing to invest in jails and prisons, and the range of alternative sanctions judges have at hand.

However, the clustering of cases by judges, then courts and political jurisdictions imposes difficult data requirements on sentencing studies, and raises statistical issues. Sentencing studies require large samples of individual criminal cases that include information on both legal and extralegal factors, identify the judges who decided them so biographical data can be appended to the analysis, and span multiple jurisdictions to ensure sufficient variance in measures of organizational and political settings. We would also like to add a temporal dimension to these studies, for example to see if the significance of race has been declining, but then we are asking for more than is available. One place to look for data is in state and federal databases developed to monitor compliance with sentencing guidelines (see below). The statistical issues to be addressed revolve around the nonindependence of all of these data elements. Earlier studies organized all of the data by defendant, treating each as a distinct unit characterized by personal, legal, and judicial variables. However, multiple regression depends on the independence of cases from one another, and the links between cases described here defy that assumption. Some may regard this as a minor point, but nonindependence overstates the significance of clustering factors, such as judges' background. Instead, researchers must use statistical techniques that account for multiple layers of relatedness across cases. Techniques for doing so are now well developed, including those that will handle the additional step of adjusting for "in–out" decisions as well (for an example incorporating both data and statistical advances see Johnson 2006).

The final development in this field is perhaps the most significant: judges no longer have much freedom in sentencing. Through the imposition of sentencing guidelines, legislatures in every state and the federal system have acted to hem in the discretionary power of judges. Some states have adopted a "presumptive sentence" for each offense type; others a grid enabling judges (or even their clerks) to trace through offense characteristics to a required sentence. Now the dependent variable in sentencing studies is essentially the extent to which outcomes deviate or not (and most do not) from the prescribed sentence. There is still some variation to be explained; every state empowers judges to make upward or downward departures from the prescribed sentences, but only under limited circumstances. In a study of Pennsylvania courts, Johnson (2006) found judges departed 17 percent of the time, "up" and "down" from the presumptive sentence in almost equal numbers. The extent to which legislatures succeeded in imposing uniformity and reducing the impact of nonprescribed factors in sentencing is variable (Spohn 2000). Some things have not changed. One is the penalty exacted for demanding a trial. In Pennsylvania, there were more downward departures for those who pled guilty, and women and whites also continued to do better than their counterparts (Kramer and Ulmer 2002). However, as a result of this political intervention, it is very difficult to generalize from the findings of past sentencing studies to the new, post-guideline world. Many of the important decisions affecting the criminal process have shifted to the legislative arena.

3 LEGISLATURES AND PRISONS

For the past twenty years, prisons and jails have been a "growth industry" in the United States. Between the early 1980s and 2003, the incarceration rate (which controls for the nation's increasing population) grew by 325 percent; growth then slowed a bit through 2005. By then, even controlling for crime, the nation's prison rate far exceeds those of other Western nations. In 2005 almost 2.2 million people were in prison or jail primarily because of new sentencing policies and the willingness of legislators (after some resistance) to spend what it took to incarcerate this many. Rising crime rates played a significant but secondary role in driving this increase before 1991—incarceration rates were higher and grew faster in states with high levels of violent crime (Greenberg and West 2001). Then a precipitous drop in crime contributed to slowing prison growth, but the number of prisoners continued to climb for another decade.

The engine driving the growing incarceration rate over this whole period was changes in sentencing policies. One goal of reformers was to make sentences more predictable. Beginning in the 1980s, many changes were made in state criminal codes to increase the predictability of time served. This included instituting "determinate sentences" that specified exact sentence lengths, rather than sentencing ranges (such as "two to five years") that the judge could use as a guideline. Along with determinant sentencing came the abolition of parole, so there would be no hope of getting out early. Some states also eliminated sentence reductions for good behavior while in prison. All of this became known as "truth in sentencing." Because states were required to adopt packages of sentencing reforms that resulted in more predictable sentences in order to qualify for federal prison construction funds, they all moved in this direction to some degree. Sentencing reformers also took on judges and prosecutors, in an attempt to keep them from awarding light sentences for serious crimes in exchange for guilty pleas. Legislatures imposed sentences that were made mandatory for specific crimes, such as those involving guns or drugs. On top of all of these changes, *longer* sentences were required under many circumstances. Repeat offenders—those with "three strikes" against them— found themselves facing very long, often lifelong, prison stays. Over time, the mandatory minimums imposed in gun and drug cases grew much longer. By the early 1990s, these policies had been consolidated and turned into ironclad formulas for the states, in the form of the sentencing guidelines described earlier (for a review, see Tonry 1996).

The reforms had their intended effect. Overall, new prisoners were tagged with longer sentences, there was a big drop in "early" releases, and average time served went up. As quickly became apparent, this vast social experiment also turned out to be very expensive. In particular, unending rounds of new prison construction soaked up state budget dollars. Many states first attempted to deal with growing inmate populations by crowding them into existing facilities. Public interest lawyers intervened, however, and federal judges were frequently appalled by the conditions of confinement that were revealed in their courtrooms. The Eighth Amendment to the Constitution, which forbids "cruel and unusual punishment," was frequently evoked in reaction to evidence of crowded, unsanitary, and dangerous living conditions in prisons. By 1992, eleven states, and individual prisons in another twenty-six, were run by the courts. In that year, thirty-seven states had more prisoners than the capacity of their prisons, and in total they needed to add more than 1,100 new beds *every week* to handle new admissions (Skogan 1995).

Research on the adoption of these policies and resulting trends in incarceration rates and spending on corrections has focused on the influence of partisan politics and of societal divisions (such as race) that have political consequences. The influential political variables include party control of legislatures and governors' mansions and the extent to which state politics is competitive. The two interact, for it appears that politicians on the right "play the crime card" more often when seats are hotly contested. Prison admissions rise in response to Republican control of state legislatures, and when "tough on crime" governors are in charge. These effects become stronger when there are large numbers of competitive legislative seats; competition combined with Republican control results in even higher incarceration rates. Further, the effect of Republican control has grown over time, as the parties have realigned themselves around race. What used to be captured in statistical models as a "Southern" regional effect on policy now is associated with the rise of Republican control of state houses (Stucky et al. 2005).

There is also a body of research on the "disciplinary" role imposed by prisons and jails on the "dangerous classes." As in the case of police strength, the presumption is that the exercise of social discipline is a more urgent matter for social and economic elites where and when racially and economically disadvantaged populations threaten their comfortable position. The size of the economically threatening population is typically measured by unemployment and poverty rates, and the extent of the tension between elites and the underclass by indicators of economic inequality. "Race threats" are indexed by the relative size of African-American and Hispanic populations. These measures are included in virtually every study of trends in incarceration. The findings are decidedly mixed, with some statistical models finding support for the threat hypothesis and others rejecting it (Greenberg and West 2001). There is some evidence that the rounds of riots the nation experienced in the 1960s and 1970s further boosted spending on corrections. Riot-related expansion of prisons would constitute an important test of the threat hypothesis, and it needs more careful exploration in case studies and aggregate arrest, sentencing, and incarceration studies.

Prisons in turn have an impact on politics. The mounting number of prisoners and ex-prisoners in American society has pushed the issue of "felon disenfranchise-ment" onto the political agenda. Large numbers of Americans are denied the right to vote by their states because of their status as convicted felons. This phenomenon is especially concentrated in the South, where some states disenfranchise as many as one in four African-American males. A recent study reports that, by selectively reducing the number of eligible voters, felon disenfranchisement probably decided the outcome of the 2000 presidential election, and over time, has provided the margin of victory in several Senate elections (Manza and Uggen 2006).

The statistical findings of research on incarceration trends are complicated by the presumably reciprocal relationship between prisons and crime. If prisons have a deterrent, crime reduction effect—which doubtless they do—it is difficult to isolate the extent to which changes in crime drive changes in the size of the prison popula-tion, when compared to the effects of other political and social factors. It also greatly complicates answering the important question: Has this investment in prisons paid off in the form of lower crime rates? In principle, incarceration affects crime through incapacitation (people in prison cannot commit free-world crimes), individual deterrence (successfully "scaring straight" those who have been to prison), and general deterrence (threatening nonoffenders sufficiently to keep them from getting into trouble in the first place). Given the size of America's investment in prisons, there may be no more important criminal justice policy question than the magnitude and cost-effectiveness of the deterrent effect of incarceration. Researchers have struggled with the issue, but there is no clear empirical consensus.

REFERENCES

GREENBERG, D., and WEST, V. 2001. State prison populations and their growth, 1971–1991. *Criminology*, 39: 615–53.

HELMS, R., and JACOBS, D. 2002. The political context of sentencing: an analysis of community and individual determinants. *Social Forces*, 81: 577–604.

JACOBS, D., and CARMICHAEL, J. T. 2002. Subordination and violence against state control agents: testing political explanations for lethal assaults against the police. *Social Forces*, 80: 1223–51.

—— and HELMS, R. E. 1997. Testing coercive explanations for order: the determinants of law enforcement strength over time. *Social Forces*, 75: 1361–92.

—— and O'BRIEN, R. M. 1998. The determinants of deadly force: a structural analysis of police violence. *American Journal of Sociology*, 103: 837–62.

JOHNSON, B. D. 2006. The multilevel context of criminal sentencing: integrating judge- and county-level influences. *Criminology*, 44: 259–98.

KRAMER, J. H., and ULMER, J. T. 2002. Downward departures for serious violent offenders: local court "corrections" to Pennsylvania's sentencing guidelines. *Criminology*, 40: 897–932.

LEE, S. J. 1994. Policy types, bureaucracy and urban policies: integrating models of urban service delivery. *Policy Studies Journal*, 22: 87–108.

LEVIN, M. 1977. *Urban Politics and the Criminal Courts*. Chicago: University of Chicago Press.

MAGUIRE, E. R., and UCHIDA, C. D. 2000. Measurement and explanation in the comparative study of American police organizations. Pp. 491–557 in *Criminal justice 2000*, vol. 4. Washington, DC: Office of Justice Programs, U. S. Department of Justice.

MANZA, J., and UGGEN, C. 2006. *Locked Out: Felon Disenfranchisement and American Democracy*. New York: Oxford University press.

MYERS, M. A., and TALARICO, S. 1987. *The Social Contexts of Criminal Sentencing*. New York: Springer-Verlag.

NARDULLI, P. F., EISENSTEIN, J., and FLEMMING, R. B. 1988. *The Tenor of Justice: Criminal Courts and the Guilty Plea Process*. Urbana: University of Illinois Press.

PETERSILIA, J. 1997. *Community Corrections: Probation, Parole, and Intermediate Sanctions*. New York: Oxford University Press.

PETERSON, R. D., and HAGAN, J. 1984. Changing conceptions of race: towards an account of anomalous findings of sentencing research. *American Sociological Review*, 49: 56–70.

SCHEINGOLD, S. 1984. *The Politics of Law and Order: Street Crime and Public Policy*. New York: Longman.

SKOGAN, W. G. 1995. Crime and the American states. Pp. 378–410 in *Politics in the American States*, ed. V. Gray, H. Jacob, and R. Albritton. Boston: Scott, Foresman/Little, Brown.

—— and FRYDL, K. 2004. *Fairness and Effectiveness in Policing: The Evidence*. Washington, DC: National Academies Press.

SPOHN, C. 2000. Thirty years of sentencing reform: the quest for a racially neutral sentencing process. Pp. 427–501 in *Criminal Justice 2000*, vol. 3. Washington, DC: National Institute of Justice.

STUCKY, T. D. 2005 Local politics and police strength. *Justice Quarterly*, 22: 139–69.

—— HEIMER, K., and LANG, J. B. 2005. Partisan politics, electoral competition and imprisonment: an analysis of states over time. *Criminology*, 43: 211–48.

TONRY, M. 1996. *Sentencing Matters*. New York: Oxford University Press.

WILSON, J. Q. 1968. *Varieties of Police Behavior*. Cambridge, Mass.: Harvard University Press.

CHAPTER 36

LAW AND POLITICAL IDEOLOGIES

JULIE NOVKOV

OTHER chapters in this volume explore the influences on the development of law and legal doctrine and how both ordinary politics and institutional environments can influence the substantive development of law on the ground. Recent scholarship, primarily in political science but in other disciplines as well, has brought ideas in as important factors in shaping the evolution of law. Few scholars would argue that law is purely a reflection of a dominant ideology. Nonetheless, studying how ideas find their way into legal institutions and how legal institutions shape ideas can give more substance to an analysis of the dynamics of interpretation. These dynamics cannot be completely explained if one focuses solely on the internal and doctrinal world of the court or on the political forces that shape judicial appointments, and recent work in political science has illuminated ideas as potent intervening influences (Kahn and Kersch 2006b).

This process is easiest to see with respect to ideologies in ascendancy in U.S. political culture. Liberalism has obviously been a major influence, and many scholars of contemporary law as well as legal history have traced its relationship to US law, a topic of analysis that goes back fairly far in the literature (see e.g. Smith 1985; Kluger 1976). As political science emerged in a disciplinary form in the early twentieth century, considerations of law and constitutionalism were a dominant strand, and this literature largely addressed the relationship between democracy and constitutionalism in legal and ideological terms. This mode of consideration fell in abeyance after the rise of behaviorism in political science, and in the 1970s the study of law by political scientists shifted toward modeling judicial behavior in the appellate courts.

More focused examination of ideologies, however, is emerging in contemporary scholarship and is promoting better understandings of how ideas that may not map perfectly within liberalism or that challenge some conceptions of liberalism nonetheless play significant roles in legal development. Analyses that take ideology seriously have traced the ideological influences on law and legal thinking and have considered legal influences on ideologies and their evolution. The element that most, if not all, of these analyses have in common is that they understand the relationship between law and ideology as an important factor in development and change. Many contemporary political scientists who take the role of ideas seriously look not only to the direct relationship between ideology and legal outcomes, but also to how legal institutions provide conduits for the translation of ideology into law and the reflection of legal discourse in ideological debates. The attention to the role of legal institutions differentiates these approaches from the earlier, more strictly doctrinally-focused discussions and breaks down the artificial separation between an ideological world outside the courthouse doors and a strictly doctri-nal—or purely political—world at the bench (see e.g. Kahn and Kersch 2006b).

This chapter will summarize some of the arguments about ideological influences on law, some arguments about the influence of law on ideology, and then reflect upon the value added by incorporating an understanding of ideology in refining doctrinal and political stories of legal change. Recognizing the role of ideology facilitates a clearer analysis of how doctrinal developments take place within political contexts and how the law interfaces with culture and values. A final speculative question is whether the courts are more porous to ideas at some historical moments than others. This chapter will sketch an argument that this question misframes the process of courts' grappling with ideas. Instead, ideas become more visible when they are in conflict in legal circles, leading to their greater salience at those moments, but ideas always intervene in legal development even when major and visible ideological clashes are not occurring in the courts.

What are some significant historical examples of ideological influence upon law and legal thinking? Two examples will be addressed here, though the reader could likely think of other candidates. In the early twentieth century, the ideological underpinnings of the emerging state had significant implications for the develop-ment of law establishing freedom of contract. In the same time frame, racial ascriptivism strongly influenced the expression of law and constitutionalism in the southern United States and shaped the relationship between the national government and the states. For both of these examples, recent work has done much to illuminate the relationship between law and ideas in the historical process of constitutional and legal change.

Before considering these examples, a brief discussion of law and ideology may be helpful to situate them. Recent scholarship on law incorporating the tools of political development has helped, in Ronald Kahn's and Kenneth Kersch's terminology, to break down the division between internal and external models of judicial decision-making (Kahn and Kersch 2006b, 16–21). Internal models that view decision-making as driven by interpretive methodology (i.e. originalism, strict construction, structuralism, and the like) cannot account for how political pressures and events outside the courthouse door influence decisions. At the same time, the purely behavioral models embraced by some political scientists rely upon placing judges according to their political standpoints along a conservative–liberal continuum and coding judicial decisions along this continuum. Such models also have a blind spot—they fail to address how the institutional dynamics and historical practices of the courts provide constraints upon both the framing and at times the outcomes of judicial decisions.

Considering ideology as a factor provides one way of bridging the gap between the internal and external world of the court (or alternatively demonstrating that the gap is not terribly meaningful). Ideological standpoints can influence judicial selection in the federal courts, but ideology can also contribute to the institutional setting of legal decision-making. Ideology provides a background set of frames and perhaps contests through which legal challenges emerge. In some instances, litigation arises as a means of promoting or challenging a particular ideology, creating a direct link between political actors and the supposedly nonpolitical institution of the courts. In other instances, ideology shapes the way courts make decisions, providing boundaries or frameworks within which decisions are made. Finally, the language of judicial decisions themselves can generate ideological change. Ideologies thus interact with judicial decision-making both through litigants' and attorneys' reliance upon them as motivating or framing legal actions as well as through judicial commitments to particular ideologies.

The claim that ideology finds a place in judicial decision-making is different from a claim that judging is inherently partisan. As the historical examples will demonstrate, rather than simply dictating outcomes in cases, the incorporation of ideology into judicial decisions affects the framing of legal ideas in judicial opinions. The role of ideas is thus subtler but has the potential for a longer-term impact if particular ideas or framings become institutionalized through their adoption as precedent. As Howard Gillman has observed, "legal principles and judicial opinions are ideological constructs in the sense that their function is to defend specific structures, processes, and practices by suggesting that they are good, natural, traditional, in the general interest, or a matter of common sense" (Gillman 1993, 16). The institutionally-based "stickiness" of ideologically derived doctrinal framings can render them resistant to change, even in times when significant changes in the partisan spectrum have occurred (see e.g. Kahn and Kersch 2006a). Thus, shifts in legal decision-making that at first glance seem like dramatic reversals or changes upon examination often rest upon a longer term process of reworking the ideological underpinnings of the policy or principle in question.

1 Contract Rights: Untangling the Role of Competing Ideologies

The era of strong contract rights in the early twentieth century in the United States illustrates this point, because it is often understood as a moment when judges simply ruled in favor of their political connections to conservative and propertied business interests. However, recent scholarship argues that early twentieth-century contract theory was itself ideologically based and rulings traced out a clear path rooted in these ideas. Further, progressive efforts to support legislation protecting workers exploited gendered ideologies underlying court doctrine on both the state and federal level.

For years, the dominant narrative about judicial decision-making in the early twentieth century presented economic ideology as a causal mechanism. Commentators beginning with Supreme Court Justice Oliver Wendell Holmes attributed many of the federal courts' rulings to an embrace and implementation of laissez-faire economic principles. This interpretation reads ideology as an external factor in judicial decision-making consciously introduced by "activist" judges seeking to promote political agendas from the bench.

Recent work in political science, however, emphasizes the historical and institutional developments that shaped the jurisprudence of the early twentieth century. Analysts who read judicial opinions and lines of precedent as ideological constructs perceive the role of ideology as an integrated factor of legal development rather than an external force exerted upon the law or brought into it through the illegitimate action of judges. Ideology shapes and responds to the ways that decisions are framed, not just in influencing outcomes, but in influencing the way these outcomes are reached and in establishing boundaries within which decisions occur. Untangling the ideological commitments within the law reveals the sources of doctrinal development and maps the contours of legal debate at crucial moments in history. Ideology is a prominent factor in determining what kinds of outcomes are possible at particular moments, and ideological struggle can provide opportunities for shifting the boundaries within which both outcomes and doctrine are produced. Such analyses require close readings of the judicial opinions in leading cases rather than simply considering the outcomes.

In the late nineteenth century, a legal ideology of state neutrality shaped the parameters of the debate over the fate of protective legislation and the general development of police powers jurisprudence (Gillman 1993). This Jacksonian-era ideology arose judicially, supporting market liberties and suppressing factionalism. The base was a concept of public purpose that legitimated general laws affecting all (white, male, and adult) citizens equally while questioning legislation that differentiated among citizens without articulating a general public interest (Gillman 1993, 54). After the Civil War, the passage of the Reconstruction Amendments, and the emergence of large-scale industrialization, this ideology of limits on the state's police powers clashed with a growing regulatory impulse at both the state and federal levels.

As the courts began to consider protective measures, they relied upon the ideological distinctions developed in the doctrine of the earlier era. The category of class legislation presented an ideological rather than a partisan or simply corporatist barrier to protective measures intended to ameliorate the worst effects of large-scale capitalism for workers (Gillman 1993, 75–81). As the twentieth century began, the established constitutional ideology increasingly inclined commentators and judges to frame efforts to regulate industrialization as illegitimate attempts to leverage class interests into factionalized public policy, even as others sought to justify the new regulations in terms that were consistent with established ideological categories. The rise of realism as filtered through existing constitutional ideology led to close considerations of the concrete relationship of regulation to the health, safety, or morality of the general public (Gillman 1993, 100–5).

This constitutional ideology stymied activists promoting protective legislation, and some turned to an alternative ideology—beliefs about the appropriate relationship between women and the state. Maternalism, the concept of women's crucial public duty to the state as the bearers and rearers of the next generation, emerged from antebellum threads of republican motherhood to gain prominence among postbellum advocates for more engagement between the state and women (Skocpol 1992). The Court endorsed the notion of women's special status by rejecting efforts to extend women's capacity for full citizenship under the Fourteenth Amendment in *Minor v. Happersett* (Siegel 2002). The reinforcement of this status in constitutional terms allowed for the manipulation of the constitutional ideology of state neutrality to allow for regulation of the terms and conditions of women's labor. As maternalism made significant social and political headway, the specific constitutionalization of the public need to protect women shaped both the political and social iterations of women's protection and constitutional doctrine itself (Novkov 2001). The Supreme Court's rulings in *Lochner v. New York* and *Muller v. Oregon* demonstrate the constitutional ideologies of cabining police power and protecting women at their heights.

Lochner is best known for its outcome—invalidating a sixty-hour per week limit on bakers' labor—and for Holmes' accusation that the Court was judicially (and illegitimately) performing the legislative act of enforcing Herbert Spencer's *Social Statics* as public policy. The case, however, perfectly represented the constitutional ideology of state neutrality as it existed in 1905. The majority opinion framed the core question of the case as whether the regulation posed "an unreasonable, unnecessary and arbitrary interference with the right of the individual ... to enter into those contracts in relation to labor which may seem to him appropriate or necessary for the support of himself and his family?" (*Lochner v. New York*, 198 U.S. 45, 56 (1905)). Determining the reasonableness of the exercise of police power rested upon the carefully constructed category of public interest, which presumed that class legislation was a threat to the health of the republic.

Muller reflected the intervention of gender into this ideology and linked constitutional conceptions of women's citizenship to constitutional understandings of the laborer's relationship to the state. This ruling, coming three years after *Lochner*, validated the state courts' consensus that protective limits on women's labor were constitutionally legitimate. The Court distinguished Oregon's law limiting female laundry workers to ten hours of labor per day from *Lochner* on the basis of women's physical, psychological, and social differences from men and the public significance of these differences. The Court relied primarily upon their roles as the bearers and raisers of the next generation, which infused their lives with inherent public significance that permitted supervision and protection by the state (*Muller v. Oregon*, 208 U.S. 412, 422 (1908)).

The Court's use of these constitutional ideologies, modeled after their embrace by state and lower federal courts, unintentionally set the agenda for those who wished to see the courts uphold for all workers the same sorts of protections they permitted for women. Legislators and advocates used the category of health, safety, and morality to justify protection, and the courts increasingly had to distinguish between laws that served the public interest and laws that provided illegitimate advantage to a particular class within society. Many reformers sought ultimately to destroy this distinction, or at least to shrink the judiciary's willingness to read laws as class legislation (Gillman 1993; Novkov 2001). But the courts ultimately had to develop an alternative constitutional ideology to address increasing industrial pressures and support for more regulatory authority on the part of the state, an ideological reconstruction that played out across a range of doctrinal areas (see e.g. Kersch 2004).

The flashpoint for this conflict and ultimate reformulation was the struggle over minimum wage laws (Lipschultz 1996; Novkov 2001; Gillman 1993). Promoters of minimum wages pursued two strategies: First, they challenged the neutrality and inherent liberty of the labor market and argued that minimum wages served the public's interest because they prevented social dependency; and second, as the federal courts became increasingly hostile, they pursued women's minimum wages. Ultimately, focus on women's particular dependency—already well established as constitutional ideology—provided the means to crush the dominant police powers paradigm.

The battle over minimum wages ignited after the Supreme Court's apparent softening in allowing limits on hours of labor to stand in *Bunting v. Oregon* in 1917. Advocates had relied upon the conjunction of a more favorable balance toward regulatory authority with gendered arguments in favor of bolstering women's weaker bargaining power with a state-based backstop to support a minimum wage for women. They were bitterly disappointed when the Court ruled in *Adkins v. Children's Hospital* in 1923 that the minimum wage interfered with women's bargaining power and constituted unwarranted class legislation. Public outcry against the ruling revealed strong opposition to the Court's continued limits on police powers, and academic and legal commentators called for change in light of the new industrialized economy (Lipschultz 1996). Finally, in 1937 in *West Coast Hotel v. Parrish*, the U.S. Supreme Court embraced a new constitutional understanding of the state's regulatory authority that decentered questions about class legislation and the proper balance between police power and public interest. The first seed of the new equal protection regime was planted in *Carolene Products'* fourth footnote only a year after the ruling in *West Coast Hotel*. Gender would no longer play a pivotal role in building inroads into the dominant constitutional ideology, and thus elite policy debates over women's capacity to operate as full autonomous citizens diminished sharply.

This example illustrates the interplay between ideology and doctrinal change. The antebellum ideology of class legislation rendered the struggle to regulate working conditions in the postbellum years significantly more difficult, as advocates had to seek ways of reworking the doctrinally embedded ideology of state neutrality to accommodate state intervention. Initially, varied attempts to crack state neutrality had limited success; primarily through the mobilization of maternalist ideology, doctrinal exceptions could be generated. Ultimately, the negotiations over competing ideological frameworks generated space within which major transformations could occur, leading to the abandonment of maternalism as a primary strategy for supporting state-based protection of laborers. Attending to the role of ideology provides a deeper understanding of why the Court produced the doctrinal principles of the *Lochner* era, how the Court abandoned class legislation and substantive due process, how the ground was cleared for modern equal protection and due process review, and why this process was contentious and time-consuming.

2 RACIAL ASCRIPTIVISM: INTERWEAVING IDEOLOGY AND DOCTRINAL DEVELOPMENT

One can also see the operation of ideology in the rise and institutionalization of white supremacy in the late nineteenth and early twentieth centuries. Again, it would be tempting to assume that this process was driven by the straightforward importation of racial ideology into the law, and that judicial decisions thus simply reflected the predominant racial hostility prevalent among white elites (see e.g. Spann 1993). Such a reading, however, would substantially overlook the courts' role in producing, legitimating, and transforming racial ideology, as well as the significance of the federal courts' ceding significant authority over race and race relations to the states.[1]

Racial ideology was thoroughly institutionalized and permeated both state and federal law at the time of the Civil War. The war, emancipation, and the process of re-creating the nation disembedded the structure of racialized constitutional ideology. Political and constitutional actors built and institutionalized the ideology of white supremacy as a substitute foundation for a state that remained committed to dualist citizenship. As Wayne Moore and Pamela Brandwein have argued, the Fourteenth Amendment and its early interpretations were critical in this process, but the Court had to choose among radically different and contingent alternative paths (Brandwein 2006; Moore 2006). During the years between 1866 and 1896, the federal and state courts worked through the potentially radical transformations grounded in the outcome of the war and the new amendments. As they did so, they participated in the construction of white supremacy as a political ideology, though they were but one institutional player in this process. Focusing on ideology, however, reveals that we should not read the final outcome backward, seeing the courts as participating in a process in which the desired conclusion was known in the 1870s and 1880s as the critical battles were being fought.

As the Waite Court, its more racially retrograde successor, and the state high courts confronted the institutional, political, and legal legacy of war and reconstruction, they traced a path that ended with *Plessy v. Ferguson*'s broad endorsement of the early twentieth-century principles that the states should be left to manage social relations among racial groups and that constitutional equality required only equality at the level of prescribed statutory outcomes or formal parity for narrowly defined political rights for African-Americans. The federal courts initiated this process with the Supreme Court's ruling in *Slaughter-House* against a broad reading of the Thirteenth and Fourteenth Amendments that nonetheless noted in dicta the amendments' primary purpose of ameliorating the political and social conditions of inequality for African-Americans (*Slaughter-House Cases*, 83 U.S. 36 (1873)). More surprising was the Alabama Supreme Court's 1872 ruling in *Burns v. State*, that the state's newly passed criminal ban on interracial

---

[1] Scholars disagree as to whether ascriptive hierarchies are a necessary and integrated element of liberal ideology or are themselves an independent and competing tradition within U.S. politics (see e.g. Michael Rogin 1988; and Rogers Smith 1985; 1997). For the purposes of this illustration of the relationship between law and ideology, this debate is beside the point, although scholars who see the traditions as separate and competing would analyze the law's struggle with ascriptive hierarchy somewhat differently than those who see liberal legalism as a crucial facilitating mechanism for the building and maintenance of a racialized state.

marriage violated the Fourteenth Amendment (48 Ala. 196 (1872)). Then, in 1879, the U.S. Supreme Court invalidated West Virginia's statutory ban on African-American jurors (*Strauder v. West Virginia*, 100 U.S. 303 (1879)).

The equivocal nature of early rulings sparked conflict, as cultural and political forces contended for the authority to shape the postwar political order. The struggle to relegitimate laws barring intimate interracial relationships was a bellwether. After Alabama's ruling against antimiscegenation laws, nine years of litigation on the state level eventually brought the issue to the U.S. Supreme Court (Novkov 2006; Pascoe 1996; Kennedy 2003; Wallenstein 2002). In its ruling in *Pace v. Alabama*, the Court established the principle that formal equal treatment by statute—in this case, the threat of identical sentences for engaging in interracial adultery, fornication, or marriage—was sufficient to avert invalidation, even if the statute explicitly used racial categories (Wallenstein 2002). Although the debate over how to deal with race in light of constitutional change was ongoing, this ruling established the approach that the Court would endorse in *Plessy* fourteen years later, facilitating the development and implementation of full-blown white supremacy as an organizing principle for Southern state governments (Novkov 2006).

Once the federal courts had signaled that they would not scrutinize the states' endorsements of racial discrimination closely, the state courts became the primary site for developing racialized legal ideology. Through the early twentieth century, they participated actively in drawing the boundaries within which Jim Crow functioned as a system of government. This hostile and repressive system nonetheless incorporated legal dynamism, and the process of racial formation continued through the interplay of individual litigants and the courts, as the Southern courts increasingly worked to sanitize the racial regime sufficiently to stave off federal intervention. As Michael Klarman and others have shown, the social fabric of Jim Crow was intimately interwoven with the network of legal regulations under nearly continuous recalibration, leading ultimately to what Aldon Morris has described as largely separate worlds for white and black Americans in the South just prior to the first stirrings of the civil rights movement (Klarman 2004; Morris 1984).

The struggles of the late nineteenth and early twentieth century over the place of African-Americans in the social and political order serve well to show how the courts incorporate emerging ideologies into their decisions, reformulating them within existing and new legal categories as they do so. This model is more complex than one that assumes that judges simply rule directly upon cases based on their own political ideological preferences. Instead, the institutions of law and legal decision-making provide a set of frameworks through which ideology is constructed and expressed. In this example, the legal requirement of equality rendered through the Reconstruction Amendments generated significant ideological struggle and triggered clashes over the meaning of citizenship and belonging. At the same time, the courts considered the fundamental structure of government under federalism and contended over the proper allocation of responsibility for defining relations among citizens in the postbellum era. The institutional structure of the legal process as well as judges' commitments to the practice of doctrinal reasoning channeled the flow of racialized ideologies and defined the process through which the accommodation in *Plessy* and the rise of the era of state-based white supremacy and national neglect were grounded. This analysis allows for a better understanding of how racial ascriptivism was reformulated around the Reconstruction Amendments and shows specifically how Jim Crow—as a legal and ideological system of governance distinct from the racial ordering of slavery—was initially established and legitimated. Focus on ideology and its relationship to development demonstrates that the legitimation of Jim Crow was a process, not simply the result of the Supreme Court's preordained approval of supremacy foreshadowed in the *Civil Rights Cases* and confirmed in *Plessy v. Ferguson.*

3 Law and Ideological Transformation

But what of the interaction between law and ideology in the other direction? Does legal change itself ever influence the formulation or transformation of ideology? Two examples illustrate how the process also works when the courts' decisions establish an ideological framework that contains and at times constrains public debate and discourse. In both cases, legal frameworks had significant impacts upon the shape of ideologies emerging from controversial issues. In the case of abortion regulation, the U.S. Supreme Court's initial framing of the right to choose abortion in *Roe v. Wade* both chose freedom of choice as the specific liberal source for the right and inadvertently set up a dynamic for opponents of abortion to limit access. In the case of affirmative action, Tom Keck shows how the emergence of conservative judicial ideology supported a right-wing embrace of rights-based color blindness as an ideological tool in efforts to dismantle racial preferences in education and employment.

Roe's much-criticized trimester framework established abortion as a legitimate choice within the First trimester of pregnancy and forbade the states from foreclosing this choice for pregnant women. *Roe* and its progeny had two significant impacts upon how struggles over reproductive freedom played out in the decades since the ruling: First, it focused support for reproductive freedom around the concept of choice; and second, it sparked a wave of regulatory efforts framed around constructions of fetal personhood, danger, and lack of information or consideration on the part of the pregnant woman. This struggle then fed back to produce and embed the new constitutional ideology of undue burden as a limit upon the states' capacity to regulate abortion.

In *Roe* itself, the Court expressed the right at stake as a "right of privacy... broad enough to encompass a woman's decision whether or not to terminate her pregnancy. The detriment that the State would impose upon the pregnant woman by denying this choice altogether is apparent" (*Roe v. Wade*, 410 U.S. 113, 153 (1973)). This framing of decision and choice foreclosed significant discussion of access (an issue settled more directly in the post-*Roe* funding cases of the late 1970s) and encouraged the liberal feminist framing of individual choice as the central rallying point through the struggles over abortion in the 1980s and 1990s. As Kristen Luker illustrates, choice played into an understanding of women as full liberal subjects imbued with individual autonomy rooted in the right to choose when and whether to reproduce (Luker 1984).

But, as Rickie Solinger has shown, the framing of choice and its privileging of liberal autonomy ultimately undermined a broader feminist commitment to full reproductive freedom. As a result of the centering of public debate around protecting the right to choose abortion, coercive control over the reproductive rights of poor women and women of color, including pressures to curtail child bearing and to give up parental rights, were not closely linked to the struggles over abortion. Abortion thus became an issue identified strongly with the rights and interests of white, middle-class men and women and their daughters, even though access to abortion remained critical for all women's capacity to control reproduction (Solinger 2005).

At the same time, *Roe* sparked the formation of widespread and active opposition in the form of a movement that quickly dubbed itself "pro-life." Pro-lifers consciously constructed their rhetoric and strategies in response to the framing of choice. Although Luker's research suggests that a different conception of women's appropriate roles was at bottom of their opposition, the public legal and popular campaign against abortion centered around cabining the scope of choice to limit abortion. Thus, the first legislative efforts promoted by pro-lifers targeted public funding for abortion, exploiting the choice framing by ensuring that the public would not be required to fund immoral choices on the part of poor women. In the abortion funding cases, the Supreme Court allowed these restrictions to stand, ruling that the federal government and the states had the right to influence the choice of whether to abort by providing financial support for pregnancy but not for abortion services (*Maher v. Roe*, 432 U.S. 464 (1977); *Harris v. McRae*, 448 U.S. 297 (1980)).

As the lower courts and ultimately the Supreme Court endorsed this view on the state and federal levels, pro-lifers endorsed other limitations within the ideological framework of choice. Teenagers, with their tenuous status as competent and autonomous liberal citizens, provided a target of opportunity, and states passed laws requiring them to seek counsel or approval from other adult decision-makers before they would be permitted to exercise the right to choose abortion (Silverstein 1999). Some states also enacted laws requiring pregnant women to inform or seek consent from their spouses before choosing abortion. States also passed laws requiring that pregnant women review information regarding fetal development before exercising choice and that they wait for at least twenty-four hours between requesting and receiving an abortion.

All of these measures invoked choice by calling into question the subjective capacity of the chooser to choose appropriately, with sufficient counsel and reflection. By emphasizing the serious nature of the choice and the problematic access to full liberal subjectivity of the chooser, pro-life activists were able to convince state legislatures and then several state high courts to accept significant limits on abortion. Debate over the appropriate conditioning of choice was the central issue in the Supreme Court's reconsideration of *Roe* in *Planned Parenthood v. Casey* in 1992.

Casey is probably best known for reaffirming the Supreme Court's commitment to supporting abortion rights, but many feminists note that the Court, in its ruling on the facial challenge to Pennsylvania's multipronged restrictive regime, upheld four of the five regulations at stake. Only one—a spousal notification requirement—was invalidated, and the Court let stand parental consent, a twenty-four-hour waiting period, mandatory review of materials concerning fetal development, and a set of reporting requirements (*Planned Parenthood v. Casey,* 505 U.S. 833 (1992)). The case also moved from *Roe's* trimester framework and strong rights-based approach to a more ambiguous and flexible standard focusing on the nature of the state regulations rather than on primary protection for choice in early pregnancy. The Court clarified that states could regulate abortion as long as the regulations did not constitute an undue burden on the right to choose.

The adoption of undue burden as a standard reinforced the ideological commitment to choice while undercutting the capacity of many women to exercise untrammeled choice. These limits were permissible, however, because the years of debate over choice had precluded a meaningful consideration of access or of the connection between abortion and a broader conception of reproductive autonomy. Further, choice itself was readily subject to conditioning on the basis that it was not fully informed or fully considered, that it was being exercised without sufficient input from all stakeholders, or that the state's interests deserved a role in its exercise. Access to abortion had always been tenuous, but the evolution of *Roe's* liberty to *Casey's* undue burden and the subsequent application of this standard enabled the most conservative states to eliminate it in practical terms or contain it completely within urban areas.

As this sketch demonstrates, the initial doctrinal expression of the right to choose abortion had significant ideological ripple effects within public, political, and legislative spheres. Establishing abortion rights as the right of full liberal subjects to choose shaped the struggle between "pro-choice" and "pro-life" activism. Pro-choicers, operating primarily through the National Organization for Women (NOW) and the National Abortion Rights Action League (NARAL), strategically focused on defensive litigation to preserve *Roe* and abortion choice, making choice the rallying cry for abortion rights while emphasizing choice as a liberal and legal concept. Embracing and defending the ideology of choice in the early post-*Roe* years encouraged liberal feminists to speak of abortion in the language of rights and not to target their analyses on the broader role that state control over reproduction has had in the lives of women, particularly poor women and women of color. The radical feminists of the women's health movement in the late 1960s and early 1970s had sidestepped the state and worked directly to provide access to services, but this kind of direct action fell largely into abeyance in the post-*Roe* context (Solinger 2005).

Roe and its centering of the individual female chooser presented a vision of liberal female subjectivity that resonated in the cultural and political debates of the 1970s over feminism and women's appropriate roles, leaving little room for effective pro-choice retrenchment as the nation turned to the right. As a result, while the right to choose abortion has remained a formal legal principle and has continued as the flashpoint for fierce political battles, on the ground that access has been limited. Further, while the cultural struggle over abortion has expanded to include access to birth control both nationally and internationally, liberal advocates for reproductive rights have been slow to link the struggle over abortion to concerns over other coercive state practices affecting the reproductive autonomy of poor women and women of color (Solinger 2005).

A final example illustrates how legal decision-making can influence the broader political and ideological context. While the rise of conservatism was not initiated by the judiciary, the contours of its modern appearance are sharply marked by the Rehnquist Court's activism (Keck 2004; on the rise of modern conservatism, see Lowndes forthcoming). As Keck observes, in certain areas, "conservative justices have sought not to abandon judicial power but to redirect its active use in conservative directions," leading to transformations in constitutional law and ultimately in public discourse (Keck 2004, 10). In constructing his theory, Keck takes seriously both the impact of how judicial decisions are framed (in addition to the substantive outcomes) and the view that ideas matter to judges and justices. His analysis of the rise of conservative judicial activism rests upon his belief that the conservatives on the Court have built a coherent constitutional vision, rather than simply deciding cases to drive outcomes that reflect the external tenor of the conservative political environment.

Keck analyzes this process in historic terms, beginning with the judicial revolution of the late 1930s and responses to it (Keck 2004). He also considers this process in a more confined way in his discussion of the Supreme Court's role in developing an ideological framework for the contours of rights-based conservatism in the context of the affirmative action debate (Keck 2006). The Center for Individual Rights (CIR), modeling its litigation strategy on the NAACP's multipronged attack on segregation, promoted the elimination of all race-conscious policies designed to benefit members of disempowered races. In order to succeed, however, the CIR had to attend to the Court's discursive constructions of the issues in question and adopt framings that would have more likelihood of success. Their policy preferences therefore incorporated ideological framings that reflected the Court's interpretations, leading them to mobilize arguments based in color blindness and equal rights for aggrieved whites rather than potential alternative reasonings (Keck 2006).

Keck pegs this process's start in Justice Powell's opinion in *Bakke*, which placed whites as injured parties at the center of concerns over affirmative action. This reasoning resonated with an emerging new racialization of whites as victims of predatory and discriminatory policies. The CIR and related groups launched aggressive efforts to locate and support white victims; this outreach contributed to shifts in white racial consciousness and the growing resonance for the right of the rhetoric of individual rights (Keck 2006, 424–5). At the same time, opponents of affirmative action focused their energies upon Powell's use of diversity as an appropriate state interest for the exercise of race-conscious programs, seeking simultaneously to limit the permissible grounds for affirmative action to actual racial injury and to render diversity a narrow and problematic justification under a strong reading of the equal protection clause (Keck 2006).

As the struggle developed and the Court continued to signal its interest in the issues by accepting *certiorari* in cases, the debate over affirmative action increasingly targeted Justices Kennedy and O'Connor, who were at the center of the Court's range of standpoints on affirmative action. In the Court's rulings in *Gratz* and *Grutter*, O'Connor's understanding of the institutional role of the U.S. Supreme Court shaped her approach to and ruling in the cases and rejected a sweeping rights-based challenge to affirmative action in principle. These rulings clearly feed back into the public sphere and provide ideological signaling devices to the advocacy groups that oppose and support affirmative action (Keck 2006).

The interplay between advocacy groups and the Court has not been merely strategic on the part of the groups, however. As Keck shows, the Court's earlier embrace of a model of white victimization became incorporated not solely in briefs and other legal filings, but in groups like CIR's efforts to recruit potential litigants and financial donations from political allies. The influence of these maneuvers goes beyond the legal sphere, mobilizing a broader group of ideological entrepreneurs not directly associated with litigation. As others loosely aligned with the anti-affirmative action movement observe the success of the rights-based framings, they have opportunities to transport the ideology to additional and perhaps unanticipated spheres, where it can influence public officials' rhetoric and public opinion on affirmative action and related issues. The ideological constructive process was co-constitutive and incorporated both internal and external dynamics and discourses, to use Kahn and Kersch's description of Supreme Court decision-making. Ideology thus played a complex role in this process, as ideas emanating from the

Court provided the boundaries within which activist groups pressed and responded, leading to a further ideological constructive process that partially incorporated and partially rejected a harder-edged conservative rights-based framing (Keck 2006, 433–6).

4 CONCLUSION

These examples—the struggle over police power and the legitimacy of labor regulations, the establishment of twentieth century white supremacy, the contest between pro-choice and pro-life forces, and conservative efforts to end affirmative action—all illustrate the relationship between law and ideology. Close readings of the cases in these areas, the institutional arrangements behind them, and the social and political dynamics driving the issues onto the courts' dockets demonstrate that ideology is not a free-floating force that independently causes judicial outcomes. A multifaceted analysis, however, also rejects the interpretation that ideology, as distinguished from doctrinal rule, plays no role in judicial decision-making. Rather, ideas are dynamic within and mediated by the legal process at several different institutional junctures.

Legal scholarship and popular discussion of the role of the judiciary at times presents a debate about when the intervention of ideology is appropriate in judicial decision-making and whether it is more apt to happen at certain historical moments than others. The early twentieth century's rulings supporting employers' liberty, the Warren Court's reworking of the modern regime of civil liberties, and the recent efforts by the U.S. Supreme Court to dismantle the Warren Court's legacy are often identified as such moments. As Barry Friedman has pointed out, these concerns often, but not always, coincide with serious considerations of the countermajoritarian implications of the judiciary's invalidating democratically passed legislation. But Friedman notes that these concerns do not necessarily correspond with moments of heightened judicial invalidations of statutes on constitutional grounds; rather, "panics" over countermajoritarian courts tend to reflect and resonate with broader issues in the contemporary political moment (Friedman 2002).

This debate misconstrues the ways that ideology is always intertwined with the legal process at the juncture of law and society. When litigants bringing or defending suits through advocacy groups are seeking not just wins in individual cases but broader political or policy-based change, the role of ideology becomes more visible. This is particularly true in instances when the interested advocacy groups seek to raise the public and political salience of judicial decisions in order to raise the courts' political stake in the outcomes. As the examples of struggles over choice, diversity, and color-blindness demonstrate, juridical concepts map readily and publicly as ideological frameworks that can drive outcomes in cases in these instances.

But the interplay between ideas and judicial institutions is always present, even when advocacy groups are not pressing for public and visible engagement with the courts. The NAACP did not take up the cause of dismantling segregation through legal means until the 1930s, and avoided the issue of interracial intimacy altogether until much later. Nonetheless, judicial considerations of the Jim Crow regime were and remained deeply ideological. Analysis of struggles over maintaining a broad prohibition on interracial intimacy reveals that the basis for such statutes was the political ideology of white supremacy, and policy-makers were quite open about this even in state constitutional debates (Novkov 2008).

In sum, ideology is relied upon, constructed, engaged, and transformed through the constitutive nature of the legal process. In legal institutions, ideology operates at the interface of state plenary and regulatory power on the one hand, and culture, politics, and society on the other. Simple models that place it either wholly inside or wholly outside the law miss the most interesting parts of the story.

References

BRANDWEIN, P. 2006. The *Civil Rights Cases* and the lost language of state neglect. Pp. 275–328 in Kahn and Kersch 2006*b*.

FRIEDMAN, B. 2002. The birth of an academic obsession: the history of the countermajoritarian difficulty, part five. *Yale Law Journal*, 112: 153–259.

GILLMAN, H. 1993. *The Constitution Besieged: The Rise and Demise of Lochner Era Police Powers Jurisprudence.* Durham, NC: Duke University Press.

KAHN, R., and KERSCH, K. 2006*a*. Introduction. Pp. 1–32 in Kahn and Kersch 2006*b*.

—— —— 2006*b*. *The Supreme Court and American Political Development.* Lawrence: University Press of Kansas.

KECK, T 2004. *The Most Activist Supreme Court in History.* Chicago: University of Chicago Press.

—— 2006. From *Bakke* to *Grutter*: the rise of rights-based conservatism. Pp. 414–42 in Kahn and Kersch 2006*b*.

KENNEDY, R. 2003. *Interracial Intimacies: Sex, Marriage, Identity, and Adoption.* New York: Pantheon.

KERSCH, K. 2004. *Constructing Civil Liberties: Discontinuities in the Development of American Constitutional Law.* Cambridge: Cambridge University Press.

KLARMAN, M. 2004. *From Jim Crow to Civil Rights: The Supreme Court and the Struggle for Racial Equality.* Oxford: Oxford University Press.

KLUGER, R. 1976. *Simple Justice: The History of* Brown v. Board of Education *and Black America's Struggle for Equality*. New York: Knopf.

LIPSCHULTZ, S. 1996. Hours and wages: the gendering of labor standards in America. *Journal of Women's History*, 8: 114–37.

LOWNDES, J. 2008. *From the New Deal to the New Right: The Southern Origins of Modern Conservatism*. New Haven, Conn.: Yale University Press.

LUKER, K. 1984. *Abortion and the Politics of Motherhood*. Berkeley: University of California Press.

MOORE, W. D. 2006. (Re)construction of constitutional authority and meaning: the Fourteenth Amendment and *Slaughter-House Cases*. Pp. 229–74 in Kahn and Kersch 2006*b*.

MORRIS, A. 1984. *The Origins of the Civil Rights Movement: Black Communities Organizing for Change*. New York: Free Press.

NOVKOV, J. 2001. *Constituting Workers, Protecting Women: Gender, Law, and Labor in the Progressive Era and New Deal Years*. Ann Arbor: University of Michigan Press.

—— 2006. *Pace v. Alabama*: interracial love, the marriage contract, and postbellum foundations of the family. Pp. 329–65 in Kahn and Kersch 2006*b*.

—— 2008. *Law, Intimacy, and the White State in Alabama, 1865–1954*. Ann Arbor: University of Michigan Press.

PASCOE, P. 1996. Miscegenation law, court cases, and ideologies of "race" in twentieth-century America. *Journal of American History*, 83: 44–69.

ROGIN, M. 1988. *Ronald Reagan, the Movie: And Other Episodes in Political Demonology*. Berkeley: University of California Press.

SIEGEL, R. B. 2002. She the people: the Nineteenth Amendment, sex equality, federalism, and the family. *Harvard Law Review*, 115: 947–1046.

SILVERSTEIN, H. 1999. Road closed: evaluating the judicial bypass provision of the Pennsylvania Abortion Control Act. *Law and Social Inquiry*, 24: 73–96.

SKOCPOL, T. 1992. *Protecting Soldiers and Mothers: The Political Origins of Social Policy in the United States*. Cambridge, Mass.: Belknap.

SMITH, R. 1985/1990. *Liberalism and American Constitutional Law*, rev. edn. Cambridge, Mass.: Harvard University Press.

—— 1997. *Civic Ideals: Conflicting Visions of Citizenship in U.S. History*. New Haven, Conn.: Yale University Press.

SOLINGER, R. 2005. *Pregnancy and Power: A Short History of Reproductive Politics in America*. New York: New York University Press.

SPANN, G. 1993. *Race against the Court: The Supreme Court and Minorities in Contemporary America*. New York: New York University Press.

WALLENSTEIN, P. 2002. *Tell the Court I Love My Wife: Race, Marriage, and Law—An American History*. New York: Palgrave.

CASES

Adkins v. Children's Hospital, 261 U.S. 525 (1923).

Bradwell v. Illinois, 83 U.S. 130 (1873).

Bunting v. Oregon, 243 U.S. 426 (1917).

Burns v. State, 48 Ala. 196 (1872).

Goesaert v. Cleary, 335 U.S. 464 (1948).

Gratz v. Bollinger, 539 U.S. 234 (2003).

Grutter v. Bollinger, 539 U.S. 306 (2003).

Harris v. McRae, 448 U.S. 297 (1980).

Lochner v. New York, 198 U.S. 45 (1905).

Maher v. Roe, 432 U.S. 464 (1977).

Minor v. Happersett, 88 U.S. 162 (1874).

Muller v. Oregon, 208 U.S. 416 (1908).

Pace v. Alabama, 106 U.S. 583 (1883).

Planned Parenthood v. Casey, 505 U.S. 833 (1992).

Plessy v. Ferguson, 163 U.S. 537 (1896).

Regents of the University of California v. Bakke, 438 U.S. 265 (1978).

Roe v. Wade, 410 U.S. 113 (1973).

Slaughter-House Cases, 83 U.S. 36 (1873).

Strauder v. West Virginia, 100 U.S. 303 (1879).

The Civil Rights Cases, 109 U.S. 3 (1883).

West Coast Hotel v. Parrish, 300 U.S. 379 (1937).

CHAPTER 37

....

COURTS AND
THE POLITICS
OF PARTISAN
COALITIONS

....

HOWARD GILLMAN

ONE of the most promising ways of integrating the study of law and courts into the mainstream of political analysis is to focus more attention on how legal institutions figure into the broader interests and agendas of other power holders. Toward this end an increasing number of scholars within political science have begun to develop what is becoming known as a "regime politics" approach to the study of courts (e.g. Clayton and May 1999). The objective behind this approach is to incorporate legal studies into a more general set of theories or hypotheses about how political regimes organize, exercise, and protect their power.

Much of the work associated with this research agenda focuses especially on the relationship between courts and party politics. The point of departure for this focus is Dahl's (1957) now classic discussion of how the U.S. Supreme Court "tends to act as part of the national governing coalition" (see also Peretti 1999, 133).

Thanks to Mark Graber, Keith Whittington, Malcolm Feeley, and Michael Bowers for helpful advice on earlier drafts of this chapter. In exchange I happily relieve them of any responsibility for existing mistakes and weaknesses in analysis and presentation.

Years ago this starting point generated research on courts and critical elections (Adamany 1980; Funston 1975; Gates 1992; Lasser 1985). However, since then, researchers have explored how the idea of "national governing coalitions" might illuminate a broader set of questions involving law and courts, including the role of courts in political systems, the determinants of judicial empowerment, the nature of judicial decision-making, and the dynamics of legal change.

This chapter reviews this emergent research tradition and organizes existing findings into clearer set of statements about how courts fit into regime politics and the dynamics of national governing coalitions. I am especially interested in highlighting research that will help us begin to think of courts not merely as platforms for the promotion of a judge's policy preferences but as institutions that are often explicitly designed to promote the goals of nonjudicial actors. I begin with some propositions that can be associated with Dahl's original argument about how courts should be expected to cooperate with the prevailing governing coalition. I then move on to research that attempts to expand and complicate Dahl's original analysis.

1 COURTS AS POLICY-MAKING PARTNERS IN A GOVERNING COALITION

The central idea behind Dahl's argument in "The Supreme Court as a National Policy Maker" was that it was unreasonable to expect federal courts to challenge an existing national majority. The logic of this argument was straightforward: In the United States, Supreme Court justices are appointed by national party leaders, and these party leaders almost always attempt to ensure that these justices are generally sympathetic to the party's political agenda. This is why presidents and senators overwhelmingly select federal judges from among their own party activists or loyalists (see Barrow, Zuk, and Gryski 1996, 15). Dahl knew that there was some belief in the 1950s that the Supreme Court could be counted on as a force for the protection of so-called "discreet and insular minorities" in the political system, but he demonstrated that the U.S. Supreme Court almost never struck down as unconstitutional a law passed by the current governing coalition. In almost every case exercises of judicial review at the national level were targeted at laws that had been passed by majorities that were no longer in power. In effect, then, judicial review was better understood as a kind of judicial repeal of inherited and nominally outdated legislation than as a check on the preferences of functioning majorities. Because the Supreme Court almost always upheld the acts of the dominant governing coalition, he suggested that the most notable political function performed by the Court was as a "legitimation" function—bestowing some measure of legitimacy on the agendas of the party in power.

Dahl's original study is now almost a half-century old, and by contemporary standards his data-collection and analysis are not especially sophisticated. Over the past few years a number of researchers with a deep knowledge of American political history have begun to extend and refine Dahl's basic thesis. For example, Graber (1998) has shown how our perception of the Marshall Court as a bastion of hard-core Federalists amidst hostile Jeffersonians misunderstands the nature of the governing coalitions in the early nineteenth century and especially the common ground between the justices and Congress. Powe's (2001) magisterial analysis of *The Warren Court and American Politics* is explicitly framed around establishing how those justices saw themselves as full partners with Great Society liberals in the Congress and how they acted, not just to legitimate congressional preferences (as with the decision to uphold the Civil Rights Act of 1964) but also to make it easier for Democratic constituencies to press their case in the political process. Similarly, Klarman (1996; 2004) has suggested that the Court's twentieth-century reputation for the protection of civil rights and liberties is overblown precisely because most commentators fail to appreciate the favorable political climate within which those decisions were made.

In his recent book, Kersch (2004) reinterpreted the traditional story of twentieth century constitutional "progress" on rights into a story about how the Court expands or contracts rights and liberties depending on the perceived imperatives of the developing regulatory state. Sometimes the expansion and contraction takes place simultaneously within different areas of the law, as with unprecedented First Amendment protections for labor picketing in the 1930s and 1940s (after the Norris–LaGuardia Act of 1932 recognized the legitimacy of the practice) and a newfound unwillingness to protect the speech rights of factory owners (after the Wagner Act attempted to protect union organizing against owner interference). More generally, Kersch revitalized Dahl's focus on legitimation by emphasizing the way in which the Court's decision-making represents the translation of a political "settlement" on the contours of a rights regime into a full-blown ideological defense of that settlement (see also Tushnet 2003 on the idea of "constitutional orders").

In an important new addition to this literature, Whittington (2005) has pointed out that "friendly" courts—that is, courts made up of judges who are sympathetic to the political agenda of the dominant national coalition—might perform a service to other power holders by helping them "overcome obstructions" to governing. Whittington's case studies of "judicial review by an allied court" focus on obstructions associated with local challenges to national authority (e.g. *McCulloch v. Maryland*, late nineteenth-century state regulatory assaults on the evolving national market, or Southern resistance to national civil rights policy), factious political coalitions (e.g. civil rights policy-making and campaign finance legislation), and the entrenched positions of competing power holders (e.g. malapportionment). This last observation builds on Klarman's (1997) earlier work on "Majoritarian Judicial Review," in which he points out that Supreme Court decisions on issues such as term limits, malapportionment, gerrymandering, the scope of political community, ballot access restrictions, campaign finance reform, minority vote dilution, and minority voting districts have more to do with reestablishing majoritarian democratic norms than with promoting a countermajoritarian difficulty.

One can accept Dahl's general thesis as a starting point without being committed to the view that the Court is always a perfectly cooperative partner. After all, as Orren and Skowronek (2004) point out, political regimes are typically characterized by "multiple orders" and patterns of "intercurrence" rather than tightly interlocking and functional pieces of a coherent system (see also Kahn and Kersch 2006). Clayton and Pickerill (2004) properly trace the origins of the Rehnquist Court's federalism jurisprudence to the evolving views of the major parties (especially the post-Reagan Republican Party) and to an overall trend in federal policy-making in the direction of a "devolution revolution." At the same time, they acknowledge that the federal laws invalidated by the Court—including the Indian Gaming Regulatory Act, the Violence Against Women Act (VAWA), the Americans With Disabilities Act (ADA), the Age Discrimination in Employment Act (ADEA), the Religious Freedom Restoration Act (RFRA), the Brady Bill, and the Gun-Free School Zones Act (GFSZA)—have been supported by Republicans and Democrats. They point out that the Court's decisions have been relatively narrow in scope and have not prevented the Congress or the states from advancing the same basic policies in other ways; and in fact, rather than challenge the Court, the Congress has frequently responded by drafting legislation that promotes the same goals but also satisfies the concerns of the justices.

As we will see, it is possible to imagine a political context within which courts can exercise power in a way that challenges the agenda of a governing coalition, at least on some issues for some period of time. However, absent a condition of divided government that prevents a unified challenge to the judiciary, it is difficult from Dahl's perspective to see how courts can remain functionally independent of the rest of the regime for any significant length of time. As Scheppele (2002) has pointed out, there was a time in the 1990s when the Hungarian Constitutional Court had earned a well-deserved reputation as an active and independent voice in Hungarian politics. However, when conservatives gained sufficient control of the rest of the political system, it was a relatively easy matter to dramatically reconfigure the Court so that it would not become a nuisance to the prevailing majority. Dahl understood that FDR was also committed to removing that particular veto point after New Dealers came to power.

2 COURTS AND THE ENHANCEMENT OF "CREDIBLE COMMITMENTS" TO FAVORED CONSTITUENCIES

Dahl's analysis of the Court and regime politics began and ended by documenting how courts rarely interfere with the governing interests of a dominant coalition. However, there are other ways to develop this argument beyond more detailed analyses of the relationships between the judiciary's overall policy agenda and the substantive agenda of coordinate power holders.

One way to further specify the argument is to link it to work in the economic analysis of law that focuses on the role that courts play in helping other power holders offer "credible commitments" to favored constituencies, or to other groups seeking reassurance that the regime will hold true to its legislative commitments. In the area of judicial politics this argument was first laid out by Landes and Posner (1975). The problem they wanted to address from a rational choice perspective was why a regime would allow courts to enforce the decisions of earlier governing majorities when those decisions no longer reflected the agenda of those in power; in other words, why was it rational for current power holders to accommodate a measure of judicial independence rather than insist that courts gut outdated (but unrepealed) laws? Their argument was that it was in the long-term interest of all legislators that judges enforce the interest-group bargains reflected in statutes. Without such a guarantee existing legislators would not be in a position to guarantee current favored constituents that their interests would be promoted and protected in new statutes—in other words, the value of statutes would be diminished because favored constituents would always worry that their statutory victories might be gutted. Judicial independence from immediate shifts in legislative alignments would mean that statutory bargains would not be hastily undone in a new political climate. As a result of judicial independence, and the "credible commitment" it brings to the political system, current legislators were in a position (in effect) to extract higher rents from their favored constituents. An independent judiciary made legislation more "valuable" than it would be in the absence of a reliable enforcement mechanism.

As Ferejohn (1999) has pointed out, "this idea is quite parallel to that found in the literature on the creation of independent central banks," which is premised on the assumption that the "median member of the legislature is willing, ex ante, to create a central bank and appoint someone more fiscally conservative than herself to run it." By extension, this same median legislator would find it rational to create and staff courts with decision-makers who are committed to norms of legality even when they run counter to the legislator's short-term political preferences.

The Landes–Posner perspective on the judiciary's contribution to regime politics has been refined and challenged over the past few decades. For example, a number of scholars have pointed out that the model is premised on the dubious empirical assumption that nominally independent judges decide cases according to the original legislature's will—an assumption that, in some respects, is in tension with some political science accounts of judicial decision-making and with what one might expect from Dahl's original thesis (Epstein 1990; Salzberger and Fenn 1999). Some have pointed out that the Landes–Posner argument is not an equilibrium because any particular legislature has an incentive to free ride (in the sense that it does best when it pressures courts but all other legislatures respect judicial independence), and that the model seems to "overpredict" judicial independence (in the sense that it is not clear how the model could account for nonindependent courts). As an alternative Stephenson (2003) has suggested that judicial review allows risk-averse political competitors to adopt positions of mutual restraint, at least when "(1) the political system is sufficiently competitive, (2) judicial doctrine is sufficiently moderate, and (3) parties are both sufficiently risk averse and forward looking." This echoes Ramseyer's (1994) earlier claim that we should see stronger efforts to maintain an independent judiciary in political systems that experience frequent change in political power but more dependent judiciaries in places (like Japan) where governing coalitions are remarkably stable. Ginsburg (2002), using data from Eastern Europe, has similarly suggested that "the extent and power of judicial review can be expected to increase relative to the degree of political uncertainty at the time of constitutional design;" thus, when political parties believe they will dominate a political system for some time, they support the creation of relatively dependent courts, and when they believe that governing coalitions will be more fluid they support more independent and powerful courts (see also Ginsburg 2003). Magalhaes (1999) uses a similar framework to explain why strong constitutional review mechanisms were developed in Spain and Portugal during their transitions to democracy while Greece became the only Southern European democracy without judicial review.

Another version of the "credible commitment" argument focuses, not on the benefits to domestic legislative constituencies, but rather on the role that strong courts can play in developing countries that are attempting to reassure international investment communities. This has led some to assume that courts might be central to "the political foundations of secure markets" (North 1990; North and Weingast 1989; Weingast 1993). While this view has been widely accepted, some recent work has called into question some of the empirical premises of the model (Sussman and Yafeh 2003; Stasavage 2002). Then again, Moustafa (2003) has demonstrated that the Egyptian regime established a relatively independent constitutional court "in order to attract desperately needed private investment after the failure of its socialist-oriented development strategy." Rather than resolve these controversies, my purpose is merely to point out how continued research on these questions would be consistent with a research agenda that seeks to make judicial power central to theories about how regimes promote their interests.

3 COURTS AS COALITION STABILIZERS

Some scholars who have challenged the Landes–Posner version of the "credible commitments" thesis have suggested that courts serve governing coalitions in ways other than by holding the regime to its previous interest-group bargains. For example, Salzberger (1993) has argued that independent judges benefit politicians because they allow elected officials to "shift blame" for unpopular collective decisions and thus help maintain political coalitions that might otherwise fragment. Voigt and Salzberger (2002) have linked this idea to a more general theory of "delegation" of decision-making authority to more insulated political institutions, such as central banks, international organizations, or courts (see also Salzberger 2001). They illustrate their argument with reference to the role of the Israeli Supreme Court in addressing issues relating to the government's policies in the occupied territories (where there is domestic political controversy both when government policies are considered too harsh and when efforts are made to respect the rights of inhabitants) and to the relation between the state and religion (an ongoing source of domestic political controversy).

This argument is very similar to Graber's (1993) path breaking discussion of "legislative deference to the judiciary," or what he called "the nonmajoritarian difficulty" in American constitutional politics. He argued that party leaders have an interest in channeling certain kinds of political disputes into the judiciary, mostly as a way of preventing elected officials from having to address issues that might otherwise threaten to divide a governing coalition. His case studies focused on slavery policy in the mid-nineteenth century, antitrust policy in the late-nineteenth and early twentieth centuries, and abortion policy in the early 1970s. More recently, McMahon (2003) has argued that FDR focused on promoting a civil rights agenda in federal courts because he worried that more explicit legislative action would threaten the New Deal coalition. Lovell (2003) has also argued that national legislators in the late nineteenth and early twentieth centuries deliberately drafted ambiguous statutes in matters of industrial relations and labor policy precisely so that they could avoid blame for making difficult choices. Hayes (2004) has focused explicitly on the question of "how political parties maintain their national coalition" by examining the ways in which the Republican Party from 1896 to 1920 used the courts to displace divisive issues and also "help reunite coalitions" following defections by progressives.

A similar pattern has been described by Moustafa (2003) in his study of Egypt's Supreme Constitutional Court. The SCC accommodated the regime's core political and economic interests by avoiding issues of state security and removing socialist-era legislation that was hampering reform efforts. "SCC rulings enabled the executive to carry out its new economic agenda and claim that it was simply respecting an autonomous rule-of-law system rather than implement sensitive reforms through more overt political channels. These regime-friendly rulings in the eco-nomic sphere gave the SCC more leverage to push a moderate reform agenda and to provide avenues of participation to progressive social activists." Then again, as we might expect, as soon as the SCC's agenda appeared to represent threats to the regime (especially by encouraging groups in civil society to develop litigation campaigns over issues the regime preferred to avoid) a series of legal and extralegal measures against the SCC and its "support structures" in civil society effectively reined in the court (although only after an unexpectedly lively struggle).

None of this is to suggest that courts always act in a perfectly functional way for their coalitions. Gates (1999) has pointed out that judicial decisions can some-times put pressure on parties in power rather than relieve the pressure. Powe (2001) noted that the same justices who were the great partners in the promotion of Great Society liberalism extended their liberalism to the rights of criminal defendants and thus helped set in motion the politics of "law and order" that Richard Nixon used so effectively against Democrats in the 1968 presidential election. Nevertheless, to say that things do not always work out as expected is compatible with observing that party leaders might view courts as useful precisely because they are in a good position to address and resolve potentially divisive controversies. After all, in 2000, Republican leaders in Congress expressed no interest in asserting their institutional prerogatives when the U.S. Supreme Court (at their invitation) claimed the authority to resolve the presidential election dispute (Gillman 2001; 2003).

4 Courts and the Imposition of National Norms on "Regional Outliers"

In his well-known critique of Dahl's study, Casper (1976) pointed out that Dahl underestimated the scope of the Court's power, and perhaps the extent of its commitment to the protection of civil rights, by excluding from his analysis Supreme Court review of state legislation. Casper's discussion certainly put the Court in a different perspective, and also helped to rehabilitate the judiciary's role in the protection of minority rights from Dahl's almost exclusive focus on major-itarian politics. But it is compatible with an argument about the Court's place in a political regime also to point out that the justices may act more aggressively against local majorities than they do against national majorities.

It was Shapiro (1980*a*) who first pointed out that the process of appealing cases to national courts made more sense if we considered it a way for national elites to impose their values on subnational units of government than if we believed that appeals were designed as an error-correction mechanism. This political purpose was served when royal judges canvassed the countryside of England after the Norman Conquest and when the King's Courts established the writ system, with its limited attention to the legal polices in play rather than to the facts of a particular case (see also Shapiro 1980*b*). This same perspective is behind Klarman's (1996, 16–17) argument that many examples of judicial review in the United States represent the imposition of national norms on "regional outliers" rather than any interesting instance of a "counter-majoritarian difficulty." The examples used by Klarman to illustrate "the justices" seizing upon a dominant national consensus and imposing it on resisting local outliers' include "*Griswold v. Connecticut* (striking down a state ban on contraceptive use, as applied to married couples); *Gideon v. Wainwright* (requiring state-appointed defense counsel in all felony cases); *Pierce v. Society of Sisters* (invalidating a state law barring children from attending private schools); *Harper v. Virginia Bd. of Elections* (invalidating a poll tax); *Coker v. Georgia* (forbidding imposition of the death penalty for the crime of rape); and *Moore v. City of East Cleveland* (invalidating legislation denying certain blood relatives the right to live in a single household)." In his analysis of the Warren Court, Powe (2001) also draws explicitly on the language of "imposing norms on regional outliers" to explain the ways in which the Court helped serve the Great Society coalition. Of course, as Klarman (1997, 10) points out, Congress can also "force local outliers to abide by national norms as well as the Court can," but this sort of legislative response is not always likely to occur when problems are relatively isolated and do not attract much national attention. By contrast, a diffuse system of hierarchically organized national courts is very well suited to take on this chore.

The fact that federal courts often attempt to impose national norms on local government does not mean that they are always successful. The federal judiciary in the early American republic often had a difficult time securing compliance from resistant state governments (Goldstein 2001). Klarman (2000) has pointed that the Supreme Court made almost no headway against problems with the way that Southern courts in the 1930s were treating black criminal defendants. The Southern resistance to *Brown v. Board of Education* has also been well documented by Rosenberg (1980) among others. When federal courts had more success, as with the White Primary cases, it was because the background political conditions were more conducive to local acceptance, and not because federal courts are capable on their own of accomplishing this mission (Klarman 2001*a*).

A similar political dynamic can be seen in research that has looked at the efforts of the European Court of Justice to impose EU law in the face of member state opposition. Cichowski (1998) has documented the battles between the ECJ to quash "lowest common denominator" domestic environmental laws and, at times, to quash more stringent environmental regulations if they obstruct free trade. ECJ has also quashed lowest common denominator laws on gender equality, with a resulting expansion of women's rights (Cichowski 2001). In a slightly different vein, Shapiro (2000) has suggested that judicial empowerment may be correlated with a regime's desire to have an institution that effectively polices federalism boundaries.

5 COURTS AND POLITICAL ENTRENCHMENT

One of the problems with Dahl's account of Supreme Court politics is that it did a very good job explaining why national courts would *uphold* acts of the national government but not a very good job of explaining judicial review targeted against the national government. One possibility is that judicial decisions that strike down national policy-making represent mere anomalies or perhaps relatively rare examples of "lag" during periods when new majorities face off against unreconstructed courts. However, it may also be the case that these circumstances are the byproduct of self-conscious efforts by national elites to "entrench" potentially vulnerable policy agendas in politically insulated courts.

Hirschl (2000; 2004) was one of the first to relate the logic of entrenchment politics to judicial empowerment. He focused on judicial empowerment in four countries that are not otherwise going through fundamental political transitions: Israel, New Zealand, the Republic of South Africa, and Canada. He argues that governing elites chose to expand judicial power in response to the rising electoral power of competing groups; in essence, like the Federalists after the election of 1800, these elites attempted to entrench their political agenda in an institution that was not accountable to an electorate. This argument bears some relationship to the Landes–Posner "credible commitment" thesis—except on this view, worried party leaders are not hoping for relatively neutral judges to give them a fair shake after others rise to power; they are hoping that judges will continue to embody the agenda of the party that appointed them. Hirschl does not think that the Landes–Posner model can explain why countries that got along just fine without expanded judicial power would suddenly adopt bills of rights and then expect judges to use them as a way of monitoring legislative activity. Hirschl also argues that judicial empowerment is primarily a governing tactic of more liberal-bourgeoisie parties, who assume that elite judges are likely to have a more cosmopolitan commitment to individualistic and secular values, including personal freedoms and economic liberty. For example, Hirschl argues that Israeli leaders representing mostly "Ashkenazi" (European) Jews adopted the Basic Law in 1992 in response to the rising power of the orthodox community, North African/Middle Eastern Jews, and immigrants from Russia and Ethiopia. After similar overviews of developments in the other countries that make up his case studies, Hirschl concludes that the general phenomenon of "juristrocracy" is best understood as neoliberal global trend whose main institutional feature is an expanded delegation of policy-making authority to relatively autonomous decision-makers (including civil service agencies and even transnational institutions such as the WTO).

Balkin and Levinson (2001) have also proposed a "theory of partisan entrenchment" as a way of understanding "how constitutional revolutions occur." In their view, federal judges "resemble Senators who are appointed for 18-year terms [the average tenure of a Supreme Court justice] by their parties and never have to face election." They define partisan entrenchment as precisely this "temporal extension of partisan representation" that is so characteristic of the tenure of federal judges, and they argue that this extension of partisan representation through presidential appointment "is the best account of how the meaning of the constitution changes over time." More specifically, they argue that the balance of power between the president and the senate often shapes whether presidents are in a position to entrench strong party ideologues or party moderates. For example, even though Justices Blackmun and Scalia were both Republicans appointed by Republican presidents, they turned out different mostly because Nixon had to get an appointment through a Democratic Congress and Reagan did not. As a rule, "judges—and particularly Supreme Court Justices—tend to reflect the vector sum of political forces at the time of their confirmation." Presidents sometimes make notorious "mistakes" but a regrettable appointment "is a familiar feature of democratic politics" whether one is talking about the judiciary or the cabinet.

In a recent article I developed and applied this perspective to the efforts of the post-Reconstruction Republican Party (Gillman 2002). I argued that by the mid-1870s party leaders had begun to abandon a commitment to black civil rights in favor of a commitment to conservative economic nationalism, and that the institutionalization of this policy was largely accomplished through an expansion of federal judicial power. The party accomplished this goal by using two brief (lame-duck) periods in which Republicans controlled the presidency and the entire Congress to pass legislation expanding the jurisdiction of federal courts (the Judiciary and Removal Act of 1875) and expanding the size and structure of federal courts (the Evarts Act of 1891). Even though Republicans lost the House of Representatives immediately after the passage of these acts they maintained control of the presidency and the Senate (sometimes with less than a majority of the popular vote for president, as in the case of Hayes in 1876 and Harrison in 1888), and with those institutions they were able to staff federal courts with conservative economic nationalists while at the same time fight off House Democratic efforts to roll back federal judicial power. More recently I have applied the same perspective to the efforts of the presidential wing of the Democratic Party after 1960 to transform the federal judiciary so that it would become an ally in promoting New Frontier/Great Society liberalism (Gillman 2006).

A number of scholars have begun to offer the same interpretation when examining the efforts of the post-Reagan New Right to transform the federal judiciary. One of the explicit goals of the Reagan Justice Department was to use judicial appointments, not simply to reverse some of the more unwelcome features of the modern judicial liberalism but also to institutionalize key features of the political agenda of the New Right, including a rollback of the scope of federal power over commerce and civil rights and an expansion in the idea of state sovereignty. The Office of Legal Policy under Reagan prepared a 199-page guide to judicial appointments, entitled *The Constitution in the Year 2000: Choices Ahead in Constitutional Interpretation*, which was premised on the assumption that "There are few factors that are more critical to determining the course of the Nation, and yet more often overlooked, than the values and philosophies of the men and women who populate the third co-equal branch of the national government—the federal judiciary" (see Johnsen 2003). The Reagan and Bush I White Houses appointed four of the five justices who became known as the "federalism five" and elevated the fifth to the position of Chief Justice. The Bush II Justice Department, staffed with many veterans of these earlier New Right battles, has also been intent on using the opportunity presented by the Republican Party's recapture of the Senate after the 2002 midterm elections to solidify conservative control of the federal judiciary; this process has led to an escalation of interparty conflict with respect to court of appeals appointment. Keck (2004) notes that these modern efforts at conservative retrenchment have been only partially successful; still, the ability of the White House in 2005 to appoint two reliable conservatives to the Supreme Court has nudged the "median" justice slightly to the right (from O'Connor to Kennedy) and also revitalized the conservative wing of the Court.

6 COURTS AS INDEPENDENT POLICY-MAKERS

The mainstream judicial behavior literature typically accepts as given that judges focus on promoting their "personal policy preferences," and this has prevented many scholars examining more carefully the defensibility of that assumption, or from specifying the particular institutional contexts within which judges are able to promote purely personal preferences (rather than regime interests more broadly). However, if one begins from a regime politics perspective—including the assumption that most judges will have a political relationship to the regime that is evident in their decision-making—then it may also make sense to ask whether there are certain circumstances or conditions that would allow judges to promote unexpected agendas.

There are a number of possible explanations, some of which have already found their way into this evolving literature. First, we might expect a degree of policy-making independence over less salient issues—that is, over issues that central decision-makers in the regime care little about. As mentioned earlier, judicial appointments are typically made with an eye on the most salient political considerations facing presidents and senators at that moment; however, because courts have jurisdiction over a boundless set of policy questions, it is inevitable that national leaders will care very little about the particular legal rules and doctrines used in resolving most routine cases. This is not to say that individual judges can always do whatever they want; the judiciary is structured as a hierarchical system, and within that system there will be efforts to standardize particular ways of addressing certain issues. But it may be reasonable to expect that cases involving less salient policy questions will not necessarily reflect any particular regime perspective (other than a general administrative concern that courts do nothing that will create unexpected problems for other power holders).

Second, it is also possible that there are certain political conditions that make it possible for judges to act with greater independence even over issues that are more salient to other power holders. A number of researchers have suggested that, in trying to explain the expansion of power by the Rehnquist Court in the 1990s, it is important to keep in mind that the Court has been operating within an extended period of divided government. This means that (*a*) signals from the regime about the appropriate policy-making agenda will be fluid and perhaps even incoherent on some issues and (*b*) it is more difficult for opponents of a given judicial policy to organize effective opposition (because the Court should have enough allies *somewhere* in the political system to ensure a veto against any serious attacks). Similarly, Klarman (1997) has showed that when the Court is not imposing national values in regional outliers it is sometimes acting when the nation is genuinely divided over an issue; in effect, the Court aligns itself with one side against the other. His examples are racial segregation in 1954, the death penalty in 1972, abortion in 1973, affirmative action in 1978, and sexual orientation in 1986; after 2000 he could have added presidential election disputes (Gillman 2001; Klarman 2001*b*).

Third, it may be possible to draw on literatures in the field of American political development for new ideas about the nature of independent decision-making by nominally dependent state institutions. Consider, for example, Carpenter's (2001) work on the postal service. For a long time it was assumed that late nineteenth-century bureaucracies acted purely in the interest of the parties in power. However, Carpenter shows how career bureaucrats created overlapping networks among their agencies and forged public reputations from mass publics, and the result was that they established some freedom from their party bosses and were thus in a position to engage in bureaucratic entrepreneurship, policy innovation, and mission expansion.

Fourth, it is possible that judges arrive at some independence by virtue of internalizing their legal training and taking seriously the distinctive institutional "mission" of the judiciary in the political system. It is a settled lesson of the literature on the "new institutionalism" that institutional settings are not merely platforms from which office holders promote exogenous agendas and interest; they are also the source of purposes, perspectives, and responsibilities that can have an autonomous influence on political behavior (Gillman 1999; Smith 1988). In a recent study of the Supreme Court's decisions since 1980, Keck (2005, 31) has argued that "the actual pattern of cases striking down recently enacted federal statutes is not easily explicable on the grounds that the justices are following the policy preferences of governing Republican elites." Keck speculates that some of this deviation can be attributed to the Court protecting its own institutional prerogatives, but also believes that the justices are often "committed to jurisprudential traditions that are relatively autonomous from ordinary politics" (see also Richards and Kritzer 2002).

Finally, it should be noted that policy-making "independence" may not always be a source of frustration for competing policy-makers. Rogers (2001) has suggested that information in judicial opinions may represent a useful "signaling game" between politically convergent legislators and judges, especially when judges are able to inform their cohort on how well laws are operating. As Whittington (2003, 452) explains, "the judiciary can provide additional information to the policy-making process that was unavailable to the legislature at the time of the initial policy decision." A court might share the legislature's policy goals but still void a law if the judicial record demonstrates that the act failed to achieve the desired objectives. Even if laws are not struck down, a judicial decision may allow courts to send signals back to legislators about whether there are unexpected problems or unanticipated consequences. Thus, in a number of ways, "a legislature benefits from the critical post-enactment examination by a friendly court," which is why it is not necessarily inconsistent with a regime politics perspective to note that judges sometimes challenge the policies of a live majority.

7 CONCLUSION

The research on courts and party politics has advanced quite a bit since Dahl first proposed that judges serve national governing coalitions primarily by upholding their lawmaking against constitutional challenges. Moving beyond this "deference" model a new generation of scholars is using this framework also to explain the sources of judicial empowerment, including the circumstances within which courts might challenge the agendas of governing majorities. Others have drawn attention to different ways in which courts might serve governing coalitions, including removing obstructions to governance, enhancing credible commitments, stabilizing partisan coalitions, imposing national norms on subnational units of government, and in some cases promoting a strategy of political entrenchment. This new body of work also gives us a better perspective on the circumstances within which judges might assert genuine autonomy in relation to the rest of the political system.

Still, although the promise of this approach has been clearly demonstrated, there are other steps that must be taken for this literature to move forward and establish greater influence in the discipline. Scholars who believe that the concept of governing coalitions is best used as an interpretive framework should develop more focused arguments about why this framework is better than others at explaining judicial politics; they will also need to defend against the suspicion that any court action might be interpreted, *post hoc*, as reflecting some political advantage to governing coalitions. Scholars who believe that this approach is a promising fount for the generation of hypotheses need to develop a collection of propositions against which the model can be tested. In order to link this empirical scholarship with traditional legal scholarship we will need to see more concerted efforts at addressing the implications of this type of analysis for our understanding of debates about the rule of law, judicial independence, and the capacity of courts to act as a bulwark for rights protection. Greater influence within political science will require more focused engagement with research traditions outside of the traditional public law canon, including work in party systems, comparative politics, and the new institutionalism.

These efforts should be encouraged. We have already seen enough to know that a focus on courts and party politics opens up the field of law and courts to a wider range of questions than has typically driven the mainstream literature on judicial behavior, and provides a platform from which scholars across various fields can begin to reintegrate courts into the broader analysis of political systems.

REFERENCES

ADAMANY, D. 1980. The Supreme Court's role in critical elections. In *Realignment in American Politics*, ed. B. Campbell and R. Trilling. Austin: University of Texas Press.

BALKIN, J., and LEVINSON, S. 2001. Understanding the constitutional revolution. *Virginia Law Review*, 87: 1045–109.

BARROW, D. J., ZUK, G., and GRYSKI, G. G. 1996. *The Federal Judiciary and Institutional Change*. Ann Arbor: University of Michigan Press.

CARPENTER, D. P. 2001. *The Forging of Bureaucratic Autonomy: Reputations, Networks, and Policy Innovation in Executive Agencies, 1862–1928*. Princeton, NJ: Princeton University Press.

CASPER, J. 1976. The Supreme Court and national policy making. *American Political Science Review*, 70: 50–63.

CICHOWSKI, R. A. 1998. Integrating the environment: the European Court and the construction of supranational policy. *Journal of European Public Policy*, 5: 387–405.

—— 2001. Judicial rulemaking and the institutionalization of the EU Sex Equality Policy. In *The Institutionalization of Europe*, ed. A. Stone Sweet, W. Sandholtz, and N. Fligstein. Oxford: Oxford University Press.

CLAYTON, C. W. 2002. The supply and demand sides of judicial policy-making (or, why be so positive about the judicialization of politics)? *Law and Contemporary Problems*, 65: 69–86.

—— and MAY, D. 1999. The new institutionalism and Supreme Court decision making: toward a political regimes approach. *Polity*, 32: 233–52.

—— and PICKERILL, M. 2004. The Rehnquist Court and the political dynamics of federalism. *Perspectives on Politics*, 2: 233–48.

DAHL, R. A. 1957. Decision-making in a democracy: the Supreme Court as a national policymaker. *Journal of Public Law*, 6: 279–95.

EPSTEIN, R. A. 1990. The independence of judges: the uses and limitations of public choice theory. *Brigham Young University Law Review*, 1990: 827–56.

FEREJOHN, J. 1999. Independent judges, dependent judiciary: explaining judicial independence. *Southern California Law Review*, 72: 353–84.

FUNSTON, R. 1975. The Supreme Court and critical elections. *American Political Science Review*, 69: 795–811.

GATES, J. B. 1992. *The Supreme Court and Partisan Realignment: A Macro- and Microlevel Perspective*. Boulder, Colo.: Westview.

—— 1999. The Supreme Court and partisan change: contravening, providing, and diffusing partisan conflict. Pp. 98–114 in *The Supreme Court in American Politics: New Institutionalist Interpretations*, ed. H. Gillman and C. W. Clayton. Lawrence: University Press of Kansas.

GILLMAN, H. 1999. The Court is an idea, not a building (or a game): interpretive institutionalism and the analysis of Supreme Court decision-making. Pp. 65–87 in *Supreme Court Decision-Making: New Institutionalist Approaches*, ed. C. W. Clayton and H. Gillman. Chicago: University of Chicago Press.

—— 2001. *The Votes That Counted: How the Court Decided the 2000 Presidential Election*. Chicago: University of Chicago Press.

—— 2002. How political parties can use courts to advance their agendas: federal courts in the United States, 1875–1891. *American Political Science Review*, 96: 511–24.

—— 2003. Judicial independence through the lens of *Bush v. Gore*: four lessons from political science. *Ohio State Law Journal*, 64: 249–64.

—— 2004. Martin Shapiro and the new institutionalism in judicial behavior studies. In *Annual Review of Political Science*, vol. 7, ed. N. W. Polsby. Portland, Ore.: Annual Reviews.

—— 2006. Party politics and constitutional change: the political origins of liberal judicial activism. In *The Supreme Court and American Political Development*, ed. R. Kahn and K. Kersch. Lawrence: University Press of Kansas.

GINSBURG, T. 2002. Economic analysis and the design of constitutional courts. *Theoretical Inquiries in Law*, 3: 49–86.

GINSBURG, T. 2003. *Judicial Review in New Democracies: Constitutional Courts in Asian Cases*. New York: Cambridge University Press.

GOLDSTEIN, L. F. 2001. *Constituting Federal Sovereignty: The European Union in Comparative Context*. Baltimore: Johns Hopkins University Press.

GRABER, M. A. 1993. The non-majoritarian difficulty: legislative deference to the judiciary. *Studies in American Political Development*, 7: 35–73.

—— 1998. Federalist or friends of Adams: the Marshall Court and party politics. *Studies in American Political Development*, 12: 229–66.

HAYS, B. D. 2004. The Supreme Court as coalition stabilizer: how political orders use the Court to maintain their national coalitions. Presented at the annual meeting of the Western Political Science Association, Portland.

HIRSCHL, R. 2000. The political origins of judicial empowerment through constitutionalization: lessons from four constitutional revolutions. *Law and Social Inquiry*, 25: 91–148.

—— 2004. *Toward Juristocracy: The Origins and Consequences of the New Constitutionalism*. Cambridge, Mass.: Harvard University Press.

JOHNSEN, D. 2003. Ronald Reagan and the Rehnquist Court on congressional power: presidential influences on constitutional change. *Indiana Law Journal*, 78: 363–412.

KAHN, R., and KERSCH, K. I. (eds.) 2006. *The Supreme Court and American Political Development*. Lawrence: University Press of Kansas.

KECK, T. 2004. *The Most Activist Supreme Court in History: The Road to Modern Constitutional Conservatism*. Chicago: University of Chicago Press.

—— 2005. Does the Court still follow the election returns? Presented at the annual meeting of the American Political Science Association.

KERSCH, K. I. 2004. *Constructing Civil Liberties: Discontinuities in the Development of American Constitutional Law*. Cambridge: Cambridge University Press.

KLARMAN, M. J. 1996. Rethinking the civil rights and civil liberties revolutions. *Virginia Law Review*, 82: 1–68.

—— 1997. Majoritarian judicial review: the entrenchment problem. *Georgetown Law Journal*, 85: 491–554.

—— 2000. The racial origins of modern criminal procedure. *Michigan Law Review*, 99: 48–97.

—— 2001a. The white primary rulings: a case study in the consequences of Supreme Court decisionmaking. *Florida State University Law Review*, 29: 55–108.

—— 2001b. *Bush v. Gore* through the lens of constitutional history. *California Law Review*, 89: 1721–66.

—— 2004. *From Jim Crow to Civil Rights: The Supreme Court and the Struggle for Racial Equality*. Oxford: Oxford University Press.

KRITZER, H. M. 2003. Martin Shapiro: anticipating the new institutionalism. Pp. 387–417 in *The Pioneers of Judicial Behavior*, ed. N. Maveety. Ann Arbor: University of Michigan Press.

LANDES, W. M., and POSNER, R. A. 1975. The independent judiciary in an interest-group perspective. *Journal of Law and Economics*, 18: 875–901.

LASSER, W. 1985. The Supreme Court in periods of critical realignment. *Journal of Politics*, 47: 1174–87.

LOVELL, G. I. 2003. *Legislative Deferrals: Statutory Ambiguity, Judicial Power, and American Democracy*. Cambridge: Cambridge University Press.

MAGALHAES, P. 1999. The politics of judicial reform in Eastern Europe. *Comparative Politics*, 31: 43–62.

McMahon, K. 2003. *Reconsidering Roosevelt on Race: How the Presidency Paved the Road to Brown*. Chicago: University of Chicago Press.

Moustafa, T. 2003. Law versus the state: the judicialization of politics in egypt. *Law and Social Inquiry*, 28: 883–930.

North, D. C. 1990. *Institutions, Institutional Change, and Economic Performance*. Cambridge: Cambridge University Press.

—— and Weingast, B. 1989. Constitutions and commitment: the evolution of institutions governing public choice in seventeenth-century Britain. *Journal of Economic History*, 49: 803–32.

Orren, K., and Skowronek, S. 2004. *The Search for American Political Development*. New York: Cambridge University Press.

Peretti, T. 1999. *In Defense of a Political Court*. Princeton, NJ: Princeton University Press.

Powe, Jr., L. A. 2001. *The Warren Court and American Politics*. Cambridge, Mass.: Belknap.

Ramseyer, M. 1994. The puzzling independence of courts: a comparative approach. *Journal of Legal Studies*, 23: 721–47.

—— and Rasmusen, E. B. 2001. Why are Japanese judges so conservative in politically charged cases? *American Political Science Review*, 95: 331–44.

Richards, M. J., and Kritzer, H. M. 2002. Jurisprudential regimes in Supreme Court decision making. *American Political Science Review*, 96: 305–20.

Rogers, J. R. 2001. Information and judicial review: a signaling game of legislative–judicial interactions. *American Journal of Political Science*, 45: 84–99.

Rosenberg, G. N. 1980. *The Hollow Hope: Can Courts Bring About Social Change?* Chicago: University of Chicago Press.

Salzberger, E. 1993. A positive analysis of the doctrine of separation of powers, or: why do we have an independent judiciary? *International Review of Law and Economics*, 13: 349–79.

—— 2001. Temporary appointments and judicial independence: theoretical analysis and empirical findings from the Supreme Court of Israel. *Israel Law Review*, 35: 481–523.

—— and Fenn, P. 1999. Judicial independence: some evidence from the English Court of Appeal. *Journal of Law and Economics*, 42: 831–47.

Scheppele, K. L. 2002. Declarations of independence: judicial reactions to political pressure. In *Judicial Independence at the Crossroads*, ed. S. B. Burbank and B. Friedman. Thousand Oaks, Calif.: Sage.

Shapiro, M. 1980a. Appeal. *Law and Society Review*, 14: 629–61.

—— 1980b. *Courts: A Comparative and Political Analysis*. Chicago: University of Chicago Press.

—— 2000. The success of judicial review and democracy. In *On Law, Politics, and Judicialization*, ed. M. Shapiro and A. Stone Sweet. Oxford: Oxford University Press.

Smith, R. M. 1988. Political jurisprudence, the "new institutionalism," and the future of public law. *American Political Science Review*, 82: 90–108.

Stasavage, D. 2002. Credible commitment in early modern Europe: North and Weingast revisited. *Journal of Law, Economics and Organization*, 18: 155–86.

Stephenson, M. C. 2003. "When the devil turns...:" the political foundations of independent judicial review. *Journal of Legal Studies*, 32: 59–89.

Sussman, N., and Yafeh, Y. 2003. Constitutions, commitment, and the historical evidence of the relation between institutions, property rights, and financial development. At http://papers.ssrn.com/sol3/papers.cfm?abstract_id=347640 (visited May 1, 2006).

TUSHNET, M. 2003. *The New Constitutional Order.* Princeton, NJ: Princeton University Press.

VOIGT, S., and SALZBERGER, E. 2002. On constitutional processes and the delegation of power. *Theoretical Inquiries in Law,* 3: 207–64.

WEINGAST, B. 1993. Constitutions as governance structures: the political foundations of secure markets. *Journal of Institutional and Theoretical Economics,* 1: 286–311.

WHITTINGTON, K. E. 2001. Taking what they give us: explaining the Court's federalism offensive. *Duke Law Journal,* 51: 477–520.

—— 2003. Legislative sanctions and the strategic environment of judicial review. *International Journal of Constitutional Law,* 1: 446–74.

—— 2005. "Interpose your friendly hand:" political supports for the exercise of judicial review by the United States Supreme Court. *American Political Science Review,* 99: 583–96.

UNDERSTANDING REGIME CHANGE: PUBLIC OPINION, LEGITIMACY, AND LEGAL CONSCIOUSNESS

SCOTT BARCLAY

SUSAN S. SILBEY

FORTY years ago, Murphy and Tanenhaus (1968) argued that courts played an important role facilitating and legitimating regime change. By their willingness to revise existing constitutional definitions, courts help political institutions pursue popular policies. The idea of court-assisted regime change resonated within political science because it appeared consistent with contemporary policy controversies. In cases such as desegregation and interracial marriage, the U.S. Supreme Court appeared to be creating openings for state and local, as well as federal, agencies to incorporate popular demands for change. The idea appeared fairly simple:

Sometimes governmental officials can meet public demands only if certain changes are made in the rules under which politics is traditionally conducted. Furthermore, the boundaries separating constitutionally permissible and impermissible behavior are typically vague. Thus, important and controversial government policies are likely to engender disputes not only about their merits but also about whether the government, or a particular set of officials can legitimately undertake a given course of action.... When it validates official decisions which may initially seem to many to violate the rules, a constitutional court thereby gives sanction to regime change. In refusing to validate such decisions, a court denies them its imprimatur of legitimacy.   (Murphy and Tanenhaus 1968, 358–9)

The requirement necessary for constitutional courts to accomplish regime change was clear: a population sufficiently aware of the role of a constitutional court to permit such a court to review and legitimate changes in rules required for new policies. Yet, because of the low level of awareness within the general population of the institutional components of the relevant constitutional court (see Caldeira and Gibson 1992, fn. 5; cf. Mondak 1991; 1994), Murphy and Tanenhaus's attractive idea of court legitimated regime change nonetheless lacked an empirically functioning mechanism.

Here we argue that contemporary research on legal consciousness offers a means to explain the role of courts in facilitating and legitimating regime changes that keep government policy consonant, to variable degrees, with transformations in material conditions and popular sentiment. The dynamic nature of legal consciousness allows courts to redefine the formal law and fundamental rules that have previously governed social interactions without precipitously affecting the long-term legitimacy of the state or its political institutions. Furthermore, popular legal consciousness allows this process to occur despite the lack of popular knowledge of the institutional components apparently required to achieve such regime change. In framing our argument, we adopt an unusual path through the literature on legal consciousness.[1] More often described as a development within sociolegal scholarship, the relevance of legal consciousness—as a concept and body of theoretically-informed empirical research—for mainstream political science has been less often explored. The extraordinary power wielded by an unelected constitutional court within a democratic republic continues to vex political scientists and legal scholars. Recent literature on legal consciousness provides a multidisciplinary perspective that offers new resources for addressing this long-standing dilemma.

1 REGIME CHANGE

For our part, we reconceptualize regime change by beginning with an assumption of political dysfunction: an inability of the existing political system to translate

[1] For reviews of the literature on legal consciousness, see Albiston (2006); Engel (1998); Ewick (2003); Garcia-Villegas (2003); Hertogh (2004); Marshall and Barclay (2003); Silbey (2001; 2005).

a popular set of demands on a policy issue into political action (Easton 1965a; 1965b). This scenario presumes that the demand for policy change can arise independent of a commensurate shift in political power within a legislature.

Although legislators respond to the groups who exercise social influence, the legislature is not a perfect reflection of the social power exercised by these various groups at a given moment. Once groups convert social influence into institutionalized bases of power, these groups are able to utilize legislative position, and the coercive power of law, to consolidate and maintain existing political and social advantage. We propose that the sources of regime change lay in the potential difference between the power being exercised by a group in ongoing struggles for legislative influence and the institutionalized power exercised through established position, office, and administrative hierarchy.

Pressure for regime change occurs because the political power currently exercised by one group, and entrenched in existing laws, no longer correlates well with the current level of social influence that the group exercises in larger society. The influence of particular social groups varies as their economic, social, or demographic resources shift. For example, by the early 1960s, white Southern Democrats exercised considerable power in the U.S. Congress and dominated the state legislatures in the South. They also used their political power to effectively institutionalize their preferences within existing state and federal laws. This political power, however, bore little relationship to their declining legitimacy in the face of the expanding civil rights movement. Despite its declining legitimacy, this group's dominant position within the existing political institutions made it difficult to dislodge it to a political status more commensurate with its social standing.

In a representative democracy, the disjuncture between institutionalized power and sociocultural status normally occurs where there is a systemic failure in the mechanisms for coordinating levels of social power with levels of political power. For example, the electoral disenfranchisement of African-Americans in most Southern states certainly precluded the effective political representation of their interests and is the most evident example of a purposive failure in U.S. representative mechanisms. A similar phenomenon occurred in the case of lesbians and gays although no specific law proscribed their electoral involvement. As Justice Brennan noted, "because of the immediate and severe opprobrium often manifested against homosexuals once so identified publicly, members of this group are particularly powerless to pursue their rights openly in the political arena" (*Rowland v. Mad River*, 470 U.S. 1009, at 1014, 1985).

A constitutional court, we argue, may be able to redefine the existing rules in order to facilitate the policies necessary to effect regime change. Courts can recognize the claims and interests voiced by the less politically powerful group and simultaneously withdraw institutional resources from the politically entrenched group. Constitutional courts can facilitate regime change because, using law as a basis, they are able to engage the claims of the less powerful when other institutions are constrained by their affiliation with the politically entrenched.

Our revised version, however, does not resolve the fundamental difficulty associated with the idea of court-sanctioned regime change: according to public opinion surveys, the level of comprehension in the general population about the Court's role is insufficient to drive this process. In the next sections, we suggest that the use of survey data as the basis for considering the nature of regime change is flawed to the extent it relies on individualistic conceptions of social action and static measures of change in policy positions to explain shifts in the Court's legitimacy. Clearly, there are serious flaws in public opinion measures as indicators of general support for regime change at any point in time (Althaus 2003; Zaller 1991; Zaller and Feldman 1992; Bennett 1988; Pierce and Rose 1974; Converse 1974; 1962). The greater problem, we claim, derives from the inability of standard survey measures to capture the dynamic cultural processes that underwrite institutional power, legitimacy, and durability, or to explain the relationship among popular opinion, policy initiatives, and regime change. We turn to the notion of legal consciousness not only to explain the processes involved in these transitions, but also to highlight the fundamental role of legal norms as a catalyst in this process. Rather than focusing on Court action and the general level of legitimacy enjoyed by the Court as an institution, we will focus on the understandings and uses of law circulating in American popular culture to explain both regime change and continuity.

2 THE MECHANISM OF CHANGE AND THE MECHANISM OF LEGITIMATION

In their definition of regime change, Murphy and Tanenhaus (1968) divided the mechanism that precipitated the *need* for regime change, a change in popular opinion, from the mechanism used to *legitimate* the action, a change in the fundamental legal rules. Their sole focus was the latter, the act of legitimation. How the population comes to the position of desiring a policy change requiring a fundamental change in the current rules is an issue Murphy and Tanenhaus never explicitly address. We deal with both.

Murphy and Tanenhaus used measures of popular opinion on the assumption that only a population that understood and embraced the rule-changing role of a constitutional court would accord sufficient legitimacy to the subsequent change to successfully institutionalize regime change. The court's legitimacy as an institution also attaches to the decisions, including the rule changes, issued by the court. Thus, Murphy and Tanenhaus focused on measures of support for the court and measures of popular understanding of the court's role in the political system.

Yet, for Murphy and Tanenhaus, the use of survey data to measure the citizenry's knowledge and understanding of the constitutional court was problematic. For example, they note that in 1949 only 17 percent of Americans could correctly offer the name of "the highest court of law in the United States" (Murphy and Tanenhaus 1968, fn. 2). Although the level of information about the highest court has presumably increased in recent years, the problem remains; a large enough cohort of individuals do not seem to possess sufficient information of the role of the constitutional court to facilitate agreement to a change in the previously accepted rules.

Political scientists have largely abandoned the search for a direct link between institutional legitimacy and the legitimation function implied by the idea of regime change (Caldeira and Gibson 1992, fn. 5). Social psychological and experimental results on courts and legitimacy (e.g. Gibson 1989; Mondak 1991; 1994; Tyler and Rasinski 1991; Tyler and Mitchell 1994; Baird 2001; see also Murphy, Tanenhaus, and Kastner 1973; Tanenhaus and Murphy 1981) raise the tantalizing possibility of this link, although political scientists have refocused their efforts on measures of diffuse support to consider how the general population views constitutional courts (e.g. Caldeira 1986; Caldeira and Gibson 1992; 1995; Gibson, Caldeira, and Baird 1998). According to Easton (1965a, 273; see Caldeira and Gibson 1992; 637), diffuse support can be characterized as a "reservoir of favorable attitudes or good will that helps members to accept or tolerate outputs to which they are opposed or the effects of which they see as damaging to their wants." Such support is more amorphous; for empirical research, it has often been translated and operationalized as "trust" (e.g. Tyler 1998), "satisfaction" (e.g. Tyler and Mitchell 1994), or "institutional commitment" (e.g. Caldeira and Gibson 1992, 638). Interestingly, these measures of diffuse support often implicitly or explicitly conflate it with legitimacy. Nonetheless, the idea of court-sanctioned regime change is also not well supported by this more capacious notion of diffuse support. For example, Caldeira and Gibson (1992, 636) "find no connection between support for specific policies and diffuse support for the Supreme Court. Instead, broad political values—commitment to social order and support for democratic norms—do a good job of predicting attitudes toward the Supreme Court."

As it currently stands, we are left with the fact that public opinion data appear either unable to support the idea of court-sanctioned regime change or, more likely, unable to measure effectively the complex individual and social mechanisms the concept is meant to capture (e.g. Bourdieu 1990, 125). Contemporary research has addressed some of these persistent dilemmas by shifting the conceptual framing. This work explores the importance of the constitutional court in regime change, and in general, through studies of the role of law and courts in daily lives of ordinary citizens, rather than through surveys of support for particular policies or institutions. Recent scholarship also shows that the public's comprehension and evaluation of issues and institutions can be, and often is, shaped by circulating cultural tropes and metaphors, as well as popular media and "opinion leaders." From more recent studies of the role of law in everyday life, we can begin to craft an alternative construction of regime change based upon legal consciousness. This concept offers the means to recognize the relationship among and shifts within popular understandings of law, courts, and regime change.

3 LEGAL CONSCIOUSNESS: DIFFUSE, DYNAMIC, AND SUBVERSIVE

The phrase, legal consciousness, is in many ways a misnomer because it implies a focus on individuals and individual minds. Unlike research on attitudes about partisan choices, policy issues, or other political preferences, research on legal consciousness does not document primarily what people think about the law "but rather *how what they think and do coalesces* into a recognizable, durable phenomena and institution we recognize as the law" (Silbey 2005, 347, our emphasis). Studies of legal consciousness seek to trace the meaning and power of law, not in the acts and decisions of constitutional courts, but in the acts and decisions of ordinary citizens and official legal agents as they go about their work and lives. Ewick and Silbey argue that the rule of law is "an emergent feature of social relations rather than an external apparatus acting upon social life. As a constituent of social interactions, the law—or what [they] call legality—embodies the diversity of the situations out of which it emerges and that it helps structure" (1998, 17). Thus legality as a structure of social action includes decisions to drive on the right side of the road in the U.S. but on the left in Australia and Japan, to threaten litigation when a neighbor's dog overturns one's garbage, to file workmen's compensation and disability claims when injured on the job, to exchange drivers' licenses and auto registration documents when in an accident, to seek a patent for an invention, to write a will in order to transfer property to charities after death, to complain about litigious citizens, to watch Court TV, as well as myriad decisions by administrative agencies, local magistrates, state or federal legislatures, and the U.S. Supreme Court.

In studies of legal consciousness, individuals and their social interactions are key elements constituting the power and legitimacy of legal institutions. Persons are not, however, conceived of as carriers of specifically targeted opinions and political directives for representative government, but rather as agents of legal continuity, change, and legitimacy as they perpetuate, invent, or resist cultural tropes, concepts, and interpretations that invoke political and legal associations. In these social interactions, individuals are behavioral and cognitive participants in the social production (and reproduction) of cultural schemas; people's verbal and corporeal expressions reinforce incrementally, transform existing, or begin the process of inventing and accepting new schema. In concert with others, people implicitly construct or reconstruct every day in multiple arenas and in multiple, often contradictory, forms the meanings we attribute to law, rules, power, and authority. Yet few of these transactions or meanings are exclusively legal, or political.

"Legal consciousness... consists of mobilizing, inventing, and amending pieces of these schemas" that refer to law and legality (Silbey 2005, 349). Since the construction and transmission of legal consciousness occur through myriad social transactions, many of which may not appear at first to have anything to do with law, individuals' thoughts and behavior are relevant only when aggregated and circulated through common or shared social meanings. "Law and legality achieve their recognizable character as 'the rule of law', despite the diversity of constituent actions and experiences... because individual transactions are crafted out of a limited array of generally available cultural schemas. These few but generally circulating schemas are not themselves fixed or immutable, but are also constantly in the making through local invocations and inventions" (Silbey 2005, 347, referencing Ewick and Silbey 1998).

The concept of legal consciousness offers conceptual and theoretical advantages to the analysis of the relationships among regime change, public opinion, and legitimacy. Unlike surveys of public opinion, studies of legal consciousness do not focus on exclusively legal or political expression to understand legal authority and legitimacy. In other words, they do not focus so close to the surface of what is to be explained, or rely entirely on what is explicitly articulated and self-conscious. Instead, research on legal consciousness (e.g. Bumiller 1988; Fleury-Steiner 2003; Fleury-Steiner and Nielsen 2006; Greenhouse 1986; Hoffman 2003; 2005; Hull 2003; Larson 2004; Marshall 2003; 2005; McCann 1994; Merry 1990; Nielsen 2000; 2002; 2004; Pelisse 2004; Sarat 1990; Yngvesson 1993) proposes that the propagation and perpetuation of cultural schemas are so embedded in everyday social transactions that individuals often fail to appreciate the normally seamless diffusion through each and every social exchange. "Law is powerful, and rules everyday life because its constructions are uncontroversial and have become normalized and habitual. Law's mediations have been sedimented throughout the routines of daily living, helping to make things move around in more or less clear ways, without having to invoke, display, or wield its elaborate and intricate procedures, especially its ultimate, physical force" (Silbey 2005). Thus, we defer to traffic lights, wear seat belts, read warning labels on appliances, and follow instructions on pharmaceutical products. These legally-mandated communications are so routinized that we no longer recall the struggles that produced the specific legal regulations and the required language. Although there are may be some who still see each one of these as a sign of a continuing political battle, the legal content is usually buried within concerns about health, safety, or prudence.

The gradual or incremental transformation of meanings and the status associated with an activity, such as where or how to drive a car, or a group, such as lesbians or African-Americans, may occur without individual or collective awareness of the scope of the transition until new signs and new norms have overtly emerged and are openly contested culturally and politically. The slow emergence of modifications in cultural schemas through everyday social exchange may help to explain why it is often impossible for survey research that asks a direct question about support for specific policies to capture the comprehensive nature of a transition in an individual's understanding. Individuals may not recognize the extent to which their interpretive schemas have been reconfigured because the shifts occur through myriad conventional, unusually unproblematic, and unreflective, transactions. The taken-for-granted norms of everyday transactions reinforce the correctness and legitimacy of the new position and, as individuals engage in social exchange, they are complicit, without planning or intention, in fostering sociocultural changes. Because law's "meanings and uses echo and resonate with other common phenomena" (Ewick and Silbey 1998, 17) through shared words and metaphors (Lakoff and Johnson 1980), legality is often only one among many institutional beneficiaries of the schema that comprise social transactions. This makes it particularly difficult to recognize gradual transitions in interpretations relevant to a specific institution or policy or law. Thus, the survey researchers' efforts to identify specific and measurable attitudes about particular issues fail to capture the extent to which there has been collective transformation of their understanding of the acceptability of the current rules.

This disjuncture between articulated opinions of individuals and collective cultural shifts may explain why some social movements often appear to burst suddenly onto the public scene. Surveys usually begin to record the articulated attitudes of individuals only when policy issues are already politically contested or even at the time when constitutional courts are already engaged in regime change. For example, the Gallup poll did not ask a question about the legalization of same-sex marriage until March 1996, when a state court ruling in Hawaii was imminent (*Baehr v. Miike*, 1996 WL 694235, 1996)—five years after the case was filed (Eskridge 2002), three years after the Hawaii Supreme Court first commented on the issue (*Baehr v. Lewin*, 852 P.2d 44, 1993), and twenty-five years after the first cases were filed on this issue in state courts (Barclay and Fisher 2006). The circulation and aggregation of the new interlaced meanings of marriage, romantic commitment, sex, sexuality, state action, and privacy seemed to have long preceded their recognition in surveys of public attitudes. Lesbian and gay relationships began to be socially acknowledged prior to any changes in the legal status of these relationships (e.g. Hull 2003).

The method of cognitive/cultural diffusion inherent in legal consciousness—through ordinary, everyday social transactions—also allows us to understand the means by which the status and legitimacy of an idea can be transformed while the political power of an opposing group may remain dominant. The transformation of old narratives and the invention of new schema through everyday transactions undermine the social power of some groups, and support the growing power of challenging groups. Eventually, the growing influence of the challenging group may aggregate at the cultural level to underwrite a transition in the rules. Importantly, the process of inventing and accepting new schema incrementally through ordinary exchange, media, and habit means that social norms and expectations may be transformed even as rules, formal laws, and officers continue to support exercises of power in a contrary direction. Legality enacted and propagated through social transaction need only be loosely tied to the position of formal law and it may directly challenge it (Ewick and Silbey 1998; 2003). In fact, the strongest statements of formal law may occur at points where there is overt contestation over the current policy because social norms and legal rules are no longer consonant. The decay in norms, and the failure of formerly accepted actions and ideas to be reproduced, brings into prominence the power inherent in legal authority and action. As the current political configuration tries to reassert the authority of these decaying norms, the disjuncture among political, legal authority and cultural norms becomes explicit.

This scenario is the setting for regime change: A portion of the population no longer enacts the current rules even as the current political configuration presses for enforcement of those rules. The subsequent change in rules in a regime change is an indication or prediction of the impending transition in political power to a new configuration representing the emerging social consensus. Similarly, the push for change in a few key policy areas is just one indicator that a transition is under way to a new social understanding of a previously outlawed activity or of a previously marginalized group. Desegregation of educational facilities and the prohibition of laws restricting interracial marriage, for example, represented recognitions that a new approach to race had already catalyzed in popular legal consciousness.

Once we conceptualize legal consciousness as participation in the construction of schemas concerning law and legal institutions, we can also understand what has often been interpreted in survey research as inconsistent and contradictory among the mass populace and between mass and elite public opinion. Consider for example Caldeira and Gibson's (1992) study in which they note a divergence between members of the general public and "opinion leaders" in the etiology of support for the Supreme Court. The mass public does not condition its support, Caldeira and Gibson suggest, on the Court's satisfaction of their policy or ideological preferences; but opinion leaders' support seems to rest on congruence in policy and principle. In their data, one is more likely to find that mass opinion may not be aligned with a regime change while the populace still voices support for the Court: Elite support is conditioned on the extent of ideological agreement, eliminating the vexing disjuncture between the regime changes and mass public opinion.

The discussion of hegemony in the research on legal consciousness also helps explain Caldeira and Gibson's findings that elite opinion leaders have more informed, consistent, and ideologically nuanced understandings of institutions and issues and condition their support on the basis of these views; the mass public does not condition its support for the Court on the basis of policy agreements. The concept of hegemony is, Silbey (1998, 287) writes, "to refer to those circumstances where representations and social constructions are so embedded" in normal social transactions and culture "as to be almost invisible." Research on legal consciousness emerged in the 1980s and 1990s specifically to explain the willingness of citizens in representative democracies to support legal institutions that did not seem to live up to their announced ambitions of equal justice, or reliably support the self-articulated interests of the mass public, just those dilemmas Caldeira and Gibson's research identified. The analytic concept of hegemony helps scholars to describe the ways in which popular and elite opinion may vary, and the mechanisms in popular culture that sustain these differences.

The term hegemony refers to situations where "both the sources of power and the forms of subordination are buried. In these transactions, no one seems to be demanding obedience, and subordinate parties appear to be normally socialized rather than compliant. . . . Social actors are thus constrained without knowing from where or whom the constraint derives" (Ewick and Silbey 2003; cf. Ewick and Silbey 1995; Silbey 1998; Haltom and McCann 2004; Silbey 2005). Power is enacted when some actors are able to shape the schemas and narratives that relatively powerless individuals subsequently help to perpetuate. The degree of power that can be exercised in the construction and diffusion of narratives within cultural schema is rarely total and most often contested, but it may nevertheless have the potential for cultural hegemony. Hegemony is evidenced in an absence: for "struggles that are no longer active, where power is dispersed through social structures and meanings are so embedded that representational and institutional struggles are no longer visible" (Silbey 2005, 333).

What Pierson (2000, 252) calls path dependence, "the causal relevance of preceding stages in a temporal sequence," may also help us to understand the hegemonic potential of common cultural schemas and legal narratives. The framing, invocation, and alteration of narratives and cultural schemas are shaped by prior social understandings and currently accepted norms. Opinion leaders adjust their actions, representations, and metaphors to fit within recognized cultural schema and diffuse new narratives in response to old criteria (see Strathern 2005; Lakoff and Johnson 1980).[2] These paths allow the purposeful reproduction of political and cultural frames over extended periods, which marginalize certain groups and/or denigrate certain ideas to the advantage of others. But those same invocations also structure resistance to this marginalization. "Since power is exercised through the patterned distribution of resources and schemas, if there is resistance to this power it must also operate through the appropriation of these selfsame structures" (Ewick and Silbey 2003, 1335; 1995).

Finally, adopting the lens of legal consciousness to understand regime change unites the mechanisms of change and legitimacy, the critical link lacking in survey measures of popular legal knowledge and institutional legitimacy. That legal consciousness is embedded in and reproduced by everyday social interactions—many of which have nothing to do with law or political institutions—is an important source of its ability to legitimate news stories and other political reports, especially those consistent with existing cultural schema. As noted, the correctness or rightness of a view is reaffirmed with every repetition in each new social interaction. But the pervasive, overlapping, nonexclusive content of commonplace cultural schemas in legal consciousness should not lead us to discount the role of the law and legality in processes of legitimation. The privileged role of law and legality in constructing social meaning (Smart 1989; Comaroff and Comaroff 1991; Ewick and Silbey 1995) and its implicit or explicit structuring of so many social interactions, enables legal institutions to use rules, laws, and social norms to move between old and new political configurations.

4 Conclusion

Beginning with a classic account of the role of the Supreme Court in American politics, we have tried to show how the institutional authority of the Court is better understood when approached through a theory of legal consciousness. This effort to synthesize heretofore divergent literatures—models of court-legitimated regime change, surveys of public opinion, empirical studies of legal consciousness—suggests routes for future research.

---

[2] As Strathern (2005, 67) writes, analogies are not relations of cause and effect. Concepts do not procreate. People carry them across domains, often because there is some argument to pursue.

We urge greater attention to pragmatism's theories of action and what sometimes is called theories of practice (Dewey 1957 [1922]; 1929; Goffman 1967; Bourdieu 1977; Giddens 1979; 1986; Connell 1987; Sewell 1992; Emirbayer 1997, 287). For nearly two centuries, social theorists have debated the mechanisms of social cohesion and change. Too often the discussion has focused on methodological techniques, mistakenly dividing scholars by mode of data collection (quantitative versus qualitative; surveys versus interviews or observation), slighting both important theoretical distinctions and the grounds of conceptual convergence. The desire to collect reliable and valid information about human action may have too quickly sacrificed the essential question: What constitutes the social (Latour 2005)? Research on legal consciousness has attempted to answer these fundamental questions by focusing on the mechanisms by which action is always transactional, never the possession, product, or indicator of an individual alone, and always part of an ongoing assembly, of slow accretion, sedimentation, and institutionalization of memes, practices, and organizational forms experienced collectively as social institutions, such as the family, a court, or the rule of law. Importantly, the mechanisms of aggregation, coagulation, or what Latour (2005) calls reassembling, are neither additive nor multiplicative. These mechanisms do not impose an intellectual's model of mind where command of information creates status and contradiction is discrediting, and where being human is understood primarily in intellectuals' terms. Research on legal consciousness neither assumes a rational actor nor sets it as a standard. The literature we have been reviewing does not assume the premises and virtues of representative democracy are institutionalized within a particular governmental structure or regime. Rather, we understand action as part of temporally unfolding sequences of perception and impulse, mediated by habit and yet enabling imaginative revision or intelligence. As Dewey wrote, " 'present' activity is not a sharp knife-blade in time. The present is complex, containing within itself a multitude of habits and impulses" (Dewey 1957 [1922], 281). More productive analyses of the citizen's participation in constructing institutional legitimacy and regime change would draw from this rich pool of theoretical insight, eschewing the narrowly conceived models of mind and action that have proved less than fruitful in advancing institutional understanding and have been so difficult to reconcile theoretically. Instead, we should build our analyses of law and legal institutions with the recognition that they are forever in the making, using what is at hand, revisable and sometimes unexpected, yet also comfortably familiar and habituated.

References

ALBISTON, C. 2006. Legal consciousness and workplace rights. In *New Civil Rights Research: A Constitutive Approach*, ed. B. Fleury-Steiner and L. B. Nielsen. Burlington, Vt.: Dartmouth/Ashgate.

ALTHAUS, S. L. 2003. *Collective Preferences in Democratic Politics: Opinion Surveys and the Will of the People.* New York: Cambridge University Press.

BAIRD, V. A. 2001. Building institutional legitimacy: the role of procedural justice. *Political Research Quarterly*, 54: 333–54.

BARCLAY, S., and FISHER, S. F. 2006. Cause lawyers and social movements, failure and success: comparing the two waves of same sex marriage litigation. In *Cause Lawyers and Social Movements*, ed. A. Sarat and S. Scheingold. Palo Alto, Calif.: Stanford University Press.

BENNETT, S. E. 1988. "Know-Nothings" revisited: the meaning of political ignorance today. *Social Science Quarterly*, 69: 476–90.

BOURDIEU, P. 1977. *Outline of a Theory of Practice*, trans. R. Nice. New York: Cambridge University Press.

—— 1990. *In Other Words: Essays Towards a Reflexive Sociology*, trans. M. Adamson. Palo Alto, Calif.: Stanford University Press.

BUMILLER, K. 1988. *The Civil Rights Society: The Social Construction of Victims.* Baltimore: Johns Hopkins University Press.

CALDEIRA, G. A. 1986. Neither the purse nor the sword: dynamics of public confidence in the Supreme Court. *American Political Science Review*, 80: 1209–26.

—— and GIBSON, J. L. 1992. The etiology of public support for the Supreme Court. *American Journal of Political Science*, 36: 635–64.

—— 1995. The legitimacy of the Court of Justice in the European Union: models of institutional support. *American Political Science Review*, 89: 356–76.

COMAROFF, J., and COMAROFF, J. L. 1991. *Of Revelation and Revolution: Christianity, Colonialism, Consciousness in South Africa*, vol. 1. Chicago: University of Chicago Press.

CONNELL, R. W. 1987. *Gender and Power.* Stanford, Calif.: Stanford University Press.

CONVERSE, P. E. 1962. Information flow and the stability of partisan attitudes. *Public Opinion Quarterly*, 26: 578–99.

—— 1974. Nonattitudes and American public opinion: comment: the status of nonattitudes. *American Political Science Review*, 68: 650–60.

COOPER, D. 1995. Local government legal consciousness in the shadow of juridification. *Journal of Law and Society*, 22: 506–26.

COWAN, D. 2004. Legal consciousness: some observations. *Modern Law Review*, 67: 928–58

DEWEY, J. 1957 *Human Nature and Conduct: An Introduction to Social Psychology.* New York: Random House; originally published 1922.

—— 1929. *The Quest for Certainty: A Study of the Relation of Knowledge and Action.* New York: Minton, Balch.

EASTON, D. 1965a. *A Systems Analysis of Political Life.* New York: Wiley.

—— 1965b. *A Framework for Political Analysis.* Englewood Cliffs, NJ: Prentice Hall.

EMIRBAYER, M. 1997. Manifesto for a relational sociology. *American Journal of Sociology*, 103: 281–317.

ENGEL, D. 1998. How does law matter in the constitution of legal consciousness? In *How Does Law Matter?* ed. B. Garth and A. Sarat. Evanston, Ill.: Northwestern University Press.

ESKRIDGE, JR., W. N. 2002. *Equality Practice: Civil Unions and the Future of Gay Rights.* New York: Routledge.

ETZIONI, A. 2000. Social norms: internalization, persuasion, and history. *Law and Society Review*, 34: 157–78.

EWICK, P. 2003. Consciousness and ideology. In *The Blackwell Companion to Law and Society*, ed. A. Sarat. Malden, Mass.: Blackwell.

—— and SILBEY, S. B. 1995. Subversive stories and hegemonic tales: toward a sociology of narrative. *Law and Society Review*, 29: 197–226.

—— —— 1998. *The Common Place of Law: Stories from Everyday Life*. Chicago: University of Chicago Press.

—— —— 2003. Narrating social structure: stories of resistance to legal authority. *American Journal of Sociology*, 108: 1328–72.

FLEURY-STEINER, B. 2003. Before or against the law? Citizens' legal beliefs and expectations as death penalty jurors. *Studies in Law, Politics, and Society*, 27: 115–37.

—— and NIELSEN, L. B. (eds.) 2006. *New Civil Rights Research: A Constitutive Approach*. Burlington, Vt.: Dartmouth/Ashgate.

GARCIA-VILLEGAS, M. 2003. Symbolic power without symbolic violence? Critical comments on legal consciousness studies in the USA. *Droit et Société*, 53: 137–62.

GIBSON, J. L. 1989. Understandings of justice: institutional legitimacy, procedural justice, and political tolerance. *Law and Society Review*, 23: 469–96.

—— and CALDEIRA, G. A. 1995. The legitimacy of transnational legal institutions: compliance, support, and the European Court of Justice. *American Journal of Political Science*, 39: 459–89.

—— —— and BAIRD, V. A. 1998. On the legitimacy of national high courts. *American Political Science Review*, 92: 343–58.

GIDDENS, A. 1979. *Central Problems in Social Theory*. Berkeley: University of California Press.

—— 1986. *The Constitution of Society: Outline of the Theory of Structuration*. Berkeley: University of California Press.

—— 1990. *The Consequences of Modernity*. Stanford, Calif.: Stanford University Press.

GOFFMAN, E. 1967. *Interaction Ritual: Essays on Face-to-Face Behavior*. Garden City, NY: Doubleday.

GREENHOUSE, C. J. 1986. *Praying for Justice: Faith, Order, and Community in an American Town*. Ithaca, NY: Cornell University Press.

HALTOM, W., and McCANN, M. 2004. *Distorting the Law*. Chicago: University of Chicago Press.

HARCOURT, B. 2000. After the "social meaning turn:" implications for research design and methods of proof in contemporary criminal law policy analysis. *Law and Society Review*, 34: 179–212.

HERTOGH, M. 2004. A "European" conception of legal consciousness: rediscovering Eugen Ehrlich. *Journal of Law and Society*, 31: 455–81.

HOFFMAN, E. A. 2003. Legal consciousness and dispute resolution: different disputing behavior at two similar taxicab companies. *Law and Social Inquiry*, 28: 691–718.

—— 2005. Dispute resolution in a worker cooperative: formal procedures and procedural justice. *Law and Society Review*, 39: 51–82.

HULL, K. E. 2003. The cultural power of law and the cultural enactment of legality: the case of same sex marriage. *Law and Social Inquiry*, 28: 629–58.

LAKOFF, M., and JOHNSON, G. 1980. *Metaphors We Live By*. Chicago: University of Chicago Press.

LARSON, E. W. 2004. Institutionalizing legal consciousness: regulation and the embedding of market participants in the securities industry in Ghana and Fiji. *Law and Society Review*, 38: 737–67.

LATOUR, B. 2005. *Reassembling the Social: An Introduction to Actor Network Theory*. New York: Oxford University Press.

MARSHALL, A.-M. 2003. Injustice frames, legality, and the everyday construction of sexual harassment. *Law and Social Inquiry*, 28: 659–90.

—— 2005. Idle rights: employees' rights consciousness and the construction of sexual harassment policies. *Law and Society Review*, 39: 83–124.

—— and BARCLAY, S. 2003. In their own words: how ordinary people construct the legal world. *Law and Social Inquiry*, 28: 617–28.

McCANN, M. 1994. *Rights at Work: Pay Equity Reform and the Politics of Legal Mobilization*. Chicago: University of Chicago Press.

MERRY, S. E. 1990. *Getting Justice and Getting Even: Legal Consciousness Among Working Class Americans*. Chicago: University of Chicago Press.

MONDAK, J. J. 1991. Substantive and procedural aspects of Supreme Court decisions as determinants of institutional approval. *American Politics Quarterly*, 19: 174–88.

—— 1994. Policy legitimacy and the Supreme Court: the sources and contexts of legitimation. *Political Research Quarterly*, 47: 675–92.

MURPHY, W. F., and TANENHAUS, J. 1968. Public opinion and the United States Supreme Court: mapping of some prerequisites for court legitimation of regime change. *Law and Society Review*, 2: 357–84.

—— —— and KASTNER, D. L. 1973. *Public Evaluations of Constitutional Courts: Alternative Explanations*. London: Sage.

NIELSEN, L. B. 2000. Situating legal consciousness: experiences and attitudes of ordinary citizens about law and street harassment. *Law and Society Review*, 34: 1055–90.

—— 2002. Subtle, pervasive, harmful: racist and sexist remarks in public as hate speech. *Journal of Social Issues*, 58: 265–80.

—— 2004. *License to Harass: Law, Hierarchy and Offensive Public Speech*. Princeton, NJ: Princeton University Press.

PELISSE, J. 2004. Time, legal consciousness, and power: the case of France's 35-hour workweek laws. Presented at the annual meeting of the Law and Society Association, Chicago.

PIERCE, J. C., and ROSE, D. D. 1974. Nonattitudes and American public opinion: the examination of a thesis. *American Political Science Review*, 68: 626–49.

PIERSON, P. 2000. Increasing returns, path dependence, and the study of politics. *American Political Science Review*, 94: 251–67.

SARAT, A. 1990. "… The law is all over:" power, resistance and the legal consciousness of the welfare poor. *Yale Journal of Law and Humanities*, 2: 343–79.

SEWELL, W. H. 1992. A theory of structure: duality, agency, and transformation. *American Journal of Sociology*, 98: 1–29.

SILBEY, S. S. 1998. Ideology, power and justice. In *Justice and Power in Sociolegal Studies*, ed. B. Garth and A. Sarat, Evanston, Ill.: Northwestern University Press.

—— 2001. Legal culture and consciousness. In *International Encyclopedia of the Social and Behavioral Sciences*, ed. P. B. Baltes and N. J. Smelser. Amsterdam: Elsevier Science.

—— 2005. After legal consciousness. *Annual Review of Law and Social Science*, 1: 323–68.

SMART, C. 1989. *Feminism and the Power of the Law*. London: Routledge.

STRATHERN, M. 2005. *Kinship, Law and the Unexpected: Relatives Are Always a Surprise.* Cambridge: Cambridge University Press.

TANENHAUS, J., and MURPHY, W. F. 1981. Patterns of public support for the Supreme Court: a panel study. *Journal of Politics,* 43: 24–39.

TYLER, T. R. 1998. Public distrust in the law: a political perspective. *University of Cincinnati Law Review,* 66: 847–75.

—— and MITCHELL, G. 1994. Legitimacy and empowerment of discretionary legal authority: the United States Supreme Court and abortion rights. *Duke Law Journal,* 43: 703–815.

—— and RASINSKI, K. 1991. Legitimacy, and the acceptance of unpopular U.S. Supreme Court decisions: a reply to Gibson. *Law and Society Review,* 25: 621–30.

WRONG, D. 1979. *Power: Its Forms, Bases and Uses.* Chicago: University of Chicago Press.

YNGVESSON, B. 1993. *Virtuous Citizens, Disruptive Subjects: Order and Complaint in a New England Court.* New York: Routledge.

ZALLER, J. 1991. Information, values, and opinions. *American Political Science Review,* 85: 1215–37.

—— and FELDMAN, S. 1992. A simple theory of the survey response: answering questions versus revealing preferences. *American Journal of Political Science,* 36: 579–616.

PART IX

INTERDISCIPLINARY APPROACHES TO LAW AND POLITICS

C H A P T E R   39

....

LAW AND SOCIETY

....

LYNN MATHER

THE study of law and society rests on the belief that legal rules and decisions must be understood in context. Law is not autonomous, standing outside of the social world, but is deeply embedded within society. While political scientists recognize the fundamentally *political* nature of law, the law and society perspective takes this assumption several steps further by pointing to ways in which law is socially and historically constructed, how law both reflects and impacts culture, and how inequalities are reinforced through differential access to, and competence with, legal procedures and institutions.

The interdisciplinary field of law and society dates to the late 1950s/mid-1960s, and the story of its early development has been told before (e.g. Levine 1990; Schlegel 1995; Garth and Sterling 1998). Its philosophical roots lie in the jurispru-dential writings of the legal realists, who saw law as a vehicle for social engineering and challenged depictions of law as apolitical and autonomous. Likewise, social scientists were highly optimistic and confident about the potential of their work to solve social problems. Law and society scholars of the 1960s were also responding to many of the burning issues (literally—from riots in Los Angeles, Detroit, and elsewhere) of the day. Dismayed and frustrated by the formalism of the legal academy and the irrelevance and narrowness of much social science, a number of legal scholars and social scientists sought to engage in research that would address current policy debates over racial discrimination, poverty, and crime. Substantial funding for empirical research on these topics from the Ford Foundation, Russell Sage, and others provided further impetus for studies that would combine social science and law. Responding to the availability of research funds and their own political and intellectual agendas, a multidisciplinary group of scholars created the

Law and Society Association in 1964. Its members were drawn primarily from sociology, political science, and law, with some representation from anthropology, psychology, history, and occasionally economics.

The law and society field welcomed a wide range of subject areas for study. At the same time, President Lyndon Johnson's War on Poverty attempted to underscore the rule of law by creating federally funded legal aid programs to increase access to justice and address problems of the urban poor. Politicians and scholars recognized that what happened in local agencies or in trial courts could be as important as what happened in Washington, DC. This opened up new topics for empirical research on legal processes and resulted in law and society studies of public defender offices, legal aid, lower courts, administrative agencies, juries, police, and prosecutors. Political scientists authored many of these works and they enjoyed the feedback from sociologists and law professors they received in the law and society community. Constitutional law scholars who supported law and society in its early days had also turned their attention away from formal doctrinal analysis of Supreme Court decisions. They focused instead on interest groups and the lower courts in an effort to understand the political and organizational dynamics in test case litigation, the difficulties of implementing the decisions of the Supreme Court, the politics of administrative agencies, and the politics of judicial selection.

With this early history in mind, what are the key characteristics of a law and society perspective? What are some of the major research contributions of this field? And what recent developments in law and society hold particular promise for scholars of law and politics today?

1 KEY CHARACTERISTICS

Law and society scholarship has typically been *multidisciplinary* or *interdisciplinary.* Although most law and society scholars have been trained in one or another established discipline, they have frequently borrowed from other disciplines in their research. For example, early empirical analyses of plea bargaining in criminal courts reflected multiple methods and theories. The studies drew upon organization theory (Blumberg 1967; Eisenstein and Jacob 1977; Feeley 1979), social learning theory (Heumann 1978), ethnography (Mather 1979), ethnomethodology (Sudnow 1965), history (Alschuler 1979; Friedman 1979), and discourse analysis (Maynard 1984). As general law and society theories emerged, for example, to explain trial courts (Shapiro 1981; Boyum and Mather 1983), legal mobilization (McCann 1994), or "why the 'haves' come out ahead" (Galanter 1974), these theories sought to integrate the perspectives of different disciplines. Such interdisciplinary work has been more common in recent years. It reflects the maturity and growth of the field as well as the development of graduate and undergraduate programs in law and society.

Second, in terms of *epistemology and methodology*, law and society emerged during the 1960s, a time of the behavioral revolution in the social sciences and an optimistic embrace of positivism. Scholars focused their work on legal processes and individual and group decision-making. The study of rules was passé, as was the study of formal institutions. Empirical studies of behavior could be qualitative or quantitative, with the former defined broadly to encompass historical or anthropological methods. Methodological debates that were fierce in political science at this time were, by contrast, relatively muted within law and society. This tendency has continued to characterize the field, with greater focus on theory and substantive results than on sophistication of the methods or an insistence on the superiority of any particular method (Engel 1999).

By the 1980s, law and society critics of positivism raised serious challenges to the paradigm and articulated postrealist, interpretive, and constitutive approaches to law (Brigham and Harrington 1989; Harrington and Yngvesson 1990; Hunt 1993). Scholars reclaimed an interest in institutions (Smith 1988; Heydebrand and Seron 1990) as well as embracing an interest in legal ideology and legal discourse (Mather and Yngvesson 1980–1; Conley and O'Barr 1990; Merry 1990). Contemporary law and society scholarship encompasses a wide range of epistemological perspectives, from the cultural studies approach of law and humanities to empirical legal studies—and everything in between.

Third, *normative, policy-relevant* concerns for justice and equality that initially drove the field remain significant even as debate continues over the best way that scholars can realize that normative commitment. Sarat and Silbey (1988) urged law and society colleagues to reject the "pull of the policy audience" in order to produce broader, more critical scholarship and to avoid reinforcing the status quo. Levine (1990) noted the long history of tension between basic and applied research in sociolegal studies, but suggested that both could be realized; theoretical work can provide policy insights and studies of specific policy reforms can generate theory. In an important exchange over postmodernism and political change, Handler (1992) chastised the new postmodern scholarship for its inattention to power structures, collective identity, and the possibilities of transformative politics (but see responses by Calavita and Seron 1992; McCann 1992). A decade later, Munger (2001) called for renewed activism along with scholarly inquiry. He observed that as the law and society "field goes global, I see a reawakening of the earlier interest in justice and equality, and in power, class, race, ethnicity, and religion" (2001, 8).

Fourth, *comparative* approaches to research questions in law and society have been a long-standing commitment of the field, even as they have sometimes been honored in the breach more than the practice (Mather 2003). The very first volume of the *Law and Society Review* contained articles on comparative family law, one by a sociologist (Cicourel 1967) and the other by anthropologists (Bohannan and Huckleberry 1967). Other important sociolegal studies examined comparative disputing processes (Abel 1974; Moore 1978; Nader and Todd 1978), comparative lawyers (Abel and Lewis 1988; Epp 1998), comparative courts (Shapiro 1981; Jacob et al. 1996), comparative regulation (Hawkins 1992; Gunningham and Rees 1997; Kagan 2001), and comparative lay participation in legal decisions (Hans 2003).

One quarter of the membership of the Law and Society Association (LSA) is non-American, and the LSA leadership has been committed to holding its annual meetings in outside of the U.S. on a regular basis. Meetings in Amsterdam (1991), Glasgow (1996), Budapest (2001), and Berlin (2007) were held jointly with the Research Committee on the Sociology of Law (the last meeting was also supported by three other non-U.S. associations). LSA meetings held in Vancouver (2002) and Montreal (2008) are cosponsored by the Canadian Law and Society Association. Political scientists in the United States regularly suggest that the field of "American politics" should really be a subset of "comparative politics," but old habits die hard. The American politics subfield operates quite independently and scholars infrequently cite across subfields. By contrast, the law and society field actively seeks connections to the empirical scholarship on law being done in other countries, connections that are facilitated by LSA networks.

Finally, while law is the central concern of law and society scholars, it is not seen as residing in a formal, separate sphere, apart from society. *Law is in society*, and most now agree with the argument Laura Nader made initially that the field should have been named "Law *in* Society" rather than law *and* society (Nader 1969). Just as political scientists have long recognized the political nature of law, sociolegal scholars add that law is also social, cultural, economic, linguistic, and ideological. Researchers engaged in empirical and theoretical work on law in society thus confront the extraordinarily messy (and some would say futile) question of how to say anything interesting or disciplined at all if in fact "the law is all over" (Sarat 1990). Scholars in the field do not agree in their response. But most identify a particular question or problem about the creation, maintenance, or change in law and seek to answer it wherever the question leads. What is important is to be self-aware in drawing the boundaries for study, as opposed to limiting a priori the scope, and to draw on other disciplines for relevant concepts, methods, or insights.

It is difficult to strictly define "the" law and society perspective for a political science audience. Some of what falls under this umbrella (e.g. courts and public policy, law and social change, regulation, judicial decision-making) is mainstream law and politics. Other law and society work may seem less so because of the individual topics studied (border patrol, divorce lawyers, film, science laboratories, lawyer jokes) or the methods used (narrative, experiments, network analysis, ethnography). Over the years law and society scholars have attempted to define the field through textbooks or edited collections; these underscore the editors' quite different perspectives on the field (Kidder 1983; Lempert and Sanders 1986; Macaulay, Friedman, and Stookey 1995; Sarat 2004).

2 Major Contributions to Law and Society Scholarship

A recent symposium of the *Law and Courts Newsletter* (Winter 2007) featured summaries of the law and society field and its relation to political science, written by seven political scientists who have long been active in this area. Readers should consult this issue for excellent descriptions of this large and robust field of study. I will concentrate on three broad areas of law and society scholarship: disputing; decision-making; and legal ideology and consciousness. I will then briefly mention other areas, while acknowledging that I am still omitting many others.

2.1 Disputing

Studies of *disputing* ask how disputes become court cases and what occurs to cases once they are in court. What are the alternatives to courts for resolving problems or disputes? Why do some conflicts become legal cases but most do not? How does understanding disputing help to explain conflict resolution and the impact of law? Both criminal and civil conflicts in the U.S. fill out a pyramid with vast numbers of grievances or injuries at the bottom, a smaller number that become disputes, even fewer that contain some kind of informal recourse to law (calling the police or a lawyer), an even smaller number with two-party legal activity (plea bargaining or negotiated settlement), and only a tiny fraction resolved by trial (Trubek 1980–1; Felstiner, Abel, and Sarat 1980–1). A large survey done in the late 1970s by the Civil Litigation Research Project (CLRP) showed that different types of civil grievances (e.g. post-divorce) were likelier than others (e.g. discrimination) to reach higher on the pyramid of legal action (Miller and Sarat 1980–1; Kritzer 1991). The empirical results of the CLRP scholars have been reported in myriad judicial process textbooks but this important, forty-year-old study has not been replicated.

Galanter's (1974) comprehensive theory exploring the use of courts by repeat players vs. one-shotters suggested multiple ways in which those experienced in legal procedures are advantaged in the legal process. Galanter also showed how disparities in the legal profession (specialization, relations with clients, legal training, etc.) further exacerbated the advantages of the repeat players. Galanter's study in the *Law and Society Review* is one of the most frequently cited law review articles of all time. A number of empirical studies since then have supported his theory (see Kritzer and Silbey 2003).

One aspect of Galanter's theory centers on the differential use of formal vs. informal mechanisms for dispute settlement by repeat players and one-shotters. That is, parties who are more familiar with legal processes know when to settle out of court and when to press on to formal trial, according to the likelihood of gain in the legal rule as opposed to a win or loss in the immediate conflict. This argument, powerfully supported by Albiston's (1999) research on litigation outcomes after the Family and Medical Leave Act, shows an important link between disputing and change in the law. Employers who were sued by employees seeking family leave ultimately "won" even when they "lost" by settling some cases out of court because employers gained important rule-making opportunities in other cases that ultimately weakened the legislation.

Another way in which disputing can be linked to change in law is through the expansion or reframing of a dispute into a new normative framework, and through the support for that expansion that parties may obtain. As Mather and Yngvesson (1980–1) suggest, legal cases are not objective events, but are socially constructed to reflect the interests of supporters of disputants, to appeal to a particular audience, and to incorporate the values and language of law. The language of law is inherently political, ordering facts and invoking norms to support one set of interests or another. By constructing claims in certain ways, one can expand the law and mobilize others in support of the new interpretation. Groups lacking in political power may succeed in attracting support for legal change through reframing issues and mobilizing support, as shown in litigation over comparable worth (McCann 1994), tobacco control (Mather 1998), and sexual harassment (Marshall 2005). A victory in litigation, even if later reversed on appeal, can aid in agenda setting and serve as a catalyst for further change.

The linkage among litigation, political order, and political change also emerges in empirical research on the use of courts over time. Filing disputes in court should be seen as an alternative to traditional forms of political participation, as Zemans (1983) argued, and indeed longitudinal study of court usage in the U.S. by McIntosh (1983) supports this view. Nevertheless, courts are not passive institutions waiting for disputes to percolate up the pyramid to become fodder for judicial decisions. Courts are institutions of the state and as such, they (or other arms of government) can and do exercise power to shape the nature and amount of litigation (Munger 1990; Harrington and Ward 1995). This general point about the power of institutions was made in law and society research some time ago. Recent battles over tort reform illustrate it well, as actions by state legislatures, Congress, and the U.S. Supreme Court have all sought to curb what business interests saw as an "explosion" of litigation.

2.2 Decision-making

A second major area of law and society research focuses on *decision-making*. Scholarship on judicial decision-making is hardly news to those interested in the politics of law, but those in law and society broadened the terrain in several ways. They examined decision-making by judges at *all* levels of court including non-lawyer judges on justice of the peace courts, those on small claims courts, misdemeanor and felony courts, civil courts, and occasionally appellate courts. Research revealed differences in sentencing severity across courts and in patterns of judicial interaction with prosecutors (Eisenstein and Jacob 1977; Eisenstein, Flemming, and Nardulli 1988). Questions about racial discrimination in trial court sentencing have been investigated numerous times, initially with some mixed results. More recently, an overview of forty different sentencing studies that controlled for offense and defendant's prior record showed clear evidence of significant race effects in judicial decisions in state and federal courts (Spohn 2000).

The impact of race has also been shown in numerous state studies of jury and prosecutorial decisions to recommend the death penalty. Jury decision-making has received a great deal of attention from sociolegal scholars. They have explored, for example, the impact of decision rules and jury size on verdicts, differences in evidence-driven vs. verdict-driven processes of deliberation, how juries compare to judges, juror assessments of credibility by race and gender of witnesses, jury assessments of corporate defendants, jury awards over time, and jury nullification (Levine 1992; Hans 2000; 2006; Sunstein et al. 2002).

Second, recognizing that over 95 percent of trial court cases settle through plea negotiations or settlement talks, without trial, sociolegal researchers examined decision-making by lawyers. They asked, for example, how, why, and when do prosecutors and defense attorneys engage in plea bargaining? Do decisions by defense attorneys vary according to whether they are privately employed or public defenders? How are lawyers' decisions to recommend particular dispositions affected by the views of their clients? The rich literature on these questions found in earlier research on plea bargaining would benefit from reexamination in order to see how legal changes on sentencing and jury selection, demographic changes in lower court personnel, increased punitiveness in the cultural and political climate, and the impact of federal anti-immigration measures on local officials, have affected the processes of negotiation in criminal courts.

Lawyers in civil cases also play important roles in dispute settlement and in the production of law. Research on lawyers representing personal injury plaintiffs (Rosenthal 1974; Genn 1987; Kritzer 2004) and divorce clients (Sarat and Felstiner 1995; Mather, McEwen, and Maiman 2001) has revealed much about lawyers' screening decisions in agreeing to represent clients, their interactions with clients, and their negotiating strategies and decisions on settlements. We also know a good deal about the strategies, problems, and goals of cause lawyers (Sarat and Scheingold 1998;

Scheingold and Sarat 2004). By contrast, we know much less about decision-making in the work of corporate lawyers, and this is also an area that deserves more research.

Research that began by simply analyzing individual decision-making soon moved to consider (and to incorporate into theory building) the context in which those decisions were made. Relevant aspects of context include, for example, institutional features, legal rules, economic structures, social networks and organization, and shared cultural values. The literature thus moved from its original behavioral focus to reflect institutional and cultural theories. Understanding and explaining the work of lawyers involves studying them within their communities of practice, including the law firm as a community or important cultural space (Kelly 1994; Mather, McEwen, and Maiman 2001). Empirical research that has demonstrated collegial influence on lawyers' decisions has been done in the areas of divorce, personal injury, criminal defense, and most recently, occupational safety and health (Schmidt 2005).

Heinz and Laumann (1982) first reported the significant differences in lawyers according to what they called the two hemispheres of the legal profession: lawyers who represent organizations or corporate entities and those who represent individual clients (and see Heinz et al. 2005 for more recent findings). Lawyers representing organizations not only have higher incomes and prestige than those representing individuals, but they work in larger firms, have fewer clients, spend less time in court, and have different educational backgrounds, social characteristics, and political values. The bifurcated profession has enormous implications for the creation and enforcement of law. For example, law and politics scholars should examine how lawyers exercise influence on law through particular communities of legal practice (Mather forthcoming). Specialization by legal field, coupled with the social stratification of the profession (with disproportionate representation in different fields by gender, race, class, and religion) and observed differences in political values by field, provide rich data for political scientists who are willing to go to lawyers' offices, rather than to courts, to see where law is made.

Finally, sociolegal scholars broadened their scope beyond judges, juries, and lawyers to include the work of less visible legal actors such as court clerks (Yngvesson 1993), health and safety inspection officers (Hawkins 2002), immigration officials (Coutin 2000), probation officers, and police (Skolnick 1994; Bell 2002). Every decision of a low-level legal official helps to shape a pattern of law interpretation and enforcement, and to construct ideas about law for the public they encounter.

Even further, law and society researchers have explored the decisions and work of *private* actors, those without official legal status but who also contribute to lawmaking and law enforcement through private ordering. Who are some of these actors? They include: real estate agents and mortgage brokers who maintain a color line in urban housing; security guards with badges and uniforms who patrol malls and parking lots; human resource officers who define the parameters of civil rights laws through their routine advice and actions in employee disputes;

mediators who help parties resolve conflicts without the expense of trial or the constraints of law. Political scientists studying the legislative process are accustomed to paying close attention to the role of private interest groups in lawmaking and administrative enforcement and have developed theories of specialized influence (e.g. the "iron triangle" for congressional subcommittees). Similarly, law and courts scholars should build on the empirical work on private ordering to better understand connections between powerful private interests and law (see e.g. Edelman and Suchman 1999).

2.3 Legal Ideology and Consciousness

Legal ideology and consciousness comprises a third major area of law and society scholarship. Decisions by the street-level bureaucrats, legal officials, and private actors discussed above matter in part because of the direct effect of their actions on people's lives: denying a mortgage; stopping and frisking a suspicious character; channeling personnel conflicts away from law. But from an ideological perspective, what is even more important for the law is the meaning conveyed by those decisions. What values reside in the categories of "suspicious" and "not suspicious" and how are they conveyed in each encounter? Law and society research reminds us that law is constructed through such categories for classification. When the clerk of a local court dismisses a citizen's grievance as not "really" a legal matter, he is making law for the court (Yngvesson 1993). Similarly, with every passage through airport security, government agents are communicating that the law of the U.S. border is different than it was before September 11; the state is more powerful, scrutinizing not only our passports and suitcases, but our belt buckles, toothpaste, and nail files.

Studies of the actuarial practices of insurance companies, for example, underline the power that comes from the rhetoric of granting or denying insurance (Simon 1988; Glenn 2000). Researchers have examined different areas of law to uncover the hidden assumptions, as in the racial bias of insurance, that privilege some people and interests over others. Numerous works document race and gender disparities that emerge from ostensibly neutral concepts or principles. As the title of one article says, "Is the 'reasonable person' a reasonable standard in a multicultural world?" (Minow and Rakoff 1998). Focus on legal ideology looks at the categories of law and how they are used, in order to reveal the process by which legal meaning is constructed. While political scientists readily acknowledge the ideology of constitutional constructs, law and society scholars analyze the narratives, taken for granted assumptions, and values in other areas of law—contracts and tort (Engel 1984), employment, property, family, and so forth.

If knowledge is power, then how do people obtain their knowledge of law? Examining the "litigation crisis" in tort law and the media coverage of the hot coffee and antitobacco lawsuits, Haltom and McCann (2004) found that the institutional conventions of news reporting combined with cultural values about the importance of personal responsibility to muffle the voices of litigation scholars and the plaintiffs' bar. Interest groups on different legal issues battle for the hearts and minds of jurors and the public. While the tort reformers played their hand in the mass media, the plaintiffs' bar chose an insider strategy of legislative and judicial lobbying. In addition to the newspapers' images of legal issues or cases, television and film provide ample material for the cultural production of law. The drama of trials, conflict between good and evil, guilt and innocence, chaos and order, all convey legal meaning that may find its way into law. Survey research on the "*CSI* effect," for example, has not revealed clear results, yet some trial attorneys are convinced that the TV show is shaping popular legal ideas. Prosecutors worry that avid watchers of *CSI*, when asked to serve on a jury, are more reluctant to convict unless there is scientific evidence.

Studies of legal consciousness explore how people's experiences and understandings of law translate into actions and how social action in turn constitutes their relation to law. For example, Ewick and Silbey (1998) conducted detailed interviews with people of diverse backgrounds and found three distinct narratives about law, each with its own normative value and structure: law as impartial, objective, and remote; law as a game shaped by self-interest and individual resources; law as a power to be resisted. Other research on legal consciousness, which examined people's experiences and understandings of how the law should respond to offensive public speech, found interesting variation in responses by race and gender (Nielsen 2004). Engel and Munger (2003) examined how people with disabilities understood and used the new rights conferred by the American for Disabilities Act. The authors concluded that individual identity was key to perceptions of, and experience with, legal rights. Scholars of law and politics should find intriguing material here to integrate with research on political participation, framing of issues, critical race theory, or feminist jurisprudence.

2.4 Other Areas of Law and Society Scholarship

Other areas of law and society scholarship may be more familiar to those in law and politics so I will mention them only briefly.

2.4.1 *Regulation and Compliance*

Studies of *regulation* and *compliance* have been a mainstay of law and society scholarship, encompassing research on compliance with Supreme Court decisions on prayer in schools, implementation of lower court orders on school busing, compliance with environmental, health and safety, or business regulations. Once a legal rule is announced, judicial decision is made, or new regulations go into effect, how do officials secure compliance? Whereas legal scholars try to draw a bright line between law and discretion, many sociolegal scholars would challenge the distinction. Law, it is argued, is constituted by the discretionary decisions that give it meaning. Instead of conceptualizing discretion as "the hole in a doughnut," surrounded by legal form, as Dworkin (1977) suggested, critics have challenged the very distinction between the two (Hawkins 1992; Pratt 1999).

Similarly, the notion of law as purely governmental regulation breaks down entirely with the proliferation of private and quasi-public actors whose support is critical for the success of any regulatory regime. In place of command and control models of regulation, some point to the empirical and normative advantages of self-regulation (Gunningham and Rees 1997). Important comparative work on regulation by Kagan (2001) identifies the very different approaches of Britain and the U.S. and critiques what he calls the "adversarial legalism" of the American system.

2.4.2 *Legal History*

One of the critical influences on the development of law and society was Willard Hurst and his focus on *legal history.* His view of law as deeply grounded in the social and economic context of its time shaped generations of scholars studying particular laws, judicial decisions, or legal movements (Simon 1999). The notion of law and society as mutually constitutive emerges clearly in much of the sociolegal historical scholarship (e.g. Gordon 1988; Hartog 2000), and especially in work on race and the law (Gomez 2004).

Friedman and Ladinsky's (1967) well-known account of the rise of workman's compensation law in the early twentieth century reflects a critical eye toward the autonomy of law. After charting the demise of the common law tort doctrine of the fellow-servant rule, they ask whether law was simply "lagging" behind society. Their answer, quite familiar to law and society scholars forty years later, was a resounding "NO." What was seen as "lag" to some was simply vested interests claiming their power. The old tort doctrine lasted as long as it did because there was no stable compromise behind its replacement. Many similar legal changes would benefit from reexamination by political scientists who have studied American political development and could bring new understandings of the political contexts for change as well as informing law and politics scholars about important areas of the common law they have overlooked.

2.4.3 *Procedural Justice*

Procedural justice questions have also been explored for decades by those interested in integrating philosophical questions of justice with psychological research and people's experiences with law. Applying the philosophical distinction between procedural and substantive justice to the legal system, psychologists hypothesized that providing fair and transparent court procedures would result in greater satisfaction and compliance regardless of the substantive outcome of their case. Tyler's (1990) work on *Why People Obey the Law* generated a large body of research testing this idea, and finding considerable support. Other researchers extended the research to litigant satisfaction in felony cases according to the perceived fairness of the procedures (Casper, Tyler, and Fisher 1988) and to acceptance of unpopular decisions of the U.S. Supreme Court (Gibson 1989; cf. Tyler and Rasinski 1991).

3 RECENT DEVELOPMENTS

Although the law and society field lacks clear boundaries to separate its interdisciplinary perspective from the other disciplines, it has significantly aided our understanding of law and politics through the various areas of research discussed here. I have already referred to some promising avenues for future research on law and politics. Let me just outline a few others.

1. Look beyond appellate courts. There has been little recent research on American trial courts, despite huge changes in the balance of federal to local legal power, a massive increase in incarceration, a wealth of quantitative data on state courts available from the National Center for State Courts, and the creation of new types of specialized courts for drugs or mental health. Further study of trial courts and tribunals in other countries would add greatly to our comparative knowledge of courts. Law and society work on international disputing through arbitration (Dezalay and Garth 1998) and on the international Tuna Court ("the world's premier fish market;" Feldman 2006, 313) show the potential for integrating norms, disputing, and law. Numerous other regional and international bodies could be studied as well to help us understand processes of law and globalization.

2. Broaden the range of legal actors to study beyond judges and beyond the arena of public law. Integrate studies of the legal profession with our understanding of courts and lawmaking. By combining the specialization of the bar with the sorting process of legal education that shapes the class, race, and gender of who enters (and remains) in corporate law, one might gain new understanding of the outcomes in different legal areas. The phrase "public law" is highly misleading given the range of public policy concerns and effects that emerge from areas of "private" law (Shapiro 1972). Private law areas of tort, property, contracts, labor, and family contain a wealth of interesting law and politics questions that would benefit from the scrutiny of political science. In punitive damages, for example, juries and trial judges were completely free (until very recent constitutional limits were imposed)

to impose civil punishments for fraud or negligence. Why not do the same kind of rigorous investigation of damage awards that has been done for criminal sentencing to explore the determinants of punitive damages?

3. Examine how people use courts, harking back to a view of litigation as a form of political participation. Integrate perspectives from identity politics, legal consciousness, critical race theory, and feminist jurisprudence, with knowledge of legal institutions and processes. Examine test case litigation to see how changed conditions and new modes of communication have altered the strategies of interest groups.

4. Popular culture involves framing problems, events, and people. Law is increasingly seen as a set of visual images in popular culture. How do those visuals affect law? Political scientists with an interest in capital punishment should consider Haney's (2005) excellent book on the death penalty. Haney combines decades of psychological research on jury decision-making in death cases with research on popular culture and public opinion to present a disturbing look at the forces that maintain capital punishment in law.

In sum, the field of law and society continues to develop in response to new restarch questions and new scholars. Political scientists contribute to, and learn from, this interdisciplinary approach to law and politics.

REFERENCES

ABEL, R. L. 1974. A comparative theory of dispute institutions in society. *Law and Society Review*, 8: 217–347.
—— and LEWIS, P. S. C. eds. (1988). *Lawyers in Society*, 3 vols. Berkeley: University of California Press.
ALBISTON, C. 1999. The rule of law and the litigation process: the paradox of losing by winning. *Law and Society Review*, 33: 869–910.
ALSCHULER, A. 1979. Plea bargaining and its history. *Law and Society Review*, 13: 211–46.
BELL, J. 2002. *Policing Hatred: Law Enforcement, Civil Rights, and Hate Crime*. New York: New York University Press.
BLUMBERG, A. S. 1967. The practice of law as a confidence game: organizational cooptation of a profession. *Law and Society Review*, 1: 15–39.
BOHANNAN, P., and HUCKLEBERRY, K. 1967. Institutions of divorce, family and the law. *Law and Society Review*, 1: 81–102.
BOYUM, K. O., and MATHER, L. 1983. *Empirical Theories About Courts*. New York: Longman.
BRIGHAM, J., and HARRINGTON, C. 1989. Realism and its consequences: an inquiry into contemporary sociological research. *International Journal of the Sociology of Law*, 17: 41–62.
CALAVITA, K., and SERON, C. 1992. Postmodernism and protest: recovering the sociological imagination. *Law and Society Review*, 26: 765–72.

CASPER, J. D., TYLER, T., and FISHER, B. 1988. Procedural justice in felony cases. *Law and Society Review,* 22: 483–507.

CICOUREL, A. V. 1967. Kinship, marriage, and divorce in comparative family law. *Law and Society Review,* 1: 103–29.

CONLEY, J. M., and O'BARR, W. M. 1990. *Rules versus Relationships: The Ethnography of Legal Discourse.* Chicago: University of Chicago Press.

COUTIN, S. B. 2000. *Legalizing Moves: Salvadoran Immigrants' Struggle for U.S. Residency.* Ann Arbor: University of Michigan Press.

DEZALAY, Y., and GARTH, B. G. 1998. *Dealing in Virtue: International Commercial Arbitration and the Construction of a Transnational Legal Order.* Chicago: University of Chicago Press.

DWORKIN, R. 1977. *Taking Rights Seriously.* Cambridge, Mass.: Harvard University Press.

EDELMAN, L., and SUCHMAN, M. 1999. When the "haves" hold court: speculations on the organizational internalization of law. *Law and Society Review,* 33: 941–92.

EISENSTEIN, J. B., FLEMMING, R. B., and NARDULLI, P. F. 1988. *The Contours of Justice: Communities and Their Courts.* Boston: Little, Brown.

—— and JACOB, H. 1977. *Felony Justice: An Organizational Analysis of Criminal Courts.* Boston: Little, Brown.

ENGEL, D. M. 1984. The oven bird's song: insiders, outsiders, and personal injuries in an American community. *Law and Society Review,* 18: 551–82.

—— 1999. Presidential Address—making connections: law and society researchers and their subjects. *Law and Society Review,* 33: 3–16.

—— and MUNGER, F. W. 2003. *Rights of Inclusion: Law and Identity in the Life Stories of Americans with Disabilities.* Chicago: University of Chicago Press.

EPP, C. R. 1998. *The Rights Revolution: Lawyers, Activists, and Supreme Courts in Comparative Perspective.* Chicago: University of Chicago Press.

EWICK, P., and SILBEY, S. S. 1998. *The Common Place of Law: Stories from Everyday Life.* Chicago: University of Chicago Press.

FEELEY, M. M. 1979. *The Process is the Punishment.* New York: Russell Sage Foundation.

FELDMAN, E. A. 2006. The Tuna Court: law and norms in the world's premier fish market. *California Law Review,* 94: 313–70.

FELSTINER, W. L. F., ABEL, R. L., and SARAT, A. 1980–1. The emergence and tranformation of disputes: naming, blaming, claiming. . . . *Law and Society Review,* 15: 631–54.

FRIEDMAN, L. M. 1979. Plea bargaining in historical perspective. *Law and Society Review,* 13: 247–60.

—— and LADINSKY, J. 1967. Social change and the law of industrial accidents. *Columbia Law Review,* 67: 50–82.

GALANTER, M. 1974. Why the "haves" come out ahead: speculations on the limits of legal change. *Law and Society Review,* 9: 95–160.

GARTH, B., and STERLING, J. 1998. From legal realism to law and society: reshaping law for the last stages of the social activist state. *Law and Society Review,* 32: 409–71.

GENN, H. 1987. *Hard Bargaining: Out of Court Settlement in Personal Injury Actions.* Oxford: Clarendon Press.

GIBSON, J. 1989. Understandings of justice: institutional legitimacy, procedural justice, and critical race theory. *Law and Society Review,* 23: 469–96.

GLENN, B. 2000. The shifting rhetoric of insurance denial. *Law and Society Review,* 34: 779–808.

GOMEZ, L. 2004. A tale of two genres: on the real and ideal links between law and society and critical race theory. Pp. 453–70 in Sarat 2004.

GORDON, R. W. 1988. The independence of lawyers. *Boston University Law Review*, 68: 1–83.

GUNNINGHAM, N., and REES, J. (eds.) 1997. Special issue. *Law and Policy*, 19 (4).

HALTOM, W., and MCCANN, M. 2004. *Distorting the Law: Politics, the Media, and the Litigation Crisis.* Chicago: University of Chicago Press.

HANDLER, J. F. 1992. Presidential address—postmodernism, protest, and the new social movement. *Law and Society Review*, 26: 697–731.

HANEY, C. 2005. *Death by Design: Capital Punishment as a Social Psychological System.* New York: Oxford University Press.

HANS, V. P. 2000. *Business on Trial: The Civil Jury and Corporate Responsibility.* New Haven, Conn.: Yale University Press.

—— (ed.) 2003. Special issue on lay participation in legal decision making. *Law and Policy*, 25 (2).

—— (ed). 2006. *The Jury System: Contemporary Scholarship.* Aldershot: Ashgate.

HARRINGTON, C. B., and WARD, D. S. 1995. Patterns of appellate litigation, 1945–1990. Pp. 206–26 in *Contemplating Courts*, ed. L. Epstein. Washington, DC: Congressional Quarterly.

—— and YNGVESSON, B. 1990. Interpretive sociolegal research. *Law and Social Inquiry*, 15: 135–48.

HARTOG, H. 2000. *Man and Wife in America: A History.* Cambridge, Mass.: Harvard University Press.

HAWKINS, K. (ed.) 1992. *The Uses of Discretion.* New York: Oxford University Press.

—— 2002. *Law as Last Resort: Prosecution Decision-Making in a Regulatory Agency.* Oxford: Oxford University Press.

HEINZ, J. P., and LAUMANN, E. O. 1982. *Chicago Lawyers: The Social Structure of the Bar.* New York: Russell Sage Foundation.

—— NELSON, R. L., SANDEFUR, R. L., and LAUMANN, E. O. 2005. *Urban Lawyers: The New Social Structure of the Bar.* Chicago: University of Chicago Press.

HEUMANN, M. 1978. *Plea Bargaining: The Experiences of Prosecutors, Judges, and Defense Attorneys.* Chicago: University of Chicago Press.

HEYDEBRAND, W., and SERON, C. 1990. *Rationalizing Justice: The Political Economy of Federal District Courts.* Albany: State University of New York Press.

HUNT, A. 1993. *Explorations in Law and Society: Toward A Constitutive Theory of Law.* New York: Routledge.

JACOB, H. et al. 1996. *Courts, Law, and Politics in Comparative Perspective.* New Haven, Conn.: Yale University Press.

KAGAN, R. A. 2001. *Adversarial Legalism: The American Way of Law.* Cambridge, Mass.: Harvard University Press.

KELLY, M. J. 1994. *Lives of Lawyers.* Ann Arbor: University of Michigan Press.

KIDDER, R. I. 1983. *Connecting Law and Society: An Introduction to Research and Theory.* Englewood Cliffs, NJ: Prentice Hall.

KRITZER, H. M. 1991. *Let's Make A Deal.* Madison: University of Wisconsin Press.

—— 2004. *Risks, Reputations, and Rewards: Contingency Fee Legal Practice in the United States.* Stanford, Calif.: Stanford University Press.

—— and SILBEY, S. S. (eds.) 2003. *In Litigation: Do the "Haves" Still Come Out Ahead?* Stanford, Calif.: Stanford University Press.

LEMPERT, R., and SANDERS, J. 1986. *An Invitation to Law and Social Science.* New York: Longman.

LEVINE, F. J. 1990. Presidential address—goose bumps and "the search for signs of intelligent life" in sociolegal studies: after twenty-five years. *Law and Society Review*, 24: 7–33.

LEVINE, J. P. 1992. *Juries and Politics*. Belmont, Calif.: Brooks/Cole.

MACAULAY, S., FRIEDMAN, L. M., and STOOKEY, J. (eds.) 1995. *Law and Society: Readings on the Social Study of Law*. New York: W. W. Norton.

McCANN, M. W. 1992. Resistance, reconstruction, and romance in legal scholarship. *Law and Society Review*, 26: 733–50.

—— 1994. *Rights at Work*. Chicago: University of Chicago Press.

McINTOSH, W. 1983. Private use of a public forum: a long range view of the dispute processing role of courts. *American Political Science Review*, 77: 991–1010.

MARSHALL, A.-M. 2005. *Confronting Sexual Harassment: The Law and Politics of Everyday Life*. Burlington, Vt.: Ashgate.

MATHER, L. 1979. *Plea Bargaining or Trial? The Process of Criminal Case Disposition*. Lexington, Mass.: Lexington Press.

—— 1998. Theorizing about trial courts: lawyers, policymaking, and tobacco litigation. *Law and Social Inquiry*, 23: 897–940.

—— 2003. Presidential address—reflections on the reach of law (and society) post 9/11: an American superhero? *Law and Society Review*, 37: 263–82.

—— Forthcoming. Bringing the lawyers back in. In *Exploring Judicial Politics*, ed. M. C. Miller. New York: Oxford University Press.

—— McEWEN, C. A., and MAIMAN, R. J. 2001. *Divorce Lawyers at Work: Varieties of Professionalism in Practice*. New York: Oxford University Press.

—— and YNGVESSON, B. 1980–1. Language, audience, and the transformation of disputes. *Law and Society Review*, 15: 775–822.

MAYNARD, D. 1984. *Inside Plea Bargaining: The Language of Negotiation*. New York: Plenum.

MERRY, S. E. 1990. *Getting Justice and Getting Even: Legal Consciousness Among Working-Class Americans*. Chicago: University of Chicago Press.

MILLER, R. E., and SARAT, A. 1980–1. Grievances, claims, and disputes: assessing the adversary culture. *Law and Society Review*, 15: 525–66.

MINOW, M., and RAKOFF, T. 1998. Is the "reasonable person" a reasonable standard in a multicultural world? Pp. 68–108 in *Everyday Practices and Trouble Cases: Fundamental Issues in Law and Society Research: Volume 2*, ed. A. Sarat, M. Constable, D. Engel, V. Hans, and S. Lawrence. Evanston, Ill.: Northwestern University Press.

MOORE, S. F. 1978. *Law as Process: An Anthropological Approach*. London: Routledge and Kegan Paul.

MUNGER, F. (ed.) 1990. Special issue on longitudinal studies of trial courts. *Law and Society Review*, 24 (2).

—— 2001. Presidential address: inquiry and activism in law and society. *Law and Society Review*, 35: 7–20.

NADER, L. 1969. Introduction. Pp. 1–10 in *Law in Culture and Society*, ed. L. Nader. Chicago: Aldine Press.

—— and TODD, H. 1978. *The Disputing Process: Law in Ten Societies*. New York: Columbia University Press.

NIELSEN, L. B. 2004. *License to Harass: Law, Hierarchy, and Offensive Public Speech*. Princeton, NJ: Princeton University Press.

PRATT, A. C. 1999. Dunking the doughnut: discretionary power, law and the administration of the Canadian Immigration Act. *Social and Legal Studies*, 8: 199–226.

Rosenthal, D. E. 1974. *Lawyer and Client: Who's In Charge?* New York: Russell Sage Foundation.

Sarat, A. 1990. "The law is all over:" power, resistance, and the legal consciousness of the welfare poor. *Yale Journal of Law and Humanities*, 2: 348–79.

—— 2004. *The Blackwell Companion to Law and Society.* Malden, Mass.: Blackwell.

—— and Felstiner, W. L. F. 1995. *Divorce Lawyers and their Clients: Power and Meaning in the Legal Process.* New York: Oxford University Press.

—— and Scheingold, S. A. (eds.) 1998. *Cause Lawyering: Political Commitments and Professional Responsibilities.* New York: Oxford University Press.

—— and Silbey, S. 1988. The pull of the policy audience. *Law and Policy*, 10: 97–166.

Scheingold, S. A., and Sarat, A. 2004. *Something to Believe In: Politics, Professionalism, and Cause Lawyering.* Stanford, Calif.: Stanford University Press.

Schlegel, J. H. 1995. *American Legal Realism and Empirical Social Science.* Durham: University of North Carolina Press.

Schmidt, P. 2005. *Lawyers and Regulation: The Politics of the Administrative Process.* Cambridge: Cambridge University Press.

Shapiro, M. 1972. From public law to public policy, or the "public" in "public law." *PS*, 5: 410–18.

—— 1981. *Courts: A Comparative and Political Analysis.* Chicago: University of Chicago Press.

Simon, J. 1988. The ideological effects of actuarial practices. *Law and Society Review*, 22: 771–800.

—— 1999. Law after society. *Law and Social Inquiry*, 24: 143–94.

Skolnick, J. H. 1994. *Justice Without Trial: Law Enforcement in Democractic Society*, 3rd edn. New York: Macmillan.

Smith, R. M. 1988. Political jurisprudence, the "new institutionalism," and the future of public law. *American Political Science Review*, 82: 89–108.

Spohn, C. C. 2000. Thirty years of sentencing reform: the quest for a racially neutral sentencing process. *Criminal Justice*, 3: 427–501.

Sudnow, D. 1965. Normal crimes: sociological features of the penal code in a public defender office. *Social Problems*, 12: 255–76.

Sunstein, C. R. et al. 2002. *Punitive Damages: How Juries Decide.* Chicago: University of Chicago Press.

Trubek, D. M. 1980–1. The construction and deconstruction of a disputes-focused approach: an afterword. *Law and Society Review*, 15: 485–501.

Tyler, T. R. 1990. *Why People Obey the Law.* New Haven, Conn.: Yale University Press.

—— and Rasinski, K. 1991. Procedural justice, institutional legitimacy, and the acceptance of unpopular U.S. Supreme Court decisions: a reply to Gibson. *Law and Society Review*, 25: 621–30.

Yngvesson, B. 1993. *Virtuous Citizens, Disruptive Subjects: Order and Complaint in a New England Court.* New York: Routledge.

Zemans, F. K. 1983. Legal mobilization: the neglected role of the law in the political system. *American Political Science Review*, 77: 690–703.

....

THE ANALYSIS OF COURTS IN THE ECONOMIC ANALYSIS OF LAW

....

LEWIS A. KORNHAUSER

ECONOMIC analyses of adjudication and positive political theories of adjudication share common methodologies. Each applies the methods of microeconomic theory and game theory to the study of adjudicatory institutions and then tests these theories econometrically. As a consequence, many analyses of courts within economic analysis of law are indistinguishable from those produced by positive political theorists; they consider how judges control, exploit, or resolve conflicts of interest among judges.

This survey emphasizes three contributions by economic analysts of law outside this common, positive, political theoretic model but which still exploit the tools of rational-choice theory. These contributions either integrate appellate decision-making within a more comprehensive model of litigant and trial behavior; assume that judges constitute a team with shared preferences; or assume that judges decide cases rather than announce or implement policies. These three elements yield a substantively different understanding of courts than the standard model of positive political theory. The assumption of shared preferences explicitly rejects the principal–agent model that is standard in PPT. The integration of appellate decision-making with other aspects of the disputing process and the shift from policies to cases are consistent with, but potentially transformative of, the standard principal–agent models of adjudication.

1 AN INTEGRATED MODEL OF ADJUDICATION

The process of adjudication begins with an injury that may yield a grievance that evolves into a dispute which itself may be settled or tried and then possibly, appealed. Political scientists have largely concentrated on judicial decision-making while scholars in law and society have concentrated on the transformation from harm to injury to grievance. Economic analysts of law, by contrast, have investigated virtually every stage of the adjudicatory process.

I focus on the literature on the influence of litigant selection on cases to be tried and appealed on the development of the law. Interest in this issue arose in part to buttress Posner's early claim (in e.g. Posner 1972) that common law legal rules were, in some sense, efficient. Rubin (1977) and Priest (1977) developed the first evolutionary models of the common law, which studied how litigant choices could drive the development of the law regardless of the preferences of the judges. Rubin[1] asserted that efficient rules will never be litigated and parties with a long-term interest in the activity will litigate inefficient rules because there is a social gain to the announcement of an efficient rule. This differential in litigation clearly implies that, over time, efficient rules, and only efficient rules, will prevail. Priest noted that a similar, though weaker, result would follow from less extreme assumptions about litigation behavior: If there are only two rules, judges announce the efficient rule p percent of the time, and the inefficient rule is litigated more often than the efficient one, the efficient rule will govern more often than p percent of the time.

These articles suggested the power of litigant selection of cases to determine the path of the law. Some subsequent articles suggested other mechanisms through which such selection might occur such as the possibilities that parties would invest more in advocating efficient legal rules and thereby make their adoption more likely (Goodman 1978) and that judges would, under reasonable assumptions, eventually announce an efficient rule as a result of learning from litigation.

---

[1] In an interesting precursor, Galanter (1974) observed that, when one party had a continuing interest in a dispute but the other party did not, the rule favored by the interested party would eventually prevail.

These models, however, are and were subject to two types of criticism. First, neither argument rests on an adequate model of the choice between settlement and litigation. The early date of these contributions makes this inadequacy unsurprising. Rubin's assumption that efficient rules are never litigated is highly implausible; often more than one legal rule is efficient and they will differ in distributional consequences. Priest's assumption therefore seems more plausible though it is not well motivated. He notes only that the frequency of litigation should rise with the surplus to be gained, but Priest's conclusion rests critically on the assumption that there are only two rules (Kornhauser 1996).

The second class of objections concerns the logic of the selection pressures. Rubin and Priest assume selection pressure that is independent of the aims of the judges. They do not, however, model it explicitly. By placing Priest's model in its natural mathematical context, Cooter and Kornhauser (1980) show by counter-example that differential litigation does not imply greater efficiency.[2] Hadfield (1992), by contrast, argued against the model of judicial learning. She showed that judges who pursue efficiency and learn from the resolution of the cases before them will still fail to announce efficient rules because the set of cases they hear represents a biased sample of the transactions governed or potentially governed by a legal rule.

The importance of these evolutionary models of the common law to the study of adjudication does not depend on the truth of the claim that the common law evolves towards efficiency. Rather, it highlights the importance of the decisions of litigants on the movement of the law. Priest and Klein (1984) provided an early and influential insight into the importance of selection pressures. They argued that only "hard" cases would be appealed.

2 TEAM MODELS OF ADJUDICATION

Models of adjudication vary along several dimensions. First, they differ in the preferences they ascribe to judges. Most positive political theory studies offer principal–agent models of adjudication in which each judge has preferences over policies and these preferences may differ. Team models, first introduced in Kornhauser (1992a; 1992b; 1995), assume that judges share a preference but differ in their information or their tasks.

Second, models of adjudication consider different judicial functions. Scholars generally ascribe two distinct functions to courts: dispute resolution and rule

---

[2] Kornhauser (1996) clarifies the argument in Cooter and Kornhauser (1980).

creation. Political science models in which judges choose policies or rules generally consider rule creation but ignore dispute resolution. Team models of adjudication, by contrast, have more often focused on the judicial function of dispute resolution. They have sought to explain judicial hierarchy in terms of error correction.

Third, the economic analysis of law has produced both structural and behavioral models of adjudication by a team. A structural model of adjudication considers the interrelation of various systemic variables such as the aggregate likelihood that a case will be appealed or if appealed, reversed. A behavioral team model, by contrast, derives these structural parameters from the decisions of rational agents.

Analysts have used both structural and behavioral models of adjudication to understand the hierarchical organization of courts. Court systems rarely have more than three tiers of courts—a trial court and two appellate courts—though some have only one or two. What explains this uniformity? Why not have more than three tiers? Why should courts be organized hierarchically at all? Several models have combined litigant selection with a team perspective to provide some insight into the hierarchical structure of courts.

Shavell (1995) offered the first formal model of error correction. It is a hybrid structural and behavioral model from a team perspective. A policy-maker must design a court structure that minimizes social costs understood as the sum of the costs of operating the judicial system and the costs of errors. Shavell considers three design choices: (1) a flat vs. a two-tiered hierarchy; (2) the structure of fees and subsidies to litigants; and (3) random review of trial judgments vs. litigant-initiated review. He identifies conditions under which an appropriate set of fees and subsidies to litigants seeking to appeal ensures that only incorrectly decided cases are appealed. From this conclusion, it follows almost immediately that litigant selection of appeals is superior to an appellate court randomly selecting cases for review.

Cameron and Kornhauser (2006) refine Shavell's analysis and connect the design of a court system more closely to litigant selection. In their structural model, the policy-maker must allocate judges among tiers in order to minimize error. They consider two questions: First, ignoring resource constraints, under what circumstances would a policy-maker want to add an additional tier? Second, given a fixed number of judges, when would the policy-maker want to reorganize the allocation of n judges among T tiers to add a T+1st tier? The answers to these questions highlight the importance of litigant selection.

The model is algebraically messy but conceptually clear. Cameron and Kornhauser show that an additional tier is desirable if the additional tier is sufficiently selective—i.e. if the ratio of the probability a wrongly decided case is appealed to the probability a correctly decided case is appealed is sufficiently large or if the ratio of the probability that, conditional on its being appealed a rightly decided case will be reversed to the rate of error in the court below is sufficiently small. This result extends Shavell's analysis; he assumes that the appellate court more often reverses wrongly decided cases than correctly decided cases. If the process is sufficiently selective—i.e. if primarily wrongly decided cases are appealed—this assumption is not necessary. Cameron and Kornhauser further show that a similar condition is sufficient to ensure that N judges in T tiers should be reorganized to add a T+1st tier.

Cameron and Kornhauser (2005a; 2006) also offer a behavioral team model of error correction in a judicial hierarchy to motivate and illuminate their structural model. They consider a judicial system with N judges and ask what hierarchical arrangement is best. They assume that judicial accuracy is a function of the amount of resources allocated per case. Prior to trial, the litigants are asymmetrically informed so that litigation rather than settlement can occur. Trial produces both a public and a private signal that may inform the trial court or the other litigant of the true state of responsibility of the defendant. They prove that, if the highest court is sufficiently accurate, then one never needs more than three tiers to ensure that all cases are correctly decided. The accuracy of the highest court ensures that only losing litigants in wrongly decided cases appeal. An interesting feature of some of the equilibria is that lower courts do not resolve cases in a Bayesian way; they do not always rule on their beliefs about the responsibility of the defendant. Rather, the lower courts hold against the informed litigant in order to exploit the power of litigant selection. This non-Bayesian procedure might be interpreted as judges adhering to the legal rule of decision.

3 MODELING ADJUDICATION: DECIDING CASES RATHER THAN CHOOSING POLICIES

Rational-choice models in political science have largely ignored the institutional detail of courts and adjudication. The models ascribe preferences over policies to judges; although judges may face constraints in acting on their preferences, the constraints derive from the presence of other political actors—either the other branches of government or judges on other courts. One might say that rational-choice theorists in political science have treated courts like legislatures, a tactic that has facilitated the transfer of methods developed for the study of Congress in particular, and legislatures in general, to adjudication.

Economic analysts of law, by contrast, have been more attentive to the institutional structures specific to courts. This attention has led some economic analysts to begin their analyses not with policies but with the rendering of judgments in cases or the announcement of rules. Adjudication is not equivalent to the announcement or implementation of policies. Rather, adjudication maps cases into outcomes for or against plaintiffs. Specifically, adjudication is a function from a *case-space* to a two-element set {0,1} that one might interpret as "judgment for defendant" and "judgment for plaintiff." The model represents a case as an n-dimensional vector; each element of the vector represents some "fact" in the case.

In this section, I develop some of the ideas and consequences of starting from case-spaces rather than policies. I begin with a discussion of doctrine because it permits a clear exposition of some of the key ideas and provides a useful contrast to approaches to doctrine in positive political theory. I then turn to models of collegiality.

3.1 Modeling Doctrine

Doctrine pervades common-law adjudication.[3] It structures the pleadings of the parties and the decisions of lower courts. Its articulation and discussion constitutes the primary subject-matter of legal education in the United States and other common law countries. Indeed, its analysis still dominates law reviews that fifty years ago would have been devoted almost exclusively to its articulation and critique.

Within the positive political theory of adjudication, however, doctrine is nearly invisible. When it does appear, it assumes a very spare, abstract character that is divorced from its actual functioning in courts. One common approach assumes that the Supreme Court has preferences over a two-dimensional space (Schwartz 1992; Cohen and Spitzer 1994; McNollgast 1995). One dimension remains the policy space over which, in the standard PPT model, the judges have preferences. The second dimension, variously called "deference" or "precedent," explicitly measures the judge's level of tolerance for deviation from her optimal policy choice. Similarly, Spiller and Spitzer (1992) model doctrine in terms of the dimensionality of the permissible policy space with the Supreme Court potentially using constitutional rulings to restrict future lower court decisions to a one-dimensional subspace.

These abstract characterizations facilitate understanding some aspects of the politics of adjudication. This approach, however, is inherently "political" and nonlegal; it makes no reference to the facts of a case or features of legal discourse that appear in an opinion. The model and even its interpretation are quite distant from the realities of day-to-day case adjudication and the practicalities of doctrine. An account of doctrine that began from these concrete practices might help to integrate legal understandings of adjudication with political ones.

---

[3] Doctrine also exists in civilian legal systems but it has a somewhat different structure and implication.

Kornhauser (1992*a*; 1992*b*), in the context of a study of the aggregation of judgments on a collegial court, offered a more concrete model of doctrine. The analysis begins with the identification of a case space. Each case is represented by a long vector of characteristics: all relevant (or potentially relevant) facts concerning the disputed events, including possibly legal actions. A(n) (extended) legal rule simply maps the case space into a two-element set {0,1} that we might interpret as {plaintiff prevails, defendant prevails}. Doctrine imposes structure on this global mapping. The framework in Kornhauser (1992*b*) considers a doctrine that has multiple causes of action. For expository purposes, however, it is clearer to consider a single cause of action. A cause of action consists of a set of *issues*. For a plaintiff to prevail on a cause of action, she must prevail on each issue. An issue is simply a map from the case space that depends only a portion (or subspace) of the case space to the set {0,1} which we may interpret as {defendant prevails on the issue, plaintiff prevails on the issue}.

Consider a simple negligence cause of action. To prevail, the plaintiff must prove that the defendant had a duty to her, that an act of the defendant caused her harm, and that the defendant acted without due care. The determination of each of these issues depends on a limited number of facts of the case. The question of duty depends on the relation of plaintiff to defendant. The question of causation depends in part on physical facts about the world. The question of negligence depends in part on the value of the activity in which defendant was engaged and the manner in which he undertook that activity. For the plaintiff to prevail, the court must resolve each of these issues in her favor.

This framework ties the empirical methods of fact pattern analysis to a theoretical model of judicial decision-making.[4] Much of the empirical literature relies on a statistical conception of fact pattern analysis—see Kort (1957), Kort and Mars (1957), Segal (1984), Segal and Spaeth (1993) Kritzer and Richards (2002; 2003; 2005). But the analytic framework fits more naturally with a Boolean interpretation of fact pattern analysis—see Kort (1963). This interpretation can be empirically implemented by categorization and regression trees as suggested by Kastellec (2005).

Cameron (1993) suggested that positive political theory adopt the set of cases or the case space rather than the policy space as the domain of study. Lax (2007) has taken up the suggestion. He argues that focus on the case space better connects decisions in specific cases to rules and rules to policies than a more abstract model that assumes that judges choose directly in a multidimensional policy space. After all, policies are represented by points in the policy space and rules by manifolds in case space. Lax does not, however, make the connection between rules and policies clear. Indeed it seems to me that the idea of a policy space, even in the legislative

---

[4] For a fuller discussion of the relation between fact pattern analysis in political science and this doctrinal framework, see Cameron and Kornhauser (2005*b*).

context, is a convenient simplification. Statutes are legal rules that also sit in case spaces and it seems reasonable to assume that legislators have basic (or primitive) preferences over these rules rather than over some ill-defined policy (and much reduced) space.

3.2 Collegiality

In most legal systems, appellate decisions are rendered by panels of more than one judge. In the federal system in the United States, for example, the first appeal is heard by a panel of three judges chosen from a larger bench; appeals to the Supreme Court of the United States are heard by the entire bench of nine justices. This inverted pyramid is typical of judicial systems throughout the world: as one moves up the judicial hierarchy, a greater number of judges resolves each case.

Collegiality raises several questions generally ignored in the legal, philosophical, and economic literature. First, why are cases decided collegially rather than by a single judge? Why, moreover, does the number of decision-makers generally increase as a case moves up the hierarchy? Second, what consequences does collegiality have for the development of the law? Does it produce a consistent body of decisions? Does it produce a coherent body of decisions? Third, how are the decisions of each judge on a panel aggregated into a decision of the court? Easterbrook (1982) raised and addressed this second set of questions. His article then spurred further research into each of the three sets of questions.

3.2.1 *Why do we have Collegiality?*

Posner (1985, 12) offered several reasons for collegiality: (*a*) multiple judges reduces the costs of poor appointments; (*b*) multiple judges reduces the power of any single judge on a court; (*c*) multiple judges permits deliberation; and (*d*) multiple judges increases productivity by dividing the labor of opinion drafting.

Kornhauser and Sager (1986) offer a more systematic analysis of the reasons for collegiality. First, they distinguished two conceptions of adjudication: the rendering of judgment and the rendition of preferences. They then suggested three different models of collegial adjudication, each of which identified a distinct standard against which to measure judicial performance. (1) If collegial courts aggregate the preferences of the judges, then *authenticity*, the extent to which the court's judgment correctly reflects the preferences of the judges, measures the quality of adjudication. (2) If collegial courts aggregate judgments, then *accuracy*, i.e. their ability to "get the right answer" however one defines the right outcome, is the appropriate criterion. (3) If collegial courts are representative institutions that seek to reach the outcome that the represented body would have reached if they deliberated and voted, then we may identify two evaluative criteria: *fit*, or the tendency to arrive at results that the represented group would have reached; and *reliability*, the absence of bad surprises. In this context, they rely on the Condorcet Jury Theorem and emphasize accuracy. Good and Tullock (1984), by contrast, offer a representation model of supreme court collegiality in which fit is the relevant value.

3.2.2 *Consistency and Coherence*

In the first model of collegiality, Easterbrook (1982) offered a simple application of Arrow's Theorem to Supreme Court adjudication. Easterbrook assumes that each case presents the Court with a choice between two legal rules to govern a particular doctrinal realm. When more than two legal rules are possible and no rule is a Condorcet winner, the Court's case law will cycle as successive cases challenge the prevailing rule with an alternative that a majority of the Court prefer.

We might however distinguish between *consistent* and *coherent* patterns of decisions. A consistent court decides identical cases identically. The definition of coherence is less clear; a court that decides coherently creates a body of law that exhibits the quality of conceptual unity. A panel of judges, each of whom had a consistent view of the law, would produce a consistent body of law; but a panel of judges, each of whom had a coherent conception of the law, need not yield a coherent body of decisions (Kornhauser and Sager 1986; Kornhauser 1992*a*).

Landa and Lax (2006) provide a formal structure and precise conception of coherence. They show that, if each judge on a collegial court decides cases on the basis of a base rule, the court, proceeding case-by-case by majority rule, may not produce a body of law that can be stated as a base rule. Thus, the development of the law may be incoherent in the sense that no judge on the court endorses the legal rule that emerges from its decisional practice.

3.2.3 *Voting on Collegial Courts*

Collegial courts present several interesting questions. Most obviously, the judgment of the court aggregates the judgments of each judge on the court. Positive political theory usually resolves complexities that arise from voting by assuming that each judge has spatial preferences over a one-dimensional policy space. As a consequence, the median voter theorem applies and the aggregation of views of the panel is unproblematic. Courts with a fixed personnel render judgments that are stable if not consistent.

A similar result may be obtained in case space rather than policy space. In the model in Lax (2004), each judge decides on the basis of well-behaved, simple rules that he calls "proper." Lax shows that if all judges have proper rules, then the body of law announced by that court is, in a sense he clearly specifies, the median of the proper rules of the judges. This result parallels the median vote rule for one-dimensional policy spaces, but Lax's formulation shows that stability is stronger in multidimensional case spaces than in multidimensional policy spaces.

Interestingly, however, the median rule of the court may differ from the rule of decision used by each judge. There is thus no single swing justice as in the policy space model.

Common-law courts do not function in the simple fashion postulated in the PPT model. The views of each judge are not aggregated through a simple vote. Actual aggregation procedures vary from common-law jurisdiction to common-law jurisdiction. In nineteenth-century England, for example, no aggregation occurred. Judges announced their views seriatim and subsequent courts and litigants had to infer the court's rule from these seriatim opinions.

In the United States, a court generally offers an opinion of the court but the aggregation process is not well defined. Kornhauser and Sager (1986) contrast two modes of aggregation: issue-by-issue and case-by-case. Unfortunately, these two aggregation methods do not always yield the same outcome. Specifically, they considered a case that presented two distinct issues for decision. Legal doctrine determines the relation between the decisions on each issue and the decision on the case. In some circumstances, the procedure the court adopts for aggregating votes will determine the outcome of the case. In *case-by-case* adjudication, each judge registers her view of how the *case* should be decided and the court aggregates these votes to reach a majority judgment. In *issue-by-issue* adjudication, each judge registers her view on each *issue* in the case should be decided; the court then aggregates the votes on each issue and applies the legal doctrine to the issue-by-issue results to reach a judgment in the case.

In fact, judicial practice in the United States is even less settled than this conflict suggests. The Supreme Court of the United States not only does not adhere to a single voting protocol, it does not have a centralized or self-conscious procedure for choosing the aggregation method. Rather, in practice, each judge counts votes as he wishes; the Court as a whole generally ignores or suppresses discussion of the aggregation procedure.

This conflict creates a "doctrinal paradox" (Kornhauser 1992*b*). A single judge decides a case by deciding each legal issue in each cause of action. To prevail on a cause of action, the plaintiff must prevail on each issue; to prevail in the case, she must prevail on at least one cause of action. On a multimember court, the two different aggregation methods may lead to different results. The doctrinal paradox is distinct from the Condorcet cycle. When the judges' orderings of outcomes (described as the vector of outcomes on each issue) yield a Condorcet cycle, issue-by-issue and case-by-case voting might not conflict. Conversely, when the judges' orderings produce a Condorcet winner over outcomes, the issue-by-issue result might differ from the case-by-case result. (Kornhauser 1992*b* provides examples; Landa and Lax 2006 derive the paradox in a formal setting.)

Analysis of the doctrinal paradox assumed that each judge voted "sincerely" on each issue regardless of the method of aggregation of the votes on the court. (Defining "sincerity" in the context of multiple-issue cases presents difficulties addressed in a different voting context in Benoit and Kornhauser (1995).) An assumption of sincerity comports well with a team model; it does not easily fit into a political model. In a political model, a self-interested, rational judge should foresee the results of sincere votes that might be detrimental to the realization of her interests.

In the agency context, one would expect judges to be sophisticated. If a court includes both sincere and sophisticated judges, the former can be manipulated by the latter. Moreover, sincere courts would be subject to frequent legislative over-rulings. As these phenomena are not generally observed, we may infer judicial sophistication (Spiller and Spitzer 1995).

4 CONCLUSION

This survey has sketched three areas in which economic analysis of law has made a distinctive contribution to the study of law and politics. First, economic analysts have embedded the study of the development of the law more fully into the complex phenomena that give rise to disputes and litigation and that characterize adjudica-tory institutions. Second, economic analysts have given formal structure and con-tent to at least some of the "legal model" often caricatured in the political science literature. Specifically, they have investigated how treating judges as a team rather than as political actors with conflicting interests influences decisions. Finally, and most importantly, economic analysts have grounded their models of adjudication in the institutional details of adjudication. They thus start not from policies but rather from judgments in individual cases that are aggregated into rules. This case-space approach has significant implications for both principal–agent and team models.

Another author, faced with similar space limitations, might emphasize either three other distinctive contributions of economic analysis of law to the study of law and politics, or the important contributions that economic analysts of law have made to the positive political theory. As a partial remedy to the limited, parochial scope of this review, I conclude with a series of references to other, related surveys of the literature in economic analysis of law.

Daughety (2000) and Spier (forthcoming a; forthcoming b) survey the literature on the choice between settlement and litigation. Cooter and Rubinfeld (1989) and Spier (forthcoming a) survey the literature on the trial process. Rubin (2004) surveys the literature on the evolution of the common law. Rubin (2000) and Kornhauser (2000a) provide surveys of different aspects of the development of the law. In addition, there is a large and rapidly growing literature on the importance of law in development.

References

Benoit, J. P., and Kornhauser, L. A. 1995. Assembly-based preferences, candidate-based procedures, and the Voting Rights Act. *Southern California Law Review*, 68: 1503–44.

Cameron, C. M. 1993. New avenues for modeling judicial politics. Wallis Institute for Political Economy Working Paper, University of Rochester.

—— and Kornhauser, L. A. 2005a. Decision rules in a judicial hierarchy. *Journal of Institutional and Theoretical Economics*, 161: 264–92.

—— —— 2005b Modeling law: theoretical implications of empirical models. Manuscript.

—— —— 2006. Appeals mechanisms, litigant selection, and the structure of judicial hierarchies. Pp. 173–204 in *Institutional Games and the Supreme Court*, ed. J. Bond, R. Flemming, and J. Rogers. Charlottesville: University of Virginia Press.

Coase, R. 1960 The problem of social cost. *Journal of Law and Economics*, 3: 1–44.

Cohen, L., and Spitzer, M. 1994. Solving the *Chevron* puzzle. *Law and Contemporary Problems*, 57: 65–110.

Cooter, R., and Kornhauser, L. A. 1980. Can litigation improve the law without the help of judges? *Journal of Legal Studies*, 9: 139–63.

—— and Rubinfeld, D. 1989. Economic analysis of legal disputes and their resolution. *Journal of Economic Literature*, 27: 1067–97.

Daughety, A. 2000. Settlement. Pp. 95–158 in *Encyclopedia of Law and Economics*, vol. 5, ed. B. Bouckaert and G. de Geest; available at http://encyclo.findlaw.com/7400book.pdf.

Easterbrook, F. H. 1982. Ways of criticizing the Court. *Harvard Law Review*, 95: 802–32.

Galanter, M. 1974. Why the "haves" come out ahead: speculations on the limits of legal change. *Law and Society Review*, 9: 95–160.

Good, I. J., and Tullock, G. 1984. Judicial errors and a proposal for reform. *Journal of Legal Studies*, 13: 289–98.

Goodman, J. C. 1978. An economic theory of the evolution of the common law. *Journal of Legal Studies*, 7: 393–406.

Hadfield, G. 1992. Bias in the evolution of legal rules. *Georgetown Law Journal*, 80: 583–616.

Hay, B., and Spier, K. 1998 Settlement of Litigation. Pp. 442–51 in *The New Palgrave Dictionary of Economics and the Law*, ed. P. Newman. London: Macmillan Reference.

Kastellec, J. P. 2005. Legal rules and the classification of Supreme Court decisions. Presented at the annual meeting of the American Political Science Association.

Kornhauser, L. A. 1992a. Modeling collegial courts I: path dependence. *International Review of Law and Economics*, 12: 169–85.

—— 1992b. Modeling collegial courts II: legal doctrine. *Journal of Law, Economics and Organization*, 8: 441–70.

—— 1995 Adjudication by a resource-constrained team: hierarchy and precedent in a judicial system. *Southern California Law Review*, 68: 1605–30.

—— 1996 Notes on the logic of legal change. In *Social Rules: Origin, Character, Logic, Change*, ed. D. Braybrooke. Boulder, Colo.: Westview.

—— 2000a. Judicial administration and organization. Pp. 27–44 in *Encyclopedia of Law and Economics*, ed. B. Bouckaert and G. de Geest; available at http://encyclo.findlaw.com/7100book.pdf.

—— 2000b. Appeal and supreme courts. Pp. 45–62 in *Encyclopedia of Law and Economics*, ed. B. Bouckaert and G. de Geest; available at http://encyclo.findlaw.com/7200book.pdf.

Kornhauser, L. A., and Sager, L. G. 1986. Unpacking the Court. *Yale Law Journal*, 96: 82–117.

Kort, F. 1957. Predicting Supreme Court decisions mathematically: a quantitative analysis of the "right to counsel" cases. *American Political Science Review*, 51: 1–12.

—— 1963. Simultaneous equations and Boolean algebra in the analysis of judicial decisions. *Law and Contemporary Problems*, 28: 143–63.

—— and Mars, D. 1957. *The Administration of Justice in Connecticut*. Storrs, Conn.: Institute of Public Service, University of Connecticut.

Kritzer, H. M., and Richards, M. J. 2002. Jurisprudential regimes in Supreme Court decision-making. *American Political Science Review*, 96: 305–20.

—— —— 2003. Jurisprudential regimes and Supreme Court decisionmaking: the *Lemon* regime and Establishment Clause cases. *Law and Society Review*, 37: 827–40.

—— —— 2005. The influence of law in the Supreme Court's search and seizure jurisprudence. *American Politics Quarterly*, 33: 33–55.

Landa, D., and Lax, J. R. 2006. Rule creation on collegial courts. Manuscript.

Lax, J. 2007. Constructing legal rules on appellate courts. *American Political Science Review*, 101: 591–604.

McNollgast 1995. Politics and the courts: a positive theory of judicial doctrine and the rule of law. *Southern California Law Review*, 68: 1631–82.

Posner, R. A. 1972. *Economic Analysis of Law*. Boston: Little, Brown.

—— 1985. *The Federal Courts: Crisis and Reform*. Cambridge, Mass.: Harvard University Press.

Priest, G. L. 1977. The common law process and the selection of efficient rules. *Journal of Legal Studies*, 6: 65–82.

—— and Klein, B. 1984. The selection of disputes for litigation. *Journal of Legal Studies*, 13: 1–55.

Rubin, P. H. 1977. Why is the common law efficient? *Journal of Legal Studies*, 6: 51–63.

—— 2000. Judge made law. Pp. 543–58 in *Encyclopedia of Law and Economics*, ed. B. Bouckaert and G. de Geest; available at http://encyclo.findlaw.com/9200book.pdf.

—— 2004. Why was the common law efficient? Emory Law and Economics Research Paper No. 04–06.

Schwartz, E. P. 1992. Policy, precedent and power: a positive theory of Supreme Court decision-making. *Journal of Law, Economics and Organization*, 8: 219–52.

Segal, J. A. 1984. Predicting Supreme Court cases probabalistically: the search and seizure cases, 1962–1981. *American Political Science Review*, 78: 891–900.

—— and Spaeth, H. J. 1993. *The Supreme Court and the Attitudinal Model*. New York: Cambridge University Press.

Shavell, S. 1995. The appeals process as a means of error correction. *Journal of Legal Studies*, 24: 379–426.

Spier, K. 2005. Economics of litigation. In *The New Palgrave Dictionary of Economics*, ed. S. Durlauf and L. Blume. London: Palgrave Macmillan.

—— 2007. Litigation. In *The Handbook of Law and Economics*, ed. A. M. Polinsky and S. Shavell. North-Holland.

Spiller, P. T., and Spitzer, M. L. 1992. Judicial choice of legal doctrines. *Journal of Law, Economics and Organization*, 8: 8–46.

—— 1995. Where is the sin in sincere? Sophisticated manipulation of sincere judicial voters (with applications to other voting environments). *Journal of Law, Economics and Organization*, 11: 32–63.

CHAPTER 41

PSYCHOLOGY AND THE LAW

TOM R. TYLER

THE legal system is a codified set of rules developed to regulate interactions and exchanges among people. The authorities who make and implement legal rules draw on a wide range of sources in seeking to understand, predict, and control human behavior. Some of these sources reflect received wisdom that is passed down within specific social and cultural traditions. In addition to cultural sources of knowledge concerning the putative causes of human behavior, there are also scientific sources that may be considered by legislators, judges, juries, and other legal decision-makers when they are creating and implementing laws. The possibility exists, therefore, that current scientific opinion about the "facts" of human nature can influence the legal system.

The range of issues that can fall within the overall intersection of law and psychology is broad. Whenever the development of law and/or the functioning of legal institutions has a psychological component, research is relevant. In some cases, the development of the law itself is based upon psychology. For example, in the famous desegregation case *Brown vs. Board of Education*, the Supreme Court cited psychological research in support of its decision that segregation was harmful. In other instances the courts have used psychology to decide whether media violence or obscenity is psychological harmful, whether adults and children have the same capacity to make reasoned choices, and many other issues. In each case legal authorities seek to base the law on an accurate knowledge of psychological facts.

In other cases the functioning of the courts and other legal institutions is linked to psychological issues. One obvious example is the operation of the courts. Jury decision-making is much studied by psychologists, and their insights shape both the structure of juries and rules about how they should function. Within trials, psychologists often provide information relevant to the introduction of evidence. This information can be related to eyewitnesses, the use of lie detectors, the introduction of recovered memories or DNA evidence, or to more clinically relevant judgments about insanity or temporary psychological disorders such as post-traumatic stress disorder or battered wife syndrome. Again, wherever psychological "facts" are relevant, psychologists provide input about research findings.

This chapter will focus on the implications of basic social psychological research for understanding human motivation in general and the specific types of motivation that lead people to obey the law and comply with legal authorities. Legal scholars and decision-makers would benefit considerably by reconceptualizing their approaches to regulation and taking into account a wider variety of instrumental and symbolic motivations, including the genuine desire to adhere to moral principles that are espoused by legitimate authorities on behalf of a just social system.

1 LAW AND THE PSYCHOLOGY OF HUMAN MOTIVATION

One of the main functions of the law is to regulate the behavior of the citizenry by maximizing the likelihood that people will comply with normative standards of conduct, i.e. with socially shared definitions of acceptable conduct as they are enshrined in rules, norms, and laws. If the law is to be effective in fulfilling its regulatory role, most citizens must obey most laws most of the time (Tyler 2006b). The need for legal authorities to secure compliance has been widely noted by legal scholars and social scientists (Fuller 1971).

Although widespread behavioral compliance is necessary to the effective functioning of society, obtaining compliance cannot be taken for granted. Because many laws restrict the ability of individual citizens to behave as they wish, people sometimes resist them. Mastrofski, Snipes, and Supina note that: "Although deference to legal authorities is the norm, disobedience occurs with sufficient frequency that skill in handling the rebellious, the disgruntled, and the hard to manage—or those potentially so—has become the street officer's performance litmus test" (1996, 272). Further, as Mastrofski et al. note, "citizens who acquiesce at the scene can renege" (1996, 283). In other words, if citizens fail to accept legal restrictions, further police intervention will eventually be required.

An important contribution of psychology is to shed light on the question of how to best motivate public rule-following behavior, both in general and with respect to specific encounters with authorities (Darley, Tyler, and Bilz 2003; Tyler 2006b). The legal system depends on obedience, and the law and police officers and judges generally expect public deference. The power of the legal system to gain cooperation is substantially increased when strategies for obtaining deference are based on an accurate model of human motivation.

1.1 The Deterrence Model

In recent decades the exercise of legal authority has become generally associated with the use of threat and punishment aimed at deterring people from engaging in criminal behavior (e.g. Kahan 1999; Nagin 1998). From this perspective, the focus is on the power of legal authorities and institutions to shape behavior by threatening to deliver (or by actually delivering) negative sanctions for rule-breaking. Within legal circles, this way of viewing the relationship between legal authorities and citizens is referred to as the "deterrence" or "social control" model, and it is this model of human behavior that—for better or worse—currently dominates law and public policy.

To implement deterrence strategies police officers carry guns and clubs, and they are empowered to threaten citizens with physical injury and incapacitation, among other penalties. The goal is to establish legal authority and, as Reiss points out, "The uniform, badge, truncheon, and arms all may play a role in asserting authority" in the effort to "gain control of the situation" (1971, 46). The police thereby seek to gain control over the individual's behavior "by manipulating an individual's calculus regarding whether 'crime pays' in any particular instance" (Meares 2000, 396). Similarly, judges attempt to influence people's acceptance of their decisions by threatening fines or jail time for failure to comply.

The notion that people's behavior with respect to the law is shaped by calculations of expected gains and losses is a core premise of rational-choice theory, which is derived from neoclassical economics (Blumstein, Cohen, and Nagin 1978; Nagin 1998). It is assumed that most people will calculate expected utilities by multiplying the probability of an outcome (e.g. getting caught for armed robbery or drunk driving) by its valence or severity. If the laws are well-calibrated, people will arrive at the desired conclusion that they should follow the law. Thus, rational self-interest is the motivational engine of the deterrence/social control model. To regulate behavior, this model suggests that decision-makers should adjust criminal sanctions to the needed level so that the expected losses associated with law-breaking will minimize the likelihood that people will break the law.

Research supports the notion that variations in the perceived certainty and severity of punishment do influence people's compliance with the law, at least to some degree (see Nagin and Paternoster 1991; Paternoster 1987; 1989; Paternoster and Iovanni 1986; Paternoster et al. 1983). Nonetheless, perceptions of the likelihood of being caught and punished have, at best, a relatively minor influence on people's behavior (MacCoun 1993; Robinson and Darley 1995; 1997; Ross 1982). Consequently, social control strategies based exclusively on a deterrence model of human behavior have had at best limited success (see also Tyler 2006a).

1.2 Problems with the Deterrence Model

The deterrence model, with all of its motivational assumptions, has had dramatic effects on the nature of American society. Consider the case of the American prison population (Haney and Zimbardo 1998). Because of the widespread belief that crime is deterred by the threat of punishment and/or the experience of punishment, a massive number of American citizens have been convicted and sentenced to serve time in American prisons. Today, the U.S. is a world leader in the proportion of citizens it holds in prison. In the year 2000 there were over 2 million Americans in jail or prison, approximately 7 percent of the overall population (United States Department of Justice 2001), far surpassing incarceration rates in Europe and elsewhere (Garland 2001).

Assuming unlimited resources on the part of law enforcement officials, there is probably nothing inherently untenable (from a purely pragmatic point of view) about controlling people's behavior through threats of punishment. One of the key problems with sanctioning systems, however, is that they require near-constant surveillance of individual behavior. And, for obvious reasons, people are strongly motivated to hide their behavior from authorities to avoid punishment. Authorities must therefore develop extensive surveillance systems for detecting rule-breaking behavior. As Meares notes, the effectiveness of "instrumental means of producing compliance always depend[s] on resource limits" (2000, 401).

Further complicating deterrence, studies consistently find that the more important issue to people who are deciding whether or not to break the law is their estimate of the likelihood of being punished for their actions and not the expected severity of their punishment (e.g. Nagin and Paternoster 1991). Consequently, societies cannot enforce rules simply by developing more and more draconian punishments. To be effective, authorities must engage in extensive surveillance strategies that increase the likelihood of detection. Effective strategies are, therefore, inevitably costly. There are no deterrence-based quick fixes that can be gained cheaply—despite the frequent suggestion among policy-makers that a few instances of dramatically severe punishment will depress crime.

Deterrence works reasonably well where society has devoted considerable resources to enforcing penalties, for example with murder. The objective risk of being caught and punished for murder is relatively high: approximately 45 percent

(Robinson and Darley 1997). The likelihood of being caught for committing a murder is high enough for deterrence to be effective in lowering the murder rate. Even in this case, however, criminals are not as sensitive to the magnitude of the penalty as they are to the estimated probability of being apprehended. As a result, capital punishment may not serve to deter murder more effectively than does life imprisonment (for differing views, see Donohue and Wolfers 2005–6; Ellsworth and Mauro 1998).

The use of surveillance systems also has deleterious effects on the social climate of groups. The use of surveillance implies distrust, which decreases people's ability to feel positively about themselves, their groups, and the system itself (Kramer and Tyler 1996). Furthermore, people may experience intrusions into their lives as procedurally unfair, leading to anger and other negative emotions often associated with perceptions of injustice (e.g. Gurr 1970; Tyler and Smith 1998). Whether surveillance works or not, then, it is demotivating and introduces new costs in terms of distrust in subsequent social interactions. Research suggests that the increasing use of deterrence strategies and social control has exerted precisely this type of negative influence on the American social climate. It has created an adversarial relationship between legal authorities and members of the communities they serve, especially with respect to racial and ethnic minority group members (Tyler and Huo 2002), leading the public to grow less compliant with the law and less willing to help the police to fight crime (Sunshine and Tyler 2003a).

2 An Alternative Model Based on Social Psychological Principles

Most legal scholarship addresses issues of motivation and rule-following in the context of deterrence and social control; that is, by imposing external constraints on people largely through the threat of punishment. Social psychology emphasizes that self-regulatory motivations can also be activated if people believe that they have an obligation to conform to the law. People who imbue the legal system with legitimacy will voluntarily abide by laws and defer to authorities (Darley et al. 2003; Jost and Major 2001; Tyler 2006b; Tyler and Blader 2000; 2005).

2.1 Commitment Based on Legitimacy and Moral Values

Ever since Kurt Lewin's (1936) field theory, social psychologists have assumed that behavior is determined by two main forces. The first is the pressure of the situation or the environment, and the second includes the motives and perceptions that the person brings to the situation. In Lewin's famous equation, behavior is understood to be a function of the person and the environment: $B = f(P, E)$. An expanded conception of the person term includes the set of social and moral values that shape the individual's thoughts and feelings about what it is ethical or normatively appropriate to do. Psychologists focus on two such values: (*a*) commitment to the notion that the rules are legitimate, and ought to be obeyed, and (*b*) the conviction that following the rules of the community is (in most cases) the morally appropriate thing to do, since the rules are consistent with one's values. From a social psychological perspective, the first step is to recognize that the legal system depends at least in part on the willingness of citizens to consent to the operation of legal authorities and actively to cooperate with them. Such cooperation is motivated by values.

2.1.1 *The Concept of Legitimacy*

Modern discussions of legitimacy are usually traced to the writings of Weber (1968) on authority and the social dynamics of authority (e.g. Zelditch 2001). Weber, like Machiavelli and others before him, argued that successful leaders and institutions use more than brute force to execute their will. More specifically, they strive to win the consent of the governed so that their commands will be voluntarily obeyed (Kelman 1969; Tyler 2006*b*). Widespread voluntary cooperation with the state and the social system allows authorities to concentrate their resources most effectively on pursuing the long term goals of society. The authorities do not need to provide incentives or sanctions to all citizens to get them to support every rule or policy they enact.

Legitimacy, according to this general view, is a quality that is possessed by an authority, a law, or an institution that leads others to feel obligated to accept its directives. It is, in other words, "a quality attributed to a regime by a population" (Merelman 1966, 548). When people ascribe legitimacy to the system that governs them, they become willing subjects whose behavior is strongly influenced by official (and unofficial) doctrine. There is a strong intellectual tradition that emphasizes the significance of developing and maintaining positive social values toward cultural, political, and legal authorities (Easton 1975; Krislov et al. 1966; Melton 1985; Parsons 1967; Tapp and Levine 1977). This work builds on the sociological tradition associated with Weber and others. According to "consensus" theories such as these, the smooth functioning of society depends on the existence of supportive attitudes and values among members of the population in general. The value of cultivating system legitimacy lies in the ability to gain voluntary deference.

While authorities can exercise power directly through the promise of rewards or the threat of punishment, such approaches to deterrence are expensive and inefficient. They may be especially problematic during times of instability or crisis, when authorities need the support of the people at a time during which they lack control over resources. An organization or society whose governance is motivated only by incentives and sanctions is at risk of disintegrating during times of trouble or change. In contrast, if a system enjoys widespread legitimacy, authorities can appeal to members based upon their shared purposes and values, providing the system with much-needed stability. From this perspective, legitimacy is a highly desirable feature of social systems (see also Tyler 2006a; Tyler and Huo 2002). The police and courts depend very heavily upon the widespread voluntary compliance of most of the citizens most of the time (Tyler 2006b). The legal system would be overwhelmed immediately if it were required to regulate the behavior of the majority citizens solely through sanctioning or the threat of sanctioning.

Research by Tyler (2006b) demonstrates that perceptions of system legitimacy do shape everyday compliance with the law, which is a conclusion that is also supported by more recent studies (Sunshine and Tyler 2003a; Tyler and Huo 2002). Furthermore, perceived legitimacy seems to have more influence on compliance than do subjective assessments of the likely risk of punishment. When people perceive the system as legitimate, they feel an intrinsic moral obligation to comply with its demands.

2.1.2 *Internalization of Moral Values*

Moral values are a second source of motivation to support or oppose the law. They are influential because they are based on internalized feelings of responsibility to follow certain personally held moral principles (see Robinson and Darley 1995; Tyler and Darley 2000). A key feature of moral values is that people feel personally obligated to adhere to them, and they feel guilty when they fail to do so. Hence, moral values—once they exist—are self-regulatory in nature; people who possess them are strongly motivated to bring their conduct into line with normative standards. The internalized sense of morality is central to the work of, among others, Freud, Weber, and Durkheim (see e.g. Sunshine and Tyler 2003b). Internalized values are self-regulating, so that people accept and act on the basis of values that produce respect for societal institutions, authorities, and rules.

The significance of morality is illustrated by research on punishment. Studies demonstrate that people's views about appropriate sentencing decisions in criminal cases are driven by moral judgments about deservingness rather than by instrumental judgments concerning how to deter future criminal conduct (Carlsmith, Darley, and Robinson 2002; Darley, Carlsmith, and Robinson 2000). People accept that a punishment is appropriate when it accords with their moral sense of what is appropriate given the level and type of wrong committed. More generally, research shows that people are more willing to comply with the law to the extent that they view it as consistent with their moral values (e.g. Robinson and Darley 1995; Tyler 2006a; Tyler and Blader 2005). As a consequence, an important question for the law is the degree to which it is believed to be congruent with public moral values. To that degree the internalized sense of morality acts as a force for law-abidingness.

2.2 Value-based Perspectives on Motivation

A value-based perspective on human motivation suggests the importance of developing and sustaining a civic culture in which people abide by the law because they feel that it is consistent with public values. Political scientists refer to this set of values as a "reservoir of support" for government and society (Easton 1975). Although it may not always be easy for authorities to maintain high reservoir levels, a value-based model is consistent with a social psychological understanding of how authorities can effectively regulate citizen behavior, maintain social order, and promote an effective, well-functioning society by developing and maintaining a culture of supportive social values that will be internalized by the citizenry.

The value-based model avoids many of the pitfalls of the deterrence model. Specifically, it does not require extensive surveillance efforts, is more sophisticated concerning the genuine causes of human behavior, engages intrinsic (and not just extrinsic) motivation, and fosters a positive social climate based on a shared commitment to moral values rather than a negative social climate based on suspicion and distrust.

2.3 Procedural Fairness as the Basis of Legitimacy

The legitimacy of authorities is an especially promising basis for the rule of law because research suggests that it is not yoked to agreement with the decisions rendered by legal authorities. If people view as legitimate only those authorities who make decisions with which they agree, or even decisions that they view as fair, it would be difficult for legal authorities to maintain their legitimacy, insofar as they are required to make unpopular decisions and to deliver unfavorable outcomes. Fortunately, from the perspective of legal authorities, studies suggest that ascriptions of legitimacy are tied to the perceived fairness of the procedures used by authorities to make decisions rather than to the favorability of outcomes per se (Lind and Tyler 1988; Thibaut and Walker 1975; Tyler 2006b; Tyler et al. 1997; Tyler and Smith 1998). To the extent that people perceive law enforcement officials as legitimate, they are significantly more willing to defer to individual authorities (Kitzman and Emery 1993; Lind et al. 1993; Tyler 2001b; Tyler and Huo 2002; Wissler 1995), and they are also more likely to be in compliance with the law in general (Kim and Mauborgne 1993; Sparks, Bottoms, and Hay 1996; Sunshine and Tyler 2003a; Tyler 2006b).

These results suggest that legal authorities may be able to maintain their legitimacy in the long term by making decisions in an ethically defensible manner. Procedural justice cues play an especially important rule in securing compliance over time (Paternoster et al. 1997; Pruitt et al. 1993). It is by now very clear that people's reactions to law and legal authorities are heavily influenced by their assessments of the fairness of legal procedures.

The procedural basis of legitimacy is especially strong with respect to public opinion concerning political and legal institutions. Studies of the presidency (Tyler, Rasinski, and McGraw 1985), the legislature (Hibbing and Theiss-Morse 1995; 2002), and the Supreme Court (Tyler and Mitchell 1994) all suggest that when citizens are evaluating government institutions they focus primarily on the fairness of the procedures by which the institution makes policies and implements its decisions. Research on work organizations also suggests that perceived legitimacy has a strong procedural basis (Tyler and Blader 2000; 2005).

The procedural basis of legitimacy on an institutional level is consistent with the argument that support for the rules of governance (i.e. procedures and institutions) is theoretically and empirically distinguishable from support for particular individuals or their policies (Rasinski, Tyler, and Fridkin 1985). In general, however, it is support for the rules of governmental operation—what Easton (1975) refers to as "diffuse system support"—that is seen as crucial to long-term governmental stability. The most reliable way of attaining real as well as ostensible legitimacy and maintaining diffuse system support for legal institutions and authorities is by establishing and protecting procedural safeguards. Indeed, the need for procedural safeguards is one of the strongest arguments for the constitutional separation of executive, representative, and judicial branches of government.

To the extent that procedures for ensuring genuine fairness are compromised, the system will begin to lose legitimacy and—over time—fail to inspire the kind of cooperation and deference that is often taken for granted during periods of stability. And, procedures also encourage deference based upon perceived congruence of moral values, since people are more likely to view policies that are fairly enacted as consistent with their moral values (Tyler and Blader 2005).

The model of motivation that dominates the law is rooted in a utilitarian conception of the person. Recent scholarship raises doubts about this model both for law, and for political science and public policy (Green and Shapiro 1994). Many legal authorities also question this model, and are actively seeking alternatives. The next generation of scholarship in law and psychology is likely to be dominated by efforts to identify and provide empirical support for alternative models upon which to based the motivation of adherence to the law, as well as rehabilitation following rule breaking.

References

BLUMSTEIN, A., COHEN, J., and NAGIN, D. 1978. *Deterrence and Incapacitation.* Washington, DC: National Academy of Sciences.

CARLSMITH, K. M., DARLEY, J. M., and ROBINSON, P. H. 2002. Why do we punish? *Journal of Personality and Social Psychology,* 83: 284–99.

DAHL, R. 1956. *A Preface to Democratic Theory.* Chicago: University of Chicago Press.

DARLEY, J. M., CARLSMITH, K. M., and ROBINSON, P. H. 2000. Incapacitation and just deserts as motives for punishment. *Law and Human Behavior*, 24: 659–83.

—— TYLER, T. R., and BILZ, K. 2003. Enacting justice: the interplay of individual and institutional perspectives. Pp. 458–76 in *The Sage Handbook of Social Psychology*, ed. M. A. Hogg and J. Cooper. London: Sage.

DONOHUE, J. J., and WOLFERS, J. 2005–6. Uses and abuses of empirical evidence in the death penalty debate. *Stanford Law Review*, 58: 791–846.

EASTON, D. 1975. A reassessment of the concept of political support. *British Journal of Political Science*, 5: 435–57.

ELLSWORTH, P. C., and GROSS, S. R. 1994. Hardening of the attitudes: Americans' views on the death penalty. *Journal of Social Issues*, 50: 19–52.

—— and MAURO, R. 1998. Psychology and law. Pp. 684–732 in *Handbook of Social Psychology*, ed. D. Gilbert, S. Fiske, and G. Lindzey. New York: McGraw-Hill.

FREY, B. S. 1994. How intrinsic motivation is crowded in and out. *Rationality and Society*, 6: 334–52.

—— and OBERHOLZER-GEE, F. 1997. The cost of price incentives. *American Economic Review*, 87: 746–55.

FULLER, L. 1971. Human interaction and the law. In *The Rule of Law*, ed. R. P. Wolff. New York: Simon and Schuster.

GARLAND, D. 2001. *The Culture of Control*. Chicago: University of Chicago Press.

GNEEZY, U., and RUSTICHINI, A. 2000. A fine is a price. *Journal of Legal Studies*, 29: 1–17.

GREEN, D. P., and SHAPIRO, I. 1994. *Pathologies of Rational Choice Theory*. New Haven, Conn.: Yale University Press.

GURR, T. R. 1970. *Why Men Rebel*. Princeton, NJ: Princeton University Press.

HANEY, C., and ZIMBARDO, P. 1998. The past and future of U.S. prison policy: twenty-five years after the Stanford prison experiment. *American Psychologist*, 53: 709–27.

HIBBING, J. R., and THEISS-MORSE, E. 1995. *Congress as Public Enemy: Public Attitudes Toward American Political Institutions*. Cambridge: Cambridge University Press.

—— —— 2002. *Stealth Democracy: Americans' Beliefs About How Government Should Work*. Cambridge: Cambridge University Press.

JOST, J. T., and MAJOR, B. 2001. Emerging perspectives on the psychology of legitimacy. Pp. 3–32 in *The Psychology of Legitimacy*, ed. J. T. Jost and B. Major. Cambridge: Cambridge University Press.

KAHAN, D. 1999. The secret ambition of deterrence. *Harvard Law Review*, 113: 413–500.

KELMAN, H. C. 1969. Patterns of personal involvement in the national system: a social-psychological analysis of political legitimacy. Pp. 276–88 in *International Politics and Foreign Policy*, ed. J. Rosenau. New York: Free Press.

KIM, W. C., and MAUBORGNE, R. A. 1993. Procedural justice, attitudes, and subsidiary top management compliance with multinationals' corporate strategic decisions. *Academy of Management Journal*, 36: 502–26.

KITZMANN, K. M., and EMERY, R. E. 1993. Procedural justice and parents' satisfaction in a field study of child custody dispute resolution. *Law and Human Behavior*, 17: 553–67.

KRAMER, R. M., and TYLER, T. R. (eds.) 1996. *Trust in Organizations*. Thousand Oaks, Calif.: Sage.

KRISLOV, S., BOYUM, K. O., CLARK, J. N., SHAEFER, R. C., and WHITE, S. O. 1966. *Compliance and the Law: A Multi-Disciplinary Approach*. Beverly Hills, Calif.: Sage.

LEWIN, K. 1936. *Principles of Topological Psychology*. New York: McGraw-Hill.

LIND, E. A., and TYLER, T. R. 1988. *The Social Psychology of Procedural Justice*. New York: Plenum.

—— KULIK, C. T., AMBROSE, M., and DE VERA PARK, M. 1993. Individual and corporate dispute resolution. *Administrative Science Quarterly*, 38: 224–51.

MACCOUN, R. J. 1993. Drugs and the law: a psychological analysis of drug prohibition. *Psychological Bulletin*, 113: 497–512.

MASTROFSKI, S. D., SNIPES, J. B., and SUPINA, A. E. 1996. Compliance on demand: the public's responses to specific police requests. *Journal of Crime and Delinquency*, 33: 269–305.

MEARES, T. L. 2000. Norms, legitimacy, and law enforcement. *Oregon Law Review*, 79: 391–415.

MELTON, G. B. 1985. The law as a behavioral instrument. *Nebraska Symposium on Motivation*, 33.

MERELMAN, R. J. 1966. Learning and legitimacy. *American Political Science Review*, 60: 548–61.

MOORE, D. A., and LOEWNSTEIN, G. 2004. Self-interest, automaticity, and the psychology of conflict of interest. *Social Justice Research*, 17: 189–202.

NAGIN, D. S. 1998. Criminal deterrence research at the outset of the twenty-first century. Pp. 1–42 in *Crime and Justice*, ed. M. Tonry, vol. 23. Chicago: University of Chicago Press.

—— and PATERNOSTER, R. 1991. The preventive effects of the perceived risk of arrest. *Criminology*, 29: 561–85.

PARSONS, T. 1967. Some reflections on the place of force in social process. In *Sociological Theory and Modern Society*, ed. T. Parsons. New York: Free Press.

PATERNOSTER, R. 1987. The deterrent effect of the perceived certainty and severity of punishment. *Justice Quarterly*, 4: 173–217.

—— 1989. Decisions to participate in and desist from four types of common delinquency. *Law and Society Review*, 23: 7–40.

—— and IOVANNI, L. 1986. The deterrent effect of perceived severity. *Social Forces*, 64: 751–77.

—— and SIMPSON, S. 1996. Sanction threat and appeals to morality. *Law and Society Review*, 30: 549–83.

—— BRAME, R., BACHMAN, R., and SHERMAN, L. W. 1997. Do fair procedures matter? The effect of procedural justice on spouse assault. *Law and Society Review*, 31: 163–204.

—— SALTZMAN, L. E., WALDO, G. P., and CHIRICOS, T. G. 1983. Perceived risk and social control: do sanctions really deter? *Law and Society Review*, 17: 457–79.

PRUITT, D. G., PEIRCE, R. S., McGILLICUDDY, N. B., WELTON, G. L., and CASTRIANNO, L. M. 1993. Long-term success in mediation. *Law and Human Behavior*, 17: 313–30.

RASINSKI, K., TYLER, T. R., and FRIDKIN, K. 1985. Exploring the function of legitimacy: mediating effects of personal and institutional legitimacy on leadership endorsement and system support. *Journal of Personality and Social Psychology*, 49: 386–94.

REISS, A. J. 1971. *The Police and the Public*. New Haven, Conn.: Yale University Press.

ROBINSON, P. H., and DARLEY, J. 1995. *Justice, Liability, and Blame*. Boulder, Colo.: Westview.

—— —— 1997. The utility of desert. *Northwestern University Law Review*, 91: 453–99.

ROSS, H. L. 1982. *Deterring the Drinking Driver*. Lexington, Mass.: Lexington Books.

SPARKS, R., BOTTOMS, A., and HAY, W. 1996. *Prisons and the Problem of Order*. Oxford: Clarendon Press.

SUNSHINE, J., and TYLER, T. R. 2003*a*. The role of procedural justice and legitimacy in shaping public support for policing. *Law and Society Review*, 37: 513–48.

—— —— 2003*b*. Moral solidarity, identification with the community, and the importance of procedural justice. *Social Psychology Quarterly*, 66: 153–65.

TAPP, J., and LEVINE, F. 1977. *Law, Justice and the Individual in Society: Psychological and Legal Issues*. New York: Holt, Rinehart, and Winston.

TENBRUNSEL, A. E., and MESSICK, D. M. 2004. Ethical fading: the role of self-deception in unethical behavior. *Social Justice Research*, 17: 223–36.

THIBAUT, J., and WALKER, L. 1975. *Procedural Justice*. Hillsdale, NJ: Erlbaum.

TYLER, T. R. 2001*a*. Trust and law-abidingness: a proactive model of social regulation. *Boston University Law Review*, 81: 361–406.

—— 2001*b*. A psychological perspective on the legitimacy of institutions and authorities. Pp. 416–36 in Jost and Major 2001.

—— 2004. Affirmative action in an institutional context: the antecedents of policy preferences and political support. *Social Justice Research*, 17: 5–24.

—— 2006*a*. Psychological perspectives on legitimacy and legitimation. *Annual Review of Psychology*, 57: 375–400.

—— 2006*b*. *Why People Obey the Law*. New Haven, Conn.: Yale University Press.

—— and BLADER, S. L. 2005. Can businesses effectively regulate employee conduct? The antecedents of rule following in work settings. *Academy of Management Journal*, 48: 1143–58.

—— —— 2000. *Cooperation in Groups: Procedural Justice, Social Identity, and Behavioral Engagement*. Philadelphia: Psychology Press.

—— BOECKMANN, R. J., SMITH, H. J., and HUO, Y. J. 1997. *Social Justice in a Diverse Society*. Boulder, Colo.: Westview.

—— CASPER, J., and FISHER, B. 1989. Maintaining allegiance toward political authorities. *American Journal of Political Science*, 33: 629–52.

—— and DARLEY, J. M. 2000. Building a law-abiding society: taking public views about morality and the legitimacy of legal authorities into account when formulating substantive law. *Hofstra Law Review*, 28: 707–39.

—— and HUO, Y. J. 2002. *Trust in the Law*. New York: Russell Sage Foundation.

—— and MITCHELL, G. 1994. Legitimacy and the empowerment of discretionary legal authority: the United States Supreme Court and abortion rights. *Duke Law Journal*, 43: 703–814.

—— RASINSKI, K., and McGRAW, K. 1985. The influence of perceived injustice on support for political authorities. *Journal of Applied Social Psychology*, 15: 700–25.

—— and SMITH, H. J. 1998. Social justice and social movements. Pp. 595–629 in Gilbert, Fiske, and Lindzey 1998.

UNITED STATES DEPARTMENT of JUSTICE 2001. Prisoners in 2000. *Bureau of Justice Statistics Bulletin*, NCJ 188207.

WEBER, M. 1968. *Economy and Society*, ed. G. Roth and C. Wittich. Berkeley: University of California Press.

WISSLER, R. L. 1995. Mediation and adjudication in the small claims court. *Law and Society Review*, 29: 323–58.

ZELDITCH, JR., M. 2001. Theories of legitimacy. Pp. 33–53 in Jost and Major 2001.

CHAPTER 42

LAW AND HISTORY

CHRISTOPHER TOMLINS

THE "critical" movement in legal studies (CLS) that flowered in the United States between 1975 and 1995 took as an early point of departure that "LAW IS POLITICS, pure and simple." This was not a methodological statement, but an insurgent exposé of the fraudulent "dichotomy between the public sphere of politics and the private sphere of law" (Schlegel 1984, 410–11). Nevertheless, certain presumptions about the best means to exposure were implicit: CLS's commitment to unmasking law as politics proceeded from an initial excoriation of "traditional" jurisprudence for its indifference to "social and historical reality." Social and historical analysis of law would reveal law as politics, past and present, amenable as such to reimagination and change.

CLS's early identification of the social and the historical as reality-based standpoints from which to address the unreality of law's conventional claims of autonomy grew out of its roots in the "Law and Society" movement, founded in the early 1960s. Their relationship did not last. By 1980, CLS had departed law and society, having rejected law and society's foundational perspective—law as dependent variable—and research practice—the ascription of objective meaning through positivist social scientific inquiry (Tomlins 2004, 386). But CLS retained its orientation to history. Arguably, historical work has been throughout the most consistent exemplar of "critical" approaches in legal studies (Gordon 1984; 1996; 1997).

The critical project's historical work and its attempts to disrupt the law/politics distinction have had considerable influence on the general development of U.S. legal history. "Much recent American legal history...has been obsessed with whether or not law is political" (Parker 2006, 518). Indeed, an obsession with politics courses throughout the field's modern development. Professional historians' first sustained engagement with law, which dates from the early 1970s (Katz 1984), came about through the study of legal institutions "in the context of political behavior and political structures" (Ernst 1998, 205). Political science has long fed the preoccupation in its application of political decision-making and institutional behavior to the analysis of legal actor and institutions, or simply in treating legal institutions *as* political institutions (Dahl 1957; Whittington 2005). The strong interest in law and legal institutions that has always marked the "American Political Development" movement within political science further replicates the preoccupation, and in effect completes the circle by according historical study prominence in its methods and conceptualizations (see e.g. Orren 1991; Gillman 1993).

In all these cases scholars are engaged in creating and then reading back onto law a conception of necessary and sufficient context—the political, the social, the economic—the terms of which will explain legal phenomena. Law is absorbed by its context, or placed in a determinate relationship to that context. Contemporary legal historians find all law at all times amenable to these strategies of critical contextualization, and indeed may feel free to move opportunistically among them because they add the further overweening context of historical time, insisting that whatever context is chosen, explanation itself can only begin once the object to be observed has been placed in its proper temporal context.

Parker (2006) has suggested that the practice of contextualizing law by something other than itself has its own point of departure. In tracing the course followed by twentieth-century legal history in its exploration of politics as an appropriate, and ultimately fully absorbing, context for law in the American case, in other words, we can isolate a prior moment when this was not the case. So doing, we can better appreciate the dynamic of legal history in the long term, and draw conclusions about what it can do, and what it cannot.

1 How We Got To Where We Are

Much of late nineteenth-century American legal thought identified "custom" as the appropriate context for law. This created a context for law out of law itself, for "custom" was a long-established legal category. Custom embodied "life"—it expressed commonalities of human action and belief in advance of law. In relation to custom, law was always running to catch up, always reforming in an attempt to capture "life" in law's crystalline form.

Custom was certainly not the only context imaginable for law in the late nineteenth century. Law's traditional craft elites conceived of law as a "science of principles," immanent and immutable, discovered and not made, studied for the particulars they might reveal. Langdellian legal science in contrast emphasized rigorous inductive investigation of legal materials (cases) to yield generalizations from which the observer could derive rules that would predict the outcome of future legal events (Schweber 1999). Here then lay competing aesthetic contexts for law—common modes of action, immanent normative universals, and scientific rules developed from rigorous observation. All, however, were self-referential; all emerged from law itself. Each could be expressed historically, but none employed history to reveal law as something other than itself, like politics or culture or society.

Change came at the turn of the century, and with it the beginnings of legal scholarship's turn to the contextualizing categories of the social/political and the temporal. The best-known statement was Oliver Wendell Holmes' famous aperçu naming "experience" corresponding to "the felt necessities of the time" as "the life of the law" (Holmes 1881); but the leading exponent was Roscoe Pound, who coined the term "sociological jurisprudence" to express the strategy of explaining law by reference to an exterior social world (Wigdor 1974; Willrich 2003, 104–15). In Pound's project, "law" was not abstract doctrinal principles but "the actual effects" of juridical activity, its measure whether it achieved the "concrete securing or realizing of human interests." Legal history should not deal with legal phenomena "apart from the economic and social history of their time" (Herget 1990, 166; Pound 1921, 196, 213; 1923, 152–65).

Here, in Pound's nutshell, we encounter what would eventually become the main current of twentieth-century U.S. legal history. Pound himself did not pursue it with much vigor; by the 1930s, largely in reaction to legal realism and the New Deal, he had returned to an "inside" narrative of law (Pound 1938). In law schools, historical scholarship remained largely descriptive and focused on doctrinal categories and legal process (Katz 1984, 458–9, 461). In history departments, if studied at all, legal history was subsumed within American colonial history and the history of the federal Constitution. In the 1920s and 1930s, external historiography of law was confined to the margins, in the work of nonconventional scholars like John W. Burgess, Charles Beard, and John R. Commons, or in highly specialized research monographs.[1]

Matters changed somewhat over the next fifteen years. Scholars who came of age during the New Deal engaged far more systematically in "enriched" contextualized explanation of law than any who had preceded them (Morris 1946; Handlin and Handlin 1947; Hartz 1948). Willard Hurst would prove the most influential of this small cohort of "new" American legal historians. Hurst's project resembled what Pound had talked of but never actually undertaken—the construction of a sociology of juridical action and institutions out of "close empirical investigations"

---

[1] Notably the monograph series *Columbia University Studies in History, Economics and Public Law*, founded in 1892.

that unpacked "law's operational ties to other components of social order" (Novak 2000, 99–100).

Hurst's initial statement described law as "passive, acted upon by other social forces, more often than acting upon them" (Hurst 1950, 4). There was much more to Hurst, however, than simple exterior causation. Constant struggles to realize self-interest generated functional sociolegal structures. As reactive mediators of outcomes these structures exhibited the short-term calculus that Hurst called "bastard pragmatism." Below lay something altogether different, not far removed (although employing a different conceptual vocabulary) from "custom." In 1950s history it became "consensus," represented in Hurst's case by incessant invocation of a homogeneous national consciousness. Consensus meant shared values produced in a collective exertion of conscious reflection. But Hurst was just as interested in consensus as unreflective habit. Hurst the historian stressed that law was not a distinct order of reality, "timeless, placeless, essential." It was "man-made," the product of human deliberation located in time (Hurst 1964, 4). But law was also made by humanity's capacity for unconscious drift and inertia.

In Hurst's scheme, law and social order met outside the strictly juridical domain. The key was the market, where consciousness intersected with the material conditions that impacted upon human needs and ambitions (Hurst 1964, 42). Law acted in the market's shadow—enabling, supplementing, and servicing market activity, balancing "the release of energy" against the accumulation of power, functions ultimately leading to a twentieth-century polity "of administrative regulation" (Novak 2000, 127; Hurst 1956). This was "modern" legal history's point of departure. No less an authority than Supreme Court Justice Byron White praised the turn from "narrow study of judicial doctrine" to "deal[ing] with the ties between law and society" (White 1971, v, vi).

At precisely this moment, however, a young assistant professor at Harvard Law School, Morton Horwitz, renewed the fight with Roscoe Pound, and this time named law, not society, as the essential terrain (Horwitz 1973).

Horwitz's target was Pound's (1938) celebratory "inside narrative" of law's internalized constancy under the tutelage of heroic judges and sympathetic legal intellectuals. He spoke out for "the real function of history"—critique—against Pound's "dominant form" in which history played "the pathetic role of justifying the world as it is" (1973, 281). Of course, by then Pound had been sidelined by the new sociolegal paradigm. But Horwitz was no less antagonistic to Hurst's history, as his immensely influential *Transformation of American Law* (1977) demonstrated. Hurst had measured outcomes by process—how effectively the goals of a presumptively shared national consciousness were realized. But process did not acknowledge social *struggle*. Asymmetric distributions of wealth and power left Horwitz skeptical of histories that represented legal innovations as responses to undifferentiated "social needs." Law's "political and redistributive" biases seemed obvious (Horwitz 1977, 266).

Transformation was an early model for critical legal history (CLH), but within a few years CLH had abandoned Horwitz's attempts to show that determinate relationships existed in historical time between legal events and socioeconomic context. Instead its adherents addressed the politics of legal knowledge, and CLH became the intellectual history of legal doctrine, whose "subversive" objective was to "take dominant legal ideologies at their own estimation and try to see how their components are assembled" (Gordon 1996, 360; for evaluative accounts see Ernst 1993; Williams 1987).

The result in the 1980s and 1990s was conceptual tension within the developing U.S. legal-historical field. The sociolegal paradigm that Hurst had exemplified remained influential in professional historical research on field-level uses of law (see e.g. McEvoy 1986). Others pursued distinct variations on the theme of a determinate relationship between context and law (see e.g. Tushnet 1981). More "constitutive" perspectives emphasizing law's impact on social, economic, and political relations followed (discussed in Grossberg 1991). All this resulted during the 1990s in an outpouring of historicizing, empirical inquiry into legal phenomena much of which explored new, non-Hurstian contexts even as it remained broadly within the sociolegal paradigm (Welke 2000). Simultaneously, some historians began to strip away the technical appurtenances that, in legal scholars' hands, had tended to inscribe a virtual autonomy on law (see e.g. Tomlins 1995).

The impact of professional historians' entry upon legal terrain as legal scholars see it has been on the whole marginal (see e.g. Ferguson 2002). This marginality responds to the actual state of affairs in the legal academy, which in the 1980s and 1990s was preoccupied by political struggles over the meaning of the rules that the juridical field produced. Within the legal academy CLH's neodoctrinalism was the dominant form legal history took.

2 THE CURRENT SCENE

By the mid-1990s, critical legal history was out of steam.[2] Its interest in dominant legal ideologies had been influential—law is an extraordinarily authoritative means to organize perception—but its deconstructive approach led to a rather dismal conclusion: The relationship between law and society was so radically underdetermined

---

[2] In 1984, Gordon conceded that critical doctrinal history remained abstract and disengaged from empirical research outside traditional scholarly law sources. "[I]f the Critics want to make [their] point convincingly, they will have to start slicing their narratives out of field-level uses of law" (1984, 120, 124–5). They never did.

that there were no "necessary consequences of the adoption of [any] given regime of rules" (Gordon 1984, 125).

Outside the critical hothouse, the conjunction of history and law has proceeded more prosaically. Contextualizing debates have been rampant—contextualizing is what historians "do." The dominion of social history in legal history research, in place since the 1960s, has been joined by cultural history (e.g. Hartog 2000). The interpretive salience of race and ethnicity, of gender and sexuality, and class is as strong in contemporary legal historical practice as in any other realm of history (see e.g. Bardaglio 1995; Stanley 1998; Davis 1999; Welke 2001; Canaday 2003; Wilson 2003). One can also observe a resurgence of perspectives relatively disfavored—political and economic history, which is to say the history of institutions (Harris 2003; Clarke 2005; Dauber 2005). Meanwhile, historians at large have become attuned to the realization that their practice—whether economic, social, cultural, intellectual, or indeed *any* kind of history—quickly enters realms of inquiry that necessarily implicate law. Add to that the continuing influence of legal pluralism in legal history, detectable in work that eschews a focus on "the law" for the conditions of existence of "legality" and the competition of distinct "legalities" in the same social space (Tomlins and Mann 2001), and one finds oneself at work in a field of immense opportunity.

But the question then arises: If law is now everywhere in history, what makes "legal history" distinctive as a historical practice?

Central to current understandings within the field is the perception that if society is "made and imagined . . . a human artifact" (Unger 1987, 1), then law is one of the most significant technologies for that inventive activity. Legal historians have tested the proposition in multiple realms of social and cultural life, through the categorizations of gender and sexuality, race and ethnicity, and class; through the design and interior relations of social and economic institutions—households, schools, plantations, factories, localities. They have moved from a perspective that stresses law's functionality as a mechanism or "arena" for the mediation of other-determined social relations to one that stresses its creativity: from law as the product or reflection of social processes to law as a means of inscribing authority on circumstance.

With all this has come a reversal of the causal assumptions that accompanied and shaped the sociolegal history of the 1970s and early 1980s. Instead of providing a social explanation of law, legal historians are pursuing legal explanations of the social. Law has become the context for society.

Willingness to reverse the causal relationship, to grant law's causal capacities, has meant a lowered threshold of interest in "the inner workings of practice and procedure." Law is taken "as a given;" as the historian focuses on "its effects on whatever surrounds it" (Mann 2001, 444–5). Mann argues that neither side of the relationship should be taken as given.

As a statement about the responsibilities of historical research, Mann's point is unexceptionable. As a methodological argument about the investigation of causation, however, the statement might appear something of a siren song. After all, one of the most durable claims of legal realism, reconstituted by CLS, is the claim that law's inner workings are indeterminate. An invitation to probe how law operates on the world through the lens of how law operates in itself looks like an invitation into a cul-de-sac. Historians are of course used to dealing with contingency. That is one reason why critical legal scholarship found history so amenable. But indeterminacy understates the fixity and resilience, the stickiness, of the regimes of rules that law sets in place. We should not assume that legally-induced structures decompose easily, or give up the pursuit of causal relationships between structures and outcomes.

And yet . . .

3 POSSIBILITIES

"Over and over again," Parker observes, historians of law have been driven to conclude that law "is a kind of politics" (2006, 518). The conclusion relies upon a propensity to comprehend law only in terms of its relation to that which is outside itself. We seem to be at an impasse. Parker's response is to ask whether the conclusion's conditioning propensity can be discarded but the insight itself retained. Two possibilities may be suggested.

The first, which departs least from current trajectories of inquiry, would focus on determining the kind of politics that law, reputedly, is. Much recent work, both theoretical and institutional, has suggested that law, in fact, displaces politics (Honig 1993; Kramer 2004). But displacing politics is itself "a kind of politics"— though not obviously or directly so until one relaxes the disciplinary and behavioral conventions that decree what "politics" is. Once relaxed, the old critical "law is politics" slogan seems superficial, but the statement itself remains interesting and becomes open to new theoretical and empirical investigation (see e.g. Dezalay and Garth 2002*a*; 2002*b*; Vauchez and Cohen 2007).

A variation on inquiry into what kind of politics law is can be found in an upsurge of interest in law's relationship to the state (see e.g. Novak 2002; Witt 2004). What does the state demand of law? What does law supply? Is *law* the health of the state? If so, is this the health of facilitation or resistance, technique or liberty (Lavi 2005)? What of sovereignty (Aleinikoff 2002)? What of emergency (Hussain 2005)? What, above all, of governance, which is to say *police* (Dubber 2005; Dubber and Valverde 2006)?

The second possibility would involve reexamining the conceptions of appropriate context to which historians and others have had resort in producing their narratives of what law is. This might lead us to further refinement in identifying the kind of politics that law is, or to identities for law that are other than politics, which would suggest that, qua law, politics has limits. Here we can turn to work by Marianne Constable. Like Parker, Constable reflects upon the drive to situate law "in an empirical social world" (2005, 9). This "sociologization" of law converges with modernist commitments to make law an instrument of social power, reinforcing a characterization of law as "sociolegal positivism" from which there seems no escape. For our purposes, Constable's work suggests two conclusions. First, when it comes to characterizing modern law, sociologization makes perfect sense. It is a way of conceiving law that indeed reveals modernity's sociolegal positivism. The trouble is, it cannot conceive of law as anything else. Constable's distinct standpoint, rhetoric, suggests two contexts for examining law outside the sociological—law's silences and law's language. Like Parker's custom, these contexts emerge from law itself. They do not contain law by describing what it "really" is or prescribing what it should be, or forecasting what it will become, but identify and hold open possibilities—what might it be (now) that sociologizing cannot discover.

The particular possibility Constable pursues is justice. This is an empirical not a conjectural exercise. Constable proceeds historically by "recall[ing] to modern law possibilities that already will have been" (2005, 12). But this practice of history is different from the professional practice with which we are familiar, the practice that preaches the completeness of the past's containment in an empirical, social world, and its epistemic and temporal severance from the present and future. A historical practice that does not "sociologize" the past, and purposefully *recalls* to the present what "already will have been," breaches both containment and severance. It implies unconventional conclusions about the extent and limits of historical time, in which all that already will have been continues to be; perhaps as a specter (Derrida 1994), or perhaps incognito, until recognized by one who will recall it (Constable 2005), or perhaps like a volcano, dormant until it "flashes up" in a moment of danger that demands our recognition (Benjamin 1968 [1940]).

4 To Conclude

The "subversive" conjunction between history and critical legal studies, with which this chapter began, has ended. No doubt work in the style of critical legal history will continue. Indeed, the (involuntary) assimilation of "virtually all history as practiced by modern historians" to critical historicism's agenda (Gordon 1997) seems to leave history of law no room to do anything else. But that in itself is a marker of intellectual exhaustion.

It is not the only marker. Recent commentary on history of law recommends eschewing philosophical inquiry into the assumptions of modern history and instead simply producing more of it, apparently believing that to the right intellect nothing can remain unknown (Whitman 2005).

There have always been futures for more of the same. Yet scholarship is not well served by complacency. As Parker and Constable separately recognize, history has philosophical limits, most importantly limits on what its object can be (see also Fasolt 2004). The goal is not to perfect our practice so that it is "really" unlimited in what it can do, but rather to know the limits of our current practices, to construct distinct forms of historical practice, to know *their* limits, and so forth. That way lies realization that what can be known is always provisional, a restoration to the past of its wildness and disorder, its seductiveness and its threats.

History's contextualizing debates are all about what context is most appropriate, what can contribute most to the exercise of "filling out our picture of the past." The task is not unimportant, and this chapter has identified some of the substantive directions that the scholarship of the last ten years would recommend. But history's debates are largely about the "how" of the task, not why to undertake it in the first place. Perhaps the latter seems self-evident: modernity's "social human being" treats the world as object or resource, and "would master it through knowledge" (Constable 2005, 175). Filling out is a means to that end. But that end is a delusion: "only a redeemed mankind receives the fullness of its past" (Benjamin 1968 [1940], 254). And precisely then, at the moment of redemption, humanity will have no further need for history, or for that matter, law. So if filling out has an end, that end can only be for its own sake, an instance of "the tendency of modern knowledge to grasp, to conceive, to master, to posit, 'to ... *plunge into* other people and other things'" (Constable 2005, 175).

Perhaps instead (while we are awaiting redemption?), history and law could be where we search not for knowledge but for something else, shards and fragments, remnants of things that hint at the possibility of a discoverable justice. If so, we must first find new ways of looking.

References

ALEINIKOFF, T. A. 2002. *Semblances of Sovereignty: The Constitution, the State and American Citizenship*. Cambridge, Mass.: Harvard University Press.

BARDAGLIO, P. W. 1995. *Reconstructing the Household: Families, Sex and the Law in the Nineteenth-Century South*. Chapel Hill: University of North Carolina Press.

BENJAMIN, W. 1968. Theses on the philosophy of history [completed 1940]. Pp. 253–64 in *Walter Benjamin: Illuminations*, ed. H. Arendt. New York: Schocken.

CANADAY, M. 2003. Building a straight state: sexuality and social citizenship under the 1944 G.I. bill. *Journal of American History*, 90: 935–57.

CLARKE, S. H. 2005. Unmanageable risks: *Macpherson v. Buick* and the emergence of a mass consumer market. *Law and History Review*, 23: 1–52.

CONSTABLE, M. 2005. *Just Silences: The Limits and Possibilities of Modern Law*. Princeton, NJ: Princeton University Press.

DAHL, R. 1957. Decision-making in a democracy: the Supreme Court as a national policy-maker. *Journal of Public Law*, 6: 275–95.

DAUBER, M. L. 2005. The sympathetic state. *Law and History Review*, 23: 387–442.

DAVIS, A. D. 1999. The private law of race and sex: an antebellum perspective. *Stanford Law Review*, 51: 221–88.

DERRIDA, J. 1994. *Specters of Marx: The State of the Debt, the Work of Mourning, and the New International*. New York: Routledge.

DEZALAY, Y., and GARTH, B. G. 2002a. *The Internationalization of Palace Wars: Lawyers, Economists, and the Contest to Transform Latin American States*. Chicago: University of Chicago Press.

—— —— 2002b. Legitimating the new legal orthodoxy. Pp. 306–34 in *Global Prescriptions: The Production, Exportation, and Importation of a New Legal Orthodoxy*, ed. Y. Dezalay and B. G. Garth. Ann Arbor: University of Michigan Press.

DUBBER, M. D. 2005. *The Police Power: Patriarchy and the Foundations of American Government*. New York: Columbia University Press.

—— and VALVERDE M. (eds.) 2006. *The New Police Science: Police Power in Domestic and International Governance*. Stanford, Calif.: Stanford University Press.

ERNST, D. R. 1993. The critical tradition in the writing of American legal history. *Yale Law Journal*, 102: 1019–76.

—— 1998. Law and american political development, 1877–1938. *Reviews in American History*, 26: 205–19.

FASOLT, C. 2003. *The Limits of History*. Chicago: University of Chicago Press.

FERGUSON, R. A. 2002. The many legalities of early America (review). *William and Mary Quarterly*, 49: 481–6.

GILLMAN, H. 1993. *The Constitution Besieged: The Rise and Demise of Lochner Era Police Powers Jurisprudence*. Durham, NC: Duke University Press.

GORDON, R. W. 1984. Critical legal histories. *Stanford Law Review*, 36: 57–125.

—— 1996. The past as authority and as social critic: stabilizing and destabilizing functions of history in legal argument. Pp. 339–87 in *The Historic Turn in the Human Sciences*, ed. T. J. McDonald. Ann Arbor: University of Michigan Press.

—— 1997. Foreword: the arrival of critical historicism. *Stanford Law Review*, 49: 1023–9.

GROSSBERG, M. 1991. Social history update: "fighting faiths" and the challenges of legal history. *Journal of Social History*, 25: 191–201.

HANDLIN, O., and HANDLIN, M. F. 1947. *Commonwealth: A Study of the Role of Government in the American Economy: Massachusetts, 1774–1861*. Cambridge, Mass.: Harvard University Press.

HARRIS, R. 2003. The encounters of economic history and legal history. *Law and History Review*, 21: 297–346.

HARTOG, H. 2000. *Man and Wife in America: A History*. Cambridge, Mass.: Harvard University Press.

HARTZ, L. 1948. *Economic Policy and Democratic Thought: Pennsylvania, 1776–1860*. Chicago: Quadrangle.

HERGET, J. E. 1990. *American Jurisprudence, 1870–1970: A History.* Houston: Rice University Press.

HOLMES, O. W. 1881. *The Common Law.* Boston: Little, Brown.

HONIG, B. 1993. *Political Theory and the Displacement of Politics.* Ithaca, NY: Cornell University Press.

HORWITZ, M. J. 1973. The conservative tradition in the writing of American legal history. *American Journal of Legal History,* 17: 275–94.

—— 1977. *The Transformation of American Law, 1780–1860.* Cambridge, Mass.: Harvard University Press.

HURST, J. W. 1950. *The Growth of American Law: The Law Makers.* Boston: Little, Brown.

—— 1956. *Law and the Conditions of Freedom in the Nineteenth-Century United States.* Madison: University of Wisconsin Press.

—— 1964. *Justice Holmes on Legal History.* New York: Macmillan.

HUSSAIN, N. 2005. *The Jurisprudence of Emergency: Colonialism and the Rule of Law.* Ann Arbor: University of Michigan Press.

KATZ, S. N. 1984. The problem of a colonial legal history. Pp. 457–89 in *Colonial British America,* ed. J. P. Greene and J. R. Pole. Baltimore: Johns Hopkins University Press.

KRAMER, L. D. 2004. *The People Themselves: Popular Constitutionalism and Judicial Review.* Oxford: Oxford University Press.

LAVI, S. J. 2005. *The Modern Art of Dying: A History of Euthanasia in the United States.* Princeton, NJ: Princeton University Press.

MANN, B. H. 2001. The death and transfiguration of early American legal history. Pp. 442–7 in Tomlins and Mann 2001.

MCEVOY, A. F. 1986. *The Fisherman's Problem: Ecology and Law in the California Fisheries, 1850–1980.* New York: Cambridge University Press.

MORRIS, R. B. 1946. *Government and Labor in Early America.* New York: Columbia University Press.

NOVAK, W. J. 2000. Law, capitalism and the liberal state: the historical sociology of James Willard Hurst. *Law and History Review,* 18: 97–145.

—— 2002. The legal origins of the modern American state. Pp. 249–83 in *Looking Back at Law's Century,* ed. A. Sarat, B. G. Garth, and R. A. Kagan. Ithaca, NY: Cornell University Press.

ORREN, K. 1991. *Belated Feudalism: Labor, the Law, and Liberal Development in the United States.* New York: Cambridge University Press.

PARKER, K. M. 2006. Context in history and law: a study of the late nineteenth century American jurisprudence of custom. *Law and History Review,* 24: 473–518.

POUND, R. 1921. *The Spirit of the Common Law.* Boston: Marshall Jones.

—— 1923. *Interpretations of Legal History.* Cambridge: Cambridge University Press.

—— 1938. *The Formative Era of American Law.* Boston: Little, Brown.

SCHLEGEL, J. H. 1984. Notes toward an intimate, opinionated, and affectionate history of the conference on critical legal studies. *Stanford Law Review,* 36: 391–412.

SCHWEBER, H. 1999. The "science" of legal science: the model of the natural sciences in nineteenth-century American legal education. *Law and History Review,* 17: 421–66.

STANLEY, A .D. 1998. *From Bondage to Contract: Wage Labor, Marriage, and the Market in the Age of Slave Emancipation.* New York: Cambridge University Press.

TOMLINS C. L. 1995. Subordination, authority, law: subjects in labor history. *International Labor and Working-Class History,* 47: 56–90.

TOMLINS C. L. 2004. History in the American juridical field: narrative, justification, and explanation. *Yale Journal of Law and the Humanities*, 16: 323–98.

—— and MANN, B. H. (eds.) 2001. *The Many Legalities of Early America*. Chapel Hill: University of North Carolina Press.

TUSHNET, M. V. 1981. *The American Law of Slavery: Considerations of Humanity and Interest*. Princeton, NJ: Princeton University Press.

UNGER, R. M. 1987. *Social Theory: Its Situation and Task*. New York: Cambridge University Press.

VAUCHEZ, A., and COHEN, A. 2007. Law, lawyers and transnational politics in the production of Europe: a symposium. *Law and Social Inquiry*, 32: 75–82.

WELKE, B. Y. 2000. Willard Hurst and the archipelago of American legal historiography. *Law and History Review*, 18: 197–204.

—— 2001. *Recasting American Liberty: Gender, Race, Law, and the Railroad Revolution*. New York: Cambridge University Press.

WHITE, B. R. 1971. Introduction. Pp. v–xi in *Law in American History*, ed. D. Fleming and B. Bailyn. Boston: Little, Brown.

WHITMAN, J. Q. 2005. The limits of history (review). *Law and History Review*, 23: 459–60.

WHITTINGTON, K. E. 2005. Congress before the *Lochner* court. *Boston University Law Review*, 85: 821–58.

WIGDOR, D. 1974. *Roscoe Pound: Philosopher of Law*. Westport, Conn.: Greenwood Press.

WILLIAMS, J. C. 1987. Critical legal studies: the death of transcendence and the rise of the new Langdells. *New York University Law Review*, 62: 429–96.

WILLRICH, M. J. 2003. *City of Courts: Socializing Justice in Progressive Era Chicago*. Cambridge: Cambridge University Press.

WILSON, S. H. 2003. *Brown* over "other white:" Mexican-Americans' legal arguments and litigation strategy in school desegregation lawsuits. *Law and History Review*, 21: 145–94.

WITT, J. F. 2004. *The Accidental Republic: Crippled Workingmen, Destitute Widows, and the Remaking of American Law*. Cambridge, Mass.: Harvard University Press.

PART X

OLD AND NEW

CHAPTER 43

THE PATH OF THE LAW IN POLITICAL SCIENCE: DE-CENTERING LEGALITY FROM OLDEN TIMES TO THE DAY BEFORE YESTERDAY

STUART A. SCHEINGOLD

COURTS in general, the U.S. Supreme Court in particular, and constitutional law are, have been, and will continue to be the intellectual center of gravity for the law and courts subfield of political science—albeit with the welcome addition in recent years of a strong element of comparative inquiry. Indeed, there was a time at the beginning of the twentieth century when they were the intellectual center of gravity of the discipline of political science. Witness the Department of Public Law and

Government at Columbia University—founded in 1880 and retaining that name at least through 1954, Columbia University's bicentennial year (Millett 1955).

Beginning in the late 1950s, however, the law and courts subfield—formerly known as public law—began to spread its wings. This is the process which I refer to as de-centering. My objective is to identify the roots, the elements, and the rewards of de-centering. I will argue that de-centering does not displace the center but augments it. As scholars in the subfield have looked beyond its intellectual center, they have enriched the collective enterprise by exploring its normative, empirical, political, and policy implications. In so doing they have laid the foundation for making mutually rewarding connections with our fellow political scientists and with interdisciplinary sociolegal scholars.

I will get the ball rolling with a solipsistic identification of the center; go on to explain what I mean by de-centering; and conclude by making my case for the virtues of thus extending the reach and the grasp of the subfield.

1 CONFESSIONS OF A CENTRIST

What I now see as the center of the law and courts subfield of political science, was seen in olden times as the entirety of public law. To convey that center which was amorphous, ill-defined, and unrelenting, I am going to share one of the clearest of my graduate school memories: *the public law workroom.* Its physical configurations come immediately and rather benignly to mind: a clean, well-lit, medium-sized room with a wall of windows on one side and heavily laden bookshelves lining the other three walls. While the room itself was benign, such was not the case for its contents, which conjure up less benign and more relevant recollections.

1.1 The Center

For me and my fellow graduate students those heavily laden bookshelves were public law. There was one section of books on the Supreme Court and constitutional law by the leading figures of that period and earlier times. Some of those who come to mind are Johns Hopkins political scientist Carl Brent Swisher, Cornell political scientist Robert Cushing, and Harvard law professor Paul Freund. I associate Swisher, Freund, and numerous others with rather crisp little volumes offering their well-respected and, ever so slightly, divergent views of the Supreme Court, the First Amendment, the Commerce Clause, and so on. There was also a complete set of the Supreme Court reports. The rest of the shelves—most of them, that is—were more alarmingly packed with law reviews that, at least in my ill-formed academic identity, took on what I now see as wildly exaggerated intellectual authority.

The contents of the public workroom, along with undergraduate classes and graduate seminars in constitutional law taught primarily by Charles Aiken and some jurisprudence taught primarily by Aiken's junior colleague, Yosal Rogat, constituted public law at Berkeley.[1] The overall configuration was simple: Public law (that forbiddingly opaque and never elucidated designation) and constitutional law were indistinguishable from one another, and from the Supreme Court. Graduate students who intended to offer a field in public law, therefore, spent an inordinate amount of time in the public law workroom hoping to become at one with the field by long-term and intense exposure to it. I suppose that it is not altogether by accident that this made us behave rather like law students, particularly first year law students. They, I am told and also have observed, spend great gobs of time in the law library—whether actually reading or just staring at their case books, whispering to friends about alternative career paths or planning brief interludes of liberation, reading the campus paper or napping. Of course, our immersion was much less intense because we were distracted by the other three fields in which we were examined (in my case international relations, comparative and American politics).

As prelims approached I became ever more anxious and, indeed, deranged about all my exams but particularly my public law exams. In part that was because, along with international relations, public law was a designated "major" field for me. But more fundamentally, it was the public law workroom that was the problem. Nobody except one's notoriously unreliable fellow students provided any indication about what was to be tested. What was I supposed to read? Please God: certainly not every article and every book in the public law workroom! But what were to be my criteria of selection? I was without a clue: no recommendations, no bibliographies—nor were prior exams made available. I was being called upon to subdue, nay *to consume*, the public law workroom and felt entirely unequal to the task. Well, to end an already too long prelude, I did somehow manage to stumble through my public law examination, which included old warhorse questions about the evolution of the Commerce Clause, the importance of the Youngstown Steel case, and the status of the First Amendment in the era of virulent anticommunism from which the country was just emerging (think of the Yates and Watkins cases).

So there you have the jumble of intellectual baggage that I packed and brought with me into the postdoctoral world of grown-ups, who are destined to consort with postadolescents, for thirty years or so. Fairly shortly thereafter, following two or three desultory years at the University of California, Davis, I had the good

---

[1] John Schaar's American political thought scholarship contributed much to what became my decentered conception of public law. Rogat later taught at the University of Chicago and Stanford law schools.

fortune to land at the University of Wisconsin where the public law workroom met the Russell Sage Foundation and I began to get my intellectual bearings. True, constitutional law continued to retain a kind of pride of place in political science even at Wisconsin for reasons having to do with undergraduate education, FTEs, jobs for graduate students, and not least of all, the esteemed scholar of constitutional law, David Fellman.

Still, there was much more going on. I was delighted to discover an interdisciplinary cadre of law and society scholars, including intellectually engaged law professors (influenced by the justly revered and renowned Willard Hurst), sociologists, historians, and philosophers. Within political science, judicial process and judicial behavior scholarship was in full bloom with the beloved Herbert Jacob and the lovable Joel Grossman showing the way to newcomers like Kenneth Dolbeare and me.

1.2 What is De-centering?

Having, I hope, firmly, if in too personal a fashion, fixed the center, I will go on in a less personal vein to introduce and in subsequent sections to explore in some detail the nature and the contribution of de-centering to the law and courts subfield.

De-centering is grounded in two propositions and the theory and research that have been derived therefrom. The first proposition is that there is no bright line between law and politics—that law and politics are inextricably linked to one another.[2] This proposition is at the core of the work now identified as *the new institutionalism*. The second proposition extends the concept of law from its formal institutions and authoritative rules to its constitutive presence in culture, politics, and civil society. This proposition is derived from research on the *legal mobilization*—efforts by individuals, interest groups, and social movements to deploy the law to serve their individual and collective purposes.

Each of these elements of the de-centered conception of law has both disciplinary and interdisciplinary roots. The starting point is outside the discipline in legal realism—originally developed and practiced in the 1930s by a small cadre of law professors from elite schools (Kalman 1996). Within the discipline and mostly within the law and courts subfield, I would identify as the patron saints of de-centering such honored figures as Jack Peltason, Victor Rosenblum, Clement Vose, Alan Westin, Walter Murphy, and John Schmidhauser. Although they would not necessarily think of themselves in these terms, I will explain below why I do.

---

[2] I had thought until recently that the law–politics distinction was a kind of historical curiosity—useful in my pursuit of the etiology of de-centering but otherwise discredited. However, a fairly recent spate of exchanges on the law and politics list-serve concerning the relative merits of the attitudinal and legal models of judicial decision-making suggest that this controversy is alive and kicking.

2 THE NEW INSTITUTIONALISM

The de-centering impact of the new institutionalism and its precursors is perhaps best captured by the idea of putting the law into its political context.[3] To do so encourages us to think systematically, rather than in an anecdotal, off-the-cuff manner, about how the "least dangerous branch" is connected to the other branches and other levels of government as a sometime reluctant player in the American polity. While thus reaching beyond courts, the new institutionalism, I will argue, remains very much court centered.

2.1 Anticipating the New Institutionalism

It would be anachronistic, at best, to identify Alan Westin as a new institutionalist. In retrospect, however, he can be seen as among the earliest precursors of the new institutionalism (cf. Clayton 1999). Westin constructed a series of portraits of leading decisions of the U.S. Supreme Court that put these cases into their political contexts. For example, he analyzed the Youngstown Steel Case not simply in terms of the limits it imposed on presidential powers in time of war but as it was embroiled in heated conflicts over the Taft–Hartley Act. President Truman was unwilling to invoke Taft–Hartley, because of the union-busting implications of its invalidation of the "closed shop" (Westin 1958). In this book and in subsequent studies Westin reminded those of us in public law that we had been trained as political scientists not as lawyers.

There followed a variety of analogous reminders. Two books on the relationships between Congress and the courts by Walter Murphy (1962) and John Schmidhauser and Harry Berg (1972) come immediately to mind, as does the innovative case book by Joel Grossman and Richard Wells (1988), students of Schmidhauser at the University of Iowa. Finally, along the same lines, and very valuable as a supplement to case books, were Schmidhauser's *The Supreme Court: Its Politics, Personalities and Procedures* (1964), Samuel Krislov's *The Supreme Court in the Political Process* (1965), and subsequently Lawrence Baum's now venerable and admirable introductory analysis, *The Supreme Court* (1989). It is worth noting that Baum was trained by Joel Grossman at the University of Wisconsin, and that Grossman was a student of Schmidhauser's at Iowa—thus, constituting along with other Wisconsin Ph.D.'s and *their* Ph.D. students, a multigenerational lineage.

---

[3] With William Twinning taking a leadership role, the "law in context" approach to sociolegal studies originated in the law faculty at Warwick University to provide an alternative to the dominant "black-letter" tradition of British legal scholarship.

This initial law-in-political-context work had, however, its own shortcomings. Largely descriptive and constructed around cases, it did not generate much in the way of explanatory generalizations, much less, testable propositions. There are important exceptions—in particular Robert Dahl's seminal article on the relationship between the Supreme Court and *law-making majorities* and some of the early research on the *impact* of Supreme Court decisions. With respect to impact research, the work of one of Dahl's Ph.D. students, William Muir, stands out. His *Prayer in the Public Schools: Law and Attitude Change* (1967) brought the Yale school of community power analysis to bear on the Supreme Court's school prayer case law. As for the Dahl article, I would say in retrospect that it more than any other piece of research prefigured the new institutionalism.

2.2 The New Institutionalism

The spirit of the new institutionalism seems reasonably clear, as do its general contours which can be readily inferred from the following notable examples.

- Howard Gillman (1995), one of the earliest practitioners of the new institutionalism, conducted historical research which successfully destabilized long-standing conventional wisdom about the Supreme Court's invocation of substantive due process standards to invalidate social reform legislation. He found, on the one hand, that substantive due process reflected "an overarching set of well-established legal doctrines and principles governing the legitimate exercise of police powers" (1995, 177). On the other hand, he went on to point out that new social conditions had overwhelmed the preconditions of freedom on which the old jurisprudence rested. By disregarding economic pressures on workers, the old jurisprudence failed to offer an adequate account of what constitutes freedom (1995, 156).
- The fluid and reciprocal character of institutional interaction is the essential message of two studies of relationship between the Supreme Court and the Congress. Even the title of Louis Fisher's *Constitutional Dialogues: Interpretation as Political Process* (1988) captures the transactional nature of interbranch relationships: constitutional meaning as the product of ongoing discursive negotiations among the three branches of the government. A similar message emerges from empirical research by George Lovell (2003) on the history of "legislative referrals." He finds reciprocal relationships that are as much about evading power as exercising it.
- Malcolm Feeley and Edward Rubin (2000) shift the terrain of inquiry to the transactions between the courts, mostly the lower courts, and the prison system. Their principal finding is that the courts have been effective agents of institutional reform—thus suggesting, at first glance, a top-down imposition of judicial

power. However, the broader message of this inquiry into judicial capabilities is that the courts were successful primarily because they were working within a broader political consensus. Rather like Lovell, Feeley and Rubin see the courts' success in prison reform as an exercise in buck passing. The courts "forced" state governments to do what they wanted to do but were, because of fiscal constraints, reluctant to undertake.

- Finally, I come to Gerald Rosenberg's *The Hollow Hope* (1991). His exhaustively researched and meticulously analyzed examination of the impact of the Supreme Court's desegregation and abortion jurisprudence leads him to conclude that the Court is almost entirely ineffectual when it comes to overcoming substantial opposition to its most important decisions. Irrespective of whether one entirely accepts his conclusions, the study exemplifies the de-centering of the new institutionalism because it so clearly embeds the Supreme Court in the political process by pursuing the way in which judicial decisions resonate, or in Rosenberg's view, fail to resonate throughout the polity.

  These examples provide only a glimpse of the complexity, the challenge, and the opportunities afforded by the new institutionalism.[4] They do, nonetheless, suggest how and why the new institutionalism has destabilized some of the conventional wisdom within the subfield by generating propositions and data that provide systematic access to the interactions between courts and the other branches of government. The courts, however, loom very large in the new institutionalism— thus suggesting that it represents an important *but reluctant* step toward de-centering. For a more thorough going exercise in de-centering, let us go on to *legal mobilization* theory and research.

3 MOBILIZING THE LAW: LEGALITY, POLITICS, AND DEMOCRACY

Individuals and groups are the primary loci of the de-centering associated with legal mobilization scholarship. Put another way, the terrain of intellectual inquiry shifts away from the interinstitutional transactions of the new institutionalism

---

[4] In conceptual terms, the new institutionalism is much more difficult to pin down. Rogers Smith (1988, 90) identifies and calls for a reconciliation of several versions of the new institutionalism. The goal of such a reconciliation is to uncover "different types of structures or institutions that, we hypothesize, constitute and empower political actors and their environments in important ways, endowing actors with specifiable constraints or capabilities or both" (quoted in Gillman and Clayton 1999, 7).

to reciprocal, if ordinarily asymmetrical transactions between formal institutions and the groups and individuals of civil society. Whereas traditional legal scholarship treats individuals and groups as consumers of a top-down system of legal rules, the legal mobilization theory and research reconstitutes these erstwhile consumers as co-producers of law.

As such legal mobilization work has contributed scope, depth, intensity, and illumination to a long-standing debate within and beyond the subfield about the relationship between legality and democracy. That contribution is the focus of the following very condensed account. I begin with a précis of classical and revisionist democratic theory; they provide the background for addressing how and why legal mobilization research has transformed and reinvigorated legality and democracy debates among law and courts and sociolegal scholars.

Initially, legal mobilization research suggested that a politics of rights could contribute to more robust and egalitarian forms of democracy. These arguments have not, however, gone unchallenged—fueled in part by a political and legal backlash against egalitarian tendencies and in part by an intellectual backlash against the politicization of legality. My objective here is not so much to take sides as to underscore the intellectual, legal, and political importance of the issues generated out of theory and research on the politics of rights.

3.1 Legal and Electoral Accountability

At the heart of the contested affinities between legality and equality are competing visions of political accountability. While I can only touch on the contentious partnership between legal and electoral accountability, enough can be said to indicate both how and why research on the mobilization of constitutional and legal rights has important implications for both the normative integrity and policy efficacy of liberal democracy.

From the perspective of classical legality *electoral accountability* is a necessary condition of democracy that becomes a sufficient condition only in combination with *legal accountability*. Without legal accountability, electoral accountability is deemed incomplete, unreliable, and self-destructive. In short, legal accountability promises protection against too much democracy—with legal rights providing insulation from intemperate egalitarian majorities. In this framing, legality is an essential feature of constitutionalism and of a thin version of liberal democracy. The protections of classical legal accountability do not, however, extend to more robust, egalitarian versions of democracy. Indeed, classical legal accountability is more the enemy than the ally of egalitarian democratic values and aspirations. As the shortcomings of electoral accountability were made increasingly clear by social scientists, so, too, were the limitations of classical legal accountability by sociolegal theorists and researchers.

Beginning in the late 1950s influential social scientists exposed the inadequacy of liberal democratic electoral accountability and, in particular, its inegalitarian implications and outcomes. For example, sociologist C. Wright Mills (1957) famously identified an entrenched and interdependent "power elite." Within political science, E. E. Schattschneider (1960), Peter Bachrach, and Morton Baratz (1970) uncovered the "mobilization of bias" in pluralist politics through which "the power elite" *covertly* suppressed opposition. Finally, and by way of example, the interdisciplinary team of Frances Piven and Richard Cloward (1972) demonstrated how and why welfare benefits were deployed to "regulate" the poor rather than to alleviate poverty and inequality. Pluralist politics was, in sum, charged with regularly striking bargains at the expense of society's most vulnerable groups.

In rough parallel, sociolegal theorists and researchers revealed the weaknesses of legal accountability. Among sociolegal *theorists*, I see the seminal figure as Philip Selznick who reacted against the positivism of the classical legality and proposed a neo-natural law alternative. Selznick argued that, properly understood, legality could provide standards for judging the content as well as the process of law (1961):

[L]aw is tested in two ways: first, against conclusions regarding the needs of man, including his need for a functioning society; second against tested generalizations as to requirements of a legal order. (1961, 101)

Clearly, the former test takes the role of natural law into matters of social justice having to do with "the welfare of man in society" (1961, 101). Subsequently, Philippe Nonet and Selznick (1978) offered a developmental analysis of legality, which stretches the reach of neo-natural law to a robust vision of egalitarian democracy.

Similarly seminal within empirical sociolegal research was Marc Galanter's "Why the Haves Come Out Ahead" (1974), in which he definitively established that despite the promise of equal justice under law, "repeat players" in the legal process have a decisive advantage over "one shotters." These repeat players are, moreover, overwhelmingly drawn from among the privileged and powerful, while one-shotters are just as overwhelmingly numbered among the inefficacious and dispossessed. Note also Joel Handler's "Controlling Official Discretion in Welfare Administration" (1966), which led the way in exposing the inadequacy of due process protections afforded welfare recipients against the mean spirited and abusive procedures of the state agencies on which they depended. This work, as well as other research on welfare dependency, demonstrated legality's complicity in welfare's regulating, rather than liberating, the poor—just as Piven and Cloward charged.

Most fundamentally, sociolegal research cast doubt on one of the mainstays of the classical canon, the much-vaunted autonomy of the law. If the "haves" do reliably come out of ahead, legal accountability, like electoral accountability, is responsive to differentials in status and material resources.[5] In short, the broader context of inequality in society compromised equality before the law—thus calling into question the underlying integrity of legal accountability as well as its status as a guardian of democracy.

3.2 The Politicization of Legal Accountability

The increasing realization that the law's emperor was at least in part unclothed led to the emergence of a politicized conception of legal accountability. Whereas classical legality celebrated the separation of law from politics, sociolegal scholarship has revealed the egalitarian opportunities provided by the politicization of legality. Specifically, sociolegal scholarship has demonstrated that by embracing, rather than evading, the inextricable connections between law and politics a politicized legality could help defeat the "mobilization of bias," which subverts electoral accountability.

Scholarship on the politicization of legal accountability has its roots in political science and, indeed, in the law and courts subfield. Victor Rosenblum's *Law as a Political Instrument* (1955) and Clement Vose's "Litigation as a Form of Pressure Group Activity" (1958) anticipated much of the work which was to follow on legal and constitutional rights as agents of political accountability. Subsequent research on legality and collective legal mobilization has demonstrated why, how, and to what extent it is possible to deploy a *politics of rights* (Scheingold 2004 [1974]; McCann 1994) to expand the reach of legality and to correct some of the shortcomings of pluralistic democracy.

However, to appreciate both the *possibilities* and *limitations* of a politics of rights, it is necessary to take into account the constitutive character of law—what one might call its cultural capacities: law as "a continuous part of social practice." From this perspective, "law enters social practices and is indeed, imbricated in them, by shaping consciousness, by making law's concepts and commands seem, if not invisible, then perfectly natural and benign" (Sarat and Kearns 1993, 31; McCann and Silverstein 1993, 133).[6] This constitutive understanding of legality can be traced to Murray Edelman's *The Symbolic Uses of Politics* (1964), to Judith Shklar's

---

[5] In addition, compliance and impact studies conducted by political scientists revealed that occasional egalitarian judicial decisions on controversial matters of public policy were regularly evaded or ignored (Canon and Johnson 1999). If the courts can not assure remedies for the rights which they articulate, the political dependence of the courts is undeniable.

[6] A primary source of the constitutive conception of law comes from the individual disputing literature and in particular from its inquiry into rights in everyday life. This research lends credence to the constitutive power, which I attributed to the myth of rights (Scheingold 1974; 2004). However, in uncovering multiple iterations of rights consciousness, the more recent work reveals rights as a fluid, contingent, and ambivalent resource (see e.g Ewick and Silbey 1998; Engel and Munger 2003).

Legalism (1964), and to law professor Thurman Arnold's seminal *The Symbols of Government* (1935).

3.3 Legality and Democracy

Research on the politicization of legality can be, without doing too much violence to its complexity, divided into three categories. In all three of them legal and constitutional rights are analyzed as contingent political resources rather than legal entitlements. Initially this work focused on the way in which the politicization of legality could, through collective political mobilization, contribute to empowering the dispossessed and enhancing the quality of egalitarian democracy. A second wave of research revealed the power of counter-mobilization and how a politics of rights could serve *inequality* as well as equality, *exclusion* as well as inclusion, and so on. Finally, there is a body of scholarship that challenges politicization—claiming that it tends to undermine democratic accountability while compromising the moral authority of the law. Let us look very briefly at each of these bodies of scholarship.

1. *Rights and collective political mobilization:* Research on collective political mobilization is situated squarely within the political process. These are studies of campaigns to deploy rights to pursue a progressive political agenda—on behalf of pay equity (McCann 1994), gays (Goldberg-Hiller 2002; Brigham 1996; Herman 1996), people with disabilities (Olson 1984), animals (Silverstein 1996), and the mentally ill (Milner 1986). This research analyzes rights as both discursive and institutional resources and also identifies the conditions and circumstances that are conducive to a successful politics of rights. These issues have also been pursued in the cause lawyering literature (see in particular Sarat and Scheingold 2006). The result is a complex, fluid, and contingent understanding of how and under what conditions rights can serve as agents for mobilizing the dispossessed and the marginalized.

2. *Counter mobilization:* Whereas the dominant message of collective mobilization research is a positive, albeit qualified, endorsement of rights as a progressive political resource, there are arguments and evidence that reveal conservative versions of, and reactions against, the politics of rights (Dudas 2003; Den Dulk 2006). As Carol Greenhouse has argued, the success of the civil rights movement has made rights appear to be not only superfluous but also actually subversive of citizenship. "Since the Brown generation has now reached middle age, the benefits of equality having been made available (so this reasoning seems to go), inequality is no longer the public's responsibility, but the lifestyle choice of intrinsically inferior citizens" (1997, 186). In short, their indeterminacy and the quid pro quos attached to rights reveal them as double agents—amenable to serving antiegalitarian as well as egalitarian purposes.

3. *The politicization debate.* The case against politicization has been formulated around the concept of adversarial legalism (Kagan 2001), which thrusts the courts and judges into policy processes that they are ill-equipped to serve effectively. That is because litigation is deemed confrontational and legalistic rather than collaborative and rational. More broadly, the courts are being called upon to respond to the cultural proclivities of Americans to seek "total justice" (Friedman 1985) and to the fragmentation of political institutions. There is, however, also research on schools (Paris 2001; Reed 1998) and prisons (Feeley and Rubin 2000) that demonstrate that courts and judges do have sufficient policy resources to act effectively as agents of institutional reform when, as is their tendency, they act in consonance and cooperation with electoral institutions.

Taken together, this body of work extends the reach of law and politics research conceptually, institutionally, politically, and professionally. Conceptually, the meaning of legality is enlarged to include what I referred to many years ago as its "symbolic life" and the way it "shapes the context in which American politics is conducted" (2004, xlix). Institutionally, the scope of legality is broadened beyond the constitution, the courts, legislative bodies, and administrative agencies into civil society. Politically, legality's relationship with and contribution to American democracy becomes intrinsic to the study of law in political science. Finally, from the point of view of the law and courts subfield, theory and research on legal mobilization offers an additional avenue for engagement within and beyond political science. It is to this last issue that I now turn by way of conclusion.

4 CONCLUSIONS

I have long been aware of efforts to increase the relevance of the law and courts subfield to political scientists more generally. It has always seemed to me that at least part of the driving force behind the development of the intense inquiry into judicial behavior was the way it demonstrated how far we have come methodologically from an outdated immersion in legal rules and legal doctrine. By demonstrating that the study of judicial behavior was amenable to statistical analysis, we could thereby prove our bona fides as card-carrying social *scientists*. I have my doubts about the effectiveness of that strategy.[7]

---

[7] These doubts were fueled and/or confirmed by a study that I initiated in 1989 during the time that I headed the organized section. The committee that I appointed to conduct the inquiry was chaired by Austin Sarat and included Kim Scheppele, Tim O'Neil, and Greg Caldeira. The only specific finding that I recall was that when asked about prominent scholars in the law and courts subfield, only Martin Shapiro was identified by "mainstream" political scientists.

But irrespective of whether the status of the subfield and its connections to the discipline were enhanced by the study of judicial behavior, the de-centering that I have been analyzing offers a new and different path to connecting with political and social science. Note to begin with that the roots of de-centering and legal mobilization are less within law and courts and more in political science and interdisciplinary sociolegal studies—nurtured by the Law and Society Association. It follows that de-centering *ipso facto* opens lines of communication with the discipline and beyond it to other social scientists and to sociolegal scholars.

For example, de-centering provides an opportunity for intellectual engagement with scholars of state theory. Specifically, the de-centering of law is consonant with, and complementary to, the fragmented conception that has become increasingly prominent in state theory (Migdal 2001). Indeed, a sociologist has recently taken state theory and research to task for ignoring law (Skrentny 2006). In short, de-centering has the potential to make the study of law and courts an integral part of international and interdisciplinary inquiry into the evolution of the state.

Insofar as this occurs, it not only bodes well for the status of the law and courts subfield by offering an opening to the mainstream of the discipline. It also provides us with a challenging research agenda.

REFERENCES

ARNOLD, T. 1962. *The Symbols of Government.* New York: Harcourt, Brace.

BACHRACH, P., and BARATZ, M. 1970. *Power and Poverty.* New York: Oxford University Press.

BAUM, L. 1989. *The Supreme Court,* 3rd edn. Washington, DC: C.Q. Press.

BRIGHAM, J. 1996. *The Constitution of Interests: Beyond the Politics of Rights.* New York: New York University Press.

CANON, B., and JOHNSON, C. 1999. *Judicial Policies: Implementation and Impact,* 2nd edn. Washington, DC: Congressional Quarterly Press.

CLAYTON, C. 1999. The Supreme Court and political jurisprudence: new and old institutionalisms. In *Supreme Court Decision-Making: New Institutionalist Aprroaches,* ed. C. Clayton and H. Gillman. Lawrence: University of Kansas Press.

DAHL, R. 1957. Decision-making in a democracy: the Supreme Court as a national policy maker. *Journal of Public Law,* 6: 279–95.

DEN DULK, K. 2006. In legal culture, but not of it: the role of cause lawyers in evangelical political mobilization. In *Cause Lawyering and Social Movements,* ed. A. Sarat and S. Scheingold. Stanford, Calif.: Stanford University Press.

DUDAS, J. 2003. Rights, resentment, and social change. Ph.D. dissertation, Department of Political Science, University of Washington.

EDELMAN, M. 1964. *The Symbolic Uses of Politics.* Urbana: University of Illinois Press.

ENGEL, D., and MUNGER, F. 2003. *Rights of Inclusion: Law and Identity in the Life Stories of Americans with Disabilities.* Chicago: University of Chicago Press.

EWICK, P., and SILBEY, S. 1998. *The Common Place of Law: Stories from Everyday Life.* Chicago: University of Chicago Press.

FEELEY, M., and RUBIN, E. 2000. *Judicial Policy Making and the Modern State: How the Courts Reformed America's Prisons*. Cambridge: Cambridge University Press.

FISHER, L. 1988. *Constitutional Dialogues: Interpretation as Political Process*. Princeton, NJ: Princeton University Press.

FELDMAN, L. 2006. *Homeless Politics: Democratic Pluralism and the Predicament of Bare Life*. Ithaca, NY: Cornell University Press.

FRIEDMAN, L. 1985. *Total Justice: What Americans Want from the Legal System and Why*. Boston: Beacon Press.

GALANTER, M. 1974. Why the "haves" come out ahead: speculations on the limits of legal change. *Law and Society Review*, 9: 95–160.

GILLMAN, H. 1995. *The Constitution Besieged: The Rise and Demise of Lochner Era Police Powers Jurisprudence*. Durham, NC: Duke University Press.

—— and CLAYTON, C. (eds.) 1999. *The Supreme Court in American Politics: New Institutionalist Interpretations*. Lawrence: University of Kansas Press.

GOLDBERG-HILLER, J. 2002. *The Limits of Union: Same-Sex Marriage and the Politics of Civil Rights*. Ann Arbor: University of Michigan Press.

GREENHOUSE, C. 1994. Courting difference: issues of interpretation and comparison in the study of legal ideologies. Pp. 91–110 in *Law and Community in Three American Towns*, ed. C. Greenhouse, B. Yngvesson, and D. Engel. Ithaca, NY: Cornell University Press.

—— 1997. A federal life: *Brown* and the nationalization of the life story. Pp. 170–89 in *Race, Law and Culture: Reflections on* Brown v. the Board of Education, ed. A. Sarat. New York: Oxford University Press.

GROSSMAN, J., and WELLS, R. 1988. *Constitutional Law and Judicial Policy Making*, 3rd edn. New York: Longman.

HANDLER, J. 1966. Controlling official discretion in welfare administration. *California Law Review*, 54: 479–510.

HERMAN, D. 1996. *Rights of Passage: Struggles for Lesbian and Gay Legal Equality*. Toronto: University of Toronto Press.

KALMAN, L. 1996. *The Strange Career of Liberal Legalism*. New Haven, Conn.: Yale University Press.

KAGAN, R. 2001. *Adversarial Legalism: The American Way of Law*. Cambridge, Mass.: Harvard University Press.

KRISLOV, S. 1965. *The Supreme Court in the Political Process*. New York: Macmillan.

LOVELL, G. 2003. *Legislative Deferrals: Statutory Ambiguity, Judicial Power, and American Democracy*. New York: Cambridge University Press.

McCANN, M. 1994. *Rights at Work: Pay Equity Reform and the Politics of Legal Mobilization*. Chicago: University of Chicago Press.

—— and SILVERSTEIN, H. 1993. Social movements and the American state: legal mobilization as a strategy for democratization. Pp. 131–43 in *A Different Kind of State? Popular Power and Democratic Administration*, ed. G. Albo, D. Langille, and L. Panitch. Toronto: Oxford University Press.

MIGDAL, J. S. 2001. *State in Society: Studying How States and Societies Transform and Constitute One Another*. New York: Cambridge University Press.

MILLETT, J. 1955. The Department of Public Law and Government. In *A History of the Faculty of Political Science: Columbia University*, ed. R. G. Hoxie. New York: Columbia University Press.

MILLS, C. 1957. *The Power Elite*. New York: Oxford University Press.

MILNER, N. 1986. The dilemmas of legal mobilization: ideologies and strategies of mental patient liberation. *Law and Policy*, 8: 105–29.

MUIR, W. 1967. *Prayer in the Public Schools: Law and Attitude Change*. Chicago: University of Chicago Press.

MURPHY, W. 1962. *Congress and the Court: A Case Study in the American Political Process*. Chicago: University of Chicago Press.

NONET, P., and SELZNICK, P. 1978. *Law and Society in Transition: Toward Responsive Law*. New York: Harper.

OLSON, S. 1984. *Clients and Lawyers: Securing Rights of Disabled Persons*. Wesport, Conn.: Greenwood Press.

PARIS, M. 2001. Legal mobilization and the politics of reform: lessons from school finance litigation in Kentucky, 1984–1995. *Law and Social Inquiry*, 26: 631–84.

PIVEN, F., and CLOWARD, R. 1972. *Regulating the Poor: The Functions of Public Welfare*. New York: Vintage.

REED, D. S. 1998. Twenty-five years after *Rodriguez*: school finance litigation and the impact of the new judical federalism. *Law and Society Review*, 32: 175–220.

ROSENBERG, G. 1991. *The Hollow Hope: Can Courts Bring About Social Change?* Chicago: University of Chicago Press.

ROSENBLUM, V. 1955. *Law as a Political Instrument*. New York: Random House.

SARAT, A., and KEARNS, T. 1993. Beyond the great divide: forms of legal scholarship and everyday life. Pp. 21–62 in *Law in Everyday Life*, ed. A. Sarat and T. Kearns. Ann Arbor: University of Michigan Press.

—— and SCHEINGOLD, S. 2006. *Cause Lawyering and Social Movements*. Stanford, Calif.: Stanford University Press.

SCHATTSCHNEIDER, E. 1960. *The Semi-Sovereign People*, New York: Holt, Rinehart and Winston.

SCHEINGOLD, S. 2004 [1974]. *The Politics of Rights: Lawyers, Public Policy and Political Change*, 2nd edn. Ann Arbor: University of Michigan Press.

SCHMIDHAUSER, J. 1964. *The Supreme Court: Its Politics, Personalities and Procedures*. New York: Holt, Rinehart and Winston.

—— and BERG, L. 1972. *The Supreme Court and Congress: Conflict and Interaction, 1945–1968*. New York: Free Press.

SELZNICK, P. 1961. Natural law and sociology. *Natural Law Forum*, 6: 84–108.

SHKLAR, J. N. 1964. *Legalism*. Cambridge, Mass.: Harvard University Press.

SKRENTNY, J. D. 2006. Law and the American state. *Annual Review of Sociology*, 32: 213–44.

SMITH, R. 1988. Political jurisprudence, the "new institutionalism," and the future of public law. *American Political Science Review*, 82: 89–108.

SILVERSTEIN, H. 1996. *Unleashing Rights: Law, Meaning, and the Animal Rights Movement*. Ann Arbor: University of Michigan Press.

VOSE, C. 1958. Litigation as a form of pressure group activity. *Annals of the American Academy of Political and Social Science*, 319: 20–31.

WESTIN, A. 1958. *The Anatomy of a Constitutional Law Case: Youngstown Sheet and Tube Co. v. Sawyer, the Steel Seizure Decision*. New York: Macmillan.

WHITTINGTON, K. E. 1999. *Constitutional Construction: Divided Powers and Constitutional Meaning*. Cambridge, Mass.: Harvard University Press.

CHAPTER 44

REFLECTIONS ABOUT JUDICIAL POLITICS

HAROLD J. SPAETH

THE year 2006 marked the golden anniversary of my receipt of the Ph.D., and the years since have resulted in an unbroken sojourn in the grove of academe. And though longevity is neither a necessary nor a sufficient condition for reflection, its existence at least provides a basis for perspective.

1 SCIENTIFIC PRECONDITIONS

In the middle of the last century, though other fields within American politics were beginning to show the first glimmerings of a behavioral—previously quantitative—focus, judicial politics remained untouched (shall I say "uncontaminated") by those then modern currents. Of course, C. Herman Pritchett had published a series of brief articles in the *American Political Science Review* and in the *Journal of Politics*, then the only two general journals of political science, culminating in 1948 with his book *The Roosevelt Court* and its twenty-five tables and two figures ("Charts"). These, though, contained only frequencies and percentages and lacked explanation.

The absence of social science theory and methodology in Pritchett's early work is only partially explained by the very limited body of relevant scholarship, but also by his adherence to the belief that the justices were not merely political actors, but were mightily constrained by the law and institutional features of courts. Indeed, in his later book, *Civil Liberties and the Vinson Court*, and in work co-authored with his student, Walter F. Murphy, he de-emphasized the voting patterns that he sharply adumbrated in *The Roosevelt Court* and echoed the then dominant view that the law and its work ways constrained judicial behavior.

Political scientists, who have done so much to put the "political" in "political jurisprudence" need to emphasize that it is still "jurisprudence." It is judging in a political context, but it is still judging; and judging is still different from legislating or administering. Judges make choices, but they are not the "free" choices of congressmen....There is room for much interpretation in the texts of constitutions, statutes, and ordinances, but the judicial function is still interpretation and not independent policy making. It is just as false to argue that judges freely exercise their discretion as to contend they have no policy function at all. Any accurate analysis of judicial behavior must have as a major purpose a full clarification of the unique limiting conditions under which judicial policy making proceeds.   (Pritchett 1969, 49)

Nonetheless, the late Glendon Schubert, indisputably the doyen of judicial behavior, described Pritchett as having "blazed a trail" (Schubert 1963), a view he never repudiated, notwithstanding Pritchett's backsliding into the morass of legalistic doublespeak.

In the passage quoted above, the assertion that judging is different from the free choices of congresspersons or administrators is simply false. Legislators and executive officials need the blessing of constitutionality to justify their actions—directly or indirectly. And though the same applies to lower court judges, state and federal, that is not true of the justices of the U.S. Supreme Court, who wield the seals of approval and disapproval. Simply consider the Court's landmark decisions: *Marbury v. Madison, M'Culloch v. Maryland, Scott v. Sandford, Plessy v. Ferguson, Brown v. Board of Education, Roe v. Wade, Bush v. Gore*, etc. Certainly the range of choices available for the resolution of these cases was at least as variegated as those available to other political actors—nay, more so.

Yet Pritchett states that the judicial function involves interpretation and "not independent policy making." What, pray tell, is the difference? Faith-based believers and fabulists assert a difference, but it is no more meaningful than that between Tweedledum and Tweedledee: the former ends in a consonant, the latter in a vowel.

That is not to say that the discretion available to political actors—including the justices—is boundless. Rather it is to say that whatever policy choice the justices make they must rationalize—i.e. justify—it through verbal interpretation. In other words, cloak the reality of choice with the rhetoric of analogical legal phraseology.

I know not what the "unique limiting conditions" are that Pritchett avers judicial policy-making must proceed under. I know even less their operational effect on American government. The typical lawsuit presents polar opposites between which choice reigns supreme: guilty or innocent, liable or not, reasonable or unreasonable. Looked at realistically, the only limitation—and it certainly does not differ from case to case—is the ability of language to justify the ultimate choice. The ultimate choice, then, becomes no more than a choice of words. And in choosing these words, the prescribed procedure is to reason inductively from example. That this is a primitive stage of mental development warrants no caviling. Little Suzie, contrary to her wishes, when told that it is bedtime, logically queries why she should go to bed when her big brother, several years older, does not.

2 MODELING

As a further prelude to the subsequent discussion of the scholarly evolution of judicial politics, reference needs be made to modeling. If present-day political science, qua science, has a buzzword meant to establish the credibility of the work of its *au courant* minions, it is "model." Any writing that does not formulate what passes conventional muster as a model is viewed askance.

Because of the complexity of human behavior and the institutions in which we function, comprehension warrants simplification. Unlike the natural world where regularity and the resulting orderliness reign supreme, disasters and other natural calamities to the contrary notwithstanding (they also follow given patterns and predictable consequences), the proclivities of individual human beings encountered in a dizzying array of social interactions beseeches explanation. Hence, models whose function it is to simplify the apparently incomprehensible real world.

Of course, *ipse dixits* in one form or another—typically religious beliefs and concomitant doctrines that rely on faith to the exclusion of reason in whole or in substantial part—serve to elucidate the human condition. But these lack intellectual intersubjectivity, the test of which is refutation; i.e. falsifiability.

Granted, one may become deeply immersed in a subject to understand it as completely as possible, but knowledge of A may tell us nothing about that which is non-A. Hence, the utility of models which focus on the simplification of reality by attempting to specify commonalities of human behavior. Generalization rather than individuation becomes the goal.

The successful model accomplishes two results: It explains behavior and it does so parsimoniously. Tension exists between these objectives. The more that is explained, the less parsimonious the model becomes. Optimal resolution occurs when variables explaining a high percentage of the behavior are emphasized and those verging on idiosyncrasy are ignored.

A relatively full account of some phenomenon—such as judicial voting—may contain a larger number of variables [than judicial attitudes]. It is axiomatic, of course, that one may explicate any phenomenon if the number of variables used in the explanation equals the number of times the phenomenon has occurred. Thus, if the reasons given for the Court's decisions in [a] term differ for each of the cases the justices decided, *we have learned nothing systematic* about the justices' voting. All we know is unique—idiosyncratic—to each case.   (Spaeth 1995, 297)

The simplification of reality that models produce precludes a judgment that they are either true or false. By definition, they are all false to some extent because they ignore minor aspects of the explained behavior. Rather than truth or falsity, the test of a model is its ranking relative to others in terms of coherence, internal consistency, in addition of explanatory ability and parsimony. These are matters of judgment, of course.

Providing objectivity to the worth of a model is its falsifiability. Falsifiable in the sense of being testable. If refutation—disconfirmation—cannot be had because, for example, the model fails to assert in a meaningful fashion the goals of a court's decisions, the ineluctable result is that any choice exercised may be deemed rational or reasonable and, hence, compatible with the model. Or, if the model stipulates precedent as the explanation for judicial behavior, and the court in question cites precedents as authority for all of its decisions, the model could not be refuted.

Ostensibly nonfalsifiable assertions may be disconfirmed if the model proposes a rigorous definition that does make refutation highly probable. In other words, models must be susceptible to scientific testing. Failure to refute the model's assumptions, notwithstanding statistical tests that make failure highly probable, obviously enhances the model's explanatory power.

Before reflecting on the past and future of the field of judicial politics, it may be parenthetically noted that much modern-day modeling—indeed, most—does not provide current scholarship an unmixed blessing. Though apparently scientific, albeit formalistically, it eschews empirical testing (e.g. Hammond et al. 2005). Ostensible reasons for this condition will be discussed at the end of this chapter.

3 SPARKS OF CONFLICT

The study of courts and their decisions began concomitantly with the organization of political scientists into a professional society at the beginning of the twentieth century under the rubric of public law. An ostensibly historical and comparative focus initially emerged as an historical–legal critique and attendant surveys of recent decisions of the U.S. Supreme Court. The major scholars of this period— Edward S. Corwin, Robert Cushman, Charles Grove Haines, and Thomas Reed Powell—structured their analyses of the Supreme Court around an historical framework. And though glimmerings of legal realism emerged, they were largely submerged in the legal and institutional context with which the field saw judicial decision-making immersed.

Given Pritchett's reassertion of the importance of law and the constraints that he argued judging imposes, the scientific study of courts made no progress during the ten years following the 1948 publication of *The Roosevelt Court* until Schubert's *Quantitative Analysis of Judicial Behavior* (1959) appeared. Methodologically sophisticated for its time and more than inchoately imbued with a testable theory of appellate court decision-making, it admirably and thoroughly laid the groundwork for the work of other productive early behavioralists, such as S. Sidney Ulmer and Harold J. Spaeth. The book extended Pritchett's bloc analysis to include measures of cohesion and adhesion; it applied game theory to the justices' decisions; and it adapted Louis Guttman's theory of cumulative scaling to the justices' policy-making behavior.

Two of Schubert's subsequent books, *The Judicial Mind: Attitudes and Ideologies of Supreme Court Justices* (1965) and *The Judicial Mind Revisited* (1974), further developed and methodologically advanced his work into a full-scale, completely behavioral theory of judicial decision-making—at least insofar as the U.S. Supreme Court was concerned.

Schubert's sociopsychological theorizing and use of cumulative scaling quickly dominated the behavioral scene, both pro and con, while his game theoretic and rational choice contributions were largely lost in the shuffle. That does not diminish the value of his deductive work, most especially his focus on the process whereby the Court selects the cases it chooses to review. The systematic study of its decision to decide bodes well to become, half a century later, a major feature of twenty-first-century judicial scholarship.

For whatever reason, Schubert's simple stimulus (case facts)–organism (the justice's attitudes)–response (votes) model positing a direct relationship between attitudes and voting caught the fancy of scholars on both sides of the behavioral fence. Traditionalists, especially, galvanized in opposition to what quickly became known as the attitudinal model, perhaps because it struck directly at the essence of legalistic work ways unlike the more intellectually complex strategizing inherent in rational-choice modeling. More specifically, if legalists failed to show that judicial votes and opinions rested on legal and constitutional considerations, their professional *raison d'être* would go aglimmering (Mendelson 1963; 1964). I recall a New York City convention panel, circa 1960, in which Schubert, surrounded by a frenzied coterie of traditionalists, out-shouted them in defending his work against a vehement antibehavioral onslaught. In a related instance, I personally was the recipient of disapproving remarks from the editor of a major journal who viewed the assertion that the justices' attitudes rather than the law motivated their votes to be disrespectful and demeaning and arrogantly unprofessional.

Accompanying intemperate criticism were more sober assertions that this new political science had been proven dysfunctional. Thus Martin Shapiro's (1993) view that the behavioral movement relegated judicial studies to an intellectual back-water of political science in large part because of its focus on the Supreme Court rather than on judicial systems writ large, domestic as well as foreign. A sample of political scientists of the same vintage ranked judicial scholarship as the least significant work of political scientists (Somit and Tanenhaus 1982, 55–6). Arguably, the low esteem of judicial scholarship was exacerbated by the spotlight that Schubert and his followers put on methodology, with the result that abstraction and abstruseness were perceived to dominate substance; e.g. Dixon (1971).

Though to my perhaps warped lights judicial scholarship today is as cutting edged as that of any subfield, it remains schizoid. The best evidence of the split is the division of judicial panels at the annual meeting of the American Political Science Association between two sections: "Law and Courts" for the scientifically inclined and "Constitutional Law and Jurisprudence" for the legally and philo-sophically oriented. ("Squishes," as they are irreverently known.) This segmenta-tion is also reflected in the panel organization of the Midwest Political Science Association, the second-largest political science association.

4 THE DOMINANCE OF PERSONAL POLICY PREFERENCES

As indicated, modeling has become the name of the game for twenty-first-century judicial scholarship. Three types may be denominated: legal, rational choice, and attitudinal. But in one sense the legal and rational-choice model may fairly be viewed as subtypes of the attitudinal model to the extent that both admit the presence of personal policy preferences in the exercise of decisional choice. This does not intimate that policy preferences dominate judicial decision-making, but rather that it is a factor that operates in a more or less untrammeled fashion in a judge's decisional calculus.

The recognition of personal policy preferences does not surprise insofar as rational-choice modeling is concerned. Choice is key to such analyses—at least among the postpositivist legal philosophers—and among such choices are the judge's personal preferences. But its recognition among the legally oriented, including historical institutionalists, rather clearly indicates that the attitudinalists have won the intellectual battle. Of course, as is the wont of losers, they put the best face possible on their defeat, and the legalists have been no exception. Sensibly unwilling to accept the moniker, "personal policy preferences," they employ "indeterminate" as their word of choice (Cross 1997). Of course, some among the legalists are true believers; and as is true of believers of whatever ilk, their behavioral—if unspoken—mantra is "don't confuse me with facts." Hence, for these persons law is determinate (e.g. Greenawalt 1992, 11; Markovits 1998, 1).

Judges, of course, continue to peddle their nostrum of nondiscretion as they have since the days of John Marshall.

Judicial power, as contradistinguished from the power of the laws, has no existence. Courts are the mere instruments of the law and can will nothing. When they are said to exercise a discretion, it is a mere legal discretion, a discretion to be exercised in discerning the course prescribed by law; and, when that is discerned, it is the duty of the court to follow it. Judicial power is never exercised to give effect to the will of the judge... (*Osborn v. Bank of the United States* 1824, 866)

Almost two centuries later, Scalia parrots his predecessor:

The very framing of the issue that we purport to decide today... presupposes a view of our decisions as *creating* the law, as opposed to *declaring* what the law already is.... To hold a governmental act as unconstitutional is not to announce that we forbid it, but that the *Constitution* forbids it. (*American Trucking Assns. v. Smith* 1990, 201)

5 LEGALISTIC MYTH-MAKING

Representing the dominant nonjudicial legal position are three leading legal philosophers, Ronald Dworkin, Bruce Ackerman, and Howard Gillman. According to Dworkin, the notion that judges freely exercise discretion is false. Although he recognizes that precedent only inclines judges to certain conclusions—that it does not require literal adherence—he nevertheless denies that judges "pick and choose amongst the principles and policies that make [up] this doctrine," or that a judge applies "extra-legal" principles "according to his own lights" (1988, 38, 39). Mind bogglingly, he asserts that precedent should be adhered to especially in cases where no precedent exists! Those who assert that judges exercise discretion in such cases err. "It remains the judge's duty, even in hard cases, to discover what the rights of the parties are, not to invent new rights retrospectively" (1988, 81). Discovery thus becomes the judge's *modus operandi*, as though the law being sought lies about in various courts' reports and requires only that a computer be directed to search and find the relevant rule.

A case that falls within the scope of an earlier decision has "enactment force" that requires judges' adherence. Novel cases, by comparison, are subject to a "gravitational force" emanating from earlier decisions that will lead the judge to the correct result (1988, 111). Though judges may differ as to the specifics of the gravitational force and though the judges' posture reflects their own intellectual and philosophical convictions, one should not conclude "that those convictions have some independent force" (1988, 118).

Admittedly, Dworkin deviates a tad from a purely legalistic perspective. Judges may differ in the their selection of relevant precedents for similar cases and appellate judges are more subject to the gravitational force of precedent than to its enactment force. But when all is said and done, the judge's basic task is to find the relevant law as though it were the proverbial needle lost in a haystack. The operative word "find" thus becomes part and parcel of the other favorite legal rationalization, "reasonableness."

Some nonlegal scholars, notably economically-minded rational-choice theorists, also buy the nondiscretionary nostrum, modeling nonempirically the possibility that legal factors explain judicial behavior (Ferejohn and Weingast 1992; Kornhauser 1992; 1995).

Political philosophers have also bought into the legal model. Bruce Ackerman (1991) argues that the Supreme Court's role over time has been to infuse the Founders' Constitution into the changes that have occurred in the United States since its inception. Thus, conservative decisions are not the result of conservative justices giving effect to their policy preferences, but rather an attempt to synthesize the meaning of the Constitution with current controversies out of the available legal materials.

Howard Gillman, the noted postpositivist, while admitting the existence of judicial policy-making, claims that law exercises a subjective influence within the mind of the judge. Thus,

A legal state of mind does not necessarily mean obedience to conspicuous rules; instead, it means a sense of obligation to make the best decision possible in light of one's general training and sense of professional obligation. On this view, decisions are considered legally motivated if they represent a judge's sincere belief that their decision represents their best understanding of what the law requires.   (2001, 486)

Under this conception, any decision may be seen as compatible with the legal model so long as judges have convinced themselves that their ruling is legally sustainable. And if any decision is so amenable, then it is not falsifiable. And if not falsifiable, then it is not scientific and can provide no valid explanation of judges' actions. Relatedly, this variant of the legal model ignores classic social-psychological findings about the human condition that demonstrate our ability to convince ourselves of the propriety, the truth, of what we believe. And though the refusal to allow facts to alter belief enters into this picture, the context of appellate court decision-making obfuscates such a refusal because plausible arguments support the contentions of parties on both sides of the controversy.

6 THE ATTITUDINAL MODEL APPLIED

The attitudinal model in its inchoate stage reacted against the formalistic jurisprudence in vogue since the time of William Blackstone, the celebrated English jurist, 200 years ago. The proto attitudinalists, labeled legal realists, asserted that lawmaking necessarily inhered in judging. Lacking clear answers as to how judges made their decisions, they called for a scientific study of law. Into this environment stepped Glendon Schubert. Drawing on the work of psychologists Clyde Coombs (1964) and Milton Rokeach (1968), he assumed that the facts in the Supreme Court's cases and the justices' attitudes could be cumulatively scaled in a left (liberal)–right (conservative) direction as evidenced by the justices' voting division. Thus, a 7-2 liberal outcome would indicate a less extreme liberal set of facts that a case decided 9-0 or 8-1. Conversely, a 4–5 decision would indicate a set of facts sufficiently conservative to produce such an outcome, but with facts not so extreme as to gain the support of the four dissenters. If a voting pattern resulted in which, for example, the two dissenters in the liberal 7-2 decision voted conservatively in all cases 6-3 to 0–9 and the liberal dissenters from the 4–5 decision also voted liberally in all liberally decided cases, a valid scale formed. Accordingly the justices could be ordinally ranked from most liberal (the sole dissenter in an 8-1 conservative decision) to most conservative (the sole dissenter in a liberal decision). Given that nine justices may combine in 510 patterns, half of which are liberal and half conservative, if the resulting pattern is one that far exceeds statistical improbability, one may confidently conclude that the hypothesized underlying variable—e.g. attitude toward national supremacy or affirmative action—explains the justices' voting. One may cavil that this procedure is circular: that the explanation of the justices' votes is based on the votes themselves. But if the replicable voting pattern far exceeds probability, the objection becomes trivial.

A not atypical nontrivial example concerns the affirmative action cases decided by a 5-4 vote during the first five terms of the Rehnquist Court (1986–90). In a 5-4 vote, the justices may combine in 126 different combinations with the resultant probability of predicting the correct one equaling 0.0079. The cumulative scale of the Rehnquist Court's affirmative actions decisions for the first five terms contains six 5-4 decisions, each of which fits perfectly into an attitudinally grounded cumulative scale (Spaeth 1995, 313). Strictly speaking, the probability of such a pattern is six times 0.0079, resulting in 0.2 preceded by 12 zeros! But given that attitudes are correctly perceived as relatively stable, it is most improbable that a Rehnquist, Scalia, or Thomas would dissent from a conservatively decided affirmative action case, or that Brennan or Marshall would dissent from one liberally decided. Taking this sort of consideration into account, a more realistic calculation of the foregoing pattern is 0.002—still highly improbable.

Subsequent work demonstrated that at least two interacting attitudes were required for social action to result (Spaeth 1972): one toward the object (typically the parties to the case, e.g. labor union, publisher, criminal defendant) and the other toward the situation in which the parties were encountered (e.g. the dominant legal issue, such as obscenity, antitrust, double jeopardy). Precision resulted by dividing the Court's cases into microanalytically discrete categories (e.g. search and seizure, right to counsel, self-incrimination) as precise as the data permit, rather than such broad areas as business, criminal procedure, federalism, or civil rights.

Though cumulative scaling was suitable for unidimensional analyses, it lacked generality. Hence, the use of multivariate techniques, such as factor analysis, multidimensional scaling, multiple regression, and probit. The latter two and their variants have proven especially useful because they enable analysts to establish the statistical relationships and the resulting probabilities between various independent (presumably explanatory) variables on the one hand and the hypothesized dependent (to be explained) variable on the other.

The formulation of multiple regression and probit obviously lends itself to modeling because of the implicit cause and effect relationship that it sets up. But it is one matter to fabricate a model and another to test it. The former requires nothing more than logic, the latter testable data.

7 RATIONAL CHOICE

William Riker, more so than any other scholar, laid the groundwork for the rational-choice model in political science (1990). Derived from economic theorizing and methodology, its application to political science operates under the rubric of positive political theory (Riker and Ordeshook 1973). A more or less common set of assumptions underlies it, the essence of which Riker stated:

Actors are able to order their alternative goals, values, tastes and strategies. This means that the relation of preferences and indifference among the alternative is transitive. . . . Actors choose from among available alternatives so as to maximize their satisfaction.   (1990, 172)

Hence, judges have the ability to rank alternative choices and such ranking can be preferentially ordered or treated indifferently.

Parenthetically, indifference is not formally a part of the attitudinal model. But there is no good reason why it should not be. Judges, no less than other decision-makers, assuredly view certain choices uncaringly. If choice must be exercised, it is between six of one and a half dozen of the other. Hence, the expectation of attitudinal consistency is unlikely. Such indifference may explain many unanimous decisions where it would appear that the justices at one end or the other of the ideological spectrum should dissent. Indifference may also attend, at least at lower court levels, many trivial decisions and trial motions. At the Supreme Court level, decisions of limited applicability, such as those involving narrow tax questions, matters of arcane civil procedure, or the preemptive effect of federal legislation, may also engender indifference.

Transitivity applies to the inherent ordering of preferences. Hence, if a justice prefers reversing a lower court decision *vel non* to affirming it, said justice should prefer granting the petition to review the case to denying it. Transitivity, of course, can be multifaceted. To take the foregoing example, if the justice is concerned that a vote to grant review may result in the Court's affirming the decision the justice wishes to reverse, denial of the petition may transitively take ascendance.

With regard to the satisfaction of which Riker speaks, no goals are ruled out. Hence, at least abstractly, rational-choice models become presumptively self-fulfil-ling prophecies. This feature is no less nonscientific than the lack of falsifiability.

The maximization of satisfaction also admits of miscalculation. Actors may lack pertinent information, or simply be misinformed. Choices contingent on the decisions of one's peers may be misguided because others' choices may be inscrutable.

In a group setting, maximizing satisfaction requires foresight. Actors need know the consequences of their decisions. As a result, rational-choice modeling may lead to strategizing, to making so-called "sophisticated" decisions rather than those of a "sincere" character. Actors may rationally view the former as the means to achieve one's wants even more satisfactorily than sincere choice. Of course, because no goals are ruled out, it may well be that certain decision-makers simply delight in playing games other than the one to which they have been appointed. We do not know whether such psychological deviltry afflicts the judicial mind, although ordinary encounters with bureaucratic behavior suggests that it is not unknown among other government officials. And, of course, lacking any assumption of behavioral consistency—unlike the attitudinal and legal models—such neurotic conduct need not be regularly manifest.

Theoretically, but without real-world support, the most powerful feature of rational choice is the concept of equilibrium, of which there are many variants. In its most simplified form, this is a stable outcome, one from which no player has an incentive to deviate. Rational-choice theorists favor hypotheses and explanations derived from logical—frequently mathematical—deductions. Given their general disinterest (aversion?) to empiricism, logical deductions need not, and commonly do not, accord with reality (e.g. Hammond et al. 2005). While the "if...then" feature of equilibrium analysis has much theoretical attraction, behaviorally disposed rational-choice scholars do not necessarily view it as key (Epstein and Knight 2000).

As applied to judicial politics, rational choice follows two different paths. Though both suffer from the Supreme Court focus that dominates most judicial work of whatever stripe, one views the Court as a largely self-contained entity, the other emphasizes Court–Congress relationships. I focus on the latter variant because the former does not substantially deviate from attitudinal work and, as a result, lacks an equilibrium emphasis. Those that do contradict the attitudinal model deal with the matter of separation of powers and specify logically, mathematically, and abstractly the extent to which the Supreme Court must defer to Congress in order that it does not override a specified decision and make policy worse from the Court's standpoint than would have occurred if the justices had behaved more sophisticatedly. This work tends to focus on a single Court decision. Elements in its analysis include abstractly derived Senate, House, and Court ideal points, and a hypothesized set of irreversible decisions that result because any movement by one chamber will necessarily worsen the position of the other. The assumption least congruent with reality that separation of powers models typically make is the readiness with which the Court will defer to congressional preferences (Segal and Spaeth 2003, 103–10).

These models' disconnection with reality is perhaps best evidenced by the fact that between February 22, 1995 and the end of the 1998 term the justices voided congressional legislation in 16 of the 21 cases in which their constitutionality was at issue: 76 percent (Segal and Spaeth 2003, 414).

8 PROS AND CONS

Comments about the backward condition of the broad field of judicial politics have been notably absent since the last decade or two of the twentieth century. But the use of *au courant* theory and methodology does not mean that the substance of judicial studies is where it ought to be.

A Supreme Court focus continues to dominate, to a lesser extent than was true during the twentieth century, however. Studies of the lower courts—especially the federal courts of appeals—are growing apace (e.g. Hettinger et al. 2006), as are occasional analyses of specialized federal courts and the district courts (e.g.

Howard 2006). The state courts, however, largely remain a *terra incognita* except for data and reports published by the National Center for State Courts in Williamsburg, Virginia.

Aiding and abetting scholarly output are the databases and attendant documentation on the federal courts housed at the University of Kentucky (www.as.uky.edu/polisci/ulmerproject). Absent these sources, systematic knowledge would depend on the resources of individual scholars rather than publicly available, reliable data. The Law and Social Sciences Program of the National Science Foundation deserves the gratitude of judicial scholars for funding these endeavors.

The availability of data on the output of the federal courts does not eliminate all deficiencies. Segmentation afflicts these courts. Only recently have scholars begun to model the federal courts as a system (Segal et al. 1995), a focus that warrants much greater emphasis.

Nor do the models discussed above flourish without blemish. Legal modelers have emphasized the inability of the attitudinal model satisfactorily to explain unanimous decisions, and preliminary analysis of the Court's agenda setting, particularly cases denied review, indicates the justices' policy preferences explain little of the Court's behavior (Hagle and Spaeth 2006). This suggests that either the legal model or rational-choice explanations may substantially explicate the decision whether or not to decide.

Apart from the failure of legal modelers to retreat from tendentiousness in favor of more systematic accounts, rational-choice theorists would do well to correlate their assumptions with the real world and test them empirically. Assumptions that the justices have complete and perfect information about congressional preferences is surely nonsense, as are suppositions that Congress incurs neither transaction nor opportunity costs when enacting legislation. Focusing on the median member ignores the reality of presidential veto, committee action, and the capacity of committee chairs to bottle up proposed legislation. Last but by no means least, the Court has the final word in its relationships with Congress and the executive branch. And in voicing the last word the Court is fully capable of making policy out of whole cloth, compatibly with its members' policy preferences, as *Bush v. Gore* (2000) so creatively attests.

References

ACKERMAN, B. 1991. *We the People.* Cambridge, Mass.: Harvard University Press.

COOMBS, C. H. 1964. *A Theory of Data.* New York: Wiley.

CROSS, F. 1997. Political science and the new legal realism: a case of unfortunate interdisciplinary ignorance. *Northwestern University Law Review*, 92: 251–327.

DIXON, R. G. 1971. Who is listening? Political science research in public law. *PS: Political Science and Politics*, 4: 19–26.

DWORKIN, R. 1988. *Takings Rights Seriously.* Cambridge, Mass.: Harvard University Press.

EPSTEIN, L., and KNIGHT, J. 2000. Toward a strategic revolution in judicial politics: a look back, a look ahead. *Political Research Quarterly*, 53: 625–66.

FEREJOHN, J., and WEINGAST, B. 1992. A positive theory of statutory interpretation. *International Review of Law and Economics*, 12: 263–98.

GILLMAN, H. 2001. What's law got to do with it? Judicial behavioralists test the "legal model" of judicial decision-making. *Law and Social Inquiry*, 6: 465–504.

GRENNAWALT, K. 1992. *Law and Objectivity.* New York: Oxford University Press.

HAGLE, T. M., and SPAETH, H. J. 2006. The presence of lower court amici as an aspect of Supreme Court agenda setting. Unpublished manuscript.

HAMMOND, T. H., BONNEAU, C. W., and SHEEHAN, R. S. 2005. *Strategic Behavior and Policy Choice on the U.S. Supreme Court.* Stanford, Calif.: Stanford University Press.

HETTINGER, V. A., LINDQUIST, S. A., and MARTINEK, W. L. 2006. *Judging on a Collegial Court: Influences on Federal Appellate Decision Making.* Charlottesville: University of Virginia Press.

HOWARD, R. M. 2006. Litigation choice, bureaucratic response, and judicial decisions: challenging tax assessments in the United States Tax Court and United States District Courts. Presented at the annual meeting of the Southern Political Science Association, Atlanta.

KORNHAUSER, L. 1992. Modeling collegial courts II: legal doctrine. *Journal of Law, Economics and Organization*, 8: 441–61.

—— 1995. Adjudication by a resource-constrained team: hierarchy and precedent in a judicial system. *Southern California Law Review*, 68: 1605–55.

MARKOVITS, R. S. 1998. *Matters of Principle: Legitimate Legal Arguments and Constitutional Interpretation.* New York: New York University Press.

MENDELSON, W. 1963. The neo-behavioral approach to the judicial process: a critique. *American Political Science Review*, 57: 597–603.

—— 1964. The untroubled world of jurimetrics. *Journal of Politics*, 26: 914–22.

PRITCHETT, C. H. 1948. *The Roosevelt Court.* New York: Mamillan.

—— 1953. *Civil Liberties and the Vinson Court.* Chicago: University of Chicago Press.

—— 1969. The development of judicial research. Pp. 27–42 in *Frontiers of Judicial Research*, ed. J. Grossman and J. Tanenhaus. New York: Wiley.

RIKER, W. H. 1990. Political science and rational choice. In *Perspectives on Positive Political Economy*, ed. J. E. Alt and K. A. Shepsle. New York: Cambridge University Press.

—— and ORDESHOOK, P. 1973. *An Introduction to Positive Political Theory.* Englewood Cliffs, NJ: Prentice Hall.

ROKEACH, M. 1968. *Beliefs, Attitudes, and Values.* San Francisco: Jossey-Bass.

SCHUBERT, G. A. 1959. *Quantitative Analysis of Judicial Behavior.* Glencoe, Ill.: Free Press.

—— 1963. *Judicial Decision Making.* New York: Free Press.

—— 1965. *The Judicial Mind: Attitudes and Ideologies of Supreme Court Justices.* Evanston, Ill.: Northwestern University Press.

—— 1974. *The Judicial Mind Revisited.* New York: Oxford University Press.

SEGAL, J. A., SONGER, D. R., and CAMERON, C. A. 1995. Decision making on the U.S. Courts of Appeals. Pp. 227–45 in *Contemplating Courts*, ed. L. Epstein. Washington: CQ Press.

SEGAL, J. A., and SPAETH, H. J. 2003. *The Supreme Court and the Attitudinal Model Revisited*. New York: Cambridge University Press.

SHAPIRO, M. 1993. Public law and judicial politics. Pp. 365–81 in *Political Science: The State of the Discipline II*, ed. A. W. Finifter. Washington, DC: American Political Science Association.

SOMIT, A., and TANENHAUS, J. 1982. *American Political Science: A Profile of a Discipline*. New York: Atherton.

SPAETH, H. J. 1972. *An Introduction to Supreme Court Decision Making*. San Francisco: Chandler.

—— 1995. The attitudinal model. Pp. 296–314 in *Contemplating Courts*, ed. L. Epstein. Washington, DC: CQ Press.

CASES

American Trucking Associations v. Smith. 1990. 496 U.S. 167.
Brown v. Board of Eduction. 1954. 347 U.S. 484.
Bush v. Gore. 2000. 531 U.S. 98.
Marbury v. Madison. 1803. 1 Cranch 137.
M'Culloch v. Maryland. 1819. 4 Wheaton 316.
Osborn v. Bank of the United States. 1824. 9 Wheaton 738.
Plessy v. Ferguson. 1896. 163 U.S. 537.
Roe v. Wade. 1973. 410 U.S. 113.
Scott v. Sandford. 1857. 19 Howard 393.

LAW AND POLITICS: THE PROBLEM OF BOUNDARIES

MARTIN SHAPIRO

LAW and politics is one of the many "law and..." movements that have arisen in recent years, the most notable of which, of course, is law and economics. All of these designations harbor a number of ambiguities, uncertainties, and tensions. The very words themselves present a major ambiguity. For the words law, economics, and politics may refer either to real-world phenomena or to the disciplines that study them. Perhaps the simplest way to look at the matter is to treat the "and" movements as marking the intersection of two disciplines. If so, it would be clearer to relabel law and politics as law and political science.

Even treated as disciplinary intersections, however, the problem remains of which way the traffic is supposed to flow. In law and economics, for instance, there is little doubt that the discipline of economics is supposed to help out the study of law and not vice versa. There are indeed economists who find that the study of law improves their study of economics, but typically they call themselves institutional economists rather than practitioners of law and economics.

In law and politics, the overt traffic pattern and the covert pattern diverge. Law professors and other legal scholars have long acknowledged the reality, if not necessarily the propriety, of the influence of politics as a real-world phenomenon upon law. For the last several generations a succession of lawyer scholars such as Jesse Choper and Richard Stewart have even acknowledged the writings of political scientists as among the sources and supports of their own arguments. Naturally this acknowledgment has been most open among constitutional and administrative law legal scholars, public law fields in which the entanglements of real-world law and politics are so palpable as to be virtually undeniable to any scholar who has moved beyond the most formal of formalisms.

Only a few of these lawyer scholars, however, are likely to label themselves as participants in a law and politics movement. In reality nearly every law school, the constitutional law and administrative law course is a law and politics course, as are many courses in environmental and other areas of regulatory law. While many a tax or property law professor may proudly proclaim him or herself a law and economics person, it is a rare constitutional or administrative law teacher who flies a law and politics flag. Most law teachers in those fields remain law, law, law professors, not "law and..." professors, no matter how much political science they absorb or teach.

So, quite unlike the traffic pattern in law and economics, the acknowledged, overt traffic flow at the law and political science intersection is largely from law to political science. Most of those who acknowledge their own membership in a law and politics movement are political scientists who claim that their knowledge of law informs and improves their practice of the discipline of political science.

If we accept the vision of law and politics as a movement of political scientists who use their knowledge of the discipline of law to improve their scholarly performance as political scientists, we lunge into the definitional vagaries and boundary uncertainties of the subfields of political science. Traditionally the subfield of political science entailing a knowledge of law was called public law, which meant constitutional law, administrative law, and a portion of international law. This set made some sense because it comprised the rules that regulate the behavior of government officials and organizations. If political science is the study of government, then a special subfield studying the rules for government was appropriate. If, however, political science is the study of politics, and politics is about the authoritative allocation of values, all sorts of law, most notably property, contract, corporation, tax, and regulatory law, have as much or more to do with allocations of value as do constitutional, administrative, and public international law. Thus the exclusive concern of political scientists with public law never made much sense.

It was not this lack of sense, however, but the "behavioral revolution" that rendered the "public law" label problematic among political scientists. The subject of study ought not to be the formal, legal rules purporting to prescribe how government officials ought to act but rather the actual, real-world behavior of officials and other politicians. And so "public law" became "judicial behavior."

Herein lies yet another rub. Why "judicial behavior?" All sorts of government officials and organs, as well as all sorts of other political actors, such as political parties, make law, are constrained by law, and implement law, not just judges and courts. Why should those political scientists who enriched their political science with cross-disciplinary legal knowledge confine themselves to the study of courts. Why "judicial behavior" and not "legal behavior?"

In terms of the historical sociology of knowledge, the answer is clear enough. Political science is largely an American discipline. The Supreme Court was a uniquely American and uniquely politically important entity because it could declare laws unconstitutional. Unlike other U.S. political organs, the Supreme Court did its politics by speaking legal discourse so you could understand it only if you spoke the language, a language no other political scientist needed to learn to speak. But even "public law" political scientists were not really native speakers of law. They had only learned, in a rather haphazard way, one of the minor, although most glamorous dialects, constitutional law. By the 1950s "public law" political science had pretty much reduced itself to the study of the constitutional law decisions of the U.S. Supreme Court. So when the behavioral revolution started to revolt against the "public law" subfield of political science, it revolted against what was there, namely, the study of the Supreme Court's constitutional law opinions, by proclaiming that what ought to be studied was not the formal prescriptions of the justices' written opinions but the real political behavior of the justices; that is, their votes in the constitutional cases. The rather grandiose title was "judicial behavior." The real study was the voting behavior of nine of the thousands of judges in the U.S. and even then their votes only in a small subset of the cases they actually voted on.

To be sure over time some expansion occurred to other courts, like the state Supreme Courts or the U.S. Courts of Appeal and even very occasionally to nonconstitutional cases. A concern for criminal trial courts arose, but that concern arose more from the subfield of urban politics than from that of judicial behavior.

Today the organized section of the American Political Science Association, seeking to move beyond the "public law" "judicial behavior" chatter, calls itself the "Law and Courts" section. Why "Courts?" Why not? There is every reason why some political scientists should devote themselves to the specialized study of courts, just as others do to legislatures and others yet to executives. What is problematic is the special association of law with courts.

This association does not appear so problematic at first glance. Courts are courts of law. They conduct their business in the language of law. They implement law, and in the course of doing so, they make a lot of law. Political scientists devoting themselves to the study of courts would be well advised to bring to that study an interdisciplinary approach enriching political science with law.

Legislatures, however, also have as one of their major activities the production of law, laws written in legal language. While little legal discourse may take place on the floor, much necessarily does in the committees actually writing those laws. Government administrators' legitimate actions are largely defined by law. They implement law. A substantial share of their business is conducted in legal language. They implement law, and in the course of doing so, they make a lot of law. Political scientists devoting themselves to specialized study of legislatures or administrators ought to be equally well advised as those who study courts to do law and political science. But most of them don't.

If we view the law and politics movement as the enrichment of political science as a discipline by the introduction of the discipline of law, then the translation of law and politics into law and courts logically is unjustified, although historically explainable. Because public law once reduced itself to the study of one variety of law handled by one court, and judicial behavior, more concerned with changing method than subject matter, at first followed suit, the next move was necessarily to expand the number and kind of courts studied and the number and kinds of law. Indeed we have not yet gone very far down that road. Most American political scientists supposedly devoted to "law and politics" still confine themselves largely to the study of the U.S. Supreme Court's constitutional decisions and the inputs to and consequences of these decisions. Any movement onward tends to be to the constitutional decisions of other higher or highest courts. There are probably more political scientists studying the constitutional law and politics of the Hungarian Supreme Court than the antitrust or bankruptcy decisions of the U.S. District courts.

Looking at the matter in a somewhat different way leads to the same ultimate issue. Most law and politics political scientists are law and courts political scientists and interested in only parts of a very few courts. Most of them are particularly interested in judicial lawmaking. If you are interested primarily in highest courts' constitutional decisions, you are likely to be most interested in judicial lawmaking, and vice versa, because judicial lawmaking is particularly dramatic and particularly easy for judges to do in their constitutional law decisions. If, however, you are a law and politics person particularly interested in judicial lawmaking, why shouldn't you be equally interested in legislative lawmaking and administrative lawmaking, particularly because such lawmaking is more often than not inextricably mixed with judicial lawmaking in the real world. Once again why law and courts and not law and legislatures and law and executives too?

The answer of law and courts people may be a quite simple one, or perhaps two quite simple ones. The first is, all of this is someone else's problem. We study courts. Obviously doing that study in an interdisciplinary law and political science way is a good idea. Perhaps people studying legislatures and executives also ought to do law and political science, but that is their problem not ours. Our problem is to move beyond studying the trunk of one elephant, and we are now proceeding to do so. Secondly, if we took as our primary allegiance not law and courts but law and politics, we would have to abandon the whole idea of subfields of political science and study everything or nearly everything political because nearly all political actors, institutions, and processes are defined and/or constrained to some degree by law and have some impact on law. Moving beyond the constitutional decisions of the U.S. Supreme Court to other law in other courts is a big enough task for us without taking on all the other subject matters of political science as well.

It seems perfectly reasonable to allow the law and courts movement to get on with its own judicial affairs so long as we see law and courts as itself a subfield of law and politics rather than conflating the two. We should be acutely aware, however, that as things stand, law and courts is far too large a proportion of law and politics. If law and politics is the flag of an interdisciplinary mode of injecting the discipline of law into political science in order to enrich political scientists' understanding of what they study, then the movement is hideously deficient outside the courts subfield of political science. Very few political scientists outside that subfield inform their work with legal knowledge. Two examples are offered here.

Congressional studies are one of the glories of American political science, having attracted many of its brightest stars. We know an enormous amount about congressional voting, internal organization and processes, committee functioning, constituency relationships, leadership, political party activity, campaigns and elections, and so on. In short, we know all about inputs to and throughputs of Congress. But very little effort has been made to discover the nature and functions of Congress by studying the proof of the pudding. It might appear obvious that one of the best ways to study what goes on in Congress would be to look at what comes out of Congress. And the principal product, unlike the products of many organs of government, is formal, distinct, relatively permanent, and readily accessible to everyone, namely the statutes Congress enacts. Yet very few Congress specialists routinely read, let alone comment upon or analyze, congressional statutes. To be sure, there is a policy studies tradition of tracking the origins, enactment, and implementation of particular public policies. Some of these studies tell us much about congressional behavior in particular instances or policy areas, but congressional specialists rarely seek to put these fragments together. No doubt there are a number of reasons for slighting congressional output, but one surely is that statutes are often highly complex legal documents whose significance is difficult to understand without the interdisciplinary skills in law and political science that few Congress scholars enjoy.

The same point can be made about political scientists who study the executive branch. It is true that administrative law often shows up as an option or even a requirement in public administration curricula. But it rarely shows up even as an option in graduate political science curricula training Ph.D's who will specialize in the study of "bureaucracy" and/or assorted areas of "regulatory politics" or the "politics of public policy." Many political scientists who specialize in public law or judicial politics study judicial lawmaking. Judges and administrators are both law implementers, subordinated to, or agents of, the statute maker. Both do and must make a good deal of law interstitially in the course of the statutory interpretation they must do in order to implement statutes. Judges and administrators as law-makers are inextricably intertwined in the course of judicial review of administra-tive action in which judges unavoidably go through the same thought processes in reviewing agency lawmaking as that in which the agencies engaged in making law. Yet only a few law and courts specialists are at home in administrative law. Few study agency lawmaking. Most confine themselves to the one area in which courts and agencies are not mutual and interacting subordinates of statutes, constitu-tional law. The major reason for this strange situation is, of course, that for the most part law and politics specialists are not law and politics but law and courts specialists and even more narrowly constitutional law and courts specialists.

Thus very few political scientists who study the major American organs making and implementing federal law, Congress and the executive, know anything much about law, and very few law and politics specialists know anything much about what Congress and the executive actually do, make and implement laws, as opposed to the constitutional limits on what they are supposed to do.

Finally, shortly before his untimely death, Herb Jacob began to complain that law and courts specialists were not paying enough attention to law in their study of courts. Given the enormous intellectual energies and resources poured into the official myth that judges only carry out the law and never make it, a lie so powerful and yet so unbelievable that it generates the endless circumlocutions, hypocrisies, and speaking silences of Supreme Court confirmation struggles, it is hardly sur-prising that law and courts political scientists have poured their energies into debunking the myth by concentrating their attention on revealing judicial discre-tion and judicial lawmaking. Here, of course, they were following on from the work of the judicial realism school of lawyer scholars. Jacobs' point was that judicial discretion, or lawmaking, or policy-making or politics, important as it was, nonetheless was highly constrained by legal rules. Political scientists studying courts ought to pay attention to constraints as well as freedoms, rules as well as discretion. Court specialists among political scientists ought to know law not only because judges expressed their discretion in legal language, but because that discretion was itself closely confined by legal rules.

From this point might be developed a different approach to law and politics from seeing it simply as an interdisciplinary intersection of the disciplines of law and political science. All political decisions may be characterized as arising out of either rule or discretion. In the real world, of course, rule and discretion are not opposites divided by a bright line but rather a spectrum arrayed from the most to the least rule-constrained. Actions by an administrative official in obedience to a very clear statutory command to do a very discrete, specific thing are at the most rule-constrained end of the spectrum but still typically entail some degree of discretion as to timing or allocation of scarce administrative capacity. No matter how specifically he is commanded to, the traffic cop cannot enforce the speeding law on all of the speeders all of the time. At the other end of the spectrum, even in polities in which the rule of law is fully established, some foreign policy decisions are almost purely discretionary. Even those decisions, however, are at the very least, made by government organs constituted by constitutional or statutory law, exercising discretion vested in them by law. Of course, in autocratic regimes, all may be at the discretion of the autocrat, but law and politics scholars really have nothing to study in regimes in which there is no law.

Admitting all this, it might be fruitful to define law and politics as a specialization in the relatively more rule-constrained aspects of political action leaving the most discretionary aspects of politics to American and comparative politics. The law and politics specialist would assist or lead where high levels of rule constraint exist because one must be able to muster, read, and understand the constraining rules in those areas in order to understand what is happening. It is the law and politics specialist who brings a skill at dealing with rules to those areas of politics where rules are most important.

To be sure, this is hardly a narrow specialization. Many areas of political activity are heavily rule-constrained, including of course judging and administration, but also elections, and in some countries, campaign financing, and so on. Yet a specialization defined in this way is more manageable than, say, one defined as concerned with the lawmaking and implementing process. For paradoxically lawmaking, although somewhat constrained by procedural rules, and like everything else by constitutional rules, is, when done by legislatures, essentially an exercise of discretion. Because administrators and judges are often secondary lawmakers highly constrained by the primary laws they seek to implement, their rulemaking does fall within the purview of law and politics under this definition. The law and politics scholar working on such secondary rulemaking, however, is warned to pay as much or more attention to the constraining rules as to the discretion. This definition of a specialization in terms of rule constraints leads us away from claiming as our terrain everything having to do with law, including making it, which becomes a specialization so broad as to cease to be a specialization.

Indeed a rule-constraint set of boundaries leads us back to the traditional designation, public law, because public law is the set of rules constraining government activity and such quasi-government activity as parties and elections. In this context, however, public law must denote not only constitutional, administrative, and public international law but also regulatory and much of welfare law. For these bodies of substantive law not only endow private actors with rights and obligations but also constrain the actions of public officials in implementing government programs. Banking law commands not only bankers to act on certain ways but also the government regulators of banks to act in certain ways.

A specialization in public law or rule constraints will, of course, spread law and politics far beyond the study of courts to that of all political actors operating in heavily rule-constrained environments, but the study of courts does fall squarely within such a bounding of law and politics. However, even if public law is broadly defined as including all of the substantive law that imposes duties on public officials, the public law label imposes artificial, indeed crippling, restraints on those law and politics scholars who seek to specialize in the study of courts. For much of what courts do lies in the realm of private not public law, and those few courts that do largely or exclusively public law are atypical. One of the typical errors of public law-oriented political scientists is to build elaborate theories about courts in general based solely on the study of a small number of very peculiar courts, that is, constitutional courts. The legitimacy of courts, a key problematic for law and courts studies, derives far more from their role as processors of disputes between private parties over property, contract, and injury than from their role in restraining other government actors. Thus the paradox that those law and politics students specializing in the study of courts ought not to see themselves as public law and courts specialists, while those law and politics specialists who wish to work on nonjudicial as well as judicial politics probably ought to confine themselves to public law, that is to the law constraining government actors, as a way of bounding a field of specialization within the study of politics as a whole.

It would appear then that it would be most convenient to view law and politics as involving two overlapping but not coterminous specializations; one, law and politics, that, growing out of the historical concern of political scientists with public law, brings an expertise in law to the political science study of highly legally constrained government behavior; the other law and courts which consciously throws off the public law boundaries to study all of the behavior of courts. Such a dual vision would have to acknowledge that law-oriented political scientists who study most of government (the activities of legislatures, executives, and parties) would be concerned with the most law-constrained actions of government while those who study courts might *actually focus on courts'* least law-constrained behavior; that is, instances of judicial lawmaking. For this paradox follows naturally if law and politics is to be a specialization in the study of those portions of politics in which a knowledge of law is most relevant.

Name Index

Abbott, K 190, 194
Abel, L K 542, 549
Abel, R L 388, 536, 544, 545, 546, 548, 549, 684, 685
Abel-Smith, B 248
Abraham, H 473
Abramowitz, A I 327, 328
Abrams, Elliot 259
Abrams, J S 231
Acheson, Dean 251, 254–5
Ackerman, B 50, 83, 86, 95, 149, 165, 236 n3, 285, 294, 578, 758, 759
Adamany, D 479, 645
Adenauer, Konrad 102 n5
Adler, M 583
Agamben, G 166, 167
Aiken, Charles 739
Albiston, C 525, 664 n1, 686
Aleinikoff, T A 729
Alexander, G J 176
Alexander, L 285, 289, 434
Alito, Samuel 27, 489, 542
Allan, T R S 288
Allende, Salvador 388
Almond, Gabriel 4
Alter, K 133, 211, 216, 217, 219, 220, 223
Althaus, S L 666
Alvarez, J E 239
Alvarez, R M 331, 335
Aman, A C 389
Amar, A R 49
Ames, B 517
Amin, Idi 238
Aquinas, St Thomas 399, 400, 401, 405, 406–7, 411
Arend, A C 197
Aristotle 167, 400, 405, 408
Arkes, H 409
Armstrong, V 493
Arnold, Thurman 747
Aron, R 235

Arps, Skadden 253
Arthurs, H W 547
Asimov, M 586
Asmal, A 236 n4
Aspin, L 479
Atkins, B 480
Auerbach, J S 386
Austin, J 189

Bachrach, P 300, 745
Baer, Harold 562
Baer, J A 439, 441 n2, 442, 443, 444, 447
Bahlul, Ali Hamza Ahmed Sulayman al 542
Baird, V A 76, 110, 667
Baker, R 84
Baker, S C 452
Baldez, L 23, 498
Balkin, J M 285, 286, 654
Balla, S J 577
Banks, C P 514
Barak, Aharon 128
Baratz, M S 300, 745
Barber, S A 288, 314
Barclay, S 528, 664 n1, 671
Bardaglio, P W 728
Baretto, M 335
Barkan, E 236
Barkow, R 24
Barnes, J 304, 373, 609
Barnett, R E 285, 286
Barro, R J 566
Barron, D 344
Barros, R 71, 92, 293
Barrow, D J 645
Barrow, J 476
Barry, B 333
Bartlett, K T 438–9
Barzilai, G 536
Bass, G J 232, 235, 240
Baum, L 21, 113, 133, 472, 478, 479, 492, 511, 513, 514, 547, 564, 741

Baumgartner, F R 600, 608
Baxi, U 85
Beach, D 216
Bealey, F 270
Beard, Charles 725
Becker, G 342
Bednar, J 84 n3, 146, 150
Beer, J E 386
Behuniak, S M 441
Beierle, T C 586, 587
Bell, D 456–7, 458, 459
Bell, Griffin 384
Bell, L 477
Bellamy, R 143
Benesh, S C 21, 506, 507, 511
Benjamin, W 730, 731
Bennett, C J 270
Bennett, S E 666
Benoit, J P 708
Benton, L 248
Bergara, M 40
Berger, R 432
Berger, S 47
Berkson, L 476
Berlusconi, Silvio 126
Berman, H J 64
Berman, S 54
Bermann, G 152
Berns, Walter 6
Berry, F S 513, 515
Berry, W D 513, 515
Bevan, G 547
Bhutto, Benazir 126
Bickel, Alexander 283, 455
Bignami, F 588
Bilz, K 713
Binder, S 477
Bird, Rose 570
Biro, M 241
Black, Barry Elton 542
Black, C L 455
Black, E 325
Black, Hugo 431, 433
Black, M 325
Blackmun, Harry A 495, 654
Blackstone, W 168–9, 274, 361, 362
Blader, S L 715, 717, 719
Bloom, A 536
Blumberg, A S 682
Blumstein, A 713
Blyth, M 54
Böckenförde, E-W 173
Bodin, J 171
Boehmke, F J 513

Bogdanor, V 281
Bohannan, P 684
Bohte, J 579, 604, 608
Bok, D 548
Boli, J 47 n2
Bolton, J R 232 n1
Bond, J R 323
Bonneau, C 479
Borgwardt, E 233 n2
Bork, R H 134, 231, 408, 469, 473
Börzel, T 216, 218
Bottoms, A 718
Boucher, R L 490, 493, 509 n6
Boudreau, C 364
Boudreaux, D 107 n9
Boulanger, C 93
Bourchier, D 86
Bourdieu, P 667, 674
Bowen, W G 548
Boyum, K O 682
Brace, P 23, 28, 30, 480, 481, 570
Bradley, C A 200
Brady, H 331
Braithwaite, J 256
Braman, E 21
Brandon, M 176
Brandwein, P 313, 391 n5, 633
Bratton, K 481
Braun, A 274
Brazier, J E 577
Brehm, J 506
Brennan, William J, Jr 432, 665
Brenner, S 22, 30, 491, 492
Brent, J 507, 512
Bressman, L 346, 349, 353, 354
Breton, A 145
Breyer, S 350, 361, 370, 558, 581
Brigham, J 316, 384, 390, 392, 524, 533, 747
Brink, D 422
Brisbin, R A, Jr 498, 507, 510, 600, 604
Brown, D 384
Brown, N J 70
Brown, W 443
Brubaker, R 334
Brudney, J J 315, 373–4
Brunell, T 216, 218
Brunner, G 93, 132
Bruun, R 533
Buchanan, J M 291
Buergenthal, T 258
Bull, H 190, 192
Bullock, A 234
Bulterman, M K 200
Bumiller, K 391, 530, 669

Bundy, McGeorge 251, 259
Burbank, S 102
Burger, Warren 41
Burgess, John W 725
Burgess, S R 49
Burke, T F 597, 602, 609
Burley, A M 147, 214
Burstein, P 533, 534
Buruma, I 232
Busch, M 220
Bush, George W 246, 469, 476, 477, 478
Bussiere, E 48, 49, 313
Butterfield, H 233
Bzdera, A 147, 150

Cahill, M L 606
Cain, P A 443
Calabresi, G 273, 431
Caldeira, G 30, 76, 110, 111, 303, 304, 473, 477, 490,
    491, 492, 493, 498, 508, 509, 512, 513, 514, 515, 516,
    664, 667, 672
Calderon, Felipe 127
Caldwell, P 172, 173, 175
Cameron, C M 22, 41 n4, 473, 490, 507, 509, 511,
    512, 600, 701–2, 704
Caminker, E 512
Canaday, M 728
Cane, P 11
Canes-Wrone, B 577
Canon, B 480, 504, 505, 506, 511, 514, 532, 600,
    601, 746 n5
Canon, P 534
Caparoso, J 217, 218
Cappelletti, M 82, 85, 100, 267, 269
Carbado, D W 462
Cardozo, B N 316
Carlin, J E 530
Carlsmith, K M 717
Carmichael, J T 616
Carothers, T 74
Carp, R 477
Carpenter, D P 577, 656
Carr, E H 192
Carrington, P D 488
Carroll, L D 550
Carrubba, C 114, 218
Carson, J L 329
Carter, Jimmy 259, 476, 477
Carter, L 381
Carter, S 473, 488
Carvajal, D 545
Casper, J 651
Cayford, J 586, 587
Chalmers, D 218

Chambliss, E 548
Champagne, A 546
Chang, R 401, 461
Charles, G-U 286
Chase, Samuel 488
Chavez, R B 67, 70, 72, 73, 75, 76, 91
Chayes, A 202
Chayes, A H 202, 232, 596, 602
Checkel, J T 202
Cheek, K 546
Cheibub, J 293
Choi, S 488
Choper, J H 143, 146, 768
Choudry, S 334
Christensen, R K 276
Christiano, C 422
Chubb, J E 146
Churchill, W S 234
Cichowski, R A 536, 595, 607, 652, 653
Cicourel, A V 684
Cincinnatus 167
Claes, M 210
Clarke, S H 728
Clausewitz, C von 229
Clayton, C W 48, 49, 55, 90, 391 n5, 644, 647, 741
Clifford, Nathan 311
Clifford, P G 310
Clinton, Bill 246, 477
Clinton, R L 83, 114
Cloward, R 745
Coffin, F M 147
Coglianese, C 387, 585, 586
Cohen, A J 389, 729
Cohen, J 713
Cohen, L 42, 353, 703
Cohen, M A 510
Coke, Lord 82–3
Cole, D 165, 177, 178
Cole, W M 198
Coleman, J 11
Colker, R 315
Comaroff, J 529, 673
Comaroff, J L 673
Commager, H S 437
Commons, John R 725
Conant, L 86, 138, 218, 536
Conley, J M 683
Connally, John 255
Connell, R W 674
Constable, M 730, 731
Coolidge, Calvin 188
Coombs, C 760
Cooper, N L 382
Cooper, P J 596, 599

Cooter, R D 38, 569, 570, 700, 708
Corkalo, Dinka 241
Cornell, D 442 n3, 443
Cortell, A P 202
Corwin, Edward 5, 756
Cotterrell, R 390
Courville, S 389
Couso, J A 70–1, 75
Coutin, S B 688
Cover, A D 26, 40
Craig, P P 272, 588
Cramer, R A 392
Cramton, R C 488
Crenshaw, K W 458, 459, 533
Crespin, M H 329
Crews, C W, Jr 585, 586
Cristi, R 173
Cross, F B 22, 27, 38, 355, 507, 511, 547, 562, 563, 565, 566, 571, 577, 758
Cruft, R 415, 420
Cuellar, M F 349, 354, 355
Culp, J M, Jr 462
Cummings, S 549
Cunningham, C D 367
Curran, B 530
Curtis, C 543
Curtis, M K 432
Cushing, Robert 738
Cushman, Robert E 5, 496, 756

Dahl, R A 64, 70, 114, 143, 474, 564, 644, 724, 742
Dai, X 201
Dalton, C 439
Daly, M 547
Damaska, M R 275
Danelski, David 6, 10, 472
Daniels, S 528
Danner, M 232
Darley, J M 713, 714, 715, 717
Dauber, M L 728
Daughety, A 708
Davis, A D 728
Davis, J W J 202, 250, 251
Davis, K 343, 346, 347
Davis, R 488, 490
Davis, S 477
Dawson, J P 273, 274
de Figueiredo, J M 37 n1, 38, 476, 563
De Gaulle, Charles 86, 170, 213
de la Garza, R O 335
de Moor, J A 248
De Witte, B 210
Dehousse, R 214

Delgado, R 456, 457, 459, 461
Den Dulk, K R 534, 747
Dennison, G M 169
Derrida, Jacques 459, 730
DeSipio, L 335
Dewan, S 549
Dewey, J 674
Dezalay, Y 248, 252, 256, 388, 547, 692, 729
Diamant, N J 536
Diamond, L 64
Diamond, Martin 6
Dicey, A V 160
DiMaggio, P J 47 n2
Ditslear, C 373–4
Diver, C 343, 349
Dix, G E 562
Dixon, R G 757
Dobbin, F 605
Dolbeare, Kenneth 740
Domingo, P 68, 72, 73
Donnelly, J 200
Donner, A 210
Donohue, J J 715
Donohue, L 177
Dotan, Y 92, 137
Douglas, William O 282
Downing, R 480
Downs, D A 447
Downs, G 192–3, 201
Drahos, P 256
Dratel, J 179, 544
Dryden, S 255
Dubber, M D 729
DuBois, P 479, 480
DuBois, W E B 451, 452
Dudas, J 534, 535, 747
Dudziak, M L 292
Duffy, H 178
Dulles, Allan 251, 257
Dulles, John Foster 251
Durkheim, Emile 121
Durr, R 111
Duvalier, J-C 'Baby Doc' 238
Dworkin, R 287, 314, 408, 422, 758–9
Dyzenhaus, D 178, 180
Dzur, A W 385

Easterbrook, F H 367, 371, 705, 706
Easton, D 665, 667, 716, 718, 719
Eberle, William 255
Edelman, L B 602, 605
Edelman, M 746
Edley, C 345

Edling, M M 292
Edmundson, W 415
Edwards, L 542
Eilperin, J 324
Eisenberg, T 528
Eisenstein, J 28, 618, 682, 687
Eisgruber, C 287
Elazar, D J 146
Elhauge, E 365–6
Elkin, S L 292
Elkind, P 547
Elkins, Z 93, 196, 270
Elliott, E D 344, 374
Ellman, L M 27
Ellsworth, P C 715
Elster, J 143, 236, 237, 239, 290
Ely, J H 153, 283, 286, 346, 455
Emery, R E 718
Emirbayer, M 674
Emrey, J A 514
Engel, D M 527 n2, 529, 530, 531, 664 n1,
    683, 689, 690, 746 n6
Epp, C R 72–3, 89, 113, 135, 309, 490,
    533–4, 595, 596, 599, 601, 607, 684
Epstein, C F 548
Epstein, D 352, 577, 579
Epstein, L 19, 23, 30, 39, 41, 70, 83, 94, 114, 133,
    175, 303, 323, 474, 476, 488, 489, 490, 493,
    494, 496, 497, 498, 512, 532, 534, 564, 763
Epstein, R A 288, 649
Erdos, D O 294
Erlanger, H S 596, 605
Ernst, D R 724, 727
Eskridge, W N, Jr 30, 36, 37, 40, 146, 149,
    354, 365, 370, 372, 373, 493, 562, 670
Espinoza, L 461
Estreicher, S 495
Ewick, P 525, 526, 530–1, 664 n1, 668,
    669, 670, 671, 672, 673, 690, 746 n6
Eykholt, M 234

Fairman, C 169
Farber, D 349, 362, 373, 460, 569
Farhang, S 28
Farina, C 344
Farrand, M 306
Fasolt, C 731
Fatovic, C 168
Fearon, J D 195 n3
Feeley, M 386, 390, 596, 601, 604 n3, 606, 682,
    742–3, 748
Feely, M 135
Feld, L 100 n3
Feldman, C 571

Feldman, E A 692
Feldman, S 666
Fellman, David 6, 740
Felstiner, W 524, 685
Fenn, P 649
Ferejohn, J 29, 36, 37, 70, 75, 88, 90, 102,
    120, 136, 143, 146, 149, 165, 167, 174, 352,
    354, 366, 372, 559, 563, 565, 580,
    648, 759
Ferguson, J 277
Ferguson, N 234
Ferguson, R A 727
Filipov, M 143, 321
Fineman, M A 444–5
Finkel, J 69, 91
Finkelman, P 306
Finley, L 440
Finn, J 177, 180
Finnemore, M 190
Finnis, J 400, 405, 411
Fiorina, M P 323, 579
Fischer, F 234
Fisher, L 169, 314, 742
Fisher, S F 671
Fiss, O 65, 507
Fitzpatrick, J 165
Fitzpatrick, P 383, 384
Fitzpatrick, S 176
Flagg, B J 455
Fleisher, R 323
Fleming, J E 288, 314
Flemming, R B 28, 477, 491, 495, 604, 608,
    618, 687
Fleury-Steiner, B 527 n2, 531, 669
Fligstein, N 155
Foley, E B 332
Foot, R 232
Forbath, W E 533
Ford, Gerald 255
Ford, R T 462
Fortna, V P 196, 202
Foster, S 454
Fraenkel, E 177
France, Anatole 439
Franck, T M 202
Frank, Jerome 22
Frankel, M 541
Frankfurter, Felix 282, 283
Franklin, D 169
Frederick II, the Great 99
Freedman, M 543
Freeman, A D 455
Freeman, J 349
Freeman, M 174

Freund, Paul 738
Frey, B S 588
Frickey, P 349, 362, 370
Fridkin, K 719
Friedman, B 30, 72, 103, 105 n7, 111 n13, 144, 147, 282, 304, 497, 566, 640
Friedman, L 748
Friedrich, Carl 6, 166, 281, 282
Fritsch, J 549
Fromkin, D 234
Frydl, K 615, 616
Frymer, P 53–4, 146, 391 n5, 535, 598
Fukuyama, F 270
Fuller, L L 381, 409, 433, 712
Funston, R 645
Furlong, S R 585

Galanter, M 528, 529, 564, 601, 682, 685–6, 699 n1, 745
Gambaro, A 275, 277
Garcia-Villegas, M 529, 536, 664 n1
Garland, D 714
Garland, M 343, 350
Garrett, E 369, 370
Garrett, G 39, 138, 147, 214–15, 365
Garth, B G 248, 252, 256, 388, 547, 681, 692, 729
Gates, J B 645, 651
Gates, S 506
Gaubatz, K T 195
Gelderen, M van 282
Gely, R 36, 37, 40, 42, 563
Genn, H 687
George, R 404 n1, 411
George, T E 19, 492, 496, 508, 509
Gerber, E R 324
Geyh, C G 570
Gibson, G 236 n4
Gibson, J L 19, 28, 76, 110, 111, 137, 664, 667, 672
Giddens, A 674
Giles, M W 28, 505, 511
Gilligan, C 440–1
Gilliom, J 525, 531, 609
Gillman, H 20, 22, 48, 49, 52, 53, 90, 302, 304, 310–11, 316, 391 n5, 628, 630, 631, 651, 654, 655, 656, 657, 724, 742, 758, 759
Gilmore, G 274
Ginsburg, R B 440, 489
Ginsburg, T 38, 39, 69, 83, 87, 90, 91, 94, 95, 109 n11, 115, 137, 649
Giuliani, Rudolph 549
Glater, J D 547
Glendon, M A 136
Glick, H 480, 513, 514
Gloppen, S 66, 72

Goffman, E 674
Golay, J F 172
Goldberg-Hillier, J 534, 747
Golden, M M 585, 586
Goldford, D J 292
Goldman, Sheldon 6, 475–6, 489
Goldschmidt, J 547
Goldsmith, J L 157, 188, 193, 194, 200, 236–7, 238
Goldstein, J 120, 122, 137, 190, 203, 219, 246
Goldstein, L F 440, 652
Goldsworthy, J 288
Golub, J 218
Good, I J 706
Goodman, J C 699
Goodman, R 197, 198
Goodstein, L 543
Gordon, R W 723, 727, 728, 730
Gordon, S 481
Gould, J B 392, 536
Gourevitch, P 241
Graber, M A 53, 83, 114, 128, 137, 286, 294, 306, 307, 308, 309, 313, 317, 391 n5, 568, 646, 650
Graham, B 480
Grande, E 276
Graziadei, M 275
Green, D P 719
Green Cowles, M 218
Greenawalt, K 758
Greenberg, D 622, 624
Greenberg, K 179, 544
Greenhouse, C J 527 n2, 530, 669, 747
Griffin, S M 286
Grodzins, M 145
Gross, O 165, 170, 175, 176
Grossback, L J 515
Grossberg, M 727
Grossman, Joel 6, 391, 471, 474, 478, 740, 741
Gruhl, J 504
Gryski, G G 645
Guarnieri, C 136, 559, 570
Gulati, M 462, 488
Gunningham, N 684, 691
Gurr, T R 715
Guzman, A 195, 220

Habermas, J 121, 135, 286, 290
Hadfield, G 700
Hafner-Burton, E M 193, 201, 202
Hagan, J 620
Hagle, T M 489, 764
Hahn, R 590
Haines, Charles Grove 5, 756
Haire, S 506, 507, 509, 510, 511, 512, 514

Halberstam, D 145, 147, 155, 156, 157
Hall, A B 5
Hall, H 480
Hall, K 475, 480
Hall, M 479, 480, 481
Hall, M G 23, 28, 30, 570
Hall, P A 47, 48, 54
Halliday, T C 546
Haltom, W 392, 528, 530, 534, 602, 609,
   672, 689, 690
Hamilton, Alexander 101, 558–9
Hamilton, J T 577
Hammond, T H 41, 42, 755, 763
Hand, Learned 282, 283
Handler, J F 533, 596, 683, 745
Handley, L 330
Handlin, M F 725
Handlin, O 725
Haney, C 714
Haney-Lopez, I 460
Hankey, L 237
Hans, V P 684, 687
Hansford, T G 22, 505
Hanssen, F A 571
Hardin, R 291
Harding, S 443
Harel, A 415
Harfst, D 343, 350, 586
Harland, C 199
Harlow, C 217, 272
Harman, Jane 542
Harrington, C B 378, 381, 383, 384, 385, 386, 387,
   388, 390, 391
Harrington, W 585
Harris, A 442–3, 457, 461, 462
Harris, B E 604, 609
Harris, C 460
Harris, J P 331
Harris, P 513, 515
Harris, R 728
Harris, W F, II 290, 292
Hart, H M, Jr 189, 360, 370, 371, 410, 454
Harter, P J 387
Hartley, R E 385, 477
Hartog, H 728
Hartz, L 725
Harvey, A 30, 497
Hatcher, L J 392, 534
Hathaway, O 193, 198, 202, 240
Hawkins, D 202, 215
Hawkins, K 684, 688, 691
Hay, W 718
Hayes, B D 650
Hayner, P 236, 240

Heinz, J P 548, 688
Heise, M 25, 563
Helfer, L R 203, 214, 219–20
Hellman, A 508
Helm, C 202
Helmke, G 26, 39 n3, 70, 86, 133, 498, 561
Helms, J 232 n1
Helms, R E 615, 619
Henderson, J 528
Hendley, K 536
Henkin, L 82, 202
Henneberger, M 542
Herget, J E 725
Herman, D 747
Hernandez, T K 462
Herrnson, P S 300
Herron, E S 66, 94
Hersh, S M 232
Hershovitz, S 288
Hertogh, M 664 n1
Herzog, D 153
Hesselink, M W 274
Hettinger, V A 28, 30, 511, 763
Heumann, M 682
Heydebrand, W 381 n1, 391, 683
Heymann, P B 550
Hibbing, J R 719
Hilbink, E 70, 76
Hill, J S 577
Hills, R M, Jr 145, 156, 159
Hines, C N 545
Hirschl, R 53, 69, 86, 90, 91, 120, 121, 123, 137, 150,
   245, 294, 309, 317, 322, 566, 653–4
Hittinger, R 400
Hobbes, Thomas 291
Hoekstra, V 507, 510
Hoffman, E A 669
Hofnung, M 92, 95, 137
Hofrichter, R 385
Hohfeld, W 415–17
Hojnacki, M 477, 479
Holdsworth, W S 169
Hollingsworth, E J 596
Holmes, L 477
Holmes, O W 143, 316, 429, 434, 629, 725
Holmes, S 143, 290
Holmes, S A 542
Honig, B 729
Hopkins, D J 204
Hor, M 179, 180
Horowitz, D L 333
Horwitz, M J 726
Hosoya, C 232
Houston, Charles Hamilton 453

Howard, J Woodward 6, 391, 472, 475, 514, 530
Howard, R M 24, 763–4
Hoxie, R G 5
Huber, G 481
Huber, J D 577, 579, 580
Huckleberry, K 684
Hudec, Robert 256
Hull, K E 548, 669, 671
Hume, David 291
Hume, R J 22, 511
Humphries Ginn, M 517
Hunt, A 385 n3, 533
Huntington, S 87, 235, 237
Huo, Y J 715, 717, 718
Hurst, Willard 691, 725, 726, 740
Hussain, N 178, 180, 729
Hussein, Saddam 128, 236, 239
Hutchings, V 474
Hutchinson, D L 461
Hyneman, Charles 6 n1

Iaryczower, M 30, 39, 70, 94
Iglesias, E M 461
Ikenberry, J 48
Iovanni, L 714
Ishiyama, J 69, 87, 89
Ishiyama-Smithey, S 87, 89
Issacharoff, S 175, 176, 326, 327, 328, 329
Iyer, T K K 172

Jackson, John 256
Jackson, R H 233, 234
Jacob, H 480, 682, 684, 687, 740, 772
Jacobi, T 41
Jacobs, D 615, 616, 619
Jacobsohn, G 86
Jacobson, G C 328
Jacobson, H K 201
Jaffa, H 409
Jaffe, L 341
Jefferson, Thomas 83
Jeffries, S 442
Jenkins-Smith, H C 598, 600, 601, 602, 608
Jensen, L 391 n5
Jinks, D 197, 198
John Paul II, Pope 412
Johnsen, D 655
Johnson, B 670
Johnson, C A 493, 504 n1, 505, 506, 511, 532, 600, 601, 746 n5
Johnson, G 673
Johnson, Lyndon B 477
Johnson, S M 581 n1
Johnson, T R 490

Johnston, M D 542
Jones, B D-M 456, 457, 458, 459, 600, 608
Jones, M A 201
Jones, P 415
Jönsson, C 219
Jordan, E C 462
Jordan, W 350
Jost, J T 715
Jupille, 217

Kabila, Laurent 238
Kagan, E 577
Kagan, R 344, 348, 350, 354, 385, 525, 528, 597, 607, 684, 691, 748
Kahan, D 713
Kahn, A 342
Kahn, P W 286
Kahn, R 391 n5, 626, 627, 628, 647
Kalman, L 284, 740
Kammen, M 316
Kapiszewski, D 67
Karl, T L 64
Karlan, P S 286, 327
Karpik, L 548
Kastner, D L 667
Katz, S N 724, 725
Katznelson, I 47
Kay, H H 440
Kearns, T R 529, 746
Keck, M E 72, 202, 240
Keck, T M 54, 284, 314–15, 391 n5, 635, 638, 639, 640, 655, 657
Keegan, J 234
Kelemen, R D 74, 86, 135, 147, 151, 215, 261, 270, 272, 595, 597
Kellum, Joseph WIlson 542
Kelly, M J 688
Kelman, H C 716
Kelsen, Hans 85, 172, 410
Kennan, G F 192 n2, 237, 246
Kennedy, A 639
Kennedy, E 171
Kennedy, J F 231, 255
Kennedy, Randall 458, 634
Keohane, R O 193, 194, 196, 220, 223
Kersch, K I 313, 391 n5, 626, 627, 628, 631, 646, 647
Kerwin, C 585, 586
Kessler, M 534
Ketcham, B 101
Kidder, R I 685
Kilroy, B 215
Kilwein, J C 507, 510, 600
Kim, W C 718
Kimball, D C 331

King, Martin Luther, Jr 523
Kingsbury, B 389
Kinsley, M 542
Kitzman, K M 718
Klarman, M J 286, 634, 646, 647, 652, 656
Klein, B 700
Klein, D E 22, 510, 511, 512, 513, 515, 565
Kleiner, M M 545
Klug, H 74
Kluger, R 626
Knight, J 30, 41, 70, 83, 94, 114, 133, 303,
    488, 493, 496, 498, 564, 763
Kobylka, J F 532
Kocs, S A 192
Koh, H H 200, 232, 246, 247
Kommers, D 11, 86, 114, 132, 516
Koremenos, B 190, 194
Kornhauser, L A 42, 512, 525, 559, 561, 596,
    609, 700, 701–2, 704, 705, 706, 707, 708, 759
Kort, F 704
Kötz, H 267
Kozinski, A 558, 560
Kramer, J H 622
Kramer, L 134, 144, 146, 288, 317, 563, 565, 729
Kramer, M 415, 417, 419, 420
Kramer, R M 715
Krasner, S D 47, 193, 236–7, 238
Kratochwil, F 196
Krisch, N 389
Krishnan, J K 534
Krislov, S 716, 741
Kritzer, H M 22–3, 304, 309–10, 498, 545, 657,
    685, 686, 687, 704
Krog, A 236 n4
Krol, J F 491, 492
Krupnick, A J 585
Krygier, M 385
Kyvig, D E 306

Ladinsky, J 479
Laitin, D D 334
Lakoff, M 670, 673
Landa, D 706, 707
Landes, W 107, 505, 514, 515, 568, 580, 648
Landis, James 341
Landman, T 198
Lane, J-E 293
Langbein, L 349
Langer, L 23, 28, 564
Larkins, C 64, 560, 561
Larson, E W 669
Larson, M S 548
Lash, K 286
Lasser, M 273

Lasser, W 645
Latour, B 383, 674
Laumann, E O 548, 688
Lavi, S J 729
Lawrence, C R 458
Lawrence, S E 534
Lawson, G 285
Lax, J R 41 n4, 42, 704, 706, 707
Lecourt, Robert 213
Lee, F E 306
Lee, S J 616
Leff, A 277
Legrand, P 271
Legro, J W 190, 202
Lehmbruch, G 146
Lehoucq, F E 331
Lempert, R O 523, 548, 685
Lenaerts, K 142, 143
Lenhardt, R A 462
Lesher, D 542
Lessig, L 514
Lev, D 72
Levi-Faur, D 270
Levin, M 619
Levine, F 530, 681, 683, 687
Levine, S 716
Levinson, D J 146, 147, 323
Levinson, S 179, 292, 305–6, 654
Levinthal, Harold 343
Lewin, K 715–16
Lewis, D E 577
Lewis, P S 684
Lijphart, A 332–3
Lillich, Richard 258
Limongi, F 293
Lind, E A 718
Lindgren, J 478
Lindquist, S A 22, 30, 147, 474, 507, 509,
    510, 512
Lipschultz, S 631, 632
Lipson, C 194
Liptak, A 545, 546, 549
Lipton, Wachtell 253
Litan, R 590
Littleton, C A 440
Liu, C 549
Livingston, W S 149
Llewellyn, K N 147
Lloyd George, David 232, 233
Lobel, J 165, 178, 598
Lobel, O 347
Locke, John 168, 291
Longman, T 240
Loughborough, Lord Chief Justice 169

Loughlin, M 284
Lovell, G I 53, 531, 535, 597, 650, 742
Loveman, B 170, 180
Lovrich, N, Jr 479
Lowenstein, D H 306, 326
Lowi, T 342, 346
Luban, D 541, 543
Lubman, S B 66, 76, 536
Luhmann, N 135
Luker, K 636
Lundberg, P J 23
Lupia, A 363
Luskin, R C 480
Lutz, D S 293, 294
Lutz, E L 202

Macaulay, S 382
McBride, Sean 257
McCann, M 392, 523, 525, 528, 529, 530, 531, 533, 534, 596, 602, 604, 609, 669, 672, 682, 686, 689, 690, 746, 747
McClain, L 441
McCloskey, Robert 6, 114, 312
McCloy, John J 251, 257
McConnell, M W 152
McCormick, J 173
MacCoun, R J 714
McCubbins, M 342, 351, 354, 363, 368–9, 577
McDonald, M P 328
McEvoy, A F 727
McEwen, C 385, 687, 688
McFeeley, N 473
McGarity, T 342, 350
McGarry, J 333
McGinnis, J 285, 286, 306
McGuire, K T 31, 110, 114, 133, 493, 498, 499, 564
McIlwain, C H 282
McIntosh, W 391
McIntyre, L 541
Mackie, G 363
MacKinnon, C 440, 441 n2, 442, 444
McLean, B 547
MacMahon, G 387
McMahon, K J 53, 650
McNollgast (McCubbins, Noll & Weingast) 22, 37, 354, 363, 367, 508, 597, 703
Macey, J 354, 371
Madison, J 67, 83, 153, 160
Madsen, C 168
Madsen, M R 213, 258
Maduro, M P 156
Maeda, K 499
Magalhaes, P C 69, 649
Magaloni, B 91

Magat, W A 585
Maguire, E R 617
Maharaj, D 545
Mahmud, T 172
Maiman, R J 385, 687, 688
Maine, Henry 121
Majone, G 150
Major, B 715
Malcolm, George 250
Maltese, J 473
Maltzman, F 30, 477, 493
Mancini, Federico 213
Mann, B H 728
Mansbridge, J 473
Manza, J 624
March, J 47, 90
March, T 525
Markesinis, B S 271
Markovits, R S 758
Marks, B 35
Marmor, A 286, 367
Mars, D 704
Marshall, A M 534, 664 n1, 669, 686
Marshall, John 82, 83, 85, 758
Marshall, T R 564
Marshall, Thurgood 432, 453, 489
Marshall, W J 35
Martin, A D 23, 111, 303
Martin, J 528
Martin, L L 194, 195, 203
Martinek, W L 21, 30, 507, 511
Marx, Karl 442
Mashaw, J 343, 346, 347, 348, 350, 355, 362, 374, 375, 586
Mason, Alpheus 6, 472
Massaro, J 473
Massicotte, L 331
Mastrofski, S D 712
Mather, L 390, 607, 682, 683, 686, 687, 688
Matsuda, M 457
Mattei, U 272, 274, 275, 277
Mattli, W 133, 147, 214
Mauborgne, R A 718
Mauro, R 715
May, D 644
Mayhew, D R 35
Maynard, D 682
Meares, T L 713, 714
Mearsheimer, J 192
Medcalf, L 533
Meernik, J 241
Melnick, R S 343, 350, 579, 597
Melone, A P 66
Melton, G B 716

Mendeloff, J 350
Mendelson, N A 585, 586
Mendelson, W 756
Méndez, J E 76
Menem, Carlos 73
Mengitsu Haile Mariam 238
Menkel-Meadow, C 548
Merelman, R J 716
Merrill, T 342, 374
Merry, S E 383, 384, 386, 389, 527 n2, 529, 530, 536, 669, 683
Merryman, J H 64
Messinger, S L 530
Metternich, K von 235
Metzger, G 347
Meyer, J W 47 n2
Michelman, F I 286
Miles, T 344
Miller, A S 169
Miller, R A 126, 391, 527, 528
Miller, R E 685
Millett, J 738
Mills, C Wright 745
Milner, N 389, 533, 603 n2, 747
Milosevic, Slobodan 128, 235, 240, 542
Ming, W R 453
Minnow, M 236
Mitchell, G 667, 719
Mitnick, B 342, 509
Mnookin, R H 525, 596, 609
Mobuto Sese Seko 238
Moe, T 342, 354, 506
Mommsen, W J 248
Mondak, J 111, 664, 667
Monroe, B L 499
Monroe, James 309
Moore, S F 383, 547
Moore, W D 633
Moorhead, R 547
Morag-Levine, N 391 n5
Moran, M J 37, 38, 342, 352
Moraski, B J 489
Moravcsik, A 69, 198, 220, 223, 240
Morgan, B 389
Morgenthau, H 192, 246
Morin, M 549
Morris, A 634
Morris, R B 725
Morrisroe, D 514
Morriss, A P 25
Morriss, J P 563
Morrow, J D 201
Morton, F L 137
Moussaoui, Zacarias 542

Moustafa, T 72, 74, 86, 291, 649
Mueller, D C 291
Muir, William 742
Müller, J-W 172, 173
Munger, F 531, 532, 683, 686, 690, 746 n6
Murphy, Frank 282
Murphy, W F 6, 10, 114, 293, 474, 496, 663–4, 666–7, 740, 741
Murrah, L 218
Musharraf, Pervez 120
Myers, M A 619

Nader, L 277, 382 n2, 523–4, 527, 684
Nader, Ralph 523
Nagel, S 480
Nagin, D S 713, 714
Nagler, J 328, 335
Nardulli, P F 28, 618, 687
Neier, A 237, 259
Nelson, B J 562, 563, 565
Nelson, D L 285
Nelson, R L 548
Nemacheck, C 473
Neuffer, E 241
Newberg, P 86
Newman, Frank 258
Ní Aoláin, F 165, 170, 175
Nicolaidis, K 149
Nielsen, L B 527 n2, 530, 531, 669
Nielson, D L 293
Nikitinsky, I 494
Nino, C S 238
Nixon, Richard M 255, 258
Nolan-Haley, J M 385 n4
Noll, R 579
Nonet, P 745
North, D 66, 108, 247, 291, 649
Norton, A 290
Nourse, V F 367, 373
Novak, W J 726, 729
Novkov, J 54, 313, 391 n5, 630, 631, 634, 641
Nyikos, S 218

O'Barr, W M 683
Obrador, Andres Manuel Lopez 127
O'Brien, D M 247, 478, 492
O'Brien, K J 536
O'Brien, R M 616
O'Connor, Sandra Day 639
Oderberg, D 400
O'Donnell, G 64, 65, 76, 236
Oeter, S 147, 150, 154
O'Gorman, H 542
O'Halloran, S 352, 577, 579

O'Leary, B 333, 334
Olsen, J 47, 90
Olson, M 108 n10, 568, 579
Olson, S M 385, 533, 536, 747
Omar, I 178
O'Neill, J 284
Oppenheimer, B I 306
Ordeshook, P C 291, 362, 761
Orfield, M W, Jr 607
Örkény, A 66
Orren, K 50–1, 54, 391 n5, 647, 724
Overby, M 473
Overton, S 330

Pacelle, R L, Jr 490
Pahlavi, M R 238
Panizza, U 559
Paris, M 604, 748
Parker, K M 723, 724, 729
Parsons, T 716
Pascoe, P 634
Pasquino, P 165, 167, 174
Paternoster, R 714, 718
Paulsen, M 178, 179
Pavlich, G 385
Peckham, R W 429, 430
Pederzoli, P 559, 570
Pedriana, N 534, 606, 609
Peerenboom, R P 64, 74, 76
Pelisse, J 669
Peltason, Jack 6, 504, 505, 740
Peltzman, S 342, 579
Pennington, K 282
Peppers, T 28, 511, 543, 546
Perea, J 461
Peretti, T J 559, 562, 563, 569, 644
Perez-Linan, A 517
Perry, B 473
Perry, H W 491, 492, 493, 508, 512
Persily, N 323, 329
Persson, T 293
Pescatore, Pierre 213
Petersilia, J 620
Peterson, R D 620
Pham, P 239
Pickerill, J M 53, 391 n5, 647
Pierce, J C 666
Pierce, R, Jr 350
Pierson, P 49, 50, 52, 54, 321, 672
Pildes, R H 120, 146, 175, 176, 322, 323, 325,
    326, 327, 329, 331, 334, 335, 347
Pinello, D R 28, 563, 565, 604
Pinheiro, S 76
Pinochet, Augusto 71, 258, 259

Pion-Berlin, D 236 n3
Pitts, J 247
Piven, F 745
Plato 412
Platt, A M 381
Pollack, M 215, 216
Pollak, L H 455
Polletta, F 533
Poole, K T 323
Popkin, M 66, 73
Posner, D 334
Posner, E A 188, 193, 194, 220 n6, 286, 346, 583
Posner, Michael 259
Posner, R 34, 107, 147, 178, 179, 355, 361, 432, 505,
    510, 550, 564, 567, 568, 579, 580, 648, 699, 705
Pospisil, L 383
Post, R 289, 315
Potter, P B 74, 76
Pound, Roscoe 8, 378, 725, 726
Powe, L A, Jr 646, 652
Powell, L F 432
Powell, M J 546
Powell, Thomas Reed 5, 314, 756
Powell, W W 47 n2
Prakash, S 285
Pressman, J L 600
Preston, E 530
Preuss, U 173
Priest, G L 699, 700
Pring, F W 534
Pritchard, A C 107 n9
Pritchett, C Herman 6, 35, 496, 752–4, 756
Prodi, Romano 127
Provine, D M 10, 41, 491
Pruitt, D G 718
Puritz, P 382

Qian, Y 84

Rabin, R 341
Rabkin, J 232 n1, 240
Radin, M 170, 362
Rakove, J 82, 83
Ramirez, F O 198
Ramraj, V 179, 180
Ramseyer, J M 30, 39, 68, 90, 109, 137,
    149, 568, 649
Randazzo, K A 66, 94
Randolph, E 152
Rappaport, M B 285, 286
Rasinski, K 667, 719
Rasmusen, E B 30, 39
Rasmussen, H 214
Ratner, S R 231

Raustiala, K 202, 220
Rawlings, R 217, 272
Rawls, J 291
Raz, J 429
Reagan, Ronald 259, 283, 343, 475, 476, 477, 489
Reddick, M 506, 511
Reed, D S 288, 294, 748
Rees, J 684, 691
Regan, D 156
Rehnquist, W 148
Reinhardt, E 220
Reiss, A J 713
Relyea, H 169
Resnick, J 276, 547, 562
Reus-Smit, C 196–7
Revesz, R L 27
Reynolds, A 333–4
Rhode, D L 439, 545, 549
Richards, M J 22–3, 304, 309–10, 498, 657, 704
Richardt, N 218
Rieff, D 232 n1
Riker, W H 146, 300, 362, 491, 761–2
Rimer, S 543
Ringquist, E J 606
Ríos-Figueroa, J 70
Risse-Kappen, T 218
Rittberger, B 294
Roach, K 179, 180
Roberts, J G 542
Roberts, J M 490, 546
Robinson, P H 714, 715, 717
Robinson, R L 462
Roche, John 6
Rodriguez, D 341, 342, 348, 351, 352, 354, 364, 365, 368–9
Rodríguez-Garavito, C A 536
Rogat, Yosal 739
Rogers, J 109 n12, 111, 114, 657
Rogin, M 633 n1
Rohde, D W 324, 549
Rokeach, M 760
Rokumoto, K 544
Romano, C 122, 219
Romero, D W 504 n3
Ron, J 203
Roo Moo-hyun 126
Roosevelt, F D 72, 282, 475
Root, Elihu 249, 250, 252
Root, H 66
Rose, D D 666
Rose-Ackerman, S 578, 581, 585, 588, 590
Rosenbaum, T 544
Rosenberg, E 250

Rosenberg, G N 30, 40, 94, 106 n8, 138, 497, 525, 532, 596, 599, 600, 603, 604 n3, 652, 743
Rosenberg, T 236 n4, 239
Rosenblum, Victor 740, 746
Rosenthal, D E 687
Rosenthal, H 323
Ross, H L 714
Rossi, J 342
Rossiter, C 167, 170, 180
Rotberg, R 236
Roxas, Manuel 250
Rubin, E 135, 346, 347, 462, 596, 601, 606, 742–3, 748
Rubin, P H 699, 700, 708
Rubin, R 542
Rubinfeld, D L 546, 708
Ruddick, S 444
Ruggie, J G 196
Ruhl, J B 347
Russell, P H 247, 558, 567, 571

Sabatier, P A 598, 599, 600, 601, 602, 603, 606, 608
Sacco, R 269
Sacks, A M 360, 370, 371, 454
Sacriste, G 213
Sager, L G 308, 705, 706, 707
Saguy, A C 606
Sala-i-Martin, X 566
Saltman, R G 330
Salzberger, E M 136, 560, 649, 650
Salzman, J 347
Samuels, D J 293
Sander, R H 547
Sanders, J 685
Sanders Romero, F 504 n3
Sandholtz, W 197
Sands, P 246, 247
Santoro, M A 232
Santos, B de 384, 536
Sarat, A 11, 72, 260, 391, 524, 527, 528, 529, 530, 534, 535, 542, 669, 683, 684, 685, 687–8, 746, 747
Sartori, G 281
Sarver, T A 517
Savchak, E 478
Scales, A M 438
Scalia, Antonin 24, 314, 360, 367, 432, 433, 654, 758
Scamardo, Robert F 543
Schaar, John 739 n1
Schacter, J S 367, 373
Schanzenbach, M M 507, 511, 517
Scharpf, F 145
Schattschneider, E 745

Schauer, F 128, 289, 304, 307–8, 309, 428, 433, 434

Scheingold, S 72, 260, 523, 526, 532–3, 534, 535, 542, 595, 599–600, 601, 603, 608, 618, 687–8, 746, 747

Scheppele, K L 66, 169, 175, 177, 179, 446, 560, 568, 647

Scherer, N 476, 477

Scheuerman, W E 165, 169

Schiller, R 342

Schimmelfennig, F 201, 294

Schkade, D 27

Schlegel, J H 681, 723

Schlesinger, R B 267, 268, 271, 276

Schmidhauser, John 740, 741

Schmidt, H 219

Schmidt, P 688

Schmitt, C 165, 171, 172

Schmitter, P C 236

Schmitz, H P 204

Schneider, C E 382

Schneider, E 441 n2, 447, 533

Schneyer, T J 546

Schoenbrod, D 346

Schönlau, J 143

Schroeder, C H 577

Schroeder, R 480

Schubert, G A 6, 10, 41, 491, 493, 496, 753, 756–7, 760

Schuck, P H 374, 585, 586

Schudson, M 523

Schultz, U 548

Schulz, H 147, 215

Schwab, G 171

Schwartz, E P 37 n1, 703

Schwartz, H 66, 76, 87, 115, 224

Schwartz, M 541

Schwartz, T 352, 577

Schwarze, J 272

Schweber, H H 292, 313, 725

Scotchmer, S 546

Scott, K 509

Scott, S V 197

Scribner, D L 70, 75

Segal, J A 20, 22, 24, 26–7, 30, 39, 40, 147, 302, 303, 304, 308, 473, 474, 476, 488, 489, 490, 492, 493, 496, 497, 498, 507, 509, 511, 512, 563, 565, 600, 704, 763, 764

Segev, T 241

Segura, G 335

Seidenfeld, M 344, 350

Seidman, M L 286, 471

Seitzer, J 171, 173

Seligson, M A 517

Sellers, J M 528

Selznick, Philip 745

Seron, C 532, 683

Sewell, W H 674

Sexton, J 495

Sforza, M 256

Shaffer, G 256

Shambayati, H 92

Shamir, R 248

Shane, P 344

Shang, W 382

Shapiro, I 719

Shapiro, M 6, 11, 48, 53, 70, 83, 84, 85, 88, 89, 90, 106, 110, 120, 135, 147, 150, 151, 212–13, 260, 272, 341, 343, 349, 350, 389, 390, 513, 524, 583, 588, 589, 597, 652, 653, 682, 684, 692, 757

Shapiro, S 11, 349, 545

Sharif, Nawaz 126

Shavell, S 510, 701

Shaw, G 548

Sheehan, R 506, 511

Sheldon, C 479

Shepsel, K 35

Shepsle, K 47, 321, 352, 362, 363, 580

Sherry, S 460

Shipan, C 29, 352, 489, 577, 579, 580

Shklar, J N 231–2, 234, 241, 746–7

Shuck, P 344

Shugart, M S 293

Shvetsova, L 70, 94, 114

Sibbitt, E C 74, 135, 261, 270, 272, 597

Sieder, R 72, 76, 120, 121

Siegal, R B 630

Siegel, R 289, 315, 455

Sieyès, E-J 171

Sikkink, K 72, 202, 204, 240, 246

Silbey, S 525, 526, 530–1, 664 n1, 668, 669, 670, 671, 672, 673, 683, 686, 690, 746 n6

Silver, A 479

Silverstein, H 526, 636, 746, 747

Silverstein, M 474

Simeon, R 333

Simmonds, N E 417

Simmons, A M 547

Simmons, B 93, 190, 194, 196, 200 n4, 201, 204, 220, 270

Simon, J 689

Simon, W H 541, 543

Simons, M 542

Sinclair, B 473

Sisk, G B 563

Sisk, G C 25

Skinner, Q 282

Skocpol, T 47, 55, 630

Skogan, W G 615, 616, 623
Skolnick, J H 688
Skowronek, S 47, 50–1, 54, 341, 647
Skrentny, J D 46 n1, 535
Slagstad, R 84
Slaughter, A-M 122, 133, 147, 200, 202, 214,
    219–20, 223, 232, 261, 389
Slotnick, E 476, 477
Smart, C 442 n3, 673
Smith, C 84, 473
Smith, D E 443
Smith, David B 543
Smith, H J 715, 718
Smith, L D 275
Smith, R M 48, 51, 626,
    633 n1, 657
Smith, T W 203
Smithey, S 69
Snidal, D 190, 194
Snipes, J B 712
Snowiss, S 82
Snyder, J L 203, 236, 238, 239
Sohn, L 258
Solberg, R S 147
Solimine, M 42, 508, 509, 514
Solinger, R 636, 638
Solum, L B 285
Solyom, L 93, 132
Solzhenitsyn, Alexander 115
Somek, A 176
Somit, A 5, 757
Songer, D R 22, 41 n4, 477, 504 n1, 505, 506, 507,
    509, 510, 511, 512, 517, 600
Spaeth, H J 6, 20, 22, 26–7, 30, 39, 40, 147,
    302, 303, 304, 308, 492, 496, 497, 498,
    563, 565, 704, 755, 756, 760–1, 763, 764
Spann, G 633
Sparks, R 718
Spence, D 577
Spier, K 708
Spill, R 481
Spill Solberg, R 514, 515
Spiller, P T 30, 36, 37, 38, 41 n4, 42, 70, 94, 353,
    563, 708
Spiro, P J 157
Spitzer, M T 37, 38, 42, 353, 703, 708
Spohn, C 622
Spriggs, J F, II 22, 30, 113, 476, 505
Sprinz, D 202
Squire, P 489
Sreenivasan, G 420
St Paul 412
Stanley, A D 728
Stasavage, D 649

Staton, J K 72, 110, 113
Staudt, N C 498
Stein, E 151, 214
Stein, J von 193, 204
Steinberg, J 326
Steinberg, R H 188, 203
Steiner, H 420
Steiner, Z S 234
Steinmetz, G 179
Steinmo, S 47, 48
Stepan, A 142, 236
Stephenson, M 91, 109, 353–4
Sterett, S M 391 n5
Sterling, J 681
Stevens, J P 432
Stevens, R 248
Stewart, P 22, 433
Stewart, R 341, 342–3, 347, 349, 389,
    578, 583, 768
Stidham, R 477
Stier, M 22
Stigler, G 342, 579
Stimson, J 114, 133, 564
Stolleis, M 172, 177
Stone, A 11, 48, 49, 86, 120, 131, 212
Stone Sweet, A 86, 120, 122, 135, 143, 147, 150, 155,
    197, 216, 218, 256, 390, 595, 684
Stookey, J 391
Storing, Herbert 6
Story, J 434
Stover, E 241
Strathern, M 673
Strauss, D A 294
Strauss, P L 374, 586
Streeck, W 52
Strickland, Tom 542
Stroessner, A 238
Strong, T 171
Strossen, N 440
Stryker, R 606, 609
Stucky, T D 617, 623
Subramanian, A 203
Sudnow, D 682
Sunshine, J 715, 717
Sunstein, C R 27, 287, 341, 343, 344, 346, 347,
    578–9, 583, 589, 590, 687
Supina, A E 712
Susskind, L 387
Sussman, N 649
Sutter, D 112
Sutton, F R 605
Svensson-McCarthy, A-L 169, 170
Swartz, M 547
Swisher, Carl 6, 738

Tabellini, G 293
Taft, William Howard 249–50
Talarico, S 619
Tallberg, J 215, 216, 218, 219
Tamanaha, B Z 64
Tanenhaus, J 5, 6, 10, 491, 493, 663–4, 666–7, 757
Tapp, J 716
Tarnopolsky, W S 156
Tarr, G A 504, 505, 571
Tate, C N 120, 131, 136, 137, 595
Tate, K 473
Taylor, A J P 237
Taylor, Charles G 128
Taylor, M M 67
Taylor, R C R 47, 48
Taylor, T 233
Teles, S M 284
Teubner, G 121, 135
Thaksin Shinawatra 126
Thaler, R H 578–9
Thayer, J B 143
Theiss-Morse, E 719
Thelen, K 47, 48, 52
Thibaut, J 718
Thomas, Clarence 24, 30, 469, 473–4
Thomas, G M 47 n2, 287
Thompson, D 236
Thucydides 229, 230
Tiberi, T 508 n5
Till, Emmett 542
Tiller, E H 27, 38, 353, 355, 476, 507, 511, 517, 563, 577
Tocqueville, A de 306–7
Todd, H L 382 n2, 684
Tokaji, D P 331, 332
Tolley, H 201, 257
Toma, E F 562
Tomasic, R 386
Tomlins, C L 723, 727, 728
Tommasi, M 30, 70, 94
Tonry, M 623
Toope, S J 190
Treanor, W M 82
Trevor-Roper, H R 234
Tribe, L H 153, 286
Trochev, A 69
Trubek, D M 389, 685
Trubek, L G 389
True, J L 608
Truman, Harry S 254–5, 313, 475
Tsebelis, G 146, 215
Tsutsui, K 193, 202
Tucker, Russell 543
Tullock, G 291, 706

Turem, Z U 388
Tushnet, M 11, 134, 143, 179, 286, 288, 456, 727
Tutu, D M 236
Twining, W 277, 741 n3
Tyler, P E 232
Tyler, T R 303 n1, 667, 712, 713, 714, 715, 716, 717, 718, 719

Uchida, C D 617
Udell, D S 549
Uggen, C 605, 624
Ullmann-Margalit, E 405
Ulmer, J T 622
Ulmer, Sidney 6, 491, 493, 756
Ungar, M 76, 224, 728
Ura, J D 108
Uribe, Alvaro 126

Valdes, F 461, 462
Vallinder, T 120, 136, 137, 595
Valverde, M 729
Vanberg, G 31, 84, 86, 89, 94, 102 n5, 105 n7, 110, 113, 114, 133, 498, 499
Vance, Cyrus 251
Vanden Burgh, R G 38 n2
Vauchez, A 213, 729
Vermeule, A 179, 286, 346, 365, 367, 374
Victor, D G 199
Vines, K 479
Vining, A 578
Vinjamuri, L 203, 236, 238, 239
Vogel, S 135
Voigt, Stefan 100 n3, 136, 291, 650
Volcansek, M 11, 85
Vose, Clement 740, 746

Wahlbeck, P J 30, 476, 506
Waldron, J 288, 290, 362, 422
Walker, C 179
Walker, L 447, 718
Walker, S 607
Walker, T 473, 505
Wallace, J E 548
Wallach, L 256
Wallenstein, P 634
Walsh, D J 513, 515, 516
Waltz, K 192
Waluchow, W 422, 423
Ward, A 546
Ward, D S 391
Warren, C 309
Wasby, S L 504, 603 n2
Wasserstrom, R 543

Watkins, F M 172
Watkins, S 547
Watson, A 269
Watson, R 480
Wattenberg, M P 323
Wawro, G 28
Weber, Max 121, 146, 381, 716
Wechsler, H 143, 144, 146, 283, 439, 454
Wedgwood, R 232 n1
Wei, S-J 203
Weidemaier, W M 383
Weiler, J H H 122, 147, 211, 214, 217
Weimer, D 578
Weingast, B 35, 37, 38, 47, 65, 66, 70, 75, 84, 108,
    111–12, 214–15, 291, 292, 342, 348, 351, 353, 354,
    363, 364, 365, 366, 372, 580, 649, 759
Weinstein, H M 241, 549
Weiss, E B 201
Welke, B Y 727, 728
Wells, Richard 741
Wenar, L 420, 421
Wendt, A 194
Wenzel, J P 31
West, R 440, 441–2
West, V 622, 624
West, W F 585, 587
Westerland, C 30
Westin, Alan 740, 741
Wheare, K C 147
Wheeler, H 282
White, Byron 431, 433, 726
Whitman, J Q 731
Whittington, K E 30, 53, 92, 102, 103, 105 n7,
    106 n8, 108, 109, 109 n12, 137, 144, 151, 284–5,
    288–9, 293, 301, 314, 316, 390, 496, 646, 657, 724
Widner, J A 72, 292
Wiegand, W 261, 272
Wigdor, D 725
Wildavsky, A 600
Wilgoren, J 549
Wilhelm II, Kaiser 233, 234
Williams, E D 547
Williams, J 440, 441 n2, 442, 727
Williams, P 457, 459, 533
Williams, R 384
Williams, W 440
Williamson, J 247

Williamson, O E 65
Willrich, M J 725
Wilson, J 3, 378, 579, 617
Wilson, S H 728
Wilson, Woodrow 250
Winston, K 385
Wishik, H R 438
Wissler, R L 718
Witmer, R 513
Witt, J F 729
Wolbrecht, C 111
Wolfe, C 405
Wolfers, J 715
Wollschlager, C 528, 547
Wood, B D 579, 604, 608
Woods, N 335
Wormuth, F D 282
Wotipka, C M 198
Wright, J R 30, 303, 304, 473, 477, 490, 491,
    492, 508, 509, 512

Yackee, J W 586
Yackee, S W 586
Yafeh, Y 649
Yalof, D 474, 488, 490
Yates, J 564
Yeltsin, Boris 39, 115, 126
Yngvesson, B 382 n2, 390, 527 n2, 530, 669,
    683, 686, 688, 689
Yoo, J 166, 178, 179, 220 n6
Yoon, A 146, 489
Young, O 200
Yutaka, S 232

Zakaria, F 64
Zaller, J 666
Zasloff, J M 188
Zedillo, Ernest 69
Zeisberg, M A 287
Zelditch, M, Jr 716
Zemans, F K 523, 527, 528, 529, 530, 686
Zeppos, N S 373
Zimbardo, P 714
Zimmermann, R 271
Zorn, C J W 30, 509 n6
Zuk, G 476, 645
Zweigert, K 267

SUBJECT INDEX

All referenced legal cases are indexed under the "cases" heading.

abdications, and emergency powers 176
abortion regulation, and ideological
    transformation 635–8
accountability:
  and agencies:
    delegation 346
    discretion 347
  and electoral accountability 744, 745
  and institutional provisions 101
  and judicial elections 479–80, 570–1
  and judicial independence 100–1, 115, 566
  and legal accountability 744, 745–6
    politicization of 746–7
  and negotiated rulemaking 387–8
  and rule of law 65
accounting firms 547
adjudication:
  and economic analysis of 698, 708
  and integrated model of 699–700
    criticisms of 700
  and litigant selection 699–700
  and modeling collegiality 705–8
    consistency and coherence 706
    reasons for collegiality 705–6
    voting on collegial courts 706–8
  and modeling doctrine 703–5
  and models of 700–1, 702–3
  and team models of 700–2
Administrative Conference of the United States
    (ACUS) 387
administrative law 340
  and agency deference 344
  and agency discretion 343
    external rules 343
    internal rules 343
  and delegation 346
  and democracy–technocracy balance 580–4
  and deregulation 344
  and discretion 347–8
  and expansion of regulatory agencies 342
  and fairness 348–9

and governance/legality trade-off 341–5
and impact of Reagan administration 344–5
and judicial review 343, 355, 589, 590
  curtailing of 344
  reasonableness review 349–51
and managerial ideology 341
and objective of 340–1, 356
as omnibus category 353
and political foundations of 351–5
  political goals 352–3
and positive political theory (PPT) 342, 345,
  353–5
and reasonableness 349–51
and regulatory process 579, 584–7
  outside United States 588–9
  public participation 585–7
  rulemaking 585–7
and response to expansion of regulatory
  agencies 342–3
and skepticism over agency performance 342
Administrative Procedure Act (1946, USA) 341,
  348, 349, 381, 387, 584–5
adversarial legalism 748
advocacy networks:
  and globalization of the law 245–6
  and social reform 601
affirmative action 548
  and ideology 635, 638–40
  and United States Supreme Court decision-
    making 760–1
Afghanistan 74
Age Discrimination in Employment Act
    (USA) 647
agencies:
  and administrative law:
    delegation 346
    discretion 347–8
    fairness 348–9
    reasonableness 349–51
  and administrative state 341
  and capture of 342

and economic case for regulation 578–9
and expansion of 342
and governance/legality trade-off 341–5
and informalism 381, 386–8
    negotiated rulemaking 386–7
and judicial review 343, 344, 355, 576, 577,
    583, 589, 590
    reasonableness review 349–51
and managerial ideology 341
and political conception of administrative
    regulation 342–3
    political goals 352–3
and power of 340, 346
and regulatory process 584–7
    outside United States 588–9
    public participation 585–7
    rulemaking 585–7
and "retail justice" 348
and skepticism over performance 342
and statutory interpretation 374–5
and strategic judicial decision-making 38
al Qaeda 544
Albania 66
alternative dispute resolution (ADR) 385–6
and informalism 384
American Bar Association 545
and influence on courts 546
and judicial recruitment 471
    lower federal courts 477–8
    United States Supreme Court 474
American Civil Liberties Union (ACLU) 237
American Political Development movement 724
American Political Science Association
    (APSA) 5, 757, 769
American Political Science Review 5
Americanization Movement 378
Americans with Disabilities Act (1991, USA)
    531, 647, 690
Americas Watch 259
amnesty, and democratization 235–9
Amnesty International 258
Andean Court of Justice 220, 223
appropriations process, and statutory
    interpretation 368–9
arbitration, international commercial 252–4
Argentina:
and judicial independence 39, 68, 70, 72,
    73, 567
and judicialization of politics 125–6
and rule of law 63
ASEAN 122
attitudinal model of judicial decision-
    making 24–6, 39–41, 756–7, 760
and judicial independence 563–4, 565

and lower courts 27–8
and United States Supreme Court 26–7,
    302–4, 496–7, 760–1
attorneys' fees, and convergence 268
Australia:
and electoral districts 330
and judicial review 84
Austria:
and emergency powers 176
and judicial review 85
autarchy 550
authoritarianism, and judicial review 92

battered woman syndrome 447–8
behavioralism 7, 752
and significance of constitutions 292–3
Belarus 66
Belgium, and federalism 142
bilateral treaties, and growth of 188–9
bills of rights:
and evolution of implications of 426
and legal immunities 417
and legal rights 425–6
and symbolic value 425, 426
Bosnia 241
Brady Bill (USA) 647
Bretton Woods institutions 255
British School of international relations 190, 192,
    196
Bulgaria 66
and judicial independence 69
business organizations, and establishment of rule
    of law 73
business regulation, and judicial decision-
    making 312–13
    see also regulation

campaign finance 324
Canada:
and Charter of Rights and Freedoms
    (1982) 125, 150
and electoral districts 330
and emergency powers 174
    delegation 175
and federalism 146
and judicial empowerment 653
and judicial independence 69
and judicial review 84, 131
and judicialization of politics 124–5, 128
and subsidiarity 154
Canadian Law and Society Association 684
Canadian Supreme Court 150
and integration 156
and subsidiarity 157

cases (USA, unless otherwise stated):
   A v Secretary of State (2005, England) 177
   Adkins v Children's Hospital (1923) 632
   Aetna Life Insurance v Lavoie (1986) 559
   American Communication Ass'n v Douds
      (1950) 313
   American Trucking Assns v Smith (1990) 758
   Argersinger v Hamlin (1972) 549
   Ash Grove Cement v FTC (1978) 343
   Atkins v Virginia (2002) 516
   Austerity Package Decisions (1995, Hungary) 125
   AZAPO (1996, South Africa) 127
   Baehr v Lewin (1993) 670
   Baehr v Miike (1996) 670
   Barber v Guardian Gra (1990, ECJ) 211, 215
   Board of Trustees of University of Alabama v
      Garrett (2001) 315
   Bonham's Case 82
   Bradley v Fisher (1872) 561
   Brown v Board of Education (1954) 283, 310,
      453–5, 504, 523, 603–4, 607, 652, 711, 753
   Brown v Legal Foundation of Washington
      (2003) 549
   Bunting v Oregon (1917) 631
   Burns v State (1872) 633–4
   Bush v Gore (2000) 753, 764
   California Democratic Party v Jones (2000) 324
   Cassis de Dijon (1979, ECJ) 211
   Chechnya Case (1995, Russia) 125
   Chevron v Natural Resource Defense Council
      (1984) 344, 374
   Chicago Police Department v Mosley (1972) 310
   Chisom v Roemer (1991) 367
   City of Boerne v Flores (1997) 315
   Civil Rights Cases (1883) 311
   Coker v Georgia (1977) 652
   Commission v Germany (1987, ECJ) 211
   Cooperative Committee on Japanese-Canadians
      v Attorney General of Canada (1946,
      Canada) 176
   Corralito Case (2004, Argentina) 126
   Costa v ENEL (1964, ECJ) 210–11, 213
   Crowell v Benson (1932) 341
   Crown Zellerbach (1988, Canada) 157
   Davis v Bandemer (1986) 327
   Dred Scott v Sandford (1856) 311, 753
   Edenfield v Fane (1993) 547
   Eisenstadt v Baird (1972) 22
   Ellison v Brady (1991) 446
   Ethyl Corp v EPA (1978) 349
   Fiji v Prasad (2001, Fiji) 126
   Florida Bar v Went for It, Inc (1993) 545
   Germany v Parliament and Council (2000,
      ECJ) 158–9

   Gideon v Wainwright (1963) 549, 652
   Goldberg v Kelly (1970) 348
   Gonzales v Oregon (2006) 150
   Gonzales v Raich (2005) 159
   Grant v Gould (1792, Great Britain) 169
   Gratz v Bollinger (2003) 639
   Grayned v City of Rockford (1972) 23, 310
   Greater Boston Television Corp v FCC
      (1971) 343
   Griswold v Connecticut (1965) 22, 433, 652
   Grutter v Bollinger (2003) 548, 639
   Hale v Committee on Character and Fitness
      (2000) 545
   Hamdan v Rumsfeld (2006) 125, 177, 307
   Hans v Louisiana (1890) 431
   Harper v Virginia Board of Elections (1966) 652
   Harris v McRae (1980) 636
   HBO v FCC (1977) 343
   Heydon's Case (1584, England) 369
   Holden v Hardy (1898) 312
   Holy Trinity Church v United States (1892) 362
   Immigration and Naturalization Service v
      Chadha (1983) 431, 433
   Johnson v California (2005) 310
   Keystone Bituminous Coal Association v
      DeBenedictis (1987) 433
   Korematsu v United States (1944) 176, 310, 453
   Lawrence v Texas (2003) 156, 516, 546
   Lee v Weisman (1992) 498
   Legal Services Corporation v Velazquez
      (2001) 549
   Lemon v Kurtzman (1971) 311
   Lochner v New York (1905) 312, 429–30, 630–1
   Maastricht Case (1993, Germany) 128
   Maher v Roe (1977) 636
   Marbury v Madison (1803) 82, 83, 114, 753
   Martin v Hunter's Lessee (1986) 434
   McCulloch v Maryland (1819) 309, 646, 753
   Meritor v Vinson (1986) 446
   Miller v California (1973) 506
   Minor v Happersett (1874) 630
   Miranda v Arizona (1966) 506
   Moore v City of East Cleveland (1977) 652
   Muller v Oregon (1908) 441, 630, 631
   NLRB v Friedman-Harry Marks Clothing Co
      (1937) 312
   NLRB v Jones & Laughlin Steel Corp (1937) 312
   Ohralik v Ohio State Bar Association
      (1978) 545
   Oncale v Sundowner Offshore Services
      (1998) 447
   Operation Dismantle (1985, Canada) 125
   Orr v Orr (1979) 439
   Osborn v Bank of the United States (1824) 758

Pace v Alabama (1883) 634
Panhandle Oil Co v Knox (1928) 434
Patriation Reference (1981, Canada) 150
Pierce v Society of Sisters (1925) 652
Planned Parenthood v Casey (1992) 637
Plaut v Spend Farm Inc (1995) 565
Plessy v Ferguson (1896) 310, 633, 635, 753
Principality of Monaco v Mississippi
    (1934) 431
Printz v United States (1997) 156
Quebec Secession Reference (1998) 128
Rasul v Bush (2004) 177
In re Gault (1967) 382
Republican Party of Minnesota v White
    (2002) 559
Roe v Wade (1973) 22, 283, 635–6, 638, 753
Roper v Simmons (2005) 546
Rowland v Mad River (1985) 665
Salazar v Davidson (2003) 327
Secession Reference (1998, Canada) 150
Slaughterhouse Cases (1873) 156, 311, 633
Southern Christian Leadership Conference v
    Louisiana Supreme Court (2001) 549
Southern Pacific Co v Jensen (1917) 316
SPUC Grog (1991, ECJ) 211
State v Kelly (1984) 447–8
State v Rusk (1981) 446
Strauder v West Virginia (1880) 311, 634
Swedish Match (2004, ECJ) 159
Tanja Kreil v Bundesrepublik (2000, ECJ) 211
TVA v Hill (1978) 368
United States v Gonzalez-Lopez (2006) 542
United States v Locke (1985) 432
United States v Lopez (1995) 158, 159
United States v Sawyer (2006) 503
United States v Shaughnessy (1955) 22
United States v Will (1980) 558
Van Gend en Loos (1962, ECJ) 210, 213
Vermont Yankee v NRDC (1978) 348
Virginia R Co v System Federation (1937) 312
Wallace v Jaffree (1984) 498
Washington, Virginia & Maryland Coach
    Co v NLRB (1937) 312
Washington v Davis (1976) 458
Washington v Glucksberg (1997) 156
West Coast Hotel v Parrish (1937) 632
West Virginia State Board of Education v
    Barnette (1943) 560
cause layering 534–5, 687
Centre for Individual Rights (CIR) 638–9
Central and Eastern Europe:
  and judicial independence 69
  and rule of law, threats to 66
Central Intelligence Agency (CIA) 257, 258

Chile 258–9
  and informalism 388
  and judicial independence 70–1, 75–6
China:
  and judicial review 83
  and rule of law 64, 76
    economic liberalization 74
    threats to 66
choice, and natural law 399–400, 401, 402
civil law systems:
  and colonialism 248
  and international law 199
  see also convergence
civil liberties, and judicialization of politics 121
Civil Litigation Research Project (CLRP) 390–1,
    528, 685
Civil Rights Act (1964, USA) 646
civil rights movement, and use of courts 598
civil society, and establishment of rule of
    law 71–3
class, and legal consciousness 530
class action litigation 535
class legislation 630
Cleveland Bar Association 545
collaboration problems, and international
    law 194
collegial courts, and adjudication models:
  and consistency and coherence 706
  and reasons for collegiality 705–6
  and voting on collegial courts 706–8
Colombia 67
colonialism:
  and globalization of the law 247–8
  and United States 249–50
    dollar diplomacy 250
Columbia University, and study of law and
    politics 4–5
commitments:
  and conceptual constitutionalism 291
  and international law 197–8
    credibility 195
  see also credible commitments
common good, and judicial independence 568–9
common law systems:
  and colonialism 248
  and doctrine 703
  and evolutionary models of 700
  and international law 199
  and litigant choices 699
  and martial law 168–9
  and prerogative power 168–9
  see also convergence
communication theory, and statutory
    interpretation 364

community empowerment, and neighborhood
    justice centers 386
comparative judicial politics 12
comparative law 10–11
    see also convergence
compliance:
    and international law 200–2
        credible commitments 195
    and law and society 690–1
    and motivation to obey law 712–13, 715–16
        deterrence model 713–14
        internalization of moral values 717
        legitimacy 716–17
        problems with deterrence model 714–15
        procedural fairness 718–19
        value-based perspectives 718
Congressional Dominance Hypothesis 37
Congressional studies 771
connection thesis 441
consociationalism 332–3
constitutional courts:
    and measuring performance of 93–5
    and strategic decision-making 39
    see also judicial review
constitutional law, and American politics 301–2
    and constitutional decision-making 314–15
        future research 316–17
    and creating agreement 306–9
        political procedures 305–6
        public policy 306–9
    and election campaigns 305–6
    and structuring disagreement 310–13
        business regulation 312–13
        jurisprudential regimes 310–11
        state neutrality 312
    and United States Supreme Court decision-
        making 302–5
        public policy-making 307–9
    and value voting 314
constitutional politics 9
constitutional review, *see* judicial review
constitutionalism:
    and conceptual constitutionalism 289–92
        constitutions as contracts 290–1
        constitutions as coordination device 291
        constitutions as credible commitment 291
        constitutions as precommitment
            devices 290
        constitutions as promises 289–90
        entrenchment of rules and
            commitments 291–2
        functions of constitutions 289, 292
    and constitutional arrangements 281
    and constraint of government power 281

and empirical constitutionalism 292–4
    constitutional change 294
    constitutional design 293
    significance of constitutions 292–3
    working of constitutions 293
and judicial independence 567–8
and liberalism 281
and normative constitutionalism 282–9
    conservative legal movement 283–4
    constitutional change 285–6
    democratic institutions 287
    dualist democracy 285
    judicial review 282–3
    judicial supremacy assumption 289
    moral inadequacy 286
    originalist theories 284–5
    post-cold war theorizing 284
    priority of democracy 288–9
    priority of substantive values 287–8
    proceduralist approach 286
    protection from self-interested
        politicians 286–7
    reconciling with democracy 284–9
    theoretical developments 284
and scholarship on 294–5
    revival of 282
constitutions, and types of 281
constructivism, and international law 194, 196–7
    and compliance with 201–2
contract rights, and ideology 629–32
contractarianism, and conceptual
        constitutionalism 290–1
convergence 267–8
    and analytical tools 277
    and attorneys' fees 268
    and binding nature of court decisions 269
    and complexity of 269
    and contradiction in 272–3
    and cultural/political context 271–2, 277
    and current debates 271–3
    and definition of 268
    and deterministic logic of 269
    and divisions over idea 271
    as dynamic process 272
    and ideological dimensions 270–1, 277
    and imperialism 278
    and judicial review 269–70
    and language 277–8
    and legal procedure 275–6
    and policy diffusion 270
    and power dynamics 270, 277
    and role of legal doctrine 274
    and sources of law 273–4
    and temporal aspects of 268–9

and trust law 274–5
and Western rule of law notion 277
cooperation problems, and international law 194
coordination, and conceptual
    constitutionalism 291
corporate law:
  and decision-making 688
  and expansion of 549
  and structure of private practice 548
Council on Foreign Relations (CFR) 250–1
counter-mobilization 534
credible commitments:
  and conceptual constitutionalism 291
  and international law 195
  and judicial independence 107–8, 569, 648–9
criminal justice system 614
  and criminal sentencing:
    alternatives to prison 619–20
    defendant characteristics 618
    determinants of severity of 618–21
    impact of judicial selection processes 619
    judge characteristics 618–19
    law and society 687
    screening processes 620
    sentence predictability 622–3
    sentencing guidelines 621–2
    statistical issues 621
  and policing 615–18
    decentralized nature of 615
    distribution of police services 616
    impact of politics 615, 617
    impact on politics 617–18
    local political culture 617
    race 615–16
    threat hypothesis 615–16
  and prisons 622–4
    deterrent effect 624
    expenditure on 623
    felon disenfranchisement 624
    impact on politics 624
    incarceration rate growth 622, 714
    political effects 623
    social disciplinary role 623–4
    threat hypothesis 623–4
crisis, see emergency powers
critical juncture:
  and exogenous shocks 50–1
  and path dependency 49–50
Critical Legal History (CLH) 726
Critical Legal Studies (CLS) 439
  and historical approach 723
  and law and society 723
  and legal history 730
  and nature of law 456, 723

and race 456–7
Critical Race Theory (CRT) 452, 455–6
  and analytical tools 459
  and emergence of 457–8
  and focus of 459–60
  and strategies of 459
  and successful establishment of 458–9
Croatia 241
Cuba, and informalism 388
cultural norms, and legal consciousness 530
custom, and law 724

de-centering, and law and courts subfield 738
  and definition of 740
  and legal mobilization 740, 743–4
  and nature of the center 738–40
  and new institutionalism 740
    examples of 742–3
    precursors of 741–2
  and opportunities presented by 749
Declaration of Sentiments and Resolutions 437
decolonization, and judicial review 85
deference, and emergency powers 176–7
delegation, and administrative law 346
democracy:
  and electoral accountability 744, 745
  and legal accountability 744, 745–6
    politicization of 746–7
  and legal structure of 321–2
    addressing group differences 332–5
    bipartisan gerrymandering 328–9
    consociationalism 332–3
    design of electoral districts 329–30
    election administration 330–2
    gerrymandering 325
    group identity 334
    integrationists 333
    partisan gerrymandering 325–7
    political parties 322–5
    power-sharing 334–5
  and legality 744, 747–8
  and normative constitutionalism:
    constitutional change 285–6
    democratic institutions 287
    dualist democracy 285
    judicial supremacy assumption 289
    moral inadequacy 286
    originalist theories 284–5
    priority of democracy 288–9
    priority of substantive values 287–8
    proceduralist approach 286
    protection from self-interested
      politicians 286–7
    reconciling with democracy 284–9

democratization:
  and amnesty 235–9
  and comparative judicial politics 12
  and focus on elections 63–4
  and horizontal accountability 65
  and human rights regimes 69
  and judicial review, establishment of 91–2
    hegemonic preservation 91
    political insurance 90–1
  and judicialization of politics 134–5
  and proliferation of new democracies 321–2
  and rule of law, establishment of 63
    civil society 71–3
    consolidation of ruling elite's power 69–70
    domestic economic factors 76
    inequality 76
    informal influences on 67
    international community 73–4
    party competition 68–9, 70
    separation of powers framework 67–71,
      74–5
    threats to 66–7
  and strategic defection 86–7
  and third wave of 87
deregulation, and administrative law 344
deterrence, and psychology of human
      motivation 713–14
  and problems with model 714–15
developmental states 248
devolution, and federalism 142
dictatorship:
  and ancient Rome 167
  and German state of exception 171
diffusion, and policy convergence 270
disabled, and legal mobilization 531
discretion:
  and administrative law 347–8
  and judicial decision-making 758
dispute resolution:
  and alternative dispute resolution (ADR) 384,
      385–6
  and international commercial
      arbitration 252–4
  and team models of adjudication 701
disputing:
  and changes in law 686
  and dispute pyramid 527–8, 685
  and law and society 685–6
  see also legal mobilization; litigation
diversion programs, and lower courts 380
doctrine, and adjudication models 703–5
dollar diplomacy 250
domestic violence 447–8
dualist democracy 285

economic analysis of law, and adjudication 698,
      708
  and integrated model of 699–700
    criticisms of 700
  and litigant selection 699–700
  and modeling collegiality 705–8
    consistency and coherence 706
    reasons for collegiality 705–6
    voting on collegial courts 706–8
  and modeling doctrine 703–5
  and models of 700–1, 702–3
  and team models of 700–2
economic development:
  and judicial independence 649
  and rule of law 63
Egypt:
  and judicial independence 70, 74, 649
    civil society 72
  and judicialization of politics 128
  and Supreme Constitutional Court 650–1
El Salvador, and judicial independence 66, 73
elections:
  and administration of 330–2
    national legislation 331–2
    partisan control 330, 331
  and democratization 63–4
  and impact of constitutional law 305–6
  and judicialization of politics 126–7
  see also gerrymandering; primary elections
Electoral College 306
electoral districts, see gerrymandering
emergency powers:
  and extra legalist approach to 165–6
  and legalist approach to 165
  and post-9/11 debate over 178–80
  and traditions of 166
    French state of siege tradition 169–70
    German state of defense 172–3
    German state of exception 171–2
    martial law 168–9
    prerogative power 168–9
    Roman legal dictatorship 167
    Roman suspension of law 167
  and use of 173–4
    delegation 174–5
    enabling acts 174–5
    judicial deference 176–7
    suspension 175–6
    targeting of 177–8
emerging democracies, see democratization
enabling acts, and emergency powers 174–5
Endangered Species Act (ESA) (USA) 368
England:
  and development of rule of law 66

and judicial independence 108
Environmental Protection Act (EPA) 606
Environmental Protection Agency (EPA) 585–6
Equal Employment Opportunities
        Commission 606
European Coal and Steel Community 209
European Commission:
    and enforcement of European law 216
    and European Court of Justice 209–10,
        218–19
    and public participation 588
European Convention on Human Rights 426
European Court of Human Rights 75
    and emergency powers 176
    and judicialization of politics 122
    and structure of democracy 322
European Court of Justice (ECJ) 75, 589
    and Barber protocol 215–16
    and comparison with other international
        courts 220–4
    and establishment of authority of 210–12
    and European integration 212
        ECJ as interlocutor 217–19
        ECJ as states' agent 214–16
        ECJ's leading role 212–14
        invocation of European law by substate
            actors 217–18
        political influences of decisions 219
        referring cases to ECJ 218–19
    and features of:
        compulsory jurisdiction 209
        European Commission references to
            209–10, 218–19
        influence of 219
        preliminary ruling mechanism 209,
            210–11
    and federalism:
        centralizing activity 150–1
        integration 156
    and foundation of 209
    and imposition of EU law 652–3
    and judicialization of politics 122
    and political autonomy of 223–4
    and strategic decision-making 39
    and subsidiarity 158–9
European Union 389
    and federalism 142
        role of judiciary 145, 147
    and subsidiarity 153
Evarts Act (1891, USA) 654
exception, state of, and emergency powers 171–2,
        173
exogenous shocks, and historical
        institutionalism 50–1

fairness:
    and administrative law 348–9
    and judicial independence 559
    and motivation to obey law 718–19
Family and Medical Leave Act (USA) 686
family law, and feminist jurisprudence 444–5
federal courts:
    and imposition of national norms 652
    and judicial decision-making 763, 764
    and recruitment to 475–8
        American Bar Association 477–8
        confirmation process 477
        diversity 476
        ideology 476–7
        interest groups 477
        party affiliation 475–6
        presidential agendas 475
federalism:
    as "constitutional" bargain 143
    and distinctive feature of 143
    and flexibility/stability balance 143
    and horizontal federalism 142, 145
        protection of state interests 145–6
    and "infant system protection" 151
    and informal centralization 146
    and integration 154–5, 156–7
    and international law 199–200
    and judicial bias 147–51
        incentives and motives 147–8
    and judicial review 83–4, 88, 146–7
    and judiciary 143–4, 160
        protection of state interests 144–7
    and legal forms of 142–3
    and legalism 160
    and legitimacy of 149
    and meaning of 142
    and origins of 142
    and subsidiarity 152–4, 157–60
        instrumental subsidiarity 153, 154
        role of courts in enforcing 154
        substantive subsidiarity 153–4
    and vertical federalism 142, 145
        protection of state interests 145
Fédération de Droit Européen (FIDE) 214
feminism, and law:
    and consciousness raising 443
    and critiques of law 437
    and equal protection doctrine 439
    and family law 444–5
    and feminist jurisprudence 438
    and feminist legal reasoning 443–4
    and gendered reality 439–43
        connection thesis 441
        difference versus domination 440–2

feminism, and law (*cont.*)
  ethic of care 441
  gender essentialism 441–2
  physical gender differences 441
  radical feminism 441–2
  sameness versus difference 440
  situation jurisprudence 442
  and impact on intellectual discourse 438
  and law as instrument of male supremacy
    437
  and male bias 438–9
  and rape 445
  and reasonable person concept 445–6
    battered woman syndrome 447–8
    domestic violence 447–8
    reasonable woman doctrine 446–7
  and result-oriented jurisprudence 439
  and second stage of 437–8
  and women's education 437–8
Fiji 126
First World War 232, 233, 234
Ford Foundation 251, 259, 681
foreign aid, and establishment of rule of
    law 73
Foreign Assistance Act (1973, USA) 258
foreign investment, and establishment of
    rule of law 74
foreign policy:
  and international law 188, 246
  and role of law 246–7
  and United States, role of lawyers 249–52
formalism:
  and arguments against 431–2
  and best case for 433–4
  and change in attitude towards 435
  and decision-making under uncertainty
    434–5
  and definition of 431
  and *Lochner v New York* (1905) 429–30
  and pejorative use of term 428–9
  and "real" formalism 430–2
  and "slippery slope" argument 434
framing 390
France:
  and Constitutional Council 49, 86
  and development of rule of law 66
  and emergency powers 174
    enabling acts 175
    state of siege 169–70
  and judicial review 86, 130, 131
free trade, and judicial review 84
French Revolution, and state of siege 169
functionalist theories, and international
    law 193–6

game theory 7
  and origins of judicial review 83
gender 630, 631–2
gender differences:
  and connection thesis 441
  and difference versus domination 440–2
  and ethic of care 441
  and gender essentialism 441–2
  and physical gender differences 441
  and sameness versus difference 440
  and situation jurisprudence 442
  see also feminism, and law
gender equality:
  and legal profession 548
  and radical feminism 441–2
  see also feminism, and law
General Agreement on Tariffs and Trade
    (GATT) 203, 255, 256
Geneva Conventions 544
German Supreme Court, and subsidiarity 158
Germany:
  and emergency powers 174
    dual state 177
    enabling acts 175
    state of defense 172–3
    state of exception 171–2
    suspension 175–6
  and federalism 142
    informal centralization 146
    integration 156
    role of judiciary 145, 147, 150
  and judicial review 85–6, 131
  and judicialization of politics 128
gerrymandering 324, 325
  and bipartisan gerrymandering 328–9
    decline in electoral competition 328
    degree of systemic harm 328–9
    role of courts 329
  and design of electoral districts 329–30
  and partisan gerrymandering 325–7
    capacity for 326–7
    defining 326
    incentives for 327
    partisan symmetry standard 326
    process-oriented constraints 326
    stability of 327
  and United States Supreme Court 327
global governance, and informalism 389
globalization of the law 245
  and advocacy networks 245–6
  and colonialism 247–8
  and domestic rule of law 245
  and human rights 257–60
  and inevitability of 245

and international commercial
    arbitration 252–4
and international trade 254–7
and internationalists 246
and legal authority 245
and scholarship of 247
and transnational norms 245–6
and transnational political and economic
    matters 245
and unilateralists 246
and United States 246–7, 259–61
    role of lawyers in foreign policy 249–52
Glorious Revolution 66
Golden Rule 401, 402
governing coalitions, and courts 645, 657–8
    as coalition stabilizers 650–1
    and credible commitments 648–9
    and imposition of national norms 651–3
    as independent policy-makers 655–7
    as policy-making partners 645–7
    and political entrenchment 653–5
    and United States Supreme
        Court 644, 645–6
group identity, and democratic structure 334
Guantánamo Bay, and United States Supreme
    Court 177
Guatemala 76
    and judicial independence 72
Gun-Free School Zones Act (USA) 647

Hague Convention in Private International
    Law 275
Hague Court of International Arbitration 252
harm, and natural law 404
Harvard Program on Negotiation 387
hegemonic preservation:
    and judicial independence 69
    and judicial review 91
hegemony:
    and legal consciousness 672
    and legal mobilization 531
Help America Vote Act (2002, USA) 331–2
historical institutionalism 7, 12
    and emergence of 46–9
        application to law and courts 48–9
        motives for 46
        new institutionalism 47
    and ideas 54–5
    and identifying independent variables 56
    and legal mobilization 535
    and political regime approach 55
    and public law scholarship:
        contemporary position 52–4
        future of 54–7

and realizing potential of 56
and theorizing 49–52
    exogenous shocks 50–1
    intercurrence of political orders 51–2
    path dependency 49–50, 52
history, and law, see legal history
horizontal accountability, and rule of law 65
human rights:
    and amnesties 237
    and democratization 69
    and globalization of the law 257–60
    and international treaty commitments 198
        compliance 201, 202
    and judicial review 81–2, 87, 88–90
Human Rights Watch 237, 259
Hungary 66
    and judicial independence 69
    and judicialization of politics 125

ideology 626–9
    and constitutionalism 626–7
    and contract rights 629–32
    and framing of legal ideas 628
    and historical institutionalism 54–5
    and judicial decision-making 24–6, 39–41,
        628–9, 640
        judicial independence 563–4, 565
        lower courts 27–8
        United States Supreme Court 26–7
    and law 640–1
    and law and society 689–90
    and law's influence on 635
        abortion regulation 635–8
        affirmative action 635, 638–40
        conservatism 638
    and legal institutions 627
    and liberalism 626
    and racial ascriptivism 632–5
    and research focus on 627
impartiality, and judicial independence 559
impeachment of judges 562
implementation:
    and international law 199–200
    and social reform decisions 600–1
India:
    and emergency powers 177
    and judicial review 85
    and judicialization of politics 128
Indian Gaming Regulatory Act (USA) 647
indifference, and judicial decision-making 762
Indonesia 72
inequality:
    and justice 549
    and legal and political accountability 744–6

inequality (*cont.*)
  and legal mobilization 529
  and rule of law 76
informalism:
  and alternative dispute resolution (ADR) 384–7
  and comparative perspective 388–9
  and global governmentality 389
  and judicial hierarchy approach 380–2
    administrative agencies 381
    flexible informal procedures 381
    lower courts 380
    scrutiny by higher authority 381–2
  and legal ordering 389–90
  and legal pluralist approach 383–4, 390
  and nature of 378
  and ongoing relationship approach 382–3
    enforcement 382–3
    privacy 382
    relationship between parties 382
  and order maintenance 378–9
  as political resource 391
  as regulatory reform 386–8
    accountability 387–8
    negotiated rulemaking 386–7
  and research on 390–1
institutionalism:
  and international law 194
  and litigation 391
  see also historical institutionalism; new
    institutionalism
institutions, and definition of 48
integration, and federalism 154–5, 156–7
integrationists, and democratic structure 333
Intellectual Property Organization 256
intellectual property rights 256
intentionalism, and statutory interpretation, *see*
    statutory interpretation
Inter-American Commission on Human
    Rights 75
Inter-American Court of Human Rights 220
  and judicialization of politics 122
Inter-American Development Bank 63
intercourt relations in United States:
  and complexity of 503
  and consensus 512
  and hierarchical organization of judiciary 504,
    507
  and information asymmetries 507
  and judicial ideology 512
  and lower court compliance with
    precedent 504–6
  and monitoring of lower courts:
    appellate review 509–10
    ideology 509, 510

    reversal 509, 510
    United States Supreme Court 507–9
  and parallel courts:
    citation practices 515–16
    diffusion of doctrine 513
    foreign court precedents 516
    judicial incentives and cues 515–16
    policy leadership 514
  and principal–agent model 506–7
    lower court decision-making 511–12
  and research on 503–4, 516–17
interest groups:
  and judicial independence 107
  and judicial recruitment 477
  and regulation 579
  and regulatory process in America 585, 586
Interest Theory of Legal Rights 417, 418–21
interlegality 383
International Association of Democratic Jurists
    (IADJ) 257
International Chamber of Commerce 246, 252
international commercial arbitration, and
    globalization of the law 252–4
International Commission of Jurists 257–8
  and emergency powers 180
international community, and establishment of
    rule of law 73–4
international courts (ICs):
  and comparison with European Court of
    Justice 220–4
  and design and caseloads of 220–3
  and effective supranational
    adjudication 219–20
  and features of 219
  and private access to 220, 223
International Criminal Court (ICC) 203, 231
  and international commercial
    arbitration 252–3
  and judicialization of politics 128
  and legitimacy crisis 233
  and political costs of action by 236–7
  and problems facing 232
  and prosecuting aggression 235
International Criminal Tribunal for Rwanda
    (ICTR) 127, 235
International Criminal Tribunal for the former
    Yugoslavia (ICTY) 127, 235, 241, 542
international law 11, 12, 203–4
  and characteristics of 187
  and compliance with 200–2
    conditions for 201
    constructivist explanations of 201–2
    domestic mechanisms 201
    first-order 200

reputation 201
  second-order 200
and effectiveness of 202–3
and enforcement of 200–1
and existence of international legal system 189
and foreign policy 188, 246
and implementation of 199–200
and political theories of 190–1
  constructivism 196–7
  constructivist 194
  human rights commitments 198
  international regimes 190, 193
  legal commitments 197–8
  rationalist/functionalist 193–6
  realism 191–3
and proliferation of bilateral/multilateral
  treaties 188–9
International Monetary Fund 63, 73, 255
international relations:
and British School 190, 192, 196
and existence of international legal system 189
and international law 188, 203–4
  compliance 200–2
  effectiveness of 202–3
  enforcement 200–1
  implementation of 199–200
and legalization of 190
and proliferation of bilateral/multilateral
  treaties 188–9
and theories of 190–1
  constructivism 196–7
  constructivist 194
  human rights commitments 198
  international regimes 190, 193
  legal commitments 197–8
  rationalist/functionalist 193–6
  realist 191–3
international trade:
and globalization of the law 254–7
and international law 203
Iran 92
Iraq 74
and support for war crimes trials 239–40
Islamic law:
and judicial review 83, 92
and judicialization of politics 128
Israel:
and judicial empowerment 653–4
and judicial independence 69
and judicial review 86
and judicialization of politics 128
Israeli Supreme Court 650
and judicialization of politics 125
Italy, and judicial review 85, 131

Japan:
and judicial independence 39, 68, 109
and judicial review 85
Jim Crow 634, 635
Jordan 74
judicial behavior, see judicial decision-making
judicial decision-making 12, 19–20, 30–1
and administrative law 351–5
and approaches to 19
and attitudinal model 24–6, 39–41, 302–4,
    563–4, 565, 756–7, 760
  lower courts 27–8
  United States Supreme Court 26–7, 496–7,
    760–1
and behavioral theory of 756
and computer-based analysis of 31
and constitutional law 302–5
  constitutional decision-making 314–15
and development of study of 755–6
and diffusion of doctrine 513
and discretion 758
and ideology 628–9, 640
  abortion regulation 635–8
  affirmative action 638–40
  contract rights 629–32
  white supremacy 632–5
and independent policy-making 655–7
and judges' good faith 20–1
and judicial independence 563–4
and judicialization of politics 132–4
and jurisprudential regimes 310–11
and law and society 687–9
and legal influences 19–20, 316
  modeling law 20–1
and legal models 304–5, 758–60
and legal realism 19
and modeling of 754–5
and nature of 316, 753
and personal policy preferences 492, 495–6,
    753–4, 757–8
and policy leadership 514
and political science 768–9
and precedent 20, 758–9
  foreign legal authorities 516
  horizontal 22–3
  lower court compliance 504–6
  United States Supreme Court 497–8
  vertical 21–2
and principal–agent framework 511–12
and rational-choice model 761–3
and recruitment processes 480–1
and separation of powers model 28–30
and strategic approaches 20
and text and intent of law 23–4

judicial decision-making (*cont.*)
    and typology of 20
    and United States Supreme Court 495–9
        attitudinal model 496–7
        policy preferences 495–6
        research methodology 498–9
    and value voting 314
    see also adjudication; strategic judicial
        decision-making
judicial empowerment 653–4
judicial independence 557–8
    and accountability 100–1, 115, 566
    and centrality in Western constitutional
        thought 99–100
    as collective action problem 112–13
    and compliance with judicial decisions 113
    and constitutional structure 105–6
    as constraint on political power 102, 115–16
        puzzle of creation by politicians 102–3, 107,
            116, 568
    and credible commitments 107–8, 568, 648
    and democratizing states 64
        civil society 71–3
        consolidation of ruling elite's power 69–70
        domestic economic factors 76
        inequality 76
        informal influences on 67
        international community 73–4
        party competition 68–9, 70, 649
        separation of powers framework 67–71,
            74–5
    and development of 66
    and disagreements over nature of 100
    and dual dimensions of 100
    and dynamic nature of 115
    and economic and political development 63
    and economic development 649
    and endogenous explanations for 106–9
        benefits for political actors 107–8
        electoral volatility 109
        interest groups 107
        "passing the buck" by politicians 108
        political credibility 107–8
        reciprocity 108–9
    and exogenous explanations for 110–12
        public support for 110–12
    and future research 116
    and governing coalition stability 650–1
    as human right 557
    and institutional provisions for 102
    and judicial accountability 100–1, 115
    and judicial recruitment 569–71
        elected judges 570–1
    and meaning of 558

    contested nature of 572
    definitional difficulties 558
    empowering function 561
    freedom from constraints of law 560–1
    independence from litigants 559
    independence from public opinion 559–60
    lack of single definition 561
    limitation to judicial actions 561
    separation of powers rationale 558–9
    and model of costs and benefits of 103–5
    and nonabsolute nature of 558
    and parliamentary systems 75
    and political costs of curbing 106, 110, 113
    and political institutions 38–9
    and reality of 562–5
        budgetary threats 562
        congressional influence 562, 563
        ideological decision-making 563–4, 565
        impact of promotion prospects 562–3
        impeachment threats 562
        independence from law 564–5
        influence of litigants 564
        influence of public opinion 564
        measurement of 563–4
        presumption of 562
        responsiveness to political changes 563
    and rights protection 559
    and rule of law 64–7, 557
    and selective resistance to 112–13
    and sources of 567–9
        concern for common good 568–9
        constitutional protections 567–8
        credible commitments 569
        customary independence 569
        economic basis 568
        political basis 568
    and strategic defection 86–7
    and strategic judicial decision-making 38–9,
        113–15
        sensitivity to political actors 114–15
        sensitivity to public attitudes 113–14
    and uncertain virtue of 566–7
judicial politics 9
    and development of study of law and
        politics 6–7
    and modeling 754–5
judicial recruitment 471
    and biases in scholarship 469
        emphasis on readily available data 470
        lack of intercourt comparisons 470, 472
        preoccupation with United States Supreme
            Court 470
    and common features of 471
    and future research 482

and ideal types of 471
and increased attention to 469
and judicial independence 569–71
  elected judges 570–1
and literature review 471–2
and lower federal courts 475–8
  American Bar Association 477–8
  confirmation process 477
  diversity 476
  interest groups 477
  party affiliation 475–6
  political ideology 476–7
  presidential agendas 475
and state judicial systems 478–81
  electoral accountability 479–80
  gubernatorial appointment 479
  impact of selection system 480–1
  merit selection system 479, 480
  nonpartisan elections 479
  partisan elections 479
and United States Supreme Court 472–4,
  488–90
  American Bar Association 474
  choice of nominees 474, 489
  confirmation process 473–4, 489–90
  nominee characteristics 473
  obstacles to study of 472
  political ideology 474
  studies of 472–3
  vacancies 488–9
judicial review:
and administrative law 343, 355
  curtailing of 344
  reasonableness review 349–51
and contrasting views of 282–3
and convergence 269–70
and definition of 81
and determination of legal rights 422–4
and emergencies 176
and explaining spread of:
  democratization 91–2
  diffusion 93
  domestic political logics 90
  federalism 88
  hegemonic preservation 91
  institutionalist approach 90
  political fragmentation 90
  political insurance 90–1
  rights ideology 88–90
  rule of law hypothesis 88
and federalism 146–7
and future research:
  authoritarian contexts 92
  comparative studies 95

ideological reasons for adopting 92–3
measuring performance 93–5
and human rights 81–2, 87, 88–90
and imposition of national norms 652
and origins and development of:
  Anglo-American natural law
    traditions 82–3
  decolonization 85
  federalism 83–4
  free trade 84
  game theory 83
  higher law 82
  international quasi-judicial review 87–8
  Marbury v Madison (1803) 83
  post-World War II Europe 85–6
  second wave 85–7
  social contract 82
  third wave democratization 87
  United States 82–4
  written constitution 82
and race 455
and regulatory agencies 343, 576, 577, 583,
  589, 590
  curtailing of 344
and spread of 81–2
and types of 130–1
  centralized/decentralized 131–2
  see also judicialization of politics
judicialization of politics 138
and ascendancy of legal discourse and
  procedures 121
and expanded scope of 120
and limited academic coverage of 120
and mega-politics (core political issues) 123,
  124–9
  corroboration of regime change 126
  definition of the polity 128
  legislative and executive prerogatives 124–6
  oversight of electoral processes 126–7
  restorative justice 127–8
and political entrenchment 653–4
and political salience of 123–4
and public policy-making:
  domestic 121–2
  international 122
  limited impact on 307–9
and reasons for:
  access rights 132
  centralized/decentralized judicial
    review 131–2
  institutional features 129–32
  judicial decision-making 132–4
  judicial will 134
  necessity of political support for 137–8

judicialization of politics (*cont.*)
  political determinants 134–8
  rights discourse 135–6
  sociopolitical trends 134–5
  standing rights 132
  strategic political maneuvering 136–7
  type of judicial review process 130–1
  and significance of 119
  and spread of 119–20
  see also judicial review; legal mobilization
Judiciary and Removal Act (1875, USA) 654
jurisprudence 13
  and politics and law 7–8
jurisprudential regimes 310–11
juristocracy 123, 138, 245, 654
Juvenile Court Reform Movement 381–2

Kantianism, and morality 402–3
Kazakhstan 66
Korea 68
Kosovo war 238
Kuwait 74

labor regulation, and contract rights 629–32
language, and convergence 277–8
Latin America, and rule of law 66–7
law and courts 769–71
  and neglect of law 772
  see also de-centering, and law and courts
     subfield
law and politics:
  and defining field of 773–4
  and development of study of 4–7
  and disciplinary traffic patterns 767–8
  and diversity of field 3–4
  and law and courts 769–71
    neglect of law 772
  and political science 767–8
    congressional studies 771
    enrichment of 770
    executive studies 771–2
    limited influence on 771
  and structure of field 7
    comparative law 10–11
    constitutional law 8–9
    constitutional politics 9
    international law 11
    judicial politics 9
    jurisprudence 7–8
    law and society 10
  see also de-centering, and law and courts
     subfield
law and society 10, 681–2
  and compliance 690–1

and construction of law 681
and contextual perspective 681
and Critical Legal Studies 723
and decision-making 687–9
and definition of 684–5
and development of field 681–2
and disputing 685–6
and key characteristics of 682–5
  comparative approaches 683–4
  epistemology 683
  interdisciplinary 682–3
  law in society 684
  methodology 683
  policy-relevant concerns 683
and legal consciousness 690
and legal history 691
and legal ideology 689–90
and procedural justice 691–2
and recent developments in 692–3
and regulation 690–1
and research areas 682
Law and Society Association 10, 682, 684
lawyers:
  and cause lawyering 534–5
  and decision-making 687–8
  and distribution across professional
     roles 547–8
  and division of private practice 548
  and establishment of rule of law 72–3
  and influence on courts 545–6
  and judicial influence on 544–5
  and market for legal representation 546–7
  and monopoly protection 545
  and multidisciplinary partnerships
     (MDPs) 547
  and status of 248–9
  and theories of legal representation 541–4
    "Adversary System Excuse" 541–2
    lawyers' amoralism 542–3
  and United States:
    prominence of 248–9
    role in foreign policy 249–52
League of Nations 246, 250
Lebanon 74
legal aid 549
legal consciousness:
  and action 674
  and construction and transmission of 669
  and cultural diffusion 671
  and cultural shifts 670–1
  and hegemony 672
  and law and society 690
  and legal mobilization 529–31
  and legality 668

and path dependency 672–3
and regime change 664, 669–73
and routinization of law 669–70
and social interactions 669
and transformation of old narratives 671
legal globalization, *see* globalization of the law
legal history 723–4
  and contemporary position of 727–9
  and contextualizing debates 731
  and critical contextualization 724
  and Critical Legal History 726
  and Critical Legal Studies 723, 730
  and development of 724–7
  and distinctiveness of 728–9
  and law and society 691
  and law as politics 729
  and law's context outside the sociological 730
  and sociologization of law 730
legal mobilization 522
  and American politics 522–3
  and approaches to 526–7
    constitutive framework 526
    cultural 526
    individual/group focus 527
    instrumental 526
  and core analytical ideas:
    actors' choice of litigation 524–5
    citizen capacity to mobilize law 525
    focus on nonofficial legal actors 523–4
    litigation as part of larger dynamic 524
  and de-centering 740, 743–4
  and definition of 523
  and group mobilization and social reform 532
    case studies 533–4
    cause lawyering 534–5
    conservative functions of law 532–3
    counter-mobilization 534
    litigation campaigns 532
  and hegemony 531
  and improved legal access 523
  and individual disputing 527
    analysis of identity and context 531–2
    challenging assumption of American
      litigiousness 528
    citizen political participation 527
    disabled 531
    disputing pyramid 527–8
    explaining reluctance to mobilize 528, 531
    legal consciousness 529–31
    resource inequalities 529
    social reform impact 605–6
  and institutional norms 601–7
    activist use of legal rights 604
    growth of administrative professions 602

    judicial restructuring of incentives 602
    organizational responses 605
    policy process 602–3
    political mobilization 603–4
    professional networks 606–7
    support structures 601–2
  and legal and political accountability
    744–6
  and legality and democracy 747–8
  and politicization of legal
    accountability 746–7
  and research on 522–3
    class action litigation 535
    cross-national studies 536
    historical institutionalism 535
    mobilization by the powerful 535
    reduced opportunities 535–6
  and social change 523
legal order 12–13
  and informalism 390
  and legal pluralism 383–4
legal pluralism
  and informalism 383–4
  and legal history 728
legal process theory, and race 452, 454–5
legal profession:
  and composition of 547–8
  and division of private practice 548, 688
  and entry standards 544–5
  and judicial influence on 544–5
  and justice 548–9
  and lawyers' influence on courts 545–6
  and legal aid 549
  and market for legal representation 546–7
  and monopoly protection 545
  and multidisciplinary partnerships
    (MDPs) 547
  and politics 550
  and representativeness of 548
  and right to representation 549
  and theories of legal representation 541–4
    "Adversary System Excuse" 541–2
    lawyers' amoralism 542–3
legal realism, and judicial decision-making 19,
    760
legal representation:
  and justice 548–9
  and legal aid 549
  and market for 546–7
  and right to 549
  and theories of 541–4
    "Adversary System Excuse" 541–2
    lawyers' amoralism 542–3
Legal Services Corporation 549

legality:
  and broadening scope of 748
  and democracy 744, 747–8
  and electoral accountability 744, 745
  and legal accountability 744, 745–6
    politicization of 746–7
legalization, *see* globalization of the law
legislative supremacy, and determination of legal
    rights 422–7
legitimacy:
  and international law 196–7
  and motivation to obey law 716–17
    procedural fairness 718–19
legitimation, and role of United States Supreme
    Court 646
lex mercatoria, and international commercial
    arbitration 252–3
liberalism:
  and constitutionalism 281
  and influence on law 626
liberalization:
  and comparative judicial politics 12
  and establishment of rule of law 74
litigation:
  and ambivalence about 595
  and institutions 391
  and law and society 685–6
  and litigant selection 699–700
  and social reform 595
  see also legal mobilization
local government, and imposition of national
    norms 651–3
Lord's Resistance Army (LRA) 239

Maastricht Treaty (1993) 215
Malaysia:
  and judicial independence 72
  and judicialization of politics 128
martial law, and common law systems 168–9
maternalism 630, 631
media, and impact of judicial decisions 603–4
mega-politics (core political issues), *see*
    judicialization of politics
Mercosur 122
Mexico:
  and election administration 331
  and judicial independence 68, 69, 70
    civil society 72
  and judicial review 84
Middle East 70
minimum wage laws 631
minority groups:
  and democratic structure 332–5
  and legal consciousness 530

  and safe districts 335
modeling, and use of 754–5
Mongolia 68
morality:
  and internalization of moral values 717
  and natural law 399, 400–1, 402–4
    free choice 403
    and law 410–11
    moral obligations 411
motivation, *see* psychology and law
multidisciplinary partnerships (MDPs) 547

National Abortion Rights Action League
    (NARAL) 637
National Association for the Advancement of
    Colored People (NAACP) 641
  Legal Defence Fund 606
National Center for State Courts 764
National Organization for Women (NOW) 637
natural law:
  and avoidance of evils 401
  and choice 399–400, 401, 402
  and harm as side effect 404
  and human goods 399, 400, 401
  and immoral choices 402
  and integral human fulfillment 401
  and intending harm 404
  and legal authority 406
  and legal enforcement of moral
    obligations 409–10
  and legal injustice 410, 411
  and legal interpretation 408–9
  and moral norms 399, 400–1, 402
  and moral obligations 411
  and morality 402–4
    free choice 403
    and law 410–11
  and political morality 405–7
  and positive law 405–7
  and practical reasoning 399–402
  and religion 412
  and rights 411
  and theoretical reasoning 400
  and unreasonableness 402
  and virtue 404–5
  and voluntariness 403–4
NDispute 387
negotiated rulemaking 386–7
  and accountability 387–8
Negotiated Rulemaking Act (1990, USA) 387
negotiating costs, and international law 194
Neighborhood Justice Centers (NJCs), and
    alternative dispute resolution
    (ADR) 385–6

neoliberalism, and negotiated rulemaking 387–8
New Deal:
  and administrative law 341
  and United States Supreme Court 282–3, 312–13
new institutionalism 47, 657
  and de-centering 740
  and examples of 742–3
  and precursors of 741–2
  and structure of democracy 321
New York Convention (1958) 252–3
New Zealand:
  and electoral districts 330
  and judicial empowerment 653
  and judicial independence 69
Nigeria 128
nongovernmental organizations (NGOs), and
    informalism 389
nonstate actors, and establishment of rule of law
  and civil society 71–3
  and international community 73–4
Norris-LaGuardia Act (1932, USA) 646
North American Free Trade Agreement
    (NAFTA) 389
  and judicialization of politics 122
  and quasi-judicial review 87
Northern Ireland 177
Norway 84
Nuremberg war crimes trial 232, 233–4

ongoing relationships:
  and alternative dispute resolution
    (ADR) 384–7
  and informalism 382–3
Open Society Institute 237
originalist theories, and normative
    constitutionalism 284–5

Pakistan 66
  and judicialization of politics 126, 128
pandectism 550
parliamentary supremacy:
  and determination of legal rights 422–7
  and modifications to 288
parliamentary systems, and judicial
    independence 75
path dependency:
  and historical institutionalism 49–50, 52
  and regime change 672–3
peace settlements, and amnesties 235–9
personal growth, and neighborhood justice
    centers 386
Peru 125
Philippines 249–50
Physicians for Human Rights 239

plea bargaining 687
Poland 69
policing 615–18
  and decentralized nature of 615
  and distribution of police services 616
  and impact of politics 615, 617
  and impact on politics 617–18
  and local political culture 617
  and race 615–16
  and threat hypothesis 615–16
political crisis, see emergency powers
political institutions, and judicial
    independence 38–9
political parties:
  and campaign finance 324
  and centrality of 322–3
  and congressional rules and practices 324
  and gerrymandering 325
    bipartisan gerrymandering 328–9
    partisan gerrymandering 325–7
    safe districts 324
  and impact of Voting Rights Act (1965)
    324–5
  and judicial recruitment 475–6
  and legal regulation of 323
  and polarization of 323–5
  and primary elections 323
    closed 323
    open 323
    United States Supreme Court decision
    on 323–4
  and structure of democracy 322–5
political party competition:
  and judicial independence 68–9, 70, 109,
    568, 649
  and judicial review 90–1
  and rule of law 68
political science:
  as American discipline 769
  and congressional studies 771
  and development of study of law and
    politics 4–7
  and executive studies 771–2
  and judicial decision-making 768–9
  and law and courts 769–71
    neglect of law 772
  and law and politics 767–8
    enrichment by 770
    limited influence of 771
  and modeling 754–5
political-action committees (PACs) 324
Portugal:
  and informalism 388
  and judicial review 84

positive political theory (PPT):
  and adjudication 698
  and administrative law 342, 345, 353–5
  and statutory interpretation 360, 361
    intentionalism 363–5
power elite 745
power relations, and rule of law 68
power-sharing 334–5
  and consociationalism 332–3
precautionary principle 589
precedent:
  and citation practices 515–16
  and judicial decision-making 20, 758–9
    horizontal 21–2
    United States Supreme Court 497–8
    vertical 22–3
  and lower court responsiveness 504–6
  and *stare decisis* 21–3, 269
  and use of foreign court precedent 516
precommitment, and conceptual
    constitutionalism 290
prerogative power, and common law
    systems 168–9
primary elections:
  and closed primaries 323
  and impact of structure on candidate
    selection 323–4
  and open primaries 323
  and political parties 323
  and United States Supreme Court 323–4
principal–agent theory:
  and adjudication 700
  and European Court of Justice 214–15, 216
  and intercourt relations 506–7
    lower court decision-making 511–12
  and judicial independence 111
prisons:
  and deterrent effect 624
  and expenditure on 623
  and felon disenfranchisement 624
  and growth in incarceration rate 622, 714
  and impact on politics 624
  and political effects on 623
  and prison reform 606–7
  and social disciplinary role 623–4
  and threat hypothesis 623–4
pro bono programs 549
procedural justice, and law and society 691–2
procedure, legal, and convergence 275–6
pro-choice movement 637–8
professional networks, and social reform 606–7
pro-life movement 636, 637
psychology and law 711–12
  and motivation to obey law 712–13, 715–16

  deterrence model 713–14
  internalization of moral values 717
  legitimacy 716–17
  problems with deterrence model 714–15
  procedural fairness 718–19
  value-based perspectives 718
public choice theory:
  and agency discretion 349
  and judicial independence 107
  and statutory interpretation 371–2
    legislative intent 362–3
    legislative process 370
public interest law firms 523
public law 3
  and behavioral revolution 769
  as problematic label 768
  and scope of 773–4
public opinion:
  and judicial independence 559–60, 564
  and support for court-sanctioned regime
    change 666–8
public participation:
  and legal mobilization 527
  and regulatory process:
    outside United States 588–9
    United States 585–7
public policy-making:
  and courts as policy-makers 655–7, 753–4
    policy preferences 492, 495–6
  and judicialization of politics:
    domestic level 121–2
    international level 122
    limited impact 307–9
purposivism, *see* statutory interpretation

race:
  and antidiscrimination law 455
  and *Brown v Board of Education* (1954) 453–5
  and comparative analysis 462
  and contestation over concept 460–1
  and Critical Legal Studies 456–7
  and Critical Race Theory 452, 455–6
    analytical tools 459
    emergence of 457–8
    focus of 459–60
    intersectionality 458
    strategies of 459
    successful establishment of 458–9
    unconscious racism 458
  and deconstruction of 461
  and differences among contemporary
    theorists 462
  and fluidity of concept 460
  and future in legal theory 462–3

and identity politics 461
and ideology 632–5
and legal and social construction of 460
and legal consciousness 530
and legal process theory 454–5
and legal profession 548
and legal scholarship 451
and policing 615–16
and pre-*Brown* era 452–3
    interwar period 453
    neglect in legal scholarship 452
    postwar period 453
rape, and feminist jurisprudence 445
rational-choice institutionalism 47
rational-choice theory:
    and democratic decision-making 579
    and judicial decision-making 761–3
    and obedience to law 713
    and regulation 591
rationalist theories, and international law
        193–6
realism:
    and amnesties 236–7
    and international law 191–3
    and war crimes tribunals 237–8
reasonableness:
    and administrative law 349–51
    and reasonable person concept 445–6
        reasonable woman doctrine 446–7
reciprocity:
    and international law 201
    and judicial independence 108–9
recruitment, *see* judicial recruitment
Red Army Faction 172
regime change:
    and judicialization of politics 126
    and legal consciousness 664, 669–73
        cultural diffusion 671
        cultural shifts 670–1
        hegemony 672
        path dependency 672–3
        transformation of old narratives 671
    and political dysfunction 664–5
    and pressure for 665
    and role of courts 663–4, 665–6
        public opinion data on support for 666–8
    and sources of 665
regime politics, and courts 644, 657–8
    as coalition stabilizers 650–1
    and credible commitments 648–9
    and imposition of national norms 651–3
    as independent policy-makers 655–7
    as policy-making partners 645–7
    and political entrenchment 653–5

regulation:
    and administrative law 580
    and American process 584–7
        public participation 585–7
        rulemaking 585–7
    and contract rights 629–32
    and cost–benefit analysis 590
    and democracy–technocracy balance 580–4
    and economic case for 578–9
    and future research 590–1
    and interest groups 579
    and judicial review 576–7, 583, 589, 590
    and law and society 690–1
    and political economy of 579–80
    and role of courts 589–90
    see also administrative law
regulatory agencies, *see* agencies
rehabilitation, and lower courts 380
religion:
    and judicial decision-making 311
    and natural law 412
Religious Freedom Restoration Act (USA) 647
reproductive rights, and abortion
        regulation 635–8
reputation-building, and international law 195
        and compliance 201
resource inequalities, and legal mobilization 529
restorative justice, and judicialization of
        politics 127–8
rights:
    and analysis of 414, 415–21
        duty 415
        Hohfeld's framework 415–17
        Interest Theory of Legal Rights 417,
            418–21
        legal claims 415
        legal disability 416
        legal immunity 416–17
        legal liabilities 416
        legal liberty 416
        legal powers 416
        Will Theory of Legal Rights 417–21
    and legal philosophy 414
        analytical/normative distinction 414
    and natural law 411
    and normative questions 414
        judicial review/legislative supremacy
            debate 422–7
        procedural issues 421
        substantive issues 421
        who determines rights 421–2
    and a politics of 746
rights discourse, and judicialization of
        politics 135–6

Romania 66
Rome (Ancient) 167
Rome, Treaty of (1957) 209
rule of law:
  and constraints on state actors and
      individuals 66
  and definition of 64
  and democratizing states 63, 64–7
    civil society 71–3
    consolidation of ruling elite's power 69–70
    domestic economic factors 76
    inequality 76
    informal influences on 67
    international community 73–4
    political party competition 68–9, 70
    separation of powers framework 67–71,
      74–5
    threats to 66–7
  and development of 66
  and horizontal accountability 65
  and judicial independence 64–7, 557
rulemaking, and regulatory process:
  and public participation, United States 585–7
  and public policy-making, outside United
      States 588–9
Russia:
  and Constitutional Court 39
    Chechnya Case (1995) 125
  and emergency powers 174, 177
  and judicial independence 70
    consolidation of ruling elite's power 69–70
    curbing of 115
  and rule of law 63
    threats to 66
Russian Revolution 176

Second World War 232
Seneca Falls Declaration 437
separation of powers:
  and establishment of rule of law 67–71, 74–5
  and judicial decision-making 28–30
    strategic decision-making 35–7
  and judicial independence 105–6, 558–9
siege powers, and emergency governance 169–70
signaling, and international law 195
situation jurisprudence 442
slavery, and development of:
  and intercurrence of political orders 51–2
  and path dependency 49–50
Small Claims Court movement 378
social cohesion 674
social reform, and law:
  and conditions for court-made law as
      instrument of:

fragmented governing structures 597, 609
  fragmented political organizations 597–8
and future research:
  legal environment 609
  limitations of rights 610
and implementation of court decisions 600–1
and law as tool of 595–6
and legal mobilization 532
  activist use of legal rights 604
  case studies 533–4
  cause lawyering 534–5
  conservative functions of law 532–3
  counter-mobilization 534
  growth of administrative professions 602
  impact of private litigation 605–6
  institutional norms 601–7
  judicial restructuring of incentives 602
  litigation campaigns 532
  organizational responses 605
  policy process 602–3
  political mobilization 603–4
  professional networks 606–7
  support structures for 601–2
and litigation 595
  practical impact of 599–600
  resource requirements 599
  securing support of judge 599
  utility of 598–600
and role of courts 596–7, 608–9
  disputed effectiveness of 607
  judicial events 596
  policy interventions 596
social transformation, and neighborhood justice
      centers 386
sociological perspectives 12
Sonnetrach 253
South Africa:
  and Constitutional Court 87
  and emergency powers 174
  and judicial empowerment 653
  and judicial independence 69, 74
  and judicialization of politics 126, 127
  and Truth and Reconciliation
      Commission 236
South Korea 126
Spain 131
Spanish American War 249
specialized courts 546
Stafford Act (USA) 175
stare decisis 269
  and judicial decision-making 21–3
  and lower court responsiveness 504–6
  see also precedent
state intervention, and contract rights 629–32

state judicial systems, and recruitment to 478–81
  and electoral accountability 479–80
  and gubernatorial appointment 479
  and impact of selection system 480–1
  and merit selection system 479, 480
  and nonpartisan elections 479
  and partisan elections 479
state neutrality 312
  and contract rights 629–31
state of siege, and French legal tradition 169–70
statutory interpretation:
  and administrative agencies 374–5
  and dynamic statutory interpretation 372
  and empirical scholarship on 373–4
  and formalism:
    arguments against 431–2
    best case for 433–4
    change in attitude towards 435
    decision-making under uncertainty 434–5
    definition of 431
    Lochner v New York (1905) 429–30
    pejorative use of term 428–9
    "real" formalism 430–2
    "slippery slope" argument 434
  and future research 361
  and institutional design 375
  and intentionalism 361–6
    communication theory 364
    difficulty in determining legislative
      intent 361–3
    intent of current legislature 365–6
    legislative materials 363–4
    manufacture of legislative history 362–3
    meaning of 361
    pivotal lawmakers 364
    positive political theory 363–5
    preference-estimating 366
    public choice objections 362–3
    understanding legislative process 365
  and natural law 408–9
  and positive political theory 360–1
  and pragmatic approach 374
  and public choice theory 371–2
    legislative intent 362–3
    legislative process 370
  and purposivism 369–72
    identification of purpose 370
    as judicial power grab 371
    mischief rule 369
    reasonable legislator assumption 370–1
  and regulatory process 589
  and renaissance of scholarship on 360
  and strategic judicial decision-making 37
  and textualism 360, 366–9

appropriations process 368–9
  canons of construction 367–9
  formalist justification 366
  incentive for precise legislation 366–7
  substantive canons 369
strategic action 12
  and judicial decision-making 20
strategic defection 86–7
strategic judicial decision-making 34–5, 42–3
  and antecedents of approach 35
  and attitudinal approach 39–41
  and constitutional courts 39
  and constraints imposed by separation of
    powers 35–7
  and decision costs 38
  and first wave studies of 35–7
  and internal strategic behavior 41–2
  and judicial independence 38–9, 113–15
    sensitivity to political actors 114–15
    sensitivity to public attitudes 113–14
  and judicialization of politics 133–4
  and relative political position 37
  and reluctance to use constitutional
    justification 37–8
  and responsiveness to Congress 36–7
  and second wave studies of 37–9
  and statutory interpretation 37
  and United States Supreme Court 496–7
  see also judicial decision-making
subsidiarity:
  and federalism 152–4, 157–60
  and versions of:
    instrumental 153, 154
    substantive 153–4
surveillance, and deterrence 714, 715
suspension, and emergency powers 175–6
Switzerland:
  and federalism 142
  and rejection of judicial review 147

Taft-Hartley Act (USA) 313
Taiwan:
  and judicial independence 68–9
  and rule of law 63
Taliban 544
Tanzania 66
  and judicial independence 72
team models of adjudication 701–2
Tellico Dam 368
Tennessee Valley Authority (TVA) 368
textualism, *see* statutory interpretation
Tokyo war crimes trial 232, 234
torture 177, 203, 544
trade, *see* international trade

Trade Act (1974, USA) 255
transaction costs:
  and international law 194
  and judicial independence 65
transitivity, and judicial decision-making 762
transnational governance, and informalism 389
transnational tribunals 119
  and judicialization of politics 122
treaties, and proliferation of bilateral/
    multilateral treaties 188–9
trust law, and convergence 274–5
truth commissions 236
Turkey 128

Uganda 239
Ukraine 176
uncertainty, and international law 194
undue burden, and abortion regulation 637
United Kingdom:
  and electoral districts 329–30
  and emergency powers 177
    Northern Ireland 177
    post-9/11 179
  and federalism 142
  and judicial independence 567, 569
  and judicialization of politics 125
United Nations Convention Against Torture 203
United Nations Convention on the Political
    Rights of Women 202
United Nations Security Council 200
United Nations Treaty Series (UNTS) 188–9
United States:
  and colonialism 249–50
    dollar diplomacy 250
  and emergency powers 174
    deference 177
    delegation 175
    enabling acts 175
    post-9/11 179
    targeting of 178
  and federalism 142
    informal vertical integration 145–6
    international law 199–200
    role of judiciary 144–5
  and foreign policy
    internationalist vs. unilateralist 246
    role of international law 188
    role of law 246–7
    role of lawyers 249–52
  and globalization of the law 246–7, 259–61
    human rights 257–60
    international commercial arbitration 252–4
    international trade 254–7
  and judicial independence 70

    civil society 72
  and judicialization of politics 119, 125
  and prominence of lawyers 248–9
United States Circuit Court Judge Nominating
    Commission 476
United States Congress:
  and influence on judiciary 38
  and overrides of Supreme Court decisions 37
United States Courts of Appeals, and judicial
    decision-making 27–8
United States Military Commission in
    Guantánamo 542
United States Supreme Court 487–8
  and administrative law 341, 348
  and agenda setting (case selection) 490–5
    attention to other actors 494
    factors affecting 508–9
    future research 494–5
    ideology of lower courts 509
    legal or jurisprudential model 491–2
    policy preferences 492
    role of litigants 493
    strategic calculations 493
  and constitutional theory 282–4
  and emergency powers 177
  and federalism 149
    integration 156
    subsidiarity 158, 159
  and formalism 429–30
  and gerrymandering 327
  and hierarchical organization of judiciary 504
  and intercourt relations:
    lower court compliance 504–6
    monitoring of lower courts 507–9
    reversal 509
  and judicial decision-making 495–9, 753
    attitudinal model 26–7, 40–1, 302–4, 496–7,
      756–7, 760–1
    compliance of lower courts 21–2
    computer-based analysis of 31
    decision-making 302–5
    foreign legal authorities 516
    jurisprudential regimes 310–11
    legal models 304–5
    policy preferences 495–6, 753–4
    precedent 497–8
    research methodology 498–9
    separation of powers model 28–30
    strategic decision-making 496–7
    value voting 314
  and judicial independence 558
  and judicial review 130
    contrasting views of 282–3
    origins of 82–4

and judicialization of politics 125
and legitimation function 646
as part of governing coalition 644, 645–6
    policy-making partner in 645–7
and political parties 323
    primary elections 323–4
and public policy-making:
    governing coalition partner 645–7
    limited impact on 307–9
and recruitment to 472–4, 488–90
    American Bar Association 474
    choice of nominees 474, 489
    confirmation process 473–4, 489–90
    nominee characteristics 473
    obstacles to study of 472
    political ideology 474
    studies of 472–3
    vacancies 488–9
and strategic decision-making:
    internal strategic behavior 41–2
    relative political position 37
    reluctance to use constitutional
        justification 37–8
    responsiveness to Congress 36–7
    sensitivity to political actors 114
    sensitivity to public attitudes 114
    separation of powers constraints 35–7
    statutory interpretation 37
and structure of democracy 322
as trustee 150
Universal Declaration of Human Rights
    (1948) 257, 557
utilitarianism, and morality 402–3

Venezuela 66
Versailles, Treaty of (1919) 233
Violence Against Women Act (USA) 647

virtue, and natural law 404–5
Voting Rights Act (1965, USA) 331
    and impact on political parties 324–5
    and power-sharing effects 334–5

Wagner Act (USA) 646
war, and laws of 229–30
war crimes tribunals 230–1
    and ad hoc nature of 231
    and amnesty 235–9
    and assigning responsibility for war 234
    and impact of 240–1
    and individual-level politics of 240
    and legitimacy of 232
    and outlawing war 233–5
    and peace vs. justice 235–40
    and powerful states 232–3
    and public opinion 240
    and relative power balance 237–8
    and shrinking ambit of 233
    as sign of lack of progress 241
    and truth commissions 236
    and victims' attitudes 239–40
    and victors' justice 231–3
Washington Consensus 247
Weimar Republic 171, 172
white supremacy, and racial ideology
    632–5
Will Theory of Legal Rights 417–21
World Bank 63, 73, 224, 247, 255
World Trade Organization (WTO) 203,
    389, 569
    and Dispute Settlement Body 200
    and globalization of the law 256
    and judicialization of politics 122

Zambia 66